Fromm

POSTCARDS FROM ENGLAND

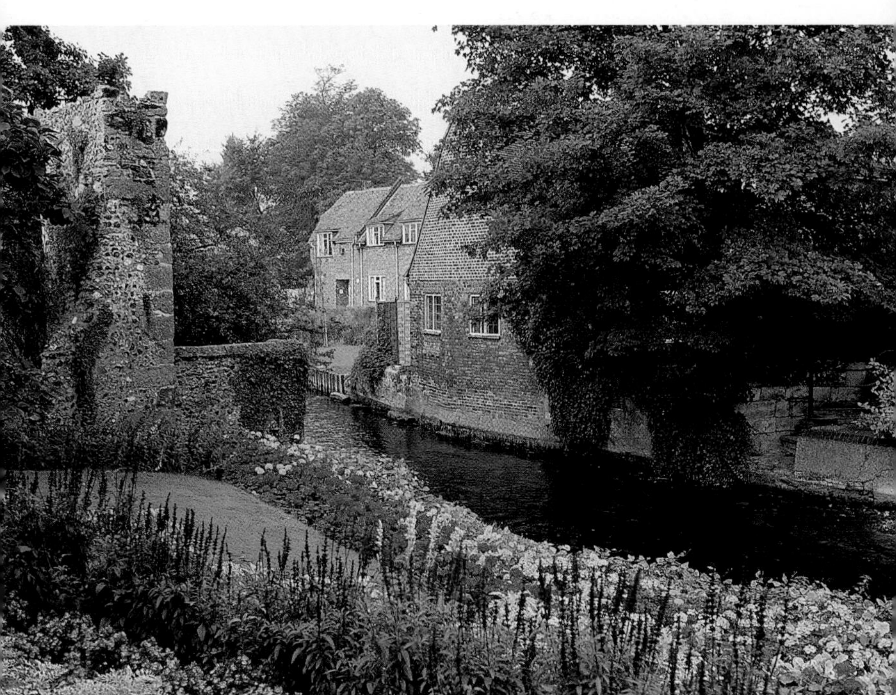

Many of England's finest country houses and gardens are found in Kent. See chapter 6.
© David W. Hamilton/The Image Bank.

Windsor Castle, just outside of London, housed English royalty for almost 1,000 years. See chapter 5. © Derek Croucher/The Stock Market.

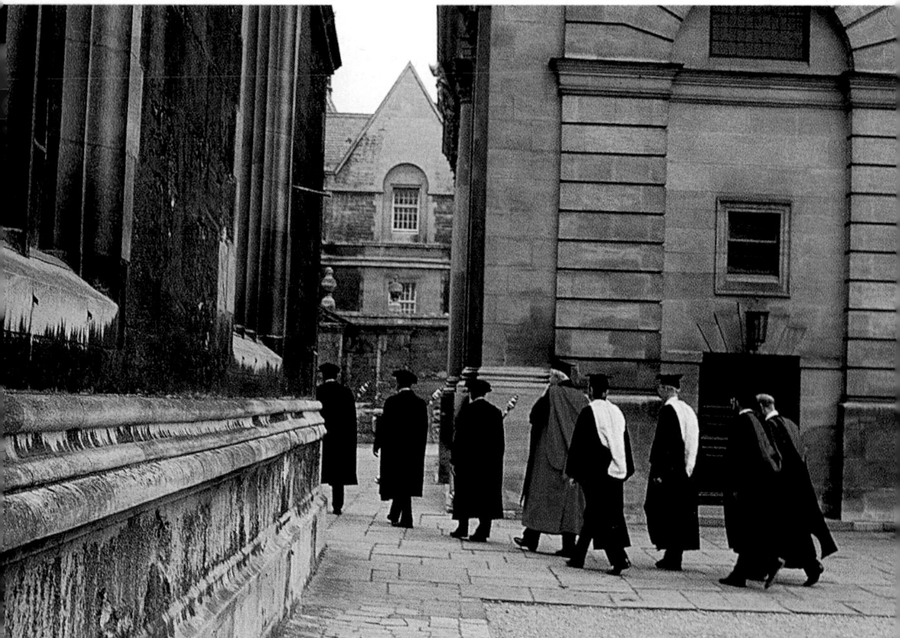

Old English tradition still thrives at Oxford University. See chapter 5. © Sally Weigand.

Big Ben, the "symbol of London," has been chiming the hour for more than 150 years. See chapter 4. © Gail Mooney/Kelly/Mooney Photography.

Bath Abbey, the "Lantern of the West," is a prime example of the Perpendicular-style cathedral. See chapter 8. © Carl Purcell.

Thatched cottages are still a common sight in the villages of Devon. See chapter 9. © Nik Wheeler Photography.

Bath's Roman aqueducts are some of the finest ruins in the country. *See chapter 8.*

Stonehenge, England's most important—and mysterious—prehistoric monument, is in Wiltshire. See chapter 8. © Matthew Weinreb/The Image Bank.

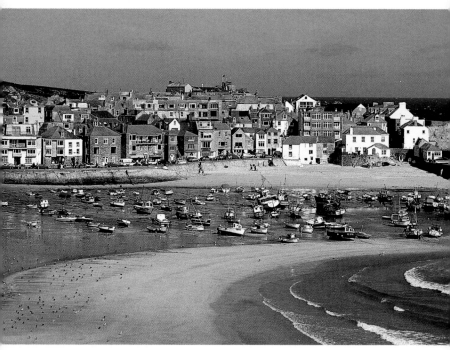

St. Ives is just one of many Cornish villages known for their fishing, sailing, and artists' colonies. See chapter 10. © Robert Holmes.

Cornwall's scenic coastline has inspired artists for centuries. See chapter 10.

Take a stroll through one of England's charming villages, such as Castle Combe in Wiltshire. See chapter 8. © Donna J. Carroll.

Mary Arden House, the girlhood home of Shakespeare's mother, in Stratford-upon-Avon. See chapter 12. © John Lawrence/Tony Stone Images.

The Bard's birthplace in Stratford-upon-Avon is a national shrine, and is filled with Shakespeare memorabilia. See chapter 12. © Tony Craddock/Tony Stone Worldwide.

Punting the River Cam in a flat-bottomed boat at Cambridge University. See chapter 13. © Hilary Wilkes/International Stock.

Sample traditional English dishes such as cottage pies, Dover sole, fish-and-chips, and Yorkshire pudding. See appendix A. © Catherine Karnow Photography.

The lush countryside of Derbyshire's Durwent River Valley in northern England. See chapter 14. © Catherine Karnow Photography.

The towns of East Anglia contain many timbered cottages and other examples of Tudor architecture. See chapter 13. © Sally Weigand.

Chatsworth House, one of the many historic mansions found in Derbyshire. See chapter 14.
© Catherine Karnow Photography.

The inspiration of many an English poet, the beautiful countryside of the Lake District offers some of the best hiking in England. See chapter 16. © Tom Stock/Tony Stone Images.

Blackpool's beaches, Disney-like attractions, and nostalgic atmosphere draw thousands of visitors each summer. See chapter 15. © Paul Thompson/International Stock.

Many of the guides at England's landmarks, such as the Tower of London's Yeoman Warders, are attractions in their own right. See chapter 4. © Catherine Karnow Photography.

Grab a pint and some local gossip at an English pub, such as this one in London. See chapter 1 for a list of our favorites throughout the country. © L.L.T. Rhodes/Tony Stone Images.

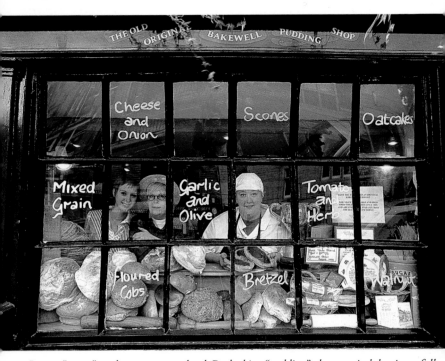

Buy a "cuppa" and a scone at a local Derbyshire "pudding" shop, or indulge in a full afternoon tea at a luxury London hotel. See chapter 3 for our favorite tea spots in London. © Catherine Karnow Photography.

Here's what the critics say about Frommer's:

"Amazingly easy to use. Very portable, very complete."

—*Booklist*

♦

"The only mainstream guide to list specific prices. The Walter Cronkite of guidebooks—with all that implies."

—*Travel & Leisure*

♦

"Complete, concise, and filled with useful information."

—*New York Daily News*

♦

"Hotel information is close to encyclopedic."

—*Des Moines Sunday Register*

Other Great Guides for Your Trip:

Frommer's Britain's Best Bike Rides

Frommer's Britain's Best-Loved Driving Tours

Frommer's England from $70 a Day

Frommer's Irreverent Guide to London

Frommer's London

Frommer's London from $85 a Day

Frommer's Memorable Walks in London

Frommer's Portable London

Frommer's Scotland

Frommer's Scotland's Best-Loved Driving Tours

Road Atlas Britain

The Unofficial Guide to London

Frommer's®

England 2001

by Darwin Porter & Danforth Prince

IDG Books Worldwide, Inc.
An International Data Group Company
Foster City, CA • Chicago, IL • Indianapolis, IN • New York, NY

About the Authors

A native of North Carolina, **Darwin Porter** was a bureau chief for the *Miami Herald* when he was 21 and was assigned to write the very first edition of a Frommer's guide devoted solely to one European country. Since then, he has written numerous best-selling Frommer's guides, notably to France, Italy, and Germany. In 1982, he was joined in his research efforts across England by **Danforth Prince,** formerly of the Paris bureau of *The New York Times,* who has traveled in and written extensively about England. Together, they are also the authors of *Frommer's London, Frommer's England from $70 a Day,* and *Frommer's Scotland.*

IDG Books Worldwide, Inc.

An International Data Group Company
919 E. Hillsdale Blvd. Suite 400
Foster City, CA 94404

Find us online at **www.frommers.com**

ISBN 0-7645-6138-3
ISSN 1055-5404

Editor: Myka Carroll
Production Editor: M. Faunette Johnston
Photo Editor: Richard Fox
Design by Michele Laseau
Staff Cartographers: John Decamillis, Roberta Stockwell, Elizabeth Puhl
Production by IDG Books Indianapolis Production Department

Special Sales

For general information on IDG Books Worldwide's books in the U.S., please call our Consumer Customer Service department at 1-800-762-2974. For reseller information, including discounts, bulk sales, customized editions, and premium sales, please call our Reseller Customer Service department at 1-800-434-3422.

Manufactured in the United States of America

5 4 3 2 1

Contents

7 Hampshire & Dorset: Austen & Hardy Country 301

8 Wiltshire & Somerset 341

9 Devon 383

10 Cornwall 415

15 The Northwest 612

16 The Lake District 645

17 Yorkshire & Northumbria 675

Appendix: England in Depth 717

Index 729

List of Maps

AN INVITATION TO THE READER

In researching this book, we discovered many wonderful places—hotels, restaurants, shops, and more. We're sure you'll find others. Please tell us about them, so we can share the information with your fellow travelers in upcoming editions. If you were disappointed with a recommendation, we'd love to know that, too. Please write to:

Frommer's England 2001
IDG Books Worldwide, Inc.
909 Third Avenue
New York, NY 10022

AN ADDITIONAL NOTE

Please be advised that travel information is subject to change at any time—and this is especially true of prices. We therefore suggest that you write or call ahead for confirmation when making your travel plans. The authors, editors, and publisher cannot be held responsible for the experiences of readers while traveling. Your safety is important to us, however, so we encourage you to stay alert and be aware of your surroundings. Keep a close eye on cameras, purses, and wallets, all favorite targets of thieves and pickpockets.

WHAT THE SYMBOLS MEAN

✪ Frommer's Favorites

Our favorite places and experiences—outstanding for quality, value, or both.

The following abbreviations are used for credit cards:

AE American Express
CB Carte Blanche
DC Diners Club
DISC Discover
ER enRoute
EC Eurocard
JCB Japan Credit Bank
MC MasterCard
V Visa

FIND FROMMER'S ONLINE

www.frommers.com offers up-to-the-minute listings on almost 200 cities around the globe—including the latest bargains and candid, personal articles updated daily by Arthur Frommer himself. No other Web site offers such comprehensive and timely coverage of the world of travel.

1 The Best of England

Planning a trip to England can present you with a bewildering array of choices. We've scoured the country in search of the best places and experiences, and in this chapter we'll share our very personal and opinionated choices. We hope they'll give you some ideas and get you started.

1 The Best Travel Experiences

- **Enjoying a Night at the Theater:** The torch passed down from Shakespeare is still burning brightly. Today, London's theater scene is acknowledged as the finest in the world. There are two major subsidized companies, the Royal Shakespeare Company, performing at the Barbican in London and at Stratford-upon-Avon, and the National Theatre on the South Bank. And fringe theater offers surprisingly good and often innovative productions staged in venues ranging from church cellars to the upstairs rooms of pubs. See chapter 4.
- **Pub Crawling:** The pursuit of the pint takes on cultural significance in England. Ornate taps fill tankards and mugs in pubs that serve as the social heart of every village and town. Quaint signs for such names as the Red Lion, the White Swan, and the Royal Oak dot the landscape and beckon you in—not only for the pint but also for the conviviality, and perhaps even the entertainment or the food.
- **Motoring Through the Cotswolds:** If *driving* means going on a determined trip from one place to another, motoring is wandering at random, and there's no better place for it than the Cotswolds, located less than 100 miles west of London. Its rolling hills and pasturelands are peppered with ivy-covered inns and honey-colored stone cottages. See chapter 11.
- **Punting on the Cam:** This is Cantabrigian English for gliding along in a flat-bottom boat, a long pole pushed into the River Cam's shallow bed, as you bypass the weeping willows along the banks, watch the strolling students along the graveled walkways, and take in the picture-postcard vistas of green lawns along the water's edge. See chapter 13.
- **Touring Stately Homes:** England has hundreds of mansions open to visitors, some of them centuries old, and we'll tell you

about dozens of them in the pages that lie ahead. The homes are often surrounded by beautiful gardens, and when the owners got fanciful, they added splashing fountains and miniature pagodas or temples.

- **Shopping for Antiques:** Whatever old treasure you're looking for, it can be found somewhere in England. We're talking Steiff teddy bears, a blunderbuss, an 1890 tin-plate toy train, an eggcup allegedly used by Queen Victoria, a first-edition English print from 1700, or the definitive Henry Harper grandfather clock. No one polishes up their antiques and curios quite as brightly as English dealers. From auction houses to quaint shops, from flea markets to country fairs, England, particularly Victorian England, is for sale.
- **Cruising on Lake Windermere:** Inspired by the lyric poetry of Wordsworth, you can board a boat at Windermere or Bowness and sail England's most famous lake. You'll see the Lake District's scenery, its tilled valleys lying in the shadow of forbidding peaks, as it was meant to be viewed—from the water. A great jaunt is the round-trip from Bowness to Ambleside, at the head of the lake, all the way back around to the village of Lakeside, at the southern tip. See chapter 16.

2 The Best of Literary England

- **Samuel Johnson's House** (London; ☎ **020/7373-3745**): The backwater at No. 17 Gough Square, situated on the north side of Fleet Street, was Johnson's home from 1749 to 1758. Here he worked on his Rambler essays and his Dictionary, and here his beloved wife, "Tetty," died in 1752. See chapter 4.
- **Keats House** (Hampstead, London; ☎ **020/7435-2062**): Most of the poet's brief life was spent in London, where he was born in 1795 in a livery stable run by his father. He moved to Hampstead in 1817, and met his fiancée, Fanny Brawne, there. In this house he coughed blood into his handkerchief. "That drop of blood is my death warrant," he said. "I must die." He left for Rome in 1820, and died there a year later. See chapter 4.
- **Jane Austen Country:** The author of *Pride and Prejudice* and *Sense and Sensibility* wrote of rural delights and a civilized society—set mainly in her beloved Hampshire. In 1809, she moved with her mother to Chawton, 50 miles south of Bath, where she lived until 1817. Her house is now a museum. Her novels *Persuasion* and *Northanger Abbey* are associated with the city of Bath, where she visited frequently in her youth and lived from 1801 to 1806. In her final year, she moved to 8 College St. in Winchester, and is buried in Winchester Cathedral. See chapters 7 and 8.
- **Stratford-upon-Avon:** Although the bard remains a mysterious figure, the folks who live in touristy Stratford gleefully peddle his literary legacy. There is Shakespeare's Birthplace, where the son of a glover was born on April 23, 1564. He died in Stratford on the same day, 52 years later. Anne Hathaway's Cottage, in the hamlet of Shottery, is also popular; Shakespeare married Hathaway when he was only 18 years old. See chapter 12.
- **Sherwood Forest:** You won't find Errol Flynn in Technicolor green tights gallivanting through a forest of mighty oaks with his merry band of men. Although most of the forest has been open grassland since the 14th century, it lives on in legend, literature, and lore as the most famous woodland in the world. At the Sherwood Forest Visitor Centre at Edinstowe, the world of Friar Tuck and Little John live on, along with Maid Marian and Alan-a-Dale. See chapter 14.
- **Grasmere** (The Lake District): William Wordsworth lived here with his sister, Dorothy, who commented on the "domestic slip of mountain" behind their

home, Dove Cottage. The cottage itself is now part of the Wordsworth Museum, displaying manuscripts and memorabilia. The poet also lived for a time at nearby Rydal Mount, just north of Ambleside (one of his descendants still owns the property), where you can see gardens landscaped by the poet himself. Throughout the region, you'll find the landscapes that inspired this giant of English romanticism, including the shores of Ullswater, where Wordsworth saw his famous "host of golden daffodils." See chapter 16.

- **Haworth** (West Yorkshire): England's second major literary pilgrimage site is the home of the Brontë Parsonage Museum. Here the famous Brontë sisters lived and spun their web of romance. Emily wrote *Wuthering Heights,* Charlotte, *Jane Eyre* and *Villette,* and even Anne wrote two novels, *The Tenant of Wildfell Hall* and *Agnes Grey,* although neither matches up to her sisters' work. See chapter 17.

3 The Best of Legendary England

- **Stonehenge** (near Salisbury, Wiltshire): The most celebrated prehistoric monument in all of Europe, Stonehenge is some 5,000 years old. Despite the "definitive" books written on the subject, its original purpose remains a mystery. Was it an astronomical observatory for a sun-worshipping cult? The romantic theory that Stonehenge was "constructed by the Druids" is nonsense, since it was completed before the Druids reached Britain in the 3rd century B.C., but legend still persists. See chapter 8.
- **Glastonbury Abbey** (Somerset): One of the great abbeys of England and once a center of culture and learning, Glastonbury quickly fell into ruins following the Dissolution of the Monasteries. One story about the abbey says that Jesus came here as a child with Joseph of Arimathea. According to another legend, King Arthur was buried at Glastonbury, which was the site of the fabled Avalon. Today, the abbey's large ruins are open to the public. See chapter 8.
- **Tintagel** (Cornwall): On the windswept Cornish coast, the castle of Tintagel is said to have been the birthplace of King Arthur. The castle was actually built much later than the Arthurian legend, around 1150. But who wants to stand in the way of a good story? No one in Cornwall, that's for sure. Tintagel merrily touts the King Arthur legend—in town you can order an Excaliburger! See chapter 10.

4 The Best of Ancient & Roman England

Stonehenge is listed in "The Best of Legendary England" category above.

- **Roman Painted House** (Dover, Kent): Called Britain's "buried Pompeii," this 1,800-year-old Roman structure has exceptionally well-preserved walls and even an under-floor heating system used by the Romans. It's best known for its unique bacchic murals. See chapter 6.
- **Avebury** (west of Marlborough, Wiltshire): Although not as famous as Stonehenge, this is one of Europe's leading prehistoric monuments. Its circle of more than 100 stones—some of them weighing in at 50 tons—is arrayed on a 28-acre site. See chapter 8.
- **Roman Baths** (Bath, Avon): Dedicated to the goddess Sulis Minerva, these baths were founded by the Romans in A.D. 75. They are among the finest Roman remains in the country and are still fed by Britain's most famous hot-water spring. The site of the Temple of Sulis Minerva has been excavated and is open for viewing. See chapter 8.

- **Corinium Museum** (Cirencester, in the Cotswolds): This regional museum contains one of the best collections of archaeological remains from the Roman occupation of Britain. You'll see Roman mosaics that have remained in Britain, along with provincial sculpture, such as figures of Minerva and Mercury. See chapter 11.
- **Hadrian's Wall** (north of England): A World Heritage Site, this wall—now in ruins—was ordered built by Hadrian, the Roman emperor, in A.D. 122 to hold back barbarian invasions from the north. Marking the far northern border of the Roman Empire, the wall stretched 73 miles from Wallsend or Wall's End north of Newcastle upon Tyne in the east all the way to Bowness-on-Solway beyond Carlisle in the west. A small fort (called a "milecastle") was added at every mile along the wall. Garrison forts, some quite large, were constructed behind the wall. A highlight is Vindolanda, the last of eight successive Roman forts that were built on a site adjacent to the wall. See chapter 17.

5 The Best of Norman & Medieval England

- **Battle** (East Sussex): This is the site of the famous Battle of Hastings (fought on October 14, 1066), in which the Normans defeated King Harold's English army. A great commemorative abbey was built here by William the Conqueror, the high altar of its church erected over the spot where King Harold fell in battle. The abbey was destroyed at the time of the Dissolution of the Monasteries, in 1538. The place where the altar stood is identified by a plaque. Some ruins and buildings remain, about which Tennyson wrote, "O Garden, blossoming out of English blood." See chapter 6.
- **Hastings Castle** (Hastings, on the south coast of England): Now in ruins, this was the first of the Norman castles erected in England (ca. 1067). The fortress was defortified by King John in 1216. An audiovisual presentation of the castle's history—shown on the grounds—includes the famous battle of 1066. See chapter 6.
- **Rye** (Sussex): Near the English Channel, and flourishing in the 13th century, this "Antient Cinque Port" was a smuggling center for centuries. Writer Louis Jennings once wrote, "Nothing more recent than a Cavalier's Cloak, Hat and Ruffles should be seen on the streets of Rye." It's one of England's best preserved towns. See chapter 6.
- **Dunster Castle** (in the West Country): This castle was built on the site of a Norman castle granted to William de Mohun of Normandy by William the Conqueror shortly after his conquest of England. A 13th-century gateway remains from the original fortress. In 1376, the castle and its lands were bought by the Luttrell family, and remained in their possession until the National Trust took it over in 1976. See chapter 8.
- **Warwick Castle:** This is one of the major sights in the Midlands. Little remains of William the Conqueror's motte and bailey castle of 1068, but much of today's external structure remains unchanged from the mid-1300s. Today, Warwick Castle is the finest medieval castle in England, lying on a cliff overlooking the Avon. Its most powerful commander in the 1400s was the earl of Warwick, who, during the War of the Roses, was called the "Kingmaker." One of the best collections of medieval armor and weapons in Europe is housed behind its walls. See chapter 12.

The Regions in Brief

NORTH SEA
SCOTLAND
Glasgow
Edinburgh
NORTHUMBERLAND NAT'L PARK
Newcastle upon Tyne
Carlisle
NORTHUMBRIA
Belfast
Solway Firth
THE LAKE DISTRICT
LAKE DISTRICT NAT'L PARK
NORTHERN IRELAND
NORTH YORK MOORS NAT'L PARK
Isle of Man
YORKSHIRE DALES NAT'L PARK
YORKSHIRE
York
IRISH SEA
Blackpool
Leeds
Liverpool Bay
Manchester
Liverpool
PEAK DISTRICT NAT'L PARK
Lincoln
Chester
THE NORTHWEST
EAST MIDLANDS
LINCOLNSHIRE
The Wash
Nottingham
Leicester
Norwich
EAST ANGLIA
Ely
Birmingham
WALES
WARWICKSHIRE
THE COTSWOLDS
Cambridge
Aldeburgh
Stratford-upon-Avon
Bedford
St. George's Channel
Woodstock
Buckingham
Dedham
Swansea
AVON
Oxford
LONDON
OXFORDSHIRE
Cardiff
Bristol
Bath
Windsor
THAMES VALLEY
Canterbury
Bristol Channel
WILTSHIRE
SURREY
KENT
Dover
EXMOOR NAT'L PARK
SOMERSET
Salisbury
HAMPSHIRE
WEST SUSSEX
EAST SUSSEX
Strait of Dover
DEVON
Southampton
Calais
DORSET
Brighton
Hastings
Portsmouth
Lyme Bay
Isle of Wight
DARTMOOR NAT'L PARK
CORNWALL
Plymouth
Land's End
Lizard Point
English Channel
Cherbourg
Le Havre
Channel Islands
FRANCE
0
50 mi
0
50 km
N

- **Fountains Abbey & Studley Royal** (southwest of Ripon, in North Yorkshire): These ruins evoke the monastic life of medieval England. The Cistercian monks constructed "a place remote from all the earth" in 1132. You'll explore the ruins as well as the Studley Royal, whose lavish 18th-century landscaping is one of the few surviving examples of a Georgian green garden. See chapter 17.

6 The Best of Tudor & Georgian England

- **Hampton Court Palace:** This is the most magnificent of a series of grand residences and royal palaces lining the River Thames west of Central London. Surrounded by rolling parkland, Hampton Court was built in grand style for Cardinal Wolsey—until Henry VIII snatched it away. Henry added the great hall in 1532, forcing laborers to toil 24 hours a day in shifts. The sheer size of the palace is amazing, and on its grounds is the world's first indoor tennis court. See chapter 4.
- **Bath:** Much magnificent 18th-century architecture remains exactly as Jane Austen once saw it, despite repeated World War II bombings. At one time Bath was the most fashionable spa in Britain. Architect John Wood (1704–54), among others, helped create a city of harmony and beauty, with landscaped terraces, famous crescents such as the Royal Crescent, and Palladian villas. See chapter 8.
- **Kenilworth Castle** (Warwickshire): Once the abode of Simon de Montfort, this castle was the setting for Sir Walter Scott's romantic novel, *Kenilworth,* first published in 1862, which recounts the supposed murder of Amy Robsart, wife of Robert Dudley, earl of Leicester. Elizabeth I had presented Kenilworth Castle to her favorite earl in 1563. The castle was destroyed after the civil war and is now in ruins. At one time the castle walls enclosed 7 acres. See chapter 12.

7 The Best of Victorian England

- **Albert Memorial** (London): If any statue symbolized an era, this flamboyant tribute to Victoria's consort, her beloved Albert (1819–61) does—it's the epitome of Victorian excess. Romantic and flamboyant, the statue depicts Albert holding a catalog of the Great Exhibition. He overlooks the South Kensington Culture Centre, his last legacy. The 14-foot-high statue, with the blessing of the queen, went into place in 1876 and was instantly described as an "outsize reliquary casket." See chapter 4.
- **Houses of Parliament** (London): No government building in England symbolizes the Victorian age like the Palace of Westminster, housing Parliament. Replacing a palace destroyed by fire in 1834, it cost £2 million to build, a princely sum at the time. The building was almost completed by 1847, and turned out to be a Gothic fantasy, its facade decorated with monarchs ranging from William the Conqueror to Queen Victoria. See chapter 4.
- **Osborne House** (southeast of East Cowes on the Isle of Wight): This was Queen Victoria and Prince Albert's most cherished residence. Constructed at Queen Victoria's own expense, it is imbued with her spirit. The rooms are a perfect period piece of Victoriana, with all their artifacts and stuffy chairs—a cozy clutter best evoked by her sitting room. Grief stricken at the death of Albert in 1861, the Queen requested that the house be kept as it was upon the death of her husband. See chapter 7.
- **Manchester:** A major inland port since 1894, Manchester long had a reputation as a blackened, foggy, and forbidding city, grim and dowdy, the worst of the

Midlands. But it's been cleaned up, and today its center is filled with masterpieces of sturdy, solid Victorian architecture, including homes built for the great industrial barons of the 19th century. See chapter 15.

- **National Railway Museum** (York): The first national museum to be built away from London is devoted to the locomotive that changed the face of Victorian England. Set in an original steam locomotive depot, the museum is filled with railway memorabilia left by the Victorians. More than 40 full-size locomotives are on display, along with the century-old Royal Saloon, in which Queen Victoria rode until her death (it's like a small hotel!). See chapter 17.

8 The Best Museums

- **The British Museum** (London): When Sir Hans Sloane died in 1753, he bequeathed to England his vast collection of art and antiquities for only £20,000 ($34,000). This formed the nucleus of the collection that would one day embrace everything from the Rosetta stone to the hotly contested Elgin marbles (Greece wants them back). It's all here—and much, much more—in one of the world's great museums. See chapter 4.
- **The National Gallery** (London): One of the world's greatest collections of Western art dazzles the eye. Every artist from Leonardo da Vinci to Rembrandt to Picasso is represented here. The gallery is especially rich in works by Renaissance artists. See chapter 4.
- **Tate Britain** (London): Two great national collections—some 10,000 works—call this gallery home. Sir Henry Tate, a sugar producer, started the nucleus of the collection with only 70 or so paintings. But the Tate has grown and grown, and was considerably enlarged when J. M. W. Turner bequeathed some 300 paintings and 19,000 watercolors to England upon his death. The Tate is also a repository of the most avant-garde modern art, with its Tate Modern directly across the river. See chapter 4.
- **The American Museum** (Claverton, 2 miles east of Bath): Housed in a neoclassical country house, this collection presents two centuries of American life and styles—including George Washington's mother's recipe for gingerbread. See chapter 8.
- **The Fitzwilliam Museum** (Cambridge): Although London dominates the museum list, there are some outstanding regional museums, including this gem near King's College. Exhibits range from paintings by Titian and Renoir to Chinese, Egyptian, and Greek antiquities. See chapter 13.
- **Walker Art Gallery** (Liverpool): One of the finest collections of European and British paintings in Britain, this gallery deserves to be better known. A nearly complete study of British paintings is displayed here, from Tudor days to the present. The gallery also owns an outstanding collection of pre-Raphaelites. See chapter 15.

9 The Best Cathedrals

- **Westminster Abbey** (London): One of the world's greatest Anglo-French Gothic buildings has witnessed a parade of English history—from the crowning of William the Conqueror on Christmas Day 1066 to the funeral of Princess Diana in 1997. With few exceptions, the kings and queens of England have all been crowned here, and many are buried here as well. See chapter 4.
- **Canterbury Cathedral:** The object of countless pilgrimages, as described in Chaucer's *Canterbury Tales,* this cathedral replaced one that was destroyed by fire

in 1067. A new cathedral, dedicated in 1130, was also destroyed by fire in 1174, when the present structure was built. Thomas à Becket, the archbishop of Canterbury, was murdered here, and his shrine was an important site for pilgrims until the Reformation. See chapter 6.

- **Winchester Cathedral:** Construction of the cathedral that dominates this ancient city and capital of old Wessex began in 1079. In time, Winchester Cathedral became England's longest medieval cathedral, noted for its 12-bay nave. Many famous people are buried here, including Jane Austen. See chapter 7.
- **Salisbury Cathedral:** The most stylistically unified of all cathedrals in England, this edifice was built between 1220 and 1265. Its landmark spire—its most striking feature—was completed in 1325. Salisbury Cathedral epitomizes the early English style of architecture. See chapter 8.
- **Durham Cathedral:** Completed between 1095 and 1133, this cathedral exemplifies Norman architecture on a broad scale. Its nave, a structure of almost majestic power, is its most notable feature. See chapter 17.
- **York Minster:** The largest Gothic cathedral north of the Alps is also among the grandest, with incredible stained-glass windows. In fact, these windows combine to create the largest single surviving collection of medieval stained glass in England. Its unusual octagonal Chapter House has a late-15th-century choir screen by William Hyndeley. See chapter 17.

10 The Best Castles, Palaces & Historic Homes

- **Woburn Abbey:** A Cistercian abbey for 4 centuries, Woburn Abbey, the seat of the dukes of Bedford, has been visited by everybody from Queen Victoria to Marilyn Monroe. You'll see Queen Victoria's bedroom, and the Canaletto room, with its 21 perspectives of Venice. The grounds, even more popular than the house, include the Wild Animal Kingdom, the best zoological collection in England after the London Zoo. See chapter 5.
- **Hatfield House** (Hertfordshire): Hatfield was the childhood home of Elizabeth I, who was under an oak tree there when she learned she had become queen of England. Hatfield remains one of England's largest and finest country houses, complete with antiques, tapestries, paintings, and even the red silk stockings Elizabeth I wore. See chapter 5.
- **Windsor Castle:** The largest inhabited stronghold in the world and England's largest castle, Windsor Castle has been a royal abode since William the Conqueror constructed a motte and bailey on the site 4 years after conquering England. Severely damaged by fire in 1992, the castle has been mainly restored. Its major attraction is the great Perpendicular Chapel of St. George's, begun by Edward IV. The chancel is known for its three-tiered stalls, which abound in misericords and ornate carvings. See chapter 5.
- **Blenheim Palace** (Woodstock): England's answer to Versailles, this extravagant baroque palace was the home of the 11th duke of Marlborough, as well as the birthplace of Sir Winston Churchill. The structure was designed by Sir John Vanbrugh, of Castle Howard fame. Sarah, the duchess of Marlborough, battled the architects and builders from the beginning, wanting "a clean sweet house and garden be it ever so small." That she didn't get—the structure measures 850 feet from end to end. Capability Brown designed the gardens. See chapter 5.
- **Knole** (Kent): Begun in 1456 by the archbishop of Canterbury, Knole is celebrated for its 365 rooms (one for each day of the year), its 52 staircases (for each

week of the year), and its 7 courts (for each day of the week). Knole, one of England's largest private houses, and set in a 1,000-acre deer park, is a splendid example of Tudor architecture. See chapter 6.

- **Penshurst Place** (Kent): One of England's most outstanding country homes, this mansion was the former residence of Elizabethan poet Sir Philip Sidney (1554–86). In its day, the house attracted literati, including Ben Jonson. The original 1346 hall has seen the subsequent addition of Tudor, Jacobean, and neo-Gothic wings. See chapter 6.
- **Hever Castle & Gardens** (Kent): This was the childhood home of Anne Boleyn, second wife of Henry VIII and mother of Queen Elizabeth I. In 1903, William Waldorf Astor, an American multimillionaire and anglophile, bought the castle, restored it, and landscaped the grounds. From the outside, it still looks like it did in Tudor times, with a moat and drawbridge protecting the castle. See chapter 6.
- **Beaulieu Abbey-Palace House** (Beaulieu, in New Forest): The home of the first Lord Montagu, Palace House blends monastic Gothic architecture from the Middle Ages with Victorian trappings. Yet many visitors consider the National Motor Museum, also on the premises and with a collection of more than 250 antique automobiles, more fascinating than the house. See chapter 7.
- **Harewood House & Bird Garden** (West Yorkshire): Edwin Lascelles began constructing this house in 1759, and his "pile" has been called an essay in Palladian architecture. The grand design involved some of the major talents of the day, including Robert Adam, Thomas Chippendale, and Capability Brown, who developed the grounds. A 4½-acre bird garden features exotic species from all over the world. See chapter 17.
- **Castle Howard** (North Yorkshire): This was Sir John Vanbrugh's grand masterpiece, and also the first building he ever designed. Many people will recognize it as the principal location for *Brideshead Revisited.* A gilt-and-painted dome tops the striking entrance, and the park around Castle Howard is one of the most grandiose in Europe. See chapter 17.

11 The Best Gardens

- **Kew Gardens** (near London): A delight in any season. Everything from delicate exotics to commonplace flowers and shrubs bloom in profusion in this 300-acre garden. It's all part of a vast lab dedicated to identifying plants from all parts of the globe, and growing some for commercial purposes. An easy trip from London, Kew Gardens possesses the largest herbarium on earth. Fabled landscape architect Capability Brown helped lay out some of the grounds. See chapter 4.
- **Wisley Garden** (Kent): Wisley Garden sprawls across 250 acres, filled with a profusion of flowers and shrubs. Maintained by the Royal Horticultural Society, it ranges from alpinelike meadows to summer carpets of flowers. In early summer, the gardens are brilliant with flowering rhododendrons. The landscaped orchid house alone is worth the trip here. See chapter 6.
- **Sissinghurst Castle Garden** (Kent): A notorious literary couple, Vita Sackville-West and Harold Nicolson, created this garden in sunny Kent. Its flamboyant parentage, unusual landscaping (the grounds were laid between the surviving parts of an Elizabethan mansion), and location just 21 miles northeast of Cranbrook make it the most intriguing garden on London's doorstep. Overrun by tourists in summer, it's lovely in autumn, when the colors are at their dramatic best. See chapter 6.

- **Stourhead** (near Shaftesbury): Outside of the Greater London area, this is the most famous garden in England. The birthplace of English landscape gardening, Stourhead is still the best-executed example of the taste for natural landscaping that swept England in the 1700s. The grounds have been compared to the painting of an old master such as Constable, but in 3-D. A wealth of flowering shrubs, trees, and beds upon beds of multihued blooms. Grottoes, bridges, and temples add to the allure. See chapter 8.
- **Hidcote Manor Garden** (near Chipping Campden, in the Cotswolds): Just outside one of the Cotswolds' most charming towns lies this stunning garden, laid out around a stone-built manor house. It's the largest garden in the Cotswolds, and one of the most intriguing in all of Britain. The garden originally bloomed under Major Lawrence Johnstone, an American horticulturist who created it in 1907. He traveled the world and brought back specimens to plant here. It shows. See chapter 11.

12 The Best Luxury Hotels

- **Brown's Hotel** (London; ☎ **020/7493-6020**): All Chippendale and chintz, Brown's was launched by the former Manservant to Lord Byron in 1837, and it's been going strong ever since. Today, it occupies 14 historic houses just off Berkeley Square, and coddles its well-heeled guests in luxury. See chapter 3.
- **The Dorchester** (London; ☎ **800/727-9820** or 020/7629-8888): Acclaimed for decades as one of the world's great hotels, this citadel of luxury is owned by one of the richest men on earth, the sultan of Brunei. With such an owner, the hotel naturally drips with opulence. After a multimillion-pound restoration, "The Dorch" is more splendid than ever. The rooftop suites are dazzling, and the Promenade, the Grill Room, the Dorchester Bar, and the Oriental Room—London's most exclusive Chinese restaurant—all deserve their acclaim. See chapter 3.
- **Chewton Glen Hotel** (New Milton, Hampshire; ☎ **01425/275341**): On the fringe of New Forest between Lymington and Bournemouth, this hotel/health-and-country club is the best place to stay in southwest England. Service, taste, and quality are its hallmarks. The health club has a stunning design, with a centerpiece swimming pool and 70 acres of manicured grounds. Guest rooms feature period furniture. And the meals served in the Marryat Room Restaurant are prepared with first-rate ingredients. See chapter 7.
- **Ston Easton Park** (near Bath; ☎ **01761/241631**): This splendid 1740 Palladian house has been massively and magnificently restored. The hotel's gardens are reason enough to stay here, but the bedrooms, with Chippendale or Hepplewhite four-poster beds, are equally worthy. Check in here for a taste of 18th-century luxury. See chapter 8.
- **Thornbury Castle** (near Bristol; ☎ **01454/281182**): Henry VIII seized this castle for a royal abode, and Mary Tudor lived here for a while. Eventually it was returned to the progeny of its original owner, the duke of Buckingham. This luxurious choice has all the elements associated with English castle living. There's even a garden for croquet. See chapter 8.
- **Gidleigh Park Hotel** (Chagford, Devon; ☎ **01647/432367**): Forty acres of grounds in the Teign valley surround a country-house hotel that is the epitome of gracious living. Every detail suggests the best of rural life: the premier antiques, those big English sofas, and floral arrangements from the hotel's gardens. All that and a reputation for fine food unequaled in the area. See chapter 9.

- **The Lygon Arms** (Broadway, Cotswolds; ☎ **01386/852255**): Dating from 1532, this fabled inn in the Cotswolds has hosted many famous guests—Charles I used to drop in, and even Oliver Cromwell spent a night here, on the eve of the Battle of Worcester. Some of the inn's antiques are listed in *The Dictionary of English Furniture.* Request one of the nine rooms in the Tudor Wing that have tilted oak floors and wooden beams. Number 20, with its massive canopied bed, is our favorite. See chapter 11.
- **Ettington Park Hotel** (Alderminster, south of Stratford-upon-Avon; ☎ **01789/450123**): From the plant-filled conservatory entrance, right up to the spacious, antique-filled bedrooms, you know you're getting something special here. The house is refurbished every year, and guests can soak up old-England country-house living in the tasteful Victorian drawing room or the richly paneled library bar. See chapter 12.
- **Sharrow Bay Country House Hotel** (Lake Ullswater, near Penrith; ☎ **017684/86301**): This gem in the Lake District is known as much for its cuisine as for its accommodations. The location alone would justify checking in: a 12-acre site, with several gardens, in a national park on bucolic Lake Ullswater, beneath Barton Fell. The lakeside dining room offers panoramic views of the water, and whether it be grilled scallops from the Kyle of Lochalsh or noisettes of English lamb, there is always something delectable on the menu here. See chapter 16.

13 The Best Moderately Priced Hotels

- **The Sanctuary House Hotel** (London; ☎ **020/7799-4044**): In a historic building close to Westminster Abbey, a brewery has converted an old building into a traditional English inn with a pub downstairs. It's like something you might find in the countryside of England, although right in the historic heart of London. The place is a bit nostalgic, just like the food served on site—all the old favorites like roast beef, Welsh lamb, and Dover sole. See chapter 3.
- **Fielding Hotel** (London; ☎ **020/7836-8305**): Named after the novelist Henry Fielding of *Tom Jones* fame, this hotel is one of the most eccentric in London. You'll either love it or hate it. Most guests love its cramped, quirky, quaint aura, and its location at Covent Garden is unbeatable. Everything is old-fashioned and traditional, but if you complain the bedrooms are too small, Smokey, the African Grey parrot, will tell you off! See chapter 3.
- **Jenkins Hotel** (London; ☎ **020/7387-2067**): Hailed by one London publication as 1 of the 10 best hotel values in town, the Jenkins was featured on the PBS *Mystery!* series *Poirot.* Those seeking a good and decent accommodation in Bloomsbury, at an affordable price, have been making their way to this address in Cartwright Gardens ever since Maggie Jenkins opened the place back in the 1920s. Rooms are small but well furnished, and some of the original Georgian charm remains. See chapter 3.
- **Collin House** (London; ☎ **020/7730-8031**): On a street of B&Bs near Victoria Station, this guest house emerges a winner. Private baths have been discreetly installed since the Victorians departed, and Collin House is a good value in high-priced London. The owners continue to improve the ambience year after year. See chapter 3.
- **Old Parsonage Hotel** (Oxford; ☎ **01865/310210**): The site dates from the 13th century, and the present building was erected in 1660. Oscar Wilde was once a guest. It's hard to find a more charming hotel with as much character in

Oxford today. Good taste, stylish comfort, fine accessories, and a clubby bar make this a winning choice. See chapter 5.

- **Howfield Manor** (west of Canterbury; ☎ **01227/738294**): This former manor house outside the cathedral city retains architectural treasures from its days as part of the Priory of St. Gregory. Bedrooms are divided between the original house and a new one. The manor is filled with character and has lots of details such as solid oak pieces and exposed beams. See chapter 6.
- **Mermaid Inn** (Rye; ☎ **01797/223065**): England's most famous smugglers' inn, the Mermaid sheltered Elizabeth I on her visit to Rye in 1573. At the time of the queen's visit, the inn had already been operating for 150 years. Still going strong, it leans heavily on English romance—old-world furnishings, some four-poster beds, and even a secret staircase. From its doorstep, the cobblestone streets of ancient Rye await exploration. See chapter 6.
- **Apsley House Hotel** (Bath; ☎ **01225/336966**): Away from the city center on the road to Bristol, this 1830 house was supposedly constructed for the duke of Wellington. Its owners have restored it and created a period house of character with an ambience of subdued elegance. See chapter 8.
- **The Rising Sun Hotel** (Lynmouth; ☎ **01598/753223**): At the mouth of the Lyn River, at the very end of a quay, this 14th-century thatched inn has uneven floors and crooked ceilings that are part of its charm. Snug, cozy, "under-the-eaves" bedrooms guarantee a good night's sleep; or you can rent Shelley's Cottage, where the poet honeymooned with his underage bride. The inn stakes out part of the river for salmon fishing. See chapter 9.
- **Bickleigh Cottage Country Hotel** (Bickleigh, Devon; ☎ **01884/855230**): This small thatched 17th-century cottage is a virtual cliché of Devonshire country charm. It has a riverside garden leading down to the much-photographed Bickleigh Bridge, where swans and ducks glide by. Inside, the cottage rooms are cozy with oak beams and old fireplaces. See chapter 9.
- **Abbey Hotel** (Penzance; ☎ **01736/366906**): Owned by Jean Shrimpton, a former international model, and her husband, Michael Cox, this small-scale hotel is charming and of high quality. Dating from 1660, it occupies the site of a 12th-century abbey overlooking Penzance Harbor. See chapter 10.
- **The Old Farmhouse Hotel** (Lower Swell; ☎ **01451/830232**): This was a working farm until the 1960s. A bar-lounge and a restaurant are in the original farmhouse, which dates from the 1500s. Some bedrooms are in converted stables, but the best rooms are in the old coach house. From here, you can rent a mountain bike and go exploring in the Cotswolds. See chapter 11.
- **Dean Court Hotel** (York; ☎ **01904/625082**): This building, dating from 1850, was originally intended to lodge the cathedral clergy of York Minster. Now this Best Western hotel lies right beneath the towers of the minster. It offers light and airy bedrooms; those at the front open onto cathedral views. See chapter 17.

14 The Best Restaurants

- **Gordon Ramsay** (London; ☎ **020/7357-4441**): The gourmet, and famous Broadway musical producer, Andrew Lloyd Webber, has proclaimed this hot, hot chef as the finest in London. Maybe that's going a bit far, but Ramsay is dazzling *tout* London with his pots and pans. Everything he does bears an innovative twist, and though he's learned from the past, he's hardly anchored there. Ramsay's restaurant is London's hot new dining destination. Try anything, but make sure you sample his "cappuccino" of white beans with grated truffles. You'll want to adopt him and take him home. See chapter 3.

- **Le Gavroche** (London; ☎ **020/7408-0881**); Long known for its top-rate French cuisine, this stellar restaurant has risen to the top again following a bit of a slump in the 90s. Go here for that grand meal and skip the trip to Paris (we don't really mean that). The menu options are a delight, with such tantalizing dishes as a cassoulet of snails with herb-seasoned frog legs. Naturally, the wine cellar is among London's finest. See chapter 3.
- **La Tante Claire** (London; ☎ **020/7823-2003**): In a swank new Knightsbridge location, Chef Pierre Koffman prepares cuisine that has been defined as one of "ravishing purity." Although it stems from French roots, this food achieves a style and quality that's rarely encountered—even in France. Koffmann manages to bring more flavor to classic Gallic dishes than one might think possible. Beautifully portioned and impeccably prepared, his legendary pig's trotters with morels is just one of his signature dishes. See chapter 3.
- **Le Manoir aux Quat' Saisons** (Great Milton, southeast of Oxford; ☎ **01844/278881**): The country-house hotel and restaurant of self-taught chef Raymond Blanc have brought him a TV series, as well as cookbooks and a school of cuisine. Although still showing intensely French loyalties, the celebrated chef now roams the world for inspiration. A new lightness, inspired mainly by Japan and the Mediterranean, is more and more evident in his creations. More meatless dishes appear on the seasonal menu, although the classics remain: sweetbread-stuffed pig's trotters, kidneys, and foie gras, even veal tongue. See chapter 5.
- **Harvey's Restaurant** (Bristol; ☎ **0117/9275034**): Chef Daniel Galmiche, who first became known while cooking in Scotland, is a formidable talent. His cuisine is French, yet like many young chefs today, he experiments with ingredients and flavors from other culinary traditions, most notably the Far East and the Mediterranean. The unusual dining room is installed in wine cellars that date from 1796, and the service is amiably informal. See chapter 8.
- **The Carved Angel** (Dartmouth; ☎ **01803/832465**): The elegant and airy Devon quayside setting is ideal for the inspired cuisine of Joyce Molyneux, doyenne of British chefs. Her imaginative and inventive technique is based on strong British tradition, but more and more, the flavors and aromas of Provence, Italy, and even Asia are appearing on the menus. A mandatory stop for foodies. See chapter 9.
- **Le Champignon Sauvage** (Cheltenham; ☎ **01242/573449**): David Everitt-Matthias has awakened the sleepy taste buds of Cheltenham. Thoroughly imbued in the French classics, he also adds more modern and lighter touches to his table d'hôte menus, the finest at this old spa. Some dishes reach into the old English repertoire, including stuffed leg of wild rabbit served with black pudding and turnip sauerkraut. His desserts are acclaimed as the most luscious in England. See chapter 11.
- **Marsh Goose** (Moreton-in-Marsh; ☎ **01608/653500**): Fans call it the Cotswolds' best-kept secret. Chef Sonya Kidney brings flair and individuality to her four-course dinner menus, with about seven or eight choices per course. All her dishes are flavorful (some evoke the Caribbean), but her roasted Cotswold lamb with eggplant and tomatoes is alone worth the trip. See chapter 11.
- **Le Talbooth** (Dedham; ☎ **01206/323150**): In Constable country, this restaurant dispenses its wares in a half-timbered Tudor building on the banks of the River Stour. In fair weather, you can dine alfresco under canvas parasols. The

English/French à la carte menu changes six times a year, and special dishes change daily, reflecting the best produce available at the market. See chapter 13.

- **Miller Howe Hotel** (Windermere; ☎ **015394/42536**): At John Tovey's Edwardian country house above Lake Windermere, the chef is renowned for his English cuisine. What makes his cooking unusual are the unexpected combinations: mashed rutabagas with cider, glazed carrots flavored with Pernod, and most definitely the cardamom ice cream. See chapter 16.

15 The Best Pubs

- **Salisbury** (London; ☎ **020/7836-5863**): Glittering cut-glass mirrors and old-fashioned banquettes, plus lighting fixtures of veiled bronze girls in flowing togas, re-create the Victorian gin-parlor atmosphere right in the heart of the West End. Theatergoers drop in for a homemade meat pie or a salad buffet before curtain time. See chapter 3.
- **Grenadier** (London; ☎ **020/7235-3074**): Arguably London's most famous pub, and reputedly haunted, the Grenadier was once frequented by the duke of Wellington's officers on leave from fighting Napoléon. It pours the best Bloody Marys in town, and fillet of beef Wellington is always a specialty. See chapter 3.
- **The Ship Inn** (Exeter; ☎ **01392/272040**): Frequented by Sir Francis Drake and Sir Walter Raleigh, this pub on St. Martin's Lane near Exeter Cathedral is the most celebrated in Devon. It still provides tankards of real ale, the same drink swilled down by the likes of Sir John Hawkins. You can also eat here; portions are large, as in Elizabethan times. See chapter 9.
- **The Cott Inn** (Dartington, near Totnes, Devon; ☎ **01803/863777**): Constructed in 1320, this is believed to be the second-oldest inn in England. It's a low, rambling two-story building of stone, cob, and plaster under a thatched roof. A gathering place for the locals of Dartington, it's a good place for a drink on a windy night, as log fires keep the lounge and bar snug. See chapter 9.
- **The Punch Bowl Inn** (Lanreath, near Looe, Cornwall; ☎ **01503/220218**): Licensed since 1620 as a pub, this was a former rendezvous for smugglers. High-backed settees and old fireplaces evoke the atmosphere of olde England. You can sample drinks in one of the kitchens—they're among the few "kitchens" in England licensed in Britain as bars. See chapter 10.
- **The Turk's Head** (Penzance, Cornwall; ☎ **01736/363093**): Dating from 1233, this durable local favorite is filled with artifacts and timeworn beams. Drinkers take their lagers into a summer garden, or retreat inside to the snug chambers when the wind blows cold. See chapter 10.
- **The Lamb Inn** (Burford; ☎ **01993/823155**): This is our favorite place for a lager in all the Cotswolds. In a mellow old house from 1430 with thick stones and mullioned and leaded windows, it's a good place to spend the night, have a traditional English meal, or else a beer. Snacks are served in the timeworn bars and lounges or in a garden in summer. See chapter 11.
- **The Black Swan** (Stratford-upon-Avon; ☎ **01789/297312**): This has been a popular hangout for Stratford players since the 18th century, and over the years we've spotted everybody from Peter O'Toole to Lord Laurence Olivier here having a drink. Locals affectionately call it "The Dirty Duck." In cool weather, an open fireplace blazes, and you can stick around if you wish and order the chef's specialty: honey-roasted duck. See chapter 12.

Planning Your Trip: The Basics

2

In the pages that follow, we'll outline the various regions of England, and explain their individual appeal to visitors. You'll also find everything you need to know about the practicalities of planning your trip in advance: finding the best airfare, deciding when to go, figuring out British currency, and more.

1 The Regions in Brief

England is a part of the United Kingdom, which is made up of England, Wales, Scotland, and Northern Ireland. Only 50,327 square miles—about the same size as New York State—England has an amazing amount of rural land and natural wilderness and an astonishing regional, physical, and cultural diversity. For a map outlining the regions of England described below, see the map on page 5 in chapter 1.

London Some 7 million Londoners live in this mammoth metropolis, a parcel of land that's more than 609 square miles. The City of London proper is merely 1 square mile, but the rest of the city is made up of separate villages, boroughs, and corporations. London's neighborhoods and outlying areas are described in chapter 3.

The Thames Valley England's most famous river runs westward from Kew to its source in the Cotswolds. A land of meadows, woodlands, attractive villages, small market towns, and rolling hillsides, this is one of England's most scenic areas. Highlights include **Windsor Castle** (Elizabeth II's favorite residence) and nearby **Eton College,** founded by a young Henry VI in 1440. **Henley,** site of the Royal Regatta, remains our favorite Thames-side town; and at the university city of **Oxford,** you can tour the colleges.

The Southeast (Kent, Surrey & Sussex) This is the land of Charles Lamb, Virginia Woolf, Sir Winston Churchill, and Henry James. Here are some of the nation's biggest attractions: **Brighton, Canterbury, Dover,** and dozens of country homes and castles—not only **Hever** and **Leeds castles,** but also **Chartwell,** the more modest abode where Churchill lived. In small villages, such as Rye and Winchelsea in Sussex, and in interesting towns like Haslemere, you discover the charm of the southeast. Almost all of the Sussex shoreline is built up, and seaside towns, such as Eastbourne and Hastings, are often tacky. In fact, although the area's major attraction is **Canterbury Cathedral,** the

Royal Pavilion at Brighton rates as an outstanding, extravagant folly. Tea shops, antiques shops, pubs, and small inns abound in the area. Surrey is essentially a commuter suburb of London and is easily reached for day trips.

Hampshire & Wiltshire Southwest of London, these two counties possess two of England's greatest **cathedrals** (Winchester and Salisbury) and one of Europe's most significant prehistoric monuments, **Stonehenge.** But there are other reasons for visiting, too. Hampshire is bordered on its western side by the woodlands and heaths of **New Forest. Portsmouth and Southampton** loom large in naval heritage. You might also want to take a ferry over to the **Isle of Wight,** once Queen Victoria's preferred vacation retreat. In Wiltshire, you encounter the beginning of the **West Country,** with its scenic beauty and monuments—Wilton House, the 17th-century home of the earls of Pembroke, and Old Sarum, the remains of what is believed to have been an Iron Age fortification.

The Southwest (Dorset, Somerset, Devon & Cornwall) These four counties are the great vacation centers and retirement havens of England. Dorset, associated with Thomas Hardy, is a land of rolling downs, rocky headlands, well-kept villages, and rich farmlands. Somerset—the Somerset of King Arthur and Camelot—offers such magical towns as **Glastonbury.** Devon has both **Exmoor and Dartmoor,** and northern and southern coastlines peppered with such famous resorts as Lyme Regis, and such villages as Clovelly. In Cornwall, you're never more than 20 miles from the rugged coastline, which ends at **Land's End.** Among the cities worth visiting in these counties are **Bath,** with its impressive Roman baths and Georgian architecture; **Plymouth,** departure point of the Mayflower; and **Wells,** site of a great cathedral.

The Cotswolds A wonderful region to tour, this is a bucolic land of honey-colored limestone villages where rural England unfolds before you like a storybook. In the Middle Ages, wool made the Cotswolders prosperous, but now they put out the welcome mat for visitors, with famously lovely inns and pubs. Start at Burford, the traditional gateway to the region, and continue on to Bourton-on-the-Water, Lower and Upper Slaughter, Stow-on-the-Wold, Moreton-in-Marsh, Chipping Campden, and Broadway. Cirencester is the uncrowned capital of the south Cotswolds, and Cheltenham is a still-elegant Regency spa. Our two favorite villages are Painswick, with its minute cottages, and Bibury, with its cluster of former weavers' cottages, Arlington Row.

Stratford & Warwick This is Shakespeare country in the Midlands, which was the birthplace of the Industrial Revolution, which made Britain the first industrialized country in the world. Its foremost tourist town is **Stratford-upon-Avon,** but also drawing visitors are **Warwick Castle,** one of England's great castles, and the ruins of **Kenilworth Castle. Coventry,** heavily bombed in World War II, is visited mainly for its outstanding modern cathedral.

Birmingham & the West Midlands The area known as the West Midlands embraces the so-called "Black Country." **Birmingham,** nicknamed "Brum," is Britain's largest city after London. The sprawling metropolis is still characterized by its overpass jungles and tacky suburbs, as well as its great piles of Victorian architecture. Urban renewal is underway. The English marshes cut through the old counties of **Shropshire** and **Herefordshire.** Ironbridge Gorge was at the heart of the Industrial Revolution, and the famous **Potteries** are in Staffordshire.

East Anglia (Essex, Cambridgeshire, Norfolk & Suffolk) East Anglia, a semicircular geographic bulge northeast of London, is the name applied to these four very flat counties. The land of John Constable is still filled with his landscapes. The Fens that broad expanse of fertile, black soil lying north of Cambridge remains our favorite district. Go there to see **Ely Cathedral. Cambridge,** with its colleges and river, is the chief attraction. The most important museum is the Fitzwilliam in Cambridge, but visitors also flock to East Anglia for the scenery and its solitary beauty fens and salt marshes and villages of thatched cottages.

The East Midlands (Derbyshire, Leicestershire, Lincolnshire, Northamptonshire & Nottinghamshire) This area encompasses some of the worst of industrial England, yet there is great natural beauty to be found, too, as well as stately homes. These include Chatsworth in Derbyshire, the seat of the dukes of Devonshire; Sulgrave Manor in Northamptonshire, the ancestral home of George Washington; and Althorp House, also in Northamptonshire, the childhood home of Diana, Princess of Wales. **Lincoln** has one of England's great cathedrals, rebuilt in the 13th and 14th centuries. Bostonians like to visit their namesake, the old seaport town of Boston. **Nottingham** recalls Robin Hood, although the deforested Sherwood Forest is obviously not what it was in the outlaw's heyday.

The Northwest Stretching from Liverpool to the Scottish border, northwest England can be a bucolic delight if you steer clear of its industrial pockets. Most people come here to follow in the footsteps of such romantic poets as Wordsworth, who wrote of the beauty of the Lake District (see below). But **Chester, Manchester,** and **Liverpool** merit stopovers along the way. The resort of **Blackpool** is big, brash, and a bit tawdry, drawing the working class of the Midlands for Coney Island–style fun by the sea. In contrast, the Roman city of Chester is a well-preserved medieval town, known for its encircling wall. And Liverpool is culturally alive and always intriguing, if only to see where the Beatles came from, but it also has a branch of London's Tate Gallery.

The Lake District The literary Lakeland evokes memories of the Wordsworths, Samuel Taylor Coleridge, John Ruskin, and Beatrix Potter, among others. **Windermere** makes the best center, but there are many others as well, including **Grasmere** and **Ambleside.** The Lake District contains some of England's most dramatic scenery.

Yorkshire & Northumbria Yorkshire will be familiar to fans of the Brontës and James Herriot. **York,** with its immense cathedral and medieval streets, is the city to visit, although more and more visitors are calling on the cities of **Leeds** and **Bradford.** Northumbria comprises **Northumberland, Cleveland, Durham,** and **Tyne** and **Wear** (the area around **Newcastle**). The whole area echoes the ancient border battles between the Scots and English. **Hadrian's Wall,** built by the Romans, is a highlight. The great cathedral at Durham is one of Britain's finest examples of Norman church architecture, and **Fountains Abbey** is among the country's greatest ecclesiastical ruins. Country homes abound; here you find **Harewood House** and **Castle Howard.**

2 Visitor Information

Before you go, you can obtain general information from **British Tourist Authority Offices:**

- In the United States: 551 Fifth Ave., Suite 701, New York, NY 10176-0799 (☎ **800/462-2748** or 212/986-2200).
- In Canada: 111 Avenue Rd., Suite 450, Toronto, ON M5R 3J8 (☎ **888/VISIT-UK** in Canada).

- In Australia: Level 16, Gateway, 1 Macquarie Place, Sydney NSW 2000 (☎ **02/9377-4400**).
- In New Zealand: Suite 305, Dilworth Building, at the corner of Queen and Customs streets, Auckland 1 (☎ **09/303-1446**).

The BTA also maintains a Web site at www.visitbritain.com, covering special interests, attractions, trip-planning tips, festivals, accommodations, and more.

For a full information pack on London, write to the **London Tourist Board,** Glen House, Victoria, Stag Place, London SW1E 5LT (☎ **020/7932-2000**). You can also call the recorded-message service, **Visitorcall** (☎ **01839/123456**), 24 hours a day. Various topics are listed; calls cost 60p ($1) per minute.

You can usually pick up a copy of ***Time Out,*** the most up-to-date source for what's happening in London, at any international newsstand. You can also check it out online at www.timeout.co.uk.

3 Entry Requirements & Customs

ENTRY REQUIREMENTS

All U.S. citizens, Canadians, Australians, New Zealanders, and South Africans must have a passport with at least 2 months validity remaining. No visa is required. The immigration officer will also want proof of your intention to return to your point of origin (usually a round-trip ticket) and visible means of support while you're in Britain. If you're planning to fly from the United States or Canada to the United Kingdom and then on to a country that requires a visa (India, for example), you should secure that visa before you arrive in Britain.

Your valid driver's license and at least one year of driving experience is required to drive personal or rented cars.

CUSTOMS

For **visitors coming to England,** goods fall into two basic categories: purchases made in a nonEuropean Union (EU) country (or bought tax-free within the EU), and purchases on which tax was paid in the European Union. In the former category, limits on imports by individuals (aged 17 and older) include 200 cigarettes, 50 cigars, or 250 grams (8.8 oz.) of loose tobacco; 2 liters (2.1 qt.) of still table wine, 1 liter of liquor (over 22% alcohol content), or 2 liters of liquor (under 22%); and 2 fluid ounces of perfume. In the latter category—items on which tax was paid in the EU—limits are much higher: An individual may import 800 cigarettes, 200 cigars, and 1 kilogram (2.2 lb.) of loose tobacco; 90 liters (23.8 gal.) of wine, 10 liters (2.6 gal.) of alcohol (over 22%), and 110 liters (29.1 gal.) of beer; plus unlimited amounts of perfume.

Returning **U.S. citizens** who have been away for 48 hours or more are allowed to bring back, once every 30 days, $400 worth of merchandise duty-free. You'll be charged a flat rate of 10% duty on the next $1,000 worth of purchases. Be sure to have your receipts handy. On gifts, the duty-free limit is $100. You cannot bring fresh foodstuffs into the United States; tinned foods, however, are allowed. For more information, contact the **U.S. Customs Service,** 1301 Constitution Ave. (P.O. Box 7407), Washington, DC 20044 (☎ **202/927-6724;** www.customs.ustreas.gov) and request the free pamphlet *Know Before You Go.*

For a clear summary of **Canadian** rules, write for the booklet *I Declare,* issued by **Revenue Canada,** 2265 St. Laurent Blvd., Ottawa K1G 4KE (☎ **613/993-0534**). Canada allows its citizens a $750 exemption, and you're allowed to bring back duty-free 200 cigarettes, 1 kilogram of tobacco, 1.5 liters of liquor, and 50 cigars. In addition, you're allowed to mail gifts to Canada from abroad at the rate of Can$60 a day, provided they're unsolicited and don't contain alcohol or tobacco (write on the package "Unsolicited gift, under $60 value"). All valuables should be declared on the Y-38 form before departure from Canada, including serial numbers of valuables you already own, such as expensive foreign cameras. *Note:* The $750 exemption can only be used once a year and only after an absence of 7 days.

The duty-free allowance in **Australia** is A$400 or, for those under 18, A$200. Personal property mailed back from England should be marked "Australian goods returned" to avoid payment of duty. Upon returning to Australia, citizens can bring in 250 cigarettes or 250 grams of loose tobacco, and 1,125 milliliters of alcohol. If you're returning with valuable goods you already own, such as foreign-made cameras, you should file form B263. A helpful brochure, available from Australian consulates or Customs offices, is *Know Before You Go.* For more information, contact **Australian Customs Services,** GPO Box 8, Sydney NSW 2001 (☎ **02/9213-2000**).

The duty-free allowance for **New Zealand** is NZ$700. Citizens over 17 can bring in 200 cigarettes, or 50 cigars, or 250 grams of tobacco (or a mixture of all three if their combined weight doesn't exceed 250 grams); plus 4.5 liters of wine and beer, or 1.125 liters of liquor. New Zealand currency does not carry import or export restrictions. Fill out a certificate of export, listing the valuables you are taking out of the country; that way, you can bring them back without paying duty. Most questions are answered in a free pamphlet available at New Zealand consulates and Customs offices: *New Zealand Customs Guide for Travelers,* Notice no. 4. For more information, contact **New Zealand Customs,** 50 Anzac Ave., P.O. Box 29, Auckland (☎ **09/359-6655**).

4 Money

The British currency is the pound sterling (£), made up of 100 pence (p), which is used throughout the United Kingdom. Notes are issued in £5, £10, £20, and £50 denominations. (A £1 note also circulates in Scotland.) Coins come in 1p, 2p, 5p, 10p, 50p, and £1.

At this writing, the price conversions in this book have been computed at the rate of $1 equals an average 61p (or £1 = $1.70). Bear in mind, however, that exchange rates can always fluctuate for a variety of reasons, so it's important to check the latest quotes before your trip so you can budget accordingly.

For the moment at least, Britain has decided not to join "Euroland," and the traditional British pound sterling is the coin of the realm. The euro, of course, is the new single European currency that officially became the currency of 11 European countries, including France, Italy, and Germany, on January 1, 1999. Euro cash will not be introduced, and the local currencies not fully replaced, however, until the year 2002.

ATMS

The ATM networks that are most widely accessible in England are **Cirrus** (☎ **800/424-7787;** www.mastercard.com/atm/) and **Plus** (☎ **800/843-7587;** www.visa.com/atms); check the back of your ATM card to see which network your bank belongs to.

Call the 800 numbers above to locate ATMs in your destination, or ask your bank for a list of overseas ATMs. Be sure to check the daily withdrawal limit before you depart, and ask whether you need a new PIN (personal ID number), since ATMs in Europe usually require a 4-digit number. Keep in mind that international withdrawal fees tend to be higher in Europe than they are in the United States, and that you'll get your money in local currency (sometimes at a very good exchange rate).

TRAVELER'S CHECKS

Traveler's checks are something of an anachronism from the days before the ATM made cash accessible at any time. These days, traveler's checks seem less necessary, but you may still prefer the security of knowing you can get a refund if your wallet is lost or stolen. (Keep a record of their serial numbers—separate from the checks, of course—so you're ensured a refund in just such an emergency.)

You can get traveler's checks at almost any bank. **American Express** offers denominations of $10, $20, $50, $100, $500, and $1,000. You'll pay a service charge ranging from 1% to 4%. You can also get American Express traveler's checks over the phone by calling ☎ **800/221-7282;** by using this number, Amex gold and platinum cardholders are exempt from the 1% fee. AAA members can obtain checks without a fee at most AAA offices.

Visa offers traveler's checks at Citibank locations nationwide, as well as several other banks. The service charge ranges between 1.5% and 2%; checks come in denominations of $20, $50, $100, $500, and $1,000. **MasterCard** also offers traveler's checks. Call ☎ **800/223-9920** for a location near you.

CREDIT CARDS

Credit cards are invaluable when traveling. They are a safe way to carry money and provide a convenient record of all your expenses. You can also withdraw cash advances from your credit cards at any bank (though you'll start paying hefty interest on the advance the moment you receive the cash, and you won't receive frequent-flyer miles on an airline credit card). At most banks, you don't even need to go to a teller; you can get a cash advance at the ATM if you know your PIN number.

Almost every credit card company has an emergency 800-number that you can call if your card is stolen. They may be able to wire you a cash advance off your credit card immediately, and in many places, they can deliver an emergency credit card in a day or two. The U.S. emergency number for **Citicorp Visa** is ☎ **800/336-8472.** American Express cardholders and traveler's check holders should call ☎ **800/221-7282** for all money emergencies. MasterCard holders should call ☎ **800/307-7309.**

EXCHANGING YOUR MONEY

It's always wise to exchange enough money before you leave home to get you from the airport to your hotel. This way, you avoid delays and the lousy rates at the airport exchange booths. When exchanging money, you're likely to get a better rate for traveler's checks than for cash.

London banks generally offer the best rates of exchange; they're usually open Monday to Friday from 9:30am to 3:30pm. Many of the "high street" branches are now open until 5pm; a handful of Central London branches are open until noon on Saturday, including **Barclays,** 208 Kensington High St., W8 (☎ **020/7441-3200**).

The U.S. Dollar & the British Pound

U.S.$	UK £	U.S.$	UK £
0.25	0.15	15	8.85
0.50	0.30	20	11.80
0.75	0.44	25	14.75
1.00	0.59	50	29.50
2.00	1.18	75	44.25
3.00	1.77	100	59.00
4.00	2.36	150	88.50
5.00	2.95	200	118.00
6.00	3.54	250	147.50
7.00	4.13	300	177.00
8.00	4.72	350	206.50
9.00	5.31	400	236.00
10.00	5.90	500	295.00

Money exchange is now also available at competitive rates at major London post offices, with a 1% service charge. Money can be exchanged during off-hours at a variety of bureaux de change throughout the city, found at small shops and in hotels, railway stations (including the international terminal at Waterloo Station), travel agencies, and airports, but their exchange rates are poorer and they charge high service fees. Examine the prices and rates carefully before handing over your dollars, as there's no consumer organization to regulate the activities of privately run bureaux de change.

Time Out recently did a survey of various exchange facilities, and American Express came out on top, with the lowest commission charged on dollar transactions. **American Express** is at 6 Haymarket, SW1 (☎ **800/221-7282** or 020/7484-9600), and other locations throughout the city. American Express charges no commission when cashing travelers checks; however, a flat rate of £2 ($3.30) is charged when exchanging the dollar to the pound. Most other agencies tend to charge a percentage rate commission (usually 2%) with a £2 to £3 ($3.30 to $4.95) minimum charge.

Other reputable firms are **Thomas Cook,** 6 Mount St., W1 (☎ **800/223-7373** or 020/7707-4501), with branches at Victoria Station, Marble Arch, and other city locations; and, for 24-hour foreign exchange, **Chequepoint,** at 548 Oxford Street, W1N 9HJ (☎ **020/7723-1005**), and other locations throughout London (hours will vary). Try not to change money at your hotel; the rates they offer tend to be horrendous.

5 When to Go

THE WEATHER

Yes, it rains, but you'll rarely get a true downpour. It's heaviest in November (2½ inches on average). British temperatures can range from 30° to 110°F but they rarely drop below 35° or go above 78°F. Evenings are cool, even in summer. Note that the British, who consider chilliness wholesome, like to keep the thermostats about 10° below the American comfort level. Hotels have central heating, but are usually kept just above the goose bump (in Brit-speak, "goose pimple") margin.

London's Average Daytime Temperature & Monthly Rainfall (inches)

	Jan	Feb	Mar	Apr	May	June	July	Aug	Sept	Oct	Nov	Dec
Temp. °F	40	40	44	49	55	61	64	64	59	52	46	42
Temp. °C	4	4	7	9	13	16	16	18	15	11	8	6
Rainfall	2.1	1.6	1.5	1.5	1.8	1.8	2.2	2.3	1.9	2.2	2.5	1.9

WHEN YOU'LL FIND BARGAINS

The cheapest time to travel to England is in the off-season: that means November 1 to December 12 and December 25 to March 14. In the last few years, the airlines have been offering irresistible fares during these periods. Weekday flights are cheaper than weekend fares (often by 10% or more).

Rates generally increase between March 14 to June 5 and in October, then hit their peak in the high travel seasons between June 6 and September 30 and December 13 and 24. July and August are also the months when most Britons take their holidays, so besides the higher prices, you'll have to deal with limited availability of accommodations and crowds.

You can avoid crowds by planning trips for November or January through March. Sure, it may be rainy and cold—but England doesn't shut down when the tourists leave! In fact, the winter season includes some of London's best theater, opera, ballet, and classical music offerings, and gives visitors a more honest view of English life. Additionally, many hotel prices drop by 20%, and cheaper accommodations offer weekly rates (unheard of during peak travel times). By arriving after the winter holidays, you can also take advantage of post-Christmas sales to buy your fill of woolens, china, crystal, silver, fashion clothing, handicrafts, and curios.

In short, spring offers the countryside at its greenest; autumn brings the bright colors of the northern moorlands, and summer's warmer weather gives rise to the many outdoor music and theater festivals. But winter offers savings across the board and a chance to see Britons going about their everyday lives largely unhindered by tourist invasions.

HOLIDAYS

England observes New Year's Day, Good Friday, Easter Monday, May Day (1st Monday in May), spring and summer bank holidays (the last Monday in May and August, respectively), Christmas Day, and Boxing Day (December 26).

England Calendar of Events

January

- **London International Boat Show.** Europe's largest boat show, held at the Earl's Court Exhibition Centre, Warwick Road. Call ☎ **01784/473377** for details. January 4 to 14.
- **Charles I Commemoration,** London. To mark the anniversary of the execution of King Charles I "in the name of freedom and democracy," hundreds of cavaliers march through central London in 17th-century dress, and prayers are said at Whitehall's Banqueting House. Last Sunday in January. Call ☎ **020/8781-9500.**

- **Chinese New Year,** London. The famous Lion Dancers in Soho perform free on the nearest Sunday to Chinese New Year. Either in late January or early February (based on the lunar calendar).

February

- **Jorvik Festival,** York. This 2-week festival celebrates this historic cathedral city's role as a Viking outpost. For more information, call ☎ **01904/621756.**

March

✪ **Crufts Dog Show,** Birmingham. The English, they say, love their pets more than their offspring. Crufts offers an opportunity to observe the nation's pet lovers doting on 8,000 dogs, representing 150 breeds. It's held at the National Exhibition Centre, Birmingham, West Midlands. Tickets can be purchased at the door. For more information, call ☎ **0121/780-4141.**

April

- **Martell Grand National Meeting,** outside Liverpool. England's premier steeplechase event takes place over a 4-mile course at **Aintree Racecourse,** Aintree (☎ **0151/5232600**). April 8.
- **London Marathon.** More than 30,000 competitors run from Greenwich Park to Buckingham Palace; call ☎ **0161/7620-4117** for information. If you'd like to take the challenge, call from May to June for an application. Mid-April.
- **Easter Parade,** London. A memorable parade of brightly colored floats and marching bands around Battersea Park.

✪ **The Shakespeare Season,** Stratford-upon-Avon. The Royal Shakespeare Company begins its annual season, presenting works by the Bard in his hometown, at the **Royal Shakespeare Theatre,** Waterside (☎ **01789/295623**). Tickets are available at the box office, or through such agents as **Keith Prowse** (☎ **800/669-8687**). April to January.

May

- **Brighton Festival.** England's largest arts festival, with some 400 different cultural events. For information, write the Brighton Tourist Information Centre (☎ **01273/292599**), 10 Bartholomew Sq., Sussex IJS 1EL. Most of May.
- **Royal Windsor Horse Show.** The country's major show-jumping presentation, held at the Home Park, Windsor, Berkshire, is attended by the queen herself. Call ☎ **01298/72272** for more information. Mid-May.

✪ **Glyndebourne Festival.** One of England's major cultural events, this festival is centered at the 1,200-seat Glyndebourne Opera House in Sussex, some 54 miles south of London. Tickets, which cost anywhere from £10 to £124 ($17 to $210.80), are available from **Glyndebourne Festival Opera Box Office,** Lewes, East Sussex BN8 5UU (☎ **01273/812321**). Mid-May to late August.

✪ **Bath International Music Festival.** One of Europe's most prestigious international festivals of music and the arts features as many as 1,000 performers at various venues in Bath. For information, contact the **Bath Festivals Trust,** 2 Midland Bridge Rd., Bath, Somerset BA2 3EQ (☎ **01225/463362**). May 19 to June 4.

- **Shakespeare Under the Stars.** The Bard's works are performed at the **Open Air Theatre,** Inner Circle, Regent's Park, NW1, in London. Take the tube to Baker Street. Performances are Monday to Saturday at 8pm;

Wednesday, Thursday, and Saturday also at 2:30pm. Call ☎ **020/7486-2431** for more information. Previews begin in late May and last throughout the summer.

- **Chelsea Flower Show,** London. The best of British gardening, with plants and flowers of the season, is displayed at the Chelsea Royal Hospital. Contact the local British Tourist Authority Office to find out which overseas reservations agency is handling ticket sales, or contact the **Chelsea Show Ticket Office,** Shows Department, Royal Horticultural Society, Vincent Square, London SW1P 2PE (☎ **020/7630-7422**). Tickets are also available through **London Ticketmaster** (☎ **020/7344-4343**). Late May.
- **Royal Academy's Summer Exhibition,** London. This institution, founded in 1768, has for some two centuries held Summer Exhibitions of living painters at Burlington House, Piccadilly Circus. Call ☎ **020/7439-7438** for more information. May 29 to August 4.
- **Chichester Festival Theatre.** Some great classic and modern plays are presented at this West Sussex theater. For tickets and information, contact the **Festival Theatre,** Oaklands Park, West Sussex PO19 4AP (☎ **01243/781312**). The season runs May to October.

June

- **Vodafone Derby Stakes.** This famous horse-racing event (the "Darby," as it's called here) is held at Epsom Downs, Epsom, Surrey. Men wear top hats and women, including the queen, put on silly millinery creations. For more details, call ☎ **01372/463072.** First week of June.
- ✪ **Trooping the Colour.** This is the queen's official birthday parade, a quintessential British event, with exquisite pageantry and pomp as she inspects her regiments and takes their salute as they parade their colors before her at the Horse Guards Parade, Whitehall. Tickets for the parade and two reviews, held on preceding Saturdays, are allocated by ballot. Applicants must write between January 1 and the end of February, enclosing a self-addressed stamped envelope or International Reply Coupon to the Ticket Office, HQ Household Division, Horse Guards, Whitehall, London SW1X 6AA. Exact dates and ticket prices will be supplied later. The ballot is held in mid-March, and only successful applicants are informed in April. Held on a day designated in June (not necessarily the queen's actual birthday). Call ☎ **020/7414-2497.**
- **Grosvenor House Art and Antique Fair,** London. This very prestigious antique fair is held at Grosvenor House, Park Lane. For information, contact Grosvenor House Art and Antiques Fair, Grosvenor House, 86–90 Park Lane, London W1A 3AA (☎ **020/7499-6363**). Ten days in mid-June.
- **Aldeburgh Festival of Music and the Arts.** The composer Benjamin Britten launched this festival in 1948. For more details on the events, and for the year-round program, write to **Aldeburgh Foundation,** High Street, Aldeburgh, Suffolk IP15 5AX (☎ **01728/452935**). Two weeks from mid- to late June.
- **Royal Ascot Week.** Although Ascot Racecourse is open year-round for guided tours, events, exhibitions, and conferences, there are 24 race days throughout the year, with the feature races being the Royal Meeting in June, Diamond Day in late July, and the Festival at Ascot in late September. For information, contact **Ascot Racecourse,** Ascot, Berkshire SL5 7JN (☎ **01344/622211**).

- **The Exeter Festival.** The town of Exeter hosts more than 150 events celebrating classical music, ranging from concerts and opera to lectures. Festival dates and offerings vary from year to year, and more information is available by contacting the Exeter Festival Office at ☎ **01392/265200;** www.exetergov.uk. June 13 to July 16.
- ✪ **Lawn Tennis Championships,** Wimbledon. Ever since players took to the grass courts at Wimbledon in 1877, this tournament has attracted quite a crowd, and there's still an excited hush at Centre Court and a certain thrill associated with being there. Savor the strawberries and cream that are part of the experience.

  Acquiring tickets and overnight lodgings during the annual tennis competitions at Wimbledon can be difficult to arrange independently. Two outfits that can book both hotel accommodations and tickets to the event include **Steve Furgal's International Tennis Tours,** 11828 Rancho Bernardo Rd., San Diego, CA 92128 (☎ **800/258-3664**), and **Championship Tennis Tours,** 8040 E. Morgan Trail, no. 12, Scottsdale, AZ 85258 (☎ **800/468-3664**). Early bookings for the world's most famous tennis tournament are strongly advised. Tickets for Centre and Number One courts are obtainable through a lottery. Write in from August to December to **A.E.L.T.C.,** P.O. Box 98, Church Road, Wimbledon, London SW19 5AE (☎ **020/8946-2244**). Outside court tickets are available daily, but be prepared to wait in line. Late June through early July.
- ✪ **City of London Festival.** This annual art festival is held in venues throughout the city. Call ☎ **020/7377-0540** for information. June and July.
- **Henley Royal Regatta,** Henley, in Oxfordshire. This international rowing competition is the premier event on the English social calendar. For more information, call ☎ **01491/578034.** Late June to early July.
- **Ludlow Festival.** This is one of England's major arts festivals, complete with an open-air Shakespeare performance within the Inner Bailey of Ludlow Castle. Concerts, lectures, readings, exhibitions, and workshops round out the offerings. From March onward, a schedule can be obtained from the box office. Write to The Ludlow Festival box office, Castle Square, Ludlow, Shropshire SY8 1AY, enclosing a self-addressed stamped envelope, or call ☎ **01584/872150.** The box office is open daily beginning in early May. June 24 to July 9.

July

- **Kenwood Lakeside Concerts.** These annual concerts on the north side of Hampstead Heath have continued a British tradition of outdoor performances for nearly 50 years. Fireworks displays and laser shows enliven the premier musical performances. The audience catches the music as it drifts across the lake from the performance shell. Concerts are held every Saturday from early July to early September. For more information call ☎ **020/8348-1286.**
- **Royal Tournament,** London. In July, Britain's armed forces put on dazzling displays of athletic and military skills at the Earl's Court Exhibition Centre, SW5. For information about performance times and tickets, call ☎ **020/7373-8141.**
- **The Proms,** London. A night at "The Proms"—the annual Henry Wood promenade concerts at Royal Albert Hall—attracts music aficionados from around the world. Staged almost daily (except for a few Sundays),

these traditional concerts were launched in 1895, and are the principal summer engagements for the BBC Symphony Orchestra. Cheering and clapping, Union Jacks on parade, banners and balloons—it's great summer fun. Mid-July through mid-September. Call ☎ **020/7589-3203.**

August

- **Cowes Week,** off the Isle of Wight. This yachting festival takes place in early August. For details, call ☎ **01983/291914.**
- **Notting Hill Carnival,** Ladbroke Grove, London. One of the largest annual street festivals in Europe, attracting more than half a million people. There's live reggae and soul music plus great Caribbean food. Two days in late August. Call ☎ **020/8964-0544** for information.

✪ **International Beatles Week,** Liverpool. Tens of thousands of fans gather in Liverpool to celebrate the music of the Fab Four. There's a whole series of concerts from international cover bands, plus tributes, auctions, and tours. **Cavern City Tours,** a local company, offers hotel and festival packages that include accommodations and tickets to tours and events, starting around £75 ($127.50) for two nights. For information, contact Cavern City Tours at ☎ **0151/2369091** or the Tourist Information Centre in Liverpool at ☎ **0151/7098111.** August 24 to 29.

- **Burghley Horse Trials,** Lincolnshire. This annual event is staged on the grounds of the largest Elizabethan house in England, Burghley House, Stamford, Lincolnshire (☎ **01780/752131**). August 31 to September 3.

September

- **Raising of the Thames Barrier,** Unity Way, SE18. Once a year, usually in September, a full test is done on this miracle of modern engineering; all 10 of the massive steel gates are raised against the low and high tides. Call ☎ **020/8854-1373** for exact date and time.
- **Horse of the Year Show,** Wembley Arena, Wembley. Riders fly from every continent to join in this festive display of horsemanship (much appreciated by the queen). The British press calls it an "equine extravaganza." It's held at Wembley Arena, outside London. For more information, call ☎ **020/8902-8833.** Late September to early October.

October

- **Cheltenham Festival of Literature.** This Cotswold event features readings, book exhibitions, and theatrical performances—all in the famed spa town of Gloucestershire. Call ☎ **01242/522878** for more details, or 01242/237377 to receive mailings about the event. Early to mid-October.

✪ **Opening of Parliament,** London. Ever since the 17th century, when the English beheaded Charles I, British monarchs have been denied the right to enter the House of Commons. Instead, the monarch opens Parliament in the House of Lords, reading an official speech that is in fact written by the government. Queen Elizabeth II rides from Buckingham Palace to Westminster in a royal coach accompanied by the Yeoman of the Guard and the Household Cavalry. The public galleries are open on a first-come, first-served basis. First Monday in October.

- **Quit Rents Ceremony,** London. At the Royal Courts of Justice, the Queen's Remembrancer receives token rents on behalf of the queen. The ceremony includes splitting sticks and counting horseshoes. Call ☎ **020/7936-6131** for more information. Late October.

- **London-Brighton Veteran Car Run.** This race begins in London's Hyde Park and ends in the seaside resort of Brighton, in East Sussex. Call ☎ **01580/893413** for more details. First Sunday in November.
- **Guy Fawkes Night,** throughout England. This British celebration commemorates the anniversary of the "Gunpowder Plot," an attempt to blow up King James I and parliament. Huge organized bonfires are lit throughout London, and Guy Fawkes, the plot's most famous conspirator, is burned in effigy. Check *Time Out* for locations. Early November.
- ✪ **Lord Mayor's Procession and Show,** The City, London. The queen has to ask permission to enter the square mile in London called the City—and the right of refusal has been jealously guarded by London merchants since the 17th century. Suffice to say that the lord mayor is a powerful character, and the procession from the Guildhall to the Royal Courts is appropriately impressive. You can watch the procession from the street; the banquet is by invitation only. Second week in November. Call ☎ **020/7606-3030.**

6 Special-Interest Vacations

BIKE TRIPS

If you're planning a bike trip on your own, you can take your two wheels on passenger trains in England if you pay a £3 ($5.10) extra charge. At the millennium Brits have rediscovered the bicycle, and by 2005 a National Cycle Network will cover 8,000 miles throughout the country. The network will run from Dover in southeast England to Inverness in the Highlands. Some 3,500 miles—known as the Millennium Route—opened in the summer of 2000.

Most routes cross old railway lines, canal towpaths, and riversides. Among the more popular routes are the Sea-to-Sea cycle Route, a 140-mile path linking the Irish Sea with the North Sea across the Pennine Hills and into the north Lake District and the Durham Dales. The Essex Cycle Route covers 250 miles of countryside, going through some of the England's most charming villages; the Devon Coast-to-Coat route runs for 90 miles in southwest England, skirting the edge of Dartmoor; the West Country Way for 248 miles links the Cornish coast to the cities of Bath and Britain, and the Severn and Thames route for 100 miles links two of Britain's major rivers.

For a free copy of "Britain for Cyclists," with information on these routes, call the British Tourist Authority at **800/462-2748** or contact the Cyclists Touring Club (see below).

The **Cyclists Touring Club,** Cotterell House, 69 Meadrow, Godalming, Surrey GU7 3HS (☎ **01483/417217**), can suggest routes and provide information. Memberships cost £25 ($42.50) a year for adults, £15 ($25.50) for those 26 and under. A family (three or more members) membership costs £40 ($68).

Himalayan Travel, 110 Prospect St., Stamford, CT 06901 (☎ **800/225-2380**), best known for its walking tours of England (see below), also offers a roster of roughly equivalent bike tours within England. They do cycling tours of the Cotswolds and Yorkshire. Cost for one week is $1,100 including breakfast, accommodations and some meals.

Vermont Bicycle Touring, P.O. Box 711, Bristol, VT 05443 (☎ **800/245-3868** or 802/453-4811), also offers tours throughout England geared to different levels of physical ability; extra guidance, assistance, and services are always available. A van transports your luggage.

FISHING

Fly-fishing was born here, and it's considered an art form. An expert in leading programs for fly-fishermen eager to experience the cold, clear waters of Britain is **Rod & Reel Adventures,** 566 Thomson Lane, Suite B6, Copperopolis, CA 95228 (☎ **800/356-6982**). Don't expect smooth salesmanship at this place, but if you persevere, someone at this company should be able to link you up with a local fishing guide who can lead you to English waters that are well stocked with trout, perch, grayling, sea bream, Atlantic salmon, and such lesser-known species as rudd and roach. Rod & Reel Adventures has contacts in the Lake District, Scotland, and the Norfolk Broads. Such streams as the Wear, the Derwent, the Copuquet, and the Till are especially prolific.

If you prefer to go it alone, contact the **British Salmon & Trout Association,** Fishmonger's Hall, London Bridge, London EC4R 9EL (☎ **020/7283-5838**), for information about British fishing regulations.

GOLF

Although the sport originated in Scotland, golf has been around in England since Edward VII first began stamping over the greens of such courses as Royal Lytham & St. Annes, in England's northwest, or Royal St. Georges, near London.

The unyielding reality is that golf in England remains a clubby sport where some of the most prestigious courses are usually reserved exclusively for members. Rules at most English golf courses tend to be stricter in matters of dress code and protocol than their equivalents in the United States.

If, however, your heart is set on enjoying a round or two on the emerald-colored turf of England, **Golf International,** 275 Madison Ave., New York, NY 10016 (☎ **800/833-1389** or 212/986-9176), can open doors for you. Golf packages in England are arranged for anywhere from 7 to 14 days and can include as much or as little golf, on as many different courses, as a participant wants. Weeklong vacations, with hotels, breakfasts, car rentals, and greens fees included, range from $2,735 per person, double occupancy, airfare not included.

Worthy competitors that operate on a less comprehensive scale than Golf International include **Adventures in Golf,** 11 Northeastern Blvd., Suite 360, Nashua, NH 03062 (☎ **603/882-8367**); and **Jerry Quinlan's Celtic Golf,** 124 Sunset Blvd., Cape May, NJ 08204 (☎ **800/535-6148**). Each of their tours is customized, and usually includes lodging in anything from simple guesthouses to five-star deluxe manor houses.

HIKING, WALKING & RAMBLING

In England and Wales alone, there are some 100,000 miles of trails and footpaths. The **Ramblers' Association,** 1–5 Wandsworth Rd., London SW8 2XX (☎ **020/7339-8500**), publishes an annual yearbook that lists some 2,500 bed-and-breakfasts near the trails; it costs £11 ($18.70). Send a check in sterling for the yearbook if you plan to order before your trip; otherwise the yearbook can be purchased in England for £4.99 ($8.50).

Alternatively, you can join an organized hiking tour. One of the longest-running tour operators is **Himalayan Travel,** 110 Prospect St., Stamford, CT 06901 (☎ **800/225-2380**). Between April and October, they offer hiking tours within seven districts of England, each configured for between 1 and 2 weeks. Participants cover between 8 and 15 miles a day within such regions as the Cotswolds, Dorset, Northumberland, Cornwall, or the Yorkshire Dales, spending the night at small inns en route. Participants should be reasonably fit, but don't have to be marathon runners. All tours include breakfast daily and overnight lodging, as well as some meals. A weeklong tour costs around $900 to $1,200 per person, double occupancy.

Wilderness Travel, Inc., 1102 Ninth St., Berkeley, CA 94710 (☎ **800/368-2794** or 510/558-2488), also specializes in treks and inn-to-inn hiking tours, plus less strenuous walking tours of Cornwall and the Cotswolds that combine transportation with walking sessions of 3 hours or less.

English Lakeland Ramblers, 18 Stuyvesant Oval, Suite 1A, New York, NY 10009 (☎ **800/724-8801** outside New York City, or 212/505-1020 within New York City; www.ramblers.com), offers 7- to 8-day walking tours for the average active person. On its Lake District tour, you'll stay and have your meals in a charming 17th-century country inn near Ambleside and Windermere. A minibus takes hikers and sightseers daily to trails and sightseeing points. Experts tell you about the area's culture and history and highlight its natural wonders. There are also tours of the Cotswolds and Scotland, as well as inn-to-inn tours and privately guided tours.

Other contenders include **Country Walkers,** P.O. Box 180, Waterbury, VT 05676 (☎ **800/464-9255**). Their "walking vacations" usually last 7 days and tend to focus on such scenic areas as the Lake District, Cornwall, and the Cotswolds. These packages include overnight accommodations at well-respected, but not excessively luxurious, three-star hotels, and the occasional manor house; most meals; and a guide who's well versed in local paths, trails, and lore. Four to 12 miles are covered each day. Prices start at $2,395 per person, double occupancy, without airfare.

HORSEBACK RIDING

You can learn to ride or brush up on your skills at **Eastern Equation,** a facility located on the Essex/Suffolk border. British Horse Society–certified instructors teach riders at a facility with a large indoor arena, a jumping course, and 30 horses and ponies of various sizes and abilities. Many trails go directly from the farm to the countryside. You can stay in a room with a private bath at the beautiful 16th-century farmhouse (subject to availability), or find accommodation in a comfortable nearby hotel Contact **Cross Country International,** P.O. Box 1170, Millbrook, NY 12545 (☎ **800/828-8768**).

There are also American companies that offer horseback-riding package tours of England. **Equitour/FITS Equestrian Tours,** P.O. Box 807, Dubois, WY 82513 (☎ **800/545-0019**), is one such firm. Formed by the 1996 merger of two well-respected tour operators based in Wyoming and California, this outfit specializes in package tours for riding enthusiasts who want to experience the horsey traditions of the land of foxes and hounds. Two types of tours can be arranged through their auspices: Stationary tours where instruction in jumping and dressage are conducted over a 7-day period at a stable beside the Bristol Channel or on the fields of Dartmoor, and "progressive" tours where treks of 4 to 10 days are conducted in Exmoor and Wales. Most riders eager to experience as wide a view of England as possible opt for the latter, spending each night at a different B&B or inn, and lodging their mounts at nearby stables. The accommodations are simple, and prices are kept deliberately low. A 4-day horseback excursion in Dartmoor that includes use of a horse and its tack, guide services, overnight accommodations, and all meals costs around $775 per person, double occupancy.

BEER & BREWERY TOURS

A Seattle-based company, **MIR Corporation,** 85 S. Washington St., Suite 210, Seattle, WA 98104 (☎ **800/424-7289**), offers 9-day Brew Tasting and Brewery Tours that include visits to such major breweries as Samuel Smith's and Young's, outside of London; the Caledonian brewery, outside of Edinburgh; and a host of lesser-known, family-owned breweries, such as Traquair House, scattered throughout the countryside. Included are frequent opportunities to taste local brew at atmospheric pubs en route. Don't expect demure sobriety during the course of this experience. Most participants quaff their first pint at least an hour before lunch and continue sampling the merchandise throughout the course of the day and evening. Prices, without airfare, begin at $1,495 per person, double occupancy. Accommodations are in unpretentious middle-bracket hotels and inns. Each tour is limited to 20 participants, and transport throughout is by train and motor coach.

UNIVERSITY STUDY PROGRAMS

You can study English literature at renowned universities such as Oxford and Cambridge during the week and then take weekend excursions to the countryside of Shakespeare, Austen, Dickens, and Hardy. While doing your course work, you can live in dormitories with other students and dine in elaborate halls or the more intimate Fellows' clubs. Study programs in England are not limited to the liberal arts, or to high-school or college students. There are many programs, some designed specifically for teachers and senior citizens (see "Tips for Seniors," later in this chapter). For more information, contact the organizations listed below or those mentioned in the section "Tips for Students," later in this chapter.

Affiliated with Richmond College, in London, **American Institute For Foreign Study,** 102 Greenwich Ave., Greenwich, CT 06830 (☎ **800/727-2437**), offers 4 weeks and up of traveling programs for high-school students, and internships and academic programs for college students. There are also programs leading to the British equivalent of an MBA.

IIE (Institute of International Education), U.S. Student Programs Division, 809 United Nations Plaza, New York, NY 10017-3580 (☎ **212/984-5400**), administers a variety of academic, training, and grant programs for the U.S. Information Agency (USIA), including the Fulbright grants. It is especially helpful in arranging enrollments for U.S. students in summer-school programs.

University Vacations, 3660 Bougainvillea Rd., Coconut Grove, FL 33133 (☎ **800/792-0100**), offers upmarket liberal-arts programs at Oxford and Cambridge universities. Courses usually last 7 to 12 days and combine lectures and excursions with dining in the intimate Fellows' Dining Rooms. Accommodations are in private rooms with available en-suite facilities in the medieval colleges. There are neither formal academic requirements nor pressure for examinations or written requirements. Its summer headquarters is Brasenose College, Oxford.

Worldwide Classrooms, P.O. Box 1166, Milwaukee, WI 53201, (www.worldwide.edu), produces an extensive listing of schools offering study-abroad programs in England, and offers a directory-like catalog for $9.95.

7 Health & Insurance

STAYING HEALTHY

You will encounter few health problems while traveling in England. The tap water is safe to drink, the milk is pasteurized, and health services are good.

The mad-cow crisis is over, but caution is always advised. (For example, it's been suggested that it's safer to eat British beef cut from the bone instead of on the bone.) Other than that, traveling to England doesn't pose any health risks.

If you need a doctor, your hotel can recommend one, or you can contact your embassy or consulate. Outside London, dial ☎ **100** and ask the operator for the local police, who will give you the name, address, and telephone number of a doctor in your area. *Note:* U.S. visitors who become ill while they're in England are only eligible for free emergency care. For other treatment, including follow-up care, you will be asked to pay.

If you suffer from a chronic illness, consult your doctor before your departure. For conditions like epilepsy, diabetes, or heart problems, wear a **Medic Alert Identification Tag** (☎ **800/825-3785;** www.medicalert.org), which will immediately alert doctors to your condition and give them access to your records through Medic Alert's 24-hour hotline. Membership is $35, plus a $15 annual fee.

Pack prescription medications in your carry-on luggage. Carry written prescriptions in generic, not brand-name form, and bring all prescription medications in their original labeled vials. Also take along copies of your prescriptions in case you lose your pills or run out.

INSURANCE

There are three kinds of travel insurance: trip-cancellation, medical, and lost luggage coverage.

Trip-cancellation insurance is a good idea if you have paid a large portion of your vacation expenses up front, say, by purchasing a package tour. (Trip-cancellation insurance costs approximately 6% to 8% percent of the total value of your vacation.) The other two types of insurance, however, don't make sense for most travelers. Rule number one: Check your existing policies before you buy any additional coverage.

Your existing **health insurance** should cover you if you get sick while on vacation (though if you belong to an HMO, you should check to see whether you are fully covered when away from home). If you need hospital treatment, most health insurance plans and HMOs will cover out-of-country hospital visits and procedures, at least to some extent. However, most make you pay the bills up front at the time of care, and you'll get a refund only after you've returned and filed all the paperwork.

Members of **Blue Cross/Blue Shield** can now use their cards at select hospitals in most major cities worldwide (☎ **800/810-BLUE** or www.bluecares.com for a list of hospitals). **Medicare** only covers U.S. citizens traveling in Mexico and Canada. For independent travel health-insurance providers, see below.

Your homeowner's insurance should cover stolen **luggage.** The airlines are responsible for $1,250 on domestic flights if they lose your luggage; if you plan to carry anything more valuable than that, keep it in your carry-on bag.

If you do require additional insurance, try one of the following companies: **Access America** (☎ 800/284-8300); **Travel Guard International** (☎ 800/826-1300); or **Travel Insured International, Inc.** (☎ 800/243-3174). Companies specializing in accident and medical care include: **MEDEX International** (☎ 888/MEDEX-00 or 410/453-6300; www.medexassist.com); and **Travel Assistance International** (Worldwide Assistance Services, Inc.; (☎ 800/821-2828 or 202/828-5894).

8 Tips for Travelers with Special Needs

TIPS FOR TRAVELERS WITH DISABILITIES

A disability shouldn't stop anyone from traveling. There are more resources out there than ever before. *A World of Options,* a 658-page book of resources for travelers with disabilities, covers a number of activities. It costs $35 ($30 for members) and is available from **Mobility International USA,** P.O. Box 10767, Eugene, OR, 97440 (☎ **541/343-1284,** voice and TDD; www.miusa.org). Annual membership for Mobility International is $35, which includes their quarterly newsletter, *Over the Rainbow.*

The Moss Rehab Hospital (☎ **215/456-9600**) has been providing friendly and helpful phone advice and referrals to disabled travelers for years through its **Travel Information Service** (☎ **215/456-9603;** www.mossresourcenet.org).

You can join **The Society for the Advancement of Travel for the Handicapped (SATH),** 347 Fifth Ave. Suite 610, New York, NY 10016 (☎ **212/447-7284;** fax 212-725-8253; www.sath.org) for $45 annually, $30 for seniors and students, to gain access to their vast network of connections in the travel industry. They provide information sheets on travel destinations, and referrals to tour operators that specialize in traveling with disabilities. Their quarterly magazine, *Open World for Disability and Mature Travel,* is full of good information and resources. A year's subscription is $13 ($21 outside the U.S.).

Travelers with disabilities may also want to consider joining a tour that caters specifically to them. One of the best operators is **Flying Wheels Travel,** 143 West Bridge (P.O. Box 382), Owatonna, MN 55060 (☎ **800/535-6790**). They offer various escorted tours and cruises, with an emphasis on sports, as well as private tours in minivans with lifts. Other reputable specialized tour operators include **Access Adventures** (☎ **716/889-9096**), which offers sports-related vacations; **Accessible Journeys** (☎ **800/TINGLES** or 610/521-0339), for slow walkers and wheelchair travelers; **The Guided Tour, Inc.** (☎ **215/782-1370**); **Wilderness Inquiry** (☎ **800/728-0719** or 612/379-3858); and **Directions Unlimited** (☎ **800/533-5343**).

Vision-impaired travelers should contact the **American Foundation for the Blind,** 11 Penn Plaza, Suite 300, New York, NY 10001 (☎ **800/232-5463** or 212/502-7600), for information on traveling with seeing-eye dogs.

Many London hotels, museums, restaurants, and sightseeing attractions have wheelchair ramps. Persons with disabilities are often granted special discounts at attractions and, in some cases, nightclubs. These are called "concessions" in Britain. It always pays to ask. Free information and advice is available from **Holiday Care Service,** Imperial Building, 2nd Floor, Victoria Road, Horley, Surrey RH6 7PZ (☎ **01293/774535;** fax 01293/784647).

The transport system, cinemas, and theaters are still pretty much off-limits, but **London Transport** does publish a leaflet called *Access to the Underground,* which gives details of elevators and ramps at individual Underground stations; call ☎ **020/7918-3312.** And the London Black Cab is perfectly suited for those in wheelchairs; the roomy interiors have plenty of room for maneuvering.

In London, the most prominent organization for information about access to theaters, cinemas, galleries, museums, and restaurants is **Artsline,** 54 Chalton St., London NW1 1HS (☎ **020/7388-2227;** fax 020/7383-2653). It offers free information about wheelchair access, theaters with hearing aids, tourist attractions, and cinemas. Artsline will mail information to North America, but it's even more helpful to contact Artsline after your arrival in London. Call between 9:30am and 5:30pm, Monday to Friday.

Another organization that cooperates closely with Artsline is **Tripscope,** The Courtyard, 4 Evelyn Rd., London W4 5JL (☎ **020/8580-7021;** fax 020/8994-3618), which offers advice on travel for persons with disabilities in Britain and elsewhere.

FOR GAY & LESBIAN TRAVELERS

England has one of the most active gay and lesbian scenes in the world, centered mainly around London. Gay bars, restaurants, and centers are also found in all large English cities, notably Bath, Birmingham, Manchester, and especially Brighton.

For starters, you may want to check out the new *Frommer's Gay & Lesbian Europe.* Other guides are *Spartacus Britain and Ireland* and *London Scene.* For up-to-the-minute activities in Britain, we recommend *Gay Times* (London). These books and others are available from **Giovanni's Room,** 1145 Pine St., Philadelphia, PA 19107 (☎ **215/923-2960;** fax 215/923-0813).

The International Gay & Lesbian Travel Association (IGLTA), (☎ **800/448-8550** or 954/776-2626; fax 954/776-3303; www.iglta.org), links travelers up with the appropriate gay-friendly service organization or tour specialist. With around 1,200 members, it offers quarterly newsletters, marketing mailings, and a membership directory that's updated quarterly. Membership often includes gay or lesbian businesses but is open to individuals for $150 yearly, plus a $100 administration fee for new members. Members are kept informed of gay and gay-friendly hoteliers, tour operators, and airline and cruise-line representatives. Contact the IGLTA for a list of its member agencies, who will be tied into IGLTA's information resources.

General gay and lesbian travel agencies include **Family Abroad** (☎ **800/999-5500** or 212/459-1800; gay and lesbian), and **Above and Beyond Tours** (☎ **800/397-2681;** mainly gay men).

There are also two good, biannual English-language gay guidebooks, both focused on gay men but including information for lesbians as well. You can get the ***Spartacus International Gay Guide*** or ***Odysseus*** from most gay and lesbian book stores, or order them from **Giovanni's Room** (☎ **215/923-2960**), or **A Different Light Bookstore** (☎ **800/343-4002** or 212/989-4850). Both lesbians and gays might want to pick up a copy of ***Gay Travel A to Z*** ($16). **The Ferrari Guides** (www.q-net.com) is yet another very good series of gay and lesbian guidebooks.

Out and About, 8 W. 19th St. #401, New York, NY 10011 (☎ **800/929-2268** or 212/645-6922) offers guidebooks and a monthly newsletter packed with good information on the global gay and lesbian scene. A year's subscription to the newsletter costs $49. ***Our World,*** 1104 North Nova Rd., Suite 251, Daytona Beach, FL 32117 (☎ **904/441-5367**) is a slicker monthly magazine promoting and highlighting travel bargains and opportunities. Annual subscription rates are $35 in the United States, $45 outside the United States.

In London, the **Lesbian and Gay Switchboard** (☎ **020/7837-7324**) is open 24 hours a day, providing information about gay-related London activities or advice in general. The **Bisexual Helpline** (☎ **020/8569-7500**) offers useful information, but only on Tuesday and Wednesday from 7:30 to 9:30pm and Saturday between 10:30am and 12:30pm. The best bookstore is **Gay's the Word,** 66 Marchmont St., WC1 (☎ **020/7278-7654;** tube: Russell Square), which is the largest such store in Britain. It is open Monday through Saturday from 10am to 6:30pm, and Sunday 2 to 6pm.

TIPS FOR SENIORS

Don't be shy about asking for discounts, but always carry some kind of identification, such as a driver's license, that shows your date of birth. Also, mention the fact that you're a senior citizen when you first make your travel reservations.

Senior citizens over 60 years old receive special 10% discounts on British Airways through its Privileged Traveler program. They also qualify for reduced restrictions on APEX cancellations. Discounts are also granted for BA tours and for intra-Britain air tickets if booked in North America.

However, in England itself, you often have to be a member of an association to obtain discounts. Public transportation reductions, for example, are available only to holders of British Pension books.

Members of the **American Association of Retired Persons (AARP),** 601 E St. NW, Washington, DC 20049 (☎ **800/424-3410** or 202/434-2277), get discounts not only on hotels but on airfares and car rentals, too. AARP offers members a wide range of special benefits, including *Modern Maturity* magazine and a monthly newsletter.

The National Council of Senior Citizens, 8403 Colesville Rd., Suite 1200, Silver Spring, MD 20910 (☎ **301/578-8800**), a nonprofit organization, offers a newsletter six times a year (partly devoted to travel tips) and discounts on hotel and auto rentals; annual dues are $13 per person or couple.

Golden Companions, P.O. Box 5249, Reno, NV 89513 (☎ **800/392-1256**), helps travelers 45-plus find compatible companions through a personal voice-mail service. Contact them for more information.

The Mature Traveler, a monthly 12-page newsletter on senior citizen travel is a valuable resource. It is available by subscription ($30 a year) from GEM Publishing Group, Box 50400, Reno, NV 89513-0400. GEM also publishes ***The Book of Deals,*** a collection of more than 1,000 senior discounts on airlines, lodging, tours, and attractions around the country; it's available for $9.95 by calling ☎ **800/460-6676.** Another helpful publication is ***101 Tips for the Mature Traveler,*** available from **Grand Circle Travel,** 347 Congress St., Suite 3A, Boston, MA 02210 (☎ **800/221-2610** or 617/350-7500; fax 617/346-6700).

Grand Circle Travel is also one of the hundreds of travel agencies specializing in vacations for seniors (347 Congress St., Suite 3A, Boston, MA 02210 (☎ **800/221-2610** or 617/350-7500)). Many of these packages, however, are of the tour-bus variety, with free trips thrown in for those who organize groups of 10 or more. Seniors seeking more independent travel should probably consult a regular travel agent. **SAGA International Holidays,** 222 Berkeley St., Boston, MA 02116 (☎ **800/343-0273**), offers inclusive tours and cruises for those 50 and older. SAGA also sponsors the more substantial **Road Scholar Tours** (☎ **800/621-2151**), which are fun-loving, but with an educational bent.

If you want something more than the average vacation or guided tour, try **Elderhostel** (☎ **877/426-8056;** www.elderhostel.org/) or the University of New Hampshire's **Interhostel** (☎ **800/733-9753**), both variations on the same theme: educational travel for senior citizens. On these escorted tours, the days are packed with seminars, lectures, and field trips, and academic experts lead all the sightseeing trips. **Elderhostel,** 75 Federal St., Boston, MA 02110-1941 (☎ **877/426-8056;** www.elderhostel.org/), arranges study programs for those aged 55 and over (and a spouse or companion of any age) in England. Most courses last about 3 weeks and many include airfare, accommodations in student dormitories or modest inns, meals, and tuition. Write or call for a free catalog, which lists upcoming courses and destinations. **Interhostel** takes travelers 50 and over (with companions over 40), and offers 2- and 3-week trips, mostly international. The courses in both these programs are ungraded, involve no homework, and often focus on the liberal arts. They're not luxury vacations, but they're fun and fulfilling.

TIPS FOR FAMILIES

On airlines, you must request a special menu for children at least 24 hours in advance. If baby food is required, however, bring your own and ask a flight attendant to warm it to the right temperature.

Arrange ahead of time for such necessities as a crib, bottle warmer, and a car seat (in England, small children aren't allowed to ride in the front seat).

If you're staying with friends and can't take advantage of amenities offered by a hotel, you can rent baby equipment from **Chelsea Baby Hire,** 83 Burntwood Lane, London SW17 OAJ (☎ **020/8540-8830**).

London's black taxi cabs can be lifesavers for families; their roomy interiors allow strollers to be lifted right into the cab without unstrapping the baby.

If you want a night out without the kids, you're in luck: London has its own children's hotel, **Pippa Popins,** 430 Fulham Road, SW6 1DU (☎ **020/7385-2458**), which accommodates children overnight in a wonderful nursery filled with lots of toys and doting caregivers. Children ages 2 to 12 can be dropped off for a 9am to 6pm session or a 4pm to 10am session. The hotel is open 7 days a week and charges £50 ($85) per session Monday through Thursday, and £60 ($102) on weekends. A 24-hour stay costs £100 ($170). Another recommended baby-sitting service in London is **Childminders** (☎ **020/7935-2049**). Baby-sitters can also be found for you at most hotels.

To find out what's on for children while you're in London, pick up the leaflet *Where to Take Children,* published by the London Tourist Board and Convention Bureau. If you have specific questions, ring **Kidsline** (☎ **020/7222-8070**) Monday to Friday between 4 and 6pm and summer holidays between 9am and 4pm, or the **London Tourist Board's** special children's information lines (☎ **0839/123-425** or 0891/505-460). Both numbers offer listings of special events and places to visit for children. The number is accessible in London only at the cost of 50p (85¢) per minute.

The newsletter, ***Family Travel Times*** is published six times a year by **TWYCH** (Travel with Your Children; **888/822-4388** or 212/477-5524), and includes a weekly call-in service for subscribers. Subscriptions are $40 a year for quarterly editions. A free publication list and a sample issue are available by calling or sending a request to the above address.

The University of New Hampshire runs **Familyhostel** (☎ **800/733-9753**), an intergenerational alternative to standard guided tours. You live on a European college campus for the 2- or 3-week program, attend lectures, seminars, go on lots of field trips, and do all the sightseeing—all of it guided by a team of experts and academics. It's designed for children (aged 8 to 15), parents, and grandparents.

TIPS FOR STUDENTS

The best resource for students is the **Council on International Educational Exchange,** or CIEE. They can set you up with an ID card (see below), and their travel branch, **Council Travel Service** (☎ **800/226-8624;** www.counciltravel.com), is the biggest student travel agency operation in the world. It can get you discounts on plane tickets, rail passes, and the like. Ask them for a list of CTS offices in major cities so you can keep the discounts flowing (and aid lines open) as you travel.

From CIEE you can obtain the student traveler's best friend, the $18 **International Student Identity Card (ISIC).** It's the only officially acceptable form of student identification, good for cut rates on rail passes, plane tickets, and other discounts. It also provides you with basic health and life insurance and a 24-hour help line. If you're no longer a student but are still under 26 you can get a GO 25 card from the same people, which will get you the insurance and some of the discounts (but not student admission prices in museums).

In Canada, **Travel CUTS,** 200 Ronson St., Ste. 320, Toronto, ONT M9W 5Z9 (☎ **800/667-2887** or 416/614-2887; www.travelcuts.com), offers similar services. **Usit Campus,** 52 Grosvenor Gardens, London SW1W 0AG (☎ **020/7730-3402;** www.usitcampus.co.uk), opposite Victoria Station, is Britain's leading specialist in student and youth travel.

9 Getting There

BY PLANE

British Airways (☎ **800/AIRWAYS;** www.british-airways.com) offers flights from 18 U.S. cities to Heathrow and Gatwick airports as well as many others to Manchester, Birmingham, and Glasgow. Nearly every flight is nonstop. With more add-on options than any other airline, British Airways can make a visit to Britain cheaper than you might have expected. Ask about packages that include both airfare and discounted hotel accommodations in Britain.

Known for consistently offering excellent fares, **Virgin Atlantic Airways** (☎ **800/862-8621;** www.fly.virgin.com) flies daily to either Heathrow or Gatwick from Boston, Newark, New Jersey, New York's JFK, Los Angeles, San Francisco, Washington's Dulles, Miami, and Orlando.

American Airlines (☎ **800/433-7300;** www.aa.com) offers daily flights to London's Heathrow from half a dozen U.S. gateways—New York's JFK (six times daily), Newark (once daily), Chicago's O'Hare and Boston's Logan (twice daily), and Miami International and Los Angeles International (each once daily).

Depending on the day and season, **Delta Air Lines** (☎ **800/241-4141;** www.delta-air.com) runs either one or two daily nonstop flights between Atlanta and Gatwick. Delta also offers nonstop daily service from Cincinnati.

Northwest Airlines (☎ **800/225-2525;** www.nwa.com) flies nonstop from Minneapolis and Detroit to Gatwick, with connections possible from other cities, such as Boston or New York.

Continental Airlines (☎ **800/231-0856;** www.flycontinental.com) has daily flights to London from Houston and Newark.

TWA (☎ **800/892-4141;** www.twa.com) flies nonstop to Gatwick every day from its hub in St. Louis. Connections are possible through St. Louis from most North American cities.

United Airlines (☎ **800/538-2929;** www.ual.com) flies nonstop from New York's JFK and Chicago's O'Hare to Heathrow two or three times daily, depending on the season. United also offers nonstop service twice a day from Dulles Airport, near Washington, D.C., plus once-a-day service from Newark, Los Angeles, and San Francisco to Heathrow.

For travelers departing from Canada, **Air Canada** (☎ **800/776-3000;** www.aircanada.ca) flies daily to London's Heathrow nonstop from Vancouver,

Montréal, and Toronto. There are also frequent direct services from Calgary and Ottawa.

From Canada, **British Airways** (☎ **800/247-9297**) has direct flights from Toronto, Montréal, and Vancouver.

For travelers departing from Australia, **British Airways** (☎ **800/247-9297**) has flights to London from Sydney, Melbourne, Perth, and Brisbane. **Qantas** (☎ **800/227-4500;** www.qantas.com) offers flights from Australia to London's Heathrow. Direct flights depart from Sydney and Melbourne. Some have the bonus of free stopovers in Bangkok or Singapore.

Departing from New Zealand, **Air New Zealand** (☎ **800/262-1234**) has direct flights to London from Auckland. These flights depart Wednesday, Saturday, and Sunday.

Short flights from Dublin to London are available through **British Airways** (☎ **800/AIRWAYS**), with four flights daily into London's Gatwick airport, and **Aer Lingus** (☎ **800/223-6537**), which flies into Heathrow. Short flights from Dublin to London are also available through **Ryan Air** (☎ **0541/569-569**) and **British Midland** (☎ **0345/554-554**).

Flying for Less: Tips for Getting the Best Airfares

- Keep your eyes peeled for **sales** in your newspaper. In the last few years, major airlines have periodically offered incredible bargains, as low as $250 round-trip from New York to London. You'll almost never see a sale during the peak summer vacation months of July and August, or during the Thanksgiving or Christmas seasons, but in spring, fall, and especially late winter, you can save a ton of money. If you already hold a ticket when a sale breaks, it may even pay to exchange your ticket, which usually incurs a $50 to $75 charge.
- If your **schedule** is flexible, ask if you can secure a cheaper fare by staying an extra day or by flying midweek. (Many airlines won't volunteer this information, so you have to ask questions and try all the possible combinations.)
- **Consolidators,** also known as bucket shops, are a good place to find low fares. Consolidators buy seats in bulk from the airlines and then sell them back to the public at prices below even the airlines' discounted rates. Their small ads usually run in the Sunday travel section at the bottom of the page. Among the most reliable companies are: **Council Travel** (☎ 800/226-8624; www.counciltravel.com) and **STA Travel** (☎ 800/781-4040; www.sta.travel.com) cater especially to young travelers, but their bargain basement prices are available to people of all ages. **Travel Bargains** (☎ 800/AIR-FARE; www.1800airfare.com) was formerly owned by TWA but now offers deep discounts on many other airlines, with a 4-day advance purchase. Other reliable consolidators include 1-800-FLY-CHEAP (www.1800flycheap.com); **TFI Tours International** (☎ 800-745-8000 or 212/736-1140), which serves as a clearinghouse for unused seats; or "rebators" such as **Travel Avenue** (☎ 800/333-3335 or 312/876-1116).
- It's possible to get some great deals on not only airfare, but hotels and car rentals as well, via the **Internet.** Among the leading travel sites are: **Arthur Frommer's Budget Travel** (www.frommers.com); **Microsoft Expedia** (www.expedia.com); **Travelocity** (www.travelocity.com); **The Trip** (www.thetrip.com); and **Smarter Living** (www.smarterliving.com), which offers a newsletter service that will send you a weekly customized e-mail summarizing the discount fares available from your departure city.

For more information on finding travel bargains on the Web, see "Planning Your Trip: An Online Directory," the next chapter in this book.

BY TRAIN FROM CONTINENTAL EUROPE

Britain's isolation from the rest of Europe led to the development of an independent railway network with different rules and regulations from those observed on the Continent. That's all changing now, but one big difference that may affect you still remains: If you're traveling to Britain from the Continent, ***your Eurail pass will not be valid when you get there.***

In 1994, Queen Elizabeth and Pres. François Mitterand officially opened the Channel Tunnel, or Chunnel, and the *Eurostar Express* passenger train began twice-daily service between London and both Paris and Brussels—a 3-hour trip. The $15 billion tunnel, one of the great engineering feats of all time, is the first link between Britain and the Continent since the Ice Age.

So if you're coming to London from say, Rome, your Eurail pass will get you as far as the Chunnel. At that point you can cross the English Channel aboard the *Eurostar,* and you'll receive a discount on your ticket. Once in England, you must use a separate BritRail pass or purchase a direct ticket to continue on to your destination.

Rail Europe (☎ **800/94-CHUNNEL;** www.raileurope.com) sells direct-service tickets on the Eurostar between Paris or Brussels and London. A round-trip fare between Paris and London costs $438 in first class and from $218 to $298 in second class. One-way unrestricted fares for passage on the Eurostar between Paris and London cost $219 in first class and $149 in second class.

In London, make reservations for **Eurostar** by calling ☎ **0345/300003;** in Paris, call ☎ **01/44-51-06-02;** and in the United States, it's ☎ **800/4-EURAIL.** Eurostar trains arrive and depart from London's Waterloo Station, Paris's Gare du Nord, and Brussels's Central Station.

BY FERRY/HOVERCRAFT FROM CONTINENTAL EUROPE

P & O Stena Lines (☎ **087/0600-0611**) operates car and passenger ferries between Dover and Calais, France (25 sailings a day; 75 minutes each way).

By far the most popular route across the English Channel is between Calais and Dover. **HoverSpeed** operates at least 12 hovercraft crossings daily; the trip takes 35 minutes. They also run a SeaCat (a catamaran propelled by jet engines) that takes slightly longer to make the crossing between Boulogne and Folkestone. The SeaCats depart about four times a day on the 55-minute voyage.

Traveling by hovercraft or SeaCat cuts the time of your surface journey from the Continent to the United Kingdom. A hovercraft trip is definitely a fun adventure, since the vessel is technically "flying" over the water. A SeaCat crossing from Folkestone to Boulogne is longer in miles, but is covered faster than conventional ferryboats make the Calais-Dover crossing. For reservations and information, call Hoverspeed (☎ **0870/5240241**). For foot passengers, a typical adult fare, with a 5-day return policy is £24 ($40.80) or half fare for children.

BY CAR FROM CONTINENTAL EUROPE

If you plan to transport a rented car between England and France, check in advance with the car-rental company about license and insurance requirements, and additional drop-off charges, before you begin.

The English Channel is crisscrossed with "drive-on, drive-off" car-ferry services, with many operating from Boulogne and Calais in France. From either of those ports, Sealink ferries will carry you, your luggage, and, if you like, your car. The most popular points of arrival along the English coast include Dover and Folkestone.

Taking a car beneath the Channel is more complicated and more expensive. Since the Channel Tunnel's opening, most passengers have opted to ride the train alone, without being accompanied by their car. The Eurostar trains, discussed above, carry passengers only; *Le Shuttle* trains carry freight cars, trucks, lorries, and passenger cars.

Count on at least £219 ($372.30) for a return ticket, but know that the cost of moving a car on Le Shuttle varies according to the season and day of the week. Frankly, it's a lot cheaper to transport your car across by conventional ferryboat, but if you insist, here's what you'll need to know: You'll negotiate both English and French customs as part of one combined process, usually on the English side of the Channel. You can remain within your vehicle even after you drive it onto a flatbed railway car during the 35-minute crossing. (For 19 minutes of this crossing, you'll actually be underwater; if you want, you can leave the confines of your car and ride within a brightly lit, air-conditioned passenger car.) When the trip is over, you simply drive off the flatbed railway car and drive off toward your destination. Total travel time between the French and English highway system is about 1 hour. As a means of speeding the flow of perishable goods across the Channel, the car and truck service usually operates 24 hours a day, at intervals that vary from 15 minutes to once an hour, depending on the time of day. Neither BritRail nor any of the agencies dealing with reservations for passenger trains through the Chunnel will reserve space for your car in advance, and considering the frequency of the traffic on the Chunnel, they're usually not necessary. For information about Le Shuttle car-rail service after you reach England, call ☎ **0990/353535**.

Duty-free stores, restaurants, and service stations are available to travelers on both sides of the Channel. A bilingual staff is on hand to assist travelers at both the British and French terminals.

BY BUS

If you're traveling to London from elsewhere in the United Kingdom, consider purchasing a **Britexpress Card,** which entitles you to a 30% discount on National Express (England and Wales) and Caledonian Express (Scotland) buses. Contact a travel agent for details.

Bus connections to Britain from the continent are generally not very comfortable, although some lines are more convenient than others. One line with a relatively good reputation is **Euroways Eurolines, Ltd.,** 52 Grosvenor Gardens, London SW1W 0AU (☎ **0990/143219**). They book passage on buses traveling twice a day between London and Paris (9 hours); three times a day from Amsterdam (12 hours); three times a week from Munich (24 hours); and three times a week from Stockholm (44 hours). On the longer routes, which employ two alternating drivers, the bus proceeds almost without interruption, taking occasional breaks for meals.

10 Package Deals & Escorted Tours

PACKAGE TOURS

Package tours are not the same thing as escorted tours. They are simply a way to buy airfare and accommodations at the same time. For popular destinations like England, they are a worthwhile option to consider, because they save you a lot of money. In many cases, a package that includes airfare, hotel, and transportation to and from the airport will cost you less than just the hotel alone would have, had you booked it yourself. That's because packages are sold in bulk to tour operators—who resell them to the public at a cost that drastically undercuts standard rates.

Packages, however, vary widely. Some offer a better class of hotels than others. Some offer the same hotels for lower prices. Some offer flights on scheduled airlines, while others book charters. In some packages, your choice of accommodations and travel days may be limited. Some packages let you choose between escorted vacations and independent vacations; others will allow you to add on just a few excursions or escorted day trips (also at lower prices than you could locate on your own) without booking an entirely escorted tour. If you spend the time to shop around, you will save in the long run.

The best place to start your search is the travel section of your local Sunday newspaper. Also check the ads in the back of national travel magazines like *Travel & Leisure, National Geographic Traveler,* and *Condé Nast Traveler*.

Liberty Travel (☎ **888/271-1584** to be connected with the agent closest to you; www.libertytravel.com), one of the biggest packagers in the Northeast, often runs a full-page ad in the Sunday papers. You won't get much in the way of service, but you will get a good deal.

American Express Vacations (☎ **800/241-1700;** www.americanexpress.com) is another option. Check out its **Last Minute Travel Bargains** site, offered in conjunction with **Continental Airlines,** (www6.americanexpress.com/travel/lastminutetravel/default.asp), with deeply discounted vacations packages and reduced airline fares that differ from the E-savers bargains that Continental emails weekly to subscribers. **Northwest Airlines** offers a similar service. Posted on Northwest's Web site every Wednesday, its **Cyber Saver Bargain Alerts** offer special hotel rates, package deals, and discounted airline fares.

Another good resource is the airlines themselves, which often package their flights together with accommodations. Among the airline packagers, your options include **American Airlines FlyAway Vacations** (☎ **800/321-2121**), **Delta Dream Vacations** (☎ **800/872-7786**), and **US Airways Vacations** (☎ **800/455-0123**). Pick the airline that services your hometown most often.

Far and away, you'll find the most options through **British Airways** (☎ **800/AIRWAYS**). Its offerings within the British Isles are more comprehensive than those of its competitors, and can be tailored to your specific interests and budget. Many of the tours, such as the 9-day all-inclusive tour through the great houses and gardens of England, include the ongoing services of a guide and lecturer. But if you prefer to travel independently, without following an organized tour, a sales representative can tailor an itinerary specifically for you, with discounted rates in a wide assortment of big-city hotels. If you opt for this, you can rent a car or choose to take the train. For a free catalog and additional information, call British Airways before you book your airline ticket, since some of the company's available options are contingent upon the purchase of a round-trip transatlantic air ticket.

ESCORTED TOURS

Some people love escorted tours. They let you relax and take in the sights while a bus driver fights traffic for you; they spell out your costs up front; and they take you to the maximum number of sights in the minimum amount of time with the least amount of hassle. If you do choose an escorted tour, you should ask a few simple questions before you buy:

1. What is the **cancellation policy?** Do they require a deposit? Can they cancel the trip if they don't get enough people? Do you get a refund if they cancel? If you cancel? How late can you cancel if you are unable to go? When do you pay in full?
2. How busy is the **schedule?** How much sightseeing do they plan each day? Do they allow ample time for relaxing by the pool, shopping, or wandering?
3. What is the **size** of the group? The smaller the group, the more flexible the itinerary, and the less time you'll spend waiting for people to get on and off the bus. Tour operators may be evasive about this, because they may not know the exact size of the group until everybody has made their reservations; but they should be able to give you a rough estimate. Some tours have a minimum group size and may cancel the tour if they don't book enough people.
4. What is included in the **price?** Don't assume anything. You may have to pay for transportation to and from the airport. A box lunch may be included in an excursion, but drinks might cost extra. Beer might be included, but wine might not. Can you opt out of certain activities, or does the bus leave once a day, with no exceptions? Are all your meals planned in advance? Can you choose your entree at dinner, or does everybody get the same chicken cutlet?

Note: If you choose an escorted tour, think strongly about purchasing travel insurance from an independent agency, especially if the tour operator asks you to pay up front. (But don't buy from the operator—talk about putting all of your eggs in one basket! Buy from one of the companies recommended in the section on Travel Insurance, earlier in this chapter.) One final caveat: since escorted tour prices are based on double occupancy, the single traveler is usually penalized.

Abercrombie & Kent (☎ **800/323-7308**), offers extremely upscale escorted tours that are loaded with luxury. Their most unusual conveyance is the *Royal Scotsman* train, which, for 1 night and 2 days, hauls participants along less frequently used railway spurs of Wiltshire, Somerset, and Devon within vintage railway cars that were fashionable around the turn of the century. Prices begin at $1,100 per person, double occupancy, for lots of local color and spit-and-polish service. Tours emphasize visits to sites of historical interest, and sometimes involve rides on buses that pick up and redeposit passengers at local railway stations.

One of Abercrombie's top rivals is **Travcoa** (☎ **800/992-2003**), which offers upscale tours by deluxe motor coach through the countryside of England and Scotland. Tours last from 14 to 24 days, include at least 3 nights in London, usually at such citadels of glamour as The Dorchester, and come with meals and virtually every other aspect of a holiday included in the price. Don't expect cost savings here: Without airfare, rates range from $6,995 to $11,995 per person double occupancy.

Other contenders in the upscale package-tour business include **Maupintour** (☎ **800/255-4266**) and **Tauck Tours** (☎ **800/468-2825**).

But not all escorted tours are so pricey. Mostly older, British folks make up a large portion of the clientele of one of the United Kingdom's largest tour operators, **Wallace Arnold Tours** (☎ **020/8686-4962** in the U.K.). Most of the company's tours last between 5 and 10 days, include lodgings at solid but not particularly extravagant hotels, most meals, and are reasonably priced from £185 ($314.50), without airfare.

U.S.-based **Trafalgar Tours** (☎ **800/854-0103**), offers affordable packages with lodgings in unpretentious but comfortable hotels. It's one of Europe's largest tour operators. There may not be a lot of frills, but you can find 8-day itineraries priced from $750 per person, double occupancy, without airfare, that include stopovers in Stratford-upon-Avon and Bath; and hotel 1-week packages at first-class hotels in London, with some money-saving coupons thrown in, for around $600 per person, double occupancy.

One of Trafalgar's leading competitors, known for offering roughly equivalent moderately priced tours through Britain, is **Globus/Cosmos Tours** (☎ **800/221-0090**).

Finally, there's **BritainShrinkers Tours.** An affiliate of BritRail, this company operates a number of escorted, full-day tours from May to the end of October to such popular places as Stratford-upon-Avon, Oxford, and the Cotswolds. All tours include transportation and sightseeing by bus. Tours usually include some free time for lunch, shopping, and exploring on your own. Tours return to London in time for dinner or the theater. Rates include entrance fees and value-added tax (VAT), but usually not the price of lunch.

BritainShrinkers offers excellent value for the money. And if you have a BritRail pass or Flexipass, you'll save up to 60% on the cost of each tour you take. Their tours can be purchased from either your travel agent or BritRail in the United States. (See "By Train," below, for more details.)

11 Getting Around

BY CAR

The British car-rental market is among the most competitive in Europe. Nevertheless, car rentals are often relatively expensive, unless you avail yourself of one of the promotional deals that are frequently offered by British Airways and others.

Since cars in Britain travel on the left side of the road, their steering wheels are positioned on the "wrong" side of the vehicle. Also keep in mind that most rental cars are manual, so be prepared to shift with your left hand; you'll pay more for an automatic—and make sure to request one when you reserve.

Most car-rental companies will accept your U.S. driver's license, provided you're 23 years old (21 in rare instances) and have had the license for more than a year. Many rental companies will grant discounts to clients who reserve their cars in advance (usually 48 hours) through the toll-free reservations offices in the renter's home country. Rentals of a week or more are almost always less expensive per day than day rentals.

When you reserve a car, be sure to ask if the price includes the 17.5% value-added tax (VAT).

Rentals are available through **Avis** (☎ 800/331-2112; www.avis.com), **British Airways** (☎ 800/AIRWAYS; www.british-airways.com), **Budget Rent-a-Car** (☎ 800/527-0700; www.budgetrentacar.com), and **Hertz** (☎ 800/654-3131; www.hertz.com). **Kemwel Holiday Autos** (☎ 800/678-0678; www.kemwel.com) is among the cheapest and most reliable of the rental agencies. **AutoEurope** (☎ 800/223-5555 in the U.S., or 0800/899893 in London; www.autoeurope.com) acts as a wholesale company for rental agencies in Europe.

Car rental rates vary even more than airline fares. The price you pay will depend on the size of the car, where and when you pick it up and drop it off, the length of the rental period, where and how far you drive it, whether you purchase insurance, and a host of other factors. A few key questions could save you hundreds of dollars.

- Are weekend rates lower than weekday rates? Ask if the rate is the same for pickup Friday morning, for instance, as it is for Thursday night.
- Is a weekly rate cheaper than the daily rate? If you need to keep the car for 4 days, it may be cheaper to keep it for 5, even if you don't need it that long.
- Does the agency assess a drop-off charge if you do not return the car to the same location where you picked it up? Is it cheaper to pick up the car at the airport compared to a downtown location?
- Are special promotional rates available? If you see an advertised price in your local newspaper, be sure to ask for that specific rate; otherwise you may be charged the standard cost. The terms change constantly, and phone operators may not volunteer information.
- Are discounts available for members of AARP, AAA, frequent-flyer programs, or trade unions? If you belong to any of these organizations, you are probably entitled to discounts of up to 30%.
- What is the cost of adding an additional driver's name to the contract?
- How many free miles are included in the price? Free mileage is often negotiable, depending on the length of your rental.
- How much does the rental company charge to refill your gas tank if you return with the tank less than full? Though most rental companies claim these prices are "competitive," fuel is almost always cheaper in town. Try to allow enough time to refuel the car yourself before returning it.

RENTAL INSURANCE Before you drive off in a rental car, be sure you're insured. Hasty assumptions about your personal auto insurance or a rental agency's additional coverage could end up costing you tens of thousands of dollars—even if you are involved in an accident that was clearly the fault of another driver.

The basic insurance coverage offered by most car rental companies, known as the **Loss/Damage Waiver (LDW)** or **Collision Damage Waiver (CDW),** can cost more than $20/day.

U.S. drivers who already have their own car insurance are usually covered in the United States for loss of or damage to a rental car, and liability in case of injury to any other party involved in an accident. But coverage probably doesn't extend outside the United States Be sure to find out whether you are covered in England, whether your policy extends to all persons who will be driving the rental car, how much liability is covered in case an outside party is injured in an accident, and whether the type of vehicle you are renting is included under your contract. (Rental trucks, sport utility vehicles, and luxury vehicles such as the Jaguar may not be covered.)

Most **major credit cards** provide some degree of coverage as well—provided they were used to pay for the rental. Terms vary widely, however, so be sure to call your credit card company directly before you rent. But though they will cover damage to or theft of your rental, ***credit cards will not cover liability,*** or the cost of injury to an outside party and/or damage to an outside party's vehicle. If you do not hold an insurance policy, or if you are driving outside the United States, you may seriously want to consider purchasing additional liability insurance from your rental company. Be sure to check the terms, however: some rental agencies only cover liability if the renter is not at fault.

Bear in mind that each credit card company has its own peculiarities. Most American Express Optima cards, for instance, do not provide any insurance.

American Express does not cover vehicles valued at over $50,000 when new, luxury vehicles such as the Porsche, or vehicles built on a truck chassis. MasterCard does not provide coverage for loss, theft, or fire damage, and only covers collision if the rental period does not exceed 15 days. Call your own credit card company for details.

DRIVING RULES & REQUIREMENTS In England, *you drive on the left* and pass on the right. Road signs are clear and the international symbols are unmistakable.

You must present your passport and driver's license when you rent a car in Britain. No special British license is needed. It's a good idea to get a copy of the *British Highway Code,* available from almost any gas station or newsstand (called a "news stall" in Britain).

Warning: Pedestrian crossings are marked by striped lines (zebra striping) on the road; flashing lights near the curb indicate that drivers must stop and yield the right of way if a pedestrian has stepped out into the zebra zone to cross the street.

ROAD MAPS The best road map is *The Ordinance Survey Motor Atlas of Great Britain,* whether you're trying to find the fastest route to Manchester or locate some obscure village. Revised annually, it's published by Temple Press and is available at most bookstores, including **W & G Foyle, Ltd.,** 113 and 119 Charing Cross Rd., London, WC2 HOEB (☎ **020/7440-3225**).

BREAKDOWNS If you are a member of AAA in the United States, you are automatically eligible for the same roadside services you receive at home. Be sure to bring your membership card with you on your trip. In an emergency, call the Automobile Association of Great Britain's emergency road service (☎ **0800/887766**). If you are not a member of AAA, you may want to join one of England's two major auto clubs—the Automobile Association (AA) and the Royal Automobile Club (RAC). Membership, which can be obtained through your car-rental agent, entitles you to free legal and technical advice on motoring matters, as well as a whole range of discounts on automobile products and services.

The **AA** is located at Norfolk House, Priestly Road, Basingstoke, Hampshire RG24 9NY (☎ **0990/500600**). The **RAC** can be contacted at P.O. Box 700, Bristol, Somerset BS99 1RB (☎ **0800/029029**).

If your car breaks down on the highway, you can call for **24-hour breakdown service** from a roadside phone. The 24-hour number to call for **AA** is ☎ **0800/887766;** for **RAC** it is ☎ **0800/828282.** All superhighways (called motorways in Britain) are provided with special emergency phones that are connected to police traffic units, and the police can contact either of the auto clubs on your behalf.

GASOLINE Called "petrol," gasoline is sold by the liter, with 4.2 liters to a gallon. Prices are much higher than Stateside, and you'll probably have to serve yourself. In some remote areas, stations are few and far between, and many are closed on Sunday.

Comparison Shop!

Many packages are available that include airfare, accommodations, and a rental car with unlimited mileage. Compare these prices with the cost of booking airline tickets and renting a car separately to see if these offers are good deals.

BY PLANE

British Airways (☎ **800/AIRWAYS**) flies to more than 20 cities outside London, including Manchester, Glasgow, and Edinburgh. Ask about the British Airways Super Shuttle Saver fares, which can save you up to 50% on travel to certain key British cities. If seats are available on the flight of your choice, no advance reservations are necessary, although to benefit from the lowest prices, passengers must spend a Saturday night away from their point of origin and fly during defined off-peak times. Flights are usually restricted to weekdays between 10am and 3:30pm, whereas most night flights are after 7pm and, in certain cases, on weekends.

For passengers planning on visiting widely scattered destinations within the United Kingdom, perhaps with a side trip to a city on Europe's mainland, British Airways' **Europe Airpass** allows discounted travel in a continuous loop to between 3 and 12 cities anywhere on BA's European and domestic air routes. Passengers must end their journey at the same point they begin it and fly exclusively on BA flights. Such a ticket (for instance, from London to Paris, then to Manchester, and finally to London again) will cut the cost of each segment of the itinerary by about 40% to 50% over individually booked tickets. The pass is available for travel to about a dozen of the most-visited cities and regions of Britain, with discounted add-ons available to most of BA's destinations in Europe as well. (This Airpass is a good bargain for round-trip travel between London and Rome, but not very practical for air travel from, say, Rome to Madrid. You'd be better off traveling between points on the Continent by full-fare airline ticket, or by train, bus, or car.)

BA's Europe Airpass must be booked and paid for at least 7 days before a passenger's departure from North America. All sectors of the itinerary, including transatlantic passage from North America, must be booked simultaneously. Some changes are permitted in flight dates (but not in destinations) after the ticket is issued. Check with British Airways for full details and restrictions.

BY TRAIN

A Eurail pass is not valid in Great Britain, but there are several special passes for train travel outside London. For railroad information, go to Rail Travel centers in the main London railway stations (Waterloo, King's Cross, Euston, and Paddington).

Americans can obtain a BritRail passes at **BritRail Travel International,** 500 Mamaroneck Ave., Suite 314, Harrison, NY 10528 (☎ **800/677-8585;** 800/555-2748 in Canada).

BRITRAIL CLASSIC PASS This pass allows unlimited rail travel during a set time period (8 days, 15 days, 22 days, or 1 month). For 8 days, the pass costs $400 in first class, $265 in "standard" class; for 15 days, $600 in first class, $400 in standard; for 22 days, $760 in first class, $505 in standard; and for 1 month, $900 in first class, $600 in standard. Senior citizens (60 and over) qualify for discounts, but only in seats within first-class—not standard class—compartments of trains. These cost $340 for 8-day passes, $510 for 15-day passes, $645 for 22-day passes, and $765 for 1-month passes. If a child age 5 to 15 is traveling with a full-fare adult, the fare is half the adult fare. Children under 5 travel free.

BRITRAIL FLEXIPASS This pass lets you travel anywhere on BritRail, and is particularly good for visitors who want to alternate travel days with blocks of uninterrupted sightseeing time in a particular city or region. Flexipasses can be used for 4 days within any 1-month period and cost $350 in first class and

Train Routes in England

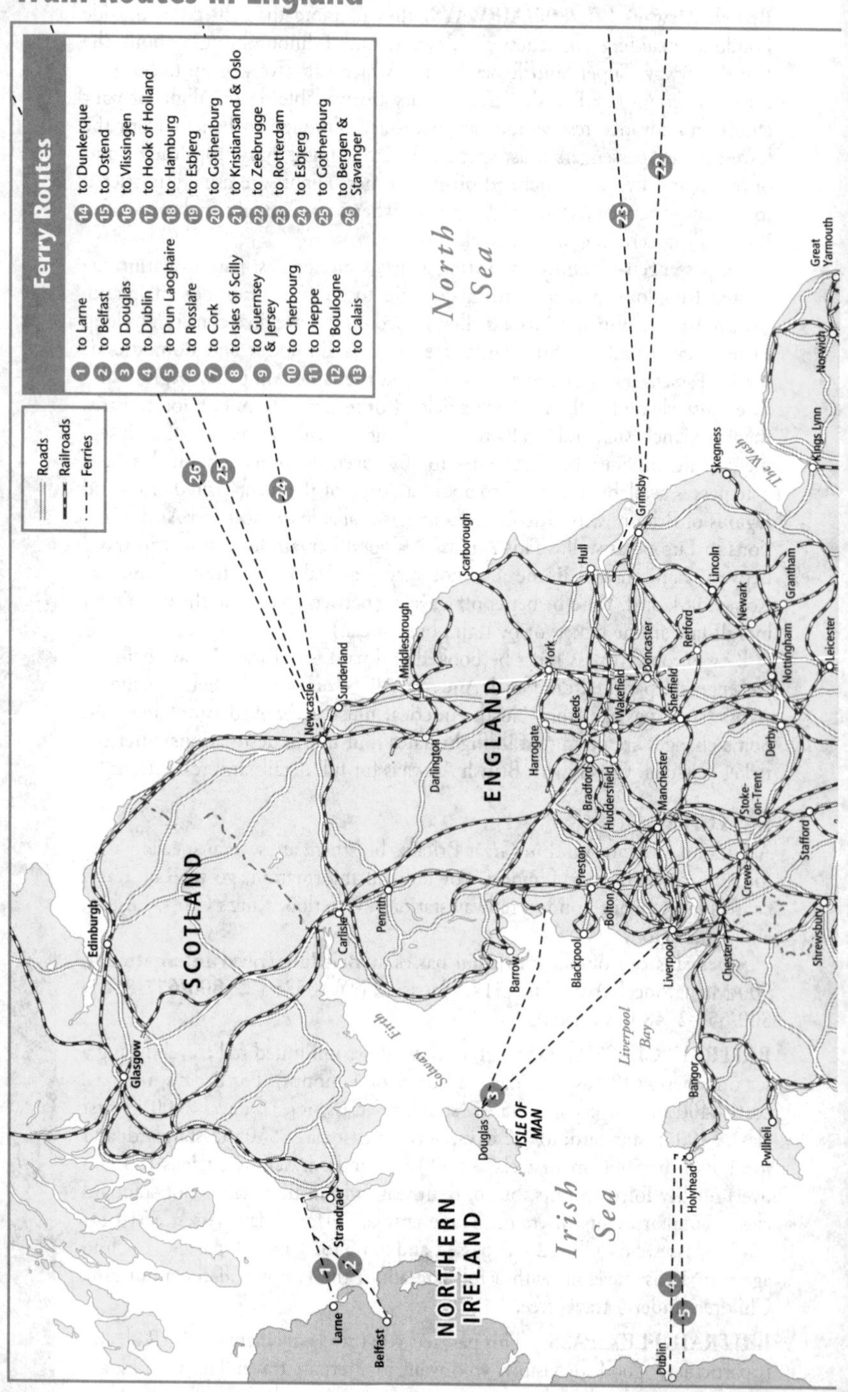

WALES
FRANCE
English Channel
Bristol Channel
Strait of Dover
Lyme Bay
ISLE OF WIGHT
CHANNEL ISLANDS
Lizard Point
London
Fishguard
Swansea
Cardiff
Newport
Hereford
Worcester
Wolverhampton
Birmingham
Walsall
Coventry
Warwick
Stratford-upon-Avon
Rugby
Kettering
Peterborough
Ely
Cambridge
Northampton
Bedford
Milton Keynes
Buckingham
Hertford
Stansted
Ipswich
Harwich
Dedham
Southend-on-Sea
Gravesend
Maidstone
Ashford
Canterbury
Northgate
Ramsgate
Dover
Hastings
Eastbourne
Royal Tunbridge Wells
Brighton
Newhaven
Worthing
Gatwick
Croydon
Guildford
Reading
Camberley
Winchester
Portsmouth
Southampton
Salisbury
Bournemouth
Poole
Weymouth
Bath
Bristol
Swindon
Oxford
Woodstock
Chipping Norton
Cheltenham
Taunton
Exeter
Torquay
Plymouth
Barnstaple
Looe
Newquay
St. Ives
Penzance
Dunkerque
Calais
The Chunnel (to Brussels & Paris)
Boulogne
Dieppe
Cherbourg
0 50 mi
0 50 km
N

$235 in standard. Seniors pay $300 in first class, and youths ages 16 to 25 pay $185 to travel standard class. Also available is a Flexipass that allows 8 days of travel within 2 months and costs $510 in first class, $340 in standard. A senior pass costs $435, the youth standard class $240. New is a Flexipass which can be used for 15 days in any 2-month period and costs $770 in first class and $515 in standard class. Seniors pay $655 in first class and youths $360 in standard class.

Train Travel from London to Principal Cities

To	Station	Typical No. of Trains Per Day	Miles	Travel Time
Bath	Paddington	25	107	1 hr. 11 min.
Birmingham	Euston/Paddington	35	113	1 hr. 37 min.
Bristol	Paddington	46	119	1 hr. 26 min.
Carlisle	Euston	10	299	3 hr. 40 min.
Chester	Euston	16	179	2 hr. 36 min.
Exeter	Paddington	17	174	1 hr. 55 min.
Leeds	King's Cross	19	185	2 hr. 12 min.
Liverpool	Euston	14	193	2 hr. 34 min.
Manchester	Euston	16	180	2 hr.27 min.
Newcastle	King's Cross	26	268	2 hr. 50 min.
Penzance	Paddington	9	305	5 hr.
Plymouth	Paddington	14	226	2 hr. 35 min.
York	King's Cross	27	188	1 hr. 57 min.

SOUTHEAST PASS If you're only planning day trips southeast of London, BritRail's Southeast Pass might make better sense than a more expensive rail pass that's valid in all parts of Britain. This pass allows unlimited travel to accessible destinations throughout BritRail's "Network Southeast," which includes Oxford, Cambridge, Dover, Canterbury, Salisbury, and Portsmouth. Frequent trains—about 41 daily from London to Brighton alone—let you leave early in the morning and return to London in time for the theater or dinner.

A Southeast Pass that's good for 3 days of travel out of any consecutive 8-day period costs $100 in first class, $70 in standard class. A Southeast Pass that's good for 4 days out of any 8-day consecutive period sells for $135 in first class and $100 in standard class. A Southeast Pass that's good for 7 days out of any 15-day consecutive period costs $180 in first class and $135 in standard class. Children under 16 pay $30 and $20 in first and standard class, respectively, for any of the three passes. The Southeast Pass must be purchased either from your travel agent or BritRail Travel International in the United States or Canada (see phone numbers above).

BY BUS

In Britain, a long-distance touring bus is called a "coach," and "buses" are taken for local transportation. There's an efficient and frequent express motorcoach network—run by National Express and other independent operators—that links most of Britain's towns and cities. Destinations off the main route can be easily reached by transferring to a local bus at a stop on the route. Tickets are relatively cheap, often half the price of rail fare, and it's usually cheaper to purchase a round-trip (or "return") ticket than two one-way fares separately.

Victoria Coach Station, on Buckingham Palace Road (☎ **020/7730-3466**), is the departure point for most large coach operators. The coach station is located just two blocks from Victoria Station. For credit card sales (MasterCard and Visa only), call ☎ **020/7730-3499** Monday to Saturday between 9am and 7pm. For cash purchases, get there at least 30 minutes before the coach departs.

National Express runs luxurious long-distance coaches that are equipped with hostesses, light refreshments, reclining seats, toilets, and no-smoking areas. Details about all coach services can be obtained by phoning ☎ **0990/808080** daily between 8am and 10pm. The National Express ticket office at Victoria Station is open from 6am to 11pm.

You might want to consider National Express's **Tourist Trail Pass,** which offers unlimited travel on their network. (This company's service is most extensive in England and Wales.) A 3-day pass costs £49 ($83.30), a 5-day pass £85 ($144.50), a 7-day pass, £120 ($204), and a 14-day pass, £187 ($317.90).

For journeys within a 35-mile radius of London, try the **Green Line** coach service, Lesbourne Road, Reigate Surrey RH2 7LE (☎ **020/8668-7261**). With a 1-day **Diamond Rover Ticket,** costing £7 ($11.90) for adults and £5 ($8.50) for children, you can visit many of the attractions of Greater London and the surrounding region, including Windsor Castle and Hampton Court. The pass is valid for 1 day on almost all Green Line coaches and country buses Monday to Friday after 9am and all day on Saturday and Sunday.

Green Line has bus routes called Country Bus Lines that circle through the periphery of London. Although they do not usually go directly into the center of the capital, they do hook up with the routes of the Green Line coaches and red buses that do.

12 Tips on Accommodations

Reserve your accommodations as far in advance as possible, even in the so-called slow months from November to April. Tourist travel to London peaks from May to October, and during that period, it's hard to come by a moderate or inexpensive hotel room.

CLASSIFICATIONS Unlike some countries, England doesn't have a rigid hotel-classification system. The tourist board grades hotels by crowns instead of stars. Hotels are judged on their standards, quality, and hospitality, and are rated "approved," "commended," "highly commended," and "deluxe." Five crowns (deluxe) is the highest rating. There is even a classification of "listed," with no crowns, and these accommodations are for the most part very modest.

In a five-crown hotel, all rooms must have a private bath; in a four-crown hotel, only 75% have them. In a one-crown hotel, buildings are required to have hot and cold running water in all the rooms, but in "listed" hotels, hot and cold running water in the rooms is not mandatory. Crown ratings are posted outside the buildings. However, the system is voluntary, and many hotels do not participate.

Many hotels, especially older ones, still lack private bathrooms for all rooms. However, most have hot and cold running water, and many have modern wings with all the amenities (as well as older sections that are less up-to-date). When making reservations, always ask what section of the hotel you'll be staying in if it has extensions.

All hotels used to include a full English breakfast of bacon and eggs in the room price, but today that is true for only some hotels. A continental breakfast is commonly included, but that usually means just tea or coffee and toast.

BED & BREAKFASTS In towns, cities, and villages throughout England, homeowners take in paying guests. Watch for the familiar bed-and-breakfast (B&B) signs. Generally, these are modest family homes, but sometimes they may be built like small hotels, with as many as 15 rooms. If they're that big, they are more properly classified as guesthouses. B&Bs are the cheapest places you can stay in England and still be comfortable.

Hometours International (☎ **800/367-4668** or 865/690-8484) will make bed-and-breakfast reservations in England, Scotland, and Wales. This is the only company to guarantee reservations for more than 400 locations in Britain. Accommodations are paid for in the United States in dollars, and prices start as low as $48 per person per night, although they can go as high as $140 per person in London. The company can also arrange for apartments in London or cottages in Great Britain that begin at $800 to $900 per week for a studio. In addition, it offers walking tours of Great Britain, with prices starting as low as $650 for 7 days, including meals, guide, and accommodation.

Reservations for bed-and-breakfast accommodations in London can also be made by writing (not calling) the **British Visitor Centre,** 1 Lower Regent St., London SW1 4PQ. Once in London, you can also visit their office (tube: Piccadilly Circus).

In addition, Susan Opperman and Rosemary Lumb run **Bed and Breakfast Nationwide,** P.O. Box 2100, Clacton-on-Sea, Essex CO16 9BW, an agency specializing in privately owned bed-and-breakfasts all over Great Britain. Host homes range from small cottages to large manor houses, as well as working farms, and the prices vary accordingly. One thing you can be sure of is that owners have been specially selected for their wish to entertain visitors from overseas. Remember that these are private homes, so hotel-type services are not available. You will, however, be assured of a warm welcome, a comfortable bed, a hearty breakfast, and a glimpse of British life. Write for a free brochure. For bookings in accommodations outside London, call ☎ **01255/831235** or fax 01255/831437, daily between 9am and 6pm.

FARMHOUSES In many parts of the country, farmhouses have one, two, even four rooms set aside for paying guests, who usually arrive in the summer months. Farmhouses don't have the facilities of most guesthouses, but they have a rustic appeal and charm, especially for motorists, as they tend to lie off the beaten path. Prices are generally lower than bed-and-breakfasts or guesthouses, and sometimes you're offered some good country home cooking (at an extra charge) if you make arrangements in advance. The British Tourist Authority will provide a booklet, *Stay on a Farm,* or you can ask at local tourist offices.

The **Farm Holiday Bureau** (☎ **1203/696909**) publishes an annual directory in early December that includes 1,000 farms and bed-and-breakfasts throughout the United Kingdom. The listings include quality ratings, the number of bedrooms, nearby attractions and activities, and prices, as well as line drawings of each property. Also listed are any special details, such as rooms with four-poster beds or activities on the grounds (fishing, for example). Many farms are geared toward children, who can participate in light chores—gathering eggs or just tagging along—for an authentic farm experience. The prices range from £16 to £45 ($27.20 to $76.50) a night and include an

English breakfast and usually private facilities. (The higher prices are for stays at mansions and manor houses.)

Another option is self-catering accommodations, which are usually cottages or converted barns that cost from £150 to £450 ($255 to $765) per week, and include dishwashers and central heating. Each property is inspected every year not only by the Farm Holiday Bureau but also by the English Tourist Board. The majority of the properties, with the exception of those located in the mountains, are open year-round.

For a copy of the directory called *Stay on a Farm,* contact the **Farm Holiday Bureau,** National Agricultural Centre, Stoneleigh Park, Warwickshire CV8 2LZ (☎ **1203/696909**). It costs £10 ($17) and may be purchased by credit card.

NATIONAL TRUST PROPERTIES The National Trust of England, Wales, and Northern Ireland, 36 Queen Anne's Gate, London SW1H 9AS (☎ **020/7222-9251**), is Britain's leading conservation organization. In addition to the many castles, forests, and gardens it maintains, the National Trust owns 235 houses and cottages in some of the most beautiful parts of England, Wales, and Northern Ireland. Some of these properties are in remote and rural locations, some have incomparable views of the coastline, and others stand in the heart of villages and ancient cities.

Most of these comfortable self-catering holiday accommodations are available for rental throughout the year. Examples include a simple former coast guard cottage in Northumbria, a gaslit hideaway on the Isle of Wight, a gem of a country house above the Old Brewhouse at Chastleton, a 15th-century manor house in a hidden corner of the Cotswolds, and a superb choice of cottages in Devon and Cornwall. Houses can be booked for a week or more. Many can be booked for midweek or weekend breaks on short notice, particularly in the autumn and winter months. National Trust properties can sleep from 2 to 12 guests, and range in price from £146 ($248.20) per week for a small rental in winter to £1,393 ($2,368.10) per week for a larger property in peak season. Prices include value-added tax. Call ☎ **01225/791199** for reservations.

Although anyone can book rentals in National Trust properties, it's worth mentioning the trust's U.S. affiliate, the **Royal Oak Foundation,** 285 W. Broadway, Suite 400, New York, NY 10013-2299 (☎ **800/913-6565** or 212/966-6565), which publishes a full-color 120-page booklet that describes all National Trust holiday rental properties, their facilities, and prices. Copies cost $5 for members, $7.50 for nonmembers. Individual annual memberships are $45, and family memberships are $70. Benefits include free admission to all National Trust sites and properties open to the public, plus discounts on reservations at cottages and houses owned by them, and air and train travel.

HOLIDAY COTTAGES & VILLAGES Throughout England, there are fully furnished studios, houses, cottages, "flats" (apartments), even trailers suitable for families or groups that can be rented by the month. From October to March, rents are sometimes reduced by 50%.

The British Tourist Authority and most tourist offices have lists available. The BTA's free *Apartments in London and Holiday Homes* lists rental agencies such as **At Home Abroad,** 405 E. 56th St., Suite 6H, New York, NY 10022 (☎ **212/421-9165;** fax 212/752-1591). Interested parties should write or fax a description of their needs, and At Home Abroad will send listings at no charge.

British Travel International (☎ **800/327-6097** or 540/298-2232; fax 540/298-2347), represents between 8,000 and 10,000 rental properties in the United Kingdom, with rentals by the week (Saturday to Saturday), and requires a 50% payment at the time of booking. A catalog with pictures of their offerings is available for a $5 fee that is counted toward a deposit. They have everything from honey-colored, thatch-roofed cottages in the Cotswolds to apartments in a British university city. The company represents about 100 hotels in London whose rates are discounted by 5% to 50%, depending on the season and market conditions, and they have listings of some 4,000 bed-and-breakfast establishments. They are also the North American representative of the United Kingdom's largest bus company, National Express.

The **Barclay International Group (BIG;** ☎ **800/845-6636;** www.barclayweb.com) specializes in short-term apartment (flat) rentals in London, and cottages in the English countryside. These rentals can be appropriate for families, groups of friends, or businesspeople traveling together, and are sometimes less expensive than equivalent stays in hotels. Apartments, available for stays as short as 1 night (although the company prefers that guests stay a minimum of 3 nights and charges a premium if your stay is shorter), are usually more luxurious than you'd imagine. Furnished with kitchens, they offer a low-cost alternative to restaurant meals. Apartments suitable for one or two occupants begin, during low season, at around $500 a week (including tax) and can go much higher for deluxe accommodations that offer many hotel-like features and amenities. For extended stays in the English countryside, BIG has country cottages in such areas as the Cotswolds, the Lake District, and Oxford, as well as farther afield in Scotland and Wales. The company can also arrange tickets for sightseeing attractions, BritRail passes, and various other "extras." They have recently established an office in England at 45 Albemarle St., London W1X 3FE (☎ **020/7495-2986;** fax 020/74992312).

At the cheaper end of the spectrum, there's **Hoseasons Holidays,** Sunway House, Lowestoft, NR32 2LW (☎ **01502/500-500**), a reservations agent based in Suffolk (East Anglia). They arrange stopovers in at least 300 vacation villages throughout Britain. Although many are isolated in bucolic regions far from any of the sites covered within this guidebook, others lie within an hour's drive of Stratford-upon-Avon. Don't expect luxury or convenience: Vacation villages in England usually consist of a motley assortment of trailers, uninsulated bungalows, and/or mobile homes perched on cement blocks. They're intended as frugal escapes for claustrophobic urbanites with children. Such a place might not meet your expectations for a vacation in the English countryside (and a minimum stay of 3 nights is usually required), but it's hard to beat the rate. A 3-day sojourn begins from £45 ($76.50) per person, double occupancy.

YOUTH HOSTELS The **Youth Hostels Association** (England and Wales) operates a network of 240 youth hostels in major cities, in the countryside, and along the coast. They can be contacted at Customer Services Department, YHA, Trevelyan House, 8 St. Stephen's Hill, St. Albans, Hertfordshire, AL1 2DY (☎ **01727/855215**), for a free map showing the locations of each youth hostel and full details, including prices.

13 Tips on Shopping

When shopping for the best buys in England, note that British goods, even products from Wales and Scotland, may offer sensational buys even when sold in England. You will also find Irish stores and Irish departments in some stores often selling merchandise at the same good value you'd find on a shopping trip to Ireland itself. Many French brands, it may come as a surprise, are less expensive in the United Kingdom than in France!

This section is an overview of England's shopping scene, including what's hot, where to get it, and how you can save money and secure value-added tax (VAT) refunds. If you're heading to London, check out chapter 4 for coverage of the capital's shopping and the famous sales.

THE BEST BUYS OF BRITAIN

When bargain hunting, focus on those goods that are manufactured in England and are liable to cost much more when exported. These include anything from The Body Shop, Filofax, or Doc Martens; many woolens and some cashmeres; most English brands of bone china; antiques, used silver, and rare books.

ANTIQUES Whether you're looking for museum-quality antiques or simply fun junk, England has the stores, the resources, the stalls, and the markets. You can shop the fanciest of upmarket shops—mostly in London, Bath, and the Cotswolds—or browse through antiques shows, markets, fairs, buildings, centers, arcades, warehouses, jumble fairs, fetes, and car boot sales throughout the country. (A car boot sale is the British version of a yard sale. Participants set up tables at an abandoned parking lot or airfield to sell their goods.)

Actually, prices are better once you get outside of London. Entire towns and areas in Britain are known to be treasure troves for those seeking anything from architectural salvage to a piece of the Holy Grail. Whereas the Cotswolds and Bath are known as charming places to shop for antiques, there are warehouses in Suffolk, Merseyside, and in the Greater Manchester (Yorkshire and Lancashire) area that aren't glamorous but offer dealers and those in the know the best buys. Serious shoppers can head directly to the Manchester area, get a car or van and just start shopping. The best hunting grounds are Boughton (right outside Chester), Liverpool, Prestwich, and Stockport. Harrogate and nearby Knaresborough are known for antiques, but offer a far more upscale scene with prices competitive to those in the Cotswolds.

AROMATHERAPY The British must have invented aromatherapy—just about every store sells gels, creams, lotions, or potions made with the right herbs and essential oils to cure whatever ails you, including jet lag. Whether it works or not is secondary to the fact that most of the British brands are half the U.S. price when bought on home soil. **The Body Shop** becomes the best store in the world at prices like these. Check out drugstore brands as well. Shoppers like the Body Shop knockoffs that **Boots The Chemist** makes, as well as their own line (sold in another part of the store) of healing foot gels. Both of these are national brands available all over the United Kingdom. In addition, some small communities have homemade brands—check out **Woods of Windsor** (in the heart of downtown Windsor) for English flower soaps, lotions, and cures.

BASIC BRIT GEAR Don't assume any bargains on woolens, cashmeres, tweeds and the like—often British quality is much higher than similar, and less expensive, goods available in the United States. If you want the best and expect it to last forever, you can't beat British-made, especially in gear that has been fine-tuned over the last century for the weather and outdoor lifestyle: from wax coats (**Barbour** is the leading status brand) to raincoats to guns (and English roses). While we can hardly put **Doc Martens** brand of shoes in the traditional Brit category, they do cost a lot less in Britain than in America. The other quintessential English accessory is the **Filofax,** sold in a variety of versions with inserts galore for 30% to 50% less than prices in the United States.

BEAUTY PRODUCTS Dime-store brands of makeup cost less than they do in the United States. The French line **Bourjois** (made in the same factories that produce Chanel makeup) costs less in London than in Paris and isn't sold in the United States; Boots makes its own Chanel knockoff line, **Number 7.**

BONE CHINA Savings actually depend on the brand, but can be as much as 50% off U.S. prices. The trick is that shipping and U.S. duties may wipe out any savings; know what you're doing before you buy—and how you plan to get it back. Don't forget that there are factory outlets that sell seconds.

DESIGNER THIS & THAT Designer clothing from any of the international makers may be less in London than in the United States or Paris, but know your prices. Often the only difference is the VAT refund, which at 15% to 17.5% is substantial. This game is also highly dependent on the value of the dollar.

While you won't get a VAT refund on used designer clothing, London has the best prices on used Chanel (and similar) clothing of any major shopping city.

HATS "Does anyone still wear a hat?," Elaine Stritch asked archly in the musical *Company.* In England, the answer is yes. Everyone wears a hat, including the queen. Hats are sold all over England in department stores and specialty stores. Resale shops are an excellent graveyard for m'lady's discards.

ROYAL SOUVENIRS Forget about investing in Diana memorabilia; word is that it won't appreciate significantly because there was so much of it. Still, royal collectibles can be cheap kitsch bought in street markets or serious pieces from coronations long past found in specialist's shops. If you're buying new for investment purposes, it must be kept in mint condition.

TAPESTRY & KNITTING For some reason, the English call needlepoint "tapestry." It's a passion, perhaps the seasonal flip side to gardening. Tapestry kits by the famous English designers, and Welsh queen of needles Elizabeth Bradley, cost a fraction of their U.S. prices when purchased anywhere in England or Wales.

Whereas England is famous for its sweaters (jumpers), what it should be famous for are the sweater kits: do-it-yourself jobs from the major designers that come with yarn, instructions, and a photo. English knitter-designers are cult heroes in Britain and do everything but knit autographs.

SHOPPING STRATEGIES

Most English towns feature a main street usually called the High Street. On this one road you'll find a branch of each of what is locally called "the High Street multiples." These are the chain stores that dominate the retail scene.

The leader among them is **Marks & Spencer,** a private label department store with high-quality goods at fair value prices; **Boots The Chemist** (a drugstore); **Laura Ashley** (less expensive in the United Kingdom); **The Body Shop** (the most popular politically correct bath and beauty statement of our times); **Monsoon** (a firm that sells hot fashion made from Far Eastern fabrics for moderate prices; they also have a dress-up division called **Twilight** and an accessories business called **Accessorize**); **Habitat** (sort of the English version of the Pottery Barn); and maybe (if you're lucky) **Past Times,** sort of a museum shop selling reproduction gifts and souvenirs. **Shelly's, Pied a Terre,** and **Hobbs** are all shoe stores selling everything from Doc Martens to expensive-looking cheap shoes. **Knickerbox** is usually found in train stations rather than on High Streets, but it's interesting nonetheless—the store sells fashion underwear at what the English call moderate prices.

ANTIQUES GALORE Napoléon was wrong, England is not a nation of shopkeepers—it's a nation of antiques collectors. Weekends are devoted to fairs and markets; evenings can be spent reading the dozens of newsstand specialty magazines geared to collectors or the plethora of books. Books in Britain are more expensive than in the United States, but the selection of titles on design, home furnishings, do-it- yourself, and collecting is staggering.

There are a number of famous antiques fairs held at certain times of the year as well as several annual big-time events that attract several thousand dealers and thousands of shoppers. Among the best outside of London are those held at the **Newark and Nottinghamshire Showgrounds** (six times a year); **Sussex Midweek Fairs,** Ardingly (six times a year); **Newmarket** (four times a year); **Shepton Mallet** (four times a year); **Cardiff International** (twice a year); and **Royal Welsh Showgrounds** (twice a year). For the exact dates of any of these events, contact **DMG County Antiques**

How to Get Your VAT Refund

To receive back a portion of the tax paid on purchases made in Britain, first ask the store personnel if they do VAT refunds and what their minimum purchase is. Once you've achieved this minimum, ask for the paperwork; the retailer will have to fill out a portion themselves. Several readers have reported that merchants have told them that they can get refund forms at the airport on their way out of the country. *This is not true.* You must get a refund form from the retailer (don't leave the store without one), and it must be completed by the retailer on the spot.

Fill out your portion of the form and then present it, along with the goods, at the customs office in the airport. Allow a half hour to stand in line. *Remember:* You're required to show the goods at your time of departure, so don't pack them in your luggage and check it; put them in your carry-on instead.

Once you have the paperwork stamped by the officials, you have two choices: You can mail the papers and receive your refund in either a British check (no!) or a credit card refund (yes!), or you can go directly to the Cash VAT Refund desk at the airport and get your refund in your hand, in cash. The bad news: If you accept cash other than sterling, you will lose money on the conversion rate. (If you plan on mailing your paperwork, try to remember to bring a stamp with you to the airport; if you forget, you can usually get stamps from stamp machines and/or the convenience stores in the terminal.)

Be advised that many stores charge a flat fee for processing your refund, so £3 to £5 may be automatically deducted from the total refund you receive. But since the VAT in Britain is 17.5%, if you get back 15%, you're doing fine.

Note: If you're traveling to other countries within the European Union, you don't go through any of this in Britain. At your final destination, prior to departure from the European Union, you file for all your VAT refunds at one time.

Fairs (☎ **01278/784912;** fax 01636/707923); or **DMG Antiques Fairs, Ltd.** (☎ **01636/702326**).

For immediate information on current antiques fairs and events, check the magazine section of the ***Sunday Times*** where you'll find the Antique Buyer's Guide, which lists fairs all over England, not just in London.

There are also continual **car boot sales,** as well as **house sales,** during which entire estates are cleaned out. There are only a few of these each year, and they become sort of voyeuristic social events; people drive for miles in order to attend. Advertisements are usually taken in magazines such as *Country Life.*

Just as house sales have boomed in recent years, the other big trend to come out of the recession is that **resale shops** are springing up all over. No one seems shy about admitting that her Chanel and Louis Feraud are secondhand. London has a lot of these shops, but many out-of-the-way towns and cities have enormous resale shops as well.

TAXES & SHIPPING Value-added tax is the British version of sales tax, but it is a whopping 17.5% on most goods. This tax is added to the total so that the price on a sales tag already includes VAT. Non–European Union residents can get back all, or most, of this tax if they apply for a VAT refund (see sidebar, "How to Get Your VAT Refund").

One of the first secrets of shopping in England is that the minimum expenditure needed to qualify for a refund on value-added tax (VAT) is a mere £50 ($85). Not every store honors this minimum (it's £100 ($170) at Harrods; £75 ($127.50) at Selfridges; £62 ($105.40) at Hermès), but it's far easier to qualify for a tax refund in Britain than almost any other country in the European Union.

Vendors at flea markets may not be equipped to provide the paperwork for a refund, so if you're contemplating a major purchase and really want that refund, ask before you fall in love. Be suspicious of any dealer who tells you there's no VAT on antiques. There didn't use to be, but there is now. The European Union has now made the British add VAT to antiques. Since dealers still have mixed stock, pricing should reflect this fact. So ask if it's included before you bargain on a price. Get to the price you're comfortable with first, then ask for the VAT refund.

VAT is not charged on goods shipped out of the country, whether you spend £50 ($85) or not. Many London shops will help you beat the VAT by shipping for you. But watch out: Shipping can double the cost of your purchase. Also expect to pay U.S. duties when the goods reach you at home.

You may want to consider paying for excess baggage (rates vary with the airline), or else have your packages shipped independently. Independent operators are generally less expensive than the airlines. Try **London Baggage,** London Air Terminal, Victoria Place, SW1 (☎ **020/7828-2400;** tube: Victoria), or **Burns International Facilities.** They are found at Heathrow Airport in Terminal 1 or at Terminal 4. For information, call **020/8745-5301.**

DUTY-FREE AIRPORT SHOPPING Shopping at airports is big business, so big business has taken over the management of some of Britain's airports to ensure that passengers in transit are enticed to buy. Terminal 4 at London Heathrow Airport is a virtual shopping mall, but each terminal has a good bit of shopping, with not a lot of crossover between brands.

Prices at the airport for items such as souvenirs and candy bars are actually higher than on the streets of London, but the duty-free prices on luxury goods are usually fair. There are often promotions and coupons that allow for pounds off at the time of the purchase.

Don't save all your shopping until you get to the airport, but do know prices on land and sea so that you know when to pounce.

14 Sightseeing Passes

There are several passes available that can cut down considerably on entrance costs to the country's stately homes and gardens. If you plan to do extensive touring, you'll save a lot of pounds by using one of these passes instead of paying the relatively steep entrance fees on an attraction-by-attraction basis.

Listed below are three organizations that offer passes waiving admission charges to hundreds of historical properties located throughout the United Kingdom. Each is a good deal, as the money you'll save on visitation to just a few of the available sites will pay for the price of the pass.

The **British National Trust** offers members free entry to some 240 National Trust sites in Britain, and more than 100 properties in Scotland. Focusing on gardens, castles, historic parks, abbeys, and ruins, sites include Chartwell, St. Michael's Mount, and Beatrix Potter's House. The membership fee includes a listing of all properties, maps, and essential information for independent tours, and listings and reservations for holiday cottages located on the protected properties.

Individual memberships cost $45 annually, and family memberships, including up to seven people, run $70, so savings on the admission charges, combined with discounts on holiday cottage reservations and British Air or BritRail travel, make this especially appealing. Visa and MasterCard are accepted.

Contact **The British National Trust,** 36 Queen Anne's Gate, London SW1H 9AS (☎ **020/7222-9251**), or **The Royal Oak Foundation,** 285 W. Broadway, no. 400, New York, NY 10013-2299 (☎ **212/966-6565**).

The **English Heritage** sells 7- and 14-day passes and annual memberships, offering free admission to more than 300 historical sites in England, and half-price admission to more than 100 additional sites in Scotland, Wales, and the Isle of Man. (Admission to these additional sites is free for anyone who renews his or her annual membership after the first year.) Sites include Hadrian's Wall, Stonehenge, and Kenilworth Castle.

Also included is free or reduced admission to 450 historic re-enactments and open-air summer concerts, a handbook detailing all properties, a map, and, with the purchase of an annual membership, events and concerts diaries, and *Heritage Today,* a quarterly magazine.

A 7-day Overseas Visitor Pass runs £12.50 ($21.25) for an adult or £27.50 ($46.75) for a family of six or less. A child accompanied by an adult goes free. A 21-day pass is £28 ($47.60) for an adult (free for a child) or £40 ($68) for a family. Annual memberships are also available with rates of £26 ($44.20) for an adult, £16 ($27.20) for those between the ages of 16 and 21, and free for a child under 16, or else £45.50 ($77.35) for a family ticket. MasterCard and Visa are accepted.

For visitor passes and membership, contact **Customer Services, English Heritage,** 429 Oxford St., London W1R 2HD (☎ **020/7973-3434**) or join directly at the site.

The Great British Heritage Pass, available through **BritRail,** allows entry to more than 500 public and privately owned historic properties, including

Shakespeare's birthplace, Stonehenge, Windsor Castle, and Edinburgh Castle. Included in the price of the pass is *The Great British Heritage Gazetteer,* a brochure that lists the properties with maps and essential information.

A pass gains you entrance into private properties not otherwise approachable. A 7-day pass costs $54, a 15-day pass is available for $75, and a 1-month pass is $102. Passes are nonrefundable, and there is no discounted children's rate. A $10 handling fee is charged additionally for each ticket issued.

To order passes, contact **BritRail Travel International, Inc.,** 500 Mamaroneck Ave., Suite 314, Harrison, NY 10528; visit BritRail's British Travel Shop at 551 Fifth Ave. (at 45th Street), New York, NY 10176; or call **800/677-8585;** www.britrail.com.

Fast Facts: England

For information on London, refer to "Fast Facts: London," in chapter 3.

Area Codes The country code for England is **44.** The area code for London is **020.**

Business Hours With many, many exceptions, business hours are Monday to Friday from 9am to 5pm. In general, stores are open Monday to Saturday from 9am to 5:30pm. In country towns, there is usually an early closing day (often on Wednesday or Thursday), when the shops close at 1pm.

Car Rentals See "Getting Around," earlier in this chapter.

Climate See "When to Go," earlier in this chapter.

Currency See "Money," earlier in this chapter.

Customs See "Entry Requirements & Customs," earlier in this chapter.

Documents Required See "Entry Requirements & Customs," earlier in this chapter.

Drugstores In Britain, they're called "chemists." Every police station in the country has a list of emergency chemists. Dial "0" (zero) and ask the operator for the local police, who will give you the name of the one nearest you.

Electricity British electricity is 240 volts AC (50 cycles), roughly twice the voltage in North America, which is 115 to 120 volts AC (60 cycles). American plugs don't fit British wall outlets. Always bring suitable transformers and/or adapters—if you plug an American appliance directly into a European electrical outlet without a transformer, you'll destroy your appliance and possibly start a fire. Tape recorders, VCRs, and other devices with motors intended to revolve at a fixed number of revolutions per minute probably won't work properly even with transformers.

Embassies & High Commissions See "Fast Facts: London," in chapter 3.

Emergencies Dial **999** for police, fire, or ambulance. Give your name, address, and telephone number and state the nature of the emergency.

Holidays See "When to Go," earlier in this chapter.

Information See "Visitor Information," earlier in this chapter, and the individual city/regional chapters that follow.

Legal Aid The American Services section of the U.S. Consulate (see "Embassies & High Commissions," under "Fast Facts: London," in chapter 3) will give you advice if you run into trouble abroad. They can advise you of your rights, and will even provide a list of attorneys (for which you'll have to pay if services are used). But they cannot interfere on your behalf in the legal processes of Great Britain. For questions about American citizens who are arrested abroad, including ways of getting money to them, telephone the **Citizens Emergency Center** of the Office of Special Consulate Services in Washington, D.C. (☎ **202/647-5225**).

Liquor Laws The legal drinking age is 18. Children under 16 aren't allowed in pubs, except in certain rooms, and then only when accompanied by a parent or guardian. Don't drink and drive. Penalties are stiff.

In England, pubs can legally be open Monday to Saturday from 11am to 11pm, and on Sunday from noon to 10:30pm. Restaurants are also allowed to serve liquor during these hours, but only to people who are dining on the premises. The law allows 30 minutes for "drinking-up time." A meal, incidentally, is defined as "substantial refreshment." And you have to eat and drink sitting down. In hotels, liquor may be served from 11am to 11pm to both residents and nonresidents; after 11pm, only residents, according to the law, may be served.

Mail Post offices and subpost offices are open Monday to Friday from 9am to 5:30pm and Saturday from 9:30am to noon.

Sending an airmail letter to North America costs 44p (75¢) for 10 grams (.35 oz.), and postcards require a 37p (65¢) stamp. British mailboxes are painted red and carry a royal coat of arms. All post offices accept parcels for mailing, provided they are properly and securely wrapped.

Pets It is illegal to bring pets to Great Britain—except with veterinary documents, and then most animals are subject to an outrageous 6-month quarantine.

Police Dial **999** if the matter is serious. Losses, thefts, and other criminal matters should be reported to the police immediately.

Safety Stay in well-lit areas and out of questionable neighborhoods, especially at night. In Britain, most of the crime perpetrated against tourists is pickpocketing and mugging. These attacks usually occur in such cities as London, Birmingham, or Manchester. Most villages are safe.

Taxes To encourage energy conservation, the British government levies a 25% tax on gasoline (petrol). There is also a 17.5% national value-added tax (VAT) that is added to all hotel and restaurant bills, and will be included in the price of many items you purchase. This can be refunded if you shop at stores that participate in the Retail Export Scheme (signs are posted in the window). See the "How to Get Your VAT Refund" box in the "Tips on Shopping" section, above.

In October 1994, Britain imposed a departure tax. Currently it is £20 ($34), but is included in the price of your ticket.

Telephone To call England from North America, dial **011** (international code), **44** (Britain's country code), the local area codes (usually three or four digits and found in every phone number we've given in this book), and the seven-digit local phone number. The local area codes found throughout this book all begin with "0"; you drop the "0" if you're calling from outside Britain, but you need to dial it along with the area code if you're calling from another city or town within Britain. For calls within the same city or town, the local number is all you need.

For **directory assistance** in London, dial **142;** for the rest of Britain, **192.**

There are three types of public pay phones: those taking only coins, those accepting only phonecards (called Cardphones), and those taking both phonecards and credit cards. At coin-operated phones, insert your coins before dialing. The minimum charge is 10p (15¢).

Phonecards are available in four values—£2 ($3.40), £4 ($6.80), £10 ($17), and £20 ($34)—and are reusable until the total value has expired. Cards can be purchased from newsstands and post offices. Finally, the credit-call pay phone operates on credit cards—Access (MasterCard), Visa, American Express, and Diners Club—and is most common at airports and large railway stations.

To make an international call from Britain, dial the international access code (**00**), then the country code, then the area code, and finally the local number. Or call through one of the following long-distance access codes: **AT&T USA Direct** (☎ 0800/890011), **Canada Direct** (☎ 0800/890016), **Australia** (☎ 0800/890061), and **New Zealand** (☎ 0800/890064). Common country codes are: USA and Canada, **1;** Australia, **61;** New Zealand, **64;** South Africa, **27.**

If you're calling **collect** or need the assistance of an international operator, dial **155.**

Caller, beware: Some hotels routinely add outrageous surcharges onto phone calls made from your room. Inquire before you call! It'll be a lot cheaper to use your own calling card number or to find a pay phone.

Time England follows Greenwich mean time (5 hours ahead of Eastern standard time), with British summertime lasting (roughly) from the end of March to the end of October. Throughout most of the year, including the summer, Britain is 5 hours ahead of the time observed on the East Coast of the United States. Because of different daylight-savings-time practices in the two nations, there's a brief period (about a week) in autumn when Britain is only 4 hours ahead of New York, and a brief period in spring when it's 6 hours ahead of New York.

Tipping For cab drivers, add about 10% to 15% to the fare shown on the meter. However, if the driver personally loads or unloads your luggage, add something extra.

In hotels, porters receive 75p ($1.30) per bag, even if you have only one small suitcase. Hall porters are tipped only for special services. Maids receive £1 ($1.70) per day. In top-ranking hotels, the concierge will often submit a separate bill showing charges for newspapers and other items; if he or she has been particularly helpful, tip extra.

Hotels often add a service charge of 10% to 15% to most bills. In smaller bed-and-breakfasts, the tip is not likely to be included. Therefore, tip for special services, such as the waiter who serves you breakfast. If several people have served you in a bed-and-breakfast, you may ask that 10% to 15% be added to the bill and divided among the staff.

In both restaurants and nightclubs, a 15% service charge is added to the bill, which is distributed among all the help. To that, add another 3% to 5%, depending on the service. Waiters in deluxe restaurants and nightclubs are accustomed to the extra 5%. Sommeliers (wine stewards) get about £1 ($1.70) per bottle of wine served. Tipping in pubs isn't common, but in wine bars, the server usually gets about 75p ($1.30) per round of drinks.

Barbers and hairdressers expect 10% to 15%. Tour guides expect £2 ($3.40), although it's not mandatory. Gas station attendants are rarely tipped and theater ushers don't expect tips.

Planning Your Trip: An Online Directory

by Lynne Bairstow

Lynne Bairstow is the co-author of *Frommer's Mexico* and the editorial director of *e-com* magazine.

Day by day, the Internet becomes more integrated into our lives—including the way we plan and book our travel. By early 2000, one in every 10 trips was being booked online, a trend that's sure to accelerate.

The Internet not only provides a wealth of destination information, but also gives you the chance to compare experiences with fellow travelers, ask experts for pre-trip advice, seek out discounted fares once accessible only to travel-industry insiders, and stay in touch via e-mail while you're away. The instant communication and storehouse of information have revolutionized the way travel is researched, reserved, and realized.

This online directory will help you take better advantage of the planning information available online, and is best used in conjunction with this book. Part 1 lists general Internet resources that can make any trip easier, such as sites for obtaining the best possible prices on airline tickets. In Part 2, you'll find some top online guides for England, including city guides, visitor information, and activities.

Please keep in mind that this is not a comprehensive list, but rather a discriminating selection to get you started. Recognition is given to sites based on their content value and ease of use, and are not paid for—unlike some Web-site rankings, which are based on payment. Finally, remember this is a press time snapshot of leading Web sites—some undoubtedly will have evolved, changed, or moved by the time you read this.

1 Top Travel-Planning Web Sites

While the Internet was once a conglomerate of sites for researching places to visit, several key companies have emerged that offer comprehensive travel planning and booking. In addition to Frommer's Online, we list the other top online travel agencies below, along with some more specialized services.

WHY BOOK ONLINE?

Online agencies have come a long way over the past few years, now providing tips for finding the best fare as well as giving you suggested dates or times to travel that yield the lowest price if your plans are at all flexible. Other sites even allow you to establish the price you're willing to pay, and then check the airlines' willingness to accept it.

Editor's Note: What You'll Find at the Frommer's Site

We highly recommend **Arthur Frommer's Budget Travel Online** (**www.frommers.com**) as an excellent travel planning resource. Of course, we're a little biased, but you'll find indispensable travel tips, reviews, monthly vacation giveaways, and online booking. Among the most popular features of this site is the regular "Ask the Expert" bulletin boards, which feature one of the Frommer's authors answering your questions via online postings.

Subscribe to Arthur Frommer's Daily Newsletter (**www.frommers.com/newsletters**) to receive the latest travel bargains and insider travel secrets in your e-mailbox every day. You'll read daily headlines and articles from the dean of travel himself, highlighting last-minute deals on airfares, accommodations, cruises, and package vacations. You'll also find great travel advice by checking our "Tip of the Day" or "Hot Spot of the Month."

Search our Destinations archive (**www.frommers.com/destinations**) of more than 200 domestic and international destinations for great places to stay, tips for traveling there, and what to do while you're there. Once you've researched your trip, the online reservations system (**www.frommers.com/booktravelnow**) takes you to Frommer's favorite sites for booking your vacation at affordable prices.

However, in some cases, these sites may not always yield the best price. Unlike a travel agent, for example, they may not have access to charter flights offered by wholesalers.

Online booking sites aren't the only places to reserve airline tickets—all major airlines have their own Web sites and often offer incentives, like bonus frequent flyer miles or Net-only discounts, when you buy online or buy an e-ticket.

The best of the travel-planning sites are now highly personalized; they store your seating preferences, meal preferences, tentative itineraries, and credit card information, allowing you to quickly plan trips or check agendas.

In many cases, booking your trip online can be better than working with a travel agent. It gives you the widest variety of choices, control, and the 24-hour convenience of planning your trip when you choose. All you need is some time—and often a little patience—and you're likely to find the fun of online travel research will greatly enhance your trip.

WHO SHOULD BOOK ONLINE?

Online booking is best for travelers who want to know as much as possible about their travel options, for those who have flexibility in their travel dates and are looking for the best price, and for bargain hunters driven by a good value, who are open-minded about where they travel.

One of the biggest successes in online travel for both passengers and airlines is the offer of last-minute specials, such as American Airlines' weekend deals or other Internet-only fares that must be purchased online. Another advantage is that you can cash in on incentives for booking online, such as rebates or bonus frequent flyer miles.

Business and other frequent travelers also have found numerous benefits in online booking, as the advances in mobile technology provide them with the ability to check flight status, change plans, or get specific directions from handheld computing devices, mobile phones, and pagers. Some sites will even e-mail or page passengers if their flight is delayed.

Online booking is increasingly able to accommodate complex itineraries, even for international travel. The pace of evolution on the Net is rapid, so you'll probably find additional features and advancements by the time you visit these sites. What the future holds for online travelers is ever-increasing personalization and customization.

TRAVEL-PLANNING & BOOKING SITES

Below are listings for the top sites for planning and booking travel. The following sites offer domestic and international flight, hotel, and rental-car bookings, plus news, destination information, and deals on cruises and vacation packages. Free (one-time) registration is required for booking.

Travelocity (incorporates Preview Travel). **www.travelocity.com; www.previewtravel.com; www.frommers.travelocity.com**

Travelocity is Frommer's online travel-planning and booking partner. Travelocity uses the SABRE system to offer reservations and tickets for more than 400 airlines, plus reservations and purchase capabilities for more than 45,000 hotels and 50 car-rental companies. An exclusive feature of the SABRE system is its **Low Fare Search Engine,** which automatically searches for the three lowest-priced itineraries based on a traveler's criteria. Last-minute deals and consolidator fares are included in the search. If you book with Travelocity, you can select specific seats for your flights with online seat maps, and also view diagrams of the most popular commercial aircraft. Its hotel finder provides street-level location maps and photos of selected hotels. With the **Fare Watcher** e-mail feature, you can select up to five routes and receive e-mail notices when the fare changes by $25 or more.

Travelocity's **Destination Guide** includes updated information on some 260 destinations worldwide — supplied by Frommer's.

Note to AOL Users: You can book flights, hotels, rental cars, and cruises on AOL at keyword: Travel. The booking software is provided by Travelocity/Preview Travel and is similar to the Internet site. Use the AOL "Travelers Advantage" program to earn a 5% rebate on flights, hotel rooms, and car rentals.

Staying Secure

More people still look online than book online, partly due to fear of putting their credit card numbers out on the Net. Secure encryption has removed this fear for most travelers. In some cases, however, it's simply easier to buy from a local travel agent who can deliver your tickets to your door (especially if your travel is last-minute or if you have special requests). You can find a flight online and then book it by calling a toll-free number or contacting your travel agent, though this is somewhat less efficient. To be sure you're in secure mode when you book online, look for a little icon of a key (in Netscape) or a padlock (in Internet Explorer) at the bottom of your Web browser.

Expedia. **expedia.com**
Expedia is Travelocity's major competitor. It offers several ways of obtaining the best possible fares: **Flight Price Matcher** service allows your preferred airline to match an available fare with a competitor; a comprehensive **Fare Compare** area shows the differences in fare categories and airlines; and **Fare Calendar** helps you plan your trip around the best possible fares. Its main limitation is that like many online databases, Expedia focuses on the major airlines and hotel chains, so don't expect to find too many budget airlines or one-of-a-kind B&Bs here.

TRIP.com. **www.trip.com**
TRIP.com began as a site geared toward business travelers, but its innovative features and highly personalized approach have broadened its appeal to leisure travelers as well. It is the leading travel site for those using mobile devices to access Internet travel information.

TRIP.com includes a trip-planning function that provides the average and lowest fare for the route requested, in addition to the current available fare. An on-site "newsstand" features breaking news on airfare sales and other travel specials. Among its most popular features are Flight TRACKER and intelliTRIP. **Flight TRACKER** allows users to track any commercial flight en route to its destination anywhere in the U.S., while accessing real-time FAA-based flight monitoring data. **intelliTRIP** is a travel search tool that allows users to identify the best airline, hotel, and rental-car rates in less than 90 seconds.

Yahoo Travel. **www.travel.yahoo.com**
Yahoo is currently the most popular of the Internet information portals, and its travel site is a comprehensive mix of online booking, daily travel news, and destination information. Their **Best Fares** area offers what it promises, plus provides feedback on refining your search if you have flexibility in travel dates or times. There is also an active section of Message Boards for discussions on travel in general and specific destinations.

TOP VACATION-PACKAGE SITES

Both **Expedia** and **Travelocity** (see above) offer excellent selections and searches for complete vacation packages. Travelers can search by destination and desired dates coupled with how much they are willing to spend. Travelocity has a valuable "Cruise Critic" function, to help would-be cruisers

Airline Web Sites

Below are the Web sites for the major airlines. These sites offer schedules, flight booking and most have pages where you can sign up for email alerts for weekend deals and other late-breaking bargains.

Air Canada **www.aircanada.com**
American Airlines **www.aa.com**
British Airways **www.british-airways.com**
Continental Airlines **www.continental.com**
Delta **www.delta-air.com**
Northwest Airlines **www.nwa.com**
TWA **www.twa.com**
United Airlines **www.ual.com**
Virgin Atlantic Airways **www.fly.virgin.com**

obtain first-hand accounts of the quality and details of a cruise from recent passengers.

Travel wholesalers, like **Apple Vacations** (**www.applevacations.com**) and **Funjet** (**www.funjet.com**), are also good starting points, but still require that the final booking be handled through a travel agent.

As travel agents tend to be more expert at sorting through the values in vacation packages, you might find **Vacation.com** (**www.vacation.com**) helpful in previewing packages and finding an appropriate agent to help you book the deal. This site represents a nationwide network of 9,800 local travel agencies that specialize in finding the best values in cruises, vacation packages, tours, and other leisure travel services.

LAST-MINUTE DEALS AND OTHER ONLINE BARGAINS

There's nothing airlines hate more than flying with lots of empty seats. The Net has enabled airlines to offer last-minute bargains to entice travelers to fill those seats. Most of these are announced on Tuesday or Wednesday and are valid for travel the following weekend, but some can be booked weeks or months in advance. You can sign up for weekly e-mail alerts at the airlines' sites (see "Airline Web Sites," above) or check sites that compile lists of these bargains, such as **Smarter Living** or **WebFlyer** (see below). To make it easier, visit a site that will round up all the deals and send them in one convenient weekly e-mail. But last-minute deals aren't the only online bargains; other sites can help you find value even if you haven't waited until the eleventh hour. Increasingly popular are travel auction sites and services that let you name the price you're willing to pay for an air seat or vacation package.

Cheap Tickets. **www.cheaptickets.com**

Cheap Tickets has exclusive deals that aren't available through more mainstream channels. One caveat about the Cheap Tickets site is that it will offer fare quotes for a route, then later show this fare is not valid for your dates of travel—most other Web sites, such as Expedia, consider your dates of travel before showing what fares are available. Despite its problems, Cheap Tickets can be worth the effort because its fares can be lower than those offered by its competitors.

✪ 1travel.com. **www.1travel.com**

Here you'll find deals on domestic and international flights, cruises, hotels, and all-inclusive resorts such as Club Med. 1travel.com's **Saving Alert** compiles last-minute air deals so you don't have to scroll through multiple e-mail alerts. A feature called "Drive a little using low-fare airlines" helps map out strategies for using alternate airports to find lower fares. And **Farebeater** searches a database that includes published fares, consolidator bargains, and special deals exclusive to 1travel.com. *Note:* The travel agencies listed by 1travel.com have paid for placement.

Bid for Travel. **www.bidfortravel.com**

Bid for Travel is another of the travel auction sites, similar to Priceline (see below), which are growing in popularity. In addition to airfares, Internet users bid on vacation packages and hotels.

Go4less.com. **www.go4less.com**

Specializing in last-minute cruise and package deals, Go4less has some excellent offers. The Hot Deals section gives an alphabetical listing by destination of super discounted packages.

LastMinuteTravel.com. **www.lastminutetravel.com**

Suppliers with excess inventory come to this online agency to distribute unsold airline seats, hotel rooms, cruises, and vacation packages. It's got great deals, but you have to put up with an excess of advertisements and slow-loading graphics.

Moment's Notice. www.moments-notice.com
As the name suggests, Moment's Notice specializes in last-minute vacation and cruise deals. You can browse for free, but if you want to purchase a trip, you have to join Moment's Notice, which costs $25. Go to World Wide Hot Deals for a complete list of special deals in international destinations.

✪ Priceline.com. travel.priceline.com
Even people who aren't familiar with many Web sites have heard about Priceline.com. Launched in 1998 with a $10-million ad campaign featuring William Shatner, Priceline lets you "name your price" for domestic and international airline tickets and hotel rooms. In other words, you select a route and dates, guarantee with a credit card, and make a bid for what you're willing to pay. If one of the airlines in Priceline's database has a fare lower than your bid, your credit card will automatically be charged for a ticket.

But you can't say when you want to fly—you have to accept any flight leaving between 6am and 10pm on the dates you selected, and you may have to make a stopover. No frequent flyer miles are awarded, and tickets are nonrefundable and can't be exchanged for another flight. So if your plans change, you're out of luck. Priceline can be good for travelers who have to take off on short notice (and who are thus unable to qualify for advance-purchase discounts). But be sure to shop around first, because if you overbid, you'll be required to purchase the ticket—and Priceline will pocket the difference between what it paid for the ticket and what you bid.

Priceline says that over 35% of all reasonable offers for domestic flights are being filled on the first try, with much higher fill rates on popular routes (New York to San Francisco, for example). It defines "reasonable" as not more than 30% below the lowest generally available advance-purchase fare for the same route.

Smarter Living. www.smarterliving.com
Best known for its e-mail dispatch of weekend deals on 20 airlines, Smarter Living also keeps you posted about last-minute bargains on everything from Windjammer Cruises to flights to Iceland.

SkyAuction.com. www.skyauction.com
An auction site with categories for airfare, travel deals, hotels, and much more.

Travelzoo.com. www.travelzoo.com
At this Internet portal, over 150 travel companies post special deals. It features a Top 20 list of the best deals on the site, selected by its editorial staff each Wednesday night. This list is also available via an e-mail list, free to those who sign up.

Know When the Sales Start

While most people learn about last-minute weekend deals from e-mail dispatches, it can pay to check the airline sites to find out precisely when they post their special fares. Because deals are limited, they can vanish within hours, sometimes minutes—often before you even read your e-mail. An example: Southwest's specials are posted at 12:01am Tuesdays (Central time). So if you're looking for a cheap flight, stay up late and check Southwest's site to grab the best new deals.

Travel Discussion Sites

One of the best sources of travel information is word-of-mouth, from someone who has just been there. Internet discussion groups are offering an unprecedented way for travelers around the globe to connect and share experiences. **Frommer's Online (www.frommers.com)** offers these message boards, as well as areas where you can pose questions to the guidebook writers themselves, in its section "Ask the Expert." **Yahoo Travel, Expedia,** and **Travelocity** are other good sources of online travel discussion groups.

The granddaddy of specialized discussions on particular topics is **Usenet,** a collection of over 50,000 newsgroups. You'll find a comprehensive listing at **Deja News (www.dejanews.com/usenet)** or at **www.liszt.com.**

WebFlyer. **www.webflyer.com**
WebFlyer is a comprehensive online resource for frequent flyers and also has an excellent listing of last-minute air deals. Click on "Deal Watch" for a round-up of weekend deals on flights, hotels, and rental cars from domestic and international suppliers.

ONLINE TRAVELER'S TOOLBOX

Veteran travelers usually carry some essential items to make their trips easier. Following is a selection of online tools to smooth your journey.

Visa ATM Locator. **www.visa.com/pd/atm/**

MasterCard ATM Locator. **www.mastercard.com/atm**
Find ATMs in hundreds of cities in the U.S. and around the world. Both include maps for some locations and both list airport ATM locations. *Tip:* You'll usually get a better exchange rate using ATMs than exchanging traveler's checks at banks, but check in advance to see what kind of fees your bank will assess for using an overseas ATM.

Intellicast. **www.intellicast.com**
Weather forecasts for all 50 states and cities around the world. Note that temperatures are in Celsius for many international destinations, so don't think you'll need that winter coat for your next trip to Athens.

✪ Mapquest. **www.mapquest.com**
The best of the mapping sites that lets you choose a specific address or destination; in seconds, it will return back a map and detailed directions. It really is easier than calling, asking, and writing down directions. The site also links to special travel deals and helpful sites.

Universal Currency Converter. **www.xe.net/currency**
See what your dollar or pound is worth in more than a hundred other countries.

2 The Top Web Sites for England

VISITOR INFORMATION

For AOL Members
AOL International: Great Britain
Keyword: Britain
A vibrant guide to the U.K. that gives you the skinny on arts, dining, nightlife and more. You can subscribe to a free online newsletter and participate in AOL's active chat areas to see what others are saying or pose a question of your own. To access the AOL London guide, type in the keyword, "London."

Check E-mail at Internet Cafes While Traveling

Until a few years ago, most travelers who checked their e-mail while traveling carried a laptop—an expensive and often technologically problematic option. Thankfully, Web-based free e-mail programs have made it much easier to check your mail.

Just open an account at any one of the numerous "freemail" providers—the original leaders continue to be **Hotmail** (**hotmail.com**), **Excite** (**www.excite.com**), and **Yahoo! Mail** (**mail.yahoo.com**), though many are available. AOL users should check out **AOL Netmail,** and **USA.NET** (**www.usa.net**) comes highly recommended for functionality and security. You can find hints, tips, and a mile-long list of freemail providers at **www.emailaddresses.com**.

Then, all you'll need to check your mail is a Web connection, easily available at Net cafes and copy shops around the world. After logging on, just call up your freemail's Internet address, enter your username and password, and you'll have access to your mail. From these sites, you can download all of your e-mail—even from office accounts—or your local or national Internet Service Provider address. There will be a section generally called "check other mail" that allows you to add the names of other e-mail servers.

The downside is that most Web-based e-mail sites allow only a maximum of 3MB capacity per mail account, which can fill up quickly. Also, message sending and receiving is not immediate; some messages may be delayed by several hours, or even days.

Internet cafes have become ubiquitous, so for a few dollars an hour you'll be able to check your mail and send messages from virtually anywhere in the world. Interestingly, Internet cafes tend to be more common in very remote areas, where they may offer the best form of access for an entire community, especially if phone lines are difficult to obtain. Surf the excellent Net Café Guide before leaving home (**www.netcafeguide.com**) for listings across the U.K. divided up by town.

✪ A2B Travel. **www.a2btravel.com**
This site focuses on helping travelers plan and book their trips. It has lots of nifty tools, such as bus, rail and ferry guides, a point-to-point mileage calculator and a guide to more than two dozen UK airports. You'll also find maps, a currency converter, and weather information.

✪ Britannia. **www.britannia.com**
This expansive site is much more than a travel guide—it's chock full of lively features, history and regional profiles, including sections on Wales and King Arthur.

UK for Visitors (About.com). **gouk.about.com/travel/gouk**
This useful gateway links to local information sites all over the country. It also offers a limited guide to hotels and restaurants, but you're better off going to a specialist for both.

GETTING AROUND

BAA: London Airports. **www.baa.co.uk**
Guides and terminal maps for Heathrow, Gatwick, Stansted and smaller airports, with info about flight arrival times, duty-free shops, airport restaurants, and information on travel into London.

Birmingham International Airport. www.bhx.co.uk
All the information you need for navigating this airport: ground transport, facilities, flight schedules for incoming flights, and more.

Eurostar. www.eurostar.com
Fares, timetables, and booking for this high-speed train, which shoots through the Chunnel to France and Belgium.

London Transport. www.londontransport.co.uk
London Transport operates the Underground (subway), city buses and river ferries. This extensive and well-designed site includes maps, fare information, and advice to help you get around London as easily and cheaply as possible. You'll find schedules for the last trains and for night buses.

✪ **RailEurope. www.raileurope.com**
This is a one-stop shopping site for European train travel, whether you're looking for fares and schedules, discount passes or a ride through the Chunnel. Also see Rick Steves' *Europe Through the Back Door* (**www.ricksteves.com**) for insider tips on Eurail passes.

The TrainLine. www.thetrainline.com
Find out schedules, book tickets and reserve seats on trains run by all the UK's privatized rail companies. This site also explains the restrictions for different ticket types.

ACCOMMODATIONS

✪ **Automobile Association-UK. www.theaa.co.uk**
This outstanding guide lists hundreds of places to stay, ranked by price and quality and with apparently objective reviews. Many of the lodgings accept online bookings. You'll also find dining information with ratings based on food, service, atmosphere and price. Most, but not all, restaurants list typical meal prices and which credit cards are accepted.

British Hotel Reservation Centre. www.bhrc.co.uk
This consolidator offers hotels and apartments in London and six other popular tourist towns, publishing the rack rate, its own price and the resultant saving. You can search by hotel name, location or closeness to attractions, and then book online.

Hotels England. www.hotelsengland.com
This site promises discounts of up to 50% but, checking prices against those quoted direct by a couple of hotels, it's more like 25%. Irritatingly, Hotels England does not list the rack rate for comparison so you should call around too.

Late Rooms. www.laterooms.com
From seaside resorts to country houses, inns and city breaks, this site offers big savings for same-day to 3-week-away bookings. The downside is that although it does give official Star and Diamond ratings, there are no independent reviews or photographs, and the site is annoyingly arranged by region not town.

Cottage Net UK. www.cottage-net.ndirect.co.uk
Referral service for 20,000 properties to rent, from thatched cottages to seaside villas, in the UK and Ireland. You can search by region, county and town and pay \$21 (£12) for three area listings with photographs, local information and the owners' contact details.

THINGS TO SEE AND DO IN ENGLAND

The Insider's Guide to Shopping. **www.inshop.co.uk**
Join up for free and get the latest news on promotions, events and sales across the capital. It will also tell you where to find the hottest items of the season, from womenswear to housewares, luggage to watches and jewelry.

Londontown.com: The Official Internet Site for London. **www.londontown.com**
A fab site from the tourist board that will get you panting to start your trip. It lists events, accommodation, attractions, pubs and living it up after dark. Daily special features include discount offers. You can download mini-area maps, by Tube stop, attraction, theater or street. And the editorial is written like a chat with a friend.

Official London Theater Guide. **www.officiallondontheatre.co.uk**
An extensive site from the Society of London Theatres, which also runs the half-price ticket booth in Leicester Square. Search by type of show, title, theater name, or date. Or simply view everything playing in London—listings include a brief summary, actors, times, prices and the date a show is guaranteed to run until.

✪ Original London Walks. **www.walks.com**
London's longest established guided walks company posts a day-by-day schedule of more than a dozen distinct tours, such as "In the Footsteps of Sherlock Holmes" or "Jack the Ripper Haunts."

This is London. **www.thisislondon.com**
This well-rounded site from the *Evening Standard* includes a frank guide to dining, drinking and clubbing. You can search for city attractions and events. And the Hot Tickets section offers independent insider advice on theater, music and comedy. Any kind words are well-earned.

✪ The 24 Hour Museum. **www.24hourmuseum.org.uk**
This excellent Web site aims to promote Britain's thousands of museums, galleries and heritage attractions—and, boy, does it do a good job. It is entertaining and downloads fast. You can search geographically or gear your holiday around one of its themed "trails" and tour Museums and the Macabre, Art Treasures of the North East, and so on.

✪ Cathedrals of Britain. **www.cathedrals.org.uk**
This well-designed site features dozens of cathedrals, organized by region. Each listing includes a couple of photos, advice for getting there and history. You could surf here to plan an entire touring vacation.

English Heritage. **www.english-heritage.org.uk**
Mouthwatering photographs and details of the hundreds of glorious historic castles, country houses, Roman sites, churches, abbeys and ancient monuments cared for by this organization all over England. A must-visit site for pre-trip planning.

The National Trust. **www.nationaltrust.org.uk**
This charity owns over 300 historic buildings and countless acres of countryside. You can search the list by area, county, name or theme, from film & TV to ghosts. The Surf the Coast section makes you want to pack a picnic and rush off to the seaside.

UK Golf. **www.uk-golf.com**
A listing of 2,000 courses throughout UK with greens fees and directions to help you get there. Despite the site's name, you'll also find listings for France, Spain and Portugal.

CITY GUIDES AND REGIONAL ATTRACTIONS

Bath.co.uk. www.bath.co.uk

This site attempts to round up accommodation, shopping, entertainment, attractions and restaurants, not always successfully as some sections claim they can find no listings. The dining guide usefully allows searching by price but does not carry reviews.

Brighton & Hove: A virtual guide. www.brighton.co.uk

A fab site with everything you need to know about this seaside town, made fashionable in the late 18th century when the dissolute Prince George built the Brighton Pavilion, and now one of funkiest places in England for shopping, clubbing and eating out.

Bristol City Council. www.bristol-city.gov.uk

Unlike the various net directories serving Bristol, this site is quick and includes interesting background on the city. The hotel, restaurant and attractions listings are nicely presented, with special sections on family fun, events on water, and so on.

Canterbury: The Official Guide. www.canterbury.co.uk

There's everything you could need to know here from accommodation and dining to shopping, attractions and events. It includes price, opening times and useful links, but no reviews and the site is slow.

Dartmoor National Park Authority. www.dartmoor-npa.gov.uk

This ancient moorland is a haven for walkers and horse-riders. Check the official Web site for accommodation, events, fact files and links to other local information sources.

Oxford. www.oxfordcity.co.uk

This very user-friendly site makes it easy to learn more about lodgings, restaurants, shops, and evening entertainment. Hotel listings are divided into price bands and link to the properties' own Web sites where you can see images and compare rates. It's also a nice orientation to the city itself and its prestigious university.

Stonehenge: Ancient Sites Directory. www.henge.demon.co.uk/wiltshire/shenge.html

Pictures of this astonishing ancient monument, directions to it, and a frank appraisal of the tourist facilities from an enthusiast. The main site lists other stone circles and barrows in England, Wales and Scotland.

Cambridge News. www.cambridge-news.co.uk/tourism

This Web site is a great source of information about one of England's most beautiful towns. It has lots of useful links, including one to Cambridge University where you'll find a fascinating, if slightly dry, history of this ancient institution.

✪ Birmingham Entertainment Guide. www.bhamentertainment.co.uk

This remarkably wide-ranging guide includes listings for restaurants, pubs, hotels, theater, and events. In the attractions section alone you'll find galleries, museums, parks, and historic sites.

Derby City Index Page. www.derbycity.com

Known as the Ghost Capital of the World, Derby claims haunted pubs, churches, inns and mills, but this site is no phantom. The listings for top attractions, pubs, museums and events are incredibly thorough and the site is nicely illustrated, offering a sense of what you can see in Derby and the dramatic Peak District.

Gloucestershire: England at its Best. www.visit-glos.org.uk
This handy guide to one of the most beautiful counties—it includes the Cotswolds, the Royal Forest of Dean and Severn Vale—features attractions, activities, events and walking tours from the local tourist information center.

Nottingham Tour. www.proweb.co.uk/~lordthorpe/nottingham/notts1.htm
This site is heavy on photos and slow to load, but it's a nice introduction to Nottingham and its legendary outlaw, Robin Hood. You'll find sections on history, the local castle, inns, the Nottingham Festival, and of course Sherwood Forest, as well as local Web links.

Peak District Tourism Online. www.peakdistrict-tourism.gov.uk/peakdistrict
Take a peak at some sights and find out where to go in Britain's first national park, from the White Peak to the Drowned Dales, and the Seven Wonders. There is information on wildlife, local activities such as caving and climbing, and hotel listings to search by price.

✪ **Stratford-upon-Avon: Shakespeare's Stratford. www.stratford.co.uk**
This site won't win any design awards but it's a wonderful resource for exploring Shakespeare's birthplace. Click on "A Visitor's Guide" for detailed information on local attractions including Warwick Castle (**www.warwick-castle.co.uk**), tips for getting around, and suggestions for lodging and dining. Click on "Shakespeare" for information about local performances and background on his life.

Blackpool: Entertainment Capital of the North. www.blackpool.gov.uk
This site has a lovely picture of Blackpool by night—much lovelier than the daytime reality. It offers some useful listings for dining, lodging, clubs, and shows, but with no reviews or links.

Chester: An official guide. www.chestercc.gov.uk/tourism
Where to stay and eat out, and what to visit in this ancient town, from the biggest uncovered Roman amphitheater in Britain, the most complete city walls, the cathedral, fab shopping and events at the local racecourse.

✪ **Hadrian's Wall. www.hadrians-wall.org**
Take a virtual walk along the wall that stretches from Bowness-on-Solway to Wall's End (north of Newcastle upon Tyne). Use this site to find out about touring the wall (there's a link to the Hadrian's Wall bus), and to figure out where to stay nearby.

Lake District. www.uk-north.com
A guide to attractions, lodging and entertainment. There are also tips on how to avoid holiday crowds and find the more secluded areas of the Lake District.

✪ **Leeds Tourism Information. www.leeds.gov.uk/tourinfo/tourinfo.html**
An all-in-one site where you can find updated events listings, hotel information and booking, and detailed information on more than a dozen museums and historic attractions. There are also tips on nearby places of interests, listings for parks and gardens, and local sports news.

✪ **Liverpool Guide. www.liverpoolguide.co.uk**
An entertaining and very comprehensive site, put together by a young local lad when he was still at school. He encourages input from Web-surfers and city visitors, some of whom he has even met up with during their holiday in Liverpool.

Manchester Online. www.manchesteronline.co.uk

News, weather, sports and what's on (events) from the *Manchester Evening News*. The paper was in the middle of creating a new tourist guide at time of writing.

Virtual Newcastle. www.newcastle-gov.uk

Click through to the About Town section for very comprehensive listings, without reviews, and essential tourist information. It also has links to other useful sites.

York: This Is York. www.thisisyork.co.uk

This site forms the *Evening Press*, combining an extensive travel guide with local news and entertainment information.

Yorkshire Dales Online. www.yorkshiredales.net

Maps and guides to this 1,769 square kilometer national park, including where to stay and what to see from rare sheep breeds to ancient fortresses.

3 Settling into London

Europe's largest city is like a great wheel, with Piccadilly Circus at the hub and dozens of communities branching out from it. Since London is such a conglomeration of neighborhoods, each with its own personality, first-time visitors may be confused until they get the hang of it. You'll probably spend most of your time in the West End, where many attractions are located, except for the historic part of London known as The City, which includes the Tower of London. This chapter will help you get your bearings.

1 Orientation

ARRIVING

By Plane

London is served by four airports. The one you'll fly into will depend on your airline's point of departure.

LONDON HEATHROW AIRPORT Heathrow, west of London, in Hounslow (☎ **020/8759-4321**), is divided into four terminals. Terminal 4 handles the long-haul and transatlantic operations of British Airways. Most transatlantic flights of U.S. airlines arrive at Terminal 3. Terminals 1 and 2 receive the intra-European flights of several European airlines.

Getting to Central London from Heathrow There is an Underground (subway) connection from Heathrow Central to the center of London; the trip takes 50 minutes and costs £3.50 ($5.95). The Heathrow Express is by far the easiest (albeit more expensive) way to get into Central London. Trains leave every 15 minutes for a 15-minute ride to Paddington Station. (And when you leave London to catch your flight home, you can even check your luggage right at the train station.) Fares are £12 ($20.40) for a regular ticket, £20 ($34) for first class. For more information, call **Heathrow Express** (☎ **0845/600-1515**). Airbuses will also take you to central London in about an hour; they cost £7 ($11.90) for adults and £3 ($5.10) for children. A taxi will cost at least £45 ($76.50). For more information about train or bus connections, call ☎ **020/7222-1234.**

GATWICK AIRPORT This smaller and more remote airport (☎ **01293/535353** for flight information) lies 25 miles south of London, in West Sussex. Some charter flights, as well as many scheduled flights on major airlines, arrive here.

Getting to Central London from Gatwick Trains leave for London every 15 minutes during the day and every hour at night; the round-trip cost is £20 ($34) for adults and half price for children ages 5 to 15 (under 5 free). There is also an express Flightline bus (no. 777) from Gatwick to Victoria Station that departs every half-hour from 6:30am to 8pm and every hour from 8 to 11pm; it costs £12 ($20.40) per person round-trip. For more information about train or bus connections, call ☎ **020/7222-1234.**

It's very expensive to take a taxi from Gatwick into central London. A taxi usually costs from £60 ($102); however, you must negotiate a fare with the driver before you get into the cab—the meter does not apply since Gatwick lies outside the Metropolitan Police District.

LONDON CITY AIRPORT Located just 3 miles east of the bustling business community of Canary Wharf and 6 miles east of The City, London City Airport (☎ **020/7646-0000**) is served by 11 airlines (Air Engiadina, Air France, Air Jet, Air UK, Augsburg Airways, CityJet, Crossair, Denimair, Lufthansa, Malmö Aviation, Sabena, and VLM) that fly from 18 cities in western Europe and Scandinavia.

Getting to Central London from London City Airport A blue-and-white bus charges £4 ($6.80) each way to take you from the airport to the Liverpool Street Station, where you can connect with rail or Underground transportation to almost any destination. The bus runs daily every 10 minutes during the hours the airport is open (approximately 6:50am to 9:20pm, except Saturday when it closes at 1pm).

There's also a shuttle bus to Canary Wharf, where trains from the Dockland Line Railway make frequent 10-minute runs to the heart of London's financial district, known as "The City." Here, passengers can catch the Underground from the Bank tube stop.

In addition, London Transport bus no. 473 goes from the City Airport to East London, where you can board any Underground at the Plaistow tube stop.

LONDON STANSTED AIRPORT Located about 50 miles northeast of London's West End, Stansted (☎ **01279/680-500**) was originally a U.S. air base during World War II, and was expanded massively in the 1980s. Most of its flights arrive from continental Europe, although it also has an increased number of charter flights from the North American mainland.

Getting to Central London from Stansted Your best bet is the Stansted Express, a train that takes you from the airport to Liverpool Street Rail and Tube Station in 45 minutes. Tickets cost £10.40 ($17.70) for adults and £5.20 ($8.85) for children. Daily service runs every 30 minutes from 5:30am to 11pm.

If you prefer the relative privacy of a taxi, you'll pay dearly for the privilege. For a ride to London's West End, they'll charge you from £45 ($76.50) for up to four passengers, and from £100 ($170) for five or six passengers. Expect the ride to take around 75 minutes during normal traffic conditions, but beware of Friday afternoons, when dense traffic may double your travel time. Our advice: stick to the Express.

BY TRAIN

Most trains originating in Paris and traveling through the Chunnel arrive at **Waterloo Station.** Visitors from Amsterdam arrive at the Liverpool Street Station, and those journeying south by rail from Edinburgh pull in at **King's Cross Station.** Each of these stations is connected to London's vast bus and Underground network, and each has phones, restaurants, pubs, luggage-storage areas, and London Regional Transport Information centers.

By Car

If you're taking a car ferry across the Channel, you can quickly connect with a motorway into London. *Remember to drive on the left.* London is encircled by a ring road. Determine which part of the city you wish to enter and follow the signs there.

Once you're in London, we don't recommend driving. Unfortunately, parking is scarce and expensive. Before you arrive in London, call your hotel and ask for advice on where to park your car.

VISITOR INFORMATION

The Britain Visitor Centre, 1 Regent St., London SW1 4XT (tube: Piccadilly Circus), caters to walk-in visitors who wait in line for information on all parts of Britain. (Telephone information has been suspended.) On the premises are a British Rail ticket office, a travel agency, a theater-ticket agency, a hotel-booking service, a bookshop, and a souvenir shop. Open Monday through Friday from 9am to 6:30pm, Saturday and Sunday from 10am to 4pm, with extended hours on Saturday from June through September.

Equally useful is the London Tourist Board's **Tourist Information Centre,** forecourt of Victoria Station, SW1 (tube: Victoria). The center deals with accommodations in all size and price categories. It also arranges for travel, tour-ticket sales, and theater reservations, and it has a shop that sells books and souvenirs. Open from Easter to October, daily from 8am to 7pm; November to Easter, Monday to Saturday from 8am to 6pm, Sunday from 9am to 4pm.

The tourist board also maintains offices at Heathrow Airport's Terminals 1, 2, and 3, Underground Concourse, and at the Liverpool Street Railway Station.

The tourist board has a 24-hour recorded information service, **Visitorcall** (☎ **01839/123456**), which, for a fee of 50p (85¢) per minute, will play a recorded message about tourist attractions that change every day.

London's Neighborhoods in Brief

The West End Neighborhoods

Mayfair Bounded by Piccadilly, Hyde Park, and Oxford and Regent streets, this is the most elegant, fashionable section of London, filled with luxury hotels, Georgian town houses, and swank shops. Grosvenor Square (pronounced *Grov*-nor) is nicknamed "Little America," because it's home to the American embassy and a statue of Franklin D. Roosevelt; Berkeley Square (pronounced *Bark*-ley) was made famous by the song, "A Nightingale Sang in Berkeley Square." At least once you'll want to dip into this exclusive section. One of the curiosities of Mayfair is **Shepherd Market,** a tiny village of pubs, two-story inns, book and food stalls, and restaurants, all sandwiched between Mayfair's greatness.

Marylebone All first-time visitors head to Marylebone, to explore Madame Tussaud's waxworks or walk along Baker Street in the make-believe footsteps of Sherlock Holmes. The streets form a near-perfect grid, with the major ones running north-south from Regent's Park toward Oxford Street. Marylebone Lane and High Street still retain some of their former village atmosphere, but this is otherwise a now rather anonymous area. At Regent's Park, you can visit Queen Mary's Gardens or, in summer, see Shakespeare performed in an open-air theater.

St. James's Often called "Royal London," St. James's is home to Elizabeth II, who lives at its most famous address, Buckingham Palace. The neighborhood begins at

Piccadilly Circus and moves southwest, incorporating Pall Mall, The Mall, St. James's Park, and Green Park; it's "frightfully convenient," as the English say, enclosing such addresses as American Express on Haymarket and many of London's leading department stores. Be sure to stop in at Fortnum & Mason, at 181 Piccadilly, the world's most luxurious grocery store.

Piccadilly Circus & Leicester Square **Piccadilly Circus** is the very heart and soul of London; its gaudy living room. The circus isn't Times Square yet, but its traffic, neon, and jostling crowds don't do anything to make it fashionable. If you want a little more grandeur, retreat to the Regency promenade of exclusive shops, the Burlington Arcade, designed in 1819.

A bit more tawdry is **Leicester Square,** a center of theaters, restaurants, movie palaces, and nightlife. It was once a chic address, but it changed forever in the Victorian era, when four towering entertainment halls were opened (even Queen Victoria came to see a circus here). In time, the old palaces changed from stage to screen; three of them still show films.

Soho These densely packed streets in the heart of the West End are famous for their gloriously cosmopolitan mix of people and trades. A decade ago, much was heard about the decline of Soho, when the thriving sex industry threatened to engulf it. That destruction has now largely been halted. Respectable businesses have returned, and chic restaurants and shops prosper; it's now the heart of London's expanding gay colony. But Soho wouldn't be Soho without a few sex shops and porn theaters.

Soho starts at Piccadilly Circus and spreads out; it's basically bordered by Regent Street, Oxford Street, Charing Cross Road, and the theaters of Shaftesbury Avenue. Carnaby Street, a block from Regent Street, was the center of the universe in the Swinging '60s, but now it's just a schlocky sideshow. Across Shaftesbury Avenue, a busy street lined with theaters, is London's **Chinatown,** centered on Gerrard Street: small, authentic, and packed with excellent restaurants. But Soho's heart—with marvelous French and Italian delicatessens, fine butchers, fish stores, and wine merchants—is farther north, on Brewer, Old Compton, and Berwick streets; Berwick is also a wonderful open-air fresh-food market. To the north of Old Compton Street, Dean, Frith, and Greek streets have fine little restaurants, pubs, and clubs, like Ronnie Scott's for jazz. The British movie industry is centered in Wardour Street.

Bloomsbury This district, a world within itself, lies northeast of Piccadilly Circus, beyond Soho. It is, among other things, the academic heart of London; here you'll find the University of London, several other colleges, and many bookstores. Despite its student population, this neighborhood is fairly staid. Its reputation has been fanned by such writers as Virginia Woolf, who lived within its bounds and became one of the unofficial leaders of a group of artists and writers known as "the Bloomsbury Group."

The heart of Bloomsbury is **Russell Square,** and the streets jutting off from the square are lined with hotels and B&Bs. Most visitors come to the neighborhood to visit the British Museum, one of the world's greatest repositories of treasures. The British TeleCom Tower (1964) on Cleveland Street is a familiar landmark.

Nearby is **Fitzrovia,** bounded by Great Portland, Oxford, and Gower streets, and reached by the Goodge Street tube. Goodge Street, with its many shops and pubs, forms the heart of the "village." Once a major haunt of artists and writers—this was the stamping ground of Ezra Pound, Wyndham Lewis, and George Orwell, among others—the bottom end of Fitzrovia is a virtual extension of Soho, with a cluster of Greek restaurants.

Holborn The old borough of Holborn, which abuts The City to the west, takes in the heart of legal London—the city's barristers, solicitors, and law clerks call it home.

London at a Glance

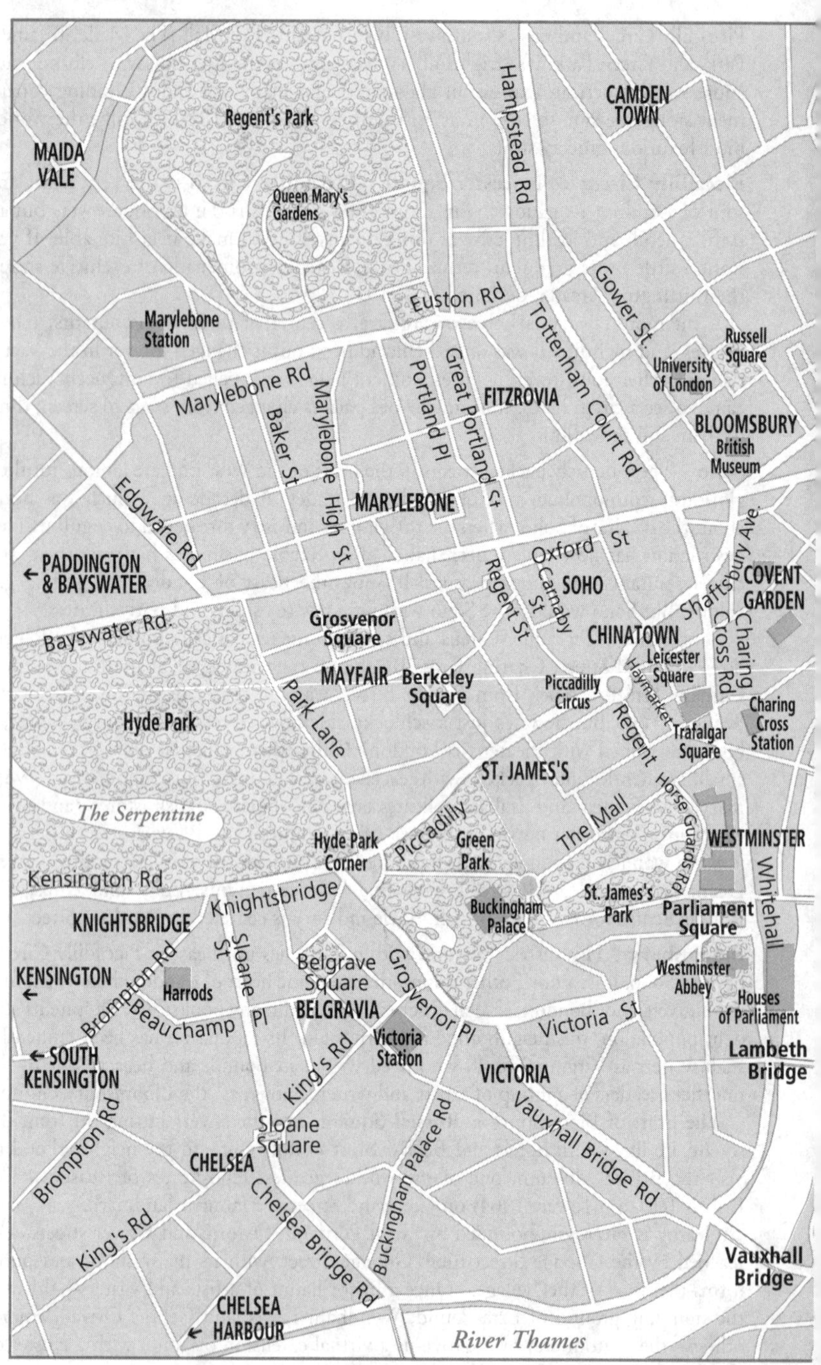

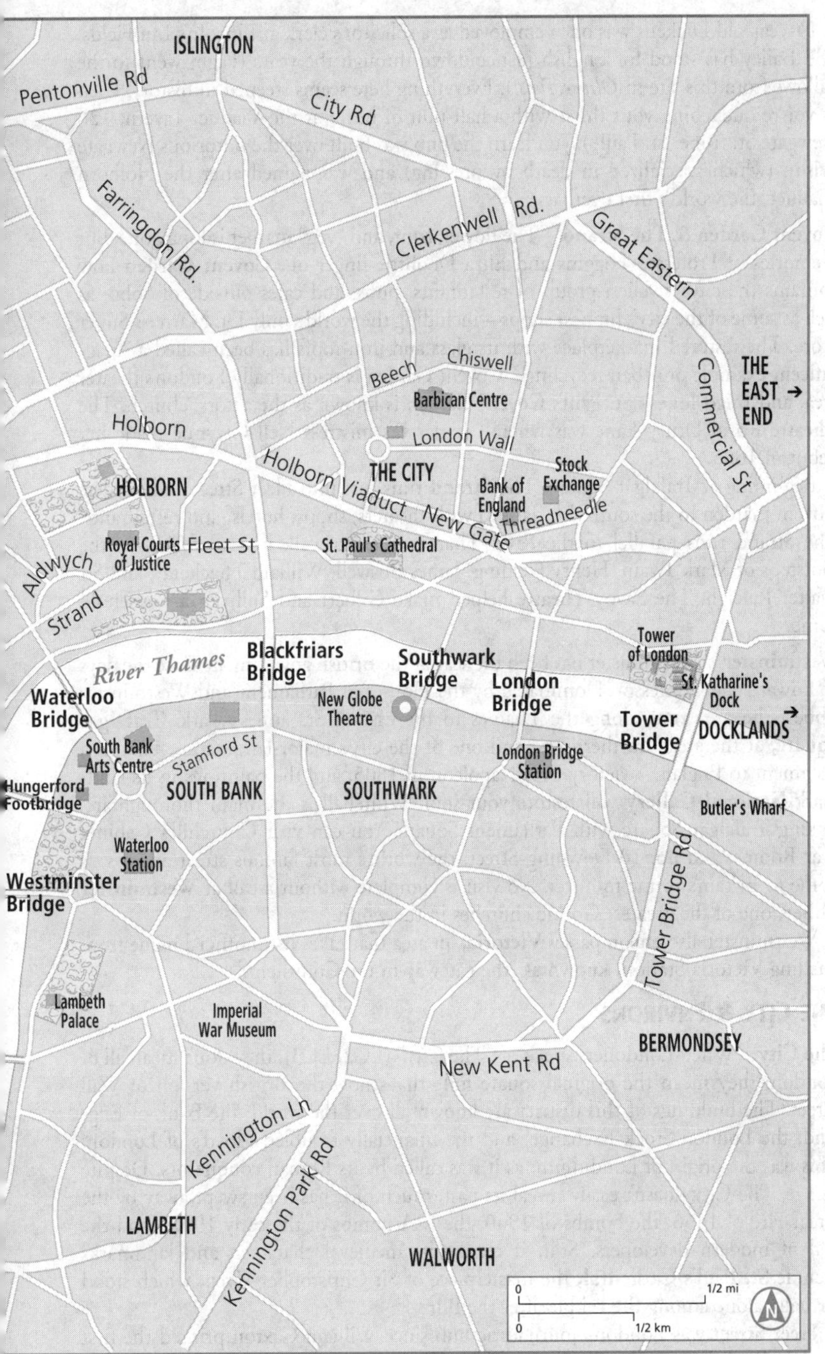
ISLINGTON
Pentonville Rd
City Rd
Farringdon Rd.
Clerkenwell Rd.
Great Eastern
Beech
Chiswell
Barbican Centre
Commercial St
THE EAST END
Holborn
London Wall
Holborn Viaduct
THE CITY
Stock Exchange
Bank of England
HOLBORN
New Gate
Threadneedle
Royal Courts of Justice
Fleet St
St. Paul's Cathedral
Aldwych
Strand
Tower of London
River Thames
Blackfriars Bridge
Southwark Bridge
London Bridge
St. Katharine's Dock
Waterloo Bridge
New Globe Theatre
Tower Bridge
DOCKLANDS
South Bank Arts Centre
Stamford St
London Bridge Station
Hungerford Footbridge
SOUTH BANK
SOUTHWARK
Butler's Wharf
Waterloo Station
Westminster Bridge
Tower Bridge Rd
Lambeth Palace
Imperial War Museum
BERMONDSEY
New Kent Rd
Kennington Ln
Kennington Park Rd
LAMBETH
WALWORTH
0
1/2 mi
0
1/2 km
N

A 14-year-old Dickens was once employed as a solicitor's clerk at Lincoln's Inn Fields. Old Bailey has stood for English justice down through the years (Fagin went to the gallows from this site in *Oliver Twist*). Everything here seems steeped in history. Even as you're quenching your thirst with a half-pint of bitter at the Viaduct Tavern, 126 Newgate St. (tube: St. Paul's), you learn the pub was built over the notorious Newgate Prison (which specialized in death by pressing) and was named after the Holborn Viaduct, the world's first overpass.

Covent Garden & The Strand The flower, fruit, and "veg" market is long gone, but memories of Professor Higgins and Eliza Doolittle linger on. **Covent Garden** now contains the city's liveliest group of restaurants, pubs, and cafes outside of Soho, as well as some of the city's hippest shops—including the world's only Dr. Marten's Super Store. The restored marketplace with its glass and iron roofs has been called a "magnificent example of urban recycling." Covent Garden is traditionally London's theater area, and Inigo Jones's St. Paul's Covent Garden is known as the actors' church. The Theatre Royal Drury Lane was where Charles II's mistress Nell Gwynne made her debut in 1665.

Beginning at Trafalgar Square, **The Strand** runs east into Fleet Street and borders Covent Garden to the south. It's flanked with theaters, shops, hotels, and restaurants. The Strand runs parallel to the River Thames, and to walk it is to follow in the footsteps of Mark Twain, Henry Fielding, James Boswell, William Thackeray, and Sir Walter Raleigh. The Savoy Theatre helped make Gilbert and Sullivan a household name.

Westminster Westminster has been the seat of the British government since the days of Edward the Confessor. Dominated by the Houses of Parliament and Westminster Abbey, the area runs along the Thames to the east of St. James's Park. **Trafalgar Square,** at the area's northern end and one of the city's major landmarks, remains a testament to England's victory over Napoléon in 1805, and the paintings in its landmark **National Gallery** will restore your soul. Whitehall is the main thoroughfare, linking Trafalgar Square with Parliament Square. You can visit Churchill's Cabinet War Rooms; and no. 10 Downing Street, the world's most famous street address, is home to Britain's prime minister. No visit is complete without a call at **Westminster Abbey,** one of the greatest Gothic churches in the world.

Westminster also encompasses **Victoria,** an area that takes its unofficial name from bustling Victoria Station, known as "the gateway to the Continent."

THE CITY & ENVIRONS

The City When Londoners speak of "The City" (EC2, EC3), they don't mean all of London; they mean the original square mile that's now the British version of Wall Street. The buildings of this district are known all over the world: the Bank of England, the London Stock Exchange, and the financially troubled Lloyd's of London. This was the origin of Londinium, as it was called by its Roman conquerors. Despite its age, The City doesn't easily reveal its past; much of it has been swept away by the Great Fire of 1666, the bombs of 1940, the IRA bombs of the early 1990s, and the zeal of modern developers. Still, it retains its medieval character, and landmarks include **St. Paul's Cathedral,** the masterpiece of Sir Christopher Wren, which stood virtually alone among the rubble after the Blitz.

Fleet Street was London's journalistic hub since William Caxton printed the first book in English here. However, most of the London tabloids have recently abandoned Fleet Street for the Docklands development across the river.

The City of London still prefers to function on its own, separate from the rest of the city; in keeping with its independence, it maintains its own **Information Centre** at St. Paul's Churchyard, EC4 (☎ **020/7332-1456**).

Docklands In the last two decades, this area—which is bordered roughly by Tower Bridge to the west and London City Airport and the Royal Docks to the east—has undergone an ambitious redevelopment. Thames-side warehouses have been converted to Manhattan-style lofts, and the neighborhood has attracted many businesses, including most of the Fleet Street newspapers, museums, entertainment complexes, shops, and an ever-growing list of restaurants.

Canary Wharf, on the Isle of Dogs, is the heart of Docklands; an 800-foot-high tower designed by Cesar Pelli, the tallest building in the United Kingdom, dominates this huge 71-acre site. The Piazza is lined with shops and restaurants. On the south side of the river at Surrey Docks, the Victorian warehouses of **Butler's Wharf** have been converted by Sir Terence Conran into offices, workshops, houses, shops, and restaurants; Butler's Wharf is also home to the Design Museum.

To get to Docklands, take the Underground to Tower Hill and pick up the **Docklands Light Railway** (☎ **020/7363-9696**), which operates Monday to Friday from 5:30am to 12:30am, with selected main routes now offering weekend service from 6am to 12:30am Saturday, and 7:30am to 11:30pm Sunday.

The East End Traditionally, this was one of London's poorest districts, and was nearly bombed out of existence by the Nazis. Hitler, in the words of one commentator at the time, created "instant urban renewal." The East End extends from the City Walls east encompassing Stepney, Bow, Poplar, West Ham, Canning Town, and other districts. The East End has always been filled with legend and lore. It's the home of the Cockney, London's most colorful character. To be a true Cockney, it's said that you must have been born "within the sound of Bow Bells," a reference to a church, St. Mary-le-Bow, rebuilt by Sir Christopher Wren in 1670. Many immigrants to London have found a home here.

South Bank Although not officially a district like Mayfair, South Bank is the setting today for the **South Bank Arts Centre,** now the largest arts center in Western Europe and still growing. Reached by Waterloo Bridge, it lies across the Thames from the Victoria Embankment. Culture buffs flock to its many galleries and halls, including the National Theatre, Queen Elizabeth Hall, Royal Festival Hall, and the Hayward Gallery. It's also the setting of the National Film Theatre and the Museum of the Moving Image (MOMI). Nearby are such neighborhoods as Elephant and Castle and **Southwark,** home to grand Southwark Cathedral. To get here, take the tube to Waterloo Station.

Central London Beyond the West End

Knightsbridge One of London's most fashionable neighborhoods, Knightsbridge is a top residential and shopping district, just south of Hyde Park. **Harrods,** on Brompton Road, is its chief attraction. Right nearby, Beauchamp Place (pronounced *Beech*-am) is one of London's most fashionable shopping streets, a Regency-era boutique-lined little street with a scattering of fashionable restaurants.

Belgravia South of Knightsbridge, this area has long been the aristocratic quarter of London, rivaling Mayfair in grandness. Although it reached the pinnacle of its prestige during the reign of Queen Victoria, it's still a chic address; the duke and duchess of Westminster, one of England's richest families, still live at Eaton Square. Its centerpiece is Belgrave Square, which was built between 1825 and 1835. When the town houses were built, the aristocrats followed—the duke of Connaught, the earl of Essex, even Queen Victoria's mother, the duchess of Kent. Chopin on holiday in 1837 was appropriately impressed: "And the English! And the houses! And the palaces! And the pomp, and the carriages! Everything from soap to the razors is extraordinary."

Chelsea This stylish Thames-side district lies south of Belgravia. It begins at Sloane Square, where flower sellers hustle their flamboyant blooms here year-round. The area has always been a favorite of writers and artists, including such names as Oscar Wilde (who was arrested here), George Eliot, James Whistler, J. M. W. Turner, Henry James, and Thomas Carlyle. Mick Jagger and Margaret Thatcher have been more recent residents, and the late Princess Diana and the "Sloane Rangers" of the 1980s gave it even more fame.

Its major boulevard is **King's Road,** where Mary Quant launched the miniskirt in the '60s and where the English punk look began. King's Road runs the entire length of Chelsea; it's at its liveliest on Saturday. The hip-hop of King's Road isn't typical of otherwise upmarket Chelsea, an elegant village filled with town houses and little mews dwellings that only successful stockbrokers and solicitors can afford to occupy.

On the Chelsea/Fulham border is **Chelsea Harbour,** a luxury development of apartments and restaurants with a private marina. You can spot its tall tower from far away; the golden ball on top moves up and down to indicate tide level.

Kensington This Royal Borough (W8) lies west of Kensington Gardens and Hyde Park and is traversed by two of London's major shopping streets, Kensington High Street and Kensington Church Street. Since 1689, when asthmatic William III fled Whitehall Palace for Nottingham House (where the air was fresher), the district has enjoyed royal associations. In time, Nottingham House became Kensington Palace, and the royals grabbed a chunk of Hyde Park to plant their roses. Queen Victoria was born here. "KP," as the royals say, was the home of Princess Diana and her two young princes for a time. Kensington Gardens is now open to the public.

Southeast of Kensington Gardens and Earl's Court, primarily residential **South Kensington** is often called "museumland" because it's dominated by a complex of museums and colleges—set upon land bought with the proceeds from Prince Albert's Great Exhibition, held in Hyde Park in 1851—that include the **Natural History Museum,** the **Victoria and Albert Museum,** and the **Science Museum;** nearby is **Royal Albert Hall.** South Kensington is also home to some fashionable restaurants and town-house hotels. One of the district's chief curiosities is the **Albert Memorial;** for sheer excess, the Victorian monument is unequaled in the world.

Earl's Court Earl's Court lies below Kensington, bordering the western half of Chelsea. For decades a staid residential district, Earl's Court now attracts a new and younger crowd (often gay), particularly at night, to its pubs, wine bars, and coffeehouses. It's long been a popular base for budget travelers (particularly Australians), thanks to its wealth of B&Bs and budget hotels, and its convenient access to central London: A 15-minute tube ride will take you into the heart of Piccadilly, via either the District or Piccadilly lines.

Once regarded as the boondocks, nearby **West Brompton** is seen today as an extension of central London. It lies directly south of Earl's Court (take the tube to West Brompton) and directly southeast of West Kensington. It also has many good restaurants, pubs, and taverns, as well as some budget hotels.

Notting Hill Increasingly fashionable Notting Hill is bounded on the north by Bayswater Road and on the east by Kensington. Hemmed in on the north by West Way and on the west by the Shepherd's Bush ramp leading to the M40, it has many turn-of-the-century mansions and small houses sitting on quiet, leafy streets, plus a growing number of hot restaurants and clubs. Gentrified in recent years, it's becoming an extension of central London.

On the north end, across Notting Hill, west of Bayswater, is the increasingly hip neighborhood known as **Notting Hill Gate;** its Portobello Road is home to one of London's most famous street markets. The area tube stops are Notting Hill Gate, Holland Park, and Ladbroke Grove.

Nearby **Holland Park** is a chichi residential neighborhood visited chiefly by the chic guests of Halcyon Hotel, one of the grandest of London's small hotels.

Paddington & Bayswater The Paddington section centers around Paddington Station, north of Kensington Gardens and Hyde Park. It's one of the major centers in London, attracting budget travelers who fill up the B&Bs in Sussex Gardens and Norfolk Square. After the first railway was introduced in London in 1836, it was followed by a circle of sprawling railway termini, including Paddington Station, which spurred the growth of this middle-class area, which is now blighted in parts.

Just south of Paddington, north of Hyde Park, and abutting more fashionable Notting Hill to the west is **Bayswater,** a sort of unofficial area also filled with a large number of B&Bs attracting budget travelers. Inspired by Marylebone and elegant Mayfair, a relatively prosperous set of Victorian merchants built homes for their families in this area

FARTHER AFIELD

Greenwich Some 4 miles from the city, Greenwich—ground zero for use in the reckoning of terrestrial longitudes—enjoyed its heyday under the Tudors. Henry VIII and both of his daughters, Mary I and Elizabeth I, were born here. Greenwich Palace, Henry's favorite, is long gone, though; today's visitors come to this lovely port village for nautical sights along the Thames, including the 1869 tea clipper *Cutty Sark.*

Hampstead This residential suburb of north London, beloved by Keats and Hogarth, is a favorite spot for weekending Londoners. Everybody from Sigmund Freud to John Le Carré has lived here, and it's still one of the most desirable districts in the Greater London area to call home. Its centerpiece is **Hampstead Heath,** nearly 800 acres of rolling meadows and woodlands with panoramic views; it still maintains its rural atmosphere even though engulfed by cityscapes on all sides. The hilltop village is filled with cafes, tearooms, and restaurants, and there are pubs galore, some with historic pedigrees. Take the Northern Line to Hampstead Heath station.

Highgate Along with Hampstead, Highgate in north London is another choice residential area, particularly on or near Pond Square and along Hampstead High Street. It's long been a desirable place to live, and Londoners used to flock to its taverns and pubs for "exercise and harmless merriment"; some still do. Today, most visitors come to see moody **Highgate Cemetery,** London's most famous cemetery—it's the final resting place of such famous figures as Karl Marx and George Eliot.

2 Getting Around

Remember that cars drive on the left, and vehicles have the right-of-way in London over pedestrians. Wherever you walk, always look both ways before stepping off a curb.

BY PUBLIC TRANSPORTATION

Transportation within London is unusually easy and inexpensive. Both the Underground (subway) and bus systems are operated by **London Transport**—with **Travel**

Information Centres in the Underground stations at King's Cross, Hammersmith, Oxford Circus, St. James's Park, Liverpool Street Station, and Piccadilly Circus, as well as in the main line stations at Euston and Victoria and in each of the terminals at Heathrow Airport. They take reservations for London Transport's guided tours and have free Underground and bus maps and other information. A **24-hour telephone information** service is available by calling ☎ **020/7222-1234.**

DISCOUNT PASSES London Transport, Travel Information Service, 55 Broadway, London SW1H 0BD also offers **Travelcards** for use on the bus, Underground, and main line service inside Greater London. Available in a number of combinations for adjacent zones, Travelcards can be purchased for periods of 7 days to a year. A Travelcard allowing travel in two zones for 1 week costs £17.60 ($29.90) for adults and £6.50 ($11.05) for children.

To purchase a Travelcard, you must present a Photocard. If you're 16 years old or older, bring along a passport-type picture of yourself when you buy your Travelcard and the Photocard will be issued free. Child-rate Photocards for Travelcards are issued only at Underground ticket offices or Travel Information Centres; in addition to a passport-type photograph, proof of age is required (a passport or birth certificate). Teenagers (14 or 15) are charged adult fares on all services unless they have one of the cards.

For shorter stays in London, consider the **One-Day Off-Peak Travelcard.** This Travelcard can be used on most bus, Underground, and main-line services throughout Greater London Monday through Friday after 9:30am and at any time on weekends and bank holidays. The Travelcard is available at Underground ticket offices, Travel Information Centres, and some newsstands. For two zones, the cost is £3.80 ($6.45) for adults and £1.90 ($3.25) for children aged 5 to 15. Children 4 and under ride free.

The **Visitor Travelcard** is worthwhile if you plan to travel a lot within Greater London. This card allows unlimited transport within all six zones of Greater London's Underground and bus network. You'll most likely travel within the first two zones of the network's boundaries, but you could travel as far as Heathrow during valid times. However, *you must buy this pass in North America;* it's not available in England. A pass good for 3 consecutive days of travel costs $31 for adults and $14 for children aged 5 to 15; a pass good for 4 consecutive days of travel costs $41 for adults, $16 for children; and a pass good for 7 consecutive days of travel costs $61 for adults, $26 for children. For more information, contact **BritRail Travel International,** 500 Mamaroneck Ave., Suite 314, Harrison, NY 10528 (☎ **800/677-8585** in the U.S., 800/555-2748 in Canada, or www.raileurope.com).

You can now buy **Carnet tickets,** a booklet of 10 single Underground tickets valid for 12 months from the issue date. Carnet tickets are valid for travel only in Zone 1 (Central London), and cost £10 ($17) for adults and £5 ($8.50) for children (up to 15). A book of Carnet tickets gives you a savings of £2 ($3.40) over the cost of 10 individual tickets. Another pass is the **Family Travelcard,** a 1-day ticket. It's a go-as-you-please card, allowing as many journeys as you wish on the tube, buses (excluding night buses) displaying the London Transport bus sign, and even the Docklands Light Railway or any rail service within the travel zones designated on your ticket. The family card is valid after 9:30am Monday through Friday, all day on weekends, and public holidays. The cost is £3 ($5.10) to £3.20 ($5.45) for adults, or 60p ($1) for children. Yet a final discount pass is the **Weekend Travel card** allowing 2 days of weekend transportation on the Underground or buses. The cost ranges from £5.70 to £6 ($9.70 to $10.20)for adults or £2.80 ($4.75) for children. These passes are available at all Underground stations.

Will you have enough stories to tell your grandchildren?

BY UNDERGROUND

Known locally as "the tube," this is the fastest and easiest way to get from place to place. All Underground stations are clearly marked with a red circle and blue crossbar. You descend by stairways, escalators, or huge elevators, depending on the depth. Some Underground stations have complete subterranean shopping arcades, and several boast high-tech gadgets such as push-button information machines.

If you have British coins, you can get your ticket at a vending machine. Otherwise, buy it at the ticket office. You can transfer as many times as you like as long as you stay in the Underground. The flat fare for one trip within the Central zone is £1.40 ($2.40). Trips from the Central zone to destinations in the suburbs range from £1.40 to £4.70 ($2.40 to $8) in most cases.

Be sure to keep your ticket, as it must be presented when you get off. If you're caught without a valid ticket, you'll be fined £10 ($17) on the spot. If you owe extra money, you'll be asked to pay the difference by the attendant.

Also keep in mind that many trains stop running at midnight (11:30pm on Sunday).

For information on the London tube system, call the London Underground at ☎ **020/7222-1234,** but expect long delays before an actual person comes to the phone. See the full-color Underground map on the inside cover of this guide.

BY BUS

The first thing you learn about London buses is that nobody just gets on them. You queue up (that is, form a single-file line) at the bus stop.

The comparably priced bus system is almost as good as the Underground, and you'll have a better view. You can pick up a free bus map at one of London Regional Transport's Travel Information Centres listed above.

London still has some of the old-style Routemaster buses, with both a driver and conductor. Once you're on the bus, a conductor will pass by your seat. You state your destination and pay the fare, receiving a ticket in return. However, this type of bus is being phased out for newer buses with only a driver. On these, you pay the driver as you enter, and exit through one of the rear doors.

As with the Underground, the fares vary according to the distance traveled. Generally, the cost is 50p to £1.20 (85¢ to $2.05), which is less than tube fares. If you travel for two or three stops, the cost is 60p ($1); longer runs within Zone 1 cost £1 ($1.70). If you want to be warned when to get off, simply ask the conductor.

Call the 24-hour hot line (☎ **020/7222-1234**) for schedules and fares.

BY TAXI

You can get a cab from a cab station or hail one on the street; if the yellow light on the roof is on, the taxi is accepting passengers. For a radio cab, call ☎ **020/7272-0272** or 020/7253-5000.

The minimum fare is £5 ($8.50) with the meter starting at £3.60 ($6.10), with increments of 20p (35¢) thereafter, based on distance or time. Each additional passenger is charged 40p (70¢). Passengers pay 10p (15¢) for each piece of luggage in the driver's compartment and any other item more than 2 feet long. Surcharges are imposed after 8pm and on weekends and public holidays. All these tariffs include value-added tax (VAT). Fares usually increase annually. We recommend tipping 10% to 15% of the fare. All taxis take all major credit cards.

If you call for a cab, the meter starts running when the taxi receives instructions from the dispatcher, so you could find £1.40 ($2.40) or more already on the meter when you step inside.

Cab sharing is permitted in London, and allows cabbies to offer rides for two to five people. The taxis accepting such riders display a sign on yellow plastic with the words shared taxi. Each of two sharing riders is charged 65% of the fare a lone passenger would be charged. Three people pay 55%, four pay 45%, and five (the seating capacity of all new London cabs) pay 40% of the single-passenger fare.

Fast Facts: London

American Express The main office is at 30-31 Haymarket, SW1 (☎ **020/7484-9670;** tube: Piccadilly Circus). Full services are available Monday to Saturday from 9am to 5:30pm. On Sunday from 10am to 5pm, only the foreign-exchange bureau is open.

Area Codes London now has only one area code: **020.** Within the city limits, you don't need to dial it, only an eight-digit number. If you're calling London from home before your trip, the country code for England is **44.** It must precede the London area code. When you're calling London from outside Britain, drop the "0" in front of the local area code.

Baby-Sitters If your hotel won't recommend a sitter, call **Childminders,** 9 Paddington St. (☎ **020/7935-3000;** tube: Baker Street). The rates are £5.80 ($9.85) per hour during the day and £4 to £5.50 ($6.80 to $9.35) per hour at night. There is a 4-hour minimum, and hotel guests pay a £10 ($17) booking fee each time they use a sitter.

Currency Exchange See "Money," in chapter 2.

Dentists For dental emergencies, call **Eastman Dental Hospital** (☎ **020/7915-1000;** tube: King's Cross).

Doctors In an emergency, contact **Doctor's Call** (☎ **07000/372255**). Some hotels also have doctors on call. **Medical Express,** 117A Harley St. (☎ **020/7499-1991;** tube: Regent's Park), is a private British clinic. If you need a prescription filled, stop by, but to fill the British equivalent of a U.S. prescription, there is sometimes a surcharge of £20 ($34) in addition to the cost of the medication. The clinic is open Monday through Friday from 9am to 6pm and on Saturday from 9:30am to 2:30pm.

Embassies & High Commissions The **U.S. Embassy** is at 24 Grosvenor Sq., W1 (☎ **020/7499-9000;** tube: Bond Street). However, for passport and visa information, go to the **U.S. Passport and Citizenship Unit,** 55-56 Upper Brook St., London, W1 (☎ **020/7499-9000,** ext. 2563 or 2564; tube: Marble Arch or Bond Street). Hours are Monday through Friday from 8:30am to 5:30pm.

The **Canadian High Commission,** MacDonald House, 38 Grosvenor Sq., W1 (☎ **020/7258-6600;** tube: Bond Street), handles visas for Canada. Hours are Monday through Friday from 8am to 4pm.

The **Australian High Commission** is at Australia House, The Strand, WC2 (☎ **020/7379-4334;** tube: Charing Cross or Aldwych). Hours are Monday through Friday from 10am to 4pm.

The **New Zealand High Commission** is at New Zealand House, 80 Haymarket at Pall Mall, SW1 (☎ **020/7930-8422;** tube: Charing Cross or Piccadilly Circus). Hours are Monday through Friday from 9am to 5pm.

The **Irish Embassy** is at 17 Grosvenor Place, SW1 (☎ **020/7235-2171;** tube: Hyde Park Corner). Hours are Monday through Friday from 9:30am to 1pm and 2:15 to 5pm.

Emergencies In London, for police, fire, or an ambulance, dial ☎ **999.**

Hospitals The following offer emergency care in London, 24 hours a day, with the first treatment free under the National Health Service: **Royal Free Hospital,** Pond Street (☎ **020/7794-0500;** tube: Belsize Park), and **University College Hospital,** Gower Street (☎ **020/7387-9300;** tube: Warren Street). Many other London hospitals also have accident and emergency departments.

Hot Lines If you're in some sort of legal emergency, call **Release** (☎ **020/7729-9904**) 24 hours a day. The **Rape Crisis Line** (☎ **020/7837-1600**), accepts calls after 6pm. **Samaritans,** 46 Marshall St. (☎ **020/7734-2800**), maintains a crisis hot line that helps with all kinds of trouble, even threatened suicides. From 9am to 9pm daily, there's a live attendant on duty to handle emergencies; the rest of the time, a series of recorded messages tells callers other phones and addresses where they can turn to for help. **Alcoholics Anonymous** (☎ **020/7833-0022**) answers its hot line daily from 10am to 10pm.

Information See "Visitor Information," earlier in this chapter.

Maps If you plan on exploring London in any depth, you'll need a detailed street map with an index, not one of those superficial overviews given away at many hotels and tourist offices. The best ones are published by Falk, and they're available at most newsstands and nearly all bookstores. And no Londoner is without a ***London A to Z,*** the ultimate street-by-street reference, available at bookstores and newsstands everywhere. One good source for maps is **W & G Foyle, Ltd.,** 113-119 Charing Cross Rd., WC2 (☎ **020/7439-8501;** tube: Leicester Square).

Police In an emergency, dial ☎ **999** (no coins are needed).

Telephone For **directory assistance** for London, dial ☎ **142;** for the rest of Britain, dial ☎ **192.** See also "Area Codes," above.

3 Accommodations

The London Tourist Board, anticipating the millennium boom, campaigned to secure another 10,000 hotel rooms by 2000. That target was met, but with few exceptions, the newly opened hotels are in districts far from the center and most of them are of the no-frills, efficient budget chain variety. In spite of these bandbox modern horrors sprouting up, some of the hoteliers have wisely decided to adapt former public or institutional buildings rather than start from scratch.

Another trend noted is a shift away from the West End as the traditional hotel stamping ground. Of course, the fact that there is a dearth of old buildings to turn into hotels in the West End is the reason for the shift toward such salubrious sections of London as Greenwich, the Docklands, and even the City.

The 1990s saw the refurbishing and modernization of many of London's hotels, so chances are you'll like your room. What you won't like is the price, and that's almost guaranteed. Even if a hotel remains scruffy and shabby, London hoteliers operating in a seller's market have little embarrassment about jacking up the price. Hotels in all price categories remain vastly overpriced as European capitals go.

As London observer Christopher Reynolds put it, "Looking for a really good price on a hotel room? Try Arizona in August, Alaska in February, or New York in about 1962. But if it's London you want to see, brace yourself."

Face it—you're just going to pay more than you'd like for a hotel room in London. London boasts some of the most famous luxury hotels in the world, such as The Ritz,

Central London Accommodations

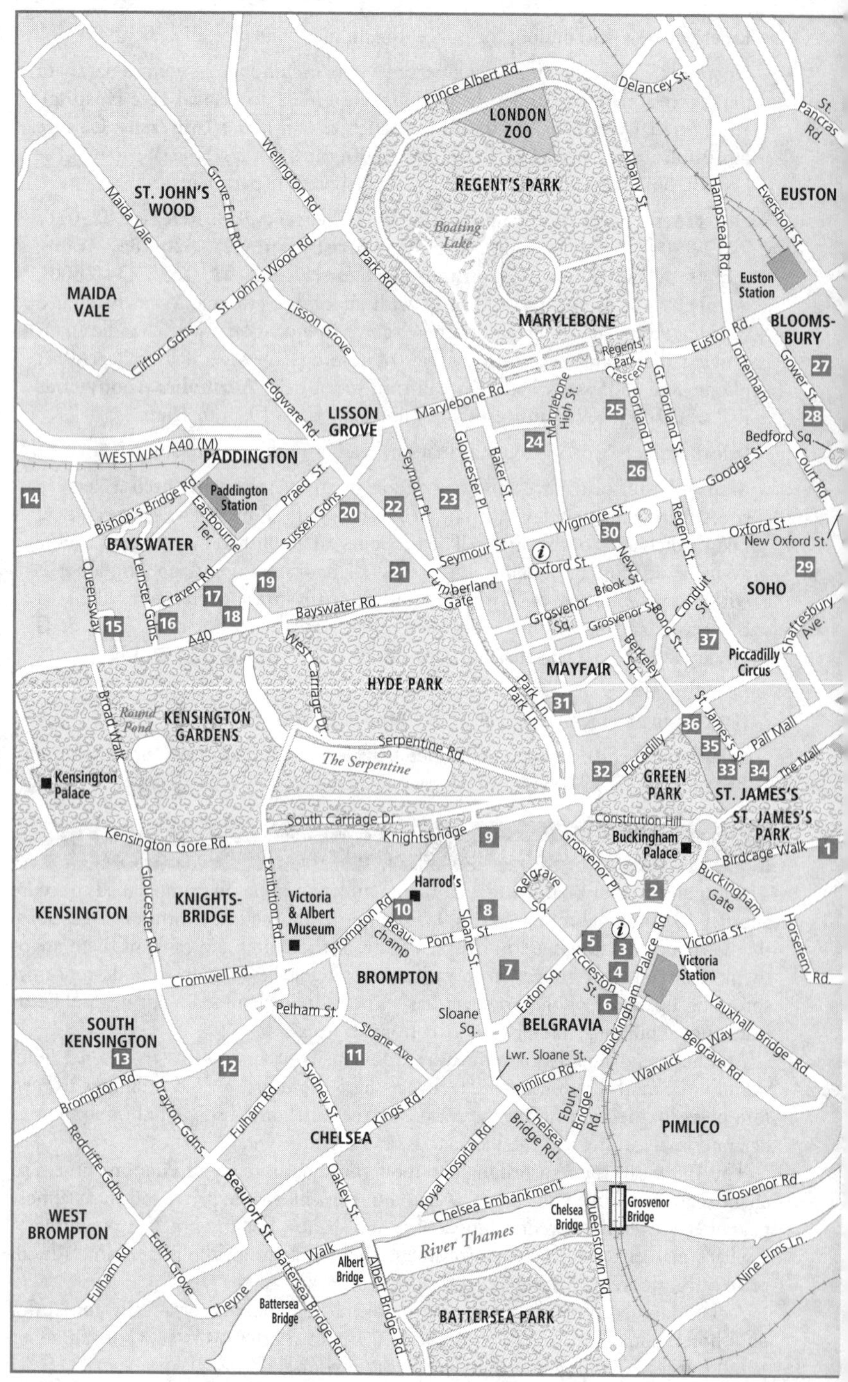

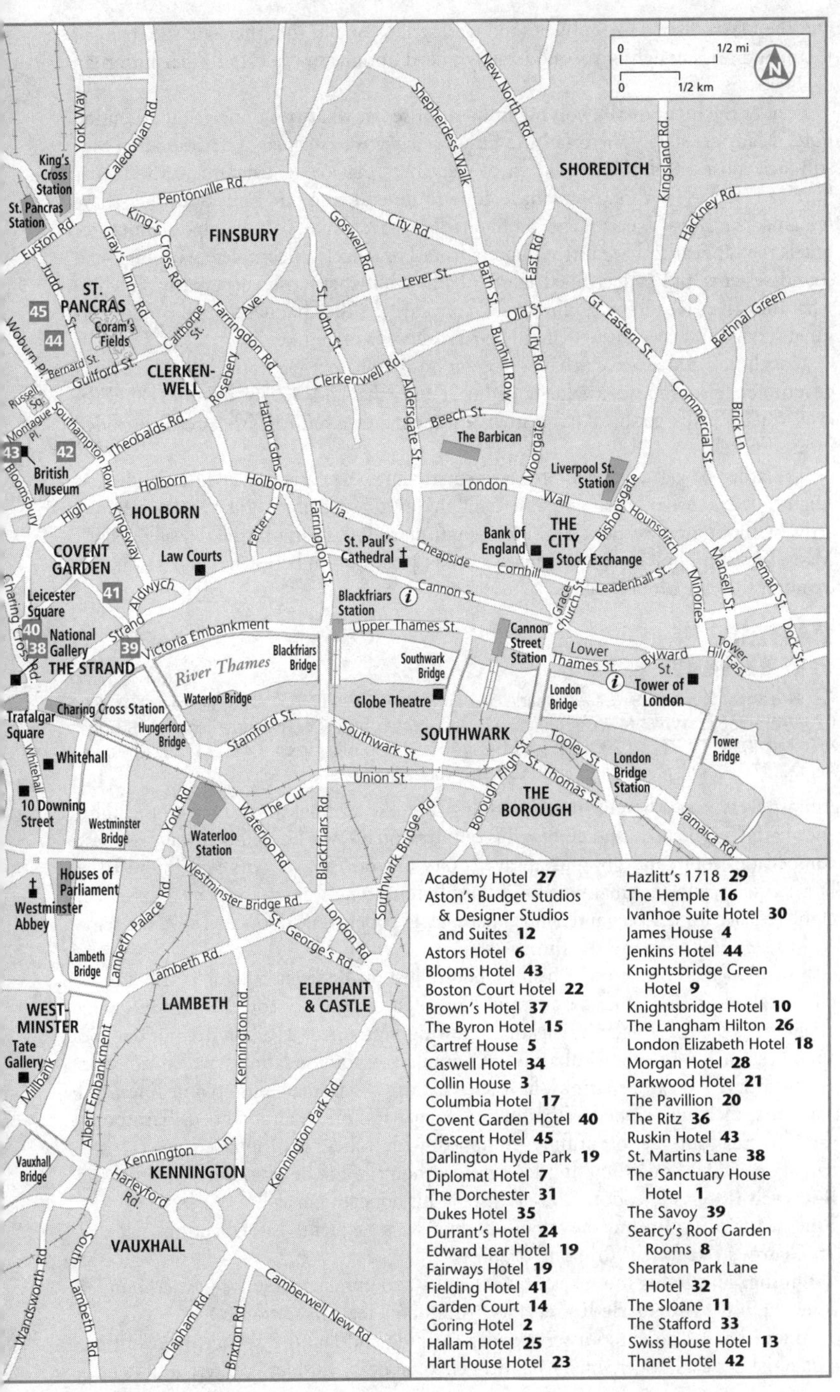

0 1/2 mi
0 1/2 km
N
SHOREDITCH
FINSBURY
ST. PANCRAS
CLERKEN-WELL
HOLBORN
COVENT GARDEN
THE STRAND
THE CITY
SOUTHWARK
THE BOROUGH
ELEPHANT & CASTLE
LAMBETH
WEST-MINSTER
KENNINGTON
VAUXHALL
King's Cross Station
St. Pancras Station
York Way
Caledonian Rd.
Pentonville Rd.
King's Cross Rd.
Euston Rd.
Gray's Inn Rd.
Judd St.
Woburn Pl.
Bernard St.
Guilford St.
Coram's Fields
Calthorpe St.
Russell Sq.
Montague Pl.
Southampton Row
Theobalds Rd.
British Museum
Bloomsbury
High Holborn
Kingsway
Farringdon Rd.
Rosebery Ave.
Hatton Gdns.
Fetter Ln.
Holborn Via.
Farringdon St.
Law Courts
Aldwych
Strand
Charing Cross Rd.
Leicester Square
National Gallery
Victoria Embankment
River Thames
Waterloo Bridge
Blackfriars Bridge
Charing Cross Station
Trafalgar Square
Hungerford Bridge
Whitehall
10 Downing Street
Westminster Bridge
Houses of Parliament
Westminster Abbey
Lambeth Bridge
Tate Gallery
Millbank
Albert Embankment
Vauxhall Bridge
Wandsworth Rd.
South Lambeth Rd.
Harleyford Rd.
Kennington Ln.
Clapham Rd.
Brixton Rd.
Camberwell New Rd.
Kennington Park Rd.
Kennington Rd.
Lambeth Rd.
Lambeth Palace Rd.
Westminster Bridge Rd.
St. George's Rd.
London Rd.
York Rd.
Waterloo Station
Waterloo Rd.
The Cut
Stamford St.
Union St.
Southwark St.
Blackfriars Rd.
Southwark Bridge Rd.
Borough High St.
St. Thomas St.
Tooley St.
London Bridge Station
Jamaica Rd.
Tower Bridge
Tower of London
Byward St.
Lower Thames St.
London Bridge
Globe Theatre
Southwark Bridge
Cannon Street Station
Upper Thames St.
Blackfriars Station
Cannon St.
St. Paul's Cathedral
Cheapside
Cornhill
Bank of England
Stock Exchange
Leadenhall St.
Gracechurch St.
Bishopsgate
Houndsditch
Minories
Mansell St.
Leman St.
Dock St.
Tower Hill East
Liverpool St. Station
London Wall
Moorgate
The Barbican
Beech St.
Aldersgate St.
Clerkenwell Rd.
St. John St.
Goswell Rd.
Lever St.
City Rd.
Old St.
Bath St.
Bunhill Row
City Rd.
East Rd.
Shepherdess Walk
New North Rd.
Kingsland Rd.
Hackney Rd.
Gt. Eastern St.
Bethnal Green
Commercial St.
Brick Ln.
Academy Hotel 27
Aston's Budget Studios & Designer Studios and Suites 12
Astors Hotel 6
Blooms Hotel 43
Boston Court Hotel 22
Brown's Hotel 37
The Byron Hotel 15
Cartref House 5
Caswell Hotel 34
Collin House 3
Columbia Hotel 17
Covent Garden Hotel 40
Crescent Hotel 45
Darlington Hyde Park 19
Diplomat Hotel 7
The Dorchester 31
Dukes Hotel 35
Durrant's Hotel 24
Edward Lear Hotel 19
Fairways Hotel 19
Fielding Hotel 41
Garden Court 14
Goring Hotel 2
Hallam Hotel 25
Hart House Hotel 23
Hazlitt's 1718 29
The Hemple 16
Ivanhoe Suite Hotel 30
James House 4
Jenkins Hotel 44
Knightsbridge Green Hotel 9
Knightsbridge Hotel 10
The Langham Hilton 26
London Elizabeth Hotel 18
Morgan Hotel 28
Parkwood Hotel 21
The Pavillion 20
The Ritz 36
Ruskin Hotel 43
St. Martins Lane 38
The Sanctuary House Hotel 1
The Savoy 39
Searcy's Roof Garden Rooms 8
Sheraton Park Lane Hotel 32
The Sloane 11
The Stafford 33
Swiss House Hotel 13
Thanet Hotel 42

and the Dorchester. The problem (and it's a serious one) is that there are too many of them, and not enough of the moderately priced options so typical of other European capitals.

Even at the luxury level, you might be surprised at what you don't get at a London hotel. Many are stately Victorian and Edwardian gems so steeped in tradition that they still lack most or all of the modern conveniences that come standard in the luxury hotels of, say, New York. Some have gone to no end to modernize, but others have remained at Boer War vintage. London does have some cutting-edge, chintz-free hotels that appear to have arrived bodily from Los Angeles—complete with high-end sound systems and gadget-filled marble baths—but they're not necessarily superior; what the others lack in streamlining and convenience, they frequently make up in personal service and spaciousness. It all depends on what you like.

Most hotels add a service charge ranging from 10% to 15% to the bill. The British government also imposes a value-added tax (VAT) that adds 17.5% to your bill. However, you'll usually get breakfast (either continental or a full English spread) included in most hotels.

It's harder to get a hotel room, particularly an inexpensive one, during July and August. Inexpensive hotels are also tight in June, September, and October. If you arrive without a reservation, begin looking for a room as early in the day as possible. Many West End hotels have vacancies, even in peak season, between 9 and 11am, but by noon they are often booked.

MAYFAIR

Very Expensive

✪ **Brown's Hotel.** 29–34 Albemarle St., London W1X 4BP. ☎ **020/7493-6020.** Fax 020/7493-9381. www.brownshotel.com. E-mail: brownshotel@brownshotel.com. 118 units. A/C MINIBAR TV TEL. £290–£355 ($493–$603.50) double; from £435 ($739.50) suite. AE, DC, MC, V. Off-site parking £35 ($59.50). Tube: Green Park.

Almost every year a hotel sprouts up trying to evoke an English country house ambience with Chippendale and chintz; this quintessential town-house hotel watches these competitors come and go, and always comes out on top. Brown's was founded by James Brown, a former manservant of Lord Byron's, who wanted to create a dignified, clublike place for discreet and genteel patrons. He opened its doors in 1837, the same year Queen Victoria took the throne.

Brown's, which occupies 14 historic houses just off Berkeley Square, is still a thorough realization of its founder's vision. The guest rooms vary considerably and are a tangible record of England's history, showing restrained taste in decoration and appointments; even the washbasins are antiques. Accommodations, which range in size from small to extra-spacious, have such extras as voice mail, dual-phone lines, and dataports; each is equipped with a luxurious mattress on an antique bed. Bathrooms vary in size, but are beautifully equipped with robes, luxurious cosmetics, and hair dryers. The hotel's inviting lounges pay homage to the past: They include the **Roosevelt Room** (Theodore Roosevelt spent his honeymoon at Brown's in 1886), the **Rudyard Kipling Room** (the famous author was a frequent visitor), and the paneled **St. George's Bar** for the drinking of spirits.

Dining: The dining room has a quiet dignity and unmatched service. Afternoon tea is served in the **Albemarle Room.** (See "Afternoon Tea," in section 5.)

Amenities: 24-hour room service, dry cleaning and laundry service, baby-sitting, secretarial services, valet, men's hairdresser, tour desk, business center; health club nearby.

✪ **The Dorchester.** 53 Park Lane, London W1A 2HJ. ☎ **800/727-9820** or 020/7629-8888. Fax 020/7409-0114. E-mail: infor@dorchesterhotel.com. 248 units. A/C MINIBAR TV TEL. £305–£335 ($518.50-$569.50) double; from £450 ($765) suite. AE, DC, MC, V. Parking £27 ($44.55). Tube: Hyde Park Corner or Marble Arch.

This is among the best hotels in London today. It has all the elegance of Claridge's, but without the upper-crust attitudes that can verge on snobbery. The Lanesborough is also a premier address, but it doesn't have the time-honored experience of "The Dorch," which has maintained a tradition of fine comfort and cuisine since it opened its doors in 1931.

Breaking from the neoclassical tradition, the most ambitious architects of the era designed a building of reinforced concrete clothed in terrazzo slabs. Within you'll find a 1930s take on Regency motifs: The monumental arrangements of flowers and the elegance of the gilded-cage promenade seem appropriate for a diplomatic reception, yet convey a kind of comfort in which guests from all over the world feel at ease.

The Dorchester boasts guest rooms outfitted with Irish linen sheets on deluxe mattresses, plus all the electronic gadgetry you'd expect from a world-class hotel, and double- and triple-glazed windows to keep out noise, along with plump armchairs, cherrywood furnishings, and, in many cases, four-poster beds piled high with pillows. The large bathrooms are equally stylish, with mottled carrara marble and Lalique-style sconces, plus hair dryers, makeup mirrors, and posh toiletries. The best rooms open onto views of Hyde Park.

Dining: The hotel's restaurant, **The Grill Room,** is among the finest dining establishments in London, and the **Dorchester Bar** is a legendary meeting place. **The Promenade,** with its glorious lush sofas, is the ideal setting to enjoy afternoon tea and watch the world go by. The hotel also offers Cantonese cuisine at **The Oriental,** London's most exclusive—and expensive—Chinese restaurant.

Amenities: 24-hour room service, dry cleaning and laundry service. The Dorchester Spa, one of the best-outfitted health clubs in London; barbershop; hairdresser; tour desk, secretarial services and baby-sitting.

✪ **Sheraton Park Lane Hotel.** Piccadilly, London W1Y 8BX. ☎ **800/325-3535** or 020/7499-6321. Fax 020/7499-1965. www.sheraton.com. 305 units. A/C MINIBAR TV TEL. £275 ($467.50) double; from £389 ($661.30) suite. AE, DC, MC, V. Parking £28 ($47.60). Tube: Hyde Park Corner or Green Park.

The most traditional of the Park Lane mansions, the Park Lane Hotel was sold in 1996 to the Sheraton Corporation, which upgraded it but maintained its quintessential Britishness. Launched in 1913, but kept empty for years, the Park Lane finally opened in 1924 under the leadership of Bracewell Smith, one of London's leading hoteliers. Today, its Silver Entrance remains an art-deco marvel that has been used as a backdrop in many films, including the classic BBC miniseries *Brideshead Revisited.*

Designed in a U shape, with a view overlooking Green Park, the hotel offers luxurious accommodations that are a surprisingly good deal—they're among the least expensive on Park Lane. Many of the suites have marble fireplaces and original marble bathrooms. The rooms have benefited from an impressive refurbishment—they're larger, and the decor is lighter in tone. All have double-glazed windows to block out noise. Some bedrooms are larger and better appointed than others, with higher ceilings and taller windows. In the more deluxe rooms, you get trouser presses and better views. The most tranquil rooms open onto the rear, but those opening onto the court are dark. Bathrooms are generally spacious and equipped with hair dryers; many units also have robes.

Dining/Diversions: On site is a **Brasserie,** serving French cuisine. A harpist plays in the **Palm Court Lounge** every Sunday and tea is served daily (see "Afternoon Tea," in section 5).

Amenities: 24-hour room service, concierge, dry cleaning and laundry service, baby-sitting, secretarial services, fitness center, beauty salon, business center, safety-deposit boxes, gift and newspaper shop, barbershop, women's salon, and Daniele Ryman Aromatherapy Shop.

INEXPENSIVE

Ivanhoe Suite Hotel. 1 St. Christopher's Place, Barrett St. Piazza, London W1M 5HB. ☎ **020/7935-1047.** Fax 020/7224-0563. www.scoot.co.uk/ivanhoe_suite_hotel. 8 units. MINIBAR TV TEL. £86 ($146.20) double, £95 ($161.50) triple. Rates include continental breakfast. AE, DC, MC, V. Tube: Bond St.

Born-to-shop buffs flock to this little hidden discovery uniquely located in a part of town off Oxford Street not known for its hotels. "It's like having my own little flatlet every time I come to London," one satisfied guest told us. Situated above a restaurant on a pedestrian street of boutiques and restaurants and close to the shop-flanked New and Old Bond streets, this town-house hotel has attractively furnished small and mid-sized singles and doubles, each with a sitting area. Each stylish room has its own entry, security video, trouser press, and beverage-making facilities along with a fridge/bar, plus a wide selection of videotapes. The newly tiled baths are small—half with a shower, half with a tub-shower combination, plus hair dryers and trouser presses. Breakfast is served in a very small area at the top of the first flight of stairs, and you can stop off for a nightcap at the corner pub, a real neighborhood locale. They offer a number of services including room service, baby-sitting, secretarial service, laundry, and sightseeing tour and theater reservations. *Note:* The four-floor hotel doesn't have an elevator.

MARYLEBONE

VERY EXPENSIVE

✪ **The Langham Hilton.** 1C Portland Place, London W1N 4JA. ☎ **800/774-1500** from the U.S., or 020/7636-1000. Fax 020/7323-2340. www.hilton.com. 379 units. A/C MINIBAR TV TEL. £280 ($476) double; £365 ($620.50) executive room; from £670 ($1,139) suite. Rates include breakfast for executive room and suite. AE, DC, MC, V. Tube: Oxford Circus.

When this extremely well-located hotel opened in 1865, it was a fashionable address for aristocrats seeking respite from their country estates. After it was bombed in World War II, it languished until the early 1990s, when Hilton International took it over. Its restoration was painstaking; today, it's Hilton's European flagship. The Langham's public rooms reflect the power and majesty of the British Empire at its apex. Guest rooms are attractively furnished and comfortable, featuring French provincial furniture and red oak trim. The small bathrooms contain hair dryers, robes, and trouser presses. And the location is still terrific: within easy reach of Mayfair and Soho restaurants and theaters and Oxford and Regent Street shopping; Regent's Park is just blocks away.

Dining/Diversions: Vodka, caviar, and champagne flow liberally at the **Tsar's Russian Bar and Restaurant.** Drinks are served in the **Chukka Bar,** a re-creation of a private polo club. The most upscale restaurant is a high-ceilinged Victorian fantasy called **Memories,** featuring patriotic nostalgia and cuisine from the far corners of the British Commonwealth. Afternoon tea is served amid the potted palms of the Edwardian-style **Palm Court.**

Amenities: 24-hour room service, concierge, health club, business center, beauty salon.

EXPENSIVE

Durrants Hotel. George St., London W1H 6BJ. ☎ **020/7935-8131.** Fax 020/7487-3510. 92 units. TV TEL. £135–£180 ($229.50–$306) double; £175 ($297.50) family room for 3; from £275 ($467.50) suite. AE, CB, MC, V. Tube: Bond St. or Baker St.

Established in 1789 off Manchester Square, this historic hotel with its Georgian-detailed facade is snug, cozy, and traditional—almost like a poor man's Brown's. We find it to be one of the most quintessentially English of all London hotels and a soothing retreat on a cold, rainy day. In the 100 years that the Miller family has owned the hotel, several neighboring houses have been incorporated into the original structure. A walk through the pine-and-mahogany–paneled public rooms is like stepping back into another time. You'll even find an 18th-century letter-writing room. The small rooms are rather bland except for elaborate cove moldings and very comfortable furnishings. They exude an aura of solidity; some are air-conditioned. Bathrooms are also tiny, but nearly all of them have both tubs and showers.

The in-house restaurant serves a full afternoon tea and satisfying French or traditional English cuisine in one of the most beautiful Georgian rooms in the neighborhood. Nineteenth-century political cartoons by a noted Victorian artist embellish the less formal breakfast room. The pub, a neighborhood favorite, has Windsor chairs, an open fireplace, and decor that hasn't changed much in two centuries. Services include 24-hour room service, laundry service, and baby-sitting.

MODERATE

Hallam Hotel. 12 Hallam St., Portland Place, London W1N 5LJ. ☎ **020/7580-1166.** Fax 020/7323-4527. 25 units. MINIBAR TV TEL. £92–£97 ($156.40–$164.90) double. Rates include English breakfast. AE, DC, MC, V. Tube: Oxford Circus.

This heavily ornamented stone-and-brick Victorian—one of the few on the street to escape the blitz—is just a 10-minute stroll from Oxford Circus. It's the property of the Baker family, brothers Grant and David, who maintain it well. The guest rooms are comfortably furnished with good beds. Some of the singles are so small they're called *cabinettes.* Several of the twin-bedded rooms are quite spacious with adequate closet space. Bathrooms are a bit cramped but have hair dryers. Guest services include concierge, dry cleaning and laundry service, express checkout, and tour desk. There is also a bar where residents gather to swap stories, and a bright breakfast room overlooking the pleasant patio.

INEXPENSIVE

Boston Court Hotel. 26 Upper Berkeley St., Marble Arch, London W1H 7PF. ☎ **020/7723-1445.** Fax 020/7262-8823. www.boston_court_hotel.com or www.smoothhound.co.ukhotels/Bostonct.html. E-mail: info@boston_court_hotel.com. 15 units (7 with shower only). TV TEL. £59–£65 ($100.30–$110.50) double with shower only, £75–£83 ($127.50–$141.10) double with bathroom; £85–£93 ($144.50–$158.10) triple with bathroom. Rates include continental breakfast. MC, V. Tube: Marble Arch.

Upper Berkeley is a classic street of B&Bs; in days of yore, it was a prestigious address, home to Elizabeth Montagu (1720–1800), "queen of the bluestockings," who defended Shakespeare against attacks by Voltaire. Today, it's a good, safe, respectable retreat at an affordable price. This no-frills hotel offers accommodations in a centrally located Victorian-era building within walking distance of Oxford Street shopping and Hyde Park. The small, basic rooms have been refurbished and redecorated with a no-nonsense decor, but with good mattresses; all have central heating, hair dryers, coffeemakers, and small refrigerators.

Edward Lear Hotel. 28–30 Seymour St., London W1H 5WD. ☎ **020/7402-5401.** Fax 020/7706-3766. www.edlear.com. E-mail: edwardlear@aol.com. 31 units (12 with bathroom). TV TEL. £64.50 ($109.65) double without bathroom, £79.50–£89.50 ($135.15–$152.15) double with bathroom; from £105 ($178.50) suite. Rates include English breakfast. MC, V. Tube: Marble Arch.

This popular hotel located one block from Marble Arch occupies a pair of brick town houses, both of which date from 1780. The western house was the London home of the 19th-century artist and poet Edward Lear, famous for his nonsense verse; his illustrated limericks adorn the walls of one of the sitting rooms. Steep stairs lead up to the cozy rooms, which are fairly small but comfortable, with firm mattresses. One major drawback: This is an extremely noisy part of London. Rooms in the rear are quieter. Bathrooms are well maintained, complete with hair dryers.

Hart House Hotel. 51 Gloucester Place, Portman Sq., London W1H 3PE. ☎ **020/7935-2288.** Fax 020/7935-8516. www.harthouse.co.uk. E-mail: reservations@harthouse.co.uk. 16 units. TV TEL. £95 ($161.50) double; £115 ($195.50) triple; £130 ($221) quad. Rates include English breakfast. AE, MC, V. Tube: Marble Arch or Baker Street.

Hart House has been a long-enduring favorite with Frommer's readers. In the heart of the West End, this well-preserved historic building (one of a group of Georgian mansions occupied by exiled French nobles during the French Revolution) lies within easy walking distance of many theaters, as well as some of the most sought-after shopping areas and parks in London. Cozy and convenient, it's run by Andrew Bowden, one of Marylebone's best B&B hosts. The rooms—done in a combination of furnishings, ranging from Portobello antique to modern—are spic-and-span, each one with a different character. Favorites include no. 7, a triple with a big bath and shower. Ask for no. 11, on the top floor, if you'd like a brightly lit aerie. Housekeeping rates high marks here, and the bedrooms are comfortably appointed with chairs, an armoire, a desk, a chest of drawers, and a good bed with a firm mattress. The small bathrooms are efficiently organized, with hair dryers. Guest services include baby-sitting, dry cleaning and laundry service, and massage service. *Literary buffs take note:* Poet Elizabeth Barrett resided at no. 99 with her family for many years.

ST. JAMES'S

VERY EXPENSIVE

✪ **Dukes Hotel.** 35 St. James's Place, London SW1A 1NY. ☎ **800/381-4702** or 020/7491-4840. Fax 020/7493-1264. www.dukeshotel.co.uk. E-mail: dukeshotel@csi.com. 89 units. A/C TV TEL. £210–£250 ($357–$425) double; from £280 ($476) suite. AE, DC, MC, V. Parking £32 ($52.80). Tube: Green Park.

Dukes provides elegance without ostentation in what was presumably someone's Upstairs–Downstairs town house. Along with its nearest competitors, the Stafford and 22 Jermyn Street, it caters to those looking for charm, style, and tradition. A hotel since 1908 (and last renovated in 1994), it stands in a quiet courtyard off St. James's Street with turn-of-the-century gas lamps that create the appropriate mood for what's coming once you walk through the front door. Each well-furnished guest room is decorated in the style of a particular English period, ranging from Regency to Edwardian. All rooms are equipped with marble baths, satellite TV, air-conditioning, and private bar, plus a luxurious mattress. Bathrooms are small, but clad in marble, with robes and hair dryers. A short walk away are Buckingham Palace, St. James's Palace, and the Houses of Parliament. Shoppers will be near Bond Street and Piccadilly.

Dining: Dukes' Restaurant is small, tasteful, and elegant, combining classic British and continental cuisine. The hotel also has a clublike bar, which is known for its rare collection of vintage ports, Armagnacs, and cognacs.

Amenities: Even though it's claustrophobically small—it was once described as England's smallest castle—Dukes offers full hotel services, including 24-hour room service, car-rental and ticket services, and photocopying and typing services, baby-sitting, dry cleaning and laundry service, a small health spa, conference rooms.

The Ritz. 150 Piccadilly, London W1V 9DG. ☎ **800/525-4800** or 020/7493-8181. Fax 020/7493-2687. www.theritzhotel.co.uk. E-mail: enquire@ritzhotel.co.uk. 131 units. A/C MINIBAR TV TEL. £285–£365 ($484.50–$620.50) double; from £430 ($731) suite. Children under 12 stay free in parents' room. AE, DC, MC, V. Parking £40 ($68). Tube: Green Park.

Built in the French-Renaissance style and opened by César Ritz in 1906, this hotel overlooking Green Park is synonymous with luxury. Marble columns and potted palms abound, and a gold-leafed statue, La Source, adorns the fountain of the oval-shaped Palm Court. After a major restoration, this hotel is better than ever. New carpeting and air-conditioning have been installed in the guest rooms, and an overall polishing has recaptured much of the Ritz's original splendor. The belle époque guest rooms, each with its own character, are spacious and comfortable. Many have elaborate gilded plasterwork and a decor of soft pastel hues. A few rooms have their original brass beds and marble fireplaces. Beds are deluxe with luxury mattresses, and the bathrooms are elegantly appointed in either tile or marble, and filled with robes, phones, deluxe toiletries, and a hair dryer.

Dining: The Ritz is still the most fashionable place in London to meet for afternoon tea at the **Ritz Palm Court** (see "Afternoon Tea," in section 5). The **Ritz Restaurant,** one of the loveliest dining rooms in the world, has been faithfully restored to its original splendor. Service is efficient yet unobtrusive, and the tables are spaced to allow the most private of conversations (perhaps the reason Edward and Mrs. Simpson dined here so frequently before they married). The Palm Court also serves coffee and breakfast. Remember, both venues are very formal and require jacket and tie for gentlemen.

Amenities: 24-hour room service, valet, laundry service, baby-sitting, concierge, turndown, in-room massage, twice-daily maid service, express checkout, salon fitness center, business center.

The Stafford. 16–18 St. James's Place, London SW1A 1NJ. ☎ **800/525-4800** or 020/7493-0111. Fax 020/7493-7121. www.thestaffordhotel.co.uk. E-mail: info@thestaffordhotel.co.uk. 81 units. A/C TV TEL. £220–£280 ($374–$476) double; from £330 ($561) suite. AE, DC, MC, V. Tube: Green Park.

This hotel is famous for its American Bar, its clubby St. James's address, its discretion, and the warmth of its Edwardian decor. The Stafford was built in the late 19th century on a cul-de-sac off one of London's most centrally located and busiest neighborhoods; it's reached via St. James's Place or by a cobble-covered courtyard designed as a mews and known today as the Blue Ball Yard. The recently refurbished hotel has retained a country-house atmosphere, with touches of antique charm and modern amenities. It's not the Ritz, but the Stafford competes well with Dukes and 22 Jermyn Street (both highly recommended as well) for a tasteful, discerning clientele. All of the guest rooms are individually decorated, reflecting the hotel's origins as a private home. Many singles contain queen-size beds. Most of the units, however, have king-size or twin beds, and some of the deluxe units also offer a four-poster. Nearly all the baths are clad in marble with tubs and stall showers, a hair dryer, and toiletries. A handful of the hotel's newest and plushest accommodations in the historically restored stable mews require a walk across the yard. These rooms are in some ways even superior to those in the main building, and much of their original style has been preserved. But no horse in the 18th century ever slept like this: Units come with electronic safes, disc and stereo systems, and quality furnishings, mostly antique reproductions.

Dining: Classic international dishes are prepared from select fresh ingredients at the elegant **Stafford Restaurant,** lit with handsome chandeliers and accented with flowers and candles. The famous **American Bar,** which brings to mind the memento-packed library of an English country house, is an especially cozy place serving light meals and cocktails.

Amenities: 24-hour room service, baby-sitting, concierge, secretarial services, laundry service, maid service, privileges at a nearby health club.

SOHO

EXPENSIVE

✪ **Hazlitt's 1718.** 6 Frith St., London W1V 5TZ. ☎ **020/7434-1771.** Fax 020/7439-1524. E-mail: reservations@hazlitts.co.uk. 23 units. TV TEL. £170 ($289) double; £250 ($425) suite. AE, DC, MC, V. Tube: Leicester Sq. or Tottenham Court Rd.

This gem, housed in three historic homes on Soho Square—the most fashionable address in London two centuries ago—is one of London's best small hotels. Built in 1718, the hotel is named for William Hazlitt, who founded the Unitarian church in Boston and wrote four volumes on the life of his hero, Napoléon; the essayist died here in 1830.

Hazlitt's is a favorite with artists, actors, media people, and models. It's eclectic, filled with odds and ends picked up at estate auctions. Some find the Georgian decor a bit spartan, but the 2,000 original prints hanging on the walls brighten it considerably. Many bedrooms have four-poster beds, and some bathrooms have their original claw-footed tubs (only one unit has a shower). If you can afford it, opt for the elegant Baron Willoughby suite, with its giant four-poster bed and wood-burning fireplace. Some of the floors dip and sway and there's no elevator, but it's all part of the charm. Some rooms are a bit small, but most of them are spacious. Most of the bathrooms have 19th-century styling with oversize tubs and old brass fittings; the showers, however, are mostly hand-held. Amenities include a concierge, 24-hour room service, baby-sitting, dry cleaning and laundry service, video rentals and a discounted rate on a car or limousine. Swinging Soho is at your doorstep; the young, hip staff will be happy to direct you to the local hot spots.

BLOOMSBURY

MODERATE

Academy Hotel. 17–21 Gower St., London WC1E 6HG. ☎ **800/678-3096** or 020/7631-4115. Fax 020/7636-3442. E-mail: academy@aol.com. 48 units. A/C TV TEL. £125–£145 ($212.50–$246.50) double; £185 ($314.50) suite. AE, DC, MC, V. Tube: Tottenham Court Rd., Goodge St., or Russell Sq.

Right in the heart of London's publishing district, the Academy attracts budding British John Grishams who haven't hit the big time yet. If you look out your window you'll see where Virginia Woolf and other literary members of the Bloomsbury Group used to pass by every day. Most of the hotel's original architectural details were preserved when these three 1776 Georgian row houses were joined. The hotel was substantially upgraded in the 1990s, with a bathroom added to every bedroom (whether there was space or not). Fourteen have a tub-shower combination; the rest have showers only. The beds, so they say, were built to "American specifications," and they assure you of a restful night's sleep. Rooms with their overstuffed armchairs and half-canopied beds sometimes evoke English country house living, but the poorer relations. The theater district and Covent Garden are within walking distance. The in-house, award-winning restaurant, Alchemy, has been recently refurbished to a much more modern design and offers a reasonably priced menu of modern European food. Other facilities include an elegant bar, a secluded patio garden, concierge, room service and dry cleaning and laundry service.

Blooms Hotel. 7 Montague St., London WC1B 5BP. ☎ **020/7323-1717.** Fax 020/7636-6498. E-mail: blooms@mermaid.co.uk. 27 units. TV TEL. £195–££205 ($331.50–$348.50) double. Extra person £45 ($76.50). Rates include English breakfast. AE, DC, MC, V. Tube: Russell Sq.

This exquisitely restored town house has a pedigree: It stands in what was formerly the grounds of Montague House (now the British Museum). It's had a distinguished, if eccentric, list of former occupants: everybody from Richard Penn, the Whig member of Parliament from Liverpool, to Dr. John Cumming, who firmly believed he'd witness the end of the world (on long winter nights, his ghostly presence has been spotted). Even though it's in the heart of London, the house evokes a country home atmosphere, complete with cozy fireplace, period art, and copies of *Country Life* in the magazine rack. Guests take morning coffee in a walled garden overlooking the British Museum. In summer, light meals are served. The small- to midsize bedrooms are individually designed with traditional elegance, in beautifully muted tones. The bathrooms here are excellent, with a hair dryer. Services include 24-hour room service, dry cleaning and laundry service, and concierge.

✪ **Morgan Hotel.** 24 Bloomsbury St., London WC1B 3QJ. ☎ **020/7636-3735.** 21 units. TV TEL. £80 ($136) double; £120 ($204) triple; £110 ($187) suite. All rates include English breakfast. MC, V. Tube: Russell Square or Tottenham Court Road.

In a row of Georgian houses, each built in the 1790s, this much-restored hotel is distinguished by its gold-tipped iron fence railings, lying a 12-minute walk from Covent Garden. The family managers do all the work themselves, and they have such a devoted following of habitués that it's hard to get a reservation in summer. Even if things are a bit cramped and the stairs rather steep, the rooms are pleasant and the atmosphere congenial. The carpeted bedrooms in this completely refurbished hotel have big beds (by British standards), dressing tables with mirrors, ample wardrobe space, hair dryers, batik bedspreads, and central heating; about 11 of the rooms have air-conditioning. Several rooms overlook the British Museum. Even though they cost more, the suites are worth the extra money if you can afford it. They're furnished tastefully with brightly polished dark English pieces, framed English prints, and decorator fabrics, all with spacious bathrooms and daily maid service.

INEXPENSIVE

Crescent Hotel. 49–50 Cartwright Gardens, London WC1H 9EL. ☎ **020/7387-1515.** Fax 020/7383-2054. 24 units, 18 with bathroom (some with shower only, some with tub only). TV TEL. £80 ($136) double with bathroom. Rates include English breakfast. MC, V. Tube: Russell Sq., King's Cross, or Euston.

Although Dorothy Sayers, John Ruskin, and Percy Bysshe Shelley no longer pass by the door, the Crescent still stands in the heart of academic London. The private square is guarded by the University of London, whose student residential halls are just across the street. You have access to the gardens, with its private tennis courts. Mrs. Bessolo and Mrs. Cockle, the managers, are the kindest hosts along the street; they view Crescent as an extension of their private home and welcome you to its comfortably elegant Georgian surroundings. Some guests have been returning for 4 decades to enjoy a range of bedrooms, from small singles with shared bathrooms to more spacious twin and double rooms with private plumbing. All rooms have beverage makers, alarm clocks, and hair dryers. Twins and doubles have private plumbing, admittedly with very tiny baths. Many rooms are singles, however, ranging in price from £40 to £60 ($66 to $99), depending on the plumbing. The good ladies will even let you do your own ironing so you'll look sharp when you go out on the town.

✪ **Jenkins Hotel.** 45 Cartwright Gardens, London WC1H 9EH. ☎ **020/7387-2067.** Fax 020/7383-3139. www.jenkinshotel.demon.co.uk. E-mail: reservations@jenkinshotel.demon.co.uk. 15 units (6 with bathroom). MINIBAR TV TEL. £68 ($115.60) double without bathroom, £78 ($132.60) double with bathroom; £90 ($153) triple with bathroom. MC, V. Rates include English breakfast. Tube: Russell Sq., King's Cross, or Euston.

Followers of the Agatha Christie TV series *Poirot* might recognize this residence—it was featured in the series. The antiques are gone and the rooms are small, but some of the original charm of the Georgian house remains—enough so that the London *Mail on Sunday* recently proclaimed it one of the "ten best hotel values" in the city. All the rooms have been redecorated, and many completely refurbished. Only a few rooms have a private bathroom, and they're quite small, but the corridor bathrooms are adequate and well maintained. Each guest room has a hair dryer. The location is great, near the British Museum, London University, theaters, and antiquarian bookshops. There are some drawbacks—no elevator and no reception or sitting room, but it's a place where you can settle in and feel at home.

Ruskin Hotel. 23–24 Montague St., London WC1B 5BH. ☎ **020/7636-7388.** Fax 020/7323-1662. 32 units (6 with bathroom). £60 ($102) double without bathroom, £80 ($136) double with bathroom; £80 ($136) triple without bathroom, £92 ($156.40) triple with bathroom. Rates include English breakfast. AE, DC, MC, V. Tube: Russell Sq., Holborn, or Tottenham Ct. Rd.

This hotel, named for author John Ruskin, has been managed for two decades by a hard-working family who enjoy a repeat clientele. They keep the place spic-and-span, but the furnishings, though polished, are worn. The mattresses, however, are good and each room has a beverage maker. Double-glazing in the front blots out the noise, but we prefer the cozy old-fashioned chambers in the rear, as they open onto a park. Sorry, no elevator. The greenery in the cellar-level breakfast room provides an elegant touch, and the breakfast is big enough to fortify you for a full day at the British Museum next door. *Insider tip:* Although the private bathrooms are ridiculously small, the shared bathrooms in the hall are generous and well-maintained—and you'll save money by opting for one of the rooms without a bathroom.

Thanet Hotel. 8 Bedford Place, London WC1B 5JA. ☎ **020/7636-2869.** Fax 020/7323-6676. www.freepages.co.uk/thanet_hotel. 16 units. TV TEL. £82 ($139.40) double with bathroom; £99 ($168.30) triple with bathroom; £108 ($183.60) quad with bathroom. Rates include English breakfast. AE, MC, V. Tube: Russell Sq.

The myriad hotels around Russell Square become peas in a pod at some point, but the Thanet stands out. It no longer charges the same rates it did when it first appeared in *England on $5 a Day,* but it's still a winning choice nonetheless, a fine address and an affordable option for those who want to be close to the British Museum, Theaterland, and Covent Garden. It's a landmark status building on a quiet Georgian terrace between Russell and Bloomsbury squares; although it was restored many times over the years, many original features remain. Third-generation hoteliers, the Orchard family offers small, comfortably furnished and well-decorated rooms with beverage makers. The beds have firm mattresses, and many units were recently redecorated. Bathrooms are very small, but neatly maintained and equipped with a hair dryer.

COVENT GARDEN

VERY EXPENSIVE

Covent Garden Hotel. 10 Monmouth St., London WC2H 9HB. ☎ **800/53-6674** in the U.S., or 020/7806-1000. Fax 020/7806-1100. www.firmdale.com. E-mail: covent@firmdale.com. 50 units. A/C MINIBAR TV TEL. £200–£255 ($340–$433.50) double; £295–£550 ($501.50–$935) suite. AE, MC, V. Tube: Covent Garden or Leicester Sq.

Constructed as a French-directed hospital around 1850, this building lay derelict for years until it was reconfigured in 1996 by hot hoteliers Tim and Kit Kemp into one of London's most charming boutique hotels, situated in one of the West End's hippest neighborhoods. *Travel and Leisure* called it one of 1997's 25 hottest places to stay in the *world.* It remains so today.

Across from Neal's Yard and behind a bottle-green facade reminiscent of a 19th-century storefront, the hotel has a welcoming lobby outfitted with elaborate marquetry furniture. Upstairs, above a dramatic stone staircase, soundproof bedrooms are lushly furnished in English style with Asian fabrics, many ornately adorned with hand-embroidered designs. Their decorative trademark? Each room has a clothier's mannequin—a lithe female form draped in the fabric that's the predominant theme of that particular room. Each comes with VCR, CD player, a luxurious mattress, two phone lines with voice mail, and marble bathrooms with double vanities, deep soaking tubs, thick towels, and a hair dryer. The young, well-mannered staff works hard to please, and succeeds—the friendly concierge walked blocks in a downpour to hail us a cab.

Dining: Permeated with a sense of 19th-century nostalgia, **Max's Brasserie** serves up very good French-English bistro fare. With high stools at the bar and crisp table linens, it's a chic place for lunch.

Amenities: 24-hour room service, concierge, secretarial services, office facilities, small gym, small video library.

St. Martins Lane. 45 St. Martins Lane, London WC2N 4HX. ☎ **020/7300-5500.** Fax 020/7300-5565. 204 units. A/C MINIBAR TV TEL. £255–£470 ($433.50–$799) double, from £650 ($1,105) suite. AE, DC, MC, V. Tube: Covent Garden.

Eccentric and irreverent, with a sense of humor, is how Ian Schrager describes his own cutting edge Covent Garden hotel which he transformed into a chic enclave from a 1960s office building. This is Schrager's first hotel outside the United States, and many guests have already fallen in love with Schrager hotels from New York to West Hollywood. The hip mix of high design and a sense of cool have been imported across the pond. Whimsical touches abound. For example, a string of daisies replaces "do not disturb" signs. Because of full spectrum dials, you can bathe your white furnishings into whatever color suits your mood. Floor-to-ceiling glass windows in every room offer a panoramic view of London, and down comforters and soft pillows ensure a good night's sleep. Some rooms are non-smoking.

Dining/Diversions: The critically acclaimed New York restaurant, **Asia de Cuba,** has now invaded London with its rum bar and seabar serving caviar, oysters, and innovative sushi and Asian seafood creations. There is also an outdoor garden restaurant, plus a 24-hour brasserie. **The Light Bar** is color-splashed and a sophisticated rendezvous.

Amenities: Business center, 24-hour concierge, 24-hour room service, supervised play area for children.

MODERATE

✪ **Fielding Hotel.** 4 Broad Court, Bow St., London WC2B 5QZ. ☎ **020/7836-8305.** Fax 020/7497-0064. 24 units. TV TEL. £100–£130 ($170–$221) double. AE, DC, MC, V. Tube: Covent Garden.

One of London's more eccentric hotels, the Fielding is cramped, quirky, and quaint, but an enduring favorite nonetheless. The hotel is named after novelist Henry Fielding of *Tom Jones* fame, who lived in Broad Court. It lies on a pedestrian street still lined with 19th-century gas lamps; the Royal Opera House is across the street. Rooms are quite small, but they're charmingly old-fashioned and traditional. Some of the units are redecorated or at least "touched up" every year. Bathrooms are minuscule, and if you want a hair dryer you'll have to request one from the front desk. Very few rooms have anything approaching a view; floors dip and sway, and the furnishings and fabrics have known better times—so be duly warned. But with a location like this, in the very heart of London, the Fielding keeps guests coming back; many love the hotel's rickety charm. There's no room service or restaurant, but breakfast is served. Be sure to introduce yourself to Smokey the African Grey parrot in the bar—he's the hotel's oldest resident.

ALONG THE STRAND

VERY EXPENSIVE

✪ **The Savoy.** The Strand, London WC2R 0EU. ☎ **800/63-SAVOY** or 020/7836-4343. Fax 020/7240-6040. www.savoy-group.co.uk. E-mail: info@the-savoy.co.uk. 207 units. A/C MINIBAR TV TEL. From £335 ($569.50) double; from £455 ($773.50) suite. AE, DC, MC, V. Parking £24 ($40.80). Tube: Charing Cross or Covent Garden.

Although not as swank as the Dorchester, this London landmark is the premier address if you want to be in the Strand and Covent Garden area. Impresario Richard D'Oyly Carte built the hotel in 1889 as an annex to his nearby Savoy Theatre, where many Gilbert and Sullivan operettas were originally staged. With eight stories of glazed tiles rising between the Strand and the Thames, it dwarfs all of its nearby competition, including the Waldorf at Aldwych and the Howard on Temple Place. Each guest room is individually decorated with solid and comfortable furniture, large closets, and an eclectic blend of antiques; 48 have their own sitting rooms. The luxurious handmade beds have top-of-the-line crisp linen clothing. Some bathrooms have shower stalls, but most have a combination shower and tub. Bathrooms are spacious with hair dryers and deluxe toiletries. The expensive river-view suites are the most sought after, and for good reason—the views are the best in London.

Dining: The world-famous **Savoy Grill** has long been popular with the theater crowd; Sarah Bernhardt was a regular. The even more elegant **River Restaurant** has tables overlooking the Thames; there's dancing to live band music in the evening. The room known as **Upstairs** specializes in champagne and seafood.

Amenities: 24-hour room service, nightly turndown, same-day dry cleaning and laundry service, secretarial service, hairdresser, news kiosk, the city's best health club—the pool has fabulous views.

WESTMINSTER/VICTORIA

EXPENSIVE

Goring Hotel. 15 Beeston Place, Grosvenor Gardens, London SW1W OJW. ☎ **020/7396-9000.** Fax 020/7834-4393. www.goringhotel.co.uk. E-mail: reception@goringhotel.co.uk. 75 units. A/C TV TEL. £195–£235 ($331.50–$399.50) double; from £230–£290 ($391–$493) suite. AE, DC, MC, V. Parking £25 ($42.50). Tube: Victoria.

For tradition and location, the Goring is our premier choice in the Westminster area—even better than the nearby Stakis London St. Ermins, its closest competitor. Located just behind Buckingham Palace, it lies within easy reach of the royal parks, Victoria Station, Westminster Abbey, and the Houses of Parliament. It also happens to offer the finest personal service of all its nearby competitors.

Built in 1910 by O. R. Goring, this was the first hotel in the world to have central heating and a private bathroom in every room. Today's well-furnished guest rooms still offer all the comforts, including refurbished bathrooms—which are most luxurious, with extra-long tubs, red marble walls, dual pedestal basins, bidets, deluxe toiletries, fluffy towels, hair dryers, and power showerheads. There is an ongoing refurbishment of all the bedrooms; the beds, in fact, are among the most comfortable in London. Preferred is one of the rooms overlooking the garden. Maintenance is so high here that some discerning English clients call it "bang up-to-date." The charm of a traditional English country hotel is evoked in the paneled drawing room, where fires crackle in the ornate fireplaces on nippy evenings. The adjoining bar overlooks the rear gardens.

Dining: At the restaurant, the chef uses only the freshest ingredients in his classic English recipes; specialties include roast breast of pheasant, rump of English lamb with bubble and squeak (cabbage and potatoes) and rosemary jus, and grilled Dover sole. The restaurant also offers one of the most extensive wine lists in London. Afternoon tea is served in the lounge.

Amenities: 24-hour room service, valet service, concierge, dry cleaning and laundry service, baby-sitting, secretarial services, free use of local health club.

Moderate

✪ **The Sanctuary House Hotel.** 33 Tothill St., London, SW1H 9LA. ☎ **020/7799-4044.** Fax 020/7799-3657. www.fullers.co.uk. E-mail: sanctuary@fullers.demon.co.uk. 33 units. A/C TV TEL. £72.50–£99.50 ($123.25–$169.15) double. AE, DC, MC, V. Parking: £20 ($34). Tube: St. James's Park.

The hotel is in an historic building close to Westminster Abbey. Only in the new London where hotels are bursting into bloom like spring daffodils would you expect to find a hotel so close to Westminster Abbey—a pub hotel, no less! It has been converted into traditional English-inn–style, with a pub downstairs and the rooms above. Rooms have a rustic feel, but they have first-rate beds along with newly restored bathrooms with fluffy towels. Downstairs a pub/restaurant, part of The Sanctuary, offers hearty old-style British meals that have ignored changing culinary fashions of the past quarter of a century. The food is excellent if you like the roast beef, Welsh lamb, and Dover sole known to Churchill's palate. Naturally, there's always plenty of brew on tap. The reception is open 24 hours a day, and they offer laundry and dry cleaning services.

Inexpensive

Astors Hotel. 110–112 Ebury St., London SW1W 9QD. ☎ **020/7730-3811.** Fax 020/7823-6728. www.astors.uk.com. E-mail: Jmevans@astors.uk.com. 22 units (12 with bathroom). TV. £60 ($102) double without bathroom, £72 ($122.40) double with bathroom; from £140 ($238) family unit with bathroom. Rates include English breakfast. MC, V. Parking £15 ($25.50) nearby. Tube: Victoria.

This well-located choice is a stone's throw from Buckingham Palace and just a 5-minute walk from Victoria's main line and Tube stations. The brick-fronted Victorian was once home to Margaret Oliphant (1828–97), a popular Victorian novelist; Noël Coward was a neighbor for 20 years, and H. G. Wells, Yeats, and Shaw called down the street at no. 153 when poet, novelist, and racy autobiographer George Moore (1852–1933) was in residence. The guests today are frugal travelers looking for a decent, affordable address in pricey London. Although more functional than glamorous, the rooms are satisfactory in every way. Each unit is fitted with a comfortable mattress, and the well-maintained bathrooms have been renewed. Since space and furnishings vary greatly, ask to take a little peek before committing yourself to a room. (As the hotel is often full, that won't always be possible.)

Caswell Hotel. 25 Gloucester St., London SW1V 2DB. ☎ **020/7834-6345.** www.hotellondon.co.uk. E-mail: manager@hotellondon.co.uk. 18 units (7 with bathroom). MINIBAR TV. £56 ($95.20) double without bathroom, £76 ($129.20) double with bathroom. Rates include English breakfast. MC, V. Tube: Victoria.

Run with consideration and thoughtfulness by Mr. and Mrs. Hare, Caswell lies on a cul-de-sac, a calm oasis in an otherwise busy area. Beyond the chintz-filled lobby, the decor is understated: There are four floors of well-furnished but not spectacular bedrooms, each with such amenities as hair dryers and beverage makers. Mattresses are worn but still have much comfort left in them. Private baths are very small units with a shower stall and few amenities except a hair dryer; however, corridor baths are adequate and well maintained. How do they explain the success of the place? One staff member said, "This year's guest is next year's business."

✪ **Collin House.** 104 Ebury St., London SW1W 9QD. ☎ and fax **020/7730-8031.** www.milford.co.uk/england/accom/h-1-3229.html. 13 units, 8 with bathroom (shower only). £62–£78 ($105.40–$132.60) double, £90 ($153) triple. Rates include English breakfast. No credit cards. Tube: Victoria.

On a street devoted in part to B&Bs—some of the finest in the vicinity of Victoria Station—Collin House emerges as a winner. Queen Victoria was halfway through her long reign when this house was constructed here. Over the years it's been changed and modified to keep abreast of the times. Private bathrooms have been discreetly installed in areas not designed for plumbing, but everything still works efficiently. Even in rooms without bathrooms, there are adequate hallway facilities. In some cases occupants of two units share a bath so there is often no waiting in line. Traffic in this area of London is heavy outside, and the front windows are not soundproofed, so be duly warned. Year after year, owners make improvements in the furnishings and carpets, and all bedrooms, which vary in size, are comfortably furnished and well maintained. Two rooms are large enough for families. A generous breakfast awaits you each morning in the basement of this no-smoking facility.

✪ **James House/Cartref House.** 108 and 129 Ebury St., London SW1W 9QD. James House ☎ **020/7730-7338;** Cartref House ☎ **020/7730-6176.** Fax 020/7730-7338. E-mail: jandchouse@compuserve.com. 21 units (11 with bath). TV. £65 ($110.50) double without bathroom, £78 ($132.60) double with bathroom; £110 ($187) quad with bathroom. Rates include English breakfast. AE, MC, V. Tube: Victoria.

Hailed by many publications, including the *Los Angeles Times,* as one of the top 10 B&B choices in London, James House and Cartref House (across the street) deserve their accolades. Derek and Sharon James have real dedication in their work, and have the ability to make everyone feel right at home, even the first-time visitor to London. They're the finest hosts in the area, and they're constantly refurbishing, so everything looks up-to-date. Each room is individually designed; some of the large ones have bunk beds that make them suitable for families, although these mattresses are a bit thin; mattresses on the other beds are firm. Maintenance is exceedingly high. Clients in rooms with a private bathroom will find somewhat cramped quarters, but each room is tidily arranged. Corridor bathrooms are adequate and frequently refurbished. The English breakfast is so generous that you might end up skipping lunch. There's no elevator, but the happy guests don't seem to mind. Don't worry about which house you're assigned; each one's a winner. You're just a stone's throw from Buckingham Palace should the Queen invite you over for tea. Smokers be warned, both houses are no-smoking environments.

IN AND AROUND KNIGHTSBRIDGE

EXPENSIVE

Knightsbridge Green Hotel. 159 Knightsbridge, London SW1X 7PD. ☎ **020/7584-6274.** Fax 020/7225-1635. E-mail: theKGHotel@aol.com. 28 units. A/C MINIBAR TV TEL. £135 ($229.50) double; £160 ($272) suite. AE, DC, MC, V. Tube: Knightsbridge.

Many return guests from around the world view this dignified 1890s structure as their home away from home. In 1966, when it was converted into a hotel, the developers were careful to retain its wide baseboards, cove moldings, high ceilings, and spacious proportions. Even without kitchens, the well-furnished suites come close to apartment-style living; all have trouser presses and hair dryers in the well-appointed marble bathrooms with fluffy towels, a hair dryer, and power showers. Most of the rooms are quite spacious, with adequate storage space. Bedrooms are often individualized—one has a romantic sleigh bed—and each comes with a deluxe mattress. This is still a solid choice, and it's just around the corner from Harrods.

Amenities: Coffee, tea, and pastries are available throughout the day; baby-sitting, dry cleaning, and laundry service.

Knightsbridge Hotel. 12 Beaufort Gardens, London SW3 1PT. ☎ **020/7589-9271.** Fax 020/7823-9692. www.knightsbridgehotel.co.uk. E-mail: reception@knightsbridgehotel.co.uk. 40 units. MINIBAR TV TEL. £135 ($229.50) double. Rates include English or continental breakfast. AE, DC MC, V. Parking free on street from 6pm to 8am. Tube: Knightsbridge.

The Knightsbridge Hotel attracts visitors from all over the world seeking a small hotel in a high-rent district. It's fabulously located, sandwiched between fashionable Beauchamp Place and Harrods, and with many of the city's top theaters and museums close at hand, including the Royal Albert Hall and Madame Tussaud's. Built in the early 1800s as a private town house, this family-run place sits on a tranquil, tree-lined square, free from traffic. Small and unpretentious, with a subdued Victorian ambience, it's been recently renovated to a high standard: All the well-furnished rooms have private bathrooms, coffeemakers, trouser presses, and safety-deposit boxes. Most bedrooms are spacious and furnished with traditional English fabrics. The best are numbers 311 and 312 at the rear, each with a pitched ceiling and a small sitting area. Bathrooms are clad in marble or tile and contain hair dryers.

Amenities: Room service, laundry and dry cleaning service, and a concierge. There's also a small health club with a steam room and a spa for guests' use.

Searcy's Roof Garden Rooms. 30 Pavilion Rd., SW1X 0HJ. ☎ **020/7584-4921.** Fax 020/7823-8694. www.searcys.co.uk/pavilion.html. E-mail: searcyrgr@aol.com. 12 units. TV TEL. £120–£130 ($204–$221) double, £160–£190 ($272–$323) apt. AE, DC, MC, V. Tube: Knightsbridge.

Searcy's, one of London's best catering firms, operates the surprise of the year: an old pumping station that has been discreetly turned into a hotel only a short hop, skip, and jump from Harrods and the boutiques of Sloane Street. At this Knightsbridge oasis, you'll press a buzzer and be admitted to a freight elevator that will carry you to the third floor. Upstairs you'll encounter handsomely furnished rooms with occasional antiques, tasteful fabrics, comfortable beds (with some canopied ones), and often a sitting alcove. Surprisingly, some of the bathtubs are placed right in the room instead of in a separate unit. Opt, if possible, for rooms 7, 14, and 15. For an extra charge, the staff will bring you a continental breakfast. Guests have use of a spacious communal kitchen, and there is also a rooftop garden.

Hotels & Dining from Knightsbridge to Kensington

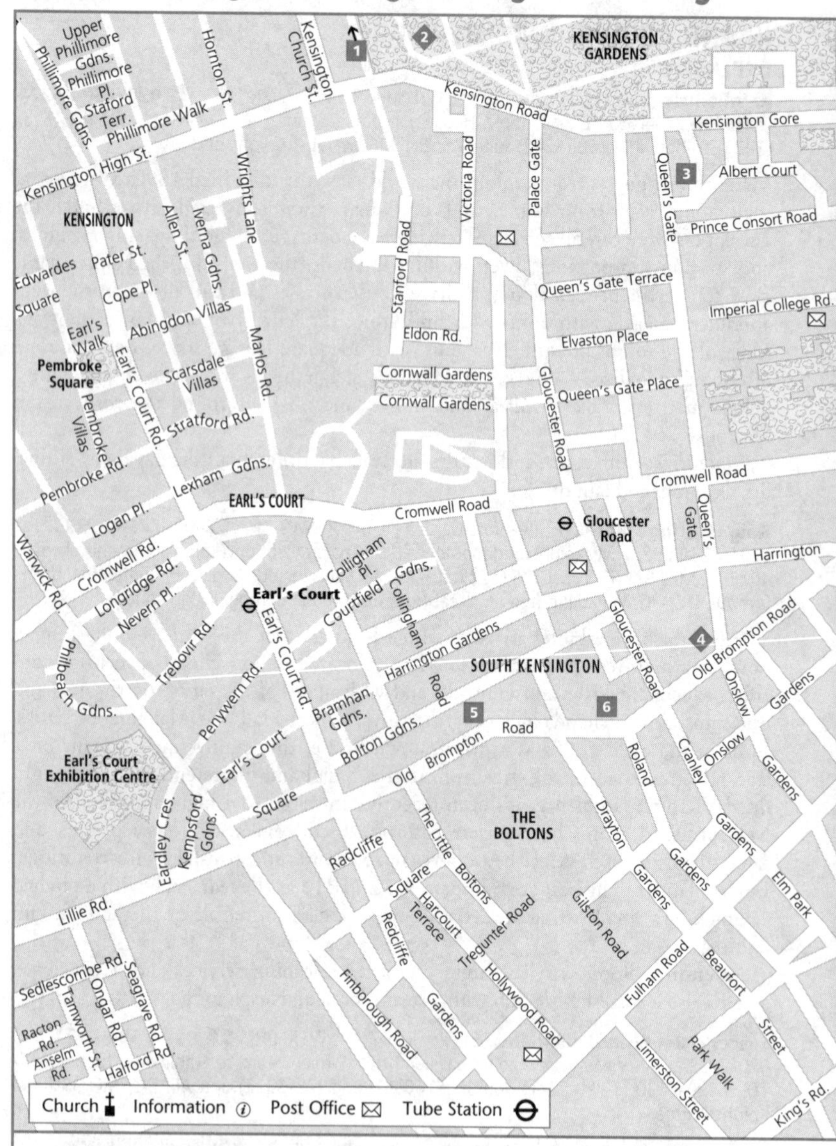

ACCOMMODATIONS ■

Aston's Budget Studios & Designer Studios & Suites **6**
Diplomat Hotel **13**
The Gore **3**
Knightsbridge Green House **17**
Knightsbridge Hotel **21**
Searcy's Roof Garden Rooms **14**
The Sloane **10**
Swiss House Hotel **5**
Vicarage Private House **1**

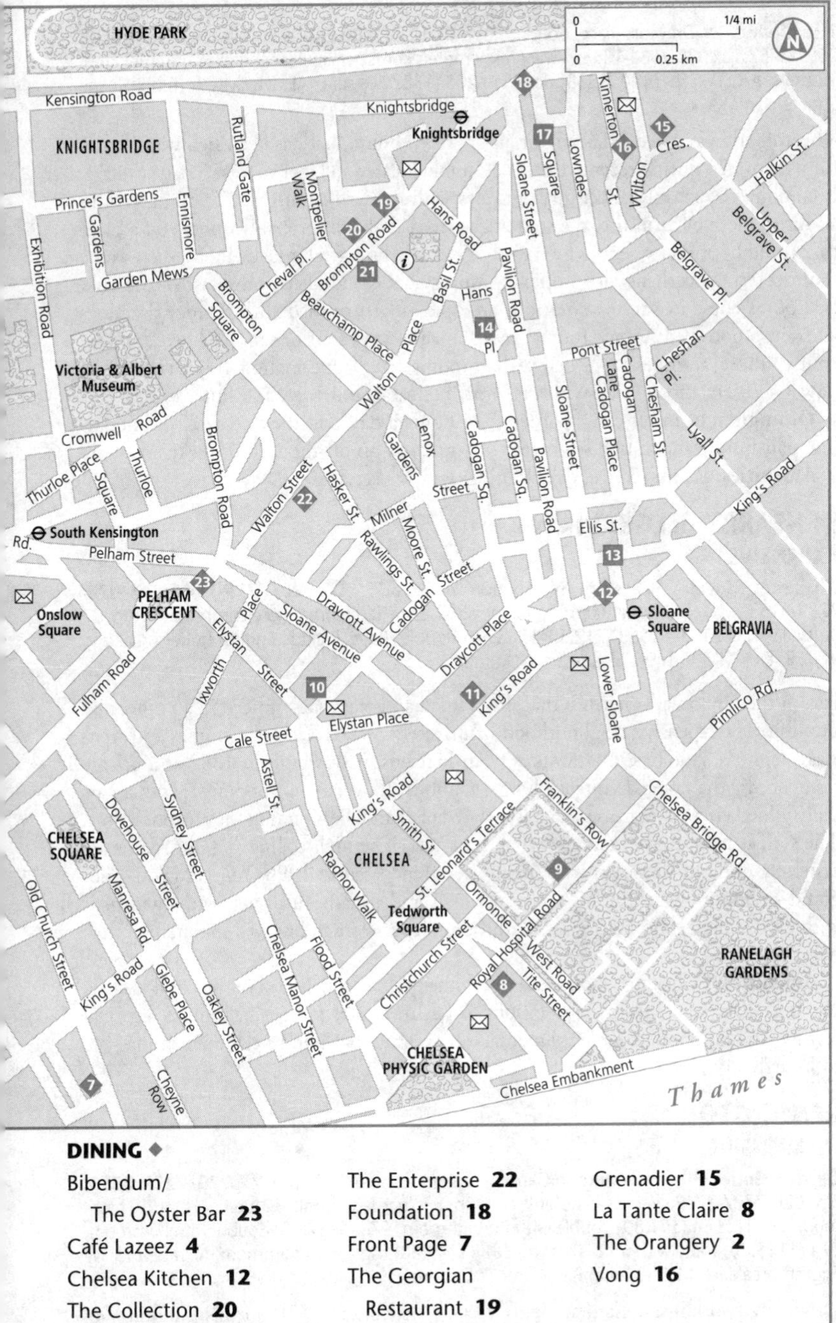

DINING ◆

Bibendum/ The Oyster Bar **23**
Café Lazeez **4**
Chelsea Kitchen **12**
The Collection **20**
English Garden **11**
The Enterprise **22**
Foundation **18**
Front Page **7**
The Georgian Restaurant **19**
Gordon Ramsey **9**
Grenadier **15**
La Tante Claire **8**
The Orangery **2**
Vong **16**

The Sloane. 29 Draycott Place, London SW3 2SH. ☎ **800/324-9960** in the U.S., or 020/7581-5757. Fax 020/7584-1348. www.premierhotels.com. E-mail: sloanehotel@BTinternet.com. 12 units. A/C TV TEL. £140 ($238) double; £225 ($382.50) suite. AE, DC, MC, V. Tube: Sloane Square.

This toff address, a red-brick Victorian-era town house that has been richly and tastefully renovated during recent years, is desirably located in Chelsea near Sloane Square. It combines worthy 19th-century antiques with modern comforts—if you happen to admire a piece of furniture, the staff at the front desk will probably quote you a price that could be attractive enough for you to actually buy it. Our favorite spot here is the rooftop terrace with its views opening onto Chelsea, ideal for breakfast or a drink. Bedrooms come in varying sizes, but are opulently furnished with flouncy draperies and sumptuous beds. Many rooms have draped four-posters or canopied beds, and, of course, those antiques. The deluxe bathrooms have combination tub and chrome power showers, mostly wall-width mirrors, luxurious toiletries, and fluffy towels.

Dining: Light meals can be ordered 24 hours a day, and the staff is accommodating, pan-European, and oh-so-discreet if you fancy an off-the-record weekend.

Amenities: Room service, dry cleaning, laundry service.

IN NEARBY BELGRAVIA

EXPENSIVE

Diplomat Hotel. 2 Chesham St., London SW1X 8DT. ☎ **020/7235-1544.** Fax 020/7259-6153. www.btinternet.com/-diplomat.hotel. E-mail: diplomat.hotel@btinternet.com. 27 units. TV TEL. £125–£155 ($212.50–$263.50) double. Rates include English buffet breakfast. AE, CB, DC, MC, V. Tube: Sloane Sq. or Knightsbridge.

Part of the Diplomat's charm is that it is a small and reasonably priced in an otherwise prohibitively expensive neighborhood of privately owned Victorian homes and first-class, high-rise hotels. Only minutes from Harrods, it was built in 1882 as a private residence by the noted architect Thomas Cubbitt. It's very well appointed, with a partially gilded circular staircase and a Regency-era chandelier framing the reception area. The staff is helpful, well mannered, and discreet. The high-ceilinged guest rooms are tastefully done in Victorian style; many were renovated in 1996. You get good—not grand—comfort here. Rooms are a bit small and usually furnished with twin beds with exceedingly good mattresses. Bathrooms are also small but well maintained with hair dryers.

Amenities: Concierge, massage service, business center, afternoon tea, and a snack menu available daily from 1 to 8:30pm. A health club is located nearby. As a special feature, the hotel offers a complimentary 15-minute back and neck Shiatsu massage to its arriving guests.

KENSINGTON

INEXPENSIVE

Garden Court. 30–31 Kensington Gardens Square, London W2 4BG. ☎ **020/7229-2553.** Fax 020/7727-2749. www.s-h-systems.co.uk/hotels/gardenc.html. 32 units, 16 with bathroom. TV TEL. £54 ($91.80) double without bathroom, £78 ($132.60) double with bathroom, £74 ($125.80) triple without bathroom, £88 ($149.60) triple with bathroom. All rates include English breakfast. MC, V. Tube: Bayswater or Queensway.

Originally two houses, Garden Court was constructed in 1870 on this tranquil Victorian garden square in the heart of the city. The houses were combined to form one efficiently run hotel near such attractions as Kensington Palace, Hyde Park, and the Portobello Antiques Market. Each year new rooms are redecorated and refurbished, although there seems to be a lack of consistency in an overall plan. Most accommodations are spacious, with good lighting, generous shelf and closet space, and comfortable but not stylish furnishings. If you're in a room without bathroom, you'll generally have to share with the occupants of only one other room. Each room is individually decorated, and "comfy" like visiting your Great Aunt. Your room will open onto the square in front or the gardens in the rear. Bathrooms were installed in areas not intended as such and tend to be very cramped. Rooms have hair dryers, and you can use the office safe. There is no elevator.

✪ **Vicarage Private Hotel.** 10 Vicarage Gate, London W8 4AG. ☎ **020/7229-4030.** Fax 020/7792-5989. www.londonvicaragehotel.com. E-mail: reception@londonvicaragehotel.com. 18 units (none with bathroom). £98 ($166.60) double with bathroom, £74 ($125.80) without bathroom; £90 ($153) triple; £98 ($166.60) family room for 4. Rates include English breakfast. No credit cards. Tube: High St. Kensington or Notting Hill Gate.

Eileen and Martin Diviney have a host of admirers on all continents. Their hotel is tops for old-fashioned English charm, affordable prices, and hospitality. Situated on a residential garden square close to Kensington High Street, not far from Portobello Road Market, this Victorian town house retains many original features. Individually furnished in a country-house style, the bedrooms can accommodate up to four. If you want a little nest to hide away in, opt for the top floor aerie (no. 19), a private retreat such as Noël Coward used to occupy before "I got rich enough to move downstairs." By the time you arrive, some small private bathrooms may be added. For the moment, guests find the corridor bathrooms adequate, and they are well maintained. Each year a few rooms are refurbished, and beds have decent mattresses. Guests meet in a cozy sitting room for conversation and to watch the telly. As a thoughtful extra, hot drinks are available 24 hours a day. In the morning, a hearty English breakfast awaits.

SOUTH KENSINGTON

EXPENSIVE

✪ **The Gore.** 189 Queen's Gate, London SW7 5EX. ☎ **800/637-7200** or 020/7584-6601. Fax 020/7589-8127. www.gorehotel.co.uk. E-mail: reservations@gorehotel.co.uk. 54 units. MINIBAR TV TEL. £171–£236 ($290.70–$401.20) double; £257 ($436.90) The Tudor Room. AE, DC, MC, V. Tube: Gloucester Rd.

Once owned by the Marquess of Queensberry's family, the Gore has been a hotel since 1892—and it's always been one of our favorites. Victorians would still feel at home here among all the walnut and mahogany, Oriental carpets, and walls covered in antique photos. The Gore has always been known for eccentricity. Each room is different, so try to find one that suits your personality. The dark-paneled Tudor Room is the most fascinating, with its gallery and fireplace. Rooms are a good value; although most are a bit small, there is still room for a sitting area. Well-maintained bathrooms have thick towels, hair dryers, and custom brass taps. Some units contain a shower stall only, although most have a tub and shower combination. Some of the plumbing wares would be familiar to Queen Victoria, but everything works smoothly. Many rooms have four-poster beds or half testers, each with a good, firm mattress. Amenities include private safes.

Dining: It's worth a trip across town to dine at renowned chef Antony Worrall Thompson's **Bistro 190,** especially for the crispy squid, the chargrilled corn-fed chicken, and the seared tuna sashimi with spicy lentil relish.

Amenities: Concierge, room service daily from 7am to 12:20am, dry cleaning and laundry service. Newspaper delivery, baby-sitting, secretarial services, and express checkout may be arranged. Access to health club next door.

Inexpensive

✪ Aston's Budget Studios & Aston's Designer Studios and Suites. 31 Rosary Gardens, London SW7 4NQ. ☎ **800/525-2810** in the U.S., or 020/7590-6000. Fax 020/7590-6060. www.astons_apartments.com. E-mail: sales@astons_apartments.com. 76 units. A/C TV TEL. Standard Studios £80 ($136) double; £120 ($204) triple; £150 ($255) quad. Designer Studios £130 ($221) double. AE, MC, V. Tube: South Kensington.

This carefully restored row of Victorian town houses offers comfortably furnished studios and suites that are among London's best values. Heavy oak doors and 18th-century hunting pictures give the foyer a rich traditional atmosphere. Accommodations range in size and style from budget to designer; every one has a compact but complete kitchenette concealed behind doors. The air-conditioned designer studios and two-room designer suites are decorated with rich fabrics and furnishings and each has its own marble bathroom with a hair dryer. Amenities include concierge, laundry service, secretarial services, guests' message line, fax machines, private catering on request, car and limousine service, and daily maid service in the designer studios and suites.

Swiss House Hotel. 171 Old Brompton Rd., London SW5 OAN. ☎ **020/7373-2769.** Fax 020/7373-4983. www.swiss-hh.demon.co.uk. E-mail: recep@swiss-hh.demon.co.uk. 16 units (15 with bath). TV TEL. £85 ($144.50) double with bathroom; £109 ($185.30) triple with bathroom; £123 ($209.10) quad with bathroom. Rates include continental breakfast. AE, DC, MC, V. Tube: Gloucester Rd.

This appealing B&B, in a Victorian row house with a portico festooned with flowers and vines in the heart of South Kensington, is close to the South Kensington museums, Kensington Gardens, and the main exhibition centers of Earl's Court and Olympia. Some of its individually designed country-style guest rooms have fireplaces, and there's enough chintz to please the most avid Anglophile. Try to avoid the rooms along the street—traffic is heavy, and even with double-glazing, they get noisy. Instead, book one of the rear bedrooms, which overlook a communal garden and have a view of the London skyline. Most of the rooms are small, but sometimes include a private safe. Bathrooms are also small but contain a hair dryer. And there's a luxury that you won't get in most B&Bs: Room service—nothing elaborate, just soups and sandwiches—is available from noon to 9pm. Additional services include baby-sitting, massage, tour desk, and laundry service.

NOTTING HILL

Expensive

The Abbey Court. 20 Pembridge Gardens, London W2 4DU. ☎ **020/7221-7518.** www.abbeycourthotel.co.uk. E-mail: info@abbeycourthotel.co.uk. 22 units. TV TEL. £135–£165 ($229.50–$280.50) double; £190 ($323) suite with four-poster bed. AE, DC, MC, V. Tube: Notting Hill Gate.

This first-rate hotel is a small white-fronted mid-Victorian town house with a flower-filled patio in front and a conservatory in back. Its recently renovated lobby has a sunny bay window and a comfortable sofa and chairs. Each room, although small, has carefully coordinated fabrics and fine furnishings, mostly 18th- and 19th-century country antiques, plus excellent mattresses. Done in Italian marble, bathrooms are equipped with a Jacuzzi bath, shower, and heated racks of towels. Light snacks and drinks are available from room service 24 hours a day and breakfast is served in the newly renovated conservatory. Kensington Gardens is a short walk away, as are the antiques stores along Portobello Road and Kensington Church Street.

Amenities: Tour desk, dry cleaning, laundry service, and concierge.

The Portobello Hotel. 22 Stanley Gardens, London W11 2NG. ☎ **020/7727-2777.** Fax 020/7792-9641. 24 units. TV TEL. £155–£260 ($263.50–$442) double. Rates include continental breakfast. AE, MC, V. Tube: Notting Hill Gate.

Mixing an eclectic medley of styles, two six-floor town houses dating from 1850 on an elegant Victorian terrace near the Portobello antiques market were combined to form a quirky property that doesn't please everybody, but has its devotees. We remember these rooms when they looked better; but although they're tattered here and there, they still have plenty of character—whimsy and a fair measure of flamboyance went into their design. Who knows what will show up in what nook? Perhaps a Chippendale, a multi-nozzle clawfoot tub, or a round bed tucked under a gauze canopy. Try for no. 16, with a full-tester bed facing the garden. Some of the cheaper rooms are so tiny they're cabin-like garrets (some consider them romantic). But some of these have been combined into large doubles. The comfortable beds are standard throughout, and most of the small bathrooms have shower stalls only. An elevator will take you as far as the third floor; after that, it's the stairs. Some rooms are air-conditioned. Don't expect top-notch service; It's erratic at best.

Dining: 24-hour bar and restaurant in the basement is a local favorite.

Amenities: Concierge, room service.

Moderate

The Gate Hotel. 6 Portobello Rd., London W11 3DG. ☎ **020/7221-0707.** Fax 020/7221-9128. www.users.globalnet.co.uk/-thegate. E-mail: gatehotel@thegate.globalnet.co.uk. 6 units. TV TEL. £80–£85 ($136–$144.50) double. Rates include continental breakfast. MC, V. Tube: Notting Hill Gate.

This antiques-hunters' favorite is the only hotel along the entire length of Portobello Road—and because of rigid zoning restrictions, it will probably remain the only one for many years to come. It was built in the 1820s as housing for farmhands working the orchards and vegetable plots at the now-defunct Portobello Farms and has functioned as a hotel since 1932. It has two cramped but cozy bedrooms on each of its three floors, plus a renovated breakfast room in the cellar. Be prepared for some *very* steep English stairs. Rooms have a bit of style and such amenities as full-length mirrors, built-in wardrobes, and excellent mattresses. Bathrooms are small but adequate; housekeeping is excellent. Especially intriguing are the wall paintings that show what the Portobello Market was in its early days: Every character looks straight from a Dickens novel. The on-site manager can direct you to the antiques markets and the attractions of Notting Hill Gate and nearby Kensington Gardens, both of which lie within a 5-minute walk.

PADDINGTON & BAYSWATER

Very Expensive

The Hempel. 31–35 Craven Hill Garden Square, London W2 3EA. ☎ **020/7298-9000.** Fax 020/7402-4666. www.hempelhotel.com. E-mail: the-hempel@easynet.co.uk. 47 units. A/C MINIBAR TV TEL. £235–£275 ($399.50–$467.50) double; from £390 ($663) suite. AE, DC, DISC, MC, V. Tube: Lancaster Gate.

Set in a trio of nearly identical 19th-century row houses, this hotel is the newest statement of flamboyant interior designer Anouska Hempel-Weinberg. Don't expect the swags, tassels, and labyrinthine elegance of her better-established hotel, Blake's—the feeling here is radically different. The Hempel manages to combine a grand Italian sense of proportion with Asian simplicity, all meant for capitalists rich enough to afford it. Its artful simplicity is like that of a Zen temple. Soothing monochromatic tones prevail. The deliberately underfurnished lobby is flanked by symmetrical fireplaces. Throughout the hotel are carefully positioned mementos from Asia, including Thai bullock carts that double as coffee tables. Bedrooms continue the minimalist theme, except for their carefully concealed battery of electronic accessories, which includes a VCR, satellite TV control, CD player, twin phone lines, and a modem hookup. The bathrooms have cut-stone walls and bathtubs, a hair dryer, deluxe toiletries, robes, slippers, and a rack of fluffy towels. The hotel mostly caters to business travelers from around the world, most of whom appreciate its tactful service and undeniably snobbish overtones.

Dining: In the cellar is an innovative restaurant and bar, **I-Thai.**

Amenities: 24-hour room service, concierge, dry cleaning and laundry service, turndown and twice-daily maid service, massage, express checkout, limited business services; baby-sitting can be arranged. Conference rooms, access to nearby health club.

EXPENSIVE

London Elizabeth Hotel. Lancaster Terrace, Hyde Park, London W2 3PF. ☎ **020/7402-6641.** Fax 020/7224-8900. www.londonelizabethhotel.co.uk. E-mail: reservations@londonelizabethhotel.co.uk. 49 units. A/C TV TEL. £115–£150 ($195.50–$255) double, £135–£250 ($229.50–$425) suite. AE, DC, MC, V. Parking £9 ($15.30). Tube: Lancaster Gate or Paddington.

This elegant and refined early Victorian town house is ideally situated overlooking Hyde Park. Despite being in the midst of all the buzz and excitement of central London, the gentle, graceful atmosphere offers a haven of charm and refinement. The hotel has just completed a restoration costing three million pounds. The place has plenty of character. Individually decorated rooms range from executive to deluxe, and are more akin to English country-house living than a hotel room in a large city. Deluxe rooms might be galleried split-level, and are fully air-conditioned; some contain four-poster beds. Executive units usually contain one double bed. Some rooms have special features such as Victorian antique fireplaces, and all contain beds with first-rate mattresses and well-shined bathrooms with hair dryers and a rack of fluffy towels. Suites have grand comfort and luxury—the Conservatory Suite, for example, houses its own veranda, part of the original conservatory of 1850.

Dining/Diversions: The hotel offers two restaurants: the intimate and elegant gourmet restaurant, **The Rose,** and the less formal yet chic **Theatre Bar.**

Amenities: 24-hour room service, concierge, private car park.

MODERATE

The Byron Hotel. 36–38 Queensborough Terrace, London W2 3SH. ☎ **020/7243-0987.** Fax 020/7792-1957. www.capricornhotels.co.uk. E-mail: byron@capricornhotels.co.uk. 45 units. A/C TV TEL. £96–£105 ($163.20–$178.50) double; £120 ($204) triple; from £135 ($229.50) suite. Rates include English/continental breakfast. AE, CB, DC, MC, V. Tube: Bayswater or Queensway.

A mostly American clientele appreciates this family-run hotel just north of Kensington Gardens for its country-house atmosphere, its helpful staff (who spend extra time with guests hoping to make their stay in London special), and the good value it offers. This is one of the best examples of a Victorian house conversion that we've seen; it was modernized without ruining its traditional appeal. The interior was recently redesigned and refurbished, and the rooms are better than ever, with ample closets, fine mattresses, tile bathrooms with hair dryers, good lighting, and extra amenities like trouser presses, coffeemakers, and safes. An elevator services all floors, and breakfast is served in a bright and cheery room. Services include concierge, room service (limited hours), dry cleaning and laundry service.

Columbia Hotel. 95–99 Lancaster Gate, London, W2 3NS. ☎ **020/7402-0021.** Fax 020/7706-4691. www.columbiahotel.co.uk/. E-mail: columbiahotel@btconnect.com. 103 units. TV TEL. £79 ($134.30) double, £102 ($173.40) triple, £120 ($204) quad. AE, MC, V. Tube: Lancaster Gate.

On the northside of Hyde Park, less than a mile from Marble Arch, five Victorian houses were linked together to form one hotel. And a good one it is. Its character much altered over the years, the complex was the American Red Cross Hospital in World War I, and after World War II became the American Officers Club in London. Since 1975, it's been the Columbia, and has been frequently improved ever since, although retaining elements of its Victorian allure. An elegant lounge, bar, and spacious breakfast room are part of the facilities, as are 24-hour laundry and room service. Extras include free overnight luggage storage. The public rooms here are so large it's like wandering the Victoria & Albert Museum; the bedrooms too are generally spacious, with high ceilings and often three to four beds. Beverage makers, hair dryers, and direct-dial phones add to the amenities list. Many of the bedrooms open onto Hyde Park, and some rooms are suited for persons with disabilities.

Darlington Hyde Park. 111–117 Sussex Gardens, London W2 2RU. ☎ **020/7460-8800.** Fax 020/7460-8828. E-mail: darlinghp@aol.com. 40 units. TV TEL. £110–£130 ($187–$221) double; £135–£145 ($229.50–$246.50) suite. Rates include continental breakfast. AE, DC, MC, V. Tube: Paddington or Lancaster Gate.

Although not flashy and lacking a full range of services, the Darlington Hyde Park is a winning choice and good value for central London. Rooms, which have been newly renovated, are in an updated Victorian style, tasteful and neat, albeit a bit short of flair. Rooms range from small to midsize, but each includes a tiny but adequate bathroom. The maintenance is good, however, and a happy blend of business people and vacationers check in here. Five bedrooms are non-smoking. The hotel restaurant serves breakfast only (continental or English). There is no bar, but guests are invited to BYOB (bring your own bottle) and drink in the lounge. A number of neighboring restaurants cater room service for the hotel; they are listed in a restaurant book found in each room. Dry cleaning and laundry service are available, and there's a health club nearby.

INEXPENSIVE

Fairways Hotel. 186 Sussex Gardens, London W2 1TU. ☎ **020/7723-4871.** Fax 020/7723-4871. www.scoot.co.uk/fairways_hotel. E-mail: fairwayshotel@compuserve.com. 17 units (10 with bathroom). TV. £68 ($115.60) double without bathroom, £74 ($125.80) double with bathroom. Rates include English breakfast. MC, V. Tube: Paddington.

Jenny and Steve Adams welcome you into one of the finest B&Bs along Sussex Gardens. Even though it doesn't enjoy the pedigree it used to, this little place near Hyde Park is still a favorite address of bargain hunters. The black-and-white town house is easily recognizable: Just look for its colonnaded front entrance with a wrought-iron balustrade stretching across the second floor. The Adams family opts for traditional charm and character whenever possible. They call their breakfast room "homely" (Americans might say "home-like"); it's decorated with photographs of the family and a collection of china. Bedrooms are attractive and comfortably furnished, each with hot and cold running water, intercom, and beverage makers. Beds are fitted with firm mattresses, and units with private bathrooms are small but tidy. Those who must share the corridor bathrooms will find them clean and well maintained. The breakfast is hearty and home cooked, fit fortification for a day of sightseeing.

Parkwood Hotel. 4 Stanhope Place, London W2 2HB. ☎ **020/7402-2241.** Fax 020/7402-1574. www.parkwoodhotel.com. E-mail: prkwd@aol.com. 18 units (12 with bathroom). TV TEL. £64.50 ($109.65) double without bathroom, £87.50 ($148.75) double with bathroom; £77 ($130.90), triple without bathroom, £97 ($164.90) triple with bathroom. Children under 13 sharing parents' room £7.50 ($12.75) Mon–Fri, free Sat and Sun. Rates include English breakfast. MC, V. Tube: Marble Arch.

Parkwood occupies one of the best locations for a good-value hotel in London: near Oxford Street and Marble Arch and just 50 yards from Hyde Park, in a section known as Connaught Village. The well-maintained, simple bedrooms have coffeemakers and radios, plus a firm mattress. The private bathrooms are small, but corridor bathrooms are adequate and well maintained. The hotel prides itself on an excellent breakfast; in fact, the menu states that if you're still hungry, you can have another meal—for free.

✪ **The Pavilion.** 34–36 Sussex Gardens, London W2 1UL. ☎ **020/7262-0905.** Fax 020/7262-1324. www.msi.com.mt/pavilion. 27 units. TV TEL. £95 ($161.50) double. Rates include breakfast. AE, DC, MC, V. Parking £5 ($8.50). Tube: Edgware Road.

Until the early 1990s, this was a rather dull, ordinary-looking B&B. Then, a team of entrepreneurs with inroads to the fashion industry took over and radically redecorated the rooms with sometimes wacky themes, turning it into an idiosyncratic little hotel. The result is a theatrical and often outrageous décor that's much appreciated by the many fashion models and music-industry buffs who regularly make this their temporary home in London. Behind a blackened 1830s Victorian facade of stock bricks and stucco, the hotel offers rooms without any particular frills, but each has a distinctive decorative style. Examples include a kitschy 1970s room ("Honky-Tonk Afro"), an Oriental bordello theme ("Enter the Dragon"), and even some with 19th-century ancestral themes. One Edwardian-style room, a gem of emerald brocade and velvet, is called "Green with Envy." Each contains tea-making facilities, a firm mattress, and they are, regrettably, rather small. Bathrooms are also small, but efficiently organized. No meals are served other than breakfast.

NEAR HEATHROW

EXPENSIVE

Hilton London Heathrow. Terminal 4, Hounslow TW6 3AF. ☎ **020/8759-7755.** Fax 020/8759-7579. www.hilton.com. E-mail: gm_heathrow@hilton.com. 395 units. A/C MINIBAR TV TEL. Sun–Thurs £110–£260 ($187–$442) double, Fri–Sat from £110 ($187) double. Suite from £430 ($731) (all week). AE, CB, DC, MC, V. Parking from £6.50 ($11.05). Tube: Piccadilly.

This eye-catching, first-class hotel with its five-story atrium evoking the feel of a hangar is linked to Heathrow's Terminal 4 by a covered walkway. A glass wall faces the runways, so you can see planes land and take off. You can take buses to Terminals 1, 2, or 3. Bedrooms are fairly standardized, but comfortably decorated with built-in wood furniture, upholstered sofas, and first-class mattresses on the beds. Bathrooms are tiled and trimmed in marble, containing a phone, a hair dryer, and a set of fluffy towels. The best accommodations are on the fifth floor with private robes and better amenities such as a private lounge with airport vistas.

Dining/Diversions: An open brasserie lies in the main lobby, and is "shaded" by umbrellas and canopies. There's also a rather good Chinese and Thai restaurant on site, plus a standup bar with a grill section, decorated with a movie theme.

Amenities: 24-hour room service, concierge, laundry and dry cleaning service, TV with flight information, automated checkout, video rentals, baby-sitting, business services.

Renaissance London Heathrow Hotel. Bath Rd., Hounslow, London TW6 2AQ. ☎ **020/8987-6363.** Fax 020/8897-1113. www.renaissancehotels.com. E-mail: 106047.3556@compuserve.com. 650 units. A/C MINIBAR TV TEL. Sun–Thurs £139 ($236.30) double, Fri–Sat £82 ($139.40) double. All-week suite from £315 ($535.50). AE, DC, MC, V. Heathrow Hopper bus service to all terminals.

This is no airport sleeping dormitory. A bustling hotel factory, it lies just inside the perimeter of the airport and is spotted just before you reach the long airport entrance tunnel. Three cantilevered concrete floors attract a bevy of international travelers. Rooms have recently been renovated and are fairly standardized and a bit small, with coffeemakers, bedside controls, inlaid wood and laminate furnishings, and first-class mattresses, along with tiled baths featuring hair dryers, marble sinks, and toiletries. We prefer the units facing the airport itself (double glazing keeps down the noise).

Dining: A brasserie serving international food overlooks the runaways, and there's also an international bar decorated with vintage aeronautical wall prints.

Amenities: 24-hour room service, concierge, laundry service, solarium, sauna, gym, health club.

MODERATE

Stanwell Hall. Town Lane, Stanwell, Staines, Middlesex TW19 7PW. ☎ **01784/252292.** Fax 01784/245250. www.rac.co.uk. 19 units (18 with bathroom). TV TEL. £100 ($170) double; £130 ($221) suite. Rates include breakfast. AE, DC, MC, V. Free parking.

This sunny Victorian house was purchased in 1951 by the Parke family, who converted it into a comfortable hotel. The cheery house with its side garden is located in a small village just minutes from Heathrow; it's perfect for business people who are tired of staying in standard airport hotels. About half the rooms have been fully renovated. The renovated rooms are comfortably furnished, papered in warm shades, and have chintz curtains covering the windows—a dramatic improvement over the washed-out, prerenovation rooms. All have coffeemakers and good mattresses. Bathrooms are efficiently organized and tidy, each with a hair dryer. **St. Anne's Restaurant,** located on the ground floor, is small but inviting and serves modern British cuisine. The bar, which is popular with locals, serves drinks and snacks at lunchtime. Basic services include limited room service, dry cleaning and laundry, and conference rooms.

NEAR GATWICK

EXPENSIVE

Hilton London Gatwick Airport. South Terminal, Gatwick Airport, West Sussex RH6 0LL. ☎ **800/HILTONS** or 01293/518080. Fax 01293/528980. www.hilton.com. E-mail: gathitwsal@hilton.com. 550 units. A/C TV TEL. £187–£240 ($317.90–$408) double; from £260 ($442) suite. AE, MC, V. Parking £10.40 ($17.70).

This deluxe five-floor hotel—Gatwick's most convenient resting place—is linked to the airport terminal with a covered walkway; an electric buggy service transports people between the hotel and airport. The most impressive part of the hotel is the first-floor lobby; its glass-covered portico rises four floors and contains a scale replica of the de Havilland Gypsy Moth airplane *Jason,* used by Amy Johnson on her solo flight from England to Australia in 1930. The reception area has a lobby bar and lots of greenery. The well-furnished, soundproofed rooms have triple-glazed windows, firm mattresses, and coffeemakers. Baths are tidily kept and equipped with a hair dryer. Recently, 123 of the rooms were refurbished, in addition to the executive floor and all their junior suites. Now 300 of the rooms have minibars, stocked upon request.

Dining/Diversions: The American-themed restaurant **Amy's** serves buffet breakfasts, lunches, and dinners. **The Garden Restaurant,** outfitted in a formal English garden theme, serves drinks and full meals. There's also the 24-hour **Lobby Bar,** plus a polo-themed watering hole aptly named the **Jockey Bar.**

Amenities: Same-day dry cleaning and laundry service, up-to-date flight information channel, 24-hour room service, salon, bank, gift shop, concierge, newspapers, baby-sitting, health club (sauna, steam room, massage room, swimming pool, gymnasium, Jacuzzi), conference rooms, business center, shopping arcade.

4 Dining

London has emerged as one of the great food capitals of the world. In the last few years, both its veteran and upstart chefs have fanned out around the globe for culinary inspiration, and have returned with innovative dishes, flavors, and ideas that London diners have never seen before—or at least not at such unprecedented rates. These chefs are pioneering a new style of cooking called "Modern British," which is forever changing, yet comfortingly familiar in many ways. They've committed to centering their dishes around local ingredients from field, stream, and air, and have become daringly innovative with traditional recipes—too much so in the view of some critics, who don't like fresh mango over their blood pudding

Traditional British cooking has made a comeback, too. The dishes that British mums have been forever feeding their reluctant families are fashionable again. Yes, we're talking British soul food: bangers and mash, Norfolk dumplings, nursery puddings, cottage pie—the works. This may be a rebellion against the excessive minimalism of the nouvelle cuisine that ran rampant over London in the 1980s, but who knows? Maybe it's just plain old nostalgia. Pig's nose with parsley-and-onion sauce may not be your idea of cutting-edge cuisine, but Simpson's-in-the-Strand is serving it for breakfast.

If you want a lavish meal, London is the place to eat it, with some of the world's top restaurants calling the city home: gourmet havens such as Le Gavroche or Chez Nico at Ninety Park Lane, and a half-dozen others you'll find reviewed in the following pages. For those of you who don't want to break the bank, we've included many affordable restaurants where you can dine really well. You'll find that London's food revolution has infiltrated every level of the dining scene—even the lowly pub has entered London's culinary sweepstakes. Believe the unthinkable: At certain pubs, you can now dine better than in many restaurants. In some, standard pub grub has given way to Modern British and Mediterranean-style fare; in others, oyster bars have taken hold.

All restaurants and cafes in Britain are required to display the prices of the food and drink they offer in a place visible from outside the establishment. Charges for service, as well as any minimum charge or cover charge, must also be made clear. The prices shown must include 17% VAT. Most of the restaurants add a 10% to 15% service charge to your bill, but you'll have to check to make sure of that. If nothing has been added to your bill, leave a 12% to 15% tip.

MAYFAIR

Very Expensive

Chez Nico at Ninety Park Lane. In Grosvenor House, 90 Park Lane, W1. ☎ **020/7409-1290.** Reservations required (at least 2 days in advance for lunch, 7 days for dinner). Fixed-price lunch £25–£40 ($42.50–$68) for 3 courses; à la carte dinner £53 ($90.10) for 2 courses, £65 ($110.50) for 3 courses. AE, DC, MC, V. Mon–Fri noon–2pm; Mon–Sat 7–11pm. Closed 10 days around Christmas/New Year's. Tube: Marble Arch. FRENCH.

Although the setting is as opulent as the cuisine, nothing takes precedence over the food here. It's the work of one of London's supreme culinary artists, the temperamental but always amusing Nico Ladenis, now assisted by Paul Rhodes, who interprets the master's culinary ideas with flair and zest. Ladenis, a former oil company executive, self-taught cook, and economist, remains one of Britain's most talked about chefs; his food is always impressive, always stylish, and he's constantly re-inventing dishes we thought he had already perfected.

As starters go, who can top his quail salad with sweetbreads, flavored with an almond vinaigrette? The main courses are a tour de force in the best post-nouvelle tradition, in which the tenets of classical cuisine are creatively and flexibly adapted to local fresh ingredients. With masterful technique, Nico's chefs dazzle with ever-changing fare, including a ravioli of langoustine that's a virtual signature dish. The chargrilled sea bass with basil purée or the Bresse pigeon are rivaled only by the work of Le Gavroche (see below). The only complaint we've ever heard about Chez Nico is that it attracts too many Michelin three-star groupies.

✪ **Le Gavroche.** 43 Upper Brook St., W1. ☎ **020/7408-0881.** Fax 020/7491-4387. Reservations required as far in advance as possible. Main courses £29.10–£38 ($49.45–$64.60); fixed-price lunch £38.50 ($65.45); menu exceptionnel, for entire table, £78 ($132.60) per person. AE, MC, V. Mon–Fri noon–2pm and 7–11pm. Tube: Marble Arch. FRENCH.

Le Gavroche has long stood for quality French cuisine, perhaps England's finest, although Michelin gives it only two stars. Though it may have fallen off briefly in the early 1990s, it's fighting its way back to the stellar ranks of Europe's French restaurants. There's always something special coming out of the kitchen of Burgundy-born Michel Roux; the service is faultless and the ambience formally chic without being stuffy.

The menu changes constantly, depending on the fresh produce that's available and the current inspiration of the chef. But it always remains classically French, although not of the "essentially old-fashioned bourgeois repertoire" that some critics suggest. There are signature dishes that have been honed over years of unswerving practice: Try, if featured, the soufflé Suissesse or *papillote* of smoked salmon. Game is often served, depending on availability. New menu options include mousseline of lobster in champagne sauce; pavé of braised turbot with red provençal wine and smoked bacon; and fillet of red snapper with caviar and oyster-stuffed tortellini. Desserts, including the sablé of pears and chocolate, are sublime. The wine cellar is among the most interesting in London, with many quality Burgundies and Bordeaux.

The fixed-price dinner has recently been replaced by the *menu exceptionnel,* which is, in essence, a tasting menu for the entire table. The menu usually consists of four to five smaller courses, followed by one or two desserts and coffee. At £78 ($132.60) per person, this may prove to be a smarter choice as opposed to the à la carte items, given the culinary options and price that the *menu exceptionnel* offers.

EXPENSIVE

✪ **Nobu.** In the Metropolitan Hotel, 19 Old Park Lane, W1. ☎ **020/7447-4747.** Reservations required. Main courses £15–£28.50 ($25.50–$48.45); sushi and sashimi £3–£4.75 ($5.10–$8.05) per piece; fixed-price menu £60 ($102). AE, DC, MC, V. Mon–Fri noon–2:15pm; Mon–Fri 6–10:15pm, Sat 6–11:15pm, Sun 6–9:45pm. Tube: Hyde Park Corner. JAPANESE.

Robert de Niro and his restaurant gang of Nobu Matsuhisa and Como Holdings have taken their New York hot spot to London, where they offer an intensely innovative and experimental Japanese cuisine. The kitchen staff is brilliant and as finely tuned as

Central London Dining

Atlantic Bar & Grill **48**
Back to Basics **27**
Belgo Central **60**
Bibendum/The Oyster Bar **7**
Birdcage **26**
The Blue Room **53**
Bow Wine Vaults **65**
British Museum Restaurant **28**
Brown's Hotel **46**
Bubbles **21**
Café Spice Namaste **67**
Chelsea Kitchen **4**
Chez Nico at Ninety Park Lane **18**
China City **58**
Circus **40**
Cittie of Yorke **63**
Coast **37**
The Collection **8**
Cork & Bottle Wine Bar **59**
Crank's in London **33**
Dumpling Inn **56**
English Garden **5**
The Enterprise **6**
Foundation **10**
Fung Shing **57**
The George **68**
The Georgian Restaurant **9**
Gordon Ramsay **3**
Greenhouse **17**
Grenadier **12**
Hard Rock Café **14**
The Ivy **55**
J Brown's Hotel **36**
La Tante Claire **2**
Lagan's Brasserie **39**
Le Gavroche **19**
Mash **25**
Mezzo **30**
Mildreds **29**
MJ Bradley's **42**
Momo **34**
Museum Tavern **62**
Nico Central **23**
Nobu **15**
North Sea Fish Restaurant **61**
Old Coffee House **49**
Palm Court at the Waldorf Meridien **69**
Palm Court Lounge **16**
Piccadilly **20**
Poons in the City **66**
Porter's English Restaurant **70**
Quaglino's **41**
Quo Vadis **31**
Red Lion **43**
Rhodes in the Square **1**
Ritz Palm Court **44**
Rules **70**
St. James Restaurant/The Fountain Restaurant **45**
Salisbury **54**
Satsuma **52**
Shampers **35**
Simply Nico **13**
Simpsons-in-The-Strand **71**
Soho Spice **32**
Sugar Club **50**
Tamarind **38**
Tate Gallery Reataurant **72**
The Titanic **55**
Union Café **22**
Villandry **24**
Vong **11**
Wilton's **47**
Ye Olde Cheshire Cheese **64**
YO! Sushi **51**

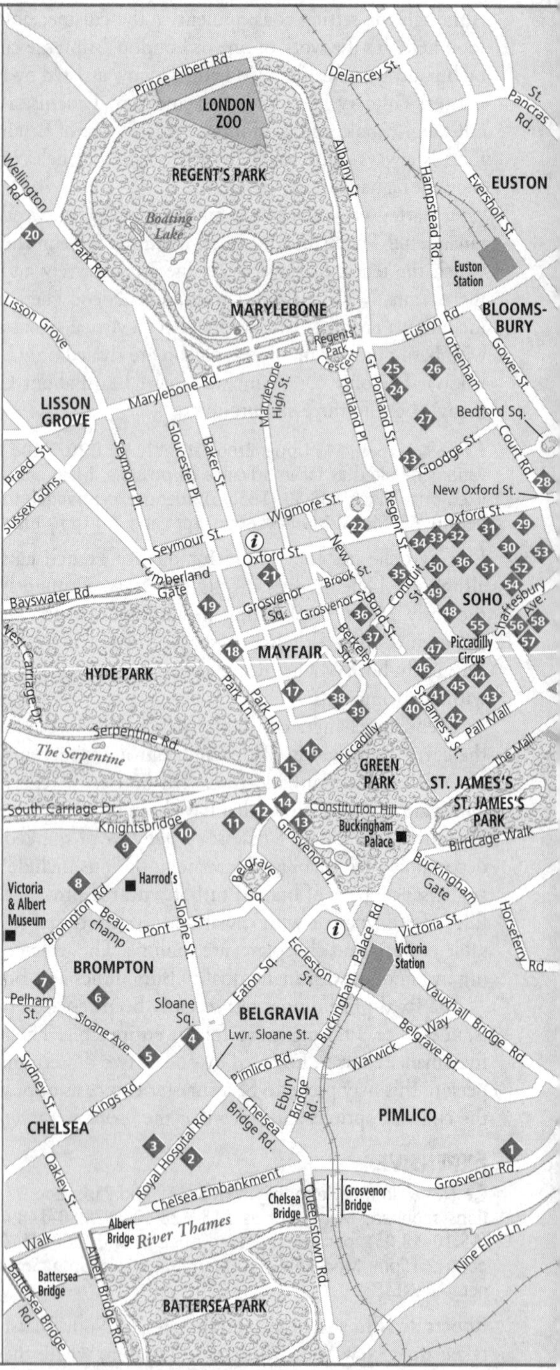

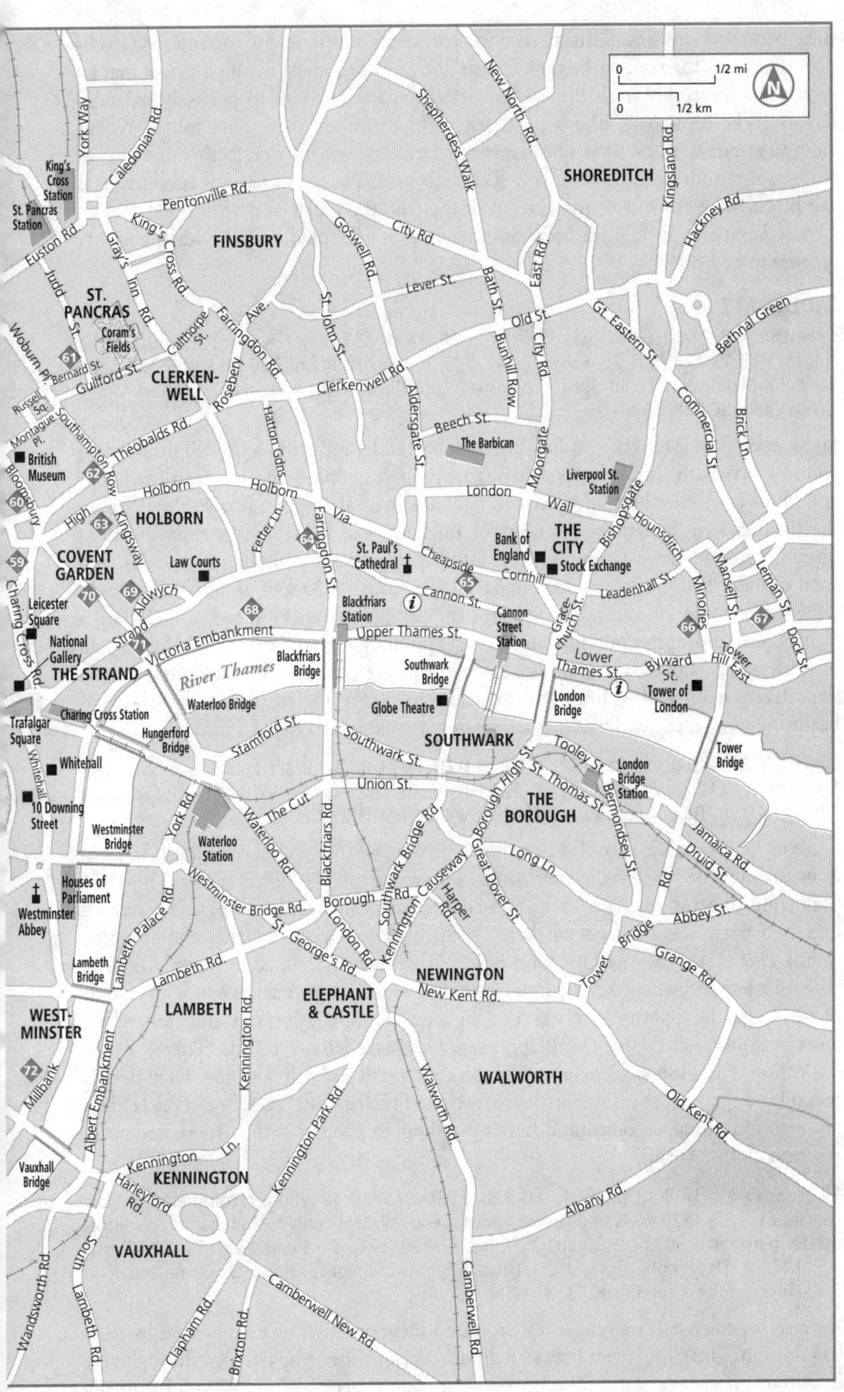
SHOREDITCH
FINSBURY
ST. PANCRAS
CLERKEN-WELL
HOLBORN
COVENT GARDEN
THE STRAND
THE CITY
SOUTHWARK
THE BOROUGH
NEWINGTON
ELEPHANT & CASTLE
LAMBETH
WEST-MINSTER
WALWORTH
KENNINGTON
VAUXHALL
River Thames
King's Cross Station
St. Pancras Station
British Museum
Coram's Fields
Law Courts
St. Paul's Cathedral
The Barbican
Liverpool St. Station
Bank of England
Stock Exchange
Blackfriars Station
Cannon Street Station
Leicester Square
National Gallery
Trafalgar Square
Charing Cross Station
Whitehall
10 Downing Street
Westminster Bridge
Houses of Parliament
Westminster Abbey
Lambeth Bridge
Vauxhall Bridge
Waterloo Bridge
Hungerford Bridge
Waterloo Station
Blackfriars Bridge
Southwark Bridge
Globe Theatre
London Bridge
London Bridge Station
Tower of London
Tower Bridge
Pentonville Rd.
Euston Rd.
York Way
Caledonian Rd.
King's Cross Rd.
Gray's Inn Rd.
Goswell Rd.
City Rd.
Shepherdess Walk
New North Rd.
Kingsland Rd.
Hackney Rd.
East Rd.
Lever St.
Bath St.
Old St.
Gt. Eastern St.
Bethnal Green
Commercial St.
Brick Ln.
St. John St.
Farringdon Rd.
Rosebery Ave.
Calthorpe St.
Judd St.
Woburn Pl.
Bernard St.
Guilford St.
Russell Sq.
Montague Pl.
Southampton Row
Theobalds Rd.
Clerkenwell Rd.
Aldersgate St.
Bunhill Row
City Rd.
Beech St.
Moorgate
Hatton Gdns.
Bloomsbury
Holborn
Holborn Via
High
Kingsway
Fetter Ln.
Farringdon St.
London Wall
Bishopsgate
Houndsditch
Cheapside
Cornhill
Leadenhall St.
Minories
Mansell St.
Leman St.
Dock St.
Aldwych
Strand
Cannon St.
Upper Thames St.
Victoria Embankment
Grace-church St.
Lower Thames St.
Byward St.
Tower Hill East
Charing Cross Rd.
Whitehall
Stamford St.
Southwark St.
Tooley St.
St. Thomas St.
Bermondsey St.
Union St.
The Cut
York Rd.
Waterloo Rd.
Blackfriars Rd.
Southwark Bridge Rd.
Borough High St.
Jamaica Rd.
Druid St.
Long Ln.
Great Dover St.
Harper Rd.
Rd.
Westminster Bridge Rd.
Borough Rd.
Southwark Causeway
Kennington Causeway
London Rd.
St. George's Rd.
Lambeth Palace Rd.
Lambeth Rd.
Tower Bridge
Abbey St.
Grange Rd.
New Kent Rd.
Kennington Rd.
Millbank
Albert Embankment
Walworth Rd.
Old Kent Rd.
Kennington Park Rd.
Kennington Ln.
Harleyford Rd.
Albany Rd.
South Lambeth Rd.
Wandsworth Rd.
Camberwell New Rd.
Clapham Rd.
Brixton Rd.
Camberwell Rd.
0 1/2 mi
0 1/2 km
N
59
60
61
62
63
64
65
66
67
68
69
70
71
72

their New York cousins. Sushi chefs don't just create sushi but gastronomic pyrotechnics. Those on the see-and-be-seen circuit don't seem to mind the high prices that go with these incredibly fresh dishes. Elaborate preparations lead to perfectly balanced flavors. Where can you find a good sea urchin tempura these days but at Nobu? Salmon tartare with caviar is a brilliant appetizer. Follow with a perfectly done fillet of sea bass in a sour bean paste or soft-shell crab rolls. The squid pasta is sublime, as is the black cod with miso, this latter dish incredibly popular and with good reason. Cold sake arrives in a green bamboo pitcher. If it's featured, finish with the savory ginger crème brûlée.

MODERATE

Greenhouse. 27A Hays Mews, W1. ☎ **020/7499-3331.** Reservations essential. Main courses £12.50–£20 ($21.25–$34). AE, DC, MC, V. Mon–Fri noon–2:30pm and 6:30–11pm; Sat 6:30–11pm; Sun 12:30–3pm and 6:30–10pm. Closed Christmas, bank holidays. Tube: Green Park. MODERN BRITISH.

Head chef Paul Merrett is quite inspired by modern British food. Grafton has a winning way with fish, if his poached skate is any example—and his deep-fried cod-and-chips is galaxies beyond what you'd get at the local chippie. But you may prefer the lip-smacking fare from the heart of England, which includes a roast breast of pheasant that Henry VIII would have loved, and grilled farmhouse pork; we're also fond of the wilted greens wrapped in bacon. The menu is backed up by a well-chosen wine list of some 20 selections. Some of the delightfully sticky desserts, including a moist bread-and-butter pudding and a ginger pudding with orange marmalade, would have pleased a Midlands grandmum. Simply conceived dishes with a resolutely British slant draw a never-ending line of satisfied customers. The ingredients are first class and beautifully prepared, without ever destroying the natural flavor of a dish.

Langan's Brasserie. Stratton St., W1. ☎ **020/7491-8822.** Reservations recommended. Main courses £12.75–£15.95 ($21.70–$27.10). AE, DC, MC, V. Mon–Fri 12:15–11:45pm; Sat 7pm–11:45pm. Tube: Green Park. TRADITIONAL BRITISH/FRENCH.

Since its heyday in the early 1980s, when it was one of the hippest restaurants in London, this upscale brasserie has welcomed an average of 700 diners a day. The 1976 brainchild of actor Michael Caine and chef Richard Shepherd, the brasserie sprawls over two noisy, see-and-be-seen floors, each filled with potted plants and spinning ceiling fans that create a 1930s kind of feel. The menu is defined as "mostly English with a French influence" and includes a spinach soufflé with anchovy sauce; croustade of quail eggs in a pastry case served with a duxelle of mushrooms and hollandaise sauce; and roast crispy duck with apple sauce and sage-lemon stuffing. There's always a selection of English fare, including bangers and mash and fish 'n' chips. Their dessert menu (and they call them desserts here instead of the English "puddings") reads like a journey into nostalgia: bread-and-butter pudding, treacle tart with custard, and apple pie with clotted cream.

✪ **Quaglino's.** 16 Bury St., SW1. ☎ **020/7930-6767.** Reservations recommended. Main courses £12–£18 ($20.40–$30.60); fixed-price menu (available only for lunch and pre-dinner theater between 5:30 and 6:30pm) 2 courses £12.50 ($21.25), 3 courses £15 ($25.50). AE, DC, MC, V. Daily noon–3pm; Mon–Thurs 5:30pm–midnight, Fri–Sat 5:30pm–1am, Sun 5:30–11pm. Tube: Green Park. CONTINENTAL.

It's vast, it's convivial, it's fun. A restaurant on these premises was established in 1929 by Giovanni Quaglino, from Italy's Piedmont. Personalities who paraded through here in ermine and pearls could fill a between-the-wars roster of Who's Who for virtually every country of Europe. In 1993, noted restaurateur and designer Sir Terence

Conran brought the place into the postmodern age with a vital new decor—eight artists were commissioned to decorate the octet of massive columns supporting the soaring ceiling. A mezzanine with a bar features live jazz every Friday and Saturday night and live piano music the rest of the week, and an "altar" in the back is devoted to the most impressive display of crustaceans and shellfish in Britain.

Everything seems to be served in bowls. Menu items have been criticized for their quick preparation and standardized format. But considering that on some nights up to 800 people might show up here for food, laughter, and gossip, the marvel is that the place functions as well as it does. That's not to say there isn't an occasional delay. Come for fun, not culinary subtlety and finesse. The menu changes often, but your choices might include goat cheese and caramelized onion tart; crab tartlet with saffron; and roasted cod and ox cheek with chargrilled vegetables. The prawns and oysters—so delectable, so fresh—are the most ordered items.

Union Café. 96 Marylebone Lane, W1. ☎ **020/7486-4860.** Reservations recommended. Main courses £10–£15 ($17–$25.50). AE, MC, V. Mon–Sat 10:30am–10:30pm. Tube: Bond St. CONTINENTAL.

After shopping till you drop along Oxford Street, restore your spirits with the quality ingredients and exceptional food served at this sleek glass-and-wood eatery. Everything from farmhouse English cheeses to free-range meat will tempt you. Rarely is any item oversauced. The natural, fresh flavors come to the fore. In most cases the fresh fish and meat are chargrilled to perfection. The pepper tuna steaks, served rare, are an exceptional taste sensation, as are the oak-smoked salmon with fresh horseradish sauce and the wild boar and apple sausage. A daily vegetarian pizza is offered, including one filled with mozzarella, spinach, tomatoes, and eggplant. If you don't want wine, you can choose some homemade drinks that might have delighted Dickens, including the elderflower cordial. Desserts such as carmelized pear cake or blood orange sorbet are worth the trek across town.

INEXPENSIVE

✪ **Crank's In London.** 8 Marshall St., W1 ☎ **020/7437-9431.** Main courses £2–£2.50 ($3.40–$4.25). No credit cards. Mon–Tues 8am–8pm; Wed–Fri 8am–9pm. Tube: Oxford Circus. VEGETARIAN.

Located just off Carnaby Street, this is the headquarters of a chain of vegetarian restaurants with seven other branches in London. Outfitted in natural wood, wicker-basket lamps, pinewood tables, and handmade ceramic bowls and plates, Crank's is completely self-service: You carry your own tray to one of the tables. Organic-white and stone-ground flour is used for breads and rolls. The uncooked vegetable salad is especially good, and there's always a hot stew of savory vegetables (with "secret" seasoning), served in a hand-thrown stoneware pot with a salad. Their couscous with asparagus is an original concoction, and their stir-fry vegetable dishes continue to draw a youthful funky crowd. Homemade honey cake, cheesecake, tarts, and crumbles are featured. Bakery goods, nuts, and general health-food supplies are sold in an adjoining shop.

Hard Rock Cafe. 150 Old Park Lane, W1. ☎ **020/7629-0382.** Main courses £8.50–£16 ($14.45–$27.20). AE, DC, MC, V. Mon–Fri 11:30am–12:30am; Sat–Sun 11:30am–1am. Closed Dec. 25–26. Tube: Green Park or Hyde Park Corner. AMERICAN.

This is the original Hard Rock, now a worldwide chain of rock-and-roll–themed, southern-cum-midwestern American roadside diners serving up good food and service with a smile. Since it was established on June 14, 1971, more than 12 million people have eaten here. Almost every night there's a line waiting to get in. The portions on the beef-laden menu are generous, and the price of a main dish includes not only a salad, but also fries or baked potatoes. The fajitas are always a good choice. The tempting dessert menu offers homemade apple pie and thick, cold shakes. There's also a good selection of beers. The collection of rock memorabilia is worth seeking out if you're a fan.

Tamarind. 20 Queen St., W1. ☎ **020/7629-3561.** Reservations required. Main courses £11.50–£18.50 ($19.55-$31.45). AE, DC, DISC, MC, V. Sun–Fri noon–3pm; Mon–Sat 6–11:30pm, Sun 6–10:30pm. Tube: Green Park. INDIAN.

Currently in favor with food critics as well as the local lunchtime business crowd, Tamarind is the hottest and most fashionable Indian restaurant in Mayfair. A small basement restaurant, it has a "tandoor window" so you can watch the chefs pull their flavorful, spicy dishes from the ovens. Chef Atul Kochhar leads a culinary brigade direct from Delhi that tries to maintain the style of cooking they knew back home, depending on the availability of spices and produce. The kitchen prides itself on its "nouvelle" dishes, but they also excel at traditional Indian fare—including fabulous breads. The monkfish marinated in saffron and yogurt is especially delectable, as is the mixed kebab platter, cooked in a charcoal-fired tandoor—these chefs are king of the kebabs. Your best bet for a curry? Opt for the prawns cooked in a five-spice mixture. Vegetarians will find a safe refuge here, especially if they go for the Dal Bukhari, a black-lentil specialty of northwest India.

ST. JAMES'S

INEXPENSIVE

Bubbles. 41 N. Audley St., W1. ☎ **020/7491-3237.** Reservations recommended. Main courses £4.50–£11.80 ($7.65–$20.05); vegetarian main courses £6–£6.50 ($10.20–$11.05). AE, DC, MC, V. Mon–Sat 11am–11pm. Tube: Bond St. BRITISH/INTERNATIONAL VEGETARIAN.

This interesting wine bar lies between Upper Brook Street and Oxford Street (in the vicinity of Selfridges). The owners attach equal importance to their food and to their impressive wine list (some wines are sold by the glass). On the ground floor, you can enjoy not only fine wines but also draft beer and liquor, along with a limited but well-chosen selection of bar food, such as smoked salmon on brown bread, or homemade steak burger with fries and salad and cheese. Downstairs, the restaurant serves both English and continental dishes, including an appealing vegetarian selection. You might begin with French onion soup, followed by bangers and mash with onion gravy or Dover sole.

PICCADILLY CIRCUS & LEICESTER SQUARE

EXPENSIVE

Coast. 26B Albemarle St., W1X 3FA. ☎ **020/7495-5999.** Reservations required. Main courses £14.50–£22.50 ($24.65–$38.25). AE, MC, V. Mon–Sat noon–3pm and 6–11:30pm. Tube: Green Park. MODERN INTERNATIONAL.

Coast is so cutting edge, so 21st-century, that you might get the feeling it strains a bit to maintain its image as one of London's hippest restaurants. Set in a former auto showroom with lots of parquet woodwork, it's painted in colors that resemble, according to your tastes, either spring green or the color of aged bilgewater, and accented with lighting fixtures that protrude like alien bug-eyes from their settings. There's only one piece of art (by the terribly fashionable artist Angela Bulloch), but it's a doozy: a drawing machine that uses a robotic arm to scribble a graph simulating the movement within the room on an electronic screen; like a giant Etch-a-Sketch, it's wiped clean when it becomes unreadable.

With all this forced hipness, we didn't really want to like this place, but it won us over with its surprisingly good food. Innovative chef Bruno Loubet is original (some say too innovative), but we liked his willingness to go where others fear to tread. He handles textures well and brings out the best of the flavors in the light cuisine, particularly the fish dishes. Loubet tempts with his seared salmon spring roll in fermented black bean aïoli, monkfish and pickled vegetable terrine, and rabbit ravioli. Of course, none of these exact items will be on the menu presented to you, because Loubet will have long changed them, but expect a surprise and a delight to your palate regardless of what he's dishing out.

✪ **Wiltons.** 55 Jermyn St., SW1. ☎ **020/7629-9955.** Reservations required. Jacket and tie required for men. Main courses £15–£30 ($25.50–$51). AE, DC, MC, V. Mon–Fri 12:30–2:30pm and 6–10:30pm; Sun 12:30–2:30pm and 6:30–10pm. Closed Sat. Tube: Green Park or Piccadilly Circus. TRADITIONAL BRITISH.

This is one of the top purveyors of traditional British cuisine and our favorite of the current bunch. Opened in 1742, this thoroughly British restaurant is known for its fine fish and game. Gourmets flock here for the best oysters and lobsters in London, and they know it's the place to go to find unusual seafood. You might begin with an oyster cocktail and follow with Dover sole, plaice, salmon, or lobster, prepared in any number of ways. In season (from mid-Aug), there are such delights as roast partridge, pheasant, or grouse; you may even be able to order widgeon, a wild, fish-eating river duck (the chef might ask you if you want it "blue" or "black," a reference to roasting times). To finish, consider a savory such as Welsh rarebit, soft roes, or anchovies; if that's too much, try the sherry trifle or syllabub.

We consistently find the service to be the most helpful in the West End. Since this is a bastion of traditionalism, however, don't show up in the latest Covent Garden fashions—you might not get in. Instead, don your oldest suit and look like you believe the Empire still exists.

MODERATE

Atlantic Bar & Grill. 20 Glasshouse St., W1. ☎ **020/7734-4888.** Reservations required. Main courses £11.50–£25 ($19.55–$42.50); fixed-price lunch £14.50 ($24.65) 3 courses. AE, DC, MC, V. Mon–Fri noon–3pm; Mon–Sat 6pm–3am, Sun 6–10:30pm. Tube: Piccadilly Circus. MODERN BRITISH.

A titanic restaurant installed in a former art deco ballroom off Piccadilly Circus, this 160-seat locale draws a trendy crowd to London's tawdry heartland. The restaurant remains cosmopolitan, and it's one of the best choices for an after-theater crowd because it closes at 3am on most nights. The original chef, Richard Sawyer, is back, serving his second tour of duty and doing much to recapture the mid-1990s chicdom the restaurant enjoyed. He is turning out a new menu that places more emphasis on organic and homegrown produce. Some dishes are quite complicated and taste as good as they sound. The menu changes every two months but is always strong on seafood and meats. For a starter, we recommend the Caesar club salad (the chicken is smoked on the premises). Memorable also is the loin of yellow fin tuna served with a wild parsley and eggplant relish with a roasted red bell pepper pesto. The desserts, however, are purposefully (and inexplicably) unsophisticated: rice pudding, poire Belle Hélène (poached pear). If you're rushed, you can drop into Dick's Bar, where they serve up everything from lamb burgers sparked with yogurt and fresh mint to Cashel blue cheese and pumpkin seeds on ciabatta bread, for a quick bite.

Circus. 1 Upper James St. W1. ☎ **020/7534-4000.** Reservations required. Main courses £11.50–£16.50 ($19.55–$28.05). Fixed-price menus before 7:30pm and 10:15pm–midnight £14.75–£16.75 ($25.10–$28.45). AE, DC, MC, V. Daily noon–2:30pm and Mon–Sat 6pm–midnight. Bar menu daily noon–1:30am. Tube: Piccadilly Circus. BRITISH/INTERNATIONAL.

A minimalist haven for power design and eating in the very heart of London, this new restaurant took over the ground floor and basement of what used to be the Granada Television building at the corner of Golden Square and Beak Street. The place evokes a London version of a Left Bank Parisian brasserie. It is especially buzzing during pre- and post-theater times, and chef Richard Lee has already acquired a fashionable following of London foodies. You may want to taste the divine skate wing with "crushed" new potatoes accompanied by a thick pesto-like medley of rocket blended with black olives. Or else try the tasty sautéed chili-flavored squid with *bok choy,* made even more heavenly with the tamarind dressing. The sorbets are a nice finish to a meal, especially the delectable mango and pink grapefruit version. Of course, if you're ravenous, there's always the velvety smooth Amaretto cheesecake with a coffee sauce. Service is a delight.

Fung Shing. 15 Lisle St., WC2. ☎ **020/7437-1539.** Reservations required. Main courses £7.50–£18 ($12.75–$30.60). Fixed-price menus £25–£35 ($42.50–$59.50). AE, DC, MC, V. Daily noon–11:30pm. Tube: Leicester Square. CANTONESE.

In a city where the competition is stiff, Fung Shing emerges as London's finest Cantonese restaurant. Firmly established as a culinary landmark, it dazzles with its array of classic Cantonese dishes as well as nouvelle Cantonese. Look for the seasonal specials, as many are sensational to the taste. The standard of cookery along with the presentation remains high. Some of the dishes may be a bit experimental for you, notably stir-fried fresh milk with scrambled egg white, but you'll feel more at home with the soft-shell crab sautéed in a light batter and served with tiny rings of red hot chili and deep-fried garlic. Chinese gourmets go here for the fried intestines, but you may prefer the hot pot of stewed duck with yam instead. The spicy whole sea bass and the stir-fried crispy chicken are worthy choices—in all, there are some 150 dishes from which to choose.

Momo. 25 Heddon St., W1. ☎ **020/7434-4040.** Reservations required 2 weeks in advance. Main courses £10.50–£16.50 ($17.85–$28.05); 2-course fixed-price lunch £12.50 ($21.25), 3-course fixed-price lunch £15.50 ($26.35). AE, DC, MC, V. Mon–Fri noon–2:30pm; Mon–Sat 7–11:30pm. Tube: Piccadilly Circus. MOROCCAN/NORTH AFRICAN.

You'll be greeted by a friendly and casual staff member clad in black and white T-shirts and fatigue pants. The setting is like Marrakesh, with stucco walls, a wood and stone floor, burning candles, and cozy banquettes. You can fill up on the freshly baked bread the waiter brings along with appetizers such as garlicky marinated olives and pickled carrots spiced with pepper and cumin. These starters are a "gift" from the chef. Other appetizers, which you'll pay for, are also tantalizing, especially the *briouat,* paper thin and very crisp triangular packets of puffed pastry that are filled with saffron-flavored chicken and other treats. One of the chef's finest specialties is *pastilla au pigeon,* a traditional poultry pie with almonds. Many diners visit for the couscous maison, among the best in London. Served in a decorative pot, this aromatic dish of raisins, meats (including merguez sausage), chicken, lamb, and chick peas is given added flavor with that powerful hot sauce of the Middle East, marissa. After all this, the refreshing cinnamon-flavored orange slices are a tempting treat for dessert.

Satsuma. 56 Wardour St., W1. ☎ **020/7437-8338.** Reservations not needed. Main courses £4.90–£13.50 ($8.35–$22.95). AE, MC, V. Daily noon–midnight. Tube: Piccadilly Circus. JAPANESE.

This is a funky Japanese canteen that's all the rage in London town. Clean lines, stark white walls, and plain long wooden tables with bench seating might suggest an upmarket youth hostel in Sweden. But patrons on the run come here not for luxury but for tasty treats at reasonable prices. It's ideal for a pre-theater visit as well. Your meal comes in a lacquered bento box on a matching tray. Try the chicken teriyaki or fresh chunks of tuna and salmon. The Chinese dumplings are excellent, as is the traditional bowl of miso soup. A specialty is a large bowl of seafood ramen, noodles swimming in a well-seasoned broth studded with mussels, scallops, and prawns. Tofu steaks are a delight, as are udon noodles mixed with wok-fried chicken and fresh vegetables. You can finish with deep-fried tempura ice cream.

The Titanic. In the Regent Palace Hotel, 12 Sherwood St., near Piccadilly Circus, W1A. ☎ **020/7437-1912.** Reservations required. Main courses £10–£11.50 ($17–$19.55). Breakfast platters £7–£12.50 ($11.90–$21.25). AE, DC, MC, V. Daily noon–2:30pm and 5:30–11:30pm. Breakfast daily 11:30pm–2:30am. Tube: Piccadilly. MODERN BRITISH.

Despite its phone number ("1912" is the year the famous ship went down) and its name, the staff is eager to point out that the nautical art deco decor is modeled after the *Queen Mary,* not *The Titanic.* Expect a large, crowded venue where tables turn over several times during the course of a night, and where food items are designed for the young at heart. Menu items include bresaola (Scottish beef cured in the Mediterranean style with olive oil and herbs); snails in garlic butter; oysters; mussels in white wine; fish 'n' chips with mushy peas; and caramelized skate. After 11:30pm, the focus moves to breakfast, presumably for night owls who have worked up an appetite at the disco, or for any transatlantic flyer suffering from jet lag and a hankering for eggs benedict, an omelet, kippers, or shirred eggs with calves liver.

INEXPENSIVE

China City. White Bear Yard, 25A Lisle St., WC2. ☎ **020/7734-3388.** Reservations recommended. Main courses £8.50–£12 ($14.45–$20.40). Fixed-price menus from £9 ($15.30). AE, MC, V. Daily noon–midnight. Tube: Leicester Sq. CANTONESE.

This gigantic Chinese hash house feeds 500 at the same time, and does so admirably well, all for a reasonable price unless you go suddenly mad and start ordering break-the-bank lobster. Take a seat at one of two glass-fronted floors furnished in a vaguely Oriental style and study the modern and classic Chinese dishes on the huge menu. This eatery is a good address to know about because it's not only central, but you can drop in for a meal, either lunch or dinner, at any time. In that sense, it's like a gigantic Chinese brasserie. Many opt for dim sum during the day, selecting more elaborate dishes in the evening, including eel fried in batter with chili, crab with glass noodles, and, if you want to go native, crispy pork belly.

✪ **Cork & Bottle Wine Bar.** 44–46 Cranbourn St., WC2. ☎ **020/7734-7807.** Reservations not accepted after 6pm. Main courses £3.95–£12.95 ($6.70–$22); glass of wine from £3.30 ($5.60). AE, DC, MC, V. Mon–Sat 11am–11:30pm; Sun noon–10:30pm. Tube: Leicester Sq. INTERNATIONAL.

Don Hewitson, a connoisseur of fine wines for more than 30 years, presides over this trove of blissful fermentation. The ever-changing wine list features an excellent selection of Beaujolais crus from Alsace, 30 selections from Australia, 30 champagnes, and a good selection of California labels. If you want something to wash down, the most successful dish is a raised cheese-and-ham pie, with a cream cheese–like filling and crisp well-buttered pastry—not your typical quiche. There's also chicken and apple salad, Mediterranean prawns with garlic and asparagus, lamb in ale, and tandoori chicken.

SOHO

EXPENSIVE

Quo Vadis. 26–29 Dean St., W1. ☎ **020/7437-9585.** Reservations required. Main courses £15–£27.50 ($25.50–$46.75). Fixed-price lunches and pre- and post-theater £14.95–£17.95 ($25.40–$30.50). AE, MC, V. Mon–Fri noon–3pm; Mon–Sat 6–11pm, Sun 6–10:30pm. Tube: Leicester Sq. or Tottenham Court Rd. MODERN BRITISH.

This hyper-trendy restaurant occupies the former apartment house of Communist patriarch Karl Marx, who would never recognize it. It was a stodgy Italian restaurant from 1926 until the mid-1990s, when its interior was ripped apart and reconfigured into the stylish, postmodern place you'll find today. The stark street-level dining room is a museum-style showcase for dozens of hyper-modern paintings by the controversial Damien Hirst and other contemporary artists. Many bypass the restaurant altogether for the upstairs bar, where Hirst has put a severed cow's head and a severed bull's head on display in separate aquariums. Why? They're catalysts to conversation, satirical odes to the destructive effects of Mad Cow Disease, and perhaps tongue-in-cheek commentaries on the flirtatious games that patrons conduct here.

Quo Vadis is associated with Marco Pierre White, but don't expect to see the temperamental culinary superstar here; as executive chef, he only functions as a consultant. Also, don't expect that the harassed and overburdened staff will have the time to pamper you; they're too preoccupied dealing with the glare of frenetic publicity. And the food? It's appealingly presented and very good, but not nearly as artful or innovative as the setting might lead you to believe. We suggest starting with the tomato and red mullet broth perfumed with basil, or the terrine of foie gras and duck confit, before moving on to the escallop of tuna with tapenade and eggplant caviar (actually eggplant and black olives puréed and seasoned, which gives it the look of caviar), or the roast chicken à la souvaroff, truffle oil, herb dumplings and vegetable broth.

MODERATE

Back to Basics. 21A Foley St., W1. ☎ **020/7436-2181.** Reservations recommended. Main courses £8.25–£14.75 ($14.05–$25.10). AE, DC, MC, V. Mon–Fri noon–3pm and 6–10pm. Tube: Oxford Circus or Goodge St. SEAFOOD.

Stefan Plaumer's Fitzrovia bistro draws discerning palates seeking some of the freshest seafood dishes in London. When the weather's fair, tables are placed outside. Otherwise, you can retreat inside to a vaguely Parisian setting with a blackboard menu and checked tablecloths. The fresh fish is served in large portions, and you may want to forego an appetizer unless you're ravenous. More than a dozen seafood dishes are offered nightly, and the fish can be broiled, grilled, baked, or poached to your specifications—no frying. Start with a bowl of tasty, plump mussels or else the sea bass flavored with fresh basil and chili oil. Brill appears delectably with green peppercorn butter, and plaice is jazzed up with fresh ginger and soy sauce. For the meat eater, there is Scotch ribeye or perhaps lamb steak. Freshly made salads accompany most meals, and an excellent fish soup is offered daily. For dessert, try either the bread pudding or freshly made apple pie.

Birdcage. 110 Whitfield St., W1. ☎ **020/7383/3346.** Reservations required as far in advance as possible. Set lunch and dinner £19.50–£32.50 ($33.15–$55.25) for 2 courses; £26.50–£36 ($45.05–$61.20) for 3 courses. AE, MC, V. Mon–Fri noon–4pm, Mon–Sat 6pm–midnight. Tube: Goodge St. THAI/FRENCH.

Small and intimate, this cozy restaurant is a celebrity favorite, attracting the likes of Madonna and Hugh Hefner. Michael Von Hruschka, darling of the media, has opened this reasonably priced restaurant decorated in a whimsical style, with everything from

Buddha to birdcages serving as props. The drink list written on delicate paper and inserted in an ostrich eggshell; everything is presented in exquisite boxes, and even the bill comes in a book. In spite of these precious touches, the cuisine is first rate, both in ingredients and preparations. Launch your meal with a coconut and lemon grass soup or the most delectable small carrot spring rolls. Vegetable couscous or a fish and banana risotto are delectable, and tiramisù is given an original touch with the addition of ginger wine. Birdcage is definitely on the see-and-be-seen circuit.

✪ **The Ivy.** 1–5 West St., WC2. ☎ **020/7836-4751.** Reservations required. Main courses £8.75–£35 ($14.90–$59.50); Sat–Sun 3-course fixed-price lunch £15.50 ($26.35) plus £1.50 ($2.55) cover charge. AE, DC, MC, V. Daily noon–3pm and 5:30pm–midnight (last order). Tube: Leicester Sq. MODERN BRITISH/INTERNATIONAL.

Effervescent and sophisticated, The Ivy has been intimately associated with the West End theater district since it opened in 1911. With its ersatz 1930s look and tiny bar near the entrance, this place is fun—and it hums with the energy of London's glamour scene. The menu may seem simple, but the kitchen has a solid appreciation for fresh ingredients and a talent for skillful preparation. Favorite dishes include white asparagus with sea kale and truffle butter; seared scallops with spinach, sorrel, and bacon; and salmon fish cakes. There's also Mediterranean fish soup and such English desserts as sticky toffee and caramelized bread-and-butter pudding. Meals are served quite late to accommodate the post-theater crowd.

Mash. 19-21 Great Portland St. W1. ☎ **020/7637-5555.** Reservations required. Main courses £9.50–£14 ($16.15–$23.80). Set lunch Sat £16.50 ($28.05). AE, DC, MC, V. Daily Mon–Fri noon–3pm and 6–11:30pm, Sat 11am–4pm, Sun 11:30am–5:30pm. Tube: Oxford Circus. MODERN CONTINENTAL.

What is it? A bar? A deli? A microbrewery? All of the above, and, oh, yes, a restaurant. Breakfast and weekend brunch are the highlights, but don't ignore dinner either. The novelty decor includes the likes of curvy "sci-fi" lines and "lizard-eye" lighting fixtures. Diners are invited into a "sunken chill out zone" designed by John Currin, a leading designer. "The food is good," one local patron informed us, "but I really come here for the mirrored loos." He left after that enigmatic statement, allowing us to launch into suckling pig with spring cannellini stew, our companion opting for one of the terrific pizzas emerging from the wood-fired oven. Ultimately, the food is the attraction here. On another occasion we returned for the fish freshly grilled over wood. It was sea bass and presented enticingly with grilled artichoke. You can also try the marinated quail with thin slices of crisp deep-fried taro root. Desserts are often startling, but be brave. An example is the rhubarb compote with a crisp polenta shortcake and a custardlike ice cream flavored with fresh basil.

Mezzo. 100 Wardour St., W1. ☎ **020/7314-4000.** Reservations required for Mezzonine. Mezzo 3-course fixed-price dinner £15.50 ($26.35). Mezzonine 3-course dinner £25–£30 ($42.50–$51). AE, DC, MC, V. Mezzo: Mon–Fri noon–3pm; Sun 12:30–3pm; Mon–Thurs 5:30pm–1am; Fri–Sat 5:30pm–3am; Sun 6–11pm. Mezzonine: Mon–Fri noon–3pm; Sat noon–4pm; Mon–Thurs 5:30pm–1am; Fri–Sat 5:30pm–3am. Tube: Piccadilly Circus. MODERN EUROPEAN/ASIAN.

This blockbuster 750-seat Soho restaurant—the latest creation of entrepreneur Sir Terence Conran—may be the biggest in Europe. The mammoth space, on the former site of rock's legendary Marquee club, has been split into several separate restaurants: Mezzonine upstairs, serving a Thai/Asian cuisine with European flair (roast marinated lamb with yogurt and cumin on flat bread); the swankier Mezzo downstairs offering a modern European cuisine, in an atmosphere of 1930s Hollywood; and Mezzo Café, where you can stop in for a sandwich.

The food is at its most ambitious downstairs, where 100 chefs work behind glass to feed up to 400 diners at a time. This is dinner as theater. Not surprisingly, the modern European cuisine tends to be uneven. We suggest the rotisserie rib of beef with red wine and creamed horseradish, or the roast cod, which was crisp-skinned and cooked to perfection. For dessert, you can't beat the butterscotch ice cream with a pitcher of hot fudge. A live jazz band entertains after 10pm from Wednesday to Saturday, and the world of Marlene Dietrich and Noël Coward comes alive again.

✪ **The Sugar Club.** 21 Warwick St. W1. ☎ **020/7437-7776.** Main courses £12–£18 ($20.40–$30.60). AE, DC, MC, V. Daily noon–3pm and 6–11pm. Tube: Piccadilly Circus or Oxford Circus. PACIFIC RIM.

Ashley Sumner and Vivienne Hayman originally launched their restaurant in Wellington, New Zealand in the mid-80s. Now after a detour at Notting Hill Gate, they have moved deep into Soho with their original chef, the talented Peter Gordon, who is known for attracting homesick Aussies with the best loin of grilled kangaroo in London (very tender with a rich piquant sauce). The restaurant is both elegant and spacious, offering a bar waiting area for diners, a separate no-smoking floor, and a kitchen open to view.

The flavors here are often stunning, as evoked by the sashimi of Iki Jimi yellowtail with a black bean and ginger salsa. The fish tastes amazingly fresh, and the flavors may startle your palate, but only in the most exciting ways. You can dig into the duck leg braised in tamarind and star anise with coconut rice, or you may sample the pan-fried turbot with spinach, sweet potato, a red-curry sauce, and onion raiata. Many of the starters are vegetarian and can be upgraded to a main course. For dessert, the blood-orange curd tart with créme fraîche is drop-dead delicious.

Villandry. 170 Great Portland St., W1. ☎ **020/7631-3131.** Reservations recommended. Main courses £11–£14 ($18.70–$23.80). AE, MC, V. Mon–Sat noon–3pm and 7–10pm. Food store Mon–Sat 8am–8pm, Sun 11am–4pm. Tube: Great Portland Street. INTERNATIONAL/ CONTINENTAL.

Food lovers and gourmands flock to this combination food store, delicatessen, and restaurant, where racks of the finest meats, cheese, and produce in the world are displayed and changed virtually every hour. And, where some of the finest of the merchandise is quickly and almost whimsically transformed into menu choices within the restaurant. The setting is an oversized Edwardian-style storefront north of Oxford Circus. Inside, the venue is artfully minimalist and immaculate—sort of a pared-down temple to the glories of fresh produce and esoteric foodstuffs. Ingredients change here so frequently that the menu is revamped and rewritten twice a day. During our latest visit, the menu proposed such perfectly crafted dishes as breast of duck with fresh spinach and a gratin of baby onions; fillets of black codfish with prosciutto, radicchio, and creamed lentils; and pan-fried turbot with deep-fried celery, artichoke hearts, and hollandaise sauce.

INEXPENSIVE

Dumpling Inn. 15a Gerrard St., W1. ☎ **020/7437-2567.** Reservations recommended. Main courses £7–£15 ($11.90–$25.50); fixed-price lunch or dinner £14–£30 ($23.80–$51). AE, MC, V. Sun–Thurs noon–11:30pm; Fri–Sat 11:30am–12:45pm. Tube: Piccadilly Circus. CHINESE.

Despite its incongruous name, this is a cool and rather elegant restaurant serving a delectable brand of Peking Mandarin cuisine that dates back almost 3,000 years and owes some of its special piquancy to various Mongolian ingredients, best represented by its savory stew called "hot pot." Regulars come here for the shark's-fin soup, the beef in oyster sauce, the seaweed and sesame-seed prawns on toast, duck with chili and black-bean sauce, and the fried sliced fish with sauce. Naturally, the specialty is dumplings; you can make a meal from the dim sum list. Portions aren't large, so you can order a good variety without fear of leftovers. Chinese tea is extra. Service is leisurely, so don't dine here before a theater date.

Mildreds. 58 Greek St., W1. ☎ **020/7494-1634.** Reservations not accepted. Main courses £5–£6.50 ($8.50–$11.05). Mon–Sat noon–11pm, Sun noon–5pm. No credit cards. Tube: Tottencourt Rd. VEGETARIAN.

Mildreds may sound like a 1940s Joan Crawford movie, but it's actually one of London's most enduring vegetarian and vegan dining spots. It was vegetarian long before such restaurants became trendy. Jane Muir and Diane Thomas worked in various restaurants together before deciding to open their own place. Today they are a success, running a busy, bustling diner with casual, friendly service. Sometimes it's a bit crowded and tables are shared. They do a delectable series of stir-fries. The ingredients going into their dishes are naturally grown, and they strongly emphasize the best produce in any given season. The menu is changed daily but features an array of homemade soups, casseroles, and salads. Organic wines are served, and the portions are very large. Save room for their desserts which are among the finest items on the menu, especially the nutmeg and mascarpone ice cream or the chocolate rum and Amaretto pudding.

Shampers. 4 Kingly St. (between Carnaby and Regent Sts.), W1. ☎ **020/7437-1692.** Reservations recommended. Main courses £6.50–£11.50 ($11.05–$19.55). AE, DC, MC, V. Mon–Sat 11am–11pm. Closed Easter and Christmas. Tube: Oxford Circus. CONTINENTAL.

For a number of years now, this has been a favorite of West End wine-bar aficionados. In addition to the street-level wine bar where platters of food are served, there's a more formal basement-level restaurant. In either section, you can order such main dishes as grilled calves liver with bacon, chips, and salad; pan-fried large prawns with ginger, garlic, and chili; and platters of assorted cheese. Salads are especially popular, including spicy chicken salad. A platter of Irish mussels cooked in a cream-and-tarragon sauce seems to be everybody's favorite. The restaurant is closed in the evening, but the bar serves an extended menu, incorporating not only the luncheon menu but also such dishes as fresh squid, tuna steak, pan-fried tiger prawns, free-range chicken, and a variety of other dishes.

Soho Spice. 124–126 Wardour St., W1. ☎ **020/7434-0808.** Reservations recommended. Main courses £8.50–£14.50 ($14.45–$24.65); set lunch £7.50 ($12.75); set dinner £15.95 ($27.10). AE, V. Sun–Thurs 11:30am–12:30pm; Fri–Sat 11:30am–3am; Sun 12:30–10:30pm. Tube: Tottenham Court Road. SOUTH INDIAN.

One of central London's most stylish Indian restaurants combines a sense of media and fashion hip with the flavors and scents of southern India. You might opt for a drink at the cellar-level bar before heading to the large street-level dining room decorated in the saffron, cardamom, bay, and pepper hues evocative of the place's piquant cuisine. There is a wide array of dishes, including a range of slow-cooked Indian tikkas that feature combinations of spices with lamb, chicken, fish, or all-vegetarian. The à la carte menu offers a variety of main courses including Jhinga Hara Pyaz, spicy queen prawns with fresh spring onions, and Paneer Pasanda, cottage cheese slices stuffed with spinach and served with almond sauce. The cuisine will satisfy traditionalists, but has a modern, nouveau-Soho flair. The presentation takes it a step above typical Indian restaurants, here or elsewhere.

YO! Sushi. 52 Poland St., W1. ☎ **020/7287-0443.** Reservations recommended. Sushi £1.50–£3.50 ($2.55–$5.95). AE, DC, MC, V. Daily noon–midnight. Tube: Oxford Circus. SUSHI.

This is London's first sushi Disneyland. In spite of the high-tech gadgets and gimmicks, the sushi is really good. If you've got a kid, and you want to indoctrinate him or her into the glories of sushi, this is the place to go. YO! Sushi has the longest sushi bar in the world, with a kaiten (conveyor belt) serving 130 guests. You can take your drink from one of the passing service robots. You're allowed to choose two pieces of sushi from five different price categories. Plates have five different colors that match the prices; lime is the cheapest, pink the most expensive. The human chefs stand behind a counter where you can order directly from them, everything from fresh clams to avocado and salmon handrolls. You can have your fill of cuttlefish, eel, shrimp, salmon roe, octopus, or whatever. Vegetarian sushi includes pickled turnip and cucumber. Wash it all down with Sapporo beer, Japanese tea, or iced or hot sake. Live footage from Japan on Sony widescreen TVs keep you amused.

BLOOMSBURY

MODERATE

British Museum Restaurant. Great Russell St., WC1. ☎ **020/7323-8256.** Main courses £6.45–£8 ($10.95–$13.60); £5.75 ($9.80) soup & baguette special. MC, V. Mon–Sat cold food 11am–4:30pm, hot food 11:30am–3pm. Tube: Holborn or Tottenham Court Rd. TRADITIONAL BRITISH.

This is the best place for lunch if you're exploring the wonders of this world-renowned museum. It's on the lobby level of the West Wing and is decorated with full-size copies of the bas-reliefs from a temple in the town of Nereid in ancient Greece. (If you want to compare, you'll find the originals in nearby galleries.) The format is self-service. A few hot specials (including a vegetarian selection) and crisp salads are made fresh every day, and there's always a good selection of fish and cold meat dishes. Try the soup and baguette special, which is changed daily. Desserts include pastries and cakes. There's also a cafe offering coffee, sandwiches, pastries, and soup.

✪ **North Sea Fish Restaurant.** 7–8 Leigh St., WC1. ☎ **020/7387-5892.** Reservations recommended. Fish platters £7.50–£16 ($12.75–$27.20). AE, DC, MC, V. Mon–Sat noon–2:30pm and 5:30–10:30pm. Tube: King's Cross, or Russell Sq. SEAFOOD.

The fish served in this bright and clean restaurant is purchased fresh every day; the quality is high, and the prices low. In the view of London's diehard chippie devotees, it's the best in town. The fish is most often served battered and deep-fried, but you can also order it grilled. The menu is wisely limited. Students from the Bloomsbury area flock to the place.

IN NEARBY FITZROVIA

EXPENSIVE

✪ **Nico Central.** 35 Great Portland St., W1. ☎ **020/7436-8846.** Reservations required. £15–£20 ($25.50–$34) set lunch, £35–£45 ($59.50–$76.50) set dinner. AE, DC, MC, V. Mon–Fri noon–2:30pm; Mon–Sat 6:30–10:30pm. Tube: Oxford Circus. FRENCH/MODERN BRITISH.

This brasserie—founded by London's legendary chef, Nico Ladenis (who spends most of his time at Chez Nico at Ninety Park Lane)—delivers earthy French cuisine that's been called "haute but not haughty" and consistently praised for its "absurdly good value." Of course, everything is handled with considerable culinary urbanity. Nearly a dozen starters—the pride of the chef—will tempt you. The menu changes seasonally and according to the chef's inspiration, but might include grilled duck served with risotto with cèpes (flap mushrooms) and parmesan; pan-fried foie gras with brioche and a caramelized orange; and braised knuckle of veal. Save room for one of the desserts—they are, in the words of one devotee, "divine."

COVENT GARDEN & THE STRAND

EXPENSIVE

Rules. 35 Maiden Lane, WC2. ☎ **020/7836-5314.** Reservations recommended. Main courses £15.95–£19.95 ($27.10–$33.90). AE, DC, MC, V. Daily noon–11:30pm. Tube: Covent Garden. TRADITIONAL BRITISH.

If you're looking for London's most quintessentially British restaurant, eat here or at Wiltons (see above). London's oldest restaurant was established in 1798 as an oyster bar; today, on the site of the original premises, it rambles through a series of antler-encrusted Edwardian dining rooms exuding patriotic nostalgia. You can order such classic dishes as Irish or Scottish oysters, jugged hare, and mussels. Game dishes are offered from mid-August to February or March: wild Scottish salmon or wild sea trout; wild Highland red deer; and game birds like grouse, snipe, partridge, pheasant, and woodcock. As a finale, the "great puddings" continue to impress decade after decade.

Simpson's-in-the-Strand. 100 The Strand (next to the Savoy Hotel), WC2. ☎ **020/7836-9112.** Reservations required. Main courses £15–£22 ($25.50–$37.40); fixed-price 2-course lunch and pre-theater dinner £14.50 ($24.65); fixed-price breakfast from £13.95 ($23.70). AE, DC, MC, V. Mon–Fri 7am–11am; Mon–Sat noon–2:30pm and 5:30–11pm; Sun noon–2pm and 6–9pm. Tube: Charing Cross or Embankment. TRADITIONAL AND MODERN BRITISH.

Simpson's is more of an institution than a restaurant—it's been in business since 1828, and as a result of a recent £2 million renovation, it's now two separate restaurants. The Grande Divan, with its army of grandly formal waiters to whom nouvelle cuisine means anything after Henry VIII, serves traditional British fare. Most diners agree that Simpson's serves the best roasts in London, an array that includes roast sirloin of beef, roast Aylesbury duckling, and steak, kidney, and mushroom pie. (Remember to tip the tailcoated carver.) For a pudding, you might order the treacle roll and custard or Stilton with vintage port.

Simpson's also serves traditional breakfasts. The most popular one, curiously enough, is called "The Ten Deadly Sins" for £15.95 ($27.10): a plate of sausage, fried egg, streaky and back bacon, black pudding, lamb's kidneys, bubble and squeak, baked beans, lamb's liver, and fried bread, mushrooms and tomatoes. That will certainly fortify you for the day.

Chequers, the new restaurant, specializes in modern British cuisine. Appetizers include tartare of Cornish crab with spiced avocado relish, dill dressed cucumber and Avruga caviar. For a main course, try the thyme-infused Gressingham breast of duck with parsnip pureé and red wine blackcurrant jus. You can finish a delectable meal with desserts that include orange crème brûlée and pear marinated in spiced red wine syrup with gingerbread ice cream. Chequers is open from Monday through Saturday, noon to 7pm. Main dish prices range from £9 to £15.75 ($15.30 to $26.80).

Jacket and tie is no longer essential; however, we do recommend smart casual attire.

MODERATE

Belgo Centraal. 50 Earlham St., WC2. ☎ **020/7813-2233.** Reservations required for the restaurant. Main courses £8.95–£20.95 ($15.20–$35.60); fixed-price menus £6–£16.95 ($10.20–$28.80). AE, DC, MC, V. Mon–Sat noon–11:30pm; Sun noon–10:30pm. Closed Christmas. Tube: Covent Garden. BELGIAN.

Chaos reigns supreme in this audacious and cavernous basement, where mussels marinière with frites and 100 Belgian beers are the *raison d'etre.* You'll take a freight elevator down past the busy kitchen and into a converted cellar, which has been divided into two large eating areas. One is a beer hall seating about 250; the menu here is the same as in the restaurant, but reservations aren't needed. The restaurant side has three nightly seatings: 5:30, 7:30, and 10pm. Between 5:30 and 8pm you can choose one of three fixed-price menus, and you pay based on the time of your order: the earlier you order, the less you pay. Although heaps of fresh mussels are the big attraction here, you can also opt for fresh Scottish salmon, roast chicken, a perfectly done steak, or one of the vegetarian specialties. Belgian stews called *waterzooi* are also served. With waiters dressed in maroon monk's habits with black aprons, barking orders into headset microphones, it's all a bit bizarre.

INEXPENSIVE

The George. 213 The Strand, WC2. ☎ **020/7427-0941.** Main courses £6.50–£10.50 ($11.05–$17.85). AE, MC, V. Mon–Fri 11am–11pm; Sat noon–3pm (food served Mon–Fri noon–3pm and 5:30–8:30pm; Sat noon–2:30pm). Tube: Temple. TRADITIONAL BRITISH.

Although its half-timbered facade would have you believe that it's older than it is, this pub was built as a coffeehouse in 1723. Set on the Strand, at the lower end of Fleet Street opposite the Royal Courts of Justice, the George is a favorite of barristers, their clients, and the handful of journalists who haven't yet moved to other parts of London. The pub's illustrious history saw Samuel Johnson having his mail delivered here during his heyday, and Oliver Goldsmith enjoying many tankards of what eventually became draught Bass. Today, the setting seems only slightly changed from those days; much of the original architecture is still intact. Hot and cold platters, including bangers and mash, fish-and-chips, steak-and-kidney pie, and lasagna, are served from a food counter at the back of the pub. Additional seating is available in the basement, where a headless cavalier is said to haunt the same premises where he enjoyed his liquor in an earlier day.

✪ **Porter's English Restaurant.** 17 Henrietta St., WC2. ☎ **020/7836-6466.** Reservations recommended. Main courses £8–£12 ($13.60–$20.40); fixed-price menu £16.50 ($28.05). AE, DC, MC, V. Mon–Sat noon–11:30pm; Sun noon–10:30pm. Tube: Covent Garden or Leicester Square. TRADITIONAL BRITISH.

In 1979 the 7th Earl of Bradford opened this restaurant, stating "it would serve real English food at affordable prices," and he has succeeded notably—and not just because Lady Bradford turned over her carefully guarded recipe for banana and ginger steamed pudding. A comfortable, two-storied restaurant with a friendly, informal, and lively atmosphere, Porter's specializes in classic English pies, including Old English fish pie; lamb and apricot; ham, leek, and cheese; and of course, bangers and mash. Main courses are so generous—and accompanied by vegetables and side dishes—that you hardly need appetizers. They have also added grilled English fare to the menu, with sirloin and lamb steaks, and pork chops. The puddings, including bread-and-butter pudding or steamed syrup sponge, are the real puddings (in the American sense); they're served hot or cold, with whipped cream or custard. The bar does quite a few exotic cocktails, as well as beers, wine, or English mead. A traditional English tea is also served from 2:30 to 5:30pm for £3.50 ($5.95) per person.

WESTMINSTER/VICTORIA

EXPENSIVE

✪ **Rhodes in the Square.** Dolphin Square, Chichester St., SW1. ☎ **020/7798-6767.** Reservations required. Set-price meals £28.50 ($48.45) for 2 courses, £31 ($52.70) for 3 courses. AE, DC, MC, V. Tues–Fri noon–2:30pm, Tues–Sat 7–10pm. Tube: Pimlico. MODERN BRITISH.

In this discreet residential district, super-chef and media darling, Gary Rhodes has done it again, opening a successful restaurant to which some of the more discerning and demanding palates of London are flocking. Rhodes has long been known for taking the most traditional of British cookery and giving it daring twists, adding new flavors and removing some of the excesses of the past, such as suet. You can always count on some delightful surprises from this major culinary talent. Start with his chicken liver parfait with foie gras, and go on to an open omelet with chunky bits of lobster topping it along with a Thermidor sauce and cheese crust. His glazed duck served with bitter orange jus tastes how this dish is supposed to, but so often doesn't. For dessert, make your selection from the British "pudding plate" that ranges from lemon meringue tart to a simple seared "carpaccio" of pineapple oozing with good flavor.

MODERATE

✪ **Simply Nico.** 48A Rochester Row, SW1. ☎ **020/7630-8061.** Reservations required. Fixed-price 2-course lunch £20.50 ($34.85), fixed-price 3-course lunch £23.50 ($39.95); fixed-price 3-course dinner £25.50 ($43.35). AE, DC, MC, V. Mon–Fri 12:30–2pm; Mon–Sat 7–11pm. Tube: Victoria or St. James's Park. FRENCH.

The brainchild of Nico Ladenis, of the much grander and more expensive Chez Nico at Ninety Park Lane, it's run by his sous-chef. In Nico's own words, it's "cheap and cheerful." We think it's the best value in town. The wood floors reverberate with the din of contented diners, who pack in daily at snug tables to enjoy the simply prepared—and invariably French-inspired—food. The fixed-price menu changes frequently, but options might include starters such as pan-fried foie gras followed by shank of lamb with parsnips, or the ever-popular monkfish.

✪ **Tate Gallery Restaurant.** Millbank, SW1. ☎ **020/7887-8877.** Reservations recommended. Main courses £12.50–£16 ($21.25–$27.20); fixed-price 2-course lunch £16.75 ($28.45); fixed-price, 3-course lunch £19.50 ($33.15). Minimum charge £16.75 ($28.45). AE, DC, MC, V. Mon–Sat noon–3pm; Sun noon–5pm. Tube: Pimlico. Bus 77 or 88. MODERN BRITISH.

This restaurant is particularly attractive to wine fanciers; it offers what may be the best bargains for superior wines anywhere in Britain. Bordeaux and Burgundies are in abundance, and the management keeps the markup between 40% and 65%, rather than the 100% to 200% added to the wholesale price in other restaurants. Wine begins at £13.50 ($22.95) per bottle, or £4.95 ($8.40) per glass. Oenophiles frequently come just for lunch, heedless of the art. The restaurant specializes in an English menu that changes about every month. Dishes might include pheasant casserole, Oxford sausage with mashed potatoes, pan-fried skate with black butter and capers, and a selection of vegetarian dishes. One critic found the staff and diners as traditional "as a Gainsborough landscape." Access to the restaurant is through the museum's main entrance on Millbank.

THE CITY

MODERATE

✪ **Café Spice Namaste.** 16 Prescot St., E1. ☎ **020/7488-9242.** Reservations required. Main courses £9.95–£14.95 ($16.90–$25.40). AE, DC, MC, V. Mon–Fri noon–3pm and 6:15–10:30pm; Sat 6:30–10pm. Tube: Tower Hill. INDIAN.

This is our favorite Indian restaurant in London, where the competition is stiff, with Tamarind also vying for top honors. It's housed in a landmark Victorian hall near Tower Bridge, just east of the Tower of London. The chef, Cyrus Todiwala, is a former resident of Goa, where he learned many of his culinary secrets. He concentrates on southern and northern Indian dishes with a strong Portuguese influence. Chicken and lamb are prepared a number of ways, from mild to spicy-hot. As a novelty, Todiwala occasionally even offers a menu of emu dishes; when marinated, the meat is rich and spicy and evocative of lamb. Other dining oddities include ostrich gizzard kebab, alligator tikka, minced moose, and blue boar. Many patrons journey here just for the complex chicken curry known as *xacutti.* A weekly specialty menu complements the long list of regional dishes. The homemade chutneys alone are worth the trip; our favorite is made with kiwi. All dishes come with fresh vegetables and Indian bread. With the exotic ingredients, the impeccable service, the warm hospitality, and the spicy but subtle flavors, this is hardly a curry hash house.

✪ **Poons in the City.** 2 Minster Lane, Minster Court, Mincing Lane, EC3. ☎ **020/7626-0126.** Reservations recommended for lunch. Fixed-price lunch and dinner £22.50–£30.80 ($38.25–$52.35); main courses £6.50–£8.50 ($11.05–$14.45). AE, DC, MC, V. Mon–Fri noon–10:30pm. Tube: Tower Hill or Meriment. CHINESE.

In 1992, Poons opened this branch in the City, less than a 5-minute walk from the Tower of London and close to other City attractions. It's modeled on the Luk Yew Tree House in Hong Kong. Main courses feature crispy aromatic duck; prawns with cashew nuts; and barbecued pork. Poons's famous *lap yuk soom* (like Cantonese tacos) has finely chopped wind-dried bacon. Special dishes can be ordered on 24-hour notice. At the end of the L-shaped restaurant is an 80-seat fast-food area and take-out counter that's accessible from Mark Lane. The menu changes every 2 weeks, and fixed-price lunches cost from £22.50 ($38.25) per person (minimum of two).

✪ **Ye Olde Cheshire Cheese.** Wine Office Court, 145 Fleet St., EC4. ☎ **020/7353-6170.** Main courses £8.95–£13.95 ($15.20–$23.70). AE, DC, MC, V. Mon–Fri noon–9:30pm, Sat noon–2:30pm and 6–11pm, Sun noon–3pm. Drinks and bar snacks daily 11:30am–11pm. Tube: St. Paul's or Blackfriars. BRITISH.

The foundation of this carefully preserved building was laid in the 13th century, and it holds the most famous of the old City chophouses and pubs. Established in 1667, it claims to be the spot where Dr. Samuel Johnson (who lived nearby) entertained admirers with his acerbic wit. Charles Dickens and other literary lions also patronized the place. Later, many of the ink-stained journalists and scandalmongers of 19th and early 20th-century Fleet Street made it their locale. You'll find six bars and two dining rooms here. The house specialties include "Ye Famous Pudding" (steak, kidney, mushrooms, and game) and Scottish roast beef with Yorkshire pudding and horseradish sauce. Sandwiches, salads, and standby favorites such as steak and kidney pie are also available, as are dishes such as Dover sole.

KNIGHTSBRIDGE

VERY EXPENSIVE

✪ **La Tante Claire.** Wilton Place, Knightsbridge, SW1. ☎ **020/7823-2003.** Reservations essential. Main courses £24–£36 ($40.80–$61.20). AE, DC, MC, V. Mon–Fri 12:30–2pm, Mon–Sat 7–11pm. Tube: Hyde Park Corner, Knightsbridge. FRENCH.

In swanky new digs, "Aunt Claire" has once again emerged as one of the stellar restaurants of London. Pierre Koffmann remains the chef behind this fabled place, a man more interested in turning out culinary fireworks than in creating a media feeding frenzy. The standards of Chef Koffmann are the benchmark other chefs aspire to. To sample perfection, dishes bringing out mouthwatering flavors and precise textures, try his now legendary ravioli langoustine or pig's trotters. (Who would have thought that the lowly pig trotter could be transformed into such a sublime concoction?) His soup made with truffles compels gourmands to shed tears of joy. His *nage de homard* (lobster) with Sauterne and fresh ginger is a culinary work of skill, as is his steamed lamb with a vegetable couscous. For dessert, his hot pistachio soufflé served with its own ice cream will linger long in your memory. The service proceeds like a perfectly trained and talented orchestra.

EXPENSIVE

✪ **Vong.** In the Berkeley Hotel, Wilton Place, SW1. ☎ **020/7235-1010.** Reservations recommended. Main courses £13.75–£26.75 ($23.40–$45.50); vegetarian main courses £10.25–£13.50 ($17.45–$22.95); tasting menu £49 ($83.30); 3-course lunch £20 ($34), 3-course, fixed-price dinner £29–£41 ($49.30–$69.70); pre- and post-theater dinner £19.50 ($33.15). AE, DC, DISC, MC, V. Mon–Sat noon–2:30pm and 6–11pm; Sun 11:30am–2:30pm and 6–9:30pm. Dim Sum available Sat–Sun 11:30am–2:30pm from £2.50 ($4.25) per plate. Pre- and post-theater dinner available 6–7pm and 10:30–11:30pm. Tube: Hyde Park. FRENCH/THAI.

Just 600 yards from Harrods, this strikingly modern restaurant on three levels is one of the chic rendezvous of London. Jean-Georges Vongerichten, the darling of New York culinary circles, has brought his award-winning French/Thai menu to London. The results here are subtle, innovative, and inspired. In a minimalist setting, you can partake of the "Black Plate," featuring samples of six starters, if you'd like a taste of everything. Other options are a perfectly roasted halibut or a lobster and daikon roll, the latter with rosemary and ginger sauce. You can virtually eat everything on the menu and be filled with wonder and admiration, especially by the crab spring roll with a vinegary tamarind dipping sauce. The sautéed foie gras with ginger and mango literally melts in the mouth. Spiced cod with curried artichokes is well worth a try. Desserts are equally exotic, especially the salad of banana and passion fruit with white-pepper ice cream.

CHELSEA

VERY EXPENSIVE

✪ **Gordon Ramsay.** 68 Royal Hospital Rd., SW3. ☎ **020/7352-4441.** Reservations essential (1 month in advance). Set lunch £28 ($47.60) for 3 courses. Set dinner £50 ($85) for 3 courses, £65 ($110.50) for 7 courses. AE, DC, MC, V. Mon–Fri noon–2:30pm and 6:45–11pm. Tube: Sloane Square. FRENCH.

One of the city's most innovative and talented chefs, Gordon Ramsay, has taken over the former premises of La Tante Claire, and this genius of a chef is serving a cuisine even more innovative and exciting than the long-established "La Tante" herself. Food critic Dominic Bradbury called Ramsay a "Captain Ahab, a dedicated monomaniac, hell-bent on cruising his kitchen until he finds his second Michelin star." Every dish from his kitchen is gratifying, reflecting subtlety and delicacy without any sacrifice to the food's natural essence. Try, for example, his celebrated cappuccino of white beans with grated truffles. His appetizers are likely to dazzle: salad of crispy pig's trotters with calf's sweetbreads, fried quail eggs, and a cream vinaigrette, or else foie gras three ways—sautéed with quince, *mi-cuit* with an Earl Grey consomme, or pressed with truffle peelings. From here, you can grandly proceed to fillet of brill poached in red wine, or else caramelized Challandaise duck cooked with dates. Desserts are equally stunning, especially the pistachio soufflé with chocolate sorbet or the passion fruit and chocolate parfait.

EXPENSIVE

✪ **Aubergine.** 11 Park Walk, SW10. ☎ **020/7352-3449.** Reservations essential and accepted up to 4 weeks in advance. Fixed-price 2-course lunch £15 ($25.50), 3-course lunch £18 ($30.60); fixed-price 3-course dinner £42.50 ($72.25); menu gourmand £55 ($93.50), truffle menu £80 ($136). AE, DC, MC, V. Mon–Fri noon–2:30pm; Mon–Sat 6:45–11pm. Tube: South Kensington. FRENCH.

"Eggplant" is luring savvy diners down to the lower reaches of Chelsea, where new chef Williams Drabble, who earned his first Michelin star in 1998, has remained true to the style and ambience of this famous establishment. Starters continue to charm and delight palates, ranging from the ravioli of crab with mussels, chili, ginger, and coriander nage, to the terrine of foie gras with confit of duck with pears poached in port. Every dish is satisfyingly flavorsome, from the warm salad of truffled vegetables with asparagus purée to the roasted monkfish served with crushed new potatoes, roasted leeks, and a red-wine sauce. Another stunning main course is a tranche of sea bass with bouillabaisse potatoes. A new dish likely to catch your eye is roasted veal sweetbreads with caramelized onion purée and a casserole of flap mushrooms. There are only 14 tables, so bookings are imperative.

MODERATE

Chelsea Kitchen. 98 King's Rd., SW3. ☎ **020/7589-1330.** Reservations recommended. Main courses £3–£5.50 ($5.10–$9.35); fixed-price menu £6 ($10.20). No credit cards. Daily 8am–11:45pm. Tube: Sloane Sq. INTERNATIONAL.

This simple restaurant feeds large numbers of Chelsea residents in a setting that's changed very little since 1961. The food and the clientele move fast, almost guaranteeing that the entire inventory of ingredients is sold out at the end of each day. Menu items usually include leek-and-potato soup, chicken Kiev, chicken parmigiana, steaks, sandwiches, and burgers. The clientele includes a broad cross-section of patrons—all having a good and cost-conscious time.

English Garden. 10 Lincoln St., SW3. ☎ **020/7584-7272.** Reservations required. Main courses £14.50–£16.50 ($24.65–$28.05); fixed-price lunch £19.50 ($33.15). AE, CB, DC, MC, V. Mon–Sat 12:30–2:30pm, Sun 12:30–2pm; Mon–Sat 7:30–11:30pm, Sun 7–10:30pm. Tube: Sloane Sq. TRADITIONAL BRITISH.

This is a metropolitan restaurant par excellence. The decor is pretty and lighthearted in the historic town house: The Garden Room is whitewashed brick with a domed conservatory roof, rattan chairs, banks of plants, and candy-pink napery. Every component of a meal here is chopped or cooked to the right degree and well proportioned. Launch into a fine feast with a caramelized red onion–and–cheddar cheesecake or mussel-and-watercress soup. For a main course, opt for such delights as roast baron of rabbit with oven-dried tomato, prunes and olive oil mash, or saddle of venison with potted cabbage. Some of these dishes sound as if they were cloned from an English cookbook of the Middle Ages—and are they ever good. Desserts, especially the rhubarb and cinnamon ice cream or the candied orange tart with orange syrup, would've pleased Miss Marple.

Front Page. 35 Old Church St., SW3. ☎ **020/7352-0648.** Main courses £6.50–£7.95 ($11.05–$13.50). AE, DISC, MC, V. Restaurant Mon–Fri noon–2:30pm; Sat–Sun 12:30–3pm; daily 7–10pm, Sun 7–9:30pm; pub Mon–Sat 11am–11pm; Sun noon–10:30pm. Tube: Sloane Sq. MODERN EUROPEAN.

Front Page is favored by young professionals who like the mellow atmosphere provided by its wood paneling, wooden tables, and pews and benches. In one section, an open fire burns on cold nights. The pub stands in an expensive residential section of Chelsea and is a good place to go for a drink or some pub grub. Check the chalkboard for the daily specials, which might include hot chicken salad, fishcakes, and smoked salmon and cream cheese on a bagel.

SOUTH KENSINGTON

EXPENSIVE

Bibendum/The Oyster Bar. 81 Fulham Rd., SW3. ☎ **020/7581-5817.** Reservations required in Bibendum; not accepted in Oyster Bar. Main courses £15–£25 ($25.50–$42.50);

fixed-price 3-course lunch £28 ($47.60); cold seafood platter in Oyster Bar £45 ($76.50) for 2. AE, DC, MC, V. Bibendum Mon–Fri noon–2:30pm and 7–11:15pm; Sat 12:30–3pm and 7–11:15pm; Sun 12:30–3pm and 7–10:15pm. Oyster Bar Mon–Sat noon–10:30pm; Sun noon–3pm and 7–10pm. Tube: South Kensington. FRENCH/MEDITERRANEAN.

In trendy Brompton Cross, this still-fashionable restaurant occupies two floors of a garage—the former home of the Michelin tire company—that's an art deco masterpiece. The white-tiled room, with stained-glass windows, streaming sunlight, and a chic clientele, is an extremely pleasant place to dine. The fabulously eclectic cuisine, known for its freshness and simplicity, is based on what's available seasonally. Dishes might include roast pigeon with celeriac purée and apple saute; rabbit with anchovies, garlic, and rosemary; or grilled lamb cutlets with a delicate sauce. Some of the best dishes are for dining *à deux:* Bresse chicken flavored with fresh tarragon, or grilled veal chops with truffle butter.

Simpler meals and cocktails are available in the **Oyster Bar** on the building's street level. The bar-style menu stresses fresh shellfish presented in the traditional French style, on ice-covered platters occasionally adorned with strands of seaweed. It's a crustacean-lover's lair.

Hilaire. 68 Old Brompton Rd., SW7. ☎ **020/7584-8993.** Reservations recommended. 2-course fixed-price lunch £18.50 ($31.45); 3 courses £21.50 ($36.55); 3-course fixed-price dinner £37.50 ($63.75); dinner main courses £13.50–£21.50 ($22.95–$36.55). AE, DC, MC, V. Mon–Fri 12:30–2:30pm; Mon–Sat 6:30–11pm. Closed bank holidays. Tube: South Kensington. CONTINENTAL.

After this former Victorian storefront was refurbished following a fire, it became one classy joint, like an elegant restaurant you might find in a town in the heart of France. It has a fitting ambience for enjoying some of South Ken's finest food. Chef Bryan Webb prepares a mixture of classical French and *cuisine moderne,* always following his own creative impulses and good culinary sense and style. The menu reflects the best of the season's offerings. A typical lunch might begin with a red-wine risotto with radicchio and sun-dried tomato pesto, followed with sautéed scallops with creamed chicory, and ending with rhubarb sorbet. At dinner, main courses might include rack of lamb with tapenade and wild garlic, or grilled tuna with Provençal vegetables. An aperitif bar, extra tables, and a pair of semi-private alcoves are in the lower dining room.

MODERATE

Café Lazeez. 93-95 Old Brompton Rd., SW7. ☎ **020/7581-9932.** Reservations recommended. Main courses £7–£15 ($11.90–$25.50). AE, DC, MC, V. Daily 1pm–midnight. Tube: South Kensington. INDIAN.

Its most devoted fans claim it's the best Indian restaurant in London, but the competition is too stiff in the category. Nonetheless, Café Lezeez surfaces near the top. Downstairs is a lively café-bar with live music such as jazz on weekends. Upstairs is the more formal restaurant. The decor reflects a sleek modern European eatery that doesn't much resemble an Indian restaurant at all. Very fresh ingredients go into the carefully prepared dishes, with all sorts of sensations assaulting your taste buds. Many discerning diners come here for the succulent and spicy meats cooked in a tandoor oven, but there is so much more if you want to experiment. The spicy lamb chops are marinated in honey and soy sauce, then baked. The lamb dishes are superb, as is a fiery but delectable chili chicken. Spicy spring lamb with okra is another chef's specialty; the rice dishes are superb, and marvelous things are done with eggplant.

The Collection. 264 Brompton Rd., SW3. ☎ **020/7225-1212.** Reservations recommended. Main courses £12–£16 ($20.40–$27.20); set-price menu £35 ($59.50). AE, DC, MC, V. Mon–Sat noon–3pm and 6:30–11pm, Sun 6–11pm. Tube: South Kensington. INTERNATIONAL/MODERN BRITISH.

This is a temple to voyeurism and the vanities, catering to the aesthetics and preoccupations of the fashion industry. It occupies an echoing warehouse; the only access is by a 30-foot underlit catwalk that emulates what you'd expect to find at a showing of next season's *couture.* Don't worry about a snobbish chill: Manager Julian Shaw is one of the most adept and humorous in London. Yummy menu items include crispy duck with *yaki soba* noodles; sesame-crusted tuna steak with sweet potatoes and *bok choi;* and pan-fried calves liver with sage and onions. Incidentally, don't overlook this site as a venue for your after-dark barhopping.

KENSINGTON

MODERATE

The Enterprise. 35 Walton St., SW3. ☎ **020/7584-3148.** Reservations accepted only for lunch. Main courses £9.65–£13.95 ($16.40–$23.70). AE, MC, V. Daily 12:30–2:30pm, Sat–Sun 12:30–3:30pm, Mon–Sat 7–11pm, and Sun 7–10:20pm (the bar is open all day). Tube: South Kensington. BRITISH/EUROPEAN.

Its proximity to Harrods attracts both regulars and out-of-towners loaded down with packages. Although the joint is cruisy at night (whatever your preference), during the day it attracts the ladies-who-lunch crowd. The kitchen serves very respectable traditional English fare as well as European favorites, all prepared with fresh ingredients. Featured dishes include fried salmon cakes with perfectly done fries and grilled steak with fries and salad. They will prepare an entrecôte with frites if that's what pleases you—actually, the juicy, properly aged, and flavorful thin French-style slice of beef is about the best you can have in London.

Foundation. Harvey Nichols Department Store (ground floor), 108–125 Knightsbridge, SW1. ☎ **020/7201-8000.** Main courses £10–£14 ($17–$23.80), 2-course set lunch (Mon–Fri and Sun) £14.50–£16.50 ($24.65–$28.05), 2-course set dinner £15–£19.50 ($25.50–$33.15). Daily noon–3:30pm and Mon–Sat 6:30–11pm. AE, DC, MC, V. Tube: Knightsbridge. CONTINENTAL/ASIAN.

Entered from Seville Street, this cavernous restaurant is in the basement of the famed department store. The setting evokes an old-fashioned nightclub with big mirrors. Behind the large bar there's a wall of cascading water. The cookery is first class and portions are generous, the prices kept within reason. The store secures very fresh seafood daily along with the choices of whatever products are good and seasonal. The breast of guinea fowl with garbanzo beans, Spanish chorizo sausage and spinach is a delight, as is the sea bass with baby fennel. Salt cod appears with truffled green beans, and linguine is served studded with fresh mussels and clams. Save room for the caramel ripple cheesecake.

NOTTING HILL

MODERATE

✪ **Bali Sugar Club.** 33A All Saints Rd., W11. ☎ **020/7221-4477.** Main courses £12–£17 ($20.40–$28.90); set lunch menu £18.50 ($31.45). AE, DC, MC, V. Daily 12:30–2:30pm and 6:30–11pm. Tube: Westbourne Park. FUSION.

The owners originally opened The Sugar Club here and achieved fame across London. But they have now moved and turned the original site into Bali Sugar, which is every bit as good as the original. They have acquired the talents of Claudio Aprile, one of Canada's most exciting and innovative young chefs. He brings an exotic, bold, and extraordinary new look to fusion cuisine which has been labeled here "Southern Hemisphere Pacific Rim Modern Mediterranean Cosmopolitan British cookery"—whatever. Claudio has created a menu using Japanese and South American ingredients to great effect. For starters, dig into his Peruvian ceviche with king prawn, coconut, lime, and sweet potato, followed by rare tuna. The taste is magical. His cured salmon is perfect and wonderfully accompanied by a side order of wasabi mash. Try also the breast of chicken integrated distinctively with an irresistibly rich fufu. The two-floor eatery is a delight with a sunken garden, and there's a separate no-smoking floor.

The Cow. 89 Westbourne Park Rd., W2. ☎ **020/7221-0021.** Reservations required. Main courses £12.20–£15.50 ($20.75–$26.35); fixed-price dinner Sun–Tues £15.50–£17.95 ($26.35–$30.50). MC, V. Mon–Sat 7–11pm and Sun 12:30–3:30pm for brunch and 7:30–10:30pm; bar daily noon–1pm. Tube: Westbourne Grove. BRITISH.

You don't have to be a young fashion victim to enjoy the superb viands served here. Tom Conran (son of entrepreneur Sir Terence Conran) holds forth nightly in this increasingly hip Notting Hill watering hole. It resembles an Irish pub, but the accents you'll hear are trustafarian rather than street-smart Dublin. With a pint of Fuller's or London Pride firmly in hand, you can linger over the modern European menu, which changes daily but is likely to include ox tongue poached in milk; or mussels in curry and cream. The seafood selections are especially delectable. "The Cow Special"—a half-dozen Irish rock oysters with a pint of Guinness or a glass of wine for £8 ($13.60)—is the star of the show. A raw bar downstairs serves other fresh seafood choices. To finish, skip the filtered coffee served upstairs (it's wretched), and opt for an espresso downstairs.

Prince Bonaparte. 80 Chepstow Rd., W2. ☎ **020/7313-9491.** Reservations required. Main courses £7–£9.50 ($11.90–$16.15). MC, V. Mon and Wed–Fri noon–11pm; Tues 5:30–10:30pm; Sun 12:30–10pm. Tube: Notting Hill Gate or Westbourne Park. INTERNATIONAL.

This offbeat restaurant serves great pub grub in what was a grungy boozer in the days before Notting Hill Gate became fashionable. The pub is filled with mismatched furniture from schools and churches; jazz and lazy blues fill the air, competing with the babble. It may seem at first that the staff doesn't have its act together, but once the food arrives, you won't care one way or the other: It's very good. The menu roams the world for inspiration: Moroccan chicken with couscous is as good or better than any you'll find in Marrakesh; seafood risotto is delicious, as is the salad of beet root, new potatoes, walnuts, and eggplant. Roast lamb, tender and juicy, appears on the traditional Sunday menu. We recommend the London Pride or Grolsch to wash it all down.

5 Afternoon Tea

Everyone should indulge in a formal afternoon tea at least once while in London. This relaxing, drawn out, civilized affair usually consists of three courses, all elegantly served on delicate china: first, dainty finger sandwiches (with the crusts cut off, of course); then fresh-baked scones served with jam and deliciously decadent clotted cream (also known as Devonshire cream); and lastly, an array of bite-size sweets. All the while, an indulgent server keeps the pot of your choice fresh at hand. Sometimes ports or aperitif are on offer for your final course. It is a quintessential British experience, and here are a few of our favorite places to indulge.

MAYFAIR

Brown's Hotel. 29–34 Albemarle St., W1. ☎ **020/7493-6020.** Reservations not accepted. Afternoon tea £19.95 ($33.90). AE, DC, MC, V. Daily 3–5:45pm. Tube: Green Park.

Along with the Ritz, Brown's ranks as one of the most chic venues for tea in London. Tea is served in the drawing room, done in English antiques, oil paintings, and floral chintz; it's an appropriate venue for such an affair. Give your name to the concierge upon arrival; he'll seat you at one of the clusters of sofas and settees or at low tables. There's a choice of 10 teas, plus sandwiches, scones, and pastries (all made in the hotel kitchens) that are rolled around on a trolley for your selection.

The Palm Court. In the Sheraton Park Lane Hotel, Piccadilly, W1. ☎ **020/7290-7328.** Reservations recommended. Afternoon tea £17 ($28.90), with a glass of Park Lane champagne £23 ($39.10). AE, DC, MC, V. Daily 3–6pm. Tube: Hyde Park Corner or Green Park.

This is one of the great London favorites for tea. Restored to its former charm, the lounge has an atmosphere straight from 1927, with a domed yellow-and-white–glass ceiling, torchieres, and palms in Compton stoneware *jardinières.* A delightful afternoon tea that includes a long list of different teas is served daily. Many guests come here after the theater for a sandwich and drink. A pianist plays every weekday afternoon.

Ritz Palm Court. In The Ritz Hotel, Piccadilly, W1. ☎ **020/7493-8181.** Reservations required at least 8 weeks in advance. Jeans and sneakers not acceptable. Jacket and tie required for men. Afternoon tea £24.50 ($41.65). AE, DC, MC, V. 2 seatings daily at 3:30 and 5pm. Tube: Green Park.

This is the most fashionable place in London to order afternoon tea—and the hardest to get into without reserving way in advance. Its spectacular setting is straight out of *The Great Gatsby,* complete with marble steps and a baroque fountain. You have your choice of a long list of teas, served with delectable sandwiches and luscious pastries.

✪ **St. James Restaurant & The Fountain Restaurant.** In Fortnum & Mason, 181 Piccadilly, W1. ☎ **020/7734-8040.** In the St. James, full tea £16.50 ($28.05). In The Fountain, full teas £11.95 ($20.30). AE, DC, MC, V. St. James, Mon–Sat 3–5pm; The Fountain, Mon–Sat 3–6pm. Tube: Piccadilly Circus.

This pair of tea salons functions as a culinary showplace for London's most prestigious grocery store, Fortnum & Mason. The more formal of the two venues, the St. James, on the venerable store's fourth floor, is a pale green and beige homage to formal Edwardian taste. More rapid, less formal, and better tuned to the hectic pace of London shoppers and London commuters is The Fountain Restaurant, on the street level, where a sense of tradition and manners is very much a part of the teatime experience, but in a less opulent setting. The quantities of food served in both venues are usually ample enough to be defined as full-fledged early suppers for most theatergoers.

PICCADILLY CIRCUS & LEICESTER SQUARE

The Blue Room. 3 Bateman St., W1. ☎ **020/7437-4827.** Reservations not accepted. Cup of tea £1.20 ($2.05), cakes and pastries 60p–£2.50 ($1–$4.25), sandwiches £3–£4.50 ($5.10–$7.65). No credit cards. Mon–Sat 9am–midnight; Sun 10am–11pm. Tube: Leicester Sq.

Nothing about this place has been patterned on the grand dame tearooms mentioned above, where tea drinking is presented as an intricate and elaborate social ritual. What you'll find here instead is a cozy, somewhat eccentric enclave lined with the artworks of some of the regular patrons, battered sofas that might have come out of somebody's college dormitory, and a gathering of likable urban hipsters to whom very little is sacred. You can enjoy dozens of varieties of tea, including herbals, served in steaming mugs. Lots of arty and eccentric types gather here during the late afternoon, emulating some of the rituals of the old-fashioned tea service but with absolutely none of the hauteur.

COVENT GARDEN & THE STRAND

MJ Bradley's. 9 King St., WC2. ☎ **020/7240-5178.** Cup of tea 95p ($1.60), sandwiches £1.85–£4.50 ($3.15–$7.65) each. AE, DC, DISC, MC, V. Daily 8am–11:30pm. Tube: Covent Garden or Charing Cross.

Although it defines itself as a coffeehouse, many of MJ Bradley's fans resolutely drop in for a cup of as many as 20 different kinds of tea, everything from Earl Grey and Assam to such herbal brews as peppermint. Outfitted like a brasserie, it manages to mingle nostalgia with modern wall sculptures. If you're hungry, consider one of the imaginative sandwiches with fillings of herb-flavored cream cheese with sun-dried tomatoes.

✪ **Palm Court at the Waldorf Meridien.** In the Waldorf Hotel, Aldwych, WC2. ☎ **020/7836-2400.** Reservations required for tea dance. Jacket and tie required for men at tea dance. Afternoon tea £18–£21 ($30.60–$35.70); tea dance £25–£28 ($42.50–$47.60). AE, DC, MC, V. Afternoon tea Mon–Fri 3–5:30pm; tea dance Sat 2:30–5pm; Sun 4–6:30pm. Tube: Covent Garden.

The Waldorf's Palm Court combines afternoon tea with afternoon dancing (the foxtrot, quickstep, and the waltz). The Palm Court is aptly compared to a 1920s movie set (which it has been several times in its long life). You can order tea on a terrace or in a pavilion the size of a ballroom lit by skylights. On tea-dancing days, the orchestra leader will conduct such favorites as "Ain't She Sweet" and "Yes, Sir, That's My Baby," as a butler in a cutaway asks if you want a cucumber sandwich.

KNIGHTSBRIDGE

✪ **The Georgian Restaurant.** On the 4th floor of Harrods, 87–135 Brompton Rd., SW1. ☎ **020/7225-6800.** High tea £17.50 ($29.75) or £23 ($39.10) with Harrods champagne per person. AE, DC, MC, V. Teatime Mon–Sat 3:30–5:15pm (last order). Tube: Knightsbridge.

As long as anyone can remember, teatime at Harrods has been one of the most distinctive features of Europe's most famous department store. A flood of visitors is somehow gracefully herded into a high-volume but nevertheless elegant room. Many come here expressly for the tea ritual, where staff haul silver pots and trolleys laden with pastries and sandwiches through the cavernous dining hall. Most exotic is Betigala tea, a rare blend from China, similar to Lapsang Souchong.

KENSINGTON

✪ **The Orangery.** In the gardens of Kensington Palace, W8. ☎ **020/7376-0239.** Reservations not accepted. Pot of tea £2 ($3.40), summer cakes and puddings £1.95–£4.25 ($3.30–$7.25), sandwiches £6 ($10.20). MC, V. Daily 10am–5pm; closing time 1/2 hour before gates close (usually between 4 and 5pm) in winter. Mar–Oct 10am–6pm; Nov–Mar 10am–4pm. Tube: High St. Kensington or Queensway.

In its way, the Orangery is the most amazing place for mid-afternoon tea in the world. Set about 50 yards north of Kensington Palace, it occupies a long and narrow garden pavilion built in 1704 by Queen Anne as a site for her tea parties. In homage to that monarch's original intentions, rows of potted orange trees bask in sunlight from soaring windows, and tea is still served amid Corinthian columns, ruddy-colored bricks, and a pair of Grinling Gibbons woodcarvings. The menu includes lunchtime soups and sandwiches, which come with a salad and a portion of upscale potato chips known as "kettle chips." There's also an array of different teas, served with high style, usually accompanied by freshly baked scones with clotted cream and jam, and Belgian chocolate cake.

6 Pubs

ST. JAMES

Red Lion. 2 Duke of York St. (off Jermy St.), SW1. ☎ **020/7930-2030.** Sandwiches £2.75 ($4.70). No credit cards. Mon–Fri 11:30am–11pm; Sat noon–11pm. Tube: Piccadilly Circus.

This little Victorian pub, with its early-1900s decorations and mirrors 150 years old, has been compared in spirit to Edouard Manet's painting *A Bar at the Folies-Bergère*. You can order pre-made sandwiches, but once they're gone you're out of luck. On Saturday, homemade fish-and-chips are also served. Wash down your meal with Ind Coope's fine ales or the house's special beer, Burton's, an unusual brew made of spring water from the Midlands town of Bourton-on-Trent.

LEICESTER SQUARE

✪ **Salisbury.** 90 St. Martin's Lane, WC2. ☎ **020/7836-5863.** Snacks from £3.50 ($5.95). AE, DC, MC, V. Mon–Sat 11am–11pm, Sun noon–10:30pm. Tube: Leicester Sq.

Salisbury's glittering cut-glass mirrors reflect the faces of English stage stars (and hopefuls) sitting around the curved buffet-style bar. A less prominent place to dine is the old-fashioned wall banquette with its copper-topped tables and art-nouveau decor. The pub's specialty—home-cooked pies set out in a buffet cabinet with salads—is really quite good and inexpensive. A hot and a cold food buffet is available at all times.

SOHO

Old Coffee House. 49 Beak St., W1. ☎ **020/7437-2197.** Main courses £2.75–£4.50 ($4.70–$7.65). No credit cards. Mon–Sat 11am–11pm, Sun noon–3pm and 7–10:30pm. Tube: Oxford Circus or Piccadilly Circus.

Once honored as "Soho Pub of the Year" by the *Good Pub Guide*, the Old Coffee House takes its name from the coffeehouse heyday of 18th-century London, when coffee was called "the devil's brew." The pub still serves pots of filtered coffee. Have a drink at the long, narrow bar, or retreat to the upstairs restaurant, where you can enjoy good pub food at lunch, including steak-and-kidney pie, one of three vegetarian dishes, scampi-and-chips, or a burger and fries.

BLOOMSBURY

Museum Tavern. 49 Great Russell St., WC1. ☎ **020/7242-8987.** Bar snacks £2.50–£6.50 ($4.25–$11.05). AE, MC, V. Mon–Sat 11am–11pm, Sun noon–10:30pm. Tube: Holborn or Tottenham Court Rd.

Across the street from the British Museum, this pub (ca. 1703) retains most of its antique trappings: velvet, oak paneling, and cut glass. It lies right in the center of the University of London area and is popular with writers, publishers, and researchers from the museum. (Supposedly, Karl Marx wrote over meals here.) Traditional English food is served with shepherd's pie, sausages cooked in English cider, and chef's specials on the hot-food menu. Cold fare includes turkey-and-ham pie, ploughman's lunch, and salads. Several English ales, cold lagers, cider, Guinness, wines, and spirits are available. Food and coffee are served all day; the pub gets crowded at lunchtime.

HOLBORN

Cittie of Yorke. 22 High Holborn, WC1. ☎ **020/742-7670.** Snacks from £3 ($5.10). AE, DC, MC, V. Mon–Sat noon–3pm and 6–10pm; Sun noon–3:30pm and 7–10:30pm. Tube: Holborn Chancery Lane.

Boasts the longest bar in all of Britain, rafters ascending to the heavens, and a long row of immense wine vats, all of which give it the air of a great medieval hall—

appropriate since a pub has existed at this location since 1430. Samuel Smiths is on tap, and the bar offers novelties such as chocolate-orange-flavored vodka.

THE CITY

Bow Wine Vaults. 10 Bow Chuchyard, EC4. ☎ **020/7248-1121.** Main courses £7.50–£15 ($12.75–$25.50). AE, DC, MC, V. Mon–Fri 11am–11pm. Tube: Mansion House, Bank or St. Paul's.

Bow Wine Vaults has existed since long before the wine-bar craze began in the 1970s. One of the most famous wine bars of London, it attracts cost-conscious diners and drinkers to its vaulted cellars for such traditional fare as deep-fried Camembert, lobster ravioli, and a mixed grill, along with fish. More elegant meals, served in the street-level dining room, include mussels in cider sauce, English wild mushrooms in puff pastry, beef Wellington, and steak with brown-butter sauce. Adjacent to the restaurant is a cocktail bar that's popular with City employees after work (open weekdays from 11:30am–8pm).

BELGRAVIA

✪ **Grenadier.** 18 Wilton Row, SW1. ☎ **020/7235-3074.** Main courses £12.95–£19.95 ($22–$33.90). AE, DC, MC, V. Mon–Sat noon–3pm and 6–10pm, Sun noon–3:30pm and 7–10:30pm. Tube: Hyde Park Corner.

Tucked away in a mews, the Grenadier is one of London's reputedly haunted pubs. Aside from the poltergeist, the basement houses the original bar and skittles alley used by the Duke of Wellington's officers on leave from fighting Napoléon. The bar is nearly always crowded. Lunch and dinner are offered daily—even on Sunday, when it's a tradition to drink Bloody Marys here. In the stalls along the side, you can order good-tasting fare based on seasonal ingredients. Well-prepared dishes include pork Grenadier and chicken and Stilton roulade. Snacks like fish and chips are available at the bar.

CHELSEA

King's Head & Eight Bells. 50 Cheyne Walk, SW3. ☎ **020/7352-1820.** Main courses £6.25–£8.75 ($10.65–$14.90). MC, V. Mon–Sat 11am–11pm, Sun noon–10:30pm. Tube: Sloane Sq.

Many distinguished personalities once lived near this historic Thames-side pub; a short stroll will take you to the former homes of Carlyle, Swinburne, and George Eliot. In other days, press gangs used to roam these parts of Chelsea seeking lone travelers to abduct for a life at sea. Today, it's popular with stage and TV celebrities as well as writers. The best English beers are served here, as well as a good selection of reasonably priced wine. The menu features homemade specials of the day, such as fish and chips, and includes at least one vegetable main dish. On Sunday, a roast of the day is served.

SOUTHWARK

The George Inn. Off 77 Borough High St., SE1. ☎ **020/7407-2056.** Main courses in the bar cost from £4.50–£6 ($7.65–$10.20); main courses in the restaurant cost from £10–£12 ($17–$20.40). AE, MC, and V. Mon–Sat 11am–11pm. Tube: Borough, London Bridge.

Preserved by the National Trust, the existing structure was built to replace the original pub, destroyed in the Great Fire. The pub's accolades date to 1598, when it was reviewed as a "faire inn for the receipt of travellers." No longer an inn, it's still a great place to enjoy Flowers Original, Boddingtons, and Restoration Ale, a brand that's specially brewed for this inn at a nearby location.

4 Exploring London

London is more eclectic and electric than it's been in years. Some even think it's surpassed New York for sheer energy, outrageous fashion, trendy restaurants, and a nightlife that's second to none.

But we don't want to mislead. Although London is more open and dynamic than it's been since 1969, it's not one giant house party. There are problems here, as elsewhere, that all the trendy restaurants and pricey boutiques in the world cannot obliterate. The gulf between rich and poor continues to widen, and violent crime, once relatively rare, is on the rise.

And although the cool youth culture is grabbing headlines, it's not all there is to London these days. What makes the city so fascinating is its cultural diversity. It seems that half the world is flocking there, not just from the far-flung former colonies of the once great British Empire, but also from Algeria, Argentina, China, and Senegal. And these recent transplants are transforming a city once maligned as a drab, stuffy metropolis with their talent and new ideas. In the London of today, where everything's changing, only the queen appears the same. (After she's gone, even the House of Windsor may be in for a shake-up.)

In this chapter, we can explore only a fraction of what's exciting in London. We went in search of what's causing the hottest buzz in shopping and nightlife, but we also provide plenty of detail about London's time-tested treasures: ancient monuments, literary shrines, walking tours, Parliament debates, royal castles, waxworks, palaces, cathedrals, and royal parks.

Note: As a rule, and unless otherwise stated on the listings below, children's prices at London attractions apply to those age 16 and under. You must be 60 years of age or older to obtain available senior-citizen discounts at some attractions. For students to get available discounted admissions they must have a valid student ID card.

Suggested Itineraries

For the first-time visitor, the question is never what to do, but what to do first.

If You Have 1 Day

Make sure to see Westminster Abbey, with its Poets' Corner inside. After you've visited the abbey, walk over to see Big Ben and the Houses of

Parliament. Also witness the Changing of the Guard at Buckingham Palace, if it's being held, and then walk over to 10 Downing St., home of the prime minister. For dinner, try a Covent Garden restaurant, such as Porter's English Restaurant. For a nightcap, head over to the Red Lion, 2 Duke of York St., in Mayfair, where you can enjoy a lager in the ultimate Victorian pub.

If You Have 2 Days

Spend your first day as above. Devote a good part of the second day to exploring the British Museum, one of the world's biggest and best museums. Spend the afternoon visiting the Tower of London and seeing the collection of crown jewels (expect slow-moving lines). For dinner, go to one of London's landmark restaurants such as Simpson's-in-the-Strand, 100 The Strand, where your favorite roast will be carved at your table.

If You Have 3 Days

Spend days 1 and 2 as above. On the third day, go to the National Gallery, facing Trafalgar Square, in the morning. Then enjoy the afternoon at Madame Tussaud's Waxworks. It's also worthwhile to walk around St. James's. In the evening, try to catch a performance at the South Bank Centre, site of the Royal Festival Hall.

If You Have 4 Days

Spend the first 3 days as above. On the morning of the 4th day, head for The City, the financial district of London in the East End, where you can explore Sir Christopher Wren's St. Paul's Cathedral. Spend a few hours strolling The City and visit a few of its many metropolitan attractions. In the late afternoon, head down King's Road in Chelsea to check out the boutiques, followed by dinner at a Chelsea restaurant.

If You Have 5 Days

On the 5th day, explore the Victoria and Albert Museum in the morning, or perhaps the Tate Gallery (you can plan to have lunch at its restaurant). Spend the rest of the afternoon wandering through the gallery enjoying its masterpieces. Finally, see where history was made during the dark days of World War II by visiting the Cabinet War Rooms at Clive Steps, where Churchill directed the British operations against the Nazis. If you haven't already crammed in as many West End shows as you can on the first 4 nights, attend the theater this final evening.

1 The Top Attractions

✪ **Tower of London.** Tower Hill, EC3. ☎ **020/7709-0765;** www.hrp.org.uk. Admission £11 ($18.70) adults, £8.30 ($14.10) students and seniors, £7.30 ($12.40) children, free for children under 5; £33 ($56.10) family ticket for 5 (but no more than 2 adults). Mar–Oct Mon–Sat 9am–5pm, Sun 10am–5pm; off-season Tues–Sat 9am–4pm, Sun and Mon 10am–4pm. Tube: Tower Hill.

This ancient fortress continues to pack in visitors because of its macabre associations with all the legendary figures who were imprisoned and/or executed here. James Street once wrote, "There are more spooks to the square foot than in any other building in the whole of haunted Britain. Headless bodies, bodiless heads, phantom soldiers, icy blasts, clanking chains—you name them, the Tower's got them." Plan on spending a lot of time here.

One-hour tours are given by the Yeoman Warders at frequent intervals, starting at 9:25am from the Middle Tower near the main entrance. The tour includes the Chapel Royal of St. Peter and Vincula (St. Peter in Chains). The last guided walk starts at

Central London Sights

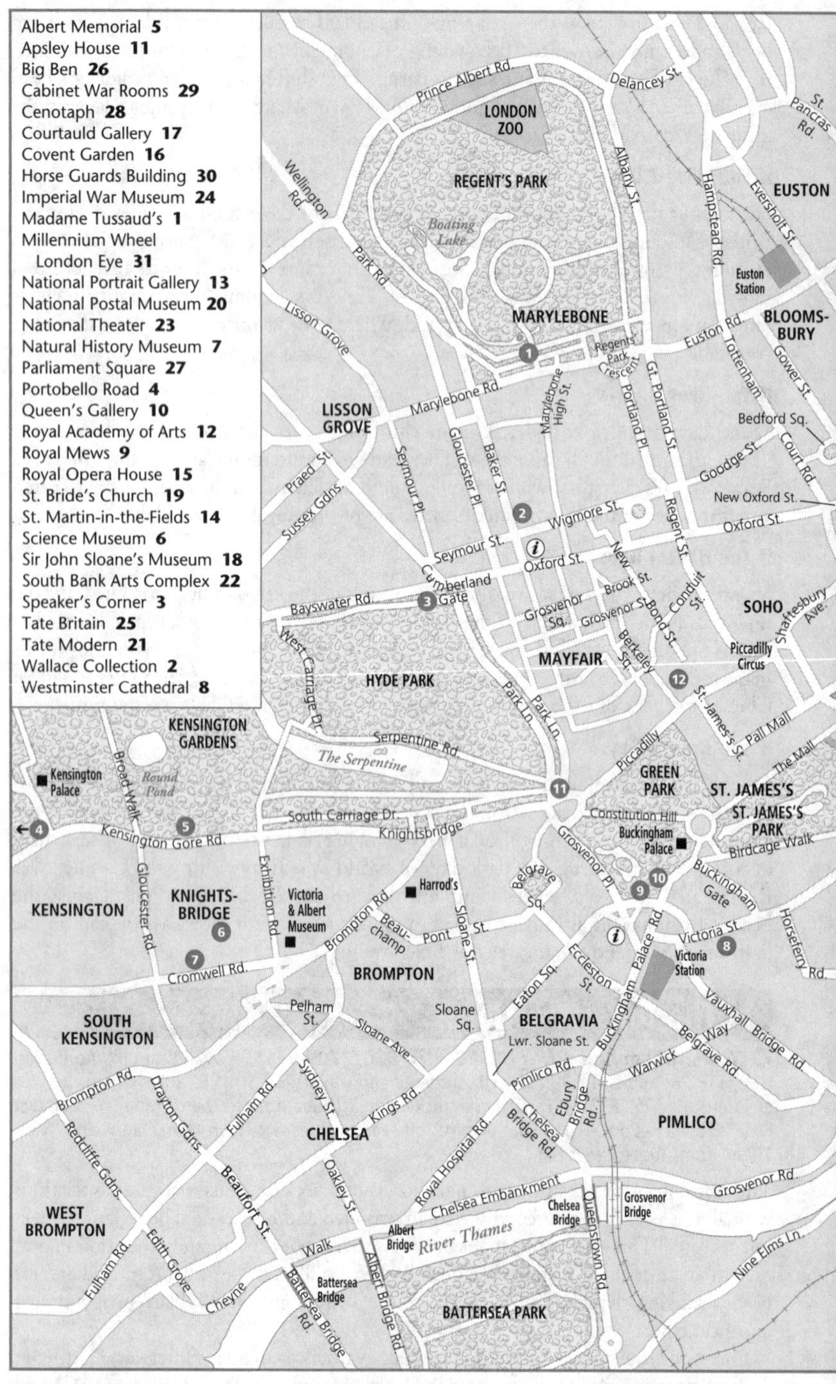

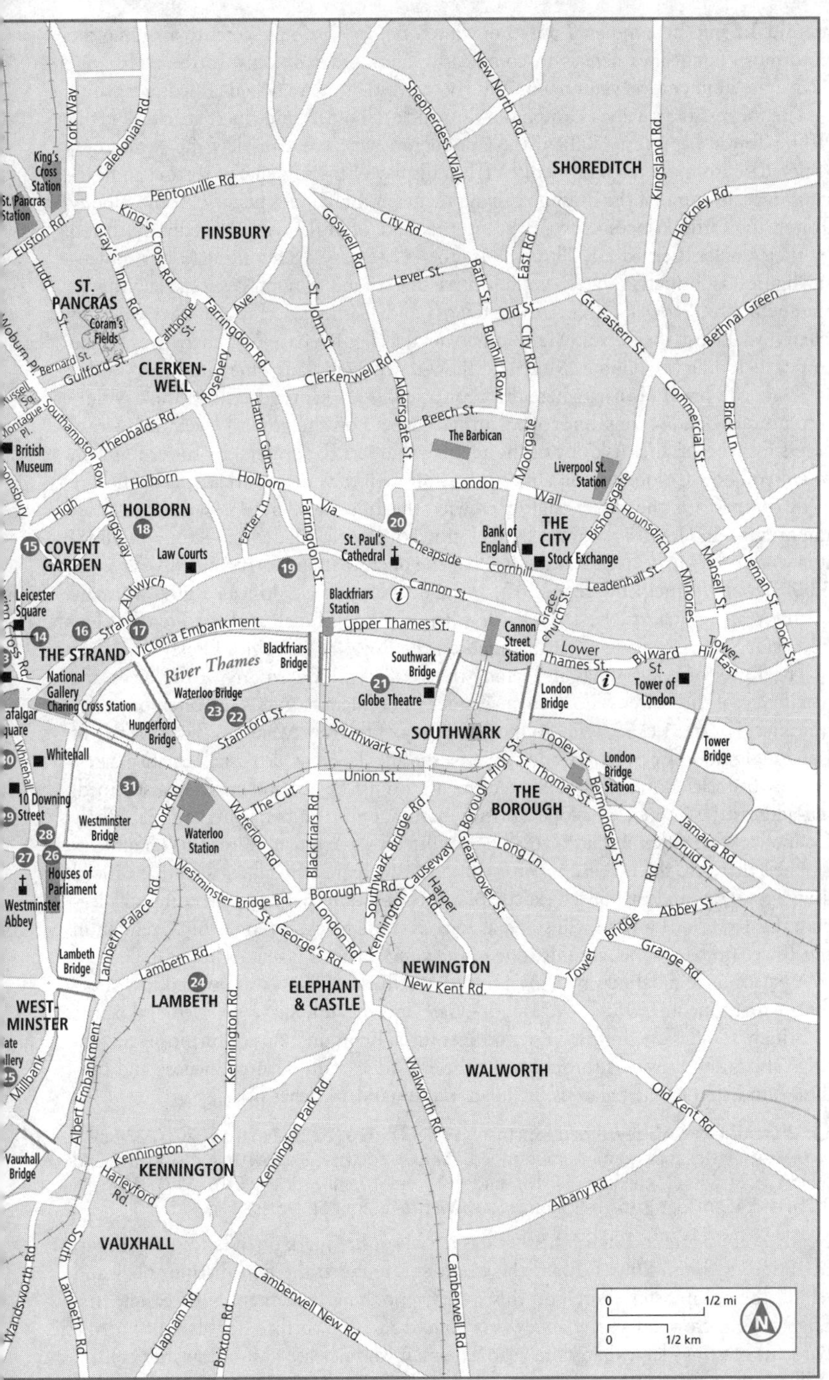

SHOREDITCH
FINSBURY
ST. PANCRAS
CLERKEN-WELL
HOLBORN
COVENT GARDEN
THE STRAND
THE CITY
SOUTHWARK
THE BOROUGH
NEWINGTON
ELEPHANT & CASTLE
LAMBETH
WEST-MINSTER
WALWORTH
KENNINGTON
VAUXHALL
York Way
Caledonian Rd.
King's Cross Station
St. Pancras Station
Pentonville Rd.
New North Rd.
Shepherdess Walk
Kingsland Rd.
Hackney Rd.
Goswell Rd.
City Rd.
East Rd.
King's Cross Rd.
Gray's Inn Rd.
Euston Rd.
Judd St.
Lever St.
Bath St.
Old St.
Gt. Eastern St.
Bethnal Green
Coram's Fields
Calthorpe St.
Farringdon Rd.
Rosebery Ave.
St. John St.
Bunhill Row
City Rd.
Bernard St.
Guilford St.
Clerkenwell Rd.
Aldersgate St.
Commercial St.
Brick Ln.
Southampton Row
Montague Pl.
Theobalds Rd.
Hatton Gdns.
Beech St.
The Barbican
Moorgate
Liverpool St. Station
British Museum
Holborn
Holborn Via.
London Wall
Bishopsgate
Houndsditch
High
Kingsway
Fetter Ln.
Farringdon St.
St. Paul's Cathedral
Cheapside
Bank of England
Stock Exchange
Cornhill
Leadenhall St.
Minories
Mansell St.
Leman St.
Law Courts
Cannon St.
Leicester Square
Aldwych
Strand
Blackfriars Station
Victoria Embankment
Upper Thames St.
Cannon Street Station
Gracechurch St.
Lower Thames St.
Byward St.
Tower Hill East
Dock St.
Blackfriars Bridge
Southwark Bridge
River Thames
National Gallery
Charing Cross Station
Waterloo Bridge
Globe Theatre
London Bridge
Tower of London
Hungerford Bridge
Stamford St.
Southwark St.
Tooley St.
London Bridge Station
Tower Bridge
Whitehall
Union St.
St. Thomas St.
Bermondsey St.
York Rd.
The Cut
Waterloo Rd.
Blackfriars Rd.
Southwark Bridge Rd.
Borough High St.
10 Downing Street
Westminster Bridge
Waterloo Station
Jamaica Rd.
Druid St.
Long Ln.
Houses of Parliament
Westminster Abbey
Westminster Bridge Rd.
Borough Rd.
London Rd.
Kennington Causeway
Harper Rd.
Great Dover St.
Rd.
Abbey St.
Lambeth Palace Rd.
St. George's Rd.
Tower Bridge Rd.
Grange Rd.
Lambeth Bridge
Lambeth Rd.
New Kent Rd.
Kennington Rd.
Millbank
Albert Embankment
Kennington Park Rd.
Walworth Rd.
Old Kent Rd.
Vauxhall Bridge
Kennington Ln.
Harleyford Rd.
Albany Rd.
Wandsworth Rd.
South Lambeth Rd.
Clapham Rd.
Brixton Rd.
Camberwell New Rd.
Camberwell Rd.
0
1/2 mi
0
1/2 km
N
14
15
16
17
18
19
20
21
22
23
24
26
27
28
31

around 3:25pm in summer, 2:35pm in winter. *Insider's tip:* The secret to avoiding the notoriously long lines here is to come early. The hordes descend in the afternoon. Arrive the moment the gates open. And try to avoid Sundays, when crowds are awful.

The fortress is actually a compound, in which the oldest and finest structure is the White Tower, begun by William the Conqueror. Here you can view the Armouries, which date from the reign of Henry VIII. A display of instruments of torture and execution recalls some of the most ghastly moments in the Tower's history. At the Bloody Tower, the Little Princes (Edward V and the duke of York) were allegedly murdered by their uncle, Richard III. Through Traitors' Gate passed such ill-fated but romantic figures as Robert Devereux, known as the second earl of Essex, a favorite of Elizabeth I. At Tower Green, Anne Boleyn and Catherine Howard, two wives of Henry VIII, lost their lives. Many other notable figures have lost their lives at the tower, including Sir Thomas More and the 9-day queen, Lady Jane Grey.

To see the **Jewel House,** where the Crown Jewels are kept, go early in the day during summer because long lines often form. Since it's on the ground level, there's easy access for wheelchairs. Ask one of the Yeoman Warders (Beefeaters) in Tudor uniform to tell you how Colonel Blood almost made off with the crown and regalia in the late 17th century. Of the three English crowns, the Imperial State Crown is the most important—in fact, it's the most famous crown on earth. Made for Victoria in 1837, it is worn today by Queen Elizabeth when she opens Parliament. Studded with some 3,000 jewels (principally diamonds), it includes the Black Prince's Ruby, worn by Henry V at Agincourt (the 1415 battle where the English defeated the French). The 530-carat Star of Africa is a cut diamond on the Royal Sceptre with Cross.

The Tower of London has an evening ritual called the **Ceremony of the Keys,** the locking up of the Tower. The Yeoman Warder will explain to guests the ceremony's significance. For free tickets, write to the Ceremony of the Key, Waterloo Block, Tower of London, London EC3N 4AB, and request a specific date, but also list alternative dates. At least 6 weeks' notice is required. All requests must be accompanied by a stamped, self-addressed stamped envelope (British stamps only) or two International Reply Coupons. With ticket in hand, you'll be admitted by a Yeoman Warder at 9:35pm.

Then there are the ravens. Six of them, plus two spares, are all registered as official Tower residents and each is fed exactly 6 ounces of rations per day. According to a legend, the Tower of London will stand as long as those black, ominous birds remain in the Tower (to be on the safe side, one of the wings of each raven is clipped).

A palace once inhabited by King Edward I in the late 1200s was opened to visitors for the first time in 1993. Above Traitor's Gate, it is the only surviving medieval palace in Britain. Guides are dressed in period costumes. Reproductions of furniture and fittings, including Edward's throne, evoke the era, along with burning incense and candles. Admission to the palace is included in the standard ticket price.

✪ **Westminster Abbey.** Broad Sanctuary, SW1. ☎ **020/7222-7110** or 020/7222-5897; www.westminster.abbey.org. Admission £5 ($8.50) adults, £3 ($5.10) for students and seniors, £2 ($3.40) children 11–18, under 11 free, family ticket £10 ($17). Mon–Fri 9:15am–3:45pm, Sat 9:15am–1:45pm. Tube: Westminster or St. James's Park.

Nearly every figure in English history has left his or her mark on Westminster Abbey. In 1065, the Saxon king, Edward the Confessor, founded the Benedictine abbey and rebuilt the old minster church on this spot, overlooking Parliament Square. The first English king crowned in the abbey was Harold in 1066, before he was killed at the Battle of Hastings later that same year. The man who defeated him, Edward's cousin, William the Conqueror, was also crowned at the abbey; the coronation tradition has continued to the present day, broken only twice (Edward V and Edward VIII). Most

Tower of London

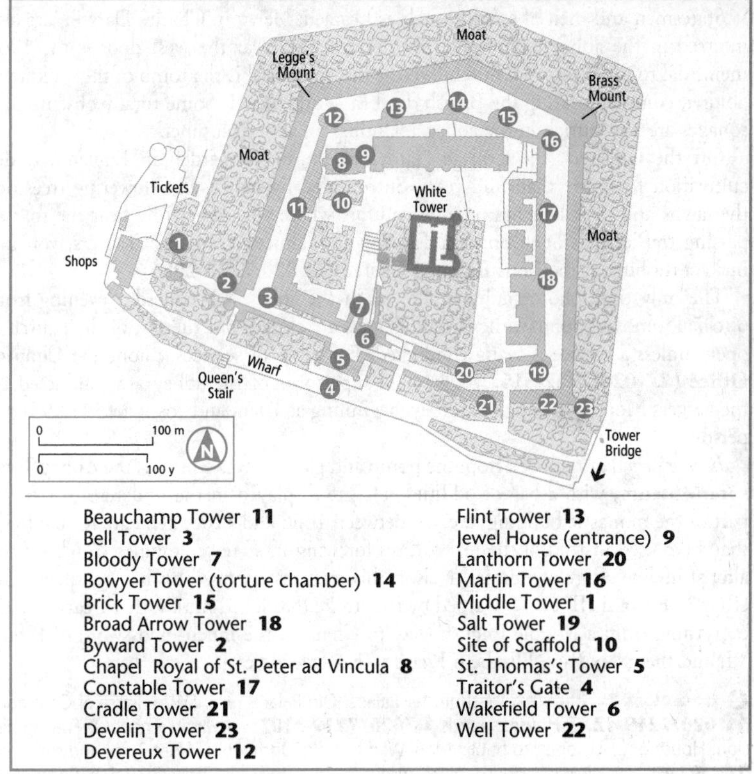

recently, in September 1997, the abbey served as the setting for the funeral of Diana, Princess of Wales.

Built on the site of the ancient lady chapel in the early 16th century, the Henry VII Chapel is one of the loveliest in Europe, with its fan vaulting, Knights of Bath banners, and Torrigiani-designed tomb of the king himself. Also here are the feuding half-sisters, ironically buried in the same tomb, Catholic Mary I and Protestant Elizabeth I (whose arch rival, Mary Queen of Scots, is entombed on the other side of the Henry VII Chapel). In one end of the chapel, you can stand on Cromwell's memorial stone and view the RAF chapel and its Battle of Britain memorial stained-glass window, unveiled in 1947 to honor the RAF.

You can also visit the most hallowed spot in the abbey, the shrine of Edward the Confessor (canonized in the 12th century). In the Saint's Chapel is the Coronation chair, made at the command of Edward I in 130 to display the Stone of Scone. Scottish kings were once crowned on this stone, which has since been returned to Scotland.

Another noted spot in the abbey is the **Poets' Corner,** to the right of the entrance to the Royal Chapel, with monuments to everybody—Chaucer, Shakespeare, "O Rare Ben Johnson" (his name misspelled), Samuel Johnson, the Brontë sisters, Thackeray, Dickens, Tennyson, Kipling, even the American Longfellow. The most stylized monument is Sir Jacob Epstein's sculptured bust of William Blake. A more recent tablet commemorates poet Dylan Thomas.

Statesmen and men of science, such as Disraeli, Newton, Charles Darwin, are also interred in the abbey or honored by monuments. Near the west door is the 1965 memorial to Sir Winston Churchill. Near this memorial is the tomb of the Unknown Soldier, commemorating the British dead in World War I. Some totally obscure personages are also buried in the abbey, including an abbey plumber.

Off the Cloisters, the College Garden is the oldest garden in England, under cultivation for more than 900 years. Surrounded by high walls, flowering trees dot the lawns and park benches provide comfort where you can hardly hear the roar of passing traffic. It is open only on Tuesday and Thursday. In the Cloisters, you can make a rubbing at the Brass Rubbing Center (☎ **020/7222-2085**).

The only time photography is allowed in the abbey is Wednesday evening from 6 to 7:45pm. On Sunday, the Royal Chapels are closed, but the rest of the church is open, unless a service is being conducted. For times of services, phone the **Chapter Office** (☎ **020/7222-5152**). Up to six supertours of the abbey are conducted by the vergers Monday through Saturday, beginning at 10am and costing £3 ($4.95) per person.

Insider's tip: Far removed from the pomp and glory of this edifice is the **Abbey Treasure Museum,** with a bag of oddities. They're displayed in the undercroft or crypt, part of the monastic buildings erected between 1066 and 1100. Here are royal effigies that were used instead of the real corpses for lying-in-state ceremonies. You'll see the almost lifelike effigy of Admiral Nelson (his mistress arranged his hair) and even the effigy of Edward III, his lip warped by the stroke that felled him. Other treats include everything from a Middle English lease to Chaucer, the much-used sword of Henry VI, and the Essex Ring Elizabeth I gave to her favorite earl.

✪ **Houses of Parliament.** Westminster Palace, Old Palace Yard, SW1. House of Commons ☎ **020/7219-4272;** House of Lords ☎ **020/7219-3107;** www.parliament.uk. Free admission. House of Lords open to public Mon–Wed from 2:30pm, Thurs from 3pm, and some Fridays (check by phone). House of Commons open to Mon–Tues 2:30–10:30pm; Wed 9:30am–10:30pm, Thurs 11:30am–7:30pm, Fri call ahead—not always open. Join line at St. Stephen's entrance. Tube: Westminster.

The Houses of Parliament, along with their trademark clock tower, are the ultimate symbol of London. They're the stronghold of Britain's democracy, the assemblies that effectively trimmed the sails of royal power. Both the House of Commons and the House of Lords are in the former royal Palace of Westminster, the king's residence until Henry VIII moved to Whitehall. The current Gothic Revival buildings date from 1840 and were designed by Charles Barry. (The earlier buildings were destroyed by fire in 1834.) Assisting Barry was Augustus Welby Pugin, who designed the paneled ceilings, tiled floors, stained glass, clocks, fireplaces, umbrella stands, and even the inkwells. There are more than 1,000 rooms and 2 miles of corridors.

The clock tower at the eastern end houses the world's most famous timepiece. **"Big Ben"** refers not to the clock tower itself, but to the largest bell in the chime, which weighs close to 14 tons and is named for the first commissioner of works.

You may observe parliamentary debates from the **Stranger's Galleries** in both houses. Sessions usually begin in mid-October and run to the end of July, with recesses at Christmas and Easter. Although we can't promise you the oratory of a Charles James Fox or a William Pitt the Elder, the debates in the House of Commons are often lively and controversial (seats are at a premium during crises). The chances of getting into the House of Lords when it's in session are generally better than for the more popular House of Commons, where even the queen isn't allowed.

The general public is admitted to the Strangers' Galleries on "sitting days." You have to join a public line outside the St. Stephen's entrance on the day in question, and

AT&T Access Numbers

Aruba	800-8000	**Czech Rep. ▲**	**00-42-000-101**
Australia	**1-800-551-155**	Egypt●(Cairo)‡	510-0200
Austria●	**0800-200-288**	France	0-800-99-0011
Bahamas	1-800-872-2881	**Germany**	**0800-2255-288**
Barbados✚	1-800-872-2881	**Greece●**	**00-800-1311**
Belgium●	**0-800-100-10**	Guam	1-800-2255-288
Bermuda✚	1-800-872-2881	**Hong Kong**	**800-96-1111**
Cayman Isl.✚	1-800-872-2881	**Hungary**	**06-800-01111**
China, PRC▲	10811	**India ✖,➤**	**000-117**
Costa Rica	0-800-0-114-114	**Ireland ✓**	**I-800-550-000**

AT&T

AT&T Direct® Service

AT&T Access Numbers

Aruba	800-8000	**Czech Rep. ▲**	**00-42-000-101**
Australia	**1-800-551-155**	Egypt●(Cairo)‡	510-0200
Austria●	**0800-200-288**	France	0-800-99-0011
Bahamas	1-800-872-2881	**Germany**	**0800-2255-288**
Barbados✚	1-800-872-2881	**Greece●**	**00-800-1311**
Belgium●	**0-800-100-10**	Guam	1-800-2255-288
Bermuda✚	1-800-872-2881	**Hong Kong**	**800-96-1111**
Cayman Isl.✚	1-800-872-2881	**Hungary**	**06-800-01111**
China, PRC▲	10811	**India ✖,➤**	**000-117**
Costa Rica	0-800-0-114-114	**Ireland ✓**	**I-800-550-000**

Israel	**1-800-94-94-949**	**Philippines** ●	**105-11**
Italy ●	**172-1011**	**Portugal** ▲	**0800-800-128**
Jamaica ●	1-800-872-2881	Singapore	800-0111-111
Japan ● ▲	**005-39-111**	**Spain**	**900-99-00-11**
Malaysia ●	**1800-80-0011**	**Switzerland** ●	**0-800-89-0011**
Mexico ● ▽	**01-800-288-2872**	Thailand ❮	001-999-111-11
Neth. Ant. ○	001-800-872-2881	**Turkey** ●	**00-800-12277**
Netherlands ●	**0800-022-9111**	**U.K.**	**0800-89-0011**
New Zealand ●	**000-911**	**U.K.**	**0800-013-0011**
Panama	800-001-0109	**Venezuela**	**800-11-120**

FOR EASY CALLING WORLDWIDE

1. Just dial the AT&T Access Number for the country you are calling from. *2.* Dial the phone number you're calling. *3.* Dial your card number.

For access numbers not listed ask any operator for **AT&T Direct®** Service. In the U.S. call 1-800-331-1140 for a wallet guide listing all worldwide AT&T Access Numbers.

Visit our Web site at: www.att.com/traveler

Bold-faced countries permit country-to-country calling outside the U.S.

- ● Public phones may require coin or card deposit to place call.
- † Outside of Cairo, dial "02" first.
- ▲ May not be available from every phone/payphone.
- ✚ Public phones and select hotels.
- ✓ Use U.K. access number in N. Ireland.
- ❮ When calling from public phones, use phones marked "Lenso."
- ▽ When calling from public phones, use phones marked "Ladatel."
- ✖ Not available from public phones.
- ➤ Available from phones with international calling capabilities or from most Public Calling Centers.
- ○ From St. Maarten or phones at Bobby's Marina, use 1-800-872-2881.

When placing an international call ***from*** the U.S., dial 1 800 CALL ATT.

Israel	**1-800-94-94-949**	**Philippines** ●	**105-11**
Italy ●	**172-1011**	**Portugal** ▲	**0800-800-128**
Jamaica ●	1-800-872-2881	Singapore	800-0111-111
Japan ● ▲	**005-39-111**	**Spain**	**900-99-00-11**
Malaysia ●	**1800-80-0011**	**Switzerland** ●	**0-800-89-0011**
Mexico ● ▽	**01-800-288-2872**	Thailand ❮	001-999-111-11
Neth. Ant. ○	001-800-872-2881	**Turkey** ●	**00-800-12277**
Netherlands ●	**0800-022-9111**	**U.K.**	**0800-89-0011**
New Zealand ●	**000-911**	**U.K.**	**0800-013-0011**
Panama	800-001-0109	**Venezuela**	**800-11-120**

FOR EASY CALLING WORLDWIDE

1. Just dial the AT&T Access Number for the country you are calling from. *2.* Dial the phone number you're calling. *3.* Dial your card number.

For access numbers not listed ask any operator for **AT&T Direct®** Service. In the U.S. call 1-800-331-1140 for a wallet guide listing all worldwide AT&T Access Numbers.

Visit our Web site at: www.att.com/traveler

Bold-faced countries permit country-to-country calling outside the U.S.

- ● Public phones may require coin or card deposit to place call.
- † Outside of Cairo, dial "02" first.
- ▲ May not be available from every phone/payphone.
- ✚ Public phones and select hotels.
- ✓ Use U.K. access number in N. Ireland.
- ❮ When calling from public phones, use phones marked "Lenso."
- ▽ When calling from public phones, use phones marked "Ladatel."
- ✖ Not available from public phones.
- ➤ Available from phones with international calling capabilities or from most Public Calling Centers.
- ○ From St. Maarten or phones at Bobby's Marina, use 1-800-872-2881.

When placing an international call ***from*** the U.S., dial 1 800 CALL ATT.

© 1/2000

Westminster Abbey

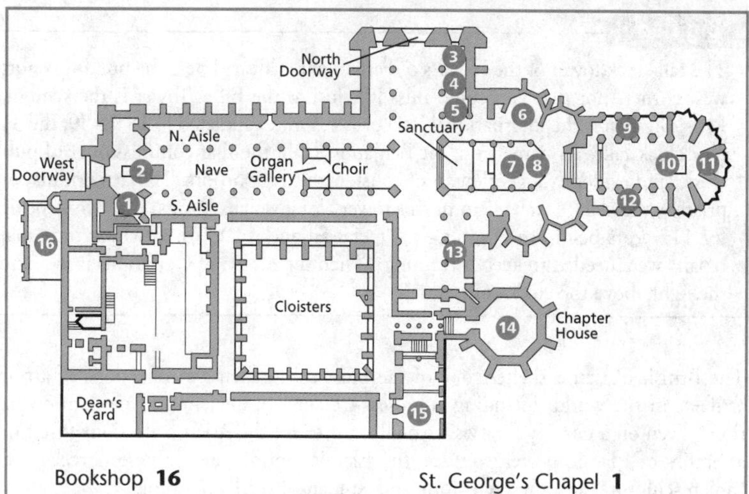

Bookshop **16**
Chapel of St. John the Baptist **6**
Chapel of St. John the Evangelist **5**
Chapter House **14**
Henry V's Chantry **8**
Poets' Corner **13**
Royal Air Force Chapel **11**
St. Andrew's Chapel **3**
St. Edward's Chapel (Coronation Chair) **7**
St. George's Chapel **1**
St. Michael's Chapel **4**
Tomb of Mary I & Elizabeth I **9**
Tomb of Henry VII **10**
Tomb of Mary Queen of Scots **12**
Tomb of the Unknown Warrior/ Memorial to Churchill **2**
Undercroft Museum **15**

there's often considerable delay before the public is admitted. The line forms on the left for the House of Commons, on the right for the Lords. You can speed matters up somewhat by applying at the American Embassy or the Canadian High Commission for a special pass, which should be issued well in advance of your trip, but this is too cumbersome for many people. Besides, the embassy has only four tickets for daily distribution, so you might as well stand in line. It's usually easier to get in after about 5:30pm; debates often continue until about 11pm. To arrange a tour before you leave home, you can write **House of Commons Information Office,** 1 Derby Gate, Westminster, London SW1A 2TT. Tours are usually conducted on Friday.

Stay tuned for developments surrounding the House of Lords, which London's tabloid newspaper portray as a bunch of "Monty Pythonesque upper-class twits." For years this house has given Britain its wit and wisdom, including a 1992 remark by the earl of Longford, "A girl is not ruined for life by being seduced—a young fellow is." Today, under Tony Blair's Labour government, the Houses of Parliament are facing radical reforms. In 1999, more than 600 of the 752 hereditary peers, often descendants of royal mistresses and ancient landowners, have been fired from the upper chamber. Britain's foreign secretary has already called the House of Lords "medieval lumber."

✪ **British Museum.** Great Russell St., WC1. ☎ **020/7323-8299** or 020/7636-1555 for recorded information; www.thebritishmuseum.ac.uk. Free admission, donations encouraged. Mon–Sat 9:30am–5:30pm, Sun 11:30am–6:30pm. Tube: Holborn or Tottenham Court Rd.

Big Ben

The tall clock tower of the Houses of Parliament is located near the building's northwest corner (not that you could miss it!). Just as the Eiffel Tower is the symbol of Paris, Big Ben is the international icon of London. Completed in 1858–59, the 316-foot clock takes its name from Sir Benjamin Hall, the first commissioner of public works and evidently a gentleman of considerable proportions. Perhaps not inappropriately, the clock mechanism in this tower along weighs 5 tons. Big Ben kept time for 117 years before succumbing to "metal fatigue" in 1976, at which time major repairs were needed to keep it running. When the House of Commons is in session, the light above the clock is lit.

The British Museum shelters one of the most comprehensive collections of art and artifacts in the world, including countless treasures of ancient and modern civilizations. Even on a cursory first visit, you'll want to see the Asian collections (the finest assembly of Islamic pottery outside the Islamic world), the Chinese porcelain, the Indian sculpture, and the Prehistoric and Romano-British collections.

Here's our advice: The museum is so vast, so overwhelming (with 2¹/₂ miles of galleries) that it's best to take a tour for 1 or 1¹/₂ hours for £6 ($10.20) on your first visit. They're offered Monday through Saturday at 10:30am, 1 and 3:15pm, or Sunday at 1, 1:30, 3:30, and 4pm. Later you can come back and examine more closely what interested you. If you have only minutes to spare for the museum, concentrate on the Greek and Rome rooms (nos. 1 through 15). They contain all the booty bought or stolen from the Empire's once far-flung colonies.

As you enter the front hall, you may want to head first to the Assyrian Transept on the ground floor, where you'll find the winged and human-headed bulls and lions that once guarded the gateways to the palaces of Assyrian kings. Nearby is the **Black Obelisk of Shalmaneser III** (858–824 B.C.) depicting Jehu, king of Israel, paying tribute. From here you can continue into the angular hall of Egyptian sculpture to see the **Rosetta stone,** whose discovery led to the deciphering of hieroglyphs.

Also on the ground floor is the Duveen Gallery, housing the **Elgin marbles,** consisting chiefly of sculptures from the Parthenon, on the Acropolis in Athens.

The classical sculpture galleries house a caryatid from the Erechtheum, also on the Acropolis, a temple started in 421 B.C. and dedicated to Athena and Poseidon. Displayed here, too, are sculptures from the Mausoleum at Halicarnassus (ca. 350 B.C.).

The Department of Medieval and Later Antiquities has its galleries on the first floor (second floor to Americans), reached by the main staircase. Of its exhibitions, the Sutton Hoo Anglo-Saxon burial ship, discovered in Suffolk, is, in the words of an expert, "the richest treasure ever dug from English soil"; it held gold jewelry, armor, weapons, bronze bowls and cauldrons, silverware, and the inevitable drinking horn of the Norse culture.

The featured attractions of the upper floor are the Egyptian Galleries, especially the **mummies.** Egyptian Room 63 is extraordinary, resembling the props for Cleopatra, with its cosmetics, domestic utensils, toys, tools, and other work. Items of Sumerian art, unearthed from the Royal Cemetery at Ur (southern Iraq), lie in a room beyond, some dating from around 2500 B.C. In the Iranian room rests "The Treasure of the Oxus," a hoard of riches, perhaps a temple deposit, dating from the 6th to the 3rd century B.C. See also the galleries of the City of Rome and its Empire, which include exhibitions of art before the Romans.

The British Museum

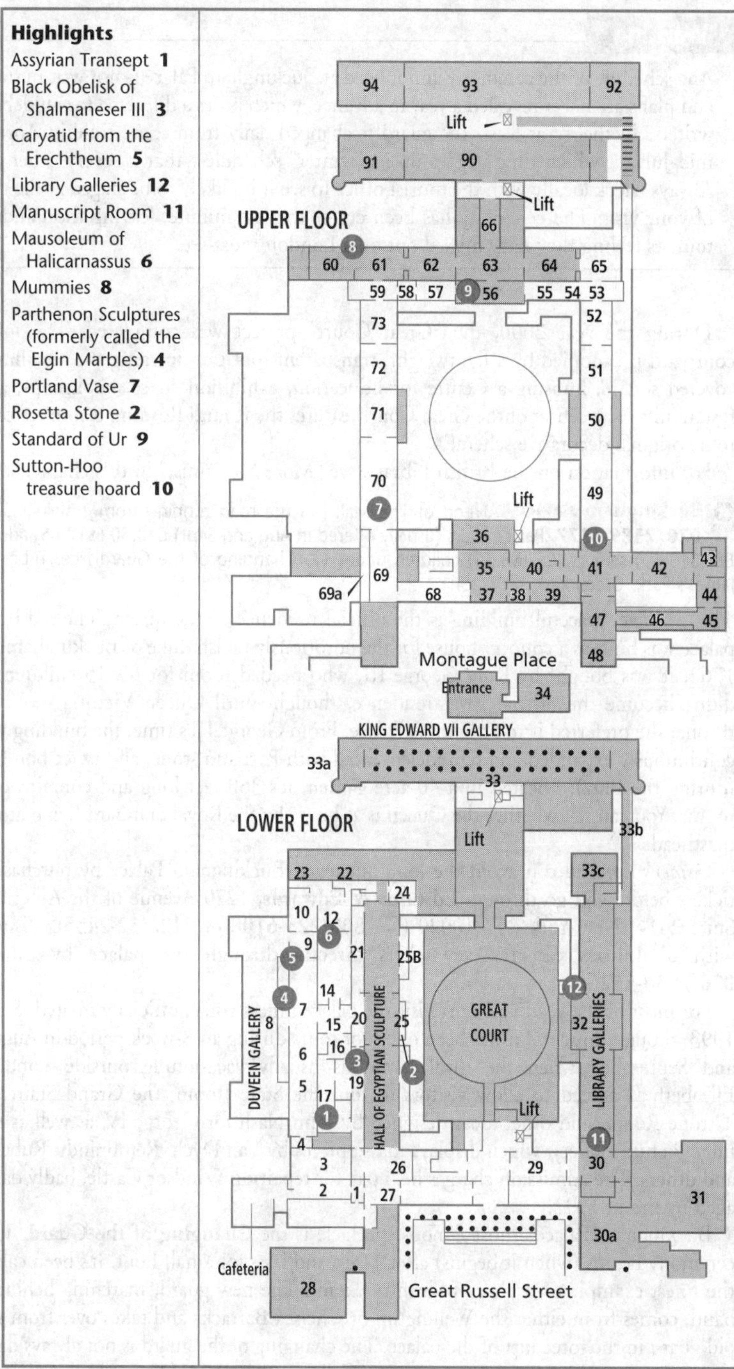

Highlights
Assyrian Transept 1
Black Obelisk of Shalmaneser III 3
Caryatid from the Erechtheum 5
Library Galleries 12
Manuscript Room 11
Mausoleum of Halicarnassus 6
Mummies 8
Parthenon Sculptures (formerly called the Elgin Marbles) 4
Portland Vase 7
Rosetta Stone 2
Standard of Ur 9
Sutton-Hoo treasure hoard 10
UPPER FLOOR
Lift
Montague Place
Entrance
KING EDWARD VII GALLERY
LOWER FLOOR
DUVEEN GALLERY
HALL OF EGYPTIAN SCULPTURE
GREAT COURT
LIBRARY GALLERIES
Cafeteria
Great Russell Street

Warning

Any schedule of the ceremony announced at Buckingham Palace is not writ in stone, and plans are never revealed a year in advance, which poses a dilemma for guidebook writers. In theory at least, the guard is changed daily from some time in April to mid-July, at which time it goes on its "winter" schedule—that is, every other day. Always check locally with the tourist office to see if it's likely to be staged at the time of your visit. The ceremony has been cut at the last minute, leaving thousands of tourists feeling they have missed out on a London must-see.

During the year 2000, the "Great Court" project was completed. The inner courtyard is canopied by a lightweight, transparent roof transforming the area into a covered square; housing a Centre for Education, exhibition space, bookshops, and restaurants. The center of the Great Court features the Round Reading Room restored to its original decorative scheme.

For information on the British Library, see "More Museums," in this chapter.

✪ **Buckingham Palace.** At end of The Mall (on the road running from Trafalgar Sq.). ☎ **020/7389-1377.** Palace tours (usually offered in Aug and Sept) £10.50 ($17.85) adults, £8 ($13.60) seniors, £5 ($8.50) children under 17. Changing of the Guard free. Tube: St. James's Park, Green Park, or Victoria.

This massive, graceful building is the official residence of the queen. The red-brick palace was built as a country house for the notoriously rakish duke of Buckingham. In 1762, it was bought by King George III, who needed room for his 15 children. It didn't become the official royal residence, though, until Queen Victoria took the throne; she preferred it to St. James's Palace. From George III's time, the building was continuously expanded and remodeled, faced with Portland stone, and twice bombed (during the Blitz). Located in a 40-acre garden, it's 360 feet long and contains 600 rooms. You can tell whether the Queen is at home by the Royal Standard flying at the masthead.

Insider's tip: You can avoid the long queues at Buckingham Palace by purchasing tickets before you go through **Edwards & Edwards,** 1270 Avenue of the Americas, Suite 2414, New York, NY 10020 (☎ **800/223-6108** or 212/332-2435). Visitors with disabilities can reserve tickets directly through the palace by calling **020/7930-5526.**

For most of the year, you can't visit the palace unless you're officially invited. Since 1993, though, much of it has been open for tours during an 8-week period in August and September, when the royal family is usually vacationing outside London. Elizabeth II agreed to allow visitors to tour the State Room, the Grand Staircase, Throne Room, and other areas designed by John Nash for George IV, as well as the huge Picture Gallery, which displays masterpieces by Van Dyck, Rembrandt, Rubens, and others. The admission charges help pay for repairing Windsor Castle, badly damaged by fire in 1992.

Buckingham Palace's most famous spectacle is the **Changing of the Guard.** This ceremony begins (when it begins) after 11am and lasts for a half hour. It's been called the finest example of military pageantry extant. The new guard, marching behind a band, comes from either the Wellington or Chelsea Barracks and takes over from the old guard in the forecourt of the palace. The changing of the guard is not always daily and varies depending on the time of year. Call ☎ **0839/123-411** to check times.

Madame Tussaud's. Marylebone Rd., NW1. ☎ **020/7935-6861;** www.madame-tussaauds.com. Admission £10.50 ($17.85) adults, £8.50 ($14.45) seniors, £7.50 ($12.75) children under 16, free for children under 5. Combination tickets including the new planetarium £12.95 ($22) adults, £9.80 ($16.65) seniors, £7 ($11.90) children under 16. Mon–Fri 10am–5:30pm, Sat–Sun 9:30am–5:30pm. Tube: Baker St.

In 1770, an exhibition of life-size wax figures was opened in Paris by Dr. Curtius. He was soon joined by his niece, Strasbourg-born Marie Tussaud, who learned the secret of making lifelike replicas of the famous and the infamous. During the French Revolution, the head of almost every distinguished victim of the guillotine was molded by Madame Tussaud or her uncle.

Whereas some of the figures on display today come from molds taken by Madame Tussaud, who continued to make portraits until she was 81, the exhibition also introduces new images of whoever is au courant. An enlarged Grand Hall continues to house years of royalty and old favorites, as well as many of today's heads of state and political leaders. In the Chamber of Horrors, you can have the vicarious thrill of walking through a Victorian London street where special effects include the shadow terror of Jack the Ripper. The instruments and victims of death penalties contrast with present-day criminals portrayed within the confines of prison. You are invited to mingle with the more current stars in the garden party, "meeting" everyone from Arnold Schwarzenegger to Elizabeth Taylor. "Super Stars" offers the latest technologies in sound, light, and special effects combined with new figures from the fields of film and sports.

One of the latest attractions to open here is called "The Spirit of London," a musical show that depicts 400 years of London's history, using special effects that include audio-animatronic figures that move and speak. Visitors take "time-taxis" that allow them to see and hear "Shakespeare" as he writes and speaks lines, to be received by Queen Elizabeth I, and to feel and smell the great fire that started in Pudding Lane in 1666.

✪ **Tate Britain.** Millbank, SW1. ☎ **020/7887-8000;** www.tate.org.uk. Free admission; special exhibitions sometimes incur a charge varying from £3–£6 ($5.10–$10.20). Daily 10am–5:50pm. Tube: Pimlico. Bus: 77A, 88, or C10.

Fronting the Thames near Vauxhall Bridge in Pimlico, the Tate looks like a smaller and more graceful relation of the British Museum. The most prestigious gallery in Britain, it houses the national collections covering British art from the 16th century to the present day. Since only a portion of the collections can be displayed at any one time, the works on view change from time to time. Because it's difficult to take in all the exhibits, we suggest that you try to schedule two visits—the first to see the classic British works, the second to concentrate on whichever section interests you more, if your time is limited.

The older works include some of the best of Gainsborough, Reynolds, Stubbs, Blake, and Constable. William Hogarth is well represented, particularly by his satirical *O the Roast Beef of Old England* (known as *The Gate of Calais*). The illustrations of William Blake, the incomparable mystical poet for such works as *The Book of Job, The Divine Comedy,* and *Paradise Lost* are here. The collection of works by J.M.W. Turner is its largest collection of works by a single artist; Turner himself willed most of the paintings and watercolors here to the nation.

Also on display are the works of many major 19th- and 20th-century painters, including Paul Nash. In the modern collections are works by Matisse, Dalí, Modigliani, Munch, Bonnard, and Picasso. Truly remarkable are the several enormous abstract canvases by Mark Rothko, the group of paintings and sculptures by

Giacometti, and the paintings of one of England's best-known modern artists, the late Francis Bacon. Sculptures by Henry Moore and Barbara Hepworth are also occasionally displayed.

Downstairs is the internationally renowned **Tate Gallery Restaurant** (see chapter 3), with murals by Whistler, as well as a coffee shop.

Tate Modern. 25 Sumner St., SE1. ☎ **020/7887-8000.** Free admission. Sun–Thurs 10am–6pm, Fri–Sat 10am–8pm. Tube: Southwark.

In the spring of 2000, the Tate opened a new gallery to display its collection of 20th- and 21st-century art. You can walk over the Millennium Bridge, a pedestrian only walk from the steps of St. Paul's over the Thames to the new gallery.

Tate Modern was converted from the former Bankside Power Station, which was designed by Sir Giles Gilbert Scott who also designed the famous British red telephone box. The architect made extensive use of glass both inside and out. A glass structure crowns the building, adding two floors to the original structure offering panoramic views of London. Galleries showing art are arranged over three levels and provide different kinds of space for display.

One of the foremost modern art museums in the world, Tate Modern will display only international modern art from 1900 to the 21st century. New art created by both British and international artists will also be displayed here. Tate Modern will rank in prestige with the Museum of Modern Art in New York or Pompidou Centre in Paris. Instead of exhibiting art chronologically and by school, Tate Modern, in a radical break from tradition, will have a thematic approach. This will allow displays to cut across movements. Photographs will be displayed for the art form that they are, including rare photographs on loan from the Victoria and Albert Museum. The top level of the gallery will be turned over to various exhibitions on loan.

✪ **National Gallery.** Northwest side of Trafalgar Sq., WC2. ☎ **020/7747-2885;** www.nationalgallery.org.uk. Free admission. Thurs–Tues 10am–6pm; Wed 10am–9pm. Tube: Charing Cross, Embankment, or Leicester Square.

In an impressive neoclassical building, the National Gallery houses one of the most comprehensive collections of Western paintings, representing all the major schools from the late 13th to the early 20th centuries. The largest part of the collection is devoted to the Italians, including the Sienese, Venetian, and Florentine masters, now housed in the Sainsbury Wing.

Insider's tip: The National Gallery has a computer information center in the Sainsbury Wing where visitors can design a personal tour map. The computer room, located in the Micro Gallery, includes 12 computer workstations open to the public. The system offers 2,200 paintings to select from, with supporting text for each one. The program includes four indexes that are cross-referenced for your convenience. Using a touch-screen computer, you can design your own personalized tour by selecting a maximum of 10 paintings that you would like to view. Once you have made your choices, you print a free personal tour map that shows your selections. There's a small charge, usually about £1 ($1.65), for printouts.

Of the early Gothic works, the *Wilton Diptych* (French or English school, late 14th century) is the rarest treasure; it depicts Richard II being introduced to the Madonna and Child by John the Baptist and the Saxon king, Edward the Confessor. A Florentine gem by Masaccio is displayed, as well as notable works by Piero della Francesca, Leonardo da Vinci, Michelangelo, and Raphael.

Among the 16th-century Venetian masters, the most notable works include a rare *Adoration of the Kings* by Giorgione, Bacchus and *Ariadne* by Titian, *The Origin of the Milky Way* by Tintoretto, and *The Family of Darius Before Alexander* by Veronese.

A number of satellite rooms are filled with works by major Italian masters of the 15th century, such as Andrea Mantegna of Padua, Giovanni Bellini, and Botticelli.

The painters of northern Europe are well represented. For example, there is Jan van Eyck's portrait of G. Arnolfini and his bride, plus Pieter Brueghel the Elder's Bosch-influenced *Adoration.*

One of the National's big drawing cards is its collection of Rembrandts. His *Self-Portrait at the Age of 34* shows him at the pinnacle of his life; his *Self-Portrait at the Age of 63* is deeply moving and revealing.

Five of the greatest of the homegrown artists—Constable, Turner, Reynolds, Gainsborough, and Hogarth—have masterpieces here, as do three giants of Spanish painting. Velázquez's portrait of the sunken-faced Philip IV, El Greco's *Christ Driving the Traders from the Temple,* and Goya's portrait of the duke of Wellington (once stolen) and his mantilla-wearing *Doña Isabel de Porcel* are on display.

Other rooms are devoted to early 19th-century French painters, such as Delacroix and Ingres; the later 19th-century French impressionists, such as Manet, Monet, Renoir, and Degas; and postimpressionists such as Cézanne, Seurat, and van Gogh.

Kensington Palace. The Broad Walk, Kensington Gardens, W8. ☎ **020/7937-9561;** www.hrp.org.uk. Admission £9.50 ($16.15) adults, £7.70 ($13.10) seniors/students, £7.10 ($12.05) children, family £29.10 ($49.45). June–Sept daily 10am–5pm; off-season Wed–Sun 10am–3pm. Tube: Queensway or Bayswater on north side of gardens; High St. Kensington on south side.

The palace is located at the far western end of Kensington Gardens; the entrance is from the Broad Walk. Kensington Palace was acquired by William III in 1689, and was remodeled by Sir Christopher Wren. George II, who died in 1760, was the last king to use it as a royal residence. You can tour parts of the palace, but many rooms are private. Princess Diana used this as her London residence, and the area in front of the palace drew tens of thousands of mourners after her death. A sea of flowers and tributes stood testament to a nation's grief.

The most interesting chamber to visit is Queen Victoria's bedroom. Here, on the morning of June 20, 1837, she was aroused from her sleep with the news that she had succeeded to the throne, following the death of her uncle, William IV. As you wander through the apartments, you'll see many fine paintings from the Royal Collection.

A special attraction is the Royal Ceremonial Dress Collection, which shows restored rooms from the 19th century, including Queen Victoria's birth room and a series of room settings with the appropriate court dress of the day.

The palace gardens adjoin Hyde Park and are open to the public for daily strolls around Round Pond, near the heart of Kensington Gardens. Also in Kensington Gardens is the ✪ Albert Memorial, honoring Queen Victoria's consort. Facing Royal Albert Hall, the statue reflects the ostentation of the Victorian era.

✪ **St. Paul's Cathedral.** St. Paul's Churchyard, EC4. ☎ **020/7236-4128;** www.stpauls.london.anglican.org. Cathedral and galleries £5 ($8.50) adults, £2.50 ($4.25) children 6–16. Guided tours £2 ($3.40); recorded tours £3–£7 ($5.10–$11.90). Free for children 5 and under. Sightseeing Mon–Sat 8:30am–4pm; galleries Mon–Sat 9:30am–4pm. No sightseeing Sun (services only). Tube: St. Paul's.

During World War II, newsreel footage reaching America showed the dome of St. Paul's Cathedral lit by fires caused by the bombings all around it. That it survived at all is a miracle, since it was badly hit twice during the early years of the Nazi bombardment of London. But St. Paul's is accustomed to calamity, having been burned down three times and destroyed once by invading Norsemen. It was during the Great Fire of 1666 that the old St. Paul's was razed, making way for a new Renaissance structure designed (after many mishaps and rejections) by Sir Christopher Wren and built between 1675 and 1710.

The classical dome of St. Paul's dominates The City's square mile. Inside, the cathedral is laid out like a Greek cross; it houses few art treasures (Grinling Gibbons's choir stalls are an exception) but many monuments, including one to the "Iron Duke," and a memorial chapel to American service personnel who lost their lives in World War II while stationed in the United Kingdom. Encircling the dome is the Whispering Gallery, so be careful what you say. In the crypt lie not only Wren, but also the duke of Wellington and Lord Nelson. A fascinating Diocesan Treasury was opened in 1981. You can climb to the very top of the dome for a spectacular 360° view of London.

Guided tours last 1½ hours and include parts of the cathedral not open to the general public. They take place Monday through Saturday at 11, 11:30am, 1:30, and 2pm. Recorded tours lasting 45 minutes are available throughout the day.

St. Paul's is an Anglican cathedral with daily services at the following times: Matins Monday through Friday at 7:30am, Saturday at 8:30am, Holy Communion Monday through Saturday at 8am and 12:30pm, and Evensong Monday through Saturday at 5pm. On Sunday, there is Holy Communion at 8 and again at 11:30am, Matins at 10:15am, and Evensong at 3:15pm. Admission charges do not apply if visitors are attending services.

Insider's tip: One of the loveliest things you can do during a spring visit to London is to saunter through the free gardens of St. Paul's when the roses are in bloom.

Victoria and Albert Museum. Cromwell Rd., SW7. ☎ **020/7938-8500;** www.vam.ac.uk. Admission £5 ($8.50) adults, £3 ($5.10) seniors, free for children under 18 and persons with disabilities. Daily 10am–5:45pm. Tube: South Kensington. Bus: C1, 14, or 74.

Located in South Kensington, this museum is one of the liveliest and most imaginative in London. It's named after the queen and her consort but not run in their spirit. The general theme here is the fine and decorative arts, but that's adhered to in a pleasantly relaxed fashion.

The medieval holdings include many treasures, such as the Eltenberg Reliquary (Rhenish, second half of the 12th century); the Early English Gloucester Candlestick; the Byzantine Veroli Casket, with its ivory panels based on Greek plays; and the Syon Cope, a highly valued embroidery made in England in the early 14th century. The Gothic tapestries, including the Devonshire ones depicting hunting scenes, are displayed in another gallery. An area devoted to Islamic art houses the Ardabil carpet from 16th-century Persia (320 knots per square inch).

The Victoria and Albert houses the largest collection of Renaissance sculpture outside Italy, including a Donatello marble relief, *The Ascension;* a small terra-cotta statue of the Madonna and Child by Antonio Rossellino; a marble group, *Samson and a Philistine,* by Giovanni Bologna; and a wax model of a slave by Michelangelo. The highlight of 16th-century art from the Continent is the marble group *Neptune with Triton* by Bernini. The cartoons by Raphael, which were conceived as designs for tapestries for the Sistine Chapel, are owned by the queen and can also be seen here. A most unusual, huge, and impressive exhibit is the *Cast Courts,* life-size plaster models of ancient and medieval statuary and architecture.

The museum has the greatest collection of Indian art outside India. It has Chinese and Japanese galleries as well. In complete contrast are suites of English furniture, metal-work, and ceramics dating beyond the 16th century, and a superb collection of portrait miniatures, including the one Hans Holbein the Younger made of Anne of Cleves for the benefit of Henry VIII, who was again casting around for a suitable wife.

St. Paul's Cathedral

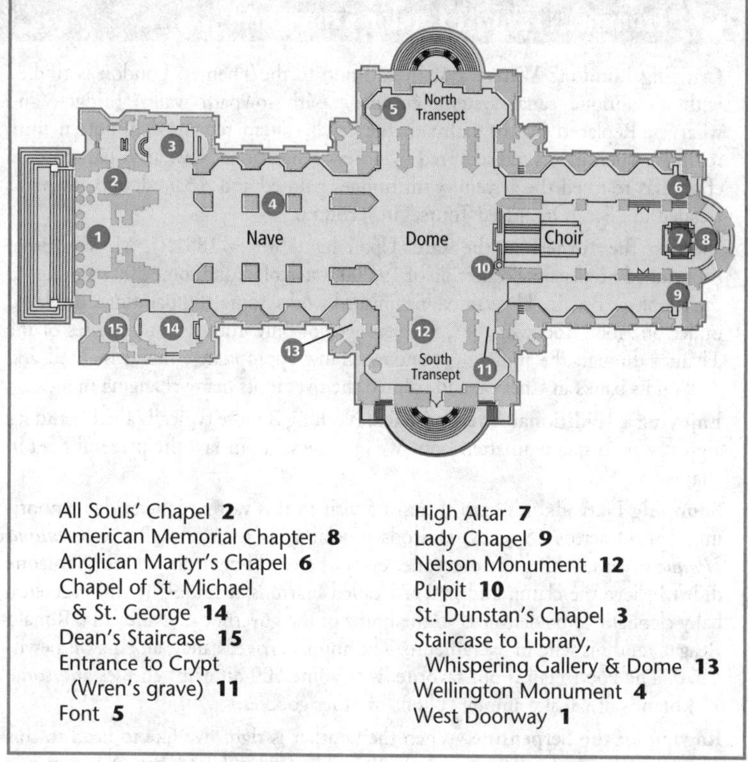

In a major redevelopment plan, the entire run of the British Galleries won't be fully open until 2001. But the museum has a lively program of changing exhibitions and displays, so there's always something new to see. The turn of the century will see the hosting of *A Grand Design: The Art of the Victoria and Albert Museum,* a celebration of the last 2,000 years of art.

A restaurant serves snacks and meals, and two museum shops sell wonderful gifts, posters, cards, and books.

Insider's tip: As incongruous it sounds, the museum hosts a jazz brunch on Sunday mornings from 11am to 3pm for only £8.50 ($14.45). Also, check out the museum's most bizarre gallery, "Fakes and Forgeries." The art impostors in this gallery are amazingly authentic—in fact, we'd judge some of them better than the old masters themselves.

Trafalgar Square. Tube: Charing Cross.

One of the landmark squares of London, Trafalgar Square honors one of England's great military heroes, Horatio, Viscount Nelson (1758–1805), who died at the Battle of Trafalgar. Although he suffered from seasickness all his life, he went to sea at the age of 12 and was an admiral at the age of 39. Lord Nelson was a hero of the Battle of Calvi in 1794 where he lost an eye, the Battle of Santa Cruz in 1797 where he lost an arm, and the Battle of Trafalgar in 1805 where he lost his life.

Frommer's Favorite London Experiences

Cruising London's Waterways. In addition to the Thames, London is riddled with an antique canal system, complete with towpath walks, bridges, and wharves. Replaced by the railroad, the canal system remained forgotten until recently, when it was rediscovered by a new generation. Now, an urban renewal effort has restored the system, with bridges painted and repaired, and towpaths cleaned up. See "Organized Tours," in section 6.

Viewing the Turners at the Tate. Upon his death in 1851, J. M. W. Turner bequeathed his personal collection of 19,000 watercolors and some 300 paintings to the people of Britain. He wanted his finished works, some 100 paintings, displayed under one roof. Today at the Tate, you get not only Turner, but glimpses of the Thames through the museum's windows. How appropriate—the artist lived and died on its banks in Chelsea, and painted the river in its many changing moods.

Enjoying a Traditional Afternoon Tea. Nothing is more typically British and it's a great way to spend an afternoon. We've suggested our favorite places for tea in chapter 3.

Shopping Harrods. It's hard to resist a visit to this vast Knightsbridge emporium. Spread across 15 acres, Harrods proclaims as its motto *Omnia Omnibus Ubique* or "everything for everyone, everywhere." They mean it, too: Someone didn't believe the claim, and in 1975 called Harrods at midnight and ordered a baby elephant to be delivered to the home of the governor of California, Ronald Reagan, and his wife in Sacramento. The animal arrived safely, albeit a bit bewildered. The Food Hall is our favorite, with some 500 different cheeses and some 163 brands of whisky among zillions of other goodies.

Rowing on the Serpentine. When the weather is right, we like to head to this 41-acre artificial lake, dating from 1730 and located in Hyde Park. A stream was dammed to create the artificial lake, whose name derives from its winding, snake-like shape. At the Boathouse, you can rent a boat by the hour. With the right companion, it's one of the most idyllic ways to spend a sunny London afternoon.

Wandering Through Covent Garden. George Bernard Shaw got his inspiration for *Pygmalion* here, where the character of Eliza Doolittle sold violets to wealthy operagoers and became a household name around the world. The old fruit and vegetable market, with its Cockney cauliflower peddlers and butchers in blood-soaked aprons, is long gone. But what's left is just as interesting: Covent Garden today is London's best example of urban renewal. There's an antiques market in the piazza on Monday, and a crafts market Tuesday through Saturday.

Watching the Sunset at Waterloo Bridge. Waterloo Bridge is the best place in London to watch the sun set over Westminster. From here, you can also see the last rays of sunlight bounce off The City spires in the East End.

Spending a Night at the West End Theater. London is the theatrical capital of the world. The live stage offers a unique combination of variety, accessibility, and economy—and a look at next year's Broadway hit.

Crawling the London Pubs. With some 5,000 pubs within the city limits, you would be crawling indeed if you tried to have a drink in each of them. Enough traditional ones remain, especially in central London, to make it worthwhile to go on a crawl, perhaps fortifying yourself with a ploughman's lunch or a plate of shepherd's pie.

The square today is dominated by a 145-foot granite column, the work of E. H. Baily in 1843. The column looks down Whitehall toward the Old Admiralty, where Lord Nelson's body lay in state. The figure of the naval hero towers 17 feet high, not bad for a man who stood 5 feet 4 inches in real life. The capital is of bronze cast from cannons recovered from the wreck of the *Royal George*. Queen Victoria's favorite animal painter, Sir Edward Landseer, added the four lions at the base of the column in 1868. The pools and fountains were not added until 1939, the last work of Sir Edwin Lutyens.

Political demonstrations still take place at the square and around the column, which has the most aggressive pigeons in London. These birds will even land on your head or perform less desirable stunts. Actually, the birds are part of a long feathery tradition, for this site was once used by Edward I (1239–1307) to keep his birds of prey. Called "Longshanks," he came here often before he died of dysentery in 1307. Richard II, who ruled from 1377 to 1399, kept goshawks and falcons here too. By the time of Henry VII, who ruled from 1485 to 1509, the square was used as the site of the royal stables. Sir Charles Barry, who designed the Houses of Parliament, created the present square in the 1830s.

To the southeast of the square, at 36 Craven St., stands a house once occupied by Benjamin Franklin when he was a general of the Philadelphia Academy (1757–74). On the north side of the square rises the National Gallery, constructed in the 1830s. In front of the building is a copy of a statue of George Washington by J. A. Houdon.

To the left of St. Martin's Place is the National Portrait Gallery, a collection of British greats (and not-so-greats)—everyone from Chaucer and Shakespeare to Captain Hook and Nell Gwynne. Also on the square is the landmark St. Martin-in-the-Fields by James Gibbs, with its towering steeple, the resting place of such figures as Sir Joshua Reynolds, William Hogarth, and Thomas Chippendale.

2 More Attractions

OFFICIAL LONDON

Whitehall, the seat of the British government, grew up on the grounds of Whitehall Palace and was turned into a royal residence by Henry VIII, who snatched it from its former occupant, Cardinal Wolsey. Whitehall extends south from Trafalgar Square to Parliament Square. Along it you'll find the Home Office, the Old Admiralty Building, and the Ministry of Defence.

Visitors today can see the **Cabinet War Rooms,** the bombproof bunker suite of rooms, just as they were when abandoned by Winston Churchill and the British government at the end of World War II. You can see the Map Room with its huge wall maps, the Atlantic map a mass of pinholes (each hole represents at least one convoy). Next door is Churchill's bedroom-cum-office, which has a bed and a desk with two BBC microphones on it for his famous speech broadcasts that stirred the nation.

The **Transatlantic Telephone Room,** its full title, is little more than a broom closet, but it housed the Bell Telephone Company's special scrambler phone, called Sig-Saly, and it was where Churchill conferred with Roosevelt. Visitors are provided with a step-by-step personal sound guide, providing a detailed account of each room's function and history.

The entrance to the War Rooms is by Clive Steps at the end of King Charles Street, SW1 (☎ **020/7930-6961;** tube: Westminster or St. James's), off Whitehall near Big Ben. Admission is £5 ($8.50) for adults, free for children 16 and under, and £3.60 ($6.10) students and seniors. The rooms are open from April to September daily, 9:30am to 6pm (last admission 5:15pm); and October through March daily, 10am to 5:30pm; they're closed during Christmas holidays. Tube: Westminster or St. James's.

At the Cenotaph (honoring both world wars' dead), turn down unpretentious **Downing Street** to the modest little town house at no. 10, flanked by two bobbies. Walpole was the first prime minister to live here, Churchill the most famous. But Margaret Thatcher was around longer than any of them.

Nearby, north of Downing Street, is the **Horse Guards Building,** Whitehall (☎ **020/7414-2396;** tube: Westminster), now the headquarters of the horse guards of the Household Division and London District. There has been a guard change here since 1649, when the site was the entrance to the old Palace of Whitehall. You can watch the Queen's Life Guards ceremony at 11am Monday through Saturday (10:30am on Sunday). You can also see the hourly smaller change of the guard, when mounted troopers are changed. And at 4pm you can watch the evening inspection, when 10 unmounted troopers and two mounted troopers assemble in the courtyard.

Across the street is Inigo Jones's **Banqueting House,** Palace of Whitehall, Horse Guards Avenue (☎ **020/7930-4179;** tube: Westminster), site of the execution of Charles I. William and Mary accepted the crown of England here, but they preferred to live at Kensington Palace. The **Banqueting House** was part of Whitehall Palace, which burned to the ground in 1698, but the ceremonial hall escaped razing. Its most notable feature today is an allegorical ceiling painted by Peter Paul Rubens. Admission to the Banqueting House is £3.60 ($6.10) for adults, £2.30 ($3.90) for children, £2.80 ($4.75) for senior citizens and students. It's open Monday through Saturday from 10am to 5pm (last admission 4:30pm). Tube: Westminster, Charing Cross, or Embankment.

LEGAL LONDON

The smallest borough in London, bustling Holborn (pronounced *Ho*-burn) is often referred to as Legal London, home of the city's barristers, solicitors, and law clerks. It also embraces the university district of Bloomsbury. Holborn, which houses the ancient **Inns of Courts**—Gray's Inn, Lincoln's Inn, Middle Temple, and Inner Temple—was severely damaged during World War II bombing raids. The razed buildings were replaced with modern offices, but the borough still retains pockets of its former days.

At the 60 or more **Law Courts** presently in use, on The Strand, all civil and some criminal cases are heard. Designed by G. E. Street, the neo-Gothic buildings (1874–82) contain more than 1,000 rooms and 3.5 miles of corridors. Sculptures of Christ, King Solomon, and King Alfred grace the front door; Moses is depicted at the back entrance. Admission is free, and the courts are open during sessions Monday to Friday from 10am to 4:30pm. No cameras, tape recorders, video cameras, or cellular phones are allowed during sessions. Tube: Holborn or Temple.

The court known as the **Old Bailey,** on Newgate Street, EC4 (☎ **020/7248-3277**), replaced the infamous Newgate Prison, once the scene of public hangings and other forms of "public entertainment." It's fascinating to watch the bewigged barristers presenting their cases to the high court judges. Entry is strictly on a first-arrival basis, and guests line up outside. Courts 1 to 4, 17, and 18, are entered from Newgate Street, and the balance from Old Bailey (the street). To get here, take the Tube to Temple, Chancery Lane, or St. Paul's. Travel east on Fleet Street, which along the way becomes Ludgate Hill. Cross Ludgate Circus and turn left to the Old Bailey, a domed structure with the figure of Justice standing atop it. Admission is free; children under 14 are not admitted, and ages 14 to 16 must be accompanied by adult. No

Official London: Westminster & Whitehall

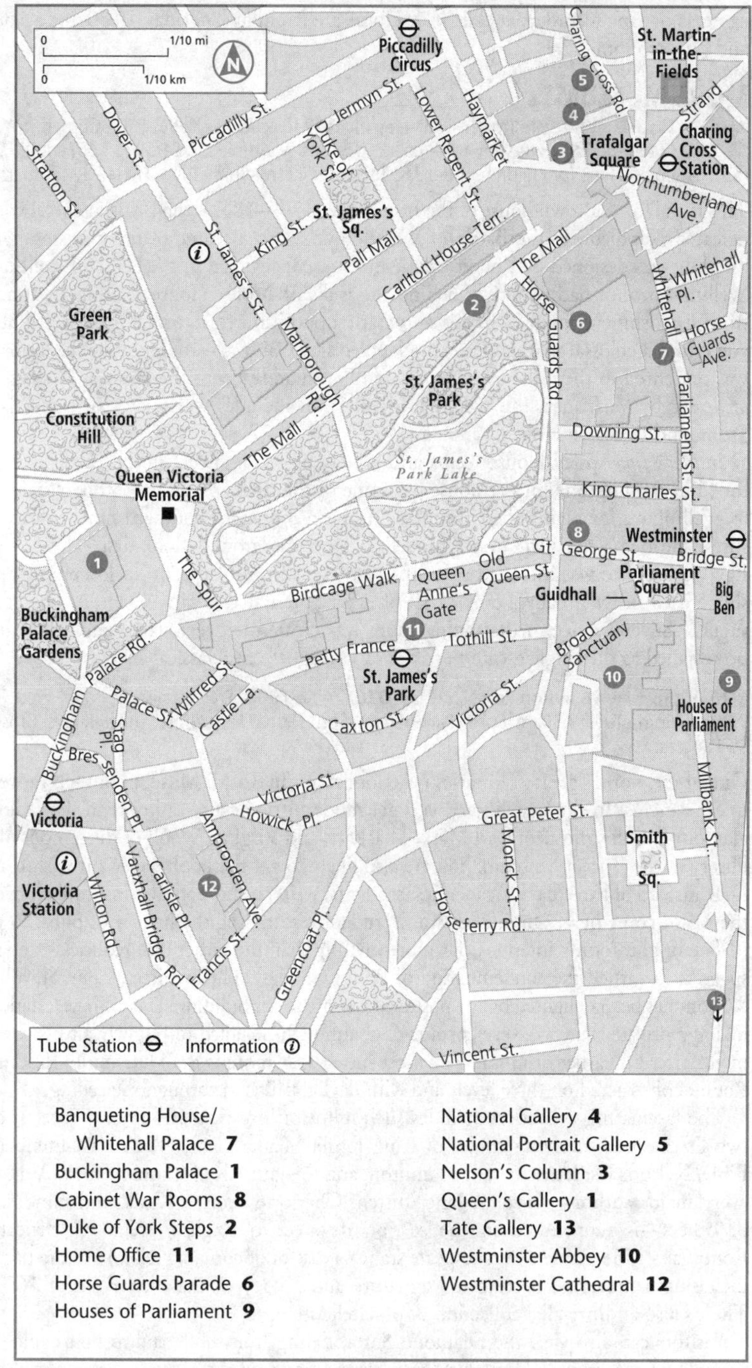

Banqueting House/
Whitehall Palace **7**
Buckingham Palace **1**
Cabinet War Rooms **8**
Duke of York Steps **2**
Home Office **11**
Horse Guards Parade **6**
Houses of Parliament **9**
National Gallery **4**
National Portrait Gallery **5**
Nelson's Column **3**
Queen's Gallery **1**
Tate Gallery **13**
Westminster Abbey **10**
Westminster Cathedral **12**

cameras or tape recorders are allowed. Hours are Monday to Friday 10:30am to 1pm and 2 to 4:30pm.

MORE MUSEUMS

Apsley House. The Wellington Museum. 149 Piccadilly, Hyde Park Corner, SW1. ☎ **020/7499-5676;** www.vam.ac.uk/collections/apsley. Admission £4.50 ($7.65) adults, £3 ($5.10) seniors. Free for children under 18. Tues–Sun 11am–5pm. Tube: Hyde Park Corner.

This is the former town house of the Iron Duke (1769–1852), the British general who defeated Napoléon at the Battle of Waterloo and later became prime minister. The building was designed by Robert Adam and was constructed in the late 18th century. Wellington once had to retreat behind the walls of Apsley House, fearing an attack from Englishmen outraged by his autocratic opposition to reform. In the vestibule, you'll find a colossal marble statue of Napoléon by Canova—ironic, to say the least; it was presented to the duke by King George IV. In addition to the famous *Waterseller of Seville* by Velázquez, the Wellington collection includes works by Correggio, Jan Steen, and Pieter de Hooch.

Insider's tip: Apsley House seems an unlikely place for silver and porcelain collectors, but Wellington's former house has some of the finest pieces in Europe. Grateful to Wellington for saving their thrones, European monarchs endowed him with treasures. Head for the Plate and China Room on the ground floor first. The Sèvres Egyptian service was intended as a divorce present from Napoléon to Josephine, but she refused it. Eventually, Louis XVIII of France presented it to Wellington. The Portuguese Silver Service in the dining room was created between 1812 and 1816: It's been hailed as the single greatest artifact of Portuguese neoclassical silver.

British Library. 96 Euston Rd., NW1. ☎ **020/7412-7000.** Free admission. Mon, Wed–Fri 9:30am–6pm, Tues 9:30am–8pm, Sat 9:30am–5pm, Sun 11am–5pm. Tube: King's Cross/ St. Pancras.

One of the world's greatest libraries is no longer at the British Museum but has moved to St. Pancras. In the new library, you get modernistic beauty rather than the fading glamour and the ghosts of Karl Marx, Thackery, and Virginia Woolf of the famous old library at the British Museum. You are also likely to get the book you want within an hour instead of three days. Academics, students, writers, and bookworms from all over the world come here. On our left was a student researching the history of pubs.

The bright, roomy interior is far more inviting than the rather dull redbrick exterior suggests (it earned the condemnation of Prince Charles). The architect, Colin St. John Wilson, has been delighted by the positive response to his building. Even Prince Charles, taking a private tour, was very encouraging, although he failed to publicly air his comments after his earlier dismissal. The most spectacular room is the Humanities Reading Room, constructed on three levels and with daylight filtered through the ceiling.

The fascinating collection includes such items of historical and literary interest as two of the four surviving copies of King John's Magna Carta (1215), a Gutenberg Bible, Nelson's last letter to Lady Hamilton, and the journals of Captain Cook. Almost every major author—Dickens, Jane Austen, Charlotte Brontë, Keats, and hundreds of others—is represented in the section devoted to English literature. Beneath Roubiliac's 1758 statue of Shakespeare stands a case of documents relating to the Bard, including a mortgage bearing his signature and a copy of the First Folio of 1623. There's also an unrivaled collection of philatelic items.

Visitors can also view the Diamond Sutra, dating from 868, said to be the oldest surviving printed book. Using headphones set up around the room, you can also hear thrilling audio snippets, even James Joyce reading a passage from *Finnegans Wake.*

Sights from Knightsbridge to Kensington

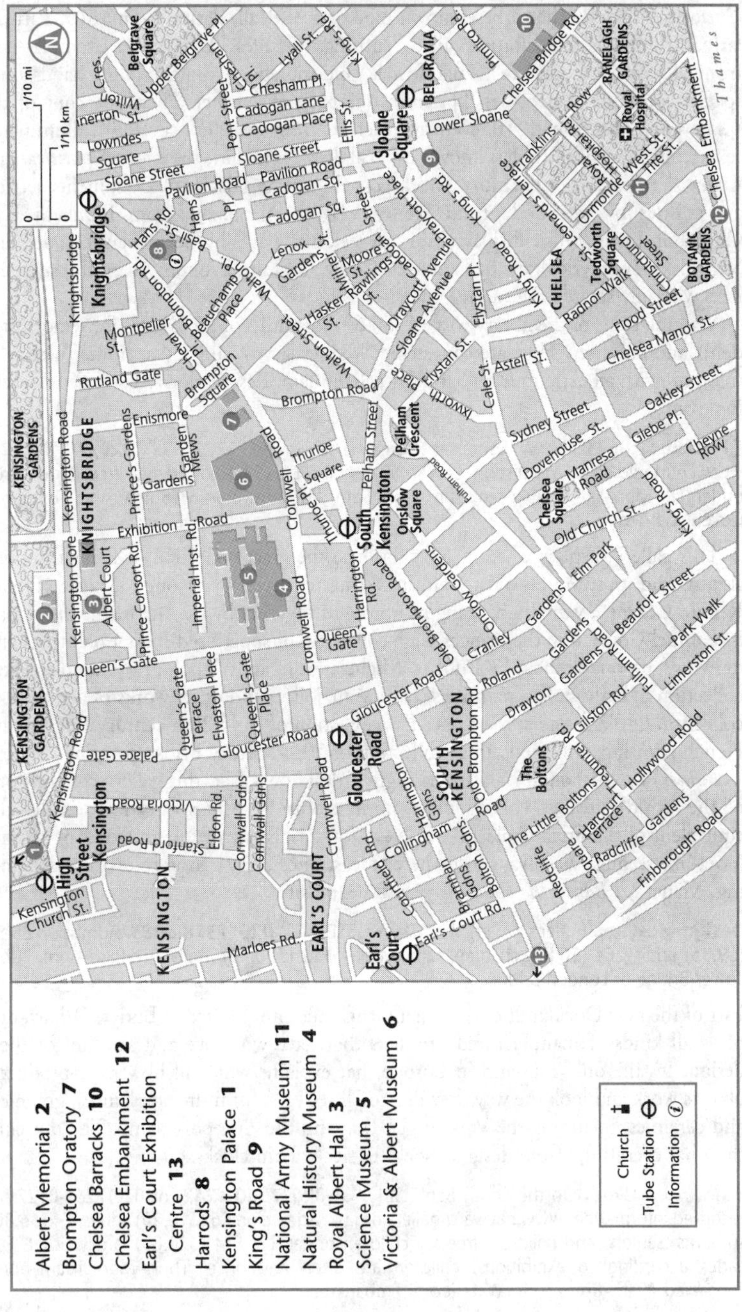

Albert Memorial 2
Brompton Oratory 7
Chelsea Barracks 10
Chelsea Embankment 12
Earl's Court Exhibition Centre 13
Harrods 8
Kensington Palace 1
King's Road 9
National Army Museum 11
Natural History Museum 4
Royal Albert Hall 3
Science Museum 5
Victoria & Albert Museum 6
Church
Tube Station
Information
KENSINGTON GARDENS
KNIGHTSBRIDGE
KENSINGTON
EARL'S COURT
SOUTH KENSINGTON
CHELSEA
BELGRAVIA
BOTANIC GARDENS
RANELAGH GARDENS
Royal Hospital
Thames

Curiosities include the earliest known tape of a birdcall, dating from 1889. Particularly intriguing is an exhibition called "Turning the Pages." You can, for example, electronically read a complete Leonardo da Vinci notebook, putting your hands on a special computer screen that flips from one page to another. There is a copy of the *Canterbury Tales* from 1410, even manuscripts from *Beowulf* (ca. 1000). Illuminated texts from some of the oldest known Biblical displays include the *Codex Sinaitticus* and *Codex Alexandrius,* 3rd-century Greek gospels. In the Historical Documents section are epistles by everybody from Henry VIII to Napoleon, from Elizabeth I to Churchill. In the music displays, you can seek out works by Beethoven, Handel, and Stravinsky, even lyric drafts by Paul McCartney and John Lennon. An entire day spent here will only scratch the surface.

Walking tours of the library cost £4 ($6.60) for adults or £3 ($4.95) for seniors, students and children. They are conducted Wednesday to Monday at 3pm, Tuesday at 6:30pm, with an extra tour on Saturday at 10:30am. Reservations are advised 3 weeks in advance.

✪ **Courtauld Gallery.** Somerset House, The Strand, WC2. ☎ **020/7873-2526;** www.courtauld.ac.uk. Admission £4 ($6.80) adults, £2 ($3.40) students, free for children under 18. Mon–Sat 10am–6pm, Sun noon–6pm; last admission 5:15pm. Tube: Temple or Covent Garden.

This gallery displays a wealth of paintings: the great collection of French impressionist and postimpressionist paintings (masterpieces by Monet, Manet, Degas, Renoir, Cézanne, van Gogh, Gauguin) brought together by the late textile industrialist Samuel Courtauld; the Princes Gate collection of superb old-master paintings and drawings, especially those by Rubens, Michelangelo, and Tiepolo; the Gambier-Parry collection of early Italian paintings, ivories, majolica, and other works of art; the Lee collection of old masters; the Roger Fry collection of early-20th-century English and French painting; and the Hunter collection of 20th-century British painting.

Insider's tip: Although it's a surprisingly little-known fact, this gallery contains one of the world's greatest collections of impressionist paintings outside Paris. It's the equivalent of the Frick Collection in New York, a display of superb works of art in a jewel-like setting. We always come here at least once every season to revisit one painting: Manet's *A Bar at the Folies-Bergère*. It's exquisite.

Design Museum. Butler's Wharf, Shad Thamas, SE1. ☎ **020/7378-6055.** Admission £5.50 ($9.35) adults, £4 ($6.80) children, family ticket £12 ($20.40). Daily 11:30am–6pm. Tube: Tower Bridge or London Bridge.

Part of the new Docklands development, this museum, located at Butler's Wharf, displays all kinds of manufactured products that have won love and acclaim for their design. It's the only museum in Europe that explains why and how mass-produced objects work and look the way they do. You'll see cars, furniture, appliances, graphics, and ceramics, including the Volkswagen Bug and the anglepoise lamp. The museum shop has everything from designer socks to sleek alarm clocks.

Hayward Gallery. On the South Bank, SE1, ☎ **020/7960-4242;** or 020/7261-0127 for recorded information. www.hayward-gallery.org.uk. Admission £6 ($10.20) adults, £4 ($6.80) students, seniors, and children, free for children under 12, £14 ($23.80) family ticket. Fee varies according to exhibitions; children are often half price. Thurs–Mon 10am–6pm, Tues–Wed 10am–8pm. Tube: Waterloo or Embankment.

Opened by Elizabeth II in 1968, this gallery presents a changing program of major contemporary and historical exhibits. It's managed by the South Bank Board, which also includes the Royal Festival Hall, the Queen Elizabeth Hall, and the Purcell Room.

An Open Sesame to Viewing

If you're coming to London to pub crawl, forget it, but if you want to become a serious museum-goer, you can save a lot of money by purchasing the London White Card. Available to individuals or families, it is a real saver pass if you plan to visit a lot of museums, including some of the major attractions of London: the Museum of Moving Image, the Victoria and Albert Museum, the Science Museum, and the Design Museum, plus a lot more. Validity ranges from 3 to 7 days. An adult 3-day costs £16 ($27.20), a 7-day card going for £26 ($44.20). Families of two adults and up to four children can purchase a 3-day card for £32 ($54.40) or a 7-day card for £50 ($85). Cards are sold at British tourist information centers, London Transport centers, airports, and various attractions. For more details, call ☎ **020/7923-0807.**

Every exhibition is accompanied by a variety of educational activities, including tours, workshops, lectures,and publications. The gallery closes between exhibitions, so call before crossing the Thames.

Imperial War Museum. Lambeth Rd., SE1. ☎ **020/7416-5000;** www.iwm.org.uk. Admission £5.20 ($8.85) adults, £4.20 ($7.15) seniors and students, £2.60 ($4.40) children; free daily 4:30–6pm. Daily 10am–6pm. Tube: Lambeth North or Elephant and Castle.

Built around 1815, this large, domed building, the former Bethlehem Royal Hospital for the Insane (or Bedlam), houses the museum's collections relating to the two world wars and other military operations since 1914. There are four floors of exhibitions, including the Large Exhibits Gallery, a vast area showing historical displays, two floors of art galleries, and a dramatic re-creation of London at war during the Blitz. You can see a Battle of Britain Spitfire, the rifle carried by Lawrence of Arabia, and Hitler's political testament, as well as models, decorations, uniforms, photographs, and paintings.

London Transport Museum. The Piazza, Covent Garden, WC2. ☎ **020/7379-6344.** Recorded info 020/7565-7299; www.hmuseum.co.uk. Admission £5.50 ($9.35) adults, £2.95 ($5) children, £13.95 ($23.70) family ticket, free for children under 5. Sat–Thurs 10am–6pm, Fri 11am–6pm (last entrance at 5:15pm). Tube: Covent Garden.

This splendidly restored Victorian building once housed the flower market. Now it's home to horse buses, motor buses, trams, trolleybuses, railway vehicles, models, maps, posters, photographs, and audiovisual displays that trace 200 years of London transport history. The story is enlivened by several interactive video exhibits—you can put yourself in the driver's seat of a bus or tube train. The fabulous gift shop sells a variety of London Transport souvenirs. Much to the glee of parents, the museum has added "kidzones"—interactive programs for children so parents can enjoy the museum without having to entertain the kids.

✪ **Museum of London.** 150 London Wall, EC2. ☎ **020/7600-3699;** www.museumoflondon.org.uk. Admission £5 ($8.50) adults, £3 ($5.10) students, and seniors, children, free. Mon–Sat 10am–5:50pm, Sun noon–5:50pm. Tube: St. Paul's or Barbican.

In the Barbican district near St. Paul's Cathedral, the Museum of London allows visitors to trace the city's history from prehistoric times to the postmodern era through relics, costumes, household effects, maps, and models. Anglo-Saxons, Vikings, Normans—they're all here, displayed on two floors around a central courtyard. The exhibits are arranged so that visitors can begin and end their chronological stroll through 250,000 years at the museum's main entrance, and exhibits have quick labels for museum sprinters, more extensive ones for those who want to study, and still more detail for scholars. It's an enriching experience for everybody—allow at least an hour for a full (but still quick) visit.

You'll see the death mask of Oliver Cromwell; the Great Fire of London in living color and sound; reconstructed Roman dining rooms with kitchen and utensils; cell doors from Newgate Prison, made famous by Charles Dickens; and an amazing shop counter with pre–World War II prices on the items. But the pièce de résistance is the lord mayor's coach, built in 1757 and weighing 3 tons. Still used each November in the Lord Mayor's Procession, this gilt-and-red horse-drawn vehicle is like a fairy-tale coach.

Free lectures on London's history are often given during lunch hours; ask at the entrance hall if one will be given the day you're here. You can reach the museum, which overlooks London's Roman and medieval walls, by going up to the elevated pedestrian precinct at the corner of London Wall and Aldersgate, 5 minutes from St. Paul's.

National Army Museum. Royal Hospital Rd., SW3. ☎ **020/7730-0717;** www.national-army-museum.ac.uk. Free admission. Daily 10am–5:30pm. Closed Good Friday, 1st Mon in May, and for some days around Christmas. Tube: Sloane Sq.

Located in Chelsea, this museum traces the history of the British land forces, the Indian army, and colonial land forces. The collection starts with 1485, the date that the Yeomen of the Guard was formed. The saga of the forces of the East India Company is also traced, from its beginning in 1602 to Indian independence in 1947. The gory and glory are all here—everything from Florence Nightingale's lamp to the cloak wrapped around the dying Gen. James Wolfe at Québec in 1759. There are also "cases of the heroes," mementos of such outstanding men as the duke of Marlborough and the duke of Wellington. But the field soldier isn't neglected either: The Nation in Arms Gallery tells the soldier's story in two world wars, including an exhibit of the British Army in the Far East from 1941 to 1945.

✪ **National Portrait Gallery.** St. Martin's Place, WC2. ☎ **020/7306-0055;** www.npg.org.uk. Free admission; fee charged for certain temporary exhibitions. Mon–Wed 10am–6pm, Thurs–Sat 10am–9pm, Sun noon–6pm. Tube: Charing Cross or Leicester Square.

The National Portrait Gallery was founded in 1856 to collect the likenesses of famous British men and women. Today, the collection is the most comprehensive of its kind in the world and constitutes a unique record of the men and women who created the history and culture of the nation. A few paintings tower over the rest, including Sir Joshua Reynold's portrait of Samuel Johnson. Among the best are Nicholas Hilliard's miniature of a handsome Sir Walter Raleigh and a full-length Elizabeth I, along with the Holbein cartoon of Henry VIII (sketched for a family portrait that hung, before it was burned, in the Privy Chamber in Whitehall Palace). You'll also see a portrait of William Shakespeare (with gold earring, no less), which is claimed to be the most "authentic contemporary likeness" of its subject of any work yet known. One of the most unusual pictures in the gallery is a group of the three Brontë sisters painted by their brother Branwell. Famous people of today, including the Baroness Thatcher, are celebrated in two floors of the most recent galleries. The portrait of Diana, the late Princess of Wales, is on the Royal Landing.

Insider's tip: The galleries of Victorian and early-20th-century portraits were radically redesigned. Occupying the whole of the first floor, they display portraits from 1837 up through the beginning of the 1960s—a remarkable span of British history.

Some of the more flamboyant personalities of the age, from the pre-Raphaelites to the Bloomsbury Group, are on show, including our two favorites—G. F. Watts's famous portrait of his great actress wife, Ellen Terry, and Vanessa Bell's portrait of her sister, Virginia Woolf.

Natural History Museum. Cromwell Rd., SW7. ☎ **020/7938-9123;** www.num.ac.uk. Admission £6.50 ($11.05) adults, £3.50 ($5.95) seniors and students, £3 ($5.10) children 5–17, free, £16 ($27.20) family ticket; free to everyone Mon–Fri after 4:30pm and Sat–Sun after 5pm. Mon–Sat 10am–5:50pm, Sun 11am–5:50pm. Tube: South Kensington.

With towers, spires, and a huge navelike hall, this terra-cotta building is a wonder in itself. The core of the collection came from Sir Hans Sloane. Today, only a fraction of the museum's natural treasures—fossils, animal- and plant-life exhibits, and minerals—can be displayed. Among the highlights are the dinosaurs in the main hall, the Human Biology exhibit that features many interactive displays, and an ecology exhibit. There's also an earthquake simulator and an insect display. The latest addition is "Earth Galleries," an exhibition outlining humankind's relationship with planet earth. Here in the exhibition "Earth Today and Tomorrow," visitors are invited to explore the planet's dramatic history from the big bang to its inevitable death.

Royal Academy of Arts. Burlington House, Piccadilly, W1. ☎ **020/7300-8000;** www.royalacademy.org.uk. Admission varies, depending on the exhibition. Daily 10am–6pm (last admission 5:30pm); Fri 10am–8:30pm (last admission 8pm). Tube: Piccadilly Circus or Green Park.

Established in 1768, the academy included Sir Joshua Reynolds, Thomas Gainsborough, and Benjamin West among its founding members. Since its beginning, each academician has had to donate a work of art, so over the years the academy has built up a sizable collection. The annual summer exhibition has been held for more than 200 years.

✪ **The Saatchi Gallery.** 98A Boundary Rd., NW8. ☎ **020/7624-8299.** Admission £4 ($6.80) adults, £2 ($3.40) students and seniors, children under 12 free. Thurs–Sun noon–6pm. Tube: St. John's Wood or Swiss Cottage.

In the world of contemporary art, this collection is unparalleled (except perhaps by New York's MOMA.) Charles Saatchi is one of Britain's greatest private collectors, and this personal museum features rotating displays from his vast holdings. Enter through the unmarked metal gateway of a former paint warehouse. The aim, as set forth by Saatchi, is to introduce new art, or art largely unseen in the United Kingdom, to a wider audience. The collection comprises more than 1,000 paintings and sculptures. Works that are not on display at the gallery are frequently on loan to museums around the world.

The main focus is on young British artwork including controversial ones, such as Damien Hirst's 14-foot tiger shark preserved in a formaldehyde-filled tank. Also on occasional exhibit is Marc Quinn's frozen "head" cast from nine pints of blood taken from the artist over several months. Art critics were shocked at Richard Wilson's art when it was introduced: 2,500 gallons of used sump oil that flooded through an entire gallery. Jenny Saville was commissioned to paint a series of paintings, which debated obesity and challenged the accepted perceptions of female beauty.

Young American and European artists are also represented, their work often controversial as well. Regardless of the exhibition on display when you visit, it's almost guaranteed to be fascinating. And if you've ever wondered what many British people think American tourists look like, catch Duane Hanson's *Tourists II* (1988). It's devastating!

Science Museum. Exhibition Rd., SW7. ☎ **020/7938-8000;** www.nmsi.ac.uk. Admission £6.50 ($11.05) adults, £3.50 ($5.95) children 5–17, free for children under 5. Free to all after 4:30pm. Daily 10am–6pm. Tube: South Kensington.

Among the most notable exhibits here are naval models; the Puffing Billy (1813), one of the oldest locomotives still in existence; Arkwright's spinning machine; Wheatstone's electric telegraph; Fox Talbot's first camera; Edison's original phonograph; the Vickers "Vimy" aircraft, which made the first Atlantic crossing in 1919; and Sir Frank Whittle's turbojet engine.

Three new galleries are designed to appeal to children. The Garden provides water, construction, sound-and-light shows, and games for 3- to 6-year-olds. The other two galleries appeal to 7- to 12-year-olds, with interactive exhibits and networked computer terminals that they can play on.

✪ **Sir John Soane's Museum.** 13 Lincoln's Inn Fields, WC2. ☎ **020/7405-2107.** Free admission (donations invited). Tues–Sat 10am–5pm; first Tues of each month 6–9pm. Tours given Sat at 2:30pm; £3 ($5.10) tickets distributed at 2pm on a first-come, first-served basis (group tours by appointment only). Tube: Holborn.

This is the former home of Sir John Soane (1753–1837), an architect who rebuilt the Bank of England (not the present structure). With his multilevels, fool-the-eye mirrors, flying arches, and domes, Soane was a master of perspective and a genius of interior space (his picture gallery, for example, is filled with three times the number of paintings a room of similar dimensions would be likely to hold). William Hogarth's satirical series, *The Rake's Progress,* includes his much-reproduced *Orgy* and *The Election,* a satire on mid-18th-century politics. Soane also filled his house with paintings and classical sculpture. On display is the sarcophagus of Pharaoh Seti I, found in a burial chamber in the Valley of the Kings. Also exhibited are architectural drawings from the collection of 30,000 in the Soane Gallery.

Wallace Collection. Manchester Sq., W1. ☎ **020/7935-0687;** www.the-wallace-collection.org.uk. Free admission. Mon–Sat 10am–5pm, Sun 2–5pm. Tube: Bond St. or Baker St.

This outstanding collection of artworks, bequeathed to the nation by Lady Wallace in 1897, is still displayed in the house of its founders. The works of art (mostly French) include important pictures by artists of all European schools. There's also sculpture, furniture, goldsmiths' work, and Sèvres porcelain, along with valuable collections of majolica and European and Asian arms and armor. Frans Hals's *Laughing Cavalier* is the most celebrated painting in the collection, but Pieter de Hooch's *A Boy Bringing Pomegranates* and Watteau's *The Music Party* are also well known.

LITERARY LANDMARKS

See the discussion of Hampstead Village in section 4, "Sights on the Outskirts," for details on Keats House. See section 1, "The Top Attractions," for details on Poet's Corner in Westminster Abbey.

Born in London in 1882, the author Virginia Woolf lived and worked in **Bloomsbury,** and set many of her works in London. Virginia spent her formative years at 22 Hyde Park Gate, off Kensington High Street, west of Royal Albert Hall. After the death of her father, the family left Kensington for Bloomsbury and settled in the area around the British Museum (upper-class Victorians at that time, however, didn't view Bloomsbury as "respectable"). From 1905, they lived first at 46 Gordon Sq., east of Gower Street and University College. It was here that the nucleus of the soon-to-be celebrated Bloomsbury Group was created, which would in time embrace Clive Bell

Bloomsbury

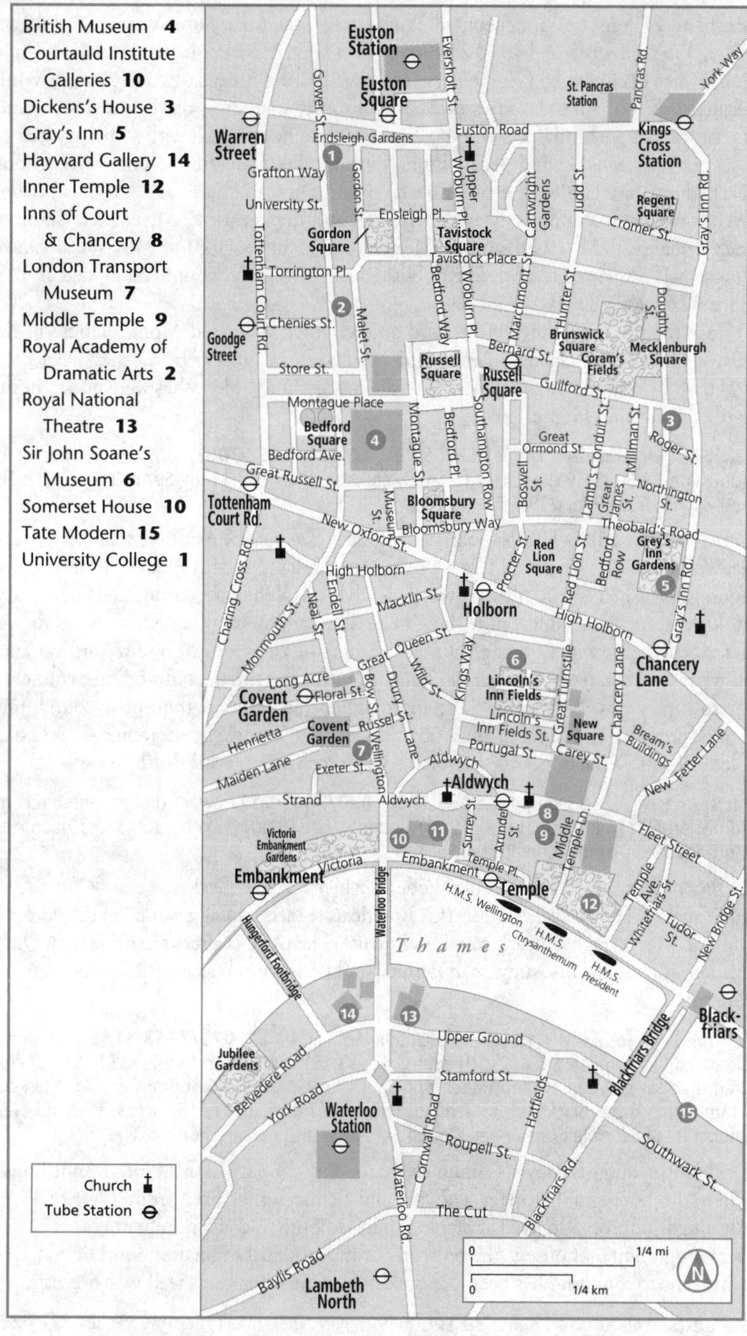

British Museum 4
Courtauld Institute Galleries 10
Dickens's House 3
Gray's Inn 5
Hayward Gallery 14
Inner Temple 12
Inns of Court & Chancery 8
London Transport Museum 7
Middle Temple 9
Royal Academy of Dramatic Arts 2
Royal National Theatre 13
Sir John Soane's Museum 6
Somerset House 10
Tate Modern 15
University College 1
Church
Tube Station
Euston Station
Euston Square
Eversholt St.
St. Pancras Station
Pancras Rd.
York Way
Kings Cross Station
Warren Street
Gower St.
Euston Road
Endsleigh Gardens
Upper Woburn Pl.
Grafton Way
Gordon St.
University St.
Ensleigh Pl.
Cartwright Gardens
Judd St.
Regent Square
Cromer St.
Gray's Inn Rd.
Gordon Square
Tavistock Square
Tavistock Place
Tottenham Court Rd
Torrington Pl.
Bedford Way
Woburn Pl.
Marchmont St.
Hunter St.
Doughty St.
Chenies St.
Malet St.
Goodge Street
Brunswick Square
Coram's Fields
Mecklenburgh Square
Bernard St.
Store St.
Russell Square
Guilford St.
Montague Place
Bedford Square
Bedford Ave.
Montague St.
Bedford Pl.
Southampton Row
Great Ormond St.
Lamb's Conduit St.
Millman St.
Roger St.
Great Russell St.
Tottenham Court Rd.
Museum St.
Bloomsbury Square
Bloomsbury Way
Boswell St.
Great James St.
Northington St.
Theobald's Road
New Oxford St.
Red Lion Square
Procter St.
Red Lion St.
Bedford Row
Grey's Inn Gardens
Charing Cross Rd
High Holborn
Endell St.
Neal St.
Macklin St.
Holborn
Monmouth St.
Great Queen St.
Wild St.
Kings Way
Lincoln's Inn Fields
Great Turnstile
Chancery Lane
Long Acre
Floral St.
Covent Garden
Bow St.
Drury Lane
Lincoln's Inn Fields St.
New Square
Bream's Buildings
Henrietta
Russel St.
Wellington
Portugal St.
Carey St.
New Fetter Lane
Maiden Lane
Exeter St.
Aldwych
Strand
Surrey St.
Arundel St.
Middle Temple Ln.
Fleet Street
Victoria Embankment Gardens
Victoria Embankment
Temple Pl.
Temple
Embankment
Waterloo Bridge
H.M.S. Wellington
H.M.S. Chrysanthemum
H.M.S. President
Temple Ave.
Whitefriars St.
Tudor St.
New Bridge St.
Thames
Hungerford Footbridge
Blackfriars
Blackfriars Bridge
Upper Ground
Jubilee Gardens
Belvedere Road
Stamford St.
York Road
Waterloo Station
Cornwall Road
Hatfields
Roupell St.
Southwark St.
Blackfriars Rd.
Waterloo Rd.
The Cut
Baylis Road
Lambeth North
0
1/4 mi
1/4 km
N

(husband of Vanessa) and Leonard Woolf, who was to become Virginia's husband. Later, Virginia went to live at 29 Fitzroy Sq., west of Tottenham Court Road, in a house once occupied by George Bernard Shaw. During the next two decades, Virginia resided at several more addresses in Bloomsbury, including on Brunswick Square, Tavistock Square, and Mecklenburg Square; these homes have either disappeared or else been altered beyond recognition. During this time, the Bloomsbury Group reached out to include the artists Roger Fry and Duncan Grant, and Virginia became friends with the economist Maynard Keynes and the author E. M. Forster. At Tavistock Square (1924–1939) and at Mecklenburg Square (1939–1940) she operated Hogarth Press with Leonard. She published her own early work here, as well as T. S. Eliot's *The Waste Land.*

To escape from urban life, Leonard and Virginia purchased Monk's House in the village of Rodmell between Lewes and Newhaven in Sussex. Here, they lived until 1941 when Virginia drowned herself in the nearby Ouse. Her ashes were buried in the garden at Monk's House.

Carlyle's House. 24 Cheyne Row, SW3. ☎ **020/7352-7087;** www.great-britain.org. Admission £3.50 ($5.95) adults, £1.75 ($3) children. Wed–Sun 11am–5pm. Tube: Sloane Sq. Bus: 11, 19, 22, 49, or 239.

From 1834 to 1881, Thomas Carlyle, author *of The French Revolution,* and Jane Baillie Welsh Carlyle, his noted letter-writing wife, resided in this modest 1708 terraced house. Furnished essentially as it was in Carlyle's day, the house is located about 3/4 of a block from the Thames, near the Chelsea Embankment along King's Road. It was described by his wife as being "of most antique physiognomy, quite to our humour; all wainscoted, carved and queer-looking, roomy, substantial, commodious, with closets to satisfy any Bluebeard." The most interesting room is the not-so-soundproof "soundproof" study in the skylit attic. It's filled with Carlyle memorabilia—his books, a letter from Disraeli, personal effects, a writing chair, even his death mask.

Dickens House. 48 Doughty St., WC1. ☎ **020/7405-2127;** www.dickensmuseum.com. Admission £4 ($6.80) adults, £3 ($5.10) students, £2 ($3.40) children, £9 ($15.30) families. Mon–Sat 10am–5pm. Tube: Russell Sq.

In Bloomsbury stands the simple abode in which Charles Dickens wrote *Oliver Twist* and finished The *Pickwick Papers* (his American readers actually waited at the dock for the ship that brought in each new installment). The place is almost a shrine for a Dickens fan; it contains his study, manuscripts, and personal relics, as well as reconstructed interiors.

✪ **Samuel Johnson's House.** 17 Gough Sq., EC4. ☎ **020/7353-3745;** www.drju.dircon.co.uk. Admission £3 ($5.10) adults, £2 ($3.40) students and seniors, £1 ($1.70) children, free for children 10 and under. Apr–Sept Mon–Sat 11am–5:30pm; Oct–Mar Mon–Sat 11am–5pm. Tube: Blackfriars or Temple. Bus from Trafalgar: 11, 15, or 23. Walk up New Bridge St. and turn left onto Fleet; Gough Sq. is tiny and hidden, north of Fleet St.

Dr. Johnson and his copyists compiled a famous dictionary in this Queen Anne house, where the lexicographer, poet, essayist, and fiction writer lived from 1748 to 1759. Although Johnson also lived at Staple Inn in Holborn and at a number of other places, the Gough Square house is the only one of his residences remaining in London. The 17th-century building has been painstakingly restored, and it's well worth a visit.

Shakespeare's Globe Theatre & Exhibition. New Globe Walk, Southwork, SE1. ☎ **020/7902-1500;** www.shakespeares-globe.org. Exhibition and tour admission £7.50 ($12.75) adults, £5 ($8.50) children 15 and under, £6 ($10.20) seniors and students. Guided tours £5 ($8.50) adults, £4 ($6.80) students and seniors, £3 ($5.10) children 15 and under. May–Sept daily 9:30am–noon, Oct–Apr daily 10am–5pm (guided tours every 30 minutes or so). Tube: Mansion House or London Bridge.

This is a re-creation of what was probably the most important public theater ever built—only yards from the site where many of Shakespeare's plays were originally staged in the 16th century. The late American filmmaker, Sam Wanamaker, worked for some 20 years to raise funds to re-create the theater as it existed in Elizabethan times, thatched roof and all. A fascinating exhibit tells the story of the Globe's re-creation in modern times, using the material (including goat's hair in the plaster), techniques, and craftsmanship of 400 years ago. The new Globe isn't actually an exact replica: It seats 1,500 patrons, not the 3,000 that regularly squeezed in during the early 1600s; and this thatched roof has been specially treated with a fire retardant. Guided tours of the facility are offered throughout the day.

See "London After Dark," later in this chapter, for details on attending a play here.

LANDMARK CHURCHES

Many of the churches listed below offer free **lunchtime concerts**—it's customary to leave a small donation. A full list of churches offering lunchtime concerts is available from the London Tourist Board.

✪ **St. Martin-in-the-Fields,** overlooking Trafalgar Square, WC2 (☎ **020/7930-0089;** tube: Charing Cross), is the Royal Parish Church. The first known church on the site dates from the 13th century, but the present classically inspired church, with its famous steeple, dates from 1726. From St. Martin's vantage position in the theater district, it has drawn many actors to its door—none more notable than Nell Gwyn, the mistress of Charles II. On her death in 1687, she was buried in the crypt. Throughout the war, many Londoners rode out uneasy nights in the crypt, while Blitz bombs rained down overhead. One, in 1940, blasted out all the windows. Today, the crypt has a pleasant restaurant, a bookshop, and a gallery. It is home to London's original **Brass Rubbing Centre** (☎ **020/7930-9306**).

St. Bride's Church, on Fleet Street (☎ **020/7353-1301;** tube: Blackfriars), is known as the church of the press. It's also a remarkable landmark: The current church is the eighth one that's stood here. Its spire has four octagonal tiers capped by an obelisk that's topped off with a ball and vane. This soaring confection (234 ft. tall) inspired the wedding cakes of a pastry cook who lived on Fleet Street in the late 17th century, it's said. The crypts are now a museum.

St. Etheldreda's, Britain's oldest Roman Catholic church, lies on Ely Place, Holborn Circus, EC1 (☎ **020/7405-1061;** tube: Farringdon or Chancery Lane), leading off Charterhouse Street at Holborn Circus. Built in 1251, it was mentioned by the Bard in both *Richard II* and *Richard III*. One of the survivors of the Great Fire of 1666, the church was built by, and was the property of, the diocese of Ely. Until this century, the landlord of Ye Olde Mitre public house near Ely Place had to obtain his license from the Justices of Cambridgeshire rather than in London, and today Ely Place is still a private road, with impressive iron gates and a lodge for the gatekeeper, all administered by six elected commissioners. The church has a distinguished musical tradition, with an 11am Latin mass on Sunday.

The spectacular brick-and-stone **Westminster Cathedral,** Ashley Place (☎ **020/7798-9055;** tube: Victoria), is the headquarters of the Roman Catholic church in Britain. Done in high Byzantine style, it's massive. One hundred different marbles compose the richly decorated interior. Mosaics emblazon the chapels and the vaulting of the sanctuary. If you climb to the top of the 273-foot-tall campanile, you'll be rewarded with a sweeping view over Victoria and Westminster.

London's Millennium Wheel

The world's largest observation wheel, the **Millennium Wheel London Eye**, Millennium Jubilee Gardens (☎ **020/7487-0294;** www.british-airways.com/londoneye), opened in February of 2000. It is the fourth tallest structure in London, offering panoramic views that extend for some 25 miles if the weather's clear. Passengers are carried in 32 "pods," a single revolution of the wheel—and the duration of the ride—taking half an hour. Along the way you'll see some of London's most famous landmarks from a bird's eye point of view.

Built by a European consortium with steel, this eye was conceived and designed by London architects Julia Barfield and David Marks. Barfield and Marks claim inspiration from both the Statue of Liberty in New York and the Eiffel Tower in Paris. Some two million visits are expected to ride the eye every year.

The eye lies close to Westminster Bridge (you can hardly miss it). Tickets for the ride are £7.45 ($12.65) for adults, £5.95 ($10.10) for seniors, and £4.95 ($8.40) for children. Hours are daily from 10am to 6pm November to March; otherwise daily from 9am to late—depending on the weather. Tube: Embankment or Waterloo.

ALONG THE THAMES

All of London's history and development is linked to this winding ribbon of water—which connects the city with the sea—from which London drew its wealth and its power. For centuries the river was London's highway and main street, and today there is a row of fascinating attractions lying on, across, and alongside the River Thames.

Some of the bridges that span the Thames are household words. London Bridge, which, contrary to the nursery rhyme, has never "fallen down," was dismantled and shipped to Arizona in 1971 and was immediately replaced by a new **London Bridge;** it ran from the Monument (a tall pillar commemorating the Great Fire of 1666) to Southwark Cathedral, parts of which date from 1207.

Its neighbor to the east is ✪ **Tower Bridge,** SE1 (☎ **020/7403-3761;** tube: Tower Hill), one of the city's most celebrated landmarks and the most photographed and painted bridge on earth. The Tower Bridge was built between 1886 and 1894 with two towers 200 feet apart, joined by footbridges that provide glass-covered walkways for the public. Exhibitions housed in the bridge's towers utilize advanced technology, including animatronic characters, video, and computers to illustrate the history of the Tower Bridge. The bridge is a photographer's dream, with interesting views of St. Paul's, the Tower of London, and in the distance, part of the Houses of Parliament.

You can visit the main engine room with Victorian boilers and steam-pumping engines, which used to raise and lower the roadway across the river. One model shows how the 1,000-ton arms of the bridge can be raised in 1½ minutes to allow ships' passage. Nowadays, electric power is used to raise the bridge, an occurrence that usually happens about once a day, more often in summer. Admission to the **Tower Bridge Experience** (☎ **020/7403-3761**) is £6.15 ($10.45) for adults and £4.15 ($7.05) for children 5 to 15, students, and senior citizens. It's free for children 4 and under. From April through October, hours are daily from 10am to 6:30pm; off-season daily 9:30am to 6pm. Last entry is 1 1/4 hours before closing. It's closed Good Friday, December 24 through 26, and January 1 through 28.

3 London's Parks & Gardens

London has the greatest system of parklands of any large city on the globe. Not as rigidly laid out as the parks of Paris, London's are maintained with a loving care and lavish artistry that puts their American equivalents to shame.

The largest of them—and one of the world's biggest—is **Hyde Park,** W2. With the adjoining Kensington Gardens, it covers 636 acres of central London with velvety lawn interspersed with ponds, flowerbeds, and trees. Hyde Park was once a favorite deer-hunting ground of Henry VIII. Running through the width is a 41-acre lake known as the Serpentine. Rotten Row, a 1½-mile sand track, is reserved for horseback riding and on Sunday attracts some skilled equestrians.

At the northeastern corner of Hyde Park, near Marble Arch, is **Speaker's Corner,** where anyone can get up and speak. The only rules: You can't blaspheme, be obscene, or incite a riot. The tradition began in 1855—before the legal right to assembly was guaranteed in 1872—when a mob of 150,000 gathered to attack a proposed Sunday Trading Bill. Orators from all over Britain have been taking advantage of it in this spot ever since.

Lovely ✪ **Kensington Gardens,** W2, blending with Hyde Park, border on the grounds of Kensington Palace. These gardens are home to the celebrated statue of Peter Pan, with the bronze rabbits that toddlers are always trying to kidnap. The Albert Memorial is also here, and you'll recall the sea of flowers and tributes left here after the death of Diana, Princess of Wales.

East of Hyde Park, across Piccadilly, stretch **Green Park** and **St. James's Park,** W1, forming an almost-unbroken chain of landscaped beauty. This is an ideal area for picnics, and one that you'll find hard to believe was once a festering piece of swamp near a leper hospital. There is a romantic lake, stocked with a variety of ducks and pelicans, descendants of the pair that the Russian ambassador presented to Charles II in 1662.

Regent's Park, NW1, covers most of the district by that name, north of Baker Street and Marylebone Road. Designed by the 18th-century genius John Nash to surround a palace of the prince regent that never materialized, this is the most classically beautiful of London's parks. The core is a rose garden planted around a small lake alive with waterfowl and spanned by humped Japanese bridges. The open-air theater and the London Zoo are here, and, as in all the local parks, there are hundreds of deck chairs on the lawns in which to sunbathe. The deck-chair attendants, who collect a small fee, are mostly college students on vacation.

The London Zoo (☎ **020/7722-3333**) is more than 150 years old. Run by the Zoological Society of London, the 36-acre garden houses some 8,000 animals, including some of the rarest species on earth. It waned in popularity the last few years, but a recent campaign won the zoo corporate sponsorship that is funding a modernization program. Zoo admission is £9 ($15.30) for adults, £7 ($11.90) for children 4 to 14, and free for children under 4. The zoo is open daily from 10am to 5:30pm (closes at 4pm from November through February). You can watch the penguins or the denizens of the aquarium being fed their lunch daily at 2:30pm. Take the tube to Camden Town or bus no. 274 or Z2 in summer only.

Battersea Park, SW11 (☎ **020/8871-7530**), is a vast patch of woodland, lakes, and lawns on the south bank of the Thames, opposite Chelsea Embankment between Albert Bridge and Chelsea Bridge. Formerly known as Battersea Fields, the present park was laid out between 1852 and 1858 on an old dueling ground. The park, which measures ¾ mile on each of its four sides, has a lake for boating, a fenced-in deer park with wild birds, and fields for tennis and football (soccer). There's even a children's zoo. The park's architectural highlight is the Peace Pagoda, built of stone and wood.

The park, open May through September daily from dawn until dusk, is not well serviced by public transportation. The nearest tube is in Chelsea on the right bank (Sloane Square); from here it's a brisk 15-minute walk. If you prefer to ride the bus, take no. 137 from the Sloane Square station, exiting at the first stop after the bus crosses the Thames.

See "Sights on the Outskirts," below, for details on Hampstead Heath and Kew Gardens.

4 Sights on the Outskirts

HAMPSTEAD HEATH & VILLAGE

Located about 4 miles north of the center of London, **Hampstead Heath,** an 800-acre expanse of high heath surrounded entirely by London, is a chain of continuous park, wood, and grassland. On a clear day you can see St. Paul's Cathedral and even the hills of Kent south of the Thames from here. For years, Londoners have come here to fly kites, sun worship, fish the ponds, swim, picnic, or jog. In good weather, it's also the site of big 1-day fairs. At the shore of Kenwood Lake, in the northern section, is a concert platform devoted to symphony performances on summer evenings. In the northeast corner, in Waterlow Park, ballets, operas, and comedies are staged at the Grass Theatre in June and July.

When the Underground came to **Hampstead Village** (tube: Hampstead) in 1907, its attraction as a place to live became widely known, and writers, artists, architects, musicians, and scientists—some from The City—came to join earlier residents. D. H. Lawrence, Rabindranath Tagore, Percy Bysshe Shelley, and Robert Louis Stevenson all once lived here, and Kingsley Amis and John Le Carré still do.

The Regency and Georgian houses in this village are just 20 minutes by tube from Piccadilly Circus. There's a palatable mix of historic pubs, toy shops, and chic boutiques along Flask Walk, a pedestrian mall. The original village, on the side of a hill, still has old roads, alleys, steps, courts, and groves to be strolled through.

✪ **Keats House.** Wentworth Place, Keats Grove, NW3. ☎ **020/7435-2062.** Free admission; donations welcome. Apr–Oct Mon–Fri 10am–1pm and 2–6pm, Sat 10am–1pm and 2–5pm, Sun and bank holidays 2–5pm; Nov–Mar Mon–Fri 1–5pm, Sat 10am–1pm and 2–5pm, Sun 2–5pm. Tube: Hampstead.

The poet lived here for only 2 years, but that was approximately two-fifths of his creative life, because he died in Rome of tuberculosis at the age of 25 (in 1821). In Hampstead, Keats wrote some of his most celebrated odes, including "Ode on a Grecian Urn" and "Ode to a Nightingale." His Regency house possesses the manuscripts of his last sonnet ("Bright star, would I were steadfast as thou art") and a portrait of him on his deathbed in a house on the Spanish Steps in Rome. Call before coming here, as the house is experiencing ongoing renovation and will be closed at random periods until 2003.

Kenwood House. Hampstead Lane, NW3. ☎ **020/8348-1286.** Free admission. Apr–Oct daily 10am–6pm; Nov–Mar daily 10am–4pm. Tube: Golders Green, then bus 210.

Kenwood House was built as a gentleman's country home and was later enlarged and decorated by the famous Scottish architect Robert Adam, starting in 1764. The house contains period furniture and paintings by Turner, Frans Hals, Gainsborough, Reynolds, and more.

Fenton House. Windmill Hill, NW3. ☎ **020/7435-3471.** Admission £4.20 ($7.15) adults, £2.10 ($3.55) children, £10.50 ($17.85) family ticket. Mar Sat–Sun 2–5pm; Apr–Oct Sat–Sun 11am–5pm, Wed–Fri 2–5pm. Closed Good Friday and Nov–Feb. Tube: Hampstead.

This National Trust property is on the west side of Hampstead Grove, just north of Hampstead Village. You pass through beautiful wrought-iron gates to reach the red-brick house in a walled garden. Built in 1693, it's one of the earliest, largest, and finest houses in the Hampstead section, and contains the outstanding Benton-Fletcher collection of early keyboard musical instruments, dating from 1540 to 1805. Occasional concerts are given.

Freud Museum. 20 Maresfield Gardens, NW3. ☎ **020/7435-2002;** www.freud.org.uk. Admission £4 ($6.80) adults, £2 ($3.40) full-time students, free for children under 12. Wed–Sun noon–5pm. Tube: Finchley Rd.

After he and his family left Nazi-occupied Vienna as refugees, Sigmund Freud lived, worked, and died in this spacious three-story house in northern London. In view are rooms with original furniture, letters, photographs, paintings, and personal effects of Freud and his daughter, Anna. In the study and library, you can see the famous couch and Freud's large collection of Egyptian, Roman, and Asian antiquities.

✪ **Highgate Cemetery.** Swain's Lane, N6. ☎ **020/8340-1834.** Western Cemetery guided tour £3 ($5.10). Eastern Cemetery, £1 ($1.70) admission, £2 ($3.40) camera pass charge (no video, hand-held cameras only). Western Cemetery, Mar–Dec guided tours only Mon–Fri at noon, 2, and 4pm, and Sat–Sun hourly 11am–4pm; Dec–Mar, tours Mon–Fri at noon, 2, and 4pm, and Sat–Sun hourly 11am–3pm; Eastern Cemetery, Apr–Oct daily 10am–5pm; Nov–Mar daily 10am–4pm. Both cemeteries closed at Christmas and during funerals. Tube: Archway, then walk through Waterlow Park. Bus: from Archway, 143, 271, or 210.

A stone's throw east of Hampstead Heath, Highgate Village has a number of 16th- and 17th-century mansions, as well as small cottages, lining three sides of the now-pondless Pond Square. Its most outstanding feature, however, is this beautiful cemetery, laid out around a huge, 300-year-old cedar tree and laced with serpentine pathways. The cemetery was so popular and fashionable in the Victorian era that it was extended on the other side of Swain's Lane in 1857. The most famous grave is that of Karl Marx, who died in Hampstead in 1883; his grave, marked by a gargantuan bust, is in the eastern cemetery. In the old western cemetery— accessible only if you take a guided tour, given hourly in summer—are scientist Michael Faraday and poet Christina Rossetti.

HAMPTON COURT

✪ **Hampton Court Palace.** ☎ **0181/781-9500;** www.hrp.org.uk. Admission £10 ($17) adults, £7.60 ($12.90) students and seniors, £6.60 ($11.20) children 5–15, free for children under 5. Gardens open year-round daily 7am–dusk (no later than 9pm), free admission to all except Privy Garden (admission £2.10/$3.55) without palace ticket during summer months). Cloisters, courtyards, state apartments, great kitchen, cellars, and Hampton Court exhibition open mid-Mar to mid-Oct daily 9:30am–6pm; mid-Oct to mid-Mar daily 9am–4:30pm. Tudor tennis court open mid-Mar to mid-Oct.

The 16th-century palace of Cardinal Wolsey can teach us a lesson: Don't try to outdo your boss, particularly if he happens to be Henry VIII. The rich cardinal did just that, and he eventually lost his fortune, power, and prestige and ended up giving his lavish palace to the Tudor monarch. Henry took over, even outdoing the Wolsey embellishments. The Tudor additions included the Anne Boleyn gateway, with its 16th-century astronomical clock that even tells the high-water mark at London Bridge. From Clock Court, you can see one of Henry's major contributions, the aptly named Great Hall, with its hammer-beam ceiling. Also added by Henry were the tiltyard, a tennis court, and kitchen.

To judge from the movie *A Man for All Seasons,* Hampton Court had quite a retinue to feed. Cooking was done in the Great Kitchen. Henry cavorted through the various apartments with his wife of the moment—everybody from Anne Boleyn to Catherine Parr (the latter reversed things and lived to bury her erstwhile spouse). Charles I was imprisoned here at one time and managed to temporarily escape his jailers.

Although the palace enjoyed prestige and pomp in Elizabethan days, it owes much of its present look to William and Mary—or rather to Sir Christopher Wren, who designed and had built the Northern or Lion Gates, intended to be the main entrance to the new parts of the palace. The fine wrought-iron screen at the south end of the south gardens was made by Jean Tijou around 1694 for William and Mary. You can parade through the apartments today, filled as they are with porcelain, furniture, paintings, and tapestries. The King's Dressing Room is graced with some of the best art, mainly paintings by old masters on loan from Queen Elizabeth II. Finally, be sure to inspect the royal chapel (Wolsey wouldn't recognize it). To confound yourself totally, you may want to get lost in the serpentine **shrubbery maze** in the garden, also the work of Sir Christopher Wren.

The gardens—including the Great Vine, King's Privy Garden, Great Fountain Gardens, Tudor and Elizabethan Knot Gardens, Board Walk, Tiltyard, and Wilderness—are open daily year-round from 7am until dusk (but not later than 9pm) and can be visited free except for the Privy Garden. A garden cafe and restaurant is in the Tiltyard Gardens.

KEW

✪ **Royal Botanic (Kew) Gardens.** Kew. ☎ **020/8940-1171;** www.rbgkew.org.uk. Admission £5 ($8.50) adults, £3.50 ($5.95) students and seniors, £2.50 ($4.25) children, family ticket £13 ($22.10). Daily 9:30am–5pm. Tube: Kew Gardens.

The Royal Botanic Gardens, better known as Kew Gardens, are among the best-known botanic gardens in Europe and offer thousands of varieties of plants. But Kew is no mere pleasure garden—it's essentially a vast scientific research center that happens to be beautiful. A pagoda, erected from 1761 to 1762, represents the "flowering" of chinoiserie. The Visitor Centre at Victoria Gate houses an exhibit telling the story of Kew, as well as a bookshop where guides to the garden are available.

The gardens, on a 300-acre site, encompass lakes, greenhouses, walks, garden pavilions, and museums, together with fine examples of the architecture of Sir William Chambers. No matter what season you visit Kew, there's always something to see, beginning with the first spring flowers and lasting through the winter, when the Heath Garden is at its best. Among the 50,000 plant species are notable collections of arum lilies, ferns, orchids, aquatic plants, cacti, mountain plants, palms, and tropical water lilies.

GREENWICH

Greenwich Mean Time is the basis of standard time throughout most of the world, and Greenwich has been the zero point used in the reckoning of terrestrial longitudes since 1884. But this lovely village—the center of British seafaring when Britain ruled the seas—is also home of the Royal Naval College, the National Maritime Museum, and the Old Royal Observatory. In dry dock at Greenwich Pier is the clipper ship *Cutty Sark.* Greenwich also has some wonderful shopping, including a famous weekend market.

Greenwich was the site of Britain's Millennium Dome for 2000, which has been billed as "the most spectacular event on earth." At least it was the largest on earth, a multimedia extravaganza that mixed education and entertainment. Most of the project's cost, estimated at more than $1.25 billion U.S. dollars, came from national lottery revenues.

GETTING THERE The extended Jubilee Line follows a new line from Green Park via Westminster, Waterloo, London Bridge, the Docklands, and North Greenwich through to Stratford in East London. Greenwich North is the largest station on the London Underground not connected to the British Rail network.

The Tube is for speed, but if you'd like to go to Greenwich the way Henry VIII did, you still can. Part of the fun of going to Greenwich, about 4 miles from the City, is getting there. The most appealing way involves boarding any of the frequent ferry-boats that cruise along the Thames at intervals that vary from every half hour (in summer) to every 45 minutes (in winter). Boats that depart from Westminster Pier (Tube: Westminster) are maintained by **Westminster Passenger Services, Ltd.** (☎ **020/7930-4097**). Boats that leave from Charing Cross Pier (Tube: Embankment) and Tower Pier (Tube: Tower Hill) are run by **Catamaran Cruises, Ltd.** (☎ **020/7987-1185**). Depending on the tides and the carrier you select, travel time varies from 50 to 75 minutes each way. Passage is £7.25 to £7.30 ($12.35 to $12.40) round-trip for adults, £3.70 to £3.95 ($6.30 to $6.70) round-trip for children 5 to 12; it's free for those under 5.

You can also take the train from Charing Cross Station. **Rail Europe** (☎ **0345/484950** in London or 800/848-7245 in the U.S.) trains take about 15 minutes to reach Greenwich from Charing Cross, costing between £1.90 to £2.90 ($3.25 to $4.95) round-trip, depending on the time of day you travel. A commuter train that can get you here is the **Docklands Light Railway** (☎ **020/7918-4000**), a tourist attraction in its own right: a narrow-gauge railway supported on stilts high above the Docklands. Passengers board the blue-and-white cars at Tower Gateway (Tube: Tower Hill) or Bank. The DLR has extended its line: The train passes above the Isle of Dogs before arriving at Island Gardens, in the Docklands, and goes on to the new stations—Lewisham, Greenwich, and Cutty Sark. The one-way fare is £1.80 ($3.05).

VISITOR INFORMATION The **Greenwich Tourist Information Centre** is at 46 Greenwich Church St. (☎ **020/8858-6376**); open daily 10am to 5pm. The Tourist Information Centre conducts **walking tours** of Greenwich's major sights. The tours, which cost £4 ($6.80), depart daily at 12:15 and 2:15pm and last 1½ to 2 hours. Advance reservations aren't required, but it's a good idea to phone in advance to find out if there have been any last-minute schedule changes.

SEEING THE SIGHTS

Most visitors flocked to Greenwich to visit the Millennium Dome in 2000, but the historic old town was a tourist attraction long before anyone ever heard of the Dome.

The **National Maritime Museum,** the **Old Royal Observatory,** and **Queen's House** stand together in a beautiful royal park, high on a hill overlooking the Thames. Combination tickets include admission to the museum and the observatory. Tickets cost £10.50 ($17.85) adults, £8.40 ($14.30) seniors. For Queen's House, tickets cost £7.50 ($12.75) adult, £6 ($10.20) seniors, £3 ($5.10) children. All three attractions are open daily from 10am to 5pm. For more information, call ☎ **020/8858-4422**; www.nmn.ac.uk.

From the days of early seafarers to 20th-century sea power, the **National Maritime Museum** illustrates the glory that was Britain at sea. The cannon, relics, ship models, and paintings tell the story of a thousand naval battles and a thousand victories, as well as the price of those battles. Look for some oddities here—everything from the dreaded cat-o'-nine-tails used to flog sailors until 1879 to Nelson's Trafalgar coat, with the fatal bullet hole in the left shoulder clearly visible. In time for the millennium, the museum spent £20 million in a massive expansion that added 16 new galleries devoted to British maritime history and improved visitor facilities.

Old Royal Observatory is the original home of Greenwich Mean Time. It has the largest refracting telescope in the United Kingdom, and a collection of historic timekeepers and astronomical instruments. You can stand astride the meridian and set your watch precisely by the falling time-ball. Wren designed the Octagon Room. Here, the first royal astronomer, Flamsteed, made his 30,000 observations that formed the basis of his *Historia Coelestis Britannica.* Edmond Halley, who discovered Halley's Comet, succeeded him. In 1833, the ball on the tower was hung to enable shipmasters to set their chronometers accurately.

Designed by Inigo Jones, **Queen's House** (1616) is a fine example of this architect's innovative style. It's most famous for the cantilevered tulip staircase, the first of its kind. Carefully restored, the house contains a collection of royal and marine paintings and other objets d'art.

Nearby is the **Royal Naval College,** King William Walk (off Romney Road; **020/8858-2154**). Designed by Sir Christopher Wren in 1696, it occupies 4 blocks named after King Charles, Queen Anne, King William, and Queen Mary. Formerly, Greenwich Palace stood here from 1422 to 1640. It's worth stopping in to see the magnificent Painted Hall by Thornhill, where the body of Nelson lay in state in 1805, and the Georgian chapel of St. Peter and St. Paul. Open daily 2:30 to 4:45pm; admission is free.

5 Especially for Kids

Kids of all ages will enjoy these attractions. For more information about what to do with children in London, call **Kidsline** (☎ **020/7222-8070**), for computerized information about current events that might interest kids. The line is open from 4 to 6pm during school-term time, and from 9am to 4pm on holidays. (However, it's almost impossible to get through.)

The London Dungeon. 28–34 Tooley St., SE1. ☎ **020/7403-7221;** www.southwark.gov.uk. Admission £9.50 ($16.15) adults, £8.50 ($14.45) students and seniors, £6.50 ($11.05) children under 15. Admission includes Judgment Day boat ride. Daily 10:30am–5pm. Tube: London Bridge.

Situated under the arches of London Bridge Station, the dungeon is a series of tableaux, more grizzly than Madame Tussaud's, that faithfully reproduce the ghoulish conditions of the Middle Ages. The rumble of trains overhead adds to the spine-chilling horror of the place. Dripping water and live rats (caged!) make for even more atmosphere. The heads of executed criminals were stuck on spikes for onlookers to observe through glasses hired for the occasion. The murder of Thomas à Becket in Canterbury Cathedral is also depicted. There's a burning at the stake, as well as a torture chamber with racking, branding, and fingernail extraction. The Great Fire of London is brought to crackling life by a computer-controlled spectacular that re-creates Pudding Lane, where the fire started.

Bethnal Green Museum of Childhood. Cambridge Heath Rd., E2. ☎ **0181/980-2415;** www.vam.ac.uk. Free admission. Sat–Thurs 10am–5:50pm. Tube: Bethnal Green.

Here you'll find displays of toys past and present. The variety of dolls alone is staggering. The dollhouses range from simple cottages to miniature mansions, complete with fireplaces, grand pianos, carriages, furniture, kitchen utensils, and household pets. In addition, the museum displays optical toys, toy theaters, marionettes, puppets, and soldiers and battle toys of both world wars. There is also a display of children's clothing and furniture.

6 Organized Tours

BUS TOURS If you're a first-time visitor and you'd like an overview, one popular choice is **The Original London Sightseeing Tour.** This 1½-hour tour on a traditional double-decker bus includes live commentary by a guide. The tour costs £12.50 ($21.25) for adults, £7.50 ($12.75) for children under 16, free for those under 5. You can hop on or hop off the bus at any point in the tour at no extra charge. The tour plus Madame Tussaud's costs from £22 ($37.40) for adults and £13.75 ($23.40) for children. You can buy tickets on the bus or from any London Transport or London Tourist Board Information Centre where you can receive a discount. Many hotel concierges also sell these tickets. You depart from various convenient points within the city, which you can decide upon when you purchase your ticket. For information or ticket purchases by phone, call ☎ **020/8877-1722.**

A double-decker air-conditioned coach in the distinctive green-and-gold livery of **Harrods,** 87–135 Brompton Rd. (☎ **020/7581-3603;** Tube: Knightsbridge), offers sightseeing tours around London. The first departure from Door 8 of Harrods is at 10:30am; afternoon tours begin at 1:30 and 4pm. Tea, coffee, and orange juice are served on board. It's £20 ($34) for adults, £10 ($17) for children under 14, free for those under 5. All-day excursions to Blenheim Palace, Windsor, Stratford-upon-Avon, and outlying areas of London are available. You can purchase tickets at Harrods, Sightseeing Department, lower-ground floor.

The Big Bus Company Ltd., Waterside Way, London SW17 (☎ **020/8944-7810**), is another alternative. It operates a 2-hour tour in summer, daily from 8:30am to 6pm (7pm in summer) with departures every 5 to 15 minutes (in winter, tours run daily from 9am to 6pm with departures every 10 to 15 minutes). Narrated tours pass by 18 sights, including all the highlights. Departure points are Marble Arch by Speakers Corner, Green Park by the Ritz Hotel, and Victoria Station (Buckingham Palace Road by the Royal Westminster Hotel). It costs £15 ($25.50) for adults, £6 ($10.20) for children. A 1-hour tour follows the same route, but only goes by 13 sights. Tickets are valid all day and you can hop on and off the bus as you wish.

BOAT TRIPS ON THE THAMES Touring boats operate on the Thames all year and can take you to various places within Greater London. Main embarking points are Westminster Pier, Charing Cross Pier, and Tower Pier, so, for example, you can take a "water taxi" from the Tower of London to Westminster Abbey.

Westminster-Greenwich Thames Passenger Boat Service, Westminster Pier, Victoria Embankment, SW1 (☎ **020/7930-4097**), concerns itself only with downriver traffic from Westminster Pier to such destinations as Greenwich (see "Attractions on the Outskirts," above). The most popular excursion departs for Greenwich (a 50-minute ride) at half-hour intervals between 10am and 4pm April to October, and between 10:30am and 5pm from June to August; from November to March, boats depart from Westminster Pier at 40-minute intervals daily from 10:40am to 3:20pm. One-way fares are £6.30 ($10.70) for adults, £3.30 ($5.60) for children under 16, senior, £5 ($8.50). Round-trip fares are £7.60 ($12.90) for adults, £3.80 ($6.45) for children, senior, £6.30 ($10.70). A family ticket for two adults and up to three children under 15 costs £16.80 ($28.55) one-way, £20 ($34) round-trip.

Westminster Passenger Association (Upriver) Ltd., Westminster Pier, Victoria Embankment, SW1 (☎ **020/7930-2062** or 020/7930-4721), offers the only riverboat service upstream from Westminster Bridge to Kew, Richmond, and Hampton Court. There are regular daily sailings from the Monday before Easter until the end of October, on traditional riverboats, all with licensed bars. Trip time, one-way, can be as little as 1½ hours to Kew and between 2½ to 4 hours to Hampton Court, depending on the tide. Cruises from Westminster Pier to Hampton Court via Kew Gardens leave daily at 10:30, 11:15am, and noon. Round-trip tickets are £10 to £14.50 ($17 to $24.65) adults, £7.50 to £12 ($12.75 to $20.40) seniors, and £5 to £9 ($8.50 to $15.30) children 4 to 14; one child under 4 accompanied by an adult goes free. Evening cruises from May to September are also available departing Westminster Pier at 7:30 and 8:30pm (9:30pm on demand) for £6.50 ($11.05) adults and £5 ($8.50) children.

WALKING TOURS **The Original London Walks,** 87 Messina Ave. (P.O. Box 1708), London NW6 4LW (☎ **020/7624-3978**). The oldest established walking-tour company in London is run by an Anglo-American journalist/actor couple, David and Mary Tucker. Their hallmarks are variety, reliability, reasonably sized groups, and—above all—superb guides, including renowned crime historian Donald Rumbelow (the leading authority on Jack the Ripper) and the author of the classic guidebook *London Walks* as well as several prominent actors (including classical actor Edward Petherbridge). Walks are regularly scheduled daily, and cost £5 ($8.50) for adults, £3.50 ($5.95) for students and seniors, and children under 15 go free. Call for schedule; no reservations needed.

Discovery Walks, 67 Chancery Lane, London WC2 (☎ **020/8530-8443;** www.Jack-the-Ripper-Walk.co.uk), are themed walks, led by Richard Jones, author of *Frommer's Memorable Walks in London.* **Stepping Out** (☎ **020/8881-2933;** www.walklon.ndirect.co.uk), offers a series of offbeat walks led by qualified historians, as does **Guided Walks in London,** 20 Denman Dr. North, London NW11 (☎ **020/7243-1097;** www.guided-walks-in-london.net/). Tours generally cost £4 to £5 ($6.80 to $8.50).

7 Shopping

THE TOP SHOPPING STREETS & NEIGHBORHOODS

There are several key streets that offer some of London's best retail stores—or simply one of everything—compactly located in a niche or neighborhood, so you can just stroll and shop.

THE WEST END The West End includes the tony Mayfair district and is home to the core of London's big-name shopping. Most of the department stores, designer shops, and multiples (chain stores) have their flagships in this area.

The key streets are **Oxford Street** for affordable shopping (start at Marble Arch tube station if you're ambitious, or Bond Street station if you just want to see some of it), and **Regent Street,** which intersects Oxford Street at Oxford Circus (tube: Oxford Circus).

While there are several branches of the private label department store **Marks & Spencer,** their Marble Arch store (on Oxford Street) is the flagship, and worth shopping for their high-quality goods. There's a grocery store in the basement and a home-furnishings department upstairs.

Regent Street has fancier shops—more upscale department stores (including the famed **Liberty of London**), multiples (**Laura Ashley**), and specialty dealers—and leads all the way to Piccadilly.

In between the two, parallel to Regent Street, is **Bond Street.** Divided into New and Old, Bond Street (tube: Bond Street) also connects Piccadilly with Oxford Street and is synonymous with the luxury trade. Bond Street has had a recent revival and is the hot address for all the international designers; **Donna Karan** has not one, but two shops here. A slew of international hotshots have their digs surrounding hers, from **Chanel** and **Ferragamo** to **Versace.**

Burlington Arcade (tube: Piccadilly Circus), the famous glass-roofed, Regency-style passage leading off Piccadilly, looks like a period exhibition and is lined with intriguing shops and boutiques. The small, smart stores specialize in fashion, jewelry, Irish linen, cashmere, and more. If you linger in the arcade until 5:30pm, you can watch the beadles, those ever-present attendants in their black-and-yellow livery and top hats, ceremoniously put in place the iron grills that block off the arcade until 9am the next morning, at which time they just as ceremoniously remove them to mark the start of a new business day. Also at 5:30pm, a hand bell called the Burlington Bell is sounded, signaling the end of trading.

Just off Regent Street (actually tucked right behind it) is **Carnaby Street** (tube: Oxford Circus), which is also having a comeback. While it no longer dominates the world of pacesetting fashion as it did in the 1960s, it's still fun to visit for teens who may need cheap souvenirs, a purple wig, or a little something in leather. There's also a convenient branch of **Boots the Chemists** here.

For a total contrast, check out **Jermyn Street,** on the far side of Piccadilly, a tiny two-block-long street devoted to high-end men's haberdashers and toiletries shops; many have been doing business for centuries. Several hold royal warrants, including **Turnball & Asser,** where HRH Prince Charles has his pj's made.

The West End leads to the theater district, so there's two more shopping areas: the still-not-ready-for-prime-time **Soho,** where the sex shops are slowly being turned into cutting-edge designer shops; and **Covent Garden,** which is a masterpiece unto itself. The original marketplace has overflowed its boundaries and eaten up the surrounding neighborhood so that even though the streets run a little higgledy-piggledy and you can easily get lost, it's fun to just wander and shop. Covent Garden is especially mobbed on Sundays.

KNIGHTSBRIDGE & CHELSEA This is the second-most famous of London's retail districts and the home of **Harrods** (tube: Knightsbridge). A small street nearby, **Sloane Street,** is chockablock with designer shops; and another street in the opposite direction, **Cheval Place,** is also lined with designer resale shops.

Walk toward Museum Row and you'll soon find **Beauchamp Place** (pronounced *Bee*-cham) (tube: Knightsbridge). The street is only one block long, but it features the kinds of shops where young British aristos buy their clothing.

Head out at the **Harvey Nichols** end of Knightsbridge, away from Harrods, and shop your way through the designer stores on Sloane Street (**Hermès, Armani, Prada,** and the like), then walk past Sloane Square and you're in an altogether different neighborhood: King's Road.

King's Road (tube: Sloane Square), the main street of Chelsea, which starts at Sloane Square, will forever remain a symbol of London in the Swinging Sixties. Today, the street is still frequented by young people, but there are fewer Mohican haircuts, "Bovver boots," and Edwardian ball gowns than before. More and more in the 1990s, King's Road is a lineup of markets and "multistores," large or small conglomerations of indoor stands, stalls, and booths within one building or enclosure.

Chelsea doesn't begin and end with King's Road. If you choose to walk the other direction from Harrods, you connect to a part of Chelsea called **Brompton Cross,**

Shipping It Home

You can ship on your flight home by paying for excess baggage (rates vary with the airline), or can have your packages shipped independently. Independent operators are generally less expensive than the airlines. Try **London Baggage,** London Air Terminal, Victoria Place, SW1 (☎ **020/7828-2400;** Tube: Victoria), or **Burns International Facilities,** at Heathrow Airport Terminal 1 (☎ **020/8745-5301**) and Terminal 4 (☎ **020/8745-7460**). But remember, you can only avoid the VAT up front if you have the store ship directly for you. If you ship via excess baggage or London Baggage, you'll still have to pay the VAT up front, and apply for a refund.

another hip and hot area for designer shops made popular when Michelin House was rehabbed by Sir Terence Conran for **The Conran Shop.**

Also seek out **Walton Street,** a tiny little snake of a street running from Brompton Cross back toward the museums. About two blocks of this three-block street are devoted to fairy-tale shops for m'lady where you can buy aromatherapy from **Jo Malone,** needlepoint, costume jewelry, or meet with your interior designer, who runs a small shop of objets d'art.

Finally, don't forget all those museums right there in the corner of the shopping streets. They all have great gift shops.

KENSINGTON & NOTTING HILL **Kensington High Street** is the new hangout of the classier breed of teen, who has graduated from Carnaby Street and is ready for street chic. While there are a few staples of basic British fashion on this strip, most of the stores feature items that stretch, are very, very short, or very, very tight. The tube station here is High Street Kensington.

From Kensington High Street, you can walk up **Kensington Church Street,** which, like Portobello Road, is one of the city's main shopping avenues for antiques. Kensington Church Street dead-ends into the Notting Hill Gate tube station, which is where you would arrive for shopping in **Portobello Road.** The dealers and the weekend market are two blocks beyond.

THE MARKETS

THE WEST END The most famous market in all of England, **Covent Garden Market** (☎ **020/7836-9136;** tube: Covent Garden), offers several different markets daily from 9am to 6:30pm (we think it's most fun to come on Sunday). It can be a little confusing, until you are here exploring it all. **Apple Market** is the fun, bustling market in the courtyard, where traders sell, well, everything. Many of the items are what the English call collectible nostalgia; they include a wide array of glassware and ceramics, leather goods, toys, clothes, hats, and jewelry. Some of the merchandise is truly unusual. Many items are handmade, with some of the craftspeople selling their own wares—except on Mondays, when the craftspeople are replaced by antiques dealers. Meanwhile, out back is **Jubilee Market** (☎ **020/7836-2139**), which is also an antiques market on Mondays. Every other day of the week, it's sort of a fancy hippie-ish market with cheap clothes and books. Out front there are a few tents of cheap stuff, except again on Monday, when antiques dealers take over here, too.

The market itself (in the superbly restored hall) offers one of the best shopping opportunities in London. The specialty shops that fill the building sell fashions and herbs, gifts and toys, books and personalized dollhouses, hand-rolled cigars, automata, and much, much more. There are bookshops and branches of famous stores (**Hamley's, The Body Shop**), and prices are kept moderate.

St. Martin-in-the-Fields Market (tube: Charing Cross) is good for teens and hipsters who don't want to trek all the way to Camden Market (see below) and can make do with imports from India and South America, crafts, and some local football souvenirs. It's located near Trafalgar Square and Covent Garden; hours are Monday through Saturday from 11am to 5pm, and Sunday noon to 5pm.

NOTTING HILL Whatever you collect, you'll find it at the **Portobello Market** (tube: Notting Hill Gate). It's mainly a Saturday happening, from 6am to 5pm. You needn't be here at the crack of dawn; 9am is fine. You just want to beat the motorcoach crowd. Once known mainly for fruits and vegetables (still sold here throughout the week), Portobello in the past four decades has become synonymous with antiques. But don't take the stall-holder's word for it that the fiddle he's holding is a genuine Stradivarius left to him in the will of his Italian great-uncle; it may just as well have been nicked from an East End pawnshop.

The market is divided into three major sections. The most crowded is the antiques section, running between Colville Road and Chepstow Villas to the south. (*Warning:* There's a great concentration of pickpockets in this area.) The second section (and the oldest part) is the "fruit and veg" market, lying between Westway and Colville Road. In the third and final section there's a flea market, where Londoners sell bric-a-brac and lots of secondhand goods they didn't really want in the first place. But looking around still makes for interesting fun.

The serious collector can pick up a copy of a helpful official guide, *Saturday Antique Market: Portobello Road & Westbourne Grove,* published by the Portobello Antique Dealers Association. It's available at most major bookstores in England, and lists where to find what, ranging from music boxes to militaria, lace to 19th-century photographs.

Note: Some 90 antiques and art shops along Portobello Road are open during the week when the street market is closed. This is actually a better time for the serious collector to shop because you'll get more attention from dealers. And you won't be distracted by the organ grinder.

NORTH LONDON If it's Wednesday, it's time for **Camden Passage** (☎ **020/7359-9969;** tube: Angel) in Islington, where each Wednesday and Saturday there's a very upscale antiques market. It starts in Camden Passage and then sprawls into the streets behind. It's on Wednesday from 8am to 4pm and Saturday from 9am to 5pm.

Don't confuse Camden Passage with **Camden Market** (very, very downtown). Camden Market (tube: Camden Town) is for teens and others into body piercing, blue hair (yes, still), and vintage clothing. Serious collectors of vintage may want to explore during the week, when the teen scene isn't quite so overwhelming. Market hours are 9:30am to 5:30pm daily, with some parts opening at 10am.

THE DEPARTMENT STORES

✪ **Fortnum & Mason.** 181 Piccadilly, W1. ☎ **020/7734-8040.** Tube: Piccadilly Circus.

The world's most elegant grocery store is a British tradition dating back to 1707. Down the street from the Ritz, it draws the carriage trade, those from Mayfair to Belgravia who come seeking such tinned treasures as pâté de foie gras or a boar's head. This store exemplifies the elegance and style you would expect from an establishment with three royal warrants. Enter and be transported to another world of deep-red carpets, crystal chandeliers, spiraling wooden staircases, and unobtrusive, tailcoated assistants.

The grocery department is renowned for its impressive selection of the finest foods from around the world—the best champagne, the most scrumptious Belgian chocolates, and succulent Scottish smoked salmon. You can wander through the four floors and inspect the bone china and crystal cut glass, find the perfect gift in the leather or stationery departments, or reflect on the changing history of furniture and ornaments in the antiques department. Dining choices include the **Patio,** the recently refurbished **St. James Restaurant, The Fountain Restaurant,** and the brand new **Salmon and Champagne Bar** (for details on taking afternoon tea here, see "Afternoon Tea," in chapter 3). After a £14 million development, Fortnum & Mason now offer exclusive and specialty ranges for the home, beauty, fashions for both women and men.

✪ **Harrods.** 87–135 Brompton Rd., Knightsbridge, SW1. ☎ **020/7730-1234.** Tube: Knightsbridge.

Harrods is an institution. As firmly entrenched in English life as Buckingham Palace and the Ascot Races, it's an elaborate emporium, at times as fascinating as a museum. Some of the goods displayed for sale are works of art, and so are the 300 departments displaying them. The sheer range, variety, and quality of merchandise are dazzling. The motto remains, "If you can eat or drink it, you'll find it at Harrods."

The whole fifth floor is devoted to sports and leisure, with a wide range of equipment and attire. Toy Kingdom is on the fourth floor, along with children's wear. The Egyptian Hall, on the ground floor, sells crystal from Lalique and Baccarat, plus porcelain. There's also a men's grooming room, an enormous jewelry department, and a fashion-forward department for younger customers. Along with the beauty of the bounty, check out the tiles and architectural touches. When you're ready for a break, you have a choice of 18 restaurants and bars. Best of all are the Food Halls, stocked with a huge variety of foods and several cafés. Harrods began as a grocer in 1849, and that's still the heart of the business.

In the basement you'll find a bank, a theater-booking service, and a travel bureau. Harrods Shop for logo gifts is on the ground floor.

Harvey Nichols. 109–125 Knightsbridge, SW1. ☎ **020/7235-5000.** Tube: Knightsbridge.

Locals call it Harvey Nicks. It has its own gourmet-food hall and fancy restaurant, on the fifth floor, and a huge store crammed with the best designer home furnishings, gifts, and fashions for all, although women's clothing is the largest segment of its business. The store does carry a lot of American designer brands; avoid them, as they're more expensive in London.

✪ **Liberty PLC.** 214–220 Regent St. ☎ **020/7734-1234.** Tube: Oxford Circus.

This is the flagship of the major British department store, which has branches all over the United Kingdom. It is celebrated for its Liberty prints. The front part of the store on Regent Street is sort of normal-looking, but don't be fooled: Outside and around back, Liberty is restored to its original Tudor splendor—whitewashed and half-timbered outside, galleries of wooden paneled salons inside. There are six floors of fashion, china, and home furnishings, as well as the famous Liberty Print fashion fabrics, upholstery fabrics, scarves, ties, luggage, and gifts.

Peter Jones. Sloane Sq., SW1. ☎ **020/7730-3434.** Tube: Sloane Sq.

Founded in 1877 and rebuilt in 1936, Peter Jones is known for household goods, household fabrics and trims, china, glass, soft furnishings, and linens. The linen department is one of the best in London.

SOME CLASSIC LONDON FAVORITES

ANTIQUES See also "The Markets," above. Portobello Road is really the prime hunting ground.

At the **Antiquarius Antiques Centre,** 131–141 King's Rd., SW3 (☎ **020/7969-1500;** tube: Sloane Square), more than 120 dealers offer specialized merchandise, such as antique and period jewelry, silver, first-edition books, boxes, clocks, prints, and paintings, with an occasional piece of antique furniture. You'll find a lot of items from the 1950s. Closed Sunday.

Alfie's Antique Market, 13–25 Church St., NW8 (☎ **020/7723-6066;** tube: Marylebone or Edgware Road), is the biggest and one of the best-stocked conglomerates of antique dealers in London, all crammed into the premises of what was built before 1880 as a department store. It contains more than 370 stalls, showrooms, and workshops scattered over 35,000 square feet of floor space. Closed Sunday and Monday. A whole antique district has grown up around Alfie's along Church Street.

BATH & BODY There are branches of **The Body Shop** seemingly everywhere. Check out the one at 375 Oxford St., W1 (☎ **020/7409-7868;** tube: Bond Street). Prices are drastically lower in the United Kingdom than they are in the United States.

Boots the Chemists has a million branches; we like the one across the street from Harrods for its convenience and size. It's at 72 Brompton Rd., SW3 (☎ **020/7589-6557;** tube: Knightsbridge). The house brands of beauty products are usually the best, be they Boots' products (try the cucumber facial scrub), Boots' versions of The Body Shop (two lines, Global and Naturalistic), or Boots' versions of Chanel makeup (called No. 7).

Stock up on essential oils, or perhaps dream pillows, candles, sachets of letters of the alphabet, and aromatherapy fans at **Culpeper the Herbalist,** 8 The Market, Covent Garden, WC2 (☎ **020/7379-6698**). There's another branch in Mayfair at 21 Bruton St., W1 (☎ **020/7629-4559**).

Floris, 89 Jermyn St., SW1 (☎ **020/7930-2885;** tube: Piccadilly Circus), stocks a variety of toilet articles and fragrances in floor-to-ceiling mahogany cabinets, which are architectural curiosities in their own right, dating from the Great Exhibition of 1851.

Neal's Yard Remedies, 15 Neal's Yard, WC2 (☎ **020/7379-7222;** tube: Covent Garden), is noted the world over for their cobalt-blue bottles. These homemade-style bath, beauty, and aromatherapy products are chichi must-haves for those who pooh-pooh The Body Shop as too common. Prices are much higher in the United States.

The Victorian perfumery called **Penhaligon's,** 41 Wellington St., WC2 (☎ **020/7836-2150;** tube: Covent Garden), offers a large selection of perfumes, aftershaves, soaps, and bath oils for women and men. Gifts include antique-silver scent bottles and leather traveling requisites.

FASHION, PART I: THE TRUE BRIT Every internationally known designer worth his or her weight in shantung has a boutique in London, but the best buys are on the sturdy English styles that last forever.

The name ✪ **Burberry,** 18–22 Haymarket, SW1 (☎ **020/7930-3343;** tube: Piccadilly Circus), has been synonymous with raincoats ever since Edward VII publicly ordered his valet to "bring my Burberry" when the skies threatened. An impeccably trained staff sells the famous raincoats, along with excellent men's shirts, sportswear, knitwear, and accessories. Raincoats are available in women's sizes and styles as well. Prices are high, but you get quality and prestige.

The finest name in men's shirts, ✪ **Hilditch & Key,** 37 and 73 Jermyn St., SW1 (☎ **020/7734-4707;** tube: Piccadilly Circus or Green Park), has been in business since 1899. The two shops on this street both offer men's clothing (including a bespoke shirt service) and women's ready-made shirts. Hilditch also has an outstanding tie collection. Shirts go for half price during the twice-yearly sales. Men fly in from all over the world for them.

Next, 20 Long Acre, WC2 (☎ **020/7930-1516;** tube: Covent Garden), a chain of "affordable fashion" stores knew its heyday when it became celebrated in the 1980s for its high street-fashion revolution. No longer at its peak (except for its mail order division), it still merits a stopover. The look is still very contemporary, with a continental flair worn not only by men and women but kids, too.

FASHION, PART II: THE CUTTING EDGE No one in the British fashion scene is hotter than the unstoppable ✪ **Vivienne Westwood,** 6 Davies St., W1 (☎ **020/7629-3757;** tube: Bond Street). While it's possible to go to more than 550 stores worldwide and purchase select Westwood pieces, her U.K. shops are the best place to find her full range of fashion designs. The flagship store at Davies Street concentrates on her couture line, or The Gold Label, as it's known. Using a wide range of uniquely British resources, Westwood creates jackets, skirts, trousers, blouses, dresses, and evening dresses. Her line features taffeta ball gowns for fall wear, made-to-measure tailored shirts, and even some Highland plaids.

The World's End branch on King's Road carries casual designs, including T-shirts, jeans, and other sportswear, and the sale shop at Conduit Street has a bit of everything: The Gold Label, her second women's line, The Red Label, and The Man Label, her menswear collection. Accessories available include women's and men's shoes, belts, and jewelry. Branches: World's End, 430 King's Rd., SW3 (☎ **020/7352-6551;** tube: Sloane Square); Vivienne Westwood, 43 Conduit St., W1 (☎ **020/7439-1109;** tube: Oxford Circus).

Miss Selfridge, 42–44 Kensington High St., W8 (☎ **020/7938-4182;** Tube: Kensington High Street) is a hip young women's clothing and accessory store that sells its own cosmetic brand, Kiss & Make-Up. For those pajama parties, there is a wide selection of sexy cotton pajamas, along with a large array of products you can't live without, including two-toned nail polish (all the rage) and a shimmery hair mascara. When you tire of all this, head for the "chill-out" zone where patrons get comfy on slick sofas while listening to the latest CDs.

Egg, 36 Kinnerton St., SW1 (☎ **020/7235-9315;** tube: Hyde Park Corner or Knightsbridge), is hot, hot, hot with fashion setters, featuring imaginatively designed, contemporary clothing by Indian textile designer Asha Sarabhai and knitwear by Eskandar. Designs created from handmade textiles from a workshop in India range from everyday dresses and coats to hand-embroidered silk coats. A line of crafts and ceramics is also available.

FASHION, PART III: VINTAGE & SECONDHAND CLOTHING *Note:* there's no value-added tax (VAT) refund on used clothing.

A London institution since the 1940s, ✪ **Pandora,** 16-22 Cheval Place, SW7 (☎ **020/7589-5289;** tube: Knightsbridge), stands in fashionable Knightsbridge, a stone's throw from Harrods. Several times a week, chauffeurs will drive up with bundles packed anonymously by the gentry of England. One woman voted best dressed at Ascot several years ago was wearing a secondhand dress acquired here. Prices are generally one-third to one-half the retail value. Outfits are usually no more than two seasons old.

For the best in original street wear from the '50s, the '60s, and the '70s, **Pop Boutique,** 6 Monmouth St., WC2 (☎ **020/7497-5262;** tube: Covent Garden), is tops. Right next to the chic Covent Garden Hotel, it has fabulous vintage wear at affordable prices—leather jackets for £45 ($74.25), for example, the equivalent selling for $300 in New York.

FILOFAX All major department stores sell Filofax supplies, but the full range is carried in their own stores. Go to the main West End branch, **The Filofax Centre,** at

21 Conduit St., W1 (☎ **020/7499-0457;** tube: Oxford Circus); it's larger and fancier than the Covent Garden branch at 69 Neal St. (☎ **020/7836-1977**), with the entire range of inserts and books, and prices that will floor you: at least half the U.S. going rate. They also have good sales; calendars for the next year go on sale very early the previous year (about 10 months in advance).

HOME DESIGN & HOUSEWARES At the **Conran Shop,** Michelin House, 81 Fulham Rd., SW3 (☎ **020/7589-7401;** tube: South Kensington), you'll find high style at reasonable prices from the man who invented it all for Britain: Sir Terence Conran. It's great for gifts, home furnishings, and table top—or just for gawking.

MUSEUM SHOPS Not only are the museums worth going to, but so are their shops. The best museum shop in London is the **Victoria and Albert Gift Shop,** Cromwell Road, SW7 (☎ **020/7938-8500;** tube: South Kensington). It sells cards, books, and the usual items, along with reproductions from the museum archives.

MUSIC The biggies in town are **Tower Records,** 1 Piccadilly Circus, W1 (☎ **020/7 439-2500;** tube: Piccadilly Circus), one of the largest tape, record, and CD stores in Europe; and its major rival, the **Virgin Megastore,** 14–16 Oxford St., W1 (☎ **020/ 7631-1234;** tube: Tottenham Court Road). You'll find whatever you're looking for at either one.

SHOES Dr. Marten makes a brand of shoe that has become so popular that now there's an entire department store selling accessories, gifts, and even clothes: **Dr. Marten's Department Store,** 1–4 King St., WC2 (☎ **020/7497-1460;** tube: Covent Garden). Teens come to worship here because ugly is beautiful, and because the prices are far better than they are in the United States, or elsewhere in Europe.

Shelly's, 266 Regent St., W1 (☎ **020/7287-0939;** tube: Oxford Circus), is the flagship of the mother of all London shoe shops, which sells hip shoes and boots for everyone from tots to grown-ups. They're famous for their Doc Martens, but there's much more—and none of it traditional.

TEAS **The Tea House,** 15A Neal St., WC2 (☎ **020/7240-7539;** tube: Covent Garden), sells everything associated with tea, tea drinking, and teatime. It boasts more than 70 quality teas and tisanes, including the best of China, India, Japan, and Sri Lanka, plus such longtime favorite English blended teas as Earl Grey. The shop also offers novelty teapots and mugs, among other items.

TOYS **Hamleys,** 188–196 Regent St., W1 (☎ **020/7494-2000;** tube: Oxford Circus), is the finest toy shop in the world—more than 35,000 toys and games on seven floors of fun and magic. A huge selection is offered, including soft, cuddly stuffed animals, as well as dolls, radio-controlled cars, train sets, model kits, board games, outdoor toys, and computer games. There's also a small branch at Covent Garden, and another at Heathrow Airport.

TRAVEL SERVICES The retail flagship of British Airways, **British Airways Travel Department Store,** 156 Regent St., W1 (☎ **020/7434-4700;** tube: Piccadilly Circus or Oxford Circus), housed on three floors, offers not only worldwide travel and ticketing, but also a wide range of services and shops, including a clinic for immunizations, a pharmacy, a bureau de change, a passport and visa service, and a theater-booking desk. The ground floor sells luggage, guidebooks, maps, and other goods.

8 London After Dark

Weekly publications such as *Time Out* and *Where* carry full entertainment listings, including information on restaurants and nightclubs. You'll also find listings in daily newspapers, notably the *Times* and the *Telegraph.*

THE THEATER

In London, you'll have a chance to see the world-renowned ✪ **English theater** on its home ground. Matinees are on Wednesday (Thursday at some theaters) and on Saturday. Theaters are closed on Sunday. It's impossible to describe all of London's theaters in this space, so below are listed just a few from the treasure trove. The biggest theatrical excitement in London today is being generated by the new Shakespeare's Globe Theatre. Since this is also a sightseeing attraction, it's previewed above in section 2.

GETTING TICKETS

If you want to see specific shows, especially hits, purchase your tickets in advance. The best method is to buy your ticket from the theater's box office, which you can do over the phone using a credit card. You'll pay the theater price and pick up the tickets the day of the show. You can also go to a reliable ticket agent (the greatest cluster is in Covent Garden), but you'll pay a fee, which varies depending on the show. You can also make theater reservations through ticket agents. In the case of hit shows, only brokers may be able to get you a seat, but you'll pay for the privilege.

With offices in London and the United States, **Keith Prowse/First Call** can reserve tickets for hit shows weeks or even months in advance. In the United States, contact them at Suite 1000, 234 W. 44th St. New York, NY 10036 (☎ **800/669-8687** or 212/398-1430; fax 212/302-4251; www.first-call.co.uk/). In London, their number is ☎ **020/7878-2081.** The fee for booking a ticket in the United States is 35%; in London, it's 20%.

For tickets and information on just about any show in London, **Edwards & Edwards** has a New York office under the name **Globaltickets,** if you'd like to arrange tickets before you go, at 1270 Avenue of the Americas, Suite 2414, New York, NY 10020 (☎ **800/223-6108** or 914/328-2150; fax 914/328-2752). They also have offices in London at the **British Visitors Center,** 1 Regents St., W1 (☎ **020/7734-4555**) or at the **Harrods** ticket desk, 87–135 Brompton Rd. (☎ **020/7589-9109**), located on the lower-ground floor opposite the British Airways desk. They'll mail tickets to your home, fax you a confirmation, or leave your tickets at the box office. Instant confirmations are available with special "overseas" rates for most shows. A booking and handling fee of up to 20% is added to the ticket price.

Another option is **Theatre Direct International (TDI)** (☎ **800/334-8457;** www.theatredirect.com), which specializes in providing London theater and Fringe production tickets. Their immediate confirmation lets you arrive in London with your tickets, or else tickets will be held for you at the box office.

London theater tickets are priced quite reasonably when compared with those in the United States. Prices vary greatly depending on the seat—from £18 to £60 ($30.60 to $102). Sometimes gallery seats (the cheapest) are sold only on the day of the performance, so you'll have to head to the box office early in the day and return an hour before the performance to queue up, since they're not reserved seats.

Many of the major theaters offer reduced-price tickets to students on a stand-by basis, but not to the general public. When available, these tickets are sold 30 minutes prior to curtain. Line up early for popular shows, as standby tickets go fast and furious. Of course, you must have a valid student ID.

Central London Theaters

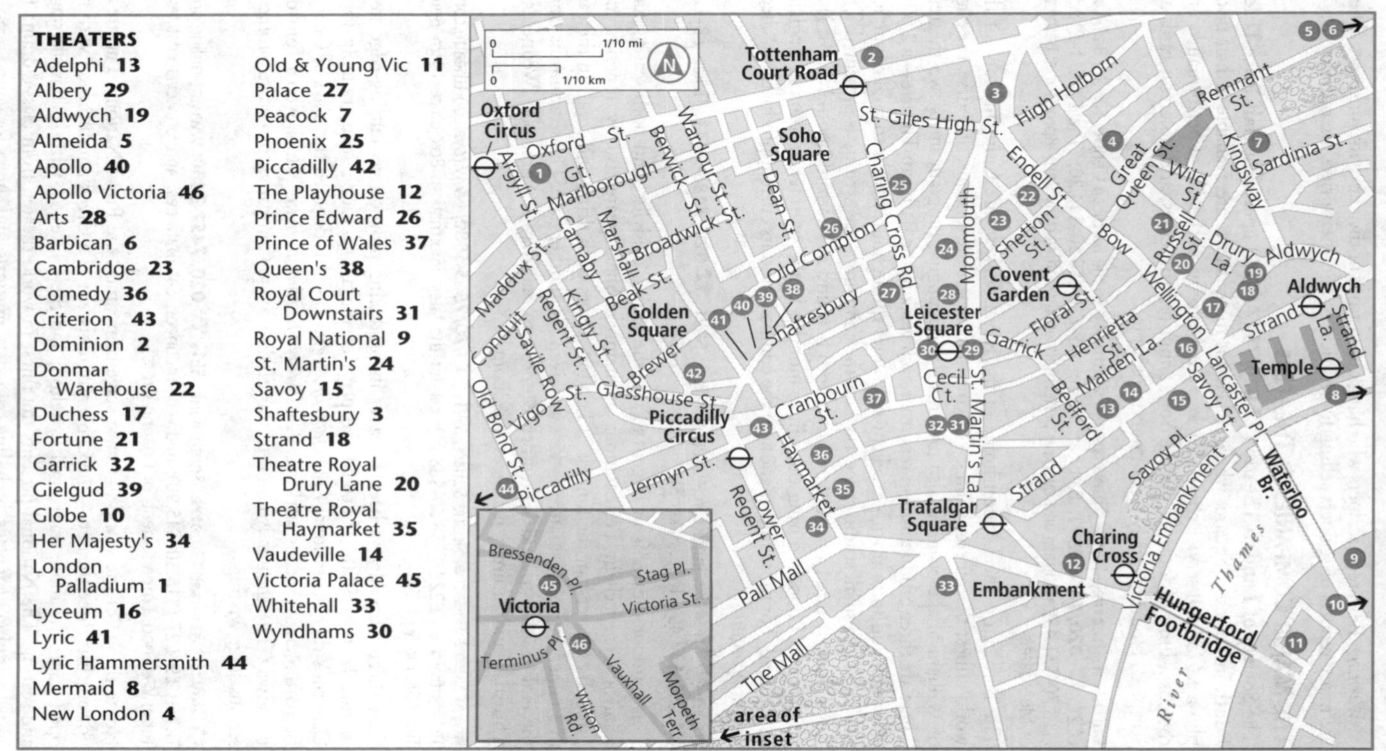

Warning: Beware of scalpers who hang out in front of theaters with hit shows. There are many reports of scalpers selling forged tickets, and their prices are outrageous.

THE MAJOR COMPANIES & THEATERS

The **Society of London Theatre** (☎ **020/7577-6700**) operates a **Half Price Ticket Booth** in Leicester Square, where tickets for many shows are available at half price, plus a £2 ($3.30) service charge. Tickets are sold only on the day of performance, and there is a limit of four per person. You cannot return tickets, and no credit cards are accepted. Hours are daily from noon to 6:30pm.

Barbican Theatre—Royal Shakespeare Company. In the Barbican Centre, Silk St., Barbican, EC2Y. ☎ **020/7638-8891.** Barbican Theatre £5–£26 ($8.50–$44.20). The Pit £11–£18.50 ($18.70–$31.45) matinees and evening performances. Box office daily 9am–8pm. Tube: Barbican or Moorgate.

The Barbican is the London home of the Royal Shakespeare Company, one of the world's finest theater companies. The core of its repertoire remains, of course, the plays of William Shakespeare. It also presents a wide-ranging program in its two theaters. There are three productions in repertory each week in the Barbican Theatre—a 2,000-seat main auditorium with excellent sight lines throughout, thanks to a raked orchestra. The Pit, a small studio space, is where the company's new writing is presented. The Royal Shakespeare Company performs both here and at Stratford-upon-Avon. It is in residence in London during the winter months; in the summer, it tours in England and abroad. For more information on the company and its current productions, check www.rsc.org.uk/.

Open-Air Theatre. Inner Circle, Regent's Park, NW1. ☎ **020/7486-2431.** Tickets £8–£22 ($13.60–$37.40). Tube: Baker St.

This outdoor theater is in Regent's Park; the setting is idyllic, and both seating and acoustics are excellent. Presentations are mainly of Shakespeare, usually in period costume. Its theater bar, the longest in London, serves both drink and food. In the case of a rained-out performance, tickets are given for another date. The season runs from the end of May to mid-September, Monday to Saturday at 8pm, plus Wednesday, Thursday, and Saturday matinees at 2:30pm.

Royal Court Theatre. Sloane Square, SW1. ☎ **020/7565-5000;** www.royalcourttheatre.com. Tickets from £5–£22.50 ($8.50–$38.25); call for the latest information. Box office 10am–6pm. Tube: Sloane Sq.

This theater has always been a leader in producing provocative, cutting-edge new drama. In the 1950s, it staged the plays of the angry young men, notably John Osborne's then-sensational *Look Back in Anger;* earlier it debuted the plays of George Bernard Shaw. A recent work was *The Beauty Queen of Leenane,* which won a Tony on Broadway. The theater is home to the English Stage Company, formed to promote serious stage writing.

✪ **Royal National Theatre.** South Bank, SE1. ☎ **020/7452-3400;** www.nt-online.org. Tickets £9–£27 ($15.30–$45.90); midweek matinees, Sat matinees, and previews cost less. Tube: Waterloo, Embankment, or Charing Cross.

Home to one of the world's greatest stage companies, the Royal National Theatre is not one but three theaters—the Olivier, reminiscent of a Greek amphitheater with its open stage; the more traditional Lyttelton; and the Cottesloe, with its flexible stage and seating. The National presents the finest in world theater, from classic drama to award-winning new plays, including comedies, musicals, and shows for young people.

There is a choice of at least six plays at any one time. It's also a full-time theater center, with an amazing selection of bars, cafés, restaurants, free foyer music and exhibitions, short early-evening performances, bookshops, backstage tours, riverside walks, and terraces. You can have a three-course meal in Mezzanine, the National's restaurant; enjoy a light meal in the brasserie-style Terrace café; or have a snack in one of the coffee bars.

Shakespeare's Globe Theatre. New Globe Walk, Bankside, SE1. ☎ **020/7902-1400.** Box office: 020/7401-9919. www.shakespeares-globe.org/IE-home.htm. Tickets £5 ($8.50) for groundlings, £5–£25 ($8.50–$42.50) for gallery seats. Tube: Mansion House.

In May 1997, the new Globe Theatre—a replica of the Elizabethan original, thatched roof and all—staged its first slate of plays *(Henry V* and *A Winter's Tale)* yards away from the site of the 16th-century theater where the Bard originally staged his work.

Productions vary in style and setting; not all are performed in Elizabethan costume. In keeping with the historic setting, there's no lighting focused just on the stage, but floodlighting is used during evening performances to replicate daylight in the theater—Elizabethan performances took place in the afternoon. Theatergoers sit on wooden benches of yore—in thatch-roofed galleries, no less—but these days you can rent a cushion to make yourself more comfortable. About 500 "groundlings" can stand in the uncovered yard around the stage, just as they did when the Bard was here. Mark Rylane, the artistic director of the Globe, wanted the theater-going experience to be as authentic as possible—he told the press he'd be delighted if the audience threw fruit at the actors, as they did in Shakespeare's time.

From May to September, the company intends to hold performances Tuesday to Saturday at 3 and 7pm, and Sunday at 4pm. There will be a limited winter schedule. In any season, the schedule may be affected by the weather, since this is an outdoor theater. Performances last 2½ to 4 hours, depending on the play.

Also in the works is a second theater, the **Inigo Jones Theatre,** based on the architect's designs from the 1600s, where plays will be staged year round. For details on the exhibition that tells the story of the painstaking re-creation of the Globe, as well as guided tours of the theatre, see "Literary Landmarks," earlier in this chapter. A new Shakespeare's Globe exhibition was opened in January 2000.

Theatre Royal Drury Lane. Catherine St., Covent Garden, WC2. ☎ **020/7494-5060.** Tickets £8–£35 ($13.60–$59.50). Box office Mon–Sat 10am–8pm. Evening performances Mon–Sat 8pm; matinees Wed and Sat 3pm. Tube: Covent Garden.

Drury Lane is one of London's oldest and most prestigious theaters, crammed with tradition—not all of it respectable. This, the fourth theater on this site, dates from 1812; the first was built in 1663. Nell Gwynne, the rough-tongued cockney lass who became Charles II's mistress, used to sell oranges under the long colonnade in front. Nearly every star of London theater has taken the stage here at some time. It has a wide-open repertoire but leans toward musicals, especially long-running hits. Guided tours of the backstage area and the front of the house are given most days at 10:30am and 12:30pm. Call ☎ **020/7494-5091** for more information.

THE REST OF THE PERFORMING ARTS SCENE

Currently, London supports five major orchestras—the **London Symphony,** the **Royal Philharmonic,** the **Philharmonia Orchestra,** the **BBC Symphony,** and the **BBC Philharmonic**—several choirs, and many smaller chamber groups and historic-instrument ensembles. Look for the **London Sinfonietta,** the **English Chamber Orchestra,** and of course the **Academy of St. Martin-in-the-Fields.** Performances are in the South Banks Arts Centre and the Barbican. For smaller recitals, there's Wigmore Hall and St. John's Smith Square.

British Music Information Centre, 10 Stratford Place, W1 (☎ **020/7499-8567;** www.bmic.co.uk), is the city's clearinghouse and resource center for serious music. The center is open Monday to Friday noon to 5pm, and provides free telephone and walk-in information on current and upcoming events. Recitals featuring 20th-century British classical compositions cost up to £5 ($8.50) and are offered here weekly, usually on Tuesday and Thursday at 7:30pm; call ahead for day and time. Since capacity is limited to 40, you may want to check early. Take the tube to Bond Street.

✪ **Barbican Centre—London Symphony Orchestra (& more).** Silk St., the City, EC2. ☎ **020/7638-8891.** Tickets £6.50–£32 ($11.05–$54.40). Box office daily 9am–8pm. Tube: Barbican or Moorgate.

The largest art and exhibition center in Western Europe, the roomy and comfortable Barbican complex is a perfect setting for enjoying music and theater. Barbican Hall is the permanent home address of the **London Symphony Orchestra** as well as host to visiting orchestras and performers, from classical to jazz, folk, and world music.

In addition to the hall and the two theaters of the Royal Shakespeare Company, Barbican Centre includes: The Barbican Art Gallery, a showcase for visual arts; the Concourse Gallery and foyer exhibition spaces; Cinemas One and Two, which show recently released mainstream films and film series; the Barbican Library, a general lending library that places a strong emphasis on the arts; the Conservatory, one of London's largest plant houses; and restaurants, cafés, and bars.

English National Opera. London Coliseum, St. Martin's Lane, WC2. ☎ **020/7632-8300;** www.eno.org/. Tickets £5–£10 ($8.50–$17) balcony, £12.50–£55 ($21.25–$93.50) upper or dress circle or stalls; about 100 discount balcony tickets sold on the day of performance from 10am. Tube: Charing Cross or Leicester Sq.

Built in 1904 as a variety theater and converted into an opera house in 1968, the London Coliseum is the city's largest theater. One of two national opera companies, the English National Opera performs a wide range of works from classics to Gilbert and Sullivan to new and experimental works, staged with flair and imagination. All performances are in English. A repertory of 18 to 20 productions is presented 5 or 6 nights a week for 11 months of the year (dark in July). Although balcony seats are cheaper, many visitors seem to prefer the upper circle or dress circle.

Royal Albert Hall. Kensington Gore, SW7 2AP. ☎ **020/7589-8212.** Tickets £3–£130 ($5.10–$221), depending on the event. Box office daily 9am–9pm. Tube: South Kensington.

Opened in 1871 and dedicated to the memory of Victoria's consort, Prince Albert, the circular building holds one of the world's most famous auditoriums. With a seating capacity of 5,200, it's a popular place to hear music by stars like Eric Clapton and Shirley Bassey. Occasional sporting events (especially boxing) figure strongly here, too.

Since 1941, the hall has been the setting for the BBC Henry Wood Promenade Concerts, known as **"The Proms,"** a concert series that lasts for 8 weeks between mid-July and mid-September. The Proms have been a British tradition since 1895. Although most of the audience occupies reserved seats, true aficionados usually opt for standing room in the orchestra pit, which affords close-up views of the musicians performing on stage. Newly commissioned works are often premiered here. The final evening of The Proms is the most traditional; the rousing favorites "Jerusalem" or "Land of Hope and Glory" echo through the hall. For tickets, call Ticketmaster (☎ **020/7344-4444**) directly.

✪ **The Royal Opera House—The Royal Ballet & the Royal Opera.** Bow St., Covent Garden, WC2. ☎ **020/7304-4000;** www.royalopera.org. Tickets £6–£150 ($10.20–$255). Box office daily 10am–8pm. Tube: Covent Garden.

Reopening in December of 1999, the Royal Ballet and the Royal Opera are at home again in a magnificently restored theater presenting world-class performances of opera and dance. Opera and ballet aficionados of yesterday hardly recognize the place, with its spectacular new public spaces, including the Vilar Floral Hall, a rooftop restaurant, and bars and shops. The entire northeast corner of one of London's most famous public squares has been transformed, finally realizing Inigo Jones's original vision for this colonnaded piazza. Regular backstage tours are possible daily at 10:30am, 12:30, and 2:30pm (not on Sunday or matinee days).

Performances of the Royal Opera are usually sung in the original language, but supertitles are projected, translating the libretto for the audience. The Royal Ballet, that ranks with top companies such as the Kirov and the Paris Opera Ballet, performs a repertory with a tilt toward the classics, including works by its earlier choreographer-directors Sir Frederick Ashton and Sir Kenneth MacMillan.

✪ **Royal Festival Hall.** On the South Bank, SE1. ☎ **020/7960-4242.** Tickets £5–£50 ($8.50–$85). Box office daily 9am–9pm. Tube: Waterloo or Embankment.

In the aftermath of World War II, the principal site of London's music scene shifted to the south bank of the Thames. Three of the most acoustically perfect concert halls in the world were erected between 1951 and 1964. They include Royal Festival Hall, the Queen Elizabeth Hall, and the Purcell Room. Together they hold more than 1,200 performances a year, including classical music, ballet, jazz, popular music, and contemporary dance. Also here is the internationally renowned **Hayward Gallery**.

Royal Festival Hall, which opens daily at 10am, offers an extensive array of things to see and do, including free exhibitions in the foyers and free lunchtime music at 12:30pm. On Friday, Commuter Jazz in the foyer from 5:15 to 6:45pm is free. The Poetry Library is open from 11am to 8pm, and shops display a wide selection of books, records, and crafts. The Festival Buffet has a wide variety of food at reasonable prices, and bars dot the foyers. The People's Palace offers lunch and dinner with a panoramic view of the River Thames. Reservations by calling ☎ **020/7928-9999** are recommended.

Sadler's Wells Theatre. Rosebery Ave., EC1. ☎ **020/7314-8800;** www.sadlers-wells.com. Tickets £7.50–£60 ($12.75–$102). Performances usually 8pm. Box office Mon–Sat 10am–8pm. Tube: Angel.

This is a premier venue for dance and opera. It occupies the site of a theater that was built in 1683, on the location of a well prized for the healing powers of its waters. In the early 1990s, the old-fashioned, turn-of-the-century theater was demolished, and construction began on an innovative new design which was completed at the end of 1998. The original facade has been retained; however, but the interior has been completely revamped to create a stylish cutting-edge theater design. The new theater offers both traditional and experimental dance.

Wigmore Hall. 36 Wigmore St., W1. ☎ **020/7935-2141.** Tickets £6–£40 ($10.20–$68). Performances nightly, plus Sun Morning Coffee Concerts and Sun concerts at 4 or 7pm. Box office Mon–Sat 10am–8:30pm; Sun varies. Tube: Bond St. or Oxford Circus.

An intimate auditorium, Wigmore Hall offers an excellent regular series of song recitals, piano and chamber music, early and baroque music, and jazz. A free list of the month's programs is available from Wigmore. A café-bar and restaurant are on the premises; a cold supper can be pre-ordered if you are attending a concert.

Outside Central London

Kenwood Lakeside Concerts. Kenwood, Hampstead Lane, Hampstead Heath, London NW3 7JR. ☎ **020/7413-1443.** Tickets for adults £9 ($15.30) for seats on the grass lawn, £11–£16 ($18.70–$27.20) for reserved deck chairs. Reductions of 12.5% for students and persons over 60. Every summer Saturday at 7:30pm from July to early Sept. Tube: Golders Green or Archway, then bus no. 210.

These band and orchestral concerts on the north side of Hampstead Heath have been a British tradition for some 50 years. In recent years, laser shows and fireworks have added to a repertoire that includes everything from rousing versions of the *1812 Overture* to jazz, and such operas as *Carmen.* The final concert of the season always features some of the Pomp and Circumstance marches of Sir Edward Elgar, everyone's favorite imperial composer. Music drifts across the lake to serenade wine-and-cheese parties on the grass.

THE CLUB & MUSIC SCENE

Cabaret & Comedy

The Comedy Store. 1A Oxendon St., off Piccadilly Circus, SW1. ☎ **020/7344-0234.** Cover £11–£15 ($18.70–$25.50). Daily from 6:30pm. Tube: Leicester Sq. or Piccadilly Circus.

This is London's most visible showcase for established and rising comic talent. Inspired by comedy clubs in the United States, this London club has given many comics their start. Today a number of them are established TV personalities. Even if their names are unfamiliar, you'll enjoy the spontaneity of live comedy performed before a British audience. Visitors must be 18 and older; dress is casual. Reserve through Ticketmaster (☎ **020/7344-4444**); the club opens 1½ hours before each show. *Insider's Tip:* Go on Tuesday when the humor is more cutting edge and topical.

Live Music

Bagley's Studios. King's Cross Freigh Depot, off York Way, N1. ☎ **020/7278-2777.** Cover £10–£20 ($17–$34). Guaranteed openings Fri–Sun 10pm–7am. Otherwise, openings depend on whatever promoter wants to book the space. Tube: King's Cross.

The premises of this place are vast, echoing, a bit grimy, and warehouse-like. Set in the bleak industrial landscapes behind King's Cross Station, its interior is radically transformed 3 nights a week into an animated rave event. Its two floors, each the size of an American football field, are divided into trios of individual rooms, with their own ambience and sound system. You'll be happiest here if you wander from room to room, searching out the site that best corresponds to your energy level at the moment. Choices will probably include sites devoted to garage, club classics as promoted by AM/FM radio, "banging" (hard house) music, and "bubbly" upbeat dance music. If you happen to be in London on a weeknight, don't assume that the place will be dark, as various social groups, including lots of East Indian social clubs, rent the place for gatherings, some of which might be open to the public. Saturday night "Freedom" parties are more fun.

Barfly Club. At the Falcon Pub, 234 Royal College St., NW1. ☎ **020/7482-4884.** Cover £7–£11 ($11.90–$18.70). Nightly 7:30p–2 or 3am, with most musical acts beginning at 8:15pm. Tube: Camden Town.

In a dingy residential neighborhood in north London, this traditional-looking pub is distinguished by the roster of rock-and-roll bands who come in from throughout the U.K. for bouts of beer and high-energy music. A recorded announcement tells fans what to expect on any given night, along with instructions on how to reach the place through a warren of narrow streets. You can get virtually anything here—which adds considerably to the sense of fun and adventure. The roster of world-class groups who were "discovered" here includes Oasis. You'll usually hear three different bands a night.

The Bull & Gate. 389 Kentish Town Rd., NW5. ☎ **020/7485-5358.** Cover £4 ($6.80). Tube: Kentish Town.

Outside central London, and smaller, cheaper, and often more animated and less touristed than many of its competitors, The Bull & Gate is the unofficial headquarters of London's pub rock scene. Indie and relatively unknown rock bands are often served up back to back by the half dozen in this somewhat-battered Victorian pub. If you like spilled beer, this is off-the-beaten-track London at its most authentic. Bands that played here and later ascended to Europe's clubby scene have included Madness, Blur, Pulp, and that 1980s music video oddity, Sigue-Sigue-Sputnik. The place operates pub hours, with music nightly from 9pm to midnight

The Rock Garden. 6–7 The Piazza, Covent Garden, WC2. ☎ **020/7240-3961.** Cover £5–£8 ($8.50–$13.60); diners enter free. Mon–Thurs 5pm–3am, Fri and Sat 5pm–5am, Sun 7pm–midnight. Bus: Any of the night buses that depart from Trafalgar Square. Tube: Covent Garden.

A long-established performance site, The Rock Garden maintains a bar and a stage in the cellar, and a restaurant on the street level. The cellar, known as The Venue, has hosted such acts as Dire Straits, Police, and U2 before their rises to stardom. Today bands vary widely, from promising up-and-comers to some who'll never be heard from again. Simple American-style fare is served in the restaurant.

Shepherd's Bush Empire. Shepherd's Bush Green W12. ☎ **020/7771-2000.** Ticket prices vary according to show. Tube: Shepherd's Bush or Goldhawk Rd.

In an old BBC television theater, with great acoustics, this is a major venue in London for big name pop and rock stars. Announcements appear in the local press. There's a capacity seating of 2,000. The box office is open Monday to Friday 10am to 6pm and Saturday from noon to 6pm.

Sound Republic. Swiss Centre at 10 Wardour St., Leicester Square W1. ☎ **020/7287-1010.** Tickets £8–£15 ($13.60–$25.50). Tube: Leicester Square.

Right in the very heart of London, this 700-seat venue books the big acts, everybody from Sinead O'Connor to Puff Daddy or the Spice Girls. This is really a music restaurant, one of the best of its type in London. The program is forever changing; call to see what's happening at the time of your visit.

Traditional English Music

Cecil Sharpe House. 2 Regent's Park Rd., NW1. ☎ **020/7485-2206.** Tickets £5–£12 ($8.50–$20.40). Box office Tues–Fri 9am–5pm. Tube: Camden Town.

CSH was the focal point of the folk revival in the 1960s, and it continues to treasure and nurture the style. Here you'll find a whole range of traditional English music and dance. Call to see what's happening.

Jazz & Blues

Ain't Nothing But Blues Bar. 20 Kingly St., W1. ☎ **020/7287-0514.** Cover Fri £3–£5 ($5.10–$8.50); Sat £3–£5 ($5.10–$8.50); free before 9:30pm. Mon–Thurs 6pm–1am, Fri–Sat 6pm–3am, Sun 7:30pm–midnight. Tube: Oxford Circus or Piccadilly Circus.

The club, which bills itself as the only true blues venue in town, features local acts and occasional touring American bands. On weekends prepare to queue. From the Oxford Circus Tube stop, walk south on Regent Street, turn left on Great Marlborough Street, and then make a quick right on Kingly Street.

Jazz Café. 5 Parkway, NW1. ☎ **020/7916-6060.** Cover £8–£20 ($13.60–$34). No charge to book a table, but you will have to order a meal. Tube: Parkway.

Afro-Latin jazz fans are hip to this club hosting combos from around the globe. The weekends, described by one patron as "bumpy jazzy-funk nights," are the best time to decide for yourself what that means. Call ahead for listings, cover, and table reservations (when necessary); opening times can vary.

100 Club. 100 Oxford St., W1. ☎ **020/7636-0933.** Cover Fri £8 ($13.60) members and non-members, Sat £8 ($13.60) members, £9 ($15.30) non-members, Sun £6 ($10.20) members and non-members. Mon–Thurs 7:45pm–midnight, Fri noon–3pm and 8:30pm–2am, Sat 7:30pm–1am, Sun 7:30–11:30pm. Tube: Tottenham Court Rd. or Oxford Circus.

Although less plush and expensive than some jazz clubs, 100 Club is a serious contender. Its cavalcade of bands includes the best British jazz musicians and some of their Yankee brethren. Rock, R&B, and blues are also on tap.

✪ **Pizza Express.** 10 Dean St., W1. ☎ **020/7439-8722.** Cover £8.50–£20 ($14.45–$34). Daily 11:30am–midnight, jazz from 7:45pm–midnight. Tube: Tottenham Court Rd.

Don't let the name fool you: This restaurant-bar serves up some of the best jazz in London by mainstream artists. While enjoying a thin-crust Italian pizza, check out a local band or a visiting group, often from the United States. Although the club has been enlarged, it's important to reserve ahead of time.

✪ **Ronnie Scott's Club.** 47 Frith St., W1. ☎ **020/7439-0747.** Cover non-member £20 ($34), member £5 ($8.50). Mon–Sat 8:30pm–3am. Tube: Leicester Sq. or Piccadilly Circus.

Inquire about jazz in London and people immediately think of Ronnie Scott's, long the European vanguard for modern jazz. Only the best English and American combos, often fronted by a top-notch vocalist, are booked here. The programs inevitably make for an entire evening of cool jazz. In the heart of Soho, Ronnie Scott's is a 10-minute walk from Piccadilly Circus along Shaftesbury Avenue. In the Main Room, you can watch the show from the bar or sit at a table, from which you can order dinner. The Downstairs Bar is more intimate; among the regulars at your elbow may be some of the world's most talented musicians. On weekends, the separate Upstairs Room has a disco called Club Latino.

606 Club. 90 Lots Rd., SW10. ☎ **020/7352-5953.** Cover Sun–Thurs £5 ($8.50), Fri–Sat £6 ($10.20). Mon–Sat 8:15pm–2am, Sun 8:15pm–midnight. Bus: 11, 19, 22, 31, 39, or C3. Tube: Earl's Court.

Located in a discreet basement site in Chelsea, the 606 presents live music nightly. Predominantly a venue for modern jazz, style ranges from traditional to contemporary. Local musicians and some very big names play here, whether planned gigs or informal jam sessions after their shows elsewhere in town. This is actually a jazz supper club in the boondocks of Fulham; because of license requirements, patrons can only order alcohol with food.

DANCE, DISCO & ECLECTIC

Bar Rumba. 26 Shaftesbury Ave., W1. ☎ **020/7287-2715.** Cover £3–£12 ($5.10–$20.40). Mon–Thurs 5pm–3:30am, Fri 5pm–4am, Sat 9pm–6am, Sun 8pm–1:30am. Tube: Piccadilly Circus.

Despite its location on Shaftesbury Avenue, this Latin bar and club could be featured in a book of "Underground London." A hush-hush address, it leans toward radical jazz fusion on some nights, phat funk on other occasions. Boasting two full bars and a different musical theme every night, Tuesday and Wednesday are the only nights you probably won't have to queue at the door. Monday's "That's How It Is" showcase features jazz, hip hop, and drum and bass; Friday's "KAT Klub" grooves with soul, R&B, and swing; and Saturday's "Garage City" buzzes with house and garage. On weeknights you have to be 18 and up; the age limit is 21 on Saturday and Sunday.

Camden Palace. 1A Camden High St., NW1. ☎ **020/7387-0428.** Cover varies, but averages Tues £5 ($8.50), Fri–Sat £7–£20 ($11.90–$34). Tues 10pm–2:30am, Fri approximately 10pm–6am, and Sat approximately 10pm–8am. Tube: Camden Town or Mornington Crescent.

Housed in a former theater built around 1910, Camden Palace draws an over-18 crowd that flocks here in trendy downtown costumes. Energy levels vary according to the night of the week, as does the music, so call in advance to see if that evening's musical program appeals to your taste. A live band performs only on Tuesday. There's a restaurant if you get the munchies.

The Cross. The Arches, Kings Cross Goods Yard, York Way, N1. ☎ **020/7837-0828.** Cover £10–£15 ($17–$25.50). Fri and Sat 10:30pm–6am. Tube: Kings Cross.

In the backwaters of Kings Cross, this club has stayed hot since 1993. London hipsters come here for private parties thrown by Rough Trade Records or Red Or Dead, or just to dance in the space's cozy brick-lined vaults. It's always party time here. Call to find out who's performing.

Diva. 43 Thurloe St., SW7. ☎ **020/7584-2000.** Cover £1.50 ($2.55). Mon–Thurs 6–11pm, Fri–Sat 6pm–3am; July–Sept also Sun noon–3pm. Tube: South Kensington.

Diva combines a first-class Italian restaurant with a dance club. So get down with your manicotti! Meals, from £8.50–£14.50 ($14.45–$24.65) per head, are mostly Neapolitan-inspired. Only restaurant patrons are allowed into the disco (where recorded music is played).

Equinox. Leicester Sq., WC2. ☎ **020/7437-1446.** Cover £5–£12 ($8.50–$20.40), depending on the night of the week. Mon–Thurs 9pm–3am, Fri–Sat 9pm–4am. Tube: Leicester Sq.

Built in 1992 on the site of the London Empire, a dance emporium that has witnessed the changing styles of social dancing since the 1700s, the Equinox has established itself as a perennial favorite. It contains nine bars, the largest dance floor in London, and a restaurant modeled after a 1950s American diner. With the exception of rave, virtually every kind of dance music is featured here, including dance hall, pop, rock, and Latin. The setting is lavishly illuminated with one of Europe's largest lighting rigs, and the crowd is as varied as London itself.

Equinox has been quite busy lately, hosting some of the U.K.'s hottest talents. Most recently, the Equinox featured those international sex symbols, the Spice Girls, Prince Harry's favorite group. Summer visitors can enjoy their theme nights, which are geared to entertaining a worldwide audience, including a once a month "Ibiza" foam party—you'll actually boogie the night away on a foam covered floor.

Hanover Grand. 6 Hanover St., W1. ☎ **020/7499-7977.** Cover £5–£15 ($8.50–$25.50). Wed–Sat 10:30pm–4am; Sat 11pm–5:30am. Tube: Oxford Circus.

Thursdays are funky and down and dirty. Fridays and Saturdays the crowd dresses up in their disco-finery, clingy and form-fitting or politicized and punk. Dance floors are always crowded, and masses seem to surge back and forth between the two levels. Age and gender is sometimes hard to make out at this cutting-edge club.

Hippodrome. Corner of Cranbourn St. and Charing Cross Rd., WC2. ☎ **020/7437-4311.** Cover £4–£12 ($6.80–$20.40). Mon–Sat 9pm–3am. Tube: Leicester Sq.

Located near Leicester Square, the popular Hippodrome is London's grand old daddy of discos, a cavernous place with a great sound system and lights to match. It was Lady Di's favorite scene in her bar-hopping days. Tacky and touristy, the 'Drome is packed on weekends.

Iceni. 11 White Horse St., W1. ☎ **020/7495-5333.** Cover Fri and Sat £10 ($17). Fri–Sat 10pm–3:30am. Tube: Green Park.

Attracting an older 20-something crowd on Fridays, and 18-to-25ers on Saturdays, this funky three-story nightclub features films, board games, tarot readings, and dancing to swing, soul, hip hop, and R&B. You can even get a manicure.

Legends. 29 Old Burlington St., W1. ☎ **020/7437-9933.** Admission £7–£15 ($11.90–$25.50). Thurs–Fri 10pm–3am, Sat 10pm–5am. Tube: Oxford Circus or Green Park.

Established in 1986, but greatly expanded in 1996, is a stylish Mayfair joint where the young Lady Dianas of the millennium might be seen. It's young at heart, chic, and sophisticated. The Beautiful People of Mayfair gather in this chrome-lined monument to glitter. Its most popular night is "Horny Thursday" with garage grooves when "devilish" dress is worn. Dancing on most nights is to funky house and garage beats.

Limelight. 136 Shaftesbury Ave., WC2. ☎ **020/7434-0572.** Cover £4–£12 ($6.80–$20.40). Mon–Thurs 10pm–3am; Fri–Sat 9pm–3:30am. Tube: Leicester Sq.

Although opened in 1985, this large dance club—located inside a former Welsh chapel that dates to 1754—has only recently come into its own. The dance floors and bars share space with plenty of cool Gothic nooks and crannies. DJs spin the latest house music.

✪ **Ministry of Sound.** 103 Gaunt St., SE1. ☎ **020/7378-6528.** Cover £12–£15 ($20.40–$25.50). Fri 10pm–6am, Sat midnight–8am. Tube: Elephant & Castle.

Removed from the city center, this club-of-the-hour is still going strong after all these years. It remains hot, hot, hot. With a large bar and an even bigger sound system, it blasts garage and house music to energetic crowds that pack the two dance floors. If the stimulants in the rest of the club have gone to your head, you can chill in the cinema room. Note: The club's cover charge is stiff, and bouncers decide who is cool enough to enter, so leave the sneakers and denim at home and slip into your grooviest and most glamorous club wear.

The Office. 3–5 Rathbone Place, W1. ☎ **020/7636-1598.** Cover £7–£9 ($11.90–$15.30). Mon–Tues noon–11:30pm; Wed–Fri noon–3am; Sat 9:30pm–3am. Tube: Tottenham Court Rd.

An eclectic club with a bureaucratic name, one of The Office's most popular nights is Wednesday's "Double Six Club," featuring easy listening and board games from 6pm to 2am. Other nights are more traditional recorded pop, rock, soul, and disco. Ambience wins out over decor.

Stringfellows. 16–19 Upper St. Martin's Lane, WC2. ☎ **020/7240-5534.** Cover £10–£15 ($17–$25.50). Mon–Thurs 7pm–3:30am, Fri and Sat 8pm–3:30am, Sun closed. Reservations recommended for restaurant. Tube: Leicester Sq. or Covent Garden.

This would-be glam club has a varied clientele and lots of velvet and gloss. In theory, it's members-only, but—at the discretion of management—non-members may be admitted. The disco has a glass dance floor and a dazzling sound-and-light system. A restaurant feeds late-night diners, and there's no charge for admission to the club if you dine in the restaurant.

The Velvet Room (formerly The Velvet Underground). 143 Charing Cross Rd., WC2. ☎ **020/7734-4687.** Cover £6–£10 ($10.20–$17). Wed–Thurs 9pm–3am, Fri–Sat 9pm–4am. Tube: Tottenham Court Rd.

The Velvet Underground was a London staple for years. Times changed and the clientele grew up—hence The Velvet Room, a more mature setting that is luxurious but not stuffy. DJs Carl Cox and others spin favorite dance hits—more laid back to better represent the new theme. The Velvet Room hasn't sacrificed a shred of cool, and still sets a standard for the next generation of Soho bar life.

✪ **Zoo Bar.** 13–18 Bear St., WC2. ☎ **020/7839-4188.** Cover £3–£10 ($5.10–$17) after 11pm (Fri and Sat after 9pm). Mon–Sat 4pm–3:30am; Sun 4–10:30pm. Tube: Leicester Sq.

The owners spent millions of pounds outfitting this club in the slickest, flashiest, and most psychedelic decor in London. If you're looking for a true Euro nightlife experience replete with gorgeous *au pairs* and trendy Europeans, this is it. Zoo Bar upstairs is a menagerie of mosaic animals beneath a glassed-in ceiling dome. Downstairs, the music is intrusive enough to make conversation futile. Clients range from 18 to 35; androgyny is the look of choice.

LATIN RHYTHMS

Cuba. 11 Kensington High St., W8. ☎ **020/7938-4137.** Cover £2–£7 ($3.40–$11.90). Mon–Sat noon–2am, Sun 2–10:30pm. Tube: High St. Kensington.

This Spanish/Cuban–style bar-restaurant, which has a music club downstairs, features live music acts from Cuba, Brazil, Spain, and the rest of Latin America. Odd as it may seem, the crowd is equal parts restaurant diners, after-work drinkers, Latinophiles, and dancers. Salsa dance classes are offered Monday and Wednesday from 7:30 to 9:30pm and Wednesday from 8 to 9:30pm. Classes cost £5 ($8.50). Happy hour is Monday to Saturday, noon to 8:30pm.

Salsa. 96 Charing Cross Rd., WC2. ☎ **020/7379-3277.** Cover Fri–Sat £4 ($6.80) after 9pm. Mon–Sat 5:30pm–2am. Tube: Leicester Sq.

This lively bar-restaurant and music club for Latin music aficionados features mostly bands from Central and South America. Dance lessons are available nightly starting at 6:30pm; live music starts at 9pm. Some of the best dancers in London strut their stuff here.

THE GAY & LESBIAN SCENE

The most reliable source of information on gay clubs and activities is the **Lesbian and Gay Switchboard** (☎ **020/7837-7324**). The staff runs a 24-hour service for information on gay-friendly places and activities. *Time Out* also carries listings on such clubs. Also a good place for finding out what's hot and hip is **Prowler Soho,** 3–7 Brewer St. Soho W1 (☎ **020/7734-4031;** Tube: Piccadilly Circus), the largest gay lifestyle store in London. (You can also buy anything from jewelry to CDs and books, fashion and sex toys.) It's open till midnight on Friday and Saturday.

The Box. 32–34 Monmouth St. (at Seven Dials), WC2. ☎ **020/7240-5828.** Daily 11am–11pm (café Mon–Sat 11am–5:30pm, Sun noon–6:30pm). Tube: Leicester Sq.

Adjacent to one of Covent Garden's best-known junctions, Seven Dials, this sophisticated Mediterranean-style bar attracts more lesbians than many of its competitors. In the afternoon, it is primarily a restaurant, serving meal-size salads, club sandwiches, and soups. Food service ends abruptly at 5:30pm, after which the place reveals its core: a cheerful, popular place of rendezvous for London's gay and countercultural crowds. The Box considers itself a "summer bar," throwing open doors and windows to a cluster of outdoor tables that attracts a crowd at the slightest hint of sunshine.

Candy Bar. 4 Carlisle St., W1. ☎ **020/7494-4041.** Cover £2–£5 ($3.40–$8.50). Club hours Mon–Thurs 8pm–midnight, Fri–Sat 8pm–2am, Sun 7–11pm. Tube: Tottenham Court Rd.

This is the most popular lesbian bar in London at the moment. It has an extremely mixed clientele from butch to fem and from young to old. There is a bar and a club downstairs. Design is simple with bright colors and lots of mirrors upstairs and darker and more flirtatious downstairs. Men are welcome as long as they are escorted by a woman.

The Complex. 1–5 Parkfield St., Islington, M1. ☎ **020/7738-2336.** Cover £8 ($13.60). Fri 10pm–4am. Tube: Angel.

On Fridays, this four-floor club is the site of Pop Starz, which has become one of the most popular nights in London. It offers a mix of indie, British pop, 1980s trash, and funk. Originally started as an alternative to the generic gay muscle boy dance parties, the once-weekly night has attracted a very mixed and loyal following.

The Edge. 11 Soho Square, W1. ☎ **020/7439-1313.** Mon–Sat 11am–1am, Sun noon–10:30pm. No cover. Tube: Tottenham Court Rd.

Few bars in London can rival the tolerance, humor, and sexual sophistication found here. The first two floors are done up with accessories that, like an English garden, change with the seasons. Dance music can be found on the high-energy and crowded lower floors, while the upper floors are best if you're looking for intimate conversation. Three menus are featured: a funky daytime menu, a café menu, and a late-night menu. Dancers hit the floors starting around 7:30pm. Clientele ranges from the flamboyantly gay to hetero pub crawlers out for a night of slumming.

First Out. 52 St. Giles High St., W1. ☎ **020/7240-8042.** Mon–Sat 10am–11pm, Sun 11am–10:30pm. Tube: Tottenham Court Rd.

First Out prides itself on being London's first (est. 1986) all-gay coffee shop. Set in a 19th-century building whose wood panels have been painted the colors of the gay liberation rainbow, the bar is intimate (that is, not particularly cruisy) and offers an exclusively vegetarian menu. Cappuccino and whiskey are the preferred libations; curry dishes, potted pies in phyllo pastries, and salads are the foods of choice. Don't expect a raucous atmosphere—some clients come here with their grandmothers. Look for the bulletin board with leaflets and business cards of gay and gay-friendly entrepreneurs.

G.A.Y. London Astoria, 157 Charing Cross Rd., WC2. ☎ **020/7734-6963.** Admission £10 ($17). Mon–Fri 10:30–4am, Sat 10:30pm–5am. Tube: Tottencourt Rd.

In spite of the name, the clientele is mixed, and on a Saturday night this could well be the most rollicking club in London. You may not find love here, but perhaps a partner for the night. If you've got the figure for it, you can strip down to your briefs or shorts and give other patrons a treat. A mammoth place, this club draws a young crowd to dance at this pop extravaganza with is mirrored disco balls. Overheard recently: One young man asked another his sexual orientation. The first young man said, "Total confusion!"

Heaven. The Arches, Villiers and Craven Sts., WC2. ☎ **020/7930-2020.** Mon, Wed 10pm–3am, Fri 10pm–6am, Sat 10:30pm–6am. Cover £3–£10 ($5.10–$17). Tube: Charing Cross or Embankment.

This club in the vaulted cellars of Charing Cross Railway Station is a London landmark. Owned by the same investors who brought the world Virgin Atlantic Airways, Heaven is one of the biggest and best-established gay venues in Britain. Painted black, and reminiscent of an air-raid shelter, the club is divided into at least four distinct areas connected by a labyrinth of catwalk stairs and hallways. Each area has a different activity going on. Heaven also has theme nights, which depending on the night are frequented by gays, lesbians, or a mostly heterosexual crowd. Thursday in particular seems open to anything, but on Saturday it's gay only. Call before you go.

Madame Jo Jo's. 8 Brewer St., W1. ☎ **020/7734-2473.** Cover £6–£22.50 ($10.20–$38.25). Daily 10pm–2am. Tube: Piccadilly Circus.

Tucked alongside Soho's most explicit girlie shows, Madame Jo Jo's also presents "girls." London's most popular transvestite showplace—an eye-popper with a decadent art nouveau interior—has attracted film directors such as Stanley Kubrick, who filmed scenes from *Eyes Wide Shut,* starring Tom Cruise, here. Other celebrities, including Hugh Grant and Mick Jagger, have dropped in to check out Jo Jo's drag cabaret. Drag shows are Thursday to Saturday nights, with outside promoters organizing entertainment on other nights.

Royal Vauxhall Tavern. 372 Kennington Lane, SE11. ☎ **020/7582-0833.** Cover Thurs–Sun £2–£4 ($3.40–$6.80). Thurs–Sat 9pm–2am, Sun 2pm–midnight. Tube: Vauxhall.

Originally an 1880s vaudeville pub frequented by London's East End working class, this place has long been a bastion of campy humor and wit. It has been a gay pub since the end of World War II. The tavern received a jolt of fame when—as legend has it—Queen Elizabeth's ceremonial carriage broke down, and the monarch stopped in for a cup of tea. Since then, "Royal" has been gleefully affixed to the name, no doubt suiting the regular queens found here. Charington, one of the largest breweries in England, recently acquired this unabashedly gay pub. Shaped like an amphitheater, the bar has a large stage area and gay themes on weekends. Friday nights are reserved for women only. Saturday is camp night, when the pub overflows with gay men fawning over their favorite cabaret acts.

Substation Soho. 1A Dean St., W1. ☎ **020/7287-9608.** Tues–Thurs 10:30pm–3:30am, Fri 10pm–5am, Sat 10pm–6am. Tube: Tottenham Court Rd.

This is a sprawling, and sometimes packed, enclave that features three bars, a dance floor with a rotating team of DJs, video screens, pool tables, and an environment where picking up a stranger is fully permissible. About 80% of the clients are gay men aged 18 to 50; the remainder are women, both gay and straight, who like the joint's tolerant sense of permissiveness. There's a cover charge that varies from £3 to £8 ($5.10 to $13.60), depending on the night of the week.

THE BAR & PUB SCENE

For additional pub listings, see chapter 3.

OUR FAVORITE BARS

American Bar. In The Savoy, The Strand, WC2. ☎ **020/7836-4343.** Smart casual—no jeans, sneakers, T-shirts. Drinks start at £7.25 ($12.35). AE, DC, MC, V. Mon-Sat 11am–11pm. Tube: Charing Cross, Covent Garden, or Embankment.

The bartender in this sophisticated gathering place is known for his special concoctions, "Savoy Affair" and "Prince of Wales," as well as what is reputedly the best martini in town. Monday to Saturday evenings, jazz piano is featured from 7 to 11pm. Near many West End theaters, the location is ideal for a pre- or post-theater drink.

Beach Blanket Babylon. 45 Ledbury Rd., W11. ☎ **020/7229-2907.** Drinks start at £6.50 ($11.05). AE, DC, MC, V. Mon–Sat noon–11pm, Sun noon–10:30pm. Tube: Notting Hill Gate.

Go here if you're looking a hot singles bar that attracts a crowd in their 20s and 30s. This Portobello joint—named after a kitschy musical revue in San Francisco—is very cruisy. The decor is a bit wacky, no doubt designed by an aspiring Salvador Dalí, who decided to make it a fairy-tale grotto (or did he mean a medieval dungeon?). It's close to the Portobello Market. Saturday and Sunday nights are the hot, crowded times to show up for bacchanalian revelry.

The Dorchester Bar. In the Dorchester, Park Lane. ☎ **020/7629-8888.** Drinks begin at £6 ($10.20). AE, DC, MC, V. Mon–Sat 11am–12:30am, Sun noon–10:30pm. Tube: Hyde Park Corner, Marble Arch or Green Park.

This sophisticated and modern bar is on the lobby level, and you'll find an international clientele, confident of its good taste and privilege. The bartender knows his stuff. The bar serves Italian snacks, lunch, and dinner. A pianist performs every evening after 7pm.

The Library. In the Lanesborough Hotel, 1 Lanesborough Place, SW1. ☎ **020/7259-5599.** Drinks begin at £6 ($10.20). AE, DC, MC, V. Mon–Sat 11am–11pm, Sun noon–10:30pm. Tube: Hyde Park Corner.

For one of London's poshest drinking retreats, head for this deluxe hotel with its high ceilings, leather chesterfields, respectable oil paintings, and grand windows. Its collection of ancient cognacs is unparalleled in London.

Lillie Langtry Bar. In the Cadogan Hotel, 75 Sloane St., SW1. ☎ **020/7235-7141.** Drinks begin at £4.50 ($7.65). AE, DC, MC, V. Daily 11am–11pm. Tube: Sloane Sq. or Knightsbridge.

Next door to Langtry's Restaurant, this 1920s-style bar epitomizes the charm and elegance of the Edwardian era. Lillie Langtry, the turn-of-the-century actress and society beauty (notorious as the mistress of Edward VII), once lived here. Oscar Wilde—arrested in this very hotel bar—is honored on the drinks menu by his favorite libation, the Hock and Seltzer. Sir John Betjeman's poem "The Arrest of Oscar Wilde at the Cadogan Hotel" tells the story. The Cadogan Cooler seems to be the most popular drink here. An international menu is served in the adjoining restaurant.

The Lobby Bar. In the Hotel One Aldwych, 1 Aldwych, WC2. ☎ **020/7300-1000.** Drinks begin at £7.50 ($12.75). AE, DC, MC, V. Mon–Sat 11am–11pm, Sun 11am–10:30pm. Tube: Temple.

This bar and the bar associated with the Axis restaurant are in London's newest five-star hotel. We advise that you check out the dramatic visuals of both before selecting your preferred nesting place for a drink or two. The Lobby Bar occupies what was built in 1907 as the very grand, very high-ceilinged reception area for one of London's premier newspapers. (It's the only part of the historically important hotel's interior that wasn't demolished during a stylish renovation in 1998.) If that setting doesn't appeal to you, check out the travertine, hardwood, and leather-sheathed bar in the Axis restaurant. The Lobby Bar is open daily from 9am to 11pm; the Axis bar is open at hours that correspond to those of the restaurant.

The Met Bar. In the Metropolitan Hotel, 10 Old Park Lane, W1. ☎ **020/7447-1000.** Members-only and hotel guests. Drinks begin at £5.50 ($9.35). AE, DC, MC, V. Mon–Sat 10am–3am, Sun 10am–10:30pm. Tube: Hyde Park Corner.

Very much the place to be seen, this has become the hottest bar in London. Mix with the elite of the fashion, TV, and the music world. A lot of American celebrities have been seen here, sipping on a martini, from Demi Moore to Courtney Cox. Despite the caliber of the clientele, the bar has managed to maintain a relaxed and unpretentious atmosphere.

The Heart of the City

Central London is chock-full of wonderful old pubs with histories almost as rich and varied as the city itself.

Black Friar. 174 Queen Victoria St., EC4. ☎ **020/7236-5650.** Drinks begin at £6.15 ($10.45). AE, MC, V. Mon–Fri 11am–11pm. Tube: Blackfriars.

The Black Friar will transport you to the Edwardian era. The wedge-shaped pub reeks of marble and bronze art nouveau, featuring bas-reliefs of mad monks, a low-vaulted mosaic ceiling, and seating carved out of gold marble recesses. It's especially popular with the City's afterwork crowd, and it features Adams, Wadsworth 6X, Tetleys, and Brakspears on tap.

Jamaica Wine House. St. Michael's Alley off Cornhill, EC3. ☎ **020/7626-9496.** Drinks begin at £2.50 ($4.25). AE, DC, MC, V. Mon–Fri 11am–11pm. Tube: Bank.

Jamaica Wine House was one of the first coffeehouses in England and, reputedly, the Western world. For years, merchants and daring sea captains came here to transact deals over rum and coffee. Nowadays, the two-level house dispenses beer, ale, lager, and fine wines, among them a variety of ports. The oak-paneled bar is on the street level, attracting a jacket-and-tie crowd of investment bankers. You can order standard but filling dishes such as a ploughman's lunch and toasted sandwiches.

Lamb & Flag. 33 Rose St., off Garrick St., WC2. ☎ **020/7497-9504.** Drinks begin at £4.50 ($7.65). No credit cards. Mon–Sat 11am–11pm, Sun noon–10:30pm. Tube: Leicester Square.

Dickens once hung out in this pub and the room itself is little changed from the days when he prowled this neighborhood. The pub has an amazing and somewhat scandalous history. Dryden was almost killed by a band of thugs outside its doors in December 1679; the pub gained the nickname the "Bucket of Blood" during the Regency era (1811–20) because of the routine bare-knuckled prizefights that broke out here. Tap beers include Courage Best and Directors, Old Speckled Hen, John Smiths, and Wadworths 6X.

Sherlock Holmes. 10 Northumberland St., WC1. ☎ **020/7930-2644.** Drinks from £4.50 ($7.65). DC, MC, V. Mon–Sat 10am–11pm, Sun noon–10:30pm. Tube: Charing Cross or Embankment.

It would be rather strange if the Sherlock Holmes was not the old gathering spot for the Baker Street Irregulars, a once-mighty clan of mystery lovers who met here to honor the genius of Sir Arthur Conan Doyle's most famous fictional character. Upstairs, you'll find a re-creation of the living room at 221B Baker Street and such "Holmesiana" as the serpent of *The Speckled Band* and the head of *The Hound of the Baskervilles*. In the upstairs dining room, you can order complete meals with wine. Try "Copper Beeches" (grilled butterfly chicken breasts with lemon and herbs). You select dessert from the trolley. Downstairs is mainly for drinking, but there's a good snack bar with cold meats, salads, cheeses, and wine and ales sold by the glass.

Ye Olde Cock Tavern. 22 Fleet St., EC4. ☎ **020/7353-8570.** Main courses £5–£6.50 ($8.50–$11.05). AE, DC, MC, V. Carvery, Mon–Fri noon–2:30am; Pub, Mon–Fri 11am–11pm. Tube: Temple or Chancery Lane.

Dating back to 1549, this tavern boasts a long line of literary patrons: Samuel Pepys mentioned the pub in his diaries; Dickens frequented it; and Tennyson referred to it in one of his poems, a copy of which is framed and proudly displayed near the front entrance. It's one of the few buildings in London to have survived the Great Fire of 1666. At street level, you can order a pint as well as snackbar food, steak-and-kidney pie, or a cold chicken-and-beef plate with salad. At the Carvery upstairs, a meal includes a choice of appetizers, followed by lamb, pork, beef, or turkey.

Ye Olde Watling. 29 Watling St., EC4. ☎ **020/7653-9971.** Main courses £6.25–£7 ($10.65–$11.90). AE, MC, V. Mon–Fri 10am–10pm. Tube: Mansion House.

Ye Olde Watling was rebuilt after the Great Fire of 1666. On the ground level is a mellow pub; upstairs is an intimate restaurant where, under oak beams and at trestle tables, you can dine on simple English main dishes for lunch. The menu varies daily, with such choices and reliable standbys as fish-and-chips, lamb satay, lasagna, fishcakes, and usually a vegetarian dish. All are served with two vegetables or salad, plus rice or potatoes.

5 The Thames Valley

The historic Thames Valley and Chiltern Hills lie so close to London that they can easily be reached by car, train, or Green Line coach. In fact, you can explore this area during the day and return to London in time to see a West End show.

The most visited historic site in England is Windsor Castle, 21 miles west of London. If you base yourself in Windsor, you can spend another day exploring some of the sights on its periphery, including Eton (which adjoins Windsor), Runnymede, and Savill Garden.

If your visit coincides with the spring social sporting season, you can head to Ascot or Henley-on-Thames for the famous social sporting events: Ascot and the Royal Regatta. Be sure to wear a hat!

There are also some great historic homes and gardens in the area, including Woburn Abbey, Hatfield House, Hughenden Manor, the Mapledurham House, and the Wellington Ducal Estate. If your time is severely limited, the two most important country mansions to visit are Woburn Abbey and Hatfield House. Woburn Abbey could consume an entire day, whereas Hatfield can be visited in a morning or afternoon.

It's not just the historic homes that make the Home Counties intriguing to visit; the land of river valleys and gentle hills makes for wonderful drives. The beech-clad Chilterns are at their most beautiful in spring and autumn. This 40-mile chalk ridge extends in an arc from the Thames Valley to the old Roman city of St. Albans in Hertfordshire. The whole region is popular for boating holidays on its 200-mile network of canals.

Oxfordshire is a land of great mansions, old churches of widely varying architectural styles, and rolling farmland. Certainly your principal reason for visiting Oxfordshire is to explore the university city of Oxford, about an hour's ride from London by car or train. It's not a good day-trip, though, because there's too much to see and do. Plan to spend the night, and then the following morning you can visit Blenheim Palace, England's answer to Versailles.

1 Windsor & Eton

21 miles W of London

Were it not for the castle, Windsor might still be a charming Thames town to visit. But because it is the home of the best-known asset the royal family possesses, it is overrun in summer by tourists who all but obscure the town's charm.

The good news is that after the disastrous fire of 1992, Windsor Castle is restored, even though some of the new designs for Windsor Castle have been called a "Gothic shocker" or "ghastly." Actually, in spite of some media criticism, a remarkable activity in restoration went on, as woodcarvers, gilders, and plasterers followed the same techniques as did their predecessors in the Middle Ages, when William the Conqueror originally built the castle. Queen Elizabeth opened the state apartments in November 1997 following a $62 million project that returned most of the ruined part of the castle to its original condition. Windsor Castle remains Britain's second-most-visited historic building, behind the Tower of London, attracting 1.2 million visitors a year.

ESSENTIALS

GETTING THERE The train from Waterloo or Paddington Station in London makes the trip in 30 minutes (you'll have to transfer at Slough to the Slough-Windsor shuttle train). There are more than a dozen trains per day, and the cost is £6.20 one way. Call **Thames Trains, Ltd.,** at ☎ **020/7620-6333** or 0345/484-950 for more information.

Green Line coaches (☎ **020/8668-7261**) no. 700 and 702 from Hyde Park Corner in London take about 1½ hours, depending on the day of the week. A same-day round-trip costs £7 ($11.90). The bus will drop you near the parish church, across the street from the castle.

If you're driving from London, take M4 west.

VISITOR INFORMATION A **Tourist Information Centre** is located across from Windsor Castle on High Street (☎ **01753/743900**). There's also an information booth in the Tourist Centre at Windsor Coach Park. Both are open Monday to Friday from 10am to 4pm, Saturday 10am to 5pm, and Sunday 10am to 4:30pm. They also book walking tours for the Oxford guild of guides.

CASTLE HILL SIGHTS

✪ **Windsor Castle.** ☎ **01753/868286** for information. Admission £10.50 ($17.85) adults, £8 ($13.60) seniors, £5 ($8.50) children 16 and under; £22.50 ($38.25) for a family of four. Mar–Oct daily 10am–5:30pm; Nov–Feb daily 10am–4pm. Last admission 1 hour before closing. Closed for periods in Apr, June, and Dec when the royal family is in residence. Call ahead and check what's open before visiting.

William the Conqueror first ordered a castle built on this location, and since his day it's been a fateful spot for English sovereigns: King John cooled his heels at Windsor while waiting to put his signature on the Magna Carta at nearby Runnymede; Charles I was imprisoned here before losing his head; Queen Bess did some renovations; Victoria mourned her beloved Albert, who died at the castle in 1861; the royal family rode out much of World War II behind its sheltering walls; and when Queen Elizabeth II is in residence, the royal standard flies. With 1,000 rooms, Windsor is the world's largest inhabited castle.

The apartments display many works of art, armor, three Verrio ceilings, and several 17th-century Gibbons carvings. Several works by Rubens adorn the King's Drawing Room and in the relatively small King's Dressing Room is a Dürer, along with Rembrandt's portrait of his mother, and Van Dyck's triple portrait of Charles I. Of the apartments, the grand reception room, with its Gobelin tapestries, is the most spectacular.

We think that the Windsor ✪ **Changing of the Guard** is a much more exciting and moving experience than the London exercises. In Windsor, the guard marches through town when the queen is in residence, stopping the traffic as it wheels into the castle to

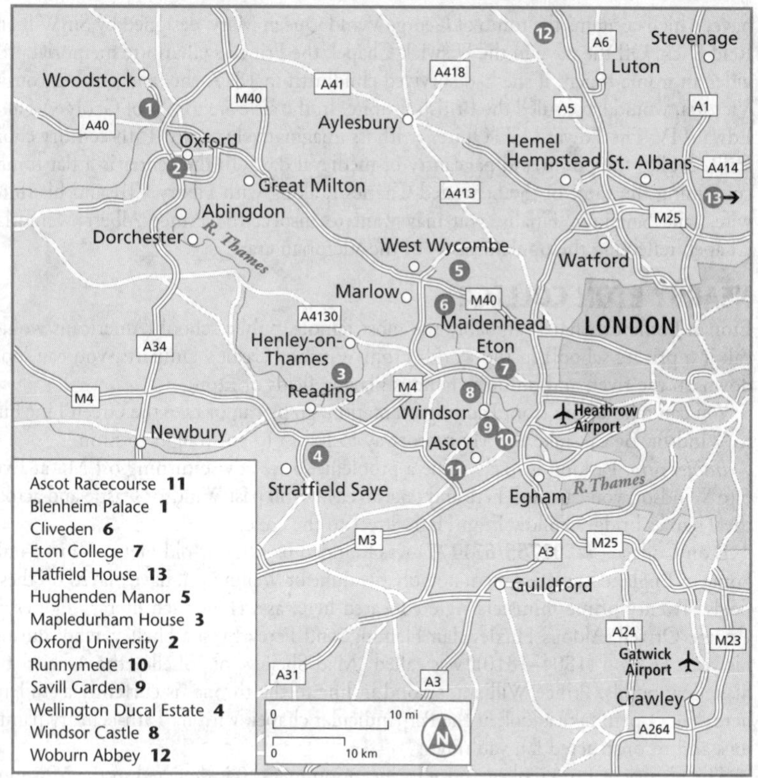

the tune of a full regimental band; when the queen is not here, a drum-and-pipe band is mustered. From April to June, the ceremony takes place daily at 11am. For the remainder of the year, the guard is changed every 48 hours weather permitting. It's best to call ☎ **01753/868286** to find out which days the ceremony will take place.

Queen Mary's Doll's House. Castle Hill. ☎ **01753/868286** or 01753/831118 for recorded information. Admission is included in entrance to Windsor Castle. Mar–Oct daily 10am–4pm; Nov–Feb daily 10am–3pm. As with Windsor Castle, it's best to call ahead to confirm opening times.

A palace in perfect miniature, the Doll's House was given to Queen Mary in 1923 as a symbol of national goodwill. The house, designed by Sir Edwin Lutyens, was created on a scale of 1 to 12. It took 3 years to complete and involved the work of 1,500 tradesmen and artists. Every item is a miniature masterpiece; each room is exquisitely furnished and every item is made exactly to scale. Working elevators stop on every floor, and there is running water in all five bathrooms.

✪ **St. George's Chapel.** Castle Hill. Admission is included in entrance to Windsor Castle. Mon–Sat 10am–4pm. Closed Sun and for a few days in mid-June.

A gem of the Perpendicular style, this chapel shares the distinction with Westminster Abbey of being a pantheon of English monarchs (Victoria is a notable exception). The present St. George's was founded in the late 15th century by Edward IV on the site of the original Chapel of the Order of the Garter (Edward III, 1348). You first enter the nave, which contains the tomb of George V and Queen Mary, designed by Sir William Reid Dick. Off the nave in the Urswick Chapel, the Princess Charlotte memorial provides an ironic touch; if she had survived childbirth in 1817, she, and not her cousin Victoria, would have ruled the British Empire. In the aisle are tombs of George VI and Edward IV. The Edward IV "Quire," with its imaginatively carved 15th-century choir stalls, evokes the pomp and pageantry of medieval days. In the center is a flat tomb, containing the vault of the beheaded Charles I, along with Henry VIII and his third wife, Jane Seymour. Finally, you may want to inspect the Prince Albert Memorial Chapel, reflecting the opulent tastes of the Victorian era.

NEARBY ETON COLLEGE

Eton is home of what is arguably the most famous public school (Americans would call it a private school) in the world. From Windsor Castle's ramparts, you can look down on the river, and onto the famous playing fields of Eton.

You can take a train from Paddington Station, go by car, or take the Green Line bus to Windsor. By car, take the M4 motorway to Exit 5 to go straight to Eton.

Insider's tip: Parking is likely to be a problem, so we advise turning off M4 at Exit 6 to Windsor; you can park here and take an easy stroll past Windsor Castle and across the Thames bridge. Follow Eton High Street to the college.

Eton College (☎ **01753/671177**) was founded by 18-year-old Henry VI in 1440. Some of England's greatest men, notably the duke of Wellington, have played on these fields. Twenty prime ministers were educated here, as well as such literary figures as George Orwell, Aldous Huxley, Ian Fleming, and Percy Bysshe Shelley, who, during his years at Eton (1804–1810), was called "Mad Shelley" or "Shelley the Atheist" by his fellow pupils. Prince William, second in line to the throne, is currently a student here. If it's open, take a look at the Perpendicular chapel, with its 15th-century paintings and reconstructed fan vaulting.

The history of Eton College since its inception in 1440 is depicted in the **Museum of Eton Life,** Eton College (☎ **01753/671177**), located in vaulted wine cellars under College Hall, which were originally used as a storehouse by the college's masters. The displays, ranging from formal to extremely informal, include a turn-of-the-century boy's room, schoolbooks, and canes used by senior boys to apply punishment they felt needful to their juniors.

Admission to the school and museum costs £2.70 ($4.60) for adults and £2 ($3.40) for children. You can also take guided tours for £4 ($6.80) or £3 ($5.10) for children. Eton College is open from Easter to October, daily from 10:30am to 4:30pm; during school term, daily from 2 to 4:30pm. However, it may close for special occasions.

MORE TO SEE & DO IN & AROUND WINDSOR

The town of Windsor is largely Victorian, with lots of brick buildings and a few remnants of Georgian architecture. In and around the castle are two cobblestone streets, Church and Market, which have antiques shops, silversmiths, and pubs. After lunch or tea, you may want to stroll along the 3-mile, aptly named **Long Walk.**

On Sunday, there are often **polo matches** in Windsor Great Park, and at Ham Common, and you may see Prince Charles playing and Prince Philip serving as umpire while the queen watches. The park is the site of the queen's occasional equestrian jaunts. On Sunday, she attends a little church near the Royal Lodge. Traditionally, she prefers to drive herself here, later returning to the castle for Sunday lunch. For more information, call the Tourist Information Centre (see above).

Savill Garden, Wick Lane, Englefield Green, Egham, and Surrey (☎ **01753/860222**) are all in **Windsor Great Park,** which is signposted from Windsor, Egham, and Ascot. Started in 1932, the 35-acre garden is one of the finest of its type in the northern hemisphere. The display starts in spring with rhododendrons, camellias, and daffodils beneath the trees; then throughout the summer there are spectacular displays of flowers and shrubs presented in a natural and wild state. It's open daily year-round (except at Christmas) from 10am to 6pm (to 4pm in winter). Admission prices vary throughout the year: from November to March, 3 for adults, £2.50 ($4.25) for seniors; in April and May, £5 ($8.50) adults, £4.50 ($7.65) for seniors, and from June to October £4 ($6.80) adults, £3.50 ($5.95) for seniors. Children 16 and under are admitted free. The location is 5 miles from Windsor along A30; turn off at Wick Road and follow the signs to the gardens. The nearest rail station is at Egham; from here you'll need to take a taxi a distance of 3 miles. There's a licensed, self-service restaurant and gift shop on the premises.

Adjoining the Savill Garden are the **Valley Gardens,** full of shrubs and trees in a series of wooded natural valleys running down to the water. It's open daily throughout the year. Entrance to the gardens is free, although parking your car costs £1.50 ($2.55) per vehicle.

Queen Victoria died on January 22, 1901, and was buried beside her beloved Prince Albert in a mausoleum at **Frogmore** (a private estate), a mile from Windsor. The prince consort died in December 1861. The house, gardens, and mausoleum are open only a few days out of the year, usually in May and August, from around 10am to 6pm. The cost for adults is £5.90 ($10.05); seniors pay £4.90 ($8.35). Call **01753/868286,** ext. 2235, for more details.

On the B3022 Bracknell/Ascot Road, outside Windsor, **Legoland,** a 150-acre theme park, opened in 1996. Although a bit corny, it's fun for the entire family. Attractions, spread across five main activity centers, include the Duplo Gardens, offering a boat ride, puppet theater, and water works, plus a Miniland, showing European cities or villages re-created in minute detail from millions of Lego bricks. The "Enchanted Forest" has treasure trails, a castle, and animals created from Lego bricks. The latest attraction is Dragon Knight's Castle, which takes you back to the days of knights and dragons, and includes a blazing dragon roller coaster. For reservations and information, call **0990/040404.** The park is open daily 10am to 6pm from mid-March through October. Admission costs £17.50 ($29.75) for adults, £11.50 ($19.55) for seniors, £14.50 ($24.65) for children 3 to 15, and is free for children 2 and under.

Three miles south of Windsor is **Runnymede,** the 188-acre meadow on the south side of the Thames, in Surrey, where it's believed that King John put his seal on the Great Charter after intense pressure from his feudal barons and lords. Today, Runnymede is also the site of the John F. Kennedy Memorial, an acre of English ground given to the United States by the people of Britain. The memorial, a large block of white stone, is hard to see from the road, but is clearly signposted and reached after a short walk. The pagoda that shelters it was placed here by the American Bar Association to acknowledge the fact that American law stems from the English system.

The historic site, to which there is free access all year, lies beside the Thames, 1/2 mile west of the hamlet of Old Windsor on the south side of the A308. If you're driving on the M25, exit at Junction 13. The nearest rail connection is at Egham, 1/2 mile away. Trains depart from London's Waterloo Station, and take about 25 minutes.

Bus & Boat Tours, Horse Rides & Guided Walks of Windsor

The tourist office can put you in touch with a Blue Badge (official) guide to lead you on a **walking tour** of town. These trained local guides cost £45 ($76.50) per hour—get together a group to split the cost. Advance booking is essential.

You can also take a 30-minute **carriage ride** up the sycamore-lined length of Windsor Castle's Long Walk. Horses with their carriages and drivers line up beside the castle waiting for fares, charging from about £18 ($30.60) for up to four passengers.

Boat tours depart from Windsor's main embarkation point along Windsor Promenade, Barry Avenue, for a 35-minute round-trip to Boveney Lock. The cost is £3.80 ($6.45) for adults, half price for children. You can also take a 2-hour tour through the Boveney Lock and up past stately private riverside homes, the Bray Film Studios, Queens Eyot, and Monkey Island, for £6 ($10.20) for adults, half price for children. There's also a 45-minute tour from Runnymede on board the *Lucy Fisher,* a replica of a Victorian paddle steamer. You pass Magna Carta Island, among other sights. This tour costs £3.80 ($6.45) for adults, half price for children. In addition, longer tours between Maidenhead and Hampton Court are offered. The boats offer light refreshments and have a well-stocked bar, plus the decks are covered in case of an unexpected shower. Tours are operated by **French Brothers, Ltd.,** Clewer Boathouse, Clewer Court Road, Windsor (☎ **01753/851900**).

Shopping

A colorful traditional English perfumery, **Woods of Windsor,** Queen Charlotte Street (☎ **01753/868125**), dates from 1770. It offers soaps, shampoos, scented drawer liners, and hand and body lotions, all prettily packaged in pastel-flower and bright old-fashioned wraps.

The Token House, High Street (☎ **01753/863263**), is the largest gathering of everyone's favorite china and crystal. Place settings in Wedgwood, Royal Albert, Minton, and Spode, plus Portmeirion bowls, Royal Dalton figurines, Waterford crystal stemware and collector plates, bowls, and vases are stacked through the airy, bright shop. **The Reject China Shop** across the street has items that sell for less, but there is no connection to The Token House.

At **Billings & Edmonds,** 132 High St., Eton (☎ **01753/861348**), you may think you've blundered into a time warp. This distinctive clothing store offers excellent traditional tailoring, suits made to order, and a complete line of cufflinks, shirts, ties, and accessories.

Asquith's Teddy Bear Shop, 33 High St., Eton (☎ **01753/831200**), appeals to your inner child with every bear imaginable, including Winnie and Paddington. Bear clothes from dungarees to Eton College uniforms mix with tinware and hatboxes covered in teddy-bear prints.

WHERE TO STAY IN THE WINDSOR AREA

During the Ascot races and Windsor Horse Show, reservations are necessary far in advance.

The Castle Hotel. 18 High St., Windsor, Berkshire SL4 1LJ. ☎ **800/225-5843** in the U.S. and Canada, or 01753/851011. Fax 01753/830244. www.Fork-holes.com. 111 units. TV TEL. £135–£195 ($229.50–$331.50) double; £215–£295 ($365.50–$501.50) suite. Children 12 and under stay free in parents' room. AE, DC, MC, V.

In the shadow of Windsor Castle, on the main street, is this solid choice with a dignified Georgian facade. It was originally built in the 15th century to shelter the workers laboring on the town's foundations and royal buildings. The grounds behind the hotel once served as the stable yard for Windsor Castle, but now they contain a modern wing, where the bedrooms are much more sterile than those in the main building. Guest rooms are equipped extras such as trouser presses. The baths are well supplied with hair dryers and a set of toiletries. The restaurant's food has improved a lot recently.

Fairlight Lodge. 41 Frances Rd., Windsor, Berkshire SL4 3AQ. ☎ **01753/861207.** Fax 01753/865963. http://fairlightlodge.webjump.com. E-mail: fairlight@hotmail.com. 10 units. TV TEL. £76–£86 ($129.20–$146.20) double; £99–£110 ($168.30–$187) family room for 2 adults and 2 children. Rates include English breakfast. AE,DC, MC, V.

Built in 1885 as the home of the mayor of Windsor, this highly rated B&B in a residential section is only a few minutes' walk south of Windsor Castle. It offers comfortable rooms complete with Victorian decor and private facilities; two have large four-poster beds. Bathrooms, though small, are efficiently organized with a shower stall. There's a fully licensed Garden Restaurant that serves affordable dinners, and caters to vegetarians and special dietary needs.

✪ **The Oakley Court Hotel.** Windsor Rd., Water Oakley, Windsor, Berkshire SL4 5UR. ☎ **01753/609988.** Fax 01628/637011. E-mail: oakleyct@atlab.co.uk. 115 units. MINIBAR TV TEL, Mon–Thurs £180 ($306) double, £310 ($527) suite; Fri–Sun £156 ($265.20) double, £350 ($595) suite. Weekend rates include breakfast. AE, DC, MC, V. Take the river road, A308, 3 miles from Windsor toward Maidenhead.

Built beside the Thames (only a 20-minute drive from Heathrow) by a Victorian industrialist, the Oakley Court has quite a sense of tradition. Today it's affiliated with the Queen's Moat House hotel chain. The building's jutting gables and bristling turrets have lent themselves to the filming of several horror movies, including the *Rocky Horror Picture Show* and *Dracula.* Recently renovated, the hotel is a comfortable place to stay—far superior to your choices in the heart of Windsor. Although the grandest public areas are in the main house, most rooms are in a pair of well-accessorized modern wings that ramble through the estate's 35 acres of parks and gardens. The spacious rooms include trouser presses; bathrooms are generous in size and clad in granite with robes, thick fluffy towels, hair dryers, and bidets, plus an array of luxurious toiletries.

Dining: The hotel restaurant, The Oak Leaf, is open for breakfast, lunch, and dinner, serving an excellent, formal cuisine.

Amenities: You can rent a boat for punting on the Thames, stroll through the extensive gardens, or order room service 24 hours a day. Recently installed facilities include a pool and Jacuzzi, plus a gym with sauna and steam room.

Royal Adelaide Hotel. 46 King's Rd., Windsor, Berkshire SL4 2AG. ☎ **01753/863916.** Fax 01753/830682. www.meridianleisure.com. E-mail: royaladelaide@meridianleisure.com. 42 units. TV TEL. £95 ($161.50) double. Rates include English breakfast. AE, DC, MC, V.

This interesting Georgian building is opposite the famous Long Walk leading to Windsor Castle, 5 minutes away. It was named for Queen Adelaide, who visited the premises during her reign, thereby dubbing it "royal." All the well-furnished rooms, which vary in size, have trouser presses, alarm clocks, and beverage makers. Rooms have recently been refurbished, and the mattresses renewed. The small bathrooms have sufficient shelf space and a hair dryer. A 3-course fixed price dinner is available for £17.50 ($29.75), but arrangements should be made in advance. The cuisine is both English and French.

Sir Christopher Wren's House Hotel. Thames St., Windsor, Berkshire SL4 1PX. ☎ **01753/861354.** Fax 01753/860172. www.wrensgroup.com. 60 units. TV TEL. Mon–Thurs £185 ($314.50) double; £275 ($467.50) suite. Fri–Sun (including breakfast) £135–£195 ($229.50–$331.50). AE, DC, MC, V. Free parking.

Designed by Christopher Wren in 1676 as his own home, this former town house occupies a prime position on the Thames. It lies between Eton and Windsor, just a 3-minute walk from the castle. Wren's oak-paneled former study is equipped with his Empire desk, a fireplace, and shield-back Hepplewhite chairs. The bay-windowed main drawing room opens onto a garden and a riverside flagstone terrace for after-dinner coffee and drinks. Some rooms have fine old furniture, and all are equipped with trouser presses and tea- and coffeemakers. Rooms come in a wide range of sizes; some have a full canopied bed, others a half-canopied bed. Bathrooms are tiled or marbled with such extras as hair dryers. Several bedrooms overlook the river. Room 2, which was Sir Christopher Wren's bedroom, is said to be haunted.

Dining: The hotel's restaurant, The Orangerie, is recommended below.

Amenities: 24-hour room service, concierge, dry cleaning/laundry, newspaper delivery, secretarial services, access to a nearby health club, business center.

Ye Harte & Garter Hotel. 31 High St., Windsor, Berkshire SL4 1PH. ☎ **01753/863426.** Fax 01753/830527. 39 units. TV TEL. £110–£180 ($187–$306) double. AE, DC, MC, V.

On Castle Hill opposite Windsor Castle, the old Garter Inn, named for the Knights of the Garter, was the setting for scenes in Shakespeare's *Merry Wives of Windsor.* The Garter burned down in the 1800s and was rebuilt as part of one hostelry that included the Harte. From the front rooms, you can watch the guards marching up High Street every morning on their way to change the guard at the castle. The recently renovated rooms are most comfortable, and rather functionally furnished, although they vary greatly in size. More expensive are the Windsor rooms, which have front views and Jacuzzis. Regardless of size or location, each has a small but well-maintained bathroom with a shower stall.

Dining: The hotel operates a carvery, plus a separate fish-and-chips restaurant and a bistro/cafe bar.

WHERE TO DINE IN WINDSOR & ETON

Many visitors prefer to dine in Eton; most of the restaurants and fast-food places along the main street of Windsor, in front of the castle, serve dreary food.

Antico. 42 High St., Eton. ☎ **01753/863977.** Reservations strongly recommended. Main courses £9.50–£17 ($16.15–$28.90). AE, DC, MC, V. Mon–Fri 12:30–2:30pm; Mon–Sat 7–10:30pm. Closed bank holidays. ITALIAN.

Eton's finest Italian restaurant, Antico serves Mediterranean food in a formal setting. People have been dining here for 200 years, although not from an Italian menu. On your way to the tiny bar you pass a cold table, displaying hors d'oeuvres and cold meats. There are many fish dishes, such as grilled fresh salmon or Dover sole, and a wide selection of pastas. The food is substantial and filling—a good value, but rarely exciting.

Gilbey's Bar and Restaurant. 82–83 High St., Eton. ☎ **01753/854921.** Reservations recommended. Main courses £9.95–£13.95 ($16.90–$23.70). AE, DC, MC, V. Mon–Tues noon–2:30pm and 6–10:30pm; Wed, Thurs, and Sun noon–10:30pm, Fri–Sat noon–11pm. MODERN BRITISH/CONTINENTAL.

Just across the bridge from Windsor, this charming place is located on Eton's main street, among the antiques shops. It is furnished with pinewood tables and old church pews and chairs, and there's a glassed-in conservatory out back. A brigade of seven chefs turns out quite good modern British dishes. Begin with one of the well-prepared soups, or a smoked-salmon-and-artichoke tart. Main dishes include pan-fried skate wing with a champagne or chili and caper risotto. For dessert, try the delicious white and dark mousse with amaretto cream.

House on the Bridge. 71 High St., Eton. ☎ **01753/860914.** Reservations recommended. Main courses from £14.95 ($25.40); fixed-price meal £22.45 ($38.15) at lunch, £32.50 ($55.25) at dinner. AE, DC, MC, V. Daily noon–3pm and 6–11pm. ENGLISH/INTERNATIONAL.

This restaurant is in a charming redbrick and terra-cotta Victorian building, adjacent to the bridge and beside the river at the edge of Eton. Near the handful of outdoor tables is an almost vertical garden whose plants cascade into the Thames. Among the well-prepared main dishes are crispy duckling with Calvados and Seville oranges, chicken supreme flavored with tarragon and served with mushrooms, and chateaubriand. Good ingredients go into the dishes, and the food, although traditionally based, has many modern touches.

✪ **The Oak Leaf Restaurant at the Oakley Court Hotel.** Windsor Rd., Water Oakley, Windsor. ☎ **01753/609988.** Reservations recommended. Table d'hôte lunch £24.50 ($41.65); table d'hôte dinner £29.50 ($50.15). AE, DC, MC, V. Daily,7am–10am, noon–2pm, and7–10pm. INTERNATIONAL.

In the mid-1990s, this chic London restaurant, known for its delectable food and sophisticated clientele, moved from central London to this new setting beside the Thames. Today, under the supervision of chef Damien Bradley, the reincarnated Oak Leaf serves a modern cuisine that might include a parfait of duck livers with a confit of red onions and mandarin oranges, or a pavé of Scottish salmon with creamed leeks served with broad beans and a red-wine shallot sauce.

The Orangerie. In Sir Christopher Wren's House Hotel, Thames St., Windsor. ☎ **01753/861354.** Main courses £14.50–£19 ($24.65–$32.30). AE, DC, MC, V. Daily 12:30–2:30pm and 6:30–10:30pm. CONTINENTAL.

This restaurant, located near the castle, is Windsor's most elegant and charming, possessing garden terraces and a conservatory. The dining room is designed a bit like a greenhouse. Chef Philip Ward selects an individual garnish to complement each well-prepared dish. For starters, try the tower of smoked salmon and asparagus. For your main course, enjoy the rosettes of spring lamb with beans, artichokes and an herb Yorkshire pudding, or the seafood platter of lobster, king prawns, crab, mussels and shrimps. There is also a variety of vegetarian dishes. At dinner a pianist entertains.

SIDE TRIPS FROM WINDSOR

If you have time to spare in the Windsor area, you can take any number of fascinating excursions. But if you can squeeze in only one, make it Hughenden Manor (see below).

HUGHENDEN MANOR: DISRAELI CALLED IT HOME

Hughenden Manor. High Wycombe. ☎ **01494/755573.** Admission £4.20 ($7.15) adults, £2.10 ($3.55) children; £10.50 ($17.85) family ticket. Garden only, £1.50 ($2.55) adults, 75p ($1.30) for children. Apr–Oct Wed–Sun 1–5pm; Mar Sat–Sun only 1–5pm. Closed Nov–Feb; Good Friday. From Windsor take the M4 (toward Reading), then A404 to A40. Continue north of High Wycombe on the A4128 for about 1½ miles. From London, catch coach no. 711 to High Wycombe, then board a Beeline bus (High Wycombe-Aylesbury no. 323 or 324).

This country manor not only gives us insight into the age of Victoria, but also acquaints us with a remarkable man: Benjamin Disraeli, one of the most enigmatic figures of 19th-century England. At age 21, Dizzy published his five-volume novel, *Vivian Grey,* anonymously. Then he went on to other things and in 1839 married an older widow for her money, although they apparently developed a most harmonious relationship. He entered politics in 1837 and continued writing novels; his later ones met with more acclaim.

In 1848, Disraeli acquired Hughenden Manor, a country house that befitted his fast-rising political and social position. He served briefly as prime minister in 1868, but his political fame rests on his stewardship as prime minister from 1874 to 1880.

He became friends with Queen Victoria who, in 1877, paid him a rare honor by visiting him at Hughenden. In 1876, Disraeli became the earl of Beaconsfield; he died a few years later in 1881. Instead of being buried at Westminster Abbey, he preferred the simple little graveyard of Hughenden Church.

Today, Hughenden houses an odd assortment of memorabilia, including a lock of Disraeli's hair, letters from Victoria, autographed books, and a portrait of Lord Byron.

West Wycombe

Snuggled in the Chiltern Hills 30 miles west of London and 15 miles northwest of Windsor, the village of West Wycombe still has an atmosphere of the early 18th century. The thatched roofs have been replaced by tiles, and some of the buildings have been replaced, but the village is still 2 centuries removed from the present day.

From Windsor, take the M4 (toward Reading), then A404 to A40. Signs to follow en route include Maidenhead, Marlow, and Oxford. If you previously visited Hughenden Manor, the village of West Wycombe lies immediately to the west.

A visit to West Wycombe wouldn't be complete without a tour of **West Wycombe Park,** seat of the Dashwood family. Now owned by the National Trust, it's of both historical and architectural interest. The house is one of the best examples of Palladian-style architecture in England. The interior is lavishly decorated with paintings and antiques from the 18th century.

In the mid-18th century, Sir Francis Dashwood began an ambitious building program at West Wycombe. His strong interest in architecture and design led Sir Frances to undertake a series of monuments and parks that are still among the finest in the country.

Sir Francis also commissioned the excavation of a cave on the estate. Its primary purpose was to serve as a meeting place for "The Knights of St. Francis of Wycombe," later known as the notorious Hellfire Club, which spent its time partying, drinking, and ravishing innocent virgins. It seems that some satanic rites also took place here—not so much to invoke Satan, as to inspire general debauchery. The cave is about a half-mile long, filled with stalactites and stalagmites, and dotted with statues of Sir Francis, his friend Lord Sandwich, and even Ben Franklin.

The house and grounds are open March through August, daily from 11am to 5pm. Admission is £4.20 ($7.15) for adults, and £2 ($3.40) for children. If you wish to visit only the grounds, the cost is £3 ($5.10). The caves are open daily from March through September from 11am to 5pm; off-season hours are only on Saturday and Sunday from 11am to 5pm. Admission is £3.50 ($5.95) for adults, or £2 ($3.40) for seniors and children. The cave tour includes stops for talks about former Hellfire members; it lasts 30 minutes. For more information, call the West Wycombe Estate Office at West Wycombe (☎ **01494/524411**), or the caves at ☎ **01494/533739.**

Other sights at West Wycombe include the **Church of St. Lawrence,** perched on West Wycombe Hill and topped by a huge golden ball. Parts of the church date from the 13th century; its richly decorated interior was copied from a 3rd-century Syrian sun temple. The view from the hill is worth the trek up. Near the church stands the **Dashwood mausoleum,** built in a style derived from Constantine's Arch in Rome.

After your tour of the park, head for **George & Dragon,** High Street (☎ **01494/464414**), for a pint or a good, inexpensive lunch. In a building that dates back to 1720, this is a former coaching inn with a cheerful log fire, a comfortable-sized bar (that nevertheless gets crowded on weekends), and an impressive oak staircase with its own ghost. There is a separate no-smoking room open to children, a children's play area, and a garden for dining outside. If you like West Wycombe and want to stay over, there are eight cozily furnished rooms with private bath, phone, and TV, costing £68 ($115.60) for a double, including breakfast.

Cliveden: Former Home of Lady Astor

Cliveden House. 10 miles northwest of Windsor. ☎ **01628/605069.** Admission to grounds £5 ($8.50) for adults; £2.50 ($4.25) for children; family ticket £12 ($20.40). Admission to house £1 ($1.70) extra. Grounds mid-Mar to Dec daily 11am–6pm. House Apr–Oct Thurs and Sun 3–6pm, 3 rooms of the mansion are open to the public, as is the Octagon Temple, with its rich mosaic interior. From Windsor, follow the M4 toward Reading to the junction at No. 7 (direction Slough West). At the roundabout, turn left onto the A4 signposted Maidenhead. At the next roundabout, turn right signposted Burnham. Follow the road for 2½ miles to a T junction with B476. The main gates to Cliveden are directly opposite.

Now a National Trust property, Cliveden House, former home of Lady Astor, stands on a constructed terrace of mature gardens high above the Thames. The estate's original mansion and sweeping lawns were created by William Winde in 1666 for the second duke of Buckingham. Later the father of King George III reared his sons here. After a fire in 1795, Sir Charles Barry, the architect of the House of Parliament, converted the house into its present gracefully symmetrical form. A soaring clock tower was added to one side as a later Victorian folly. When the house was sold by the duke of Southerland to the Astors in 1893, Queen Victoria lamented the passage. The house remained part of the Astor legacy until 1966, a repository of a notable collection of paintings and antiques.

The surrounding **gardens** have a distinguished variety of plantings, ranging from Renaissance-style topiary to meandering forest paths with vistas of statuary and flowering shrubs. Garden features are a rose garden, a magnificent parterre, and an amphitheater where "Rule Britannia" was played for the first time. There are 375 acres of garden and woodland to explore.

The manor also accepts paying guests, and it's a spectacular place to stay, as we've described below.

Where to Stay & Dine

✪ **Cliveden House.** Cliveden, Taplow, Maidenhead, Berkshire SL6 0JF. ☎ **01628/668561.** Fax 01628/661837. www.clivedenhouse.co.uk. 38 units. TV TEL. £290–£565 ($493–$960.50) double. AE, DC, MC, V.

Lady Astor's former estate is one of the most beautiful and luxurious hotels in England. Often acclaimed as "hotel of the year" by various rating services in England, this majestic property was home to a Prince of Wales and a scattering of dukes before the Astors moved in. It was also a setting for the infamous Profumo scandal of the 1960s, which shook the Empire.

Rooms are sumptuous, each furnished in impeccable taste. The baths are among the finest we've ever seen in England. Less preferred are the recently added rooms in the Clutton Wing. Nothing (except perhaps renting Lady Astor's bedroom itself) is more elegant here than walking down to the river and boarding a hotel boat for a champagne cruise before dinner. In the morning you can go horseback riding on the 376-acre estate along the riverbank. A traditional English breakfast is served in the Terrace Dining Room.

Dining: The main drawing room of the house is now the Terrace Dining Room, with panoramic views. Classical French and modern and traditional English cuisine are served here. The wild mushrooms and grilled leeks in a truffle sauce would surely have pleased Lady Astor herself. You can also dine at Waldo's, a showcase for a talented chef, Gary Jones, who specializes in contemporary British cuisine. There's also a conservatory dining room in the original walled garden.

Amenities: A luxurious Pavilion Spa with separate steam rooms for men and women, plus indoor and outdoor pools, a gym, and a beauty treatment room.

THE COTTAGE WHERE MILTON WROTE *PARADISE LOST*

The modern residential town of **Gerrards Cross** is often called the Beverly Hills of England, as it attracts many wealthy Londoners, among others. To the north of it is **Chalfont St. Giles,** where the poet John Milton lived during the Great Plague in 1665. To reach it, take the A355 north from Windsor bypassing Beaconsfield until you come to the sign-posted cutoff for Chalfont St. Giles to the east.

Chalfont St. Giles is today a typical English village, although its history goes back to Roman times. The charm of the village is in its center, with shops, pubs, and cafes clustered around the green and the village pond.

The 16th-century **John Milton's Cottage,** Chalfont St. Giles (☎ **01494/872313**), is the site where the great poet completed *Paradise Lost* and started *Paradise Regained.* Its four rooms contain many relics and exhibits devoted to Milton. It is open March through October, Tuesday through Sunday from 10am to 1pm and 2 to 6pm, charging adults £2 ($3.40) and children £60 ($102).

2 Ascot

28 miles W of London

While following the royal buck hounds through Windsor Forest, Queen Anne decided to have a racecourse on Ascot Heath. The first race meeting at Ascot, which is directly south of Windsor at the southern end of Windsor Great Park, was held in 1711. Since then, the Ascot Racecourse has been a symbol of high society as pictures of the royal family, including the Queen and Prince Philip, have been flashed around the world. Ladies: Be sure to wear a hat.

GETTING THERE

Trains travel between Waterloo in London and Ascot Station, which is about 10 minutes from the racecourse. The trip takes about 1 hour, and service is about every 30 minutes during the day. For rail information, call ☎ **0345/484950** in the United Kingdom, or ☎ **01603/764776** in the United States.

Buses frequently depart from London's Victoria Coach Station. Call ☎ **0990/808080** for more information.

If you're driving from Windsor, take A332 west.

THE ASCOT RACECOURSE

The **Ascot Racecourse,** High Street (☎ **01344/622211**), England's largest and most prestigious course, is open throughout the year, although no races are held during March. The facility hosts 24 days of racing yearly. The highlight of the Ascot social season is the above-mentioned **Royal Meeting (or Royal Week),** when many women wear fancy hats and white gloves. There is also excellent racing on De Beers Diamond Day (4th Sat in July) and during the Festival at Ascot (last Sat and Sun in Sept), when the prize money usually exceeds £1 million per event.

You can buy tickets for one of three distinctly different observation areas, known locally as "enclosures." These include the Members' Enclosure, which during the Royal Meeting (4 days in June) is known as the Royal Enclosure. Also available are Tattersall's Enclosure, largest of the three; and the Silver Ring, which does not enjoy direct access to the paddocks and has traditionally been the site of most of Ascot's budget seating. Except during the Royal Meeting, newcomers can usually secure viewing space in the Member's Enclosure, but only if they call ahead to confirm that space is available. Tickets cost £16 to £27 ($27.20 to $45.90) for seats in the Member's Enclosure, £11 to £16 ($18.70 to $27.20) in the Grandstand and Paddock, and £6 to £10 ($10.20 to $17) in the Silver Ring. Prices depend on the race and the season. Children 16 and under are admitted free if accompanied by an adult, and there is free supervised daycare for children under 8.

Advance bookings for guaranteed seating in the most desirable areas during the most popular races can be arranged beginning January 1 every year. Write for tickets to the Secretary's Office, Ascot Racecourse, Ascot, Berkshire SL5 7JN. For admission to the Royal Enclosure, write to Her Majesty's Representative, Ascot Office, St. James's Palace, London SW1. First-timers usually have difficulty being admitted to the Royal Enclosure, since their application must be endorsed by someone who has been admitted to the Royal Enclosure at least eight times before. Credit cards are accepted by calling ☎ **01344/876456.** Car parking is free except on June 22, July 27, and the Festival Meeting in September.

WHERE TO STAY & DINE

Berystede Country House Hotel. Bagshot Rd., Sunninghill Ascot, Berkshire SL5 9JH. ☎ **01344/623311.** Fax 01344/872301. 91 units. TV TEL. £165 ($280.50) double; from £200 ($340) suite. AE, DC, MC, V. Free parking. Take the A330 1 1/2 miles south of Ascot.

This hotel just south of Ascot is a Victorian fantasy of medieval towers, steeply pitched roofs, and a landscaped garden. Drawing race-goers and businesspeople, it also caters to conferences (at which time it's best avoided). The rooms, with their high ceilings and chintz, evoke a private country house. Recently refurbished bedrooms are decorated in period styles, most often Victorian. The best rooms are in the main house because they are more spacious and better decorated. Most of the rooms are in a more modern annex with less character. Most rooms have a tub and shower; 36 bedrooms are designated no-smoking.

Brockenhurst. Brockenhurst Rd., S. Ascot, Berkshire SL5 9HA. ☎ **01344/621912.** Fax 01344/873252. www.brockenhurst.com. 15 units. TV TEL. £89–£100 ($151.30–$170) double. Rates include continental breakfast. AE, DC, MC, V.

A small, tastefully refurbished 1905 Edwardian hotel of charm and distinction, Brockenhurst is conveniently situated near shops and the train station. The most expensive rooms are called "executive" and include whirlpool baths, trouser presses, and hair dryers in the well-appointed bathrooms. Regardless of location, bedrooms are generally spacious. The hotel has a bar and offers a room-service menu. The owners serve mainly English and French cuisine, and, if given 24 hours' notice, will try to prepare a meal of your choice. This is a very good alternative to the pricey Royal Berkshire or Berystede.

The Royal Berkshire. London Rd., Sunninghill, Ascot, Berkshire SL5 OPP. ☎ **01344/623322.** Fax 01344/627100. www.hilton.com. 63 units. TV TEL. £200 ($340) double; from £250 ($425) suite. AE, DC, MC, V. Free parking. Take A322 2 miles northeast of Ascot.

This is a prestigious and elegant hotel with a rich history. Built in Queen Anne style in 1705, it housed the Churchill family for many years. The stylish rooms are divided between the main house and an annex. While the annex rooms are furnished well, they aren't equal to those in the main building. Rooms are spacious with thick carpeting and large comfortable beds, plus marble baths with thick towels, robes, and hair dryers. If you want the character of old England, opt for the main building, although the annex rooms are exceedingly comfortable as well, each redecorated in 1996.

Dining: Many people visit only for a meal in the Stateroom Restaurant, which overlooks the hotel lawns and gardens. The food, some of the finest in the area, is prepared with quality ingredients and often with artistic flair. The menu changes frequently and offers contemporary English dishes.

3 Henley-on-Thames & the Royal Regatta

35 miles W of London

At the eastern edge of Oxfordshire, Henley-on-Thames, a small town and resort on the river at the foothills of the Chilterns, is the headquarters of the ✪ **Royal Regatta,** held annually in late June and early July. Henley, which lies on a stretch of the Thames that's known for its calm waters, unobstructed bottom, and predictable currents, is a rower's mecca. The regatta, which dates back to the first years of Victoria's reign, is the major competition among international oarspeople who find it both challenging and entertaining.

The Elizabethan buildings, the tearooms, and the inns along the town's High Street will live up to your preconception of an English country town. Henley-on-Thames is an excellent (though pricey) stopover en route to Oxford; its fashionable inns are far from cheap.

ESSENTIALS

GETTING THERE Trains depart from London's Paddington Station but require a change at the junction in Twyford. More than 20 trains make the journey daily; the trip takes about an hour. For rail information, call ☎ **0345/484950** in the United Kingdom or ☎ 01603/764776 in the United States.

About 10 buses depart every day from London's Victoria Coach Station for Reading. From Reading, take local bus 328 or 329 to Henley. These buses depart every half hour. Call **0990/808080** for more information.

If you're driving from London, take M4 toward Reading to Junction 819, then head northwest on A4130.

VISITOR INFORMATION The **Tourist Information Centre** is at Town Hall, Market Place (☎ **01491/578034**). It's open daily from 10am to 7pm; in winter the center closes at 4pm.

THE HENLEY ROYAL REGATTA

The Henley Royal Regatta, held the first week in July, is one of the country's premier racing events. If you want a close-up view from the Stewards' Enclosure, you'll need a guest badge, which is only obtainable through a member. In other words, you have to know someone to obtain special privileges, but admission to the Regatta Enclosure is open to all. Information is available from the Secretary, Henley Royal Regatta, Henley-on-Thames, Oxfordshire RG9 2LY (☎ **01491/572153**).

During the annual 5-day event, up to 100 races will be organized each day, with starts scheduled as frequently as every 5 minutes. This event is open only to all-male crews of up to nine at a time. In late June, rowing events for women are held at the 3-day Henley Women's Regatta.

If you want to float on the waters of the Thames yourself, stop by the town's largest and oldest outfitter, **Hobbs & Sons, Ltd.,** Station Road Boathouse (☎ **01491/572035**), established in 1870. Open daily from April to October, their armada of watercraft includes rowboats that rent for between £7.50–£10 ($12.75–$17) per hour. Motorboats can be rented for £18–£35 ($30.60–$59.50) per hour. On the premises, a chandlery shop sells virtually anything a boat crew could need, as well as souvenir items like straw boater's hats and commemorative T-shirts.

MUSEUM CELEBRATING THE THAMES

The River and Rowing Museum, Mill Meadows (☎ **01491/415610**), celebrates the Thames and those oarsmen and oarswomen who row upon it. Opened by Queen Elizabeth in 1998, the $28 million museum, designed by English architect David Chipperfield, is the finest of its kind in Britain. A short walk south of Henley Bridge, it opens onto the banks of the Thames. The Rowing Gallery follows the saga of rowing from the days of the Greeks. It's all here: models of Arctic whaleboats in the 1700s, elaborate Venetian gondolas fit for a doge, and coastal lifeboats that pulled many a victim from the cold waters of the North Sea. In a more modern exhibit, you'll find the boat in which British oarsmen captured the gold medal in the Olympic games at Atlanta in 1996. The museum reaches out to embrace the saga of the Thames itself and the history of the regatta in Henley in particular. The museum is open Monday to Friday 10am to 5pm, Saturday and Sunday 10:30am to 5pm, charging an admission of £4.95 ($8.40).

WHERE TO STAY & DINE IN THE AREA

It's impossible to find a room during the Royal Regatta, unless you've made reservations months in advance.

Red Lion Hotel. Hart St., Henley-on-Thames, Oxfordshire RG9 2AR. ☎ **01491/572161.** Fax 01491/410039. 26 units. TV TEL. £125 ($212.50) double. AE, MC, V.

This ivy-covered coaching inn (ca. 1531) near Henley has a guest list that reads like a hall of fame: Johnson and Boswell, George IV (who, it is said, consumed 14 mutton chops one night), and Charles I. You can book the room in which Princess Grace stayed when her brother Jack was competing in the Royal Regatta in 1947. Most of the well-furnished rooms overlook the Thames. Bedrooms are midsize to spacious, each with a small but well-organized private bath with a shower stall.

Dining: Guests congregate in the low-beamed bar and take meals in the restaurant. The last dinner is served at 10pm, but 24-hour room service is provided. The menu is English with a French twist. The chef selects local produce each morning to prepare a "market-fresh" repertoire.

Amenities: Laundry service.

Stonor Arms. Stonor, by A4130 on B480 near Henley-on-Thames, Oxfordshire RG9 6HE. ☎ **01491/638866.** Fax 01491/638863. www.stonor-arms.co.uk. E-mail: stonorarms.hotel@virgin.net. 10 units. TV TEL. £125–£155 ($212.50–$263.50) double. Rates include breakfast. AE, MC, V.

For the area's finest dining and accommodations, head to the village of Stonor, 4 miles north of Henley. The village pub dates from the 1700s. Chef Stephen Morris, backed up by a hardworking and talented staff, prepares such fine food that he often attracts Londoners. For those who wish to stay over, a wing of rooms is handsomely furnished, often with antiques. You get grand comfort here, from fine bed linen to the roomy and well-equipped bathrooms, with a hair dryer and a set of thick towels. Cots for children can be added to most rooms.

Dining: Open daily for breakfast, lunch and dinner, the Stonor Restaurant offers main courses from £11.95 to £28 ($20.30 to $47.60). The cuisine is mainly English, with some French and Italian influences. Main dishes change nightly but might include roast partridge with onions and turnips, or a supreme of cod served with potatoes, lentils, and peppered sweet breads. Fresh produce is used whenever possible, and the fish is brought in from Cornwall. You can dine outdoors in summer.

SIDE TRIPS FROM HENLEY

A Romantic Boat Trip to a Historic Home

Mapledurham House. ☎ **01189/723350.** Admission to house and mill £6 ($10.20) adults, £3 ($5.10) children 5–14, free for children 4 and under. Easter–Sept Sat–Sun and bank holidays 2–5pm; the mill opens at 2pm. Closed Oct–Easter. From Henley-on-Thames, head south along A4155 toward Reading. At the junction with A329 head west. Mapledurham is signposted from this road. Or take the boat trip described below.

The Blount family mansion lies beside the Thames in the unspoiled village of Mapledurham. In the house, you'll see the Elizabethan ceilings and the great oak staircase, as well as the portraits of the two beautiful sisters with whom the poet Alexander Pope, a frequent visitor here, fell in love. The family chapel, built in 1789, is a fine example of modern gothic architecture. Cream teas with homemade cakes are available at the house. On the grounds, the last working water mill on the Thames still produces flour.

The most romantic way to reach this lovely old house is to take the boat that leaves the promenade next to Caversham Bridge at 2pm on Saturday, Sunday, and bank holidays from Easter to September. The journey upstream takes about 45 minutes, and the boat leaves Mapledurham again at 5pm for the return trip to Caversham. This gives you plenty of time to walk through the house. The round-trip boat ride from Caversham costs £4 ($6.80) for adults and £2.95 ($5) for children. Further details about the boat can be obtained from **Thames Rivercruises Ltd.,** Pipers Island, Bridge Street, Caversham Bridge, Reading (☎ **01189/481088**).

The Wellington Ducal Estate

Stratford Saye House. 1 mile west of Reading, beside the A33 to Basingstoke. ☎ **01256/882882.** Admission £5.50 ($9.35) adults, £2.95 ($5) children 5–15; free for children under 5. Combined ticket for Stratford Saye and Wellington Country Park £6.50 ($11.05) adults, £3.50 ($5.95) children. June, July, and Aug Wed–Sun 11am–4:30pm. From Henley, head south along A1455.

This combined house and country park provides obvious tangible evidence of the fortune of the duke of Wellington and his descendants. The complex's centerpiece is the Stratford Saye House. This has been the home of the dukes of Wellington since 1817, when the 17th-century house was bought for the Iron Duke to celebrate his victory over Napoléon at the Battle of Waterloo. A grateful Parliament granted a large sum of money for its purchase. Many memories of the first duke remain in the house, including his billiard table, battle spoils, and pictures. The funeral carriage that once rested in St. Paul's Cathedral crypt is on display. In the gardens is the grave of Copenhagen, the charger ridden to battle at Waterloo by the first duke. There are also extensive landscaped grounds, together with a tearoom and gift shop.

Although extensive parks and gardens surround Stratford Saye, all except those immediately adjacent to the house are closed to the public. If you're looking for greenery and lovely landscaping, you'll find it 3 miles away, on the opposite side of the A33 highway, at the **Wellington Country Park.**

Wellington Country Park. Riseley, Reading, Berkshire RG7 1SP. ☎ **01189/326444.** Admission £4 ($6.80) adults, £2 ($3.40) children 5–16; free for children under 5. Combined ticket for Stratford Saye and Wellington Country Park £6.50 ($11.05) adults, £3.50 ($5.95) children. Park and exhibits Mar 1–Oct 31 daily 10am–5:30pm.

Under the same administration as Stratford Saye, this is a favorite place for the locals to picnic and stroll, since it has a nice lake and miles of well-maintained walking paths.

But there's a handful of attractions inside as well: The park contains a riding school, a miniature steam railway, a deer park, and the Thames Valley Time Trail, a walk-through series of exhibits related to the geology of the region and the dinosaurs that once inhabited it.

MARLOW: RETREAT OF THE *COMPLEAT ANGLER*

This Thames-side town, 35 miles northwest of London and 8 miles east of Henley-on-Thames, is a miniature version of the better-known Henley. To reach it from Henley, take route 4155 and just follow the signs. Many prefer its more pastoral look to the larger Henley.

The town stands on a great loop of the riverbank between Maidenhead and Oxford. Here, along this middle reach of the Thames, is some of the most beautiful rural scenery in England, a land of green fields and deep woods, of stately mansions and parks. It was in these surroundings that Izaak Walton wrote his immortal work on fishing, *The Compleat Angler,* which was published in 1655. On the south bank of the river facing Marlow itself stood the inn in which he stayed. That inn still stands, and is named after his work.

Where to Stay & Dine

✪ **The Compleat Angler Hotel.** Marlow Bridge, Bisham Rd., Marlow, Buckinghamshire S17 IRG. ☎ **01628/484444.** Fax 01628/486388. 65 units. TV TEL. £225–£250 ($382.50–$425) double; from £295–£495 ($501.50–$841.50) suite. AE, DC, MC, V.

This hotel of charm and character blends architectural eras, including Queen Anne, Regency, Georgian, and Victorian. It occupies an emerald swath of lawns stretching down to the banks of the Thames. It's had a long and distinguished list of guests, including Percy Shelley and his wife, Mary, along with Dame Nellie Melba (for whom the peach dessert was named), J. M. Barrie (author of *Peter Pan*), F. Scott Fitzgerald, and Noël Coward. The hotel is a well-organized and impeccably polite center of English chintz, predictably elegant bars, and very fine dining. Each of the rooms is outfitted a lot like those found in a private country home, with antiques or reproductions and plush, comfortable beds. The more expensive rooms look out on the Thames. The finest accommodations are in a modern wing with balconies overlooking the rushing weir. Modern bathrooms with separate showers are the order of the day.

4 Oxford: The City of Dreaming Spires

54 miles NW of London; 54 miles SE of Coventry

A walk down the long sweep of The High, one of the most striking streets in England; a mug of cider in one of the old student pubs; the sound of May Day dawn when choristers sing in Latin from Magdalen Tower; students in traditional gowns whizzing past on rickety bikes; towers and spires rising majestically; nude swimming at Parson's Pleasure; the roar of a cannon launching the bumping races; a tiny, dusty bookstall where you can pick up a valuable first edition—all that is Oxford, home of one of the greatest universities in the world.

Romantic Oxford is still here, but to get to it, you'll also have to experience the bustling and crowded city that is also Oxford. You may be surprised by the never-ending stream of polluting buses and the fast-flowing pedestrian traffic—the city core feels more like London than once-sleepy Oxford. Surrounding the university are suburbs that keep growing, and not in a particularly attractive manner.

At any time of the year, you can enjoy a tour of the colleges, many of which represent a peak in England's architectural history, as well as a valley of Victorian contributions. The Oxford Tourist Information Centre (see below) offers guided walking tours daily throughout the year. Just don't mention the other place (Cambridge) and you shouldn't have any trouble. Comparisons between the two universities are inevitable: Oxford is better known for the arts, Cambridge more for the sciences.

The city predates the university—in fact, it was a Saxon town in the early part of the 10th century. By the 12th century, Oxford was growing in reputation as a seat of learning, at the expense of Paris, and the first colleges were founded in the 13th century. The story of Oxford is filled with conflicts too complex and detailed to elaborate here. Suffice it to say, the relationship between town and gown wasn't as peaceful as it is today. Riots often flared, and both sides were guilty of abuses. Nowadays, the young people of Oxford take out their aggressiveness in sporting competitions.

Ultimately, the test of a great university lies in the caliber of the people it turns out. Oxford can name-drop a mouthful: Roger Bacon, Sir Walter Raleigh, John Donne, Sir Christopher Wren, Samuel Johnson, William Penn, John Wesley, William Pitt, Matthew Arnold, Lewis Carroll, Harold Macmillan, Graham Greene, A. E. Housman, T. E. Lawrence, and many others.

ESSENTIALS

GETTING THERE Trains from Paddington Station reach Oxford in 1¼ hours. Service is every hour. A cheap, same-day round-trip ticket costs £14.20 ($24.15). For more information, call ☎ **0345/484950.**

Oxford CityLink provides coach service from London's Victoria Station (☎ **020/7824-0056**) to the Oxford Bus Station. Coaches usually depart about every 20 minutes during the day; the trip takes approximately 1¾ hours. A same-day round-trip ticket costs £7.50 ($12.75).

If you're driving, take M40 west from London and just follow the signs. Traffic and parking are a disaster in Oxford, and not just during rush hours. However, there are four large park-and-ride parking lots on the north, south, east, and west of the city's ring road, all well marked. Parking is free at all times, but from 9:30am on and all day Saturday, you pay £60 ($102) for a bus ride into the city, which drops you off at St. Aldate's Cornmarket or Queen Street to see the city center. The buses run every 8 to 10 minutes in each direction. There is no service on Sunday. The parking lots are on the Woodstock road near the Peartree traffic circle, on the Botley road toward Farringdon, on the Abingdon road in the southeast, and on A40 toward London.

VISITOR INFORMATION The **Oxford Tourist Information Centre** is at Gloucester Green, opposite the bus station (☎ **01865/726871**). The center sells a comprehensive range of maps, brochures, and souvenir items, as well as the famous Oxford University T-shirt. It provides hotel booking services for £2.50 ($4.25). Guided walking tours leave from the center daily (see below). Open Monday through Saturday from 9:30am to 5pm and Sunday and bank holidays in summer from 10am to 3:30pm.

GETTING AROUND Competition thrives in Oxford transportation, and the public benefits with swift, clean service by two companies. The **Oxford Bus Company,** 395 Cowley Rd. (☎ **01865/785400**), has green Park and Ride buses that leave from four parking lots in the city using the north-south or east-west routes. A round-trip costs £1.30 ($2.20). Their CityLink buses are blue and travel to London, Heathrow, and Gatwick. The company's red CityLink buses cover 15 routes in all suburbs, with a day pass allowing unlimited travel for £1.80 ($3.05). Weekly and monthly passes are available. The competition, **Stagecoach,** Unit 4, Horsepath, Cowley (☎ **01865/772250**), uses blue-and-cream minibuses and red-and-gray coaches. City buses leave from

Oxford

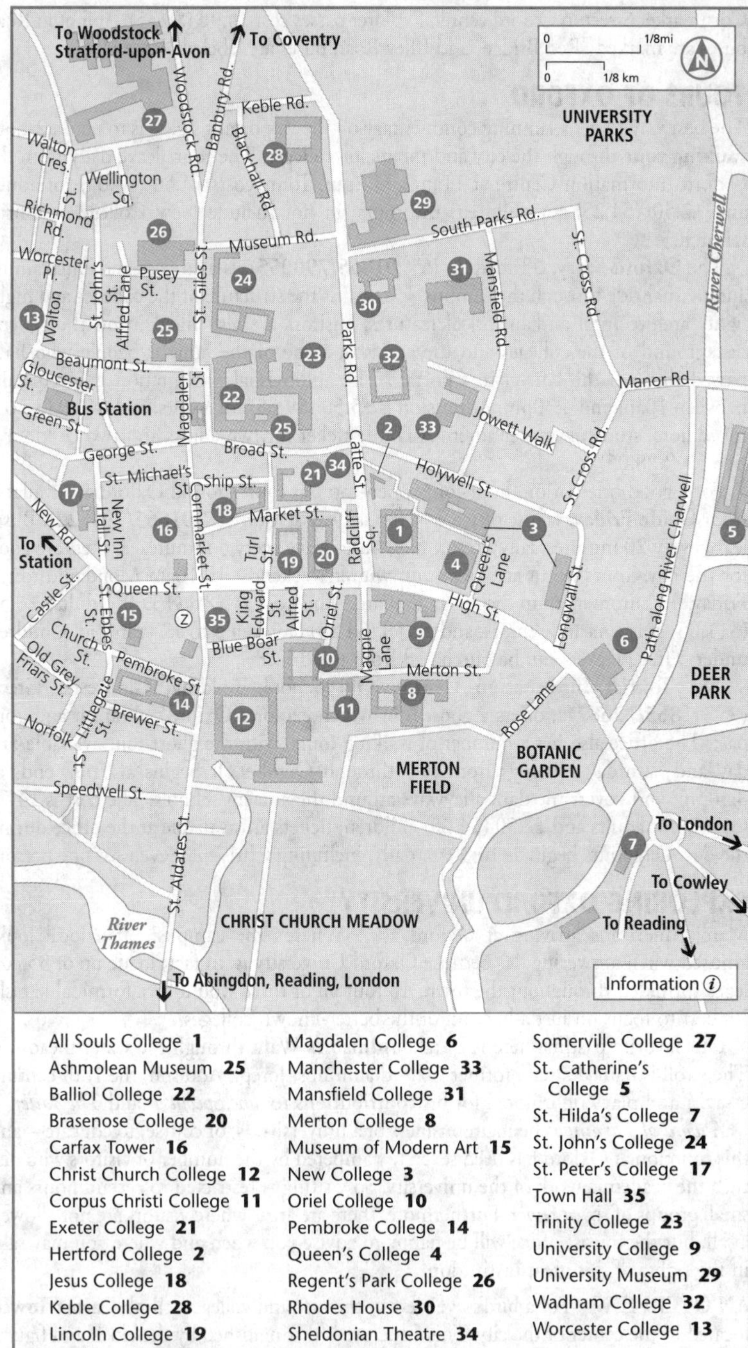
To Woodstock
Stratford-upon-Avon
To Coventry
0
1/8mi
0
1/8 km
N
UNIVERSITY PARKS
Keble Rd.
Banbury Rd.
Woodstock Rd.
Blackhall Rd.
Walton Cres.
Wellington Sq.
Richmond Rd.
Walton St.
South Parks Rd.
St. Cross Rd.
River Cherwell
Museum Rd.
Worcester Pl.
Pusey St.
St. John's St.
Alfred Lane
St. Giles St.
Mansfield Rd.
Parks Rd.
Beaumont St.
Gloucester St.
Magdalen St.
Manor Rd.
Bus Station
Green St.
Jowett Walk
George St.
Broad St.
Catte St.
St. Michael's St.
Ship St.
Holywell St.
New Inn Hall St.
Cornmarket St.
Market St.
Turl St.
Radcliff Sq.
St. Cross Rd.
Path along River Charwell
New Rd.
To Station
Queen's Lane
Longwall St.
Queen St.
Castle St.
St. Ebbes St.
King Edward St.
Alfred St.
Oriel St.
High St.
Church St.
Blue Boar St.
Magpie Lane
Old Grey Friars St.
Pembroke St.
Merton St.
DEER PARK
Littlegate St.
Brewer St.
Rose Lane
Norfolk St.
MERTON FIELD
BOTANIC GARDEN
Speedwell St.
To London
St. Aldates St.
To Cowley
River Thames
CHRIST CHURCH MEADOW
To Reading
To Abingdon, Reading, London
Information
All Souls College 1
Ashmolean Museum 25
Balliol College 22
Brasenose College 20
Carfax Tower 16
Christ Church College 12
Corpus Christi College 11
Exeter College 21
Hertford College 2
Jesus College 18
Keble College 28
Lincoln College 19
Magdalen College 6
Manchester College 33
Mansfield College 31
Merton College 8
Museum of Modern Art 15
New College 3
Oriel College 10
Pembroke College 14
Queen's College 4
Regent's Park College 26
Rhodes House 30
Sheldonian Theatre 34
Somerville College 27
St. Catherine's College 5
St. Hilda's College 7
St. John's College 24
St. Peter's College 17
Town Hall 35
Trinity College 23
University College 9
University Museum 29
Wadham College 32
Worcester College 13

Cornmarket Street in Oxford center. Explorer passes cost £4.90 ($8.35). Abington Road buses are marked "Red Bridge" and Iffley Road buses are labeled "Rose Hill."

TOURS OF OXFORD

The best way to get a running commentary on the important sights is to take a 2-hour **walking tour** through the city and the major colleges. The tours leave daily from the Oxford Information Centre at 11am and 2pm. Tours costs £4.50 ($7.65) for adults and £2.50 ($4.25) for children; the tours do not include New College or Christ Church.

The **Oxford Story,** 6 Broad St. (☎ **01865/790055**), is a concise and entertaining audiovisual ride through the campus. It explains the structure of the colleges and highlights architectural and historical features. Visitors are also filled in on the general background of the colleges and the antics of some of the famous people who have passed through the University's portals. The audiovisual presentation is given daily between 10am and 4:30pm. Admission is £5.50 ($9.35) for adults, and £4.50 ($7.65) for seniors, students and children. A family ticket for two adults and two children is £16.50 ($28.05).

For a good orientation, hour-long, open-top bus tours around Oxford are available from **Guide Friday,** whose office is at the railway station (☎ **01865/790522**). Buses leave every 20 minutes daily; in summer, buses leave every 5 minutes. Tickets are good for the day. Tours begin at 9:30am on winter weekends, 10:10am Monday through Friday. In summer, tours begin at 9:30am. The cost is £8 ($13.60) adults, £6.50 ($11.05) students and seniors, and £2.50 ($4.25) children 5 to 12 years old. Children under 5 free. Tickets can be purchased from the driver.

The **Tourist Information Centre,** Old School Building, Gloucester Green (☎ **01865/726871**), offers a ghost tour which explores Oxford's ghoulish and gory past. The office also has a number of walking tours, with the ghost tour available Friday and Saturday evenings from July through October. It begins at 7pm, ends at 8:30pm, and covers the dark alleyways around the ancient schools. The cost is £4.50 ($7.65) for adults and £2.50 ($4.25) children; tickets are available at the office during the day. Day tours begin at 10:30am daily, including Christmas, even for one person.

EXPLORING OXFORD UNIVERSITY

Many Americans arriving at Oxford ask, "Where's the campus?" If a local looks amused when answering, it's because Oxford University is, in fact, made up of 35 colleges sprinkled throughout the town. To tour all of these would be a formidable task. It's best to focus on just a handful of the better-known colleges.

Our favorite pastime here is to take **Addison's Walk** through the water meadows. The stroll is named after a former Oxford alumnus, Joseph Addison, the 18th-century essayist and playwright noted for his contributions to *The Spectator* and *The Tatler.*

A word of warning: The main business of a university, is, of course, to educate—and this function at Oxford has been severely hampered by the number of visitors who disturb the academic work of the university. So visiting is restricted to certain hours and small groups of six or fewer. Furthermore, there are areas where visitors are not allowed at all, but the tourist office will be happy to advise you when and where you may take in the sights of this great institution.

AN OVERVIEW For a bird's-eye view of the city and colleges, climb **Carfax Tower,** located in the center of the city. This structure is distinguished by the clock and figures that strike the quarter hours. Carfax Tower is all that remains from St. Martin's Church, where William Shakespeare once stood as godfather for William Davenant, who also became a successful playwright. A church stood on this site from 1032 until 1896. The tower used to be higher, but after 1340 it was lowered, following complaints from the university to Edward III that townspeople threw stones and fired arrows at students during town-and-gown disputes. Admission is £1.20 ($2.05) for adults, £60 ($102) for children. The tower is open year-round. From April through October, hours are daily from 10am to 5:30pm. Off-season hours are Monday through Saturday from 10am to 3:30pm. The tower is closed from Christmas Eve until January 2. Children under 5 are not admitted. For information, call ☎ **01865/792653.**

✪ **Christ Church** Begun by Cardinal Wolsey as Cardinal College in 1525, Christ Church (☎ **01865/276492**), known as the House, was founded by Henry VIII in 1546. Facing St. Aldate's Street, Christ Church has the largest quadrangle of any college in Oxford. Tom Tower houses Great Tom, the 18,000-pound bell referred to earlier. It rings at 9:05pm nightly, signaling the closing of the college gates. The 101 times it peals originally signified the number of students in residence at the time the college was founded. Although the student body has grown significantly, Oxford traditions live on forever. There are some interesting portraits in the 16th-century Great Hall, including works by Gainsborough and Reynolds. There's also a separate portrait gallery.

The college chapel was constructed over a period of centuries, beginning in the 12th century. (Incidentally, it's not only the college chapel, but also the cathedral of the diocese of Oxford.) The cathedral's most distinguishing features are its Norman pillars and the vaulting of the choir, dating from the 15th century. In the center of the great quadrangle is a statue of Mercury mounted in the center of a fishpond. The college and cathedral can be visited between 9am and 5:30pm, though times vary. It's best to call before you visit. The entrance fee is £3 ($5.10) adults and £2 ($3.40) for children.

MAGDALEN COLLEGE Pronounced *Maud*-lin, Magdalen College, High Street (☎ **01865/276000**), was founded in 1458 by William of Waynflete, bishop of Winchester and later chancellor of England. Its alumni range from Wolsey to Wilde. Opposite the botanic garden, the oldest in England, is the bell tower, where the choristers sing in Latin at dawn on May Day. Charles I, his days numbered, watched the oncoming Roundheads from this tower. Visit the 15th-century chapel, in spite of many of its latter-day trappings. Ask when the hall and other places of special interest are open. The grounds of Magdalen are the most extensive of any Oxford college; there's even a deer park. You can visit from Easter to November, daily between noon and 6pm; Off-season daily between 2 and 6pm. Admission is £2 ($3.40), but it's charged only from Easter to November.

MERTON COLLEGE Founded in 1264, Merton College, Merton Street (☎ **01865/276310**), is among the three oldest colleges at the university. It stands near Corpus Christi College on Merton Street, the sole survivor of Oxford's medieval cobbled streets. Merton College is noted for its library, built between 1371 and 1379 and said to be the oldest college library in England. There was once a tradition of keeping some of its most valuable books chained. Now only one book is so secured to illustrate that historical custom. One of the library's treasures is an astrolabe (an astronomical instrument used for measuring the altitude of the sun and stars) thought to have belonged to Chaucer. You pay £1 ($1.70) to visit the ancient library as well as the Max Beerbohm Room (the satirical English caricaturist who died in 1956). The library and college are open Monday through Friday from 2 to 4pm and Saturday and Sunday from 10am to 4pm. It's closed for one week at Easter and at Christmas, and at weekends during the winter.

UNIVERSITY COLLEGE University College, High Street (☎ **01865/276602**), is the oldest one at Oxford and dates from 1249, when money was donated by an ecclesiastic, William of Durham (the old claim that the real founder was Alfred the Great is more fanciful). The original structures have all disappeared, and what remains today represents essentially the architecture of the 17th century, with subsequent additions in Victoria's day as well as in more recent times. The college's most famous alumnus, Shelley, was "sent down" for his part in collaborating on a pamphlet on atheism. However, all is forgiven today, as the romantic poet is honored by a memorial erected in 1894. The hall and chapel of University College can be visited during vacations. Call ahead to arrange a time to visit.

NEW COLLEGE New College, New College Lane, off Queen's Lane (☎ **01865/279555**), was founded in 1379 by William of Wykeham, bishop of Winchester and later lord chancellor of England. His college at Winchester supplied a constant stream of students. The first quadrangle, dating from before the end of the 14th century, was the initial quadrangle to be built in Oxford and formed the architectural design for the other colleges. In the antechapel is Sir Jacob Epstein's remarkable modern sculpture of Lazarus and a fine El Greco painting of St. James. One of the treasures of the college is a crosier (pastoral staff of a bishop) belonging to the founding father. In the garden, you can stroll among the remains of the old city wall and the mound. The college (entered at New College Lane) can be visited Easter to October, daily between 11am and 5pm; off-season daily between 2 and 4pm. Admission is £2 ($3.40) from Easter to October and free off-season.

PUNTING

Punting on the River Cherwell remains the favorite outdoor pastime in Oxford. At Punt Station, **Cherwell Boathouse,** Bardwell Road (☎ **01865/515978**), you can rent a punt (flat-bottom boat maneuvered by a long pole and a small oar) for £8 to £10 ($13.60 to $17) per hour, plus a £40 to £50 ($68 to $85) deposit. Similar charges are made for punt rentals at Magdalen Bridge Boathouse. Punts are rented from mid-March to mid-October, daily from 10am until dusk. However, hours of operation seem to be rather informal; you're not always guaranteed that someone will be here to rent you a boat, even if the punt itself is available.

SHOPPING

Golden Cross, an arcade of first-class shops and boutiques, lies between Cornmarket Street and the Covered Market (or between High Street and Market Street). Parts of the colorful gallery date from the 12th century. Many buildings remain from the medieval era, along with some 15th- and 17th-century structures. The market also has a reputation as the Covent Garden of Oxford, where live entertainment takes place on Saturday mornings in summer. In the arcade shops you'll find a diverse selection of merchandise, including handmade Belgian chocolates, specialty gifts, clothing for both women and men, and luxury leather goods.

In its way, **Alice's Shop,** 83 St. Aldate's (☎ **01865/723793**), played an important role in English literature. Set within a 15th-century building that has housed some kind of shop since 1820, it functioned as a general store (selling brooms, hardware, and the like) during the period that Lewis Carroll, at the time a professor of mathematics at Christ Church College, was composing *Alice in Wonderland.* It is believed to have been the model for important settings within the book. Today, the place is a favorite stopover of Lewis Carroll fans from as far away as Japan, who gobble up commemorative pencils, chess sets, party favors, bookmarks, and in rare cases, original editions of some of Carroll's works.

The **Bodleian Library Shop,** Old School's Quadrangle, Radcliffe Square, Broad Street (☎ **01865/277216**), specializes in Oxford souvenirs, from books and paperweights to Oxford banners and coffee mugs.

Castell & Son (The Varsity Shop), 13 Broad St. (☎ **01865/244000**), is the best outlet in Oxford for clothing emblazoned with the Oxford logo or heraldic symbol. Choices include both whimsical and dead-on-serious neckties, hats, T-shirts, sweatshirts, pens, bookmarks, beer and coffee mugs, and cuff links. It's commercialized Oxford, but it's still got a sense of relative dignity and style.

WHERE TO STAY IN & AROUND OXFORD

Accommodations in Oxford are limited, although recently, motels have sprouted on the outskirts—good for those who want modern amenities. In addition, if you've got a car, you may want to consider country houses or small B&Bs on the outskirts of town; they're the best choices in the area if you don't mind commuting.

Bedrooms, albeit expensive ones, are also provided at the Bath Place Hotel and Le Manoir aux Quat' Saisons (reviewed under "Where to Dine," below).

The **Oxford Tourist Information Centre,** Gloucester Green, behind the bus bays (☎ **01865/726871**), operates a year-round room-booking service for a £2.50 ($4.25) fee, plus a 10% refundable deposit. If you'd like to seek lodgings on your own, the center has a list of accommodations, maps, and guidebooks.

VERY EXPENSIVE

✪ **Old Parsonage Hotel.** 1 Banbury Rd., Oxford OX2 6NN. ☎ **01865/310210.** Fax 01865/311262. www.oxford-hotels-restaurant.co.uk. E-mail: oldparsonage@dial.pipax.com. 30 units. TV TEL. £150–£200 ($255–$340) double; £200 ($340) suite. Rates include English breakfast. AE, DC, MC, V. Bus no. 7.

This extensively renovated hotel, near St. Giles Church and Keble College, is so old it looks like an extension of one of the ancient colleges. Originally a 13th-century hospital, it was restored in the early 17th century. In the 20th century a modern wing was added, and in 1991 it was completely renovated and made into a first-rate hotel. The rooms are individually designed but not large, with such amenities as satellite TV, hair dryers, and phones in the bathrooms. The marble rooms are air-conditioned; all the suites and some rooms have sofa beds with fine mattresses. The rooms open onto the private gardens, and 10 of them are on the ground floor.

Dining/Diversions: The Parsonage Bar serves everything from cappuccino to mixed drinks, and you can order from a well-prepared menu of continental and English food from 7am until 11pm. There's also 24-hour room service.

The Randolph. Beaumont St., Oxford, Oxfordshire OX1 2LN. ☎ **800/225-5843** in the U.S. and Canada, or 01865/247481. Fax 01865/791678. 109 units. TV TEL. £155–£175 ($263.50–$297.50) double; from £225 ($382.50) suite. AE, DC, MC, V. Parking £10 ($17). Bus no. 7.

Since 1864, the Randolph has overlooked St. Giles, the Ashmolean Museum, and the Cornmarket. The hotel is an example of how historic surroundings can be combined with modern conveniences to make for elegant accommodations. The lounges, although modernized, are cavernous enough for dozens of separate and intimate conversational groupings. The furnishings are traditional, and all rooms have hair dryers and hot-beverage makers. Some rooms are quite large; others are a bit cramped. The double glazing on the windows appears inadequate to keep out the noise of midtown traffic. In this price range, we'd opt first for the Old Parsonage before checking in here.

Dining/Diversions: The hotel's Spires Restaurant presents both a time-tested English and a modern cuisine. There's also a wine bar with an entrance off the street. The Chapters Bar has a tradition-laden atmosphere.

Studley Priory Hotel. Main St., Horton-cum-Studley, Oxfordshire OX33 1AZ. ☎ **800/525-4800** in the U.S. and Canada, or 01865/351203. Fax 01865/351613. www.studley-priory.co.uk. E-mail: sphres@studley-priory.co.uk. 18 units. TV TEL. £140–£250 ($238–$425) double; £275 ($467.50) suite. Rates include English breakfast. AE, DC, MC, V. From Oxford, drive to the end of Banbury Rd. At the traffic circle, take the 3rd exit (toward London). Go approximately 3^1/$_2$ miles. At the next traffic circle, take the 1st exit (signposted Horton-cum-Studley) and travel 4^1/$_2$ miles. Go through the estate and stay on the same road until you come to "staggered crossroads." Go straight across, signposted Horton-cum-Studley, 2^1/$_2$ miles. This road will bring you right into the village; the hotel is at the top of the hill on the right-hand side.

The Studley Priory Hotel, the best country house hotel in Oxford, may be remembered by those who saw the movie *A Man for All Seasons.* The former Benedictine priory, a hotel since 1961, was used in background shots as the private residence of Sir Thomas More. It's a stunning example of Elizabethan architecture, although it originally dates from the 12th century. Located on 13 acres of wooded grounds and occupied for around 300 years by the Croke family, the manor is 7 miles from Oxford. It's built of stone in the manorial style, with large halls, long bedroom wings, and gables with mullioned windows. The rooms are very large and the furnishings tasteful. Bed sizes range from a standard double to a master four-poster if you want to feel like Henry VIII. Little extras include a beverage tray with homemade crackers. Other than a suite, the best accommodations are the "master doubles," furnished in 16th-century style with antiques. Bathrooms are modern with adequate shelf space and a hair dryer. Room service is provided all day. Even if you're not staying over, you may want to visit for lunch or dinner. Getting here is a bit complicated, so be armed with a good map when you strike out from Oxford.

EXPENSIVE

Eastgate Hotel. 23 Merton St., The High St., Oxford, Oxfordshire, OX1 4BE. ☎ **0870/400-8201.** Fax 01865/791681. www.heritage-hotels.com. 64 units. TV TEL. £155 ($263.50) double; £185 ($314.50) suite. AE, DC, MC, V. Bus nos. 3, 4, 7, 52.

The Eastgate, built on the site of a 1600s structure, stands within walking distance of Oxford College and the city center. Recently refurbished, it offers modern facilities while retaining somewhat the atmosphere of an English country house. The bedrooms are well worn but still cozy, range in size from small to medium, and contain beverage makers. Mattresses are replaced as needed, and the bathrooms have minimum space and a tidy maintenance. The newly opened Café Boheme, offers reasonably priced French fare, complemented by an impressive selection of wines. Many undergraduates frequent the bar.

✪ **Old Bank Hotel.** 92–94 High St., Oxford OX1 4BN. ☎ **01865/579-9599.** Fax 0186/579-9598. www.oxford-hotels-restaurants.co.uk. 44 units. A/C TV TEL £160–£170 ($272–$289) double, from £195 ($331.50) suite. Rates include English breakfast. AE, DC, DISC, MC, V. Bus: 7.

Located on Oxford's main street and surrounded by some of its oldest colleges and sights, the building dates back to the 18th century and was once a bank. The first hotel created in the center of Oxford in 135 years, it opened late in 1999. The bedrooms are comfortably and elegantly appointed, often opening onto views. A combination of velvet and shantung silk-trimmed linen bedcovers give the accommodations added style. Every marble bathroom has power showers and hair dryers, along with deluxe toiletries. The building features a collection of 20th-century British art handpicked by the owners.

Dining/Diversions: The hotel has a dynamic restaurant, Alto Bar & Grill, serving an Italian-influenced cuisine in a contemporary setting. If weather permits, tables are placed on a terrace with a view of a small garden.

Amenities: Concierge, 24-hour room service, laundry/dry cleaning.

Weston Manor. Weston-on-the-Green, Oxfordshire OX6 8QL. ☎ **01869/350621.** Fax 01869/350901. 36 units. TV TEL. £135 ($229.50) double; £179–£199 ($304.30–$338.30) suite. Rates include English breakfast. AE, DC, MC, V. Drive 6 miles north of Oxford on A34.

Ideal as a center for touring the district (Blenheim Palace is only 5 miles away), this 13-acre manor, owned and run by the Osborn family, has existed since the 11th century; portions of the present building date from the 14th and 16th centuries. The estate is the ancestral home of the earls of Abingdon and Berkshire. It was also an abbey until Henry VIII abolished the abbeys and assumed ownership of the property. Of course, there are ghosts: Mad Maude, the naughty nun who was burned at the stake for her "indecent and immoral" behavior, returns to haunt the Oak rooms. Prince Rupert, during the English Civil War, hid from Cromwell's soldiers in one of the fireplaces, eventually escaping in drag as the "maiden of the milk bucket."

The reception lounge is dominated by a Tudor fireplace and a long refectory table. Most of the rooms are spacious and furnished with antiques (often four-poster beds), old dressing tables, and chests. Bedrooms are divided between the main house and a former coach that was skillfully converted and turned into well-equipped guest rooms. Regardless of the location, each bedroom is first-rate with extremely comfortable beds and fine linen, plus a modernized bathroom that has adequate shelf space and good maintenance. Six bedrooms are set aside for nonsmokers.

Dining: The Great Hall is one of the most beautiful dining rooms in England, with an open-rafter and beamed ceiling, a minstrels' gallery, and a wrought-iron chandelier. The English food is first-rate and the selection of classic wines diverse.

Amenities: In warm weather, you can enjoy an outdoor heated swimming pool surrounded by gardens, a squash court, and a croquet lawn.

MODERATE

Oxford Moat House. Godstow Rd., Wolvercote Roundabout, Oxford, Oxfordshire OX2 8AL. ☎ **01865/489988.** Fax 01865/310259. 155 units. TV TEL. £95–£140 ($161.50–$238) double. AE, DC, MC, V. Bus no. 60.

This is a good choice if you have a car; it's 2 miles north of the city center, and hidden from traffic at the junction of A40 and A34. It attracts a lot of business travelers, but also visitors. It's a good base for exploring not only Oxford but the Cotswolds, which are within easy reach. The M40 motorway is just an 8-mile drive away. Rooms are motel-like, with standard furnishings that are comfortable and spacious. Each has pay-per-view movies, a trouser press, and a kettle. Some 30 bedrooms are set aside for nonsmokers. Bathrooms are nothing special but have adequate shelf space. The moat house has some of the best facilities in the area, including a 9-hole mini-golf course, a fully equipped gym, heated indoor swimming pool, squash courts, a sauna, solarium, a health and beauty clinic, and billiards table. The Oxford Blue Restaurant has a full carvery, which is one of the better food values in the area, plus an à la carte menu. There's also a sports bar serving food.

Inexpensive

Dial House. 25 London Rd., Headington, Oxford, Oxfordshire OX3 7RE. ☎ and fax **01865/769944.** www.oxfordcity.co.uk/accom/dialhouse. E-mail: dialhouse@aol.com. 8 units. TV. £60 ($99) double. MC, V. Bus nos. 2, 2A, 7, 7A, or 22.

Two miles east of the heart of Oxford, beside the main highway leading to London, is this country-style house originally built between 1924 and 1927. Graced with mock Tudor half-timbering and a prominent blue-faced sundial (from which it derives its name), it has cozy and recently renovated rooms, each equipped with a teamaker. Bathrooms are small but have a hair dryer. Most of them have a shower only, but a few offer a combination tub and shower. The owners, the Morris family, serve only breakfast in their bright dining room. No smoking.

Tilbury Lodge Private Hotel. 5 Tilbury Lane, Eynsham Rd., Botley, Oxford, Oxfordshire OX2 9NB. ☎ **01865/862138.** Fax 01865/863700. http://localhost/hotels/tilbury. 9 units. TV TEL. £70–£75 ($119–$127.50) double. Rates include English breakfast. MC, V. Bus nos. 4A, 4B, or 100.

On a quiet country lane about 2 miles west of the center of Oxford, this small hotel is less than a mile from the railway station, where hotel staff will pick you up to save you the walk. Eddie and Eileen Trafford accommodate guests in their well-furnished and comfortable rooms. The most expensive room has a four-poster bed. Rooms vary in size but most are cozy with adequate space. Baths, although tiny, are well kept, usually with a shower stall. The guest house also has a Jacuzzi and welcomes children.

WHERE TO DINE

Very Expensive

✪ **Le Manoir aux Quat' Saisons.** Great Milton, Oxfordshire. ☎ **01844/278881.** Reservations required. Main courses £30–£44 ($49.50–$72.60); lunch menu du jour £32.50 ($55.25); lunch or dinner menu gourmand £79 ($134.30). AE, DC, MC, V. Daily 12:15–2:15pm and 7:15–10:15pm. Take Exit 7 off M40 and head along A329 toward Wallingford; look for signs for Great American Milton Manor about a mile after. FRENCH.

Some 12 miles southeast of Oxford, Le Manoir aux Quat' Saisons offers the finest cuisine in the Midlands. The gray- and honey-colored stone manor house was originally built by a Norman nobleman in the early 1300s, and over the years attracted many famous visitors. The connection with France has been masterfully revived by the Gallic owner and chef, Raymond Blanc. His reputation for comfort and cuisine attracts guests from as far away as London.

You can enjoy such creative treats such as roasted squab and foie gras ravioli with wild mushrooms; roasted grouse in a blackberry and red wine sauce; or a truly delectable roasted breast of Barbary hen duck with figs and fennel seeds and a pan-fried foie gras. Each dish is an exercise in studied perfection.

Accommodations are also available here. The gabled house was built in the 1500s and improved and enlarged in 1908. An outdoor swimming pool, still in use, was added much later. Each very pricey room—rates are £230 to £550 ($391 to $935) double—is decorated boudoir-style with luxurious beds and linens, ruffled canopies and high-quality antique reproductions, plus deluxe bathrooms with thick towels and a hair dryer.

Expensive

Cherwell Boathouse Restaurant. Bardwell Rd. ☎ **01865/552746.** Reservations recommended. Fixed-price dinner from £20.50 ($34.85); Sun lunch £19.50 ($33.15). AE, DC, MC, V. Tues–Sat noon–2pm and 6–9:30pm, Sun noon–2pm. Closed Dec 24–30. Bus: Banbury Road. FRENCH/ENGLISH.

This Oxford landmark on the River Cherwell is owned by Anthony Verdin, who is assisted by a young crew. An intriguing fixed-price menu is offered, and the cooks change the fare every 2 weeks to take advantage of the availability of fresh vegetables, fish, and meat. There is a very reasonable, even exciting, wine list. Children are charged half price. In summer, the restaurant also serves on the terrace. Enjoy such starters as warm salad of pigeon breast or toasted pine nuts and cranberry dressing. For a main, you may opt for a tress of sole and salmon with squid pasta and a tomato and herb salsa, or a free range loin of pork with port and prunes. For dessert, indulge on the lemon and almond roulade. The style is sophisticated yet understated, with a heavy reliance on quality ingredients that are cooked in such a way that natural flavors are always preserved.

Elizabeth. 82 St. Aldate's St. ☎ **01865/242230.** Reservations recommended. Main courses £13.25–£18.75 ($22.55–$31.90); lunch £16 ($27.20). AE, DC, MC, V. Tues–Sun 12:30–2:30pm and 6:30–11pm, Sun 7–10:30pm. Closed Good Friday and Christmas week. Bus no. 7. FRENCH/CONTINENTAL.

This restaurant is named after its original owner, a matriarch who founded this stone-sided house opposite Christ Church College in the 1930s. Today, you're likely to find a well-trained staff from Spain, serving beautifully presented dishes in the French style. The larger of the two dining rooms displays reproductions of paintings by Goya and Velázquez and exudes a restrained dignity; the smaller room is devoted to Alice in Wonderland designs inspired by Lewis Carroll. Recommended dishes include the chicken breast in butter with cognac, white wine and cream; the chateaubriand; grilled fillet steak with Madeira and mushroom sauce; and the beef Stroganoff. The dishes prepared here aren't so much a study in fashionable concepts in cuisine, but focus more on quality produce, hearty flavors, excellent preparation, and artistic presentation.

Moderate

✪ **Le Petit Blanc.** 71–72 Walton St. ☎ **01865/510999.** Reservations recommended. Main courses £7.95–£14 ($13.50–$23.80); fixed-price lunch £15 ($25.50). AE, CB, DC, MC, V. Mon–Sat noon–3pm and 6–11pm; Sun noon–3pm and 6:30–10pm. FRENCH/MEDITERRANEAN.

The biggest culinary news in Oxford has been the return of Raymond Blanc (of Le Manoir aux Quat' Saisons fame; see above) with another Le Petit Blanc. (A previous one proved disappointing.) However, Monsieur Blanc is a more wizened restaurateur now, and this buzzing brasserie is up and running—and doing just fine. A former piano shop has been converted into a stylish place offering a menu that promises something for every palate. Here you can get a taste of the famous chef's creations without the high prices of his famed Le Manoir aux Quat' Saisons, though here he keeps the menu fairly straightforward, with a great emphasis on fresh ingredients.

The food is wholesome and delicious, based on authentic provincial French cuisine, complemented by Mediterranean and Asian accents. The crab and lobster spring roll with spicy fig compote will get you going, if you didn't opt for the goat's cheese and thyme soufflé with apple and watercress salad. For mains, the braised rabbit with sweet onion tarte tatin and flap mushrooms, or the Oxford sausage and parsleyed mash, Madeira and sweet onion sauce are superb. The desserts are first rate, especially the raspberry soufflé.

Inexpensive

Al-Shami. 25 Walton Crescent. ☎ **01865/310066.** Reservations recommended. Main courses £7.50–£12 ($12.75–$20.40); fixed-price menu £15 ($25.50). MC, V. Daily noon–midnight. LEBANESE.

Ideal for meals all afternoon and late into the evening, this Lebanese restaurant has awakened the sleepy taste buds of Oxford. Many diners don't go beyond the appetizers, since they comprise more than 35 delectable hot and cold selections—everything from falafel to a salad made with lamb's brains. Charcoal-grilled chopped lamb, chicken, or beef constitute most of the main-dish selections. In between, guests nibble on raw vegetables. Desserts are chosen from the trolley, and vegetarian meals are also available.

✪ **Browns.** 5–11 Woodstock Rd. ☎ **01865/511995.** Main courses £7–£14 ($11.90–$23.80); afternoon tea £1.30–£2.35 ($2.20–$4). Mon–Sat 11am–11:30pm; Sun noon–11:30pm. Bus 2 Or 7. ENGLISH/CONTINENTAL.

Oxford's busiest and most bustling English brasserie suits all groups, from babies to undergraduates to grandmas. A 10-minute walk north of the town center, it occupies the premises of five Victorian shops whose walls were removed to create one large, echoing, and very popular space. A thriving bar trade (where lots of people seem to order Pimms) makes the place an evening destination in its own right.

A young and enthusiastic staff serves traditional English cuisine. Your meal might include meat pies, hot salads, burgers, pastas, steaks, and poultry. Afternoon tea here is a justly celebrated Oxford institution. Reservations are not accepted, so if you want to avoid a delay, arrive here during off-peak dining hours.

OXFORD AFTER DARK

THE PERFORMING ARTS

Highly acclaimed orchestras playing in truly lovely settings mark the Music at Oxford series at the **Oxford Playhouse Theatre,** Beaumont Street (☎ **01865/798600**). The autumn season runs from mid-September to December, the winter season from January to April, the spring-summer season from May to early July. Tickets range from £8 to £22 ($13.60 to $37.40). Classical music is performed by outstanding groups such as the European Union Chamber Orchestra, the National Symphony of the Ukraine, the Canterbury Musical Society, the Bournmouth Symphony, and the Guild Hall String Ensemble of London. All performances are held in the Sheldonian Theatre, a particularly attractive site, designed by Sir Christopher Wren, with paintings on the ceiling.

The Apollo, George Street (☎ **01865/243041** or 01865/244544 for ticket reservations), is Oxford's primary theater. Tickets are £5 to £50 ($8.50 to $85). A continuous run of comedy, ballet, drama, opera, and even rock contributes to the variety. The Welsh National Opera often performs, and The Glyndebourne Touring Opera appears regularly. Advance booking is recommended, although some shows may have tickets the week of the performance. Don't try for tickets for popular shows on the same day.

At the **Oxford Playhouse,** Beaumont Street (☎ **01865/798600**), performances at the Oxford Playhouse range from Shakespeare to modern comedy and drama. Tickets are £6 to £22 ($10.20 to $37.40). They are open most nights year-round, except some Sundays and the week after Christmas.

Insider's tip: For some of the best productions in England, with some of the most talented actors, ask at the tourist office about summer performances in some of the college gardens. These used to be student productions, but increasingly are being taken over by professional companies. There are two Shakespeare troupes as well as other groups. Ticket costs are significantly less here than you'd find for a comparable experience elsewhere.

Pubs with a Pedigree

Every college town the world over has a fair number of bars, but few can boast local watering holes with such atmosphere and history as Oxford.

A short block from The High, overlooking the north side of Christ Church College, **The Bear Inn,** on Alfred Street (☎ **01865/721783**), is an Oxford landmark, built in the 13th century and mentioned time and time again in English literature. The Bear brings together a wide variety of people in a relaxed way. You might talk with a raja from India, a university don, or a titled gentleman who's the latest in a line of owners that goes back more than 700 years. Some former owners developed an astonishing habit: clipping neckties. Around the lounge bar you'll see the remains of thousands of ties, which have been labeled with their owners' names.

Even older than the Bear is **The Turf Tavern,** 4 Bath Place (off Holywell Street; ☎ **01865/243235**), on a very narrow passageway near the Bodleian Library. The pub is reached via St. Helen's Passage, which stretches between Holywell Street and New College Lane. (You'll probably get lost, but any student worth his beer can direct you.) Thomas Hardy used the place as the setting for *Jude the Obscure.* It was "the local" of the future U.S. president, Bill Clinton, during his student days at Oxford. In warm weather, you can choose a table in any of the three separate gardens that radiate outward from the pub's central core. For wintertime warmth, braziers are lighted in the courtyard and in the gardens. A separate food counter, set behind a glass case, displays the day's fare—salads, soups, sandwiches, and platters of chili con carne, and so on. Local ales (including one named Headbanger, with a relatively high alcohol content) are served, as well as a range of wines.

Just outside of town, hidden away some 2½ miles north of Oxford, **the Trout Inn,** 195 Godstow Rd., Wolvercote (☎ **01865/302071**), is a private world where you can get ale and beer and standard fare. Have your drink in one of the historic rooms, with their settles, brass, and old prints, or go out in sunny weather to sit on a stone wall. On the grounds are peacocks, ducks, swans, and herons that live in and around the river and an adjacent weir pool; they'll join you if you're handing out crumbs. Take an arched stone bridge, architecture with wildly pitched roofs and gables, add the Thames River, and you have the Trout. The Smoking Room, the original 12th-century part, complements the inn's relatively "new" 16th-century bars. Daily specials are featured, and there's a cold-snack bar. Hot meals are served all day in the restaurant; salads are featured in summer, and there are grills in winter. On your way there and back, look for the view of Oxford from the bridge. Take bus 520 or 521 to Wolvercote, then walk ½ mile; it's also fun to bike here from Oxford.

THE CLUBS: BLUES, JAZZ & "CELTIC ROCK"

As a sign of the times, **Freud,** Walton Street at Great Clarendon Street (☎ **01865/311171**), has turned a 19th-century church, stained-glass windows and all, into a jazz and folk club with an expansive array of drink choices. The cover charge is £4 ($6.80) after 10pm on Friday and Saturday.

The **Old Fire Station,** 40 George St. (☎ **01865/794494**), covers all the bases, including live entertainment, a bar, theater, art museum, and a new science museum called Curiosity, with a light show and other exhibits. The restaurant, open daily at 11am, serves breakfast until 9pm, with free coffee, tea, and toast. Music cover charges begin at 9pm and are £4 to £6 ($6.80 to $10.20) nightly. Offerings change nightly but include 1970s disco, blues, jazz, and local bands.

The **Zodiac,** 190 Crowley Rd. (☎ **01865/726336**), presents everything from easy listening to "Celtic Rock." The cover varies from £3 to £10 ($5.10 to $17) depending on the group featured. It's open usually from about 7:30pm to 2am Monday through Friday; 9pm to 2am Saturday; closed Sunday. Club ownership is shared by some major English bands, and local and big-name bands are featured along with DJs, so call ahead to be sure of what you're getting.

The Pub Scene

These places are all good choices for affordable meals, too.

The Head of the River, Abingdon Road at Folly Bridge, near the Westgate Centre Mall (☎ **01865/721600**), is operated by Fuller Smith and Turner, a family brewery. It's a lively place where they offer true traditional ales and lagers, along with very good sturdy fare. In summer, guests sit by the river and can rent a punt or a boat with an engine. Five rooms, all with bath and overlooking the river, are available for £75 ($127.50) in summer, including breakfast, newspaper, and parking.

Jolly Farmers, 20 Paradise St. (☎ **01865/7973759**), offers real ale, several lagers, and stout, year-round, including Stella, Bass, and Murphy's. There's occasional entertainment, and it is always busy.

At **The Eagle and Child,** 49 Saint Giles St. (☎ **01865/310154**), literary history suffuses the dim, paneled alcoves and promotes a sedate atmosphere. For at least a quarter of a century, it was frequented by the likes of C. S. Lewis and J. R. R. Tolkien. In fact, *The Chronicles of Narnia* and *The Hobbit* were first read aloud at this pub. Known as the "Bird and Baby," this hallowed ground still welcomes the local dons, and the food is good. It's a settled, quiet place to read the newspapers and listen to classical music on CDs.

The King's Arms, 40 Holywell St. (☎ **01865/242369**), hosts a mix of students, gays, and professors. One of the best places in town to strike up a conversation, the pub, owned by Young's Brewery, features six of the company's ales along with visiting lagers and bitters that change periodically.

5 Woodstock & Blenheim Palace

62 miles NW of London; 8 miles NW of Oxford

The small country town of Woodstock, the birthplace in 1330 of the Black Prince, the ill-fated son of King Edward III, lies on the edge of the Cotswolds. Some of the stone houses here were constructed when Woodstock was the site of a royal palace. This palace had so suffered the ravages of time that its remains were demolished when Blenheim Palace was built. Woodstock was once the seat of a flourishing glove industry.

ESSENTIALS

GETTING THERE Take the train to Oxford (see "Essentials," in section 4). The Gloucester Green bus (no. 20) leaves Oxford about every 30 minutes during the day. The trip takes just over a half hour. Call **Stagecoach** at ☎ **01865/772250** for details. If you're driving, take A44 from Oxford.

VISITOR INFORMATION The **Tourist Information Centre** is on Hensington Road (☎ **01993/811038**), open Monday through Saturday in summer from

9:30am to 5:30pm; November through February, 10am to 5pm, and on Sunday 1 to 5pm year round.

ONE OF ENGLAND'S MOST MAGNIFICENT PALACES

✪ **Blenheim Palace.** ☎ **01993/811091.** Admission £9 ($15.30) adults, £7 ($11.90) seniors and children 16–17, £4.50 ($7.65) children 5–15; free for children under 5. Family ticket £22.50 ($38.25). Daily 10:30am–5:30pm. Last admission 4:45pm. Closed Nov to mid-Mar.

The extravagantly baroque Blenheim Palace is England's answer to Versailles. Blenheim is the home of the 11th duke of Marlborough, a descendant of John Churchill, the first duke, who was an on-again, off-again favorite of Queen Anne's. In his day (1650–1722), the first duke became the supreme military figure in Europe. Fighting on the Danube near a village named Blenheim, Churchill defeated the forces of Louis XIV, and the lavish palace of Blenheim was built for the duke as a gift from the queen. It was designed by Sir John Vanbrugh, who was also the architect of Castle Howard; the landscaping was created by Capability Brown. The palace is loaded with riches: antiques, porcelain, oil paintings, tapestries, and chinoiserie.

North Americans know Blenheim as the birthplace of Sir Winston Churchill. The room in which he was born is included in the palace tour, as is the Churchill exhibition, four rooms of letters, books, photographs, and other relics. Today, the former prime minister lies buried in Bladon Churchyard, near the palace.

Insider's tip: The **Marlborough Maze,** 600 yards from the palace, is the largest symbolic hedge maze on earth, with an herb and lavender garden, a butterfly house, and inflatable castles for children. Also, be sure to look for the Castle's gift shops, tucked away in an old palace dairy. Here you can purchase a wide range of souvenirs, handicrafts, and even locally made preserves.

WHERE TO STAY & DINE

The Bear Hotel. Park St., Woodstock, Oxfordshire OX20 1SZ. ☎ **01993/811511.** Fax 01993/813380. www.heritage-hotels.com. E-mail: bear@forte-hotels.com. 44 units. TV TEL. £145–£155 ($246.50–$263.50) double; £190–£200 ($323–$340) suite. AE, DC, MC, V.

The Bear Hotel is one of the six oldest coaching inns in England, dating from the 16th century. The half-stone structure is located in the center of Woodstock. Look for the signs in front with the picture of a huge brown bear. Richard Burton and Elizabeth Taylor, at the height of their tempestuous romance in the '60s, stayed in the Marlboro suite, an attractively decorated sitting room with a minibar, plus a bedroom and bath. According to legend, one of the chambers of the hotel is haunted. Modern amenities are combined with antiques in the rooms, which have hair dryers and trouser presses. Rooms come in a variety of sizes and styles, but each offers grand comfort; six of the rooms contain four-posters. Bedrooms have recently been refurbished, and the hotel continues to maintain high standards of innkeeping. Blazing hearth fires are found throughout the hotel when the days and nights are cool.

Dining: You can relax in the bar or enjoy a drink in the lounge. Traditional English dishes are served in the dining room.

✪ **Feathers.** Market St., Woodstock, Oxfordshire OX20 1SX. ☎ **01993/812291.** Fax 01993/813158. www.feathers.co.uk. E-mail: enquiries@feathers.co.uk. 22 units. TV TEL. £120–£185 ($204–$314.50) double; £235–£310 ($399.50–$527) suite. Rates include English breakfast. AE, DC, MC, V.

Just a short walk from Blenheim Palace, Feathers dates from the 17th century, and has been an inn since the 18th century. The bedrooms in this beautifully furnished hotel are individually decorated. Some units have draped awnings over the beds, whereas the best and most spacious contain four-posters. The bathrooms are luxuriously clad in marble, with thick bathrobes, a hair dryer, deluxe toiletries, and a set of fluffy towels. The two lounges have wood fires. A multitude of stuffed birds (from which the house took its name) adorns the bar; from here you can go into the delightful garden in the courtyard.

Dining: The modern British cuisine at Feathers is the best in the area, even better than that served at the Bear. Whether you're here for lunch or for a candlelit dinner, you're sure to enjoy the well-prepared dishes. In summer, you can have a light lunch or afternoon tea in the courtyard garden. Moderately priced set menus are served daily at lunch and dinner.

TWO FAVORITE LOCAL PUBS

The **Star Inn** (☎ **01993/811373**) has three locally brewed real ales from which to choose: Tetleys, Wadworth 6X, and Marston's Pedigree. You can enjoy the requisite bar munchies as well as full dinners. The management boasts that its half-shoulder of lamb is the tenderest around because of the slow cooking process. You can also pick and choose from a hot and cold buffet that features salads and sandwich fixings.

The **King's Head** is tucked away at 11 Park Lane (☎ **01993/812164**) in Woodstock. Tourists seem to like the "potato pub," as the locals call it, though it's a bit hard to find. The name comes from the wide variety of stuffed potato skins that the pub serves. Enjoy these with a real ale; the owners are sure to have a different specialty ale every month. If you come for dinner, a three-course meal, which may include fish, ribs, or homemade lasagna, costs about £9 ($15.30).

6 Aylesbury

46 miles NW of London; 22 miles E of Oxford

Aylesbury has retained much of its ancient charm and character, especially along the narrow Tudor alleyways and in the 17th-century architecture of the houses in the town center. Among the more interesting structures is St. Mary's Church, which dates from the 13th century and features an unusual spirelet. The 15th-century King's Head Public House, a National Trust property, has seen many famous faces in its time, including Henry VIII, who was a frequent guest while he was courting Anne Boleyn.

The market, which has been an integral part of the town since the 13th century, is still a thriving force in Aylesbury life, with markets held on Wednesday, Friday, and Saturday, and a flea market on Tuesday. During the 18th and 19th centuries, ducks were the most famous commodity of the Aylesbury market. The pure white ducks were a delicacy for the rich and famous of London and were much desired for their dinner tables. The demand for the Aylesbury duck declined in the 20th century, although not before the breed became threatened with extinction. Today, however, most ducks found on restaurant menus are raised elsewhere and the threat to the Aylesbury duck has subsided. The ivory fowl are now enjoyed more for their beauty than their flavor.

ESSENTIALS

GETTING THERE Aylesbury is 1 hour by train from London's Marylebone Station, or 25 minutes off the M25 via A41. For rail information, call ☎ **0345/484950** in the United Kingdom or 01603/764776 in the United States.

VISITOR INFORMATION The **Aylesbury Tourist Information Centre,** 8 Bourbon St. (☎ **01296/330559**), is open April to October from 9:30am to 5pm Monday through Saturday. From November to March, hours are Monday through Saturday from 10am to 4:30pm.

SEEING THE SIGHTS

Aylesbury is blessed with an abundance of interesting architecture. If you aren't busy spending money at the market, you may want to stroll through the town to see the houses and buildings that line the streets. **Hickman's Almshouses** and the **Prebendal Houses** are structures that date from the 17th century; you can walk by after enjoying tea at St. Mary's Church, which is just down the road.

Buckinghamshire County Museum. Church St. ☎ **01296/331441.** Admission to main museum £1 ($1.70) adults, children free; Children's Gallery £3.50 ($5.95) adults, £2 ($3.40) children. Mon–Sat 10am–5pm, Sun 2–5pm.

This museum is located in two buildings, a house and grammar school both dating from the 18th century. The newest addition to the recently refurbished museum is the Roald Dahl Children's Gallery. Dahl's children's books, especially *Charlie and the Chocolate Factory* and *James and the Giant Peach,* come to life as visitors ride in the Great Glass Elevator or crawl inside the Giant Peach. The hands-on exhibits don't stop upon entering the main museum, however. Innovative displays focusing on the cultural heritage of Buckinghamshire are interactive and touchable. Advance arrangements are necessary for the Children's Gallery because of the large number of school groups that visit.

Oak Farms Rare Breeds Park. Off the A41 on the way to Broughton. ☎ **01296/415709.** Admission £2.50 ($4.25) adults, £1.50 ($2.55) ages 16 and under. Wed–Sun 10am–5pm. Closed Nov to mid-Feb.

While you're in the area, you'll of course want to see those famous **Aylesbury ducks,** and this is the best place to catch sight of the once-threatened species. The traditional working farm is home to a variety of animals, from sheep to pigs, many of which are rare breeds. Guests can hand-feed special food to the animals and take a picnic of their own to enjoy. There's also a nature trail.

Waddesdon Manor. Bicester Rd. ☎ **01296/653211.** Admission to house and grounds £10 ($17) adults, £7.50 ($12.75) children; grounds only, £3 ($5.10) adults, £1.50 ($2.55) children. House open Apr 1–Oct 31 Thurs–Sun and bank holidays 11am–4pm; also Wed 11am–4pm in July–Aug. Grounds and aviary Mar 3–Dec 24 Wed–Sun and bank holidays 10am–5pm.

Built by Baron Ferdinand de Rothschild in the 1870s, the manor features French Renaissance architecture and a variety of French furniture, carpets, and porcelain. Eighteenth-century artwork by several famous English and Dutch painters is exhibited, and there are, of course, wine cellars. In the surrounding gardens, an aviary houses exotic birds. On the premises is a restaurant and gift shop, both featuring a vast assortment of Rothschild wines.

WHERE TO STAY

The Courtyard Hotel. Aston Clinton, near Aylesbury, Buckinghamshire HP22 5HP. ☎ **01296/630252.** Fax 01296/631250. 20 units. TV TEL. £68 ($115.60) double. Rates include continental breakfast. AE, MC, V.

This former coaching inn is believed to date from the end of the 18th century. It stands unobtrusively by the road, 4 miles from Aylesbury, off the A41 leading south to London. A mossy brick structure with a Georgian portico, it is coolly elegant, with an ancient bar featuring an inglenook fireplace. Former stables around a flower-filled courtyard have been turned into a block of rooms, with luxuriously appointed baths, plus sitting areas and a blend of antique and reproduction furniture. Some rooms have four-poster beds. Rooms are spacious and divided between the main building and an annex, which is equally good. There is a set of fluffy towels in each bathroom, and a coffeemaker in each room.

✪ **Hartwell House.** Oxford Rd., Aylesbury, Buckinghamshire HP17 8NL. ☎ **01296/747444.** Fax 01296/747450. www.hartwell-house.com. E-mail: info@hartwell-house.com.46 units. TV TEL. £215–£375 ($365.50–$637.50) double; £400–£550 ($680–$935) suite. AE, MC, V.

One of London's great showcase country estates and a member of Relais & Châteaux, Hartwell House lies just 2 miles southwest of Aylesbury (the nearest rail station) on A418, near the village of Stone, and about 20 miles from Oxford or an hour's drive from Heathrow. It stands on 90 acres of landscaped parkland. As you enter the house, you're transported back to another era, and can enjoy a medley of architectural styles, ranging from the 16th through the 18th centuries. The home was built for the Hampden and Lee families, ancestors of the Confederacy's Gen. Robert E. Lee. You can wander from the morning room to the oak-paneled bar, pausing in the library where a former tenant, the exiled Louis XVIII, signed the document returning him to the throne of France. This property stands on the Vale of Aylesbury.

Rooms are as regal as the prices. The stellar accommodations literally ooze with comfort, charm, and character, even those recently built in a converted stable block. Many of the rooms have garden views. Bedrooms are sumptuous, filled with luxury and comfort, rich fabrics, huge beds with deluxe mattresses, plus luxurious bathrooms with hair dryers.

Dining: The chef cooks with an international flair, using fresh regional ingredients, backed up by a supreme wine list. It's worth the trip here just to try the roast breast of Aylesbury duck with a duck confit flavored with cumin.

Amenities: The Hartwell Spa, modeled on an orangery inspired by Sir John Soane, the early-19th-century architect, is set in landscaped gardens, with a large swimming pool and a fitness center, along with a beauty salon and solarium. The house also has two all-weather tennis courts.

WHERE TO DINE

✪ **Bottle & Glass.** In the hamlet of Gibralter, 5 miles southeast of Aylesbury beside route A418. ☎ **01296/748488.** Reservations recommended. Main courses £7–£15 ($11.90–$25.50). AE, DC, MC. V. Daily noon–2pm; Mon–Fri 7–9pm, Sat 7–10pm. From Aylesbury, follow the signs to Oxford, following Route A418 for 5 miles southwest of Aylesbury. ENGLISH.

Because of its lavish sense of charm and nostalgia, no one seems to mind the short trek to this bucolic reminder of Olde England. The setting is a 1660s thatch-roofed cottage that functioned as a rough-and-tumble village pub until the mid-1990s. Around 1995, members of the Southwood family upgraded the food and service rituals to the point where most of its business today derives from a restaurant trade that draws visitors in from throughout the nearby region. No one will mind if you drop in just for a pint, but if you're hungry, menu items focus on old-fashioned but flavorful dishes that helped fortify the Empire builders of the early 20th century. Examples include bangers and mash, smoked salmon with horseradish sauce; garlic mushrooms; ribeye steaks; and grilled Dover sole served as simply as possible—only with lemon-flavored butter.

AYLESBURY AFTER DARK

The **Hobgoblin,** Kingsbury Square (☎ **01296/415100**), has been in service as a pub for only a couple of years, but this structure was built in 1742. Among the on-tap offerings are house ales, Hobgoblin and Wychwood, as well as John Smith's, and there is also a full bar. Snack food is available, as are such distractions as pool tables, TVs, and video games. Sunday nights there's live jazz (no cover). On weekends, the second floor opens as a dance club called **Merlin's.** Hours are Wednesday, Friday and Saturday from 10pm to 2:30am, with a cover charge of £5 ($8.50) on Friday and Saturday only.

7 St. Albans

27 miles NW of London; 41 miles SW of Cambridge

Dating back 2,000 years, today's cathedral city of St. Albans was named after a Roman soldier who was the first Christian martyr in England. Medieval pilgrims made the trek to visit the shrine of St. Alban, and visitors today still find the ancient cathedral city and the surrounding countryside inspiring.

Peter Rabbit was created in this county by Beatrix Potter, and George Bernard Shaw found inspiration in the view from his countryside home near Ayot St. Lawrence. As you explore St. Albans and its nearby attractions, you'll be treading in the footsteps of the Good Queen Bess and Henry VIII, who passed through before you.

Although today industry has crept in and Greater London keeps getting greater and greater, St. Albans is situated at the center of what was known as "the market basket of England." The 1,000-year-old tradition of the street market continues as merchants of every kind set up colorful stalls to display their goods. The market is held on Wednesday and Saturday, and is one of the largest in the southeast.

Tourism has also become very important to the town, since it is near the M25 and the M1 and on the way to many historic homes and attractions. St. Albans itself is home to several museums, well-preserved Roman ruins, and beautiful gardens.

ESSENTIALS

GETTING THERE St. Albans is easily reached from London. North London Railways leaves from London's Kings Cross Station every 40 minutes. The rail connection, ThamesLink, takes you from London to St. Albans in just 17 minutes. From London, Green Line coach no. 724 also runs to St. Albans frequently. For rail information, call ☎ **0345/484950.** For bus information, dial ☎ **020/86687261.**

If you're driving, take M25 Junction 21A or 22; M1 Junctions 6, 7, or 9; and A1(M) Junction 3.

VISITOR INFORMATION The **Tourist Information Centre** is at the Town Hall, Market Place (☎ **01727/864511**). From Easter through October, its hours are Monday through Saturday from 9:30am to 5:30pm; off-season hours are Monday through Saturday from 10:30am to 4:30pm. From the end of July until mid-September, the office is also open most Sundays from 10am to 4pm.

EXPLORING THE TOWN

The Association of Honorary Guides, a trained group of local volunteers, provides **guided walks.** These include a tour of the Roman Verulamium and the Medieval Town, a ghost walk, and a coaching-inn walking tour. In addition to prebooked tours, free public guided walks are available on Sunday; the tour begins at 3pm at the clock tower. Guides are also available on Sunday at the Verulamium Museum and Roman

Theatre to give short talks on a number of topics concerning the Romans and their time in the area. Full details can be obtained from the Tourist Information Centre (see above) or from the **Tours Secretary** (☎ **01727/833001**).

The **Cathedral of St. Albans,** Holywell Hill and High Street (☎ **01727/860780**) is still known as "The Abbey" to the locals, even though Henry VIII dissolved it as such in 1539. Construction of the cathedral was launched in 1077, making it one of the early Norman churches of England. The bricks, especially visible in the tower, came from the old Roman city of Verulamium, located at the foot of the hill. The nave and west front date from 1235.

The new chapter house, the first modern building beside a great medieval cathedral in the country, was opened by the queen in 1982. The structure houses an information desk, gift shop, and restaurant. There is also a video detailing the history of the cathedral that you can view for £1.50 ($2.55).

St. Albans Cathedral and the chapter house are generally open daily from 9am to 5:45pm. In addition to church services, there are often organ recitals that are open to the public. The church's choir can sometimes be heard rehearsing, if they're not on tour.

The **Verulamium Museum at St. Michael's** (☎ **01727/751810**) stands on the site of the ancient Roman city of the same name. Here you'll view some of the finest Roman mosaics in Britain as well as re-created Roman rooms. Part of the Roman town hall, a hypocaust, and the outline of houses and shops are still visible in the park that surrounds the museum. The museum is open year-round Monday through Saturday from 10am to 5:30pm and Sunday from 2 to 5:30pm. Admission is £3 ($5.10) for adults, £1.70 ($2.90) for seniors and children, and £7.50 ($12.75) for a family ticket. By car, Verulamium is a 10-minute drive from Junction 21A on M25; it is also accessible from Junctions 9, or 6 on M1; follow the signs for St. Albans and the Roman Verulamium. Taking a train to St. Albans City Station will put you within 2 miles of the museum.

Just a short distance from Verulamium is the **Roman Theatre** (☎ **01727/ 835035**). The structure is the only theater of the period that is open to visitors in Britain. You can tour the site daily between 10am and 5pm (4pm in winter). Admission is £1.50 ($2.55) for adults, £1 ($1.70) for seniors and students, and 50p (85¢) for children.

The **Museum of St. Albans,** Hatfield Road (☎ **01727/819340**), details the history of St. Albans from the departure of the Romans to the present day. The Museum of St. Albans is open Monday through Saturday from 10am to 5pm and Sundays from 2 to 5pm. Admission is free. It is located in the city center on A1057 Hatfield Road and is a 5-minute walk from St. Albans City Station.

From St. Albans, you can visit **Gorhambury,** (☎ **01727/855000**) a classic mansion built in 1777. The private home, owned by the earl and countess of Verulam, contains 16th-century enameled glass and historic portraits. It's open May to September from 2 to 5pm on Thursday only. Admission for adults is £4 ($6.80), £2.50 ($4.25) for children, and £2 ($3.40) for seniors. Gorhambury is located 2½ miles west of St. Albans near the A5. From the Verulamium Museum, cross Bluehouse Hill Road; the house is about a mile up a private drive.

Batchwood's 18-hole golf course is one of the finest public courses in the country. The Batchwood Indoor Tennis Centre, which has four indoor courts plus outdoor courts, has professional coaches available for all play levels. Both the golf and the tennis center are located on the grounds of the Batchwood Hall mansion on **Batchwood Drive** (☎ **01727/844250**).

SHOPPING

The twice-weekly **street market,** held every Wednesday and Saturday on St. Peters Street, is defined by its frantic pace. In contrast, modern off-street precincts and small specialty shops in St. Albans combine to create a unique, laid-back atmosphere the rest of the week.

The Past Times Shop, 33 Market St. (☎ **01727/812817**), sells items that cover 12 historic eras. Here you'll find books on historic places, jewelry, clothes, and CDs featuring music from a variety of time periods.

For antiques, visit **By George,** 23 George St. (☎ **01727/853032**). St. Albans' largest antiques center, the building also houses a tearoom and crafts arcade. **Forget-Me-Not Antiques,** 27 High St. (☎ **01727/848907**), specializes in jewelry, especially Victorian name brooches. At **St. Albans Antique Centre,** 9 George St. (☎ **01727/844233**), up to 20 dealers gather to sell their goods. You can browse through the furniture and collectibles, then have a light snack in the tearoom or tour the gardens.

WHERE TO STAY

The Black Lion Inn. St. Michael's Village, Fishpool St., St. Albans, Hertfordshire AL3 4SB. ☎ **01727/851786.** Fax 01727/859243. 16 units, 14 with bathroom. £50 ($85) double without bathroom, £55 ($93.50) double with bathroom. AE, MC, V.

This is the finest pub hotel in the area, and one of the best bargains. A former bakery built in 1837, it lies in the most colorful part of town, St. Michael's Village, where bustling coaches from London once arrived. Bedrooms are utterly simple and plain and, although a bit cramped, are well maintained, each with a small bathroom with rather thin towels. Owners Barry, Tony, and Royal Scott, all brothers, also welcome you to their Giovanni's Italian Restaurant, which is known locally for wishing you a *buon appetito* with its robust Italian cuisine made with fresh ingredients.

✪ **St. Michael Manor.** St. Michael's Village, Fishpool St., St. Albans, Hertfordshire AL3 4RY. ☎ **01727/864444.** Fax 01727/848909. E-mail: manor@stalbans.co.uk. 23 units. TV TEL. £145–£235 ($246.50–$399.50) double; £275 ($467.50) suite. Special weekend rate from £185 ($314.50) per day (minimum of 2 nights), with half board. Rates include English breakfast. AE, MC, V.

Set on 5 acres of beautifully maintained lakeside gardens, the Manor was built in 1586 but was recently upgraded and refurbished. Constructed on medieval fortifications, the hotel stands in award-winning gardens with an abundance of wildlife. It's hard to imagine you're in a city. The rooms are individually decorated with fine antique pieces. Each one has a certain charm; there's no bad choice among them. Rooms are stocked with everything from mineral water to a teddy bear to sleep with. Mattresses are of the finest quality with crisp bed linens, and the bathrooms are luxurious, with robes, a pumice stone, a rack of thick towels, and even a family of plastic ducks for your bath.

Dining: The Manor also has a superb restaurant, the Terrace Room, with an ornate Victorian conservatory overlooking the floodlit lawns, that offers the very best seasonally prepared regional English cooking. There's also 24-hour room service. A fixed-price lunch costs £15.75–£19.95 ($26.80–$33.90); fixed-price dinner ranges from £23–£29.50 ($39.10–$50.15).

Sopwell House. Cottonmill Lane, St. Albans, Hertfordshire AL1 2HQ. ☎ **01727/864477.** Fax 01727/844741. E-mail: sopwell@stalbans.co.uk. 92 units. TV TEL. £144.75–£154.75 ($246.10–$263.10) double; £184.75 ($314.10) suite. Reduced weekend rates from £109.75 ($186.60) double. Child £10 ($17) extra. AE, DC, MC, V.

This place is in a neck-to-neck competition with St. Michael Manor (see above), although Sopwell has more facilities. A private mansion from the days of George III, it once belonged to Lord Louis Mountbatten and has seen its share of royal heads. Now converted into a hotel of taste, charm, and character, it occupies nearly a dozen acres 2 miles southeast of the city center. Avoid it if it's hosting a conference, but at other times you can enjoy the grace of an English country house. From the drawing room to the library, public rooms are elegant and comfy. Some of the bedrooms are equipped with four-poster beds and have a traditional feel, whereas others are more contemporary. Regardless, the decor is tasteful, rather chic, and handsomely coordinated. All rooms are accompanied by amenity-filled marble baths with "power showers," fluffy towels, scales, and a hair dryer. For a review of the hotel's restaurant (Magnolia Conservatory), see below.

Amenities: Indoor swimming pool, Jacuzzi, gym, sauna, spa with sun beds, hair salon.

WHERE TO DINE

Magnolia Conservatory. In the Sopwell House Hotel, Cottonmill Lane. ☎ **01727/864477.** Reservations recommended. Fixed-price lunches £14.95–£18.95 ($25.40–$32.20); fixed-price dinner £24.95 ($42.40); main courses £13–£23.50 ($22.10–$39.95). AE, DC, MC, V. Sun–Fri 12:30–2:30pm; Mon–Sat 7:30–9:30pm. FRENCH/ENGLISH.

Consistently serving the best food in the area, this restaurant lies beneath a glass roof that's pierced with a trio of magnolias whose leaves gracefully arch into the open air outside. The ambience is light, elegant, upscale, and inviting, partly because of its formal and well-trained staff, and partly because the food is more sophisticated, and prepared with more flair, than anywhere else in town. You might begin with an award-winning version of seared scallops with polenta, served with a marmalade of fresh cherry tomatoes and angel-hair pasta. Main courses change with new chef Warren Jones' inspiration, but we enjoyed the supreme of guinea fowl filled with a mousseline of wild mushrooms and served on a rösti of parsnips. Dessert anyone? With your significant other (it's served only for two), sample the Sopwell Symphony, a degustation of half a dozen of the chef's favorite desserts, arranged on the same platter.

Also on the premises is an upscale pub that's open Monday to Friday from 11am to 10pm. The food it serves is a lot more down-home, but also a lot cheaper.

THEATER PERFORMANCES

St. Albans' nightlife is centered around its theaters. The Company of Ten, which has its base at the **Abbey Theatre,** Westminster Lodge, Holywell Hill (☎ **01727/857861**), is one of the leading amateur dramatic companies in Britain. The troupe presents 10 productions each season in either the well-equipped main auditorium or a smaller studio. Performances begin at 8pm; tickets cost from £4.50 to £7 ($7.65 to $11.90). **The Maltings Arts Theatre,** in the Maltings Shopping Center (☎ **01727/844222**), presents performances based on literature—from Shakespeare to modern novels. Plays are generally presented only once and begin at 8pm on Thursday, Friday, and Saturday. Tickets are £2 to £9 ($3.40 to $15.30).

SIDE TRIPS FROM ST. ALBANS

✪ **Hatfield House.** 6 miles east of St. Albans on A414. ☎ **01707/262823** for information. Admission £6.20 ($10.55) adults, £3.10 ($5.25) children. Mar 25–Sept 26, Tues–Thurs noon–4pm, Sat–Sun 1–4:30pm, and bank holiday Mondays 11am–4:30pm. Closed Good Friday. From St. Albans, take A414 east and follow the brown signs that lead you directly to the estate. By bus, take the University bus from St. Albans City Station. Hatfield House is directly across from Hatfield Station.

Hatfield was a part of the lives of both Henry VIII and his daughter Elizabeth I. In the old palace, built in the 15th century, Elizabeth romped and played as a child. Although Henry was married to her mother, Anne Boleyn, at the time of Elizabeth's birth, the marriage was later nullified (Anne lost her head and Elizabeth her legitimacy). Henry would also stash away his oldest daughter, Mary Tudor, at Hatfield. But when Mary became queen of England and set about earning the dubious distinction of "Bloody Mary," she found Elizabeth to be a problem. For a while she kept her in the Tower of London, but eventually let her return to Hatfield. In 1558, Elizabeth learned of her succession to the throne of England while at Hatfield.

Only the banqueting hall of the original Tudor palace remains; the rest of the house is Jacobean. The structure that exists today has much antique furniture and many tapestries and paintings, as well as three often-reproduced portraits, including the ermine and rainbow portraits of Elizabeth I. The Great Hall is suitably medieval, complete with a minstrel's gallery. One of the rarest exhibits is a pair of silk stockings, said to have been worn by Elizabeth herself, the first woman in England to don such apparel. The park and the gardens are also worth exploring. Luncheons and teas are available from 11am to 5pm in the converted coach house in the Old Palace yard.

Elizabethan banquets are staged in the banqueting hall of the Old Palace Tuesday, and Thursday through Saturday, with much gaiety and music. Guests are invited to drink in an anteroom, then join the long tables for a feast of five courses with continuous entertainment from a group of Elizabethan players, minstrels, and jesters. Wine is included in the cost of the meal, but you're expected to pay for your before-dinner drinks yourself. The best way to get here from London for the feast is to book a coach tour for an inclusive fee starting at £44 ($74.80). The Evan Evans agency has tours leaving from Mount Royal Hotel, Cockspur Street, and Herbrand Street in London. The coach returns to London after midnight. If you get here under your own steam, the cost is £31.50 ($53.55) on Tuesday, £33 ($56.10) on Friday, and £35.50 ($60.35) on Saturday. For private reservations, call ☎ **01707/262055.**

Shaw's Corner. In the village of Ayot St. Lawrence. ☎ **01438/820307.** Admission £3.40 ($5.80) adults, £1.75 ($3) children. Apr–Oct Wed–Sun and bank holidays 1–5pm. From St. Albans, take B651 to Wheathampstead. Pass through the village, go right at the roundabout, and take the first left turn. A mile up on the left is Brides Hall Lane, which leads to the house.

George Bernard Shaw lived here from 1906 to 1950. The utilitarian house, with its harsh brickwork and rather comfortless interior, is practically as he left it at his death. In the hall, for example, his hats are still hanging, as if ready for him to don one. Shaw wrote 6 to 8 hours a day, even when he'd reached his 90s. Evidence of his longtime relationship with the written word is obvious throughout the house; one of his old typewriters is even still in position. Shaw, of course, was famous for his eccentricities, his vegetarianism, and his longevity. And, of course, for his vast literary output, the most famous of which remains *Pygmalion,* on which the musical *My Fair Lady* was based.

Mosquito Aircraft Museum. On the grounds of Salisbury Hall, just off the main M25 London-St. Albans Rd. ☎ **01727/822051.** Admission £4.25 ($7.25) adults; £1.25 ($2.15) children 5–16, seniors, and students with identification; free for children under 5. Mar–Oct Tues, Thurs, and Sat 2–5:30pm; Sun and bank holidays 10:30am–5:30pm. Take M25 Junction 22 at London Colney about 5 miles south of St. Albans. The museum is on the B556.

This is the oldest aircraft museum in Britain. The hall where the de Havilland Aircraft Company developed the "Mosquito," known as the most versatile aircraft of World War II, is no longer open to the public. However, the museum displays more than 20 types of aircraft, including modern military and civil jets, along with aircraft engines and other memorabilia. Several of the displays are hands-on exhibits.

8 Woburn Abbey: England's Great Georgian Manor

44 miles N of London

Aside from Windsor Castle, the most visited attraction in the Home Counties is Woburn Abbey, which is so spectacular you should try to visit even if you have to miss all the other historic homes described in this chapter. The great 18th-century Georgian mansion has been the traditional seat of the dukes of Bedford for more than three centuries.

TOURING THE ESTATE

✪ **Woburn Abbey.** 1/2 mile from the village of Woburn, which is 13 miles southwest of Bedford. ☎ **01525/290666.** Admission £7.50 ($12.75) adults, £6.50 ($11.05) seniors, £3 ($5.10) children. House Mar 21–Sept 26 Mon–Sat 11am–4:30pm, Sun 10am–4:45pm; Jan 1–Mar 20 Sat–Sun and bank holidays 11am–5pm. Park Mon–Sat 10am–4:30pm, Sun 10am–4:45pm. In summer, travel agents can book you on organized coach tours out of London. Otherwise, if you're driving, take the M1 (motorway) north to Junction 12 or 13, where Woburn Abbey directions are signposted.

In the 1950s, the present duke of Bedford opened Woburn Abbey to the public to pay off his debt of millions of pounds in inheritance taxes. In 1974, he turned the estate over to his son and daughter-in-law, the marquess and marchioness of Tavistock, who reluctantly took on the business of running the 75-room mansion. And what a business it is, drawing hundreds of thousands of visitors a year and employing more than 300 people to staff the shops and grounds.

Its state apartments are rich in furniture, porcelain, tapestries, silver, and a valuable art collection, including paintings by Van Dyck, Holbein, Rembrandt, Gainsborough, and Reynolds. Of all the paintings, one of the most notable is the Armada Portrait of Elizabeth I. Her hand rests on the globe, as Philip's invincible armada perishes in the background.

Queen Victoria and Prince Albert visited Woburn Abbey in 1841; Victoria's Dressing Room displays a fine collection of 17th-century paintings from the Netherlands. Among the oddities and treasures at Woburn Abbey are a Grotto of Shells, a Sèvres dinner service (gift of Louis XV), and a chamber devoted to memorabilia of "The Flying Duchess." The wife of the 11th duke of Bedford, she was a remarkable woman who disappeared on a solo flight in 1937 (coincidentally, the same year as Amelia Earhart); the duchess was 72 years old at the time.

Today, Woburn Abbey is surrounded by a 3,000-acre deer park that includes the famous Père David deer herd, originally from China and saved from extinction at Woburn. The **Woburn Safari Park** has lions, tigers, giraffes, camels, monkeys, Przewalski's horses, bongos, elephants, and other animals.

NEARBY SHOPPING & AFTERNOON TEA

In a wonderful old building, **Town Hall Antiques,** Market Place (☎ **01525/290950**), is a treasure trove of collectibles and antiques, including some early English porcelain and pieces from the 1940s. Some unusual commemorative items are also sold, such as an array of Victorian, Georgian, and Edwardian memorabilia. There's something here to suit a wide range of pocketbooks, including clocks, Victorian jewelry, brass, copper, and "kitchenalia."

When it's teatime, head to **Copperfields,** Woburn (☎ **01525/290464**), located inside a B&B with low-beamed ceilings that add to its intimacy and charm. There is no set tea, but a pot of tea with clotted cream and a cake is £3.50 ($5.95). Baked goods include scones, and chocolate, lemon, Victoria sponge, carrot, coffee, and fruitcakes, as well as daily specials. The tearoom is open daily, but it's a good idea to call on weekends between January and Easter, since it might be closed if business is slow.

WHERE TO STAY

Bedford Arms. 1 George St., Woburn, Bedfordshire MK17 9PX. ☎ **01525/290441.** Fax 01525/290432. 53 units. MINIBAR TV TEL. £120–£148 ($204–$251.60) double; £180 ($306) suite. Children under 16 stay free in parents' room. AE, MC, V.

After visiting the abbey, head here for food and lodging at the gates of the estate. This Georgian coaching inn has a checkered history that blends the old and new. Tastefully modernized, it preserves a certain mellow charm. Guests are housed in one of several well-furnished and beautifully maintained rooms, which were refurbished in 1995. A more recent block provides "executive bedrooms," which don't have the charm of the older units, but are more up-to-date and comfortable. Each room has a small bathroom with adequate shelf space and good maintenance.

Dining/Diversions: The 90-seat Georgian dining room was designed by Henry Holland, architect of Woburn Abbey. Adjacent to the restaurant is the Tavistock Bar, a good place for a pint, with its exposed old beams as well as its inglenook fireplace. There is also a more elegant and modern cocktail bar.

WHERE TO DINE

Paris House. Woburn Park (2¼ miles southeast of Woburn on A4012). ☎ **01525/290692.** Reservations required. Fixed-price dinner £45–£48 ($76.50–$81.60); set lunch £26 ($44.20). AE, DC, MC, V. Tues–Sat noon–2pm and 7–10pm, Sun noon–2pm. Closed Feb. CONTINENTAL.

This reconstructed timbered house stands in a park where you can see deer grazing. The black-and-white timbered building originally stood in Paris where it was constructed for the Great Exhibition 1878, but it was torn down and transplanted, timber by timber, to Woburn. Since 1983, it has been the domain of Bedfordshire's finest chef, Peter Chandler, who was the first English apprentice of the legendary Roux brothers. Chandler has brought his own innovative touch to the dishes served here. He still regularly visits France for new ideas, and is known for his use of the freshest of seasonal ingredients. Try his delectable marinated Cajun prawns, delicately spiced savory, or his duck confit in a black currant and orange sauce. The chef is rightly known for his *tulipe en fantaisie,* a sugar-fairy fantasy with fruit and ice cream.

6 Kent, Surrey & Sussex

Lying to the south and southeast of London are the shires (counties) of Kent, Surrey, and Sussex—fascinating areas within easy commuting distance of the capital.

In **Kent,** Canterbury is the major highlight and makes the best base for exploring the area. Dover, which is Britain's historic gateway to the Continent, is famed for its white cliffs, and is another convenient option. This county is on the fringes of London, yet is far removed in spirit and scenery. Since the days of the Tudors, cherry blossoms have enlivened the fertile landscape. Orchards and hop fields abound, earning Kent the title of "the garden of England"—and in England, the competition's tough. Kent suffered severe destruction during World War II, since it was the alley over which the *Luftwaffe* flew in its blitz of London. But despite much devastation, it's still filled with interesting old towns and castles.

In fact, Kent boasts some of Europe's grandest mansions. If your time is limited, seek out the big four: **Knole,** one of the largest private houses of England, a great example of Tudor architecture; **Hever Castle,** dating from the end of the 13th century, a gift from Henry VIII to the "great Flanders mare," Anne of Cleves; **Penhurst Place,** a magnificent English Gothic mansion, and one of the outstanding country houses of Britain; and lovely **Leeds Castle,** near Maidstone, dating from A.D. 857. Although it doesn't compare with these grand castles, Chartwell House also merits a visit because of the man who used to call it home: Sir Winston Churchill. For more advice on how to tour these homes, refer to "Kent's Country Houses, Castles & Gardens," in section 6.

With the continuing expansion of London's borders, it's a wonder that the tiny county of **Surrey** hasn't been gobbled up and turned into a sprawling suburb. Yet its countryside remains unspoiled, even though many people commute from homes here to jobs in London (you're only about 45 minutes to an hour away).

If King Harold hadn't loved **Sussex** so much, the course of English history might have been changed forever. Had the brave Saxon waited longer in the north, he could have marshaled more adequate reinforcements before striking south to meet the Normans. But Duke William's soldiers were ravaging the countryside he knew so well, and Harold rushed down to counter them.

Harold's enthusiasm for Sussex is understandable. The landscape rises and falls like waves. The county is known for its woodlands, from which came the timbers to build England's mighty fleet in days gone by. The shires lie south of London and Surrey, bordering Kent in the east, Hampshire in the west, and opening directly onto the English Channel, where the coast is dotted with seaside towns.

Like the other sections in the vulnerable south of England, Sussex was the setting of some of the most significant events in English history. Apart from the Norman landings at Hastings, the most life-changing transformation occurred in the 19th century, as middle-class Victorians flocked to the seashore, pumping new spirit into Brighton and even old Hastings.

The old towns and villages of Sussex, particularly Rye and Winchelsea, are far more intriguing than the seaside resorts. No Sussex village is lovelier than Alfriston (and the innkeepers know it, too); Arundel is noted for its castle; and the cathedral city of Chichester is a mecca for theater buffs. The old market town of ✪ **Battle** was the setting for the Battle of Hastings in 1066.

Where to base yourself in Sussex? The best option is Brighton, since it has a wide choice of hotels, restaurants, and nightclubs. There's more excitement here at "London by the Sea" than at Hastings. If you're seeking old-English charm and village life, head instead to Alfriston or Rye.

1 Canterbury

56 miles SE of London

Under the arch of the ancient West Gate journeyed Chaucer's knight, solicitor, nun, squire, parson, merchant, miller, and others—spinning tales. They were bound for the shrine of Thomas à Becket, archbishop of Canterbury, who was slain by four knights of Henry II on December 29, 1170. (The king later walked barefoot from Harbledown to the tomb of his former friend, where he allowed himself to be flogged in penance.) The shrine was finally torn down in 1538 by Henry VIII, as part of his campaign to destroy the monasteries and graven images. But Canterbury, by then, had already become an attraction.

The medieval Kentish city on the River Stour is the ecclesiastical capital of England. The city was once completely walled, and many traces of its old fortifications remain. Canterbury was inhabited centuries before the birth of Jesus Christ. Although its most famous incident was the murder of Becket, the medieval city witnessed other major events in English history, including Bloody Mary's order to burn nearly 40 victims at the stake. Richard the Lion-Hearted returned this way from crusading, and Charles II passed through on the way to claim his crown.

Canterbury pilgrims still continue to arrive today, except now they're called day-trippers and they overrun the city and its monuments. It's amazing that the central core of the city is as interesting and picture-perfect as it is, considering the enormous damage caused by the Nazi blitz of 1941. The city has an active university life—mainly students from Kent—and an enormous number of pubs. And its High Street is filled with shoppers in from the country. We suggest exploring Canterbury in the early morning or the early evening, after the busloads have departed.

ESSENTIALS

GETTING THERE There is frequent train service from Victoria, Charing Cross, Waterloo, and London Bridge stations. The journey takes 1½ hours. For rail information, call ☎ **0345/484950.**

The bus from Victoria Coach Station takes 2 to 3 hours and leaves every half hour. For schedules, call ☎ **0870/2433711.**

If you're driving from London, take A2, then M2. Canterbury is signposted all the way. The city center is closed to cars, but it's only a short walk from several parking areas to the cathedral.

VISITOR INFORMATION A few doors away from St. Margaret's Church, the **Canterbury Tourist Information Centre,** 34 St. Margaret's St., Canterbury CT1 2TG (☎ **01227/766567**), sells a useful guidebook, *National Travelguide,* for £10.99 ($18.70). It's open daily from 9:30am to 5:30pm April through October, and daily 9:30am to 5pm November through March.

GETTING AROUND BY BIKE Dutch touring bikes, small, folding bikes, and mountain bikes can be rented at the **House of Agnes Hotel,** 71 St. Dunstan's St., Canterbury (☎ **01227/472185**). A simple map comes with each bike, and an Ordinance Survey map of East Kent is offered for £2.50 ($4.25). A credit card or £50 ($85) deposit is required for city bikes.

SEEING THE SIGHTS

✪ **Canterbury Cathedral.** 11 The Precincts. ☎ **01227/762862.** Admission £3 ($5.10) adults, £2 ($3.40) children. Guided tours, based on demand, £3 ($5.10) adults, £2 ($3.40) children. Mon–Sat 9am–5pm, Sun 12:30–3pm and 4:30–5:30pm.

The foundation of this splendid cathedral dates from A.D. 597, but the earliest part of the present building is the great Romanesque crypt built around A.D. 1100. The monastic "quire" erected on top of this at the same time was destroyed by fire in 1174, only 4 years after the murder of Thomas à Becket on a dark December evening in the northwest transept, which is still one of the most famous places of pilgrimage in Europe. The destroyed "quire" was immediately replaced by a magnificent early Gothic one, the first major expression of that architectural style in England.

The cathedral is noteworthy for its medieval tombs of royal personages, such as King Henry IV and Edward the Black Prince, as well as numerous archbishops. To the later Middle Ages belong the great 14th-century nave and the famous central "Bell Harry Tower." The cathedral stands on spacious precincts amid the remains of the buildings of the monastery—cloisters, chapter house, and Norman water tower—which have survived intact from Henry VIII's dissolution to the present day.

Becket's shrine was destroyed by the Tudor king, but the site of that tomb is in Trinity Chapel, near the high altar. The saint is said to have worked miracles, and the cathedral has some rare stained glass depicting those feats.

But the most miraculous event is that the windows escaped Henry VIII's agents of destruction as well as Hitler's bombs. The windows were removed as a precaution at the beginning of the war. During the war, a large area of Canterbury was flattened, but the main body of the church was unharmed. However, the cathedral library was damaged during a German air raid in 1942. The replacement windows of the cathedral were blown in, which proved the wisdom of having the medieval glass safely stored away.

OTHER ATTRACTIONS

The Canterbury Tales. 23 St. Margaret's St. (off High St., near the cathedral). ☎ **01227/454888.** Admission £5.50 ($9.35) adults, £4.60 ($7.80) seniors and students, £4.60 ($7.80) children 5–16; free for children 4 and under. Family ticket £17.50 ($29.75). Mar–June 9:30am–5:30pm; Sept–Oct daily 9am–5:30pm; July–Aug daily 10am–4:30pm; Nov–Feb daily 10am–4:30pm.

One of the most visited museums in town re-creates the pilgrimages of Chaucerian England through a series of medieval tableaux. Visitors are handed headsets with

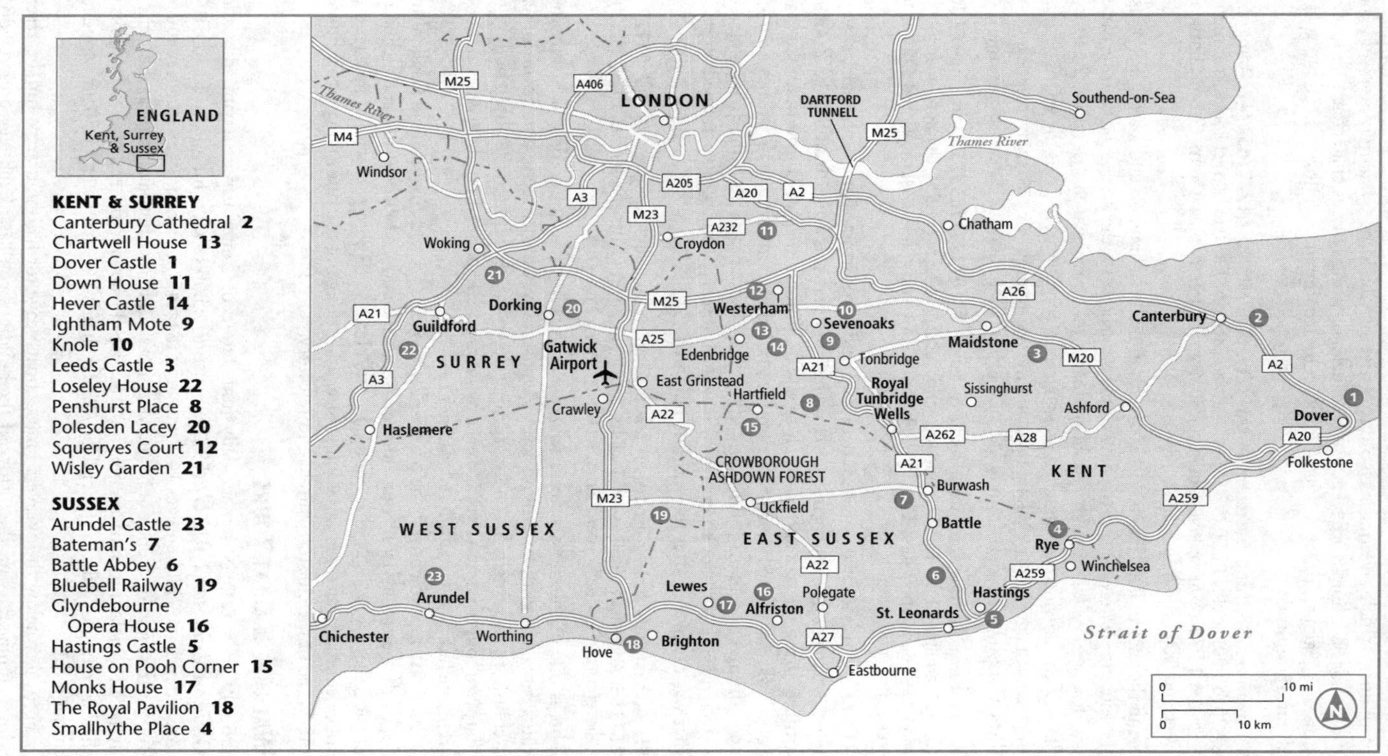

ENGLAND
Kent, Surrey & Sussex
KENT & SURREY
Canterbury Cathedral 2
Chartwell House 13
Dover Castle 1
Down House 11
Hever Castle 14
Ightham Mote 9
Knole 10
Leeds Castle 3
Loseley House 22
Penshurst Place 8
Polesden Lacey 20
Squerryes Court 12
Wisley Garden 21
SUSSEX
Arundel Castle 23
Bateman's 7
Battle Abbey 6
Bluebell Railway 19
Glyndebourne Opera House 16
Hastings Castle 5
House on Pooh Corner 15
Monks House 17
The Royal Pavilion 18
Smallhythe Place 4
LONDON
DARTFORD TUNNEL
Southend-on-Sea
Thames River
Thames River
Windsor
Woking
Croydon
Chatham
Guildford
Dorking
Westerham
Sevenoaks
Canterbury
Maidstone
SURREY
Gatwick Airport
Edenbridge
Tonbridge
East Grinstead
Hartfield
Royal Tunbridge Wells
Sissinghurst
Ashford
Dover
Folkestone
Crawley
Haslemere
CROWBOROUGH ASHDOWN FOREST
Burwash
KENT
Uckfield
Battle
WEST SUSSEX
EAST SUSSEX
Rye
Winchelsea
Lewes
Polegate
Alfriston
Arundel
Hastings
St. Leonards
Chichester
Worthing
Hove
Brighton
Eastbourne
Strait of Dover
M25
A406
M4
A205
A3
A20
A2
M23
A232
A26
M25
A21
A25
M20
A2
A3
A21
A22
A262
A28
A20
A21
M23
A259
A22
A259
A27
0
10 mi
0
10 km
N

earphones, which give oral recitations of five of Chaucer's *Canterbury Tales* and the murder of St. Thomas à Becket. Audiovisual aids bring famous characters to life, and stories of jealousy, pride, avarice, and love are recounted. A tour of all exhibits takes about 45 minutes.

Canterbury Heritage Museum of the City. Stour St. ☎ **01227/452747.** Admission £2.30 ($3.90) adults, £1.50 ($2.55) students and seniors, £1.10 ($1.85) children. Year-round Mon–Sat 10:30am–5pm; June–Oct Sun 1:30–5pm. Last entry time is 4pm. Closed Christmas week and Good Friday.

Set in the ancient Poor Priests' Hospital with its medieval interiors and soaring oak roofs, the museum features award-winning displays to showcase the best of the city's treasures and lead the visitor through crucial moments that have shaped Canterbury's history. State-of-the-art video, computer, and hologram technology transports the visitor back in time to such events as the Viking raids and the wartime Blitz. Collections include a huge display of pilgrim badges from medieval souvenir shops and the Rupert Bear Gallery.

Canterbury Roman Museum. Butchery Lane. ☎ **01227/785575.** Admission £2.30 ($3.90) adults, £1.50 ($2.55) students and seniors, £1.15 ($1.95) children. Year-round Mon–Sat 10am–5pm; June–Oct Sun 1:30–5pm. Last entry time is 4pm. Closed Christmas week and Good Friday.

The museum is located beneath street level and is constructed around actual archaeological excavations. Interactive computer shows and the actual handling of Roman artifacts bring the past to life for all ages. The Roman town of Durovernum Cantiacorum was established shortly after Emperor Claudius's invasion of the area in A.D. 43 and continued to flourish for nearly 400 years. Visitors can follow the archaeologists' detective work through an excavated Roman-house site containing patterned mosaics that was discovered after the wartime bombing.

St. Augustine's Abbey. Corner of Lower Chantry Lane and Longport Rd. ☎ **01227/767345.** Admission £2.50 ($4.25) adults, £1.90 ($3.25) students and seniors, £1.30 ($2.20) children. Apr–Sept daily 10am–6pm; Oct–Mar daily 10am–dusk.

This is one of the most historic religious centers in the country, of which only the ruins remain, mostly at ground level. Augustine was buried here, along with other archbishops and Anglo-Saxon kings. Adjacent to the remains are the abbey buildings that were converted into a royal palace by Henry VIII and used briefly by several monarchs, including Elizabeth I and Charles I.

In an attempt to convert the Saxons, Pope Gregory I sent Augustine to England in 597. Ethelbert, the Saxon King, allowed Augustine and his followers to build a church outside the city walls, and it endured until Henry VIII tore it down. In its day, the abbey church rivaled the cathedral in size, and enough of the ruins remain to conjure the whole of the cloister, church, and refectory.

Walking & Boat Tours

From Easter to early November, daily guided tours of Canterbury are organized by the **Guild of Guides** (☎ **01227/459779**), costing £3.50 ($5.95) for adults, £3 ($5.10) for students and children over 14, and £8.50 ($14.45) for a family ticket. Meet at the Tourist Information Centre at 34 St. Margaret's St., in a pedestrian area near the cathedral, daily (including Sun) at 2pm from the end of March to the end of October. From the beginning of July to the end of August there's also a tour at 11:30am Monday through Saturday.

From just below the Weavers House, boats leave for half-hour **trips on the river** with a commentary on the history of the buildings you pass. Umbrellas are provided to protect you against inclement weather.

Canterbury

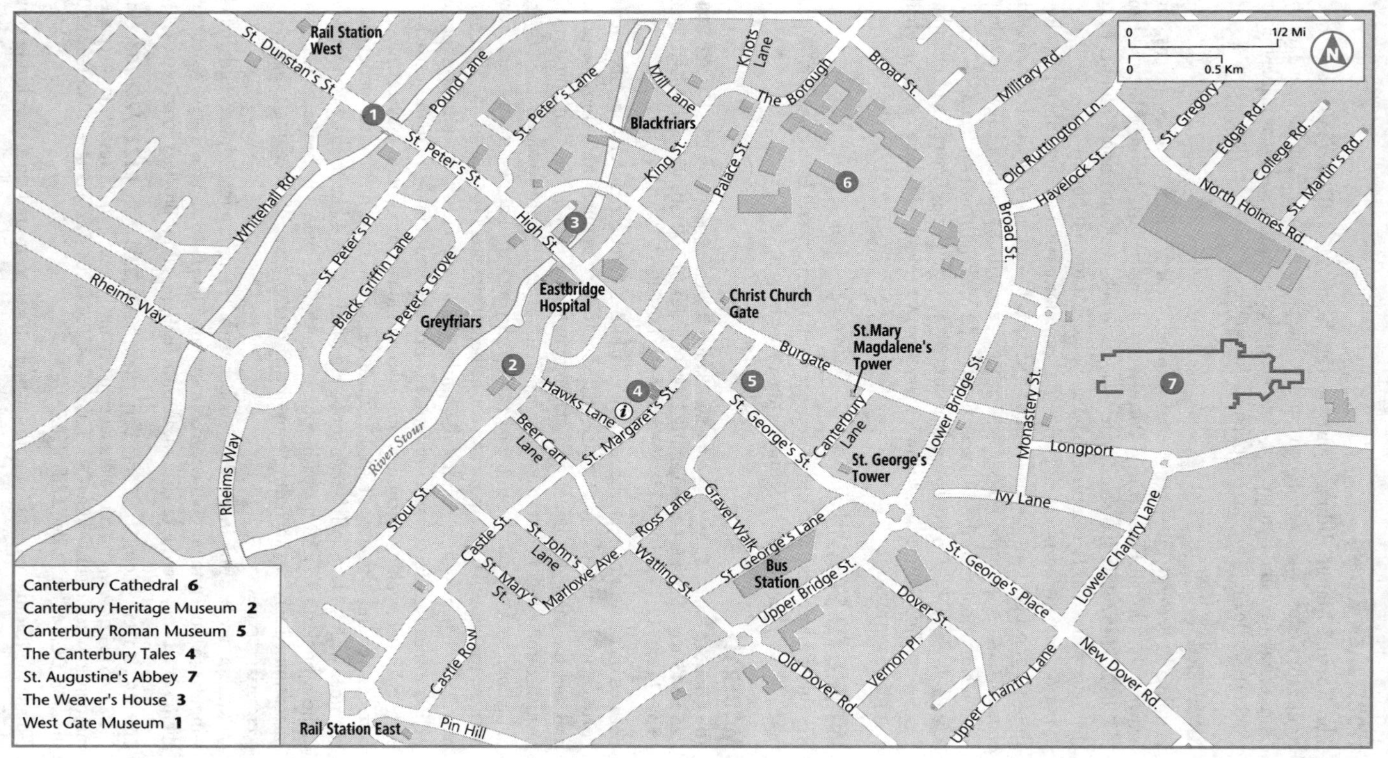

Rail Station West
St. Dunstan's St.
Pound Lane
St. Peter's Lane
Mill Lane
Blackfriars
Knots Lane
The Borough
Broad St.
Military Rd.
0 1/2 Mi
0 0.5 Km
N
St. Peter's St.
King St.
Palace St.
Old Ruttington Ln.
Havelock St.
St. Gregory
Edgar Rd.
College Rd.
St. Martin's Rd.
North Holmes Rd.
Whitehall Rd.
St. Peter's Pl.
Black Griffin Lane
St. Peter's Grove
High St.
Broad St.
Rheims Way
Greyfriars
Eastbridge Hospital
Christ Church Gate
St.Mary Magdalene's Tower
Burgate
Lower Bridge St.
Monastery St.
Hawks Lane
St. Margaret's St.
St. George's St.
Canterbury Lane
St. George's Tower
Longport
Beer Cart Lane
River Stour
Ivy Lane
Stour St.
Castle St.
St. John's Lane
Ross Lane
Gravel Walk
St. George's Lane
Lower Chantry Lane
St. Mary's St.
Marlowe Ave.
Watling St.
Bus Station
Upper Bridge St.
Dover St.
St. George's Place
Castle Row
Old Dover Rd.
Vernon Pl.
Upper Chantry Lane
New Dover Rd.
Rail Station East
Pin Hill
Canterbury Cathedral 6
Canterbury Heritage Museum 2
Canterbury Roman Museum 5
The Canterbury Tales 4
St. Augustine's Abbey 7
The Weaver's House 3
West Gate Museum 1

Horseback Riding

The **Bursted Manor Riding Centre** in Pett Bottom (☎ **01227/830568**) is open from 9am to dusk Tuesday through Sunday. The last lesson is at 7pm on weekdays and 6pm on Saturday and Sunday. A 1-hour group lesson or hack ride is available for £18 ($30.60). A Boxing Day hunt is open to the public.

Shopping

Handmade pottery (vases, mugs, and teapots in earth colors of blues, greens, and browns) is sold at **Canterbury Pottery,** 38 Burgate, just before Mercury Lane (☎ **01227/452608**). It is sturdy fare that wears well, including house-number plates that take two weeks to complete, but can be mailed to your home.

Put on your tweed jacket and grab your pipe for a trip to a secondhand **Chaucer Bookstop,** 6 Beer Cart Lane (☎ **01227/453912**), with first editions (both old and modern), out-of-print books, special leather-bound editions, and a large selection of local history books. At the **Chaucer Centre,** 22 St. Peter's St. (☎ **01227/470379**), *The Canterbury Tales* in book and tape formats join all things Chaucerian, including *Canterbury Tales* T-shirts, St. Justin jewelry from Cornwall, Ellesmere cards, and balls and plates for juggling.

WHERE TO STAY

In spite of all its fame as a tourist destination, Canterbury still lacks a really first-class hotel. What you get isn't bad, but it's not state-of-the-art.

Moderate

The Chaucer Hotel. 63 Ivy Lane (off Lower Bridge St.), Canterbury, Kent CT1 1TU. ☎ **800/225-5843** in the U.S. and Canada, or 01227/464427. Fax 01227/450397. www.heritagehotels.com. 42 units. TV TEL. £105 ($178.50) double. AE, DC, MC, V.

Located on a historic street, the recently refurbished **Chaucer Hotel,** a member of the Forte chain, lies in a Georgian house that stands a few minutes' walk from the cathedral and the Micawber house made famous in *David Copperfield.* Your comfortably furnished room will lie at the end of a labyrinth of stairs, narrow hallways, and doors. (The hotel staff will carry your luggage and park your car.) The best rooms, with views over the rooftops of Canterbury and the cathedral, are nos. 60, 61, and 65. All rooms, however, are named in a wonderfully quirky way that honors former archbishops as well as some of Chaucer's racier pilgrims. Units range from mid-size to most spacious, each chamber evoking a country inn. Accommodations contain such extras as a coffeemaker and a trouser press. The most elegant room is no. 16, the honeymoon chamber with a Henry VIII–style four-poster bed. If you'd like to share a room with a ghost, book no. 62. All the bathrooms are fairly large with a heated rack. The hotel offers limited services, including baby-sitting (prebooked), dry cleaning/laundry, and secretarial services.

You can have a drink in the Pilgrim's Bar, with its Regency mantelpieces and French windows that open to outdoor terraces in summer. The hotel also has a good restaurant, the **63 Ivy Lane,** serving English meals until 9:30pm, and it provides room service.

County Hotel. High St., Canterbury, Kent CT1 2RX. ☎ **01227/766266.** Fax 01227/451512. www.macdonaldhotel.co.uk/county-hotel. E-mail: reservations@county.macdonald-hotels.co.uk. 73 units. TV TEL. £120–£130 ($204–$221) double; £195 ($331.50) suite. AE, DC, MC, V. Parking £2.50 ($4.25).

This is the leading hotel in Canterbury itself. It's been around since the closing years of Victoria's reign, with a recorded history going back to the end of the 12th century.

The time-mellowed atmosphere is exemplified by the residents' lounge on the second floor, with its old timbers and carved antiques. The hotel is constantly refurbished. Its sumptuous suite is the best room in Canterbury. There are also a dozen period rooms with either Georgian or Tudor four-poster beds; opt for these if available. Rooms have thoughtful extras, such as hospitality trays, trouser presses, fruit baskets, and mineral water. Beds are four-poster, half-tester, or carved oak. Baths are tiled and contain a hair dryer.

For fine dining, go to Sully's restaurant, the hotel's air-conditioned dining room (see "Where to Dine," below). For snacks, vegetarian specialties, salads, and hot dishes, the coffee shop may be your best bet. For cocktails, try the Tudor Bar. The hotel also offers 24-hour room service.

Falstaff Hotel. 8–10 St. Dunstan's St., Canterbury, Kent CT2 8AF. ☎ **01227/462138.** Fax 01227/463525. 32 units. TV TEL. £100 ($170) double. AE, DC, MC, V.

Located 400 yards from the West Station, this is a classic Canterbury choice, complete with a flagstone-covered courtyard that retains its sense of history. Next to the Westgate Tower, it has its own parking lot, and easy access to the M2 and M20.

Many of the small, cozy rooms evoke olde England with their polished oak tables, leaded glass windows, and original ceiling beams; most have solid modern furniture. Many of the units are large enough to accommodate small families, and most of the accommodations are designated no-smoking. Public rooms are as cozy as the bedrooms, and even if you aren't staying here, you might want to drop in for a drink at The Falstaff Tap, an ale-and-cider house on the grounds. There is also a comfortable lounge and a good, no-smoking restaurant offering standard English fare prepared with fresh ingredients. The Falstaff's high tea is one of the best in Canterbury.

✪ **Howfield Manor.** Chartham Hatch (2 miles from Canterbury along the A28 Ashford Rd.), Canterbury, Kent CT4 7HQ. ☎ **01227/738294.** Fax 01227/731535. www.howfield.invictanet.com.uk. E-mail:enquiries@howfield.invictanet.co.uk 15 units. TV TEL. £100 ($170) double, £110 ($187) suite. Rates include English breakfast. AE, MC, V. Take the A28 2¼ miles from Canterbury.

Once part of the estate of the Priory of St. Gregory, this is one of the most charming country manors near Canterbury. It's not plush, but it's a good and reliable choice, with enough beams and private nooks to please the traditionalist.

Set on 5 acres of rolling meadows, the house offers snug, attractive rooms with alarm clocks, trouser presses, and solid comfort. Rooms in the original house have more character (exposed beams), whereas rooms in the new wing are larger and furnished with solid oak pieces. All units offer comfortable beds. Baths are small but well appointed with a hair dryer. For a recommendation of the manor's restaurant, Old Well, see "Where to Dine," below.

Ebury Hotel. 65–67 New Dover Rd., Canterbury, Kent CT1 3DX. ☎ **01227/768433.** Fax 01227/459187. www.ebury-hotel.co.uk 15 units. TV TEL. £79 ($134.30) double; £95 ($161.50) triple; £105 ($178.50) quad. Rates include English breakfast. AE, MC, V. Closed Dec 14–Jan 16. Follow the signs to A2, Dover Rd., on left-hand side south of the city.

One of the finest B&Bs in Canterbury, this gabled Victorian house stands on 2 acres of gardens at the edge of the city, within easy walking distance of the city center. It's important to reserve in advance. Built in 1850, it's composed of two separate houses that were joined several years ago; the management also rents flats on a weekly basis. The accommodations are roomy and pleasantly decorated. The rooms range from small to medium, each with traditional styling and containing coffeemakers and small baths, mainly with a tub and shower combination, plus a hair dryer. The hotel has a heated, indoor swimming pool and spa, as well as a spacious lounge and a licensed restaurant serving good English meals prepared with fresh vegetables. Charcoal-grills and dishes based on family recipes are especially good.

Slatters. St. Margaret's St., Canterbury, Kent CT1 2TR. ☎ **01227/463271.** Fax 01227/764117. www.placestosay.com/canterbury-slatterhotel. E-mail: slatters@netcomuk.co.uk. 29 units. TV TEL. £65 ($110.50) double. Rates include English breakfast. AE, DC, MC, V.

In the heart of Canterbury, 200 yards from the cathedral, this building is historic but the rooms are motel-like. Most of them convert into sitting areas with armchairs during the day. Each is furnished with a trouser press and a welcome tray with everything you need to make tea or coffee. The hotel is in the process of modernizing all its rooms and fitting them with better and more comfortable mattresses. Bathrooms are small and compact. The fully licensed French restaurant offers an international menu. Bar snacks are also available at lunchtime.

INEXPENSIVE

Cathedral Gate Hotel. 36 Burgate, Canterbury, Kent CT1 2HA. ☎ **01227/464381.** Fax 01227/462800. E-mail: cgate@cgate.demon.co.uk. 24 units, 12 with bathroom. TV TEL. £44–£54 ($74.80–$91.80) double without bathroom, £79–£81 ($134.30–$137.70) double with bathroom. Rates include continental breakfast. AE, DC, MC, V.

For those who want to stay close to the cathedral and perhaps have a view of it, there is no better choice. Built in 1438, adjoining Christchurch Gate and overlooking the Buttermarket, this former hospice was one of the first fashionable teahouses in England in the early 1600s, and the interior reveals many little architectural details of that century. The rooms are modestly furnished, with sloping floors and massive oak beams. You'll sleep better than the former pilgrims who often stopped over here, sometimes crowding in as many as six and eight in a bed. Rooms with bath have a shower stall and hair dryer; otherwise corridor baths are adequate and you rarely have to wait in line for your turn at them.

Lunchtime bar snacks and dinner are served. The menu is a deliciously sinful throwback to the 1960s—Lancashire hot pot, Cornish pasties, steak and kidney pie, and treacle sponge with custard and cream for dessert. An in-house bar is licensed to serve residents. A courtyard garden with cathedral views is available for guests. The hotel is a 10-minute walk from the train station.

Three Tuns Inn. 24 Watling St. (just off Castle St.), Canterbury, Kent CT1 2UD. ☎ **01227/767371.** Fax 01227/785962. 6 units, 4 with bath. TV TEL. £35 ($59.50) double without bath, £50 ($85) double with bath. AE, DC, MC, V.

In the center of town, this old-fashioned inn derives most of its business from its exceptionally busy pub. Upstairs are a handful of antique bedrooms, which impart a feeling of old-world charm. The inn occupies a fine 15th-century building on the site of an ancient Roman theater. William and Mary, who later became king and queen of England, stopped here in 1679. You can even stay in the room they stayed in—it's attractively furnished and has a four-poster bed. All the accommodations have recently been refurbished, although they still evoke somewhat the aura of the 15th century. Some rooms have a tub and shower combination, but occupants of two units must share a corridor bath. The pub downstairs serves a buffet-style "tavern fare" lunch daily.

A NEARBY PLACE TO STAY

The Old Coach House. Dover Rd., Barham, Kent. ☎ **01227/831218.** Fax 01227/831932. 7 units. TV TEL. £40 ($68) double. MC, V.

The inn stands halfway between Canterbury and Dover on the A2 (southbound), which makes it ideal for exploring, shopping, country walking, or horse riding. A coaching inn in the 19th century, it is now run as a relaxed French country auberge by chef-patron Jean-Claude Rozard and his English wife, Angela. Rooms are a bit small, like a pub hotel, but each has a small bath with a shower stall.

The award-winning restaurant offers a wide range of dishes from local game in season to fresh fish, such as turbot, bass, grilled lobster, and Dover sole. Jean-Claude also offers an imaginative and extensive wine cellar. You truly feel you have crossed the Channel here when you sip French Chardonnay, eat French bread spread with butter from little brown pots, and partake of *moules à la marinière* (mussels cooked in gravy with onions).

WHERE TO DINE

Duck Inn. Pett Bottom, near Bridge. ☎ **01227/830354.** Reservations recommended. Main courses £9–£15 ($15.30–$25.50); 2-course fixed-price lunch Mon–Fri £7.95 ($13.50). AE, MC, V. Daily noon and 7–10pm. Drive 5 miles outside Canterbury near the village of Bridge on the road to Dover. ENGLISH.

Once called the Woodsmen Arms, this restaurant became known as the Duck Inn because of its low door. (As you entered the establishment, the clientele would shout "Duck!") Set in the Pett Bottom valley in a 16th-century structure, it offers traditional English fare. Although there are bar and restaurant areas, diners can sit outdoors in the English country garden during the summer. The menu posted on two chalkboards changes weekly, although a few standard English favorites remain on a permanent basis. For your main course, the menu may include game pies (in season), and some duck preparation is always on the menu. James Bond fans will appreciate this place's location; according to the film *You Only Live Twice,* 007 grew up next door to the Duck Inn.

Old Well Restaurant. At Howfield Manor, Chartham Hatch. ☎ **01227/738294.** Reservations recommended. Main courses £9.95–£16.95 ($16.90–$28.80). AE, MC, V. Daily noon–2pm and 7–9pm. CONTINENTAL.

At this country manor (see Howfield Manor above), nonresidents and guests can enjoy a cuisine served in the chapel part of the manor, dating from 1181. The old well can still be seen; monks drew their water here. Head chef James Wealinds and his brigade create a market-fresh cuisine that's prepared daily. The excellent food is backed up by a homelike atmosphere, friendly service, and a well-chosen wine list. You might start with a smoked haddock and parsley fish cake, and proceed on to sirloin steak with a red onion gravy. Arrive early to enjoy a drink in the Priory Bar, with its trompe l'oeil murals and a real "priesthole" (the bar staff will be delighted to explain what that means, just to get the conversation rolling).

Sully's. In the County Hotel, High St. ☎ **01227/766266.** Reservations recommended. Fixed-price lunch £17–£20 ($28.90–$34) for 3 courses, set dinner £23–£29.50 ($39.10–$50.15). AE, DC, MC, V. Daily 24 hours. ENGLISH/CONTINENTAL.

This restaurant is located in the city's most distinguished hotel. Although the place is without windows and the decor is a bit dated (ca. 1965), the seating and comfort level are first-rate. Considering the quality of the ingredients, the menu offers good value. You can always count on a selection of plain, traditional English dishes, but try one of the more imaginatively conceived platters instead. We recommend the grilled lemon sole, or the roasted pheasant breast with kumquats served on lentils with caramelized apple and a mellow curry cream.

Tuo e Mio. 16 The Borough. ☎ **01227/761471.** Reservations recommended, especially at lunch; call ☎ **01227/472362.** Main courses £7.50–£20 ($12.75–$34); lunch £2.50–£7.50 ($4.25–$12.75). AE, DC, MC, V. Tues 7–10:45pm, Wed–Sun noon–2pm and 7–10:45pm. Closed Mon, the last 2 weeks in Aug, and the last 2 weeks in Feb. ITALIAN.

Tuo e Mio is a bastion of zesty Italian cookery. Signor R. P. M. Greggio, known locally as "Raphael," sets the style and plans the menu at his casual and long-standing bistro. Some dishes are standard, including the pastas, beef, and veal found on most Italian menus, but the daily specials have a certain flair, based on the freshest ingredients available on any given day. Try the fish dishes, including skate, which is regularly featured. A selection of reasonably priced Italian wines accompanies your meal.

CANTERBURY AFTER DARK

The **Gulbenkian Theatre,** University of Kent, Giles Lane (☎ **01227/769075**), is open during school terms (except Cricket Week, the 1st week in Aug) and offers a potpourri of jazz and classical productions, dance, drama, comedy, and a mix of new and student productions. Check newspapers for schedules; tickets cost £4 to £12 ($6.80 to $20.40).

The **Marlowe,** The Friars (☎ **01227/787787**), is Canterbury's only commercial playhouse. It's open year-round and offers drama, jazz and classical concerts, and contemporary and classical ballet. Tickets cost from £10 to £30 ($17 to $51).

A favorite local pub, **Alberry's Wine & Food Bar,** 38A St. Margaret's St. (☎ **01227/452378**), offers live music, mostly jazz, played by local and student groups. Cover charges range from £2 to £3 ($3.40 to $5.10). The menu offers affordable daily specials and light snacks at lunch and dinner.

A laid-back student hangout, **The Cherry Tree,** 10 White Horse Lane (☎ **01227/451266**), offers a wide selection of beers, including Bass Ale on draft, Cherry Tree ale, three traditional lagers, and four bitters. The atmosphere is clubby, filled with casual conversation. If you visit for lunch, you'll find a 32-item menu—the best pub menu in town—plus three types of ploughman's lunch. On Sundays they offer a traditional English roast for £5 ($8.50).

Another good choice on your Canterbury pub crawl is **The Flying Horse,** 1 Dover St. (☎ **01227/463803**), which attracts a garrulous mix of young and old. This 16th-century pub bridges generations from oldsters to the hip student crowd. A weekly quiz night stirs the conversation.

2 The White Cliffs of Dover

76 miles SE of London; 84 miles NE of Brighton

In Victoria's day, Dover basked in popularity as a seaside resort, but today it's known as a port for cross-Channel car and passenger traffic between England and France (notably Calais). Dover was one of England's most vulnerable and easy-to-hit targets during World War II; repeated bombings destroyed much of its harbor. Dover has become more important since the opening of the Channel Tunnel (Chunnel) in 1994.

Unless you're on your way to France or want to use Dover as a base for exploring the surrounding countryside, you can skip a visit here. Dover has always been rather dull except for those white cliffs. Even its hotels are second-rate; many people prefer to stay in Folkestone, about 10 miles to the southwest.

ESSENTIALS

GETTING THERE Frequent trains run between Victoria Station or Charing Cross Station in London and Dover daily from 5am to 10pm. You arrive in Dover at

Priory Station, off Folkestone Road. During the day, two trains per hour depart Canterbury East Station heading for Dover. For rail information, call ☎ **0345/484950.**

Frequent buses leave throughout the day—daily 7:30am to 11pm—from London's Victoria Coach Station bound for Dover. Call ☎ **0990/808080** for schedules. The local bus station is on Pencester Road (☎ **01304/240024**). Stagecoach East Kent provides daily bus service between Canterbury and Dover.

If you're driving from London, head first to Canterbury (see "Essentials," in section 1), then continue along A2 southeast until you reach Dover, on the coast.

VISITOR INFORMATION The Tourist Information Centre is on Townwall Street (☎ **01304/205108**). It's open daily from 9am to 6pm, July and August 8am to 7:30pm.

EXPLORING DOVER

You'll get your best view of the famous ✪ **white cliffs** if you're arriving at Dover by ferry or hovercraft from Calais. Otherwise, you could walk out to the end of the town's Prince of Wales pier, the largest of the town's western docks. The cliffs loom above you. Or you could drive 5 miles east of Dover to the pebble-covered beaches of the fishing hamlet of Deal. Here, a local fisher might take you on an informal boat ride.

Dover Castle. Castle Hill. ☎ **01304/211067** or 01304/201628. Admission £6.90 ($11.75) adults, £3.50 ($5.95) children under 15, £6 ($10.20) seniors and students, £17.30 ($29.40) family. Apr–Sept daily 10am–6pm (last tour at 5pm); Oct daily 10am–5pm (last tour at 4pm); Nov–Mar daily 10am–4pm (last tour at 3pm). Bus no. 90 bound for Deal.

Rising nearly 400 feet above the port is one of the oldest and best-known castles in England. Its keep was built at the command of Becket's fair-weather friend, Henry II, in the 12th century. The ancient castle was called back to active duty as late as World War II. The "Pharos" on the grounds is a lighthouse built by the Romans in the first half of the 1st century. The Romans first landed at nearby Deal in 54 B.C., but after 6 months they departed and didn't return until nearly 100 years later, in A.D. 43, when they stayed and occupied the country for 400 years. The castle houses a military museum and a film center, plus "Live and Let's Spy," an exhibition of World War II spying equipment.

Secret War Time Tunnels. Dover Castle, Castle Hill. ☎ **01304/211067** or 01304/201628. Admission free with castle admission. Open same days and hours as the castle. Last tour leaves 1 hr. before castle closing time. Bus no. 90 bound for Deal.

These secret tunnels, used during the evacuation of Dunkirk in 1940 and the Battle of Britain, can now be explored on a guided tour. The tunnels were originally excavated to house cannons to be used (if necessary) against an invasion by Napoléon. Some 200 feet below ground, they were the headquarters of Operation Dynamo, when more than 300,000 troops from Dunkirk were evacuated. Once forbidden ground to all but those with the strongest security clearance, the networks of tunnels can now be toured. You can stand in the very room where Ramsey issued orders; experience the trauma of life in an underground operating theater; and look out over the English Channel from the hidden, clifftop balcony, just as Churchill did during the Battle of Britain.

✪ **Roman Painted House.** New St. ☎ **01304/203279.** Admission £2 ($3.40) adults, 80p ($1.35) senior and children 16 and under. Apr–Sept Tues–Sun 10am–5pm.

This 1,800-year-old Roman structure, called Britain's "buried Pompeii," has exceptionally well-preserved walls and an under-floor heating system. It's famous for its unique bacchic murals and has won four national awards for presentation. Brass-rubbing is also offered. You'll find it in the town center near Market Square.

Deal Castle. On the seafront. ☎ **01304/372762.** Admission £3 ($5.10) adults, £2.20 ($3.75) seniors, £1.50 ($2.55) children. Apr–Oct daily 10am–6pm; Oct–Mar Wed–Sun 10am–4pm. Closed Dec 24–26.

Deal Castle is just 1 mile north of Walmer Castle and is a quarter mile south of the Deal town center, 5 miles from Dover. A defensive fort built around 1540, it's the most spectacular example of the low, squat forts constructed by Henry VIII. Its 119 gun positions made it the most powerful of his defense forts. Centered around a circular keep surrounded by two rings of semicircle bastions, the castle was protected by an outer moat. The entrance was approached by a drawbridge with a portcullis. The castle was damaged by bombs during World War II, but has been restored to its early form. A free videotape of the castle is included in the admission charge.

WHERE TO STAY

The Churchill. Waterloo Crescent, Dover, Kent CT17 9BP. ☎ **01304/203633.** Fax 01304/216320. www.bestwestern.co.uk. E-mail: reservations@bestwestern.co.uk. 68 units. TV TEL. £80 ($136) double; £93 ($158.10) triple or quad. AE, DC, MC, V.

Dover's most consistently reliable hotel is composed of an interconnected row of town houses built to overlook the English Channel in the 1830s. After World War I, the premises were transformed into a hotel, and in 1994 it was completely refurbished after being acquired by the Henley Lodge hotel chain. There's a seafront balcony, a glass-enclosed front veranda, and tranquil rooms, each with beverage maker. Ranging from small to spacious, many bedrooms offer uninterrupted views of the coast of France. **Eurotunnel travelers** find comfort in the compact bathrooms with hair dryers and shower stalls. The restaurant, Winston's, serves an international menu at lunch and dinner daily. The hotel lies close to the eastern and western docks and the Hoverport for travel to and from France and Belgium.

Forte Posthouse Dover. Singledge Lane, Whitifield, near Dover CT16 3LF. ☎ **0870/4009024.** Fax 01304/825576. 68 units. MINIBAR TV TEL. £69 ($117.30) double. AE, DC, MC, V. Free parking. Lies adjacent to the Whitifield exit of the A2 motorway.

Set 3 miles north of Dover's Center, within a semi-industrial maze of superhighways and greenbelts, this is a member of a national chain that was custom-built as a motel in the 1970s. Bedrooms are carefully positioned so that most of them overlook lawns (and a view of the motorway), fields, and a children's playground next door. Each room is functional and comfortable; bathrooms are extremely compact but tidily maintained. On the premises is a big-windowed, greenhouse-style restaurant, **The Traders,** that's open daily for lunch and dinner. Includes a bar. Lunch is likely to cost £12 ($20.40); dinner, £18.50 ($31.45).

✪ **Wallett's Court.** West Cliffe, St. Margaret's at Cliffe, Dover, Kent CT15 6EW. ☎ **01304/852424.** Fax 01304/853430. www.wallettscourt.com. E-mail: wallettscourt@compuserve.com. 17 units. TV TEL. £75–£120 ($127.50–$204) double. Rates include breakfast. AE, DC, MC, V. Closed 2 weeks at Christmas. Follow A258 for 1½ miles east from the center of Dover (signposted Deal). Wallett's Court is signposted off the A258.

Surrounded by fields and gardens, within a tiny hamlet that's 1½ miles east of Dover, this property was rebuilt in the Jacobean style in the 1400s, on a foundation that dated from the time of the Norman conquest of England. In 1975, in seriously dilapidated condition, it was bought and restored by members of the Oakley family. The setting, near clifftops overlooking the English Channel, is savored by bird watchers and hill climbers. Each of the carefully restored bedrooms features a different decorative theme, with the more expensive ones containing four-poster beds. Some lie within a barn that was comfortably converted into living quarters. Richly accessorized, each has a vivid Edwardian country house motif and lots of mementos. The bathrooms, though small, are neatly organized with a hair dryer and adequate shelf space. There's a restaurant on the premises that's separately recommended in "Where to Dine," below.

WHERE TO DINE

Britannia. 41 Townwall St. ☎ **01304/203248.** Main courses £4.95–£12 ($8.40–$20.40). MC, V. Restaurant daily noon–2:30pm and 6–9pm. Pub Mon–Sat 11am–11pm, Sun noon–10:30pm. INTERNATIONAL.

If you gravitate to typically English, pub-style meals, try this restaurant, whose windows overlook the ferry terminal and the many ships arriving from Calais and Boulogne. Its well-maintained facade has a bow window with lots of gilt and brass nautical accents. The popular pub is on the ground floor and the restaurant on the upper level. The fare is very standard, typical of what you'd get if you stopped to eat along a motorway in England. Try a prawn cocktail or a pâté to start, followed by rump steak or a mixed grill. There's a selection of vegetarian dishes. Dover sole is a specialty, available at market prices. Three TVs in the pub will keep sports fans satisfied.

Topo Gigio. 1–2 King St. ☎ **01304/201048.** Reservations recommended. Pizzas £4.50–£6.50 ($7.65–$11.05); main courses £8–£16 ($13.60–$27.20). AE, DC, MC, V. Winter daily noon–2:30pm. Summer daily noon–10:30pm. ITALIAN.

Established by an Italian entrepreneur from Vicenza, this restaurant was named after the most famous cartoon character in Italy, Topo Gigio, a Mickey Mouse look-alike. Located a short walk from Dover's market square, in a setting accented with brick arches and a wood-burning pizza oven, it serves 15 types of pastas, 16 types of pizzas, and steak, chicken, veal, and fish dishes prepared Italian-style or any way you request. The restaurant's staff and clientele tend to be animated and energetic, which makes an outing here lighthearted and fun. The food's not gourmet, but it's satisfying and filling.

Wallett's Court. West Cliffe, St. Margaret's at Cliffe. ☎ **01304/852424.** Reservations recommended. Main courses £15.50–£21 ($26.35–$35.70); 3-course fixed-price dinner £27.50–£35 ($46.75–$59.50). AE, DC, MC, V. Sun–Fri noon–2pm and daily 7–9pm. Closed 1 week at Christmas. BRITISH/INTERNATIONAL.

One of the most appealing restaurants in the district lies within a half-timbered Jacobean-era manor house, grandly restored over 15 years by Chris Oakley and his family. Within a dining room that's exemplary for its sense of history, you can enjoy dishes such as leek and potato soup; a Kentish huntsman's platter (terrine of game served with apple jelly); salmon with a champagne and shallot sauce; or Scottish Angus beef with a wine and tarragon sauce. The menu changes every month, but meals are always relatively formal, well prepared, and in most cases, very appealing.

3 The Ancient Seaport of Rye

62 miles SE of London

"Nothing more recent than a Cavalier's Cloak, Hat and Ruffles should be seen on the streets of Rye," said Louis Jennings. This ancient town, formerly an island, flourished in the 13th century. In its early days, ✪ **Rye** was a smuggling center, its residents sneaking in contraband from the marshes to stash away in little nooks.

But the sea receded from Rye, leaving it perched like a giant whale out of water, 2 miles from the Channel. Attacked several times by French fleets, Rye was practically razed in 1377. But it rebuilt itself successfully, in full Elizabethan panoply. When Queen Elizabeth I visited in 1573, she was so impressed that she bestowed upon the town the distinction of Royal Rye. This has long been considered a special place and over the years has attracted famous people, such as novelist Henry James.

Its narrow cobblestone streets twist and turn like a labyrinth, and jumbled along them are buildings whose sagging roofs and crooked chimneys indicate the town's medieval origins. The town overflows with sites of architectural interest.

Neighboring Winchelsea has also witnessed the water's ebb. It traces its history from Edward I and has experienced many dramatic moments, such as sacking by the French. In the words of one 19th-century writer, Winchelsea is "a sunny dream of centuries ago." The finest sight of this dignified residential town is a badly damaged 14th-century church containing a number of remarkable tombs.

ESSENTIALS

GETTING THERE From London, the Southern Region Line offers trains south from Charing Cross or Cannon Street Station, with a change at Ashford, before continuing on to Rye. You can also go via Tunbridge Wells with a change in Hastings. Trains run every hour during the day, arriving at the Rye Train Station off Cinque Ports Street. The trip takes 1½ to 2 hours. Call ☎ **0345/484950** for schedules and information.

You'll need to take the train to get to Rye, but once there you'll find buses departing every hour on the hour for many destinations, including Hastings. Various bus schedules are posted on signs in the parking lot. For bus information on connections in the surrounding area, call ☎ **01797/223053.**

If you're driving from London, take M25, M26, and M20 east to Maidstone, going southeast along A20 to Ashford. At Ashford, continue south on A2070.

VISITOR INFORMATION The **Rye Tourist Office** is in the Heritage Centre on the Strand Quay (☎ **01797/226696**). It's open daily from March to the end of October from 9am to 5:30pm; November until February, weekdays from 10am to 4pm and Saturday and Sunday from 10am to 4pm. The Heritage Centre houses a free exhibition and is also home to **Story of Rye,** a sound-and-light show depicting more than 700 years of Rye's history. Adults pay £2 ($3.40), seniors and students £1.50 ($2.55), and children £1 ($1.70).

EXPLORING THE AREA

In Rye, the old town's entrance is **Land Gate,** where a single lane of traffic passes between massive, 40-foot-high stone towers. The parapet of the gate has holes through which boiling oil used to be poured on unwelcome visitors, such as French raiding parties.

Rye has had potteries for centuries and today is no exception, with a number of outlets in town. The best potteries include the **Rye Pottery,** Ferry Road (☎ **01797/223038**); **Rye Tiles,** Wishward Street (☎ **01797/223038**); **David Sharp Ceramics,** The Mint (☎ **01797/222620**); **Iden Pottery,** Conduit Hill (☎ **01797/226920**); and the **Cinque Ports Pottery,** Conduit Hill (☎ **01797/222033**), where you can see the potters at work during the week. The town also abounds in antiques and collectibles shops and new and used bookstores.

St. Mary's Parish Church. Church Square. ☎ **01797/224935.** Admission to tower £2 ($3.40) adults, £1 ($1.70) children. Contributions appreciated to enter the church. June–Aug daily 9am–7pm; off-season daily 9am–4pm.

One notable historical site is the mid-12th-century church with its 16th-century clock flanked by two gilded cherubs (known as Quarter Boys because of their striking of the bells on the quarter hour). The church is often referred to as "the Cathedral of East

Sussex" because of its expansive size and ornate beauty. If you're brave, you can climb a set of wooden stairs and ladders to the bell tower of the church for an impressive view.

Lamb House. West St. (at the top of Mermaid St.). ☎ **01797/890651.** Admission £2.50 ($4.25) adults, £1.25 ($2.15) children. Wed and Sat 2–6pm. Closed Nov–Mar.

Henry James lived at Lamb House from 1898 to 1916. Many James mementos are scattered throughout the house, which is set in a walled garden. Its previous owner rushed off to join the gold rush in North America but perished in the Klondike, and James was able to buy the freehold for a modest £2,000 ($3,400). Some of his well-known books were written here. In *English Hours,* James wrote: "There is not much room in the pavilion, but there is room for the hard-pressed table and tilted chair—there is room for a novelist and his friends."

Rye Castle Museum. Gungarden. ☎ **01797/226728.** Admission £1.50 ($2.55) adults, £1 ($1.70) students and senior citizens, 50p (85¢) children. Apr–Oct daily 10:30am–5:30pm; Nov–Mar Sat–Sun 10:30am–4pm.

This stone fortification was constructed around 1250 by King Henry III to defend the coast against attack by the French. For 300 years it was the town jail but has long since been converted into a museum. In 1996, the Medieval Tower was restored.

Smallhythe Place. Smallhythe (on B2082 near Tenterden, about 6 miles north of Rye). ☎ **01580/762334.** Admission £3.10 ($5.25) adults; £1.50 ($2.55) children; £7.50 ($12.75) family ticket. Apr–Oct Sat–Wed 1–5:30pm. Take bus no. 312 from Tenterden or Rye.

On the outskirts of Winchelsea, this was for 30 years the country house of Dame Ellen Terry, the English actress acclaimed for her Shakespearean roles, and who had a long theatrical association with Sir Henry Irving; she died in the house in 1928. This timber-framed structure, known as a "continuous-jetty house," was built in the first half of the 16th century and is filled with Terry memorabilia—playbills, props, makeup, and a striking display of costumes. An Elizabethan barn, adapted as a theater in 1929, is open to view on most days.

WHERE TO STAY

Some of the best rooms in Rye are at the Benson Hotel on East Street; see "Where to Dine," below for a review of its restaurant.

Durrant House Hotel. Market St. (off High St.), Rye, E. Sussex TN31 3LA. ☎ **01797/223182.** Fax 01797/226940. E-mail:kingslands@compuserve.com. 7 units, 2 with washbasins only, 6 with bath or shower. TV. £50 ($85) double without shower, £60 ($102) double with shower; £80 ($136) suite. Rates include English breakfast. MC, V.

This beautiful Georgian house is set on a quiet residential street at the end of Market Street. The hotel's charm and character are enhanced by a cozy lounge with an arched, brick fireplace. The renowned artist Paul Nash lived next door until his death in 1946; in fact, his celebrated view, as seen in his painting *View of the Rother,* can be enjoyed from the River Room, a four-poster bedroom suite. Bedrooms range from small to medium in size; occupants of two rooms must share a corridor bath. At one time, the house was used as a relay station for carrier pigeons; these birds brought news of the victory at Waterloo.

The George. High St., Rye, E. Sussex TN31 7JP. ☎ **01797/222114.** Fax 01797/224065. 22 units. TV TEL. Mon–Thurs £90 ($153) double. Fri–Sun (minimum of 2 nights required) £100 ($170). AE, DC, MC, V.

This coaching inn has a long history dating from 1575. In the 18th century it drew a diverse clientele: some traveling by horse-drawn carriage, others by boat between

London and France. The half-timbered architecture charms a visitor like no other small inn in the region (except the Mermaid, which has even more of an antique atmosphere). Some of the timbers may be from the wreck of an English ship broken up in Rye Harbour after the defeat of the Spanish Armada. Bedrooms are snug, furnished in traditional English country-house style. Two accommodations are large enough for family use, although most units are a bit small. Five bedrooms are designated as no-smoking. Each of the compact bathrooms has adequate shelf space. You can enjoy moderately priced meals in its old-fashioned restaurant.

Hope Anchor Hotel. Watchbell St., Rye, E. Sussex TN31 7HA. ☎ **01797/222216.** Fax 01797/223796. E-mail: hopeandanchor@cdg.co.uk. 13 units, 12 with bathroom. TV TEL. £50 ($85) double with bathroom. Rates include English breakfast. MC, V.

At the end of a cobblestone street, on a hill dominating the town, stands this 17th-century hostelry, which enjoys panoramic views of the surrounding countryside and overlooks the Strand Quay, where impressive yachts can be seen at their moorings. Oak beams and open fires in winter make this a most inviting place to spend a few days. The comfortable bedrooms all have beverage makers; two feature four-poster beds and have recently been refurbished. Bedrooms range from small to mid-size; baths are small, and often come with a tub and shower combination.

Bar meals are served at lunch and in the evening, and the Hope Anchor Restaurant serves a standard English cuisine, featuring fresh fish caught locally.

✪ **Mermaid Inn.** Mermaid St. (between West St. and The Strand), Rye, E. Sussex TN31 7EU. ☎ **01797/223065.** Fax 01797/225069. 31 units, 29 with private bathroom. TV TEL. £136–£154 ($231.20–$261.80) double. Rates include English breakfast. AE, DC, MC, V.

When Elizabeth came to Rye and the Mermaid in 1573, the inn had already been operating for nearly 150 years. The Mermaid Inn is one of the most famous of the old smugglers' inns of England, known to that band of cut-throats, the real-life Hawkhurst Gang, as well as to Russell Thorndike's fictional character, Dr. Syn. (One of the present rooms, in fact, is called Dr. Syn's Bedchamber, and is connected by a secret staircase, stowed away in the thickness of the wall, to the bar.) This place, with its Elizabethan associations and its traditional touches, remains one of the most romantic, old-world inns in Sussex. The most sought-after rooms are in the building overlooking the cobblestone street. Five units have four-poster beds. The accommodations vary considerably in their shape and size; some are quite large although others are a bit cramped, as befits a building of this age. Comfort is the keynote, regardless of room assignment. Six of the units are spacious enough for use by a small family. Bathrooms are compact but have good maintenance.

Dining: The hotel restaurants specialize in attractively priced, fresh food—freshly caught local fish, Marsh lamb, Sussex beef, and an abundance of locally grown vegetables. Traditional beers are also on tap.

White Vine House. High St., Rye, E. Sussex TN31 7JF. ☎ **01797/224748.** Fax 01797-223599. 6 units. TV. £60–£100 ($102–$170) double. £130 ($221) family room. Rates include English breakfast. AE, DC, MC, V.

The winner of several awards for the beauty of its small front garden and the quality of its restoration, this charming house was originally built in 1568. Restored from an almost derelict shell in 1987, and recently refurbished by its new owners, the creeper-clad inn carefully maintains the Georgian detailing of the formal public rooms and the Tudor-style wall and ceiling beams of the antique bedrooms. The soft beds with fine linens are most comfortable, and the tiny baths are tidily maintained.

Dining: An in-house restaurant, strictly for nonsmokers, serves reasonably priced dinners. The cuisine is healthy and home-styled, with a reduced-fat content. Everything is prepared from the finest local ingredients, from meat to dairy. Even the fish, when possible, comes from Rye boats.

WHERE TO DINE

Our preferred spot for teatime is the **Swan Cottage Tea Rooms,** 41 The Mint, High St. (☎ **01797/222423**), dating from 1420 and situated on the main street. This black and white half-timbered building is one of the most historic in town. We gravitate to the room in the rear because of its big brick fireplace. Delectable pastries and freshly made cakes await you along with a selection of teas, including Darjeeling, Earl Grey, Pure Assam, and others.

✪ **Flushing Inn.** 4–5 Market St., ☎ **01797/223292.** Reservations recommended. Fixed-price meal from £15.50 ($26.35) at lunch, £24.50–£40 ($41.65–$68) at dinner. AE, DC, MC, V. Wed–Mon noon–2pm; Wed–Sun 7–9pm. Closed 1st 2 weeks in Jan. SEAFOOD/ENGLISH.

This is the best restaurant in Rye. This 16th-century inn has preserved the finest of the past, including a wall-size fresco dating from 1544 that depicts a menagerie of birds and heraldic beasts. A rear dining room overlooks a flower garden. A special feature is the Sea Food Lounge Bar, where sandwiches and plates of seafood are available. You can begin with the justifiably praised hors d'oeuvres—a fine selection of smoked fish and shellfish. Main dishes range from locally caught Rye Bay plaice to an old-fashioned loin of English lamb prepared with honey and lavender.

Besides these lunches and dinners, gastronomic evenings are held at regular intervals between October and April. One of these specialty meals costs £50 ($85) per person, including your aperitif, wine, and after-dinner brandy. Fine-wine evenings cost £50–£60 ($85-$102) per person.

In addition, the owners have constructed a luxurious accommodation known as the John Lester Suite within the 15th-century building. It costs £170 ($289) for two persons per night, which includes dinner and a full English champagne breakfast.

The Landgate Bistro. 5–6 Landgate. ☎ **01797/222829.** Reservations required on weekends. Main courses £9–£14 ($15.30–$23.80); fixed-price menu (Tues–Thurs) £15.90 ($27.05). AE, DC, MC, V. Tues–Fri 7–9:30pm, Sat 7–10pm (closing time may vary). MODERN BRITISH.

People come from miles around to dine in this pair of interconnected Georgian shops whose exteriors are covered with "mathematical tiles" (18th-century simulated brick, applied over stucco facades to save money). Inside, Toni Ferguson-Lees and her partner, Nick Parkin, offer savory modern British cuisine. Skillfully prepared dishes might include braised squid with white wine, tomatoes, and garlic; Dover sole; and grilled English lamb with butter beans, bacon, and fresh basil.

4 1066 & All That: Hastings & Battle

Hastings: 45 miles SW of Dover; 63 miles SE of London Battle: 34 miles NE of Brighton; 55 miles SE of London

The world has seen bigger skirmishes, but few are as well remembered as the Battle of Hastings in 1066. When William, duke of Normandy, landed on the Sussex coast and lured King Harold (already fighting Vikings in Yorkshire) southward to defeat, the destiny of the English-speaking people was changed forever.

The actual battle occurred at what is now Battle Abbey (8 miles away), but the Norman duke used Hastings as his base of operations. You can visit the abbey, and then have a cup of tea in Battle's main square, and then you can be off, as the rich countryside of Sussex is much more intriguing than this sleepy market town.

Present-day Hastings is a little seedy and run-down. If you're seeking an English seaside resort, head for Brighton instead.

ESSENTIALS

GETTING THERE Daily trains run hourly from London's Victoria Station or Charing Cross to Hastings. The trip takes 1½ to 2 hours. The train station at Battle is a stop on the London-Hastings rail link. For rail information, call ☎ **0345/484950.**

Hastings is linked by bus to Maidstone, Folkestone, and Eastbourne, which has direct service with scheduled departures. **National Express** operates regular daily service from London's Victoria Coach Station. If you're in Rye or Hastings in summer, several frequent buses run to Battle. For information and schedules, call ☎ **0990/808080.**

If you're driving from the M25 ring road around London, head southeast to the coast and Hastings on A21. To get to Battle, cut south to Sevenoaks and continue along A21 to Battle via A2100.

VISITOR INFORMATION In Hastings, the **Hastings Information Centre** is at Queen's Square, Priory Meadow (☎ **01424/781111**). It's open October to March Monday through Saturday from 10am to 5pm and on Sunday from 10am to 4:30pm; April to September daily from 9:30am to 6pm.

In Battle, the **Tourist Information Centre** is at 88 High St. (☎ **01424/773721**), and is open April through September daily from 10am to 6pm; off-season Monday through Saturday from 10am to 4pm and on Sunday from 10am to 2pm.

EXPLORING THE HISTORIC SITES

✪ **Battle Abbey.** At the south end of Battle High St. (a 5-minute walk from the train station). ☎ **01424/773792.** Admission £4 ($5.95) adults, £2 ($3.40) children, £3 ($5.10) seniors and students. Apr–Sept daily 10am–6pm; Oct daily 10am–5pm; Nov–March daily 10am–4pm.

King Harold, last of the Saxon kings, fought bravely here, not only for his kingdom but for his life. As legend has it, he was killed by an arrow through the eye, and his body was dismembered. To commemorate the victory, William the Conqueror founded Battle Abbey; some of the construction stone was shipped from his own lands at Caen in northern France.

During the Dissolution of the Monasteries from 1538 to 1539 by King Henry VIII, the church of the abbey was largely destroyed. Some buildings and ruins, however, remain in what Tennyson called "O Garden, blossoming out of English blood." The principal building still standing is the Abbot's House, which is leased to a private school for boys and girls and is open to the general public only during summer holidays. Of architectural interest is the gatehouse, which has octagonal towers and stands at the top of Market Square. All of the north Precinct Mall is still standing, and one of the most interesting sights of the ruins is the ancient Dorter Range, where the monks once slept.

The town of Battle flourished around the abbey; even though it has remained a medieval market town, many of the old half-timbered buildings have regrettably lost much of their original character because of stucco plastering carried out by past generations.

Insider's tip: This is a great place for the kids. There's not only a themed play area here, but at the gate a daily activity sheet is distributed. You can relax with a picnic or stroll in the parkland that once formed the monastery grounds.

✪ **Hastings Castle.** Castle Hill Rd., West Hill. ☎ **01424/781112.** Admission £3 ($5.10) adults, £2.40 ($4.10) seniors and students, £2 ($3.40) children. Easter–Sept daily 10am–5pm; Oct–Easter daily 11am–3:30pm. Take the West Hill Cliff Railway from George St. to the castle for 70p ($1.20), 40p (70¢) for children.

In ruins now, the first of the Norman castles built in England sprouted on a western hill overlooking Hastings, around 1067. Precious little is left to remind us of the days when proud knights, imbued with a spirit of pomp and spectacle, wore bonnets and girdles. The fortress was defortified by King John in 1216 and was later used as a church. Owned by the Pelham dynasty from the latter 16th century to modern times, the ruins have been turned over to Hastings. There is now an audiovisual presentation of the castle's history, including the famous battle of 1066. From the mount, you'll have a good view of the coast and promenade.

✪ **The Hastings Embroidery.** The Sussex Hall, White Rock Theatre, White Rock Rd. ☎ **01424/781000.** Admission £2 ($3.40) adults, £1 ($1.70) children and senior citizens. Tues–Sun 11am–4pm.

One of the finest places of modern needlework in Britain is proudly displayed in the theater of a municipal building in the center of town. Crafted by students and teachers at London's **Royal School of Needlework** in London, during the early 1960s, it traces 900 years of English history through a richly embroidered series of panels—27 of them in all. Measuring a total width of 243 feet, they depict 81 historic scenes, including pivotal moments in the country's greatest moments and legends between 1066 and coronation of Elizabeth II. They include: the murder of Thomas à Becket, King John signing the Magna Carta, the Black Plague, Chaucer's pilgrims going to Canterbury, the Battle of Agincourt with the victorious Henry V, the War of the Roses, the Little Princess in the Tower, Bloody Mary's reign, Drake's *Golden Hind,* the arrival of Philip II's ill-fated armada, Guy Fawkes's Gunpowder Plot, the sailing of the *Mayflower,* the disastrous plague of 1665, the great London fire of 1666, Nelson at Trafalgar, the Battle of Waterloo, the Battle of Britain, and the D-day landings at Normandy. Also exhibited is a scale model of the battlefield at Battle, with William's inch-high men doing in Harold's model soldiers.

SEASIDE AMUSEMENTS

Linked by a 3-mile promenade along the sea, Hastings and St. Leonards were given a considerable boost in the 19th century by Queen Victoria, who visited several times. Neither town enjoys such royal patronage today; rather, they do a thriving business with English families on vacation. Hastings and St. Leonards have the usual shops and English sea-resort amusements.

Smugglers Adventure. St. Clements Caves, West Hill. ☎ **01424/422964.** Admission £4.50 ($7.65) adults, £2.90 ($4.95) children, £12.95 ($22) family. Apr–Sept daily 10am–5:30pm; Oct–Mar daily 11am–4:30pm. Take the West Cliff Railway from George St. to West Hill for 70p ($1.20) adults, 40p (70¢) for children.

Here you can descend into the once-secret underground haunts of the smugglers of Hastings. In these chambers, where the smugglers stashed their booty away from Customs authorities, you can see an exhibition and museum, a video in a theater, and take a subterranean adventure walk with 50 life-size figures, along with dramatic sound and lighting effects.

WHERE TO STAY

IN HASTINGS

Beauport Park Hotel. Battle Rd. (A2100), Hastings, E. Sussex TN38 8EA. ☎ **01424/851222.** Fax 01424/852465. 23 units. TV TEL. £110–£120 ($187–$204) double; £125

($212.50) suite. Rates include English breakfast. AE, DC, MC, V. Bus: 4 or 5 from Hastings. Head 3 1/2 miles northwest of Hastings, to the junction of A2100 and B2159.

This hotel has a cozy country-house aura, and is more intimate and hospitable than The Royal Victoria (reviewed below). Originally the private estate of General Murray, former governor of Québec, the building was destroyed by fire in 1923 and rebuilt in the old style. It's surrounded by beautiful gardens; the Italian-style grounds in the rear feature statuary and flowering shrubbery. Rooms range from mid-size to large, and some are fitted with elegant four-poster beds. Nine bedrooms are set aside for non-smokers. Each beautifully maintained bathroom contains a hair dryer. The self-contained Forest Lodge is equipped with a double, twin, children's room, living area, and kitchen, and is available for £140 ($238).

Dining: The hotel offers well-prepared and handsomely arranged meals. Some of the produce comes from the hotel's own gardens. There's a fixed-price lunch and dinner.

Amenities: The parklike grounds offer an outdoor pool, putting green, and tennis, badminton, and croquet.

The Royal Victoria. Marina, St. Leonards, Hastings, E. Sussex TN38 OBD. ☎ **01424/445544.** Fax 01424/721995. www.uk-travelguide.co.uk/royal-vic-hotel. E-mail: reception@royal-vic-hotel.demons.co.uk. 52 units. TV TEL. £95–£115 ($161.50–$195.50) double. Children 15 and under stay free in parents' room. Rates include English breakfast. AE, DC, MC, V.

This seafront hotel, constructed in 1828, has the most impressive architecture in town and offers the best accommodations in Hastings or St. Leonards. It has welcomed many famous visitors, including its namesake, Queen Victoria herself. Many of the elegant and comfortably appointed rooms have separate lounge areas and views of the English Channel and Beachy Head. Many of the bedrooms are extremely large; all of them look as if Laura Ashley traipsed through, as evoked by dozens of half-tester beds in English chintz. Many of the accommodations are large enough for family suites, and a number of them are duplexes. Some of the units are wheelchair accessible. Bathrooms are roomy and fitted with a hair dryer.

Dining: The hotel restaurant serves a fine cuisine; even if you're not staying here, reserve a table. Bar snacks are served from Monday to Saturday. Both traditional and international cuisine are offered, and the all-you-can-eat Sunday carvery is well attended, with its choice of succulent English roasts.

In Battle

The George Hotel. 23 High St., Battle, E. Sussex TN33 OEA. ☎ **01424/774466.** Fax 01424/774853. 20 units. TV TEL. £65 ($110.50) double, £85 ($144.50) double with half board. Rates include breakfast. AE, DC, MC, V.

Although there has been some kind of inn on this site for more than 600 years, the hotel that stands here today dates from 1739. Much renovated since then, the George combines modern comfort with a historic building. The owners offer well-furnished, although rather nondescript, rooms with hot-beverage facilities. The hotel has a comfortable bar, with a full menu.

✪ **Netherfield Place.** Netherfield Rd., Battle, E. Sussex TN33 9PU. ☎ **01424/774455.** Fax 01424/774024. www.netherfieldplace.co.uk. E-mail: reservations@netherfieldplace.co.uk. 14 units. TV TEL. £125–£165 ($212.50–$280.50) double. Rates include English breakfast. AE, DC, MC, V. Closed Dec 15–Jan 15. Take the A2100 1 3/4 miles northwest of Battle.

Built in 1924 on 30 acres of parkland, this is by far the best place to stay in Battle. The symmetrical wings of this brick-fronted neo-Georgian mansion extend toward flowering gardens on all sides. Once you pass beneath the cornices of the entrance, you'll discover a world of exceedingly comfortable bedrooms and sunny panoramas.

The Pomeroy Room, with a four-poster bed, is the most desirable accommodation. Bedrooms come in a range of shapes and sizes, from cozy rooms with dormers on the top floor to very spacious chambers closer to the ground. Thoughtful extras include fresh fruit, flowers, mineral water, and books. Bathrooms are well appointed with bathrobes, fluffy towels, and a hair dryer.

Dining: You can enjoy tea or a drink in the glassed-in lounge overlooking the trees outside. The international cuisine is good, prepared with fresh, wholesome produce. Fresh fruit and vegetables come from the hotel's garden.

WHERE TO DINE

Röser's. 64 Eversfield Place, Hastings. ☎ **01424/712218.** Reservations required. Main courses £16–£21 ($27.20–$35.70); fixed-price lunch £21 ($35.70) fixed-price dinner £24 ($40.80) Tues–Fri. AE, DC, MC, V. Tues–Fri noon–2pm; Tues–Sat 7–10pm. Closed first 2 weeks in Jan. and last 2 weeks in June. FRENCH.

This is a pleasant culinary surprise in the gastronomic wasteland of southern England. The restaurant, in a Victorian row house, is a showcase for chef Gerald Röser, the best chef in East Sussex. Menu choices, which change about every 3 weeks, might include medallions of venison in a savory red wine sauce; fresh, locally caught sea bass served Mediterranean-style; and, in season, wild-boar chop with lentil sauce. Service is first-rate, as is the wine list.

Victoria's Tea Room (D-Day's). 19 Courthouse St., Hastings Old Town. ☎ **01424/465-205.** Cream teas £2.50 ($4.25); sandwiches £1.50–£2 ($2.55–$3.40). No credit cards. Mon–Sat 10am to 4:30 or 5pm; Sun noon–4:30pm.

Courthouse Street in Hasting's Old Town has attracted as many as 17 antiques stores in recent years, creating a kind of mecca for antique buyers. Their hub and centerpiece, and site of endless cups of up to 20 varieties of tea, is this combination tea room and antiques store. The owners, D-Day White (who was born on the day of the famous invasion in Normandy) and Beverly, have transformed their 18th-century premises into the coziest tearoom in town, and filled its nether regions with an intriguing collection of period furniture and "collectible junk" that includes everything from Victorian sideboards to gas masks from World War I. The place is especially appealing when the wind and rain blow in from the Channel.

5 Royal Tunbridge Wells

36 miles SE of London; 33 miles NE of Brighton

Dudley Lord North, courtier to James I, is credited with the accidental discovery in 1606 of the mineral spring that led to the creation of a fashionable resort. Over the years, the "Chalybeate Spring" became known for its curative properties and was the answer for everything from too many days of wine and roses to failing sexual prowess. It's still possible to take the waters today.

The spa resort reached its peak in the mid-18th century under the foppish patronage of Beau Nash (1674–1761), a dandy and final arbiter on how to act, what to say, and even what to wear (for example, he got men to remove their boots in favor of stockings). Tunbridge Wells continued to enjoy a prime spa reputation up through the reign of Queen Victoria, who used to vacation here as a child, and in 1909 Tunbridge Wells received its Royal status.

Today, the spa is long past its zenith. But the town is a pleasant place to stay—it can be used as a base for exploring the many historic homes in Kent (see section 6); it's very easy, for example, to tour Sissinghurst and Chartwell from here.

The most remarkable feature of the town itself is **The Pantiles,** a colonnaded walkway for shoppers, tea drinkers, and diners, built near the wells. If you walk around town, you'll see many other interesting and charming spots. Entertainment is presented at the Assembly Hall and Trinity Arts Centre.

ESSENTIALS

GETTING THERE Two to three trains per hour leave London's Charing Cross Station during the day bound for Hastings, but going via the town center of Royal Tunbridge Wells. The trip takes 50 minutes. For rail information, call ☎ **0345/484950.** There are no direct bus links with Gatwick Airport or London. However, there is hourly service during the day between Brighton and Royal Tunbridge Wells (call ☎ **0345/696996** for the bus schedule). You can purchase tickets aboard the bus.

If you're driving from London, after reaching the ring road around London, continue east along M25, cutting southeast at the exit for A21 to Hastings.

VISITOR INFORMATION The **Tourist Information Centre,** Old Fish Market, The Pantiles (☎ **01892/515675**), provides a full accommodations list and offers a room-reservations service. Open from 9am to 5pm Monday through Saturday (9am to 6pm in summer), and 10am to 4pm Sunday.

WHERE TO STAY

The Russell. 80 London Rd., Royal Tunbridge Wells, Kent TN1 1DZ. ☎ **01892/544833.** Fax 01892/515846. www.russell-hotel.com. E-mail: info@russell-hotel.com. 24 units. TV TEL. £70–£80 ($119–$136) double; from £82 ($139.40) suite. Rates include English breakfast. Discounts usually offered during slow periods. AE, DC, MC, V.

One of the best-recommended hotels at the spa is the Russell, which is composed of three 1875 row-houses that were joined and transformed into a hotel in 1920. Most of the bedrooms in this Victorian pile are spacious and have extras such as an iron and ironing board. 10 rooms are set aside for nonsmokers. The most luxurious way to stay here is in one of five luxury suites in a separate annex, complete with kitchenette. Bathrooms are compact and fitted with adequate shelf space, a set of fluffy towels, and a hair dryer. Overlooking Tunbridge Wells's Common (central square), the hotel is a short walk from the main shopping district. The in-house restaurant features mostly regional dishes and boasts an extensive wine list.

The Spa Hotel. Mt. Ephraim, Royal Tunbridge Wells, Kent TN4 8XJ. ☎ **800/528-1234** in the U.S., or 01892/520331. Fax 01892/510575. www.spahotel.co.uk. E-mail: info@spahotel.co.uk. 71 units. TV TEL. £95–£150 ($161.50–$255) double. Children 13 and under stay free in parents' room. AE, DC, MC, V. From The Pantiles, take Major Yorks Rd.

Standing on 15 acres, this building dates from 1766; once a private home, it was converted to a hotel in 1880, and remains the town's leading hotel to this day. This is the kind of old-fashioned place where many guests check in for long stays. They find bedrooms of various sizes and shapes, as was the custom of buildings like this in the 19th century. All bedrooms are individually furnished, and come with beverage makers; many offer panoramic vistas. Thirteen accommodations are set aside for nonsmokers. Bathrooms are compact and well organized.

Dining/Diversions: The Chandelier Restaurant serves a combination of English and French cuisine. The hotel's most impressive feature is its large lounge with Corinthian columns, although the Equestrian Bar is a cozier retreat.

Amenities: Beauty salon, health club, dance studio, a half-mile jogging track, a sauna, a solarium, tennis courts, and an indoor swimming pool.

WHERE TO DINE

✪ **Thackeray's House.** 85 London Rd. (at the corner of Mt. Ephraim Rd.). ☎ **01892/ 511921.** Reservations required. Main courses £10–£20 ($17–$34); 2-course lunch £13.50 ($22.95). MC, V. Tues–Sun 12:30–2pm; Tues–Sat 7–9pm. ENGLISH/FRENCH.

Thackeray's serves the finest food in town. You get a little history here as well, since this 1660 house was once inhabited by novelist William Makepeace Thackeray, who wrote *Tunbridge Toys* here. Bruce Wass, the owner-chef, worked at one of our favorite restaurants in London, Odin's, before coming here to set up his own place. He has created an elegant atmosphere, backed by attentive service, for his specialties. Care goes into all his dishes, and many have flair, including an occasional salad of preserved duck with quail's eggs. He reaches perfection with roasted saddle of rabbit with grilled polenta and red cabbage, or best end of lamb with dijon mustard and herb-crusted roast garlic.

6 Kent's Country Houses, Castles & Gardens

Many of England's finest country houses, castles, and gardens are in Kent. This is where you'll find the palace of Knole, a premier example of English Tudor-style architecture; Hever Castle, once the childhood home of Anne Boleyn, and later the home of William Waldorf Astor; Leeds Castle, a spectacular castle with ties to America; and Penshurst Place, a stately home which was a literary salon of sorts during the first half of the 17th century. It is said to have inspired Ben Jonson to write one of his greatest poems. Kent also has a bevy of homes that once belonged to famous men but have since been turned into intriguing museums, such as Chartwell, where Sir Winston Churchill lived for many years, and Down House, where Charles Darwin wrote his still-controversial book *On the Origin of Species.* Here you can amble down the same path the naturalist trod every evening.

It would take at least a week to see all of these historic properties—more time than most visitors have. When you make your choices, keep in mind that Knole, Hever, Penshurst, Leeds, and Chartwell are the most deserving of your attention.

We have found the guided tours to some of Kent's more popular stately homes too rushed and too expensive to recommend. Each attraction can be toured far more reasonably on your own. Because public transportation into and around Kent can be awkward, we advise driving from London, especially if you plan to visit more than one place in a day. Accordingly, this section is organized as you might drive it from London. However, if it's possible to get to an attraction via public transportation, we've included that information in the individual listings below.

If you only have a day, you might want to confine your time to Chartwell, former home of Winston Churchill; and Knole, one of England's largest private estates with a vast complex of courtyards and buildings.

An entire second day is needed to visit Leeds Castle and Hever Castle. Note that Leeds allows morning visits. (Most castles and country homes in Kent can only be visited in the afternoon.) That means that you can see Leeds in the morning, then tour Hever Castle that afternoon.

If you have more time for castle-hopping, visit Canterbury Cathedral on the morning of your 3rd day, then tour Penshurst Place in the afternoon. (See section 1 of this chapter for details on Canterbury.) Penshurst is one of the finest Elizabethan houses in England, and its Baron's Hall is one of the greatest interiors to have survived from the Middle Ages.

Two other notable attractions are Sissinghurst Castle Garden and Ightham Mote, a National Trust property dating from 1340. They are open afternoons during the week, and mornings Saturday and Sunday.

✪ **Chartwell.** Near the town of Edenbridge. ☎ **01732/868381.** Admission to house, garden, and studio only £5.50 ($9.35); family tickets are £13.75 ($23.40). Mar 27–Oct 31 11am–5:30pm; Nov 1–Dec 19 11am–4pm (closed Mon–Tues). Closed Dec 20–Mar 26. If you're driving from London, head east along M25, taking the exit to Westerham. Drive 2 miles south of Westerham on B2026 and follow the signs.

This was the late prime minister's home from 1922 until his death. Although not as grand as his birthplace (Blenheim Palace), Chartwell has preserved its rooms as the Conservative politician left them—maps, documents, photographs, pictures, personal mementos, and all. Two rooms display gifts that the prime minister received from people all over the world. There is also a selection of many of his well-known uniforms, including his famous "siren-suits" and hats. Many of Churchill's paintings are displayed in a garden studio. You can see the garden walls that the prime minister built with his own hands and the pond where he sat to feed the Golden Orfe. A restaurant on the grounds serves from 10:30am to 5pm on days when the house is open.

Québec House. At the junction of Edenbridge and Sevenoaks rds. (A25 and B2026). ☎ **01959/562206.** Admission £2.50 ($4.25) adults, £1.25 ($2.15) children. Apr–Oct Sun and Tues only, 2–6pm.

This square, redbrick gabled house was the boyhood home of Gen. James Wolfe, who led the English in their victory over the French in the battle for Québec. Wolfe was born in Westerham on January 2, 1727, and lived here until he was 11 years old. A National Trust property, Québec House contains an exhibition about the capture of Québec and memorabilia associated with the military hero. See, for example, Wolfe's traveling canteen which comes complete with a griddle, frying pans, and decanters, evoking the life of an 18th-century officer on a campaign.

Squerryes Court. 1/2 mile west of the center of Westerham (10 minutes from Exit 6 or Exit 5 on the M25). ☎ **01959/562345.** Admission to house and grounds £4 ($5.95) adults, £3.60 ($6.10) seniors and students, £2.30 ($3.90) children under 14. Grounds only £2.40 ($4.10) adults, £2.10 ($3.55) seniors, £1.40 ($2.40) children under 14. End of Mar–Sept Wed and Sat–Sun, grounds are open noon–5:30pm, house 1:30–5:30pm. Take A25 just west of Westerham and follow the signs.

Built in 1681, and owned by the Warde family for 250 years, this still-occupied manor house has pictures and relics of General Wolfe's family. A house on this site was occupied by the de Squerie family from 1216 until the mid-15th century. The family restored the formal gardens, dotting the banks surrounding the lake with spring bulbs, herbaceous borders, and old roses to retain its beauty year-round, and returned the rooms to their original uses. You can enjoy the fine collection of old-master paintings from the Italian, 17th-century Dutch, and 18th-century English schools, along with antiques, porcelain, and tapestries, all acquired or commissioned by the family in the 18th century. The military hero received his commission on the grounds of the house—the spot is marked by a cenotaph.

Down House. On Luxted Rd., in Downe. ☎ **01689/859119.** Admission £5.50 ($9.35) adults, £4.10 ($6.95) students and seniors, £2.80 ($4.75) children. Apr–Oct Wed–Sun 10am–6pm; Nov–Mar daily 10am–4pm. Closed Dec. 24–26. From Westerham, get on A233 and drive 5 1/2 miles south of Bromley to the village of Downe. Down House is 1/4 mile southeast of the village. From London's Victoria Station, take a train (available daily) to Bromley South, then go by bus no. 146 (Mon–Sat only) to Downe or to Orpington by bus no. R2.

Here stands the final residence of the famous naturalist Charles Darwin. In 1842, upon moving in, he wrote, "House ugly, looks neither old nor new." Nevertheless, he lived there "in happy contentment" until his death in 1882. The drawing room, dining room, billiard room, and old study have been restored to the way they were when Darwin was working on his famous, and still controversial, book *On the Origin of Species,* first published in 1859. The garden retains its original landscaping and a glass house, beyond which lies the Sand Walk or "Thinking Path," where Darwin took his daily solitary walk.

✪ **Knole.** 5 miles north of Tonbridge, at the Tonbridge end of the town of Sevenoaks. ☎ **01732/462100.** Admission to house £5 ($8.50) adults, £2.50 ($4.25) children; family pass £12.50 ($21.25). Admission to gardens £1 ($1.70) adults, 50p (85¢) children. House Apr 1–Nov 1 Wed–Sat noon–4pm, Sun and bank holiday Mon 11am–5pm, Thurs 2–5pm. Gardens open only first Wed of the month in May–Sept 11am–4pm; last admission at 3pm. Park is open daily to pedestrians and open to cars only when the house is. Closed Nov 1–Easter. To reach Knole from Chartwell, drive north to Westerham, pick up A25, and head east for 8 miles. Frequent train service is available from London (about every 30 minutes) to Sevenoaks, and then you can take the connecting hourly bus service, a taxi, or walk the remaining 1½ miles to Knole.

Begun in the mid-15th century by Thomas Bourchier, archbishop of Canterbury, and set in a 1,000-acre deer park, Knole is one of the largest private houses in England and is one of the finest examples of pure English Tudor-style architecture.

Henry VIII liberated the former archbishop's palace from the church in 1537. He spent considerable sums of money on Knole, but there is little record of his spending much time here after extracting the place from the reluctant Archbishop Cranmer; history records one visit in 1541. It was a royal palace until Queen Elizabeth I granted it to Thomas Sackville, first earl of Dorset, whose descendants have lived here ever since. (Virginia Woolf, often a guest of the Sackvilles, used Knole as the setting for her novel *Orlando.*)

The house covers 7 acres and has 365 rooms, 52 staircases, and 7 courts. The elaborate paneling and plasterwork provide a background for the 17th- and 18th-century tapestries and rugs, Elizabethan and Jacobean furniture, and the collection of family portraits. The building was given to the National Trust in 1946.

Insider's tip: If you want to see a bed that's to die for, check out the state bed of James II in the King's Bedroom. And, although most people don't know this, you can actually take afternoon tea at Knole. From the early 17th century, the tearooms here were used as a brew house where beer and ale were brewed regularly. Today, you can enjoy a pot of tea with scones, jam, and cream, or else devour one of their gâteaux such as carrot-and-walnut sponge topped with a cream-cheese-and-lemon-juice icing.

Ightham Mote. ☎ **01732/810378.** Admission £5 ($8.50) adults, £2.50 ($4.25) children; family ticket £12.50 ($21.25); free for children under 5. Mon and Wed–Fri 11:30am–5:30pm, Sun and bank holiday Mon 11am–5:30pm; last admission at 5pm. Closed Nov–Mar. Drive 6 miles east of Sevenoaks on A25 to the small village of Ivy Hatch; the estate is 2½ miles south of Ightham; it's also signposted from A227.

Dating from 1340, Ightham Mote was extensively remodeled in the early 16th century, and remodeling is still going on. The chapel with its painted ceiling, timbered outer wall, and ornate chimneys reflects the Tudor period. You'll cross a stone bridge over a moat to its central courtyard. From the Great Hall, known for its magnificent windows, a Jacobean staircase leads to the old chapel on the first floor, where you go through the solarium, which has an oriel window, to the Tudor chapel.

Unlike many other ancient houses in England that have been occupied by the same family for centuries, Ightham Mote passed from owner to owner, with each family

Touring Leeds Castle: "The Loveliest in the World"

Once described by Lord Conway as the loveliest castle in the world, Leeds Castle (☎ **01622/765400**) dates from A.D. 857. Originally constructed of wood, it was rebuilt in 1119 in its present stone structure on two small islands in the middle of the lake; it was an almost impregnable fortress before the importation of gunpowder. Henry VIII converted it to a royal palace.

The castle has strong ties to America through the sixth Lord Fairfax who, as well as owning the castle, owned 5 million acres in Virginia and was a close friend and mentor of the young George Washington. The last private owner, the Hon. Lady Baillie, who restored the castle with a superb collection of fine art, furniture, and tapestries, bequeathed it to the Leeds Castle Foundation. Since then, the royal apartments, known as *Les Chambres de la Reine* (the queen's chambers), in the Gloriette, the oldest part of the castle, have been open to the public. The Gloriette, the last stronghold against attack, dates from Norman and Plantagenet times, with later additions by Henry VIII.

Within the surrounding parkland is a wildwood garden and duckery where rare swans, geese, and ducks abound. The redesigned aviaries contain a superb collection of birds, including parakeets and cockatoos. Dog lovers will enjoy the Dog Collar Museum at the gate house, with a unique collection of collars dating from the Middle Ages. A 9-hole golf course is open to the public. The Culpepper Garden is a delightful English country flower garden. Beyond are the castle greenhouses, with the maze centered on a beautiful underground grotto and the vineyard recorded in the *Domesday Book.* It is once again producing Leeds Castle English white wine.

Insider's tip: Hurried visitors overlook the Aviary, but it's really special. Opened by Princess Alexandra in 1988, it houses a collection of more than 100 rare species of birds. It aims not only at conservation, but also at successful breeding—to reintroduce endangered species into their original habitats.

From March to October, the park is open daily from 10am to 5pm; the castle, daily from 11am to 5:30pm. From November to February, the park is open daily from 10am to 3pm; the castle, daily from 10:15am to 3:30pm. The castle and grounds are closed on the last Saturday in June and the first Saturday in July before open-air concerts. Admission to the castle and grounds is £9.30 ($15.80) for adults and £6 ($10.20) for children. Students and senior citizens pay £6.80

leaving its mark on the place. When the last private owner, an American who was responsible for a lot of the restoration, died, he bequeathed the house to the National Trust, which chose to keep the Robinson Library laid out as it was in a 1960 edition of *Homes & Gardens.*

Groombridge Place Gardens. Groombridge. ☎ **08192/861444.** Admission £7.50 ($12.75) adults, £6.50 ($11.05) seniors and children. Apr–Oct daily 9am–6pm.

Right outside the spa resort of Royal Tunbridge Wells stands these 17th-century formal gardens, with a vineyard and woodland walks. Part of the complex includes an "Enchanted Forest," an ancient woodland in which the artist, Ivan Hicks, designed a series of "interactive" gardens, using natural objects, native wild flowers, mirrors, and glass to create a mysterious, surreal ambience. The White Rose Garden is compared favorably to that at the fabled Sissinghurst. The English Knot Garden is based on

($11.55). For the grounds only, it's £7.30 ($12.40) adults, £4.30 ($7.30) senior citizens and students, and £4.30 ($7.30) children. Car parking is free, with a free ride on a fully accessible minibus available for those who cannot manage the half-mile-or-so walk from the parking area to the castle.

Trains run frequently from London's Victoria Station to Maidstone. Buses run weekdays from London's Victoria Coach Station to Maidstone, 36 miles to the southeast. If you're driving, from London's ring road, continue east along M26 and M20. The castle is 4 miles east of Maidstone at the junction of the A20 and the M20 London-Folkestone roads.

Snacks, salads, cream teas, and hot meals are offered daily at a number of places on the estate, including Fairfax Hall, a restored 17th-century tithe barn, and the Terrace Restaurant, which provides a full range of hot and cold meals.

Kentish Evenings are presented in Fairfax Hall on the first Saturday of the month throughout the year (except in Aug), starting at 7pm with a cocktail reception, then a private guided tour of the castle. Guests feast on a five course banquet, starting with smoked salmon mousse, followed by broth and roast beef carved at the table, plus seasonal vegetables. A half bottle of wine is included in the overall price of £42 ($71.40) per person. During the meal, musicians play appropriate music for the surroundings and the occasion. Advance reservations are required, made by calling the castle. Kentish Evenings finish at 12:30am, so it's best to stay overnight nearby.

Instead of driving back late at night, you can spend the night at **Grangemoor/Grange Park,** 4–8 St. Michael's Rd. (off Tonbridge Road), Maidstone, Kent ME16 8B5 (☎ **01622/677623;** fax 01622/678246), which are two buildings facing each other across the street. Grangemoor is the main accommodation, with 38 well-furnished rooms, each with private bath, phone, and TV. The cost is £52 ($88.40) for a double, Monday through Thursday, and £50 ($85) on other nights, including an English breakfast. Across the street, Grange Park has only 12 rooms but is similarly furnished, renting for £48 ($81.60) a night, including an English breakfast. Both places are located in a tranquil residential area that's close to the center of Maidstone. There is also a Tudor-style bar and restaurant, offering a three-course meal for £13.50 ($22.95). Children are welcome in both the bar and restaurant area.

paneling in the drawing room of an English country house. In the Fern Valley huge Jurassic plants are as old as time. At the center is Groombridge Place, built on the site of a 12th-century castle and one of the most beautiful moated manor houses in England. Sir Christopher Wren, or so it is believed, helped with the architecture. The palace was built in 1662 by one of the courtiers to King Charles II, Philip Packer. Sir Arthur Conan Doyle was a regular visitor to the house to take part in seances, and the manor was the setting for the Sherlock Holmes mystery, *The Valley of Fear*.

✪ **Penshurst Place.** 6 miles west of Tonbridge. ☎ **01892/870307.** Admission to house and grounds £6 ($10.20) adults, £4 ($5.95) children ages 5–16. Grounds only £4.50 ($7.65) adults, £3.50 ($5.95) children ages 5–16. Children 4 and under enter free. Apr–Oct daily, house noon–5:30pm, grounds 11am–6pm; Nov Sat–Sun only, house noon–5:30pm, grounds 11am–6pm. Closed Nov–Feb. From M25 Junction follow A21 to Tonbridge, leaving at the Tonbridge (North) exit; then follow the brown tourist signs. The nearest mainline station is Tonbridge.

Stately Penshurst Place is one of Britain's outstanding country houses. It is also one of England's greatest defended manor houses, standing in a peaceful rural setting that has changed little over the centuries. In 1338, Sir John de Pulteney, four times lord mayor of London, built the manor house whose Great Hall still forms the heart of Penshurst. The boy king, Edward VI, presented the house to Sir William Sidney, and it has remained in that family ever since. In the first half of the 17th century, Penshurst was known as a center of literature and attracted such personages as Ben Jonson, who was inspired by the estate to write one of his greatest poems.

The Nether Gallery, below the **Long Gallery,** which has a suite of ebony-and-ivory furniture from Goa, houses the Sidney family collection of armor. You can also see the splendid state dining room. In the Stable Wing is a toy museum, with playthings from past generations. On the grounds are nature and farm trails plus an adventure playground for children.

✪ **Hever Castle & Gardens.** ☎ **01732/865224.** Admission to castle and gardens £7.80 ($13.25) adults, £6.60 ($11.20) seniors and students, £4.20 ($7.15) children ages 5–14. Family ticket (2 adults, 2 children) £19.80 ($33.65). Garden only £6.10 ($10.35) adults, £5.20 ($8.85) seniors and students, £4 ($5.95) children ages 5–16. Family ticket £16.20 ($27.55). Children 4 and under enter free. Gardens daily 11am–6pm; castle daily noon–6pm. Closed Dec–Feb. To get here, follow the signs northwest of Royal Tonbridge Wells; it's 3 miles southeast of Edenbridge, midway between Sevenoaks and East Grinstead, and 30 minutes from Exit 6 of M25.

Hever Castle dates from 1270, when the massive gate house, the outer walls, and the moat were first constructed. Some 200 years later, the Bullen (or Boleyn) family added a comfortable Tudor dwelling house inside the walls. Hever Castle was the childhood home of Anne Boleyn, the second wife of Henry VIII and mother of Queen Elizabeth I.

In 1903, William Waldorf Astor acquired the estate and invested time, money, and imagination in restoring the castle, building the "Tudor Village," and creating the gardens and lakes. The Astor family's contribution to Hever's rich history can be appreciated through the castle's collections of furniture, paintings, and objets d'art, as well as the quality of its workmanship, particularly in the wood carving and plasterwork.

The gardens are ablaze with color throughout most of the year. The spectacular Italian Garden contains statuary and sculpture dating from Roman to Renaissance times. The formal gardens include a walled Rose Garden, fine topiary work, and a maze. There's a 35-acre lake and many streams, cascades, and fountains.

✪ **Sissinghurst Castle Garden.** ☎ **01580/715330.** Admission £6 ($10.20) adults, £3 ($5.10) children. Apr to mid-Oct Tues–Fri 1–6:30pm, Sat–Sun and Good Friday 10am–5:30pm. The garden is 53 miles southeast of London and 15 miles south of Maidstone. It's most often approached from Leeds Castle, which is 4 miles east of Maidstone at the junction of the A20 and the M20 London-Folkestone roads. From this junction, head south on B2163 and A274 through Headcorn. Follow the signposts to Sissinghurst.

These spectacular gardens, which are situated between surviving parts of an Elizabethan mansion, were created by one of England's most famous and dedicated gardeners, Bloomsbury writer Vita Sackville-West, and her husband, Harold Nicolson. In spring, the garden is resplendent with flowering bulbs and daffodils in the orchard.

The white garden reaches its peak in June. The large herb garden, a skillful montage that reflects her profound plant knowledge, has something to show all summer long, and the cottage garden, with its flowering bulbs, is at its finest in the fall. Meals are available in the Granary Restaurant. The garden area is flat, so it is wheelchair accessible; however, only two wheelchairs are allowed at a time.

7 Historic Mansions & Gardens in Dorking & Guildford

Dorking, birthplace of Lord Laurence Olivier, lies on the Mole River at the foot of the North Downs. Within easy reach are some of the most scenic spots in the shire, including Silent Pool, Box Hill, and Leith Hill.

The guildhall in Guildford, a country town on the Wey River, has an ornamental projecting clock that dates from 1683. Charles Dickens claimed that High Street, which slopes to the river, was one of the most beautiful in England.

ESSENTIALS

GETTING THERE Frequent daily train service takes 35 minutes from London's Victoria Station to Dorking. The train to Guildford departs from London's Waterloo Station and takes 40 minutes. For rail information, call ☎ **0345/484950.**

Green Line buses (no. 714) leave from London's Victoria Coach Station daily, heading for Kingston with a stop at Dorking. The trip takes 1 hour. National Express operates buses from London's Victoria Coach Station daily, with a stopover at Guildford on its runs from London to Portsmouth. For schedules, call ☎ **0990/808080.** It's usually more convenient to take the train.

If you're driving to Dorking, take A24 south from London. If you're driving to Guildford from London, head south along A3.

VISITOR INFORMATION The **Guildford Tourist Information Centre** is at 14 Tunsgate (☎ **01483/444333**). It's open October through April, Monday through Saturday from 9:30am to 5pm, and from May through September, Monday through Saturday from 9am to 6pm and 10am to 5pm on Sunday.

THE TOP SIGHTS

✪ **Wisley Garden.** Wisley (near Ripley, just off M25, Junction 10, on the A3 London-Portsmouth road). ☎ **01483/224234.** Admission £5 ($8.50) adults, £2 ($3.40) children 6–16; free for children 6 and under. Mon–Fri 10am–dusk; Sat 9am–dusk.

This is one of the great gardens of England. Every season of the year, this 250-acre garden has a profusion of flowers and shrubs, ranging from the alpine meadow carpeted with wild daffodils in spring, Battleston Hill brilliant with rhododendrons in early summer, the heather garden's colorful foliage in the fall, and a riot of exotic plants in the greenhouses in winter. Recent developments include model gardens and a landscaped orchid house. This garden is the site of a laboratory where botanists, plant pathologists, and entomologists experiment and assist amateur gardeners. A large gift shop stocks a wide range of gardening books.

Polesden Lacey. A few miles from Great Bookham, off the A246 Leatherhead-Guildford road. ☎ **01372/452048.** Admission £3 ($5.10) adults; £1.50 ($2.55) children ages 6–17; free for children 5; family ticket £7.50 ($12.75). Grounds daily 10am–6pm. House Easter–Oct Wed–Sun 1:30–5:30pm, except on bank holiday Mon, when hours are 11am–5:30pm.

This former Regency villa was built in 1824. It houses the Greville collection of antiques, paintings, and tapestries. In the early part of this century it was enlarged to become a comfortable Edwardian country house when it was the home of a celebrated hostess, Mrs. Ronald Greville, who frequently entertained royalty from 1906 to 1939. The estate consists of 1,400 acres. Stroll the 18th-century garden, lined with herbaceous borders and featuring a rose garden and beech trees.

Loseley House. Loseley Park (2$^1/_2$ miles southwest of Guildford). ☎ **01483/304440.** Admission £5 ($8.50) adults; £4 ($5.95) students and, seniors; £3 ($5.10) children. June–Aug Wed–Sat 2–5pm.

This beautiful and historic Elizabethan mansion visited by Queen Elizabeth I, James I, and Queen Mary has been featured on TV and in numerous films. Its works of art include paneling from Henry VIII's Nonsuch Palace, period furniture, a unique carved chalk chimneypiece, magnificent ceilings, and cushions made by the first Queen Elizabeth. Lunches and teas are served in the Courtyard Restaurant from 11am to 5pm.

WHERE TO STAY & DINE

IN DORKING

Burford Bridge Hotel. Box Hill, Dorking, Surrey RH5 6BX. ☎ **01306/884561.** Fax 01306/887821. 57 units. TV TEL. Mon–Thurs £165 ($280.50) double, Fri–Sun £80 ($136) double. AE, DC, MC, V. Take the A24 1$^1/_2$ miles north of Dorking.

The Burford Bridge Hotel is the best in Dorking, offering stylish living in a rural town. At the foot of beautiful Box Hill, the hotel has many historical associations. Keats completed "Endymion" here in 1817; Wordsworth and Robert Louis Stevenson also visited the hotel occasionally. You get the best of both the old and the new, including a tithe barn (ca. 1600). Twenty of the bedrooms have been recently refurbished, with more slated for renewal. Bathrooms are compact with a minimum of shelf space and a hair dryer. The restaurant serves good English food, and a bar opens onto a flowered patio with a fountain. In summer, you can enjoy the garden swimming pool and frequent barbecues.

White Horse Hotel. High St., Dorking, Surrey, RH4 1BE. ☎ **800/225-5843** in the U.S. and Canada, or 01306/881138. Fax 01306/887241. www.heritagehotels.com. 69 units. TV TEL. Mon–Thurs £135 ($229.50) double, Fri–Sun £78 ($132.60) double. B&B rates £78 ($132.60) per person Mon–Thurs, AE, MC, V.

This member of the Forte chain, just 10 miles from Gatwick Airport, is supposed to have been the home of the "Marquis of Granby" in the *Pickwick Papers.* Dickens was known to have frequented the bar parlor. Several bedrooms have recently been refurbished but all are comfortable and well maintained with beverage makers. Some units are in a rather sterile modern annex. Bathrooms are small, with minimal shelf space and a hair dryer. Called "the most interesting house in Dorking," the inn has a restaurant, as well as the Pickwick Bar that offers a moderately priced table d'hôte dinner. The hotel also has a rose garden and can arrange a temporary membership in a nearby sports club with its own swimming pool.

IN GUILDFORD

Forte Posthouse Hotel. Egerton Rd., Guildford, Surrey GU2 5XZ. ☎ **01483/574444.** Fax 01483/302960. 165 units. MINIBAR TV TEL. £129 ($219.30) double; £159 ($270.30) suite. AE, MC, V. Head about 2 miles southwest of the center of Guildford, just off A3.

It's only been around for a decade, but a feeling of heritage is conveyed by its natural red-elm joinery, marble floors, and landscaped grounds. The bedrooms incorporate both living and sleeping areas, and all are equipped with beverage makers. Both business travelers and visitors fill the attractively decorated bedrooms, which are generally mid-size. Four are set aside for nonsmokers. The hotel has recently added 20 new units, each better appointed and larger than the older rooms. Bathrooms are compact but with adequate shelf space. The needs of guests with disabilities have been taken into consideration. The hotel has an in-house restaurant called Junctions that serves modern cuisine in a relaxed, informal setting. There's also a health and fitness club with an indoor heated swimming pool and a sun terrace.

Inn on the Lake. Ockford Rd., Godalming, Surrey GU7 1RH. ☎ **01483/419997.** Fax 01483/410852. 17 units. TV TEL. £70 ($119) double. Rates include English breakfast. AE, DC, MC, V. From Guildford, take A3100 south for 3 miles.

This haven of landscaped gardens with ducks drowsing on pools beside the lake is only 3 miles from Guildford. The rooms are decorated with pretty country prints and tasteful furniture, all with tea- and coffeemakers. Thoughtful extras include magazines and sewing kits, plus trouser pressers. Six accommodations have spa baths and private balconies. All the compact bedrooms are well equipped with a set of thick towels and a hair dryer. Excellent snacks are served in a real old-world bar, where some of the timbers date from Tudor times. More substantial dinners (fixed-price menus for Sunday lunch only) are offered, plus à la carte with a varied selection of grills, English favorites, and continental dishes. Room service is available. The house, listed in the *Domesday Book,* has Tudor, Georgian, and Victorian associations. A postwar addition blends more or less gracefully into the complex.

WHERE TO SHARE A PINT

The Jolly Farmer, Millford (☎ **01483/538779**), is a riverside pub, rebuilt in 1913, with a large conservatory and a terraced garden along the River Wey. It offers traditional pub food with homemade specials served daily at lunch and dinner; bar snacks are available all day. A variety of real ales are on tap. Children are welcome until 9pm.

The White House, 8 High St. (☎ **01483/302006**), is another riverside pub, with a conservatory overlooking a lovely waterside garden. Pub grub is available at lunch and dinner; sandwiches are offered all day. They serve traditional London ales aged in barrels.

The **Forger and Firkin,** 55 Woodbridge Rd. (☎ **01483/578999**), is Guildford's only brewpub, producing five ales and offering brewery tours. They also offer traditional English dishes.

8 Haslemere

42 miles SW of London; 37 miles NW of Brighton

In this quiet, sleepy town, early English musical instruments are made by hand and an annual music festival is the town's main drawing card. Over the years, the Dolmetsch family has been responsible for the acclaim that has come to this otherwise unheralded little Surrey town, which lies in the midst of some of the shire's finest scenery.

GETTING THERE

Haslemere is an hour's train ride from Waterloo Station in London. For rail information, call ☎ **0345/484950.**

There is no bus service from London to Haslemere because the train service is so excellent. Once in Haslemere, local buses connect the town to such nearby villages as Farnham and Grayshott.

If you're driving, from Guildford (see "Essentials," in section 7), continue south on A3100, going via Godalming and branching onto A286.

THE HASLEMERE FESTIVAL

In the center of Haslemere rises one of Surrey's most prominent theaters, **Haslemere Hall,** Bridge Road, Haslemere, Surrey GU27 2AS (☎ **01428/642161**). Throughout the year, it presents concerts, musical comedies, and serious dramas, the programs of which change about every month. Throughout the year, someone will usually be on hand to sell tickets and answer questions Monday through Friday from 9am to 1pm and Saturday from 9am to noon.

One of Surrey's musical highlights occurs for 6 days in mid-July, when the Haslemere Festival attracts music aficionados from throughout Europe. At that time, concerts are arranged and administered by civic leaders and members of the family of the festival's founder, Dr. Carl Dolmetsch, the world famous musicologist. They present a program of 16th-, 17th-, and 18th-century chamber music. The music is produced on harpsichords, violas da gamba, recorders, violins, and lutes that either date from those centuries or are reproductions faithfully crafted by the Dolmetsch family in their Haslemere workshops. During the festival, there is a Saturday matinee beginning at 3:15pm; evening performances start at 7:30pm. Tickets range from £8 to £14 ($13.60 to $23.80), depending on seat location and event.

Well-intentioned musicians and music lovers are allowed to visit the **Dolmetsch workshops,** set on the village outskirts, by phoning ahead for a mutually convenient time of arrival. Don't think of it as an outing to a museum; it's a visit to an arts-conscious factory of international renown where musical instruments are manufactured to centuries-old standards. For information, contact **Dolmetsch Musical Instruments,** Unit 1B Unicorn Trading Estate, Weydown Road, Haslemere, Surrey, GU27 1DN (☎ **01428/643235**).

WHERE TO STAY & DINE

✪ **Lythe Hill Hotel.** Petworth Rd., Haslemere, Surrey GU27 3BQ. ☎ **01428/651251.** Fax 01428/644131. www.lythehill.co.uk. E-mail: lythe@lythehill.co.uk. 41 units. TV TEL. £120 ($204) double; £160–£180 ($272–$306) suite. AE, DC, MC, V. Take B2131 1¹/₂ miles east from Haslemere.

This former farmhouse on the outskirts of Haslemere, with parts dating from 1475, is situated on 20 acres of parkland overlooking National Trust woodlands—just an hour from London, Heathrow, and Gatwick. Across the courtyard is the main hotel, with luxuriously appointed bedrooms and suites, as well as an English restaurant. In the black-and-white-timbered farmhouse are five elegant period units with marble-tile baths. One has a four-poster bed from 1614. Regardless of your room assignment, you live in ultimate comfort here. Bathrooms feature quality toiletries, bathrobes, and a hair dryer.

Dining: Downstairs in the farmhouse is the renowned Auberge de France Restaurant, offering a classic French cuisine served by candlelight. Specialties include turbot, *tournedos de bœuf* (small fillet of beef), and a cellar of fine wines.

9 Chichester

31 miles W of Brighton; 69 miles SW of London

Chichester might have been just a market town if the Chichester Festival Theatre had not been born there. One of the oldest Roman cities in England, Chichester draws a crowd from all over the world for its theater presentations. Although it lacks other attractions besides theater, the town makes a good base for exploring a history-rich part of southern England.

ESSENTIALS

GETTING THERE Trains depart for Chichester from London's Victoria Station once every hour during the day. The trip takes 1¹/₂ hours. However, if you visit Chichester to attend the theater, plan to stay over—the last train back to London is at 9pm. For rail information, call ☎ **0345/484950.**

Buses leave from London's Victoria Coach Station once a day. For schedules, call ☎ **0990/808080.**

If you're driving from London's ring road, head south on A3, turning onto A286 for Chichester.

VISITOR INFORMATION The **Tourist Information Centre,** 29A South St. (☎ **01243/775888**), is open Monday through Saturday from 9:15am to 5:15pm, and from April to September, Sunday from 10am to 4pm.

THE CHICHESTER FESTIVAL THEATRE

Only a 5-minute walk from the Chichester Cathedral and the old Market Cross, the 1,400-seat theater, with its apron stage, stands on the edge of Oaklands Park. It opened in 1962, and its first director was none other than Lord Laurence Olivier. Its reputation has grown steadily, pumping new vigor and life into the former walled city, although originally many irate locals felt the city money could have been better spent on a swimming pool instead of a theater.

The ✪ **Chichester Festival Theatre,** built in the 1960s, offers plays and musicals during the summer season, from May to September, and in the winter and spring months, orchestras, jazz, opera, theater, ballet, and a Christmas show for the entire family.

The **Minerva,** built in the late 1980s, is a multifunctional cultural center that includes a theater plus dining and drinking facilities. The Minerva Studio Theatre and the Chichester Festival Theatre are managed by the same board of governors but show different programs and different plays.

Theater reservations made over the telephone will be held for a maximum of 4 days (call ☎ **01243/781312**). It's better to mail inquiries and checks to the Box Office, Chichester Festival Theatre, Oaklands Park, Chichester, West Sussex PO19 4AP. MasterCard, Visa, and American Express are accepted. Season ticket prices range from £5.50 to £22.50 ($9.35 to $38.25). Unreserved seats, sold only on the day of performance, cost £6.50 to £7.50 ($11.05 to $12.75).

A RACETRACK

One of the most famous sports car racing courses in the world, **Goodwood Motor Circuit** (☎ **01243/755055**), reopened in 1998 near Chichester. It has been restored to its look 50 years ago. The course became dangerous for faster cars and was retired as an active track in the 1960s, as the 2.4-mile circuit was never modernized. Now, that is part of its charm, offering a chance to relive the days when courageous drivers raced Jaguars or Ferraris on tracks enveloped by cornfields and hay bales. The course is now used for special exhibition races featuring historic sports cars from the 50s and 60s. The track can be reached by taking the A3 to Milford and the A283 to Petwork, then the A285 to Halnaker, following the signposts from there. Call to see if any exhibitions are being staged during your visit to the area.

SEEING THE SIGHTS NEARBY

In addition to the sights listed below, you might want to stop in nearby **Bosham,** which is primarily a sailing resort and one of the most charming villages in West Sussex. It's 4 miles west of Chichester on A259, and there's good bus service between the two towns. Bosham was the site where Christianity was first established on the Sussex coast. The Danish king, Canute, made it one of the seats of his North Sea empire, and it was the home of a manor (now gone) of the last of England's Saxon kings, Harold, who sailed from here to France on a journey that finally culminated in the invasion of England by William the Conqueror in 1066.

Bosham's little **church** was depicted in the Bayeux Tapestry. Its graveyard overlooks the boats, and the church is filled with ship models and relics, showing the villagers' link to the sea. A daughter of King Canute is buried inside. Near the harbor, it is reached by a narrow lane.

Roman Palace. North of A259, off Salthill Rd. (signposted from Fishbourne; 1½ miles from Chichester). ☎ **01243/785859.** Admission £4.40 ($7.50) adults, £2.30 ($3.90) children, £11.50 ($19.55) family ticket. Nov–Oct daily 10am–5pm (to 6pm in Aug); mid-Feb and Nov daily 10am–4pm; Dec to mid-Feb weekends only 10am–4pm. Buses stop regularly at the bottom of Salthill Rd., and the museum is within a 5-minute walk of British Rail's station at Fishbourne.

This is what remains of the largest Roman residence yet discovered in Britain. Built around A.D. 75 in villa style, it has many mosaic-floored rooms and even an underfloor heating system. The gardens have been restored to their original 1st-century plan. The story of the site is told both by an audiovisual program and by text in the museum. Guided tours are offered twice a day. (See what an archaeological dig in July 1996 unearthed.)

Weald & the Downland Open Air Museum. At Singleton, 6 miles north of Chichester on A286 (the London rd.). ☎ **01243/811348.** Admission £5.20 ($8.85) adults, £2.50 ($4.25) children; family ticket £14 ($23.80). Mar–Oct daily 10:30am–6pm; Nov–Feb Wed and Sat–Sun 10:30am–4pm. Bus no. 60 from Chichester.

In the beautiful Sussex countryside, historic buildings, saved from destruction, are reconstructed on a 40-acre downland site. The structures show the development of traditional building from medieval times to the 19th century, in the weald and downland area of southeast England.

Exhibits include a Tudor market hall, a working water mill producing stoneground flour, a blacksmith's forge, plumbers' and carpenters' workshops, a toll cottage, a charcoal burner's camp, and a 19th-century village school. A "new" reception area with shops and offices is set in Longport House, a 16th-century building rescued from the site of the Channel Tunnel.

WHERE TO STAY IN THE AREA

Marriott Goodwood Park Hotel & Country Club. Goodwood, Chichester PO18 0QB. ☎ **01243/775537.** Fax 01243/520120. www.marriott.com/marriott/pmegs. 96 units. TV TEL. £80–£130 ($136–$221) double. Rates include breakfast. AE, DC, MC, V.

Goodwood House was the home to the dukes of Richmond for more than 300 years. The hotel now located on these grounds was built in the 1786 style of the original Goodwood House. Bedrooms have been refurbished and upgraded, and easily qualify as the best in the area. Some of the rooms open onto panoramic views; all have beverage makers. Sixty-six accommodations are set aside for nonsmokers. Each bathroom is equipped with a hair dryer and efficient shower bath.

Dining: The restaurant serves a fixed-price lunch for £15.95 ($27.10) and a fixed-price dinner for £22.95 ($39). The cuisine is of a high international standard, with the use of fresh, local ingredients when possible. It is closed for lunch on Saturdays. There is also a cafe/bar serving light snacks.

Amenities: There are many leisure activities available, from horseshoes to golf on an 18-hole course.

✪ **Millstream Hotel Bosham Lane.** Bosham, Chichester, W. Sussex PO18 8HL. ☎ **01243/573234.** Fax 01243/573459. 33 units. TV TEL. £115 ($195.50) double; rates include English breakfast. Double room and half board available for £120–£140 ($204–$238). AE, DC, MC, V. Bus: Bosham bus from Chichester. Take the road to the village of Bosham and its harbor, off A27.

The Millstream was originally built in the 1700s to provide food and accommodation for the people and horses who traveled through Sussex from other parts of England. Located 5 miles south of Chichester, the hotel is in the hamlet of Bosham, with its beautiful harbor. Behind a facade of weathered yellow bricks, the hotel exudes a sense of history. The rooms, modern in style, have recently been redecorated and upgraded.

Dining/Diversions: There's a cocktail bar and an adjacent restaurant, where you can order such dishes as beef Wellington and roast Sussex lamb with fresh herbs or Selsey crab.

Ship Hotel. North St., Chichester, W. Sussex PO19 1NH. ☎ **01243/778000.** Fax 01243/788000. 34 units. TV TEL. £109 ($185.30) double. Rates include English breakfast. AE, DC, MC, V.

One of the classic Georgian buildings of the city, the Ship is only a few minutes' walk from the cathedral, the Chichester Festival Theatre, and many fine antiques shops. It was built as a private house in 1790 for Adm. Sir George Murray and still retains an air of elegance and comfort. A grand Adam staircase leads from the main entrance to the bedrooms, which are all named after historic ships. Many of the rooms have recently been refurbished. Extras include a coffeemaker in each room.

Dining/Diversions: Hornblower's Lounge, relatively formal with its own fireplace and rows of books, is an elegant place for a drink. Murray's Restaurant offers good value for the money and features a three-course dinner menu for £18.95 ($32.20) every evening.

✪ **The Spread Eagle Hotel.** South St., Midhurst, W. Sussex GU29 9NH. ☎ **01730/816911.** Fax 01730/815668. www.hshotels.co.uk. E-mail: fleming@virgin.net. 39 units. TV TEL. £125–£205 ($212.50–$348.50) double; £205 ($348.50) suite. Rates include English breakfast. AE, DC, MC, V. Midhurst bus from Chichester.

This 1430 inn, and the market town of Midhurst, are so steeped in history that the room you sleep in and the pavement you walk on have a thousand tales to tell. The rooms here are medieval in character, with beams, small mullioned windows, and unexpected corners. The most elegant have four-poster antique beds, fireplaces, and 500-year-old wall paneling. Most rooms have a shower and tub combination plus a hair dryer. The eagle in the lounge is the actual one from the back of Hermann Göring's chair in the Reichstag. It was acquired for its apt illustration of the hotel's name.

Dining/Diversions: Flickering candles on gleaming tables light this dining hall. The lounge, with its timbered ceiling, is where Elizabeth I and her court may have watched festivities taking place in the Market Square outside.

Amenities: The old has been enhanced by the new with the addition of a health, beauty, and leisure club.

WHERE TO DINE IN THE AREA

Comme ça. 67 Broyle Rd. (a 5-minute walk from the town center). ☎ **01243/788724.** Reservations required. Tues–Sat main courses £10.45–£13.50 ($17.75–$22.95), 2-course lunch £15 ($25.50), 3-course lunch £18.95 ($32.20); Sun 3-course lunch £16.75 ($28.45). MC, V. Tues–Sun 12:15–2pm; Tues–Sat 6–9:30pm. FRENCH.

This is the best French restaurant in town—in fact, the best restaurant, period. The unpretentious decor blends old Victorian and Edwardian prints with objets d'art. The theme continues in the new garden room leading through French doors to an enclosed patio and garden. In summer, you'll want to dine out here, although in winter, a log fire in the inglenook fireplace welcomes you to the bar.

Try delights of the field, river, and forest such as baked fresh Scottish salmon or roasted breasts of pigeons served with armagnac and tarragon sauce. Only the finest-quality ingredients are used. All menus have vegetarian dishes, and special dietary requirements can also be catered to.

White Horse. 1 High St., Chilgrove. ☎ **01243/535219.** Reservations required on weekends. Fixed-price meals £22.50 ($38.25) for 2 courses; £24.50 ($41.65) for 3 courses. AE, MC, V. Tues–Sun noon–3pm and Tues–Sat 6–10pm. Closed Feb, the last week in Oct, and Dec 25–26. Head 6½ miles north of Chichester on B2141 to Petersfield. ENGLISH/FRENCH.

The wine cellar at this informally elegant country restaurant is one of the most comprehensive in Britain. This is partly because of the careful attention the owners pay to the details of their 18th-century inn, whose patina has been burnished every day since it was first built in 1765. The menu is heavy on local game in season, bought from people known by the owners. Menu choices include roast breast of pheasant on a bed of celeriac puree, and roast lamb in a reduced sauce.

A bed-and-breakfast is now available at the adjoining **Forge Cottage,** Chilgrove, Chichester, West Sussex, PO18 QHX (☎ **01243/535333;** fax 01243/535363).

10 Arundel Castle

21 miles W of Brighton; 58 miles SW of London

The small town of Arundel in West Sussex nestles at the foot of one of England's most spectacular castles. Without the castle, it would be just another English market town. The town was once an Arun River port, and its residents enjoyed the prosperity of considerable trade and commerce. Today, however, the harbor traffic has been replaced with buses filled with tourists.

ESSENTIALS

GETTING THERE Trains leave hourly during the day from London's Victoria Station. The trip takes 1¼ hours. For rail information, call ☎ **0345/484950.**

Most bus connections are through Littlehampton, opening onto the English Channel west of Brighton. From Littlehampton, you can leave the coastal road by taking bus no. 11, which runs between Littlehampton and Arundel hourly during the day. If you're dependent on public transportation, the Tourist Information Centre (see below) keeps an update on the possibilities.

If you're driving from London, follow the signs to Gatwick Airport and from there head south toward the coast along A29.

VISITOR INFORMATION The **Tourist Information Centre,** 61 High St. (☎ **01903/882268**), is open from April through October, Monday through Friday from 9am to 5pm and on weekends from 10am to 5pm; off-season Monday through Friday from 10am to 3pm and weekends from 10am to 3pm.

SEEING THE SIGHTS

✪ **Arundel Castle.** On Mill Rd. ☎ **01903/883136.** Admission £7 ($11.90) adults, £6 ($10.20) seniors, £4.50 ($7.65) children 5–15, free for children 4 and under. Family ticket £19 ($32.30). Apr–Oct Sun–Fri noon–5pm. Closed Nov–Mar.

The ancestral home of the dukes of Norfolk, Arundel Castle is a much-restored mansion of considerable importance. Its legend is associated with some of the great families of England—the Fitzalans and the powerful Howards of Norfolk. This castle received worldwide exposure when it was chosen as the backdrop for *The Madness of King George* (it was "pretending" to be Windsor Castle in the film).

Arundel Castle has suffered destruction over the years, particularly during the civil war, when Cromwell's troops stormed its walls, perhaps in retaliation for the 14th earl of Arundel's (Thomas Howard) sizable contribution to Charles I. In the early 18th century, the castle had to be virtually rebuilt, and in late Victorian times it was remodeled and extensively restored again. Today it's filled with a valuable collection of antiques, along with an assortment of paintings by old masters, such as Van Dyck and Gainsborough.

Surrounding the castle, in the center off High Street, is a 1,100-acre park whose scenic highlight is Swanbourne Lake.

Arundel Cathedral. London Rd. ☎ **01903/882297.** Free admission, but donations appreciated. Daily 9:30am–dusk. From the town center, continue west from High St.

A Roman Catholic cathedral, the Cathedral of Our Lady and St. Philip Howard stands at the highest point in town. A. J. Hansom, the inventor of the Hansom taxi, built it for the 15th duke of Norfolk. However, it was not consecrated as a cathedral until 1965. The interior includes the shrine of St. Philip Howard, featuring Sussex wrought-iron work.

On the street level, adjacent to the rooms housing the tourist information office, is the **Heritage of Arundel Museum.** It displays memorabilia, antique costumes, and historic documents relating to the history of Arundel and its famous castle.

WHERE TO STAY IN THE AREA

✪ **Amberley Castle Hotel.** Amberley, near Arundel, W. Sussex BN18 9ND. ☎ **800/525-4800** in the U.S., or 01798/831992. Fax 01798/831998. www.amberleycastle.co.uk. 20 units. TV TEL. £145–£300 ($246.50–$510) double. Rates include English breakfast. AE, DC, MC, V. Take B2139 north of Arundel; the hotel is 1 1/2 miles southwest of Amberley.

The best place for food and lodging is near the village of Amberley. Joy and Martin Cummings offer accommodations in a 14th-century castle with sections dating from the 12th century. Elizabeth I herself held the lease on this castle from 1588 to 1603, and Cromwell's forces attacked it during the civil war. Charles II visited the castle on two occasions. Each of the sumptuous rooms, all doubles, is named after a castle in Sussex, and each has a private Jacuzzi bath as well as a video library. Bedrooms are the ultimate in English country house luxury, here you can choose from a four-poster, a twin four-poster, or a brass double bed. Baths are generous in with their shelf space.

Dining: You don't have to stay here to dine in the 12th-century Queen's Room Restaurant, the area's finest dining room (reserve ahead). The cuisine is classic French and traditional English. Service is daily from 7 to 10am for breakfast and from 7 to 9:30pm for dinner.

Norfolk Arms. 22 High St., Arundel, W. Sussex BN18 9AD. ☎ **01903/882101.** Fax 01903/884275. www.forestdale.com. E-mail: nka@forestdale.com 34 units. TV TEL. £110 ($187) double. Rates include breakfast. AE, DC, MC, V.

A former coaching inn, the Norfolk Arms is on the main street just a short walk from the castle. It's the best place to stay if you want to be in the market town itself. The lounges and dining room are in the typically English country-inn style. The hotel has been restored with many modern amenities blending with the old architecture. The bedrooms are handsomely maintained and furnished, each with personal touches. Rooms vary considerably in size, from small to spacious. Some rooms lie in a separate modern wing overlooking the courtyard. Four bedrooms are large enough for small families. Each unit comes with a small bath with a shower stall.

Dining: In the restaurant, you can order good but standard English food. When available, fresh local produce is offered. You can also order set dinners, which include many traditional English dishes.

Portreeves Acre. 2 Causeway, Arundel, W. Sussex BN18 9JJ. ☎ **01903/883277.** 3 units. TV. £38–£42 ($64.60–$71.40) double. Rates include English breakfast. No credit cards.

When this modern, 2-story house was built by a local architect within a stone's throw of the ancient castle and rail station, it caused much local comment. Today the glass-and-brick edifice is the property of Charles and Pat Rogers. Double guest rooms are on the ground floor and have views of the flowering acre in back. Each bedroom is well organized and includes a small bath with a shower stall. The property is bordered on one side by the River Arun.

WHERE TO DINE

China Palace. 67 High St. ☎ **01903/883702.** Reservations recommended on weekends. Main courses £6–£9 ($10.20–$15.30); fixed-price 3-course dinner for 2 £33 ($56.10). AE, MC, V. Daily noon–2:15pm and 6pm–midnight. BEIJING/SZECHUAN.

The most prominent Chinese restaurant in the region has an elaborately carved 17th-century ceiling, imported by a former owner long ago from a palace in Italy. The interior decorations include the artfully draped sails from a Chinese junk. It's located across the road from the crenellated fortifications surrounding Arundel's castle. The Beijing and Szechuan cuisine includes such classic dishes as Peking duck, king prawns Kung Po, and lobster with fresh ginger and spring onions.

✪ **Queens Room Restaurant.** In the Amberley Castle Hotel, Amberley, near Arundel. ☎ **01798/831992.** Reservations required. 3-course fixed-price dinner £35 ($59.50); 2-course lunch £12.50 ($21.25). AE, DC, MC, V. Daily noon–2pm and 7–9:30pm. ENGLISH/CONTINENTAL.

There is no contest: the best cuisine in the Arundel area is served at this previously recommended hotel. The chef has raided England's culinary past for inspiration, but has given his dishes modern interpretations. We especially admire his use of natural ingredients found in the area—wild Southdown rabbit, lavender, lemon thyme, and nettles. The menu changes frequently, though the special menu of the day is always alluring. The gourmet Castle Cuisine menu is worth driving across Sussex to enjoy. One recent menu contained not only poached halibut with smoky soy broth, but a roasted guinea fowl with sweet potato fondant. The intermediate course was a quince-and-gin water-rice (where else can you find that these days?). Desserts such as a warm gratin of orange and dark chocolate with Grand Marnier sabayon make a perfect finish. The staff is attentive, friendly, yet warmly informal, and there's a well-chosen wine list.

11 Brighton: London by the Sea

52 miles S of London

Brighton was one of the first of the great seaside resorts of Europe. The Prince of Wales (later George IV), the original swinger who was to shape so much of its destiny, arrived in 1783; his presence and patronage gave immediate status to the seaside town.

Fashionable dandies from London, including Beau Brummell, turned up. The construction business boomed as Brighton blossomed with charming and attractive town houses and well-planned squares and crescents. From the Prince Regent's title came the voguish word *Regency,* which was to characterize an era, but more specifically refers to the period between 1811 and 1820. Under Victoria, and despite the fact that she cut off her presence, Brighton continued to flourish.

But earlier in this century, as the English began to discover more glamorous spots on the Continent, Brighton lost much of its old joie de vivre. People began to call it "tatty," and it began to feature the usual run of fun-fair-type English seaside amusements. However, that state of affairs changed long ago, owing largely to the huge number of Londoners who moved in (some of whom now commute); the invasion has made Brighton increasingly lighthearted and sophisticated today. It now attracts a fair number of gay vacationers, and a beach east of town has been set aside for nude bathers (Britain's first such venture).

ESSENTIALS

GETTING THERE Fast trains (41 a day) leave from Victoria or London Bridge Station and make the trip from London in 55 minutes. For rail information, call ☎ **0345/484950.** Buses from London's Victoria Coach Station take around 2 hours.

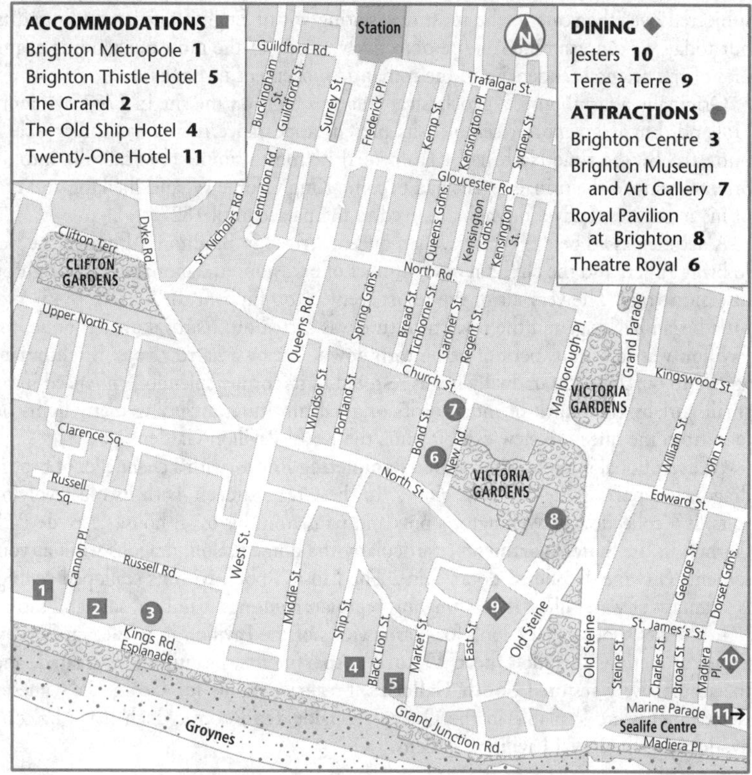

If you're driving, M23 (signposted from central London) leads to A23, which takes you into Brighton.

VISITOR INFORMATION At the **Tourist Information Centre,** 10 Bartholomew Sq. (☎ **01273/292599**), opposite the town hall, you can make hotel reservations, reserve tickets for National Express coaches, and pick up a list of current events. It's open Monday to Friday 9am to 5pm; and Saturday 10am to 4pm. From March to October on Sundays 10am to 4pm.

GETTING AROUND The **Brighton Borough Transport** serves both Brighton and Hove with frequent and efficient service. Local fares are only 70p ($1.15), and free maps giving the company's routes are available at the Tourist Information Centre (see above). You can also call the company directly at **01273/886200.**

SPECIAL EVENTS If you're here in May, the international **Brighton Festival** (☎ **01273/292599**), the largest arts festival in England, features drama, literature, visual art, dance, and concerts ranging from classical to rock. A festival program is available annually in February for those who want to plan ahead.

THE ROYAL PAVILION

✪ **The Royal Pavilion at Brighton.** ☎ **01273/290900.** Admission is £4.90 ($8.35) adults, £3.55 ($6.05) seniors and students, £3 ($5.10) children ages 5–15; free for children 4 and under. June–Sept daily 10am–6pm; Oct–May daily 10am–5pm. Closed Dec 25–26.

Among the royal residences of Europe, the Royal Pavilion at Brighton, a John Nash version of an Indian Moghul's palace, is unique. Ornate and exotic, it has been subjected over the years to the most devastating wit of English satirists and pundits, but today we can examine it more objectively as one of the most outstanding examples of the oriental tendencies of the romantic movement in England.

Originally a farmhouse, a neoclassical villa was built on the site in 1787 by Henry Holland, but it no more resembled its present appearance than a caterpillar does a butterfly. By the time Nash had transformed it from a simple classical villa into an oriental fantasy, the prince regent had become King George IV, and the king and one of his mistresses, Lady Conyngham, lived in the palace until 1827.

A decade passed before Victoria, then queen, arrived in Brighton. Although she was to bring Albert and the children on a number of occasions, the monarch and Brighton just didn't mix. The very air of the resort seemed too flippant for her. By 1845, Victoria began packing, and the royal furniture was carted off. Its royal owners gone, the Pavilion was in serious peril of being torn down, but by a narrow vote, Brightonians agreed to purchase it. Gradually it was restored to its former splendor, enhanced in no small part by the return of much of its original furniture, including many items on loan from the queen. A new exhibit tours the Royal Pavilion Gardens.

Of exceptional interest is the domed **Banqueting Room,** with a chandelier of bronze dragons supporting lily-like glass globes. In the Great Kitchen, with its old revolving spits, is a collection of Wellington's pots and pans from his town house at Hyde Park Corner. In the **State Apartments,** particularly the domed salon, dragons wink at you, serpents entwine, lacquered doors shine. The Music Room, with its scalloped ceiling, is a fantasy of water lilies, flying dragons, reptilian paintings, bamboo, silk, and satin.

In the first-floor gallery, look for Nash's views of the Pavilion in its elegant heyday. Other attractions include **Queen Victoria's Apartments,** beautifully re-created, and the impressively restored **South Galleries,** breakfast rooms for George IV's guests. Refreshments are available in the Queen Adelaide Tea Room, which has a balcony overlooking the Royal Pavilion Gardens.

SEASIDE AMUSEMENTS & ACTIVE PURSUITS

The beaches at Brighton aren't sandy; they're pebbly, and unfortunately, the waters are polluted. So, instead of swimming, most visitors to Brighton sunbathe, promenade along the boardwalk, play video arcade games, drink in local pubs and "caffs," and generally enjoy the sea air. Beachfront areas are more for the promenade crowd, which often consists of gay men and women.

Brighton is also the site of Britain's first officially designed clothing-optional beach, located a short walk west of the Brighton Marina. Local signs refer to it as simply "Nudist Beach." Telescombe Beach, frequented mostly by gay men and lesbians, lies 4½ miles to the east of the Palace Pier.

You can't miss the **Palace Pier,** a somewhat battered late Victorian iron structure jutting seaward toward France. Built between 1889 and 1899 and renovated during the early 1990s, it's lined with somewhat tacky concessions and a late-night crowd that's a bit more sinister than the one that frequents it during the day. The older West Pier is a rusting, abandoned hulk, a solitary reminder of forgotten steam-age pleasures and seafront holidays, with a beach in front that's sometimes used as a rendezvous point for gay men.

If you want to rent or charter a boat, stop by the Brighton Marina, at the intersection of A259 and King's Cliff Parade (☎ **01273/693636**). There's good fishing at the marina as well, but the breakwaters near Hove may be better because there aren't as many boats or swimmers in that area.

One of the best and most challenging 18-hole golf courses around is the **East Brighton Golf Club,** Roedean Road (☎ **01273/604838**). A less challenging 18-hole course is the **Hollingbury Park Golf Club,** Ditching Road (☎ **01273/552010**). Buses from the **Old Steine** are available to both courses.

An indoor pool, diving pool, learner's pool, solarium, and water slide are all available daily at the **Prince Regent Swimming Complex,** Church St. (☎ **01273/685692**).

If you enjoy wagering on the horses, the **Brighton Races** are held frequently between April and October at the **Brighton Racecourse,** Race Hill (☎ **01273/603580**). An admission fee is charged.

SHOPPING

Mall rats head for **Churchill Square,** Brighton's spacious shopping center, which has major chain stores. The shopping center runs from Western Road to North Street (about 2 miles long) and offers many inexpensive shops and stalls with great buys on everything from antiques to woolens. On Saturdays, there are many more antique exhibits and sidewalk stalls.

Regent Arcade, which is located between East Street, Bartholomew Square, and Market Street, sells artwork, jewelry, and other gift items, as well as high-fashion clothing.

Everyone raves about the shopping on **The Lanes,** although you may find them too quaint. The Lanes are a closely knit section of alleyways off North Street in Brighton's Old Town; many of the present shops were formerly fishers' cottages. The shopping is mostly for tourists, and, while you may fall for a few photo ops, you'll find that the nearby **North Laine**—between The Lanes and the train station—is the area for up-and-coming talent and for alternative retail. Just wander along a street called Kensington Gardens to get the whole effect. There are innumerable shops located in The Lanes with antique books and jewelry, and many boutiques are found in converted backyards on Duke Lane just off Ship Street. In the center of The Lanes is Brighton Square, which is ideal for relaxing or for people-watching near the fountain on one of the benches or from a cafe-bar.

On Sunday, Brighton has a good **flea market** in the parking lot of the train station. On the first Tuesday of each month there's the **Brighton Racecourse Antiques and Collectors Fair** (9am to 3pm) with about 300 stalls.

While browsing around the **Brighton Marina,** bargain hunters can find brand-name goods at discount prices at **Merchants Quay Factory Outlet Shopping** (☎ **01273/693636**), with everything from pottery to books, and designer clothes to perfumes. There are many stores to visit at the Brighton Marina. One is **Edinburgh Crystal** (☎ **01273/818702**) where you can find cut-glass decanters, vases, glasses, canteens of cutlery, and more. Another is **Leave It to Jeeves** (☎ **01273/818585**). Here they have old photographs of the local area, illustrations, prints, and a complete framing service.

In addition to its malls and shopping complexes, Brighton also abounds in specialty shops. One of our favorites is the finest gift shop in Brighton, **The Pavilion Shop,** East Street, Brighton (☎ **01273/292798**), next door to The Royal Pavilion. Here you can purchase many gift and home-furnishing items in the style of the design schools that created the look (from Regency to Victorian) at The Royal Pavilion. Also available are books, jams, needlepoint kits, notebooks, pencils, stencil kits, and other souvenirs.

WHERE TO STAY

Gay travelers should refer to "Brighton's Gay Scene," later in this section, for a selection of gay-friendly accommodations.

VERY EXPENSIVE

Brighton Metropole. 106 King's Rd., Brighton, E. Sussex BN1 2FU. ☎ **01273/775432.** Fax 01273/207764. www.stakis.co.uk. E-mail: reservations@stakis.co.uk. 326 units. TV TEL. £160–£226 ($272–$384.20) double; £243–£465 ($413.10–$790.50) suite. Rates include English breakfast. AE, DC, MC, V. Parking £5 ($8.50) . Bus nos. 1, 2, or 3.

Originally built in 1889, with a handful of its rooms housed in a postwar addition, the Brighton Metropole is the largest hotel in Brighton and one of the city's top three or four hotels (although it's not as grand as the Grand). This hotel, with a central seafront location, often hosts big conferences. The recently refurbished rooms are comfortable, with movies, hair dryers, trouser presses, and beverage makers. Rooms are generous in size with key-card locks and roomy sitting areas. The spacious bathrooms include a hair dryer and faux marble vanities. Only the suites have minibars, bedside controls, and robes.

Dining/Diversions: There's an array of dining and drinking choices, among them the Arundel and Windsor restaurants.

Amenities: On the premises is a leisure club, including an indoor swimming pool.

Brighton Thistle Hotel. King's Rd., Brighton, E. Sussex BN1 2GS. ☎ **01273/206700.** Fax 01273/820692. E-mail:brighton@thistle.co.uk 204 units. A/C MINIBAR TV TEL. £170–£200 ($289–$340) double; £350 ($595) suite. Children under 17 stay free in parents' room. AE, DC, MC, V. Bus nos. 1, 2, or 3.

This relatively modern hotel is one of the finest accommodations in the south of England, topped in Brighton only by the Grand. Rising from the seafront, just minutes from the Royal Pavilion, it has been luxuriously designed for maximum comfort. Rooms tend to be large but are often blandly decorated in a sort of international modern style. Each is exceptionally comfortable, with small sitting areas and long desks. Tile baths come with a hair dryer, deluxe toiletries, and even rubber ducks to play with in your bath.

Dining/Diversions: The Promenade restaurant, overlooking the sea, has an imaginative and well-planned menu. Guests and nonresidents can enjoy lunch or dinner here daily. There's also a coffee shop and a bar.

Amenities: 24-hour room service, laundry, baby-sitting, valet parking. The hotel has the best athletic facilities in town—a gym, indoor heated swimming pool, solarium, and sauna.

✪ **The Grand.** King's Rd., Brighton, E. Sussex BN2 1FW. ☎ **01273/224300.** Fax 01273/224321. www.grandbrighton.co.uk. E-mail: reservations@grandbrighton.co.uk. 200 units. A/C TV TEL. £210–£300 ($357–$510) double; from £600 ($1,020) suite. Rates include English breakfast. AE, CB, DC, MC, V. Parking £11 ($18.70). Bus nos. 1, 2, or 3.

This is Brighton's premier hotel. The original Grand was constructed in 1864 and entertained some of the most eminent Victorians and Edwardians. This landmark was massively damaged in a 1984 terrorist attack on Margaret Thatcher and other key figures in the British government. Mrs. Thatcher narrowly escaped, although several of her colleagues were killed, and entire sections of the hotel looked as if they had been hit by an air raid. The incident gave the present owners, De Vere Hotels, the challenge to create a new Grand, and frankly, the new one is better than the old. It's the most elegant Georgian re-creation in town.

You enter via a glassed-in conservatory and register in a grandiose public room, with soaring ceilings and elaborate moldings. The rooms, of a very high standard, are generally spacious with many amenities, including hospitality trays and trouser presses. The sea-view rooms have minibars and new beds and furniture. There are also "romantic rooms" with double whirlpool baths and some rooms equipped with additional facilities for travelers with disabilities. All standard rooms have been refurbished with new bathrooms, each with a hair dryer.

Dining/Diversions: Both British and continental cuisine are served in the King's Restaurant. The kitchen uses superb ingredients. The restaurant serves set menus throughout the week, followed by a Saturday-night dinner-dance with live music. The Victoria Bar is an elegant rendezvous, and Midnight Blues is the most sophisticated club at the resort.

Amenities: Hobden's Health Spa (complete with spa pool, steam room, sauna, solarium, and massage and exercise arena), hair salon, beautician, 24-hour room service, laundry, baby-sitting.

MODERATE

Old Ship Hotel. King's Rd., Brighton, E. Sussex BN1 1NR. ☎ **01273/329001.** Fax 01273/820718. www.brighton.co.uk/hotels/oldship. E-mail:oldship@paramount-hotels.co.uk 152 units. TV TEL. For 1 night from £99–£145 ($168.30–$246.50) double; from £200 ($340) suite. For 2–4 nights from £70 ($119) double; from £120 ($204) suite. Children under 12 stay free in parents' rooms. Rates include English breakfast. AE, DC, MC, V. Parking £10 ($17). Bus nos. 1, 2, or 3.

First used as an inn in 1559, this hotel, a favorite among conference groups, is the largest and best of Brighton's middle-priced choices. The place is proud of its pedigree, and was once the site of royal gatherings and society balls. Most of the hotel's structure dates from the 1880s, and despite many subsequent modernizations, there's still a sense of its old-time late Victorian origins. Nearly two-thirds of the accommodations are nicely furnished, with modern bathrooms; the rest are still somewhat dowdy. The east wing has the most smartly furnished rooms. This may be Brighton's oldest hotel, but it's managed to stay abreast of the times in comfort. Try to stay for more than one night; prices drop if you do.

There are comfortable sea-view lounges, an oak-trimmed bar, and a spacious sea-facing restaurant, the Royal Escape, that naturally specializes in seafood. Meals are nicely prepared and copious.

Topps Hotel. 17 Regency Sq., Brighton, E. Sussex BN1 2FG. ☎ **01273/729334.** Fax 01273/203679. 15 units. MINIBAR TV TEL. £84–£129 ($142.80–$219.30) double. Rates include English breakfast. AE, CB, DC, MC, V. Parking £9.20 ($15.65). Bus: 1, 2, 3, 5, or 6.

This cream-colored hotel enjoys a diagonal view of the sea from its position beside the sloping lawn of Regency Square. Each of the differently shaped and individually furnished accommodations has a radio and a trouser press. In February of 1999, the owners began a gradual refurbishment of all the bedrooms. Except for the singles, most of the rooms have a fireplace. Try, if available, for a unit with a four-poster bed and a private balcony opening onto a view of the sea. Rooms have such extras as a coffeemaker, plus a small bath with a hair dryer.

INEXPENSIVE

Paskins Hotel. 19 Charlotte St., Brighton, E. Sussex BN2 1AG. ☎ **01273/601203.** Fax 01273/621973. 19 units, 16 with shower. TV TEL. £50 ($85) double without shower, £65 ($110.50) double with shower; £85 ($144.50) double with 4-poster bed. Children 10 and under sharing with 2 adults are charged £10 ($17). Rates include English breakfast. AE, DC, MC, V. Bus: 7 or 52.

This well-run small hotel is only a short walk from the Palace Pier and Royal Pavilion. The rates depend on the plumbing and furnishings; the most expensive units are fitted with four-poster beds. Bedrooms are individually decorated with contemporary styling. Each room has a coffeemaker and a trouser press. Bathrooms are compact but tidily maintained, with a shower stall. Recent upgrading has made this one of the more charming B&B properties in Brighton. A friendly, informal atmosphere prevails, and the freshly cooked English breakfast, served in a cozy room, is one of the best in town. For a special rendezvous with someone, retreat to the snug little bar.

Regency Hotel. 28 Regency Sq., Brighton, E. Sussex BN1 2FH. ☎ **01273/202690.** Fax 01273/220438. 13 units, 9 with shower, 1 suite with bathroom. TV TEL. £75 ($127.50) double without shower, £88 ($149.60) double with shower; £125 ($212.50) Regency suite with bath. Rates include English breakfast. AE, DC, MC, V. Parking £12 ($20.40). Bus: 1, 2, 3, 5, or 6.

This typical 1820 Regency town house was once the home of Jane, dowager duchess of Marlborough, and great-grandmother of Sir Winston Churchill. It was skillfully converted into a family-managed hotel with a licensed bar and modern comforts. Each bedroom has a coffeemaker, and many rooms enjoy window views across the square and out to the sea. Bedrooms are non-smoking, although you can smoke in the lounge bar. Rooms come in a variety of shapes and sizes, but each is well furnished with such extras as bedside radios. Bathrooms are small and equipped with a hair dryer. The Regency Suite has a half-tester bed (1840) and antique furniture, along with a huge bow window dressed with ceiling-to-floor swagged curtains and a balcony facing the sea and West Pier. The Regency is only a few minutes' walk from the Conference Center and only an hour by train or car from Gatwick Airport.

✪ **Twenty-One Hotel.** 21 Charlotte St., Marine Parade, Brighton, E. Sussex BN2 1AG. ☎ **01273/686450.** Fax 01273/695560. www.smoothhound.co.uk/hotels/21.html. E-mail: room@the21.co.uk. 7 units. TV TEL. £45–£60 ($76.50–$102) double; £75–£95 ($127.50–$161.50) suite. Rates include English breakfast. AE, DC, MC, V. Bus: 7 or 52.

The most sophisticated of Brighton's smaller hotels, this early Victorian white house is a block from the sea. The owner, Mr. Jung, has completely renovated it. All individually designed rooms now have handmade four-poster beds, and there is new carpeting everywhere, including the bathrooms. The best rooms are the "classics," including a twin green room with two single four-poster beds, a double champagne room decorated in blue and gold with light-pine furnishings, and a double-oak room in rich, deep colors of green and red with a floral design. In addition to the usual amenities (beverage maker, hair dryers), there are toiletries, crackers, sweets, and mineral water in the rooms. Some rooms even have a small fridge. Mr. Jung is well on his way to reaching his goal of owning the best B&B in Brighton.

In Nearby Hove

The Dudley. Lansdowns Place, Hove, Brighton, E. Sussex BN3 1HQ. ☎ **01273/736266.** Fax 01273/729802. 71 units. TV TEL. £107 ($181.90) double. AE, DC, MC, V. Bus nos. 2 or 5.

Near the seafront in Hove, the Dudley—completely redecorated in 1995—is just a few blocks from the resort's bronze statue of Queen Victoria. Going up marble steps, you register within view of 18th-century antiques and oil portraits of Edwardian-era debutantes. The large, high-ceilinged public rooms emphasize the deeply comfortable chairs and the chandeliers. The bedrooms offer coffeemakers, tall windows, and conservatively stylish furniture. Bedrooms are usually mid-size with walnut furnishings, brass lamps, and trouser presses. Bathrooms are well appointed with hair dryers, a bidet, baths with marble basins, and heated racks holding towels. You must pass through a bar to reach the entrance to the dining room, which offers traditional and modern British cuisine. The hotel also offers laundry, baby-sitting, and 24-hour room service.

Sackville Hotel. 189 Kingsway, Hove, Brighton, E. Sussex BN3 4GU. ☎ **01273/736292.** Fax 01273/731598. 45 units. TV TEL. £50–£100 ($85–$170) double; suite (daily) £90 ($153). Rates include English breakfast. AE, DC, MC, V. Bus: 1, 2 and 5.

Its lime- and cream-colored neo-baroque facade was built across the road from the beach in 1902. Today, in a comfortably updated form, the Sackville welcomes visitors with high-ceilinged bedrooms featuring big windows, sea views, and Queen Anne furnishings. Bedrooms range from small to spacious, but each has a well-worn though still comfortable mattress resting on a good bed, plus a compact and tidily maintained bathroom with a shower stall. Eight units have terraces.

A large ground-floor dining room offers a warm, masculine formality, with views of the sea and good service and food. An adjacent bar, Winston's, is filled with photographs of Churchill in war and peace.

WHERE TO DINE

The **Mock Turtle Tea Shop,** 4 Pool Valley (☎ **01273/327380**), is a small but busy tearoom that has many locals stopping by to gossip and take their tea. They offer only a few sandwiches, but the varieties of cakes, flapjacks, tea breads, and light, fluffy scones with homemade preserves are dead-on. Everything is made fresh daily. The most popular item is the scones with strawberry preserves or whipped cream. They also serve a wide variety of good teas.

EXPENSIVE

China Garden. 88 Preston St. (in the town center off Western Rd.). ☎ **01273/325124.** Reservations recommended. Main courses £6–£30 ($10.20–$51); fixed-price menu from £18 ($30.60). AE, DC, MC, V. Mon–Tues noon–10:30pm, Wed–Sun noon–11:30pm. Closed Dec 25–26. BEIJING/CANTONESE.

The menu at the China Garden is large and satisfying. It may not be ready for London, and it's certainly pricey, but it's the brightest in town, with many classic dishes deftly handled by the kitchen staff. Dim sum (a popular luncheon choice) is offered only until 4pm. Try crispy sliced pork Szechuan-style, or Peking roast duck with pancakes.

La Marinade. 77 St. George's Rd., Kemp Town (off King's Cliff along the seafront). ☎ **01273/600992.** Reservations recommended. Main courses £17–£20 ($28.90–$34). AE, DC, MC, V. Tues–Sat 7–10pm. FRENCH.

The cuisine, inspired by Normandy and Brittany, shows a certain subtle preparation. You get a nice range of sensitively cooked dishes; care has been taken to preserve natural flavors. Begin with grilled sardine fillets on leek vinaigrette. The white-butter sauce on our fish dish was just as good as that served in the Loire Valley; you may prefer the Sussex rack of lamb Provençal. Complete the meal with one of the delicious desserts, such as the chocolate delice with orange sorbet.

Old Ship Hotel Restaurant. In the Old Ship Hotel, King's Rd. ☎ **01273/329001.** Reservations recommended. Main courses £12–£15 ($20.40–$25.50). AE, DC, MC, V. Sun–Fri 12:30–2:30pm and daily 7–9:30pm. Bus: 1, 2, or 3. ENGLISH.

A longtime favorite, the Old Ship Restaurant, in the center of town, enjoys an ideal location on the waterfront. Whenever possible, locally caught fish appears on the menu, from Dover sole to panfried red bream fillet. Try such dishes as Magret duck breast, served sliced with a shallot and orange confit and a juniper and red-currant jus. Vegetables, which accompany the main dishes, are always fresh and cooked "new style." Sometimes local dishes such as turkey from Sussex appear on the menu, but with a French sauce. The wine list is excellent. Stop in the adjoining pub for a before- or after-dinner drink.

One Paston Place. 1 Paston Place (near the waterfront off King's Cliff). ☎ **01273/606933.** Reservations required. Main courses £15.50–£17.50 ($26.35–$29.75); fixed-price 2-course lunch £14.50 ($24.65); fixed-price 3-course lunch £16.50 ($28.05). AE, DC, MC, V. Tues–Sat 12:30–2pm and 7:30–10pm. Closed 2 weeks in Jan and 2 weeks in Aug. FRENCH.

Mark (the chef) and Nicole Emmerson offer a wisely limited menu based on the freshest of ingredients available at the market. You might begin with a delectable almond-coated quail and parsnip pancake, then move on to a savory anchovy-studded sea bass with grilled stuffed squid and a lemon and basil couscous. Vegetarian dishes are also available. For dessert try the sumptuous almond and amaretto soufflé with apricot coulis.

MODERATE

English's Oyster Bar and Seafood Restaurant. 29–31 East St. ☎ **01273/327980.** Reservations recommended. Main courses £10.95–£25 ($18.60–$42.50); fixed-price menus £9.95 ($16.90) for 3 courses (not available after 7pm on Fri and Sat). AE, DC, MC, V. Mon–Sat noon–10pm, Sun 12:30–9:30pm. SEAFOOD.

This popular seafood restaurant occupies a trio of very old fisher's cottages and was founded at the turn of the century. Owned and operated by the same family since the end of World War II, it sits in the center of town, near Brighton's bus station. For years, diners have enjoyed native oysters on the half shell, hot seafood platter with hollandaise sauce and garlic butter, fried Dover sole, and fresh, locally caught plaice. The newly refurbished upstairs dining area incorporates murals depicting Edwardian dinner and theater scenes. In summer, guests can dine alfresco on the terrace.

INEXPENSIVE

✪ **Terre à Terre.** 71 East St., ☎ **01273/729051.** Reservations recommended. Main courses £9–£10 ($15.30–$17). DC, MC, V. Tues–Sun noon–10:30pm. VEGETARIAN/VEGAN.

The finest vegetarian restaurant on the south coast of England, this is a truly outstanding choice even if you're a carnivore. You dine in a trio of spacious rooms in vivid colors, and everything has a bustling brasserie aura. The cooks roam the world for inspiration in the preparation of their delectable dishes. Sushi, couscous, pizza—it's all here and does it ever taste good, especially the Spanish-inspired selection of "tapas." Just to get you going, and to give you an idea of what to expect, select as an appetizer a perfectly textured baked Spanish custard with a deliciously crisp and caramelized topping, adorned with a well-ripened passion fruit. Breads are Italian, and the house wine is organic French. Children's helpings are available.

BRIGHTON AFTER DARK

Brighton offers lots of entertainment options. You can find out what's happening by picking up the local entertainment monthly, the *Punter,* and by looking for *What's On,* a single sheet of weekly events posted throughout the town.

There are two theaters that offer drama throughout the year: the **Theatre Royal,** New Road (☎ **01273/328488**), which has pre-London shows, and the **Gardner Arts Center** (☎ **01273/685861**), a modern theater-in-the-round, located on the campus of Sussex University, a few miles northeast of town in Falmer. Bigger concerts are held at **Brighton Centre,** Russell Road (☎ **08709/009100**), a 5,000-seat facility featuring mainly pop-music shows.

Nightclubs also abound. Cover charges range from free admission (most often on early or midweek nights) to £7 ($11.90), so call the clubs to see about admission fees and updates in their nightly schedules, which often vary from week to week or season to season.

The smartly dressed can find their groove at **Steamers,** King's Road (☎ **01273/775432**), located in the Metropole Hotel, which insists on stylish casual attire. The **Paradox,** West Street (☎ **01273/321628**), is a popular club that features Gay Night on Monday, and **The Escape Club,** 10 Marine Parade (☎ **01273/606906**), home to both gay and straight dancers, has two floors for dancing, and offers different music styles on different nights of the week.

One of the best hunting grounds for dance clubs is **Kingswest,** a King's Road complex that houses two clubs featuring a blend of techno, house, and disco. **Event II** (☎ **01273/732627**) sports more than $1 million worth of lighting and dance-floor gadgetry.

Gloucester, Gloucester Plaza (☎ **01273/699068**), has a variety of music through the week, from '70s to '80s music to alternative and groove. For a change of pace, visit **Casablanca,** Middle Street (☎ **01273/321817**), which features jazz with an international flavor.

Pubs are a good place to kick off the evening, especially the **Colonnade Bar,** New Road (☎ **01273/328728**), which has been serving drinks for more than 100 years. The pub gets a lot of theater business because of its proximity to the Theatre Royal. **Cricketers,** Black Lion Street (☎ **01273/329472**), is worth a stop because it's Brighton's oldest pub, parts of which date from 1549. The **Squid and Starfish,** 77 Middle St. (☎ **01273/727114**), is a good place to meet fellow travelers from the neighboring Backpacker's Hostel; and beachside drinking lures them to **Cuba,** 160 King's Rd. (☎ **01273/770505**), and also to **Fortune of War,** 157 King's Rd. (☎ **01273/205065**), which attracts those who don't want to do their drinking at Cuba.

H. J. O'Neils, 27 Ship St. (☎ **01273/827621**), is an authentic Irish pub located at the top of The Lanes. A stop here will fortify you with traditional Irish pub grub, a creamy pint of Guinness, and a sound track of folk music. Of course, they make the best Irish stew in town.

BRIGHTON'S GAY SCENE

After London, Brighton has the most active gay scene in England. Aside from vacationers, it's home to gay retirees and executives who commute into central London by train. The town has always had a reputation for tolerance and humor, and according to the jaded owners of some of the town's 20 or so gay bars, there are more drag queens living within the local Regency town houses than virtually anywhere else in England.

But the gay scene here is a lot less glittery than in London. And don't assume that the south of England is as chic as the south of France. Its international reputation is growing, but despite that, gay Brighton remains thoroughly English, and at times, even a bit dowdy.

GAY-FRIENDLY PLACES TO STAY

Brighton Court Craven Hotel. 2 Atlingworth St., Brighton BN2 1PL. ☎ **01273/607710.** 11 units, all with showers. TV. Mon–Thurs £36 ($61.20) double, Fri–Sun £38 ($64.60) double. Rates include breakfast. MC, V.

This three-story hotel isn't particularly exciting and doesn't have many facilities, but it's the cheapest option we recommend, and it has an atmosphere of casual permissiveness. It's proud of a clientele that's almost 100% gay, and mostly male. Breakfasts are served communally, with all the traditional English accompaniments, and there's a bar. Bedrooms are rather bare-bones: you stay here for the camaraderie—not grand comfort.

Coward's Guest House. 12 Upper Rock Gardens, Brighton BN2 1QE. ☎ **01273/692677.** 6 units, 2 with shower, all with toilet. £45–£60 ($76.50–$102) double. Rates include full English breakfast. MC, V.

Originally built in 1807, this five-story Regency-era house is extremely well maintained. Inside, Jerry and his partner, Cyril (who's a cousin of the late playwright and bon vivant Noël Coward), welcome only gay men of all degrees of flamboyance. Don't expect any frills in the rooms—they're conservative, standard rooms you might find in any modern hotel across Britain. Although there are very few amenities, a number of gay bars and watering holes lie nearby.

New Europe. 31–32 Marine Parade, Brighton BN2 1TR. ☎ **01273/624462.** Fax 01273/624575. 33 units. TV TEL. £45–£50 ($76.50–$85) double. Rates include breakfast. AE, DC, MC, V.

Hands-down, this is the largest, busiest, and most fun gay hotel in Brighton. First, it's a bona fide hotel, not a B&B as most of Brighton's other gay-friendly lodgings are. Unlike many of its competitors, it welcomes women, even though very few of them tend to be comfortable (there are two very loud, very male bars on the premises). Because of the high-jinx and raucousness that sometimes float up from the bars below, rooms can sometimes be noisy, but are nonetheless comfortable, clean, and unfrilly. If you want the staff to camp it up for you before your arrival (adding balloons, champagne, flowers, and streamers), someone on the staff will, for a fee, be happy to comply.

Gay-Friendly Restaurants

Every restaurant in town grew accustomed to gay clients long, long ago, but one spot actively caters to gay patrons.

Jesters. 87 St. James St. (near the New Europe Hotel). ☎ **01273/624233.** Main courses £6.50–£12 ($11.05–$20.40). AE, MC, V. Mon–Fri 5:30–10pm, Sat–Sun noon–10pm.

Large and busy, Jesters is refreshingly unpretentious. Everything about the place, including the alert attentions of a kindly matriarch directing the traffic flow near the entrance, evokes a traditional and very busy English restaurant, with one important exception: Its clientele is almost exclusively gay. You'll find mostly English food (trout, salmon, pork, beef, and vegetarian items) and a few Italian dishes like lasagna, spaghetti Bolognese, and cannelloni.

Gay Nightlife

A complete, up-to-date roster of the local gay bars is available in any copy of G-Scene magazine (☎ **01273/749947**), distributed free in gay hotels and bars throughout the south of England.

See also "Brighton After Dark," above, for a few popular dance clubs.

Doctor Brighton's Bar, 16 Kings Rd., The Seafront (☎ **01273/328765**), is the largest and most consistently reliable choice. The staff expends great energy on welcoming all members of the gay community into its premises. In their words, "We get everyone from 18-year-old designer queens to 50-year-old leather queens, and they, along with all their friends and relatives, are welcome." Originally built around 1750, with a checkered past that includes stints as a smuggler's haven and an abortion clinic, it also has more history, and more of the feel of an old-time Victorian pub than any of its competitors. It's open Monday to Saturday from 11am to 11pm, Sunday from noon to 10:30pm. Since there's no real lesbian bar in town, gay women tend to congregate at Doctor Brighton's.

Two of the town's busiest and most flamboyant gay bars, **Legends** and **Schwarz,** lie within the previously recommended New Europe Hotel. The one with the longer hours is Legends, a pubby, clubby bar with a view of the sea that's open to the public daily from noon to 11pm, and to residents of the New Europe Hotel and their guests till 5am. Legends features cross-dressing cabarets three times a week (Tues and Thurs at 9pm, Sun afternoons at 2:30pm), when tweedy-looking English matrons and diaphanous Edwardian vamps are portrayed with loads of tongue-in-cheek satire and humor. Schwarz is a cellar-level denim and leather joint that does everything it can to encourage its patrons to wear some kind of uniform. Schwarz is open only Friday and Saturday from 10pm to 2am, and charges a£2 ($3.40) cover.

The Marlborough, 4 Princes St. (☎ **01273/570028**), has been a staple on the scene for years. Set across from the Royal Pavilion, this is a Victorian-style pub with a cabaret theater on its second floor. It remains popular with the gay and, to a lesser degree, straight community. A changing roster of lesbian performance art and both gay and straight cabaret within the second-floor theater is presented.

Wanna go dancing? The largest and usually most frenetic gay disco in the south of England is **Club Revenge,** 32-34 Old Steine (☎ **01273/606064**). Combining architectural elements from the Victorian, art deco, and postdisco eras, with a sweeping view over the amusement arcades of the Palace Pier, it has two floors, multiple bars, and a clientele that includes every conceivable subculture within the gay world. Open Monday to Saturday from 9pm to 2am, it charges a 5 to £6 ($10.20) cover.

A SIDE TRIP FROM BRIGHTON TO KIPLING'S HOMETOWN

"Heaven looked after it in the dissolute times of mid-Victorian restoration and caused the vicar to send his bailiff to live in it for 40 years, and he lived in peaceful filth and left everything as he found it," wrote Rudyard Kipling.

He was writing of **Bateman's (☎ 01435/882302),** the 17th-century ironmaster's house in the village of Burwash, on A265, the Lewes-Etchingham road, some 27 miles northeast of Brighton, close to the border with Kent. Born in Bombay, India, in 1865, Kipling loved the countryside of Sussex, and the book that best expressed his feelings for the shire is *Puck of Pook's Hill,* written in 1906. The following year he won the Nobel Prize for literature. He lived at Bateman from 1902 until his death in 1936. His widow died 3 years later at the dawn of World War II, and she left the house to the National Trust.

Kipling is known mainly for his adventure stories, such as *The Jungle Book* (1894) and *Captains Courageous* (1897). He is also remembered for his tales concerning India, including *Kim* (1901). He lived in America after his marriage to Caroline Balestier in 1892. But by 1896, he had returned to the south of England, occupying a house at Rottingdean, a little village on the Sussex Downs, 4 miles east of Brighton. Here he wrote the famous line: "What should they know of England who only England know?" In a steam-driven motorcar, Kipling and Caroline set out to explore Sussex, of which they were especially fond. Although the population of Rottingdean was only that of a small village, they decided at some point that it had become too crowded. In their motorcar one day they spotted Bateman's, which was to become a final home for both of them. "It is a good and peaceable place standing in terraced lawns nigh to a walled garden of old red brick, and two fat-headed oasthouses with redbrick stomachs, and an aged silver-grey dovecot on top," Kipling wrote.

The Burwash city fathers invited Kipling to unveil a memorial to the slain of World War I, and he agreed. It's in the center of town at the church. Kipling said that visitors should "remember the sacrifice." Both the church and an inn across the way appear in the section of *Puck of Pook's Hill* called "Hal o' the Draft." The famous writer and son of Anglo-Indian parents died in London, and was given an impressive funeral before burial in the Poets' Corner at Westminster Abbey.

The interior of Bateman's is filled with Asian rugs, antique bronzes, and other mementos the writer collected in India and elsewhere. Kipling's library is quite interesting. The house and gardens are open April through October, Saturday through Wednesday from 11am to 5:30pm. Admission is £5 ($8.50) for adults, £2.50 ($4.25) for children.

12 Alfriston & Lewes

60 miles S of London

Nestled on the Cuckmere River, Alfriston is one of the most beautiful villages of England. It lies northeast of Seaford on the English Channel, near the resort of Eastbourne and the modern port of Newhaven. During the day, Alfriston is overrun by coach tours (it's that lovely, and that popular). The High Street, with its old market cross, looks just like what you would always imagine a traditional English village to be. Some of the old houses still have hidden chambers where smugglers stored their loot (alas, the loot is gone). There are also several old inns.

Only about a dozen miles away along A27 toward Brighton, is the rather somber market town of Lewes. (Thomas Paine lived at Bull House on High Street, in what is now a restaurant.) Since the home of the Glyndebourne Opera is only 5 miles to the east, it's hard to find a place to stay, even in Lewes, during the renowned annual opera festival.

ESSENTIALS

GETTING THERE Trains leave from London's Victoria Station and London Bridge Station for Lewes. One train per hour makes the 1¼-hour trip daily. Trains are more frequent during rush hours. For rail information, call ☎ **0345/484950.** There is no rail service to Alfriston.

Buses run daily to Lewes from London's Victoria Coach Station, although the 3-hour trip has so many stops that it's better to take the train. Call ☎ **0990/808080** for schedules.

A bus runs from Lewes to Alfriston every 30 minutes. It's operated by **The East Sussex County Busline** and is called Local Rider no. 125. For bus information and schedules in the area, call ☎ **01273/474747.** The bus station at Lewes is on East Gate Street in the center of town.

If you're driving, head east along M25 (the London ring road), cutting south on A26 via East Grinstead to Lewes. Once at Lewes, follow A27 east to the signposted turnoff for the village of Alfriston.

VISITOR INFORMATION The **Tourist Information Centre** is in Lewes at 187 High St. (☎ **01273/483448**). In season, from Easter until the end of October, hours are Monday through Friday from 9am to 5pm, Saturday 10am to 5pm, and Sunday 10am to 2pm. Off-season hours are Monday through Friday only, from 10am to 2pm.

THE GLYNDEBOURNE OPERA FESTIVAL

In 1934, a group of local opera enthusiasts established an opera company based in the hamlet of Glyndebourne, which is 1½ miles east of Lewes and 5 miles northwest of Alfriston. The festival has been running ever since, and is now one of the best regional opera companies in Britain.

In 1994, the original auditorium was demolished, and a dramatic modern glass, brick, and steel structure, designed by noted English architect Michael Hopkins, was built adjacent to some remaining (mostly ornamental) vestiges of the original building. The new auditorium is known for its acoustics.

Operas are presented here only between mid-May and late August, and the productions tend to be unusual works.

For information, contact the **Glyndebourne Festival,** P.O. Box 2624, Glyndebourne (Lewes), E. Sussex BN8 5UW (☎ **01273/812321**). You can call the box office at ☎ **01273/813813.** Tickets range from £10 to £118 ($17 to $200.60). You can usually get last-minute tickets because of cancellations by season ticket holders. But if you want to see a specific show, it's a good idea to buy a ticket several months in advance. Credit Card orders (Visa and MasterCard) are accepted, and there is an additional postage charge if you have the tickets delivered to you. And it's fun to pack your own champagne picnic to enjoy before the performance; you can stock up from shops in Lewes.

To get to the theater from Lewes, take the A26 to the B2192, following the signs to Glynde and Glyndebourne. From Alfriston, follow the hamlet's main street north of town in the direction of highway A27, then turn left following signs first to Glynde, then to Glyndebourne.

EXPLORING THE TWO TOWNS

Lewes has a particularly impressive range of specialty shops, galleries, and craft centers. Our favorite is the **Old Stables Craft Center,** Market Lane (☎ **01273/475433**).

Drusilla's Park. About 1 mile outside Alfriston, off A27. ☎ **01323/870656.** Admission £7.60 ($12.90) adults, £6 ($10.20) seniors, £6.50 ($11.05) children 3–12. Daily 10am–5pm (until 4pm in winter). Closed Dec 24–26.

This fascinating but not-too-large park has a flamingo lake, Japanese garden, and unusual breeds of some domestic animals, among other attractions. The park is perfect for families with children. Check out the newly converted £85,000 bat house, where a family of 20 Rodrigues fruit bats have taken up residence. With a wing span of about 3 feet, and rich golden brown fur, they are one of the most beautiful and rarest bat species in the world.

Anne of Cleves House. 52 Southover High St., Lewes. ☎ **01273/474610.** Admission £2.50 ($4.25) adults, £2.30 ($3.90) students and seniors, £1.20 ($2.05) children. Apr–Nov Mon–Sat 10am–5:30pm, Sun noon–5pm. Dec–Mar Tues, Thurs, and Sat 10am–5:30pm. Bus no. 123.

This half-timbered house was part of Anne of Cleves's divorce settlement from Henry VIII, but Anne never lived in the house and there's no proof that she ever visited Lewes. Today it's a museum of local history, cared for by the Sussex Archaeological Society. The museum has a furnished bedroom and kitchen and displays of furniture, local history of the Wealden iron industry, and other crafts.

Museum of Sussex Archaeology. 169 High St., Lewes. ☎ **01273/486290.** Joint admission ticket to both castle and museum £3.70 ($6.30) adults, £1.90 ($3.25) children, £3.20 ($5.45) students and seniors; family ticket £10.50 ($17.85). Both sites Mon–Sat 10am–5:30pm, Sun 11am–5:30pm. Closed Christmas Day and Boxing Day. Bus no. 27, 28, 121, 122, 166, 728, or 729.

Lewes, of course, matured in the shadow of its **Norman castle.** Adjacent to the castle is this museum, where a 20-minute audiovisual show is available by advance request. Audio tours of the castle are also available.

WHERE TO STAY

IN ALFRISTON

Dean's Place Hotel. Seaford Rd., Polgate, East Sussex BN26 5TW. ☎ **01323/87048.** Fax 01323/870918. 36 units. TV TEL. Summer £108–£174 ($183.60–$295.80) double. Off-season £54.50–£87.50 ($92.65–$148.75). Rates include breakfast. AE, MC, V. On the 2nd roundabout after Lewes take the 3rd exit for Alfriston and Drusilla's Zoo. Pass through Alfriston to the south side. The hotel is on the left hand side of the road.

For English country house living, all at a reasonable price, Dean's Place dates back to the 1300s, although much improved and architecturally altered over the years. Set in landscaped gardens with a putting green and croquet lawn, it is a cliché of English country charm with creeper-covered walls. There's even a swimming pool outdoors if the weather's fair (which it often isn't). Bedrooms come in a variety of sizes, but each is comfortably appointed with firm beds and good plumbing. The staff is polite and helpful, and you can enjoy the good-tasting food during your two-day minimum stay here. You will find the location convenient for visits to Lewes and Brighton, among other places, during your second day here.

Riverdale House. Seaford Rd., Alfriston, East Sussex BN26 5TR. ☎ **01323/871038.** 6 units. TV. £45 ($76.50) double. Rates include breakfast. AE, MC, V.

Set on a hill overlooking the town, this small B&B is one of the finest in the area. A restored Victorian home, it offers handsomely furnished bedrooms in various sizes. Most of them open onto lovely countryside views including a well-kept garden in front. Riverdale also has a large conservatory where guests socialize or else enjoy the reading material. Breakfast is the only meal served, but traditional English meals are just a short walk away at one of the local pubs or dining rooms.

The Star Inn. High St., Alfriston, E. Sussex BN26 5TA. ☎ **01323/870495.** Fax 01323/870922. 34 units. TV TEL. £112 ($190.40) double. AE, DC, MC, V.

The Star Inn—the premier place to stay—occupies a building dating from 1450, although it was originally founded in the 1200s to house pilgrims en route to Chichester and the shrine of St. Richard. Located in the center of the village, its carved front remains unchanged. The lounges are on several levels, a forest of old timbers. We infinitely prefer the rooms in the main building, which have far more character even though they've been altered and renovated over the years. Out back is a more sterile motel wing, with studio rooms. Bedrooms vary in size and style, but each one in the main building is well maintained with an old-world aura. All the bedrooms, including those in the motel wing, contain a small bath.

White Lodge Country House Hotel. Sloe Lane (a 5-minute walk from the village center off A27), Alfriston, E. Sussex BN26 5UR. ☎ **01323/870265.** Fax 01323/870284. 17 units. TV TEL. £105–£146 ($178.50–$248.20) double; £150 ($255) suite. Rates include English breakfast. AE, MC, V. Bus: Southdown no. 712.

This converted private home is opulently furnished and situated amid 5 acres of gardens. The public rooms are outfitted like French salons, with carved 18th- and 19th-century antiques, many of them gilded. Bronze statues inspired by classical Greek myths are placed about. Each of the beautifully furnished rooms has a trouser press and countryside views. There is an English provincial country style aura to the rooms, which are usually mid-size. Each is individually decorated and adorned with plenty of sofas and armchairs. Bathrooms are roomy and have deluxe toiletries and a hair dryer.

Dining: The daytime dining room is French, with Louis XV furniture centered around a chiseled fireplace of violet-tinged marble. Dinner is served below the reception area in an Edwardian room. Three and four-course lunches and dinners are offered daily. Menu specialties include smoked salmon, grilled Dover sole, and, in season, marinated venison. The cooking is sturdy and reliable, almost home-style.

IN LEWES

Shelleys Hotel. High St., Lewes, E. Sussex BN7 1XS. ☎ **01273/472361.** Fax 01273/483152. 19 units. TV TEL. £140–£250 ($238–$425) double; £210 ($357) suite. AE, DC, MC, V.

The earl of Dorset owned this 1526 manor house before it was sold to the Shelley family, wealthy Sussex landowners (and relatives of the poet Percy Bysshe Shelley). Radical changes were made to the architecture in the 18th century. A complete refurbishment in 1994 turned the hotel into a rather luxurious country-house retreat. There are traditional details throughout, such as the family coat of arms in the central hall. Nowadays, the standards of the management are reflected in the fine antiques, the bowls of flowers, the paintings and prints, the well-kept gardens, and most importantly, the helpful staff. The bedrooms are personal, individually furnished, usually spacious, and most comfortable. Room 11 has a 16th-century frieze of bacchanalian figures and a design of entwining grapes and flowers. Each unit has such extras as three telephones, coffeemakers, plus well-appointed baths with a hair dryer and spotless maintenance.

Dining: The chef often manages to surprise and delight, with, perhaps, a salad of wood pigeon and braised quails (laced with a tarragon and truffle vinaigrette), followed by steamed sea bass with oranges and lemons in white wine or venison terrine with poached figs. In the rear is a sun terrace and lawn for tea and drinks; horse chestnuts and copper beech shade the grounds. There's also a lounge with its blazing fireplace.

WHERE TO DINE

IN ALFRISTON

Around teatime, head for **The Tudor House,** on Alfriston's High Street (☎ **01323/870891**). The well-lit interior has two tearooms that provide a calm setting for afternoon tea. Cheese, ham-and-cheese, and egg-salad sandwiches and muffins, Danish, scones, and a variety of cakes are served. Afternoon tea costs £2.75 to £4.25 ($4.70 to $7.25), sandwiches £2.50 to £2.95 ($4.25 to $5), and cakes and pastries from £1.25 ($2.15). Hours are daily from 10am to 5pm.

Moonrakers. High St. ☎ **01323/870472.** Reservations essential on weekends. Main courses £8.50–£15 ($14.45–$25.50); fixed-price menus £12.95–£15.95 ($22–$27.10). AE, MC, V. Mon–Sat 7–10pm, Sun noon–3:30pm. Closed first 2 weeks in Jan. ENGLISH.

The welcome is warm at this charming 16th-century restaurant with old beams, an inglenook fireplace, and a convenient location in the heart of town. The cuisine is well prepared, with market-fresh ingredients. Dishes might include salmon in puff pastry with prawn and creamy vermouth stuffing; English lamb with port and red currant sauce; and a dessert specialty of sticky toffee pudding. The restaurant has a comprehensive wine list and a polite staff. Logs burn brightly in the fireplace during winter, and in summer there's a flowering patio for outside dining. The two dining rooms are reserved, respectively, for smokers and nonsmokers.

IN LEWES

Pailin. 20 Station St. ☎ **01273/473906.** Main courses £5.50–£7.50 ($9.35–$12.75); fixed-price lunch or dinner £13 ($22.10). AE, DC, MC, V. Mon–Sat noon–2:30pm and 6:30–10:30pm. Closed Nov 5 and Dec 25–26. THAI.

Spicy hot Thai food has come to Lewes, though some of the fiery hot dishes have been toned down for English taste buds. Begin perhaps with the lemon chicken soup with lemongrass, followed by a crab-and-prawn "hot pot." A special favorite with locals is the barbecued marinated chicken, which is served with a spicy but delectable sweet-and-sour plum sauce. Vegetarian meals are served, and children are welcome and given small portions at reduced prices.

A SIDE TRIP FROM LEWES: VIRGINIA WOOLF'S HOME & THE BLUEBELL RAILWAY

The small downland village of **Rodmell** lies midway between Lewes and the port of Newhaven on C7. It's known for **Monks House,** a National Trust property that was bought by Virginia and Leonard Woolf in 1919, and was their home until his death in 1969. Much of the house was furnished and decorated by Virginia's sister, Vanessa Bell, and the artist Duncan Grant.

The house has extremely limited visiting hours: from the first Saturday in April until the last Wednesday in October, and then only on Wednesday and Saturday from 2 to 5:30pm. Admission is£2.50 ($4.25) adults, £1.25 ($2.15) children 5 and up, and free for children 4 and under. More information is available by calling the headquarters of the **National Trust** in East Sussex (☎ **01892/890651**).

Rodmell also has a 12th-century church, a working farm, and a tiny Victorian school still in use. Take Southdown bus no. 123 from the Lewes rail station.

The trail of Virginia Woolf also leads to **Charleston Farmhouse,** along A27 at Charleston, near Firle, 6 miles outside Lewes (☎ **01323/811265**), the former country residence of Virginia's sister, Vanessa Bell, and the artist, Duncan Grant. They were the glittering faces of the nice artistically influential "Bloomsbury Group" early in the 20th century. Preserved rather much as they left it, the property is filled with mementos and is open to guided tours only. A more abbreviated tour costs £5.50 ($9.35), a longer "connoisseur" tour going for £6.50 ($11.05). The trust that runs the property also has changing exhibitions and sponsors an annual literary and arts festival. Dates vary so call for information.

The all-steam **Bluebell Railway** starts at Sheffield Park Station near Uckfield in East Sussex (☎ **01825/722370**), on A275 between East Grinstead and Lewes. The name is taken from the spring flowers that grow alongside the track, running from Sheffield Park to Kingscote. It's a delight for railway buffs, with locomotives dating from the 1870s through the 1950s, when British Railways ended steam operations. You can visit locomotive sheds and a small museum, then later patronize the bookshop or have lunch in a large buffet, bar, and restaurant complex. The round-trip is 1½ hours as the train wanders through a typical English countryside. It cost £7.40 ($12.60) for adults, £3.70 ($6.30) for children 3–15 years, with a family ticket going for £19.90 ($33.85). Trains run daily from May to September, and Saturday and Sunday the rest of the year.

7

Hampshire & Dorset: Austen & Hardy Country

This countryside is reminiscent of scenes from Burke's *Landed Gentry,* from fireplaces where stacks slowly deplete as logs burn, to wicker baskets of apples freshly picked from a nearby orchard. Old village houses, now hotels, have a charming quality. Beyond the pear trees, on the crest of a hill, you'll find the ruins of a Roman camp. A village pub, with two rows of kegs filled with varieties of cider, is where the hunt gathers.

You're in Hampshire and Dorset, two shires jealously guarded by the English as special rural treasures. Everybody knows of Southampton and Bournemouth, but less known is the hilly countryside farther inland. You can travel through endless lanes and discover tiny villages and thatched cottages untouched by the industrial invasion.

Jane Austen wrote of Hampshire's firmly middle-class inhabitants, all doggedly convinced that Hampshire was the greatest place on earth. Her six novels, including *Pride and Prejudice* and *Sense and Sensibility,* earned her a permanent place among the pantheon of 19th-century writers, and unexpected popularity among 1990s film directors and producers. Her books provide an insight into the manners and mores of the English who soon established a powerful empire. Although the details of the life she described have now largely faded, the general mood and spirit of the Hampshire she depicted remains intact. You can visit her grave in Winchester Cathedral and the house where she lived, Chawton Cottage (see reviews in section 1, below).

Hampshire encompasses the South Downs, the Isle of Wight (Victoria's favorite retreat), and the naval city of Portsmouth. More than 90,000 acres of the New Forest were preserved by William the Conqueror as a private hunting ground, and even today this vast woodland and heath is ideal for walking and exploring. Although Hampshire is filled with many places of interest, for our purposes we've concentrated on two major areas: Southampton, for convenience, and Winchester, for history.

Dorset is Thomas Hardy country. Some of its towns and villages, although altered considerably, are still recognizable from his descriptions. "The last of the great Victorians," as he was called, died in 1928 at age 88. His tomb occupies a position of honor in Westminster Abbey.

One of England's smallest shires, Dorset encompasses the old seaport of Poole in the east and Lyme Regis (known to Jane Austen) in the west. Dorset is a southwestern county and borders the English Channel. It's known for its cows, and Dorset butter is served at many an afternoon tea. This is mainly a land of farms and pastures, with plenty of sandy heaths and chalky downs.

The most prominent tourist center of Dorset is the Victorian seaside resort of Bournemouth. If you don't stay here, you can try a number of Dorset's other seaports, villages, and country towns; we mostly stick to the areas along the impressive coastline. And Dorset, as the frugal English might tell you, is full of bargains.

Where to stay? You'll find the most hotels, but not the greatest charm, at the seaside resort of Bournemouth. (More intriguing than Bournemouth is the much smaller Lyme Regis, with its famed seaside promenade, the Cobb, a favorite of Jane Austen and a setting for *The French Lieutenant's Woman.*) If you're interested in things maritime, opt for Portsmouth, the premier port of the south and the home of HMS *Victory,* Nelson's flagship. For the history buff and Jane Austen fans, it's Winchester, the ancient capital of England, with a cathedral built by William the Conqueror. Winchester also makes a good base for exploring the countryside.

The best beaches are at Bournemouth, set among pines with sandy beaches and fine coastal views, and Chesil Beach, a 20-mile-long bank of shingle running from Abbottsbury to the Isle of Portland great for beachcombing. However, the most natural spectacle is New Forest itself, 145 square miles of heath and woodland, once the hunting ground of Norman kings.

1 Winchester

72 miles SW of London; 12 miles N of Southampton

The most historic city in all of Hampshire, Winchester is big on legends, since it's associated with King Arthur and the Knights of the Round Table. In the Great Hall, which is all that remains of Winchester Castle, a round oak table, with space for King Arthur and his 24 knights, is attached to the wall but all that spells is undocumented romance. What is known, however, is that when the Saxons ruled the ancient kingdom of Wessex, Winchester was the capital.

The city is also linked with King Alfred, who is believed to have been crowned here and is honored today by a statue. The Danish conqueror Canute came this way too, as did the king he ousted, Ethelred the Unready (Canute got his wife, Emma, in the bargain).

Of course, Winchester is a mecca for Jane Austen fans. You can visit her grave in Winchester Cathedral (Emma Thompson did, while working on her adapted screenplay of *Sense and Sensibility*), as well as Chawton Cottage, Jane Austen's house, which is 15 miles east of Winchester.

Its past glory but a memory, Winchester is essentially a market town today, lying on the downs along the Itchen River. Although Winchester hypes its ancient past, the modern world has arrived, as evidenced by the fast food, reggae music, and the cheap retail-clothing stores that mar its otherwise perfect High Street.

ESSENTIALS

GETTING THERE From London's Waterloo Station there is frequent daily train service to Winchester. The trip takes 1 hour. For rail information, call ☎ **0345/484950.** Arrivals are at Winchester Station, Station Hill northwest of the city center. **National Express** buses leaving from London's Victoria Coach Station depart regularly for Winchester during the day. The trip takes 2 hours. Call ☎ **0990/808080** for schedules and information.

Hampshire & Dorset

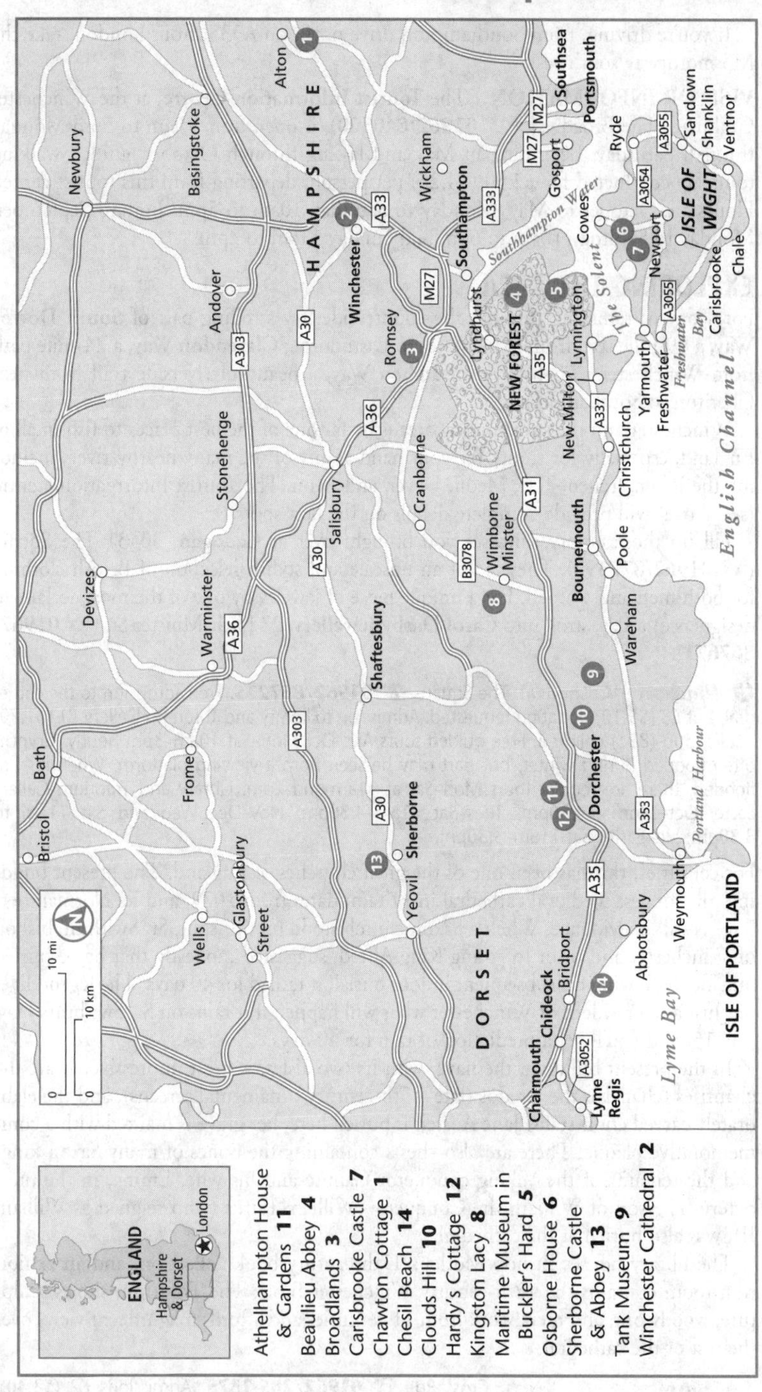

If you're driving, from Southampton drive north on A335; from London, take the M3 motorway southwest.

VISITOR INFORMATION The **Tourist Information Centre,** at the Winchester Guildhall, The Broadway (☎ **01962/840500**), is open from 10am to 5pm Monday through Saturday. Beginning in May and lasting through October, guided walking tours are conducted for £2.50 ($4.25) per person, departing from this tourist center. Hours are October to May, Monday to Saturday 10am to 5pm; June to September, Monday to Saturday 10am to 6pm and Sunday 11am to 2pm.

EXPLORING THE AREA

For a day of rambling through the countryside, try strolling part of **South Downs Way,** a 99-mile trail from Winchester to Eastbourne; **Clarendon Way,** a 24-mile path from Winchester to Salisbury; or **Itchen Way,** a beautiful riverside trail from near Cheriton to Southampton.

Winchester and the surrounding area is by far one of the best places to fish in all of England, especially for trout. Try your hand at any of the many nearby rivers including the Rivers Itchen, Test, Meon, Dever, and Avon. The Tourist Information Centre (see above) will provide complete details on the best spots.

Fill up those empty suitcases you brought over at **Cadogan,** 30–31 The Square (☎ **01962/877399**). They've got an upscale and stylish selection of British clothing for both men and women. For a unique piece of jewelry by one of the most acclaimed designers of today, stroll into **Carol Darby Jewellery,** 23 Little Minster St. (☎ **01962/867671**).

✪ **Winchester Cathedral.** The Square. ☎ **01962/857225.** Free admission to the cathedral, but £3 ($5.10) donation requested. Admission to library and Triforium Gallery £1 ($1.70) adults, 50p (85¢) children. Free guided tours Apr–Oct Mon–Sat 10am–3pm hourly. Crypt is often flooded during winter, but part may be seen from a viewing platform. When it's not flooded, there are regular tours Mon–Sat at 11am and 2pm. Library and Triforium Gallery Easter–Oct Mon 2–4:30pm, Tues–Sat 11am–4:30pm; Nov–Dec Wed and Sat 11am to 3:30pm; Jan–Easter Sat 11am–3:30pm.

For centuries, this has been one of the great churches of England. The present building, the longest medieval cathedral in Britain, dates from 1079, and its Norman heritage is still in evidence. When a Saxon church stood on this spot, St. Swithun, bishop of Winchester and tutor to young King Alfred, suggested modestly that he be buried outside. Following his subsequent indoor burial, it rained for 40 days. The legend lives on: Just ask a resident of Winchester what will happen if it rains on St. Swithun's Day, July 15, and you'll get a prediction of rain for 40 days.

In the present building, the nave, with its two aisles, is most impressive, as are the chantries (chapels), the reredos (late–15th-century ornamental screens), and the elaborately carved choir stalls. Jane Austen is buried here; her grave is marked with a commemorative plaque. There are also chests containing the bones of many Saxon kings and the remains of the Viking conqueror Canute and his wife, Emma, in the presbytery. The son of William the Conqueror, William Rufus (who reigned as William II), was also buried at the cathedral.

The library houses Bishop Morley's 17th-century book collection, and an exhibition room contains the 12th-century Winchester Bible. The Triforium shows sculpture, woodwork, and metalwork from 11 centuries and affords magnificent views over the rest of the cathedral.

The Hospital of St. Cross. Cross Rd. ☎ **01962/285-1375**. Admissions £2 ($3.40). May–Sept daily 9:30am–5pm; off-season daily 10:30am–3:30pm.

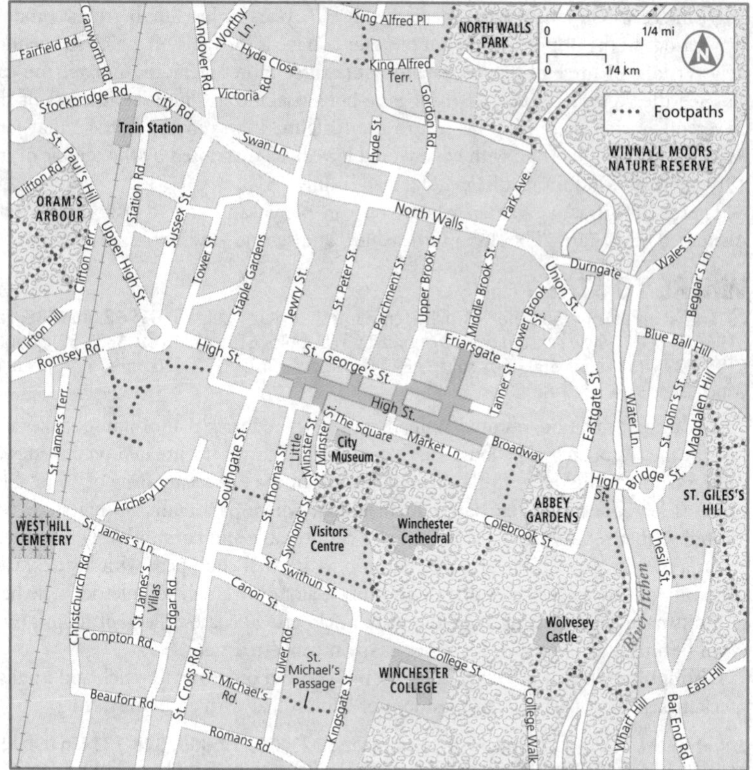

The hospital was founded in 1132 and is the oldest charitable institution in the entire country. It was established by Henri du Blois, the grandson of William the Conqueror, as a link for social care and to supply life's necessities to the local poor and famished travelers. It continues the tradition of providing refreshments to visitors. Simply stop at the Porter's Lodge for a Wayfarer's Dole and you'll receive some bread and ale. St. Cross is set in the beautiful scenery that inspired Keats and Trollope, and is still the home of 25 brothers, whose residence is on one side of the historic landmark.

Winchester College. 7 College St. ☎ **01962/285-1375.** Admission £2.50 ($4.25). Mon–Sat 10am–1pm and 2–5pm, Sun 2–5pm.

Winchester College was founded by William of Wykeham, Bishop of Winchester and Chancellor to Richard II, and was first occupied in 1394. Its buildings have been in continuous use for 600 years. The structures vary from Victorian Tudor Gothic to the more modern trimmings of the New Hall designed in 1961. The Chapel Hall, kitchens, and the Founder's Cloister all date back to the 14th century. In the 17th century buildings were added on the southside including a schoolroom constructed between 1683 and 1687.

OUTSIDE OF WINCHESTER

✪ **Chawton Cottage.** Chawton. ☎ **01420/83262.** Admission is £2.50 ($4.25) adults, 50p (85¢) children 8–18. Open Mar–Dec daily 11am–4:30pm, and Sat and Sun Jan–Feb daily 11am–4:30pm. Closed December 25–26. 1 mile southwest of Alton off A31 and B3006, 15 miles east of Winchester.

You can see where Jane Austen spent the last 7½ years of her life, her most productive period. In the unpretentious but pleasant cottage is the table on which she penned new versions of three of her books and wrote three more, including *Emma.* You can also see the rector's George III mahogany bookcase and a silhouette likeness of the Reverend Austen presenting his son to the Knights. It was in this cottage that Jane Austen became ill in 1816 with what would have been diagnosed by the middle of the 19th century as Addison's disease. She died in July 1817.

There's an attractive garden where you can picnic and an old bake house with Austen's donkey cart. A bookshop stocks new and secondhand books.

WHERE TO STAY

✪ **Lainston House.** Sparsholt, Winchester, Hampshire SO21 2LT. ☎ **01962/863588.** Fax 01962/776672. www.lainston.com. 37 units. TV TEL. £145–£195 ($246.50–$331.50) double; £185–£295 ($314.50–$501.50) suite. AE, DC, MC, V. Take A272 3½ miles northwest of Winchester.

The beauty of this fine, restored William and Mary redbrick manor house strikes visitors as they approach via a long, curving, tree-lined drive. It's situated on 63 acres of rolling land and linked with the name Lainston in the *Domesday Book* of 1086. Elegance is keynote inside the stately main house, where panoramically big suites are located. Other rooms, less spacious but also comfortable and harmoniously furnished, are in a nearby annex built in 1990. Bathrooms are well equipped, with heated racks containing fluffy towels, hair dryers, and robes, along with deluxe toiletries. The better units have large dressing areas and walk-in closets. The latest block of rooms, each room beautifully appointed, is a series of six in converted stables.

Dining: In either of the two dining rooms, you can order such French and English specialties as roast partridge or roast loin of lamb rolled with an herb stuffing.

Royal Hotel. St. Peter St., Winchester, Hampshire SO23 8BS. ☎ **800/528-1234** in the U.S., or 01962/840840. Fax 01962/841582. www.The-Royal.com. E-mail: resv@royal.com. 75 units. TV TEL. £89.50 ($152.15) double; £113.50 ($192.95) suite. AE, DC, MC, V.

This fine old hotel, a comfortable choice, was built at the end of the 17th century as a private house. It was used by Belgian nuns as a convent for 50 years before being turned into a hotel, quickly becoming the center of the city's social life. It's only a few minutes' walk from the cathedral, yet it still enjoys a secluded position. A modern extension overlooks gardens, and all rooms have traditional English styling. Bedrooms in the main house are more traditional than those in the modern wing, but each accommodation, regardless of room assignment, is well appointed. Some two dozen rooms are designated for nonsmokers. Meals are served in a small, formal dining room with a view of the private garden. Amenities include shoe cleaning, valet service, and 24-hour room service.

Stratton House. Stratton Rd., St. Giles Hill, Winchester, Hampshire SO23 0JQ. ☎ **01962/863919.** Fax 01962/842095. www.accomodata.co.uk/340999.htm. E-mail: strattongroup@btinternet.com. 10 units. TV. £58–£60 ($98.60–$102) double. Rates include English breakfast. MC, V. Closed Dec 24–27. Free pickup available from the train or bus station.

This lovely old Victorian house (ca. 1890) is situated on an acre of St. Giles Hill, overlooking the city. It's about a 5- to 10-minute walk from the city center. All the comfortably furnished rooms have beverage makers. Improvements are made yearly in the small to medium-size bedrooms. Bathrooms are small with medium-size towels; hair dryers can be requested from the reception. A three-course evening meal can be arranged. There is ample parking in a private courtyard.

✪ **Wykeham Arms.** 75 Kingsgate St., Winchester, Hampshire SO23 9PE. ☎ **01962/853834.** Fax 01962/854411. 13 units. MINIBAR TV TEL. £79.50 ($135.15) double in original building, £95 ($161.50) double in extension, £117.50 ($199.75) suite. Rates include English breakfast. AE, CB, DC, MC, V.

This is one of our longtime favorites in Winchester, known to almost everyone in town for its food and bar facilities. It lies behind a 200-year-old brick facade in the historic center of town, near the cathedral. The rooms are traditionally furnished with antiques or reproductions and such lighthearted touches as fresh flowers and baskets of potpourri. Six rooms were recently added in a 16th-century building that faces the original hotel. Most of the bedrooms are a bit small but attractively appointed. The annex contains the most luxurious accommodations, and these rooms are more spacious. The large modern bathrooms are equipped with a hair dryer. A large suite with a cozy fire-warmed sitting room and upstairs bedroom is also available. These rooms overlook the Winchester College Chapel, and have the same amenities as the original rooms. A filling breakfast, complete with fresh-squeezed orange juice, is served in a charming dining area in the main house.

The Wykeham Arms is especially known for its paneled pub and restaurant, where carefully flavored food is served in historic surroundings. Lunches are informal affairs with pub snacks and platters. Evening meals are more elaborate.

WHERE TO DINE

✪ **Hotel du Vin & Bistro.** 14 Southgate St., Winchester, Hampshire SO23 9EF. ☎ **01962/841414.** Reservations recommended. Main courses £11–£15 ($18.70–$25.50). AE, DC, MC, V. Daily noon–2pm and 7–9:30pm. ENGLISH/CONTINENTAL.

A touch of chic has come to sleepy Winchester with the opening of a bistro in this town-house hotel that dates from 1715 and has a walled garden. Gerard Basset and Robin Hutson learned their lessons well at the exclusive Chewton Glen (see "Where to Stay Around New Forest," in section 4) before embarking on their own enterprise. They wisely hired James Martin as chef, and he delivers the finest food served in Winchester today. The bistro food is excellent and a good value. The menu always features regional ingredients: Try the Torbay sole Filet served with spinach and potato galette, with a mushroom, white wine and cream sauce. The sommelier (Basset himself) has collected the finest wine list in the county.

You can also stay overnight in one of the 23 rooms decorated with a wine theme. The quite comfortable rooms have good beds, antiques, TVs, and state-of-the-art bathrooms. It costs from £85 to £185 ($144.50 to $314.50) per room.

Nine The Square. 9 Great Minster St. ☎ **01962/864004.** Reservations recommended. Main courses £7.50–£16.50 ($12.75–$28.05). AE, DC, MC, V. Mon–Sat noon–2pm and 7–10pm. ITALIAN.

Winchester's long-reigning best restaurant, now seriously challenged by the Hotel du Vin & Bistro, has an enviable view of the cathedral. Diners may either head upstairs to the comfortably formal restaurant or sit at street level, where dining tables are scattered near the sometimes crowded stand-up bar. The food is beautifully prepared and served with fresh ingredients. A typical starter is bruschetta with goat cheese and sun-dried tomatoes. For the main course, try the especially delectable crab and salmon ravioli.

WINCHESTER AFTER DARK

The place to go is **The Porthouse,** Upper Brook Street (☎ **01962/869397**), a pub-cum-nightclub, sprawling across three floors. Different nights have different themes, from karaoke to retro music from the 1960s through the 1980s. On Friday, the 25-plus crowd takes over. The only cover, ranging from £3 to £5 ($5.10 to $8.50), is charged on Thursday, Friday, and Saturday nights after 9pm. There's a ground-floor pub where lunch is served.

2 Portsmouth & Southsea

75 miles SW of London; 19 miles SE of Southampton

Virginia, New Hampshire, and even Ohio may have a Portsmouth, but the forerunner of them all is the old port and naval base on the Hampshire coast, seat of the British navy for 500 years. German bombers in World War II leveled the city, hitting about nine-tenths of its buildings. But the seaport was rebuilt admirably and now aggressively promotes its military attractions. It draws visitors interested in the nautical history of England as well as World War II buffs.

Its maritime associations are known around the world. From Sally Port, the most interesting district in the Old Town, countless naval heroes have embarked to fight England's battles. That was certainly true on June 6, 1944, when Allied troops set sail to invade occupied France.

Southsea, adjoining Portsmouth, is a popular seaside resort with fine sands, lush gardens, bright lights, and a host of vacation attractions. Many historic monuments can be seen along the stretches of open space, where you can walk on the Clarence Esplanade, look out on the Solent Channel, and view the busy shipping activities of Portsmouth Harbour.

ESSENTIALS

GETTING THERE Trains from London's Waterloo Station stop at Portsmouth and Southsea Station frequently throughout the day. The trip takes 2 hours. Call ☎ **0345/484950.**

National Express coaches operating out of London's Victoria Coach Station make the run to Portsmouth and Southsea every 2 hours during the day. The trip takes 2 hours and 20 minutes. Call ☎ **0990/808080** for information and schedules.

If you're driving from London's ring road, drive south on A3.

VISITOR INFORMATION The **Tourist Information Centre,** at The Hard in Portsmouth (☎ **01705/826722**), is open daily April to September from 9:30am to 5:45pm, and October to March daily from 9:30am to 5:15pm.

EXPLORING PORTSMOUTH & SOUTHSEA

You might want to begin your tour on the Southsea front, where you can see a number of **naval monuments.** These include the big anchor from Nelson's ship *Victory*, plus a commemoration of the officers and men of HMS *Shannon* for heroism in the Indian Mutiny. An obelisk with a naval crown honors the memory of the crew of HMS *Chesapeake,* and a massive column, the Royal Naval Memorial, honors those lost at sea in the two world wars. A shaft is also dedicated to men killed in the Crimean War. There are also commemorations of those who fell victim to yellow fever in Queen Victoria's service in Sierra Leone and Jamaica.

Southsea Common, between the coast and houses of the area, known in the 13th century as Froddington Heath and used for army bivouacs, is a picnic and play area today. Walks can be taken along Ladies' Mile if you tend to shy away from the common's tennis courts, skateboard and roller-skating rinks, and other activities.

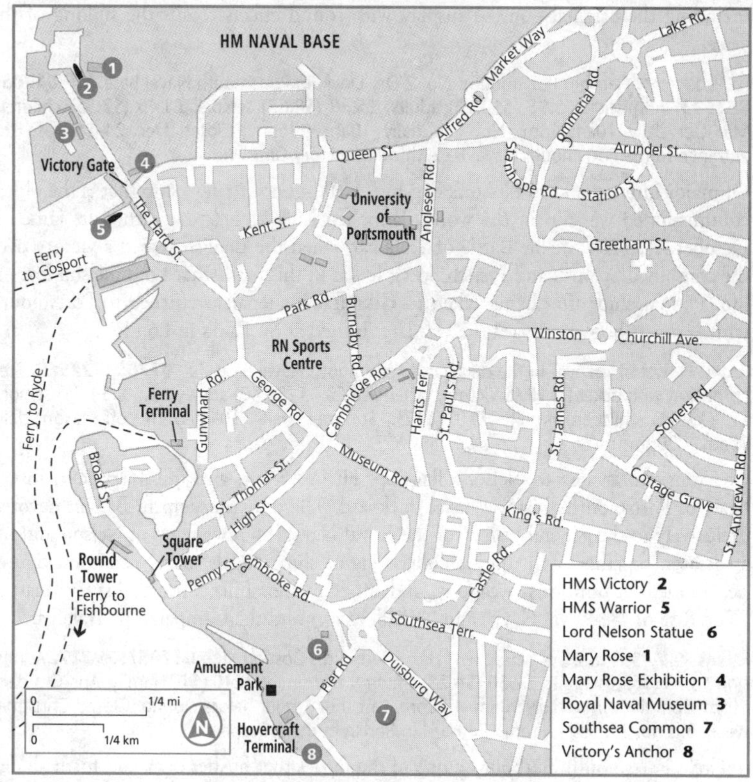

Maritime Attractions in Portsmouth

You can buy a ticket that admits you to the HMS *Victory,* the *Mary Rose,* the HMS *Warrior 1860,* and the Royal Naval Museum. It costs £11.90 ($20.25) for adults, £10.40 ($17.70) for senior citizens, and £8.90 ($15.15) for children.

✪ **The Mary Rose Ship Hall and Exhibition.** College Rd., Portsmouth Naval Base. ☎ **01705/750521.** Admission £5.95 ($10.10) adults, £5.20 ($8.85) seniors, £4.45 ($7.55) children and students. Daily 10am–5pm. Closed Dec 25. Use the entrance to the Portsmouth Naval Base through Victory Gate and follow the signs.

The *Mary Rose,* flagship of the fleet of King Henry VIII's wooden men-of-war, sank in the Solent Channel in 1545 in full view of the king. In 1982, Prince Charles watched the *Mary Rose* break the water's surface after more than four centuries on the ocean floor, not exactly in shipshape condition, but surprisingly well preserved nonetheless. Now the remains are on view, but the hull must be kept permanently wet.

The hull and the more than 20,000 items brought up by divers constitute one of England's major archaeological discoveries. On display are the almost-complete equipment of the ship's barber-surgeon, with cabin saws, knives, ointments, and plaster all ready for use; long bows and arrows, some still in shooting order; carpenters' tools; leather jackets; and some fine lace and silk. Close to the Ship Hall is the *Mary Rose* Exhibition, where artifacts recovered from the ship are stored. It features an audio-visual theater and a spectacular two-deck reconstruction of a segment of the ship, including the original guns. A display with sound effects recalls the sinking of the vessel.

HMS *Victory*. Flagship Portsmouth. No. 2 Dry Dock, in Portsmouth Naval Base. ☎ **01705/861533.** Admission £5.95 ($10.10) adults, £5.20 ($8.85) seniors, £4.45 ($7.55) children. Mar–Oct daily 10am–5pm; Nov–Feb daily 10am–4:30pm. Closed Dec 24–25. Use the entrance to the Portsmouth Naval Base through Victory Gate.

Of major interest is Lord Nelson's flagship, a 104-gun, first-rate ship that is the oldest commissioned warship in the world, launched May 7, 1765. It earned its fame on October 21, 1805, in the Battle of Trafalgar, when the English scored a victory over the combined Spanish and French fleets. It was in this battle that Lord Nelson lost his life. The flagship, after being taken to Gibraltar for repairs, returned to Portsmouth with Nelson's body on board (he was later buried at St. Paul's in London).

Royal Naval Museum. In the dockyard, Portsmouth Naval Base. ☎ **01705/727562.** Free admission with ticket for HMS Victory; otherwise £3.75 ($6.40) adults, £2.50 ($4.25) seniors, £2 ($3.40) children; family £10 ($17). Summer daily 10am–5pm; off-season daily 10am–4:30pm.

The museum is next to Nelson's flagship, HMS *Victory,* and the *Mary Rose,* in the heart of Portsmouth's historic naval dockyard. The only museum in Britain devoted exclusively to the general history of the Royal Navy, it houses relics of Nelson and his associates, together with unique collections of ship models, naval ceramics, figureheads, medals, uniforms, weapons, and other memorabilia. Special displays feature "The Rise of the Royal Navy" and "HMS *Victory* and the Campaign of Trafalgar."

Royal Navy Submarine Museum. Haslar Jetty Rd., Gosport. ☎ **01705/529217.** Admission £3.75 ($6.40) adults, £2.50 ($4.25) children and seniors, £10 ($17) family. Apr–Oct daily 10am–5pm; Nov–Mar daily 10am–4:30pm. Last tour 1 hour before closing. Closed Christmas week. Bus no. 19. Ferry: From The Hard in Portsmouth to Gosport.

Cross Portsmouth Harbour by one of the ferries that bustles back and forth all day to Gosport. Some departures go directly from the station pontoon to HMS *Alliance* for a visit to the submarine museum, which traces the history of underwater warfare and life from the earliest days to the present nuclear age. Within the refurbished historical and nuclear galleries, the principal exhibit is HMS *Alliance,* and after a brief audiovisual presentation, visitors are guided through the boat by ex-submariners. Midget submarines, not all of them English, including an X-craft, can be seen outside the museum.

More Attractions

Charles Dickens's Birthplace Museum. 393 Old Commercial Rd. (near the center of Portsmouth, off Mile End Rd./M275 and off Kingston Rd.). ☎ **01705/827261.** Admission £2 ($3.40) adults, £1.50 ($2.55) seniors, £1.20 ($2.05) students; free for children 12 and under. Daily 10am–5:30pm. Closed Nov–Mar.

The 1804 small terrace house, in which the famous novelist was born in 1812 and lived for a short time, has been restored and furnished to illustrate the middle-class taste of the southwestern counties of the early 19th century.

Southsea Castle. Clarence Esplanade, Southsea. ☎ **01705/827261.** Admission £2 ($3.40) adults, £1.50 ($2.55) seniors, £1.20 ($2.05) students and ages 13–18; free for children 12 and under. Apr–Oct daily 10am–5:30pm; Closed Nov–March.

A fortress built of stones from Beaulieu Abbey in 1545 as part of King Henry VIII's coastal defense plan, the castle is now a museum. Exhibits trace the development of Portsmouth as a military stronghold, as well as the naval history and the archaeology of the area. The castle is in the center of Southsea near the D-Day Museum.

D-Day Museum. Clarence Esplanade (on the seafront), Southsea. ☎ **01705/827261.** Admission £4.75 ($8.05) adults, £3.60 ($6.10) seniors, £2.85 ($4.85) children and students, £12.35 ($21) family of 4, children under 5 free. Daily 10am–5:30pm. Closed Dec 24–26.

Right next door to Southsea Castle, this museum, devoted to the Normandy landings, displays the Overlord Embroidery, which shows the complete story of Operation Overlord. The appliquéd embroidery, believed to be the largest of its kind (272 ft. long and 3 ft. high), was designed by Sandra Lawrence and took 20 women of the Royal School of Needlework 5 years to complete. There's a special audiovisual program with displays, including reconstructions of various stages of the mission. You'll see a Sherman tank in working order, jeeps, field guns, and even a DUKW (popularly called a Duck), an incredibly useful amphibious truck that operates on land and sea.

Portsmouth City Museum. ☎ **01705/827261.** Free admission. Daily 10am–5:30pm.

This museum explains the history of Portsmouth; some areas are audiovisual, and there are two exhibitions (galleries) that change throughout the year. Permanent displays are devoted to the history of Portsmouth through the ages. An example would be a dining room set up in the 1950s with the furnishings and atmosphere of the time.

Portsmouth (Cumberlin) Natural History Museum. ☎ **01705/827261.** Admission £2 ($3.40) adults, £1.60 ($2.70) seniors, £1.50 ($2.55) children and students over 13, family ticket £5.40 ($9.20). Daily 10am–5:30pm.

This museum is mainly for children, as it documents the history of Portsmouth and how it has developed from the age of the dinosaurs and changed over the years.

Portchester Castle. On the south side of Portchester off A27 (between Portsmouth and Southampton, near Fareham). ☎ **01705/378291.** Admission £2.70 ($4.60) adults, £2.10 ($3.55) seniors, £1.50 ($2.55) children 5–15; free for children 4 and under. Apr–Oct daily 10am–6pm; Nov–Mar daily 10am–4pm.

On a spit of land on the northern side of Portsmouth Harbour are the remains of this castle, plus a Norman church. Built in the late 12th century by King Henry II, the castle is set inside the impressive walls of a 3rd-century Roman fort built as a defense against Saxon pirates when this was the northwestern frontier of the declining Roman Empire. By the end of the 14th century, Richard II had modernized the castle and had made it a secure small palace. Among the ruins are the hall, kitchen, and great chamber of this palace.

WHERE TO STAY

Portsmouth Marriott. North Harbour, Cosham (2 miles southeast of Portsmouth's center, at the junction of A3 and M27), Portsmouth, Hampshire PO6 4SH. ☎ **800/228-9290** in the U.S. and Canada, or 01705/383151. Fax 01705/388701. 170 units. TV TEL. £59–£102 ($100.30–$173.40) double; £128 ($217.60) suite. AE, DC, MC, V. Take the bus marked Cosham from Portsmouth's center.

Located a short walk from the ferryboat terminal for ships arriving from Le Havre and Cherbourg in France, this 7-story building towers above everything in its district. Originally built as a Holiday Inn in 1980, it was acquired by Marriott in 1992 and refurbished in 1997. The bedrooms are comfortable and modern. Bedrooms have the aura of a quality motel, double or king size mattresses. Some 86 rooms are set aside for nonsmokers. All the small bathrooms come with plenty of toiletries. A cocktail lounge and a restaurant serve breakfast, lunch, and dinner. Facilities include an atrium-style swimming pool, gym equipment, a sauna, spa bath, and solarium.

Royal Beach Hotel. South Parade, Southsea, Portsmouth, Hampshire PO4 ORN. ☎ **01705/731281.** Fax 01705/817572. 117 units. TV TEL. £74 ($125.80) double; £105 ($178.50) suite. Rates include English breakfast. AE, DC, MC, V.

The balconied Victorian facade of this hotel, directly east of Southside Common, rises above the boulevard running beside the sea. Restored by its owners, the hotel's interior decor ranges from contemporary to full-curtained traditional, depending on the room. However, it doesn't stack up with the nearby Marriott. Each of the bedrooms has been renovated with built-in furniture and equipped with such extras as a trouser press and a tea- and coffemaker. Twenty rooms are set aside for nonsmokers. The small bathrooms are supplied with a hair dryer. Rooms are slated for refurbishment in 2000.

In Nearby Wickham

✪ **The Old House Hotel.** The Square, Wickham, Fareham, Hampshire PO17 5JG. ☎ **01329/833049.** Fax 01329/833672. 8 units. TV TEL. £75 ($127.50) double. AE, DC, MC, V. Bus no. 69 from Fareham. Head 9 miles west from Portsmouth on the M27 motorway; exit at number 10. The village is 2 miles north of the junction of B2177 and A32.

A handsome early Georgian (1715) structure, the Old House is surrounded by low, medieval timber structures around the square. The paneled rooms on the ground and first floors of the hotel contrast with the beamed bedrooms on the upper floors, once the servants' quarters. All eight bedrooms have period furniture, many pieces original antiques. All the prettily decorated bedrooms have warm, comfortable beds. Bathrooms are big enough to have a stand-up shower as well as a tub.

The restaurant occupies what was once a timber-frame outbuilding with stables, adjacent to a garden overlooking the Meon River; it serves French provincial cuisine.

Where to Dine

Bistro Montparnasse. 103 Palmerston Rd., Southsea. ☎ **02392/816754.** Reservations recommended. 2-course lunch £12 ($20.40), 3-course lunch £15 ($25.50). 2-course dinner £18.50 ($31.45); 3-course dinner £23.50 ($39.95). AE, MC, V. Tues–Sat noon–2pm and 7–10pm. Southsea bus. Follow the signs to the D-Day Museum, and at the museum turn left and go to the next intersection; the restaurant is on the right. BRITISH/FRENCH.

Serving the best food in the area, this bistro offers a welcoming atmosphere and background music to get you in the mood. Fresh produce is delicately prepared in the well-rounded selection of dishes here. The cooking is familiar fare but well executed. Although the menu changes, you might try the roast rack of lamb with a walnut and herb crust. Homemade breads and fresh fish, caught locally, are the specialties.

3 Southampton

87 miles SW of London; 161 miles E of Plymouth

For many North Americans, England's number-one passenger port, home base for the *QE2,* is the gateway to Britain. Southampton is a city of sterile wide boulevards, parks, and dreary shopping centers. During World War II, some 31.5 million men set out from here (in World War I, more than twice that number), and Southampton was repeatedly bombed, destroying its old character. Today, the rather shoddy downtown section represents what happens when a city's architectural focus is timeliness rather than grace. There's not much to see in the city itself but there's a lot on the outskirts. If you're spending time in Southampton between ships, you may want to explore some of the major sights of Hampshire nearby (New Forest, Winchester, the Isle of Wight, and Bournemouth, in neighboring Dorset).

Its supremacy as a port dates from Saxon times when the Danish conqueror Canute was proclaimed king here in 1017. Southampton was especially important to the Normans and helped them keep in touch with their homeland. Its denizens were responsible for bringing in the bubonic plague, which wiped out a quarter of the English

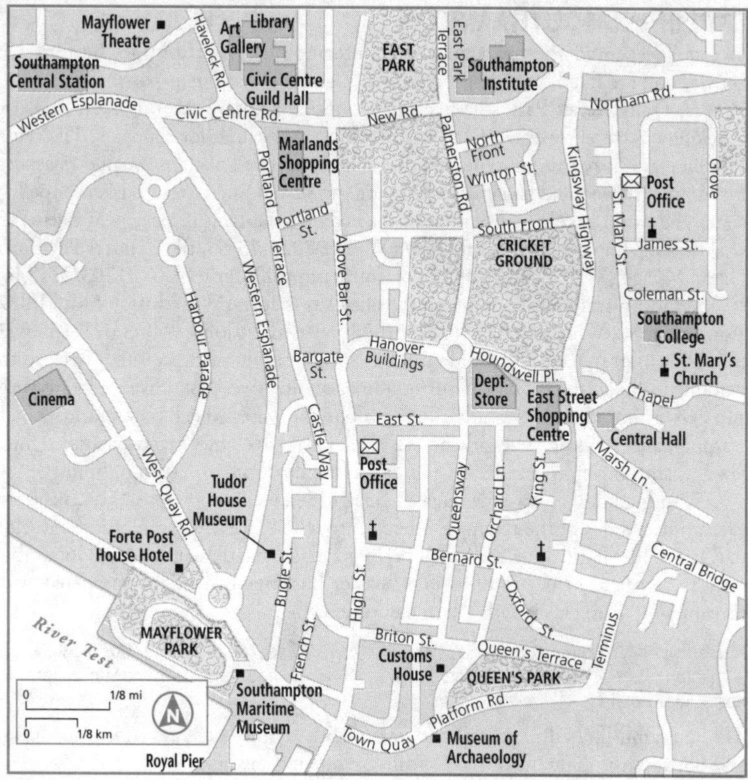

population in the mid-14th century. On the Western Esplanade is a memorial tower to the Pilgrims, who set out on their voyage to the New World from Southampton on August 15, 1620. Both the *Mayflower* and the *Speedwell* sailed from here but were forced by storm damages to put in at Plymouth, where the *Speedwell* was abandoned.

In the spring of 1912, the "unsinkable" White Star liner, the 46,000-ton *Titanic,* sailed from Southampton on its maiden voyage. Shortly before midnight on April 14, while steaming at 22 knots, the great ship collided with an iceberg and sank to the bottom of the icy Atlantic. The sinking of the *Titanic,* subject of the Oscar-winning box office smash of 1997, is one of the greatest disasters in maritime history, as 1,513 people perished.

ESSENTIALS

GETTING THERE Trains depart from London's Waterloo Station several times daily. The trip takes just over an hour. Call ☎ **0345/484950.**

National Express operates hourly departures from London's Victoria Coach Station. The trip takes 2½ hours. Call ☎ **0990/808080** for information and schedules.

If you're driving, take M3 southwest from London.

VISITOR INFORMATION The **Tourist Information Centre,** 9 Civic Centre Rd. (☎**01703/8022-1106**), is open Monday to Wednesday and Friday and Saturday from 9am to 5pm, and Thursday from 10am to 5pm; closed Good Friday and Easter Monday, Christmas, December 26, and New Year's Day.

EXPLORING SOUTHAMPTON

Ocean Village and the town quay on Southampton's waterfront are bustling with activity and are filled with shops, restaurants, and entertainment possibilities.

West Quay Retail Park, the first phase of Southampton's £250 million Esplanade development, recently opened and has become a major hub for shoppers. The central shopping area is pedestrian-only, and tree- and shrub-filled planters provide a backdrop for summer flowers and hanging baskets. You can sit and listen to the buskers or perhaps watch the world parade by from one of the nearby restaurants or pavement cafes. For a vast array of shops, try the **Town Quay** (☎ **023/8023-4397**), the **Canutes Pavilion** at Ocean Village (☎ **023/8022-2835**), or **Southampton Market** (☎ **01703/221736**).

The most intriguing shopping on the outskirts is at the **Whitchurch Silk Mill,** 28 Winchester St., Whitchurch (☎ **01256/892065**). Admission £2.50 ($4.25) adults, £2 ($3.40) seniors, £1 ($1.70) children, £6 ($10.20) family ticket. Visitors flock to this working mill, located in colorful surroundings on the River Test. Historic looms weave silk here as in olden days, and visitors can observe water-wheel–powered machinery, warping, and winding. The gift shop sells silk on the roll, ties, scarves, handkerchiefs, jewelry, and souvenirs. Hours are Tuesday to Sunday from 10:30am to 5pm.

City tour guides offer a wide range of **free guided walks** and regular **city bus tours.** Free guided walks of the town are offered throughout the year on Sunday and Monday at 10:30am and June to September twice daily at 10:30am and 2:30pm. Tours start at Bargate. For details of various boat or bus trips that might be offered at the time of your visit, check with the tourist office.

Museum of Archaeology. God's House Tower, Winkle St. ☎ **023/8063-5904.** Free admission. Tues–Fri 10am–noon and 1–5pm, Sat 10am–noon and 1–4pm, Sun 2–5pm. Bus nos. 2, 6, 8, or 13.

The museum, housed in part of the town's 15th-century defenses, traces the history and portrays the daily life of the Roman, Saxon, and medieval eras.

Southampton Maritime Museum. The Wool House, Town Quay. ☎ **023/8022-3941.** Free admission. Apr–Sept, Tues–Sat 10am–5pm, Sun 2–5pm; Oct–Mar, Tues–Sat 10am–4pm, Sun 1–4pm. Closed bank holiday Mondays, Christmas, and Boxing Day. Bus nos. 2, 6, 8, or 13.

This museum is housed in an impressive 14th-century stone warehouse with a magnificent timber ceiling. Its exhibits trace the history of Southampton, including a model of the docks as they looked at their peak in the 1930s. Also displayed are artifacts from some of the great ocean liners whose home port was Southampton.

The most famous of these was the fabled *Titanic,* which was partially built in Southampton and sailed from this port on its fateful, fatal voyage. James Cameron's box office smash, which retells the story of the ship's sinking, has also increased traffic to the relatively small *Titanic* exhibit at the museum as well. It features photographs of the crew (many of whom were from Southampton) and passengers, as well as letters from passengers, Capt. Edward Smith's sword, and a video with a dated interview with the fallen captain plus modern interviews with survivors.

WHERE TO STAY

Finding a place to stay right in Southampton isn't as important as it used to be. Very few ships now arrive, and the places to stay just outside the city are generally better. For more choices in the area, refer to "Where to Stay Around New Forest," in section 4.

Highfield House Hotel. 119 Highfield Lane, Portswood (off Portswood Rd.), Southampton, Hampshire SO17 1AQ. ☎ **023/8035-9955.** Fax 023/8058-3910. 66 units. TV TEL. Sun–Thurs £85 ($144.50) double; Fri–Sat £55 ($93.50) double. Rates include English breakfast. AE, DC, MC, V. Bus nos. 11 or 13.

In a residential area on the northern outskirts of the city, this modern hotel offers comfortable but lackluster accommodations and efficient service. Conference and business travelers often book the small to medium-size rooms; 20 rooms are rented to nonsmokers. The small bathrooms won't make *Architectural Digest*, but they are adequate for the job, with showers. Its restaurant, Hamilton's, serves a standard à la carte menu complemented by a comprehensive wine list.

✪ **De Vere Grand Harbour Hotel.** W. Quay Rd., Southampton, Hampshire S015 1AG. ☎ **023/8063-3033.** Fax 023/8063-3066. www.devere.com. E-mail:grand.harbour@devere-hotels.com 172 units. MINIBAR TV TEL. £170–£195 ($289–$331.50) double; £270–£395 ($459–$671.50) suite. Rates include breakfast. AE, DC, MC, V.

If you must stay in town, and if you can afford it, this is the most comfortable place to be. Completed in 1994, the five-story structure, sheathed in granite and possessing a dramatically tilted glass facade, is the most exciting hotel to be built in Southampton since World War II. Some 30 of the brightly painted bedrooms have air-conditioning. Most of the bathrooms are filled with amenities, including separate walk-in showers and granite vanities. Extra bathroom amenities include a hair dryer, both hand-held and overhead showers, and robes in the executive rooms only. Bedrooms range from midsize to spacious, with a pair of armchairs and traditional polished wood surfaces, plus snug beds. About nine of the rooms are equipped for persons with disabilities.

Dining: The more formal of the hotel's two restaurants is Allerton's, with somewhat mediocre food. More boisterous is Brewster's, an informal bistro.

Amenities: 24-hour room service, laundry, baby-sitting, indoor swimming pool with a separate indoor pool for children, gym, spa bath, steam room, sauna.

The Dolphin. 35 High St., Southampton, Hampshire SO14 2HN. ☎ **023/8033-9955.** Fax 023/8033-3650. 73 units. TV TEL. £85 ($144.50) double; £105 ($178.50) suite. Children under 16 stay free in their parents' room. AE, DC, MC, V. Bus nos. 2, 6, or 8.

This bow-windowed Georgian coaching house in the center of the city was Jane Austen's choice, and Thackeray's, too. Even Queen Victoria visited via her horse-drawn carriage. If you want tradition, this is your best bet. The rooms vary widely in size, but are generally spacious and well equipped with such extras as a trouser press. Bedrooms are being refurbished as part of an ongoing restoration program that includes the installation of fresh quality mattresses. Three rooms are large enough for families. English meals at the Thackeray Restaurant are quite good, and drinks are served in the Nelson Bar.

Forte Post House. Herbert Walker Ave., Southampton, Hampshire SO15 1HJ. ☎ **800/225-5843** in the U.S. and Canada, or 023/8033–0777. Fax 023/8033-2510. 128 units. TV TEL. £69–£99 ($117.30–$168.30) double. AE, DC, MC, V. Bus nos. 2, 6, or 8.

This 10-floor high-rise across from Mayflower Park was built near the new docks to overlook the harbor, but is only 5 minutes away from the city center. The rooms are standard but generally spacious, with built-in furniture and picture-window walls. Rooms have recently been refurbished and upgraded with better quality mattresses. There is only one unit with facilities for persons with disabilities. Bathrooms are routine motel-style tiled affairs. They're not big on amenities but adequate for the job. Among the facilities of the hotel are an indoor swimming pool, a Jacuzzi, a full gym, and a lounge. The Trader Bar adjacent to the restaurant offers an intimate atmosphere.

WHERE TO DINE

Ennios. Town Quay Rd. ☎ **023/8022-1159.** Reservations recommended. Main courses £8.50–£14 ($14.45–$23.80). AE, DC, MC, V. Mon–Sat 11:30am–3pm and 6:30–midnight. Bus nos. 2, 6, or 8. ITALIAN.

The best restaurant in Southampton, Ennios was designed by Scottish-born architect John Geddes as a warehouse and boatyard. At the time, the sea came up to its foundations and boats could unload their cargoes directly into its cavernous interior. Today, although the exterior is rustic and weathered, its interior is stylish. The restaurant's wine cellar, with 600-year-old walls, once part of the medieval wall that ringed Southampton, has an extensive list of Italian wines as well as some French and New World labels. Meals feature typical pastas, as well as farm-fresh venison. Freshly caught fish is listed daily on a blackboard. The restaurant, informal wine bar, and brasserie are much favored by local businesspeople at lunch and by relatively informal diners in the evening.

The Red Lion. 55 High St. ☎ **023/8033-3595.** Main courses 5.50–6.50; pub snacks 2.50–3.50. AE, DC, MC, V. Daily noon–2:30pm and 7–9:30pm. Pub: Daily noon–11:30–pm. Bus 1, 2, 6, or 8 ENGLISH.

One of the few architectural jewels to have survived World War II, this pub has its roots in the 13th century (as a Norman cellar), but its high-ceilinged and raftered Henry V Court Room is from Tudor times. The room was the scene of the trial of the earl of Cambridge and his accomplices, Thomas Grey and Lord Scrope, who were condemned to death for plotting against the life of the king in 1415. Today the Court Room is adorned with coats-of-arms of the noblemen who were peers of the condemned trio. The Red Lion is a fascinating place for a drink and a chat. Typical pub snacks are served in the bar, whereas in the somewhat more formal restaurant section the well-seasoned specialties include an array of steaks (including sirloin), stews, roasts, and fish platters.

A SIDE TRIP TO BROADLANDS: HOME OF THE LATE EARL OF MOUNTBATTEN

Broadlands. 8 miles northwest of Southampton in Romsey, on A31. ☎ **01794/505010.** Admission £5.50 ($9.35) adults, £4.70 ($8) students and seniors, £3.85 ($6.55) children 12–16; free for children 11 and under. Noon–5:30pm. Open daily from June 12 to Sept 1. Closed early Sept to early June.

Broadlands was the home of the late Earl Mountbatten of Burma, who was assassinated in 1979. Earl Mountbatten, who has been called "the last war hero," lent the house to his nephew, Prince Philip, and Princess Elizabeth as a honeymoon haven in 1947, and in 1981 Prince Charles and Princess Diana spent the first nights of their honeymoon here.

Broadlands is now owned by Lord Romsey, Earl Mountbatten's eldest grandson, who has created a fine exhibition and audiovisual show that depicts the highlights of his grandfather's brilliant career as a sailor and statesman. The house, originally linked to Romsey Abbey, was transformed into an elegant Palladian mansion by Capability Brown and Henry Holland. Brown landscaped the parkland and grounds.

4 The New Forest

95 miles SW of London; 10 miles W of Southampton

Encompassing about 92,000 acres, the New Forest is a large tract created by William the Conqueror, who laid out the limits of this then-private hunting preserve. Successful poachers faced the executioner if they were caught, and those who hunted but missed had their hands severed. Henry VIII loved to hunt deer in the New Forest, but he also saw an opportunity to build up the British naval fleet by supplying oak and other hard timbers to the boatyards at Buckler's Hard on the Beaulieu River.

Today, you can visit the old shipyards and also the museum, with its fine models of men-of-war, pictures of the old yard, and dioramas showing the building of these ships, their construction, and their launching. It took 2,000 trees to construct one man-of-war. A motorway cuts through the area, and the once-thick forest has groves of oak trees separated by wide tracts of common land that's grazed by ponies and cows, hummocked with heather and gorse, and frequented by rabbits. But away from the main roads, where signs warn of wild ponies and deer, you'll find a private world of peace and quiet.

ESSENTIALS

GETTING THERE On the train, go to Southampton (see "Essentials," in section 3), where rail connections can be made to a few centers in the New Forest. Where the train leaves off, bus connections can be made to all the towns and many villages. Southampton and Lymington have the best bus connections to New Forest villages.

If you're driving, head west from Southampton on A35.

VISITOR INFORMATION The information office is at the **New Forest Visitor Centre,** Main Car Park, Lyndhurst (☎ **01703/282269**), which is open daily from 10am to 6pm April to September, and daily from 10am to 5pm from October to March.

SEEING THE SIGHTS

✪ **Beaulieu Abbey–Palace House.** Beaulieu, on B3056 in the New Forest (5 miles southeast of Lyndhurst and 14 miles west of Southampton). ☎ **01590/612345.** Admission £9.25 ($15.75) adults, £8 ($13.60) seniors and students, £6.50 ($11.05) children 4–16; free for children 3 and under, £29.50 ($50.15) family (2 adults and up to 3 children). May–Sept daily 10am–6pm; Oct–Apr. daily 10am–5pm. Closed Dec 25. Buses run from the Lymington bus station Mon–Sat; Sun you'll need a taxi or car.

The abbey and house, as well as the National Motor Museum, are on the property of Lord Montagu of Beaulieu (pronounced *Bew*-ley). A Cistercian abbey was founded on this spot in 1204, and the ruins can be explored today. The Palace House was the great gatehouse of the abbey before it was converted into a private residence in 1538. It is surrounded by gardens.

The **National Motor Museum,** one of the best and most comprehensive automotive museums in the world, with more than 250 vehicles, is on the grounds and is open to the public. Famous autos include four land-speed record holders, among them Donald Campbell's Bluebird. The collection was built around Lord Montagu's family collection of vintage cars. A special feature is called "Wheels." In a darkened environment, visitors can travel in specially designed "pods" that carry up to two adults and one child along a silent electric track. They move at a predetermined but variable speed, and each pod is capable of rotating almost 360°. Seated in these, you'll view displays (with sound and visual effects) spanning 100 years of motor development without the fatigue of standing in line. For further information, contact the visitor reception manager at the John Montagu Building (☎ **01590/612345**).

Maritime Museum. Buckler's Hard. ☎ **01590/616203.** Admission £2 ($3.40) adults, £1.50 ($2.55) students and seniors, £1 ($1.70) children, £9 ($15.30) family. Easter–Sept daily 10am–6pm, Oct–Easter daily 10am–4:30pm.

Buckler's Hard, a historic 18th-century village 2½ miles from Beaulieu on the banks of the River Beaulieu, is where ships for Nelson's fleet were built, including the admiral's favorite, *Agamemnon,* as well as *Eurylus* and *Swiftsure.* The Maritime Museum highlights the village's shipbuilding history as well as Henry Adams, master shipbuilder; Nelson's favorite ship; Buckler's Hard and Trafalgar; and models of Sir Francis

Chichester's yachts and items of his equipment. The cottage exhibits re-create 18th-century life in Buckler's Hard you can stroll through the New Inn of 1793 and a shipwright's cottage of the same period, or look in on the family of a poor laborer at home.

The walk back to Beaulieu, 2½ miles along the riverbank, is well marked through the woodlands. During the summer, you can take a 20-minute cruise on the River Beaulieu in the present *Swiftsure,* an all-weather catamaran cruiser.

WHERE TO STAY AROUND THE NEW FOREST

Balmer Lawn Hotel. Lyndhurst Rd., Brockenhurst, Hampshire SO42 7ZB. ☎ **01590/623116.** Fax 01590/623864. www.blh.co.uk. E-mail: BLH@btinternet.com. 55 units. TV TEL. £120 ($204) double. Rates include English breakfast. AE, DC, DISC, MC, V. Take A337 (Lyndhurst-Lymington road) about half a mile outside Brockenhurst.

This hotel, about a 10-minute walk from Brockenhurst's center in a woodland location, was originally built as a modest private home during the 17th century and was later enlarged into an imposing hunting lodge. During World War II, it was a military hospital. (Within the past decade, significant numbers of overnight guests here have spotted the ghost of one of the white-coated doctors with his stethoscope, still roaming the hotel's first floor.) The hotel has a pleasant and humorous staff (which refers to the ghost as "Dr. Eric"). There is a good range of bedrooms here, in all shapes and sizes, but each has an individual character; bathrooms are small. Nearly all the bedrooms are designated as nonsmoking. Request, if available, a room with a view of the forest. There are three family bedrooms, and children up to 16 stay free in their parents' room.

Dining: There's a newly refurbished bar and lounge, where informal bar snacks are offered at lunchtime. More formal, well-prepared meals are available in the restaurant at night.

Amenities: Two swimming pools (one indoor, one outdoor), gym, sauna, Jacuzzi, two indoor squash courts, and an all-weather tennis court.

Carey's Manor. Lyndhurst Rd., Brockenhurst, Hampshire SO42 7RH. ☎ **01590/623551.** Fax 01590/622799. www.newforest-hotels.co.uk. 79 units. TV TEL. £129 ($219.30) double; £179 ($304.30) suite. Rates include English breakfast. AE, DC, MC, V. From the town center, head toward Lyndhurst on A337.

This manor house dates from Charles II, who used to come here when Carey's was a hunting lodge. Greatly expanded in 1888, the building became a country hotel in the 1930s. It's about a 90-minute drive from London. Much improved in recent years, the old house is still filled with character, possessing mellow, timeworn paneling and carved oak staircase. Each bedroom, whether in the restored main building or in the garden wing, has a tub or shower, hair dryer, and trouser press. Six rooms contain an old-fashioned four-poster bed, but whether your room does or not, it will still have a firm bed with cozy comfort.

Dining: The hotel serves good food—modern British and French cuisine.

Amenities: Carey's is ideal as a resort, with an indoor swimming pool, gym, solarium, and sauna, all on 5 acres of landscaped grounds.

✪ **Chewton Glen Hotel.** Christchurch Rd., New Milton, Hampshire BH25 6QS. ☎ **01425/275341.** Fax 01425/272310. www.chewtonglen.com. E-mail: reservations@chewtonglen.com. 55 units. TV TEL. £235–£385 ($399.50–$654.50) double; £455–£665 ($773.50–$1,130.50) suite. AE, DC, MC, V. After leaving the village of Walkford, follow signs off A35 (New Milton-Christchurch Rd.), through parkland.

A gracious country house on the fringe of the New Forest, Chewton Glen, within easy reach of Southampton and Bournemouth, is the finest place to stay in southwest England (with princely rates to match). In the old house, the magnificent staircase leads to well-furnished double rooms opening onto views of the spacious grounds. In the new wing, you will find yourself on the ground level with French doors opening onto your own private patio. Accommodations vary widely, coming in different shapes, sizes, and periods, but each is equipped with a double or twin bed. Attic accommodations and some of the newly refurbished rooms contain air conditioners. The best accommodations are the "Croquet Lawn Rooms," as they open onto the greens and have big private balconies or terraces. The baths in all rooms are luxurious, with hair dryers, deluxe toiletries, and separate power showers in large stalls. Log fires burn and fresh flowers add fragrance; the garden sweeps down to a stream and then to rhododendron woods.

Dining: In the dining room, the standards of cooking and presentation are high. Particular emphasis is placed on fresh ingredients. The chef favors a modern cuisine, complemented by excellent sauces and velvety smooth desserts.

Amenities: Open-air heated swimming pool and an indoor swimming pool, indoor and outdoor tennis courts, 9-hole golf course, health club, sauna, Jacuzzi, 24-hour room service, valet and laundry service.

Country House Hotel New Park Manor. Lyndhurst Rd., Brockenhurst, Hampshire SO42 7QH. ☎ **01590/623467.** Fax 01590/622268. E-mail:enquiries@newparkmanorhotel.co.uk 24 units. TV TEL. £110–£160 ($187–$272) double; £150–£180 ($255–$306) suite for 2. Rates include breakfast. AE, CB, DC, MC, V. Head 2 miles north off A337 (Lyndhurst-Brockenhurst rd.) toward the New Forest Show Ground.

This former royal hunting lodge, dating from the days of William the Conqueror and a favorite of Charles II, is the only hotel in the New Forest itself. Although it's now a modern country hotel, the original rooms have been preserved, including such features as beams and in some rooms open log fires. Since its purchase in 1998 by the Countess Von-Essen, the hotel has been much improved, and each room is individually furnished, including a honeymoon suite complete with a four-poster bed. Most rooms have a view overlooking the forest. Bathrooms are small but well organized, with a hair dryer.

Dining: The candlelit restaurant, with its log fire, offers a fine table d'hôte menu which is regularly changed. The chef often uses fresh garden produce, which is complemented by a good wine list.

Amenities: There's a swimming pool in a sheltered corner of the garden (heated in summer) and a hard tennis court. Horseback-riding from the hotel's stables is available.

The Crown Hotel. 9 High St., Lyndhurst, Hampshire SO43 7NF. ☎ **01703/282922.** Fax 01703/282751. 39 units. MINIBAR TV TEL. £120 ($204) double; £164 ($278.80) suite. Rates include English breakfast. AE, DC, MC, V. Bus nos. 56 or 56A. Exit the M27 motorway at Junction 1 and drive 3 miles due south.

Although the present building is only 100 years old, there has been a hostelry here on the main street of the New Forest village of Lyndhurst for centuries. For generations it has remained a favorite of visitors to the New Forest, who delight in its gardens, where afternoon tea is served, or its roaring fireplace in winter. Bedrooms are most inviting, often medium in size or spacious, but each furnished in the classic tradition of an English country house, with features such as a four-poster bed in many cases. Some rooms are more modern in character, with padded headboards and fine furnishings. Each room has a trouser press, and small bathrooms are modern and have such amenities as a hair dryer.

Dining: Much local produce, including venison, is used in the dining room, where the food is not only good, but reasonable in price. Locals flock here for Sunday lunch. The hotel also does substantial bar meals.

Lyndhurst Park Hotel. High St., Lyndhurst, Hampshire SO43 7NL. ☎ **01703/283923.** Fax 01703/283019. 59 units. TV TEL. £95 ($161.50) double. Rates include English breakfast. AE, DC, MC, V. Bus nos. 56, 56A or X1.

This is a large Georgian country house set on 5 acres of beautiful gardens. Located at the point on the edge of town where Lyndhurst meets the New Forest, this hotel often attracts conferences. Much of it remains characteristically rustic, although filled with modern comforts. Bedrooms are medium in size and extremely well kept, often coming with brass headboards crowning the fine English beds. Bathrooms are tiled and fully carpeted.

Dining: There is a bar, plus an oak-paneled restaurant, where a wide selection is offered at lunch and dinner.

Amenities: Outdoor heated swimming pool, all-weather tennis court.

Master Builders House Hotel. Buckler's Hard, Beaulieu, Hampshire SO42 7XB. ☎ **01590/616253.** Fax 01590/616297. www.themasterbuilders.co.uk. E-mail: res@hemasterbuilders.co.uk. 25 units. TV TEL. Summer £145–£195 ($246.50–$331.50) double; winter £96–£148 ($163.20–$251.60) double. Rates include breakfast. Half board £175–£225 ($297.50–$382.50) double in summer, £175–£225 ($297.50–$382.50) double in winter. AE, MC, V.

About 2½ miles south of Beaulieu, in the historic maritime village of Buckler's Hard, this 17th-century redbrick building was once the home of master shipbuilder Henry Adams, who incorporated many of his shipbuilding techniques into the construction of this lovely old house. Views from some of the bedrooms overlook the grass-covered slipways that, centuries ago, were used to ease newly built ocean vessels into the calm waters of the nearby river.

Most of the hotel's comfortable and conservatively decorated accommodations are in a modern wing, built after World War II. If you like the creaky floorboards and charm of old-world England, opt for one of the six old-fashioned bedrooms in the main house. If you want better amenities and more space, select a room in the purpose-built annex; these are plainer, but better equipped. Bedrooms vary in size and shape; most are equipped with king-size beds and contain such thoughtful touches as mineral water. Bathrooms are small but efficiently organized with luxury toiletries and a hair dryer. The hotel's historic core is devoted to the Yachtsman Buffet Bar and to the restaurant. Here, wide windows overlook the busy river.

Montagu Arms. Palace Lane, Beaulieu, Hampshire, SO42 7ZL. ☎ **01590/612324.** Fax 01590/612188. www.newforest-hotels.co.uk. E-mail: enquiries@montagu-arms.co.uk. 24 units. TV TEL. £125–£135 ($212.50–$229.50) double; £175–£195 ($297.50–$331.50) suite. Rates include English breakfast. AE, DC, MC, V.

The core of this historic coaching inn was built in the 1700s to supply food and drink to the teams of laborers who hauled salt from the nearby marshes to other parts of England. The garden walls were built with stones salvaged from Beaulieu Abbey after it was demolished by Henry VIII. Equally important is the hexagonal column supporting a fountain in the hotel's central courtyard—one of six salvaged, according to legend, from the ruined abbey's nave. Each bedroom is individually decorated in an English country-house tradition, and come in a range of shapes and sizes, but all have extras including a trouser press and a writing desk. Many units contain a traditional four-poster bed. The small bathrooms are beautifully maintained, with a hair dryer.

Dining: On the premises is an oak-beamed dining room, serving traditional English food. The oldest part of the inn is its pub, which continues to serve food and ale to visitors who appreciate its well-oiled patina and sense of history.

WHERE TO DINE

Simply Poussin. The Courtyard, at the rear of 49–55 Brookley Rd., Brockenhurst. ☎ **01590/623063.** Reservations recommended 1 month in advance on weekends. 2-course lunch £15.50 ($26.35), 3-course lunch £23 ($39.10); 2-course dinner £22.50 ($38.25), 3-course dinner £30 ($51). MC, V. Tues–Sat noon–2pm; Tues–Sat 7–10pm. GAME/FISH.

Serving the best food in the area, Le Poussin is located in what was originally a 19th-century stable and workshop. To reach it, pass beneath the arched alleyway (located midway between nos. 49 and 55 Brookley Rd.) and enter the stylishly simple premises directed by English-born chef Alexander Aitken and his wife, Caroline.

Amid a decor accented with framed 19th-century poems and illustrations celebrating the pleasures of poultry, the staff will offer fish and game dishes whose ingredients usually come fresh from the nearby New Forest. Try the "Fruits of the New Forest"—individually cooked portions of pigeon, wild rabbit, hare, and venison, encased in puff pastry and served with game sauce. Dessert choices change seasonally but usually include a lemon tart with lime sorbet, or a passion-fruit soufflé.

5 The Isle of Wight

91 miles SW of London; 4 miles S of Southampton

The Isle of Wight is known for its sandy beaches and its ports, long favored by the yachting set. The island has attracted such literary figures as Alfred, Lord Tennyson, and Charles Dickens. Tennyson wrote his beloved poem "Crossing the Bar" en route across the Solent from Lymington to Yarmouth. A vacation on the island sounds a bit dated, although many British families come here just to relax and enjoy the natural beauty. You may want to come just for the day. Some parts are rather tacky, especially Sandown and Shanklin, although other areas out on the island are still tranquil and quite beautiful.

The Isle of Wight is compact in size, measuring 23 miles from east to west, 13 miles from north to south. **Ryde** is the railhead for the island's transportation system. **Yarmouth** is something else—a busy little harbor providing a mooring for yachts and also for one of the lifeboats in the Solent area.

Cowes is the premier port for yachting in Britain. Henry VIII ordered the castle built here, but it's now the headquarters of the Royal Yacht Squadron. The seafront, the Prince's Green, and the high cliff road are worth exploring. Hovercraft are built in the town, which is also the home and birthplace of the well-known maritime photographer Beken of Cowes. In winter, everyone wears oilskins and wellies, leaving a wet trail behind them.

Newport, a bustling market town in the heart of the island, is the capital and has long been a favorite of British royalty. Along the southeast coast are the twin resorts of **Sandown,** with its new pier complex and theater, and **Shanklin,** at the southern end of Sandown Bay, which has held the British annual sunshine record more times than any other resort. Keats once lived in Shanklin's Old Village. Farther along the coast, **Ventnor** is called the "Madeira of England" because it rises from the sea in a series of steep hills.

On the west coast are the many-colored sand cliffs of **Alum Bay.** The Needles, three giant chalk rocks, and the Needles Lighthouse, are the farther features of interest at this end of the island. If you want to stay at the western end of Wight, consider **Freshwater Bay.**

ESSENTIALS

GETTING THERE A direct train from London's Waterloo Station to Portsmouth deposits travelers directly at the pier for a ferry crossing to the Isle of Wight; ferries are timed to meet train arrivals. Travel time from London to the arrival point of Ryde on the Isle of Wight (including ferry-crossing time) is 2 hours. One train per hour departs during the day from London to Portsmouth. For rail information, call ☎ **0345/484950.**

Drive to Southampton (see "Essentials," in section 3) and take the ferry, or leave Southampton and head west along A35, cutting south on A337 toward Lymington on the coast, where the ferry crossing to Yarmouth (Isle of Wight) is shorter than the trip from Southampton.

Red Funnel operates a vehicle ferry service from Terminal 1 in Southampton to East Cowes; the trip takes 55 minutes. An inclusive round-trip fare (valid for 5 days) costs from £38 to £60 ($64.60 to $102) for four persons, depending on the season. More popular with train travelers from Waterloo Station in London is a Hi-Speed passenger-only catamaran operating from the Town Quay Terminal 2 in Southampton, going to West Cowes; the trip takes 22 minutes. A day return fare costs £9.80 ($16.65) for adults and £4.90 ($8.35) for children. For ferry departure times, call ☎ **01703/334010.**

The White Line ferry operates between Portsmouth and Ryde, taking 20 minutes and costing £7 ($11.90) for adults and £3.50 ($5.95) for children, round-trip day return. Daytime departures are every 30 minutes in summer and every 60 minutes in winter. A final option involves a Hovercraft that travels from Southsea (Portsmouth's neighbor) to Ryde, charging £8.40 ($14.30) for adults and £4.20 ($7.15) for children for day return. For information on departure times and schedules, call ☎ **0800/343333** for car-ferries, ☎ **01983/811000** for the Hovercraft, or ☎ **0990/827744** for the White Line passenger ferries.

GETTING AROUND Visitors can explore the Isle of Wight just for the day on the Island Explorer bus service. Tickets may be purchased on the bus, and you can board or leave the bus at any stop on the island. The price of a Day Rover is £6.25 ($10.65) for adults and £3.15 ($5.35) for children. It also entitles you to passage on the island's only railway, which runs from the dock at Ryde to the center of Shanklin, a distance of 8 miles. For further information, call **Southern Vectis** at **01983/827005.**

VISITOR INFORMATION The **information office** is at 67 High St., Shanklin (☎ **01983/862942**). It's open Monday to Saturday, March through mid-July and September through October from 9am to 6pm, mid-July through August from 9am to 8:45pm, and November through March from 10am to 4pm. It's best to call first, as these hours are subject to change.

QUEEN VICTORIA'S FAVORITE RESIDENCE & A MEDIEVAL CASTLE

✪ **Osborne House.** A mile southeast of East Cowes. ☎ **01983/200022.** House and grounds £6.90 ($11.75) adults, £5.20 ($8.85) seniors, £3.50 ($5.95) children. Admission to grounds only £3.50 ($5.95) adults, £2.60 ($4.40) seniors, £1.80 ($3.05) children. Apr–Sept daily 10am–6pm (house closes at 5pm); Oct daily 10am–5pm. Nov to mid-Dec and Feb–Mar, Sun–Thurs 10am–2:30pm (guided tours only). Closed mid-Dec to Jan. Bus nos. 4 or 5.

Queen Victoria's most cherished residence was built at her own expense. Prince Albert, with his characteristic thoroughness, contributed to many aspects of the design of the Italian-inspired mansion, which stands amid lush gardens, right outside the village of Whippingham. The rooms have remained as Victoria knew them, right down to the French piano she used to play and all the cozy clutter of her sitting room.

Grief-stricken at the death of Albert in 1861, she asked that Osborne House be kept as it was, and so it has been. Even the turquoise scent bottles he gave her, decorated with cupids and cherubs, are still in place. It was in her bedroom at Osborne House that the queen died on January 22, 1901.

Carisbrooke Castle. Carisbrooke, 1¼ miles southwest of Newport. ☎ **01983/522107.** Castle and museum £4.50 ($7.65) adults, £3.40 ($5.80) seniors and students, £2.30 ($3.90) children. Apr–Sept daily 10am–6pm; Oct 10am–5pm; Nov–Mar daily 10am–4pm. Bus no. 91A.

This fine medieval castle lies in the center of the Isle of Wight. During one of the most turbulent periods of English history, Charles I was imprisoned here, far from his former seat of power in London, by Cromwell's Roundheads in 1647. On the castle premises is the 16th-century Well House, where during periods of siege, donkeys took turns treading a large wooden wheel connected to a rope that hauled up buckets of water from a well. Accessible from the castle's courtyard is a **museum** ☎ **01983/523112**) with exhibits pertaining to the social history of the Isle of Wight and the history of Charles I's imprisonment.

WHERE TO STAY

Biskra Beach Hotel. 17 St. Thomas's St., Ryde, Isle of Wight PO33 2DC. ☎ **01983/567913.** Fax 01983/616976. www.biskra-hotel.com. E-mail: info@biskra-hotel.com. 14 units. MINIBAR TV TEL. £55–£90 ($93.50–$153) double. Rates include English breakfast. AE, MC, V.

You'll find some of the best dining on the island at Biskra House, which also offers rooms. This place has a welcoming country house feel thanks to its new owners. Nothing is overly decorated or overblown here, but there is much comfort. Bedrooms are small but inviting. The most expensive double in the house has a private balcony with views over the Solent. Complete refurbishment of all the bedrooms is ongoing, and the bathrooms, though small, are equipped with a hair dryer, and a tub with a handheld shower. Enjoy the panoramic views in the garden terrace while you sip cocktails, or have a meal. For a more intimate candlelit dinner, the restaurant offers an imaginative international cuisine.

Bourne Hall Country Hotel. Luccombe Rd., Shanklin, Isle of Wight PO37 6RR. ☎ **01983/862820.** Fax 01983/865138. E-mail:bhch@dialstark.net. 30 units. TV TEL. £64–£94 ($108.80–$159.80) double. Rates include half board and transfers. AE, DC, MC, V.

Many visitors prefer to base themselves at Shanklin because of its old village with its thatched cottages and the Chine, two of the island's leading attractions. At Bourne Hall, they receive a warm welcome from the owners, who have one of the area's best-equipped hotels, complete with two swimming pools, a sauna, and a Jacuzzi. The hotel stands on its own grounds of nearly 3 acres adjoining open farmland. Bedrooms are furnished in a delightful English country-house style. Some of the bedrooms have recently been redecorated, and even those which haven't are still in fine shape. Each small bathroom is well maintained and comes with a hair dryer. All contain a shower. The hotel is noted for its generous and varied cuisine, using local produce whenever possible.

Clarendon Hotel and Wight Mouse Inn. Newport Rd. (B3399; 50 yd. off Military Rd.), Chale, Isle of Wight PO38 2HA. ☎ and fax **01983/730431.** www.trad-inns.co.uk/clarendon. E-mail: wightmouse@aol.com. 12 units. TV TEL. £78 ($132.60) double; £98 ($166.60) suite for 2. Children ages 9–12 stay with parents for £24.50 ($41.65), ages 4–9 £14 ($23.80), children 3 and under free. Rates include English breakfast. DC, MC, V.

The Clarendon is a cheerful place to spend the night. This old coaching inn lies on the most southerly part of the island, where the vegetation is almost tropical. From here, you can see over the Channel to the mainland coast. Although a bit small, each of the bedrooms is prettily decorated in an English country house style, with private baths (usually with a tub and shower combination). Each room is also equipped with a coffeemaker.

The pub, the Wight Mouse Inn, is open all day every day for ample hot meals and drinks; they serve a large selection of beers, real ales, and 365 scotch whiskies, including their own famous Wight Mouse whisky. Live entertainment is provided nightly year-round. Traditional English dishes are served in the more formal Clarendon Restaurant.

Hotel Ryde Castle. The Esplanade, Ryde, Isle of Wight PO33 1JA. ☎ **01983/563755.** Fax 01983/566906. 20 units. TV TEL. £60–£80 ($102–$136) double. Rates include English breakfast. AE, DC, MC, V.

This historic seafront castle looking out on the Solent makes a fine base for exploring the island. The castle, dating from the 16th century, has been added to over the centuries. Field Marshall Montgomery stayed here before the D-Day landings. With its crenellated ivy-clad exterior and its well-kept public rooms, the hotel attracts families as well as single visitors. Bedrooms, small to medium in size, have an inviting aura with traditional British styling. Comfort is the keynote here, and each room comes with a coffeemaker. Some accommodations have a more romantic aura and a four-poster bed. Each has a small private bath. Kids can hang around at the children's play area.

The hotel dining room makes full use of locally caught fresh fish and island farm products. The family bar/lounge offers inexpensive snacks for lunch.

Luccombe Chine House. Luccombe Chine, Shanklin, Isle of Wight PO37 6RH. ☎ **01983/862037.** 6 units. TV. £40–£50 ($68–$85) per person. Rates include English breakfast. MC, V. Closed Dec–Jan. Bus no. 12A. Take A3055 (Shanklin-Ventnor Rd.) to the signposted private driveway. Children not accepted.

Luccombe Chine House is situated on some 10 acres of grounds opening onto Luccombe Bay. Each room is immaculately kept and well furnished; all have four-poster beds and beverage makers. All rooms are individually decorated and come in a variety of shapes and sizes. The owners are constantly upgrading the decor. All the small bathrooms include a hair dryer. The lounge is comfortable and homelike, with an inglenook fireplace and a well-stocked honor bar. There is a small brook that cascades through the gardens down to the sea. It's a good base from which to explore the Isle of Wight.

St. Catherine's Hotel. 1 Winchester Park Rd., Sandown, Isle of Wight PO36 8HJ. ☎ **01983/402392.** Fax 01983/402392. www.smoothhound.co.uk/hotels/stcather.html. E-mail:stcathhotel@hotmail.com 19 units. TV TEL. £48–£51 ($81.60–$86.70) double. Rates include English breakfast. MC, V.

Just a few minutes' walk from Sandown's sandy beach, leisure center, and pier complex, with its sun lounges and theater and Sandown railway station, St. Catherine's was built in 1860 of creamy Purbeck stone and white trim for the dean of Winchester College. A modern extension was added for streamlined and sunny bedrooms, which have duvets over firm mattresses, white furniture, and built-in headboards. Baths are small. The brightly redecorated lounge has matching draperies at the wide bay windows. There are card tables and a small library of books. Adjacent to the library is a cozy, fully stocked bar and a spacious, comfortable dining room, serving high-quality, well-priced English food.

WHERE TO DINE

The Cottage. 8 Eastcliff Rd., Shanklin Old Village. ☎ **01983/862504.** Reservations recommended. Main courses £10.50–£38 ($17.85–$64.60). AE, DC, MC, V. Tues–Sun noon–2pm and Tues–Sat 7:30–9:45pm. Closed Feb to mid-Mar and Oct to mid-Nov. ENGLISH/FRENCH.

This restaurant is in a 200-year-old stone-sided cottage that's set among thatch-covered buildings in the center of Shanklin. Inside, two floors of pink and blue dining rooms are accented by lace tablecloths and heavy oak beams. For starters try the delicious avocado Ritz. As a main course, you could enjoy such treats as braised guinea fowl smothered in a port and apricot sauce, or Dover sole pan-fried with lemon butter. For the more adventurous, try the ostrich, pan-fried and served with a green peppercorn sauce. Two lounges accommodate smokers. The garden and courtyard are open in summer for drinks.

6 Bournemouth

104 miles SW of London; 15 miles W of the Isle of Wight

The south-coast resort at the doorstep of the New Forest didn't just happen: It was carefully planned and executed—a true city in a garden. Flower-filled, park-dotted Bournemouth is filled with an abundance of architecture inherited from those arbiters of taste, Victoria and her son, Edward. (The resort was discovered back in Victoria's day, when sea bathing became an institution.) Bournemouth's most distinguished feature is its chines (narrow, shrub-filled, steep-sided ravines) along the coastline.

Bournemouth, along with neighboring Poole and Christchurch, forms the largest urban area in the south of England. It makes a good base for exploring a historically rich part of England; on its outskirts are the New Forest, Salisbury, Winchester, and the Isle of Wight.

ESSENTIALS

GETTING THERE An express train from London's Waterloo Station takes 2 hours, with frequent service throughout the day. For schedules and information, call ☎ **0345/484950.** Arrivals are at the Bournemouth Rail Station, on Holden Surst Road.

Buses leave London's Waterloo Station every 2 hours during the day, heading for Bournemouth. The trip takes 2½ hours. Call ☎ **0990/808080** for information and schedules.

If you're driving, take M3 southwest from London to Winchester, then A31 and A338 south to Bournemouth.

VISITOR INFORMATION The **information office** is at Westover Road (☎ **01202/451731**). From May through September, it's open Monday through Saturday from 9am to 7pm, Sunday from 10am to 4pm; from September through May, hours are Monday through Saturday from 9:30am to 5:30pm.

EXPLORING THE AREA

Of Bournemouth's nearly 12,000 acres, about 1/6 consists of green parks and flower beds such as the **Pavilion Rock Garden,** which is perfect for a stroll. The total effect, especially in spring, is striking and helps explain Bournemouth's continuing popularity with the garden-loving English.

The resort's amusements are varied. At the **Pavilion Theatre,** you can see West End–type productions from London. The **Bournemouth Symphony Orchestra** is justly famous in Europe. And there's the usual run of golf courses, band concerts, variety shows, and dancing.

And of course, this seaside resort has a spectacular beach—7 miles of uninterrupted sand stretching from Hengistbury Head to Alum Chine. Most of it is known simply as **Bournemouth Beach,** although its western edge, when it crosses over into the municipality of Poole, is called **Sandbanks Beach.** Beach access is free, and you can swim where a pair of blue flags indicate that the water's fine. The flags also signify the highest standards of cleanliness, management, and facilities. A health-conscious, no-smoking zone now exists at Durley Chine, East Beach, and Fisherman's Walk. Fourteen full-time lifeguards patrol the shore and the water; they are helped by three volunteer corps during the busiest summer months. The promenade is traffic-free during the summer. There are two piers, one at Boscombe and the other at Bournemouth.

Amenities at the beach include beach bungalows, freshwater showers, seafront bistros and cafes, boat trips, rowboats, pedalos, jet skis, and Windsurfers. Cruises run in the summer from Bournemouth Pier to the Isle of Wight.

The traffic-free town center with its wide avenues is elegant but by no means stuffy. Entertainers perform on the corners of streets that are lined with boutiques, cafes, street furniture, and plenty of meeting places. Specialized shopping is found mainly in the suburbs—Pokesdown for antiques and collectibles, Westbourne for individual designer fashion and home accessories. Victorian shopping arcades can be found in both Westbourne and Boscombe.

The Shelley Rooms. Beechwood Ave., Boscombe. ☎ **01202/303571.** Free admission. Tues–Sun 2–5pm.

True romantics and die-hard fans of Percy Bysshe Shelley should take time to see this small museum and study room, housed in Boscombe Manor, the one-time home of Shelley's son, Sir Percy Florence Shelley. The rooms are devoted to the works of the great poet and his circle. Collections are built primarily around works written during the last few months of Shelley's life when he lived in San Terenzo, Italy.

Exploring Nearby Wareham

This historic little town on the Frome River 2 miles west of Bournemouth is an excellent center for touring the South Dorset coast and the Purbeck Hills. See the remains of early Anglo-Saxon and Roman town walls, plus the Saxon church of St. Martin, with its effigy of T. E. Lawrence (Lawrence of Arabia), who died in a motorcycle crash in 1935. His former home, **Clouds Hill** ☎ **01929/405616**), lies 7 miles west of Wareham (1 mile north of Bovington Camp) and is extremely small. It's open only April to October, on Wednesday, Thursday, Friday, and Sunday from noon to 5pm, and bank holiday Mondays from noon to 5pm. Admission is £2.30 ($3.90); free for children 4 and under.

Tank Museum. In the village and army base of Bovington Camp. ☎ **01929/405096.** Admission £6.90 ($11.75) adults, £4.50 ($7.65) children 5–16; £6 ($10.20) seniors; £18.30 ($31.10) family. Daily 10am–5pm.

Aficionados of military history should head to this installation maintained by the British military. Among the dozens of rare and historic armed vehicles are exhibitions and memorabilia on the life of T. E. Lawrence (Lawrence of Arabia).

Poole & Christchurch

True history buffs usually head 5 miles west to Poole, or 5 miles east to Christchurch, both of which predated Bournemouth by thousands of years. Both have large but shallow harbors, which were favored by the ancient Romans.

Waterfront Museum. High St., Poole. ☎ **01202/262600.** July–Aug admission £4 ($6.80) adults, £2.85 ($4.85) children ages 5–16; free for children under 5. Apr–June and Sept–Oct admission £2 ($3.40) adults, £1.35 ($2.30) children. Apr–Oct Mon–Sat 10am–5pm, Sun noon–5pm; Nov–Mar Mon–Sat 10am–3pm, Sun noon–3pm.

This museum celebrates the nautical influences that made the region great, with exhibits about the effects of seafaring commerce since the days of the ancient Romans.

Christchurch Priory Church. Quay Rd., Christchurch. Year-round Mon–Sat 9:30am–5pm, Sun 2:15–5pm.

The present monastic church was begun in 1094 on a site where there has been a church since A.D. 700. It is famous for the "Miraculous Beam," Norman nave and Turreet, monks' quire with its Jesse reredos and misericords, Lady Chapel, chantries, 15th-century bell tower, and St. Michael's loft, once a school but now a museum.

Red House Museum. Quay Rd., Christchurch. ☎ **01202/482860.** Admission £1 ($1.70) adults, 60p ($1) seniors and children. Tues–Sat 10am–5pm, Sun 2–5pm.

This museum occupies a redbrick building originally constructed in 1764 as a workhouse. In 1951, a civic-minded resident donated his extensive collection of archaeological and cultural artifacts to form the basis of the town's most visible public monument. An art gallery on the premises sells paintings, and exhibits showcase the region's cultural and social history.

WHERE TO STAY

VERY EXPENSIVE

Carlton Hotel. Meyrick Rd., E. Overcliff, Bournemouth, Dorset BH1 3DN. ☎ **01202/552011.** Fax 01202/299573. 74 units. TV TEL. £100–£200 ($170–$340) double; from £200 ($340) suite. Rates include half board. AE, DC, MC, V.

This is more of a resort than an ordinary hotel. The Carlton sits atop a seaside cliff lined with private homes and other hotels. This Edwardian pile, opening onto panoramic views, is the best place to stay in Bournemouth. It exudes a 1920s aura, with rather opulent public rooms. Extensively renovated, most bedrooms are spacious and open onto panoramic views of the sea. Regardless of your room assignment expect Bournemouth's ultimate in comfort. Many of the soothing rooms have marbled wallpaper, mottled mirrors, and armchairs. Bathrooms are generous in size, each equipped with a hair dryer.

Dining/Diversions: The Carlton boasts a luxury restaurant and cocktail bar, and elegant lounges.

Amenities: 24-hour room service, laundry and a swimming pool. Trained staff operate a health and beauty spa, featuring a sudsy whirlpool, a gymnasium, sauna, Jacuzzi, and tanning beds.

Norfolk Royale Hotel. Richmond Hill, Bournemouth, Dorset BH2 6EN. ☎ **01202/551521.** Fax 01202/299729. 95 units. MINIBAR TV TEL. £135 ($229.50) double; £195 ($331.50) suite. Children up to the age of 12 stay free in their parents' room. AE, MC, V.

One of the oldest and most prestigious hotels in town, located a few blocks from the seafront and the central shopping area, recently underwent a major £5 million renovation program, restoring it to its former Edwardian elegance, with a two-tier cast-iron veranda. Nevertheless, we think it still plays second fiddle to both the Carlton and the Royal Bath. It's like a country estate, with a formal entrance and a rear garden and fountain shaded by trees. The rooms and suites have been luxuriously appointed with the styles of the Edwardian period blending with modern comforts. Under new owners, the bedrooms have been considerably upgraded and improved. The bathrooms are of good size, each equipped with a hair dryer.

Amenities: Among the hotel's special features are the swimming pool covered with a glass dome and the Orangery restaurant set in the terraced gardens.

✪ **Royal Bath Hotel.** Bath Rd., Bournemouth, Dorset BH1 2EW. ☎ **01202/555555.** Fax 01202/554158. E-mail:royal.bath@devere-hotels.com 140 units. TV TEL. £160–£180 ($272–$306) double; £245 ($416.50) junior suite, £310 ($527) twin/double suite. Rates include English breakfast. AE, DC,MC, V. Parking £7.50 ($12.75).

This early Victorian version of a French château, with towers and bay windows looking out over the bay and Purbeck Hill, opened on June 28, 1838, the very day of Victoria's coronation. After the adolescent Prince of Wales (later Edward VII) stayed here, the hotel added "Royal" to its name. Over the years it has attracted everybody from Oscar Wilde to Rudolf Nureyev and the great prime minister Disraeli. In amenities and style, it is in a neck-and-neck race with the Carlton. It's located in a 3-acre garden where cliff-top panoramas open onto the sea. The mostly spacious bedrooms are furnished with a certain English style and grace, and the larger rooms have sitting areas. Most bedrooms have been recently refurbished, and the bathrooms, though a bit small, are well maintained, each with a hair dryer.

Dining: The hotel has two restaurants: the Garden Restaurant and Oscar's (reviewed below). The resident band plays for a dinner-dance most Saturday evenings.

Amenities: There's a sauna, as well as Swedish massages and special diets. In its cliff-top gardens is a heated kidney-shaped swimming pool.

Swallow Highcliff Hotel. 105 St. Michael's Rd., W. Cliff, Bournemouth, Dorset BH2 5DU. ☎ **01202/557702.** Fax 01202/293155. www.swallowhotels.com. 157 units. MINIBAR TV TEL. £140 ($238) double; from £245 ($416.50) suite. Rates include English breakfast. AE, DC, MC, V.

This 1888 cliff-side hotel is one of the best in Bournemouth, rivaled only by the Carlton and Royal Bath. The high-ceilinged interior has been tastefully renovated. A funicular elevator takes guests from the hotel to the seaside promenade. Many of the bedrooms have beautiful views of the sea. Each is traditionally furnished in elegant English style, and is located either in the main building or in coast-guard cottages built in 1912. The generally spacious rooms (there are some small units upstairs) include such additional amenities as irons and ironing boards and small refrigerators. Most of the mid-size bathrooms have a tub and shower combination along with a hair dryer.

Dining: An elegant restaurant serves well-prepared food in a grand manner, with formal service.

Amenities: The leisure club offers a heated swimming pool, tennis court, sauna, solarium, putting green, and game room.

Expensive

✪ **Langtry Manor Hotel.** 26 Derby Rd. (north of Christchurch Rd., A35), E. Cliff, Bournemouth, Dorset BH1 3QB. ☎ **01202/553887.** Fax 01202/290115. www.langtrymanor.com. E-mail: lillie@langtrymanor.com. 26 units. MINIBAR TV TEL. £119.50 ($203.15) double; £159.50 ($271.15) suite for 2. Rates include English breakfast. AE, DC, MC, V.

This is a much more atmospheric choice and run with a more personal touch than are the Carlton and Norfolk Royale. The Red House, as it was originally called, was built in 1877 for Lillie Langtry, as a gift from Edward VII to his favorite mistress. The house contains all sorts of reminders of its illustrious inhabitants, including initials scratched on a windowpane and carvings on a beam of the entrance hall. On the half-landing is the peephole through which the prince could scrutinize the assembled company before coming down to dine, and one of the fireplaces bears his initials. The bedrooms, each a double, range from ordinary twins to the Lillie Langtry Suite, Lillie's own room, with a four-poster bed and a double-heart–shaped bathtub; or you can rent the Edward VII Suite, furnished as it was when His Royal Highness lived in this spacious room. Bathrooms are tiled and beautifully maintained, each with a hair dryer.

Dining: The Lillie Langtry dining hall offers traditional English fare. A three-course dinner is served Sunday through Friday. On Saturday night, staff in period dress present an Edwardian banquet.

The Mansion House. 7–11 Thames St., Poole (4 miles west of Bournemouth), Dorset BH15 1JN. ☎ **01202/685666.** Fax 01202/665709. E-mail: mansionhouse@btinternet.com. 32 units. TV TEL. Mon–Thurs £120 ($204) double. Fri–Sun £100 ($170) double. Rates include English breakfast. AE, DC, MC, V.

In nearby Poole, The Mansion House was built more than 200 years ago by an English entrepreneur. The neoclassical detailing and fan-shaped windows are the pride and well-maintained joy of the owners.

A pair of bars are decorated with formal and rustic themes. An upstairs lounge and the graciously furnished bedrooms provide plenty of quiet, well-decorated corners for relaxation. The building has been extended to provide roomy and inviting accommodations, each individually decorated with comfortable furnishings. Most of the bathrooms have a tub and shower combination, each with a hair dryer. Excellent modern English cuisine is served.

✪ **The Priory Hotel.** Church Green, Wareham, Dorset BH20 4ND. ☎ **01929/551666.** Fax 01929/554519. www.thepriortyhotel.co.uk. E-mail:reception@theprioryhotel.co.uk. 19 units. TV TEL. £115–£240 ($195.50–$408) double; £240 ($408) suite. Rates include English breakfast. AE, DC, MC, V.

This hotel, 2 miles west of Bournemouth in Wareham, beside the River Frame and near the village church, has a well-tended garden adorned by graceful trees. Inside, a paneled bar and a lounge filled with antiques open onto views of the lawn. The rooms are individually decorated (often with fine antiques) and offer much comfort. Some of the accommodations are in a well-crafted annex. Most of the small bathrooms contain a tub and shower combination, and each comes with a hair dryer and a set of thick towels. The hotel's restaurant is a gem. Dishes are cooked to order, and every effort is made to use the abundant local produce.

Inexpensive

Sunnydene. 11 Spencer Rd., Bournemouth, Dorset BH1 3TE. ☎ **01202/552281.** 10 units, 7 with bathroom. TV. £36 ($61.20) double without bathroom, £44 ($74.80) double with bathroom. Rates include breakfast. No credit cards. Bus nos. 121 or 124.

This Victorian private hotel is in a substantial gabled house on a tree-lined road between the Central Station and Bournemouth Bay. The rooms are carpeted and centrally heated. There is hot and cold running water in all the bedrooms, although seven of them have a small bathroom equipped with a shower stall. Otherwise, corridor baths are adequate and are frequently refreshed so they'll be inviting for the next guest. All the beds have much comfort, but not a lot of frills. The hotel is licensed, and drinks and other refreshments are served in the sun lounge.

Westcliff Hotel. 27 Chine Crescent, W. Cliff, Bournemouth, Dorset BH2 5LB. ☎ **01202/551062.** Fax 01202/315377. 30 units. TV TEL. £52–£84 ($88.40–$142.80) double. Rates include English breakfast. Half board £32–£42 ($54.40–$71.40) per person. MC, V.

This hotel, a 5-minute walk from the town center, near Durley Chine, was once the luxurious south-coast home of the duke of Westminster, who had it built in 1876. Now run by the Blissert family, the hotel draws lots of repeat business. All the comfortably furnished and well-maintained rooms have beverage makers. As befits a former private home, bedrooms come in various shapes and sizes, but each is fitted with a good bed plus a small bathroom with adequate shelf space. You can order bar snacks or complete dinners at the hotel's art-deco restaurant. There's a large garden and a parking area, and facilities include a sauna, Jacuzzi, solarium, and swimming pool.

WHERE TO DINE

Oscar's. In the Royal Bath Hotel, Bath Rd. ☎ **01202/555555.** Reservations required. Main courses £17.50–£25 ($29.75–$42.50); fixed-price meal £16.50 ($28.05) at lunch, £30 ($51) at dinner. AE, DC, MC, V. Daily 12:30–2pm and 7:30–10pm. FRENCH.

Sporting Oscar Wilde mementos, this restaurant is located cliff-side, offering panoramic views of the sea. The chef, John Wood, presents à la carte dishes as well as fixed-price menus. The excellent appetizers might include a terrine of salmon scallops and king prawns with a saffron and basil jelly. The imaginative main courses might include filet of steamed bass with sesame crust, cucumber noodles, mussels and lemongrass jus; or Dorset lamb enhanced with zucchini duxelle bay flavored jus, and dauphinoise of celeriac and potatoes.

✪ **Sophisticats.** 43 Charminster Rd. ☎ **01202/291019.** Reservations recommended. Main courses £13–£15 ($22.10–$25.50). AE, DC, MC, V. Daily noon–2:30pm and 6–11:30pm. FRENCH/INTERNATIONAL.

Among the leading restaurants in town is this longtime favorite. Located in a shopping area about 1½ miles north of Bournemouth, Sophisticats tempts its diners with its excellent fresh fish, and you can order any number of veal and beef dishes (sometimes the latter will be prepared in the Indonesian style). Also served are game in season and fresh farm duckling with sauces. Appetizers are filled with flavor and texture, and a highly desirable finish to a meal is a dessert soufflé (but let the waiter know in time).

BOURNEMOUTH AFTER DARK

A choice of major art venues offers great performances throughout the year. **International Centre's Windsor Hall** hosts leading performers from London, the **Pavilion** puts on West End musicals as well as dancing with live music, and the **Winter Gardens,** the original home and favorite performance space of the world-famous Bournemouth Symphony Orchestra, offer regular concerts. Program and ticket information for all three of these venues is available by calling ☎ **01202/456456.**

EN ROUTE TO DORCHESTER: A 17TH-CENTURY MANSION

Kingston Lacy. At Wimborne Minster, on B3082 (Wimborne-Blandford road), 1½ miles west of Wimborne. ☎ **01202/883402.** Admission to the house, garden, and park £6 ($10.20) adults, £3 ($5.10) children. Garden only £2.50 ($4.25) adults, £1.25 ($2.15) children. Sat–Wed noon–5:30pm; park daily 11am–6pm. Closed Nov–Mar.

An imposing 17th-century mansion set on 250 acres of wooded park, Kingston Lacy was the home for more than 300 years of the Bankes family. They entertained such distinguished guests as King Edward VII, Kaiser Wilhelm, Thomas Hardy, George V, and Wellington. The house displays a magnificent collection of artwork by Rubens, Titian, and Van Dyck. There's also an important collection of Egyptian artifacts.

The present structure was built to replace Corfe Castle, the Bankes family's home that was destroyed in the civil war. During her husband's absence while performing duties as chief justice to King Charles I, Lady Bankes led the defense of the castle, withstanding two sieges before being forced to surrender to Cromwell's forces in 1646 because of the actions of a treacherous follower. The keys of Corfe Castle hang in the library at Kingston Lacy.

7 Dorchester: Hardy's Home

120 miles SW of London; 27 miles W of Bournemouth

Thomas Hardy, in his 1886 novel *The Mayor of Casterbridge,* gave Dorchester literary fame. Actually, Dorchester was notable even in Roman times, when Maumbury Rings, the best Roman amphitheater in Britain, was filled with the sounds of 12,000 spectators screaming for the blood of the gladiators. Today it's a sleepy market town that seems to go to bed right after dinner.

ESSENTIALS

GETTING THERE Trains run from London's Waterloo Station each hour during the day. The trip takes 2½ hours. For rail information, call ☎ **0345/484950.** Dorchester has two train stations, the South Station at Station Approach and the West Station on Great Western Road. For information about both, call ☎ **0345/484950.**

Several **National Express** coaches a day depart from London's Victoria Coach Station heading for Dorchester. The trip takes 3 hours. Call ☎ **0990/808080** for information and schedules.

If you're driving from London, take M3 southwest, but near the end take A30 toward Salisbury where you connect with A354 for the final approach to Dorchester.

VISITOR INFORMATION The **Tourist Information Centre** is at Unit 11, Antelope Walk (☎ **01305/267992**). It's open April to October, Monday through Saturday from 9am to 5pm; May to September, Sunday from 10am to 2pm; and November to March, Monday through Saturday from 9am to 4pm.

SEEING THE SIGHTS

One mile east of Dorchester is **Stinsford Church,** where Hardy's heart is buried. His two wives are buried there as well. To get to the church, officially called the Church of St. Michael, follow the signs from Dorchester for the Kingston Maurward Agricultural College, then just before the entrance gates to the college, turn right, following the signs toward the Stinsford Church.

The best place for tea in this bustling market town is the **Potter Inn,** 19 Durngate St. (☎ **01305/260312**), with a blue and white interior, and also a small herb-and-flower garden out back with several tables. Many guests stop in for some of the delectable ice creams such as butter pecan, but a proper sit-down tea is served for £3 ($4.95). You can also order freshly made sandwiches, cakes, scones, and pastries.

✪ **Athelhampton House & Gardens.** On A35, 5 miles east of Dorchester. ☎ **01305/848363.** Admission £5.25 ($8.90) adults, £1.50 ($2.55) children. Mar–Oct Sun–Fri 10:30am–5pm; Nov–Feb Sun only 10:30am–5pm. Take the Dorchester-Bournemouth Rd. (A35) east of Dorchester for 5 miles.

This is one of England's great medieval houses, the most beautiful and historic in the south, lying a mile east of Puddletown. Thomas Hardy mentioned the place in some of his writings but called it Athelhall. It was begun during the reign of Edward IV on the legendary site of King Athelstan's palace. A family home for more than 500 years, it's noted for its 15th-century Great Hall, Tudor great chamber, state bedroom, and King's Room.

In 1992, a dozen of the house's rooms were damaged by an accidental fire caused by faulty wiring in the attic. However, skilled craftspeople restored all the magnificent interiors.

Insider's tip: Although many visitors come to see the house, the gardens are even more inspiring. Dating from 1891, they are full of vistas, and their beauty is enhanced by the River Piddle flowing through and by fountains. These walled gardens contain the famous topiary pyramids and two pavilions designed by Inigo Jones. You'll see fine collections of tulips and magnolias, roses, and lilies, and also a 15th-century dovecote. Yes, they were often visited by Thomas Hardy.

Dorset County Museum. High West St. (next to St. Peter's Church). ☎ **01305/262735.** Admission £5.50 ($9.35) adults, £2.20 ($3.75) children 5–16, £2 ($3.40) seniors, £8.20 ($13.95) family; free for children 4 and under. July–Aug daily 10am–5pm; Sept–June Mon–Sat 10am–5pm. Closed Good Friday, Christmas Day.

This museum has a gallery devoted to memorabilia of Thomas Hardy's life. In addition, you'll find an archaeological gallery with displays and finds from Maiden Castle, Britain's largest Iron Age hill fort, plus galleries on the geology, local history, and natural history of Dorset.

Hardy's Cottage. Higher Bockhampton (3 miles northeast of Dorchester and 1/2 mile south of Blandford Road/A35). ☎ **01305/262366.** Admission £2.60 ($4.40). Sun–Thurs 11am–5pm. Closed Nov–Mar.

Thomas Hardy was born in 1840 at Higher Bockhampton. His home, now a National Trust property, may be visited by appointment. Approach the cottage on foot—it's a 10-minute walk—after parking your vehicle in the space provided in the woods. Write in advance to Hardy's Cottage, Higher Bockhampton, Dorchester, Dorset DT2 8QJ, England, or call the number above.

WHERE TO STAY & DINE IN & AROUND DORCHESTER

Kings Arms Hotel. 30 High East St., Dorchester, Dorset DT1 1HF. ☎ **01305/265353.** Fax 01305/260269. 33 units. TV TEL. £45–£50 ($76.50–$85) double; £65.50 ($111.35) suite. AE, MC, V.

In business for more than three centuries, the Kings Arms has great bow windows above the porch and a swinging sign hanging over the road, a legacy of its days as a coaching inn. It's still the best place to stay within Dorchester's center, although there are superior lodgings on the outskirts. An archway leads to the courtyard and parking area at the back of the hotel. All the comfortably furnished rooms have beverage makers. Most of the bedrooms are small to medium in size, and have been modernized while still retaining a traditional English aura. Baths are tiled and rather cramped. Henry's Table, a premier pub restaurant, is also on the premises.

✪ **Summer Lodge.** Summer Lane, Evershot, Dorset DT2 0JR. ☎ **01935/83424.** Fax 01935/83005. www/summerlodgehotel.com. E-mail: reservations@summerlodgehotel.com. 17 units. TV TEL. £235–£345 ($399.50–$586.50) double. Rates include English breakfast, afternoon tea, and 5-course dinner and newspaper. AE, DC, MC, V. Head north from Dorchester on A37.

In this country-house hotel 15 miles north of Dorchester, the resident owners, Nigel and Margaret Corbett, provide care, courtesy, and comfort. Once home to the heirs of the earls of Ilchester, the country house, in the village of Evershot, stands on 4 acres of secluded gardens. Evershot appears as Evershed in *Tess of the D'Urbervilles,* and author Thomas Hardy (that name again) designed a wing of the house. More recently, Summer Lodge hosted many of the stars of the locally filmed *Sense and Sensibility,* including Emma Thompson.

In this relaxed, informal atmosphere, the bedrooms have views either of the garden or over the village rooftops to the fields beyond. The hotel is regularly redecorated and recarpeted, and a new kitchen has been added. The bedrooms are individually decorated and have many comforts as reflected by such extras as hot-water bottles, fresh flowers, and racks of magazines. Most of the bathrooms have a tub and shower combination along with a hair dryer. Although centrally heated, the hotel offers log fires in winter. Guests sit around the fire getting to know each other in a convivial atmosphere.

Dining/Diversions: The chefs specialize in properly prepared traditional English dishes, emphasizing homegrown and local produce. In addition to the dining room, with its French windows opening onto a terrace, the Corbetts have a bar.

Amenities: Heated outdoor pool, an all-weather tennis court, and a croquet lawn.

Yalbury Cottage Country House Hotel and Restaurant. Lower Bockhampton, near Dorchester, Dorset DT2 8PZ. ☎ **01305/262382.** Fax 01305/266412. E-mail: yalbury.cottage@virgin.net.uk. 8 units. TV TEL. £130 ($221) double. Rates include half board. MC, V. Head 2 miles east of Dorchester (A35) and watch for signs to Lower Bockhampton.

This thatch-roofed cottage with inglenooks and beamed ceilings is in a small country village within walking distance of Thomas Hardy's cottage and Stinsford Church. The cottage is some 300 years old, and was once home to a local shepherd and the keeper of the water meadows. A mile to the north is Thorncombe Wood (home to badgers, deer, and many species of birds), which offers a pleasant stroll and a chance to see Hardy's birthplace, which is tucked in under the edge of the woods. The bedrooms overlook the English country garden beyond, reflecting a mood of tranquillity. The bedrooms have pinewood furniture in the English cottage style. Each has beverage maker, hair dryer, and other small touches for guests' added comfort. Bedrooms received considerable refurbishing in 1999, and are now more comfortable than ever, with particularly fine mattresses. Bathrooms are well appointed and clad in tiles.

Dining: The restaurant is open in the evenings only and nonresidents are welcome. Well-flavored sauces and lightly cooked fresh vegetables enhance traditional English and continental dishes.

8 Dorset's Coastal Towns: Chideock, Charmouth & Lyme Regis

Chideock & Charmouth: 157 miles SW of London; 1 mile W of BridportLyme Regis: 160 miles SW of London; 25 miles W of Dorchester

Chideock is a charming village hamlet of thatched houses with a dairy farm in the center. About a mile from the coast, it's a gem of a place for overnight stopovers, and even better for longer stays. You may be tempted to explore the countryside and the rolling hills.

On Lyme Bay, Charmouth, like Chideock, is another winner. A village of Georgian houses and thatched cottages, Charmouth provides some of the most dramatic coastal scenery in West Dorset. The village is west of Golden Cap, which, according to adventurers who measure such things, is the highest cliff along the coast of southern England.

Also on Lyme Bay, near the Devonshire border, the resort of Lyme Regis is one of the most attractive centers along the south coast. For those who shun big, commercial resorts, Lyme Regis is ideal—it's a true English coastal town, but with a mild climate. Seagulls fly overhead, the streets are steep and winding, and walks along Cobb Beach are brisk. The views, particularly of the craft in the harbor, are so photogenic that John Fowles, a longtime resident of the town, selected it as the site for the 1980 filming of his novel *The French Lieutenant's Woman.*

During its heyday, the town was a major seaport. Later, Lyme developed into a small spa, including among its visitors Jane Austen. She wrote her final novel, *Persuasion* (published posthumously and based partly on the town's life), after staying here in 1803 and 1804.

ESSENTIALS

GETTING THERE The nearest train connection to Chideock and Charmouth is Dorchester (see "Essentials," in section 7). Buses run frequently throughout the day, west from both Dorchester and Bridport.

To get to Lyme Regis, take the London-Exeter train, getting off at Axminster and continuing the rest of the way by bus. For rail information, call ☎ **0345/484950.** Bus no. 31 runs from Axminster to Lyme Regis (one coach per hour during the day). There's also **National Express** bus service (no. 705) that runs daily in summer at 9:50am from Exeter to Lyme Regis, taking 1³/₄ hours. Call ☎ **0990/808080** for schedules and information.

If you're driving to Chideock and Charmouth from Bridport, continue west along A35. To get to Lyme Regis from Bridport, continue west along A35, cutting south to the coast at the junction with A3070.

VISITOR INFORMATION In Lyme Regis, the **Tourist Information Centre,** at Guildhall Cottage, Church Street (☎ **01297/442138**), is open November through March, Monday through Friday from 10am to 4pm and Saturday from 10am to 2pm; in April, daily from 10am to 5pm; May through September, Monday through Friday from 10am to 6pm and Saturday and Sunday from 10am to 5pm; and October, daily from 10am to 5pm.

EXPLORING THE TOWNS

Chideock and Charmouth are the most beautiful villages in Dorset. It's fun to stroll through them to see the well-kept cottages, well-manicured gardens, and an occasional 18th- or 19th-century church. Charmouth, more than Chideock, boasts a small-scale collection of unusual antiques shops. Both villages are less than a mile from the western edge of **Chesil Beach,** one of the Hampshire coast's most famous (and longest) beaches. Although it's covered with shingle (sharp rocks), and hard on your feet if you go bathing, the beach nonetheless provides 5 miles of sweeping views toward France.

Today in Lyme Regis, one of the town's most visible characters is ✪ **Richard J. Fox,** three-time world champion Town Crier who, although retired, still does **guided walks.** Famed for his declamatory delivery of official (and sometimes irreverent) proclamations, he followed a 1,000-year-old tradition of newscasting. Dressed as Thomas Payne, a dragoon who died in Lyme Regis in 1644 during the civil war, Mr. Fox leads visitors on a 1¹/₂-hour walk around the town every Tuesday at 3pm, beginning at The Guildhall (mentioned below). No reservations are necessary, and the price is £2 ($3.40) for adults and £1.50 ($2.55) for children. He can be reached on the premises of **Country Stocks,** 53 Broad St. (☎ **01297/443568**). This shop sells such wares as sweets, antiques, and gifts and is open daily from 10am to 5pm (open till 6:30pm in summer).

Another famous building is **The Guildhall,** Bridge Street (call the tourist office for information), whose Mary and John Wing (built in 1620) houses the completed sections of an enormous tapestry woven by local women. Depicting Britain's colonization of North America, it's composed of a series of 11-by-4-foot sections, each of which took a team of local women 2 years to weave. Admission is free, but if anyone wants to add a stitch to the final tapestry as a kind of charitable donation, it costs £1.50 ($2.55). It's open Monday through Friday from 10am to 4pm, but only if someone is working on the tapestry.

The surrounding area is a fascinating place for botanists and zoologists because of the predominance of blue Lias, a sedimentary rock well suited to the formation of fossils. In 1810, Mary Anning (at the age of 11) discovered one of the first articulated ichthyosaur skeletons. She went on to become one of the first professional fossilists in England. Books outlining walks in the area and the regions where fossils can be studied are available at the local information bureau.

WHERE TO STAY & DINE

IN CHIDEOCK & CHARMOUTH

✪ **Chideock House Hotel.** Main St., Chideock, Dorset DT6 6JN. ☎ **01297/489242.** Fax 01297/489184. www.chideockhousehotel.com. E-mail: anna@chideockhousehotel.com. 9 units, 8 with bathroom. TV TEL. £60–£80 ($102–$136) double with bathroom. Rates include English breakfast. £100–£120 ($170–$204) double with half-board. AE, MC, V. Bus no. 31 from Bridport.

In a village of winners, this 15th-century thatched house is the prettiest. The house was used by the Roundheads in 1645, and the ghosts of the village martyrs still haunt it, since their trial was held here. Located near the road, with a protective stone wall, the house has a garden in back, and a driveway leads to a large parking area. The beamed lounge, recently face-lifted, has two fireplaces, one an Adam fireplace with a wood-burning blaze on cool days. The bedrooms range in size and have beverage makers; superior rooms have a hair dryer, dressing gowns, and toiletries.

The restaurant, serving both French and English cuisine, offers dinner nightly; lunch is also served in season. There's even homemade ice cream.

White House. 2 Hillside, The Street, Charmouth, Dorset DT6 6PJ. ☎ **01297/560411.** Fax 01297/560702. 10 units. TV TEL. £100–£110 ($170–$187) double. Rates include English breakfast and 5-course table d'hôte. AE, DC, MC, V. Closed Nov–Jan, but open for Christmas and New Year's Day. Bus no. 31 from Bridport.

The White House is the best place to stay in Charmouth. This Regency home, with its period architecture and bow doors, is well preserved and tastefully furnished. Chris Poole and Joel Kassirer took this place, constructed in 1827, and made it comfortable, with touches such as electric kettles in their handsomely furnished bedrooms. Rooms range in size from small to medium, and include such thoughtful extras as complimentary decanters of sherry in the room and homemade shortbread. Bathrooms are small but have a combination tub and shower.

For dinner, home-cooked dishes, with a selection of carefully chosen wines, are offered. West Country regional dishes are featured, including, for example, Dorset honeyed duckling. Five-course dinners begin at £18.50 ($31.45).

IN LYME REGIS

Alexandra Hotel. Pound St., Lyme Regis, Dorset DT7 3HZ. ☎ **01297/442010.** Fax 01297/443229. www.lymeregis.co.uk. E-mail: alexandra@lymeregis.co.uk. 27 units. TV TEL. £85–£122 ($144.50–$207.40) double. Rates include English breakfast. AE, DC, MC, V.

Built in 1735, this hotel is situated on a hill about 5 minutes from the center of Lyme Regis. Today, it has the best bedrooms and amenities of any inn in town, although it lacks the personal charm of Kersbrook Hotel and Restaurant (reviewed below). In bedrooms once occupied by such "blue bloods" as Dowager Countess Poulett or Duc du Stacpoole, you sleep in grand comfort in the handsome beds. Most rooms command superb sea views over Lyme Regis and the Cobb. Expect such extras as thermostatic heating and coffeemakers, along with small but beautifully maintained private baths with a hair dryer. It's been discreetly modernized around its original character. Both table d'hôte and à la carte meals are offered in the hotel's excellent dining room, with dinner costing from £15 ($25.50). The bar has been entirely renovated.

Kersbrook Hotel and Restaurant. Pound Rd., Lyme Regis, Dorset DT7 3HX. ☎ and fax **01297/442596.** 10 units. TV. £84.50–£114.40 ($143.65–$194.50) double. Rates include breakfast. AE, MC, V. Closed Dec–Jan.

Built of stone in 1790, and crowned by a thatch roof, the Kersbrook sits on a ledge above the village (which provides a panoramic view of the coast), on 1½ acres of gardens landscaped according to the original 18th-century plans. The public rooms have been refurnished with antique furniture, re-creating old-world charm with modern facilities. All of the small to medium-size bedrooms have a certain 17th-century charm, with furnishings ranging from antique to contemporary. Rooms are provided with coffeemakers, and bathrooms are tidily maintained with adequate shelf space and a hair dryer.

The hotel is justifiably proud of its pink, candlelit restaurant, serving dinner nightly and offering an extensive wine list. The chef is a culinary artist. Traditional English and French cuisine is served, with dinner costing from £16.50 ($28.05).

Royal Lion. Broad St., Lyme Regis, Dorset DT7 3QF. ☎ **01297/445622.** Fax 01297/445859. 30 units. TV TEL. £70–£86 ($119–$146.20) double with breakfast; £90–£100 ($153–$170) double with breakfast and dinner. AE, DC, MC, V.

This hotel was built in 1610 as a coaching inn, growing throughout the years to incorporate oak-paneled bars, lounges, and comfortably up-to-date bedrooms. Situated in the center of town on a hillside climbing up from the sea, the hotel features country-inspired furnishings and such venerable antiques as the canopied bed that was used regularly by Edward VII when he was Prince of Wales. Bedrooms are divided between the main house, where the traditionally furnished rooms have more character and fireplaces, and a more recent modern wing where the rooms have contemporary furnishings and the added advantage of a private terrace with a sea view. Bathrooms are small but efficiently organized.

On the premises is an indoor heated swimming pool, a Jacuzzi, a sauna, a minigym, a game room, a cocktail lounge, and a pub with an open fireplace. Bar snacks are dispensed daily at lunch; dinner is available nightly in the restaurant.

9 Sherborne

128 miles SW of London; 19 miles NW of Dorchester

A little gem of a town with well-preserved medieval, Tudor, Stuart, and Georgian buildings still standing, Sherborne is in the heart of Dorset, surrounded by wooded hills, valleys, and chalk downs. It was here that Sir Walter Raleigh lived before his fall from fortune.

ESSENTIALS

GETTING THERE Frequent trains depart from London's Waterloo Station throughout the day. The trip takes 2 hours. For rail information, call ☎ **0345/484950.**

There is one **National Express** coach departure daily from London's Victoria Coach Station. Call ☎ **0990/808080** for information and schedules.

If you're driving, take M3 west from London, continuing southwest on 303 and B3145.

VISITOR INFORMATION The **Tourist Information Centre,** on Digby Road (☎ **01935/815341**), is open mid-March to mid-October, Monday to Saturday from 9:30am to 5:30pm, and mid-October to mid-March, Monday to Saturday from 10am to 3pm.

EXPLORING SHERBORNE

In addition to the attractions listed below, you can go to **Cerne Abbas,** a village south of Sherborne, to see the Pitchmarket, where Thomas and Maria Washington, uncle and aunt of American president George Washington, once lived.

Sherborne Old Castle. Castleton, off A30, 1/2 mile east of Sherborne. ☎ **01935/ 812730.** Admission £1.60 ($2.70) adults, £1.10 ($1.85) seniors and students, 80p ($1.35) children 5–16, free for children 4 and under. Apr–Oct daily 10am–6pm; Nov–Mar Wed–Sun 10am–4pm. Follow the signs 1 mile east from the town center.

The castle was built by the powerful Bishop Roger de Caen in the early 12th century, but it was seized by the crown at about the time of King Henry I's death in 1135 and Stephen's troubled accession to the throne. The castle was given to Sir Walter Raleigh by Queen Elizabeth I. The gallant knight built Sherborne Lodge in the deer park close by (now privately owned). The buildings were mostly destroyed in the Civil War, but you can still see a gatehouse, some graceful arcades, and decorative windows.

Sherborne Castle. Cheap St. (off New Rd. 1 mile east of the center). ☎ **01935/813182.** Castle and grounds £5 ($8.50) adults, £2.50 ($4.25) children 3–15 years, £4.50 ($7.65) seniors, £12.50 ($21.25) family ticket (2 adults, 2 children); grounds only £2.50 ($4.25) adults, £1.25 ($2.15) children. Apr 1–Oct 31, Tues, Thurs, Sat–Sun, and bank holidays 12:30–5pm. Last admission 4:30pm.

Sir Walter Raleigh built this castle in 1594, when he decided that it would not be feasible to restore the old castle to suit his needs. This Elizabethan residence was a square mansion, to which later owners added four Jacobean wings to make it more palatial. After King James I had Raleigh imprisoned in the Tower of London, the monarch gave the castle to a favorite Scot, Robert Carr, and banished the Raleighs from their home. In 1617, it became the property of Sir John Digby, first earl of Bristol, and has been the Digby family home ever since. The mansion was enlarged by Sir John in 1625, and in the 18th century the formal Elizabethan gardens and fountains of the Raleighs were altered by Capability Brown, who created a serpentine lake between the two castles. The 20 acres of lawns and pleasure grounds around the 50-acre lake are open to the public. In the house are fine furniture, china, and paintings by Gainsborough, Lely, Reynolds, Kneller, and Van Dyck, among others.

✪ **Sherborne Abbey.** Abbey Close. ☎ **01935/812452.** Free admission but donations for upkeep welcomed. Apr–Sept daily 8:30am–6pm; Oct–Mar daily 8:30am–4pm.

One of the great churches of England, this abbey was founded in A.D. 705 as the Cathedral of the Saxon Bishops of Wessex. In the late 10th century, it became a Benedictine monastery, and since the Reformation it has been a parish church. It's famous for its fan-vaulted roof, added by Abbot Ramsam at the end of the 15th century; this was the first fan vault of wide span erected in England. Inside are many fine monuments, including Purbeck marble effigies of medieval abbots as well as Elizabethan "four-poster" and canopied tombs. The baroque statue of the earl of Bristol stands between his two wives and dates from 1698. A public school occupies the abbey's surviving medieval monastic buildings and was the setting for the classic film *Good-bye, Mr. Chips,* starring Robert Donat.

WHERE TO STAY & DINE

Eastbury Hotel. Long St., Sherborne, Dorset DT9 3BY. ☎ **01935/813131.** Fax 01935/817296. 15 units. TV TEL. £79–£89 ($134.30–$151.30) double. Rates include English breakfast. AE, MC, V.

This Georgian town-house hotel, Sherborne's best, is situated in its own walled garden near the 8th-century abbey and the two castles. Built in 1740 during the reign of

George II, it has a traditional ambience, with its own library of antiquarian books. Beautifully restored, it still retains its 18th-century character. Bedrooms are named after flowers and are handsomely maintained and decorated. Rooms are small to medium in size, and bright and inviting, furnished in a traditional way and often graced with the addition of fresh flowers. The bathrooms are tidily maintained with shelf space, a hair dryer, and robes. After a restful night's sleep, you can sit outside and enjoy the well-kept garden. The best fresh English produce is served in the dining room, which has an extensive wine list.

Sherborne Hotel. Horsecastles Lane (near the A30 rd. and about 1 mile west of Sherborne's center), Sherborne, Dorset DT9 6BB. ☎ **01935/813191.** Fax 01935/816493. 59 units. TV TEL. Sun–Thurs £59.50 ($101.15) double, Fri–Sun £49.50 ($84.15) double. AE, DC, MC, V.

Built of red brick in 1969, this two-story hotel lies near a school and a scattering of factories and houses. Although popular with business travelers, it's more elegant than a typical roadside hotel, with more amenities than might be expected and easy access to Sherborne's historic center. Attracting both business travelers and visitors, the hotel gets high marks for quality. Its bedrooms, small to medium in size, are too functional to be the most glamorous in the area. Thirty of the accommodations are reserved for nonsmokers, and 11 of the rooms are spacious enough for small families. The small baths are tidily kept. There's a bar on the premises, and Castles Restaurant, where fixed-price three-course dinners cost from £19 ($32.30), and affordable lunches are also served. The staff is efficient and helpful.

10 Shaftesbury

100 miles SW of London; 29 miles NE of Dorchester

The origins of this typical Dorsetshire market town date from the 9th century, when King Alfred founded the abbey and made his daughter the first abbess. King Edward the Martyr is buried here, and King Canute died in the abbey but was buried in Winchester. Little now remains of the abbey, but the ruins are beautifully laid out. The museum adjoining St. Peter's Church at the top of Gold Hill provides a good idea of what the ancient Saxon hilltop town was like.

Today, ancient cottages with thatched roofs and tiny paned windows line the steep cobbled streets, and modern stores compete with the outdoor market on High Street and the cattle market off Christy's Lane. The town is an excellent center from which to visit Hardy Country (it appears as Shaston in *Jude the Obscure*), Stourhead Gardens, and Longleat House. (The gardens and house are covered in chapter 8.)

Much of Shaftesbury's charm hearkens back to the agrarian days of bucolic old England. A promenade on **Gold Hill,** a steep cobbled hill, is lined on one side with those thatched cottages so evocative of British wholesomeness. Traffic is prohibited on the road, except for residents of the houses near the top.

Equally nostalgic are the ruins of **Shaftesbury Abbey,** Park Walk, whose boundaries flank one edge of Gold Hill. Founded in A.D. 888 by King Alfred—who appointed his daughter, Aethlgeofu, as its first abbess—it was closed during the Dissolution of the Monasteries in 1539 by Henry VIII and later fell into ruin. Over the centuries, its stones were used widely for other building projects throughout the town, including those houses on Gold Hill. Excavations of the site continue to this day, but during warm weather, from April 1 to October 30, you can visit the abbey daily from 10am to 5pm. Admission is £1 ($1.70) for adults, 70p ($1.20) for students and seniors, and 40p (70¢) for children under 14.

ESSENTIALS

GETTING THERE There is no direct train access, so you'll have to take the Exeter train leaving from London's Waterloo Station to Gillingham in Dorset, where a 4-mile bus or taxi ride to Shaftesbury awaits you. Trains from London run every 2 hours. For rail information, call ☎ **0345/484950.**

Bus connections are possible from London's Victoria Coach Station once a day. There are also two or three daily connections from Bristol, Bath, Bournemouth, and Salisbury. The Tourist Information Centre (see below) keeps up-to-date transportation hookups in the area.

If you're driving, head west from London on M3, continuing along A303 until the final approach by A350.

VISITOR INFORMATION The **Tourist Information Centre,** 8 Bell St. (☎ **01747/853514**), is open daily April through October from 10am to 5pm; from November through March hours are 10am to 1pm from Monday to Wednesday and 10am to 5pm from Thursday to Saturday.

WHERE TO STAY & DINE IN & AROUND SHAFTESBURY

King Alfred's Kitchen, 15 High St. (☎ **01747/852147**), is the best place in town for tea, lying in an antique house with low ceiling beams. At the top of Gold Hill, this building with its fireplaces and old benches dates from the 15th century. Afternoon tea costs £3.50 ($5.95), and you can also order a selection of sandwiches, cakes, scones, and pastries.

✪ **Plumber Manor.** Hazelbury Bryan Rd. (off A357), Sturminster Newton, Dorset DT10 2AF. ☎ **01258/472507.** Fax 01258/473370. E-mail: book@plumbermanor.com. 16 units. TV TEL. £95–£140 ($161.50–$238) superior double. Rates include English breakfast. AE, DC, MC, V. Closed Feb.

This Jacobean manor house on 600 acres of farmland has been the home of the Prideaux-Brune family since the early 17th century. The present inhabitants, Richard Prideaux-Brune and his wife, Alison, are the hosts at this lovely old place, treating everyone as a houseguest and creating a family atmosphere. Downstairs, a large hall from which the staircase rises is decorated with family portraits. Upstairs, a gallery leads to some of the bedrooms, which have views of the gardens and the countryside. The others, in a long, low stone barn across the courtyard from the stable block (large umbrellas are provided to make the crossing if necessary), are well designed, with wide window seats, views over the gardens, and well-chosen furnishings. If you want old-English style and traditional character, opt for one of the rooms in the main house. Your other choice is a room in the former barn, which has been skillfully converted to offer more spacious units. Bathrooms are a bit small but come with a hair dryer.

Dining: There's a bar to serve the restaurant, made up of three connecting dining rooms, where guests can sample the excellent cooking of Brian Prideaux-Brune, Richard's brother. Three-course dinners start from £20 ($34). Try the beef Wellington or chicken with lemon and tarragon. All main courses are served with fresh vegetables.

Royal Chase Hotel. Royal Chase Roundabout (at the junction of A30 and A350), Shaftesbury, Dorset SP7 8DB. ☎ **01747/853355.** Fax 01747/851969. E-mail:royalchasehotel@btinternet.com 34 units. TV TEL. £95–£105 ($161.50–$178.50) double. AE, DC, MC, V.

This was once a button-making factory, and later a monastery, but now it's a delightfully informal hotel. It's your best choice within the town of Shaftesbury. The bedrooms are comfortably furnished and well equipped. The cells for monks are long gone, and the current bedrooms range from small to spacious and are divided into standard rooms and "Crown Rooms," the latter being more expensive, elegant, and better furnished. Nonetheless, all of them have good mattresses and quality linens. Thirteen units are spacious enough for small families, and 10 bedrooms are rented only to nonsmokers. Bathrooms are small but have a hair dryer.

Dining/Diversions: A meal in the elegant Byzant Restaurant, which begins at £22 ($37.40), includes several regional dishes such as local trout, seasonal game, and venison marinated in sherry. Dinner is served nightly. A more informal restaurant, the Country Restaurant, serves light meals, snacks, and children's favorites throughout the day. They serve Thomas Hardy's Ale, featured in the Guinness Book of Records as the strongest beer available in a bottle. Even for less fanatical drinkers, the bar, dominated by an open-kitchen range and decorated with Dorsetshire bygones, is an attraction.

Amenities: Indoor swimming pool.

8

Wiltshire & Somerset

For our look at the "West Countree," we move into Wiltshire and Somerset, two of the most historic shires of England. Once you reach this area of pastoral woodland, London seems far removed. For a total preview of the West Country, you will also want to visit Devon and Cornwall (see chapters 9 and 10).

Most people agree that the West Country, a loose geographical term, begins at **Salisbury,** with its early English cathedral that has a 404-foot pinnacle. Nearby is **Stonehenge,** England's oldest prehistoric monument. (Both Stonehenge and Salisbury are in Wiltshire.) When you cross into Wiltshire, you'll be entering a country of chalky, grassy uplands and rolling plains. Much of the shire is agricultural, and a large part is pastureland.

Somerset has some of the most beautiful scenery in England. The undulating limestone hills of Mendip and the irresistible Quantocks are especially lovely in spring and fall. Somerset opens onto the Bristol Channel, with Minehead serving as its chief resort. The shire is rich in legend and history, possessing particularly fanciful associations with King Arthur and Queen Guinevere, Camelot, and Alfred the Great. Its villages are noted for the tall towers of their parish churches.

You may find yourself in a vine-covered pub, talking with the regulars and sampling Somerset's famous cider, or perhaps you'll stroll through a large estate in the woods surrounded by bridle paths and sheep walks (Somerset was once a great wool center). Or maybe you'll settle down in a 16th-century thatched stone farmhouse set in the midst of orchards in a vale.

Somerset also encompasses the territory around the old port of **Bristol** and the old Roman city of **Bath,** known for its abbey and spa water, lying beside the river Avon.

The two best places to base yourself while you explore the area are Bath and Salisbury. From Salisbury, you can visit Stonehenge and **Old Sarum,** the two most fabled ancient monuments in the West Country. Yet some say visiting the stones at **Avebury** is a much more personal experience. And **Glastonbury,** with its once-great abbey that is now a ruined sanctuary, may be one of Britain's oldest inhabited sites. The greatest natural spectacle in the area is **Exmoor National Park,** once an English royal hunting preserve, stretching for 265 square miles on the north coast of Devon and Somerset. There are also many terrific country houses and palaces in this region, including **Wilton House,** the site of 17th-century staterooms designed by Inigo Jones. The other two major attractions, **Longleat House** and the fabled gardens at **Stourhead,** can be visited in a busy day while you're based at Bath.

1 Salisbury

90 miles SW of London; 53 miles SE of Bristol

Long before you've even entered Salisbury, the spire of its cathedral will come into view—just as John Constable captured it on canvas. The 404-foot pinnacle of the early English and Gothic cathedral is the tallest in England.

Salisbury, or New Sarum, lies in the valley of the Avon River. Filled with Tudor inns and tearooms, it is the only true city in Wiltshire. It's an excellent base for visitors anxious to explore Stonehenge or Avebury, and, unfortunately, they tend to visit the cathedral and then rush on their way. But the old market town is an interesting destination in its own right, and if you choose to linger here for a day or two, you'll find that its pub-to-citizen ratio is perhaps the highest in the country.

ESSENTIALS

GETTING THERE **Network Express trains** depart for Salisbury hourly from Waterloo Station in London; the trip takes 2 hours. Sprinter trains offer fast, efficient service every hour from Portsmouth, Bristol, and South Wales. There is also direct rail service from Exeter, Plymouth, Brighton, and Reading. For rail information, call ☎ **0345/484950** in the United Kingdom.

If you're driving from London, head west on M3 to the end of the run, continuing the rest of the way on A30.

Three **National Express** buses per day run from London, Monday through Friday. On Saturday and Sunday, 3 buses depart Victoria Coach Station for Salisbury. The trip takes 2½ hours. Call ☎ **0990/808080** for schedules and information.

VISITOR INFORMATION The **Tourist Information Centre** is at Fish Row (☎ **01722/334956**), and is open October through April, Monday through Saturday from 9:30am to 5pm; in May, Monday through Saturday from 9:30am to 5pm and Sunday 10:30am to 4:30pm; in June and September, Monday through Saturday from 9:30am to 6pm and Sunday 10:30am to 4:30pm; and in July and August, Monday through Saturday from 9:30am to 7pm and on Sunday from 10:30am to 5pm.

GETTING AROUND If you'd like to bike out to Stonehenge, go to **Hayball's Cycle Shop,** 26–30 Winchester St. (☎ **01722/411378**), which rents mountain bikes for £9 ($15.30) per day. For an extra £2.50 ($4.25) you can keep the bike overnight. A £25 ($42.50) deposit is required. A 7-day rental is £55 ($93.50). Hours are daily 9am to 5pm.

SPECIAL EVENTS The Salisbury St. George's Spring Festival in April is a traditional medieval celebration of the city's patron saint. You can witness St. George slaying the dragon in the Wiltshire mummers play and see acrobats and fireworks.

With spring comes the annual **Salisbury Festival** (☎ **01722/323883,** or 01722/320333 for the box office). The city drapes itself in banners, and street theater—traditional and unexpected—is offered everywhere. There are also symphony and chamber music concerts in Salisbury Cathedral, children's events, and much more. It takes place from mid-May through the beginning of June.

At the end of July, you can see **The Salisbury Garden and Flower Show,** Hudson's Field (☎ **0118/947-8996**). This is a treat for gardening enthusiasts: There's a floral marquee packed with Chelsea exhibits, as well as display gardens created especially for

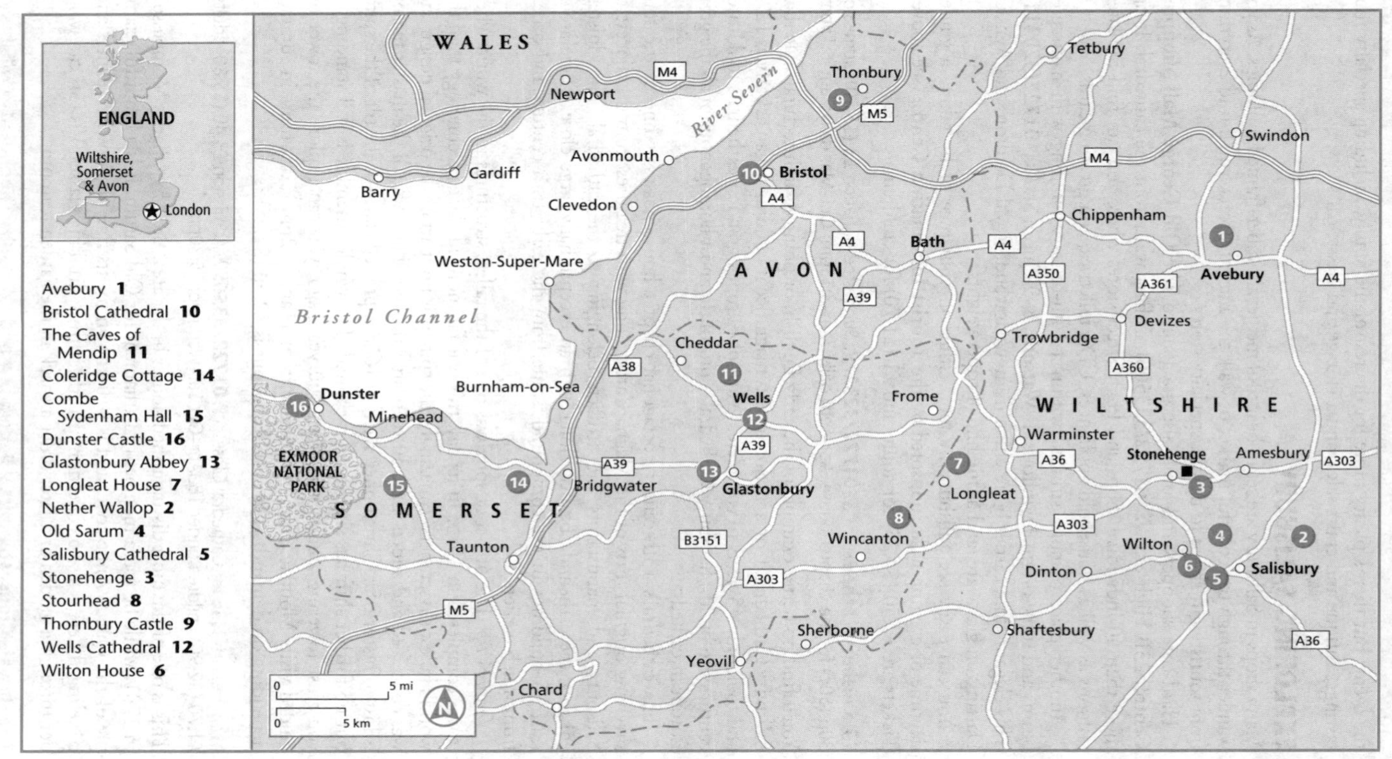

ENGLAND
Wiltshire, Somerset & Avon
London
Avebury 1
Bristol Cathedral 10
The Caves of Mendip 11
Coleridge Cottage 14
Combe Sydenham Hall 15
Dunster Castle 16
Glastonbury Abbey 13
Longleat House 7
Nether Wallop 2
Old Sarum 4
Salisbury Cathedral 5
Stonehenge 3
Stourhead 8
Thornbury Castle 9
Wells Cathedral 12
Wilton House 6
WALES
Newport
Cardiff
Barry
Avonmouth
Clevedon
Weston-Super-Mare
River Severn
Bristol Channel
Thonbury
Bristol
Tetbury
Swindon
Chippenham
Bath
Avebury
A V O N
Devizes
Trowbridge
Cheddar
Wells
Frome
W I L T S H I R E
Warminster
Stonehenge
Amesbury
Dunster
Minehead
Burnham-on-Sea
EXMOOR NATIONAL PARK
S O M E R S E T
Bridgwater
Glastonbury
Longleat
Wincanton
Wilton
Salisbury
Dinton
Taunton
Sherborne
Shaftesbury
Yeovil
Chard
M4
M5
A4
A39
A38
A350
A361
A360
A36
A303
B3151
0
5 mi
0
5 km

the event. But there's plenty more for the rest of the family, including specialty food tastings, antique and crafts sales, and a vintage and classic car show.

EXPLORING SALISBURY

Many shops in Salisbury are set in beautiful medieval timber-framed buildings. As you wander through the colorful market or walk the ancient streets, you'll find everything from touristy gift shops to unique specialty stores.

Hard-core shoppers and locals also gravitate to **The Old George Mall Shopping Centre,** 23B High St. (☎ **01722/333500**), a short walk from the cathedral. It has more than 40 individual shops and High Street stores where you can find the latest fashions as well as household appliances, CDs, toiletries, and greeting cards.

Another place of note, situated within a 14th-century building with hammered beams and some original windows, is **Watsons,** 8–9 Queen St. (☎ **01722/320311**). This elegant store carries bone china from Wedgwood, Royal Doulton, and Aynsley, Dartington glassware, and a fine line of paperweights.

You can easily see Salisbury by foot, either on your own or by taking a guided daytime or evening walk sponsored by the **Tourist Information Centre** (see above). Tickets are £2.50 ($4.25) for adults and £1 ($1.70) for children.

✪ **Salisbury Cathedral.** ☎ **01722/323279.** Suggested donation £3 ($5.10); admission 30p (50¢) for the chapter house. Apr–Sept daily 7am–8:15pm; Oct–Mar daily 7am–6:15pm.

You'll find no better example of the early English, or pointed, architectural style than Salisbury Cathedral. Construction on this magnificent building began as early as 1220 and took only 45 years to complete. (Most of Europe's grandest cathedrals took three centuries to build.) Salisbury Cathedral is one of the most homogenous of all the great European cathedrals.

The cathedral's 13th-century octagonal chapter house possesses one of the four surviving original texts of the Magna Carta, along with treasures from the diocese of Salisbury and manuscripts and artifacts belonging to the cathedral. The cloisters enhance the cathedral's beauty, along with an exceptionally large close. There are at least 75 buildings in the compound, some from the early 18th century and others from much earlier.

Insider's tip: The 404-foot spire was one of the tallest structures in the world when it was completed in 1315. In its day, this was far more advanced technology than the world's tallest skyscrapers. Amazingly, the spire was not part of the original design and was conceived and added some 30 years after the rest. The name of the master mason is lost to history. Sir Christopher Wren in 1668 expressed alarm at the tilt of the spire, but no further shift has since been measured. The whole ensemble is still standing; if you trust towering architecture from 700 years ago, you can explore the tower on guided visits Monday through Saturday from 11am to 2pm (extra tours in summer depending on demand). The cost of the tour is £2.50 ($4.25).

Mompesson House. Cathedral Close. ☎ **01722/335659.** Admission £3.40 ($5.80) adults, £1.70 ($2.90) children under 18. Apr–Oct Sat–Wed noon–5:30pm.

This is one of the most distinguished houses in the area. Built by Charles Mompesson in 1701, while he was a member of Parliament for Old Sarum, it is a beautiful example of the Queen Anne style, and is well known for its fine plasterwork ceilings and paneling. There is also a collection of 18th-century drinking glasses. Visitors can wander through a garden and later order a snack in the garden tearoom.

The Royal Gloucestershire, Berkshire, and Wiltshire Regiment (Salisbury) Museum—Redcoats in the Wardrobe. The Wardrobe, 58 The Close, Salisbury, Wiltshire. ☎ **01722/414536.** Admission £2.20 ($3.75) adults, £2 ($3.40) senior citizens, 50p (85¢)

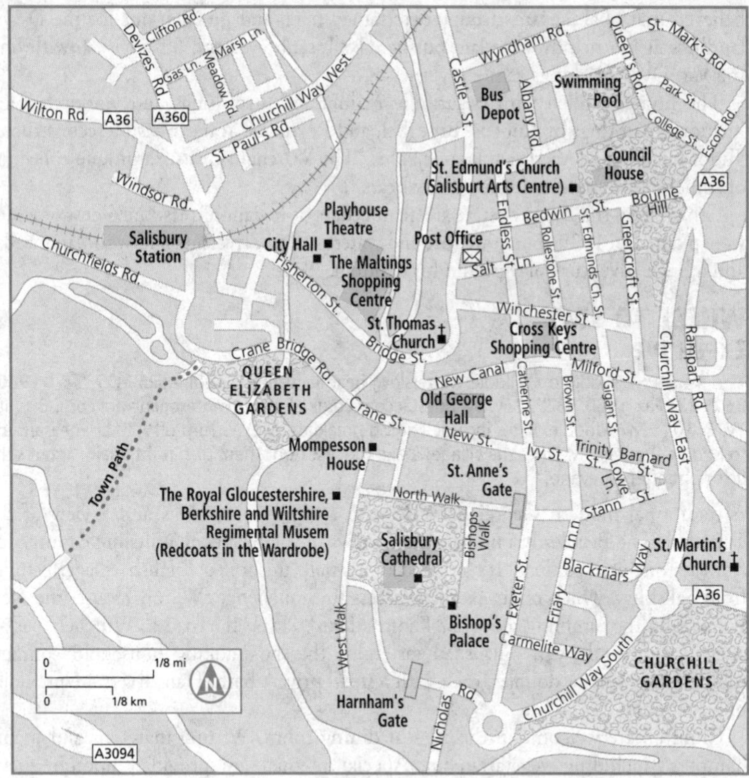

children. Feb–Mar and Nov to mid-Dec Tues–Sun 10am–4:30pm; Apr–Oct daily 10am–4:30pm.

The elegant house in which the museum's collections are displayed dates from 1254 and contains exhibits covering three centuries of military history. Visitors can relax in the garden leading to the River Somerset (with views made famous by Constable) and enjoy homemade fare from the Redcoats Tea Rooms.

SIGHTS NEARBY

✪ **Old Sarum.** 2 miles north of Salisbury off A345 on Castle Rd. ☎ **01722/335398.** Admission £2 ($3.40) adults, £1.50 ($2.55) seniors, £1 ($1.70) children. Apr–Sept daily 10am–6pm; Oct daily 10am–5pm; Nov–Mar daily 10am–4pm. Bus nos. 3, 5, 6, 7, 8, and 9 run every 20 minutes during the day from the Salisbury bus station.

Believed to have been an Iron Age fortification, Old Sarum was used again by the Saxons, and flourished as a walled town into the Middle Ages. The Normans built a cathedral and a castle here; parts of the old cathedral were taken down to build the city of New Sarum (Salisbury).

Wilton House. 3 miles west of Salisbury on A30. ☎ **01722/746729.** Admission £6.75 ($11.50) adults, £4 ($6.80) children 5–15; free for children under 5. Price inclusive of grounds. Easter–Oct daily 10:30am–5:30pm (last entrance at 4:30pm).

The home of the earls of Pembroke is in the town of Wilton. It dates from the 16th century, but has undergone numerous alterations, most recently in Victoria's day. It is noted for its 17th-century staterooms by the celebrated architect Inigo Jones. It is believed that Shakespeare's troupe entertained here, and preparations for the D-Day landings at Normandy were laid out here by Eisenhower and his advisers, with only the Van Dyck paintings as silent witnesses.

The house is filled with beautifully maintained furnishings and world-class art, including paintings by Rubens, Brueghel, and Reynolds. You can visit a reconstructed Tudor kitchen and Victorian laundry plus "The Wareham Bears," a unique collection of some 200 miniature dressed teddy bears.

Growing on the 21-acre estate are giant cedars of Lebanon trees, the oldest of which were planted in 1630. There are rose and water gardens, riverside and woodland walks, and a huge adventure playground for children.

WHERE TO STAY

EXPENSIVE

The Beadles. Middleton, Middle Winterslow, near Salisbury, Wiltshire SP5 1QS. ☎ **01980/862922.** Fax 1980/862922. www.guestaccom.co.uk/ E-mail: winterbead@aol.com. 3 units. TV. £110 ($187) double. Rates include English breakfast. MC, V. Turn off A30 at Pheasant Inn to Middle Winterslow. Enter the village, make the first right then, turn right again, and it's the first right after "Trevano."

A traditional modern Georgian house with antique furnishings and a view of the cathedral, The Beadles has unobstructed views of the beautiful Wiltshire countryside from its one-acre gardens. It's situated in a small, unspoiled English village, 8 miles from Salisbury, which offers excellent access to Stonehenge, Wilton House, the New Forest, and the rambling moors of Thomas Hardy. Even the road to Winchester is an ancient Roman byway. Furnished tastefully, this no-smoking household contains rooms with twins or doubles, each with a small private bath. Hair dryers are provided upon request.

Children are welcome in the 12-seat dining room. Writing materials and picnic hampers (including vegetarian and special menus) are provided upon request. Warm-weather meals are served on the patio or in the conservatory, and a pre-dinner drink is free. Owners David and Anne Yuille-Baddeley delight in providing information on the area.

Grasmere House. 70 Harnham Rd., Salisbury, Wiltshire SP2 8JN. ☎ **01722/338388.** Fax 01722/333710. www.grasmerehotel.com. E-mail: grasmerehotel@mistral.co.uk. 20 units. TV TEL. £95–£115 ($161.50–$195.50) double. Rates include English breakfast. AE, DC, MC, V. Take A3094 1 1/2 miles from the center of town.

Grasmere House stands near the confluence of the Nadder and Avon Rivers on 1 1/2 acres of grounds. Constructed in 1896 for Salisbury merchants, the house still suggests a family home. The original architectural features were retained as much as possible, including a "calling box" for servants in the dining room. A conservatory bar overlooks the cathedral, as do three luxurious rooms. Four rooms are in the original house, with the remainder in a new wing. Each room has a distinctive character and often opens onto a scenic view. Two accommodations are suitable for guests with disabilities. Four units are reserved for nonsmokers, and two accommodations are large enough for families. Each bathroom comes with a hair dryer.

Dining: The house also operates a good restaurant, popular with locals and residents alike. Steaks are a specialty, served in any number of ways, ranging from flambéed to *au poivre* (with pepper).

Red Lion Hotel. 4 Milford St., Salisbury, Wiltshire SP1 2AN. ☎ **800/528-1234** in the U.S., or 01722/323334. Fax 01722/325756. www.the-redlion.co.uk. E-mail: reception@the-redlion.co.uk. 54 units. TV TEL. £104–£125 ($176.80–$212.50) double; £119.50–£125 ($203.15–$212.50) suite. AE, DC, MC, V.

Since the 1300s, the Red Lion has been accommodating wayfarers from London on their way to the West Country. This Best Western–affiliated hotel no longer reigns supreme in town (we prefer the White Hart and The Rose and Crown), but it's a fine choice and somewhat more affordable than those two. Cross under its arch into a courtyard with a hanging, much-photographed creeper, a red lion, and a half-timbered facade, and you'll be transported back to an earlier era.

This antique-filled hotel is noted for its unique clock collection, which includes a skeleton organ clock in the reception hall. Each small to medium-size bedroom is individually furnished, with a beverage maker and a hair dryer. Six rooms are reserved for nonsmokers, and two units are spacious enough for families. The most expensive rooms have four-poster beds.

Dining: Many locals know the hotel for its restaurant, which serves continental and English cuisine daily at lunch and dinner. It has a wattle-and-daub wall that dates from 1230.

✪ **The Rose and Crown.** Harnham Rd., Salisbury, Wiltshire SP2 8JQ. ☎ **01722/399955.** Fax 01722/339816. 28 units. TV TEL. £115–£145 ($195.50–$246.50) double; £158 ($268.60) suite. AE, DC, MC, V. Take A3094 1 1/2 miles from the center of town.

This half-timbered, 13th-century gem stands with its feet almost in the River Avon, and beyond the water you can see the tall spire of the cathedral. Because of its tranquil location, it's our top choice. You can easily walk over the arched stone bridge to the center of Salisbury from here in 10 minutes. The lawns and gardens between the inn and the river are shaded by old trees, and chairs are set out so you can enjoy the view and count the swans. The inn, part of the Queen's Moat House hotel chain, has both a new and an old wing. The new wing is modern, but the old wing is more appealing, with its sloping ceilings and antique fireplaces and furniture. Bedrooms in the main house range from small to medium in size, though those in the new wing are more spacious and better designed. Each has a beverage maker and trouser press. Bathrooms, though small, include a shower and tub combination.

Dining/Diversions: You can dine on fine English fare while overlooking the river. Across the courtyard are two taverns with oak beams and log fires.

Amenities: 24-hour room service, laundry.

White Hart. 1 St. John St., Salisbury, Wiltshire SP1 2SD. ☎ **870/400-1825.** Fax 01722/412761. www.heritage-hotels.com. E-mail: heritagehotels-salisbury.white-hart@forte-hotels.com. 68 units. TV TEL. £115 ($195.50) double. AE, DC, MC, V.

Combining the best of old and new, the White Hart has been a Salisbury landmark since Georgian times. Its classic facade is intact, with tall columns crowning a life-size hart. The older accommodations are traditional, and a new section has been added in the rear, opening onto a large parking area. All of the units were refurbished in 1995. New-wing units are tastefully decorated; although rooms in the main building have more style and character, many of these are quite small. Twenty-eight rooms are set aside for nonsmokers. Bathrooms are a bit small in many cases.

Dining: You can enjoy a before-dinner drink, followed by a meal of modern English fare, in the White Hart Restaurant.

MODERATE

The Kings Arms Hotel. 7A–11 St. Johns St., Salisbury, Wiltshire SP1 2SB. ☎ **01722/327629.** Fax 01722/414246. 17 units. TV TEL. £55–£75 ($93.50–$127.50) double. Rates include continental breakfast. AE, MC, V.

This former coaching inn, which is in the black-and-white Tudor style, features an old pub sign out front and a royalty theme throughout. A special attraction is the

William-and-Mary four-poster room. The other rooms are cozy and well kept, with traditional styling. Each bedroom is individually decorated, and often full of charm and character. There are several accommodations containing an old-fashioned four-poster bed, and some units are large enough for families. Baths are generally small but tidily maintained. Three rooms are set aside for nonsmokers. No one seems to know the age of the inn, although it's generally acknowledged to be older than the cathedral. Conspirators helping Charles II flee to France were thought to have met here in the mid-17th century.

The hotel has a good restaurant, Pippins, which serves Anglo-French meals. Warm yourself in front of the open fire in winter or enjoy a pint of ale in the oak-beamed pub anytime.

Inexpensive

The New Inn & Old House. 39–47 New St., Wiltshire SP1 2PH. ☎ **01722/327679.** Fax 01722/334651. E-mail: newinn@rjspicer.easynet.co.uk. 5 units. TV. £49.50–£65.50 ($84.15–$111.35) double. Rates include continental breakfast. AE, MC, V.

This upscale B&B is one of the finest in Salisbury, but, despite its name, it isn't new at all. It's a 15th-century building whose walled garden backs up to the cathedral-close wall. Although small, bedrooms are cozy and traditional, with a tea- and coffeemaker. Most units have a tub and shower combination, others only a shower. The center of the inn is the serving bar, which is a common center for three outer rooms: one, a tiny sitting area; another, a tavern with high-backed settles (benches) and a fireplace; and a third, a lounge. Food and drink are available to nonresidents all day for reasonable prices. No smoking.

Wyndham Park Lodge. 51 Wyndham Rd., Salisbury, Wiltshire SP1 3AB. ☎ **01722/416517.** Fax 01722/328851. E-mail: wyndham@wyndham51 freeserve.co.uk. 4 units. TV. £40–£42 ($68–$71.40) double; £60 ($102) family room for 3. Rates include English breakfast. No credit cards.

From this appealing Victorian 1880 house, it's an easy walk to the heart of Salisbury and its cathedral, and about a 5-minute walk to a swimming pool and the bus station. The small- to medium-sized rooms are comfortably furnished with Victorian and Edwardian antiques. They have either one double or two twin beds and contain beverage makers. Only one unit has a tub and shower combination, the rest an efficient shower. Reservations are recommended.

A Nearby Place to Stay for Agatha Christie Fans

Eight miles east of Salisbury is the little village of **Nether Wallop** (not to be confused with Over Wallop or Middle Wallop, also in the same vicinity). Agatha Christie fans should note that it's the fictitious town of St. Mary Mead, Miss Marple's home, in PBS's *Miss Marple* mysteries. It's 12 miles from Stonehenge and 10 miles from Winchester, on a country road between A343 and A30.

If you'd like to stay over—and perhaps solve a murder if one occurs during your visit—consider the following choice.

The Great Barn. In the nearby village of Stockbridge. ☎ **01264/782142.** E-mail: rquaife@btinternet.com. 2 units. TV. £28 ($47.60) single; £42 ($71.40) double. Rates include breakfast. No credit cards.

There are only two rooms, one a single, the other a double, both with private bath. Set in the heart of the village, this is a highly unusual two-story private home. In 1990, it was converted from the premises of a 16th-century barn. Accommodations are small and simple but tidy, and the hospitality is quite warm and inviting.

A Choice in Nearby Dinton

✪ **Howard's House.** Teffont Evias, near Salisbury, Wiltshire SP3 5RJ. ☎ **01722/716392.** Fax 01722/716820. www.howardshousehotel.co.uk. E-mail: paulfirmin@howardshousehotel.co.uk. 9 units. TV TEL. £125–£145 ($212.50–$246.50) double. Rates include English breakfast. AE, DC, MC, V. Take A36 and A30 west of Salisbury for 10½ miles; it's on B3089.

On a lane opposite the Black Horse, this partial 17th-century dower house, one of the most appealing small hotels and restaurants in the area, stands in a medieval hamlet. Much care is lavished on the decor here, and there are fresh flowers in every public room and bedroom. Most bedrooms are spacious in size, and one room is large enough for a family. The hotel has attractive gardens, and on chilly nights log fires burn.

Dining: Even if you don't stay here, consider stopping by for a three-course dinner (call to reserve a table first). There are ample choices on the fixed-price menu, such as grilled sirloin steak with a pepper ragout and horseradish béarnaise. Chilled mango mousse with marinated strawberries makes a splendid dessert. Lunch is also served on Sunday.

WHERE TO DINE

The best restaurants are not in Salisbury itself but on the outskirts—at either the Silver Plough at Pitton (see below for details) or Howard's House at Teffont Evias (see above). See also "Salisbury After Dark," below, for a selection of pubs offering affordable fare.

Foodies should stop in at **David Brown Food Hall & Tea Rooms,** 31 Catherine St. (☎ **01722/329363**). They carry the finest fresh foods—meats, cheeses, breads, and other baked goods—making it a terrific place to put together a picnic.

Harper's Restaurant. 6–7 Ox Row, Market Sq. ☎ **01722/333118.** Reservations recommended. Main courses £6.90–£12.50 ($11.75–$21.25); 2-course fixed-price meal £8.50 ($14.45) at lunch and dinner. AE, DC, MC, V. Mon–Sat noon–2pm; daily 6–9:30pm (10pm on Sat). Closed Sun in Oct–May. ENGLISH/INTERNATIONAL.

The chef-owner of this place prides himself on specializing in "real food"—homemade, simple, and wholesome. The pleasantly decorated restaurant is on the second floor of a redbrick building at the back end of Salisbury's largest parking lot, in the center of town. Within the same all-purpose dining room, you can order from two different menus, one featuring affordable bistro-style platters, including beefsteak casserole with "herbey dumplings." A longer menu, listing items that take a bit more time to prepare, includes all-vegetarian pasta diavolo, or spareribs with french fries and rice.

Salisbury Haunch of Venison. 1 Minster St. ☎ **01722/322024.** Main courses £8.55–£12.95 ($14.55–$22); bar platters for lunches, light suppers, and snacks £5–£7 ($8.50–$11.90). AE, DC, MC, V. Daily noon–2:30pm; Mon–Sat 6:30–9:30pm. Pub Mon–Sat 11am–11pm, Sun noon–3pm and 7–10:30pm. Closed Christmas and Easter. ENGLISH.

Right in the heart of Salisbury, this creaky-timbered, 1320 chophouse serves excellent dishes, especially English roasts and grills. Stick to its specialties and you'll rarely go wrong. Begin perhaps with a tasty warm salad of venison sausages with garlic croutons, then follow with the time-honored roast haunch of venison with parsnips and juniper berries. Other classic English dishes are served as well, including grilled Barnsley lamb chops with "bubble and squeak" (cabbage and potatoes).

In Nearby Pitton

Silver Plough. White Hill, Pitton, near Salisbury. ☎ **01722/712266.** Reservations recommended. Main courses £6.95–£16.95 ($11.80–$28.80); bar platters £3.95–£12.95 ($6.70–$22). AE, DC, MC, V. Restaurant, Mon–Sat 11am–3pm and 6–11pm; Sun noon–2:30pm and 7–10:30pm. Pub, daily 11am–3pm and Mon–Sat 6–11pm, Sun 7–10:30pm. Take A30 5 miles east of Salisbury; it's at the southern end of the village of Pitton. ENGLISH.

Built as a stone-sided farmhouse 150 years ago, the Silver Plough is now a charming and accommodating country pub with an attached restaurant specializing in fish and game dishes. Snacks are available in the bar. In the somewhat more formal dining room, the chef prepares such dishes as fresh Dorset mussels in a white wine, garlic, and cream sauce, and breast of chicken with leeks and mushrooms. The management makes its guests feel at home.

SALISBURY AFTER DARK

The **Salisbury Playhouse,** Malthouse Lane (☎ **01722/320117,** or 01722/320333 for the box office), produces some of the finest theater in the region. Food and drink are available from the bar and restaurant to complete your evening's entertainment.

The City Hall, Malthouse Lane (☎ **01722/334432** or 01722/327676 for the box office), has a program of events to suit most tastes and ages in comfortable surroundings. A thriving entertainment center, it attracts many of the national touring shows in addition to local amateur events, exhibitions, and sales, thus providing good entertainment at a reasonable price.

The Salisbury Arts Center, Bedwin Street (☎ **01722/321744**), housed within the former St. Edmund's Church, offers a wide range of performing and visual arts. A typical program contains a broad mix of music, contemporary and classic theater, and dance performances, plus cabaret, comedy, and family shows. Regular workshops are available for all ages in arts, crafts, theater, and dance. The lively cafe-bar is a pleasant meeting place.

Many a Salisbury pub crawl begins at the **Haunch of Venison** (see above). Another good pub is **The Pheasant** on Salt Lane, near the bus station (☎ **01722/320675**), which attracts locals as well as visitors on their way to Stonehenge. Snacks, ploughman's lunches, and hot pub grub, including meat pies, are served all day. It's all washed down with a goodly assortment of ales. To cap the night, head for the **Avon Brewery Inn,** 75 Castle St. (☎ **01722/327280**), which is decorated like a Victorian saloon from the gay 1890s, and has an idyllic garden setting overlooking the River Avon. It offers some of the tastiest and most affordable food in town.

2 Prehistoric Britain: Stonehenge & Avebury

✪ **Stonehenge.** At the junction of A303 and A344/A360. ☎ **01980/623108** for information. Admission £4 ($6.80) adults, £3 ($5.10) seniors and students, £2 ($3.40) children. June–Aug daily 9:30am–7pm; Mar 16–May and Sept–Oct 15 daily 9am–5pm; Oct 16–Mar 15 daily 9:30am–4pm. If you're driving, head north on Castle Rd. from the center of Salisbury. At the first roundabout (traffic circle), take the exit toward Amesbury (A345) and Old Sarum. Continue along this road for 8 miles and then turn left onto A303 in the direction of Exeter. You'll see signs for Stonehenge, leading you up A344 to the right. It's 2 miles west of Amesbury.

This huge circle of lintels and megalithic pillars, believed to be approximately 5,000 years old, is the most important prehistoric monument in Britain.

Some visitors are disappointed when they see that Stonehenge is nothing more than concentric circles of stones. But perhaps they don't understand that Stonehenge represents an amazing engineering feat, since many of the boulders, the bluestones in particular, were moved many miles (perhaps from southern Wales) to this site.

The widely held view of 18th- and 19th-century romantics that Stonehenge was the work of the Druids is without foundation. The boulders, many weighing several tons, are believed to have predated the arrival in Britain of the Celtic culture. Recent excavations continue to bring new evidence to bear on the origin and purpose of Stonehenge. Controversy surrounds the prehistoric site, especially since the publication of *Stonehenge Decoded* by Gerald S. Hawkins and John B. White, which maintains that Stonehenge was an astronomical observatory—that is, a Neolithic "computing machine" capable of predicting eclipses.

Your ticket permits you to go inside the fence surrounding the site that protects the stones from vandals and souvenir hunters. You can go all the way up to a short rope barrier, about 50 feet from the stones.

A full circular tour around Stonehenge is possible. A modular walkway was introduced to cross the archaeologically important avenue, the area that runs between the Heel Stone and the main circle of stones. This enables visitors to complete a full circuit of the stones and to see one of the best views of a completed section of Stonehenge as they pass by. This is an excellent addition to the informative audio tour.

Wilts & Dorset (☎ **01722/336855**) runs several buses daily (depending on demand) from Salisbury to Stonehenge, as well as buses from the Salisbury train station to Stonehenge. The bus trip to Stonehenge takes 40 minutes, and a round-trip ticket costs £4.80 ($8.15) for adults and £2.40 ($4.10) for children 5 to 14 (4 and under free).

✪ **Avebury.** On A361 between Swindon and Devizes (1 mile from the A4 London-Bath road). The closest rail station is at Swindon, 12 miles away, which is served by the main rail line from London to Bath. For rail information, call ☎ **0345/484950.** A limited bus service (no. 49) runs from Swindon to Devizes through Avebury.

One of the largest prehistoric sites in Europe, Avebury lies on the Kennet River, 7 miles west of Marlborough and 20 miles north of Stonehenge. Some visitors say visiting Avebury, in contrast to Stonehenge, is a more organic experience—you can walk right up and around the stones, as there's no fence keeping you away. Also, the site isn't mobbed with tour buses.

Visitors can walk around the 28-acre site at Avebury, winding in and out of the circle of more than 100 stones, some weighing up to 50 tons. The stones are made of sarsen, a sandstone found in Wiltshire. Inside this large circle are two smaller ones, each with about 30 stones standing upright. Native Neolithic tribes are believed to have built these circles.

Wilts & Dorset (☎ **01722/336855**) has two buses (nos. 5 and 6) that run between the Salisbury bus station and Avebury, three times a day from Monday through Saturday and twice daily on Sunday. The one-way trip takes 1 hour and 40 minutes. Round-trip tickets are £4.80 ($8.15) adults and £2.40 ($4.10) children 5 to 14 (4 and under free).

Also here is the **Alexander Keiller Museum** (☎ **01672/539250**), which houses one of Britain's most important archaeological collections, including material from excavations at Windmill Hill and Avebury, and artifacts from other prehistoric digs at West Kennet, Long Barrow, Silbury Hill, West Kennet Avenue, and the Sanctuary. The museum is open April to October daily from 10am to 6pm, November to March from 10am to 4pm. Admission is £1.70 ($2.90) for adults and 80p ($1.35) for children.

WHERE TO DINE NEAR AVEBURY

Stones Restaurant. High St. near the Great Barn Museum. ☎ **01672/539514.** Main courses £3–£7 ($5.10–$11.90), hot buffet lunch £6.95 ($11.80). MC, V. Apr–Oct daily 10am–6pm (serving hot food noon–2:30pm); Nov–Mar Sat–Sun 10am–5pm.

This restaurant has been a hit ever since it was opened within a converted Victorian stable block by an archaeologist, Dr. Michael Pitts. They specialize in organically grown food prepared in original ways and sold at reasonable prices. Their hot lunch platters, which change daily, might include spiced chili with fried peppers served with a mixture of wild, tamargue, and white rice; or the mason's lunch (two cheeses, hand-churned butter, an apple, and homemade bread, pickles, and crackers). Pastries, coffee, fruit juices, bottled beer, cold quiche, snacks, and Welsh and English cheeses are available throughout the day. Especially attractive is the mid-afternoon cream tea served with whole-wheat scones and clotted cream from Cornwall. The owners travel abroad every winter bringing back their culinary inspirations from Asia and the Pacific.

3 Bath: Britain's Most Historic Spa Town

115 miles W of London; 13 miles SE of Bristol

In 1702, Queen Anne made the trek from London to the mineral springs of ✪ **Bath,** thereby launching a fad that was to make the city the most celebrated spa in England.

The most famous name connected with Bath was the 18th-century dandy Beau Nash, who cut a striking figure as he made his way across the city, with all the plumage of a bird of paradise. This polished arbiter of taste and manners made dueling déclassé. While dispensing (at a price) trinkets to the courtiers and aspirant gentlemen of his day, Beau was carted around in a sedan chair.

The 18th-century architects John Wood the Elder and his son provided a proper backdrop for Nash's considerable social talents. These architects designed a city of stone from the nearby hills, a feat so substantial and lasting that Bath today is the most harmoniously laid-out city in England. During Georgian times, this city, on a bend of the River Avon, was to attract a following of leading political and literary figures, such as Dickens, Thackeray, Nelson, and Pitt. Canadians may already know that General Wolfe lived on Trim Street, and Australians may want to visit the house at 19 Bennett St., where their founding father, Admiral Phillip, lived. Even Henry Fielding came this way, observing in *Tom Jones* that the ladies of Bath "endeavour to appear as ugly as possible in the morning, in order to set off that beauty which they intend to show you in the evening."

And even before its Queen Anne, Georgian, and Victorian popularity, Bath was known to the Romans as Aquae Sulis. The foreign legions founded their baths here (which you can visit today) to ease their rheumatism in the curative mineral springs.

Remarkable restoration and careful planning have ensured that Bath retains its handsome look today. The city suffered devastating destruction from the infamous Baedeker air raids of 1942, when Luftwaffe pilots seemed more intent on bombing historical buildings than in hitting any military target.

After undergoing major restoration in the postwar era, Bath today has somewhat of a museum look, with the attendant gift shops. Its parks, museums, and architecture continue to draw hordes of visitors, and because of this massive tourist invasion, prices remain high. It's one of the high points of the West Country and a good base for exploring Avebury.

ESSENTIALS

GETTING THERE Trains leave London's Paddington Station bound for Bath once every half hour during the day. The trip takes about 1¼ hours. For rail information, call ☎ **0345/484950.**

One **National Express** coach leaves London's Victoria Coach Station every 2 hours during the day. The trip takes 2½ hours. Coaches also leave Bristol bound for Bath, and make the trip in 50 minutes. For schedules and information, call ☎ **0990/808080.**

Drive west on M4 to the junction with A4, on which you continue west to Bath.

VISITOR INFORMATION The **Bath Tourist Information Centre** is at Abbey Chambers, Abbey Church Yard (☎ **01225/477101**), next to Bath Abbey. It's open June through September, Monday through Saturday from 9:30am to 6pm, Sunday 10am to 4pm; off-season, Monday through Saturday from 9:30am to 5pm and Sunday from 10am to 4pm.

GETTING AROUND One of the best ways to explore Bath is by bike. Rentals are available at **Avon Valley Cycle Shop** (☎ **01225/442442**), behind the train station. It's open daily from 9am to 5:30pm, charging £14 ($23.80) per day, depending on the bike. A bond of £350 ($595) can be put on credit card.

SPECIAL EVENTS Bath's graceful Georgian architecture provides the setting for one of Europe's most prestigious international festivals of music and the arts, the ✪ **Bath International Music Festival.** For 17 days in late May and early June each year, the city is filled with more than 1,000 performers. The festival focuses on classical music, jazz, new music, and the contemporary visual arts, with orchestras, soloists, and artists from all over the world. In addition to the main music and art program, there are walks, tours, and talks, plus free street entertainment, a free Festival Club, and opening-night celebrations with fireworks. For detailed information, contact the **Bath Festivals Box Office,** 2 Church St., Abbey Green, Bath BA1 1NL (☎ **01225/463362**).

SEEING THE SIGHTS

You'll want to stroll around to see some of the buildings, crescents, and squares in town. The **North Parade** (where Goldsmith lived) and the **South Parade** (where English novelist and diarist Frances Burney once resided) represent harmony, and are the work of John Wood the Elder. He also designed beautiful **Queen Square,** where both Jane Austen and Wordsworth once lived. Also of interest is **The Circus,** built in 1754, as well as the shop-lined **Pulteney Bridge,** designed by Robert Adam and often compared to the Ponte Vecchio of Florence.

The younger John Wood designed the **Royal Crescent,** an elegant half-moon row of town houses (copied by Astor architects for their colonnade in New York City in the 1830s). At **No. 1 Royal Crescent** (☎ **01225/428126**), the interior has been redecorated and furnished by the Bath Preservation Trust to look as it might have toward the end of the 18th century. The house is located at one end of Bath's most magnificent crescent, west of the Circus. Admission is £4 ($6.80) for adults and £3.50 ($5.95) for children, seniors, and students; a family ticket is £10 ($17). Open mid-February to October, Tuesday to Sunday from 10:30am to 5pm, and November, Tuesday to Sunday from 10:30am to 4pm (last admission 30 min. before closing); closed Good Friday.

Free 1¾-hour walking tours are conducted throughout the year by **The Mayor's Honorary Society** (☎ **01225/477786**). Tours depart from outside the Roman Baths

Monday through Friday at 10:30am and 2pm, Sunday at 2:30pm, and from May through September, Tuesday, Friday, and Saturday at 7pm.

Jane Austen Tours take you in the footsteps of the author and her characters. Conducted only once a week, tours begin at Abbey Lace Shop, York Street (☎ **01225/463030**). The cost is £3 ($5.10) per person, and departures are every Saturday at 2:30pm. To tour Bath by bus, you can choose among several tour companies. Among the best is **Patrick Driscoll,** Elmsleigh, Bathampton (☎ **01225/462010**), with tours that are more personalized than most.

Bath's newest attraction, the **Jane Austen Centre,** 40 Gay St. (☎ **01225/443-000**), is located in a Georgian town house on an elegant street where Miss Austen once lived. Exhibits and a video convey a sense of what life was like in Bath during the Regency period. The center is open Monday to Saturday 10am to 5pm and Sunday 10:30am to 5:30pm. Admission is £4 ($7).

River Avon boat cruises depart from a pier adjacent to the Pulteney Bridge (directly across the water from the Parade Gardens). Cruises last 50 minutes and are priced £4.50 ($7.65) for adults, and £2.25 ($3.80) for children. They're offered from Easter to October via two boats maintained by **The Boating Station** (☎ **01225/466407**).

✪ **Bath Abbey.** Orange Grove. ☎ **01225/422462.** £2 ($3.40) donation requested. Admission to the Heritage Vaults, £2 ($3.40) adults, £1 ($1.70) students, children, and seniors. Abbey, Apr–Oct Mon–Sat 9am–6pm; Nov–Mar Mon–Sat 9am–4:30pm; year-round Sun 1–2:30pm and 4:30–5:30pm. The Heritage Vaults, Mon–Sat 10am–4pm.

Built on the site of a much larger Norman cathedral, the present-day abbey is a fine example of the late Perpendicular style. When Queen Elizabeth I came to Bath in 1574, she ordered a national fund to be set up to restore the abbey. The west front is the sculptural embodiment of a Jacob's Ladder dream of a 15th-century bishop. When you go inside and see its many windows, you'll understand why the abbey is called the "Lantern of the West." Note the superb fan vaulting, with its scalloped effect. Beau Nash was buried in the nave and is honored by a simple monument totally out of keeping with his flamboyant character. The Bath Abbey Heritage Vaults opened in 1994 on the south side of the abbey. This subterranean exhibition traces the history of Christianity at the abbey site since Saxon times.

✪ **The Pump Room & Roman Baths.** In the Bath Abbey churchyard. ☎ **01225/477785.** Admission £6.90 ($11.75) adults, £6 ($10.20) seniors, £4 ($6.80) children. Apr–Sept daily 9am–6pm; Oct–Mar Mon–Sat 9:30am–5pm.

Founded in A.D. 75 by the Romans, the baths were dedicated to the goddess Sulis Minerva; in their day, they were an engineering feat. Even today they're among the finest Roman remains in the country, and are still fed by Britain's most famous hot-spring water. After centuries of decay, the original baths were rediscovered during Queen Victoria's reign. The site of the Temple of Sulis Minerva has been excavated and is now open to view. The museum displays many interesting objects from Victorian and recent digs (look for the head of Minerva).

Coffee, lunch, and tea, usually with music from the Pump Room Trio, can be enjoyed in the 18th-century pump room, overlooking the hot springs. There's also a drinking fountain with hot mineral water that tastes horrible.

Theatre Royal. Sawclose. ☎ **01225/448844.** Tickets £7–£25 ($11.90–$42.50). Box office Mon–Sat 10am–8pm. Shows Mon–Wed at 7:30pm, Thurs–Sat at 8pm; Wed and Sat matinees at 2:30pm.

Theatre Royal, located next to the new Seven Dials development, was restored in 1982 and refurbished with plush seats, red carpets, and a painted proscenium arch and ceiling;

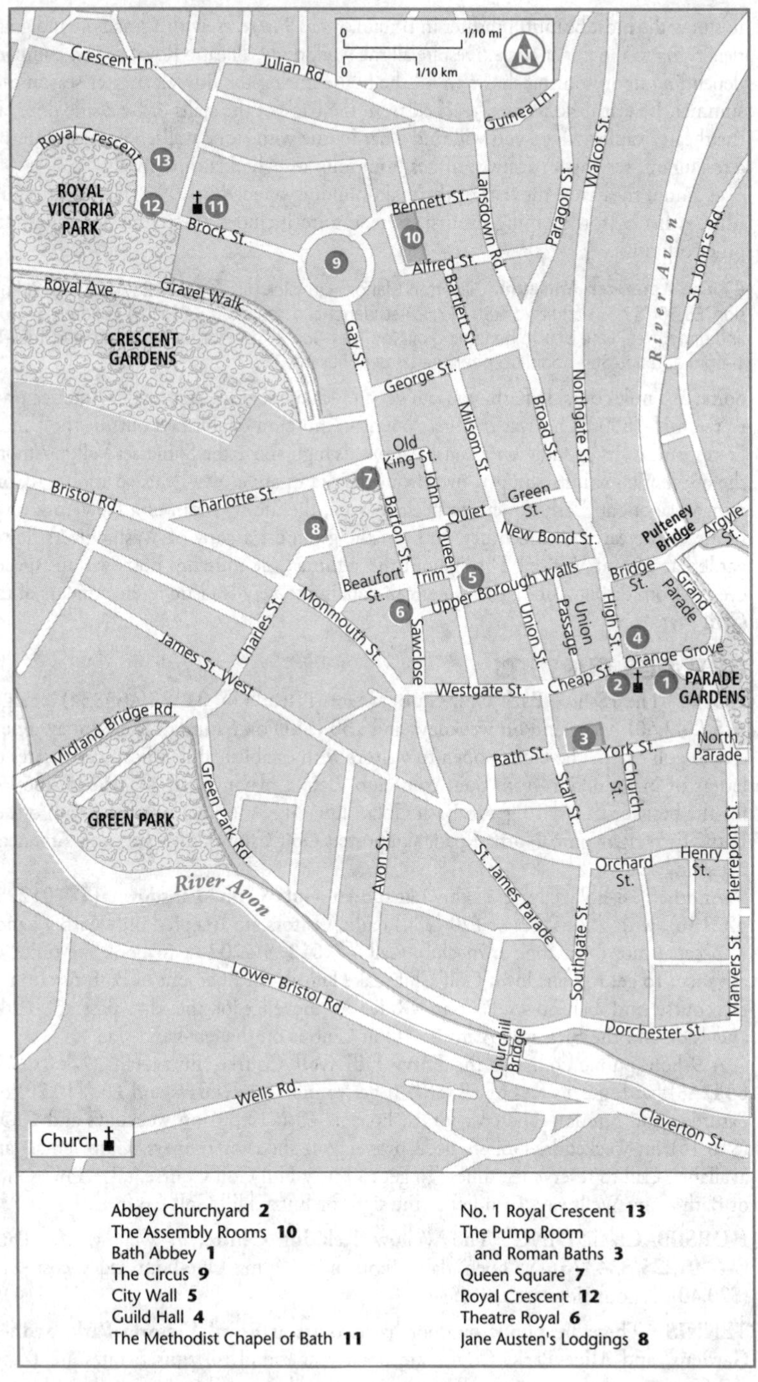

Abbey Churchyard **2**
The Assembly Rooms **10**
Bath Abbey **1**
The Circus **9**
City Wall **5**
Guild Hall **4**
The Methodist Chapel of Bath **11**
No. 1 Royal Crescent **13**
The Pump Room and Roman Baths **3**
Queen Square **7**
Royal Crescent **12**
Theatre Royal **6**
Jane Austen's Lodgings **8**

it is now the most beautiful theater in Britain. It has 940 seats, with a small pit and grand tiers rising to the upper circle. Despite all the work done, Theatre Royal has no company, depending upon touring shows to fill the house during the 8-week theater season each summer. Beneath the theater, reached from the back of the stalls or by a side door, are the theater vaults, where you will find a bar in one with stone walls. The next vault has a restaurant, serving an array of dishes from soup to light á la carte meals.

A studio theater at the rear of the main building opened in 1996. The theater publishes a list of forthcoming events; its repertoire includes West End shows, among other offerings.

✪ **The American Museum.** Claverton Manor, Bathwick Hill. ☎ **01225/460503.** Admission £5.50 ($9.35) adults, £4.50 ($7.65) students and seniors, £3 ($5.10) children 5–16, 4 and under free. Late Mar to beginning of Nov Tues–Sun 2–5pm for the museum, and Tues–Fri 1–6pm and Sat–Sun noon–6pm for the garden. Bus no. 18.

Some 2½ miles outside Bath, you can get an idea of what life was like in America prior to the mid-1800s. This was the first American museum established outside the United States, and it sits proudly on extensive grounds high above the Somerset Valley. Among the authentic exhibits shipped over from the States are a New Mexico room, a Conestoga wagon, an Early American beehive oven, the dining room of a New York town house of the early 19th century, and (on the grounds) a copy of Washington's flower garden at Mount Vernon. Throughout the summer, the museum hosts various special events, from displays of Native American dancing to very realistic re-enactments of the Civil War.

OUTDOOR PURSUITS

GOLF The 18-hole **Bath Golf Club,** at North Road (☎ **01225/463834**), charges £25 ($42.50) per round on weekdays and £30 ($51) on Saturday and Sunday. There are no golf carts. The club is open to visitors with established handicap certificates or letters of introduction from their own club. Before playing, call ☎ **01225/466953** for the best tee times. To get to Bath Golf Club, take A36 (Warminster Road) out of Bath. Turn right onto North Road, signposted Golf Club, University, and American Museum.

Another 18-hole course is the **Lansdown Golf Club,** Lansdown (☎ **01225/422138**), with greens fees of £20 ($34) daily. Visitors are accepted only with a handicap certificate from their own club. Call ☎ **01225/420242** to book tee times in advance. To get to Lansdown Golf Club, take Lansdown Road out of Bath toward the racecourse and Lansdown Park-and-Ride. At the edge of the city, pass the Park-and-Ride and the Blathway Arms; the Golf Club is on the left-hand side.

A 9-hole public course is the **Entry Hill Golf Course,** Entry Hill (☎ **01225/834248**), with greens fees of £5 ($8.50) per round on weekdays and £6 ($10.20) on Saturday and Sunday. The cost for 18 holes is £8 ($13.60) on weekdays and £9.50 ($16.15) on weekends. Golfers need proper golf shoes or trainers. Club rentals are available. Call to reserve tee times. To get to Entry Hill Golf Course, take A367 south of Bath along Wellsway. Turn left at the sign for Entry Hill Golf Course.

HORSEBACK RIDING **The Wellow Trekking Centre,** in Wellow, near Bath (☎ **01225/834376**), is open daily 9:30am to 4pm. One-hour rides cost £12 ($20.40), 2-hour rides are £20 ($34).

TENNIS There are public outdoor hard courts at **Royal Victoria Park, Sydney Gardens,** and **Alice Park.** Courts are open year-round till sunset; rates are £4.50 ($7.65) per person per hour. All courts are centrally located and marked on the city map available from the Tourist Information Centre at Abbey Chambers. For racquet and ball rentals or more information, contact **Excel Tennis** (☎ **01225/425066**).

SHOPPING

Bath is loaded with markets and fairs, antique centers, and small shops. There are literally hundreds of opportunities to buy (and ship) anything you want (including the famous spa waters, which are for sale by the bottle). Prices are traditionally less than in London but more than in the British boonies.

The whole city is basically one long, slightly uphill shopping area. It's not defined by one High Street, as are so many British towns—if you arrive by train, don't be put off by the lack of scenery. Within 2 blocks are several shopping streets. The single best day to visit, if you are a serious shopper intent on hitting the flea markets, is Wednesday.

The Bartlett Street Antiques Centre, Bartlett Street (☎ **01225/466689**), encompasses 60 dealers and 160 showcases displaying furniture, silver, antique jewelry, paintings, toys, military items, and collectibles. Another option is the **Great Western Antiques Centre,** Bartlett Street (☎ **01225/424243**), with 30 dealers. Here you can find costumes, costume jewelry, trains and other railway items, lace and linens, porcelain and glass, music boxes, canes, and much more.

Walcot Reclamation, 108 Walcot St. (☎ **01225/444404**), is Bath's salvage yard. This sprawling and appealingly dusty storeroom of 19th-century architectural remnants is set 1/4-mile northeast of the town center. Its 20,000-square-foot warehouse offers pieces from demolished homes, schools, hospitals, and factories throughout south England. Mantelpieces, panels, columns, and architectural ornaments are each departmentalized into historical eras. Items range from a complete, dismantled 1937 Georgian library crafted from Honduran mahogany to objects costing around £7 ($11.90) each. Anything can be shipped by a battery of artisans who are trained in adapting antique fittings for modern homes.

The largest purveyor of antique coins and stamps in Bath, **The Bath Stamp & Coin Shop,** 12–13 Pulteney Bridge (☎ **01225/463073**), offers hundreds of odd and unusual numismatics. Part of the inventory is devoted to Roman coins, some of which were unearthed in archaeological excavations at Roman sites near Bath.

Poppy & Scorpio, 16 Northgate (☎ **01225/465320**), offers elegant and conservatively stylish women's clothing, mostly from such German and Continental names as Betty Barclay, Basler, Bianca, Lucia, Hucke, Jobis, and Tru.

Near Bath Abbey, the **Beaux Arts Gallery,** 13 York St. (☎ **01225/464850**), is the largest and most important gallery of contemporary art in Bath, specializing in well-known British artists including Ray Richardson, John Bellany, and Nicola Bealing. Closely linked to the London art scene, the gallery occupies a pair of interconnected, stone-fronted Georgian houses. Its half dozen showrooms exhibit objects beginning at £24 ($40.80).

The very upscale **Rossiter's,** 38–41 Broad St. (☎ **01225/462227**), sells very traditional English tableware and home decor items. They'll ship anywhere in the world. Look especially for the display of Moorcraft ginger jars, vases, and clocks, as well as the Floris perfumes.

Whittard of Chelsea, 14 Union Passage (☎ **01225/483529**), is the most charming and unusual tea emporium in Bath. Inside, you'll find strainers, traditional table and tea services (plus a large selection of offbeat teapot designs), tea biscuits, tea cozies, tea caddies, and teas from all parts of what used to be the Empire. Looking for a fabulously exotic tea to wow your friends with back home? How about monkey-picked oolong—a Chinese tea made from plants so inaccessible their leaves can only be gathered by trained monkeys!

WHERE TO STAY

VERY EXPENSIVE

✪ **Bath Spa Hotel.** Sydney Rd. (east of the city, off A36), Bath, Somerset BA2 6JF. ☎ **01225/444424.** Fax 01225/476825. www.bathspahotel.com. E-mail: fivestar@bathspa.u-net.com. 98 units. MINIBAR TV TEL. Sun–Thurs £179–£209 ($304.30–$355.30) double; £260–£359 ($442–$610.30) suite for 2. Fri–Sat £224–£259 ($380.80–$440.30) double; £309–£386 ($525.30–$656.20) suite for 2. AE, DC, MC, V.

This stunning restored 19th-century mansion is a 10-minute walk from the center of Bath. Behind a facade of Bath stone, it lies at the end of a tree-lined drive on 7 acres of landscaped grounds, with a Victorian grotto and a Grecian temple. In its long history, it had served many purposes (once a hostel for nurses) before being returned to its original grandeur. The hotel uses log fireplaces, elaborate moldings, and oak paneling to create country-house charm. The rooms are handsomely furnished and most of them are spacious. Most beds are doubles, and some even offer an old-fashioned four-poster. The marble baths are among the city's finest, each with hand-held and fixed showers, deluxe toiletries and a hair dryer.

Dining: Vellore, the hotel restaurant, offers continental cuisine. You're given immaculate service and superb food and wine with a fixed-price dinner or Sunday lunch. A second venue, the Alfresco Restaurant, offers a Mediterranean-style menu. In summer, guests can dine outside in an informal garden with a fountain.

Amenities: 24-hour room service, valet and laundry service, beauty treatments, hairdressing salon, indoor swimming pool, children's nursery, beauty-treatment rooms, and a health and leisure spa.

Fountain House. 9–11 Fountain Buildings, Lansdown Rd., Bath, Somerset BA1 5DV. ☎ **01225/338622.** Fax 01225/445855. 13 units. MINIBAR TV TEL. £137 ($232.90) 1-bedroom suite; £260 ($442) 2-bedroom suite. No credit cards. Parking £5 ($8.50) .

On the northern edge of the city center, the buildings that comprise these serviced flats are a trio of 1735 Georgian neoclassic structures. The flats stand within 100 yards of Milsom Street, the city's main shopping and historic thoroughfare.

Each of these self-catering serviced flats is decorated with original or reproduction antiques, lots of color-coordinated chintz, at least one bedroom, a sitting room, and all the electronic equipment you'd expect at home. The living space is generous, and bathrooms are of a high standard. Every flat has a kitchen where you can prepare your own meals.

The Priory Hotel. Weston Rd., Bath, Somerset BA1 2XT. ☎ **01225/331922.** Fax 01225/448276. E-mail: 106076.1265@compuserve.com. 28 units. TV TEL. £210 ($357) standard double; £300 ($510) deluxe room. Rates include English breakfast. AE, DC, MC, V.

Converted from one of Bath's Georgian houses in 1969, the Priory is situated on 2 acres of formal and award-winning gardens with manicured lawns and flower beds. The hotel reopened in the spring of 1997, vastly refurbished and more inviting than ever. The rooms are furnished with antiques; our personal favorite is Clivia (all rooms are named after flowers or shrubs), a nicely appointed duplex in a circular turret. Rooms range from medium in size to spacious deluxe units, the latter with views, large sitting areas and generous dressing areas. Each has a lovely old-English bed, often half-tester; bathrooms are beautifully kept, with a set of deluxe toiletries.

Dining: The restaurant consists of two separate dining rooms, one in a small salon in the original building; the others have views over the garden. The menu is varied and reflects seasonal availability. Grouse, partridge, hare, and venison are served in season in several recipes, as is the succulent lamb, roasted with herb-flavored bread crumbs. Sunday brings traditional roasted meats.

Amenities: Indoor and outdoor swimming pools, croquet lawn, health club, Jacuzzi, sauna, concierge, 24-hour room service, dry cleaning/laundry, baby-sitting.

✪ **The Queensberry Hotel.** Russel St., Bath, Somerset BA1 2QF. ☎ **800/323-5463** in the U.S., or 01225/447928. Fax 01225/446065. www. bathqueensberry.com. E-mail: queensberry@dial.pipex.com. 29 units. TV TEL. £135–£220 ($229.50–$374) double. Rates include continental breakfast. AE, MC, V. Parking £1 ($1.70) per hour.

A gem of a hotel, this early Georgian-era town house has been beautifully restored by Stephen and Penny Ross. In our view, it is now among the finest places to stay in a city where the competition for restored town house hotels is fierce. The marquis of Queensberry commissioned John Wood the Younger to build this house in 1772. Rooms—often spacious but usually medium in size—are delightful, each tastefully decorated with antique furniture and such thoughtful extras as fresh flowers. Bathrooms are well kept with a good shower and a hair dryer.

Dining: At the hotel you can dine at the exceptional Olive Tree, offering contemporary English cuisine. See "Where to Dine," below.

✪ **Royal Crescent Hotel.** 16 Royal Crescent, Bath, Somerset BA1 2LS. ☎ **888/2954710** in the U.S., or 01225/823333. Fax 01225/339401. www.royalcrescent.co.uk. 45 units. A/C TV TEL. £195–£295 ($331.50–$501.50) double; from £395 ($671.50) suite. DC, MC, V.

This special place stands proudly in the center of the famed Royal Crescent. Long regarded as Bath's premier hotel (before the arrival of the even better Bath Spa), it has attracted the rich and famous. The bedrooms, including the Jane Austen Suite, are lavishly furnished with such amenities as four-poster beds and Jacuzzi baths. Each room is individually designed and offers such comforts as bottled mineral water, fruit plates, and other special touches. Bedrooms, generally quite spacious, are elaborately decked out with thick wool carpeting, silk wall coverings, and antiques, each with a superb and rather sumptuous bed. Bathrooms are equally luxurious with hair dryers and robes.

Dining: Excellent English cuisine is served in the Brasserie Restaurant (reservations are essential), which offers fixed-price lunches and dinners daily. The continental cuisine is imaginative, with ever-so-polite and formal service.

Amenities: Health club, steam room, Jacuzzi, car-rental desk, beauty salon, concierge, room service, dry cleaning/laundry, baby-sitting.

EXPENSIVE

Francis Hotel. Queen Sq., Bath, Somerset BA1 2HH. ☎ **800/225-5843** in the U.S., and Canada, or 01225/424257. Fax 01225/319715. E-mail: heritagehotels-bath.francis@forte-hotels.com. 94 units. TV TEL. £129–£149 ($219.30–$253.30) double; £204–£284 ($346.80–$482.80) suite. AE, DC, MC, V.

An integral part of Queen Square, the Francis is an example of 18th-century taste and style, but we find it too commercial and touristy. Originally consisting of six private residences dating from 1729, the Francis was opened as a private hotel by Emily Francis in 1884 and has offered guests first-class service for more than 100 years. Many of the well-furnished and traditionally styled bedrooms overlook Queen Square, named in honor of George II's consort, Caroline. Rooms range in size from rather small to medium, with either twin or double beds. Accommodations in the older building have more charm, especially the upper floor. Bathrooms are small but equipped with a hair dryer and heated racks holding towels.

Dining/Diversions: There's a cocktail bar and The Square Restaurant, which offers a wide array of both British and international food.

MODERATE

Pratt's Hotel. S. Parade, Bath, Somerset BA2 4AB. ☎ **01225/460441.** Fax 01225/448807. E-mail: hotel@prattshotel.demon.co.uk. 46 units. TV TEL. £100 ($170) double. Children under 15 sharing a room with 2 adults stay free. Rates include English breakfast. AE, DC, MC, V. Parking £8.50 ($14.45).

Once the home of Sir Walter Scott, Pratt's was built in the heady days of Beau Nash. Functioning as a hotel since 1791, it's become part of the legend and lore of Bath. Several elegant terraced Georgian town houses were joined together to form this complex with a very traditional British atmosphere. Rooms are individually designed and equipped with hair dryers and trouser presses. As is typical of a converted private home, bedrooms range from small to spacious (the larger ones are on the lower floors). Regardless of their dimensions, the rooms are furnished in a comfortable though utilitarian style, with small but efficiently organized bathrooms. The hotel is also known for offering good food, a range of English and French dishes.

INEXPENSIVE

✪ **Apsley House Hotel.** 141 Newbridge Hill, Bath, Somerset BA1 3PT. ☎ **01225/336966.** Fax 01225/425462. www.apsleyhouse.co.uk. E-mail: info@apsleyhouse.co.uk. 9 units. TV TEL. £85 ($144.50) double; £115 ($195.50) suite. Rates include English breakfast. DC, MC, V. Take A4 to Upper Bristol Rd. fork right at the traffic signals into Newbridge Hill, and turn left at Apsley Rd.

This charming and stately building, just 1 mile west of the center of Bath, dates from 1830, during the reign of William IV. In 1994, new owners refurbished the hotel, filling it with country-house chintzes and a collection of antiques borrowed from the showrooms of an antique store they own. (Some of the furniture in the hotel is for sale; inquire further about the details.) Style and comfort are the keynote here, and all the relatively spacious bedrooms are inviting, appointed with plush beds. Extra features include radio alarm clocks, trouser press, hair dryers, and beverage makers.

✪ **Badminton Villa.** 10 Upper Oldfield Park, Bath, Somerset BA2 3JZ. ☎ **01225/426347.** Fax 01225/420393. www.SmoothHound.co.uk/hotels/badmintn.html. E-mail: badmintonvilla@cableinet.co.uk. 5 units. TV. £62 ($105.40) double; £70 ($119) triple. Rates include English breakfast. MC, V. Bus no. 14.

Located about 1/2 mile south of the city center, this house was built in 1883 as part of a suburban development that is now an extremely desirable place to live. Constructed of honey-colored blocks of Bath stone, it lies on a hillside with sweeping views over the world-famous architecture of Bath. In 1992, John and Sue Barton transformed it from a villa in disrepair to one of the most charming small hotels in Bath. Furnishings are an eclectic but unpretentious mix of objects gathered by the Burtons during their travels. The small to medium-sized bedrooms feature double-glazed windows and new carpeting throughout. Bathrooms have a tub or an upgraded shower, plus a hair dryer. There's also a three-tiered garden with patio.

✪ **Bath Tasburgh Hotel.** Warminster Rd., Bathampton, Bath, Somerset BA2 6SH. ☎ **01225/425096.** Fax 01225/463842. www.bathtasburgh.co.uk. E-mail: hotel@bathtasburgh.demon.co.uk. 12 units. TV TEL. £72–£98 ($122.40–$166.60) double; £92 ($156.40) triple; £112 ($190.40) quad. Rates include English breakfast. AE, DC, MC, V. Bus no. 4.

Set about 1 mile east of Bath center, amid 7 acres of parks and gardens, this spacious Victorian country house was built in 1890. The redbrick structure contains a large glassed-in conservatory, original marble fireplaces, stained-glass windows, and antiques. Bedrooms are elegantly decorated, often with half-tester beds, and most have sweeping panoramic views. Each contains a beverage maker, and four rooms have four-poster beds. Bathrooms are excellent, many with a tub and shower combination, and each with a hair dryer. The Avon and Kennet Canal runs along the rear of the property, and guests enjoy summer walks along the adjacent towpath.

Dukes' Hotel. 53–54 Great Pulteney St., Bath, Somerset BA2 4DN. ☎ **01225/463512.** Fax 01225/483733. 23 units. TV TEL. £70–£100 ($119–$170) double; £120–£140 ($204–$238) family room. Rates include English breakfast. AE, MC, V. Bus no. 18.

A short walk from the heart of Bath, this 1780 building has been completely restored and rather elegantly furnished and modernized, both in its public rooms and its bedrooms. Many of the original Georgian features, including cornices and moldings, have been retained. Rooms, ranging from small to medium, are exceedingly comfortable, including such amenities as an electric trouser press. All of the bathrooms are small but efficiently arranged with adequate shelf space and a hair dryer. Guests can relax in a refined drawing room or patronize the cozy bar. A traditional English menu is also offered.

Laura Place Hotel. 3 Laura Place, Great Pulteney St., Bath, Somerset BA2 4BH. ☎ **01225/463815.** Fax 01225/310222. 8 units. TV TEL. £69–£90 ($117.30–$153) double; £115 ($195.50) family suite. Rates include English breakfast. AE, MC, V. Free parking. Bus nos. 18 or 19.

Built in 1789, this hotel has won a civic award for the restoration of its stone facade, and it lies within a 2-minute walk of the Roman Baths and Bath Abbey. This very formal hotel has been skillfully decorated with antique furniture and fabrics evocative of the 18th century. The bedrooms here are exceedingly cozy in the best tradition of an English B&B. Baths are small, usually with a shower stall instead of a tub, but have adequate shelf space.

Number Ninety Three. 93 Wells Rd., Bath, Somerset BA2 3AN. ☎ **01225/317977.** 4 units. TV. £40–£55 ($68–$93.50) double; £60–£75 ($102–$127.50) triple. Rates include English breakfast. No credit cards. Bus nos. 3, 13, 14, 17, or 23; ask for Lower Wells Rd. stop. Free parking.

This small, well-run guest house is a traditional B&B, British style. The small to medium-sized bedrooms have soft, cozy beds, and the owners undertake a continuing program of maintenance and redecoration in the slower or winter months. Bathrooms are small with a shower stall and a hair dryer. Its owner is a mine of local information. The elegant Victorian house serves a traditional English breakfast, and it is within easy walking distance from the city center and the rail and National Bus stations. Evening meals are available by prior arrangement. No smoking.

Sydney Gardens Hotel. Sydney Rd., Bath, Somerset BA2 6NT. ☎ **01225/464818.** Fax 01225/484347. www.sydneygardens.uk. 6 units. TV TEL. £69–£75 ($117.30–$127.50) double; £95 ($161.50) triple. Rates include English breakfast. AE, MC, V.

This spot is reminiscent of the letters of Jane Austen, who wrote to friends about the long walks she enjoyed in Sydney Gardens, a public park just outside the city center, a 15- to 20-minute walk away. In 1852 an Italianate Victorian villa was constructed here of gray stone on a lot immediately adjacent to the gardens. Three rooms have twin beds and the other three have 5-foot-wide double beds. Each accommodation is individually decorated with an English country-house charm. Amenities include hair dryers and beverage makers. No meals except breakfast are served, but the center of town and many restaurants are nearby. There's a footpath running beside a canal for leisurely strolls. No smoking.

In Nearby Hinton Charterhouse

Homewood Park. Hinton Charterhouse, Bath, Somerset BA3 6BB. ☎ **01225/723731.** Fax 01225/723820. www.homewoodpark.com. E-mail: res@homewoodpark.com. 19 units. £139–£177 ($236.30–$300.90) double; £209–£249 ($355.30–$423.30) suite. Rates include English breakfast. AE, CB, DC, MC, V. Take A36 (Bath-Warminster Rd.) 6 miles south of Bath.

This small, family-run hotel, set on 10 acres of grounds, was built in the 18th century and enlarged in the 19th. Overlooking the Limpley Stoke Valley, it's a large Victorian house with grounds adjoining the 13th-century ruin of Hinton Priory. You can play tennis and croquet in the garden. Riding and golfing are available nearby, and beautiful walks in the Limpley Stoke Valley lure guests. Each of the small to mid-size rooms is luxuriously decorated, and include a coffeemaker and a hair dryer. Most overlook the award-winning gardens and grounds or offer views of the valley.

Dining: Visitors come here for the cuisine, served in a dining room facing south, overlooking the gardens. The French and English cooking is prepared with skill and flair.

In Nearby Ston Easton

✪ **Ston-Easton Park.** Ston Easton, Somerset BA3 4DF. ☎ **01761/241631.** Fax 01761/241377. www.stoneaston.co.uk. E-mail: stoneastonpark@stoneaston.co.uk. 21 units, 1 cottage suite, 7 state rooms. TV TEL. £185–£315 ($314.50–$535.50) double; £320 ($544) cottage suite; £325 ($552.50) state room. Children under 7 not accepted. AE, DC, MC, V. Lies 12 miles south of Bath; follow A39 south until you see the signposted turnoff to the hamlet of Ston Easton.

This is one of the great country hotels of England. From the moment you pass a group of stone outbuildings and the century-old beeches of the 30-acre park—just up the road from Farrington Gurney—you know you've come to a very special place. The mansion was created in the mid-1700s from the shell of an existing Elizabethan house, and in 1793 Sir Humphry Repton designed the landscape. In 1977, after many years of neglect, Peter and Christine Smedley acquired the property and poured money, love, and labor into its restoration.

The tasteful rooms are filled with flowers and antiques, and feature spacious, sumptuous beds. A gardener's cottage was artfully upgraded from a utilitarian building to contain a pair of intensely decorated and very glamorous suites. In addition to the cottage suite, plus the "standard and deluxe" rooms of the main house, there are half a dozen "state rooms," four of which have four-poster beds, and all of which contain lavish but genteel decor. Bathrooms are equally luxurious, with deluxe toiletries and a hair dryer. This is English country house living at its grandest.

Dining: A grand formal dining room displays museum-quality oil portraits and exquisite attention to detail. The chef prepares superb food, offering imaginative menus.

In Nearby Hunstrete

Hunstrete House. Hunstrete, Chelwood, near Bristol, Somerset BS18 4NS. ☎ **01761/490490.** Fax 01761/490732. www.hunstretehouse.co.uk. E-mail: uscr@hunstretehouse.co.uk. 23 units. TV TEL. £130 ($221) double; £180 ($306) superior double; £230 ($391) suite. Half board £250 ($425) double; £300 ($510) suite for 2. Rates include English breakfast. AE, DC, MC, V. Take A4 about 3 1/2 miles west of Bath, then A368 another 3 1/2 miles toward Weston-super-Mare.

This fine Georgian house, a member of Relais & Châteaux, is situated on 92 acres of private parkland. Six units are in the Courtyard House, attached to the main structure and overlooking a paved courtyard with an Italian fountain. Swallow Cottage, which adjoins the main house, has its own private sitting room, double bedroom, and bath.

Units in the main house are decorated with antiques, and all have sitting areas with armchairs and sofas. Awaiting you are many little extras such as a selection of magazines and a decanter of sherry. Bathrooms are also luxurious and include a hair dryer. There is a heated swimming pool in the garden. Part of the pleasure of staying at Hunstrete is the contemporary and classic cuisine.

WHERE TO DINE

The best place for afternoon tea is **The Pump Room & Roman Baths** (see "Seeing the Sights," above). Another choice, just a 1-minute walk from the Abbey Church and Roman Baths, is **Sally Lunn's House,** 4 North Parade Passage (☎ **01225/461634**), where visitors have been eating for more than 1,700 years. For £4.78 ($8.15) you can get the Fantastic Sally Lunn Cream Tea, which includes toasted and buttered scones served with strawberry jam and clotted cream, along with your choice of tea or coffee.

Café Retro, York Street (☎ **01225/339347**), serves a variety of teas and coffees. You can order a pot of tea for £1 ($1.70), or a large cappuccino for £1.40 ($2.40) and add a tea cake, scone, or crumpet for £1 ($1.70).

Beaujolais. 5 Chapel Row, Queen Sq. ☎ **01225/423417.** Reservations recommended. 2- and 3-course lunches £8–£10.50 ($13.60–$17.85); 3-course dinner £25 ($42.50). AE, MC, V. Mon–Sat noon–2:30pm and 6–11pm. FRENCH.

This is the best-known bistro in Bath, maintaining its old regulars, but also attracting new admirers every year. Diners are drawn to the honest fare and good value. The house wines are modestly priced. Begin with grilled monkfish served with a creamy white sauce, then followed with roast partridge or duck confit. Also served is a wide variety of vegetarian dishes, one of which is a mushroom and spinach combination.

One area of the restaurant is reserved for nonsmokers. Persons with disabilities will appreciate the wheelchair access, and parents can order special helpings for children.

The Hole in the Wall. 16 George St. ☎ **01225/425242.** Reservations recommended for weekdays and required Sat. Main courses £8.50–£14.50 ($14.45–$24.65); 2-course lunch £7.50 ($12.75); 3-course dinner £22 ($37.40). AE, MC, V. Mon–Sat noon–2pm and 6–10pm. MODERN ENGLISH/FRENCH.

This much-renovated Georgian town house is owned by Gunna and Christopher Chown, whose successful restaurant in Wales has already received critical acclaim. The menu choices change frequently, according to the inspiration of the chef and the availability of ingredients. Begin with such delights as a foie gras and duck-liver terrine with pistachio and red-onion marmalade. Proceed into a taste sensation with breast of free-range chicken with wild mushrooms and leeks; or pan-fried fillets of red mullet with a yellow pepper sauce. Desserts are often a surprise—say, rhubarb parfait with a confit of ginger.

✪ **Lettonie.** 35 Kelston Rd. ☎ **01225/44676.** Set lunch £20–£25 ($34–$42.50); fixed-price dinner £47.50 ($80.75). AE, DC, MC, V. Tues–Sat noon to 2pm and 7–9:30pm. FRENCH.

Moving here from Bristol, this restaurant quickly became the talk of Bath. Sian and Martin Blunos have won an entire coterie of new admirers among the savvy foodies of Bath with their French-inspired cuisine. Their food seems to grow more elegant with every bite. One of our favorite appetizers is lobster-stuffed ravioli, but you might also sample the pan-fried foie gras with orange zest and shallots. Each dish is the result of time-consuming preparation in the kitchen, but the results are worth it as reflected by their roast noisette of lamb with garlic fritters or the steamed brill with wild mushrooms, bacon, and onions in a red-wine jus. The desserts are worth saving room for, especially the pear mousse with toffee ice cream or the hot caramel sponge tart.

The Moon and Sixpence. 6A Broad St. ☎ **01225/460962.** Reservations recommended. Main courses £9–£14 ($15.30–$23.80); fixed-price lunch £8.75 ($14.90); fixed-price dinner £24 ($40.80). AE, MC, V. Daily noon–2:30pm; Mon–Thurs 5:30–10:30pm, Fri–Sat 5:30–11pm, Sun 6–10:30pm. INTERNATIONAL.

One of the leading restaurants and wine bars of Bath, The Moon and Sixpence occupies a stone structure east of Queen Square. The food may not be as good as that served at more acclaimed choices, including The Hole in the Wall, but the value is unbeatable. At lunch, a large cold buffet with a selection of hot dishes is featured in the wine bar section. In the upstairs restaurant overlooking the bar, full service is offered. Main courses are likely to include fillet of lamb with caramelized garlic or roast breast of duck with Chinese vegetables. Look for the daily specials on the continental menu.

The Olive Tree. In the Queensberry Hotel, Russel St. ☎ **01225/447928.** Reservations highly recommended. Main courses £11–£19.50 ($18.70–$33.15); 3-course fixed-price lunch £14.50 ($24.65); 3-course fixed-price dinner £22 ($37.40). MC, V. Mon–Sat noon–2pm and 7–10pm, Sun 7–9pm. MODERN ENGLISH/MEDITERRANEAN.

Stephen and Penny Ross operate one of the most sophisticated little restaurants in Bath. Stephen uses the best local produce, with an emphasis on freshness. The menu is changed to reflect the season, with game and fish being the specialties. You might begin with grilled scallops with truffled potatoes and chive dressing, or mussels steamed with tomatoes and pesto butter. Then you could proceed with roast squab pigeon, salsify purée, and crispy parsnip; or grilled Aberdeen Angus rump fillet, creamed onions and rosemary on a red-wine-and-peppercorn jus. Stephen is also known for his desserts, which are likely to include such treats as a hot-chocolate soufflé or an apricot and almond tart.

Popjoy's Restaurant. Sawclose. ☎ **01225/460494.** Reservations recommended. Main courses £15–£19.50 ($25.50–$33.15); 3-course fixed-price lunch £14 ($23.80). AE, DC, MC, V. Mon–Sat noon–2:30pm and 6–11pm. MODERN BRITISH/CONTINENTAL.

Owned by Tomi and Nany Gretener, these two dining rooms are located on separate floors of the Georgian home (ca. 1720) where Beau Nash and his mistress, Julianna Popjoy, once entertained their friends and set the fashions of the day. Inventiveness and a solid technique go into many of the dishes. The food is unpretentious and generally quite satisfying. Menu choices may include guinea-fowl and wood pigeon terrine wrapped in smoked bacon and served with an apricot and raison compote, or lightly grilled tiger prawns marinated in coriander, lime and chili served on watercress with a passion fruit dressing.

Woods. 9–13 Alfred St. ☎ **01225/314812.** Reservations recommended. Main courses £10–£18 ($17–$30.60); fixed-price lunches £8 ($13.60); fixed-price dinners £12.50–£16.50 ($21.25–$28.05). MC, V. Mon–Sat noon–3pm and 6–11pm. MODERN ENGLISH.

Named after John Wood the Younger, architect of Bath's famous Assembly Room, which lies across the street, this restaurant is run by horse-racing enthusiast David Price and his French-born wife, Claude. A fixed-price menu is printed on paper, whereas the seasonal array of à la carte items are chalked onto a frequently changing blackboard. Good bets include grilled goats cheese with cherry tomatoes and pesto or chicken cooked with apricots.

BATH AFTER DARK

To gain a very different perspective of Bath, you may want to take the **Bizarre Bath Walking Tour** (☎ **01225/335124**), 1½ hour improvisational tour of the streets during which the tour guides pull pranks, tell jokes, and behave in a humorously annoying manner toward tour-goers and unsuspecting residents alike. It's a seasonal affair, running nightly at 8pm from Easter through September. No reservations are necessary; just show up, ready for anything, at the Huntsman Inn at North Parade Passage. The cost of the tour is £3.50 ($5.95); £3 ($5.10) for students and children.

After your walk, you may need a drink, or want to check out the local club and music scene. At **The Bell,** 103 Walcot St. (☎ **01225/460426**), music ranges from jazz and country to reggae and blues on Monday and Wednesday nights and Sunday at lunch. On music nights, the band performs in the center of the long, narrow 400-year-old room.

The two-story **Hat and Feather,** 14 London St. (☎ **01225/425672**), has live musicians or DJs playing funk, reggae, or dance music nightly. **The Hush,** The Paragon (☎ **01225/446288**), offers music at the cutting edge of the English scene Monday through Saturday nights, with a cover of £3 ($5.10) after 10pm.

SIDE TRIPS FROM BATH

LACOCK: AN 18TH-CENTURY VILLAGE

From Bath, take the A4 about 12 miles to the A350, then head south to Lacock, a National Trust village showcasing English architecture from the 13th through the 18th centuries.

Unlike many villages that disappeared or were absorbed into bigger communities, Lacock remained largely unchanged because of a single family, the Talbots, who owned most of it and preferred to keep their traditional village traditional. Turned over to the National Trust in 1944, it's now one of the best-preserved villages in all of England with many 16th-century homes, gardens, and churches. Notable is **St. Cyriac Church,** Church Street, a Perpendicular-style church built by wealthy wool merchants between the 14th and 17th centuries.

Lacock Abbey, High Street (☎ **01249/730227**), founded in 1232 for Augustinian canonesses, was updated and turned into a private home in the 16th century. It fell victim to Henry VIII's Dissolution, when, upon establishing the Church of England, he seized existing church properties to bolster his own wealth. Admission for all church properties is £6 ($10.20) for adults and £3 ($5.10) for children, family ticket £16.50 ($28.05). Open Easter through October, daily from 11am to 5pm.

While on the grounds, stop by the medieval barn, home to the **Fox Talbot Museum** (☎ **01249/730459**). It was here that William Henry Fox Talbot carried out his early experiments with photography, making the first known photographic prints in 1833. In his honor, the barn is now a photography museum featuring some of those early prints. Open daily, March through October from 11am to 5:30pm. Admission is £3.50 ($5.95) for adults, £2 ($3.40) children.

Where to Stay

At the Sign of the Angel. Church St., Lacock, Chippenham, Wiltshire SN15 2LA. ☎ **01249/730230.** Fax 01249/730527. 10 units. TV TEL. £99–£137.50 ($168.30–$233.75) double. Rates include English breakfast. AE, MC, V.

This ancient inn was built in the 14th century by a wool merchant. The rooms at the inn are quiet, and split between the main building and a 17th-century garden cottage. Each guest room is distinctly decorated with a host of antiques. One room has a magnificently carved Spanish bed that is said to have belonged to Isambard Kingdom Brunel, the famous railway and canal builder. Some rooms are standard and rather small, others are more spacious—no. 12, for example, has a four-poster bed and no. 3 is a generously-size superior room with a very large bed. Bathrooms have adequate shelf space and a tub or shower.

Dining: The inn's restaurant offers good, moderately priced meals in an atmosphere where you expect to see Shakespeare walk through the door at any moment.

Where to Dine

The George Inn. 4 West St., Lacock, Wiltshire SN15 2LH. ☎ **01249/730263.** Main courses £6.50–£12.50 ($11.05–$21.25). MC, V. Mon–Fri 10am–2:30pm and 5pm–11pm; Sat–Sun 10am–11pm. ENGLISH.

Housed in a building that has been used as a pub since 1361, The George Inn has been modernized since then, and is run today by John Glass. It still maintains many of its vestiges from the past—uneven floors, a large open fireplace with a dog-wheel once used for spit roasting—and has an extensive garden used as a dining area in the summer. There's even a children's playground. About 30 daily specials are chalked onto a blackboard in addition to a regular menu of fish, meat, and vegetarian dishes. Two of the most popular desserts are bread-and-butter pudding and sticky toffee pudding.

John Glass's wife, Judy, runs a B&B out of the family farmhouse. **The Lower Home Farm** (☎ **01225/790045**) has three double rooms, each with a private bath, that start at £40 ($68) per night, including English breakfast. The grounds are made up of 100 acres of gardens, with plenty of walks, and even a lake. It all adds up to a peaceful and serene setting. No credit cards are accepted at the farm, but rates include taxi service to The George Inn, from which guests can walk to all the attractions in this National Trust village.

CASTLE COMBE

Once voted England's prettiest village, the financially disastrous *Dr. Doolittle* was filmed here, and the 15th-century Upper Manor House, used as Rex Harrison's residence in the movie, is its most famous site. The entire village, though, can just about be absorbed in a glance. Consisting of one street lined with cottages (known simply as "The Street"), it is the quintessential sleepy village. It's easily explored in a morning or afternoon, before moving on to your next destination. Located 10 miles northeast of Bath, take A46 north 9.5 kilometers (6 miles) to A420, then head east to Ford, following the signs north to Castle Combe. From Lacock, take A350 north to Chippenham, then get on A420 west and follow the signs.

Where to Stay & Dine

Manor House Hotel & Golf Club. Castle Combe, Wiltshire SN14 7HR. ☎ **01249/782206.** Fax 01249/782159. www.exclusivehotels.co.uk. E-mail: enquiries@manor-house.co.uk. 45 units. TV TEL. £120–£350 ($204–$595) double. AE, DC, MC, V.

The house and accompanying estate date from the 14th-century and once served as the baronial seat in Castle Combe. The main building and its accompanying cottages sit regally on 47 acres of gardens, with wooded trails, a lake, and an 18-hole golf course. South of the manor flows the trout-stocked River Bybrook, where fishing is permitted. Bedrooms come in a variety of sizes, and some have four-poster beds. You can stay either in the main house or else in a row of original stone cottages on the grounds. The latter have recently been upgraded to meet the standards of the main house. Eight rooms are large enough for families. Bathrooms are superbly kept with a hair dryer and a set of fluffy towels.

Dining/Amenities: 24-hour restaurant (formal attire for dinner), room service, bar, swimming pool, and tennis courts.

4 Bristol

120 miles W of London; 13 miles NW of Bath

Bristol, the largest city in the West Country, is just across the Bristol Channel from Wales and is a good place to base yourself for touring western Britain. This historic inland port is linked to the sea by 7 miles of the navigable River Avon. Bristol has long been rich in seafaring traditions and has many links with the early colonization of America. In fact, some claim that the new continent was named after a Bristol town clerk, Richard Ameryke. In 1497, John Cabot sailed from Bristol, and pioneered the discovery of the northern half of the New World.

Although Bath is much more famous as a tourist mecca, Bristol does have some attractions, like a colorful harbor life, that make it at least a good overnight stop in your exploration of the West Country.

ESSENTIALS

GETTING THERE Bristol Airport (☎ **01275/474444**) is conveniently situated beside the main A38 road, just over 7 miles from the city center.

Rail services to and from the area are among the fastest and most efficient in Britain. **British Rail** runs very frequent services from London's Paddington Station to each of Bristol's two main stations: Temple Meads in the center of Bristol, and Parkway on the city's northern outskirts. The trip takes 1¼ hours. For rail information, call ☎ **0345/484950.**

National Express buses depart every hour during the day from London's Victoria Coach Station, making the trip in 2½ hours. For more information and schedules, call ☎ **0990/808080.**

If you're driving, head west from London on the M4.

VISITOR INFORMATION The **Tourist Information Centre** is at St. Nicholas Church, St. Nicholas Street (☎ **0117/9260767**). In winter, it's open Monday through Saturday from 9:30am to 5:30pm and Sunday 11am to 4pm; 9:30am to 5:30pm in summer.

EXPLORING THE TOWN

Guided **walking tours** are conducted in summer and last about 1½ hours. They depart from Neptune's Statue on Saturday at 2:30pm and on Thursday at 7pm. Guided tours are also conducted through Clifton, a suburb of Bristol, which has more Georgian houses than Bath. Consult the Tourist Information Centre (see above) for more information.

The **Clifton Suspension Bridge,** spanning the beautiful Avon Gorge, has become the symbol of the city of Bristol. Originally conceived in 1754, it was not completed until more than 100 years later, in 1864. The architect, Isambard Kingdom Brunel, died five years before the completion of the bridge. His fellow engineers continued on with his vision, completing the bridge as a memorial to him. There is a visitor center located in a former Victorian hotel just 200 meters from the bridge where you can see a superbly intricate scale model of Brunel's bridge, as well as an exhibition outlining the story of its construction. The visitor center is open daily from Easter to September from 10am to 5:50pm and from October to Easter Monday to Friday from 11am to 4pm and on Saturday and Sunday from 11am to 5pm. Admission cost is £1.50 ($2.55) for adults, £1 ($1.70) for seniors, and 80p ($1.30) for children under 16 years.

SS Great Britain. City Docks, Great Western Dock. ☎ **0117/9260680.** Admission £6.25 ($10.65) adults, £5.25 ($8.90) senior citizens, £3.75 ($6.40) children, £18 ($30.60) family ticket. Apr–Oct daily 10am–5:30pm; Nov–Mar daily 10am–4:30pm. Bus no. 511 from city center, a rather long haul.

In Bristol, the world's first iron steamship and luxury liner has been partially restored to its 1843 appearance, although it's still a long way from earning its old title of a "floating palace." This vessel, which weighs 3,443 tons, was designed by Isambard Brunel, a Victorian engineer.

Incidentally, in 1831 (at the age of 25), Brunel began a Bristol landmark, Suspension Bridge, over the 250-foot-deep Somerset Gorge at Clifton.

Bristol Cathedral. College Green. ☎ **0117/9264879.** Free admission; £2 ($3.40) donation requested. Daily 8am–6pm. Bus nos. 8 or 9.

Construction of the cathedral, once an Augustinian abbey, was begun in the 12th century, and the central tower was added in 1466. The chapter house and gatehouse are good examples of late Norman architecture. The cathedral's interior was singled out for praise by Sir John Betjeman, the late poet laureate.

In 1539, the abbey was closed and the incomplete nave was demolished. The building was turned into the Cathedral Church of the Holy and Undivided Trinity in 1542. In 1868, plans were drawn up to complete the nave to its medieval design. The architect, G. E. Street, found the original pillar bases, so that the cathedral is much as it would have been when it was still the abbey church. J. L. Pearson added the two towers at the west end and further reordered the interior.

The eastern end of the cathedral, especially the choir, gives the structure a unique place in the development of British and European architecture. The nave, choir, and aisles are all of the same height, making a large hall. Bristol Cathedral is the major example of a "hall church" in Great Britain and one of the finest anywhere in the world.

St. Mary Redcliffe Church. 12 Colston Parade. ☎ **0117/9291487.** Free admission. Daily 8am–5pm.

The parish church of St. Mary Redcliffe is one of the finest examples of Gothic architecture in England. Queen Elizabeth I, on her visit in 1574, is reported to have described it as "the fairest, goodliest and most famous parish church in England," and Thomas Chatterton, the boy poet, called it "the pride of Bristol and the western land." The American Chapel houses the tomb and armor of Adm. Sir William Penn, father of Pennsylvania's founder.

Theatre Royal. King St. ☎ **0117/9493993.** Box office 0117/9877877. Tickets £7–£23 ($11.90–$39.10). Any City Centre bus.

Built in 1766, this is now the oldest working playhouse in the United Kingdom. It is the home of the Bristol Old Vic. Backstage tours leave from the foyer. Tours are run Friday and Saturday at 12:30pm (Fri only in Aug) and cost £3 ($5.10) for adults and £2 ($3.40) for children and students under 19. Call the box office for the current schedule.

SHOPPING

Many major shops are now open on Sunday.

The biggest shopping complex is **Broadmead,** mainly pedestrianized with branches of all High Street stores, plus cafes and restaurants. Many specialty shops are found at **Clifton Village,** in a Georgian setting where houses are interspaced with parks and gardens. Here you'll find a wide array of shops selling antiques, arts and crafts, and designer clothing. Opened in 1991, the **Galleries** is a totally enclosed mall, providing three levels of shopping and restaurants. The **St. Nicholas Markets** opened in 1745, and are still going strong, selling antiques, memorabilia, handcrafted gifts, jewelry, and haberdashery. The **West End** is another major shopping area, taking in Park Street, Queen's Road, and Whiteladies Road. These streets are known for their clothing outlets, bookstores, and unusual gift items from around the world, as well as wine bars and restaurants.

Spending the Night in a Tudor Castle

Twelve miles north of Bristol, Thornbury is known for its genuine Tudor castle, which is now a hotel. Many of the crenellations and towers were built in 1511. It was the last defensive castle ever constructed in England, and its owner was beheaded by Henry VIII for certain words spoken in haste. Henry confiscated the lands and, to celebrate, stayed here for 10 days with Anne Boleyn in 1535. Later, Mary Tudor spent three years of her adolescence here.

Today, you can stay at ✪ **Thornbury Castle** (☎ **01454/281182;** fax 01454/416188) and step back into history. The castle is surrounded by thick stone walls, trees, vineyards, and gardens. After you check in, you reach the 19 bedrooms and 2 suites by way of stone and spiral staircases. Every room is filled with character, and is superbly fitted with fine furniture and many amenities, including televisions and telephones; eight have four-posters. Each has a deluxe mattress and a sumptuous bath. At night, the baronial public rooms are lit by candle.

Rates, which include continental breakfast, are £135 to £260 ($229.50 to $442) for a double; £195 to £350 ($331.50 to $595) for the suites. American Express, Diners Club, MasterCard, and Visa are accepted. To get there from Bristol, take the B4061; continue downhill to the monumental water pump, bear left, and continue for 300 yards.

We also recommend Thornbury for its cuisine. French and English dishes highlight the menus at the hotel's three dining rooms. Chef Steven Black changes the menu daily and uses only the best and freshest ingredients to prepare his innovative meals. Dishes might include boned wood pigeon with mangold, and a dark green-leaf vegetable of the mangel-wurzel plant, which many consider superior to spinach. He also takes care to create some very English desserts, such as treacle tart with Cornish clotted cream. The good wine list is especially strong on Bordeaux and Burgundy. You can even sample Thornbury Castle's own wine, made from the Muller-Thurgua vines in the castle's vineyards.

Even if you're not staying at the hotel, you can call for reservations in the dining room. The two-course main menu, available daily from noon to 2pm, costs £16.50 ($28.05); for three courses £19.50 ($33.15). Dinner goes for £39.50 ($67.15) per person and is served from 7 to 9:30pm daily.

The best antique markets are **The Bristol Antique Centre,** Brunel Rooms, Broad Plain, **Clifton Antiques Market** and **New Antiques Centre,** the Mall in Clifton, and **Clifton Arcade,** Boyces Avenue, also in Clifton. Both Clifton outlets are closed on Monday but The Bristol Antique Centre is open daily, including Sunday.

WHERE TO STAY

EXPENSIVE

Bristol Marriott. Lower Castle St., Bristol, Somerset BS1 3AD. ☎ **800/228-9290** in the U.S. and Canada, or 0117/9294281. Fax 0117/9225838. 289 units. A/C TV TEL. Mon–Thurs £95–£125 ($161.50–$212.50) double; £100–£150 ($170–$255) suite. Fri–Sun from £68 ($115.60) double. AE, DC, MC, V. Bus no. 9.

In the heart of town at the edge of Castle Park, this modern 11-story hotel is one of Bristol's tallest buildings, and it's far superior to the Hilton in amenities, style, and comfort. Many improvements have been undertaken, since this place used to be a rather ordinary Holiday Inn. It attracts many business travelers, as well as foreign tourists. The comfortable rooms are conservatively modern. Bedrooms offer a high level of comfort, especially those on the more expensive executive floor with its own lounge. Bathrooms have tubs and power showers, as well as adequate shelf space. Public areas are stylish and spacious—all in the upscale traditions of the Marriott chain.

Dining: The more elegant of the hotel's two restaurants is the Château. Less formal is the Brasserie, where platters of British and continental food are served.

Amenities: Heated indoor swimming pool, fully equipped health club.

Grand Hotel. Broad St., Bristol, Somerset BS1 2EL. ☎ **0117/9291645.** Fax 0117/9227619. 182 units. TV TEL. £110–£133 ($187–$226.10) double; £165–£175 ($280.50–$297.50) suite. Discount (minimum of 2 consecutive nights Fri–Sun): £98 ($166.60) double, including half board. AE, DC, MC, V. Bus nos. 8 or 9.

This Victorian grand hotel sits in the commercial heart of town, adorned with rows of fan-shaped windows and intricate exterior cornices. Inside there are lavishly ornate crystal chandeliers and a good many Victorian details. The rooms are more conservative and modern than the public areas. Most of the bedrooms are a bit on the small side except for the spacious executive rooms at the front of the structure. One wing is reserved exclusively for female guests. Rooms have such extras as fresh flowers, an iron and ironing board, a beverage maker, and a private phone.

Dining/Diversions: There are two bars (one with a nautical theme), and a pair of comfortable restaurants, including The Brass Nails, which serves good fixed-price dinners (the White Lion is less formal and less expensive).

Jarvis International Bristol. Redcliffe Way, Bristol, Somerset BS1 6NJ. ☎ **0117/9260041.** Fax 0117/9230089. 201 units. TV TEL. £120 ($204) double; £150 ($255) suite. AE, DC, MC, V.

Situated conveniently amid the commercial bustle of the center of town, this modern hotel offers a good, safe haven for the night (though some readers have commented that the pealing bells of St. Mary Redcliffe, next door, kept them awake). The six-story Hilton is designed in a rather bland international style. Two floors of the bedrooms here are designated as no-smoking. Bedrooms range from small to medium and include mostly double beds, and such extras as beverage makers, trouser presses, and desks with luggage benches. Bathrooms are clad in marble and contain hair dryers and bathrobes.

Dining: Its split-level restaurant, The Kiln, is located inside the brick-lined walls of a former 16th-century glass kiln refurbished in the style of a French brasserie, and serves English and French specialties.

INEXPENSIVE

Alandale Hotel. 4 Tyndall's Park Rd., Clifton, Bristol, Somerset BS8 1PG. ☎ **0117/9735407.** Fax 0117/9237965. 15 units. TV TEL. £58 ($98.60) double. Rates include English breakfast. MC, V. Bus nos. 8 or 9.

This elegant early Victorian house retains many of its original features, including a marble fireplace and ornate plasterwork. Note the fine staircase in the imposing entrance hall. The hotel is under the supervision of Mr. Burgess, who still observes the old traditions of personal service. A full English breakfast is served in the dining room. There is a Victorian aura in the bedrooms, which range from small to medium; each room contains a beverage maker. Baths are small, but contain a hair dryer.

Oakfield Hotel. 52–54 Oakfield Rd., Clifton, Bristol, Somerset BS8 2BG. ☎ **0117/9733643.** Fax 0117/9744141. 27 units, none with private bathroom. TV. £38.50 ($65.45) double. Rates include English breakfast. No credit cards. Bus nos. 8 or 9.

Instead of finding lodging in the center of Bristol, many visitors head for the leafy Georgian suburb of Clifton, 1 mile north, near the famous Suspension Bridge. This impressive 1840s guest house is on a quiet street, and everything is kept spick-and-span under the watchful eye of Mrs. P. Hurley. Each room has hot and cold running water and central heating, although the furnishings are modest. The mattresses are a bit thin, but are still comfortable. Rooms contain such extras as a coffeemaker, and bathrooms, though small, are adequate for the job. For another £7.50 ($12.75) you can enjoy a simple dinner.

WHERE TO DINE

✪ **Harvey's Restaurant.** 12 Denmark St. ☎ **0117/9275034.** Reservations required. Main courses £17–£20 ($28.90–$34); fixed-price lunch £17.95–£21.95 ($30.50–$37.30); fixed-price dinner £39.95–£46.95 ($67.90–$79.80). AE, DC, MC, V. Mon–Fri noon–2pm; Mon–Sat 7–10:45pm. BRITISH/FRENCH.

This restaurant is one of the finest in this part of England. It's located in medieval cellars that have belonged to Harvey's of Bristol, famous for Harvey's Bristol Cream sherry, since 1796. Chef-manager Daniel Galmiche serves modern classic French cuisine under continuing and award-winning standards. Try zesty and flavorful creations such as pan-fried foie gras with apple and raisins for a starter, followed by pan-fried filet of beef with truffle mashed potatoes and mushrooms in a Beaujolais sauce, or roast farm pigeon with sautéed potatoes and an herb and sherry vinegar sauce. A special dessert is the gratinated pink grapefruit with saffron-and-honey ice cream. The menu is complemented by an extensive wine list, with the red wines of Bordeaux a particular specialty.

The adjoining historic cellars accommodate Harvey's Wine Museum, with collections of English 18th-century drinking glasses, antique decanters, corkscrews, bottles, silverware, and furniture. The museum is open daily, and there are regular guided tours with tutored tastings. Restaurant patrons can usually browse in the museum before their meal.

Michael's. 129 Hotwell Rd. ☎ **0117/9276190.** Reservations required for Sat dinner, and recommended at other times. Main courses £10–£20 ($17–$34). AE, DC, MC, V. Sun noon–3pm; Mon–Sat 7–10pm. From city center, take Anchor Rd., left lane becomes Hotwell Rd. FRENCH/MODERN ENGLISH.

This charming and popular restaurant is near Clifton on a highway leading toward the Somerset Gorge. Its pleasant bar is decorated like an Edwardian parlor, and the dining room is bright and inviting. The fixed-price menus are imaginative and change according to the seasonal produce. The restaurant also caters to vegans; the vegetarian meals offer a selection of four to five dishes. The service is informal and enthusiastic. If you want a cigarette, stick to the bar.

BRISTOL AFTER DARK

Bath may be more stiff and formal, but Bristol clubs and pubs are more laid-back, drawing more working-class Brits than yuppies.

Some of the best pubs are along King Street, especially **Llandoger Trow,** 5 King St. (☎ **0117/926-0783**), with its mellow West Country ambience. If you'd like to meet up with some students, their favorite watering hole is the **Lord Byron,** 2 Bryon Place (☎ **0117/929-9322**).

Lakota, 6 Upper York St. (☎ **0117/942-6193**), off Stokes Croft, is a club known for its all-night "groove parties," with a funk soundtrack. However, the cover is a bit steep, ranging from £5 to £25 ($8.50 to $42.50), depending on what's featured that night.

In a converted freight steamer moored on the Grove, **Thelka** (☎ **0117/929-3301**) is a venue where acid jazz rains down. The other leading venues for jazz are **The Old Duke,** King Street (☎ **0117/929-7137**), and the **Bebop Club** at The Bear, Hotwell Road (☎ **0117/987-7796**). The leading comedy club is **Jester's**, Cherdeham Road (☎ **0117/909-6655**). Cover charges for the clubs range from £3 to £6.50 ($5.10 to $11.05), but can vary depending on the entertainment offered.

5 Wells & the Caves of Mendip

123 miles SW of London; 21 miles SW of Bath

To the south of the Mendip Hills, the cathedral town of Wells is a medieval gem. Wells was a vital link in the Saxon kingdom of Wessex—important long before the arrival of William the Conqueror. Once the seat of a bishopric, it was eventually toppled from its ecclesiastical hegemony by the rival city of Bath. But the subsequent loss of prestige has paid off handsomely for Wells today: After experiencing the pinnacle of prestige, it fell into a slumber—and much of its old look was preserved.

Many visitors come only for the afternoon or morning, look at the cathedral, then press on to Bath for the evening. But though it's rather sleepy, Wells' old inns make a tranquil stopover.

ESSENTIALS

GETTING THERE Wells has good bus connections with surrounding towns and cities. Take the train to Bath (see "Essentials," in section 3 of this chapter) and continue the rest of the way by Badgerline bus no. 175. Departures are every hour Monday through Saturday and every 2 hours on Sunday. Both no. 376 and 378 buses run between Bristol and Glastonbury every hour daily. Call ☎ **01179/553231** for bus schedules and information.

If you're driving, take M4 west from London, cutting south on A4 toward Bath and continuing along A39 into Wells.

VISITOR INFORMATION The **Tourist Information Centre** is at the Town Hall, Market Place (☎ **01749/672552**), and is open daily November to March from 10am to 4pm and April to October from 9:30am to 5:30pm.

SEEING THE SIGHTS

After a visit to the cathedral, walk along its cloisters to the moat-surrounded **Bishop's Palace.** The Great Hall, built in the 13th century, is in ruins. Finally, the street known as the **Vicars' Close** is one of the most beautifully preserved streets in Europe.

Easily reached by heading west out of Wells, the Caves of Mendip are two exciting natural attractions: the great caves of Cheddar and Wookey Hole; see below.

✪ **Wells Cathedral.** In the center of town. ☎ **01749/674483.** Admission free, but donations of £4 ($6.80) adults, £2.50 ($4.25) seniors, £1 ($1.70) students and children appreciated. Daily 7am–6pm or 8:30pm in summer.

Begun in the 12th century, this is a well-preserved example of early English architecture. The medieval sculpture (six tiers of statues recently restored) of its west front is without equal. The western facade was completed in the mid-13th century. The landmark central tower was erected in the 14th century, with the fan-vaulting attached later. The inverted arches were added to strengthen the top-heavy structure.

Much of the stained glass dates from the 14th century. The fan-vaulted Lady Chapel, also from the 14th century, is in the decorated style. To the north is the vaulted chapter house, built in the 13th century and recently restored. Look also for a medieval astronomical clock in the north transept.

Wookey Hole Caves & Paper Mill. Wookey Hole, near Wells. ☎ **01749/672243.** 2-hour tour £7 ($11.90) adults, £3.50 ($5.95) children 16 and under, £19 ($32.30) family ticket. Apr–Oct daily 10am–5:30pm; Nov–Mar daily 10:30am–4:30pm. Closed Dec 17–25. Follow the signs from the center of Wells for 2 miles. Bus nos. 172 from Wells.

Just 2 miles from Wells, you'll first come upon the source of the Axe River. In the first chamber of the caves, as legend has it, is the Witch of Wookey turned to stone. These caves are believed to have been inhabited by prehistoric people at least 60,000 years ago. A tunnel, opened in 1975, leads to the chambers unknown in early times, and previously accessible only to divers.

Leaving the caves, you follow a canal path to the mill, where paper has been made by hand since the 17th century. Here, the best-quality handmade paper is made by skilled workers according to the tradition of their ancient craft. Also in the mill are "hands-on vats," where visitors can try their hand at making a sheet of paper, and an Edwardian Penny Pier Arcade where new pennies can be exchanged for old ones with which to play the original machines. Other attractions include the Magical Mirror Maze, and an enclosed passage of multiple image mirrors.

Cheddar Showcaves & Gorge. Cheddar, Somerset. ☎ **01934/742343.** Admission £7.50 ($12.75) adults, £5 ($8.50) children 6–15, 5 and under free. Easter–Sept daily 10am–5pm; Oct–Easter daily 10:30am–4:30pm. Closed Dec 24–25. From A38 or M5, cut onto A371 to Cheddar village.

A short distance from Bath, Bristol, and Wells is the village of Cheddar, home of cheddar cheese. It lies at the foot of Cheddar Gorge, within which are the Cheddar Caves, underground caverns with impressive formations. The caves are more than a million years old, including Gough's Cave, with its cathedral-like caverns, and Cox's Cave, with its calcite sculptures and brilliant colors. The Crystal Quest is a dark walk "fantasy adventure" taking you deep underground, and in the Cheddar Gorge Heritage Centre is displayed a 9,000-year-old skeleton. You can also climb Jacob's Ladder for clifftop walks, and Pavey's Lookout Tower for views over Somerset—on a clear day you may even see Wales.

Adults and children over 12 years of age can book an Adventure Caving expedition for £7.50 ($12.40), which includes overalls, helmets, and lamps. Other attractions include local craftspeople at work, ranging from the glassblower to the sweets maker, plus the Cheddar Cheese & Cider Depot.

Chewton Cheese Dairy. Priory Farm, Chewton Mendip. ☎ **01761/241666.** Admission free. Guided tour £2.50 ($4.25) adults, £2 ($3.40) senior citizens, £1.50 ($2.55) children 4–14, 3 and under free. General admission free. Daily 9am–5pm. Head 6 miles north of Wells on the A39 Bristol–Wells rd.

The dairy is owned by Lord Chewton, and visitors are welcome to watch through the viewing window in the restaurant as the traditional cheese-making process is carried out most mornings. A video presentation is featured in a spacious screening room. Guided tours are offered daily April to October at 11:30am, 12:15, 1, and 1:45pm. Although the dairy is open on Sunday and Thursday, there are no cheese-making demonstrations then. You can purchase a "truckle" (or wheel) of mature cheddar to send home. The restaurant offers coffee, snacks, farmhouse lunches, and cream teas.

WHERE TO STAY

✪ **Star Hotel.** 18 High St., Wells, Somerset BA5 2SQ. ☎ **01749/670500.** Fax 01749/672654. 12 units. TV TEL. £60–£67 ($102–$113.90) double. Rates include English breakfast. AE, DC, MC, V.

The Star had its origins sometime in the 16th century but is most closely associated with the great coaching era, though the hotel front was restored in the Georgian period.

The cobbled carriageway, still preserved, leads to the dining room—once the stables. The refurbished but simply furnished rooms have been modernized, yet retain their old charm. Bedrooms are cozy, and come in a number of different sizes and shapes. Rooms have small baths with adequate shelf space and a hair dryer.

The inn has a good reputation for traditional British fare. Seasonal à la carte dishes are presented, plus a full selection of wines.

The Swan Hotel. 11 Sadler St., Wells, Somerset BA5 2RX. ☎ **800/528-1234** in the U.S. and Canada, or 01749/678877. Fax 01749/677647. www.heritagehotels.co.uk. E-mail: swan@heritagehotels.co.uk. 38 units. TV TEL. £95–£105 ($161.50–$178.50) double. Rates include English breakfast. AE, DC, MC, V.

Set behind a stucco facade on one of the town's main streets, this place was originally built in the 15th century as a coaching inn. Today, facing the west front of Wells Cathedral, it is the best of the inns within the town's central core. Rooms vary in style and size; a third of the rooms in this old-fashioned inn have four-poster beds. Bathrooms are small, but have a combination shower and tub. The spacious and elegant public rooms stretch out to the left and right of the entrance. Both ends have a blazing and baronial fireplace and beamed ceilings.

WHERE TO DINE

Market Place Hotel Restaurant. Market Place. Wells, Somerset BA5 2RW. ☎ **01749/672616.** Lunch £6.50–£12 ($11.05–$20.40); main courses £9.50–£12.50 ($16.15–$21.25). AE, MC, V. Daily 12:30–2pm and 7–9:30pm. BRITISH.

This is one of the top places to dine in Wells. The menu is limited but usually well chosen. Starters might include Maryland crab cakes with leeks and sliced or home-cured salmon basted in a citrus dressing. Main courses run the gamut—everything from pan-fried fillet of sea bass with "crushed" potatoes to supreme of chicken with Parma ham and a tomato-herb sauce.

The hotel also rents 34 rooms, each furnished in a contemporary style, with private bath. Rates range from £79.50 to £95 ($135.15 to $161.50) for a double, including an English breakfast.

6 Glastonbury Abbey

136 miles SW of London; 26 miles S of Bristol; 6 miles SW of Wells

Glastonbury may be one of the oldest inhabited sites in Britain. Excavations have revealed Iron Age lakeside villages on its periphery (some of the discoveries that were dug up can be seen in a little museum on High Street). After the destruction of its once-great abbey, the town lost prestige; today it is just a market town with a rich history. The ancient gatehouse entry to the abbey is a museum, and its principal exhibit is a scale model of the abbey and its community buildings as they stood in 1539, at the time of the dissolution.

Where Arthurian myth once held sway, there's now a subculture of mystics, spiritualists, and hippies, all drawn to the kooky legends whirling around the town. Glastonbury is England's New Age center, where Christian spirituality blends with druidic beliefs. The average visitor arrives just to see the ruins and the monuments, but the streets are often filled with people trying to track down Jesus, if not Arthur and Lancelot.

ESSENTIALS

GETTING THERE Go to Taunton, which is on the London-Penzance line that leaves frequently from London's Paddington Station. For rail information, call ☎ **0345/484950.** From Taunton, you'll have to take a bus the rest of the way. Take the Southern National bus (no. 17) to Glastonbury, between Monday and Saturday. There are six departures per day, and the trip takes 1 hour. Call **Southern National** at ☎ **01823/272033** for details.

You could also leave London's Paddington Station for Bristol Temple Meads, and go the rest of the way by Badgerline bus no. 376. It runs from Bristol via Wells to Glastonbury every hour Monday through Saturday; on Sunday, the schedule is reduced to every 3 hours. The trip takes 2 hours. For information about Badgerline bus service, call ☎ **01179/553231.**

One **National Express** bus a day (no. 403) leaves London's Victoria Coach Station at 6:30pm and arrives in Glastonbury at 10pm. For more information and schedules, call ☎ **0990/808080.**

If you're driving, take M4 west from London, then cut south on A4 via Bath to Glastonbury.

VISITOR INFORMATION The **Tourist Information Centre** is at The Tribunal, 9 High St. (☎ **01458/832954**). It's open Easter through September, Sunday to Thursday from 10am to 4pm, Friday and Saturday from 10am to 4:30pm; off-season, Sunday to Thursday from 10am to 4pm, Friday and Saturday 10am to 4:30pm.

SEEING THE SIGHTS

✪ **Glastonbury Abbey.** ☎ **01458/832267** for information. www.glastonburyabbey.com. Admission £3 ($5.10) adults, £2.50 ($4.25) students and seniors, £1 ($1.70) children 5–16 years, £6.50 ($11.05) family ticket. Daily 10am–5pm.

Though it's no more than a ruined sanctuary today, Glastonbury Abbey was once one of the wealthiest and most prestigious monasteries in England. It provides Glastonbury's claim to historical greatness, an assertion augmented by legendary links to such figures as Joseph of Arimathea, King Arthur, Queen Guinevere, and St. Patrick.

It is said that Joseph of Arimathea journeyed to what was then the Isle of Avalon, with the Holy Grail in his possession. According to tradition, he buried the chalice at the foot of the conical Glastonbury Tor, and a stream of blood burst forth. You can scale this more than 500-foot-high hill today, on which rests a 15th-century tower.

Joseph, so it goes, erected a church of wattle in Glastonbury. (The town, in fact, may have had the oldest church in England, as excavations have shown.) And at one point, the saint is said to have leaned against his staff, which was immediately transformed into a fully blossoming tree; a cutting alleged to have survived from the Holy Thorn can be seen on the abbey grounds today—it blooms at Christmastime. Some historians have traced this particular story back to Tudor times.

Another famous chapter in the story, popularized by Tennyson in the Victorian era, holds that King Arthur and Queen Guinevere were buried on the abbey grounds. In 1191, the monks dug up the skeletons of two bodies on the south side of the Lady Chapel, said to be those of the king and queen. In 1278, in the presence of Edward I, the bodies were removed and transferred to a black marble tomb in the choir. Both the burial spot and the shrine are marked today.

A large Benedictine Abbey of St. Mary grew out of the early wattle church. St. Dunstan, who was born nearby, was the abbot in the 10th century and later became archbishop of Canterbury. Edmund, Edgar, and Edmund "Ironside," three early English kings, were buried at the abbey.

In 1184, a fire destroyed most of the abbey and its vast treasures. It was eventually rebuilt, after much difficulty, only to be dissolved by Henry VIII. Its last abbot, Richard Whiting, was hanged at Glastonbury Tor. Like the Roman forum, the abbey was used as a stone quarry for years.

Today, you can visit the ruins of the chapel, linked by an early English "Galilee" to the nave of the abbey. The best-preserved building on the grounds is a 14th-century octagonal Abbot's Kitchen, where oxen were once roasted whole to feed the wealthier pilgrims.

Somerset Rural Life Museum. On the Abbey Farm on Chilkwell St. ☎ **01458/831197.** Admission £2.50 ($4.25) adults; £2 ($3.40) students; £1 ($1.70) children and seniors; family ticket £6 ($10.20). Apr–Oct Tues–Fri 10am–5pm, Sat–Sun 2–6pm; Nov–Mar Tues–Sat 10am–3pm.

The history of the Somerset countryside since the early 19th century is chronicled here. Its centerpiece is the abbey barn, built around 1370. The magnificent timbered room, stone tiles, and sculptural details (including the head of Edward III) make it special. There is also a Victorian farmhouse comprising exhibits that illustrate farming in Somerset during the "horse age" as well as domestic and social life in Victorian times. In summer, there are demonstrations of butter making, weaving, basketwork, and many other traditional craft and farming activities, which are rapidly disappearing.

WHERE TO STAY

The George & Pilgrims. 1 High St., Glastonbury, Somerset BA6 9DP. ☎ **01458/831146.** Fax 01458/832252. 13 units. TV TEL. £60–£85 ($102–$144.50) double. Rates include English breakfast. AE, DC, MC, V.

One of the few pre-Reformation hostelries still left in England, this inn in the center of town once offered hospitality to Glastonbury pilgrims. Its facade looks like a medieval castle, with stone-mullioned windows with leaded glass. Some of the rooms were formerly monks' cells; others have four-poster beds, veritable carved monuments of oak. You may be given the Henry VIII Room, from which the king watched the burning of the abbey in 1539. Rooms come in a variety of shapes and sizes, as befits a hotel of this vintage. Some of the bedrooms have recently been refurbished; others are slated for some work. Nonetheless, all the present mattresses are most comfortable. Some of the rooms have just a shower, others a tub and shower combined.

The building's original kitchen now functions as a bar, where you can enjoy a pint beneath the span of old oak beams. Nearby is a brasserie, specializing in English and continental food (see "Where to Dine," below).

Number 3 Hotel. 3 Magdalene St., Glastonbury, Somerset BA6 9EW. ☎ **01458/832129.** Fax 01458/834227. 5 units (with tub or shower). TV TEL. £70–£80 ($119–$136) double. Rates include continental breakfast. AE, DC, MC, V. Closed Dec–Jan.

This small property, adjoining the Glastonbury ruins, has been recently refurbished. Housed in a Georgian structure, the double rooms are all tastefully and individually decorated and have beverage makers. The bathrooms are small, but well organized with a hair dryer and a set of fluffy towels.

WHERE TO DINE

The Brasserie. In the George & Pilgrims Hotel, 1 High St. ☎ **01458/831146.** Reservations recommended. Main courses £7–£9 ($11.90–$15.30). AE, DC, MC, V. Daily noon–2:30pm and 7–9:30pm. ENGLISH/CONTINENTAL.

This is a solid, reliable choice in a town not known for its dining. There's a reasonably priced à la carte menu with the chef's special of the day posted on blackboards. Dishes may include peppered soup, warm avocado and walnuts in a light Stilton sauce, and vegetarian choices such as broccoli-and-cream-cheese bake or vegetable Stroganoff with a timbale of saffron and wild rice.

7 Longleat House & Stourhead Gardens

If you're driving, you can visit both Longleat and Stourhead in one busy day. Follow the directions to Longleat given below, then drive 6 miles down B3092 to Stourton, a village just off the highway, 3 miles northwest of Mere (A303), to reach Stourhead.

✪ **Longleat House and Safari Park.** ☎ **01985/844400.** Admission to Longleat House £6 ($10.20) adults, £4 ($6.80) children. Safari Park £6 ($10.20) adults, £5 ($8.50) children. Special exhibitions and rides require separate admission tickets. Passport tickets for all of Longleat's attractions £13 ($22.10) adults, £11 ($18.70) children. House open Apr–Oct daily 10am–6pm, Nov–Easter daily 10am–4pm. Park open mid-Mar to Oct 31 daily 10am–6pm (last cars admitted at 5:30pm or sunset). From Bath or Salisbury, take the train or bus to Warminster; then take a taxi or Davron Coach no. 53, the local bus, to Longleat (about 10 min.). You'll have to walk the last 2 miles from the bus stop up the road to Longleat House. Driving from Bath, take A36 south to Warminster; then follow the signposts to Longleat House. From Salisbury, take A36 north to Warminster, following the signposts to Longleat House.

A magnificent Elizabethan house built in the early Renaissance style, Longleat House was owned by the seventh marquess of Bath. On first glimpse it's romantic enough, but once you've been inside, it's hard not to be dazzled by the lofty rooms and their exquisite paintings and furnishings.

From the Elizabethan Great Hall and the library to the State Rooms and the grand staircase, the house is filled with all manner of beautiful things. The walls of the State Dining Room are adorned with fine tapestries and paintings, whereas the room itself has displays of silver and plate. The library represents the finest private collection in the country. The Victorian kitchens are open, offering a glimpse of life "below the stairs" in a well-ordered country home. Various exhibitions are mounted in the stable yard.

Adjoining Longleat House is **Longleat Safari Park.** The park hosts several species of magnificent and endangered wild animals, including rhinoceros and elephants, which are free to roam these bucolic surroundings. Here you can walk among giraffes, zebras, camels, and llamas, and view lions and tigers, as well as England's only white tiger, from your car. You can also ride on a safari boat around the park's lake to see gorillas and to feed sea lions. You can see the park by train for a railway adventure, or visit the tropical butterfly garden.

The park provides plenty of theme–park-like thrills as well, including an Adventure Castle, Doctor Who exhibition, and the world's longest maze, **The Maze of Love.** Commissioned by the marquess of Bath and designed by Graham Burgess, the maze was inspired by the Garden of Love in Villandry, France, and Botticelli's painting *Primavera.* It lies between Longleat House and the Orangery, and at first appears to be a traditional parterre with gravel paths and small leafed box hedging; it's only on closer examination that its amorous shapes become apparent. The most obvious ones are the four giant hearts and a pair of women's lips, but there are many more. Love's symbolic flower, the rose, has been planted in the beds, and climbing roses trail over the heart-shaped arches. More than 1,300 rose bushes have been planted with names that enhance the symbolic story: First Kiss, Eve, Seduction, and more. The Maze of Love will not open to the public until Valentine's Day, 2000, but visitors can view it from either end in the meantime, enjoying the scent of its roses in summer.

While you're here take a ride in the **Airborne I,** a giant passenger balloon. This ride for visitors of all ages takes you up in a balloon gondola to a height of some 400 feet, from which you can enjoy panoramic views over Longleat House and its gardens, the Maze, and the Safari Park, as well as the wider Wiltshire and Somerset countryside. There are also facilities for access by travelers in wheelchairs.

✪ **Stourhead.** ☎ **01747/841152.** Mar–Oct, admission £4.60 ($7.80) adults, £2.60 ($4.40) children; off-season, £3.50 ($5.95) adults, £2.60 ($4.40) children. Daily 9am–7pm (or until dusk). Take the Gillingham-bound train from Bath. In Gillingham, switch to Southern National bus no. 58 or no. 58A, both of which go directly to Stourhead, about a 20-minute trip. There's a direct bus from Bath, but it only runs on the first Sat of each month. The return journey is via Frome. From Salisbury, bus service is very limited; however, you can take bus no. 26 to Hindon or Tewesbury, where you'll have to change buses to Stourton.

In a country of superlative gardens and gardeners, Stourhead is the most fabled of all. It's certainly the most celebrated example of 18th-century English landscape gardening. But more than that, it's a delightful place to wander—among its trees, flowers, and colorful shrubs, bridges, grottoes, and temples are tucked away, almost-hidden. Although Stourhead is a garden for all seasons, it is at its most idyllic in summer when the rhododendrons are in full bloom.

A Palladian house, Stourhead was built in the 18th century by the Hoare banking family, which created 100 acres of prime 18th-century landscaped gardens, complete with classical temples, lakes, and grottos. Henry Hoare II (1705–85), known as "Henry the Magnificent," contributed greatly to the development of the landscape of this magnificent estate.

The Temple of Flora was the first building in the garden, designed by the architect Henry Flitcroft in 1744. The wooden seats are copies of those placed near the altar where images of pagan gods were laid. Marble busts of Marcus Aurelius and Alexander the Great can be seen in the niches on the wall.

The Grotto, constructed in 1748, is lined with tufa, a water-worn limestone deposit. The springs of the Stour flow through the cold bath where a lead copy of the sleeping Ariadne lies. In a cave beyond her, the white lead statue of the River God is seen dispensing justice to the waves and to the nymphs who inhabit his stream.

The Pantheon was built in 1753 to house Rysbrack's statues of Hercules and Flora and other classical figures. The temple was originally heated through brass grilles. The nearby Iron Bridge replaced a wooden one in 1860.

In 1765, Flitcroft built the Temple of Apollo, the route to which takes the visitor over the public road via a rock-work bridge constructed in the 1760s. The Apollo Temple is copied from a round temple excavated at Baalbec: The statues that used to be in the niches are now on the roof of Stourhead House. The Turf Bridge was copied from Palladio's bridge in Vicenza.

The Bristol High Cross dates from the early 15th century and commemorates the monarchs who benefited the city of Bristol. It was removed from Bristol and set up by Henry Hoare at Stourhead in 1765.

The house at Stourhead, designed by Colen Campbell, a leader in the Palladian revival, was built for Henry Hoare I between 1721 and 1725. It closely resembles the villas Palladio built for wealthy Venetians. The magnificent interior hosts an outstanding library and picture gallery and a wealth of paintings, art treasures, and Chippendale furniture.

The three fine redbrick-walled terraces were built in the early-19th century to supply cut flowers, fresh fruit, salads, and vegetables to the mansion house. They were in use up to the deaths of Sir Henry and Lady Alda Hoare in 1947.

The lower combined a herbaceous garden with a peach and vine house. The pool was part of an irrigation system fed by rainwater from the greenhouses and stable yard.

Henry Hoare II's 18th-century redbrick folly, **Alfred's Tower,** is another feature at Stourhead. It sits 160 feet above the borders of Wiltshire, Somerset, and Dorset and has 221 steps. **The Obelisk** was built between 1839 and 1840 of Bath stone, and replaced the original of Chilmark stone constructed by William Privet for Henry Hoare in 1746.

The plant center is situated near the entrance to the main parking lot in part of the Old Glebe Farm—a small estate dairy farm. This was a working farm until the early 1970s. Now it's a place where visitors can buy plants they've just seen in the garden.

Lunches and suppers are served at the **Spread Eagle Inn,** near the entrance to the garden. Boxes are available to order for picnics in the grounds and garden. The Spread Eagle is noted for dinner in the evening, and for its Sunday lunches in the autumn, winter and spring. A self-service buffet is available in the Village Hall tearoom.

8 Dunster & Exmoor National Park

184 miles W of London; 3 miles SE of Minehead

The village of Dunster, in Somerset, lies near the eastern edge of Exmoor National Park. It grew up around the original Dunster Castle, constructed as a fortress for the de Mohun family, whose progenitor came to England with William the Conqueror. The village, about 4 miles from the Cistercian monastery at Cleeve, has an ancient priory church and dovecote, a 17th-century gabled yarn market, and little cobbled streets dotted with whitewashed cottages.

ESSENTIALS

GETTING THERE The best rail link is to travel to Minehead via Taunton, which is easily reached on the main London-Penzance line from Paddington Station in London. For rail information, call ☎ **0345/484950.** From Minehead, you have to take a taxi or bus to reach Dunster.

At Taunton, you can take one of the seven **Southern National** coaches (no. 28) (☎ **01823/272033**), leaving hourly Monday through Saturday; there is only one bus on Sunday. Trip time is 1 hour and 10 minutes. Buses (no. 38 or 39) from Minehead stop in Dunster Village at the rate of one per hour, but only from June to September. Off-season visitors must take a taxi.

If you're driving from London, head west along M4, cutting south at the junction with M5 until you reach the junction with A39, going west to Minehead. Before your final approach to Minehead, cut south to Dunster along A396.

VISITOR INFORMATION Dunster doesn't have an official tourist office, but **Exmoor National Park Visitor Centre** is found at Dunster Steep (☎ **01643/821835**), 2 miles east of Minehead. It's open Easter to October daily from 10am to 5pm, plus limited hours in winter.

EXPLORING THE AREA

✪ **Dunster Castle.** On A396 (just off A39). ☎ **01643/821314.** Admission to castle and grounds £5.40 ($9.20) adults, £2.80 ($4.75) children, family ticket £13.80 ($23.45); to grounds only £2.90 ($4.95) adults, £1.30 ($2.20) children, family ticket £6.90 ($11.75). Castle Apr–Sept Sat–Wed 11am–5pm, Oct Sat–Wed 11am–4pm. Grounds Jan–Mar and Oct–Dec daily 11am–4pm, Apr–Sept daily 10am–5pm. Take bus no. 38 or 39 from Minehead.

Dunster Castle is on a tor (high hill), from which you can see Bristol Channel. It stands on the site of a Norman castle granted to William de Mohun of Normandy by William the Conqueror shortly after the conquest of England. The 13th-century gateway, built by the de Mohuns, is all that remains of the original fortress. In 1376, the castle and its lands were bought by Lady Elizabeth Luttrell; her family owned it until it was given to the National Trust in 1976, together with 30 acres of surrounding parkland.

The first castle was largely demolished during the civil war. The present Dunster Castle is a Jacobean house constructed in the lower ward of the original fortifications in 1620, then rebuilt in 1870 to look like a castle. From the terraced walks and gardens, you'll have good views of Exmoor and the Quantock Hills.

Some of the outstanding artifacts within are the 17th-century panels of embossed painted and gilded leather depicting the story of Antony and Cleopatra, and a remarkable allegorical 16th-century portrait of Sir John Luttrell (shown wading naked through the sea with a female figure of peace and a wrecked ship in the background). The 17th-century plasterwork ceilings of the dining room and the finely carved staircase balustrade of cavorting huntsmen, hounds, and stags are also noteworthy.

EXMOOR NATIONAL PARK

Between Somerset and Devon, along the northern coast of England's southwest peninsula, is Exmoor National Park, an unspoiled plateau of lonely moors. One of the most cherished national parks in Britain, it includes the wooded valleys of the rivers Exe and Barle, the Brendon Hills, a sweeping stretch of rocky coastline, and such sleepy but charming villages as **Culbone, Selworthy, Parracombe,** and **Allerford.** Bisected by a network of heavily eroded channels for brooks and streams, the park is distinctive for its lichen-covered trees, gray-green grasses, gorse, and heather. The moors reach their highest point at Dunkery Beacon, 1,707 feet above sea level.

Exmoor National Park is one of the smallest in Britain, yet it contains one of the most beautiful coastlines in England. Softly contoured, without the dramatic peaks and valleys of other national parks, the terrain is composed mostly of primeval layering of sandstone slate. Although noteworthy for its scarcity of trees, the terrain encompasses a limited handful of very old oak groves, which are studied by forestry experts for their growth patterns.

On clear days, the coast of South Wales, 20 miles away, can be spotted across the estuary of the Bristol Channel. The wildlife that thrives on the park's rain-soaked terrain includes a breed of wild pony (the Exmoor pony), whose bloodlines can be traced from ancient species.

Although there are more than 700 miles of walking paths in the park, most visitors stay on the **coastal trail** that winds around the bays and inlets of England's southwestern peninsula or along some of the shorter **riverside trails.**

The park's administrative headquarters is located within a 19th-century workhouse in the village of Dulverton, in Somerset, near the park's southern edge. A program of walking tours is offered at least five times a week, to anyone who's interested. Themes include Woodland Walks, Moorland Walks, Bird Watching Excursions, and Deer Spottings. Most of the tours last from 4 to 6 hours, and all are free, with an invitation to donate. Wear sturdy shoes and rain gear.

For the *Exmoor Visitor* brochure, which lists events, guided walks, and visitor information, contact the **Exmoor National Park Visitor Centre,** Dulverton, Somerset TA22 9EX (☎ **01398/323841**). It's open daily between Easter and the end of October from 10am to 5pm, and 10:30am to 2:30pm through the winter.

NEARBY SIGHTS

Combe Sydenham Hall. Monksilver. ☎ **01984/656284.** Admission £5 ($8.50) adults, £2 ($3.40) children. Country Park, Easter–Sept Sun–Fri 9am–4:30pm; courtroom and gardens, May–Sept at 2pm for guided tours only, Mon and Thurs–Fri. From Dunster, drive on A39, following signs pointing to Watchet and/or Bridgwater. On the right, you'll see a minor zoo, Tropiquaria, at which you turn right and follow the signs pointing to Combe Sydenham.

This hall was the home of Elizabeth Sydenham, wife of Sir Francis Drake, and it stands on the ruins of monastic buildings that were associated with nearby Cleeve Abbey. Here you can see a cannonball that legend says halted the wedding of Lady Elizabeth to a rival suitor in 1585. The gardens include Lady Elizabeth's Walk, which circles ponds originally laid out when the knight was courting his bride-to-be. The valley ponds fed by springwater are full of rainbow trout (ask about getting fly-fishing lessons). You can also take a woodland walk to Long Meadow, with its host of wildflowers. Also to be seen are a deserted hamlet, whose population reputedly was wiped out by the black death, and a historic corn mill. In the hall's tearoom, smoked trout and pâté are produced on oak chips, as in days of yore, and there is a shop, working bakery, and car park.

Coleridge Cottage. 35 Lime St., Nether Stowey, near Bridgwater. ☎ **01278/732662.** Admission £2.60 ($4.40) adults, £1 ($1.70) children. Apr 1–Oct 1 Tues–Thurs and Sun 2–5pm. From Minehead, follow A39 east about 30 miles, following the signs to Bridgwater. About 8 miles from Bridgwater, turn right, following signs to Nether Stowey.

The hamlet of Nether Stowey is on A39, north of Taunton, across the Quantock Hills to the east of Exmoor. The cottage is at the west end of Nether Stowey on the south side of A39.

Here you can visit the home of Samuel Taylor Coleridge, where he penned "The Rime of the Ancient Mariner." During his 1797 to 1800 sojourn here, he and his friends, William Wordsworth and sister Dorothy, enjoyed exploring the Quantock woods. The parlor and reading room of his National Trust property are open to visitors.

WHERE TO STAY & DINE IN THE AREA

Curdon Mill. Vellow, Williton, Somerset, TA4 4LS. ☎ **01984/656522.** Fax 01984/656197. 8 units (with tub or shower). TV. £60–£80 ($102–$136) double. Rates include English breakfast. AE, MC, V.

Situated on a 200-acre farm 5 miles northeast of Dunster, this guest house, a former mill, sports a 100-year-old water wheel made by the local ironworks. Daphne and Richard Criddle own this place, offering home-style food and accommodations. The individually decorated rooms are small to mid-sized and include tea- and coffeemakers. The small bathrooms are equipped with a hair dryer. Mrs. Criddle serves English fare, including venison, roast lamb, and pheasant. All the food is homemade and may include a few French-style dishes "when the inspiration strikes."

Luttrell Arms. 32–36 High St., Dunster, Somerset TA24 6SG. ☎ **01643/821555.** Fax 01643/821567. 27 units. TV TEL. £90–£140 ($153–$238) double. Dinner, bed-and-breakfast rates, Mar–June and Sept–Oct £45 ($76.50) per person per night; July–Sept £70 ($119) per person per night; Nov–Feb £50 ($85) per person per night. 2-night minimum stay required for the Nov–Feb rate. AE, DC, MC, V.

This is simply the best choice around. There has been a hostelry for weary travelers on this site for more than 600 years. This hotel is the outgrowth of a guest house the Cistercian abbots at Cleeve had built in the village of Dunster. It was named for the Luttrell lords of the manor, who bought Dunster Castle and the property attached to it in the 14th century. It has, of course, been updated with modern amenities, but from its stone porch to the 15th-century Gothic hall with hammer-beam roof, it still retains a feeling of antiquity. Bedrooms range in size and are attractively decorated in keeping with the hotel's long history; four of them have four-poster beds. Rooms in a section called the "Latches" are cottagelike in style, with tight stairways and narrow corridors. One room is big enough for use by a family, and in nine of the bedrooms there is a no-smoking policy. Baths are small, but have a shower and tub combination.

Dining/Diversions: A lounge is upstairs, whereas downstairs you can enjoy a drink in the timbered Tudor bar, with its large inglenook fireplace (this was once the kitchen). The dining room offers a varied menu; depending on the season, you might choose guinea fowl or baked sugared ham with Somerset cider sauce. Bar food is also offered.

9 Devon

The great patchwork-quilt area of southwest England, part of the "West Countree," abounds in cliff-side farms, rolling hills, foreboding moors, semitropical plants, and fishing villages that provide some of the finest scenery in England. You can pony trek across moor and woodland, past streams and sheep-dotted fields, or relax at a local pub to soak up atmosphere and ale.

The British approach sunny Devon with the same kind of excitement normally reserved for hopping over to the Continent. Especially along the coastline—the English Riviera—the names of the seaports, villages, and resorts are synonymous with holidays in the sun: Torquay, Clovelly, Lynton-Lynmouth. Devon is a land of jagged coasts—the red cliffs in the south face the English Channel. In South Devon, the coast from which Drake and Raleigh set sail, tranquility prevails, and on the bay-studded coastline of North Devon, pirates and smugglers found haven.

Almost every village is geared to accommodate visitors. But many small towns and fishing villages don't allow cars to enter; these towns have parking areas on the outskirts, and then it's a long walk to reach the center of the harbor area. From mid-July to mid-September the most popular villages are quite crowded, so make reservations for a place to stay well in advance.

Along the south coast, the best bases from which you can explore the region are Exeter, Plymouth, and Torquay. Along the north coast, we suggest Lynton-Lynmouth. The area's most charming village (with very limited accommodations) is Clovelly. The greatest natural spectacle is the Dartmoor National Park, northeast of Plymouth, a landscape of gorges and moors filled with gorse and purple heather—home of the Dartmoor pony.

If you're taking the bus around Devon, Stagecoach Devon and Western National bus lines combine to offer a discounted **"Key West Ticket."** Adults can enjoy unlimited use of the lines at these rates: £15 ($25.50) for 3 days or, £27 ($45.90) for 7 days. For families (two adults and two children 5 to 15 years old), a 3-day ticket at £30 ($51) and a 7-day ticket costs £49 ($83.30). You can plan your journeys from the maps and timetables available at any **Western National/Devon General** office when you purchase your ticket (☎ **01752/222666**). For further information, contact **Stagecoach Devon Ltd.**, Paris Street, Exeter Devon FX1 2JP (☎ **01392/427711**).

1 Exeter

201 miles SW of London; 46 miles NE of Plymouth

Exeter was a Roman city founded in the 1st century A.D. on the banks of the River Exe. Two centuries later it was encircled by a mighty stone wall, traces of which remain today. Conquerors and would-be conquerors, especially Vikings, stormed the fortress in later centuries; none was more notable than William the Conqueror, who brought Exeter to its knees on short notice.

Under the Tudors, the city grew and prospered. Sir Walter Raleigh and Sir Francis Drake were two of the striking figures who strolled through Exeter's streets. In May 1942, the Germans bombed Exeter, destroying many of its architectural treasures. The town was rebuilt, but the new, impersonal-looking shops and offices can't replace the Georgian crescents and the black-and-white-timbered buildings with their plastered walls. Fortunately, much was spared, and Exeter still has its Gothic cathedral, a renowned university, some museums, and several historic houses.

Exeter is a good base for exploring both Dartmoor and Exmoor national parks, two of the finest England has to offer. It's also a good place to spend a day—there's a lot to do in what's left of the city's old core.

ESSENTIALS

GETTING THERE **Exeter Airport** (☎ **01392/367433**) serves the southwest, offering both charter and scheduled flights. Lying 5 miles east of the historic center of Exeter, it has scheduled flights to and from Belfast, Jersey, Dublin, and the Isles of Scilly, but no direct flights from London.

Trains from London's Paddington Station depart every hour during the day. The trip takes 2½ hours. For rail information, call ☎ **0345/484950** in the United Kingdom. Trains also run once an hour during the day between Exeter and Plymouth; the trip takes 1¼ hours. Trains often arrive at Exeter Central Station on Queen Street, next to Northernhay Gardens, or else at Exeter St. David's Station at St. David's Hill.

A **National Express** coach departs from London's Victoria Coach Station every 2 hours during the day; the trip takes 4 hours. You can also take bus no. 38 or 39 between Plymouth and Exeter. During the day two coaches depart per hour for the 1-hour trip. For information and schedules call ☎ **0990/808080**.

If you're driving from London, take M4 west, cutting south to Exeter on M5 (junction near Bristol).

VISITOR INFORMATION The **Tourist Information Centre** is at the Civic Centre, Paris Street (☎ **01392/265700;** fax 01392/265260). It's open Monday through Saturday from 9am to 5pm, and from June to October, on Sunday from 10am to 4pm.

SPECIAL EVENTS A classical music lover's dream, the **Exeter Festival,** held for 3 weeks in July, includes more than 150 events, ranging from concerts and opera to lectures. Festival dates and offerings vary from year to year, and more information is available by contacting the **Exeter Festival Office,** Civic Center (☎ **01392/265200;** www.exeter.gov.uk).

EXPLORING EXETER

Just off "The High," at the top of Castle Street, stands an impressive **Norman Gatehouse** from William the Conqueror's castle. Although only the house and walls survive, the view from here and the surrounding gardens is panoramic.

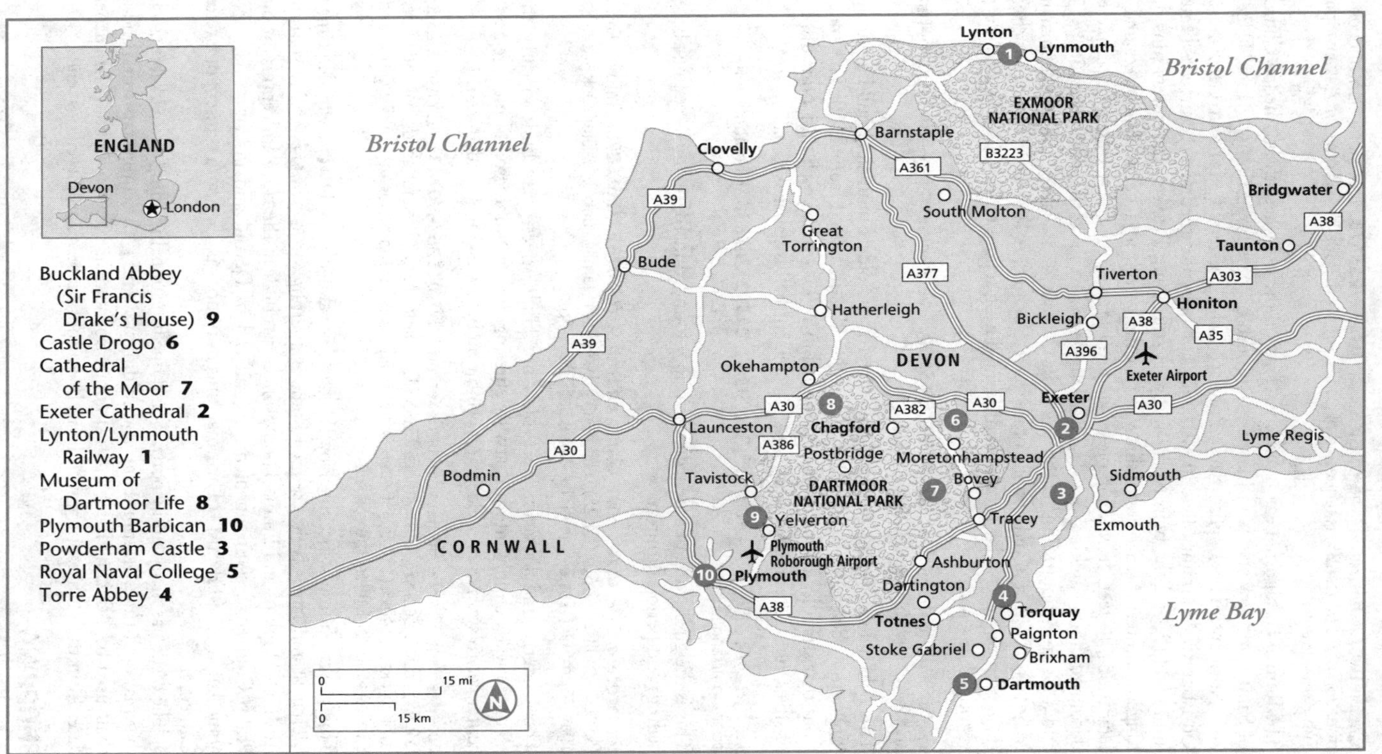
ENGLAND
Devon
London
Buckland Abbey
(Sir Francis
Drake's House) 9
Castle Drogo 6
Cathedral
of the Moor 7
Exeter Cathedral 2
Lynton/Lynmouth
Railway 1
Museum of
Dartmoor Life 8
Plymouth Barbican 10
Powderham Castle 3
Royal Naval College 5
Torre Abbey 4
Bristol Channel
Bristol Channel
Lyme Bay
EXMOOR
NATIONAL PARK
DARTMOOR
NATIONAL PARK
DEVON
CORNWALL
Lynton
Lynmouth
Barnstaple
Clovelly
South Molton
Bridgwater
Taunton
Great
Torrington
Bude
Tiverton
Honiton
Hatherleigh
Bickleigh
Exeter Airport
Okehampton
Exeter
Launceston
Chagford
Postbridge
Moretonhampstead
Lyme Regis
Bodmin
Tavistock
Bovey
Tracey
Sidmouth
Exmouth
Yelverton
Plymouth
Roborough Airport
Plymouth
Ashburton
Dartington
Totnes
Torquay
Paignton
Stoke Gabriel
Brixham
Dartmouth
A39
A39
A361
B3223
A38
A303
A377
A38
A35
A396
A30
A30
A382
A30
A30
A386
A38
0
15 mi
0
15 km
N

✪ **Exeter Cathedral.** 1 The Cloisters. ☎ **01392/255573.** Free admission, though a donation of £2.50 ($4.25) is requested of adults. Mon–Fri 7:30am–6:15pm, Sat 7:30am–5pm, Sun 8am–7:30pm.

The Roman II Augusta Legion made its camp on the site where the Cathedral Church of Saint Peter now stands in Exeter. It has been occupied by Britons, Saxons, Danes, and Normans. The English Saint Boniface, who converted northern Germany to Christianity, was trained here in A.D. 690. The present cathedral structure was begun around 1112, and the twin Norman towers still stand. Between the towers runs the longest uninterrupted true Gothic vault in the world, at a height of 66 feet and a length of 300 feet. It was completed in 1369, and is the finest existing example of decorated Gothic architecture. The Puritans destroyed the cathedral cloisters in 1655, and a German bomb finished off the twin Chapels of St. James and St. Thomas in May 1942. Now restored, it's one of the prettiest churches anywhere. Its famous choir sings evensong every day except Wednesday during school term. On school holidays, visiting choirs perform.

Exeter Guildhall. High St. ☎ **01392/265500.** Free admission. Mon–Fri 10:30am–1pm and 2–4pm. It's best to call before visiting.

This colonnaded building on the main street is the oldest municipal building in the kingdom—the earliest reference to the guildhall is in a deed from 1160. The Tudor front that straddles the pavement was added in 1593. Inside you'll find a fine display of silver, plus a number of paintings. The ancient hall is paneled in oak.

St. Nicholas Priory. The Mint, off Fore St. ☎ **01392/265858.** Free admission. Call for opening arrangements.

This is the guest wing of a Benedictine priory founded in 1070. You'll see fine plaster ceilings and period furniture.

Underground Passages. Boots Corner, off High St. ☎ **01392/265887.** Admission £3.50 ($5.95) adults, £2.50 ($4.25) children, £10 ($17) family ticket. Easter–Oct Mon–Sat 10am–5pm; Oct–Easter Tues–Fri 2–5pm, Sat 10am–5pm.

The Underground Passages, accessible from High Street, were built to carry the medieval water supply into the city. By entering the new underground interpretation center, visitors can view a video and exhibition before taking a guided tour.

Powderham Castle. In Powderham, Kenton. ☎ **01626/890243.** Admission £5.85 ($9.95) adults, £4.35 ($7.40) seniors, £2.95 ($5) children 5–17; free for children 4 and under, family ticket £14.65 ($24.90). Easter–Oct Sun–Fri 10am–5:30pm. Take the A379 Dawlish rd. 8 miles south of Exeter; the castle is signposted.

This private house is occupied by the countess and earl of Devon, who let Ismail Merchant and James Ivory use their home as a setting for *Remains of the Day,* starring Anthony Hopkins and Emma Thompson. It was built in the late 14th century by Sir Philip Courtenay, sixth son of the second earl of Devon, and his wife, Margaret, granddaughter of Edward I. Their magnificent tomb is in the south transept of Exeter Cathedral.

The castle has many family portraits and fine furniture, including a remarkable clock that plays full tunes at 4pm, 8pm, and midnight, some 17th-century tapestries, and a chair used by William III for his first council of state at Newton Abbot. The chapel dates from the 15th century, with hand-hewn roof timbers and carved pew ends.

SHOPPING

Exeter has long been famous for its silver. If you seek, ye shall find old Exeter silver, especially spoons, still sold in local stores. The best merchant for this is **William Burford,** 1 Bedford St. (☎ **01392/254901**). You can find spoons dating from before

In Search of the Traditional Devonshire Cream Tea

Cream teas will always be associated with Devon. How did they come about? Think back to the traditional Devonshire farmer's wife laboring away on a faraway grange. These matriarchs perfected the medieval process of simmering at very low temperatures a batch of whole cow's milk, sometimes for a day or two, to create the region's famous Devonshire clotted cream. Silken-textured and rich, with just enough acidity to perk up the taste buds, it isn't clotted at all. It's a very English, very urbane, and very perishable version of what the French call crème fraîche.

What should accompany your clots of cream? A scone, preferably one that's just come out of the oven and, it is hoped, one made without baking soda. The resulting, slightly bitter, slightly sour taste seems to go better with the tangy cream. Preserves? Don't even think of asking for anything except strawberry preserves.

The tea itself seems to be less crucial than the above-mentioned items that accompany it. Most Devonites opt for strong, simple Indian tea, eschewing the more delicate Chinese blends as something too fancy to muck about with.

Here are our favorite spots to pause and take your afternoon tea with clotted cream while you're exploring the byways and primrose paths of Devon.

While visiting the coastal towns of Devon, dart inland to **Honeybees,** High Street (☎ **01404/43392**), in the town of Honiton, long famous for its lace made a century ago. The brick-fronted tearoom with a large bay window is known for its cream teas and "squidgy cakes." From Exeter, take A30 straight into Honiton.

Southeast of Exeter, follow the A376 through Exmouth to **The Cozy Teapot,** Fore Street (☎ **01395/444016**), in Budleigh Salterton. A cozy brick building, this tearoom is tucked away just past a small bridge with running water. It serves the best Devon cream tea in the area. You get bone china, lace cloths on the tables, and homemade cakes, too.

Our favorite name for a tearoom is **Four and Twenty Blackbirds,** 43 Gold St., Tiverton (☎ **01884/257055**), reached by following the Old Road (now called A396) from Exeter straight into Tiverton to the north. The black-and-white-timbered tearoom stands in a sunken square. An assortment of set teas and tea breads and homemade cakes await you.

the 19th century; look for the three-castle mark of Exeter to be sure you're getting the real thing.

David Trivett Jewelry, 13A Guildhall Precinct (☎ **01392/276224**), carries antique jewelry as well as secondhand designer jewelry. They also carry original designs by artisans who work in the store, or can create a piece that you have designed.

There are a number of antique dealers in Exeter. At least six are on the Quay off Western Way. **The Quay Gallery Antiques Emporium** (☎ **01392/213283**) houses 10 dealers who sell furniture, porcelain, metalware, and other collectibles. **The Antique Centre** on the Quay (☎ **01392/493501**) has 20 dealers.

The Edinburgh Woolen Mill, 23 Cathedral Yard (☎ **01392/412318**), carries a large selection of woolen goods, including kilts, Aran jumpers, tartan travel rugs, and quality wool suits for women.

There is also a daily market on Sidwell Street, Exeter's version of an American flea market.

WHERE TO STAY

EXPENSIVE

Rougemont Thistle. Queen St. (opposite the central train station), Exeter, Devon EX4 3SP. ☎ **01392/254982.** Fax 01392/420928. 90 units. TV TEL. £113 ($192.10) double; £160–£180 ($272–$306) suite. AE, DC, MC, V.

Although its history is far less impressive than that of the Royal Clarence Hotel (see below), this great, old-fashioned, rambling Victorian hotel (which was renovated fairly recently) is also a traditional choice for those who want to stay in the center of town. Its small to medium bedrooms are comfortably furnished in a modern style. Thirteen accommodations are reserved for nonsmokers.

Dining/Diversions: Guests gather in the Adam-style Drake's Bar for drinks. A good stock of wine comes from the cellar, which, incidentally, was once a debtors' prison.

Royal Clarence Hotel. Cathedral Yard, Exeter, Devon EX1 1HD. ☎ **01392/319955.** Fax 01392/439423. 57 units. TV TEL. £100–£155 ($170–$263.50) double; from £145 ($246.50) suite. Rates include English breakfast if stay is longer than 1 night. AE, DC, MC, V.

We think the Royal Clarence has far more tradition and style than the sometimes better rated and more recently built Forte Crest at Southernhay East, or the Rougemont Thistle on Queen Street. It dates from 1769 and escaped the Nazi blitz. Just a step away from the cathedral, it offers individually furnished rooms in Tudor, Georgian, or Victorian styling. Each has such amenities as movies, trouser press, hair dryer, and tea- or coffeemaker. Six rooms are large enough for families, and 16 units are set aside for nonsmokers.

Dining: The Raleigh Restaurant serves excellent West Country fare such as sautéed breast of pheasant or the chef's nightly roast.

Amenities: 24-hour room service.

MODERATE

Buckerell Lodge Hotel. Topsham Rd., Exeter, Devon EX2 4SQ. ☎ **800/528-1234** in the U.S. and Canada, or 01392/221111. Fax 01392/491111. 53 units. TV TEL. £69–£75 ($117.30–$127.50) double. AE, DC, MC, V. Bus: K, T, or R. Take B3182 1 mile southeast, off Junction 30 of M5.

The house originated in the 12th century, but it has been altered and changed beyond recognition over the years. The exterior is a symmetrical and severely dignified building with a Regency feel. Often hosting business travelers, it's also a tourist favorite, especially in summer. The bedrooms, in a range of styles and sizes, are well decorated and nicely equipped. The best rooms are the executive accommodations in the main house, although most bedrooms are in a more sterile modern addition. Fifteen rooms are reserved for nonsmokers, and two are large enough to accommodate families.

Raffles Restaurant is one of the area's finer dining choices. The specialities are fresh fish, game, steaks, and poultry, but the menu always includes something for the vegetarian.

Gipsy Hill. Gipsy Hill Lane, via Pinn Lane, Monkerton, Exeter, Devon EX1 3RN. ☎ **01392/465252.** Fax 01392/464302. E-mail: gipsyhill@eclipse.co.uk. 37 units. TV TEL. £75–£95 ($127.50–$161.50) double. Rates include English breakfast. AE, MC, V. Bus: T.

This late Victorian country house stands on the eastern edge of the city and is close to the airport. (It's especially convenient if you're driving, as it's within easy reach of M5 Junction 30.) Bedrooms, ranging from small to medium, are comfortably appointed; some have four-poster beds. Six bedrooms are set aside for nonsmokers, and five accommodations are large enough for families. Bedrooms have more tradition and

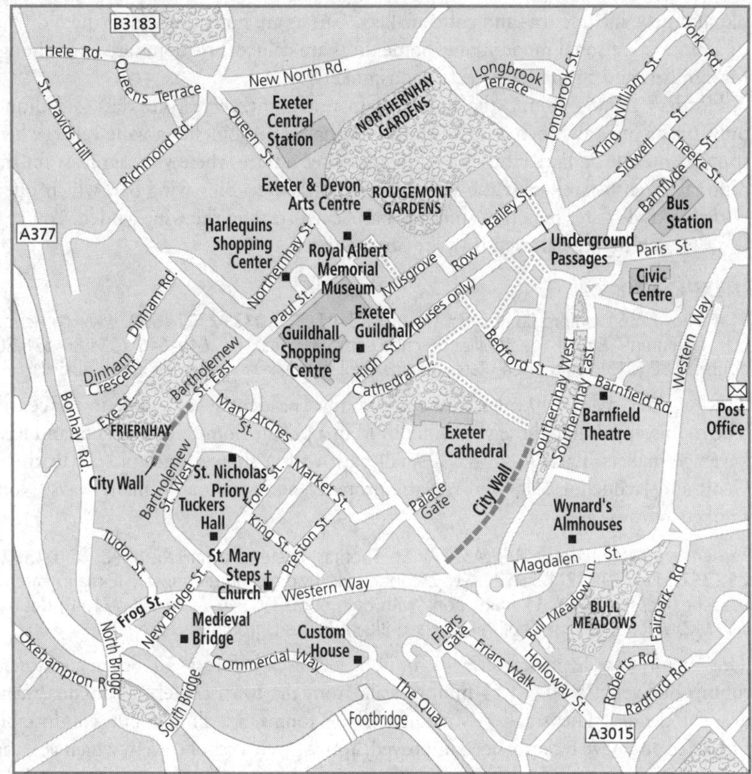

ambience in the main house, and the other 17 rooms are located in an annex. A restaurant on the premises serves both British and continental dishes, with meals beginning at £16.50 ($28.05).

✪ **St. Olaves Court Hotel.** Mary Arches St. (off High St.), Exeter, Devon EX4 3AZ. ☎ **800/ 544-9993** in the U.S. or 01392/217736. Fax 01392/413054. www.olaves.co.uk. E-Mail: info@olaves.co.uk. 15 units. TV TEL. Mon–Thurs £90–£100 ($153–$170) double; Fri–Sun £70–£80 ($119–$136) double. Rates include continental breakfast. AE, DC, MC, V.

This is our favorite. The location is ideal, within a short walk of the cathedral—you can hear the church bells. A Georgian mansion, it was constructed in 1827 by a rich merchant as a home. The house has been discreetly furnished, in part with antiques. Each of the bedrooms has a beverage maker, trouser press, hair dryer, and what the English call a "hospitality tray." Some units have Jacuzzis. The hotel features excellent English cuisine in its Golsworthy Restaurant (see "Where to Dine," below for a full review).

White Hart Hotel. 65–66 South St., Exeter, Devon EX1 1EE. ☎ **01392/279897.** Fax 01392/250159. 50 units. TV TEL. Mon–Thurs £94 ($159.80) double. Fri–Sun £60–£64 ($102–$108.80) double. Rates include English breakfast. AE, DC, MC, V.

The White Hart Hotel, in the center of town, was a coaching inn in the 17th and 18th centuries and is one of the oldest inns in the city. The hotel is a mass of polished wood, slate floors, oak beams, and gleaming brass and copper. The rooms, which combine old and new, include tea- and coffeemakers. Guests are housed in either the old wing or a more impersonal modern one. Some units are deluxe. Six rooms are large enough for families, and 11 are reserved for nonsmokers.

Hostler's Dining Room, the hotel's main restaurant, serves breakfast and dinner only, plus a Sunday lunch with all the trimmings. The hotel has a wine cellar, which supplies the Ale & Port House (a bar with waiter service where you can feast on traditional English fare), plus the well-known Bottlescreu Bills wine bar, which offers beefsteak-and-oyster pie or, in summer, barbecued steak in the wine garden. You may want to stop by the bar even if you're not a guest.

INEXPENSIVE

Claremont. 36 Wonford Rd., Exeter, Devon EX2 4LD. ☎ **01392/274699.** www.conscribe.com/claremont. E-mail: geoffself@conscribe.com. 3 units. TV. £44–£46 ($74.80–$78.20) double; £80 ($136) suite for 4. Rates include English breakfast. No credit cards. Bus: H.

This Regency-style 1840 town house is in a quiet residential area, close to the center. The rooms, much like those you would find in a private home, are well kept and have beverage makers. Each room has a small bath with a shower unit and a hair dryer. Geoff and Jacqueline Self, who run the property, assist visitors in many ways. Nonsmokers only, please.

Lea-Dene. 34 Alphington Rd. (A3777), St. Thomas, Exeter, Devon EX2 8HN. ☎ **01392/257257.** Fax 01392/427952. www.scoot.co.uk./leadene_guest_house/. E-mail: karen@Leadene.freeserve.co.uk. 11 units, none with bathroom. TV. £40–£42 ($68–$71.40) double. DC, MC, V. Rates include English breakfast. Blue minibus D from the center.

This Victorian-style guest house was built of red brick before 1930. Set in a southern suburb of Exeter, a 10- to 15-minute walk from the town center, it contains many original details. The small- to medium-sized rooms are simply but comfortably furnished and have recently been improved. You're given a set of towels, which you can use in one of the corridor baths with other guests. Maintenance is good here, and the price for Exeter represents good value. Owners Karen and Chris Rogers offer a hearty breakfast.

Park View Hotel. 8 Howell Rd., Exeter, Devon EX4 4LG. ☎ **01392/271772.** Fax 01392/253047. www.parkviewhotel.freeserve.co.uk. E-mail: philbatho@parkviewhotel.freeserve.co.uk. 15 units, 10 with bathroom. TV TEL. £38 ($64.60) double without bathroom, £47 ($79.90) double with bathroom. Rates include English breakfast. AE, MC, V.

This hotel lies near the heart of town and the train station. A landmark Georgian house, it offers comfortably but plainly furnished rooms, ranging in size from small to medium. There is regular upgrading of the decor here to keep the standards high. Rooms with private bath usually have a shower (only one has a tub and shower combination). Occupants of bathless rooms will find the public baths convenient and well maintained. Guests take their breakfast in a cozy room opening onto the hotel's garden. Breakfast is the only meal served, but the staff will prepare a packed lunch for touring.

IN NEARBY BICKLEIGH

Perhaps the finest way to enjoy the cathedral city of Exeter, especially if you have a car, is to stay on the outskirts, 10 to 19 miles from the heart of the city. In the Exe Valley, 4 miles south of Tiverton and 10 miles north of Exeter, lies Bickleigh, a hamlet with a river, an arched stone bridge, a millpond, and thatch-roofed cottages—the epitome of English charm and one of the finest spots in all of Devon.

✪ **Bickleigh Cottage Country Hotel.** Bickleigh Bridge, Bickleigh, Devon EX16 8RJ. ☎ **01884/855230.** 9 units. £45 ($76.50) double. Rates include English breakfast. MC, V. Closed Nov–Mar. Bus no. 55 from Exeter.

This thatched, 17th-century hotel has a riverside garden that leads down to the lovely Bickleigh Bridge, where swans and ducks glide by. Inside, the rooms are small, possessing oak beams and old fireplaces. Everything is comfortably cozy—like visiting your great-aunt. This is especially true when you snuggle into your comfortable bed for the evening. Each unit comes with a small private bath; half have a tub and shower, and half have a shower only. Mr. and Mrs. Stuart Cochrane, the owners, provide good and nourishing meals. The raspberries and gooseberries come fresh from the garden and are topped with generous portions of Devonshire cream.

WHERE TO DINE

Golsworthy Restaurant. In the St. Olaves Court Hotel, Mary Arches St. ☎ **01392/217736.** Reservations recommended. Main courses £14.50–£19.50 ($24.65–$33.15); fixed-price "light lunch" £12.50 ($21.25); fixed-price lunch or dinner £15.50 ($26.35). AE, DC, MC, V. Mon–Fri noon–2pm; daily 6:30–9:30pm. CONTINENTAL.

This is Exeter's finest restaurant. Guests enjoy a before-dinner drink in a paneled bar that overlooks a verdant garden. The cuisine reflects the sophisticated palate of the congenial owners and includes grilled fillet of beef and veal with vegetables and baby onions, baked scallop of salmon with langoustine mousse wrapped in filo pastry with saffron butter sauce, or a variety of vegetarian dishes.

Lamb's. 15 Lower North St. ☎ **01392/254269.** Reservations recommended. Main courses £11–£16.80 ($18.70–$28.55); fixed-price 2-course lunch £15 ($25.50); fixed-price 2-course dinner (Tues–Thurs only) £15 ($25.50); fixed-price 3-course dinner (Fri–Sat) £23 ($39.10). AE, MC, V. Tues–Fri noon–2pm; Tues–Sat 7–10pm. BRITISH.

The only serious challenger to Golsworthy in recent years is this winning candidate, run by a creative chef named Carolyn Seath. Housed on two floors of a town house from the 1700s, the restaurant exudes a warm, friendly welcome. The cookery is innovative but not flashy. Only quality ingredients go into the dishes, which include lobster and monkfish tart with hollandaise sauce. The desserts are sometimes memorable. The wine list is reasonably balanced, and not at all overpriced.

✪ **The Ship Inn.** St. Martin's Lane. ☎ **01392/272040.** Reservations recommended. Restaurant main courses £6–£12 ($10.20–$20.40). Pub platters £2–£4.50 ($3.40–$7.65). MC, V. Restaurant Mon–Fri noon–3pm and 6–9:30pm. Sat 11am–11pm. Pub Mon–Sat 11am–11pm, Sun noon–10:30pm. ENGLISH.

The Ship Inn was often visited by Sir Francis Drake, Sir Walter Raleigh, and Sir John Hawkins, and even today, it still provides tankards of real ale, lager, and stout. A large selection of snacks is offered in the bar every day, whereas the restaurant upstairs provides more substantial English fare. At either lunch or dinner, you can order French onion soup, whole grilled lemon sole, five different steaks, and more. Portions are large, as in Elizabethan times.

EXETER AFTER DARK

Exeter is a lively university town offering an abundance of classical concerts and theater productions, as well as clubs and pubs. For information concerning cultural events and theaters, the **Exeter Arts Booking and Information Centre,** Princesshay (☎ **01392/211080**), open daily from 9:30am to 5pm, provides a monthly brochure of upcoming events and sells tickets.

An abundance of concerts, opera, dance, and film can be found year-round at the **Exeter & Devon Arts Centre,** Bradninch Place, Gandy St. (☎ **01392/667080**), and Exeter University's **Northcott Theatre,** Stocker Road (☎ **01392/256182**), which is also home to a professional theater company.

On the club scene, head to **Volts,** The Quay (☎ **01392/211347;** info line 01392/435820), a two-story club featuring funk, soul, dance, and alternative tunes on the first floor, and The Hot House, playing classic pop music on the second floor. The crowd here is young, and there's a full bar and fast food available. The cover charge varies from free to £5 ($8.50).

Attracting a more diverse crowd, **The Warehouse/Boxes Disco,** Commercial Road (☎ **01392/259292**), is another split club, with different musical styles featured throughout the week. The cover charge varies from free to £4 ($6.80) before 11pm, and £6 ($10.20) afterward which gets you into both clubs.

Catering to Exeter's gay scene, **Liberty's,** Bartholomew Street (☎ **01392/275623**), hosts a Women's Social Group (no men allowed) on the first and third Wednesday of each month, a mixed gay and straight crowd for '70s and '80s dance music on Fridays, and a largely gay crowd for dancing on Saturdays. Cover is £3 ($5.10).

Pubs vary from the ancient and haunted to haunts of folk-music fans, with the Turks Head, High Street (☎ **01392/256680**), offering a bit of local color, since it's housed in a 600-year-old dungeon allegedly haunted by the Turks who were tortured and killed here. The first two floors are unchanged from that bygone era, but the top three floors were turned into the existing pub more than 450 years ago. It was a favorite hangout and scribbling spot of Charles Dickens, whose favorite chair is still on display. Today, it's a lively pub with a computerized juke box and a fast-food menu.

Well House Tavern, Cathedral Close (☎ **01392/319953**), is part of the Royal Clarence Hotel. It's housed in a building believed to have been constructed in the 14th century, although the Roman well in the basement predates that estimate. It, too, is said to be haunted—only the ghost here, affectionately called Alice, is said to be good-spirited when she appears in her flowing white dress. Join Alice and the other regulars for a pint or a light meal.

Featuring a great view of the canal, **Double Locks,** Canal Banks (☎ **01392/256947**), welcomes a varied crowd, largely students. It features live music with no cover charge two or three evenings a week, and you can get traditional pub grub to go with your pint. Although spaciously spread through a Georgian mansion, the **Imperial Pub,** New North Road (☎ **01392/434050**), is friendly to frugal travelers, with the cheapest brand-name beer in town, starting at £1.35 ($2.30), and a fast-food menu.

2 Dartmoor National Park

213 miles SW of London; 13 miles W of Exeter

This national park lies northeast of Plymouth, stretching from Tavistock and Okehampton on the west to near Exeter in the east, a granite mass that sometimes rises to a height of 2,000 feet above sea level. The landscape offers vistas of gorges with rushing water, gorse, and purple heather ranged over by Dartmoor ponies—a foreboding landscape for the experienced walker only.

In Dartmoor, you'll find 500 miles of foot- and bridle paths and more than 90,000 acres of common land with public access. The country is rough, and on the high moor you should always make sure you have good maps, a compass, and suitable clothing and shoes.

ESSENTIALS

GETTING THERE Take the train down from London to Exeter (see "Essentials," in section 1), then use local buses to connect you with the various villages of Dartmoor.

Transmoor Link, a public transport bus service, usually operates throughout the summer and is an ideal way to get onto the moor. Information on the Transmoor Link and on the bus link between various towns and villages on Dartmoor is available from the **Transport Coordination Centre** (☎ **01392/382800**).

If you're driving, Exeter is the most easily reached gateway. From here, continue west on B3212 to such centers of Dartmoor as Easton, Chagford, Moretonhampstead, and North Bovey. From these smaller towns, tiny roads—often not really big enough for two cars—cut deeper into the moor.

VISITOR INFORMATION The main source of information is the **Dartmoor National Park Tourist Information Centre,** Town Hall, Bedford Square, Tavistock (☎ **01822/612938**). It will book accommodations within a 15-mile radius for 3 to £3.50 ($5.95). It's open April through October Monday-Saturday from 10am to 5pm and in summer on Sunday also from 10am to 5pm. From November to March, it's open on Monday, Tuesday, Friday, and Saturday from 10am to 4pm.

EXPLORING THE MOORS

This region is as rich in myth and legend as anywhere else in Britain. Crisscrossed with about 500 miles of bridle paths and hiking trails and covering about 360 square miles (180 of which comprise the Dartmoor National Park), the moors rest on a granite base with numerous rocky outcroppings.

The Dartmoor National Park Authority (DNPA) runs **guided walks** of varying difficulty, ranging from 1½ to 6 hours for a trek of some 9 to 12 miles. All you have to do is turn up suitably clad at your selected starting point. Details are available from DNP information centers or from the **Dartmoor National Park Authority,** High Moorland Visitor Centre, Tavistock Road, Princetown (near Yelverton) PL20 6QF (☎ **01822/890414**). Guided tours cost £2 ($3.40) for a 2-hour walk, £3 ($5.10) for a 3-hour walk, £3.50 ($5.95) for a 4-hour walk, and £4 ($6.80) for a 6-hour walk. These prices are subsidized by the national parks services.

Throughout the area are stables where you can arrange for a day's trek across the moors. For **horseback riding** on Dartmoor, there are too many establishments to list. All are licensed, and you are accompanied by an experienced rider/guide. The moor can be dangerous since sudden fogs descend on treacherous marshlands without warning. Prices are around £9 ($15.30) per hour, £14 ($23.80) for a half day, and £25 ($42.50) for a full day. Most riding stables are listed in a useful free publication, *The Dartmoor Visitor,* which also provides details on guided walks, places to go, accommodations, local events, and articles about the national park. *The Dartmoor Visitor* is obtainable from DNP information centers and tourist information centers or by mail. Send an International Reply Coupon to the DNPA headquarters (address above).

CAMPING IN THE PARK

A few official campsites exist, but many campers prefer the open moor for the night. Since the moor is privately owned land, seek permission before camping. Only 1 night in a single spot is permitted. Campsites include **Ashburton Caravan Park,** Waterleat, Ashburton (☎ **01364/652552**); **River Dart Country Park,** Holne Park, Ashburton (☎ **01364/652511**); and **Yertiz Caravan and Camping Park,** Exeter Road, Okehampton (☎ **01837/52281**). Most sites are open from April through September, and charges begin at £3 ($5.10) per person.

CHAGFORD: A GOOD BASE FOR EXPLORING THE PARK

218 miles SW of London; 13 miles W of Exeter; 20 miles NW of Torquay

Six hundred feet above sea level, Chagford is an ancient town; with moors all around, it's a good base from which to explore north Dartmoor. Chagford overlooks the Teign River in its deep valley and is itself overlooked by the high granite tors. There's good fishing in the Teign. From Chagford, the most popular excursion is to Postbridge, a village with a prehistoric clapper bridge.

Surrounded by moors, romantic Chagford is one of the best bases for exploring the often forlorn but romantic north Dartmoor. It's also Sir Francis Drake country.

To get here, take a train to Exeter (see "Essentials," in section 1), and then catch a local bus to Chagford (Transmoor Link National Express bus no. 82). If you're driving from Exeter, drive west on A30, then south on A382 to Chagford.

EXPLORING THE TOWN

When it's teatime, drop in at **Whiddons,** High Street (☎ **01647/433406**), which is decorated with fresh flowers in summer. They have freshly baked scones and delectable cucumber sandwiches. After tea, drop in at the Church of St. Michael nearby, where a spurned lover killed Mary Whiddon on her wedding day (later fictionalized in R. D. Blackmore's classic *Lorna Doone*).

✪ **Sir Francis Drake's House.** Buckland Abbey, Yelverton. ☎ **01822/853607.** Admission £4.50 ($7.65) adults, £2.25 ($3.80) children. Apr–Oct Fri–Wed 10:30am–5:30pm; Nov–Mar Sat–Sun 2–5pm. Last admission 45 min. before closing. Go 3 miles west of Yelverton off A386.

Constructed in 1278, Sir Francis Drake's House was originally a Cistercian monastery. The monastery was dissolved in 1539 and became the country seat of sailors Sir Richard Grenville and, later, Sir Francis Drake. The house remained in the Drake family until 1946, when the abbey and grounds were given to the National Trust. The abbey is now a museum and houses exhibits including Drake's drum, banners, and other artifacts.

Castle Drogo. 4 miles northeast of Chagford and 6 miles south of the Exeter-Okehampton Rd. (A30). ☎ **01647/433306.** Admission (castle and grounds) £5.40 ($9.20) adults, £2.60 ($4.40) children; (grounds only) £2.60 ($4.40) adults, £1.35 ($2.30) children. Apr–Oct Sat–Thurs 11am–5:30pm; grounds daily 10:30am–dusk. Take A30 and follow the signs.

This massive granite castle, in the hamlet of Drewsteignton some 17 miles west of Exeter, was designed and built between 1910 and 1930 by the architect Sir Edwin Lutyens, then at the height of his powers, for his client, Julius Drewe. It was the last private country house built in the United Kingdom on a grand scale. Although constructed of granite and castellated and turreted like a medieval castle from the age of chivalry, it was never intended to be a military stronghold. The castle occupies a bleak but dramatic position high above the River Teign, with views sweeping out over the moors.

The tour covers an elegant series of formal rooms designed in the best tradition of the Edwardian age. There are two restaurants and a buffet-style tearoom on the premises.

Insider's tip: The castle is so overpowering it's easy to forget the secluded gardens. But they are wonderful, including a sunken lawn enclosed by raised walkways, a circular croquet lawn (sets are available for rent), geometrically shaped yew hedges, and a kiddies playroom based on a 1930s residence.

WHERE TO STAY & DINE

Easton Court Hotel. Easton Cross, Chagford, Devon TQ13 8JL. ☎ **01647/433469.** Fax 01647/433654. E-mail: stay@easton.co.uk. 8 units. TV TEL. £90 ($153) double. Rates include

English breakfast. MC, V. Closed Jan. Take A382 1 1/2 miles northeast of Chagford. Bus no. 359 from Exeter.

Ever since it was established as a hotel in the 1920s, this Tudor house has drawn many literary and theatrical celebrities. It's best known as the place where Evelyn Waugh wrote *Brideshead Revisited.* The atmosphere here is very English country house: an ancient stone house with a thatched roof, an inglenook where log fires burn, and a high-walled flower garden. The bedrooms are snug and comfortable, and range in size from small to medium. The rooms are appointed with coffeemakers and excellent mattresses on the English beds where the greats of yesteryear slept. Most rooms open onto views.

Dining: British and international dishes are served, including coq au vin, steak-and-mushroom pie, guinea fowl. Meals, available to nonresidents who reserve, cost £22 ($37.40) and up.

✪ **Gidleigh Park Hotel.** Gidleigh Rd. (2 miles outside town), Chagford, Devon TQ13 8HH. ☎ **01647/432367.** Fax 01647/432574. www.gidleigh.com. E-mail: gidleighpark@gidleigh.co.uk. 14 units, 1 cottage. TV TEL. £385–£475 ($654.50–$807.50) double; £515 ($875.50) cottage for 2, £675 ($1,147.50) cottage for 4. Rates include English breakfast, morning tea, newspaper, dinner, service, and tax. MC, V. To get here from Chagford Sq., turn right onto Mill St. at Lloyds Bank. After 150 yds, turn right and go down the hill to the crossroads. Cross straight over onto Holy St., following the lane passing Holy St. Manor on your right and shifting into low gear to negotiate 2 sharp bends on a steep hill. Over Leigh Bridge, make a sharp right turn into Gidleigh Park. A 1/2-mile drive will bring you to the hotel.

This Tudor-style hotel, a Relais & Châteaux member, is the country house supreme, the finest and most elegant place to stay in the Dartmoor area. The hotel lies in the Teign Valley, opening onto panoramic vistas of the Meldon and Nattadon Hills. Its American owners, Kay and Paul Henderson, have renovated and refurnished the house with flair and imagination. Most of the bedrooms are on the second floor and are reached by a grand staircase. Bedrooms are roomy and furnished in the most elegant English country house tradition. Half-testers usually crown the sumptuous English beds, and each of the well-appointed bathrooms has a set of toiletries. The hotel has a three-room thatched cottage with two bathrooms across the river, 350 yards from the hotel, available for two to four people.

Dining: Excellent meals are served in the dining room. The menu changes daily and the kitchen uses only the best and freshest products. Dining here is a memorable experience. In fact, this restaurant is one of the best in the West Country, and its wine list has received numerous awards.

Great Tree Hotel. Sandy Park, Chagford, Devon TQ13 8JS. ☎ **01647/432491.** Fax 01647/432562. www.soft.net.uk/greattree. E-mail: nigel@greattree.softnet.co.uk. 10 units. TV TEL. £79–£98 ($134.30–$166.60) double. Rates include English breakfast. AE, DC, MC, V. Take A30 to the traffic circle at Whiddon Down and drive 2 1/2 miles south on A382.

Formerly an old hunting lodge, the Great Tree Hotel is located on 25 acres of private grounds. The bedrooms are country style, with tea- and coffeemakers and hair dryers. Rooms range from small to spacious, and entire blocks are rejuvenated every year, keeping standards high. Beverly and Nigel Eaton-Gray, the proprietors, offer a five-course dinner prepared with homegrown produce; the cost is £25 ($42.50). English and continental meals are served in their Whitewater Restaurant. There are bar snacks at lunch and Devonshire cream teas on the terrace, or by the log fire in winter.

OTHER TOWNS IN & AROUND DARTMOOR

Some 13 miles west of Exeter, the peaceful little town of **Moretonhampstead** is perched on the edge of Dartmoor. Moretonhampstead contains an old market cross and several 17th-century colonnaded almshouses.

The much-visited Dartmoor village of **Widecombe-in-the-Moor** is only 7 miles from Moretonhampstead. The fame of the village of Widecombe-in-the-Moor stems from an old folk song about Tom Pearce and his gray mare, listing the men who were supposed to be on their way to Widecombe Fair when they met with disaster. Widecombe also has a parish church worth visiting. Called the **Cathedral of the Moor,** with a roster of vicars beginning in 1253, the house of worship in a green valley is surrounded by legends. When the building was restored, a wall plate was found bearing the badge of Richard II (1377–99), the figure of a white hart. The town is very disappointing, tacky, and unkempt in spite of its fame.

The market town of **Okehampton** owes its existence to the Norman castle built by Baldwin de Bryonis, sheriff of Devon, under orders from his uncle, William the Conqueror, in 1068, just 2 years after the conquest. The Courtenay family lived here for many generations until Henry VIII beheaded one of them and dismantled the castle in 1538.

Museum of Dartmoor Life, at the Dartmoor Centre, 3 West St., Okehampton (☎ **01837/52295**), is housed in an old mill with a water wheel and is part of the Dartmoor Centre, a group of attractions around an old courtyard. Also here are working craft studios, a Victorian Cottage Tearoom, and a tourist information center. Museum displays cover all aspects of Dartmoor's history from prehistoric times, including some old vehicles—a Devon box wagon of 1875 and a 1922 Bullnose Morris motorcar. There's a reconstructed cider press, and a blacksmith. The museum is open October to Easter, Monday through Friday from 10am to 4pm, and from Easter to October, Monday through Saturday from 10am to 5pm. It also opens on Sunday from June through September. Admission is £2 ($3.40) for adults, £1.80 ($3.05) for seniors, £1 ($1.70) for children, and £5.60 ($9.50) for a family ticket (2 adults, 2 children).

Let yourself drift back in time to the days when craftspeople were the lifeblood of thriving communities. Basket weavers, wood turners, and potters are among the traditional crafters that can still be seen throughout the area. Indulge yourself with some genuine Devon pieces of craftsmanship. In the Dartmoor National Park in West Devon, you'll find that **The Yelverton Paperweight Centre,** Leg O'Mutton (☎ **01822/854250**), presents an impressive display of more than 800 glass paperweights for sale along with paintings of Dartmoor scenes.

For an interesting outdoor shop, **The Kountry Kit,** 22–23 West St., Tavistock (☎ **01822/613089**), carries all the best names in gear and outerwear. It also is a clearinghouse of name-brand seconds.

WHERE TO STAY & DINE IN THE AREA

The Castle Inn. Lydford, near Okehampton (1 mile off A386), Devon EX20 4BH. ☎ **01822/820241.** Fax 01822/820454. E-mail: castle1lyd@aol.com. 9 units. £57–£74 ($96.90–$125.80) double. Special Country Breaks (any 2 nights): £182–£216 ($309.40–$367.20), including breakfast and dinner. AE, DC, MC, V.

The Castle Inn is a 16th-century structure next to Lydford Castle, midway between Okehampton and Tavistock. The inn, with its pink facade and row of rose trellises, is the hub of the village. The owners have maintained the character of the commodious old rustic lounge. One room, called the "Snug," has a group of high-backed oak settles arranged in a circle. The bedrooms are not large but are attractively furnished, often with mahogany and marble Victorian pieces. There's an equal split between bathrooms with a shower only and those with a tub and shower combination.

The Foresters' Bar serves a standard lunch and dinner daily, as well as bar snacks. The fixed-price dinner is an especially good buy.

Cherrybrook Hotel. On B3212 between Postbridge and Two Bridges, Yelverton, Devon PL20 6SP. ☎ and fax **01822/880260.** 7 units, all with shower. TV. £55 ($93.50) double. Rates include English breakfast. No credit cards. Closed Dec 22–Jan 2.

Cherrybrook Hotel is a small family-run hotel in the center of the Dartmoor National Park, on the high moor but within easy driving distance of Exeter and Plymouth. It was built in the early 19th century by a prince regent's friend who received permission to enclose a large area of the Dartmoor forest for farming. The lounge and bar with their beamed ceilings and slate floors are a reminder of those times. Andy and Margaret Duncan rent small- to medium-sized rooms with a traditional decor, often with a granite fireplace. Some of the bedrooms are redecorated each year. Bathrooms contain a shower stall. You can also dine here, paying £16.50 ($28.05) for a four-course dinner and coffee.

Holne Chase Hotel. Two Bridges Rd., Ashburton, near Newton Abbot (off the main Ashburton-Princetown rd., between the Holne Bridge and New Bridge), Devon TQ13 7NS. ☎ **01364/631471.** Fax 01364/631453. www.holne-chase.co.uk. E-mail: info@holne-chase.co.uk. 17 units. TV TEL. £125–£160 ($212.50–$272) double; from £165 ($280.50) suite. Rates include English breakfast. Discount packages available. AE, MC, V.

The Holne Chase Hotel is a white-gabled country house, 3 miles northwest of the center of town, within sight of trout- and salmon-fishing waters. You can catch your lunch and take it back to the kitchen to be cooked. Although the mood of the moor predominates, Holne Chase is surrounded by trees, lawns, and pastures—a perfect setting for walks along the Dart. The house is furnished in period style; a stable block has been converted into four sporting lodges. Rooms come in various shapes, sizes, and styles; some have their original fireplaces and four-poster beds, ideal for a romantic interlude. If you get assigned a room in the stable, don't be disappointed, as these are really delightful split-level suites. All the comforts of English country living are found here. Seven rooms are large enough for families.

Dining: The cooking combines the best of English fare with specialty dishes that are made all the better whenever produce from the gardens or fresh fish from the Dart River and Torquay are used. Devon beef and lamb are also featured. The old cellars hold a nice selection of wine.

Lewtrenchard Manor. Lewdown, Devon EX20 4PN. ☎ **01566/783256.** Fax 01566/783332. E-mail: s&j@lewtrenchard.co.uk. 9 units. TV ☎ £105 ($178.50)double, £150–£165 ($255–$280.50) suite. Rates include English breakfast. AE, DC, MC, V.

On the northwest edges of Dartmoor, near the popular touring center of Okehampton, this is a 17th-century English house with a certain charm and grace. It was at one time the residence of the Victorian hymn writer, the Rev. Sabine Baring Gould (hardly a household name today). It is set in a garden so lovely it is open to the general public as part of the National Gardens Scheme. Lovely walks are possible in several directions. As is typical of its time, the house features oak paneling, beautifully detailed ceilings, and antiques. Rooms come in various shapes and sizes, but each is exceedingly comfortable. The hotel also operates an excellent restaurant on site, specializing in a British and continental cuisine.

3 Torquay: The English Riviera

223 miles SW of London; 23 miles SE of Exeter

In 1968, the towns of Torquay, Paignton, and Brixham joined to form "The English Riviera" as part of a plan to turn the area into one of the super three-in-one resorts of Europe. The area today—the birthplace of mystery writer Agatha Christie—opens onto 22 miles of coastline and 18 beaches. Palm trees even grow here!

Fans of the British comedy *Fawlty Towers,* the television series that made Torquay and the English Riviera known the world over, might be disappointed to learn that it wasn't filmed in Torquay at all, but rather in one of the Home Counties closer to London. (The hotel that served as the comedy's set has since burned down.) Regardless, Torquay continues to be identified with the series, which was inspired by John Cleese's sojourn in Torquay during one of his tours of duty with the Monty Python team.

Torquay is set against a backdrop of the red cliffs of Devon, with many sheltered pebbly coves. With its parks and gardens, including numerous subtropical plants, it's often compared to the Mediterranean. At night, concerts, productions from the West End, vaudeville shows, and ballroom dancing keep the vacationers and many honeymooners entertained.

ESSENTIALS

GETTING THERE The nearest connection is Exeter Airport (see "Essentials," in section 1), 40 minutes away. Frequent trains run throughout the day from London's Paddington Station to Torquay, whose station is at the town center on the seafront. The trip takes 2½ hours. For rail information, call ☎ **0345/484950.**

National Express coach links from London's Victoria Coach Station leave every 2 hours during the day for Torquay. For information and schedules, call ☎ **0990/808080.**

If you're driving from Exeter, head west on A38, veering south at the junction with A380.

VISITORS INFORMATION The **Tourist Information Centre** is at Vaughan Parade (☎ **01803/297428**); open Monday through Saturday from 9am to 5pm.

PALM TREES & AGATHA CHRISTIE

This resort is known for offering one of the balmiest climates in Britain. It's so temperate, because of its exposure to the Gulf Stream, that subtropical plants such as palm trees and succulents thrive.

Torre Abbey. Kings Dr. (¼ mile east of Torquay's center). ☎ **01803/293593.** Admission £3 ($5.10) adults, £1.50 ($2.55) children. Easter or Apr 1 (whichever is earlier) to Oct 31 daily.

Originally built as a monastery in 1196, then converted into a private home in the 16th century, it has long been associated with Torquay's leading citizens. Today, the Torquay Town Council maintains it as a museum. The museum features a room outfitted in a close approximation of **Agatha Christie's private study.** After the mystery writer's death, her family donated for display her Remington typewriter, many of her original manuscripts, an oil portrait of Ms. Christie as a young woman, family photographs, and more.

Oldway Mansion. Torbay Rd., in Preston, near Paignton (a short drive south of the center of Torquay on the main Paignton-Torquay rd.). ☎ **01803/207933.** Tours available Easter–Oct between 10am and 1pm for £1 ($1.70). Admission free without guided tour. Year-round Mon–Fri 9am–5pm; Apr–Oct also Sat 9am–5pm and Sun 2–5pm.

You'll see the conspicuous consumption of England's gilded age here. The mansion was built in 1874 by Isaac Merritt Singer, founder of the sewing-machine empire, and his son, Paris, enhanced its decor, massive Ionic portico, and 17 acres of Italianate gardens. The mansion's eclectic decor includes a scaled-down version of the Hall of Mirrors in the Palace of Versailles. During its Jazz Age heyday, Oldway served as a rehearsal space and performance venue for Isadora Duncan, who was having a not terribly discreet affair with Paris.

WHERE TO STAY

EXPENSIVE

✪ **The Imperial.** Park Hill Rd., Torquay, Devon TQ1 2DG. ☎ **800/225-5843** in the U.S. and Canada, or 01803/294301. Fax 01803/298293. www.paramount.hotels.co.uk. E-mail: imperialtorquay@paramount.hotels.co.uk. 153 units. TV TEL. £128–£170 ($217.60–$289) double; from £250 ($425) suite. Rates include English breakfast, use of sporting facilities, and dancing in the ballroom Mon–Sat. AE, DC, MC, V. Garage parking £5 ($8.50); free parking lot.

This leading five-star hotel in the West Country dates from the 1860s, but a major refurbishing has kept it abreast of the times and way ahead of all its competition. It sits on 5½ acres of subtropical gardens opening onto rocky cliffs, with views of the Channel. You'll be following the example of some of the characters of Agatha Christie if you check in here. She called it the Esplanade in *The Rajah's Emerald,* the Castle in *Partners in Crime,* and the Majestic in *Peril at End House.* Inside is a world of soaring ceilings, marble columns, and ornate plasterwork—enough to make a former visitor, Edward VII, feel at home. Rooms are studies in grand living, with beautiful reproduction pieces, striped wallpaper, upholstered seating, and elegant mattresses on quality beds. Many have private balconies suspended high above a view that encompasses offshore islands with black rocks and sheer sides. Bathrooms are grandly appointed with deluxe toiletries and a hair dryer.

Dining: The elegant Regatta Restaurant serves British and international dishes, supplemented by a fine wine list, at lunch and dinner daily (reserve for dinner).

Orestone Manor. Rockhouse Lane, Maidencombe, Torquay, Devon TQ1 4SX. ☎ **01803/328098.** Fax 01803/328336. E-mail: reservations@orestone.co.uk. 18 units. TV TEL. £110–£160 ($187–$272) double. Rates include English breakfast. Winter discounts available. AE, MC, V. Closed 2 weeks in Jan. Drive 3½ miles north of Torquay on B379. Free parking.

Sometimes the best way to enjoy a bustling seaside resort is from afar, nestling in a country home. Orestone Manor is in nearby Maidencombe, a small village north of Torquay. In one of the loveliest valleys in South Devon, this gabled manor house, constructed in the early 19th century as a private home, enjoys a tranquil rural setting, situated on 2 acres of well-landscaped gardens. The bedrooms are handsomely furnished and offer beverage makers. Since this was once a country lodge, all the bedrooms have an individual character and aren't just square boxes. Each unit has a good-size bath or shower and a hair dryer. The most desirable units open onto sea views.

Dining: The restaurant offers a fixed-price dinner, which is always well prepared using only fresh ingredients.

Palace Hotel. Babbacombe Rd., Babbacombe, Torquay, Devon TQ1 3TG. ☎ **01803/200200.** Fax 01803/299899. 141 units. TV TEL. £110–£130 ($187–$221) double; £180–£200 ($306–$340) suite for 2. Rates include English breakfast. AE, DC, MC, V. Parking £5 ($8.50) for garage spaces. From the town center take B3199 east. Bus no. 32.

This 1921 hotel was built when life was experienced on a grand scale, an attitude that's reflected by the spacious public rooms with their molded ceilings and columns. With all of its recent improvements, the hotel should be able to enter the next century in a premier position. It's luxurious through and through. The bedrooms are well furnished, with extras as beverage makers and hair dryers. The hotel occupies 25 choice acres of real estate in Torquay, sweeping down to Anstey's Cove.

Amenities: Both indoor and outdoor swimming pools along with indoor and outdoor tennis courts, two indoor squash courts, a 9-hole golf course.

INEXPENSIVE

Colindale. 20 Rathmore Rd., Chelston, Torquay, Devon TQ2 6NY. ☎ **01803/293947.** 8 units with bathroom. £40–£44 ($68–$74.80) double. Rates include English breakfast. AE, DC, MC, V. Free parking.

This hotel is a good choice, and it's about as central as you'd want: It opens onto King's Garden, within a 5-minute walk of Corbyn Beach and a 3-minute walk from the railway station. There's a cocktail bar and a residents' lounge and dining room offering a fixed-price dinner for £11.50 ($19.55). Rooms are cozily furnished, coming in a range of sizes and shapes, each in a Victorian style. Accommodations contain such extras as beverage makers, and come with a private shower. Colindale is one of a row of attached brick Victorian houses, with gables and chimneys. It's set back from the road, with a parking lot in front.

Craig Court Hotel. 10 Ash Hill Rd., Castle Circus, Torquay, Devon TQ1 3HZ. ☎ **01803/294400.** Fax 01803/212525. www.craigcourthotel.co.uk. E-mail: info@craigcourt-hotel.co.uk. TV. £41–£47 ($69.70–$79.90) double. Rates include English breakfast. Special packages available. No credit cards. Take St. Marychurch Rd. (signposted St. Marychurch, Babbacombe) from Castle Circus (the town hall), make the first right onto Ash Hill Rd., go 200 yd., and the hotel is on the right.

This hotel is in a large Victorian mansion with a southern exposure that lies a short walk form the heart of town. Owner Ann Box's modernized rooms, many with private facilities, offer excellent value. Bedrooms tend to be small and cozy, each with a compact private bath with a shower. In addition to enjoying the good, wholesome food served here, guests can also make use of a lounge or an intimate bar opening onto the grounds. A four-course dinner costs £10 ($17).

Homers. Warren Rd., Torquay, Devon TQ2 5TN. ☎ **01803/213456.** Fax 01803/213458. www.homers-hotel.co.uk. E-mail: homers@tinyonline.co.uk. 15 units. TV TEL. £70–£80 ($119–$136) double; £100 ($170) suite. Rates include English breakfast. AE, DC, MC, V. Turn left from the Sea Front along the front (inside lane) straight up the hill; Warren Rd. is on the right (it's a very tight turn by St. Luke's Church).

The solid Victorian walls of this house were originally built in the 1850s as the summer vacation home of a mining magnate. In 1994, new owners Gerald Clarke and Guy Mansell began a gradual renovation of each bedroom, leaving many family antiques in place along with old-fashioned homey touches. Bedrooms come in various shapes and sizes, each with a compact bathroom with a shower stall. Set near the top of steeply inclined gardens overlooking Tor Bay, the hotel has a restaurant, Les Ambassadeurs. Here, evening meals are prepared only with fresh ingredients, and the chef caters to people with special dietary needs, including vegetarians.

WHERE TO DINE

Mulberry House. 1 Scarborough Rd., Torquay, Devon TQ2 5UJ. ☎ **01803/213639.** Reservations required. Main courses £15.50–£17.50 ($26.35–$29.75), 3-course lunch £7.95 ($13.50). No credit cards. Wed–Sun noon–2pm and 7:30–9:30pm. From the Sea Front, turn up Belgrave Rd.; Scarborough Rd. is the first right. Bus no. 32. ENGLISH.

Lesley Cooper is an inspired cook, and she'll feed you well in her little dining room, seating some two dozen diners at midday. The restaurant is situated in one of

Torquay's Victorian villas, facing a patio of plants and flowers, with outside tables for summer lunches and afternoon teas. Vegetarians will find comfort here, and others can feast on Lesley's smoked ham rissoles, honey-roasted chicken, or grilled natural fried fillets of sole with tartar sauce. Traditional roasts draw the Sunday crowds. The choice is wisely limited so that everything served will be fresh.

You can even stay here in one of three bedrooms, each comfortably furnished and well kept, with private bath. Bed-and-breakfast charges from £25 ($42.50) per person daily make this one of the best bargains of the whole area.

Remy's. 3 Croft Rd. ☎ **01803/292359.** Reservations required. Fixed-price menu £17.85 ($30.35). MC, V. Tues–Sat 7:30–9:30pm. From the Sea Front, head north on Shedden Hill. Bus no. 32. FRENCH.

The finest nonhotel restaurant in Torquay, Remy's serves good food at reasonable prices, offering a fixed-price three-course menu that changes daily. French owner and chef Remy Bopp sets great store by his ingredients, whether they be fresh fish from a local fishmonger or vegetables from the market. Everything is homemade, including the bread, ice cream, sorbet, and pastries. Guests can also enjoy his carefully selected group of French wines. The food is straightforward and rarely overdone, beginning with the pâté of the chef (garlic, herbs, and pork), and moving on to such main dishes as roast chicken in an orange sauce or lamb's kidneys in a mustard sauce.

TORQUAY AFTER DARK

There are seven theaters in town, all open year-round, offering everything from Gilbert and Sullivan and tributes to Sinatra and Nat King Cole, to Marine Band-concerts and comedy shows. Among the most active of the theaters are the **Palace Theatre,** Palace Avenue, Paignton (☎ **01803/665-800**); the **Princess Theatre,** Torbay Road (☎ **01803/290-290**).

Fifteen area nightclubs cater to everyone from teenyboppers to the gay scene, but dancing rules the town, and there's virtually nowhere to catch live club acts. Among the better dance clubs are **Claires,** Torwood Street (☎ **01803/211-097**), for its Thursday, Friday-and Saturday-night house music, with a cover charge varying from £2 to £6 ($3.40 to $10.20), depending on the DJ; and the **Monastery**, Torwood Gardens Road (☎ **01803/292-929**), on Saturday, the only night this club opens its doors. You can definitely get your fill of hip-hop and electronica here as the dancing starts at midnight and doesn't end until 7am.

4 Totnes

224 miles SW of London; 12 miles NW of Dartmouth

One of the oldest towns in the West Country, the ancient borough of Totnes rests quietly in the past, seemingly content to let the Torquay area remain in the vanguard of the building boom. On the River Dart, upstream from Dartmouth, Totnes is so totally removed in character from Torquay that the two towns could be in different countries. Totnes has several historic buildings, notably the ruins of a Norman castle, an ancient guildhall, and the 15th-century Church of St. Mary, constructed of red sandstone. In the Middle Ages the town was encircled by walls; the North Gate serves as a reminder of that period.

ESSENTIALS

GETTING THERE Totnes is on the main London-Plymouth line. Trains leave London's Paddington Station frequently throughout the day. For rail information, call ☎ **0345/484950.**

Totnes is served locally by the Western National and Devon General bus companies (☎ **01752/222555** in Plymouth for information about individual routings).

If you're driving from Torquay, head west on A385.

Many visitors approach Totnes by river steamer from Dartmouth. Contact **Dart Pleasure Craft,** River Link (☎ **01803/834488**), for information.

VISITOR INFORMATION The **Tourist Information Centre** is at the Plains (☎ **01803/863168**). It's open Monday to Friday from 9:30am to 12:30pm and 1:30 to 4:30pm.

EXPLORING TOTNES

Totnes is known for its colorful **markets,** staged year-round in the center of town at Civic Square, on Friday mornings and early afternoons. On Tuesdays from May through September, many vendors wear Elizabethan costumes. You may want to wander throughout the town enjoying its old bookstores, antique shops, and other gifts.

The Elizabethan Museum. Fore St. ☎ **01803/863821.** Admission £1.50 ($2.55) adults, £1 ($1.70) seniors, 25p (45¢) children. Easter–Oct Mon–Fri 10:30am–5pm.

This 16th-century home of a wealthy merchant houses furniture, costumes, documents, and farm implements of the Elizabethan age. One room is devoted to local resident Charles Babbage (1792–1871), a mathematician and inventor. He invented a calculating machine whose memory capacity categorized it as an early version of the computer. His other inventions included the ophthalmoscope, a speedometer, and the cowcatchers later used to nudge cows off the tracks of railways around the world.

Totnes Castle. Castle St. ☎ **01803/864406.** Admission £1.60 ($2.70). Apr–Oct daily 10am–6pm; off-season, daily 10am–4pm.

Crowning the hilltop at the northern end of High Street, this castle was built by the Normans shortly after their conquest of England. It's one of the best examples of motte-and-bailey construction remaining in the United Kingdom. Although the outer walls survived, the interior is mostly in ruins.

Totnes Guildhall. Ramparts Walk. ☎ **01803/862147.** Admission 75p ($1.30) adults, 25p (45¢) children. Easter–Oct Mon–Fri 10:30am–1pm and 2–4pm.

This is the symbol of Totnes. Originally built as a priory (monastery) in 1553, it contains an old gaol (jail), a collection of civic memorabilia, and the table Oliver Cromwell used to sign documents during his visit to Totnes in 1646.

WHERE TO STAY IN THE TOTNES AREA

✪ **The Cott Inn.** Dartington, near Totnes (on the old Ashburton-Totnes turnpike), S. Devon TQ9 6HE. ☎ **01803/863777.** Fax 01803/866629. 6 units. TV TEL. £65 ($110.50) double. Rates 10% lower Oct–Easter. Extra person £15 ($25.50) per night. AE, MC, V. Free parking. Bus: X80 travels from Totnes to Dartington, but most people take a taxi for the 1½-mile journey.

Built in 1320, this hotel is the second-oldest inn in England. It's a low, rambling two-story building of stone, cob, and plaster, with a thatched roof and 3-foot-thick walls. The owners rent low-ceilinged double rooms upstairs, with modern conveniences. The recently refurbished rooms come in all shapes and sizes, and include private baths with shower stalls. The inn is a gathering place for the people of Dartington, and you'll feel the pulse of English country life here.

You'll surely be intrigued with the tavern, where you can also order a meal. A buffet is laid out at lunchtime, priced according to your choice of dish. Dinner features local produce prepared in interesting ways; scallops, duck, steak, or fresh salmon may be available. Even if you're not staying over, you may want to drop by the pub (five beers are on draft).

Gabriel Court Hotel. Stoke Gabriel, near Totnes, S. Devon TQ9 6SF. ☎ **01803/782206.** Fax 01803/782333. E-mail: obeacom@aol.com 19 units. TV TEL. £80 ($136) double; £109 ($185.30) family room for 3. Rates include English breakfast. AE, DC, MC, V. Exit the A38 at Buckfastleigh, taking A384 to Totnes, then A385 to Paignton; approximately 1 mile out of Totnes, turn right at the sign to Stoke Gabriel.

In nearby Stoke Gabriel, the Gabriel Court is a manor house that was owned by the same family from 1487 until 1928, when it was converted into a hotel. Michael and Eryl Beacom, the proprietors, offer good value and hospitality. The hotel, overlooking a pretty village on the banks of the River Dart, stands in a terraced Elizabethan garden, with a heated swimming pool and a lawn tennis court. Each of the bedrooms is in a modern extension that was converted from a hayloft; most have bath and shower combinations, and all offer hair dryers. The Gabriel Court enjoys a good reputation for its well-cooked English food, enhanced by fruit and vegetables from its own garden, as well as trout and salmon from the Dart. The hotel has a bar, and in winter log fires make the restful lounges cozy retreats.

Royal Seven Stars Hotel. The Plains, Totnes, S. Devon TQ9 5DD. ☎ **01803/862125.** Fax 01803/867925. www.smoothhound.co.uk/hotels/royal7.html. 16 units, 14 with bathroom. TV TEL. £62 ($105.40) double without bath, £66–£76 ($112.20–$129.20) double with bath. Children under 16 £12.50 ($21.25). Rates include English breakfast. AE, DC, MC, V.

A historic former coaching inn in the center of Totnes, the Royal Seven Stars largely dates from 1660. The hotel overlooks a square in the town center, near the banks of the River Dart. The interior courtyard, once used for horses and carriages, is now enclosed in glass, with an old pine staircase. Decorated with antiques, paintings, and the hotel's own heraldic shield, the courtyard forms an inviting entrance to the inn. The bedrooms have been modernized and have built-in furniture and a hot beverage maker. Two rooms have four-poster beds. Each compact bathroom has a shower stall.

WHERE TO DINE

When it's teatime, **Greys Dining Room,** 96 High St. (☎ **01803/866369**), sets out its fine silver and china to welcome you in an atmosphere of wood paneling and antiques. About 40 different teas along with homemade cakes and scones will invite you to extend the afternoon.

Brutus Room. In the Royal Seven Stars Hotel. ☎ **01803/862125.** Reservations recommended. Main courses £5.50–£10 ($9.35–$17); 4-course table d'hôte with coffee and value-added tax (VAT) £18.50 ($31.45); lunch buffet £4–£6 ($6.80–$10.20). DC, MC, V. Daily 8am–9:30pm; noon–2:15pm and 7–9:30pm. ENGLISH.

For the kind of cuisine that pleased Grandpa, this 1660 old coaching inn delivers quite well. You can stick with the four-course table d'hôte menu or order à la carte. Begin with battercrisp mushrooms with garlic mayonnaise, or the soup of the day. Main dishes always two-fisted selections such as a grilled sirloin, grilled lemon sole, or a respectable halibut steak. Vegetables of the day are fresh and well prepared. Finish in the British manner with blue Stilton cheese or perhaps a fruit tart—homemade, of course. At last, a place that still serves belle Hélène, an old-fashioned pear dessert. The adjoining Saddle Room bar has a wide range of ales, wine, and spirits.

5 Dartmouth

236 miles SW of London; 35 miles SE of Exeter

At the mouth of the Dart River, this ancient seaport is the home of the Royal Naval College. Traditionally linked to England's maritime greatness, Dartmouth sent out the young midshipmen who saw to it that "Britannia ruled the waves." You can take a river steamer up the Dart to Totnes (book at the kiosk at the harbor); the scenery along the way is panoramic, as the Dart is Devon's most beautiful river. Dartmouth's 15th-century castle was built during the reign of Edward IV. The town's most noted architectural feature is the Butter Walk, which lies below Tudor houses. The Flemish influence in some of the houses is pronounced.

ESSENTIALS

GETTING THERE Dartmouth is not easily reached by public transport. Trains run to Totnes (see "Essentials," in section 4) and Paignton. There is one bus a day from Totnes to Dartmouth. Call ☎ **01752/222666** for schedules.

If you're driving from Exeter, take A38 southwest, cutting southeast to Totnes on A381; then follow A381 to the junction with B3207.

Riverboats make the 10-mile run from Totnes to Dartmouth, but these trips depend on the tide and operate only from Easter to the end of October. See Totnes, above, for details on obtaining boat schedules.

VISITOR INFORMATION The **Tourist Information Centre** is at the Engine House, Mayors Avenue (☎ **01803/834224**), and is open April to October, Monday to Saturday from 9:30am to 5:30pm and Sunday from 10am to 4pm (off-season Mon–Sat from 9:30am–4pm).

EXPLORING DARTMOUTH

Many visitors come to Dartmouth for the bracing salt air and a chance to explore the surrounding marshlands, which are rich in bird life and natural beauty. The historic monuments here are steeped in much of the legend and lore of Channel life and historic Devon.

The town's most historic and interesting church is **St. Petrox,** on Castle Road, a 17th-century Anglican monument with an ivy-draped graveyard whose tombstones evoke the sorrows of Dartmouth's maritime past. The church is open daily from 7am to dusk.

It's also worth walking through the waterfront neighborhood known as **Bayard's Cove,** a cobbled, half-timbered neighborhood that's quite charming. Set near the end of Lower Street, it prospered during the 1600s thanks to its ship-repair services. In 1620 its quays were the site for repairs of the Pilgrims' historic ships, the Speedwell and the Mayflower, just after their departure from Plymouth.

Dartmouth Castle. Castle Rd. (1/2 mile south of the town center). ☎ **01803/833588.** Admission £2.90 ($4.95) adults, £2.20 ($3.75) seniors, £1.50 ($2.55) children. Apr–Sept daily 10am–6pm; Oct 10am–5pm; Nov–Mar Wed–Sun 10am–4pm.

Originally built during the 15th century, the castle was later outfitted with artillery and employed by the Victorians as a coastal defense station. A tour of its bulky ramparts and somber interiors provides insight into the changing nature of warfare throughout the centuries, and you'll see sweeping views of the surrounding coast and flatlands.

Dartmouth Museum. In the Butter Walk. ☎ **01803/832923.** Admission £1 ($1.70) adults, 50p (85¢) senior and children. Mar–Oct Mon–Sat 11am–5pm; rest of the year Mon–Sat noon–3pm.

This is the region's most interesting maritime museum, focusing on the British Empire's military might of the 18th century. Built between 1635 and 1640, it's set amid an interconnected row of 17th-century buildings—The Butter Walk—whose overhanging, stilt-supported facade was originally designed to provide shade for the butter, milk, and cream sold there by local milkmaids. Today, the complex houses the museum, as well as shops selling wines, baked goods, and more.

WHERE TO STAY

Dart Marina Hotel. Sandquay, Dartmouth, Devon TQ6 9PH. ☎ **01803/832580.** Fax 01803/835040. 50 units. TV TEL. £126–£170 ($214.20–$289) double; £156–£200 ($265.20–$340) suite for 2. Rates include half board. AE, DC, MC, V.

This hotel sits at the edge of its own marina, within a 3-minute walk from the center of town. It was originally built as a clubhouse for local yachties late in the 19th century, and was then enlarged and transformed into a hotel just before World War II. It does not have as much charm or character as the Royal Castle. The bar, the new riverside terrace, and each bedroom afford a view of yachts bobbing at anchor in the Dart River; about 14 bedrooms have private balconies. The small- to medium-sized bedrooms have coffeemakers. Fifteen rooms are set aside for nonsmokers

Royal Castle Hotel. 11 The Quay, Dartmouth, Devon TQ6 9PS. ☎ **01803/833033.** Fax 01803/835445. E-mail: enquiry@r-castle-hotel.co.uk. 25 units. TV TEL. £86–£136 ($146.20–$231.20) double. Rates include English breakfast. AE, MC, V.

A coaching inn on the town quay since 1639, the Royal Castle Hotel has hosted Sir Francis Drake, Queen Victoria, Charles II, and Edward VII. Horse-drawn carriages (as late as 1910) dispatched passengers in a carriageway, now an enclosed reception hall. The glassed-in courtyard, with its winding wooden staircase, has the original coaching horn and a set of 20 antique spring bells connected to the bedrooms. Many rooms open off the covered courtyard, and the rambling corridors display antiques. River-view rooms are the most sought after. All units have been recently restored and have central heating. Some are air-conditioned, and six units offer a Jacuzzi. Several contain a four-poster bed, and each is individually decorated, although all reflect the age of the building. Four accommodations are large enough for families.

Dining/Diversions: The meals, taken in the restaurant under a beautiful Adam ceiling, are excellent, in the best English tradition. A favorite place to settle in is the Galleon Bar, once two old kitchens, with double fireplaces and large hand-hewn beams said to have been salvaged from Spanish Armada ships. There's another pub-style bar, with settles (benches), that's popular with the locals. Guests lounge on the second floor in a room with a bay window overlooking the harbor.

WHERE TO DINE

✪ **The Carved Angel.** 2 S. Embankment. ☎ **01803/832465.** Reservations recommended. Main courses £18–£21 ($30.60–$35.70); 3-course fixed-price meals £30 ($51) at lunch, £40 ($68) at dinner. MC, V. Tues–Sun noon–2:30pm; Tues–Sat 7–9:30pm. Closed Jan 1–Feb 15. CONTINENTAL.

The best restaurant in town, the stylishly simple Carved Angel is on the riverfront. The building's half-timbered, heavily carved facade rises opposite the harbor. Inside, there's a statue of a carved angel (hence the name).

The cooking is both innovative and interesting, more akin to the creative cuisine of the continent than to the traditional cookery of England. Appetizers range from crawfish bisque to chicken liver parfait with red-onion confit and toasted brioche. Main dishes include roasted salt cod with bacon, leeks and olives and pan-fried fillet of steak with pepperonata and celeriac chips. It's worth saving room for the kumquat bavarois with poached rhubarb in ginger syrup.

Carved Angel Café. 7 Foss St. ☎ **01803/834842.** Reservations not necessary. Lunch main courses £6–£6.75 ($10.20–$11.50); dinner main courses £7.50 ($12.75) each. MC, V. Mon–Fri noon–3pm; Thurs–Sat 6:30–10pm. MC, V. ENGLISH.

This is the low-budget cafe and brasserie that's associated with the upscale and pricey **The Carved Angel.** You are guaranteed a well-prepared, fairly priced meal that's presented in an environment reeking of bucolic charm and traditional English wholesomeness. Menu items are listed on a blackboard, and change every day according to the seasonality of the ingredients and the inspiration of the chef. Good cooking is the rule here, as evoked by such dishes as tagliatelle with broccoli and blue cheese and such desserts as lemon-flavored cheesecake. Soups are rich and nutritious, and there are always at least three traditional "puddings" available for dessert. The restaurant is fully licensed.

Horn of Plenty. In the Tamar View House, Gulworthy, Tavistock, Devon PL19 8JD. ☎ **01822/832528.** Reservations recommended. £21.50 ($36.55) fixed-price lunch; £23.50 ($39.95) potluck menu Mon; £35 ($59.50) fixed-price dinner (Tues–Sun). AE, MC, V. Tues–Sun noon–2pm; daily 7–9pm. Closed Dec 25. Drive 3 miles west of Tavistock on A390. INTERNATIONAL.

As you drive from Tavistock to Callington, you'll see a small sign pointing north along a leafy drive to a solid Regency house where the owners operate what the French call a restaurant *avec chambres*. It was built by the duke of Bedford in the early 1800s as a private home. After a day of touring the country, guests enjoy well-prepared dinners at this award-winning restaurant, which might include terrine of duck foie de gras with sweet-and-sour leeks as an appetizer, followed by the fresh fish of the day. Even though all meals are fixed-price arrangements, there is a choice in each category.

You can stay in one of the spacious, warm, and elegant bedrooms (10 in all) that have been installed over the old stables of the house. With a continental breakfast included, doubles range from £115 to £200 ($195.50 to $340). All accommodations have TVs, beverage maker, phones, and well-stocked minibars.

A FAVORITE LOCAL PUB

Just a 2-minute walk from Bayard's Cove is one of our favorite pubs, **The Cherub,** 13 Higher St. (☎ **01803/832571**). It was originally built in 1380 as the harbormaster's house. Today this charming pub is a great place to drink and dine on simple traditional British platters and bar snacks. There's a more formal dining room upstairs that serves a number of fish dishes, steaks, lamb, and duck.

6 Plymouth

242 miles SW of London; 161 miles SW of Southampton

The historic seaport of Plymouth is more romantic in legend than in reality. But this was not always so—during World War II, greater Plymouth lost at least 75,000 buildings to Nazi bombs. The heart of present-day Plymouth, including the municipal civic center on the Royal Parade, has been entirely rebuilt; however, the way it was rebuilt is the subject of much controversy.

For the old part of town, you must go to the Elizabethan section, known as **The Barbican,** and walk along the quay in the footsteps of Sir Francis Drake (once the mayor of Plymouth). From here, in 1577, Drake set sail on his round-the-world voyage. The Barbican also holds special interest for visitors from the United States: it was the final departure point of the Pilgrims in 1620. The two ships, Mayflower and Speedwell, that sailed from Southampton in August of that year put into Plymouth after they suffered storm damage. Here, the Speedwell was abandoned as unseaworthy and the Mayflower made the trip to the New World alone.

ESSENTIALS

GETTING THERE Plymouth Airport lies 4 miles from the center of the city. **Brymon Airways** (☎ **01752/772752**) has direct service from the London airports, Heathrow and Gatwick, to Plymouth.

Frequent trains run from London's Paddington Station to Plymouth in 3 to $3^1/_2$ hours. For rail information, call ☎ **0345/484950** in the U.K. The **Plymouth Train Station** lies on North Road, north of the Plymouth Center. Western National Bus no. 83/84 runs from the station to the heart of Plymouth.

National Express has frequent daily bus service between London's Victoria Coach Station and Plymouth. The trip takes $4^1/_2$ hours. Call ☎ **0990/808080** for schedules and information.

If you're driving from London, take M4 west to the junction with M5 going south to Exeter. From Exeter, head southwest on A38 to Plymouth.

VISITOR INFORMATION The **Tourist Information Centre** is at the Island House, The Barbican (☎ **01752/264849**). A second information center, **Plymouth Discovery Centre,** is at Crabtree Marsh Mills, Plymouth (☎ **01752/266030**). Both are open from Easter to October Monday through Saturday from 9am to 5pm and Sunday from 10am to 4pm, and from November to Easter Monday to Friday 9am to 5pm and Saturday from 10am to 4pm.

SEEING THE SIGHTS

To commemorate the spot from which the *Mayflower* sailed for the New World, a white archway, erected in 1934 and capped with the flags of Great Britain and the United States, stands at the base of Plymouth's West Pier, on The Barbican. Incorporating a granite monument that was erected in 1891, the site is referred to as both the Mayflower **Steps** and the **Memorial Gateway.**

The **Barbican** is a mass of narrow streets, old houses, and quay-side shops selling antiques, brass work, old prints, and books. It's a perfect place for strolling and browsing through shops at your leisure.

Fishing boats still unload their catch at the wharves, and passenger-carrying ferryboats run short harbor cruises. A trip includes views of Drake's Island in the sound, the dockyards, naval vessels, and The Hoe from the water. A cruise of Plymouth Harbour costs £4 ($6.80) for adults and £2 ($3.40) for children. Departures are February through November, with cruises leaving every half hour from 10:30am to 3pm daily. These **Plymouth Boat Cruises** are booked at 8 Anderto Rise, Millbrook, Torpoint (☎ **01752/822797**).

New Street Gallery. 38 New St., The Barbican. ☎ **01752/221450.** Free admission. Mon noon–4pm, Tues–Sat 10am–5pm. Bus no. 39.

This gallery specializes in contemporary arts and crafts, with changing exhibitions of paintings and ceramics. It's a 5-minute walk from the town center in Plymouth's historic Barbican, near the *Mayflower* Steps.

Plymouth Gin Distillery. Black Friars Distillery, 60 Southside St. ☎ **01752/665292.** Admission £2.75 ($4.70) adults, £2.25 ($3.80) children 10–18, free for children 9 and under. Mon–Sat 10:30am–5pm. Closed Christmas–Easter. Bus no. 54.

These premises, one of Plymouth's oldest surviving buildings, were where the Pilgrims met before sailing for the New World. Plymouth Gin has been produced here for 200 years on a historic site that dates from a Dominican monastery built in 1425. There are public guided tours. A Plymouth Gin Shop is on the premises.

Prysten House. Finewell St. ☎ **01752/661414.** Admission 70p ($1.20) adults, 30p (50¢) children. Mon–Sat 10am–4pm.

Built in 1490 as a town house close to St. Andrew's Church, this is now a church house and working museum. Reconstructed in the 1930s with American help, it displays a model of Plymouth in 1620 and tapestries depicting the colonization of America. At the entrance is the gravestone of the captain of the U.S. brig *Argus,* who died on August 15, 1813, after a battle in the English Channel.

WHERE TO STAY

Astor Hotel. 14–22 Elliott St., The Hoe, Plymouth, Devon PL1 2PS. ☎ **01752/225511.** Fax 01752/251994. www.peelhotel.com. 55 units. TV TEL. £45–£80 ($76.50–$136) double. Rates include English breakfast. AE, DC, MC, V. Free parking overnight, £3.50 ($5.95) permit parking nearby.

The hotel building was originally constructed during the Victorian era as the private home of a prosperous sea captain. In 1987, it underwent a major restoration, and today it has comfortable bedrooms, each with a coffeemaker. A few accommodations are spacious, others a bit small, but each has a small compact bathroom with a shower stall. On the premises are well-decorated public lounges and a cozy and accommodating bar, open to guests and the public alike. The hotel's restaurant serves fixed-price menus at lunch and dinner.

Duke of Cornwall Hotel. Millbay Rd., Plymouth, Devon PL1 3LG. ☎ **01752/266256.** Fax 01752/600062. 72 units. TV TEL. £94.50 ($160.65) double. Rates include English breakfast. AE, DC, MC, V.

The Duke of Cornwall Hotel is a Victorian Gothic building that survived bombings in World War II. Constructed in 1863, it was regarded by Sir John Betjeman as the finest example of Victorian architecture in Plymouth. The refurbished bedrooms all have hair dryers, trouser presses, and coffeemakers. Some rooms contain antique four-poster beds. Twenty rooms are set aside for nonsmokers, and six are large enough for families. The hotel dining features rather standard British and continental selections.

Forte Posthouse. Cliff Rd., The Hoe, Plymouth, Devon PL1 3DL. ☎ **01752/662828.** Fax 01752/660974. 106 units. MINIBAR TV TEL. £75 ($127.50) double. Weekend break rates (including dinner and breakfast) £37–£45 ($62.90–$76.50) per person. AE, DC, MC, V.

This 9-story hotel, built in 1970, is situated on a hilltop above the bay and hosts an equal amount of business and leisure travelers. The hotel has comfortable rooms, all but a dozen of which face the sea. Each unit has an iron and a coffeemaker. Most rooms are a bit small, but bathrooms have adequate shelf space and a shower stall. On the premises is a pub, a free-form, heated outdoor pool (open daily May–Sept), and the **Seasons Restaurant** with wide-angle views of the sea.

Plymouth Hoe Moat House Hotel. Armada Way, Plymouth, Devon PL1 2HJ. ☎ **01752/639988.** Fax 01752/673816. 211 units. A/C TV TEL. £110–£135 ($187–$229.50) double, suite £140 ($238) all week. AE, DC, MC, V. Parking £3.50 ($5.95) for duration of stay.

One of the most distinguished hotels in the West Country, overlooking the harbor and The Hoe, the Plymouth Moat House rises like a midget high-rise. The good-size rooms are well furnished with long double beds, and have wide picture windows, tea- and coffeemakers, trouser presses, and hair dryers in the compact bathrooms. Baby-sitting is available. A covered swimming pool is on the grounds, and there's a sauna, solarium, gym, dance studio and beauty spa.

In Elliott's Restaurant, with its panoramic sea views, both à la carte and a table d'hôte menu are served. Seafood is a specialty, some of the catch brought fresh each day from The Barbican.

Novotel Plymouth. Marsh Mills, Plymouth, Devon PL6 8NH. ☎ **800/221-4542** in the U.S., or 01752/221422. Fax 01752/223922. E-mail: h0508@accor-hotels.com. 100 units. TV TEL. £65–£86.50 ($110.50–$147.05) double. Children 16 or under stay free in parents' room. AE, DC, MC, V. Bus nos. 21 or 51.

Novotel Plymouth, a 10-minute drive from the town center beside the A38, is convenient if you're driving, and also if you're traveling with children. With landscaped gardens and plenty of parking, it offers an ample number of soundproofed rooms. Bedrooms are a bit small and bandbox-like and the compact baths are motel standard with a shower stall. Two children under 16 sharing a room with their parents also receive free breakfast. There's a swimming pool and a children's play area. A brasserie is open daily from 6am to midnight.

WHERE TO DINE

The Plymouth Arts Centre Restaurant, 38 Looe St. (☎ **01752/660060**), offers one of the most filling and down-home vegetarian meals in town. Prices range from £2 to £6 ($3.40 to $10.20), and it's also ideal for a snack. You can even see a movie downstairs if you'd like. Food is served Monday from 10am to 2pm and Tuesday through Saturday from 10am to 8pm.

✪ **Chez Nous.** 13 Frankfort Gate. ☎ **01752/266793.** Reservations required. Fixed-price lunch and dinner £34 ($57.80). AE, DC, V. Tues–Fri 12:30–2pm; Tues–Sat 7–10:30pm. Closed first 3 weeks in Feb and Sept. FRENCH.

The most distinguished restaurant in Plymouth is Chez Nous, situated directly off Western Approach. Owner and chef Jacques Marchal borrows heavily from the past, but also expresses his creative talent. His type of cooking is called *la cuisine spontanée*—using fresh produce that changes with the seasons. Look for the specials of the day on the chalkboard menu. Accompanied by a classic and predominantly French wine list, the food is likely to include scallops steamed with ginger, bouillabaisse, and duck breast on a bed of lentils. Fish, generally, is the preferred main dish to order here. Fresh, quality ingredients are a hallmark of the cuisine.

Queen Anne Eating House. 2 White Lane, The Barbican. ☎ **01752/262101.** Main courses £4.95–£11 ($8.40–$18.70); cream teas £2.60 ($4.40). MC, V. Daily noon–3:30pm, Tues–Sun 6:30–9:30pm. Bus: 54. ENGLISH.

Next to the Barbican Craft Centre, this bow-fronted, white-painted 1790s place suggests a nautical inspiration with its solid oaken furniture. The food is plentiful and wholesome, with such fare as roast beef and Yorkshire pudding, roast fish from local markets, and other hot meals. Service is fast and polite. If you're not looking for a full meal, try a Devonshire cream tea (served all day) with homemade scones.

7 Clovelly

240 miles SW of London; 11 miles SW of Bideford

This is the most charming of all Devon villages and one of the main attractions of the West Country. Starting at a great height, the village cascades down the mountainside. Its narrow, cobblestone High Street makes driving impossible. You park your car at the top and make the trip on foot; supplies are carried down by donkeys. Every step of the way provides views of tiny cottages, with their terraces of flowers lining the main street. The village fleet is sheltered at the stone quay at the bottom.

The major sight of Clovelly is Clovelly itself. Charles Kingsley once wrote, ". . . it is as if the place had stood still while all the world had been rushing and rumbling past it." The price of entry to the village (see below) includes a guided tour of a fisherman's cottage as it would have been at the end of the 1800s. For the same price, you can also visit the **Kingsley Exhibition.** Author of *Westward Ho!* and *Water Babies,* Kingsley lived in Clovelly while his father was curate at the church. This exhibition traces the story of his life.

Right down below the Kingsley Exhibition—and our shopping note for the town—is a **Craft Gallery** where you have a chance to see and buy a wide variety of works by local artists and craftspeople. Once you've reached the end, you can sit and relax on the quay, taking in the views and absorbing Clovelly's unique atmosphere from this tiny, beautifully restored 14th-century quay.

Once you've worked your way to the bottom, how are you supposed to get back up? Those in good shape will climb all the way back up the impossibly steep cobbled streets to the top and the parking lot. For those who can't make the climb up the slippery incline, go to the rear of the Red Lion Inn and queue up for a Land Rover. In summer, the line is often long, but considering the alternative, it's worth the wait.

To avoid the tourist crowd, stay out of Clovelly from around 11am until teatime. When the midday congestion here is at its height, visit nearby villages such as Bucks Mills (3 miles to the east) and Hartland Quay (4 miles to the west).

ESSENTIALS

GETTING THERE From London's Paddington Station, trains depart for Exeter (see above) frequently. At Exeter, passengers transfer to a train headed for the end destination of Barnstaple. Travel time from Exeter to Barnstaple is 1¼ hours. From Barnstaple, passengers transfer to Clovelly by bus.

From Barnstaple, about one bus per hour, operated by either the Red Bus Company or the Filers Bus Company, goes to Bideford. The trip takes 40 minutes. At Bideford, connecting buses (with no more than a 10-minute wait between the arrival and the departure) continue on for the 30-minute drive to Clovelly. Two Land Rovers make continuous round-trips to the Red Lion Inn from the top of the hill. The Clovelly Visitor Centre (see below) maintains up-to-the-minute transportation information about how to get to Clovelly, depending on your location.

If you're driving from London, head west on M4, cutting south at the junction with M5. At the junction near Bridgwater, continue west along A39 toward Lynton. A39 runs all the way to the signposted turnoff for Clovelly.

VISITOR INFORMATION Go to the **Clovelly Visitor Centre** (☎ **01237/431781**), where you'll pay £2.50 ($4.25) for the cost of parking, use of facilities, entrance to the village, and an audiovisual theater admission, offering a multi-projector show tracing the story of Clovelly back to 2000 B.C. Also included in the price is a tour of a fisherman's cottage and admission to the **Kingsley Exhibition** (see above). Open Monday through Saturday from 9am to 5pm April through June, daily 10am to 4pm October through March, and daily from 9am to 6pm July through September.

WHERE TO STAY & DINE

New Inn. High St., Clovelly, N. Devon EX39 5TQ. ☎ **01237/431303.** Fax 01237/431636. 21 units, 8 with bathroom. £35–£45 ($59.50–$76.50) double without bathroom; £68–£82 ($115.60–$139.40) double with bathroom. Rates include English breakfast. AE, MC, V.

About halfway down High Street is the village pub, a good meeting place at sundown. It offers the best lodgings in the village, in two buildings on opposite sides of the steep street (but only a 12-foot leap between their balconies). Eight rooms have TVs and phones. Each room is relatively small but comfortable, and two are large enough for a family. Only a few have a small private bath with a shower stall. Corridor baths are adequate, however, and you rarely have to wait in line. If you're driving, you can park in the lot at the entrance to the town. It's advisable to pack a smaller overnight bag, since your luggage will have to be carried down (but is returned to the top by donkey).

This little country inn is also recommended for meals in the oak-beamed dining room. The local fare, including Devonshire cream, is featured whenever possible. Locally-caught lobsters are also prepared by the chef.

Red Lion. The Quay, Clovelly, Devon EX39 5TF. ☎ **01237/431237.** Fax 01237/431044. 11 units. TV TEL. £81–£100 ($137.70–$170) double. Rates include English breakfast. AE, MC, V.

At the bottom of the steep cobbled street, right on the stone seawall of the little harbor, Red Lion occupies the prime position in the village. Rising three stories with gables and a courtyard, it's actually an unspoiled country inn, where life centers around an antique pub and village inhabitants, including sea captains, who gather to satisfy their thirst over pints of ale. Most rooms look directly onto the sea with spectacular views, and they have recently been refurbished. Many are small, but two are spacious enough for a family. Dinner is available in the sea-view dining room with a choice of main dishes, some of which always include fresh local fish, and then a selection from the dessert trolley.

EN ROUTE TO LYNTON-LYNMOUTH: A STAY ON A WORKING FARM

Halmpstone Manor. Chittlehampton Rd., Bishop's Tawton, Barnstaple, N. Devon EX32 OEA. ☎ **01271/830321.** Fax 01271/830826. www.halmpstone.free-online.co.uk. E-mail: charles@halmpstone.freeonline.co.uk. 5 units. TV TEL. £100–£140 ($170–$238) double. Rates include English breakfast. AE, DC, MC, V. From Clovelly, take the A39 east for 30 to 45 minutes, turning off the A39 when you see signs for Chittlehampton. About 2 miles after the turnoff, you'll see signs pointing to Halmpstone Manor.

In the countryside, this working farm is operated by Charles and Jane Stanbury. Originally built in the 11th century as a manor house with 22 rooms, the structure has diminished in size because of two fires that occurred in the 15th and 16th centuries. The edifice was rebuilt in 1701 in its present form, with 15th-century paneling located in the dining room and high ceilings in the four-poster bedrooms. Family heirlooms are scattered throughout, and all the rooms have beverage-makers and trouser presses. The spacious bedrooms are a regal statement of English taste, luxuriously furnished with either four-poster or brass and coronet beds, along with deluxe bathrooms with toiletries.

Dining: Mrs. Stanbury once worked at the prestigious restaurant Le Gavroche in London, and she brings some of that experience to her dining table. She offers a menu based on French and modern English fare made with fresh local ingredients, including dishes such as Fillet of Devonshire steak with black peppers, mushrooms and a cream sauce, and roasted local duckling with orange sauce, fresh vegetables, and potatoes. For dessert, try the sticky toffee pudding with butterscotch sauce. A six-course dinner costs £25 ($42.50) for guests and £32.50 ($55.25) for everyone else.

8 Lynton-Lynmouth

206 miles W of London; 59 miles NW of Exeter

The north coast of Devon is particularly dramatic in Lynton, a village some 500 feet high, which is a good center for exploring the Doone Valley and the part of Exmoor that overflows into the shire from neighboring Somerset. The Valley of the Rocks, west of Lynton, offers the most panoramic scenery.

ESSENTIALS

GETTING THERE The town is rather remote, and the local tourist office recommends that you rent a car to get here. However, local daily trains from Exeter arrive at Barnstaple. For rail information, call ☎ **0345/484950.**

From Barnstaple, bus service is provided to Lynton at a frequency of one about every 2 hours. Call ☎ **01598/752225** for schedules.

If you're driving, take M4 west from London to the junction with M5, then head south to the junction with A39. Continue west on A39 to Lynton-Lynmouth.

VISITOR INFORMATION The **Tourist Information Centre** is at the Town Hall, Lee Road (☎ **01598/752225**), and is open Easter through October daily from 8:30am to 6pm and from November through Easter from 10am to 4pm Monday through Saturday.

SEEING THE SIGHTS

Lynton is linked to its twin, Lynmouth—located about 500 feet below—near the edge of the sea, by one of the most celebrated **railways** in Devon. The century-old train uses no electricity and no power. Instead, the railway covers the differences in distance and altitude by means of a complicated network of cables and pulleys, allowing cars to travel up and down the face of the rocky cliff. The length of the track is 862 feet with a gradient of 1 inch, which gives it a vertical height of approximately 500 feet. The two passenger cars are linked together with two steel cables, and the operation of the lift is on the counterbalance system, which is simply explained as a pair of scales where one side, when weighted by water ballast, pulls the other up. The train carries about 40 passengers at a time for 50p (85¢) adults, 30p (50¢) children. Trains depart daily from February to October, at 2- to 5-minute intervals, from 9am to 7pm. From November through March, the train is shut down.

The East Lyn and West Lyn rivers meet in Lynmouth, a popular resort with the British. For a **panoramic view** of the rugged coastline, you can walk on a path halfway between the towns that runs along the cliff. From Lynton, or rather from Hollerday Hill, you can look out onto Lynmouth Bay, Countisbury Foreland, and Woody Bays in the west. From Hollerday Hill, the view encompasses the Valley of Rocks, formed during the Ice Age by towering rock formations with names such as "The Devil's Cheesewring," and its centerpiece, Castle Rock, which is renowned for its resident herd of wild goats.

From Lynmouth harbor, there are regular boat trips along what the English have dubbed "The Heritage Coast" of North Devon. You can cruise past nesting colonies of razorbills, guillemots, dunlin, and kittiwakes, with the gulls soaring in the thermals by the highest sea cliffs in England.

Other activities in the locale include fishing, putting, bowls, tennis, pony trekking, and golf courses lying within a 20-mile radius. The Tourist Information Centre (see above) also keeps abreast of the various outdoor pursuits (which change seasonally) available at the time of your visit.

WHERE TO STAY & DINE

Bath Hotel. Sea Front, Lynmouth, N. Devon EX35 6EL. ☎ **01598/752238.** www.torslynmouth.co.uk. E-mail: bathhotel@torslynmouth.co.uk. 24 units. TV TEL. £58–£80 ($98.60–$136) double. Rates include English breakfast. AE, DC, MC, V. Closed Dec–Jan and weekdays in Nov and Feb.

Despite this hotel's functional appearance, its small, almost-obliterated core dates from the 16th century. Most of what a visitor will see, however, is a solidly built structure that dates from the 1880s, set in a prominent position between the busy coastal road and the towering cliffs. All but a few of the small and cozy bedrooms offer views over the water, and each has an adjoining private bath. Well-prepared fixed-price meals are served in the hotel's restaurant.

Hewitt's Hotel and Restaurant. The Hoe, N. Walk, Lynton, Devon EX35 6HJ. ☎ **01598/752293.** Fax 01598/752489. 8 units. TV TEL. £100–£140 ($170–$238) double; £70–£130 ($119–$221) serviced apartment. Rates include English breakfast. MC, V.

Hewitt's Hotel and Restaurant is named for Sir Thomas Hewitt, who helped construct the funicular railway that links the twin resorts. In the 1860s, he also built a home for himself, and today that place is one of the most successful small hotels in Lynton. Situated on some 27 acres, it opens onto the beautiful vistas of Lynmouth Bay (best enjoyed while seated on a sunny terrace). The old house is filled with architectural character, as exemplified by its grand staircase, time-mellowed paneling, antiques, and stained-glass windows. All rooms are comfortably appointed; some have private balconies. Many rooms have panoramic views across the channel to the Welsh coastline. All bedrooms are no-smoking. The hotel is "for all seasons" and has a country-house atmosphere. It's a perfect Agatha Christie set.

Dining: The quality of the bar lunches is far above average, and dinner is among the best served at the resort. In fact, since only guests can dine, it's reason enough to stay here. You won't be overcharged either; a 3-course fixed-price meal costs £28.50 ($48.45). A medley of British and continental dishes is served.

✪ **The Rising Sun Hotel.** The Harbour, Lynmouth, N. Devon EX35 6EQ. ☎ **01598/753223.** Fax 01598/753480. www.risingsunlynmouth.co.uk. E-mail: risingsunlynmouth@easynet.co.uk. 16 units, 1 cottage. TV TEL. £90–£140 ($153–$238) double; £140 ($238) Shelley's Cottage for 2. Rates include English breakfast. AE, DC, MC, V.

The Rising Sun Hotel is a thatched inn right at the end of the quay at the mouth of the Lyn River. You can bask in the wonder and warmth of an inn that has been in business for more than 600 years. Most of the rooms, with crazy levels and sloping ceilings, offer views of the water, the changing tides, and bobbing boats. The ceilings are low and the floorboards creak at this lovely old place. Behind the inn, halfway up the cliff, a tiny garden brightens with flowers in summer. The owner has refurbished the place and he has rooms available nearby in Shelley's Cottage, where the poet honeymooned in 1812. R. D. Blackmore wrote part of *Lorna Doone* while staying at the hotel. Two rooms have four-poster beds, and each unit comes with a coffeemaker plus a compact private bath that has either a shower stall or a tub and shower combination.

Dining: It's a delight to dine at the Rising Sun since everything is 101% British in the dining room, with its deeply set window and fireplace. See the original 14th-century fireplace in the bar.

Tors Hotel. Lynmouth, Lynton, N. Devon EX35 6NA. ☎ **01598/753236.** Fax 01598/752544. 35 units. TV TEL. £70–£110 ($119–$187) double. Rates include English breakfast. AE, DC, MC, V. Closed Jan–Feb.

Set high on a cliff, the Tors Hotel opens onto a view of the coastline and the bay. It was built in 1895 in the fashion of a Swiss château, with more than 40 gables, Tyrolean balconies jutting out to capture the sun (or the moon), and some 30 chimneys. The interior has been modernized, and much attention has been lavished on the comfortable bedrooms, five of which are large enough for families. There's a heated swimming pool.

WHERE TO DINE

The Greenhouse Restaurant. 6 Lee Rd., Lynton. ☎ **01598/753358.** Reservations required. Main courses £7.95–£16.95 ($13.50–$28.80). AE, MC, V. Feb–Apr and Oct–Nov Sat–Thurs 9am–9pm, May–Sept Sat–Thurs 9am–10pm. Closed Dec–Jan INTERNATIONAL.

Established in 1890 as a tearoom, this pink-and-gray Victorian restaurant perched atop a 500-foot cliff offers a panoramic view of the Bristol Channel through its all-glass front. A nautical theme carries through the restaurant, and the bar actually has a water wheel built into it. Owners Chris and Anjali Peters serve a large menu that's about as varied as you're likely to find anywhere—a result, they say, of the fact that he's part Indian and she's part Chinese. Whatever the reason, offerings range from British to American, Chinese, Indian, Italian, and beyond. Locals and tourists alike appreciate the results and flock here to dine on main courses like the popular prawn *jalsrezi* (succulent shrimp in a spicy, medium-hot curry sauce); fresh local trout with almonds and herbs; vegetable moussaka; or a 12-ounce chicken breast in cheese-and-ham sauce. Many dishes are made with fresh local seafood, and there are more than a dozen vegetarian choices. If you're in the mood for something lighter, you can choose from several salads, soups, and sandwiches.

Cornwall 10

The ancient duchy of Cornwall is in the extreme southwestern part of England, often called "the toe." This peninsula is a virtual island—culturally if not geographically. Encircled by coastline, it abounds in rugged cliffs, hidden bays, fishing villages, sandy beaches, and sheltered coves where smuggling was once rampant. Although many of the little seaports with hillside cottages resemble towns along the Mediterranean, Cornwall retains its own distinctive flavor.

The ancient land had its own language until about 250 years ago, and some of the old words (*pol* for pool, *tre* for house) still survive. The Cornish dialect is more easily understood by the Welsh than by those who speak the queen's English.

We suggest basing yourself at one of the smaller fishing villages, such as East or West Looe, Polperro, Mousehole, or Portloe, where you'll experience the true charm of the duchy. Many of the villages, such as St. Ives, are artists' colonies. Except for St. Ives and Port Isaac, some of the most interesting places lie on the southern coast, often called the Cornish Riviera. However, the north coast has its own peculiar charm as well. The majestic coastline is studded with fishing villages and hidden coves for swimming, with Penzance and St. Ives serving as the major meccas. A little further west is Land's End, where England actually comes to an end. There are also the Isles of Scilly, 27 miles off the Cornish coast, with only five islands inhabited out of more than 100. Here you'll find the Abbey Gardens of Tresco, 735 acres with 5,000 species of plants.

1 The Fishing Villages of Looe & Polperro

Looe: 264 miles SW of London; 20 miles W of Plymouth. Polperro: 271 miles SW of London; 6 miles SW of Looe; 26 miles W of Plymouth

The ancient twin towns of East and West Looe are connected by a seven-arched stone bridge that spans the river. Houses on the hills are stacked one on top of the other in terrace fashion. In each fishing village you can find good accommodations.

The old fishing village of Polperro is reached by a steep descent from the top of a hill from the main road leading to Polperro. You can take the 4½-mile cliff walk from Looe to Polperro, but the less adventurous will want to drive. However, in July and August you're not allowed to take cars into town unless you have a hotel reservation, in order to prevent traffic bottlenecks. There's a large parking area, which charges according to the length of your stay. For those unable to walk, a horse-drawn bus will take visitors to the town center.

Fishing and sailing are two of the major sports in the area, and the sandy coves, as well as **East Looe Beach,** are spots for sea bathing. Beyond the towns are cliff paths and chalky downs worth a ramble. Looe is noted for its shark fishing, but you may prefer simply walking the narrow, crooked medieval streets of East Looe, with its old harbor and 17th-century guildhall.

Polperro is one of the handsomest villages in Cornwall, and parts of it hark back to the 17th century. The village is surrounded by cliffs.

ESSENTIALS

GETTING THERE Daily trains run from Plymouth to Looe, and rail connections can also be made from Exeter (Devon) and Bristol (Avon). Most visitors drive to Polperro, but the nearest main-line station is at Liskeard, less than 4 hours from London's Paddington Station, with a branch line to Looe. Taxis meet incoming trains to take visitors to the various little villages in the area. For rail information in the area, call ☎ **0345/484950.**

Local bus companies have various routings from Plymouth into Looe. Ask at the Tourist Information Centre in Plymouth for a schedule (see chapter 9). You can take a local bus to Polperro from Liskeard or Looe.

If you're driving to Looe from Plymouth, take A38 west, then B3253. To get to Polperro, follow A387 southwest from Looe.

VISITOR INFORMATION The **Tourist Information Centre** is at the Guildhall, Fore Street (☎ **01503/262072**), and is open in summer only, daily from 10am to 2pm, and in winter on Saturdays only from 10am to 2pm.

WHERE TO STAY & DINE IN & AROUND LOOE

Commonwood House and Cottages. St. Martin's Rd. (the main Plymouth-Looe rd., B3253), E. Looe, Cornwall PL13 1LP. ☎ **01503/262929.** Fax 01503/262632. www.commonwood.co.uk. E-mail: commonwood@compuserve.com. 11 units, 8 cottages. TV TEL. £64–£76 ($108.80–$129.20) double; £240–£715 ($408–$1,215.50) cottage per week. Rates include English breakfast. AE, MC, V. Closed Christmas (except for cottages).

A family operated, country-house hotel on the edge of town at the entrance to Looe, it's about a 5-minute walk from the harbor and the center of the resort. Commonwood Manor stands on a wooded hillside surrounded by 6 acres of private woodlands overlooking the Looe River Valley. Units are spacious and fitted with soft twin or king-size beds. Rooms have beverage makers, hair dryers, and small bathrooms, usually with a tub and shower combination. Guests can also enjoy a dip in the heated swimming pool. The meals are good, prepared with fresh ingredients.

Fieldhead Hotel. Portuan Rd., Hannafore, W. Looe, Cornwall PL13 2DR. ☎ **01503/262689.** Fax 01503/264114. www.chycor.co.uk/fieldhead. E-mail: field.head@virgin.net. 14 units. TV TEL. £64–£85 ($108.80–$144.50) double. Rates include English breakfast. AE, MC, V.

The Fieldhead, originally built in 1896 as a private home, is now one of the area's best hotels. Commanding a view of the sea, it is situated on 2 acres of gardens, with a heated outdoor swimming pool. The rooms have a high standard of traditional furnishings and are continually maintained, with beverage makers in every room. Rooms, often medium in size but some are spacious, are warm and inviting, most of them opening onto panoramic views of St. George's Island and the bay. Each has a compact private bath. Two rooms are large enough for families. You'll also find views of the bay

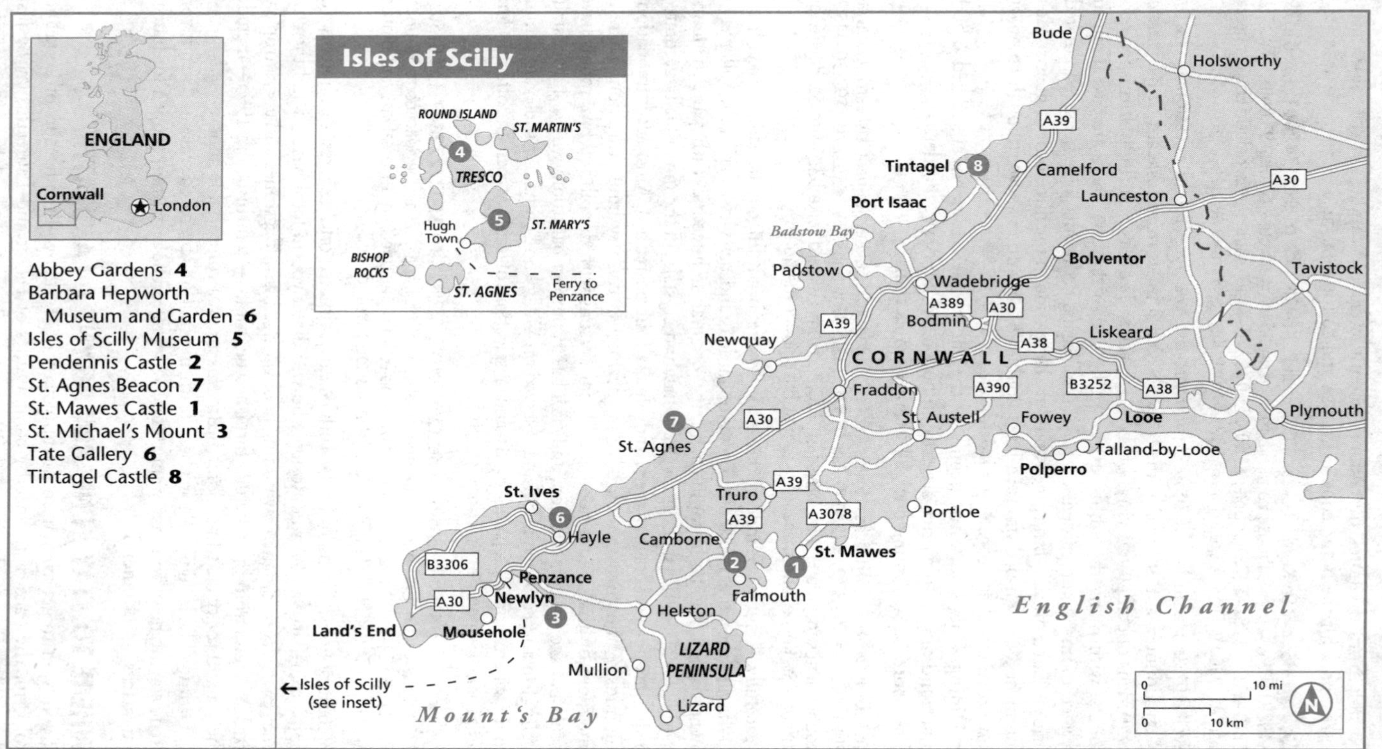
ENGLAND
Cornwall
London
Abbey Gardens 4
Barbara Hepworth Museum and Garden 6
Isles of Scilly Museum 5
Pendennis Castle 2
St. Agnes Beacon 7
St. Mawes Castle 1
St. Michael's Mount 3
Tate Gallery 6
Tintagel Castle 8
Isles of Scilly
ROUND ISLAND
ST. MARTIN'S
TRESCO
Hugh Town
ST. MARY'S
BISHOP ROCKS
ST. AGNES
Ferry to Penzance
Bude
Holsworthy
A39
Tintagel
Camelford
A30
Launceston
Port Isaac
Badstow Bay
Bolventor
Padstow
Wadebridge
Tavistock
A389
A30
Bodmin
A39
Newquay
Liskeard
A38
CORNWALL
Fraddon
A390
B3252
A38
Plymouth
St. Austell
Fowey
Looe
A30
St. Agnes
Talland-by-Looe
Polperro
A39
Truro
St. Ives
A3078
Portloe
A39
Hayle
Camborne
St. Mawes
B3306
Penzance
Falmouth
A30
Newlyn
Helston
English Channel
Land's End
Mousehole
LIZARD PENINSULA
Mullion
Isles of Scilly (see inset)
Lizard
Mount's Bay
0
10 mi
0
10 km

possible from the hotel's restaurant, where flowers and candles on the tables add a festive note for the home-cooked English and continental cuisine.

✪ **Well House.** St. Keyne, Liskeard, Cornwall PL14 4RN. ☎ **01579/342001.** Fax 01579/ 343891. www.thewellhouse.co.uk. E-mail: enquiries@wellhouse.co.uk. 9 units. TV TEL. £110–£160 ($187–$272) double; £160–£200 ($272–$340) suite. Rates include English breakfast. AE, MC, V. From Liskeard, take B3254 to St. Keyne, 3 miles away.

Well House is another of those *restaurants avec chambres* found occasionally in the West Country, and it's one of the best. Located 3 miles from Liskeard, it has 5 acres of gardens opening onto vistas of the Looe Valley. It offers beautifully furnished bedrooms, with many thoughtful extras, such as fresh flowers. There are two beautiful terrace rooms at the garden level. All the elegant bedrooms have been redecorated; price is based on size, but some rooms are large enough for three or four guests. Most rooms have a twin bed or else a large double. All bathrooms, even though compact, have adequate shelf space and a hair dryer.

Dining: Guests flock here mainly for the fine cuisine. Set menus are offered at both lunch and dinner; the price depends on how many courses you order.

Amenities: Swimming pool, all-weather tennis court.

The Old Rectory Country House Hotel. Duloe Rd., St. Keyne, near Liskeard, Cornwall PL14 4RL. ☎ **01579/342617.** Fax 01579/342293. 8 units. TV. £55–£70 ($93.50–$119) double. Rates include English breakfast. MC, V. From Liskeard, take B3254 to St. Keyne, go through St. Keyne, and make a left turn at the sign for the hotel.

Peacefully secluded 5 miles from Looe in the beautiful countryside of southeast Cornwall, the hotel overlooks 3 acres of gardens and has views across the valley. The owners' high standards complement the original architecture with paneled doors, marble fireplaces, Persian rugs, velvet sofas, and crystal. All the individually decorated bedrooms have beverage makers, and often a four-poster bed. Most accommodations are midsize and cozily comfortable in the English country house tradition. There is one room on the ground floor suitable for persons with disabilities. Five rooms have a tub and shower combination, and each has a compact bathroom with a shower stall.

English and continental cuisine is served on Wedgwood china in the elegant dining room where home-prepared meals and a selection of table wines are offered. The restaurant is open only to hotel guests.

Talland Bay Hotel. Talland-by-Looe, Cornwall PL13 2JB. ☎ **01503/272667.** Fax 01503/ 272940. www.smoothhound.co.uk/hotels/tallandb.html. E-mail: tallandbay@aol.com. 19 units. TV TEL. £124–£192 ($210.80–$326.40) double. Rates include English breakfast and dinner. AE, DC, MC, V. Closed Jan. Take A387 4 miles southwest of Looe.

A country house dating from the 16th century, situated on 2½ acres, this hotel is the domain of Barry and Annie Rosier, who will direct you to local beaches and the croquet lawn. Its rectangular swimming pool is ringed with flagstones and a semitropical garden. Views from the tastefully furnished bedrooms—refurbished in 1995—include the sea and rocky coastline. Some bedrooms are in a comfortable annex.

Dining: The food is the area's best, featuring skillfully prepared seafood. Even if you aren't staying here, you may want to reserve a table. The restaurant is open for lunch, bar snacks, and dinner daily.

WHERE TO STAY IN NEARBY PELYNT & LANREATH

If you want to get away from the busy activity of the two little harbors of Looe and Polperro, the pace of the nearby communities of Pelynt and Lanreath may be just right. The sleepy little village of Pelynt is just 3 miles north of Polperro. Peaceful

Lanreath lies just 6 miles away from Polperro off the road to West Looe. Most visitors take a car or taxi from the Looe train station. The two places listed here rank among England's major inns of character.

Jubilee Inn. Jubilee Hill, Pelynt (4 miles from Looe, 3 miles from Polperro), Cornwall PL13 2JZ. ☎ **01503/220312.** Fax 01503/220920. E-mail:rickard@jubileeinn.freeserve.co.uk 12 units. TV TEL. £65 ($110.50) double. Rates include English breakfast. MC, V.

Built in the 16th century, this inn takes its name from Queen Victoria's Jubilee celebration, when it underwent restoration. It's a comment on, rather than a monument to, the past. A glass-enclosed circular staircase, built to serve as a combined tower and hothouse, takes you to the bedrooms. All but the three newest rooms have excellent 19th-century furnishings. Most rooms are mid-size, although two are large enough for families, and include a hair dryer.

The dining room is elegantly Victorian, with mahogany chairs and tables. Vegetables come fresh from the inn's own garden. Both lunch and dinner are served in the bar or in the dignified dining room.

✪ **The Punch Bowl Inn.** Lanreath, near Looe, Cornwall PL13 2NX. ☎ **01503/220218.** Fax 01503/220788. 18 units. TV. £45–£75 ($76.50–$127.50) double. Rates include English breakfast. MC, V. From Polperro, take B3359 north.

First licensed in 1620, the Punch Bowl has since served as a courthouse, coaching inn, and rendezvous for smugglers. Today its old fireplaces and high-backed settees, as well as its bedrooms (some with four-posters), provide hospitality. Many bedrooms are quite small, although they come in various shapes and sizes, each with a small, compact bath fitted with a shower stall and adequate shelf space. There's a modern lounge and a TV room.

Even if you're not stopping over, you may sample the fare or drinks in one of the kitchens (actually bars—they're among the few "kitchens" licensed in Britain as "bars"). In the Stable Restaurant, with its Tudor beams, you order dinner from a menu that includes everything from a bowl of soup to steak.

WHERE TO DINE IN POLPERRO

The Kitchen. Fish na Bridge. ☎ **01503/272780.** Reservations required. Main courses £11–£16 ($18.70–$27.20). MC, V. Tues–Sun 7–9:30pm. Closed Oct–Easter. SEAFOOD.

This pink cottage about halfway down to the harbor from the parking area was once a wagon-builder's shop; it's now a restaurant offering good English cooking, with everything homemade from fresh ingredients. The menu changes seasonally and prominently features local fresh fish. Typical dishes include Fowey sea trout with lemon-and-herb butter and breast of duckling with blueberry-and-Drambuie sauce. Many vegetarian dishes are offered as main courses.

Nelson's Restaurant. Saxon Bridge. ☎ **01503/272366.** Reservations advised. Main courses £13.95–£16.50 ($23.70–$28.05); 3-course table d'hôte lunch or dinner £13 ($22.10); gourmet table d'hôte £25 ($42.50). AE, MC, V. Wed–Fri and Sun noon–1:45pm; Tues–Sun 7–9:45pm. Closed mid-Jan to mid-Feb. SEAFOOD.

Situated in the lower reaches of Polperro, near the spot where the local river meets the sea, this is the only structure in town specifically built as a restaurant. It features succulent preparations of regional fish and shellfish that arrive fresh from local fishing boats. The menu changes daily, but usually includes fresh crab, Dover sole, fresh lobster, and many other exotic fish. Fresh meat, poultry, and game, all from local suppliers, are also available, and are prepared exceedingly well. There's also a lower deck featuring a cafe-bar and bistro. A comprehensive wine list boasts some fine vintages.

2 St. Mawes

300 miles SW of London; 2 miles E of Falmouth; 18 miles S of Truro

Overlooking the mouth of the Fal River, St. Mawes seems like a port on the French Riviera: It's sheltered from northern winds, and subtropical plants can grow here. From the town quay, you can take a boat to Frenchman's Creek and Helford River, as well as other places. St. Mawes is noted for its sailing, boating, fishing, and yachting, and half a dozen sandy coves lie within a 15-minute drive from the port. The town, built on the Roseland Peninsula, makes for interesting walks because of its colorful cottages and sheltered harbor.

GETTING THERE

Trains leave London's Paddington Station for Truro several times a day. The trip takes 4½ hours. For rail schedules and information, call ☎ **0345/484950.** Passengers transfer at Truro to one of the two buses that make the 45-minute bus trip from Truro to St. Mawes. It's much easier to take a taxi from either Truro or, even better, from the village of St. Austell, which is the train stop before Truro.

Buses depart from London's Victoria Coach Station several times a day for Truro. The bus takes 6 hours. For bus schedules and more information, call ☎ **0990/808080.**

If you're driving, to reach St. Mawes, turn left off A390 (the main road along the southern coast of Cornwall), at a junction 4 miles past St. Austell, onto the Tregony road, which will take you into St. Mawes.

A ferry travels to St. Mawes from both Falmouth and Truro, but schedules are erratic, varying with the tides and the weather conditions.

WHERE TO STAY & DINE

✪ **Hotel Tresanton.** St. Mawes, Cornwall TR2 5DR. ☎ **01326/270055.** Fax 01326/270053. E-mail: infor@tresanton.com. 26 units. TV TEL. £180–£250 ($306–$425) double. Rates include English breakfast. AE, MC, V.

Laura Ashley and the designer of an ocean liner must have combined talents to create this country house hotel, which lies above the sea overlooking the fishing harbor. Tresanto has quickly replaced Idle Rocks and Rising Sun as the premier address of town. The whole place casts an aura of a chic house party, 1930s style. A glamorous hotel, Tresanto offers a combination of beautiful old and new furnishings in its spacious, airy bedrooms. The views from the bedrooms are among the most panoramic along the coast, which you'll want to explore on long walks above *Rebecca*-like cliffs. The preferred units are numbers 22 through 27, each with its own terrace overlooking the churning waters.

The hotel offers a large front terrace, which has exceptional nighttime views of the lights in the twinkling harbor, and a 50-seat movie theater where you can watch films on a rainy day, and the staff will even serve you popcorn. As if all this weren't enough, the hotel has hired Barry Zomfrillo, who worked with Marco Pierre White (London's greatest chef) to spark up the tastebuds of St. Mawes. This master chef uses the finest seafood in the area along with the best of seasonal ingredients.

The Idle Rocks. Tredenham Rd., St. Mawes, Cornwall TR2 5AN. ☎ **01326/270771.** Fax 01326/270062. E-mail: idlerocks@talk21.com. 24 units. £90–£180 ($153–$306) double. Rates include half board. AE, MC, V. Parking available in the town parking lot; cost will be refunded.

The best place to stay is this solid old building, right on the seawall, sporting gaily colored umbrellas and tables all along the terrace. Water laps at the wall, and the site

Trekking the Cornish Coast

Much of Cornwall is an evocatively barren landscape, composed of gray rocks, weathered headlands jutting seaward, and very few trees. The weather alternates between bright sunshine and the impenetrable fogs for which the English Channel is famous.

The land and seascapes provide a scenic backdrop for hiking around the Cornish peninsula's coastline. The government maintains a clearly signposted coastal path more than 600 miles long that skirts the edge of the sea, following the tortured coastline from Minehead (in Somerset, near Dunster) to Poole (in Dorset, near Bournemouth). En route, the path crosses some of the least developed regions of southern England, including hundreds of acres of privately owned land as well as the northern border of the Exmoor National Park. Throughout, there is a sense of ancient Celtic mysticism and existential loneliness. Low-lying gorse, lichens, and heathers characterize the vegetation. In marked contrast to the windblown uplands, verdant subtropical vegetation grows in the tidal estuaries of the Fowey, Fal, Helford, and Tamar rivers.

Your options for exploring the coasts of Cornwall, Devon, and Dorset are numerous. It's a full 4 to 6 weeks of hard trekking to do the whole thing, though most people just pick a short section for a day hike. Although the route is sometimes arduous, no special equipment other than sturdy shoes, good stamina, and waterproof clothing is required.

You may also want to pick up a locally researched and annually revised book: The South West Way Association's *The Complete Guide to the South West Coast Path—Great Britain's Longest Trail.* This book divides the 600-mile coast path into manageable segments, rates them for degrees of difficulty, and contains a comprehensive accommodations section with addresses of pubs, bed-and-breakfasts, inns, hotels, and campsites en route. The book can be ordered from the **South West Way Association,** 1 Orchard Dr., Kingskerswell, Newton Abbot, Devon, England TQ12 5DG (☎ and fax **01752/896237**), or at **Windlestraw,** Penquit, Ermington, Devon, England PL21 0LU (☎ **0183/873061**), at a cost of £8 ($13.60) including postage.

The loneliness of the Cornish moors could be marred by hundreds of other people with exactly the same idea during Britain's school holidays. If possible, schedule your visit for relatively quiet periods, and remember that the weather between late October and early May is rainy, foggy, and windy—romantic, but no fun for hiking.

opens onto views over the river and the constant traffic of sailing boats and dinghies. Most rooms have sea or river views, and they're equipped with central heating, beverage makers, intercoms, and compact baths. The 17 units in the main hotel building charge higher rates. Rooms range in size from small to medium, although those in the nearby Bohella House (an annex) are more spacious. Four rooms tout balconies and four-poster beds, and six rooms are large enough for families.

Dining/Diversions: The bar serves tasty lunch snacks, including fresh seafood caught locally.

Amenities: Golf is available at the Truro Golf Club at reduced greens fees. There's also room service from 8am to 11pm, concierge, and baby-sitting.

The Rising Sun. The Square, St. Mawes, Cornwall TR2 5DJ. ☎ **01326/270233.** Fax 01326/270198. 9 units. TV TEL. From £30–£100 ($51–$170) double. Rates include English breakfast. MC, V.

Converted from four 17th-century fishing cottages, with a flower-draped flagstone terrace out front, this colorful seafront inn in the center of town exudes charm. Known as one of Cornwall's best inns, it offers recently refurbished bedrooms that are functional and cozy, each with tea- and coffeemaker. The small to midsize bedrooms are graced with specially commissioned watercolors by local artists. Each small bathroom includes adequate shelf space.

Dining/Diversions: Owned by the St. Austell Breweries, the inn houses one of St. Mawes's busiest pubs on its ground floor. This is a rustically appealing place with stone accents, a fireplace, and bar snacks. The inn's restaurant—a dignified room adjacent to the pub—has a reputation for good food, and you might want to try it even if you don't stay at the hotel.

EN ROUTE TO PENZANCE: THE LIZARD PENINSULA

The southernmost point in England is the Lizard, a remarkable spot with jagged rocks reaching out into the sea where cormorants and gulls fish. The Lizard is the lesser known of Cornwall's two peninsulas—most people are more familiar with Land's End. The Lizard has great beaches, small villages, coastal walks, and craft studios. Some of the best beaches are at the coves at Poldhu and Kynance.

Some folks claim that the Lizard is "the most Cornish place" in Cornwall. It was the last place where the Cornish language was spoken before the language was modernized. Most of the places to stay and eat are in the village of Mullion.

To get here, driving from Falmouth, take A395 west to the junction with A3083, which you take south to Lizard Point.

3 Penzance

280 miles SW of London; 77 miles SW of Plymouth

This little harbor town, which Gilbert and Sullivan made famous, is at the end of the Cornish Riviera. It's noted for its moderate climate (it's one of the first towns in England to blossom with spring flowers), and for the summer throngs that descend for fishing, sailing, and swimming. Overlooking Mount's Bay, Penzance is graced in places with subtropical plants including palm trees.

Those characters in *The Pirates of Penzance* were not entirely fictional. The town was raided by Barbary pirates, destroyed in part by Cromwell's troops, sacked and burned by the Spaniards, and bombed by the Germans. In spite of its turbulent past, it offers tranquil resort living today.

The most westerly town in England, Penzance makes a good base for exploring Land's End, the Lizard peninsula, St. Michael's Mount, the old fishing ports and artists' colonies of St. Ives, Newlyn, Mousehole, and even the Isles of Scilly.

ESSENTIALS

GETTING THERE Ten express trains depart daily from Paddington Station in London for Penzance. The trip takes 5½ hours. Call ☎ **0345/484950.**

The **Rapide,** run by National Express from Victoria Coach Station in London (☎ **0990/808080**), costs £27 ($45.90) for the one-way trip from London, which takes about 8 hours. The buses have toilets and reclining seats, and a hostess dispenses coffee, tea, and sandwiches.

Drive southwest across Cornwall on A30 all the way to Penzance.

VISITOR INFORMATION The **Tourist Information Centre** is on Station Road (☎ **01736/362207**). It's open from the end of May to September, Monday to Friday from 9am to 5pm, Saturday from 9am to 4pm, and Sunday from 10am to 1pm; from October to May, hours are Monday to Friday from 9am to 5pm and Saturday from 10am to 1pm.

SEEING THE SIGHTS AROUND PENZANCE

✪ **Castle on St. Michael's Mount.** On St. Michael's Mount, Mount's Bay. ☎ **01736/710507.** Admission £4.40 ($7.50) adults, £2.20 ($3.75) children. Apr–Oct Mon–Fri 10:30am–4:45pm (open weekends in summer); Nov–Mar Mon, Wed, and Fri by conducted tour only, which leaves at 11am, noon, 2, and 3pm, weather and tide permitting. Bus: 20, 21, or 22 from Penzance to Marazion, the town opposite St. Michael's Mount. Parking £1 ($1.70).

Rising about 250 feet from the sea, St. Michael's Mount is topped by a part medieval, part 17th-century castle; it's 3 miles east of Penzance and is reached at low tide by a causeway. At high tide, the mount becomes an island, reached only by motor launch from Marazion. In winter, you can go over only when the causeway is dry.

A Benedictine monastery, the gift of Edward the Confessor, stood on this spot in the 11th century. The castle now has a collection of armor and antique furniture. There's a tea garden on the island, as well as a National Trust restaurant, both open in summer. The steps up to the castle are steep and rough, so wear sturdy shoes. To avoid disappointment, call the number listed above to check on the tides, especially during winter.

Minack Theatre. Porthcurno. ☎ **01736/810694.** Theater tickets £6.50 ($11.05) adults; £3.25 ($5.50) children; tour tickets £2.50 ($4.25) adults, £1.80 ($3.05) seniors, £1 ($1.70) children. Exhibition hall, Oct–Mar daily 10am–4pm; Apr–Sept 9:30am–5:30pm. Performances, end of May to mid-Sept, matinees Wed and Fri at 2pm, evening shows Mon–Fri at 8pm. Leave Penzance on A30 heading toward Land's End; after 3 miles, bear left onto B3283 and follow the signs to Porthcurno.

One of the most unusual theaters in southern England, this open-air amphitheater was cut from the side of a rocky Cornish hill near the village of Porthcurno, 9 miles southwest of Penzance. Its legendary creator was Rowena Cade, an arts enthusiast and noted eccentric, who began the theater after World War I by physically carting off much of the granite from her chosen hillside. On the premises, an exhibition hall showcases her life and accomplishments. She died a very old woman in the 1980s, confident of the enduring appeal of her theater to visitors from around the world.

Up to 750 visitors at a time can sit directly on grass- or rock-covered ledges, sometimes on cushions if they're available, within sight lines of both the actors and a sweeping view out over the ocean. Experienced theatergoers sometimes bring raincoats for protection against the occasional drizzle. Theatrical events are staged by repertory theater companies that travel throughout Britain, and are likely to include everything from Shakespeare to musical comedy.

WHERE TO STAY

✪ **Abbey Hotel.** Abbey St., Penzance, Cornwall TR18 4AR. ☎ **01736/366906.** Fax 01736/351163. www.abbey/hotel.co.uk. E-mail: glyn@abbeyhotel.fsnet.co.uk. 8 units. TV. £95–£150 ($161.50–$255) double; £150–£220 ($255–$374) suite. Rates include English breakfast. Dinner £24 ($40.80) per person extra. AE, MC, V.

This charming, small-scale hotel occupies a stone-sided house that was erected in 1660 on the site of a 12th-century abbey that was demolished by Henry VIII. It's located on a narrow side street on raised terraces that overlook the panorama of Penzance Harbour. Behind the hotel is a medieval walled garden that was part of the original abbey.

The bedrooms are stylishly furnished with English country-house flair. The hotel has been considerably upgraded, with new baths, showers, and beds. Rooms contain such extras as coffeemakers, and the bathrooms have a shower stall or else a tub and shower combination. The owners, Michael and Jean Cox, bring vitality, style, and charm to the hotel business. Mrs. Cox is the former international model Jean Shrimpton.

On the premises is a restaurant, where herbs from the garden flavor some of the food. Sample dinner dishes include homemade soups, mackerel pâté, fresh local fish, and roast joint. Everything is fresh and delicately cooked.

The Georgian House. 20 Chapel St., Penzance, Cornwall TR18 4AW. ☎ and fax **01736/365664.** www.theaa.co.uk/hotels. 11 units, 9 with bathroom. TV TEL. £38 ($64.60) double without bathroom, £42 ($71.40) double with bathroom. Rates include English breakfast. AE, MC, V.

This former home of the mayors of Penzance, reputedly haunted by the ghost of a Mrs. Baines who owned it hundreds of years ago, has been completely renovated into an intimate hotel. The bright, cozy rooms all have hot- and cold-water basins, hair dryers, and tea- and coffeemakers. All the rooms are small to medium in size; most units contain a small private bath with a shower stall. Otherwise, the corridor baths are adequate. The Abbey is better, but this one is quite good too. The house is centrally heated, with a comfortable reading lounge, a licensed bar with a nautical motif, and an intimate dining room, where good Cornish meals are served from April through October.

Tarbert Hotel. 11–12 Clarence St., Penzance, Cornwall TR18 2NU. ☎ **01736/363758.** Fax 01736/331336. www.tarbert-hotel.co.uk. E-mail: reception@tarbert-hotel.co.uk. 12 units. TV TEL. £58–£70 ($98.60–$119) double. Rates include English breakfast. AE, MC, V. Closed Dec 23–Jan 26.

This dignified granite-and-stucco house lies about a 2-minute walk northwest of the town center. The rooms are small to mid-size, and some retain their original high ceilings and elaborate cove moldings. Each is equipped with a teamaking facility and comfortable furniture. Recent improvements include a new reception area, a completely refurbished bar and lounge, and a sun patio.

A restaurant, specializing in fresh seafood brought in by local fishing boats, serves fixed-price evening meals every night. During the day, bar lunches are served to residents, and there's also a licensed bar with an extensive wine list and draft beer. A sample menu item is swordfish steak with a sun-dried tomato and black olive sauce.

WHERE TO DINE

The Nelson Bar, in the Union Hotel on Chapel Street in Penzance (☎ **01736/362319**), is known for its robust pub grub and collection of Nelsoniana. It's the spot where the admiral's death at Trafalgar was first revealed to the English people. Lunch and dinner are served daily.

Harris's Restaurant. 46 New St. ☎ **01736/364408.** Reservations recommended. Main courses £14.50–£19.50 ($24.65–$33.15). AE, MC, V. Tues–Sat noon–2pm; Tues–Sun 7–10pm. Closed 3 weeks in winter. FRENCH/ENGLISH.

Down a narrow cobblestone street off Market Jew Street, this warm, candlelit place has a relaxed atmosphere and is your best bet for a meal. A beacon of light against the culinary bleakness of Penzance, Harris's offers dining in two small rooms. The seasonally adjusted menu emphasizes local produce, including seafood and game. Dishes might include roast wild venison with caraway seeds, or John Dory in a bed of fresh spinach with a white wine and saffron sauce.

✪ **The Turk's Head.** 49 Chapel St. ☎ **01736/363093.** Main courses £5.95–£10 ($10.10–$17); bar snacks £2.50–£5 ($4.25–$8.50). AE, MC, V. Daily 11am–3pm and 5:30–11pm (bar daily 11am–3pm and 5:30–11pm). From the rail station, turn left just past Lloyd's Bank. ENGLISH.

Dating from 1233, this inn is reputed to be the oldest in Penzance. It serves the finest food of any pub in town. In summer, drinkers overflow into the garden. Inside, the inn is decorated in a mellow style, as befits its age, with flatirons and other artifacts hanging from its timeworn beams. Meals include fishermen's pie, local seafood, and chicken curry, and prime quality steaks including rib eye. See the chalkboards for the daily specials.

4 The Isles of Scilly

27 miles WSW of Land's End

Several miles off the Cornish coast, the ✪ **Scilly Isles** are warmed by the Gulf Stream to the point where semitropical plants thrive. In some winters they never see signs of frost. They're the first landfall most oceangoing passengers see on journeys from North America. Charles, the Prince of Wales (who is the duke of Cornwall as well) makes regular visits to Scilly, which he regards as a jewel in the duchy of Cornwall's crown.

There are five inhabited and more than 100 uninhabited islands in the group. Some are only a few square miles, whereas others, such as the largest, St. Mary's, encompass some 30 square miles. Three of these islands—Tresco, St. Mary's, and St. Agnes—attract visitors from the mainland. Early flowers are the main export and tourism is the main industry.

The Isles of Scilly figured prominently in the myths and legends of the ancient Greeks and Romans, and in Celtic legend they were inhabited entirely by holy men. There are more ancient burial mounds on these islands than there are anywhere else in southern England, and artifacts have clearly established that people lived here more than 4,000 years ago. Today there's little left of this long history for the visitor to see.

St. Mary's is the capital, with about seven-eighths of the total population of all the islands, and it's here that the ship from the mainland docks at Hugh Town. However, if you'd like to make this a day visit, we recommend the helicopter flight from Penzance to Tresco, the neighboring island, where you can enjoy a day's walk through 735 acres, mostly occupied by the Abbey Gardens.

ESSENTIALS

GETTING THERE You can fly by plane or helicopter. **Isles of Scilly Skybus Ltd.** (☎ **01736/785220**) operates two to eight flights per day, depending on the season, between Penzance's Land's End Airport and Hugh Town on St. Mary's Island. Flight time on the eight-passenger fixed-wing planes is 20 minutes each way. The round-trip fare is £57 ($96.90) for same-day return, and £59 ($100.30) if you plan to stay overnight.

There's also a helicopter service maintained by **British International Helicopters** at the Penzance Heliport Eastern Green (☎ **01736/363871** for recorded information), which operates, weather permitting, up to 26 helicopter flights, Monday through Saturday, between Penzance, St. Mary's, and Tresco. Flight time is 20 minutes from Penzance to either island. A same-day round-trip fare is £64 ($108.80), rising £69 to £96 ($117.30 to $163.20) if you spend a night or more on the island. A bus, whose timing coincides with the departure of each helicopter flight, runs to the heliport from the railway station in Penzance for a cost of £1 ($1.70) per person each way.

The rail line ends in Penzance (see "Getting There," in section 3, above).

Slower, but more cadenced and comtemplative, is a ship leaving from the **Isles of Scilly Travel Centre,** on Quay Street in Penzance (tel. **0845/7105555** toll free from anywhere in the UK, or 01736/362009). It departs at least 6 days a week between April and October, requiring 2 hours and 40 minutes for the segment between Penzance and Hugh Town, with an additional 20 or so minutes for the second leg of the trip, which is from hugh Town to Tresco. It departs Monday to Friday at 9:15am, returning from St. Mary's at 4:30pm. Saturday departures usually follow the Monday to Friday timing, but not always, as the managers sometimes add a second Saturday sailing to accommodate weekend holidaymakers, depending on the season. Between November and March, service is extremely limited, sometimes nonexistent. Depending on the time of year, a same-day round-trip ticket from Penzance to St. Mary's costs £30 to £34 ($51 to $57.80) for adults and £15 to £17 ($25.50 to $28.90) for children 15 and under. The continuation of the trip (the segment from St. Mary's to Tresco) costs an additional £6 to £8 ($10.20 to $13.60) for adults and £3 to £4 ($5.10 to $6.80) for children, depending on the season.

VISITOR INFORMATION **St. Mary's Tourist Information Office** is at Porthcressa Bank, St. Mary's (☎ **01720/422536**). It's open April through October Monday to Saturday from 8:30am to 6pm; Sunday 10am to 1pm; November through March, Monday to Friday from 8:30am to 5pm and Saturday from 10am to 1pm.

For information about Tresco's boat schedules, possible changes in hours and prices at the Abbey Gardens, and other matters, call ☎ **01720/422849.**

TRESCO

No cars or motorbikes are allowed on Tresco, but bikes can be rented by the day; the hotels use a special wagon towed by a farm tractor to transport guests and luggage from the harbor.

For the best selections of island crafts, visit **Phoenix,** Portmellon Ind Est, St. Mary's (☎ **01720/422900**). At this studio, you can watch original artifacts being made into stained glass. The shops also sell a wide assortment of gifts, including jewelry and leaded weights.

The **Isles of Scilly Perfumery,** Porthloo Studios, St. Mary's (☎ **01720/423304**), a 10-minute walk from the center of Hugh Town, is packed with intriguing gifts made from plants grown on the isles—everything from a delicate shell-shaped soap to fine fragrances, cosmetics, potpourri, and other accessories.

✪ **Abbey Gardens.** ☎ **01720/422849.** Admission £5.50 ($9.35) adults; free for children 13 and under. Daily 10am–4pm.

The gardens are the most outstanding feature of Tresco, started by Augustus Smith in the mid-1830s. When he began his work, the area was a barren hillside, a fact visitors now find hard to believe.

The gardens are a nature-lover's dream, with more than 5,000 species of plants from 100 different countries. The old abbey, or priory, now in ruins, was allegedly founded by Benedictine monks in the 11th century, although some historians date it from A.D. 964. Of special interest in the gardens is Valhalla, a collection of nearly 60 figure-heads from ships wrecked around the islands; the gaily painted figures from the past have a rather eerie quality, each one a ghost with a different story to tell.

After a visit to the gardens, take a walk through the fields, along paths, and across dunes thick with heather. Flowers, birds, shells, and fish are abundant. Birds are so fearless that they'll land within a foot or so of you and feed happily.

WHERE TO STAY & DINE

✪ **Island Hotel Tresco.** Old Grimsby, Tresco, Isles of Scilly, Cornwall TR24 0PU. ☎ **01720/422883.** Fax 01720/423008. E-mail: islandhotel@tresco.co.uk. 48 units. TV TEL. £88–£130 ($149.60–$221) per person double; £130–£220 ($221–$374) per person suite. Rates include breakfast and dinner. AE, MC, V. Closed Nov to early Mar.

This is the finest hotel in the Scillies, located at Old Grimsby near the northeastern shore of Tresco. It was established in 1960 when a late–19th-century stone cottage was enlarged with conservatory-style windows and a series of long and low extensions. Today, the plant-filled interior feels almost Caribbean. Some rooms overlook the sea, others face inland. All are comfortably furnished with easy chairs, storage spaces, beverage makers, and hair dryers. Bedrooms range from medium to spacious, and nearly two dozen of them are large enough for families. The hotel is noted for its subtropical garden.

Dining: Nonguests can drop by for dinner; expect to spend about £34 ($57.80) for a five-course evening meal.

New Inn. Tresco, Isles of Scilly, Cornwall TR24 0QQ. ☎ **01720/422844.** Fax 01720/423200. 14 units. TV TEL. £57–£89 ($96.90–$151.30) per person double. Rates include half board. MC, V.

Composed of an interconnected row of 19th-century fisher's cottages and shops, the New Inn is situated at the center of the island, beside its unnamed main road. The rooms are tastefully decorated in a modern style in blue and creamy yellow hues; each features matching twin or double beds, and tea- and coffeemakers. The more expensive units offer sea views.

Dining/Diversions: The place is known for its pub; it offers an outdoor area for those who'd like to picnic or drink a glass of ale alfresco. Inside, the bar is a meeting place for locals and visitors alike. Lunch snacks are available, as are fixed-price dinners served nightly for £21.50 ($36.55). The pictures in the bar show many of the ships that sank or foundered around the islands in the past, as well as some of the gigs used in pilotage, rescue, smuggling, and pillage.

Amenities: Heated outdoor swimming pool.

ST. MARY'S

To get around St. Mary's, cars are available but hardly necessary. The **Island Bus Service** charges £2 ($3.40) from one island point to another; children ride for half fare.

Bicycles are one of the most practical means of transport. **Buccabu Bicycle Rentals,** Porthcressa, St. Mary's (☎ and fax **01720/422289**), is the only bike-rental outfit. They stock "shopper's cycles" with three speeds, "hybrid" bikes with 6 to 12 speeds, and 18-speed mountain bikes. All are available at prices that range from £4 to £6 ($6.80 to $10.20) daily. A sum of £10 ($17) is required for a deposit.

Isles of Scilly Museum, on Church Street in St. Mary's (☎ **01720/422337**), illustrates the history of the Scillies from 2500 B.C., with drawings, artifacts from wrecked ships, and assorted relics discovered on the islands. A locally themed exhibit changes annually. It's open Easter to October, Monday to Saturday from 10am to noon and 1:30 to 4:30pm, and June to September, also daily from 7:30 to 9pm; off-season, only on Wednesday from 2 to 4pm. Admission is £1 ($1.70) for adults and £.10 (15¢) for children.

Where to Stay

Carnwethers Country House. Pelistry Bay, St. Mary's, Isles of Scilly, Cornwall TR21 0NX. ☎ and fax **01720/422415.** 10 units. £45–£55 ($76.50–$93.50) per person. Rates include English breakfast and dinner. No credit cards. Closed Oct–Mar.

Pelistry Bay, a secluded part of St. Mary's Island northeast of the airport, has a well-sheltered sandy beach, and this modernized farmhouse stands here on top of a hill looking out to fields, beach, and the sea. You can walk at low tide across to the nearby uninhabited island of Tolls. The guest-house rooms are spotless, warm, and comfortable. Some of the beds are four-posters. The units also contain beverage makers and a hair dryer. The main lounge is divided into two parts, one is for conversation and reading, the other has a library filled with books about the island.

Dining/Diversions: Dinner, served at 6:30pm, includes fresh local produce and homegrown vegetables; a limited choice of traditional English fare is offered. Breakfast is a substantial meal, the marmalade being a particular pride of the house. There's also a well-stocked bar.

Amenities: The house has its own grounds with a croquet lawn, and a heated outdoor swimming pool operates from May through September. A sauna and a game room are also available.

Star Castle Hotel. The Garrison, St. Mary's, Isles of Scilly TR21 0JA. ☎ **01720/422317.** Fax 01720/422343. www.starcastlescilly.demon.co.uk. E-mail: recipt@starcastlescilly.demon.co.uk. 34 units. TV TEL. £63–£108 ($107.10–$183.60) per person. Rates include half board. MC, V (accepted only with 3% surcharge). Closed Nov to mid-Mar.

This hotel was originally built as a castle in 1593 to defend the Isles of Scilly against Spanish attacks in retaliation for the 1588 defeat of the armada. The hotel has views out to sea, as well as over the town and the harbor. The great kitchen has a huge fireplace where a whole ox could be roasted. A young Prince of Wales (later King Charles II) took shelter here in 1643 when he was being hunted by Cromwell and his parliamentary forces. In 1933, another Prince of Wales officiated at the opening of the castle as a hotel—the man who succeeded to the throne as King Edward VIII but was never crowned. The 18 rooms in the garden annex are extra large units opening directly onto the gardens. Eight double rooms and five single rooms are in the castle. The rooms in the castle are full of more character, including four-poster beds and beamed ceilings, although the garden apartments are more spacious and comfortable. Seventeen rooms are large enough for families.

Dining: Lunches tend to be simple pub-style platters, and orders are accepted in the cellar bar. Dinners are more elaborate, with most of the vegetables coming from the hotel's large gardens.

Amenities: There's a glass-covered, heated swimming pool, and the garden has many sheltered places for you to relax.

ST. AGNES

St. Agnes lies farther southwest than any other community in Britain and, luckily, remains relatively undiscovered. Much of the area is preserved by the Nature Conservancy Council. Since the main industries are flower farming and fishing, there is little pollution and visitors can enjoy crystal-clear waters that are ideal for snorkeling and diving. Little traffic moves on the single-track lanes crossing the island, and the curving sandbar between St. Agnes and its neighbor, the island of Gugh, is one of the best beaches in the archipelago. The coastline is diverse and a walker's paradise. A simple trail leads to any number of sandy coves, granite outcroppings, flower-studded heaths and meadows, even a freshwater pool. Sunsets are always romantic and are followed by a brilliant showcase of the night sky. This is a place of endless natural wonderment that is truly soothing.

A boat departs from the quay at St. Mary's every day at 10:15am, 12:15pm, and 2pm, requiring a 15- to 20-minute transfer to St. Agnes, for a round-trip charge of about £5.20 ($8.85). Boats return on a schedule determined by the tides, usually at 2:15 and again at 4:45pm. The day's transportation schedule is chalked onto a blackboard on the quay at St. Mary's daily. Schedules generally allow you to visit St. Agnes for the day. The boats are operated by two family-run companies: **Briar Boating** (☎ **01720/422886**) and **Hicks Boating** (☎ **01720/422541**).

WHERE TO STAY

Coastguards. St. Agnes, Isles of Scilly, Cornwall TR22 0PL. ☎ **01720/422373.** 3 units. £30–£32 ($51–$54.40) per person. Rates include half board. No credit cards. Closed last 2 weeks in Dec.

The home of Danny and Wendy Hick has excellent sea views from its location near St. Warna's Cove. One of their double rooms has two beds, and there are beverage makers in the rooms. Accommodations are in two adjacent and roomy cottages, and furnished simply but pleasantly with interesting objects. Rooms have a shower stall and housekeeping is excellent. There's no choice on the daily menu, but special diets are catered to if advance notice is given. The price of half board depends on whether you order a two- or four-course evening meal.

WHERE TO DINE

The Turks Head. St. Agnes, Isles of Scilly, Cornwall TR22 0PL. ☎ **01720/422434.** Main courses £4.50–£9 ($7.65–$15.30). AE, MC, V. Daily 10:30am–11pm. Pub Mon–Sat 11am–11pm, Sun noon–10:30pm. Nov–Mar call for times. ENGLISH.

In a solid-looking building that was originally constructed in the 1890s as a boathouse, this is the only pub on the island. Prominently located a few steps from the pier, it's run by John and Pauline Dart, who serve pub snacks and solid fare, including steaks and platters of local fish. The pub is the second building after the arrival point of the ferryboats from St. Mary's. There's also a twin-bedded room with shower for rent here, costing £26.50 ($45.05) per person.

5 Newlyn, Mousehole & Land's End

Newlyn: 1 mile S of Penzance; Mousehole: 3 miles S of Penzance, 2 miles S of Newlyn; Land's End: 9 miles W of Penzance

Reached by traveling through some of Cornwall's most beautiful countryside, Land's End is literally the end of Britain. The natural grandeur of the place has been somewhat marred by theme-park-type amusements, but the view of the sea crashing against rocks remains undiminished. If you want to stay in the area, you can find accommodations in either Newlyn or Mousehole, two lovely Cornish fishing villages. If you visit in July and August, you'll need reservations far in advance, as neither Newlyn nor Mousehole has enough bedrooms to accommodate the summer hordes.

GETTING THERE

From London, journey first to Penzance (see "Getting There," in section 3), then take a local bus for the rest of the journey (Bus A to Mousehole and Bus no. 1 to Land's End). There is frequent service throughout the day.

If you're driving from Penzance, take the B3315 south.

NEWLYN

From Penzance, a promenade leads to Newlyn, another fishing village of infinite charm on Mount's Bay. In fact, its much-painted harbor seems to have more fishing craft than that of Penzance. The late Stanhope Forbes founded an art school in Newlyn, and in the past few years the village has achieved a growing reputation for its artists' colony, attracting both serious painters and Sunday sketchers. From Penzance, the old fishing cottages and crooked lanes of Newlyn are reached by bus.

WHERE TO STAY & DINE

Higher Faugan Hotel. Chywoone Hill, Newlyn, Penzance, Cornwall TR18 5NS. ☎ **01736/362076.** Fax 01736/351648. 11 units. TV TEL. £65–£136 ($110.50–$231.20) double. Rates include English breakfast. Children under 12 stay free in parents' room. AE, DC, MC, V. Take B3315 3/4 mile south of Penzance.

The structure was built in 1904 by painter Alexander Stanhope Forbes, whose work is now in demand, as is that of his wife, Elizabeth Adela Forbes, and many other artists from the "Newlyn" school. The spacious building's granite walls, big windows, and steep roofs are surrounded by 10 acres of lawn, garden, and woodland, all of which can be covered on foot by adventurous visitors. The traditionally furnished rooms come in a variety of shapes and sizes, and most of them contain a double or twin bed. Extras include a beverage maker, and each room has a compact bath with a shower stall and a hair dryer.

Amenities include a heated outdoor swimming pool, a putting green, a hard tennis court, a billiards room, and a dining room serving beautifully prepared English and continental specialties.

MOUSEHOLE

The Cornish fishing village of Mousehole (pronounced Mou-sel) attracts hordes of tourists, who, fortunately, haven't changed it too much. The cottages still sit close to the harbor wall; the fishers still bring in the day's catch; the salts sit around smoking tobacco, talking about the good old days; and the lanes are as narrow as ever. About the most exciting thing to happen here was the arrival in the late 16th century of the Spanish galleons, whose sailors sacked and burned the village. In a sheltered cove of Mount's Bay, Mousehole today has developed as the nucleus of an artists' colony.

WHERE TO STAY & DINE IN THE AREA

Carn Du Hotel. Raginnis Hill, Mousehole, Cornwall TR19 6SS. ☎ and fax **01736/731233.** 7 units. TV. £50–£70 ($85–$119) double. Rates include English breakfast. AE, MC, V. Take B3315 from Newlyn past the village of Sheffield (1 1/2 miles) and bear left toward Castallack; after a few hundred yards, turn left to Mousehole, which is signposted; coming down the hill, the Carn Du is on the left facing the sea.

Twin bay windows gaze over the top of the village onto the harbor with its bobbing fishing vessels. The hotel's rooms (all doubles or twins) offer radios and much comfort. Five rooms were recently redecorated. Each unit comes with a beverage maker, and most units have a shower stall, although two come with a tub and shower combination. The owners will arrange sporting options for active vacationers, but won't mind if you prefer to sit and relax.

Moderately priced meals are straightforward and fresh, usually accompanied by a bottle of wine from the cellars. You can have a drink in one of the lounges.

Lamorna Cove Hotel. Lamorna Cove, Penzance, Cornwall TR19 6XH. ☎ **01736/731411.** 12 units. TV TEL. £39.50 ($67.15) per person. Rates include English breakfast. £59.50 ($101.15) per person with breakfast and dinner. AE, MC, V. Take a taxi from Penzance.

Situated near one of the most perfect coves in Cornwall, only 5 miles south of Penzance but seemingly inaccessible down a winding, narrow road, this hotel was skillfully terraced, after months of blasting, into a series of rocky ledges that drop down to the sea. The hotel offers a rocky garden that clings to the cliff sides and surrounds a small swimming pool and a sun terrace overlooking the sea. The cozy, small to mid-size bedrooms have sea views. Each is furnished in a lovely old-fashioned way. Accommodations have a beverage maker and a hair dryer. No smoking.

Dining: The dining room is in the old chapel, and a public lounge is furnished with comfortable chairs, centered around a wintertime log fire, with many pictures and antiques. Even if you don't stay at the hotel, stop in for one of its well-recommended, affordable meals or bar snacks.

The Lobster Pot Hotel and Restaurant. Mousehole, Cornwall TR19 6QX. ☎ **01736/731251.** Fax 01736/731140. 23 units. TV TEL. June–Sept £40–£50 ($68–$85) per person double. Feb–May and Oct–Dec £35–£45 ($59.50–$76.50) per person double. Rates include English breakfast. MC, V. Closed Jan. Open weekends only in Feb.

Tasteful, nostalgic, and charming, this little hotel is housed in four adjacent former fishers' cottages near the water's edge of Mousehole. In addition to the main hotel, guests are housed in Clipper House, Gull's Cry, or Harbour's Edge. Seven rooms open onto sea views across the harbor and Mount's Bay beyond. The comfortably furnished bedrooms include such amenities as tea- or coffeemakers, trouser presses, and hair dryers. The hotel has been upgraded so many times that poet Dylan Thomas wouldn't recognize the place (he stayed here in 1937 on his honeymoon). Each accommodation is fitted with a small compact bath with a shower stall. Families are especially welcome.

Dining: Even if you don't stay here, The Lobster Pot is one of the best dining choices in town. A fixed-price dinner costs £15.50 ($26.35), or you can order à la carte, especially if you want to partake of the chef's specialty, freshly caught lobster (when available). It can be prepared virtually any way you want: steamed, grilled, Newburg, or Thermidor.

The Ship Inn. S. Cliff, Mousehole, Penzance, Cornwall TR19 6QX. ☎ **01736/731234.** 3 units. TV. £50 ($85) double. Rates include English breakfast. No credit cards.

This charming pub is located on the harbor in this fishing village. The exterior has a stone facade and the interior has retained much of the original rustic charm with its black beams and paneling, granite floors, built-in wall benches, and, of course, a nautical motif decorating the bars. The rooms, offering views of the harbor and the bay, have window seats. Although the rooms are simply furnished, they all have hair dryers and beverage makers. Rooms tend to be small but are cozy, each with a compact bathroom with a shower stall. Bar snacks are served during the day, and there's an affordable dinner menu, with mains costing from £6 to £12 ($10.20 to $20.40).

LAND'S END

Craggy Land's End is where England comes to an end. America's coast is 3,291 miles west of the rugged rocks that tumble into the sea beneath Land's End. Some enjoyable cliff walks and panoramic views are available here.

WHERE TO STAY & DINE

Land's End Hotel. Land's End, Sennen, Cornwall TR19 7AA. ☎ **01736/871844.** Fax 01736/871599. E-mail:landshotel@aol.com 33 units. TV TEL. £40–£50 ($68–$85) per person. Rate includes breakfast. AE, MC, V.

This hotel is situated behind a white facade in a complex of buildings rising from the rugged landscape at the end of the main A30 road, the very tip of England. The hotel has a panoramic cliff-top position, and is exposed to the wind and sea spray. The rooms are attractively furnished and well maintained. Rooms range from small to spacious, especially the premier or family rooms. Many contain a four-poster, but each offers beverage makers. Some rooms are reserved for nonsmokers. Bathrooms are small but have adequate shelf space and a hair dryer.

Dining: Much of the hotel's business comes from the many day visitors who stop by for a snack or cup of coffee in one of the three restaurants. Bar meals are served daily from noon to 2pm, and a cafeteria remains open all day. In the evening, more formal meals are served, mostly to hotel guests.

6 The Artists' Colony of St. Ives

319 miles SW of London; 21 miles NE of Land's End; 10 miles NE of Penzance

This north-coast fishing village, with its sandy beaches, narrow streets, and well-kept cottages, is England's most famous artists' colony. The artists settled in many years ago and have integrated with the fishers and their families. They've been here long enough to have developed several schools or "splits," and they almost never overlap—except in the pubs. The old battle continues between the followers of the representational and the devotees of the abstract in art, with each group recruiting young artists all the time. In addition, there are the potters, weavers, and other craftspeople—all working, exhibiting, and selling in this area.

St. Ives becomes virtually impossible to visit in August, when you're likely to be trampled underfoot by busloads of tourists, mostly the English themselves. However, in spring and early fall the pace is much more relaxed.

ESSENTIALS

GETTING THERE There is frequent service throughout the day between London's Paddington Station and the rail terminal at St. Ives. The trip takes 5½ hours. Call ☎ **0345/484950** for schedules and information.

Several coaches a day run from London's Victoria Coach Station to St. Ives. The trip takes 7 hours. Call ☎ **0990/808080** for schedules and information.

If you're driving, take A30 across Cornwall, heading northwest at the junction with B3306, heading to St. Ives on the coast. During the summer, many streets in the center of town are closed to vehicles. You may want to leave your car in the Lelant Saltings Car Park, 3 miles from St. Ives on A3074, and take the regular train service into town, an 11-minute journey. Departures are every half hour. It's free to all car passengers and drivers, and the parking charge is £8 to £10 ($13.60 to $17) per day. You can also use the large Trenwith Car Park, close to the town center, for £1.50 ($2.55) and then walk down to the shops and harbor or take a bus that costs 40p (70¢) per person.

VISITOR INFORMATION The **Tourist Information Centre** is at the Guildhall, Street-an-Pol (☎ **01736/796297**). From January to mid-May and from late September through December, hours are Monday through Thursday from 9:30am to 5:30pm and Friday from 9:30am to 5pm. From April to mid-May, open Saturdays also from 10am to 1pm. From mid-May to June, hours are Monday through Saturday from 9:30am to 5:30pm and Sunday from 10am to 1pm. In July and August, hours are Monday through Saturday from 9:30am to 6pm and Sunday from 10am to 1pm. For the first 3 weeks of September, hours are Monday through Saturday from 9:30am to 5:30pm, and Sunday 10am to 1pm.

SEEING THE SIGHTS

✪ **Tate Gallery St. Ives.** Porthmear Beach. ☎ **01736/796226.** Admission £3.90 ($6.65) per adult, including 1 child under 16; £2.30 ($3.90) seniors and students 16 or older. Sept–June Tues–Sun 10:30am–5:30pm, July–Aug daily 10:30am–5:30pm. Closed Dec 24–25.

This branch of London's famous Tate Gallery exhibits changing groups of work from the Tate Gallery's preeminent collection of St. Ives painting and sculpture, dating from about 1925 to 1975. The gallery is administered jointly with the Barbara Hepworth Museum (see below). The collection includes works by artists associated with St. Ives, including Alfred Wallis, Ben Nicholson, Barbara Hepworth, Naum Gabo, Peter Lanyon, Terry Frost, Patrick Heron, and Roger Hilton. All the artists whose works are shown here had a decisive effect on the development of painting in the United Kingdom in the second half of the 20th century. About 100 works are on display at all times.

Boasting dramatic sea views, the museum occupies a spectacular site overlooking Porthmear Beach, close to the home of Alfred Wallis and to the studios used by many of the St. Ives artists.

✪ **Barbara Hepworth Museum and Garden.** Barnoon Hill. ☎ **01736/796226.** Admission £3.50 ($5.95) adults, £1.80 ($3.05) children. Sept–June Tues–Sun 10:30am–5:30pm, July–Aug daily 10:30am–5:30pm. Closed Dec 24–25.

Dame Barbara Hepworth lived at Trewyn from 1949 until her death in 1975 at the age of 72. In her will she asked that her working studio be turned into a museum where future visitors could see where she lived and created her world-famous sculpture. Today, the museum and garden are virtually just as she left them. On display are about 47 sculptures and drawings, covering the period from 1928 to 1974, as well as photographs, documents, and other Hepworth memorabilia. You can also visit her workshops, housing a selection of tools and some unfinished carvings.

WHERE TO STAY

Garrack Hotel and Restaurant. Burthallan Lane, Higher Ayr, St. Ives, Cornwall TR26 3AA. ☎ **01736/796199.** Fax 01736/798955. E-mail: garrack@accuk.co.uk. 18 units. TV TEL. £58–£80 ($98.60–$136) per person. Rates include English breakfast. AE, DC, MC, V. Take B3306 to the outskirts of St. Ives; after passing a gas station on the left, take the 3rd road left toward Portmeor Beach and Ayr and after 200 yd. look for the hotel sign. Frequent minibus service.

This vine-covered hotel, once a private home, commands a panoramic view of St. Ives and Porthmear Beach from its 2-acre knoll at the head of a narrow lane. It's one of the friendliest and most efficiently run small, mid-priced hotels on the entire coast, with every room furnished in a warm, homey manner. Most of the units are midsize, but two rooms are large enough to accommodate families; one is suitable for persons with disabilities. The small bathrooms include a hair dryer.

Amenities: In addition to the swimming pool and its whirlpool spa, there is a sauna, solarium, changing rooms, exercise equipment, and a patio for sunbathing. A small bar overlooks the bay. There is a launderette.

Pedn-Olva Hotel. The Warren, St. Ives, Cornwall TR26 2EA. ☎ **01736/796222.** Fax 01736/797710. 35 units. From £42–£51 ($71.40–$86.70) person double. Rates include English breakfast. Half board £55–£65 ($93.50–$110.50) per person. MC, V. Parking £3 ($5.10).

The panoramic view of the bay afforded from its restaurant and lounges is the outstanding feature of this establishment. It was originally built in the 1870s as the home of the paymaster for the local mines, before being transformed into a hotel in the

1930s. The rooms are furnished in a modern style, with comfortable twin or double beds. Most of the accommodations open onto panoramic views across the bay. Seven of the rooms are in a less desirable annex where the chambers are more sterile and lack the character of the main building. Five rooms are large enough for families. There are sun terraces with lounges, umbrellas, and a swimming pool for those who don't want to walk down the rocky path to Porthminster Beach. If you crave solitude, however, scramble down the rocks to sunbathe just above the gentle rise and fall of the sea.

Porthminster Hotel. The Terrace, St. Ives, Cornwall TR26 2BN. ☎ **01736/795221.** Fax 01736/797043. 46 units. TV TEL. £103–£139 ($175.10–$236.30) double. Rates include half board. AE, DC, MC, V.

This leading Cornish Riviera resort, the town's best address, stands on the main road into town amid a beautiful garden and within easy walking distance of Porthminster Beach. Large and imposing, the Porthminster is a traditional choice for visitors to St. Ives. With its 1894 Victorian architecture, it's warm and inviting. The spacious rooms are well furnished, although with a bland decor. Over the years the bedrooms have been considerably upgraded, and the standard of comfort is high here.

Amenities: Facilities include a sun lounge, a solarium, a sauna, and a swimming pool that's open from June to September.

WHERE TO DINE

Garrack Hotel and Restaurant. In the Garrack Hotel, Burthallan Lane, Higher Ayr. ☎ **01736/796199.** Fax 01736/798955. E-mail: garrack@accuk.co.uk. Reservations recommended. Fixed-price dinner £23.50 ($39.95). AE, DC, MC, V. Daily 7–9pm. Frequent minibus service. ENGLISH/INTERNATIONAL.

The dining room at the Garrack Hotel produces excellent cuisine and, whenever possible, uses fresh ingredients from their own garden. The hotel dining room, which is open to nonguests, offers a set dinner, plus a cold buffet or snacks at the bar. The menu features some of the best English dishes, such as roast shoulder of lamb with mint sauce, plus a wide sampling of continental fare, such as roast roulade of salmon with sesame crust and a cucumber sauce. Live lobsters swim in the seawater tank—until they're removed for preparation and cooked to order. Cheese and dessert trolleys are at your service.

EN ROUTE TO PORT ISAAC

The stretch of coastline between St. Ives and Port Isaac doesn't have the charm of Cornwall's eastern coast. The fastest way to get to Port Isaac is to take the A30 northeast. However the B3301, hugging close to the Atlantic Ocean, is the more scenic route.

Heading north along B3301, your first stop will be the estuary town of **Hayle,** once known for its tin and copper mines, but now a beach resort with miles of sand fronting the often wind-tossed Atlantic. Going north from here, the first attraction is **St. Agnes Beacon** (it's signposted). This is the most panoramic belvedere along this wild stretch of north Cornish coastline. At 628 feet, you can see all the way from Trevose Head in the northeast to St. Michael's Mount in the southwest—that is, if the weather's clear. It's often rainy and cloudy.

The first town of any importance is **Newquay,** a resort with sandy beaches at the foot of the cliffs, opening onto a sheltered bay. Taking its name from the new quay built in 1439, it attracts everyone from young surfers to elderly ladies who check into the B&Bs along the harbor for long stays. Newquay is a rather commercial town, lacking the charm of St. Ives or Port Isaac, but its beaches attract families in summer. At night, its pubs fill up with rowdy surfers ready to party.

If you'd like to stay over in Newquay, we recommend the **Bristol Hotel,** Narrowcliff (☎ **01637/875181;** fax 01637/879347). E-mail: hotelbristol.nqy@btinternet.com. This redbrick hotel overlooking the beach has 76 well-furnished rooms that cost £100 to £110 ($170 to $187) per night, including English breakfast. This friendly and inviting place is popular with families. Facilities include an indoor swimming pool, sauna, and solarium; American Express, Diners Club, MasterCard, and Visa are accepted.

Back on the road again, you'll reach the next important stop, **Padstow.** This town has a long and ancient history. It reached its heyday in the 19th century when it was an important port. Unfortunately, ships became too big to pass the sand bar (called "The Doom Bar") at the estuary mouth. Walk along its quay-lined harbor and explore its narrow streets. At the end of the quay stands **St. Petroc's Church** and **Prideaux Place,** a Tudor house with 18th-century battlements.

Try to arrive in Padstow in time for lunch, because a restaurant—simply called **"Seafood,"** at Riverside (☎ **01841/532700**)—offers the best cuisine along this stretch of coastline. Here, Rick Stein selects the best "fruits of the sea," which he crafts into French-influenced dishes such as grillade of monkfish and Dover sole with a sauce vierge of garlic, sun-dried tomatoes, and herbs. Stein also rents 26 rooms above the restaurant, the bistro, and the coffee shop for £85 to £145 ($144.50 to $246.50) double per night including breakfast; two have private balconies opening onto harbor views. The bar is open all day; lunch is served from noon to 1:30pm; and dinner is served from 7 to 10pm daily, except Sunday when they are closed; Master Card and Visa accepted.

7 Port Isaac

266 miles SW of London; 14 miles SW of Tintagel; 9 miles N of Wadebridge

Port Isaac remains the most unspoiled fishing village on the north Cornish coastline, in spite of large numbers of summer visitors. By all means, wander through its winding, narrow lanes, gazing at the whitewashed fishing cottages with their rainbow trims.

ESSENTIALS

GETTING THERE Bodmin is the nearest railway station. It lies on the main line from London (Paddington Station) to Penzance (about a 4- or 4½-hour trip). Call ☎ **0345/484950.** Many hotels will send a car to pick up guests at the Bodmin station or you can take a taxi. If you take a bus from Bodmin, you'll have to change buses at Wadebridge, and connections are not good. Driving time from Bodmin to Port Isaac is 40 minutes.

A bus to Wadebridge goes to Port Isaac about six times a day. It's maintained by the Prout Brothers Bus Co. Wadebridge is a local bus junction to many other places in the rest of England.

If you're driving from London, take M4 west, then drive south on M5. Head west again at the junction with A39, continuing to the junction with B3267, which you follow until you reach the signposted cutoff for Port Isaac.

WHERE TO STAY & DINE

✪ **Port Gaverne Hotel.** Port Gaverne, Port Isaac, Cornwall PL29 3SQ. ☎ **01208/880244.** Fax 01208/880151. E-mail: pghotel@telinco.co.uk. 17 units. TV TEL. £70–£110 ($119–$187) double. Rates include English breakfast. AE, DC, MC, V.

Built in the 17th century as a coastal inn for fishermen needing a rest from their seagoing labors, Port Gaverne, ½ mile east of Port Isaac, today caters to vacationing families and couples. It's the port's best bet for food and lodgings. The small to mid-size bedrooms are traditionally furnished. The small bathrooms have adequate shelf space and a hair dryer. The hotel boasts a sheltered cove for boating and swimming and can arrange shark fishing, pony trekking, golf, and country hikes. Its painted facade is draped with vines, and inside you'll find a duo of atmospheric bars for relaxing beside a fireplace (one of them is a modified baking oven). Clusters of antiques and early photographs of Cornwall add somewhat bittersweet touches.

Dining: Dinners are served by candlelight and include locally caught lobster, fish, or crab in season, as well as locally raised lamb and beef. Bar snacks are also available.

Slipway Hotel. The Harbour Front, Port Isaac, Cornwall PL29 3RH. ☎ **01208/880264.** E-mail: slipway@easynet.co.uk. 12 units, 10 with bathroom. TEL. £48–£56 ($81.60–$95.20) double without bathroom, £64–£72 ($108.80–$122.40) double with bathroom; £88–£100 ($149.60–$170) suite. Rates include English breakfast. AE, MC, V. Closed Jan to mid-Feb.

Originally built in 1527, with major additions made in the early 1700s, this waterside building has seen more uses than any other structure in town, serving as everything from fishing cottages to the headquarters of the first bank here. The building was once a lifeboat station for rescuing sailors stranded on stormy seas. The bedrooms are cozy, with comfortable beds and compact baths with shower stalls.

Dining/Diversions: This hotel is best known for its restaurant, where ultrafresh seafood is a constant favorite. Its main dining room contains a minstrel's gallery and lies adjacent to a popular bar known to virtually everyone in town. At lunch, only bar snacks are served. Dinner is more elaborate, featuring fish imported directly from the nets of local fishers. Menu choices include one of the most elaborate seafood platters in town.

8 Tintagel Castle: King Arthur's Legendary Lair

264 miles SW of London; 49 miles NW of Plymouth

On a wild stretch of the Atlantic coast, ✪ **Tintagel** is forever linked with the legends of King Arthur, Lancelot, and Merlin. So compelling was this legend that medieval writers treated it as a tale of chivalry, even though the real Arthur, if he lived, probably did so around the time of the Roman or Saxon invasions. (Some scholars have speculated that if Arthur existed at all, he might not have been a king, but a warlord; his reign may have lasted 3 decades, leading native Britons who were fighting off the Saxon invasion.)

Despite its universal adoption throughout Europe, it was in Wales and southern England that the legend initially developed and blossomed. The story was polished and given a literary form for the first time by Geoffrey of Monmouth around 1135. Combining Celtic myth and Christian and classical symbolism (usually without crediting his sources), Geoffrey forged a fictional history of Britain whose form, shape, and elevated values were centered around the mythical King Arthur. Dozens of other storytellers embellished the written and oral versions of the tale.

The Arthurian legend has captured the imagination of the British people like no other. Arthur supposedly still lies sleeping, ready to rise and save Britain in its greatest need. The version of the legend by Sir Thomas Malory has become the classic, but there were many others: Edmund Spenser's in the Tudor period; John Milton's in the 17th century; Tennyson's, William Morris's, and Swinburne's in the Victorian age; and T. H. White's and C. S. Lewis's in the 20th century, not to mention the many film treatments.

The legend of King Arthur gained considerable credibility in August 1998 when a stone bearing a Latin inscription referring to King Arthur was uncovered at the ancient ruined castle in Tintagel where he was supposed to have been born. The piece of slate, 14 inches by 10 inches, was found in a drain at the castle. For Arthur fans this is the find of a lifetime and is all that is needed to verify the existence of the King.

The 13th-century ruins of the castle that stand here—built on the foundations of a Celtic monastery from the 6th century—are popularly known as King Arthur's Castle. They stand 300 feet above the sea on a rocky promontory, and to get to them you must take a long, steep, tortuous walk from the parking lot. In summer, many visitors make the ascent to Arthur's Lair, up 100 rock-cut steps. You can also visit Merlin's Cave at low tide.

The castle is 1/2 mile northwest of Tintagel. It's open April to October daily from 10am to 6pm (from mid-July through mid-Aug until 7pm); November to March daily from 10am to 4pm. Admission is £2.90 ($4.95) for adults, £2.20 ($3.75) for students and senior citizens, and £1.50 ($2.55) for children. For information, call ☎ **01840/770328.**

ESSENTIALS

GETTING THERE The nearest railway station is in Bodmin, which lies on the main rail line from London to Penzance. From Bodmin, you'll have to drive or take a taxi for 30 minutes to get to Tintagel (there's no bus service from Bodmin to Tintagel). For railway inquiries, call ☎ **0345/484950.**

If you want to take a bus, you'll travel from London to Plymouth. One bus a day travels from Plymouth to Tintagel, at 4:20pm, but it takes twice the time (2 hours) required for a private car (which only takes about 50 minutes), since the bus stops at dozens of small hamlets along the way. For bus schedule information, call ☎ **01209/719988.**

If you're driving, from Exeter, head across Cornwall on A30, continuing west at the junction with A395. From this highway, various secondary roads lead to Tintagel.

VISITOR INFORMATION Tourist information is available at the **Municipal Building,** Boscawen Street, in Truro (☎ **01872/274555**); from Easter to November, hours are Monday through Friday from 9am to 5:30pm and Saturday from 9:30am to 5:30pm; from November to Easter it's Monday through Friday from 9:30am to 5pm.

WHERE TO STAY & DINE IN TINTAGEL

Bossiney House Hotel. Bossiney Rd., Bossiney, Tintagel, Cornwall PL34 0AX. ☎ **01840/770240.** Fax 01840/770501. www.cornwell-online.co.uk/bossiney. E-mail: bossineyhh@eclipse.co.uk. 20 units. TV. £56–£66 ($95.20–$112.20) double. Rates include English breakfast. AE, DC, MC, V. Closed Dec–Jan. Take B3263 1/2 mile northeast of Tintagel.

The hotel, in its inviting location, is comfortable, but not as tranquil or idyllic as the accommodations at somewhat more expensive Trebrea Lodge (see below). Bedrooms range from small to mid-size, with streamlined modern styling. The small bathrooms are efficiently organized with a hair dryer and a combination tub and shower (or else a shower stall). A big English breakfast and other well-prepared, affordable meals are served in the dining room, which offers a panoramic view out over the lawns. There is a well-stocked bar/lounge with a fine view of the surrounding meadows. On the grounds is a Scandinavian log chalet with a heated swimming pool, a sauna, and a solarium.

Old Borough House. Bossiney, Tintagel, Cornwall PL34 0AY. ☎ **01840/770475.** E-mail: jjimbo9@compuserve.com. 5 units, 4 with shower, 1 with private bathroom. £60 ($102) double. Rates include English breakfast. MC, V. Walk north from the ruins of Tintagel Castle for 10 min.

Run by the Rayner family, this Cornish house has thick stone walls, low ceiling beams, and an illustrious history dating back to 1558. Most of what stands today was completed in the late 1600s, when it served as the residence for the mayor of Bossiney, the hamlet in which it's situated. The accommodations are cozy, antique, and very comfortable. Many of the bedrooms have been recently refurbished and upgraded. Each unit contains a beverage maker. There's a sitting room with a TV for guests' use, and, if you request in advance, affordable evening meals are available.

Trebrea Lodge. Trenale, near Tintagel, Cornwall PL34 0HR. ☎ **01840/770410.** Fax 01840/770092. 7 units, with tub or shower. TV TEL. £84–£94 ($142.80–$159.80) double. Rates include English breakfast. AE, MC, V. From Tintagel, take the Boscastle rd. and turn right at the Roman Catholic church; make another right at the top of the lane.

Although its more than 600 years old, Trebrea Lodge reflects the charm of a small Cornish manor house of the Georgian period. Although not fancy in any way, it is the best choice in Tintagel. The public rooms are all furnished with antiques, as are the rooms, one of which boasts a grand four-poster bed. All bedrooms have tea- or coffeemakers. Each small bathroom has a hair dryer and either a tub or shower combination or a shower stall. The rooms open onto uninterrupted views over the countryside to the Atlantic Ocean.

A fixed-price menu, costing £23 ($39.10), is served in an oak-paneled dining room where all the food is prepared by Sean Devlin, one of the owners, using fresh local ingredients to produce both traditional English and continental dishes.

11 The Cotswolds

Lying between Oxford and the River Severn, about a 2-hour drive west of London, the pastoral ✪ **Cotswolds** occupy a stretch of grassy limestone hills, deep ravines, and barren plateaus known as *wolds,* Old English for "God's high open land." Ancient villages with names like Stow-on-the-Wold, Wotton-under-Edge, and Moreton-in-Marsh dot this bucolic area, most of which is in Gloucestershire, with portions in Oxfordshire, Wiltshire, and Worcestershire.

Made rich by wool from their sheep, the landowners here invested in some of the finest domestic architecture in Europe, distinctively built of honey-brown Cotswold stone. The gentry didn't neglect their spiritual duties, for some of the simplest Cotswold hamlets have churches that, in style and architectural detail, seem far beyond their modest means.

You'll also see some thatched cottages in the Cotswolds, which are fiercely protected by local bylaws, yet are endlessly impractical because of their need for frequent repair, maintenance, and replacement. (They also cost a fortune to insure against fire!) More common are the Cotswolds roof shingles fashioned from split slabs of stone, which required massive buttressing from medieval carpenters as a means of supporting the weight of the roof. Buildings erected since the 1700s, however, usually have slate roofs.

You'll really want to rent a car and drive through the Cotswolds at your own pace. This way, you can spend hours viewing the land of winding goat paths, rolling hills, and sleepy hamlets. One of the reasons to visit the Cotswolds is to take advantage of its natural beauty. Play a round of golf on a scenic course, go fishing, or better yet, take a ramble across a meadow where sheep graze or alongside a fast-flowing stream.

Mobbed by tourists, Broadway, with its 16th-century stone houses and cottages, is justifiably the most popular base for touring this area, but we suggest you also head for Bibury, Painswick, or other small villages to capture the true charm of the Cotswolds. You'll find the widest range of hotels and facilities in Cheltenham, once one of England's most fashionable spas, with a wealth of Regency architecture. And families might head to Birdland, in Bourton-on-the-Water, where you can see some 1,200 birds of 361 different species.

BIKING & HIKING THROUGH THE COTSWOLDS

Biking the country roads of the Cotswolds is one of the best ways to experience the quiet beauty of the area. **Country Lanes,** 9 Shaftesbury St., Fordingbridge, Hampshire SP6 1JF (☎ **01425/655022**), offers visitors that opportunity.

The company rents 21-speed bicycles fully equipped with mudguards, a water bottle, lock and key, a rear carrier rack, and, of course, safety helmets.

Their recommended day trips are self-guided, so you can ride at your own pace. You'll get an easy-to-follow route sheet. As you explore, you'll pass manor farms and pretty cottages of honey-colored stone. Several villages are also along the path, and the Hidcote Manor Garden is a perfect spot to relax if your legs tire of pedaling. The 10-, 20-, or 28-mile trips all end at the Manor House Hotel, a former 16th-century coaching inn at Moreton-in-Marsh. Here, you'll be served afternoon tea in the garden. The £25 ($42.50) price includes everything mentioned above. Advanced booking is essential; call ☎ **01608/650065** to reserve by credit card.

This is also one of the most famous regions of England for hiking. With such a large area in which to ramble, it's a good idea to know where you are (and aren't) welcome. The **Cotswold Voluntary Wardens Service,** Shire Hall, Gloucester (☎ **01451/862000**), offers free brochures highlighting trails and paths.

The Wayfarers, 172 Bellevue Ave., Newport, RI 02840 (☎ **800/249-4620**), sponsors about 10 Cotswold walks a year from April through October. The cost of most tours is $2,090 per person, including snacks, meals during the walk, and admission to attractions.

If you'd like to walk and explore on your own without a guide, you can get data from the Cheltenham Tourist Information Center (☎ **01242/522878**). The center sells a Cotswold Way map.

1 Tetbury

113 miles W of London; 27 miles NE of Bristol

In the rolling Cotswolds, Tetbury was out of the tourist mainstream until the heir to the British throne and his beautiful bride took up residence at the Macmillan Place, a Georgian building on nearly 350 nearby acres. Then, crowds from all over the world came here to catch a glimpse of Prince Charles riding horses and Princess Di shopping in the village. (Today, folks keep an eye out for Charles and Camilla Parker-Bowles, who are occasionally spotted driving by en route to their homes.) Although it cannot be seen from the road, the nine-bedroom Windsor mansion, **Highgrove,** is 1½ miles southwest of Tetbury on the way to Westonbirt Arboretum.

Tetbury itself has a 17th-century market hall and a number of antique shops and boutiques. The town's inns weren't cheap before royalty moved in, and the prices certainly have not dropped since then.

ESSENTIALS

GETTING THERE Frequent daily trains run from London's Paddington Station to Kemble, 7 miles east of Tetbury. For more information and schedules, call ☎ **0345/484950.** You can then take a bus from there to Tetbury.

National Express buses leave from London's Victoria Coach Station with direct service to Cirencester, 10 miles northeast of Tetbury. For more information and schedules, call ☎ **0990/808080.** Several buses a day connect Cirencester to Tetbury.

If you're driving from London, take the M40 northwest to Oxford, continuing along A40 to the junction with A429. Drive south to Cirencester, where you connect with A433 southwest into Tetbury.

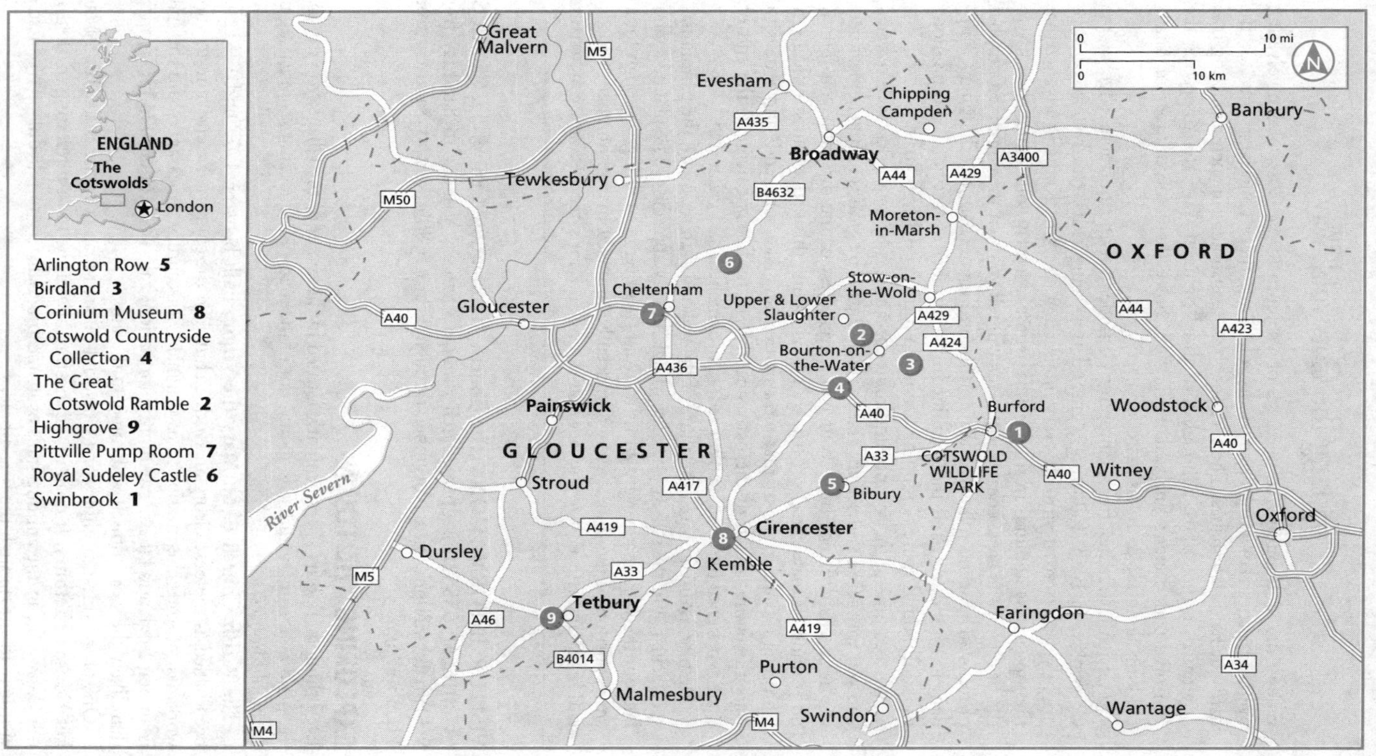
ENGLAND
The Cotswolds
London
Arlington Row 5
Birdland 3
Corinium Museum 8
Cotswold Countryside Collection 4
The Great Cotswold Ramble 2
Highgrove 9
Pittville Pump Room 7
Royal Sudeley Castle 6
Swinbrook 1
0
10 mi
0
10 km
Great Malvern
M5
Evesham
Chipping Campden
Banbury
A435
Broadway
A44
A429
A3400
Tewkesbury
M50
B4632
Moreton-in-Marsh
OXFORD
Cheltenham
Gloucester
A40
Upper & Lower Slaughter
Stow-on-the-Wold
A429
A44
A423
A424
Bourton-on-the-Water
A436
A40
Painswick
Burford
Woodstock
A40
GLOUCESTER
A33
COTSWOLD WILDLIFE PARK
A40
Witney
River Severn
Stroud
A417
Bibury
Oxford
A419
Cirencester
Dursley
Kemble
A33
M5
Tetbury
Faringdon
A46
A419
B4014
Purton
A34
Malmesbury
Swindon
Wantage
M4
M4

Hiking the Cotswold Way

One of the underpublicized pleasures of a sojourn in the Cotswolds involves an overland pedestrian ramble, the Cotswold Way, that's conceived only for the hardy or hardy wannabes. The idea for the establishment of such a walking trail originated in the 1950s, although formalized rights of way interconnecting the 104-mile path weren't finalized until 1968. Since then, the number of hikers trekking along the path has increased every year.

The path stretches from Chipping Campden, at the northern edge of the Cotswolds, to Bath, following a meandering route that's clearly marked with bright yellow signs at virtually every intersection en route. Know in advance that the topography abounds in rolling hills, whose interplay contributes so richly to the beauty of the area. Local statisticians will tell you that the combined number of feet you'll ascend following the northbound route (Bath to Chipping Campden) is 13,300 feet, and the combined total number of feet you'll ascend along the southbound route (Chipping Campden to Bath) is 12,900 feet.

We recommend the southbound route, because it's by far the less well-traveled and you won't find yourself in "traffic jams" caused by groups of hikers meandering at speeds different from your own. Regardless of the direction you follow, don't underestimate the effort it takes to walk along this path: Tourist officials in Chipping Campden report that most participants take between 7 and 8 days to walk the entire stretch of the path, and that many hikers emerge at the end of their experience blistered, sunburned, rain-drenched, and exhausted.

Despite its discomforts, the allure of the walking path is potent, the panoramas spectacular, and the sense of medieval England very appealing. The planners who laid out the walk made every effort to avoid "road verge" walking, although for a small portion of the route, you will indeed be funneled to the shoulder of roads and highways. (Be alert to the fact that in England, for safety reasons, pedestrians

VISITOR INFORMATION The **Tourist Information Centre,** 33 Church St. (☎ **01666/503552**), is open March through October, Monday to Saturday from 9:30am to 4:30pm, and November through February, Monday to Saturday from 11am to 2pm.

EXPLORING THE TOWN

Everything in Tetbury is conveniently located in the center of the village; you can easily spend a morning wandering in and out of the many antiques shops and gazing up at the old houses.

The **Parish Church of St. Mary the Virgin,** built between 1777 and 1781, has been hailed as the best Georgian Gothic church in the country. Extensive restoration work has returned the interior to its original 18th-century appearance, and the spire is among England's tallest. For more information, call ☎ **01666/502333;** it's more than likely the vicar himself will come on the line.

One of the finest examples of a Cotswold-pillared market house is the 1655 **Market House of Tetbury.** It's still in use, hosting one of the most interesting markets in the Cotswolds, in the antique stalls of its meeting hall. Try to schedule a Wednesday visit here to sift through the bric-a-brac.

are usually instructed to walk on the right side of the road, facing the oncoming traffic.) Most of the route, however, avoids traffic arteries completely, guiding you through forests and fields, along rocky escarpments where views sweep out over medieval wool villages, and along the periphery of historic villages. Whether you opt to detour a quarter-mile or so into any of at least a dozen historic villages en route depends on your level of interest, your time, and your energy.

What is the order, southbound, of the historic hamlets and monuments you'll pass through, or near, as you meander along the route? They include Broadway, Hailes, Winchcombe, Cleeve Hill, Seven Springs Crossroads, Crickley Hill, Painswick, Dursley, Wotton-under-Edge, Hawkesbury Upton, and Tormarton, with a terminus a short distance outside of Bath.

If you're interested in navigating your way along this trail, any tourist office at any village in the Cotswolds contains shelves groaning under the weight of the ordinance maps and specialized walking tour guides that cover all aspects of the Cotswold Way. One of the best of them is *The Cotswold Way Handbook and Accommodations List,* published by the English Ramblers' Association, which sells for £2 ($3.40) at dozens of shops en route. You can pre-order the guide by writing to the **English Rambler's Association,** Tudor Cottage, Berrow, Malvern, Worcestershire WR136JJ, England. Additional information can be obtained from the tourist office of Chipping Campden, Bath, or Broadway, or by calling the **Cotswold Voluntary Warden Service** at ☎ **01451/862000.** Bring a raincoat, sturdy shoes, and a sense of humor. If you collect souvenirs, you'll have plenty to choose from en route, as the experience is not without its share of touristy overtones. Hundreds of shops will sell you an official-looking certificate announcing the way you've walked the path, as well as T-shirts, postcards, commemorative ashtrays, and beer mugs.

After the market, head for **Chipping Steps.** The Chipping (market) was for centuries the site of "mop fairs," where farmhands and domestic staff offered themselves for employment. Many of the surrounding buildings have medieval origins.

Another place to explore is **Gumstoll Hill,** one of Tetbury's most ancient streets and now famous for its annual Woolsack Races. Legend has it that at the bottom of the hill, there was a pool where scolding wives and other miscreants were tied to a ducking stool and plunged underwater for punishment.

The Police Bygones Museum, Old Court House, 63 Long St., situated in the former police station and magistrates court, is worth a peek. The old cells house a collection of relics from centuries of Cotswold law enforcement. The location and hours are the same as the Tourist Information Centre (see above).

Chavenage House. 2 miles northwest of Tetbury. ☎ **01666/502329.** Admission £3 ($5.10) adults, £1.50 ($2.55) children. May–Sept Thurs and Sun 2–5pm; also open on Easter and bank holiday Mondays.

Aside from its fine Cromwell-era tapestries, furniture, and artifacts, this Elizabethan country house is worth a visit for its rich history and legends.

The drama started with Col. Nathaniel Stephens, who owned the house during the English civil war and met with an unfortunate demise while living here. He was persuaded by Cromwell, who was a relative by marriage, to vote for the impeachment of King Charles. This angered Stephens's daughter to the point that she cursed him. Soon after, Stephens died, and it is rumored that his ghostly form was seen as it was driven away from Chavenage by a headless coachman wearing royal vestments. The house has been used as a location shoot for several BBC television productions, including Agatha Christie's *Hercule Poirot.*

ANTIQUES SHOPS & GALLERIES

As in so many English villages, Tetbury's shopping centers abound with antiques and collectibles.

Day Antiques, 5 New Church St. (☎ **01666/502413**), specializes in oak and country furniture and also has a collection of early pottery and metalware.

Antiquing the 'Wolds

If ever there were an English fantasy, it's to drive the country back roads of the Cotswolds, to stay in a manor-house hotel, and spend your days browsing the villages, ignoring the touristy teddy-bear shops and concentrating on the antiques shops densely packed into these old market towns.

There aren't many bargains in these towns, but it makes for lovely browsing, for days spent strolling, searching, studying, and munching ice-cream cones. Few stores sell inexpensive or junky antiques, although there are some great rummage sales on the weekends (ask your hotel for directions to the nearest and the best if you are into cheap thrills).

For the most part, antiques in the Cotswolds are about patina and provenance—really serious stuff. Most of the dealers are members of Britain's leading antiques associations (like the British Antiques Dealers Association—BADA) so that stores displaying this logo in their window have reputations to safeguard and will only sell you the best merchandise. Naturally, the best is pricey.

There is also the **Cotswold Antique Dealer's Association** (CADA), which publishes a free brochure of members and will happily guide you toward shippers and even hotels. Write to the Secretary, CADA, Barcheston Manor, Shipston-on-Stour, Warwickshire CV36 5AY, England (☎ **01451/870028**).

Each of the Cotswolds' villages usually has an antiques center in the heart of town, with a variety of dealers. There's usually also a cafe here or a place for tea, and clean bathrooms. They do not charge an entrance fee and are often open on Sundays. Bigger towns, such as Burford, have several antiques centers.

Most of the towns are laid out in traditional style, with retail centered on the High Street. Unlike the rest of England, most of the Cotswolds' towns are not overrun with multiples on their High Streets. The most expensive stores are clustered in the center of the High Street. The further from this center, the less the rent and the more likely the possibility of finding affordable antiques shops.

The best town in the Cotswolds, especially for antiques shoppers, is **Stow-on-the-Wold;** there's far more to it than a High Street, and it's as charming as can be. **Moreton-in-Marsh** is an unusual town; its High Street is Roman and unusually wide. You'll have quite a hike if you shop your way through town on both sides of the street to take in all the shops.

Some of the Cotswolds towns have been turned into tourist traps over the years; many shops in the area sell an artful mix of reproductions, foreign imports, and Asian junk. Buyers beware.

Most of the other antiques dealers are located on Long Street in the city center. These include several shops that specialize in furniture, such as **Breakspeare Antiques,** 36 Long St. (☎ **01666/503122**), which carries mahogany pieces from the 18th and early 19th centuries and walnut pieces from as far back as the 17th century. **Country Homes,** 30 Long St. (☎ **01666/502342**), sells restored pine furniture from England, Ireland, and Europe, and **Gales Antiques,** 52 Long St. (☎ **01666/502686**), features English and French provincial furnishings. For good quality porcelain, try **Dolphin Antiques,** 48 Long St. (☎ **01666/504242**). The **Antiques Emporium,** at the Old Chape, Long Street (☎ **01666/505281**), gathers stock from 40 dealers in 1,750 square feet of showrooms; you're almost guaranteed to find something you like.

There are also several art galleries in Tetbury. The **Connoisseurs Gallery,** 2 Chipping Court Shopping Mall (☎ **01666/503155**), has prints, sculpture, blown glass, and other works created exclusively by artists in residence. **Natural Wood Framing,** Eight Bells Gallery, 14 Church St. (☎ **01666/505070**), specializes in sporting art, and **Tetbury Gallery,** 18 Market Place (☎ **01666/503412**), carries Victorian watercolors and oils and limited-edition prints.

WHERE TO STAY

✪ **Calcot Manor.** Calcot, near Tetbury, Gloucestershire GL8 8YJ. ☎ **800/987-7433** in the U.S., or 01666/890391. Fax 01666/890394. E-mail: reception@calcotmanor.com. 27 units. TV TEL. £125–£180 ($212.50–$306) double. Rates include early morning tea and continental breakfast. AE, DC, MC, V. Take A4135 3½ miles west of Tetbury.

Although The Close in town has a more refined atmosphere (see below), this inn is the finest place on the outskirts. The thick stone walls of the main house shelter a flowering terrace where tea and drinks are served in good weather. The rooms are furnished with antiques and modern conveniences; two are equipped with whirlpool baths, and one has a four-poster bed. Bedrooms range from mid-size to spacious, and some rooms, specially designed for families, are located in a refurbished granary near the main house. Bathrooms have a hair dryer. The building has indoor and outdoor play areas for children in addition to child monitors in each room. Views from many of the rooms encompass the Cotswold countryside.

Dining: The hotel restaurant serves some of the area's finest meals, with continental touches gathered from the proprietors' catering experience in Switzerland and France.

Amenities: Baby-sitting, open-air swimming pool, 2 tennis courts and limited room service.

✪ **The Close.** 8 Long St., Tetbury, Gloucestershire GL8 8AQ. ☎ **01666/502272.** Fax 01666/504401. 15 units. TV TEL. £120–£200 ($204–$340) double. Rates include English breakfast. AE, MC, V.

The Close, which dates from 1596 and takes its name from a Cistercian monastery that was on this site, is the town's premier inn. Once the home of a wealthy wool merchant, the house was built of Cotswold stone, with gables and stone-mullioned windows. The ecclesiastical windows in the rear overlook a garden with a reflecting pool, a haven for doves. Most rooms are spacious and handsomely furnished with antiques. Baths are tidily maintained and have adequate shelf space.

Dining: Before-dinner drinks are served in the Georgian room with a domed ceiling. Dining is in one of two rooms. The cooking is superb, and an à la carte menu offers specialty dishes (see "Where to Dine," below).

Amenities: Access to nearby health club, car-rental desk, concierge, room service, dry cleaning/laundry, baby-sitting.

The Snooty Fox. Market Place, Tetbury, Gloucestershire GL8 8DD. ☎ **01666/502436.** Fax 01666/503479. www.hatton-hotels.co.uk. E-mail: res@snooty-fox.co.uk. 12 units. TV TEL. £90–£145 ($153–$246.50) double. Rates include English breakfast. AE, DC, MC, V.

This desirable hotel in the commercial heart of Tetbury was originally a 16th-century coaching inn. Despite its name, it's a lot less snooty than The Close and is a popular local rendezvous. Three rooms have antique beds with canopies, and the rest are comfortably and tastefully furnished in a more modern style. Each room is equipped with radio, trouser press, and beverage makers. The small to very spacious bedrooms are filled with English country house luxury, including sumptuous beds. Each bathroom is warm and welcoming, with a hair dryer and luxury toiletries.

Dining/Diversions: There's a popular bar inside, with an amusing caricature of a Snooty Fox in full riding regalia. The restaurant is one of the most elegant in town.

WHERE TO DINE

✪ **The Close Restaurant.** In The Close, 8 Long St. ☎ **01666/502272.** Reservations required. Main courses around £22.50 ($38.25); fixed-price lunch £16 ($27.20); fixed-price dinner £29.50 ($50.15). AE, MC, V. Daily noon–2pm and 7–10pm. ENGLISH.

This is a dining room of distinction, set with exquisite porcelain, silver, and glass that reflects the sumptuous but discreet atmosphere and friendly service. While sipping champagne on the terrace, take time to peruse the imaginative menu, which is complemented by the town's best wine list.

The à la carte menu is seasonally adjusted to take advantage of the best market-fresh ingredients. Starters and main courses reach out for the finest catch or harvest in England's fields and streams. An example is pressed terrine of foie gras and Bathhurst pigeon with a paprika biscuit and shallot marmalade. Main courses are likely to feature local venison, pan-fried sea bream, or fillet of Scottish salmon. Desserts sometimes reach back in England's culinary attic for inspiration, such as a parsnip-and-Cotswold-honey soufflé with whisky and lime ice.

2 Cirencester

89 miles W of London; 16 miles S of Cheltenham; 17 miles SE of Gloucester; 36 miles W of Oxford

Cirencester is the unofficial capital of the Cotswolds, a throwback to the Middle Ages, when it flourished as the center of the great Cotswold wool industry. Then known as Corinium, five roads converged here during the Roman occupation. In size, it ranked second only to London. Today, it is chiefly a market town and a good base for touring. (And don't worry about how to pronounce *Cirencester.* There's disagreement even among the English. Say *Siren*-cess-ter and you won't be too far off.)

ESSENTIALS

GETTING THERE Cirencester has no railway station, but trains depart several times a day from London's Paddington Station for the 80-minute trip to Kemble, which is 4 miles southwest of Cirencester. You may have to transfer trains at Swindon. For schedules and information, call ☎ **0345/484950.** From Kemble, a bus travels to Cirencester four to five times a day.

National Express buses leave from London's Victoria Coach Station with direct service to Cirencester. For schedules and information, call ☎ **0990/808080.**

If you're driving from London, take the M40 northwest to Oxford, continuing along A40 to the junction with the A429, which you'll take south to Cirencester.

VISITOR INFORMATION The **Tourist Information Centre** is at Corn Hall, Market Place (☎ **01285/654180**). It's open April through October, Monday from 9:45am to 5pm and Tuesday to Saturday from 9:30am to 5pm. From November through March it closes at 5pm.

EXPLORING CIRENCESTER

Cirencester has some of the greatest walks and scenic views of any town in the Cotswolds. And you don't have to go miles out of town to enjoy these strolls—they are easily reached from the center at Market Place. On the grounds of the Cirencester Parish Church (see below), attractive trees and shrubs highlight a well-manicured landscape. You can see swans and wild fowl on the River Churn and the lake, even remnants of the town's Roman walls. For a great stroll, take the riverside walk alongside the Churn from Barton Lane to the Abbey Grounds. If you want more, head west from Market Place until you reach **Cirencester Park,** 3,000 acres of parkland with woodland walks. The park is open daily for horseback riding and walking. Pedestrian access is from Cecily Hill (no vehicles).

Brewery Arts Centre. Brewery Ct. ☎ **01285/657181.** Free admission. Year-round Mon–Sat 10am–5pm.

The living heart of this arts complex is the workshop area of 15 resident craft workers who produce everything from baskets to chandeliers. Other components of the center include three galleries with exhibitions in both crafts and fine art, a theater, education classes, a shop selling the best in British craft work, a cafe-bar, and a coffeehouse.

✪ **Corinium Museum.** Park St. ☎ **01285/655611.** Admission £2.50 ($4.25) adults, £2 ($3.40) seniors, £1 ($1.70) students, 80p ($1.35) children, £5 ($8.50) family ticket. Mon–Sat 10am–5pm, Sun 2–5pm. Closed Mon in winter.

The museum houses one of the finest collections of archaeological remains from the Roman occupation, found locally in and around Cirencester. Mosaic pavements excavated on Dyer Street in 1849 and other mosaics are the most important exhibits. Provincial Roman sculpture, including such figures as Minerva and Mercury, pottery, and artifacts salvaged from long-decayed buildings, provide a link with the remote civilization that once flourished here. The museum has been completely modernized to include full-scale reconstructions and special exhibitions on local history and conservation.

Cirencester Parish Church. Market Place. ☎ **01285/659317.** Free admission; donations invited. Mon–Fri 10am–5pm; Sun 2:30–5:30pm.

A church may have stood on this spot in Saxon times, but the present building overlooking the Market Place in the town center dates from Norman times and Henry I. In size, it appears more like a cathedral than a mere parish church, with a variety of styles, largely Perpendicular, as in the early-15th-century tower. Among the treasures inside are a 15th-century "wineglass" pulpit and a silver-gilt cup given to Queen Anne Boleyn two years before her execution. In the Trinity Chapel, you can rub some great 15th-century brasses.

SHOPPING

For antiques in Cirencester, try **William H. Stokes,** The Cloisters, 6/8 Dollar St. (☎ **01285/653907**), which specializes in furniture, tapestries, and other items from the 16th and 17th centuries. **Rankine Taylor Antiques,** 34 Dollar St. (☎ **01285/652529**), sells items from the 17th, 18th, and early 19th centuries, including silver, glass, and furniture.

The arts complex known as the **Brewery Arts,** Brewery Court (☎ **01285/657181**), has 15 independent workshops of area craftspeople ranging from jewelers and weavers to basket makers. There are three galleries and a craft shop recognized by the Crafts Council that sells many of the artists' wares.

WHERE TO STAY & DINE IN & AROUND CIRENCESTER

Tatyan's, 27 Castle St. in Cirencester (☎ **01285/653529**), is a great place to dine. It serves Peking, Hunan, and Szechuan specialties, with nearly a dozen prawn dishes on the large menu. For a pint, head for the town favorite, the **Slug & Lettuce,** 17 West Market Place (☎ **01285/653206**), a friendly pub enjoyed by locals and students alike, with out-of-towners predominating in summer. It has the most convivial after-dark scene in town.

The Jarvis Fleece Hotel. Market Place, Cirencester, Gloucestershire GL7 2NZ. ☎ **01285/658507.** Fax 01285/651017. 30 units. TV TEL. Sun–Thurs £94 ($159.80) double; £109 ($185.30) suite. Fri–Sat (including English breakfast) £99 ($168.30) double; £119 ($202.30) suite. AE, DC, MC, V.

The half-timbered facade here hints at origins as an Elizabethan coaching inn, but it was enlarged by the Georgians and today has had many modernizations. The comfortable rooms feature old-fashioned hints of yesteryear, including quilts and conveniences such as radios and coffeemakers. Rooms range from small to mid-size, each containing small baths with a shower stall.

Dining: The staff prepares modern English dinners served in a formal dining room. À la carte lunches are offered in the Shepherd's Bar. A flowering courtyard offers a pleasant place to dine on warm days.

The Pear Tree at Purton. Church End, Purton, near Swindon, Wiltshire SN5 9ED. ☎ **01793/772100.** Fax 01793/772369. E-mail: peartreepurton@msn.com. 18 units. TV TEL. £95 ($161.50) double; £115–£135 ($195.50–$229.50) four-poster room or suite. Rates include English breakfast. AE, DC, MC, V. Closed Dec 26–30. It's 8 miles southeast of Cirencester, 3 miles from Junction 16 of the M4, and 5 miles from Swindon. To get here from Cirencester, follow route B419 in the direction of Swindown. Turn left when signs point to Cricklade, and from here, follow the signs to Purton.

This English country hotel/restaurant, set on 7½ acres, offers individually decorated rooms equipped with trouser presses, free sherry, and mineral water. All accommodations (three with four-poster beds) have views of the traditional Victorian garden and countryside. Rooms come in various shapes and sizes. Each is named after a character associated with the village of Purton—Anne Hyde, for example, mother of Queen Mary and Queen Anne. Bathrooms are well supplied with a hair dryer and toiletries. The Cotswold stone house was formerly the vicarage for the twin-towered parish Church of St. Mary.

Dining: The owners, Francis and Anne Young, run the best restaurant in the area. The cuisine is inspired by France, although the recipes and cooking are distinctly English. The best seasonal produce is featured, including local lamb and pork. Seafood is brought fresh from Devon, and many of the herbs used to flavor the dishes come from the establishment's own garden. Dining is in an attractive conservatory, with service daily from noon to 2:30pm and 7 to 9pm. Lunch is not served on Saturday. Reservations are required.

Stratton House Hotel. Gloucester Rd., Cirencester, Gloucestershire GL7 2LE. ☎ **01285/651761.** Fax 01285/640024. 41 units. TV TEL. £100–£120 ($170–$204) double. Rates include English breakfast. AE, DC, MC, V. Take A417 1¼ miles northwest of Cirencester.

Built in several stages throughout the 18th century, with a modern wing added in the 1990s, this inviting country house is part Jacobean and part Georgian. It is surrounded by beautiful grounds with a walled garden and herbaceous borders. The large and well-furnished rooms have beverage makers and trouser presses. Two-thirds of the rooms are in the modern wing—designer-decorated, with an aura evoking a traditional private English country house. Bathrooms are small but tidily maintained. Nineteen accommodations are no-smoking.

Dining: The dining and drawing rooms have some fine antique furniture and oil paintings. At dinner, there is a choice of traditional British dishes, and in winter, log fires blaze in a timbered-beam bar.

3 Painswick

4 miles N of Stroud; 107 miles W of London; 10 miles SW of Cheltenham; 15 miles NW of Cirencester

This sleepy stone-built Cotswold wool town vies with Bibury for the title of the most beautiful in the Cotswolds. Painswick is a dream of England of long ago, the perfect escape from a string of dull market towns too often encountered. Its mellow gray stone houses and inns date from as early as the 14th century.

A visit to Painswick at any time of the year would be idyllic, in spite of the "day-trippers" and tourist buses, but there are two special occasions that make it an especially wonderful destination. One is the town's Victorian Market Day in early July. You can contact **Visitor Information** (see below) for the exact day, which is announced in the late spring. The other big occasion is the Clipping Feast (see "Special Events," below).

ESSENTIALS

GETTING THERE Trains depart from London's Paddington Station several times a day for Stroud, the nearest railway station, 3 miles away. The trip takes from 1½ to 2 hours, and you may have to change trains at Swindon. For rail information, call ☎ **0345/484950.** From Stroud, buses run to Painswick, some as frequently as once every hour. Many taxis also wait at the Stroud railway station.

Buses depart from Bath heading toward Cheltenham on Wednesday and Saturday, stopping in Painswick (and many other small towns) along the way. For schedules, call ☎ **0990/808080.**

If you're driving from Cirencester, continue west along A419 to Stroud, then head north on A46 to Cheltenham and Painswick.

VISITOR INFORMATION The Painswick **Tourist Information Centre** is at the Painswick Library, Stroud Road (☎ **01452/813552**), and is open April through September, Monday to Saturday from 10am to 6pm. These hours are true at least in theory, but the staff volunteers manning the office don't always show up. In that case, you can visit the more reliably open tourist office at Stroud, located in Subscription Rooms, George Street (☎ **01453/765768**). Hours are Monday to Saturday 10am to 4:30pm October to March and 10am to 5:30pm April to September.

SPECIAL EVENTS The ✪ **Clipping Feast** of Painswick, also referred to as the Clipping Ceremony, is an unusual, early medieval ceremony that anthropologists suspect may have begun in the dim Celtic prehistory of Britain. Every September, a month that coincides with the harvest ceremonies of the pagans, adults and as many children as can be mustered hold hands in a circle around St. Mary's Anglican Church. The circle moves first one way, then the other, and the participants sing hymns and pray out loud in a celebration of thanksgiving. Participants and observers come from all over the region to take part in this important rite.

EXPLORING THE TOWN

The charm of this town comes from its mellow Cotswold architecture with stone-built houses. Funded by wealthy farmers and merchants in the era when fluffy wool was called "white gold," the houses of Painswick represent a peak at English domestic architecture. The architecture is best seen by walking around New Street in the center of the village. This has to be one of the most misnamed streets in England, as it dates from 1450 and there isn't anything new about it.

You can wander into a pocket of charm by visiting the gardens of **Painswick House,** Gloucester Street, Route B4073, Painswick Stroud (☎ **01452/813204**), about 1/2 mile west of the town center. Built by Charles Hyett in 1734 and enlarged in 1830, this mansion had been home to eight generations of the same family until Lord and Lady Dickinson departed in 1999. The new owners may not allow visitors to wander through their home (check locally), and their rococo gardens are not the biggest, but are among the most cozily charming in the Cotswolds. You're allowed to visit between May and August 31, daily from 11am to 5pm; August 31 through November, Wednesday to Sunday from 11am to 5pm; December through February, daily 11am to 5pm; and February through May, Wednesday through Sunday 11am to 5pm. Admission is £3.30 ($5.60) for adults, £1.75 ($3) for children, and £3 ($5.10) for seniors and students. A family ticket is sold for £8.75 ($14.90).

If you have an itch to shop, stop by **Dennis French** on New Street (☎ **01452/814195**). He sells woodcrafts influenced by William Morris designs.

St. Mary's Church, the centerpiece of the village, was originally built between 1377 and 1399, and reconstructed into its present form in 1480. Its churchyard contains 99 massive yew trees, each of which is at least 200 years old. Local legend states that no matter how hard well-meaning gardeners have tried, they've never been able to grow more than 99 of them.

WHERE TO STAY

Cardynham House. The Cross, Painswick, Gloucestershire GL6 6XX. ☎ **01452/814006.** Fax 01452/812321. 9 units. TV. £69 ($117.30) double. Rates include breakfast. MC, V. Minimum stay of 2 nights Fri–Sun.

Set adjacent to St. Mary's Church, in the heart of Painswick, this small but choice house was begun in 1498, and was later enlarged, thanks to beams that were salvaged from the remains of a wrecked ship from the Spanish Armada. Carol Keyes, the owner, has outfitted the interior with lots of cozy accessories (tartan blankets, leather armchairs, antique books) that fit in well with a stylish hodgepodge of cabinets, wide floorboards, and an intricate network of ceiling beams built by the Elizabethans and the Jacobeans. Bedrooms are cramped but cozy, each with a different theme (Arabian Nights and Medieval Garden are good examples). One of them is a bit larger than the others, and enjoys exclusive access to a 16-foot indoor swimming pool, wherein you can swim against the current by throwing a switch for the simulation of a flowing stream. There's a pub next door, and every Tuesday to Saturday, from 7 to 10pm, the breakfast room ("The March Hare Dining Room") is transformed into a restaurant that specializes in Thai food. The only option is a set menu, priced at £19 ($32.30), wherein such dishes as spicy lemongrass soup, red or green curries, and such flavors as coconut and coriander mingle freely in an otherwise very English setting.

Painswick Hotel. Kemps Lane, Painswick, Gloucestershire GL6 6YB. ☎ **01452/812160.** Fax 01452/814059. www.massey.co.uk. E-mail: reservations@painswickhotel.com. 20 units. TV TEL. £120–£165 ($204–$280.50) double. Rates include Cotswold breakfast. AE, MC, V.

The best inn in the area, this beautiful, completely refurbished Georgian house behind the Painswick parish church was once a vicarage and is encircled by terraces of formal gardens. Many of your fellow readers have reported that a stay here was the highlight of their Cotswold tour. In accommodation, cuisine, and service, it merits a major detour. The bedrooms are what you dream about when you contemplate a stay in the Cotswolds. You'll feel like Henry VIII or Elizabeth I when you crawl in for the night in one of the luxurious four-poster beds. The bedrooms are enhanced by antiques, period furnishings, and objets d'art. The bathrooms are splendid, with plenty of fine toiletries. Thoughtful extras include baskets of fresh fruit, mineral water, books, and magazines about the English countryside.

Dining: The hotel's chefs are well trained, often from the continent, and they turn out some of the finest cuisine in the area, a medley of English and continental dishes. Reservations are required, and the fixed-price menu, served at lunch and dinner, ranges from £20.50 to £24.50 ($34.85 to $41.65). The menus change daily, but always emphasize fresh local products. The wine list is expansive and reasonably priced.

Amenities: Concierge, car-rental desk, room service, dry cleaning/laundry, baby-sitting.

WHERE TO DINE

The Country Elephant. New St. ☎ **01452/770872.** Reservations required. Main courses £14.95–£15.50 ($25.40–$26.35); fixed-price lunch £13 ($22.10); fixed-price dinner £20 ($34). AE, DC, MC, V. Tues–Sun noon–2pm and Tues–Sat 7–10pm. INTERNATIONAL.

Housed in a centrally located building crafted from Cotswold stone, this excellent restaurant serves some of the most imaginative and best food in town, even superior to that of the Painswick Hotel. Many guests enjoy a predinner drink near the open fireplace of the heavily beamed bar.

The cuisine is well crafted—based only on the freshest of produce—and served in relaxed surroundings, including a summer garden. Begin with one of the delightful appetizers—perhaps terrine of sweetened leeks with smoked salmon and Chablis vinaigrette. The kitchen shines when preparing such dishes as Cornish cod lightly flaked with truffles and parsley potatoes with a wasabi dressing, or Bresse chicken with a timbale of wild rice.

OWLPEN MANOR: A JOURNEY TO BRIGADOON

As beautiful as Painswick is, there is a place even more lovely. It's the hamlet of ✪ **Owlpen Manor** near Dursley, lying immediately to the south of Painswick, off the beaten track. "Owlpen in Gloucestershire" has been called the British version of Brigadoon, an English Shangri-la. Vita Sackville-West in 1941 rhapsodized, "Ah, what a dream is there." Even Prince Charles, who lives nearby at Highgrove, called it "the epitome of an English village," with its population of 35 lucky souls.

The hamlet centers on a medieval church, an Elizabethan manor, and a collection of stone-built cottages. In the center, you can stroll through the gardens of the triple-gabled manor, constructed between 1450 and 1720. You can visit daily from April through October from 2 to 5pm, paying £5 ($8.50) to see the antique-filled house or else just £4 ($6.80) to stroll through the beautifully kept grounds. There's also a restaurant on site, Cyder Press, serving typically English food.

Insider's Tip: You can actually rent one of these cottages if you fall in love with the Cotswolds and want to hang out for a while. Several have been luxuriously converted into guest accommodations, including a studio in the old Tithe Barn or else our favorite, "Summerfield Cottage," opening onto a murmuring brook—it's a cliché picture postcard of the Cotswolds. Weekly rentals range from £225 to £800 ($382.50 to $1,360), although you can sometimes slip in for a 2-day break costing £85 ($144.50) for two persons.

This fairy-tale hamlet is overseen by Nicholas Mader, a descendant of Sir Geoffrey and Lady Mader, fabled Pre-Raphaelite art patrons. For information about visits to the manor and its grounds, the village itself, or cottage rentals, call ☎ **01453/860261.** In the United States you can call The London Connection at ☎ **801/393-9120** for more data. From Painswick, go south on A45—signposted Stroud—until you come to the junction on A419. At that point, turn south on B4066 in the direction of Uley and follow the signposts to Owlpen Manor.

4 Cheltenham

99 miles NW of London; 9 miles NE of Gloucester; 43 miles W of Oxford

Legend has it that the Cheltenham villagers discovered a mineral spring by chance when they noticed pigeons drinking from a spring and observed how healthy they were (the pigeon has been incorporated into the town's crest). King George III arrived in 1788 and launched the town's career as a spa.

Cheltenham today remains one of England's most fashionable spas, and many visitors come just to see its gardens from spring to autumn. The architecture is mainly Regency, with lots of ironwork, balconies, and verandas. Attractive parks and open spaces of greenery make the town especially inviting. The main street, the Promenade, has been called the most beautiful thoroughfare in Britain. Rather similar are Lansdowne Place and Montpellier Parade (with caryatids separating its stores, Montpellier Walk is one of England's most interesting shopping centers).

ESSENTIALS

GETTING THERE Twenty-one trains depart daily from London's Paddington Station for the 2-hour-and-15-minute trip. You may have to change trains at Bristol or Swindon. For schedules and information, call ☎ **0345/484950.** Trains between Cheltenham and Bristol take only an hour, with continuing service to Bath.

National Express offers nine buses daily from London's Victoria Coach Station to Cheltenham. The ride takes about 2½ hours. For schedules and information, call ☎ **0990/808080.**

If you're driving from London, head northwest on the M40 to Oxford, continuing along A40 to Cheltenham.

VISITOR INFORMATION The **Tourist Information Centre,** 77 Promenade (☎ **01242/522878**), is open September through June, Monday to Saturday from 9:30am to 5:15pm; July and August, Monday to Friday from 9:30am to 6pm, Saturday from 9:30am to 5:15pm, and Sunday from 10am to 2pm in July only.

SPECIAL EVENTS The **International Festival of Music** and the **Festival of Literature** take place each year in July and October, respectively, and attract internationally acclaimed performers and orchestras.

EXPLORING THE TOWN

Pittville Pump Room. East Approach Dr., Pittville Park. ☎ **01242/523852.** Free admission. Apr–Sept Wed–Mon 10am–4:30pm; Oct–Mar Wed–Mon 11am–4pm. From the town center, take Portland St. and Evesham Rd.

Cheltenham Waters are the only natural, consumable alkaline waters in Great Britain and are still taken at one of the spa's finest Regency buildings. The Pittville Pump Room is open Sundays from the end of May until the end of September for a host of activities, including lunch, afternoon cream teas, live classical music, landau carriage rides around the city, and brass bands playing in Pittville Park.

Cheltenham Art Gallery & Museum. Clarence St. ☎ **01242/237431.** Free admission. Mon–Sat 10am–5:20pm. Closed bank holidays.

This gallery houses one of the foremost collections of the Arts and Crafts movement, notably the fine furniture of William Morris and his followers. One section is devoted to Edward Wilson, Cheltenham's native son, who died with Captain Scott in the Antarctic in 1912. The gallery is located near Royal Crescent and the Coach Station.

Everyman Theatre. Regent St. ☎ **01242/572573.** Admission £4.50–£20 ($7.65–$34), depending on the event. Box office on performance days Mon–Sat 9:30am–8:30pm, Sun 5:30–8:30pm.

Cheltenham is the cultural center of the Cotswolds, a role solidified by the Everyman Theatre. Designed in the 1890s as an opera house by Frank Matcham, Victorian England's leading theater architect, it retains its ornate cornices, sculpted ceilings, and plush velvets despite extensive renovations to its stage and lighting facilities. The theater has recently begun to attract some of England's top dramatic companies. Shakespeare, musicals, comedies, and a variety of other genres are performed in the small (658-seat) but charming hall.

SHOPPING

The different quarters that make up Cheltenham's shopping district turn shopping into an unusually organized event. Start in the **Montpellier quarter** for a host of individual boutiques and an abundance of craft and specialty shops. Then, continue to the nearby **Suffolk quarter** to find most of the town's antiques stores.

And an enjoyable short stroll to the **Promenade** will take you by stores featuring attractive clothing and shoes, as well as several bookstores. From the Promenade, take Regent Street to **High Street,** which is mostly pedestrian-only, and you'll find several brand-name department stores in the **Beechwood Shopping Centre.**

The **weekly market** is in the Henrietta Street car park on Thursday and in Coronation Square on Friday. Weather permitting, markets open around 9am and close toward 4pm.

The **Courtyard,** on Montpellier Street in the heart of the Montpellier quarter, has become an award-winning shopping mall that offers a fun blend of shops specializing in unique fashion, furniture, and gift items. A good mix of restaurants, cafes, and wine bars rounds out the mall. **Hoopers** (☎ **01242/527505**) is a quality department store devoted to designer clothes for men and women. It also has a perfumery, hair and beauty salon, and fully air-conditioned restaurant.

Cavendish House, the Promenade (☎ **01242/521300**), is a long-established shopping landmark, housing two restaurants, a hair and beauty salon, an immense cosmetic and jewelry hall, and departments devoted to fine fashion, housewares, and furniture.

HITTING THE LINKS

The **Cotswold Hills Golf Club,** Ullenwood, Cheltenham (☎ **01242/515263**), is open year-round. The only requirements at this par-71 golf course are a reasonable standard of play, your own clubs, and no jeans or sneakers. Greens fees on weekdays are £25 ($42.50) for 18 holes and £30 ($51) unlimited play; £30 ($51) for 18 holes and £35 ($59.50) unlimited play on Saturday and Sunday.

The **Tewkesbury Park Golf and Country Club,** Lincoln Green Lane, Tewkesbury, 12 miles north of Cheltenham (☎ **01684/295405**), is a par-73 course requiring a reasonable standard of play, a golf bag, and no jeans, sneakers, or club sharing. Clubs are available for rent at £10 ($17). Greens fees for 18 holes are £20 ($34) weekdays and £35 ($59.50) Friday to Sunday.

Gloucestershire Golf and Country Club, Matson Lane, Gloucester (☎ **01452/411331** or 01452/525653), is a par-70 course that requires a reasonable standard of play and disallows jeans and sneakers, though tailored shorts are okay. Club rentals are available for £7 ($11.90). Eighteen holes costs £19 ($32.30) weekdays, £25 ($42.50) Saturday and Sunday.

WHERE TO STAY

Central Hotel. 7–9 Portland St., Cheltenham, Gloucestershire GL52 2NZ. ☎ **01242/582172** or 01242/524789. 14 units, 6 with shower. TV TEL. £42 ($71.40) double without bathroom, £52 ($88.40) double with shower. Rates include English breakfast. AE, DC, MC, V.

Within easy reach of Cheltenham's range of attractions, this hotel consists of a pair of stone houses that were originally built in the 1700s and then combined. Today, it's a family run hotel, with a street-level public house. Meals are served in the bar for under £10 ($17) each. The small comfortable bedrooms are conservatively modern, with everything you need to make tea. The private baths are compact; the public baths are adequately maintained, and you rarely have to wait in line.

✪ **The Greenway.** Shurdington, near Cheltenham, Gloucestershire GL51 5UG. ☎ **800/543-4135** in the U.S., or 01242/862352. Fax 01242/862780. 19 units. TV TEL. £165–£215 ($280.50–$365.50) double. Rates include English breakfast. AE, CB, DC, MC, V. Take A46 less than 4 miles southwest of Cheltenham.

An elegant and beautifully furnished former Elizabethan manor house in a garden setting, this is an ivy-clad Cotswold showpiece. Restored with sensitivity, Greenway rents rooms in both its main house and a converted coach house. Bedrooms, mid-size to spacious, are rather sumptuously outfitted. Bathrooms have deluxe toiletries, a hair dryer, and bathrobes. This is the best English country house living in the area.

Dining: The dining room is elegantly appointed with an extension added in the Victorian conservatory style. The cooking is superb, using quality produce and good, fresh ingredients that are handled deftly. Lunch is served from 12:30 to 2pm Sunday to Friday, and dinner from 7:30 to 9:30pm Monday to Saturday; dinner is only served between 7:30 and 8pm on Sunday. The modern British cuisine is now better than ever. Service is formal, on target, and polite.

Amenities: Access to nearby health club, car-rental desk, concierge, dry cleaning/laundry, limited room service.

Hotel de la Bere and Country Club. Southam, Cheltenham, Gloucestershire GL52 3NH. ☎ **01242/237771.** Fax 01242/236016. 57 units. TV TEL. £100 ($170) double. Half board (2-night minimum required) £39 ($66.30) per person. AE, DC, MC, V. Take B4632 3 miles northeast of town.

This 16th-century Cotswold-stone building near the Cheltenham racecourse has been owned by the de la Bere family for three centuries. They converted it into a hotel in 1972 and have made every effort to ensure that it retains its original charm. All rooms are furnished to preserve their individual character. Twenty rooms have recently been refurbished. Rooms range in size, and have double or king-size beds. Five rooms have double four-poster beds, and all have coffemakers. Bathrooms come with shower stalls and a hair dryer.

Dining: The restaurant, the Elizabethan Room, and the Royalist Room are all paneled in oak. The impressive menu uses fresh seasonable ingredients. The hotel restaurant doesn't serve lunch except on Sunday; dinner, however, is offered nightly.

Amenities: Health club, sauna, tennis courts, car-rental desk, concierge, 24-hour room service, dry cleaning/laundry, baby-sitting, outdoor heated pool.

✪ **Hotel on the Park.** Evesham Rd., Cheltenham, Gloucestershire GL52 2AH. ☎ **01242/518898.** Fax 01242/511526. www.hotelonthepark.co.uk. E-mail: stay@hotelonthepark.co.uk. 12 units. TV TEL. £94.50–£114.50 ($160.65–$194.65) double; from £124.50 ($211.65) suite. AE, DC, MC, V.

Opened in 1991, in what was formerly an 1830s private villa, this is one of the most talked-about hotels in town. It is located among similar terraced buildings in the once-prominent village of Pittville Spa, a half mile north of Cheltenham's town center. Owned and operated by Darryl and Lesley-Anne Gregory, who undertook most of the Regency-inspired interior design, it has received several awards. Each bedroom is named after a prominent 19th-century visitor who came here shortly after the villa was built. Comfortable and high-ceilinged, the rooms have stylish accessories and a tasteful assortment of antique and reproduction furniture. Bedrooms are beautifully appointed, with thoughtful extras such as sherry and mineral water. Four rooms are rented to nonsmokers. Bathrooms are laudable, each roomy with deluxe toiletries.

Dining: The hotel dining room, called simply the Restaurant, is in the classic Regency style.

Amenities: Access to nearby health club, car-rental, room service, dry cleaning/laundry, baby-sitting, courtesy car.

Lawn Hotel. 5 Pittville Lawn, Cheltenham, Gloucestershire GL52 2BE. ☎ or fax **01242/526638.** 9 units. TV. £40–£45 ($68–$76.50) double. Rates include English breakfast. No credit cards. Bus nos. 1A, 2A, or 3A.

Built in 1830 with a stucco exterior, this elegant landmark Regency house lies just inside the iron gates leading to Pittville Park and the Pump Room. Owned by the Armitage family, it offers pleasantly decorated rooms with tea-making equipment. Each has a small bath with a shower stall and adequate shelf space. Evening meals can be arranged, beginning at £7.50 ($12.75) per person. The hotel is convenient to the town center and its Promenade, about a 10-minute walk away.

WHERE TO DINE

✪ **Le Champignon Sauvage.** 24–26 Suffolk Rd. ☎ **01242/573449.** Reservations required. 2-course fixed-price lunch £16.50 ($28.05); 3-course fixed-price lunch £18.50 ($31.45); 2-course fixed-price dinner Tues–Fri £32 ($54.40); 3-course fixed-price dinner Mon–Fri £37 ($62.90). AE, DC, MC, V. Tues–Sat 12:30–1:30pm and 7:30–9pm. FRENCH/ENGLISH.

This is among the culinary highlights of the Cotswolds. David Everitt-Matthias, a chef of considerable talent, wisely limits the selection of dishes every evening for better quality control. Some evenings he allows his imagination to roam a bit, so dining here is usually a pleasant surprise. You might begin with light cauliflower soup flavored with cumin. Main courses might include braised lamb dumplings with roasted carrots and shallots. Matthias was recently named the dessert chef of the year in England, so be sure to try one of the acclaimed sweet treats. Choices include iced liquorice parfait with damson sorbet, and baked caramel cheesecake with caramelized banana.

Le Petit Blanc. In the Queen's Hotel. The Promenade. ☎ **01242/266800.** Reservations required. Main courses £8–£14.50 ($13.60–$24.65). Set lunch or dinner £12.50–£14 ($21.25–$23.80) for 2 courses. Set dinner 6–7:30pm only. AE, DC, MC, V. Daily noon–3pm; Mon–Sat 6–11pm, Sun 6–10:30pm. FRENCH.

Already a bit of a dining legend in Oxford, this offspring has invaded Cheltenham and is waking up the sleepy tastebuds of the old-fashioned spa. Under the guidance of master chef Raymond Blanc, a local chef, Stephen Nash, is rather inspired in a brasserie mode with brushed steel tables, bench seating, and a hip staff. Knowledgeable and attentive, the staff presents you with beautifully prepared food based on the day's freshest and the best from the market. You might start with something classical, such as Oxford sausages with onion gravy and chips, or something more modern, perhaps salmon niçoise flavored with a mustard and pesto. Superb in every way is the sautéed asparagus with rocket and balsamic dressing. For a main, opt for a roast monkfish wrapped in Parma ham and served with pesto noodles that are "divine," in the words of one diner. Save room for the pineapple and kirsch parfait with a thin layer of meringue and a side helping of mango coulis.

CHELTENHAM AFTER DARK

The major venue for entertainment is the **Everyman Theatre** (see above), which is the premier sightseeing attraction of Cheltenham. But there's a lot more theater at the **Playhouse,** Bath Road (☎ **01242/522852**), with new local, amateur productions of drama, comedy, dance, and opera being staged at the dizzying pace of every 2 weeks. Tickets are £5–£8.50 ($8.50–$14.45). **Axiom Centre for the Arts,** 57–59 Winchcombe St. (☎ **01242/253183**), is a venue for working artists, musical performance, and traveling exhibitions. The complex houses studio spaces, two galleries featuring works by local artists, a theater specializing in fringe productions, a cafe-bar, and **The Back Bar,** the only local spot for live music, with entertainment Thursday to Saturday and Monday to Tuesday. Bands range from indie to jazz. On Saturday, they break out the turntables with DJs playing an eclectic dance mix. There's usually only a cover charge when bands play.

You can choose your groove at **Embassy,** St. James Square (☎ **01242/527700**); upstairs is generally soul and R&B, whereas downstairs features house and techno Thursday and Friday nights from 10pm to 2am, and Saturday nights from 9:30pm to 2am. The cover charge ranges from £1 to £2 ($1.70 to $3.40), depending on the night.

A SIDE TRIP TO ROYAL SUDELEY CASTLE

Royal Sudeley Castle. In the village of Winchcombe (6 miles northeast of Cheltenham). ☎ **01242/602308.** Admission £6.20 ($10.55) adults, £5.20 ($8.85) seniors, £3.20 ($5.45) children 5–15 years, £17 ($28.90) family ticket. Apr–Oct daily 10am–5:30pm; off-season Tues–Sun 10am–5:30pm. From Cheltenham, take the regular bus to Winchcombe and get off at Abbey Terrace. Then, walk the short distance along the road to the castle. If you're driving, take the B4632 north out of Cheltenham, through Prestbury, and up Cleve Hill to Abbey Terrace, where you can drive right up to the castle.

This 15th-century structure is one of England's finer stately homes. It has a rich history that begins in Saxon times, when the village was the capital of the Mercian kings. Later, Catherine Parr, the sixth wife of Henry VIII, lived and died here. Her tomb is in a chapel on the grounds, which include a host of formal gardens like the Queen's Garden, now planted with old-world roses and dating to the time of Catherine Parr. While exploring the gardens, you're sure to see the waterfowl and flamboyant peacocks that call Sudeley home. For the past 30 years, Lady Ashcombe, an American by birth, has owned the castle and welcomed visitors from the world over. The castle houses many works of art by Constable, Turner, Rubens, and Van Dyck, among others, and has several permanent exhibitions, magnificent furniture and glass, and many artifacts from the castle's past. In the area to the right of the keep, as you enter the castle, workshops are devoted to talented local artisans who continue to use traditional techniques to produce stained glass, textiles, wood and leather articles, and marbled paper.

5 Bibury

86 miles W of London; 30 miles W of Oxford; 26 miles E of Gloucester

On the road from Burford to Cirencester, Bibury is one of the loveliest spots in the Cotswolds. In fact, the utopian romancer of Victoria's day, poet William Morris, called it England's most beautiful village. In the Cotswolds, it is matched only by Painswick for its scenic village beauty and purity. Both villages are still unspoiled by modern intrusions.

GETTING THERE

About five trains per day depart from London's Paddington Station for the 1-hour-10-minute trip to Kemble, the nearest station, 13 miles south of Bibury. Some will require an easy change of train in Swindon (the connecting train waits just across the tracks). For schedules and information, call ☎ **0345/484950.** There are no buses from Kemble to Bibury, but most hotels will arrange transportation if you ask in advance.

Five buses leave London's Victoria Coach Station daily for Cirencester, 7 miles from Bibury. For schedules and information, call ☎ **0990/808080.** There are no connecting buses into Bibury, but local hotels will send a car, and taxis are available.

If you're driving from London, take the M4 to Exit 15, head toward Cirencester, then follow A33 (on some maps this is still designated as B4425) to Bibury.

EXPLORING THE TOWN

On the banks of the tiny Coln River, Bibury is noted for **Arlington Row,** a group of 17th-century gabled cottages protected by the National Trust. These houses were originally built for weavers. They are its biggest and most-photographed attraction, but it's rude to peer into the windows, as many do, because people still live here.

To get a view of something a bit out of the ordinary for the Cotswolds, check out **St. Mary's Parish Church.** As the story goes, the wool merchants who had the power and the money in the area were rebuilding the churches. However, they did not finish the restoration to St. Mary's, and, as a result, much of the original Roman-style architecture has been left intact. The 14th-century decorated-styled windows have even survived the years. This is an often overlooked treasure.

The once-prosperous mill has been silenced and converted into the **Cotswold Country Museum** (☎ **01451/860715**), where visitors are treated to a host of antiquated wagons and machines once used in the area, and a variety of display rooms that illustrate the way people used to handle day-to-day existence. It was recently combined with the **Cotswold Countryside Collection** (see below) to form the **Cotswold Heritage Center.** Open April through November, Monday to Saturday from 10am to 5pm. Admission to the heritage center is £2.50 ($4.25) for adults, £2 ($3.40) for seniors, £1 ($1.70) for students, and 80p ($1.35) for children 5–16. Free for age 4 and under. A family ticket covering 2 adults and 2 children is £5 ($8.50).

WHERE TO STAY & DINE

Bibury Court Hotel. Bibury, Gloucestershire GL7 5NT. ☎ **01285/740337.** Fax 01285/740660. 20 units. TV TEL. £110 ($187) double; £150 ($255) suite. Rates include continental breakfast and VAT. AE, DC, MC, V.

This Jacobean manor house was built by Sir Thomas Sackville in 1633 (parts of it date from Tudor times). Sackville, an illegitimate son of the first Earl of Dorset, launched a family dynasty. His family occupied the house for several generations. Through the female line it passed to the Cresswells, who, eventually, owing to a disputed will and years of litigation, sold the house in the last century to Lord Sherborne. (Charles Dickens is said to have written *Bleak House* with this case in mind.) The house was a residence until it was turned into a hotel in 1968.

You enter the 8 acres of grounds through a large gateway, and the lawn extends to the Coln River. The structure is built of Cotswold stone, with many gables, huge chimneys, and a formal graveled entryway. Many rooms have four-poster beds, original oak paneling, and antiques. Bedrooms are furnished in old English style, but have modern comforts, plus bathrooms with a shower and tub combination (one has a shower stall instead). Rooms come in a range of sizes, and two are large enough for families.

Dining: Meals are quite special. Dinners are slightly more extravagant than the more reasonably priced bar lunches. After tea and biscuits in the drawing room, walk across the lawn along the river to a little church.

The Swan. Bibury, Gloucestershire GL7 5NW. ☎ **01285/740695.** Fax 01285/740473. www.swanhotel.co.uk. 18 units. TV TEL. £165–£265 ($280.50–$450.50) double. Rates include English breakfast. AE, MC, V.

Well managed, upscale, and discreet, this hotel and restaurant—the finest in the village—originated as a riverside cottage in the 1300s, was greatly expanded throughout the centuries, and received its latest enlargement and refurbishment in the early 1990s. Owners Alex and Liz Furtek outfitted parts of the interior in a cozily overstuffed mode reminiscent of World War II. There's an elegant bar and wood-burning fireplaces. An automatic "pianola" (player piano) provides music in the lobby. The bedrooms are outfitted with antique furniture and an individualized decor. Rooms vary in size, and each contains an elegant bed with soft linens and a beautifully maintained private bath. One accommodation is large enough for a family.

Dining: An informal brasserie with outdoor courtyard seating is open daily from 10am to 10pm for coffee, drinks, snacks, and platters of food. There's also a more formal restaurant specializing in modern British food. It's open daily for dinner only and Sunday lunch. You may enjoy Bibury trout from a nearby river.

6 Burford

76 miles NW of London; 20 miles W of Oxford

Built of Cotswold stone and serving as a gateway to the area, the unspoiled medieval town of Burford is largely famous for its Norman church (ca. 1116) and its High Street lined with coaching inns. Burford was one of the last of the great wool centers, the industry bleating out its last breath during Queen Victoria's day. Be sure to photograph the bridge across the Windrush River where Queen Elizabeth I once stood. As the antiques shops along High Street will testify, Burford today is definitely equipped for tourists.

The River Windrush, which toward Burford is flanked by willows through meadows, passes beneath the packhorse bridge and goes around the church and away through more meadows. Strolling along its banks is one of the most delightful experiences in the Cotswolds.

ESSENTIALS

GETTING THERE Many trains depart daily from London's Paddington Station to Oxford, a 45-minute trip. For schedules and information, call ☎ **0345/484950.** From Oxford, passengers walk a very short distance to the entrance of the Taylor

Institute, from which about three or four buses per day make the 30-minute run to Burford.

A **National Express** bus runs from London's Victoria Coach Station to Burford several times a day, with many stops along the way. It's a 2-hour ride. For schedules and information, call ☎ **0990/808080.**

If you're driving from Oxford, head west on A40 to Burford.

VISITOR INFORMATION The **Tourist Information Centre** is at the Old Brewery on Sheep Street (☎ **01993/823558**) and is open November to February Monday to Saturday from 10am to 4:30pm; March to October Monday to Saturday from 9:30am to 5:30pm.

SEEING THE SIGHTS

Approaching Burford from the south, you'll experience one of the finest views of any ancient market town in the country. The main street sweeps down to the River Windrush, past an extraordinary collection of houses of various styles and ages. Burford's ancient packhorse bridge is still doing duty at the bottom of the hill. The hills opposite provide a frame of fields and trees and, with luck, panoramic skies.

Although the wool trade has long since vanished, most of Burford remains unchanged in appearance, with its old houses in the High Street and nearby side streets. Nearly all are built of local stone. Like many Cotswold towns, Burford has a Sheep Street, with many fine stone-built houses covered with roofs of Stonesfield slate. Burford Church (ca. 1175) is almost cathedral-like in proportion. It was enlarged throughout succeeding centuries until the decline of the wool trade. Little has changed here since about 1500.

Traders and vendors still set up their stalls under the Tolsey on Friday, where from the 12th century the guild has collected tolls from anyone wishing to trade in the town. It still stands at the corner of Sheep Street. On the upper floor is the minor Tolsey Museum, where you can see a medieval seal bearing Burford's insignia, the "rampant cat."

Two miles south of Burford on A361 lies the **Cotswold Wildlife Park** (☎ **01993/823006**). The 120 acres of gardens and forests around this Victorian manor house have been transformed into a jungle of sorts, with a Noah's Ark consortium of animals ranging from voracious ants to rare Asiatic lions. Children can romp around the farmyard and the adventure playground. A narrow-gauge railway runs from April to October, and there are extensive picnic areas plus a cafeteria. Hours are Easter through September daily from 10am to 7pm; off-season daily 10am to 5pm. Admission is £5.80 ($9.85) for adults, £3.80 ($6.45) for seniors and children 3 to 16, and free for children 2 and under.

And before you leave Burford, we suggest a slight detour to **Swinbrook,** a pretty village by the Windrush River immediately to the east. It's best known as the one-time home of the fabled Mitford sisters. Visit the local parish church to see the grave of writer Nancy Mitford and the impressive tiered monuments to the Fettiplace family.

On High Street in Burford, you'll find several antiques shops, including **Manfred Schotten Antiques,** The Crypt, 109 High St. (☎ **01993/822302**). Sporting antiques and collectibles, they also carry library and club furniture. **Jonathan Fyson Antiques,** 50/52 High St. (☎ **01993/823204**), carries English and continental furniture and porcelain, glass, and brass items. On Cheltenham Road, **Gateway Antiques** (☎ **01993/823678**) has a variety of items displayed in large showrooms. English pottery, metalware, and furniture dominate the inventory. Unique arts and crafts items and interesting decorative objects are fun to browse through, even if you don't buy.

WHERE TO STAY

✪ **Bay Tree Hotel.** 12–14 Sheep St., Burford, Oxfordshire OX18 6LW. ☎ **01993/822791.** Fax 01993/823008. www.cotswold-inns-hotels.co.uk. 21 units. TV TEL. £135 ($229.50) double; £210 ($357) suite. Rates include English breakfast. AE, DC, MC, V.

This is the best and most atmospheric of Burford's many interesting old inns. The house was built for Sir Lawrence Tanfield, the unpopular lord chief baron of the Exchequer to Elizabeth I. The house has oak-paneled rooms with stone fireplaces, and a high-beamed hall with a minstrel's gallery. 20th-century comforts have been discreetly installed in the tastefully furnished rooms, which are mostly midsized. Some of the accommodations are in a comfortable annex, although the chambers in the main building, nine in all, have more character. Try to get a room overlooking the terraced gardens at the rear of the house.

Dining: The hotel has a country-style bar, The Woolsack, offering guests and visitors a choice of light lunches. The head chef is known for his tempting menus, with dishes based on local and seasonal produce. The 65-seat restaurant overlooks the gardens and retains all of its original charm. The delightful conservatory is now the residents' lounge.

Golden Pheasant Hotel. 91 High St., Burford, Oxfordshire OX18 4QA. ☎ **01993/823223.** Fax 01993/822621. 12 units. TV TEL. £75–£85 ($127.50–$144.50) double. Rates include English breakfast. AE, MC, V.

The Golden Pheasant was the 15th-century home of a prosperous wool merchant, but it began serving food and drink in the 1730s when it was used both to brew and serve beer. Today, it's the second best place to stay in town (it lacks the rich furnishings of the best, the Bay Tree Hotel, reviewed above). Like many of its neighbors, the Golden Pheasant is capped with a slate roof and fronted with hand-chiseled stones. The rooms are cozy; one has a four-poster bed. Accommodations come in a range of sizes, many of them a bit small. Each one, nonetheless, is stylishly appointed with period furniture. One room is large enough for a family and all but one come with a shower and tub combination (one has a shower stall).

Dining: Inside, a candlelit restaurant serves both French and English specialties. The new bar also merits a visit.

✪ **The Lamb Inn.** Sheep St., Burford, Oxfordshire OX18 4LR. ☎ **01993/823155.** Fax 01993/822228. 15 units. TV TEL. £100–£120 ($170–$204) double. Rates include English breakfast. MC, V.

This thoroughly Cotswold house was solidly built in 1430 with thick stones, mullioned and leaded windows, many chimneys and gables, and a slate roof now mossy with age. Vying with the Bay Tree in antique furnishings, it opens onto a stone-paved rear garden, with a rose-lined walk and a shaded lawn. The bedrooms are a mixture of today's comforts and antiques. Rooms vary in size, and each has a compact bath with a tub and shower combination (one has a shower stall), and a hair dryer. The public living rooms have heavy oak beams, stone floors, window seats, Oriental rugs, and fine antiques.

Dining: Light lunches and snacks are served in the bars and lounges or in the garden in summer. Dinner, as well as a traditional Sunday lunch, are offered in the dining room with a garden view. See below for our review.

WHERE TO DINE

After you've browsed through the antiques shops, head to **Burford House** (☎ **01993/823151**) for tea. This old Cotswold favorite serves daily from 8am to 5pm. Freshly baked goods, including flans, scones, cakes, and muffins, will tempt you.

Lamb Inn Restaurant. Sheep St. ☎ **01993/823155.** Reservations recommended for dinner. 2-course fixed-price menu £24 ($40.80); 3-course fixed-price menu £29 ($49.30); Sun lunch £19 ($32.30); bar lunches from £6 ($10.20). MC, V. Mon–Sat noon–2pm, Sun 12:30–1:30pm; daily 7–9:30pm. ENGLISH/CONTINENTAL.

A meal in this pretty pillared restaurant is the perfect way to cap off a visit to Burford. Good pub lunches dominate the agenda at midday, whereas dinners are more formal, candlelit affairs. The evening menu is beautifully cooked and served. You might begin with cream of broccoli and blue cheese soup before moving on to rack of lamb with parsnip, sage and a port sauce, or medallions of venison with sautéed red cabbage and a beetroot coriander sauce.

The pub here attracts folks from all walks of life. They seem to adore its mellow atmosphere and charm. Guinness, cider, and a carefully chosen collection of ales, including a local brew, Wadworth, are on tap.

7 Bourton-on-the-Water

85 miles NW of London; 36 miles NW of Oxford

Its fans define it as the quintessential Cotswold village, with a history going back to the Celts. Residents fiercely protect the heritage of 15th- and 16th-century architecture, even though their town is singled out for practically every bus tour that rolls through the Cotswolds. Populated in Anglo-Saxon times, Burton-on-the-Water developed into a strategic outpost along the ancient Roman road, Fosse Way, that traversed Britain from the North Sea to St. George's Channel. During the Middle Ages, its prosperity came from wool, which was shipped all over Europe. During the Industrial Revolution when the greatest profits lay in finished textiles, it became a backwater as a producer of raw wool—albeit with the happy result for us that it was never "modernized," and its traditional appearance was preserved.

You'll feel like Gulliver voyaging to Lilliput when you arrive in this scenic Cotswold village on the banks of the Windrush River. Its mellow stone houses, its village greens on the banks of the water, and its bridges have earned it the title of "Venice of the Cotswolds." Don't expect gondoliers, however. This makes a good stopover, if not for the night, at least as a place to enjoy a lunch and a rest along the riverbanks. Afterwards, you can take a peek inside St. Lawrence's Church in the center of the village. Built on the site of a Roman temple, it has a crypt from 1120 and a tower from 1784.

GETTING THERE

Trains go from London's Paddington Station to nearby Moreton-in-Marsh, a trip of 2 hours. For schedules and information, call ☎ **0345/484950.** From here, take a Pulhams Bus Company coach 6 miles to Bourton-on-the-Water. Trains also run from London to Cheltenham and Kingham; while somewhat more distant than Moreton-in-Marsh, both have bus connections to Bourton-on-the-Water.

National Express buses run from Victoria Coach Station in London to both Cheltenham and Stow-on-the-Wold. For schedules and information, call ☎ **0990/808080.** Pulhams Bus Company operates about four buses per day from both towns to Bourton-on-the-Water.

If you're driving from Oxford, head west on A40 to the junction with A429 (Fosse Way). Take it northeast to Bourton-on-the-Water.

LILLIPUT, THE BIRDS, VINTAGE CARS & MORE

Within the town are a handful of minor museums, each of which was established from idiosyncratic collections amassed over the years by local residents. They include the **Bourton Model Railway Exhibition and Toy Shop** (☎ **01451/820686**) and **Birdland,** described below.

After you've seen them, stop by the quaint little tearoom called **Small Talk,** on High Street (☎ **01451/821596**). It's full of dainty lace and fine china and appetizing scones and pastries. Sit at a table overlooking the water and enjoy a pot of tea and some good conversation.

Birdland. Rissington Rd. ☎ **01451/820480.** Admission £4 ($6.80) adults, £3 ($5.10) seniors, £2.50 ($4.25) children 4–14; children under 4 free. Apr–Oct daily 10am–5pm; Nov–Mar daily 10am–4pm.

This handsomely designed attraction is set on 8½ acres of field and forests on the banks of Windrush River, about a mile east of Bourton-on-the-Water. It houses about 1,200 birds representing 361 species, many of them on exhibition for the first time. Included is the largest and most varied collection of penguins in any zoo, with glass-walled tanks that allow observers to appreciate their agile underwater movements. There's also an enviable collection of hummingbirds. Birdland has a picnic area and a children's playground in a wooded copse.

Cotswold Motor Museum. The Old Mill. ☎ **01451/821255.** Admission £2 ($3.40) adults, £1 ($1.70) children. Feb–Nov daily 10am–6pm.

This museum is actually in a historic water mill from the 1700s. It has fun displays of cars, bikes, caravans from the 1920s, toys, and the largest collection of advertising signs in Europe. Visitors can also see village shops from the past.

Cotswold Perfumery. Victoria St. ☎ **01451/820698.** Admission £1.75 ($3) adults, £1.50 ($2.55) children and seniors. Mon–Sat 9:30am–5pm, Sun 10:30am–5pm. Closed Dec 25–26.

This permanent perfume exhibition details the history of the perfume industry and also focuses on its production. There's an audiovisual show in a "smelly vision" theater, a perfume quiz, a perfume garden full of plants grown exclusively for their fragrance, and a genealogy chart that can be used by visitors to select their own personal perfume. Perfumes are made on the premises and sold in the shop.

The Model Village at the Old New Inn. High St. ☎ **01451/820467.** Admission £2.50 ($4.25) adults, £2 ($3.40) seniors, £1.75 ($3) children. Daily 9am–6pm or dusk in summer; daily 10am–4pm in winter.

Beginning in the 1930s, a local hotelier, Mr. Morris, whiled away some of the doldrums of the Great Depression by constructing a scale model (1:9) of Bourton-on-the-Water as a testimony to its architectural charms. This isn't a tiny and cramped display set behind glass—the model is big enough so you can walk through this near-perfect and most realistic model village.

Cotswold Countryside Collection. Fosse Way, Northleach (Cotswold District Council). ☎ **01451/860715.** Admission to Cotswold Heritage Center £2.50 ($4.25) adults, £1 ($1.70) students, 80p ($1.35) children 5–16, free 4 and under, £5 ($8.50) family ticket. Apr–Oct Mon–Sat 10am–5pm, Sun 2–5pm; Nov–Dec Sat 10am–4pm.

This museum of rural life is actually located off the A40 between Burford and Cheltenham. It was recently combined with the Cotswold Country Museum (see above) to form the Cotswold Heritage Center. You can see the Lloyd-Baker collection of agricultural history, including wagons, horse-drawn implements, and tools. A Cotswold gallery records the social history of the area. "Below Stairs" is an exhibition of laundry, dairy, and kitchen implements. The museum was once a house of correction, and its history is displayed in the reconstructed cell block and courtroom.

WHERE TO STAY & DINE

Chester House Hotel. Victoria St., Bourton-on-the-Water, Cheltenham, Gloucestershire GL54 2BU. ☎ **01451/820286.** Fax 01451/820471. www.bizare.demon.co.uk/chester. E-mail: juliand@chesterhouse.u-net.com. 22 units. TV TEL. £75–£103 ($127.50–$175.10) double. Rates include continental or English breakfast. AE, DC, MC, V. Closed mid-Dec to early Feb.

This 300-year-old Cotswold-stone house, built on the banks of the Windrush River, is conveniently located in the center of town. It blends an old building with a row of stables converted into a hotel with comfortable rooms. Many of the small to mid-size bedrooms have been redecorated. Room amenities include a beverage maker. Bathrooms are small and compact, but with adequate shelf space. Most of them have a tub and shower combination, and some of them are also equipped with a hair dryer. The hotel also has an intimate bar and a restaurant offering reliable English cuisine, including Cotswold lamb.

✪ **Dial House Hotel.** The Chestnuts, High St., Bourton-on-the-Water, Gloucestershire GL54 2AN. ☎ **01451/822244.** Fax 01451/810126. www.dialhousehotel.com. E-mail: info@dialhouse.com. 14 units. TV TEL. £104 ($176.80) double. Rates include breakfast. AE, MC, V.

Our top choice in the area, this 1698 house is constructed from yellow Cotswold stone and stands in the heart of the village center. Peter and Lynn Boxhall, your hosts, offer not only a nostalgic retreat but some of the best cuisine in the area.

Set on 1½ acres of manicured gardens, the house overlooks the Windrush River. The Boxhalls have restored all of the rooms, giving each accommodation an individual character, some with four-poster beds. Three bedrooms are nonsmoking. Two of the rooms, as charming as those in the main building, are in a converted coach house. Most of the rooms are spacious, although style, shape, and size vary. Most of the compact bathrooms have a tub and shower combination (the rest a shower stall). Log fires burn on chilly nights, and there are two small dining rooms, one with an inglenook fireplace.

Dining: Under oak beams and on flagstone floors, your candlelit table is the setting for modern British dishes, the best of local game and fish. Try pink salmon fish cakes with a pink champagne sauce or medallions of pork with a pistachio and apricot stuffing. Nonresidents can dine here but should call first for a reservation.

The Old Manse Hotel. Victoria St., Bourton-on-the-Water, Cheltenham, Gloucestershire GL54 2BX. ☎ **01451/820082.** Fax 01451/810381. www.oldenglish.co.uk. 15 units. TV TEL. £65–£85 ($110.50–$144.50) double. Rates include English breakfast. AE, MC, V.

An architectural gem, this hotel sits in the center of town by the river that wanders through the village green. Built of Cotswold stone in 1748, with chimneys, dormers, and small-paned windows, it has been modernized inside. Rooms are mid-size and cozy, like those you'd find in your favorite great-aunt's home. The small bathrooms have adequate shelf space.

Dining: Dining is a treat in Le Jardin du Vin, serving dinner daily from 6:30 to 9:30pm. Typical dishes include such appetizers as homemade venison sausage or sautéed breast of pigeon, followed by Dover sole, stuffed Bibury trout, and roast English lamb. Sometimes roast pheasant is featured.

Old New Inn. High St., Bourton-on-the-Water, Cheltenham, Gloucestershire GL54 2AF. ☎ **01451/820467.** Fax 01451/810236. www.ourworld.compuserve.com/homepages/old-new-inn. E-mail: old-new-inn@compuserve.com 19 units, 17 with bathroom. TV. £76 ($129.20) double. Rates include English breakfast. MC, V.

The Old New Inn is a landmark in the village. On the main street, overlooking the river, it's a good example of Queen Anne design (the miniature model village in its garden is reviewed above). Hungry or tired travelers are drawn to the old-fashioned comforts and cuisine of this most English inn. The rooms are comfortable, with homelike furnishings and soft beds. The bedrooms contain such amenities as a coffeemaker. Some of the rooms are spacious, especially if they have a four-poster, but most are small and lie in a cottage annex. Baths have shower stalls and adequate shelf space.

Nonresidents are also welcome here for meals; a 2-course fixed-price lunch costs £10 ($17) and a 2-course fixed-price dinner costs £15.50 ($26.35). You may want to spend an evening in the redecorated pub-lounge either playing darts or chatting with the villagers.

The Great Cotswold Ramble

A walking tour between the villages of Upper and Lower Slaughter, with an optional extension to Bourton-on-the-Water, is one of the most memorable in England. It's a mile each way between the Slaughters, or 2½ miles from Upper Slaughter to Bourton-on-the-Water. This walk could take between 2 and 4 hours.

The architecture of Upper and Lower Slaughter is so unusual that you're likely to remember this easy hike for many years. By striking out on foot, you also avoid at least some of the traffic that taxes the nerves and goodwill of local residents during peak season. En route, you're likely to glimpse the waterfowl that inhabit the rivers, streams, and millponds that crisscross this much-praised region.

A well-worn footpath known as **Warden's Way** meanders beside the edge of the swift-moving River Eye. From its well-marked beginning in Upper Slaughter's central car park, the path passes sheep grazing in meadows, antique houses crafted from local honey-colored stone, stately trees arching over ancient millponds, and footbridges that have endured centuries of foot traffic and rain.

The rushing river powers a historic mill on the northwestern edge of Lower Slaughter. In quiet eddies, you'll see ample numbers of waterfowl and birds, including wild ducks, gray wagtails, mute swans, coots, and Canadian geese.

Most visitors turn around at Lower Slaughter, but Warden's Way continues another 1½ miles to Bourton-on-the-Water by following the Fosse Way, route of an ancient Roman footpath. The path leaves the river's edge and strikes out across cattle pastures in a southerly direction. Most of it from Lower Slaughter to Bourton-on-the-Water is covered by tarmac; it's closed to cars, but ideal for walking or biking. You're legally required to close each of the several gates that stretch across the footpath.

Warden's Way will introduce you to Bourton-on-the-Water through the hamlet's northern edges. The first landmark you'll see will be the tower of St. Lawrence's Anglican Church. From the base of the church, walk south along The Avenue (one of the hamlet's main streets) and end your Cotswold ramble on the Village Green, directly in front of the War Memorial.

You can follow this route in reverse, but parking is more plentiful in Upper Slaughter than in Lower Slaughter.

8 Upper & Lower Slaughter

Midway between Bourton-on-the-Water and Stow-on-the-Wold are two of the prettiest villages in the Cotswolds: Upper and Lower Slaughter. Don't be put off by the name—"Slaughter" is actually a corruption of *de Sclotre,* the name of the original Norman landowner. Houses here are constructed of honey-colored Cotswold stone, and a stream meanders right through the street, providing a home for free-wandering ducks, which beg scraps from kindly passersby. Upper Slaughter has a fine example of a 17th-century Cotswold manor house.

The **Old Mill,** in Lower Slaughter (☎ **01451/820052**), is a sturdy 19th-century stone structure built on the River Eye with the sole purpose of grinding out flour. The river still turns the massive water wheel that powers this Victorian flour mill today. Visitors can enjoy an ice-cream parlor and tearoom while visiting the mill.

GETTING THERE

Lower Slaughter and Stow-on-the-Wold are 4 miles apart. From Stow, take A429 (the Main Fosse Way) and follow signs to Cirencester and Bourton-on-the-Water. Turn off the highway when you see signs to Upper and Lower Slaughter. The road will then divide, and you can pick which hamlet you want to head to.

WHERE TO STAY & DINE

✪ **Lords of the Manor Hotel.** Upper Slaughter, near Cheltenham, Gloucestershire GL54 2JD. ☎ **01451/820243.** Fax 01451/820696. E-mail: lordofthemanor@btinternet.com. 27 units. TV TEL. £138 ($234.60) standard double; £138–£295 ($234.60–$501.50) old rectory bedrooms; £295 ($501.50) suite. Rates include English breakfast. AE, DC, MC, V. Take A429 18 miles north of Cheltenham.

A 17th-century house set on several acres of rolling fields, the Lords of the Manor has gardens with a stream featuring brown trout. A quintessentially British hotel of great style and amenities, it's a showplace. It may be modernized, but it successfully maintains the quiet country-house atmosphere of 300 years ago. Half the rooms are in a converted old barn and granary, and many have lovely views. Bedrooms come in various sizes, some quite large, although most of them are midsize. Each has a high standard of comfort and elegant beds with sumptuous linens. The deluxe bathrooms have a hair dryer.

Dining: The walls in the lounge bar are hung with family portraits of the original lords of the manor. Another bar overlooks the garden. The country atmosphere is carried into the dining room as well, with its antiques and mullioned windows. The well-prepared dishes are all fresh and home cooked.

✪ **Lower Slaughter Manor.** Lower Slaughter, near Cheltenham, Gloucestershire GL54 2HP. ☎ **01451/820456.** Fax 01451/822150. 18 units. TV TEL. £175–£375 ($297.50–$637.50) double. Rates include English breakfast. AE, DC, MC, V. Take A429 turnoff at the sign for The Slaughters, and drive 1/2 mile; manor is on right as you enter the village. No children under 12.

Built in 1658, Lower Slaughter Manor was owned by Sir George Whitmore, high sheriff of Gloucestershire. Today, it's one of the great inns of the Cotswolds, although its charms are matched in every way by Lords of the Manor (see above). It remained in the same family until 1964 when it was sold as a private residence. Standing on its own private grounds, it has spacious and sumptuously furnished rooms, some with four-poster beds. Bedrooms in the main building have more old English character, although those in the annex are equally comfortable and include the same amenities.

Dining: The inn was always a solid dining choice, but it's improved its offerings even further under new head chef Alan Dann, who cooks in the modern French style, using the best English produce. Beef and lamb come from specially bred stock in

Scotland, the smoked salmon is wild, and the fish are mainly from inshore fishing boats docked at Brixham. The wine list now extends to 500 selections, with emphasis on New York and French vintages.

Amenities: Room service is available from the inn's excellent restaurant. Indoor heated swimming pool, sauna, room service, dry cleaning/laundry service.

9 Stow-on-the-Wold

9 miles SE of Broadway; 10 miles S of Chipping Campden; 4 miles S of Moreton-in-Marsh; 21 miles S of Stratford-upon-Avon

As you pass along through Shakespeare's "high wild hills and rough uneven ways," you arrive at Stow-on-the-Wold, its very name evoking the elusive spirit of the Cotswolds, one of the greatest sheep-rearing districts of England. Lying 800 feet above sea level, it stands on a plateau where "the cold winds blow," or so goes the old saying. This town prospered when Cotswold wool was demanded the world over. Stow-on-the-Wold may not be the cognoscenti's favorite—Chipping Campden takes that honor—but it's even more delightful as it has a real Cotswold town atmosphere.

The town lies smack in the middle of the Fosse Way, one of the Roman trunk roads that cut a swath through Britain. Kings have passed through here, including Edward VI, son of Henry VIII, and they've bestowed their approval on the town. Stagecoaches stopped off here for the night on their way to Cheltenham.

A 14th-century cross stands in the large Market Square, where you can still see the stocks where "offenders" in the past were jeered at and punished by the townspeople who threw rotten eggs at them. The final battle between the Roundheads and the Royalists took place outside Stow-on-the-Wold, and mean old Cromwell incarcerated 1,500 Royalist troops in St. Edward's Market Square.

The square today teems with pubs and outdoor cafes. But leave the square at some point and wander at leisure along some of the narrowest alleyways in Britain. When the summer crowds get you down, head in almost any direction from Stow to surrounding villages that look like sets from a Merchant/Ivory film.

ESSENTIALS

GETTING THERE Several trains run daily from London's Paddington Station to Moreton-in-Marsh (see below). For schedules and information, call ☎ **0345/484950.** From Moreton-in-Marsh, Pulhams Bus Company makes the 10-minute ride to Stow-on-the-Wold.

National Express buses also run daily from London's Victoria Coach Station to Moreton-in-Marsh, where you can catch a Pulhams Bus Company coach to Stow-on-the-Wold. For schedules and information, call ☎ **0990/808080.** Several Pulhams coaches also run daily to Stow-on-the-Wold from Cheltenham.

If driving from Oxford, take A40 west to the junction with A424, near Burford. Head northwest along A424 to Stow-on-the-Wold.

VISITOR INFORMATION The **Tourist Information Centre** is at Hollis House, The Square (☎ **01451/831082**). It's open Easter through October Monday to Saturday from 9:30am to 5:30pm, Sunday from 10:30am to 4:30pm; November through mid-February Monday to Saturday from 9:30am to 4:30pm; mid-February to Easter Monday to Saturday 9:30am to 5pm.

ANTIQUES HEAVEN

Don't be fooled by the village's sleepy, country-bucolic setting: Stow-on-the-Wold has developed over the last 20 years into the antique-buyer's highlight of Britain and has at least 60 merchandisers scattered throughout the village and its environs.

Set within four showrooms inside an 18th-century building on the town's main square, **Anthony Preston Antiques, Ltd.,** The Square (☎ **01451/831586**), specializes in English and French furniture, including some very large pieces such as bookcases, and decorative objects that include paperweights, lamps, paintings on silk, and small objects designed to add a glossy accent to carefully contrived interior decors.

Located on Church Street, **Baggott Church Street, Ltd.** (☎ **01451/830370**), is the smaller, and perhaps more intricately decorated, of two shops founded and maintained by a well-regarded local antiques merchant, Duncan ("Jack") Baggott, a frequent denizen at estate sales of country houses throughout Britain. The shop contains four showrooms loaded with furniture and paintings from the 17th to the 19th century.

More eclectic and wide-ranging is Baggott's second shop, **Woolcomber House,** on Sheep Street (☎ **01451/830662**). Among the largest retail outlets in the Cotswolds, it contains about 17 rooms that during the 16th century functioned as a coaching inn, but today are lavishly decorated, each according to a particular era of English decorative history.

Covering about half a block in the heart of town, **Huntington's Antiques Ltd.,** Church Street (☎ **01451/830842**), contains one of the largest stocks of quality antiques in England. Wander at will through 10 ground-floor rooms, then climb to the second floor where a long gallery and a quartet of additional showrooms bulge with refectory tables, unusual cupboards, and all kinds of finds.

After you've shopped till you drop, the best place for tea is a lovely cottage home that goes by the name of **Tea at the Peggums,** on Church Street (☎ **01451/830102**). The place usually sells out well before closing, so get here early. Menu items include a choice of teas and tasty tea breads, scones, and other pastries.

WHERE TO STAY & DINE

Fosse Manor Hotel. Fosse Way, Stow-on-the-Wold, Cheltenham, Gloucestershire GL54 1JX. ☎ **01451/830354.** Fax 01451/832486. 22 units. TV TEL. £118 ($200.60) double; £160 ($272) suite. Rates include English breakfast. "Bargain Breaks" (2-night minimum required): £78–£105 ($132.60–$178.50) per person, including half board. AE, CB, MC, V. Take A429 1½ miles south of Stow-on-the-Wold.

Although lacking the charm of the Grapevine, Fosse Manor is at least the second best in town, even more inviting than the Stow Lodge. The hotel lies near the site of an ancient Roman road that used to bisect England. Its stone walls and neo-Gothic gables are almost concealed by strands of ivy. From some of the high stone-sided windows, you can enjoy a view of a landscaped garden with a sunken lily pond and an old-fashioned sundial. Inside, the interior is conservatively modern, with homey bedrooms. Some are large enough for a family, others have a four-poster bed. Three of the bedrooms, equal in comfort to the main building, are on the ground floor of a converted house on the grounds. Bathrooms are small but well organized. There's a plushly upholstered bar and a dining room where dinners cost £25 ($42.50).

The Grapevine Hotel. Sheep St., Stow-on-the-Wold, Cheltenham, Gloucestershire GL54 1AU. ☎ **800/528-1234** in the U.S. and Canada, or 01451/830344. Fax 01451/832278. www.vines.co.uk. E-mail: enquiries@vines.co.uk. 22 units. TV TEL. £55–£93.50 ($93.50–$158.95) per person. Rates include breakfast. "Bargain Breaks" (2-night minimum): £75.50–£95.50 ($128.35–$162.35) per person, including half board. AE, DC, MC, V. Free parking.

Facing the village green, The Grapevine mixes urban sophistication with reasonable prices, rural charm, and intimacy. It's the best inn in town, although it doesn't have the charm and grace of Wyck Hill House on the outskirts (see below). It was named after the ancient vine whose tendrils shade and shelter the beautiful conservatory restaurant. Many of the bedrooms have been recently redecorated, and all contain beverage makers. Each bedroom varies in size—some quite small—but comfort is the keynote here. Ten rooms are in a comfortably appointed annex, and lack the character of the rooms in the main building. Each unit comes with a small bath, most with a tub and shower combination.

Dining: The reading room, comfortable lounge, and cozy bar with Victorian accessories create a warm ambience for tea, bar snacks, or dinner. Full meals feature English, French, and Italian cuisine and are served from 7 to 9:15pm daily. Bar snacks are served at midday. Dinners are more elaborate, beginning at £26 ($44.20) for a three-course menu, and including seared smoked salmon with herb brioche and a marmalade of caper and onion followed by roasted melon pearls served in a ginger-yogurt topped pastry. The restaurant has a balmy Mediterranean feel.

✪ **The Old Farmhouse Hotel.** Lower Swell, Stow-on-the-Wold, Cheltenham, Gloucestershire GL54 1LF. ☎ **01451/830232.** Fax 01451/870962. E-mail: oldfarm@globalnet.co.uk. 13 units, 12 with private bathroom. TV TEL. £22.50–£35 ($38.25–$59.50) per person double without bathroom, £39–£45 ($66.30–$76.50) per person double with bathroom; £49 ($83.30) per person suite. Rates include English breakfast. MC, V. Take B4068 1 1/2 miles west of Stow-on-the-Wold.

This small, intimate hotel in the heart of the Cotswolds was converted from a 16th-century farmhouse. It's been completely refurbished and the original fireplaces restored. The relaxed atmosphere, together with excellent food and wine, have made this a popular stop for visitors, so reserve well in advance. Two accommodations under the eaves share a bath, and all units vary in shape and size because of the building's farmhouse origin. Most of them have a small bath with a shower stall.

Dinner is served daily from 7pm, with last orders taken at 9pm. The table d'hôte menu is changed daily. The hotel has a secluded walled garden.

Stow Lodge Hotel. The Square, Stow-on-the-Wold, Cheltenham, Gloucestershire GL54 1AB. ☎ **01451/830485.** Fax 01451/831671. www.stowlodge.com. 21 units. TV TEL. £63–£93 ($107.10–$158.10) double. Rates include English breakfast. DC, MC, V.

Stow Lodge dominates the marketplace but is set back far enough to avoid too much noise. Its gardens, honeysuckle growing over the stone walls, diamond-shaped windows, gables, and many chimneys capture the best of country living, even though you're right in the heart of town. The ample, well-furnished, nonsmoking rooms vary in size and have radios, central heating, and beverage makers. The main building has more character, although some equally comfortable rooms are in a converted coach house (most of these are on the ground floor level). Bathrooms are small but contain a hair dryer.

Dining: Arrange to have your afternoon tea out back by the flower garden. In the lounge, logs burn in a 200-year-old stone fireplace. À la carte dinners, priced from £11 to £18 ($18.70 to $30.60), are served daily from 7 to 9pm and are likely to feature poached salmon steak, grilled local trout, various steaks, and roast duckling with a choice of sauces.

✪ **Wyck Hill House.** Burford Rd., Stow-on-the-Wold, Cheltenham, Gloucestershire GL54 1HY. ☎ **01451/831936.** Fax 01451/832243. www.wrensgroup.com. 32 units. TV TEL. £150–£220 ($255–$374) double; £250 ($425) suite. Rates include English breakfast. AE, MC, V. Drive 2 1/2 miles south of Stow-on-the-Wold on A424.

Parts of this otherwise Victorian country house on 100 acres of grounds and gardens date from 1720, when its stone walls were first erected. It was discovered in the course of recent restoration that one wing of the manor house rests on the foundations of a Roman villa. Today, it is the showcase country inn of this area, although not nearly the equal of the premier houses in Upper and Lower Slaughter (see section 8). The opulent interior adheres to 18th-century authenticity with room after room leading to paneled libraries and Adam sitting rooms. The well-furnished bedrooms are in the main hotel, in the coach-house annex, or in the orangery. All are of equal comfort with varying sizes. Bathrooms are state of the art.

Dining: Excellent food is served here, with a fixed-price lunch costing from £13.50 ($22.95). A set dinner starts from £30 ($51) per meal.

10 Moreton-in-Marsh

83 miles NW of London; 4 miles N of Stow-on-the-Wold; 7 miles S of Chipping Campden; 17 miles S of Stratford-upon-Avon

This is no swampland as the name implies. Marsh derives from an old word meaning "border," so you won't be wading through wetlands to get here. Moreton is a real Cotswold market town that is at its most bustling on Tuesday morning when farmers and craftspeople who live in the surrounding area flood the town to sell their wares and produce. Some of the scenes that take place then are evocative of the classic film, *Brigadoon*.

An important stopover along the old Roman road, Fosse Way, as well as an important layover for the night for stagecoach passengers, Moreton-in-Marsh has one of the widest High Streets in the Cotswolds. Roman legions trudged through here centuries ago, but today visitors and antiques shops have replaced them.

The town is still filled with records of its past, including a Market Hall on High Street, built in Victorian Tudor style in 1887, and Curfew Tower on Oxford Street dating from the 17th century. Its bell was rung daily until the late 19th century.

For a fascinating lesson on birds of prey, stop by the **Cotswold Falconry Centre,** Batsford Park (☎ **01386/701043**). These great birds are flown daily by experienced falconers for visitors to see first-hand the remarkable speed and agility of eagles, hawks, owls, and falcons. It's open daily from 10:30am to 5pm. Flying displays are daily at 11:30am, 1:30, 3, and 4:30pm. Admission is £3.50 ($5.95) for adults, £1.50 ($2.55) for children 4 to 14 (free 3 and under).

Touted as a Cotswold farm with a difference, **Sleepy Hollow Farm Park,** 32 Sleepy Hollow Farm Park (☎ **01386/701264**), is a great place for children and adults to explore. This plot of land is the home of many rare and unusual farm animals that coexist with an array of interesting wild animals, including a family of otters, and ever-curious raccoons. Admission is £3.25 ($5.50) adults, £2.50 ($4.25) seniors, and £1.75 ($3) children (free 2 and under). It is open daily from 10:30am to 6pm Easter through September.

GETTING THERE

Trains run from London's Paddington Station to Moreton-in-Marsh, a nearly 2-hour trip. For schedules and information, call ☎ **0345/484950. National Express** buses run from London's Victoria Coach Station to Moreton-in-Marsh daily. For schedules and information, call ☎ **0990/808080.**

If you're driving from Stow-on-the-Wold (see above), take A429 north.

WHERE TO STAY

Manor House Hotel. High St., Moreton-in-Marsh, Gloucestershire GL56 0LJ. ☎ **01608/650501.** Fax 01608/651481. 39 units, 1 family suite. TV TEL. £90 ($153) double; £135 ($229.50) suite. Rates include English breakfast. AE, DC, MC, V.

The town's best hotel, the Manor House comes complete with its own ghost, a secret passage, and a moot room used centuries ago by local merchants to settle arguments over wool exchanges. On the main street, it's a formal yet gracious house, and its rear portions reveal varying architectural periods of design. Inside are many living rooms, one especially intimate with leather chairs and a fireplace-within-a-fireplace, ideal for drinks and swapping "bump-in-the-night" stories. The rooms are tastefully furnished, often with antiques or fine reproductions. Many have fine old desks set in front of window ledges, with a view of the garden and ornamental pond. The cozy bedrooms vary in size, most often small to medium, but each has a bath with excellent maintenance and adequate shelf space.

Dining/Diversions: The bar, with its garden view through leaded Gothic windows, is a favorite nook. Reliably good evening meals in the dining room are candlelit.

Amenities: The hotel has a heated indoor pool, a spa bath, and a sauna.

Redesdale Arms. High St., Moreton-in-Marsh, Gloucestershire GL56 0AW. ☎ **01608/650308.** Fax 01608/651843. 20 units. TV TEL. £45.50 ($77.35) per person double. AE, MC, V.

Although the Manor House is better appointed and more comfortable, this is one of the largest and best-preserved coaching inns in Gloucestershire. Originally established around 1774 as the Unicorn Hotel, it functioned around 1840 as an important link in the Bath-to-Lincoln stagecoach routes, offering food and accommodations to both humans and horses during the arduous journey. Since then, the inn has been considerably upgraded, with modernized and comfortably furnished bedrooms, but much of the old-fashioned charm remains intact. The small to mid-size bedrooms are appointed with either twin or double beds. Each has a compact bathroom with a shower stall.

Dining/Diversions: Guests gravitate to the bar, where drinks are served in front of a 6-foot-high stone fireplace. During nice weather, tables are set up in a sheltered courtyard. The inn is especially well known for its meals and its modern British cuisine, although it offers no serious competition to Marsh Goose or Annie's restaurants (see below).

The White Hart Royal Hotel. High St., Moreton-in-Marsh, Gloucestershire GL56 0BA. ☎ **01608/650731.** Fax 01608/650880. 19 units. TV TEL. £68 ($115.60) double. Rates include English breakfast. AE, MC, V.

A mellow old Cotswold inn graced by Charles I in 1644, the White Hart provides modern amenities without compromising the personality of yesteryear. It long ago ceased being the premier inn of town but it's still a comfortable place to spend the night. The well-furnished rooms all have a few antiques mixed with basic 20th-century pieces. Much of the original character of the small to mid-size bedrooms remains intact, but you get comfort here, not a lot of style.

Dining/Diversions: The bar is built of irregular Cotswold stone. You can enjoy drinks in front of the 10-foot open fireplace. Lunches are informal affairs served in the hotel's pub. Dinners are more elaborate sit-down events, with three-course table d'hôte menus from £12.50 ($21.25).

WHERE TO DINE

Annie's. 3 Oxford St. ☎ **01608/651981.** Reservations recommended. Main courses £15.50–£21 ($26.35–$35.70). AE, DC, MC, V. Mon–Sat 7–9:30pm. Closed 3 weeks from late Jan to early Feb. ENGLISH/FRENCH.

In the heart of town, on a side street that merges with the old Roman Fosse Way, lies this stone-sided three-story house whose walls are 300 to 400 years old. For over a decade, David and Anne Ellis have prepared ample portions of English and French country cuisine, garnering enthusiastic responses from weekending Londoners.

The cooking is very straightforward and honest, with dishes standing out for their true flavors and not disguised with heavy sauces. David's tomato-and-rosemary soup is a refreshing beginning, as are the tiger prawns wrapped in filo pastry, pan fried with chili, garlic, and spring onions. Appealing main courses are adjusted to make use of the freshest ingredients on the market, and might include rack of lamb with a spiced herb crust and Madeira sauce. Fresh vegetables are served with each main dish. Freshly made desserts are also offered.

✪ **Marsh Goose.** High St. ☎ **01608/653500.** Reservations recommended. Lunch main courses £10–£14 ($17–$23.80); 3-course fixed-price lunch on Sun £17 ($28.90); 3-course fixed-price dinner £30 ($51). AE, DC, MC, V. Wed–Sat 12:30–2:30pm; Tues–Sat 7:30–9:30pm; Fri–Sat 7:30–10pm. MODERN BRITISH.

The food here is among the best in The Cotswolds. Despite its unique allure and country-house elegance, this restaurant is very much an outpost of young and sophisticated Londoners away for a weekend in the country. The unusual cuisine is modern British, with good doses of Caribbean fare thrown in. Examples include roasted Cotswold lamb with eggplant and tomatoes; and grilled medallions of monkfish on celeriac puree with an orange-and-chive cream sauce. A favorite dessert is the hot dark-chocolate soufflé with white-chocolate sauce. There's an exceptionally cozy bar area with ceiling beams and an open fireplace for before-dinner drinks.

11 Broadway

15 miles SW of Stratford-upon-Avon; 93 miles NW of London; 15 miles NE of Cheltenham

This is the showcase village of the Cotswolds. If you don't mind the coach tours of summer, this is the most attractive spot to anchor into for the night. Many of the prime attractions of the Cotswolds, including Shakespeare Country, are close at hand. Flanked by honey-colored stone buildings, its High Street is a gem, remarkable for its harmonious style and design from a point overlooking the lovely Vale of Evesham.

Don't come here seeking a lot of museums and attractions. Show-stopping Broadway is its own attraction. When you see wisteria and cordoned fruit trees covering 17th-century cottages, fronted by immaculately maintained gardens, you'll understand why Henry James found it "delicious to be in Broadway."

ESSENTIALS

GETTING THERE Rail connections are possible from London's Paddington Station via Oxford. The nearest railway stations are at Moreton-in-Marsh (7 miles away) or at Evesham (5 miles away). For schedules and information, call ☎ **0345/484950.** Frequent buses arrive from Evesham, but one has to take a taxi from Moreton.

One bus departs daily from London's Victoria Coach Station to Broadway, a 2½-hour ride. For schedules and information, call ☎ **0990/808080.**

If you're driving from Oxford, head west on A40, then take A434 to Woodstock, Chipping Norton, and Moreton-in-Marsh.

VISITOR INFORMATION The **Tourist Information Centre** is at 1 Cotswold Ct. (☎ **01386/852937**), open February through December Monday to Saturday from 10am to 1pm and 2 to 5pm.

SEEING THE SIGHTS

The **High Street** is one of the most beautiful in England—perhaps the most beautiful. Many of its striking facades date from 1620 or a century or two later. The most famous facade is that of the **Lygon Arms,** High Street (☎ **01386/852255**), a venerable old inn. It's been serving wayfarers since 1532, and it stands on its own 3 acres of formal gardens. Even if you're not staying here, you might want to visit for a meal or a drink.

You might also seek out **St. Eadurgha's Church,** a place of Christian worship for more than 1,000 years. It's located just outside Broadway on Snowshill Road, and is open most days, though with no set visiting hours. If it's closed at the time of your visit, a note on the porch door will tell you what house to go to for the key. There are occasional Sunday services here.

Also along the street you can visit the **Broadway Teddy Bear Museum,** 76 High St. (☎ **01386/858323**), a showcase shop for teddy-bear and doll artisans. The site is also the setting for a unique museum displaying hundreds of antique and collectors' teddy bears, toys, and dolls. This 18th-century stone shop offers a historical look at the world of teddy bears, ranging from Steiff to Pooh. Bears from all leading manufacturers are also for sale. Hours are daily from 10am to 5pm. Admission is £1.50 ($2.55) for adults, £1 ($1.70) for children under 14 and senior citizens.

On the outskirts of Broadway stands the **Broadway Tower Country Park** on Broadway Hill (☎ **01386/852390**), a "folly" created by the fanciful mind of the sixth Earl of Coventry. Today, you can climb this tower on a clear day for a panoramic vista of 12 shires. It's the most sweeping view in the Cotswolds. The tower is open from early April to late October daily from 10:30am to 5pm. Admission is £3.20 ($5.45) for adults, £2.20 ($3.75) for children. There's also a family ticket costing £9 ($15.30). You can also bring the makings for a picnic here and spread it out for your lunch in designated areas.

South of Broadway, a final attraction is **Snowshill Manor,** at Snowshill (☎ **01386/852410**), a house that dates mainly from the 17th century. It was once owned by an eccentric, Charles Paget Wade, who collected virtually everything he could between 1900 and 1951. Queen Mary once remarked that Wade himself was the most remarkable artifact among his entire flea market. There's a little bit of everything here: Flemish tapestries, toys, lacquer cabinets, narwhal tusks, mousetraps, and cuckoo clocks—a glorious mess, like a giant attic of the 20th century. The property, owned by the National Trust, is open April through October, Wednesday through Sunday from noon to 5pm and Monday in July and August. Admission is £5.50 ($9.35) per person or £13.80 ($23.45) for a family ticket.

WHERE TO STAY

Broadway Hotel. The Green, Broadway, Worcestershire WR12 7AA. ☎ **01386/852401.** Fax 01386/853879. www.cotswolds-inns-hotels.co.uk/ E-mail: bookings@cotswold-inns-hotels.co.uk. 20 units. TV TEL. £110–£125 ($187–$212.50) double. Rates include English breakfast. AE, DC, MC, V.

Right on the village green and one of the most colorful places in Broadway, this converted 15th-century house keeps its old-world charm while providing modern comforts. All the recently refurbished rooms have beverage makers and central heating. One room has a four-poster bed. Some guests seek out the more private bedrooms on the ground floor of a separate building, with its own direct access to the garden. All except one bedroom has a tub and shower combination along with a hair dryer.

Dining/Diversions: The cooking is fine, the service personal, the dining room attractive. The comfortable cocktail bar is well stocked. Locals claim that if you're keeping an eye on costs, the bar is the best lunch place in Broadway. Lunches are served daily from noon to 2pm. Dinner in the main dining room is served daily, featuring English specialties such as fish, duckling, or venison.

✪ **Buckland Manor Hotel.** Buckland, near Broadway, Worcestershire WR12 7LY. ☎ **01386/852626.** Fax 01386/853557. www.relaischateaux.fr/buckland. E-mail: buckland@relaischateaux.fr 13 units. TV TEL. £215–£355 ($365.50–$603.50) double. Rates include early morning tea and English breakfast. AE, DC, MC, V. Take B4632 about 2 miles south of Broadway, into Gloucestershire. No children under 12.

The Lygon Arms (see below) reigned supreme in Broadway for so long that people thought it had squatters' rights to the title of top inn in town, both for food and lodging. But along came Buckland Manor on the outskirts, topping The Lygon Arms in every way, especially in cuisine. This imposing slate-roofed manor house is ringed with fences of Cotswold stone. The core of the manor house was erected in the 13th century, with wings added in succeeding centuries, especially the 19th century. The Oak Room, with a four-poster bed and burnished paneling, occupies what used to be a private library. Leaded windows in the room overlook gardens and grazing land with Highland cattle and Jacob sheep. Some of the large bedrooms have four-poster beds and fireplaces, but all come with sumptuous beds. Each of the oversized bathrooms contains at least one antique, as well as carpeting. The bathrooms use water drawn from the hotel's own spring.

Dining: French-inspired meals are served in the elegant dining room with a baronial fireplace. (You don't have to be a guest to dine here.) Service is daily for breakfast, lunch, and dinner. The chef concocts his imaginative cuisine from first-rate ingredients. He creates happy marriages such as langoustines with shredded root vegetables. You dine in elegance with impeccable service.

Collin House Hotel and Restaurant. Collin Lane, Broadway, Worcestershire WR12 7PB. ☎ **01386/858354.** Fax 01386/858697. www.broadway-cotswolds.co.uk. E-mail: collin.house@virgin.net. 6 units. £92 ($156.40) standard double, £102 ($173.40) four-poster bedroom. Rates include English breakfast. MC, V. From Broadway, follow the signs to Evesham before turning right at the roundabout onto Collin Lane; the hotel is a mile west of Broadway off A44.

On a country lane, this 16th-century Cotswold stone farmhouse has been transformed into a hotel set amid 8 acres of gardens and orchards. The cozy rooms are named for flowers that grow here in profusion. Large structural timbers, private baths, and mullioned windows make them attractive; Wild Rose, with its sloped ceiling, is the most romantic. The bedrooms range in size and have recently been refurbished. Bathrooms are well appointed and supplied with hair dryers.

Dining: Traditional English food, flavorfully and freshly prepared, is served by candlelight nightly from 7 to 9pm. Lunch is served daily from noon to 2:30pm, either in the bar (inexpensively) or in the more formal dining room.

Dormy House. Willersey Hill, Broadway, Worcestershire WR12 7LF. ☎ **01386/852711.** Fax 01386/858636. www.johansen.com. E-mail: reservations@dormyhouse.co.uk. 49 units. TV TEL. £146 ($248.20) double; £174 ($295.80) four-poster room; £186 ($316.20) suite. Rates include English breakfast. AE, DC, MC, V. Closed Dec 24–27. Take A44 2 miles southeast of Broadway.

This manor house, high on a hill above the village, boasts views in all directions. Its panoramic position has made it a favorite place whether you're seeking a meal, afternoon tea, or lodgings. Halfway between Broadway and Chipping Campden, it was created from a sheep farm. The owners transformed it, furnishing the 17th-century farmhouse with a few antiques, good soft beds, and full central heating; they also extended these amenities to an old adjoining timbered barn, which they converted into studio rooms with open-beamed ceilings. Some rooms have four-poster beds. Each spacious room comes with a tub and shower or just a tub in the compact bathrooms. Bowls of fresh flowers adorn tables and alcoves throughout the hotel. The hotel's Tapestry Restaurant is well recommended; see our review below.

✪ **The Lygon Arms.** High St., Broadway, Worcestershire WR12 7DU. ☎ **01386/852255.** Fax 01386/858611. www.savoy-group.co.uk. E-mail: lygon@cotswoldmkt.clara.co.uk. 65 units. TV TEL. £178–£225 ($302.60–$382.50) double; from £285 ($484.50) suite. Value-added tax (VAT) extra. Rates include continental breakfast. AE, MC, V.

Despite the challenge of Buckland Manor, this many-gabled structure with mullioned windows still basks in its reputation as one of the great old English inns. It opens onto a private rear garden, with 3 acres of lawns, trees, and borders of flowers, stone walls with roses, and nooks for tea or sherry. The oldest portions date from 1532 or earlier, and additions have been made many times since then. King Charles I reputedly drank with his friends in one of the oak-lined chambers, and later, his enemy Oliver Cromwell slept here the night before the Battle of Worcester. Today, many but not all the bedrooms are in the antique style; a new wing offers more of a 20th-century feel. Each room is furnished with a radio, a trouser press, and a sumptuously comfortable bed. Bathrooms are kept in prime condition, each with a hair dryer.

Dining: You dine in the oak-paneled Great Hall, with a Tudor fireplace, a vaulted ceiling, and a minstrel's gallery.

Amenities: 24-hour room service; laundry service; a country club adjoins the old inn. A health club and many leisure facilities are available here, including a large swimming pool and a sauna.

Olive Branch Guest House. 78 High St., Broadway, Worcestershire WR12 7AJ. ☎ **01386/853440.** Fax 01386/859070. www.theolivebranch.u-net.com. E-mail: clive@theolivebranch.u-net.com. 8 units, 7 with tub or shower. TV. £50 ($85) double with tub or shower. Rates include English breakfast. AE, MC, V.

In the heart of an expensive village, this is a terrific bargain. The house, dating from the 16th century, retains its old Cotswold architectural features. Behind the house is a large-walled English garden and parking area. Guests are given a discount for purchases at the owners' attached antiques shop. Tea- and coffeemakers are in each room, and hair dryers and irons are available upon request. Furnishings are basic, but comfortable, and the bathrooms are tiny.

WHERE TO DINE

The best place in Broadway for a cup of tea is **Tisanes,** The Green (☎ **01386/852112**). The shop offers perfectly blended teas with a variety of sandwiches and salads.

The Tapestry Restaurant. In Dormy House, off the A44, Willersey Hill, Broadway. ☎ **01386/852711.** Reservations recommended. Lunch main courses (Mon–Fri) £7–£11 ($11.90–$18.70), set-price Sun lunch £19.50 ($33.15); dinner main courses £15.50–£21 ($26.35–$35.70); fixed-price dinner £30.50 ($51.85), gourmet six-course fixed-price dinner £35 ($59.50). AE, DC, MC, V. Sun–Fri 12:30–2pm; daily 7–9:30pm. MODERN BRITISH.

Set 2 miles from the center of Broadway, beside the highway leading to Moreton-in-Marsh and Oxford, this is one of the most charming and well-managed restaurants in the region. It's elegant, but not as formal and stuffy as some competitors. The setting is as pastoral as a painting by Constable. You'll dine within a room ringed with Cotswold stone (where there are areas for smokers) or within an adjacent glass-sided conservatory (no smoking here).

Chef Alan Cutler turns out an intelligent and interesting cuisine. You might order an appetizer of fine slices of parma ham with a tomato and basil dressing, or a salad of avocado and pear; followed by roast rib of prime Scottish beef with a confit of shallots and a red wine sauce; and a dessert of hot vanilla soufflé with a warm dark chocolate sauce. The cellar houses a superb collection of wines.

12 Chipping Campden

36 miles NW of Oxford; 12 miles S of Stratford-upon-Avon; 93 miles NW of London

The wool merchants have long departed, but the architectural legacy of honey-colored stone cottages—financed by their fleecy "white gold"—remains to delight the visitor today. Try to tie in a stopover here as you rush from Oxford to Stratford-upon-Avon. Chipping Campden lies 36 miles northwest of Oxford, 12 miles south of Stratford-upon-Avon, and 93 miles northwest of London.

On the northern edge of the Cotswolds, it opens onto the dreamy Vale of Evesham that you've seen depicted in a thousand postcards. Except for the heavy traffic in summer, the main street still looks as it did centuries ago—in fact, the noted British historian, G. M. Trevelyan called it "the most beautiful village street now left in the island." And so it is even today. You can tie in a visit here on the same day you visit Broadway, lying 4 miles to the west.

Arriving through beautiful Cotswold landscapes—called "seductive" by some—you come upon this country town, whose landmark is the soaring tower of the Church of St. James. You'll see it for miles around. Constructed in the Perpendicular style by the town's wool merchants in the 15th century, it is one of the finest churches in the Cotswolds.

The town's long High Street is curved like Oxford's and it's lined with stone houses dating from the 16th century. A hundred years later Chipping Campden was one of the richest wool towns of England. The Campden Trust, a determined group of dedicated conservationists, has preserved the town the way it should be.

Of special interest is the Silk Mill, Sheep Street, open Monday to Saturday 9am to 5pm. The Guild of Handicrafts was established here in 1902, practicing such skills as bookbinding and cabinetmaking. It folded in 1920 but has been revived today with a series of craft workshops.

ESSENTIALS

GETTING THERE Trains depart from London's Paddington Station for Moreton-in-Marsh, a 1½- to 2-hour trip. For schedules and information, call ☎ **0345/484950.** A bus operated by Castleway's travels the 7 miles from Moreton-in-Marsh to Chipping Campden five times a day. Many visitors opt for a taxi from Moreton-in-Marsh to Chipping Campden.

The largest and most important nearby bus depot is Cheltenham, which receives service several times a day from London's Victoria Coach Station. For schedules and information, call ☎ **0990/808080.** From Cheltenham, Barry's Coaches are infrequent and uncertain, departing three times per week at most. Call Gloucester Coach Station (☎ **01452/527516**), for details.

If you're driving from Oxford, take A40 west to the junction with A424. Follow it northwest, passing by Stow-on-the-Wold. The route becomes A44 until you reach the junction with B4081, which you take northeast to Chipping Campden.

VISITOR INFORMATION The **Tourist Information Centre** is at 2 Rosary Ct., High Street (☎ **01386/841206**). It's open daily from 10am to 5pm.

SEEING THE SIGHTS

In 1907, American horticulturist Maj. Lawrence Johnstone created ✪ **Hidcote Manor Garden,** 4 miles northeast of Chipping Campden and 9 miles south of Stratford-upon-Avon (☎ **01386/438333**). Set on 10 acres, this masterpiece is composed of small gardens, or rooms, that are separated by a variety of hedges, old roses, rare shrubs, trees, and herbaceous borders. April through October, the garden is open Monday, Wednesday, Thursday, Saturday, and Sunday from 11am to 6pm. During June and July, the garden is also open on Tuesday from 11am to 7pm. Last admission is at 6pm or 1 hour before sunset. Admission is £5.60 ($9.50) adults, £2.80 ($4.75) children, £14 ($23.80) family ticket.

Insider's tip: In summer, Shakespeare is performed on the Theatre Lawn; there is no more memorable experience in the Cotswolds than watching *A Midsummer's Night Dream* performed here on a balmy evening in July.

The poet, artist, and craftsman William Morris (1834–96) called the Cotswold countryside home for most of his life. The worldwide Arts and Crafts movement he led in the late 19th century continues to inspire artists and craftspeople in this area.

At the studio of **D. T. Hart,** The Guild, The Silk Mill, Sheep Street (☎ **01386/841100**), silver is expertly smithed by descendants of George Hart, an original member of the Guild of Handicraft, in the original Ashbee workshop. **Robert Welch Studio Shop,** Lower High Street (☎ **01386/840522**), is where Robert Welch has been crafting silverware, stainless steel, and cutlery for more than 40 years. **Martin Gotrel,** The Square (☎ **01386/841360**), designs and makes fine contemporary and traditional jewelry.

Campden Needlecraft Centre, High Street (☎ **01386/840583**), is widely known as one of the leading specialist embroidery shops in England with an interesting selection of embroidery and canvas work as well as fabrics and threads. If antiques and antiques hunting are your passion, visit **School House Antiques,** High Street (☎ **01386/841474**), or **The Barn Antiques Centre,** Long Marston on the Stratford-upon-Avon Road (☎ **01789/721399**). For new, secondhand, and antiquarian books, look up **Campden Bookshop,** High Street (☎ **01386/840944**), or **Draycott Books,** 1 Sheep St. (☎ **01386/841392**).

WHERE TO STAY & DINE

✪ **Charingworth Manor Hotel.** Charingworth, near Chipping Campden, Gloucestershire GL55 6NS. ☎ **01386/593555.** Fax 01386/593353. 26 units. TV TEL. £150–£275 ($255–$467.50) double. Rates include English breakfast. AE, DC, MC, V. Take B4035 3 1/4 miles east of Chipping Campden.

In nearby Charingworth, this elegant country home is even more luxurious than Cotswold House in town. It's the showpiece of the area. A manor has stood on this spot since the time of the *Domesday Book.* The present Tudor-Jacobean house, in honey-colored stone with slate roofs, has 55 acres of grounds. In the 1930s, it was host to such illustrious guests as T. S. Eliot. The old-world charm of the place has been preserved, in spite of modernization. Each spacious room is luxuriously furnished, both in its use of antiques and English fabrics, and offers amenities that include a trouser press and room safe. Many of the period rooms have four-poster beds. Bathrooms are state of the art and come with a hair dryer. Guests can also wander through a well-manicured garden.

Dining: There's a fixed-price dinner in the elegant restaurant of the hotel. Excellent ingredients are deftly handled in the kitchen to create a French and English menu. Game is often featured, and the wine list is carefully chosen.

Amenities: 24-hour room service, laundry service. A modern Leisure Spa consists of a luxurious indoor heated pool built in Romanesque style, a sauna, steam room, solarium, and billiards room, plus there's an all-weather tennis court on the grounds.

✪ **Cotswold House Hotel.** The Square, Chipping Campden, Gloucestershire GL55 6AN. ☎ **01386/840330.** Fax 01386/840310. 15 units. TV TEL. £170 ($289) double; £190 ($323) four-poster bed. Rates include English breakfast. AE, MC, V.

This is the best place to stay in town. A stately, formal Regency house dating from 1800, right in the heart of the village opposite the old wool market, Cotswold House sits amid 1½ acres of tended, walled gardens with shaded seating. Note the fine winding Regency staircase in the reception hall. The bedrooms are furnished with themes ranging from Gothic to French to military. Extra touches in the bedrooms include fresh flowers and mineral water. All the bathrooms, though small, are beautifully maintained with a hair dryer.

Dining: The restaurant serves first-class English and French food in a formal, elegant room, or in Forbes Brasserie, open daily from 9:30am to the last orders at 11pm. Light dishes and meals are served here.

Kings Arms Hotel. The Square, Chipping Campden, Gloucestershire GL55 6AW. ☎ **01386/840256.** Fax 01386/841598. 10 units. TV TEL. £65 ($110.50) double. Rates include English breakfast. AE, MC, V.

Dating from the late 1600s, and renovated many times, most recently in 1998, this partly Georgian building in the center of town has its own garden, which provides many of the fresh vegetables used in its meals. All the accommodations are well tended, pleasantly furnished, and spotlessly clean. Each comes with a tidy bath, most with a tub and shower combination, and a hair dryer. The inn enjoys a good reputation for its cooking. Bar meals are served in the pub, or else you can dine more formally, enjoying a fixed-price dinner or Sunday lunch.

Noel Arms Hotel. High St., Chipping Campden, Gloucestershire GL55 6AT. ☎ **01386/840317.** Fax 01386/841136. 26 units. TV TEL. £105–£125 ($178.50–$212.50) double. Rates include English breakfast. AE, DC, MC, V.

This old coaching inn has been famous in the Cotswolds since the 14th century. Charles II rested here in 1651 after his defeat at the Battle of Worcester. Tradition is kept alive in the decor, which includes fine antiques, muskets, swords, and shields. Twelve rooms date from the 14th century; the others, comfortably furnished and well appointed, are housed in a modern wing built of Cotswold stone. Rooms range from small to mid-size, and those in the older part of the hotel have more style, although comfort is perhaps better in the more modern annex, where the units are more spacious.

Dining/Diversions: There's a private sitting room for residents, but you may prefer the lounge with its 12-foot-wide fireplace. The restaurant offers an extensive menu, with an international wine list. The three-course Sunday lunch is well attended, by both locals and visitors. Typical English dishes are featured, and the hotel's tavern attracts a crowd that enjoys its real ales, malt whiskies, open fires, and Cotswold-stone walls.

12 Shakespeare Country & the Heart of England

After London, Shakespeare Country is the most popular destination in England for North Americans. Many who don't recognize the county name, Warwickshire, know its foremost tourist town, Stratford-upon-Avon, birthplace of Shakespeare and one of the great meccas for writers, readers, and playgoers from around the world.

Shakespeare's hometown is the best center for touring this part of England. You'll want to take in some theater while in Stratford-upon-Avon and branch out for day trips—notably to Warwick Castle in nearby Warwick, to Kenilworth Castle, and to Coventry Cathedral.

And then you have the heart of England at your doorstep. The adventure can begin in nearby Birmingham, England's second largest city. Although abandoned warehouses and bleak factories remain, this industrial city, like the rest of England, is being spruced up. It may even surprise you. From here, you can branch out to any number of lovely old market towns and bucolic spots. There's the scenic Malverns, the historic town of Shrewsbury, and Worcester, of Royal Worcester Porcelain fame. Those who are truly passionate about porcelain flock to the fabled Potteries to visit towns like Stoke-on-Trent. Here, factory and outlet shops sell Wedgwood, Portmeirion, and other fine brands of English tableware at a discount.

1 Stratford-upon-Avon

91 miles NW of London; 40 miles NW of Oxford; 8 miles S of Warwick

Crowds of tourists overrun this market town on the Avon River during the summer. In fact, today, ✪ **Stratford** aggressively hustles its Shakespeare connection—everybody seems to be in business to make a buck off the Bard. However, the throngs dwindle in winter, when you can at least walk on the streets and seek out the places of genuine historic interest.

Aside from the historic sites, the major draw for visitors is the **Royal Shakespeare Theatre,** where Britain's foremost actors perform during a long season that lasts from early April until late January. Other than the theater, Stratford is rather devoid of any rich cultural life, and you may want to rush back to London after you've seen the literary pilgrimage sights and watched a production of *Hamlet.* But Stratford-upon-Avon is also a good center for trips to Warwick Castle, Kenilworth Castle, and Coventry Cathedral (see below).

Warwickshire

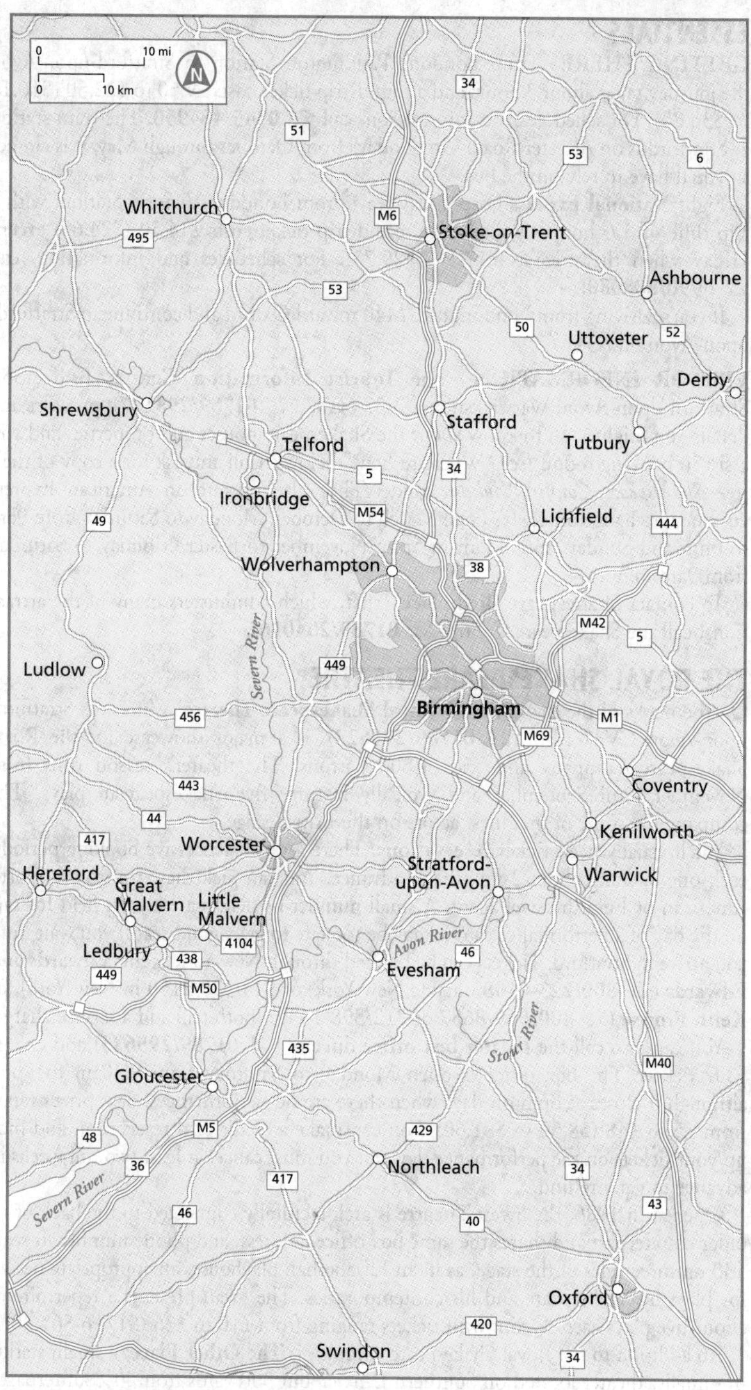

ESSENTIALS

GETTING THERE From London's Paddington Station to Stratford-upon-Avon the journey takes about 3 hours and a round-trip ticket costs £9.50 to £22.50 ($16.15 to $38.25). For schedules and information, call ☎ **0345/484950.** The train station at Stratford is on Alcester Road. On Sundays from October through May, it is closed, so you'll have to rely on the bus.

Eight **National Express** buses a day leave from London's Victoria Station, with a trip time of 3½ hours. A single-day round-trip ticket costs £14.50 ($24.65) except Friday when the price is £17.50 ($29.75). For schedules and information, call ☎ **0990/808080.**

If you're driving from London, take M40 toward Oxford and continue to Stratford-upon-Avon on A34.

VISITOR INFORMATION The **Tourist Information Centre,** Bridgefoot, Stratford-upon-Avon, Warwickshire, CV37 6GW (☎ **01789/293127**), provides any details you might wish to know about the Shakespeare houses and properties and will assist in booking rooms (see "Where to Stay," below). Call and ask for a copy of their free *Shakespeare Country Holiday* guide. They also operate an American Express currency-exchange office. It's open March to October, Monday to Saturday from 9am to 6pm and Sunday from 11am to 5pm; November to Easter, Monday to Saturday from 9am to 5pm.

To contact **Shakespeare Birthplace Trust,** which administers many of the attractions, call the Shakespeare Centre (☎ **01789/204016**).

THE ROYAL SHAKESPEARE THEATRE

On the banks of the Avon, the ✪ **Royal Shakespeare Theatre,** Waterside, Stratford-upon-Avon CV37 6BB (☎ **01789/295623**), is a major showcase for the Royal Shakespeare Company and seats 1,500 patrons. The theater's season runs from November until September and typically features five Shakespearean plays. The company has some of the finest actors on the British stage.

You'll usually need **ticket reservations.** There are two successive booking periods, each one opening about 2 months in advance. You can pick these up from a North American or English travel agent. A small number of tickets are always held for sale on the day of a performance, but it may be too late to get a good seat if you wait until you arrive in Stratford. Tickets can be booked through New York agents **Edwards and Edwards** (☎ **800/223-6108** outside New York, or 914/328-2150 in New York), or **Keith Prowse** (☎ **800/669-8687** or 212/398-1430). Both will add a service charge.

You can also call the **theater box office** directly (☎ **01789/295623**) and charge your tickets. The box office is open Monday to Saturday from 9:30am to 8pm, although it closes at 6pm on days when there are no performances. Seat prices range from £5 to £48 ($8.50 to $81.60). You can make a credit-card reservation and pick up your tickets on the performance day, but you must cancel at least two full weeks in advance to get a refund.

Opened in 1986, the **Swan Theatre** is architecturally connected to the back of its older counterpart and shares the same box office, address, and phone number. It seats 430 on three sides of the stage, as in an Elizabethan playhouse, an appropriate design for plays by Shakespeare and his contemporaries. The Swan presents a repertoire of about five plays each season, with tickets ranging from £10 to £36 ($17 to $61.20).

An addition to the Royal Shakespeare complex is **The Other Place,** a small, starkly minimalist theater located on Southern Lane, about 300 yards from its counterparts.

It was redesigned in 1996 as an experimental workshop theater without a permanent stage; seats can be radically repositioned (or removed completely) throughout the theater. A recent examples was a "promenade production" of *Julius Caesar,* in which the actors spent the whole play moving freely among a stand-up audience. Tickets are sold at the complex's main box office and generally range from £10 to £19 ($17 to $32.30) each, but prices are subject to change.

Within the Swan Theatre is a **painting gallery,** which has a basic collection of portraits of famous actors and scenes from Shakespeare's plays by 18th- and 19th-century artists. It also operates as a base for **guided tours** with lively running commentary through the world-famous theaters. Guided tours are conducted at 1:30 and 5:30pm, and four times every Sunday afternoon, production schedules permitting. Tours cost £4 ($6.80) for adults and £3 ($5.10) for students, seniors, or children. Call ahead for tour scheduling, which is subject to change.

SEEING THE SIGHTS

Besides the attractions on the periphery of Stratford, there are many Elizabethan and Jacobean buildings in town, many of them administered by the **Shakespeare Birthplace Trust.** One ticket—costing £12 ($20.40) for adults, £11 ($18.70) for seniors and students, and £6 ($10.20) for children—lets you visit the five most important sights. You can also buy a family ticket to all five sights (good for 2 adults and 3 children) for £29 ($49.30)—a good deal. Pick up the ticket if you're planning to do much sightseeing (obtainable at your first stopover at any one of the Trust properties).

Guided tours of Stratford-upon-Avon leave from near the **Guide Friday Tourism Centre,** Civic Hall, Rother Street (☎ **01789/294466**). In summer, open-top double-decker buses depart every 15 minutes daily from 9:30am to 6:30pm. You can take a 1-hour ride without stops, or you can get off at any or all of the town's five Shakespeare properties. Although the bus stops are clearly marked along the historic route, the most logical starting point is the sidewalk in front of the Pen & Parchment Pub, at the bottom of Bridge Street. Tour tickets are valid all day so you can hop on and off the buses as many times as you want. The tours cost £8 ($13.60) for adults, £6.50 ($11.05) for seniors or students, and £2.50 ($4.25) for children under 12 and £18.50 ($31.45) family ticket.

✪ **Shakespeare's Birthplace.** Henley St. (in the town center near the post office, close to Union St.). ☎ **01789/204016.** Admission £5.50 ($9.35) adults, £5 ($8.50) students and seniors, £2.50 ($4.25) children; £29 ($49.30) family ticket (2 adults, 3 children) for all 5 Shakespeare-related houses. Mar 20–Oct 19 Mon–Sat 9am–5pm, Sun 9:30am–5pm; off-season Mon–Sat 9:30am–4pm, Sun 10am–4pm. Closed Dec 23–26.

The son of a glover and whittawer (leather worker), the Bard was born on St. George's day, April 23, 1564, and died on the same date 52 years later. Filled with Shakespeare memorabilia, including a portrait and furnishings of the writer's time, the Trust property is a half-timbered structure, dating from the early 16th century. The house was bought by public donors in 1847 and preserved as a national shrine. You can visit the living room, the bedroom where Shakespeare was probably born, a fully equipped kitchen of the period (look for the "babyminder"), and a Shakespeare Museum, illustrating his life and times. Later, you can walk through the garden. You won't be alone: It's estimated that some 660,000 visitors pass through the house annually.

Built next door to commemorate the 400th anniversary of the Bard's birth, the modern **Shakespeare Centre** serves both as the administrative headquarters of the Birthplace Trust and as a library and study center. An extension houses a visitor center, which acts as a reception area for all those coming to the birthplace.

✪ **Anne Hathaway's Cottage.** Cottage Lane, Shottery. ☎ **01789/292100.** Admission £3.90 ($6.65) adults, £1.60 ($2.70) children; £29 ($49.30) family ticket (2 adults, 3 children) for all 5 Shakespeare-related houses. Mar 20–Oct 19 Mon–Sat 9:30am–5pm, Sun 9:30am–5pm; off-season Mon–Sat 9:30am–4pm, Sun 10am–4pm. Closed Dec 23–26. Take a bus from Bridge St. or walk via a marked pathway from Evesham Place in Stratford across the meadow to Shottery.

Before she married Shakespeare, Anne Hathaway lived in this thatched, wattle-and-daub cottage in the hamlet of Shottery, 1 mile from Stratford-upon-Avon. It's the most interesting and the most photographed of the Trust properties.

The Hathaways were yeoman farmers, and the cottage provides a rare insight into the life of a family in Shakespearean times. The Bard was only 18 when he married Anne, who was much older. Many of the original furnishings, including the courting settle and utensils, are preserved inside the house, which was occupied by descendants of Shakespeare's wife's family until 1892. After visiting the house, you'll want to linger in the garden and orchard.

New Place/Nash's House. Chapel St. ☎ **01789/204016.** Admission £3.50 ($5.95) adults, £1.90 ($3.25) children; £29 ($49.30) family ticket (2 adults, 3 children) for all 5 Shakespeare-related houses. Mar 20–Oct 19 Mon–Sat 9:30am–5pm, Sun 10am–5pm; Oct 20–Mar 19 Mon–Sat 10am–4pm, Sun 10:30–4pm. Closed Dec 23–26. Walk west down High St.; Chapel St. is a continuation of High St.

Shakespeare retired to New Place in 1610 (a prosperous man by the standards of his day) and died here 6 years later. Regrettably, the house was torn down, so only the garden remains today. A mulberry tree planted by the Bard was so popular with latter-day visitors to Stratford that the garden's owner chopped it down. The mulberry tree that grows here today is said to have been planted from a cutting of the original tree.

You enter the gardens through Nash's House (Thomas Nash married Elizabeth Hall, a granddaughter of the poet). Nash's House has 16th-century period rooms and an exhibition illustrating the history of Stratford. The popular Knott Garden adjoins the site and represents the style of a fashionable Elizabethan garden.

Mary Arden's House and the Shakespeare Countryside Museum. Wilmcote. ☎ **01789/204016.** Admission £5 ($8.50) adults, £2.50 ($4.25) children; family ticket £14 ($23.80). Mar 20–Oct 19 Mon–Sat 9:30am–5pm, Sun 10am–5pm; off-season Mon–Sat 10am–4pm, Sun 10:30am–4pm. Closed Dec 23–26. Take the A3400 (Birmingham) for 3 1/2 miles.

Reputedly this Tudor farmstead was the girlhood home of Shakespeare's mother—or so claimed an 18th-century entrepreneur. There is no definite evidence to prove she lived here, but the house contains country furniture and domestic utensils. In the barns, stable, cowshed, and farmyard, you'll find an extensive collection of farming implements illustrating life and work in the local countryside from Shakespeare's time to the present.

Visitors can also see the neighboring Glebe Farm, whose interior evokes farm life in late Victorian and Edwardian times. Light refreshments are available, and there is a picnic area.

Hall's Croft. Old Town (near Holy Trinity Church). ☎ **01789/292107.** Admission £3.50 ($5.95) adults, £1.90 ($3.25) children; £29 ($49.30) family ticket (2 adults, 3 children) for all 5 Shakespeare-related houses. Mar 20–Oct 19 Mon–Sat 9:30am–5pm, Sun 10am–5pm; off-season Mon–Sat 10am–4pm, Sun 10:30–4pm. Closed Dec 23–26. To reach Hall's Croft, walk west from High St., which becomes Chapel St. and Church St. At the intersection with Old Town, go left.

It was here that Shakespeare's daughter Susanna probably lived with her husband, Dr. John Hall. Hall's Croft is an outstanding Tudor house with a beautiful walled garden, furnished in the style of a middle-class home of the time. Dr. Hall was widely

Stratford-upon-Avon

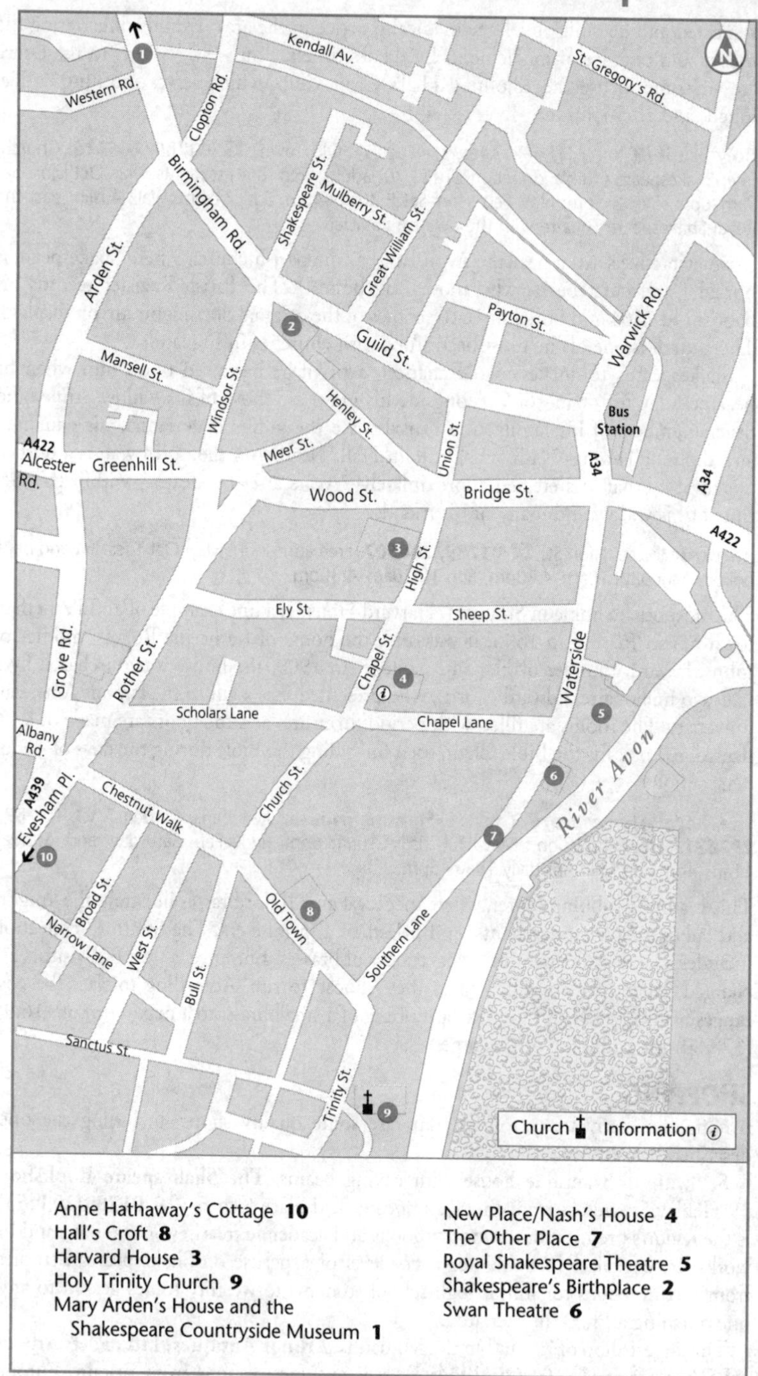

respected and he built up a large medical practice in the area. Exhibits illustrating the theory and practice of medicine in Dr. Hall's time are on view. Visitors to the house are welcome to use the adjoining Hall's Croft Club, which serves morning coffee, lunch, and afternoon tea.

Holy Trinity Church (Shakespeare's Tomb). Old Town. ☎ **01789/266316.** Church, free; Shakespeare's tomb, donation £1 ($1.70) adults, 50p (85¢) students. Mar–Oct Mon–Sat 9am–6pm, Sun 2–5pm; Nov–Feb Mon–Sat 8:30am–4pm, Sun 2–5pm. Walk 4 min. past the Royal Shakespeare Theatre with the river on your left.

In an attractive setting near the Avon River is the parish church where Shakespeare is buried ("and curst be he who moves my bones"). The Parish Register records his baptism in 1564 and burial in 1616 (copies of the original documents are on display). The church is one of the most beautiful parish churches in England.

Shakespeare's tomb lies in the chancel, a privilege bestowed upon him when he became a lay rector in 1605. Alongside his grave are those of his widow, Anne, and other members of his family. You can also see the graves of Susanna, his daughter, and those of Thomas Nash and Dr. John Hall. Nearby on the north wall is a bust of Shakespeare that was erected approximately 7 years after his death—within the lifetime of his widow and many of his friends.

Harvard House. High St. ☎ **01789/204507.** Free admission. May–Oct Tues–Sat and bank holiday Mondays 10am–4:30pm, Sun 10:30am–4:30pm.

The most ornate home in Stratford, Harvard House is a fine example of an Elizabethan town house. Rebuilt in 1596, it was once the home of Katherine Rogers, mother of John Harvard, founder of Harvard College. In 1909, the house was purchased by a Chicago millionaire, Edward Morris, who presented it as a gift to the famous American university. The rooms are filled with period furniture, and the floors are made of local flagstone. Look for the Bible Chair, used for hiding the Bible during the days of Tudor persecution.

The Royal Shakespeare Theatre Summer House. Avonbank Gardens. ☎ **01789/297671.** Free admission. May–Oct daily 10am–6pm; Nov–Feb Saturday and Sunday 11am–4pm and Mar–Apr daily 10am–5pm.

This is a brass-rubbing center, where medieval and Tudor brasses illustrate the knights and ladies, scholars, merchants, and priests of a bygone era. The Stratford collection includes a large assortment of exact replicas of brasses. Entrance is free, but visitors are charged depending on which brass they choose to rub. According to size, the cost ranges from 95p ($1.60) to make a rubbing of a small brass, to a maximum of £16.95 ($28.80) for a rubbing of the largest.

SHOPPING

Among the many tacky tourist traps are some quality shops, including the ones described below.

Set within an antique house with ceiling beams, **The Shakespeare Bookshop,** 39 Henley St., across from the Shakespeare Birthplace Centre (☎ **01789/293453**), is the region's premier source for textbooks and academic treatises on the Bard and his works. It specializes in books for every level of expertise on Shakespearean studies, from picture books for junior-high-school students to weighty tomes geared to anyone pursuing a Ph.D. in literature.

The largest shop of its kind in the Midlands, **Arbour Antiques, Ltd.,** Poets Arbour, off Sheep Street (☎ **01789/293493**), sells antique weapons from Britain, Europe, India, and Turkey. If you've always hankered after a full suit of armor, this place can sell you one.

Everything in the **Pickwick Gallery,** 32 Henley St. (☎ **01789/294861**), is a well-crafted work of art produced by copper or steel engraving plates, or printed by means of a carved wooden block. Hundreds of botanical prints, landscapes, and renderings of artfully arranged ruins, each suitable for framing, can be purchased. Topographical maps of regions of the United Kingdom are also available if you're planning on doing any serious hiking.

At **The National Trust Shop,** 45 Wood St. (☎ **01789/262197**), you'll find textbooks and guidebooks describing esoteric places in the environs of Stratford, descriptions of National Trust properties throughout England, stationery, books, china, pewter, and toiletries.

The **Trading Post,** 1 High St. (☎ **01789/267228**), occupies three floors of an Elizabethan house said to have been occupied by one of Shakespeare's daughters as an adult. It's jam-packed with an assortment of kitschy and nostalgic gift items.

A SIDE TRIP TO RAGLEY HALL

Ragley Hall. Near Alcester (9 miles from Stratford-upon-Avon). ☎ **01789/762090.** Admission to the house, garden, and park £5 ($8.50) adults, £4.50 ($7.65) seniors, £3.50 ($5.95) children, £17 ($28.90) family. Admission to park and gardens only, £4 ($6.80) adults, £3.50 ($5.95) seniors, £3 ($5.10) children, £12.50 ($21.25) family ticket. Apr–Oct Thurs–Fri and Sun Noon–5pm, Sat 11am–3:30pm (gardens 10am–6pm). You must drive or go by taxi, since there's no good bus service. Ragley Hall is located off A435 or A46 to Evesham, about 1 1/2 miles southwest of the town of Alcester. There is easy access from the main highway network, including the M40 from London.

A magnificent 115-room Palladian country house built in 1680, Ragley Hall is the home of the earl and countess of Yarmouth. The house has been restored and appears much as it did during the early 1700s. Great pains have been taken to duplicate colors and, in some cases, the original wallpaper patterns. The pictures, furniture, and works of art that fill the vast and spacious rooms represent 10 generations of collecting by the Seymour family. Ragley Hall may be a private home, but it has a museumlike quality, and many of its artifacts have great historical importance. The most spectacular attraction is the lavishly painted south staircase hall. Muralist Graham Rust painted a modern *trompe l'oeil* work depicting the Temptation. A new mural in the tearoom depicts a Victorian kitchen and the characters who inhabit it.

WHERE TO STAY

During the long theater season, you'll need reservations way in advance. The **Tourist Information Centre** (☎ **01789/293127**) (part of the national "Book-a-Bed-Ahead" service) will help find an accommodation for you in the price range you're seeking. The fee for room reservations is 10% of your first night's stay (B&B rate only), which is deductible from your final bill.

VERY EXPENSIVE

✪ **Welcombe Hotel.** Warwick Rd., Stratford-upon-Avon, Warwickshire CV37 0NR. ☎ **01789/295252.** Fax 01789/414666. www.welcombe.co.uk. E-mail: sales@welcombe.co.uk. 68 units. TV TEL. £175 ($297.50) double; £260–£295 ($442–$501.50) suite. Rates include English breakfast. AE, DC, MC, V. Take A439 1 1/2 miles northeast of the town center.

For a formal, historic hotel, there is none better in Stratford. The Welcombe is rivaled only by Ettington Park at Alderminster (see below). One of England's great Jacobean country houses, it's a 10-minute ride from the heart of Stratford-upon-Avon. Situated on 157 acres of grounds, its keynote feature is an 18-hole golf course. Guests gather for afternoon tea or drinks on the rear terrace, with its Italian-style garden and steps leading down to flower beds. The public rooms are heroic in size, with high mullioned windows providing views of the park. Regular bedrooms—some seemingly big enough for tennis matches—are luxuriously furnished; however, those in the garden wing, while comfortable, are small. The accommodations most recently refurbished and most up to date are found in the Trevelyan and Garden wings. The rooms with the greatest character of old England are found in the main house. Many of the bedrooms have four-poster beds. The bathrooms are clad in marble or else tiled, and are furnished with toiletries and a hair dryer.

Dining: The restaurant offers a traditional mix of French and English dishes, although fine cuisine is not the major reason to check in here.

Amenities: 24-hour room service, laundry/dry cleaning, baby-sitting, secretarial services, courtesy car. Sports fans gravitate to the golf course and tennis courts.

EXPENSIVE

Alveston Manor Hotel. Clopton Bridge (off B4066), Stratford-upon-Avon, Warwickshire CV37 7HP. ☎ **800/225-5843** in the U.S. and Canada, or 0870/4008181. Fax 01789/414095. www.stratforduponavon.co.uk/alveston.htm. 114 units. TV TEL. £140 ($238) double; £240 ($408) suite. AE, DC, MC, V.

This black-and-white timbered manor is perfect for theatergoers; it's just a 2-minute walk from the Avon River. The Welcombe and Ettington Park on the outskirts may have cornered the deluxe trade, but the Alveston, along with the Shakespeare (see below), are the most atmospheric choices within the town itself. The hotel has everything from an Elizabethan gazebo to Queen Anne windows. Mentioned in the *Domesday Book,* the building predates the arrival of William the Conqueror. The 19 rooms in the manor house will appeal to those who appreciate old slanted floors, overhead beams, and antique furnishings. Other accommodations—full of tour groups—are in a three-decades-old motel-like wing. Furnishings here are fresher, but the ambience is lacking. Most of the rooms have standard twins, and most baths include a shower and tub. The lounges are in the manor; there's a view of the centuries-old tree at the top of the garden—said to have been the background for the first presentation of *A Midsummer Night's Dream.*

Dining/Diversions: Meals are served in the softly lit Manor Restaurant. This is not, however, for the serious foodie or an intimate meal (bus tours stop here). The bar never closes, and is the best place in Stratford for a drink at any time.

The Arden Thistle Hotel. 44 Waterside, Stratford-upon-Avon, Warwickshire CV37 6BA. ☎ **01789/294949.** Fax 01789/415874. E-mail: stratford.uponavon@thistle.co.uk. 62 units. TV TEL. £135 ($229.50) double. AE, DC, MC, V.

Theatergoers flock here, since The Arden is across the street from the main entrance of the Royal Shakespeare and Swan theaters. The Thistle chain completely refurbished the interior after buying the hotel in 1993. Its redbrick main section dates from the Regency period, although over the years a handful of adjacent buildings were included and an uninspired modern extension added. Today, the interior has a lounge and bar; Bards, a dining room with bay windows; a covered garden terrace; and comfortable but narrow bedrooms with trouser presses and beverage makers. Most rooms are graced with a two- or four-poster bed. The small bathrooms have a hair dryer. A fixed-price dinner of pretty run-of-the-mill English and continental fare is served in the restaurant.

Moat House Stratford. Bridgefoot, Stratford-upon-Avon, Warwickshire CV37 6YR. ☎ **01789/279988.** Fax 01789/298589. 251 units. TV TEL. £140 ($238) double; £220 ($374) suite. AE, DC, MC, V.

The Moat House stands on 5 acres of landscaped lawns on the banks of the River Avon near Clopton Bridge. Although lacking the charm of the Alveston Manor or the

Shakespeare, this modern hotel offers fine amenities and facilities. It is one of the flagships of the Queen's Moat House, a British hotel chain, and was built in the early 1970s and last renovated in 1995. The hotel hosts many conferences, so don't expect to have the place to yourself. Every bedroom has a high standard of comfort—bathrooms with generous shelf space, large mirrors, tea- and coffeemakers, and a hair dryer.

Dining/Diversions: The hotel restaurant features a standard British and continental menu, and the Riverside Restaurant offers a carvery of hot and cold roasts. You can drink in the Champions Bar and in the Terrace Nightspot, a disco open only on Friday and Saturday. There is a £10 ($17) cover after 10pm.

Amenities: 24-hour room service, laundry service, a leisure complex that includes a swimming pool.

Shakespeare. Chapel St., Stratford-upon-Avon, Warwickshire CV37 6ER. ☎ **800/225-5843** in the U.S. and Canada, or 0870/400-8182 or 01789/294771. Fax 01789/415411. 74 units. TV TEL. £165 ($280.50) double; £198 ($336.60) suite. Children up to 16 stay free in parents' room. AE, DC, MC, V.

Filled with historical associations, the original core of this hotel, which dates from the 1400s, has seen many additions in its long life. Quieter and plusher than the Falcon, it is equaled within the central core of Stratford only by Alveston Manor. Residents relax in the post-and-timber–studded public rooms, within sight of fireplaces and playbills from 19th-century productions of Shakespeare's plays.

The bedrooms are named in honor of noteworthy actors, Shakespeare's plays, or Shakespearean characters. The oldest are capped with hewn timbers, and all have modern comforts. Even the newer accommodations are at least 40 to 50 years old and have rose-and-thistle patterns carved into many of their exposed timbers. The bedrooms are equipped with tea- and coffeemakers and trouser presses. Bathrooms range in size, but each is equipped with a hair dryer.

Dining: The hotel restaurant, the David Garrick, serves well-prepared lunches and dinners.

Amenities: 24-hour room service and laundry service.

MODERATE

Dukes. Payton St., Stratford-upon-Avon, Warwickshire CV37 6UA. ☎ **01789/269300.** Fax 01789/414700. www.astanet.com/get/dukes.htl. 22 units. TV TEL. £69.50–£115 ($118.15–$195.50) double. Rates include English breakfast. AE, DC, MC, V. No children under 12.

Located in the center of Stratford north of Guild Street, this little charmer was formed when two Georgian town houses were united and restored. It's a good place to escape the crowds that overrun such hotels as the Falcon. The family operated inn has a large garden and is close to Shakespeare's birthplace. The public areas and bedrooms are attractive, having been restored to an impressive degree of comfort and coziness. The furniture is tasteful, much of it antique. All the small to mid-size bedrooms and compact baths have recently been refurbished. Most bathrooms have a tub and shower combination (some with just a shower stall), and all come with a hair dryer. Dukes also serves a good English and continental cuisine.

Falcon. Chapel St., Stratford-upon-Avon, Warwickshire CV37 6HA. ☎ **01789/279953.** Fax 01789/414260. 84 units. TV TEL. £110 ($187) double; £135 ($229.50) suite. AE, DC, MC, V.

Located in the heart of Stratford, the Falcon blends the very old and the very new. The inn was licensed a quarter of a century after Shakespeare's death. A sterile 1970s bedroom extension is connected to its rear by a glass passageway. The recently upgraded bedrooms in the mellowed part have oak beams, diamond leaded-glass windows, some antique furnishings, and good reproductions. Each room includes an electric trouser press and a beverage maker, but not enough soundproofing to drown out the BBC on your next-door neighbor's telly. Rooms in the newer section are still comfortable, with the same amenities, but are more sterile in tone. Carved headboards crown fine beds. The small baths come with shower stalls. Some are rather unsightly with brown linoleum floors and plastic tub enclosures.

The comfortable lounges, also recently upgraded, are some of the finest in the Midlands. In the intimate Merlin Lounge is an open copper-hooded fireplace where coal and log fires are kept burning under beams salvaged from old ships (the walls are a good example of wattle and daub, typical of Shakespeare's day). The Oak Bar is a forest of weathered beams, and on either side of the stone fireplace is the paneling removed from the poet's last home, New Place.

Forte Post House. Bridgefoot, Stratford-upon-Avon, Warwickshire CV37 7LT. ☎ **800/225-5843** in the U.S. and Canada, or 0870/400-8183 or 01789/266761. Fax 01789/414547. 68 units. MINIBAR TV TEL. £89–£95 ($151.30–$161.50) double, £109–£115 ($185.30–$195.50) executive room. AE, DC, MC, V.

An 18th-century Georgian facade with tall, narrow windows fronts this hotel, which looks out over the swans of Avon near Clopton Bridge. The complex is surrounded by gardens on a low, flat area beside a canal, a 5-minute drive south of the Royal Shakespeare Theatre leading toward Oxford. The hotel is on par with The White Swan and Dukes. It is well priced and a decent choice if your expectations are not too demanding. The bedrooms—most of them in a redbrick extension—are modern and tastefully furnished. Amenities include a trouser press and beverage maker. Accommodations have a chain-motel sterility but are comfortable nonetheless. Bathrooms are compact with a shower stall and a hair dryer.

The River Bar offers a view of the planting outside. The Swan Nest Restaurant serves à la carte dinners in a room lined with early-19th-century paintings.

Grosvenor House Hotel. 12–14 Warwick Rd., Stratford-upon-Avon, Warwickshire CV37 6YT. ☎ **01789/269213.** Fax 01789/266087. 67 units. TV TEL. £104.50 ($177.65) double. AE, DC, MC, V.

A pair of Georgian town houses, built in 1832 and 1843, respectively, were joined to form this hotel, which is one of the second-tier choices of Stratford on equal footing with Dukes or the Arden Thistle. Situated in the center of town, with lawns and gardens to the rear, it is a short stroll from the intersection of Bridge Street and Waterside, allowing easy access to the Avon River, Bancroft Gardens, and the Royal Shakespeare Theatre. All small to mid-size bedrooms have trouser presses and tea- and coffeemakers. Bathrooms are compact but well maintained, with a hair dryer. The informal bar (open until midnight) and terrace offer relaxation before or after you lunch or dine in the large restaurant, whose floor-to-ceiling windows face the gardens.

The White Swan. Rother St., Stratford-upon-Avon, Warwickshire CV37 6NH. ☎ **01789/297022.** Fax 01789/268773. 41 units. TV TEL. £85 ($144.50) double. Children up to 16 stay half-price in parents' room. Rates include English breakfast. AE, DC, MC, V.

This cozy, intimate hotel is one of the most atmospheric in Stratford and is, in fact, the oldest building here. In business for more than a century before Shakespeare appeared on the scene, it competes successfully with the Falcon in offering an ancient atmosphere. The gabled medieval front would present the Bard with no surprises, but the modern comforts inside would surely astonish him, even though many of the rooms have been preserved. Bedrooms vary in shape and size, and all are comfortable but generally lack style. Except for an occasional four-poster or half-tester bed, most are twins or doubles. Amenities include a trouser press. Bathrooms are compact with a hair dryer and shower stalls. The hostelry has a spacious restaurant where good food is served. The bar is a popular meeting place (see "The Best Places for a Pint," below).

Inexpensive

Sequoia House. 51–53 Shipston Rd., Stratford-upon-Avon, Warwickshire CV37 7LN. ☎ **01789/268852.** Fax 01789/414559. www.stratford-upon-avon.co.uk/sequoia.htm. E-mail: info@sequoiahotel.co.uk. 24 units. TV TEL. £69–£79 ($117.30–$134.30) double without bathroom, £85 ($144.50) double with bathroom. Rates include English breakfast. AE, DC, MC, V.

This hotel has its own beautiful garden on 3/4 of an acre across the Avon opposite the theater, conveniently located for visiting the major Shakespeare properties of the National Trust. Renovation has vastly improved the house, which was created from two late Victorian buildings. In its price range, bedrooms—ranging from small to mid-size—are some of the most comfortable in town, with upholstered chairs, desk space, and a beverage maker. Bathrooms are small but tidy, with a hair dryer. Guests gather in a lounge that has a licensed bar and an open Victorian fireplace. The hotel also has a private parking area.

Stratheden Hotel. 5 Chapel St., Stratford-upon-Avon, Warwickshire CV37 6EP. ☎ and fax **01789/297119.** 9 units. TV TEL. £62–£70 ($105.40–$119) double. Rates include English breakfast. MC, V.

A short walk north of the Royal Shakespeare Theatre, the Stratheden Hotel is tucked away in a desirable location. Built in 1673, and currently the oldest-remaining brick building in the town center, it has a tiny rear garden and top-floor rooms with slanted, beamed ceilings. Under the ownership of the Wells family for the past quarter century, it has improved again in both decor and comfort with the addition of fresh paint, new curtains, and good beds. You can make a piping hot cup of tea any time of day or night. The small bathrooms have a shower stall.

The dining room, with a bay window, has an overscale sideboard that once belonged to the "insanely vain" Marie Corelli (1855–1924), an eccentric novelist, poet, and mystic, and a favorite author of Queen Victoria. You can see an example of her taste: a massive mahogany tester bed in room four.

Victoria Spa Lodge. Bishopton Lane (1 1/2 miles north of the town center where A3400 intersects A46), Stratford-upon-Avon, Warwickshire CV37 9QY. ☎ **01789/267985.** Fax 01789/204728. 7 units. TV. £55–£60 ($93.50–$102) double; £75–£85 ($127.50–$144.50) family suite. Rates include English breakfast. MC, V.

Opened in 1837, the year Queen Victoria ascended to the throne, this was the first establishment to be given her name. This lodge was originally a spa frequented by the queen's eldest daugher, Princess Vicky. Accommodating hosts Paul and Dreen Tozer offer tastefully decorated bedrooms. The comfortable rooms range from small to mid-size; amenities include a beverage maker. The small baths are neatly organized with a shower stall and hair dryer. A full English breakfast or a vegetarian alternative is served in a cheerful antique-furnished dining room. No smoking.

Nearby Places to Stay

✪ **Ettington Park Hotel.** Alderminster, near Stratford-upon-Avon, Warwickshire CV37 8BU. ☎ **01789/450123.** Fax 01789/450472. 48 units. TV TEL. £185 ($314.50) double; £275–£350 ($467.50–$595) suite. Rates include English breakfast. AE, DC, MC, V. Drive 5 miles south along A3400 just past Alderminster, then take 2nd left (signposted) into Ettington Park.

This Victorian Gothic mansion is one of the most sumptuous retreats in Shakespeare Country, on par with the Welcombe Hotel. It opened as a hotel in 1985, but has a history that spans more than 9 centuries. The land is a legacy of the Shirley family, whose 12th-century burial chapel stands near the hotel. Like a grand private home, the hotel boasts baronial fireplaces, a conservatory, and a charming staff. The Adam ceilings, stone carvings, and ornate staircases have all been beautifully restored. A new wing, assembled with the same stone and neo-Gothic carving of the original house, stretches toward a Renaissance-style arbor entwined with vines. In the bedrooms, the most modern comforts are concealed behind antique facades. Guest rooms are spacious and elegantly decorated. The best units are the deluxe doubles, which are more spacious than the standard units and open onto garden views. Some of the rooms are fitted with old-fashioned four-posters, whereas others have king or double beds. Bathrooms have a hair dryer, Victorian-style tiling, robes, deluxe toiletries, and thick towels. Stay clear of the bookcase in the library; the ghost is very temperamental.

Dining: In the dining room, the cuisine is a medley of English and French specialties featured in fixed-price dinners.

Amenities: 24-hour room service, laundry, indoor swimming pool, tennis.

Mary Arden Inn. The Green, Wilmcote, Stratford-upon-Avon, Warwickshire CV37 9XJ. ☎ **01789/267030.** Fax 01789/204875. www.oldenglish.co.uk. 12 units. TV TEL. £55 ($93.50) double, £75 ($127.50) suite. Rates include English breakfast. AE, MC, V. Take A3400 3½ miles northwest of Stratford.

Shakespeare's mother, Mary Arden, lived in the tiny village of Wilmcote, some 3½ miles northwest of Stratford. Actually an upgraded village pub-hotel, this place offers not only appealing and well-furnished bedrooms at moderate prices, but also good meals. The inn is relatively unpretentious and offers a welcome respite from the hordes in the center of Stratford. Amenities include beverage makers, and a four-poster room with a Jacuzzi is available. Some of the rooms are quite small, others more midsize. Bathrooms are very small with a minimum of shelf space.

Homemade hot and cold bar snacks and meals are served in the popular beamed bar with an open fire and the original well. The bar offers four real ales at lunch and in the evening. Guests can eat outdoors in the large garden with a sun terrace in summer. There is also a restaurant that serves breakfast, lunch, and dinner with an à la carte menu.

WHERE TO DINE

After visiting the birthplace of Shakespeare, pop across the street for tea at **Mistress Quickly,** Henley Street (☎ **01789/295261**). This airy tearoom is tremendously popular, but the very attentive staff more than compensates for the throngs of patrons that grace its doors. Choose from an array of tea blends, cream teas, and various gateaux, pastries, and tea cakes—all freshly baked in their own kitchen.

EXPENSIVE TO MODERATE

The Boathouse. Swan's Nest Lane. ☎ **01789/297733.** Reservations recommended. Main courses £10.50–£16.50 ($17.85–$28.05); fixed-price lunch £12.95 ($22); fixed-price dinner £25 ($42.50). DC, MC, V. Wed–Fri noon–2pm; Mon–Fri 7–10pm; Sat 6–10pm. ENGLISH.

The only restaurant set on the Avon, this charming choice is reached from the town center by crossing Clopton Bridge toward Oxford and Banbury. The place is still a working boathouse, and you can rent punts and rowing boats for an intimate view of the Avon. A gondola ferry service transports patrons to the theater if you'd like to dine here before watching one of Shakespeare's plays. The cooking is robust and hearty. Try such main courses as sautéed calf's liver with a delicious bubble and squeak (yes, that old horror of boiled potatoes and cabbage), which tastes wonderful here. You may also opt for venison on a bed of leeks or a tempura of codfish served with a sun-dried tomato pesto sauce.

The Box Tree Restaurant. In the Royal Shakespeare Theatre, Waterside. ☎ **01789/403415.** Reservations required. Matinee lunch £16.50 ($28.05); dinner £25.50–£26.50 ($43.35–$45.05). AE, MC, V. Thurs–Sat noon–2:30pm; Mon–Sat 5:30pm–midnight. FRENCH/ITALIAN/ENGLISH.

This restaurant enjoys the best location in town—right in the theater itself, with glass walls providing an unobstructed view of swans on the Avon. You can purchase an intermission snack feast of smoked salmon and champagne, or dine by flickering candlelight after the performance. Many dishes, such as apple-and-parsnip soup, are definitely old English; others reflect a continental touch, such as fried polenta with fillets of pigeon and bacon. For your main course, you might select Dover sole, pheasant supreme, or roast loin of pork. Homemade crème brûlée is an old-time favorite at The Box Tree. There's a special phone for reservations in the theater lobby.

The Greek Connection. 1 Shakespeare St. ☎ **01789/292214.** Reservations recommended. Main courses £9.95–£17.50 ($16.90–$29.75). DC, MC, V. Daily noon–2:30pm in summer; daily 5:30–11pm year-round. GREEK/INTERNATIONAL.

Situated in the heart of Stratford, within a 3-minute walk of Shakespeare's birthplace, the Greek Connection occupies what was formerly a Methodist chapel built in 1854 (it also functioned for a brief period as an automobile museum). A warm welcome awaits you here, along with authentic Greek cuisine, live Greek music, and dancing nightly. Chefs Spiros and George serve a variety of Greek and international dishes (some vegetarian). We are especially fond of their moussaka.

INEXPENSIVE

Hussain's. 6A Chapel St. ☎ **01789/267506.** Reservations recommended. Main courses £6–£11 ($10.20–$18.70). AE, MC, V. Daily 12:30–2:30pm and 5pm–midnight. INDIAN.

This restaurant has many admirers—it's one of the brighter spots on the bleak culinary landscape hereabouts. The owner has chosen a well-trained, alert staff, which welcomes guests, advising them about special dishes. You can select from an array of northern Indian dishes, many from the tandoor, plus various curries with lamb or prawn. There is a three-course lunch from 12:30 to 2:30pm for £5.95 ($10.10). There is a 10% discount on pre- and post-theater dinners. Hussain's is across from the Shakespeare Hotel and historic New Place.

The Opposition. 13 Sheep St. ☎ **01789/269980.** Reservations recommended. Main courses £6–£15 ($10.20–$25.50). MC, V. Mon–Sat noon–2pm; Mon–Sat 5–11pm, Sun 5–9:30pm. INTERNATIONAL.

Located in the heart of Stratford within a 16th-century building, this refreshingly unpretentious restaurant serves up good bistro cooking at reasonable prices. Menu choices include breast of chicken with banana roasted in lime butter, basmati rice with a mild curry sauce, or salmon fish cakes served on a bed of spinach.

Russons. 8 Church St. ☎ **01789/268822.** Reservations required. Main courses £6.50–£15 ($11.05–$25.50). AE, MC, V. Tues–Sat 11:30am–2pm and 5:30–10pm. INTERNATIONAL.

Since the theater is a short stroll away, this is a great place for a preshow meal. The restaurant is housed in a 400-year-old building and the two simply furnished dining rooms both feature inglenook fireplaces. The menu changes regularly to reflect the availability of seasonal ingredients. Fresh seafood is the specialty here. Daily specials are posted on a blackboard, and include rack of lamb, guinea fowl, and numerous vegetarian dishes. Finish with one of the delicious homemade desserts.

THE BEST PLACES FOR A PINT

✪ **The Black Swan ("The Dirty Duck").** Waterside. ☎ **01789/297312.** Reservations required for dining. Main courses £6–£15 ($10.20–$25.50); bar snacks £2.45–£7.50 ($4.15–$12.75). MC, V (in the Grill Room only). Pub, Mon–Sat 11am–11pm, Sun noon–10:30pm. Grill Room, Tues–Sun noon–2:30pm, Mon–Sat 6:30–11:30pm. ENGLISH.

Affectionately known as The Dirty Duck, this has been a popular hangout for Stratford players since the 18th century. The wall is lined with autographed photos of its many famous patrons. The front lounge and bar crackles with intense conversation. Typical English grills, among other dishes, are featured in the Dirty Duck Grill Room, although no one has ever accused it of serving the best food in Stratford. You'll have a choice of a dozen appetizers, most of which would make a meal in themselves. In fair weather you can have drinks in the front garden and watch the swans glide by on the Avon.

The Garrick Inn. 25 High St. ☎ **01789/292186.** Main courses £4.95–£9.95 ($8.40–$16.90). MC, V. Meals daily noon–9pm. Pub Mon–Sat 11am–11pm, Sun noon–10:30pm. ENGLISH.

Near Harvard House, this black-and-white timbered Elizabethan pub has an unpretentious charm. The front bar is decorated with tapestry-covered settles, an old oak refectory table, and an open fireplace that attracts the locals. The back bar has a circular fireplace with a copper hood and mementos of the triumphs of the English stage. The specialty is homemade pies such as steak and kidney or chicken and mushroom.

The White Swan. In The White Swan hotel, Rother St. ☎ **01789/297022.** Dinner reservations recommended. Bar snacks £2–£5 ($3.40–$8.50); 3-course fixed-price dinner £16.95 ($28.80). AE, DC, MC, V. Morning coffee daily 10am–noon; self-service bar snacks daily 12:30–2pm; afternoon tea daily 2–5:30pm; dinner daily 6–9pm. ENGLISH.

In the town's oldest building you'll find this atmospheric pub, with cushioned leather armchairs, oak paneling, and fireplaces. You're likely to meet amiable fellow drinkers, who revel in a setting once enjoyed by Will Shakespeare himself when it was known as the Kings Head. At lunch, you can partake of the hot dishes of the day, along with fresh salads and sandwiches.

2 Warwick: England's Finest Medieval Castle

92 miles NW of London; 8 miles NE of Stratford-upon-Avon

Most visitors come to this town just to see Warwick Castle, the finest medieval castle in England. Some combine it with a visit to the ruins of Kenilworth Castle (see below), but the historic center of ancient Warwick has a lot more to offer.

Warwick cites Ethelfleda, daughter of Alfred the Great, as its founder. But most of its history is associated with the earls of Warwick, a title created by the son of William the Conqueror in 1088. The story of those earls—the Beaumonts, the Beauchamps (such figures as "Kingmaker" Richard Neville)—makes for an exciting episode in English history.

A devastating fire swept through the heart of Warwick in 1694, but a number of Elizabethan and medieval buildings still survive, along with some fine Georgian structures from a later date.

ESSENTIALS

GETTING THERE Trains run frequently between Stratford-upon-Avon and Warwick. Call ☎ **0345/484950** for schedules and information.

One **Stagecoach** bus per hour departs Stratford-upon-Avon during the day. The trip takes 15 to 20 minutes. Call the tourist office (☎ **01789/293127**) for schedules.

Take A46 if you're driving from Stratford-upon-Avon.

VISITOR INFORMATION The **Tourist Information Centre** is at The Court House, Jury Street (☎ **01926/492212**), and is open daily from 9:30am to 4:30pm; closed December 24 to 26 and January 1.

SEEING THE SIGHTS

✪ **Warwick Castle.** ☎ **01926/406600.** Admission £9.75 ($16.60) adults, £5.95 ($10.10) children 4–16, £7 ($11.90) seniors; free for children 4 and under. Mar–Nov daily 10am–6pm; Dec–Feb daily 10am–5pm. Closed Christmas Day.

Perched on a rocky cliff above the Avon River in the town center, a stately late–17th-century–style mansion is surrounded by a magnificent 14th-century fortress, the finest medieval castle in England. Even 3 hours may not be enough time to see everything. Surrounded by gardens, lawns, and woodland, where peacocks roam freely, and skirted by the Avon, Warwick Castle was described by Sir Walter Scott in 1828 as "that fairest monument of ancient and chivalrous splendor which yet remains uninjured by time."

The first significant fortifications were built here in 914 by Ethelfleda, daughter of Alfred the Great. William the Conqueror ordered the construction of a motte-and-bailey castle in 1068, 2 years after the Norman Conquest. The mound is all that remains today of the Norman castle, which was sacked by Simon de Montfort in the Barons' War of 1264.

The Beauchamp family, the most illustrious medieval earls of Warwick, are responsible for the appearance of the castle today, and much of the external structure remains unchanged from the mid-14th century. When the castle was granted to Sir Fulke Greville by James I in 1604, he spent £20,000 (an enormous sum in those days) converting the existing castle buildings into a luxurious mansion. The Grevilles have held the earl of Warwick title since 1759, when it passed from the Rich family.

The staterooms and Great Hall house fine collections of paintings, furniture, arms, and armor. The armory, dungeon, torture chamber, ghost tower, clock tower, and Guy's tower create a vivid picture of the castle's turbulent past and its important role in the history of England.

The private apartments of Lord Brooke and his family, who in recent years sold the castle to Tussaud's Group, are open to visitors. They house a display of a carefully reconstructed Royal Weekend House Party of 1898. The major rooms contain wax portraits of important figures of the time, including a young Winston Churchill. In the Kenilworth bedroom, the likeness of the Prince of Wales, who later became King Edward VII, reads a letter. The duchess of Marlborough prepares for her bath in the red bedroom. Among the most lifelike of the figures is a little uniformed maid bending over to test the temperature of the water running into a bathtub.

You can also see the Victorian rose garden, a re-creation of an original design from 1868 by Robert Marnock. Near the rose garden is a Victorian alpine rockery and water garden.

St. Mary's Church. Church St. ☎ **01926/400771.** Free admission; donations accepted. Apr–Sept daily 10am–6pm; Oct–Mar daily 10am–4pm. All buses to Warwick stop at Old Sq.

Destroyed in part by the fire of 1694, this church, with its rebuilt battlemented tower and nave, is among the finest examples of late-17th- and early-18th-century architecture. The Beauchamp Chapel, spared from the flames, encases the Purbeck marble tomb of Richard Beauchamp, a well-known earl of Warwick who died in 1439 and is commemorated by a gilded bronze effigy. Even more powerful in his day than King Henry V, Beauchamp has a tomb that's one of the finest remaining examples of Perpendicular-Gothic style from the mid-15th century. The tomb of Robert Dudley, earl of Leicester, a favorite of Elizabeth I, is against the north wall. The Perpendicular-Gothic choir dates from the 14th century, and the Norman crypt and the chapter house are from the 11th century.

Lord Leycester Hospital. High St. ☎ **01926/491422.** Admission £2.95 ($5) adults, £2.25 ($3.80) students and seniors, £1.75 ($3) children. Easter–Oct Tues–Sun 10am–5pm; Nov–Easter Tues–Sun 10am–4pm.

The great fire also spared this group of half-timbered almshouses at the West Gate. The buildings were erected around 1400, and the hospital was founded in 1571 by Robert Dudley, earl of Leicester, as a home for old soldiers. It's still used by ex-service personnel and their spouses. On top of the West Gate is the attractive little chapel of St. James, dating from the 12th century but renovated many times since. Closed to the public since 1903, the gardens in back of the hospital were recently restored. Nathaniel Hawthorne wrote of his visits to the gardens in 1855 and 1857. Based on his observations, the gardens were restored as he wrote of them.

Warwickshire Museum. Market Hall, The Market Place. ☎ **01926/412500.** Free admission. Mon–Sat 10am–5:30pm, Sun May–Sept 11am–5pm. From Jury St. in the town center, take a right onto Swan St., which leads to the museum.

This museum was established in 1836 to house a collection of geological remains, fossils, and an exhibit of amphibians from the Triassic period. There are also displays illustrating the history, archaeology, and natural history of the county, including the famous Sheldon tapestry map.

St. John's House Museum. St. John's, at the crossroads of the main Warwick-Leamington Rd. (A425/A429) and the Coventry Rd. (A429). ☎ **01926/412021.** Free admission. Tues–Sat (and bank holidays) 10am–5:30pm, and from Easter–Sept Sun 2–5pm.

At Coten End, not far from the castle gates, this early-17th-century house has exhibits on Victorian domestic life. A schoolroom is furnished with original 19th-century furniture and equipment. During the school term, Warwickshire children dress in period costumes and learn Victorian-style lessons. Groups of children also use the Victorian parlor and the kitchen. Since it's impossible to display more than a small number of items at a time, a study room is available where you can see objects from the reserve collections. The costume collection is a particularly fine one, and visitors can study the drawings and photos that make up the costume catalog. These facilities are available by appointment only. Upstairs is a military museum, tracing the history of the Royal Warwickshire Regiment from 1674 to the present.

WHERE TO STAY

Many people prefer to stay in Warwick and commute to Stratford-upon-Avon, though the accommodations here are not as special as those at Stratford.

Hilton National Warwick/Stratford. Warwick Bypass (A429 Stratford Rd.), Warwick, Warwickshire CV34 6RE. ☎ **800/445-8667** in the U.S. and Canada, or 01926/499555. Fax 01926/410020. 181 units. TV TEL. £155 ($263.50) double. AE, DC, MC, V. Take A429 2 miles south of Warwick (7 miles north of Stratford-upon-Avon). Junction 15 off M40 from London.

Although it's outside of town, the Hilton is the best choice in the area. Lying at the junction of a network of highways, it's popular with business travelers and hosts many conferences for local companies. But tourists also find that its comfort and easy-to-find location make it a good base for touring Warwick and the surrounding regions. It's a low-rise modern design with a series of interconnected bars, lounges, and public areas, a heated indoor swimming pool, fitness room, and solarium. Room furnishings are bland but comfortable. Most of the rooms are mid-size, and rather motel-like in quality. Bathrooms are compact and neatly arranged. The hotel's Sonnetts Restaurant offers a three-course carvery lunch and dinner, and there is 24-hour room service.

Lord Leycester Hotel (Calotels). 17 Jury St., Warwick, Warwickshire CV34 4EJ. ☎ **01926/491481.** Fax 01926/491561. 51 units. TV TEL. £59.50 ($101.15) double. Rates include English breakfast. AE, DC, MC, V.

This affordable choice lies within walking distance of the castle and the other historic buildings of Warwick. In 1726, this manor house belonged to Lord Archer of Umberslade; in 1926, it was finally turned into this modest hotel. The rooms are small but offer reasonable comfort for the price with decent double or twin beds. Each is equipped with a trouser press and beverage maker. Bathrooms are also small with a shower stall. A small English menu is offered in the dining room, and snacks are available 24 hours a day in Alexander's Bar. There's a large parking lot at the rear of the hotel.

Tudor House Inn & Restaurant. 90–92 West St. (opposite the main Warwick Castle car park, 1/2 mile south of town on A429), Warwick, Warwickshire CV34 6AW. ☎ **01926/495447.** Fax 01926/492948. 11 units, 8 with bathroom or shower. TV TEL. £65 ($110.50) double. Rates include English breakfast. AE, DC, MC, V.

At the edge of town, on the main road from Stratford-upon-Avon to Warwick Castle, is a 1472 timbered inn. It's one of the few buildings to escape the fire that destroyed High Street in 1694. Off the central hall are two large rooms, each of which could be the setting for an Elizabethan play. All the simply furnished bedrooms have washbasins, and two contain doors only 4 feet high. Rooms are small to mid-size; the small bathrooms are equipped with a hair dryer, and most of them have a tub and shower combination. In the corner of the lounge is an open turning staircase. Bar snacks are available, and the restaurant offers a standard English and continental menu.

WHERE TO DINE

When you're ready to take a break from sightseeing, it's hard to beat the ancient ambience of tea at **Brethren's Kitchen,** Lord Leycester Hospital (☎ **01926/491422**). This tearoom is part of a 16th-century hospital the earl established in the year 1571. It has cool stone floors and wonderful exposed oak beams. Indian, Chinese, and herbal teas are all available, as well as scones with fresh cream, sponge cake, and fruit cake. Closed February and Mondays, but open on bank holidays.

Charlottes Restaurant. 6 Jury St. Tel. **(0192/498930)**. Main courses £7.95–£12.95 ($13.50–$22). AE, DC, MC, V. Mon–Sat 10am–5pm, Wed–Sat 7:30–10pm and Sun 11am–5pm. MODERN BRITISH/ITALIAN

The setting for this old-fashioned restaurant in an English home overlooking a small flower garden. The cuisine borrows freely from both Britain and the continent, and the unpretentious welcome is among the finest in Warwick. Launch yourself into your meal with a freshly made soup of the day served with crusty Cotswold bread, or perhaps the mixed antipasti. Several freshly made pastas are featured daily, including one with a fresh pesto sauce. Fresh fish is prepared and served to order (we recently enjoyed a delicious whole sea bass perfectly served with lemon, parsley, garlic, olive oil, and a chili dressing). Homemade fish cakes are also good, as are the local fresh vegetables. The venison in green peppercorn sauce is a delight. Desserts are changed daily. On Sunday the kitchen staff prepares a traditional roast beef dinner with Yorkshire pudding and all the trimmings.

Fanshaw's Restaurant. 22 Market Place. ☎ **01926/410590.** Reservations recommended. Main courses £8–£25 ($13.60–$42.50). Set menus £13–£16 ($22.10–$27.20). AE, MC, V. Mon–Sat 6:30–10pm. BRITISH/FRENCH.

In the heart of Warwick, at the edge of the city's commercial center, this restaurant occupies a late Victorian building enlivened by flowered window boxes. Inside, there are only 32 seats within a well-maintained, rather flouncy dining room lined with mirrors. A well-trained staff serves food from a menu that changes every 2 months, and that usually includes sirloin steak; fillet of beef Wellington-style, with a red wine and shallot sauce; and breast of pheasant with a shiitake and oyster mushroom brandy sauce. Especially elegant, usually offered during game season, is a brace of quail with a hazelnut and apricot stuffing.

Findon's Restaurant. 7 Old Sq. ☎ **01926/411755.** Reservations recommended. Set lunches £5.95–£13.95 ($10.10–$23.70); set dinners £15.95 ($27.10). AE, DC, MC, V. Mon–Sat noon–2pm and 7–9:30pm. BRITISH.

The building is authentically Georgian, constructed in 1700. You'll dine surrounded by original stone floors and cupboards, within a setting for only 43 diners to dine in snug comfort. Michael Findon, owner and sometime chef, works hard at orchestrating a blend of traditional and modern British cuisine. The set menus include such dishes as a sauté of pigeon breast with red wine and celery, followed by a suprême of cod with lemon and prawn butter and deep-fried parsley. À la carte meals might include pave of beef with basil crust and game jus, or fillet of sea bass with a fumet of lime. Consider a lunchtime visit to this place, when a two-course "plat du jour" includes a soup of the day followed by such platters as venison sausages with a mustard sauce and fresh vegetables (or a suitable vegetarian substitute), all for only £5 ($8.50), a great deal considering that's about what you'd pay for a mediocre lunch in a local pub.

3 Kenilworth Castle

102 miles NW of London; 5 miles N of Warwick; 13 miles N of Stratford-upon-Avon

The big attraction in the village of Kenilworth, an otherwise dull English market town, is Kenilworth Castle—and it's reason enough to stop here.

ESSENTIALS

GETTING THERE **InterCity** train lines make frequent and fast connections from London's Paddington and Euston stations to either Coventry or Stratford-upon-Avon. For schedules and information, call ☎ **0345/484950.** Midland Red Line buses make regular connections from both towns to Kenilworth.

If you're driving from Warwick, take A46 toward Coventry.

VISITOR INFORMATION The **Tourist Information Centre** is in the village at the Kenilworth Library, 11 Smalley Place (☎ **01926/852595**). It's open Monday, Tuesday, Thursday, and Friday from 9:30am to 7pm, and Saturday from 9:30am to 4pm.

THE MAGNIFICENT RUINS OF KENILWORTH CASTLE

✪ **Kenilworth Castle.** Admission £3.50 ($5.95) adults, £2.60 ($4.40) seniors, £1.80 ($3.05) children 5–16; free for children under 5. ☎ **01926/852078.** Good Friday to Oct daily 10am–6pm; other months daily 10am–4pm. Closed Jan 1 and Dec 24–26.

The castle was built by Geoffrey de Clinton, a lieutenant of Henry I. At one time, its walls enclosed an area of 7 acres, but it is now in magnificent ruins. Caesar's Tower, with its 16-foot-thick walls, is all that remains of the original structure.

Edward II was forced to abdicate at Kenilworth in 1327 before being carried off to Berkeley Castle in Gloucestershire, where he was undoubtedly murdered. In 1563,

Elizabeth I gave the castle to her favorite, Robert Dudley, earl of Leicester. He built the gatehouse, which the queen visited on several occasions. After the civil war, the Roundheads were responsible for breaching the outer walls and towers and blowing up the north wall of the keep. This was the only damage inflicted following the earl of Monmouth's plea that it be "Slighted with as little spoil to the dwellinghouse as might be."

The castle is the subject of Sir Walter Scott's romance, *Kenilworth.* In 1957, Lord Kenilworth presented the decaying castle to England, and limited restoration has since been carried out.

WHERE TO STAY

Clarendon House Hotel. 6–8 Old High St., Kenilworth, Warwickshire CV8 1LZ. ☎ **01926/857668.** Fax 01926/850669. 31 units. TV TEL. £75 ($127.50) double. Rates include English breakfast. MC, V.

A family-run hotel and restaurant, the Clarendon House is in the old part of Kenilworth. The oak tree around which the original alehouse was built in 1430 is still supporting the roof of the building today. The bedrooms vary greatly in size, but each is tastefully decorated with a comfortable bed—usually a double or twins. Baths are small and compact.

Before the evening meal, guests gather in the Royalist Retreat Bar and lounges. The hotel's Cromwell's Bistro restaurant is housed in what was once the inn's stable. The oddly timbered room is decorated with antique maps and armor, constant reminders that a Cromwellian garrison once stayed at the inn during a siege of Kenilworth Castle. In season, you can dine on such specialties as jugged hare or pheasant *georgienne* (marinated in Madeira wine with oranges, grapes, and walnuts).

WHERE TO DINE

Restaurant Bosquet. 97A Warwick Rd. ☎ **01926/852463.** Reservations recommended. Main courses £16–£17 ($27.20–$28.90); 3-course lunch or dinner £25 ($42.50). AE, MC, V. Tues–Sat 7–9pm. Closed 1 week for Christmas and the last 3 weeks in Aug. FRENCH.

This narrow, stone-fronted town house from the late Victorian age is a culinary oasis. It's owned and operated by French-born Bernard Lignier, who does the cooking, and his English wife, Jane, who supervises the dining room. The à la carte menu changes every 2 months and might include such offerings as terrine of wild duck with foie gras and truffles, and a dessert specialty known as an *assiette* of chocolates.

4 Coventry

100 miles NW of London; 20 miles NE of Stratford-upon-Avon; 18 miles SE of Birmingham; 52 miles SW of Nottingham

Coventry has long been noted in legend as the ancient market town through which Lady Godiva took her famous ride in the buff (giving rise to the term Peeping Tom). The veracity of the Lady Godiva story is hard to pin down. It's been suggested that she never appeared nude in town, but was the victim of scandalmongers. Coventry today is a Midlands industrial city. The city was partially destroyed by German bombers during World War II, but the restoration is miraculous.

ESSENTIALS

GETTING THERE Trains run every half hour from London's Euston Station to Coventry (trip time: 1 hour, 15 minutes). For schedules and information, call ☎ **0345/484950.**

From London's Victoria Coach Station, buses depart every hour throughout the day for the 2-hour trip. From Stratford, bus no. X-16 runs from the town's bus station every hour for Coventry's bus station at Pool Meadow, Fairfax Street. This bus takes 60 to 90 minutes, and stops at Kenilworth and Warwick enroute. For schedules and information, call ☎ **0990/808080.**

VISITOR INFORMATION The **Coventry Tourist Office,** Bayley Lane (☎ **01203/832303**), is open Easter to mid-October, Monday to Friday from 9:30am to 5pm, and Saturday-Sunday from 9:30 to 4:30pm; mid-October to Easter, Monday to Friday from 9:30am to 4:30pm, and Saturday and Sunday from 9:30am to 4:30pm.

TOURING COVENTRY CATHEDRAL

Coventry Cathedral. Priory Row. ☎ **01203/227597.** Suggested donation of £2 ($3.40) to cathedral. Admission to tower £1 ($1.70) adults, 50p (85¢) children; to visitor center £1.25 ($2.15) adults, 75p ($1.30) children ages 6–16, free for children under 6. Cathedral Easter–Sept daily 8:30am–6pm; Oct–Easter daily 9:30am–5pm. Visitor center Easter–Oct Mon–Sat 10am–4pm.

Consecrated in 1962, Sir Basil Spence's controversial Coventry Cathedral is the city's main attraction. The cathedral is on the same site as the 14th-century Perpendicular building, and you can visit the original tower. Many locals maintain that the structure is more likely to be appreciated by the foreign visitor, since Brits are more attached to traditional cathedral design. Some visitors consider the restored site one of the most poignant and religiously evocative modern churches in the world.

Outside is Sir Jacob Epstein's bronze masterpiece, *St. Michael Slaying the Devil.* Inside, the outstanding feature is the 70-foot-high altar tapestry by Graham Sutherland, said to be the largest in the world. The floor-to-ceiling abstract stained-glass windows are the work of the Royal College of Art. The West Screen (an entire wall of stained glass installed during the 1950s) depicts rows of stylized saints and prophets with angels flying around among them.

In the undercroft of the cathedral is a visitor center, where a 20-minute documentary film is shown more or less continually. Also within the visitor center is the Walkway of Holograms, whose otherwise plain walls are accented with three-dimensional images of the stations of the cross created with reflective light. One of the most evocative objects here is a charred cross wired together by local workmen from burning timbers that crashed to the cathedral's floor during the Nazi bombing. An audiovisual exhibit on the city and church includes the fact that 450 aircraft dropped 40,000 firebombs on the city in 1 day.

5 Birmingham

120 miles NW of London; 25 miles N of Stratford-upon-Avon

England's second-largest city may lay claim fairly to the title "Birthplace of the Industrial Revolution." It was here that James Watt first used the steam engine with success to mine the Black Country. Watt and other famous 18th-century members of the Lunar Society regularly met under a full moon in the nearby Soho mansion of manufacturer Matthew Boulton. Together Watt, Boulton, and other "lunatics," as Joseph Priestly, Charles Darwin, and Josiah Wedgwood cheerfully called themselves, launched the revolution that thrust England and the world into the modern era.

Today, this brawny, unpretentious metropolis still bears some of the scars of industrial excess and the devastation of the Nazi Luftwaffe bombing during World War II. But there's been an energetic building boom in recent years, and Brummies have

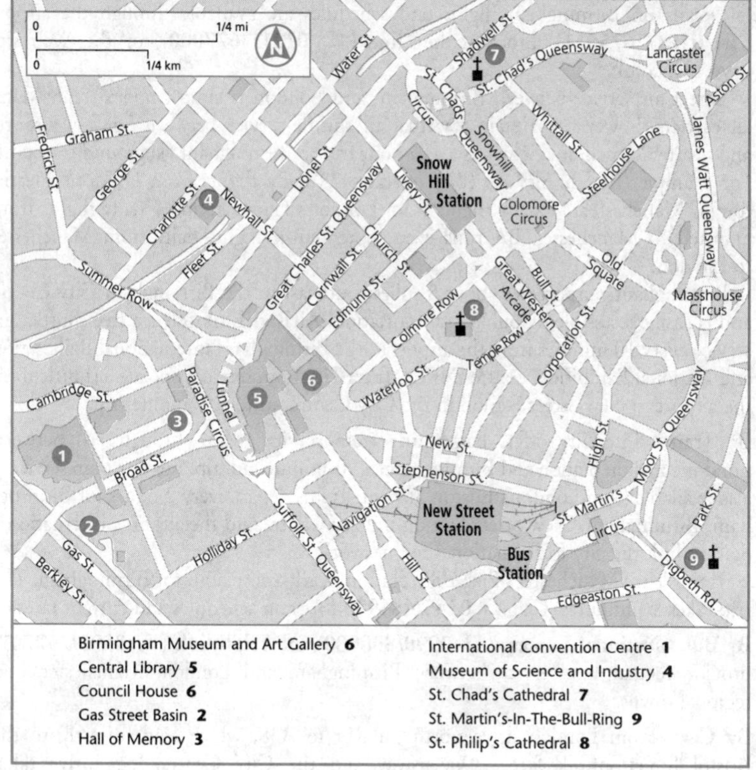

nurtured the city's modern rebirth by fashioning Birmingham into a convention city that hosts 80% of all trade exhibitions in the United Kingdom.

Birmingham has worked diligently in recent decades to overcome the blight of overindustrialization and poor urban planning. New areas of green space and the city's cultivation of a first-rate symphony and ballet company, as well as art galleries and museums, have all made Birmingham more appealing.

Although not an obvious tourist highlight, Birmingham serves as a gateway to England's north. With more than one million inhabitants, Birmingham serves up a vibrant nightlife and restaurant scene. Its three universities, 6,000 acres of parks and nearby pastoral sanctuaries, and restored canal walkways also offer welcome quiet places.

ESSENTIALS

GETTING THERE **By Plane** Three major international carriers fly transatlantic flights directly to **Birmingham International Airport (BHX)** from four North American gateways. **British Airways** (☎ **800/AIRWAYS** in the U.S. and Canada, or 0345/222111) has daily direct flights from Toronto and New York's JFK airport. **American Airlines** (☎ **800/882-8880**) flies nonstop 7 days a week from Chicago's O'Hare Airport and Birmingham. **Continental Airlines** (☎ **800/525-0280**) flies a 183-passenger 757 every evening from Newark, New Jersey, to Birmingham, departing at 8pm. Flight time is 6 hours, 45 minutes.

Details on Birmingham flights and schedules are available through the airport (☎ **0121/7675511**), brochure hot line (☎ **0121/7677000**), or the Web site www.bhx.co.uk.

Direct air service between Birmingham and London is almost nonexistent. Many air carriers, however, maintain a virtual air shuttle service between London airports and nearby Manchester, which is a 1½-hour trip to Birmingham via ground transport. For example, British Airways (BA) operates 28 daily flights from London's Heathrow to Manchester, 17 daily flights from London's Gatwick, and 6 daily flights from Stansted to Manchester. BA runs even more return flights daily from Manchester to London.

Birmingham's airport lies about 8 miles southeast of the Birmingham City Centre and is easily accessible by public transportation. **AirRail Link** offers a free shuttle bus service every 10 minutes from the airport to the Birmingham International Rail Station and National Exhibition Centre (NEC). **InterCity** train services operate a shuttle from the airport to New Street Station in the City Centre, just a 10-minute trip.

By Train InterCity offers half-hourly train service (Mon through Fri) between London's Euston Station and Birmingham, a 90-minute rail trip. Regular train service is also available from London's Euston Station. Trains depart every 2 hours for Birmingham. Birmingham's New Street Station in City Centre and the airport's International Station link the city to the national rail network.

Trains leave Manchester's Piccadilly Station nearly every hour for Birmingham. The trip takes 90 minutes. Call ☎ **0345/484950** for train schedules and current fares.

By Bus **National Express** (☎ **0990/808080**) and **Flightlink** (☎ **0990/757747**) provide regular bus service between Birmingham and London, Manchester, and regional towns.

By Car From London drive north on M5 to A38, which leads directly to the Bristol Street/Suffolk Street Queensway and the City Centre. The drive takes about 2 to 2½ hours, depending on traffic conditions. Parking is available at various city locations. Contact **National Car Parks** (☎ **0121/7677861**) for parking lot locations.

VISITOR INFORMATION The **Birmingham Convention & Visitor Bureau** (BCVB), 2 City Arcade, near New Street in the City Centre (☎ **0121/6432514**), is open Monday through Saturday from 9:30am to 5:30pm. The BCVB assists travelers in arranging accommodations, obtaining theater or concert tickets, and planning travel itineraries. The BCVB also operates offices at the National Exhibition Centre, International Convention Centre, and at 130 Colmore Rd., Victoria Square (☎ **0121/6936300**).

GETTING AROUND Birmingham's City Centre hosts a number of attractions within easy walking distance. **Centro** (☎ **0121/2002700**) provides information on all local bus and rail service within Birmingham and the West Midlands area. A **Day Saver Pass** costs £2.50 ($4.25) and is an economical way to use the Centro bus and local train system. A weekly **Centro Card** costs £18.50 ($31.45). Exact change is required on one-way local bus and train trips.

Centro (☎ **0121/2002700**) links Birmingham and surrounding Midland towns with regular bus service. Taxis queue at various spots in City Centre, rail stations, and the National Exhibition Centre. Travelers can also ring up radio cab operators such as **BB's** (☎ **0121/6933333**) and **Beaufort Cars** (☎ **0121/7844444**).

EXPLORING BIRMINGHAM

Stephenson Place, at the intersection of New and Corporation streets, is a good starting point for sampling the attractions of City Centre. A 5-minute stroll along New Street leads to Victoria Square, where **Council House,** Colmore Row (☎ **0121/3032040**), the city's most impressive Victorian building, anchors the piazza. Built in 1879, it is still the meeting place for the Birmingham City Council and an impressive example of the Italian Renaissance style.

Along Broad Street is the **Gas Street Basin** (☎ **0121/2369811**). Operated by Second City Canal Cruises, it forms the hub of the 2,000-mile canal network that runs in all directions from Birmingham to Liverpool, London, Nottingham, and Gloucester. From the Basin, you can take a cruise along the canals, or just walk by the towpaths.

Just a 10-minute walk from City Centre is the **Jewelry Quarter** at 75–79 Vyse St. (☎ **0121/5543598**). This complex includes more than 100 jewelry shops. The skill of the jeweler's craft can be viewed at the Discovery Centre's restored Smith and Pepper factory displays or by visiting shop workbenches that still produce most of the jewelry made in Britain. A unique time capsule of the ancient craft of jewelry making and working with precious metals, the quarter offers bargain-hunters the opportunity to arrange repairs, design a custom piece, or just browse. Admission to the Discovery Centre is £2.50 ($4.25), seniors £2 ($3.40). It is open Monday through Friday from 10am to 4pm and Saturday from 11am to 5pm.

Birmingham Museum and Art Gallery. Chamberlain Sq. ☎ **0121/3032834.** Free admission. Special exhibition charge. Mon–Thurs and Sat 10am–5pm, Fri 10:30am–5pm, Sun 12:30–5pm.

Known chiefly for its collection of pre-Raphaelite paintings (including works by Ford Maddox Brown, Dante Gabriel Rossetti, Edward Burne-Jones, and Holman Hunt), the gallery also houses exceptional paintings by English watercolor masters from the 18th century. The BMAG is instantly recognized by its "Big Brum" clock tower.

Barber Institute of Fine Arts. University of Birmingham (just off Edgbaston Park Rd., near the University's East Gate, 2½ miles south of City Centre). ☎ **0121/4147333.** Free admission. Mon–Sat 10am–5pm, Sun 2–5pm. Bus nos. 61, 62, or 63 from City Centre.

Don't be put off by the stark, stone-and-brick building that houses the Barber Institute collection. Some critics consider it the finest small art museum in England and the equal of any museum outside London. The choice selection of paintings includes works by Bellini, Botticelli, Brueghel, Canaletto, Delacroix, Gainsborough, Gauguin, Guardi, Murillo, Renoir, Rubens, Turner, van Gogh, and Whistler.

The Black Country Museum. Tipton Rd., Dudley (3 miles north of the Junction 2 exit on the M5). ☎ **0121/5579643.** Admission £7.50 ($12.75) adults, £6.50 ($11.05) seniors, £4.50 ($7.65) children. Family ticket £20 ($34). Mar–Oct daily 10am–5pm, Nov–Feb Wed–Sun 10am–4pm.

Much of the area immediately surrounding Birmingham is called the Black Country (after the black smoke that billowed over the city and its environs during the iron-working era). That period is best preserved at the Black Country Museum in Dudley, a town about 10 miles northwest of Birmingham. The museum occupies a sprawling landscape in the South Staffordshire coal fields, an early forge of the Industrial Revolution, and it re-creates what it was like to work and live in the Black Country of the 1850s. An electric tramway takes visitors to a thick underground coal seam, and trolleys move through a reconstructed industrial village with a schoolhouse, anchor forge, rolling mill, working replica of a 1712 steam engine, and trade shops.

WHERE TO STAY

EXPENSIVE

Hyatt Regency. 2 Bridge St., Birmingham B1 2JZ. ☎ **800/400-3319** in the U.S. and Canada, or 0121/6431234. Fax 0121/6162323. E-mail: hrbirm@hrb.co.uk. 319 units. MINIBAR TV TEL. Mon–Fri £125–£170 ($212.50–$289) double, Sat–Sun £85 ($144.50) double; from £215 ($365.50) suite. AE, DC, MC, V.

The town's premier choice, this sheer, 24-story, glass-skinned hotel, linked by footbridge to the Convention Centre, affords one of the best views of Birmingham from its upper floors. In the heart of Birmingham, it opens onto a canal-side setting with a glazed atrium that's the epitome of elegance and style. Rooms are tastefully appointed with modern furnishings, marble-floored baths, and an open design. Bedrooms, mainly midsize, conform to international Hyatt standards of overall good comfort. Windsor-styled armoires conceal minibars and TVs. Most beds are king or twins, and there are plain marble slabs for desks, plus such extra amenities as beverage makers and trouser presses. Baths are first rate, with makeup mirrors, deluxe toiletries and scales. The best accommodations are in the Regency Club, with its own lounge on the 22nd floor.

Dining: Even if you're not a guest, consider a meal at Number 282, nicknamed "The Brasserie on Broad Street." Its menu incorporates the day's news headlines, and reflects the very freshest of market ingredients. Here, the fish-and-chips is made with deep-fried monkfish. For a change, the chips are made with sweet potatoes.

Amenities: Secretarial services, health club, conference rooms.

New Hall Country House Hotel. Walmley Rd., Royal Sutton, Coldfield, W. Midlands B76 1QX. ☎ **0121/3782442.** Fax 0121/3784637. E-mail: new.hall@thistle.co.uk. 60 units. TV TEL. £136–£375 ($231.20–$637.50) double; £330–£375 ($561–$637.50) suite. AE, DC, MC, V.

Set amid 26 acres of private gardens, only 7 miles northeast of the city, this place claims to be the oldest moated manor house in England, complete with inviting formal gardens. Guest rooms feature marble-tile baths and English country furnishings. The most luxurious and desirable accommodations are in the antique part of the house, which opens onto a view of the moat. However, most of rooms are in a more modern wing built around a courtyard. The rooms in the annex are equally comfortable but lack the style and the authentic grandeur of the other bedrooms. Thoughtful extras in the rooms count a lot here, including free sherry and homemade crackers. Bathrooms are first rate with robes and hair dryers.

Dining: The formal restaurant is an elegant oak-paneled, no-smoking room with an award-winning menu of classic English offerings.

Amenities: Meeting rooms, a tennis court, a 9-hole par-3 golf course, and a croquet lawn.

MODERATE

The Apollo Hotel. Hagley Rd., Edgbaston, Birmingham B16 9RA. ☎ **0121/4550271.** Fax 0121/4562394. 126 units. TEL. £85–£105 ($144.50–$178.50) double; from £159 ($270.30) suite. AE, DC, MC, V. Take Exit 3 from the M5, or Exit 6 from the M6.

A 5-minute drive from City Centre, this hotel offers comfortable modern rooms, a restaurant, and a location convenient to the convention centers or the countryside. Rooms are often a bit cramped, but all are equipped with twin or double beds, trouser presses, and beverage makers. Bathrooms are small but tidily organized, with a shower stall and a hair dryer. Double-glazed windows cut down noise. The suites are a good value here, as they incorporate a minibar, private kitchen, and their own dining and lounge facilities. The Rib Room restaurant offers rich country English fare.

Jonathans. 16–24 Wolverhampton Rd., Oldbury (at the crossroads of A456 and A4123, just off Exit J2 or 3 on the M5), Birmingham B68 OLH. ☎ **0121/4293757.** Fax 0121/4343107. www.jonathans.co.uk. E-mail: bookings@jonathans.co.uk. 55 units. MINIBAR TV. £98–£125 ($166.60–$212.50) double; from £125 ($212.50) suite. Rates include English breakfast. AE, DC, MC, V.

Filled with Victorian antiques, this charming choice features two highly rated restaurants, a tavern, and plenty of business amenities, all set within a classic 19th-century country-house hotel 5 miles from New Street Station in City Centre. Jonathans derives its name from its two owners, each of whom is named Jonathan (one cooks and the other attends to guests). Visitors enjoy a sojourn back to the 1880s, right down to the mock Victorian street, and the secret boardroom tucked behind a book-lined dining-room wall. The bedrooms are spacious—really like suites—and each is furnished individually with antiques and quaint Victoriana or—in the words of one visitor—"artifacts carefully chosen to give homely familiarity." (The Brits use homely to mean homelike.) Bathrooms feature thick towels and a hair dryer.

INEXPENSIVE

Ashdale House Hotel. 39 Broad Rd., Acock's Green B27 7UX. ☎ **0121/7063598.** Fax 0121/7063598. 9 units, 4 with bathroom. TV. £38 ($64.60) double without bathroom, £44 ($74.80) double with bathroom. Rates include English breakfast. MC, V.

A spacious Victorian terrace house, this is one of Birmingham's best B&Bs. Your hosts, David and John, invite you to use their library with television. The cozy rooms range from small to mid-size, and rooms with bath contain a shower stall and adequate shelf space; the corridor baths are well maintained for those who must share. Organic produce is offered at breakfast along with some vegetarian choices. Naturally in such an ecofriendly environment, smoking isn't allowed. It's a very inviting and homelike place for an affordable stay in Birmingham.

Awentsbury Hotel. 21 Serpentine Rd., Selly Park B29 7HU. ☎ and fax **0121/4721258.** 16 units, 11 with shower. TV TEL. £46 ($78.20) double without shower, £54 ($91.80) double with shower. Rates include English breakfast. AE, DC, MC, V. Take the A38 from City Centre for about 2 miles, turn left at Bournebrook Rd., then take the 1st right onto Serpentine Rd.

University and Pebble Mill Studio visitors will find this lodging convenient and comfortable. The place is kept spick-and-span, and the rooms, while not stylish, are acceptable in every other way, with beverage makers. Two of the rooms are large enough for families. Rooms are small to mid-size, each fitted with a rather thin mattress, although the beds are reasonably comfortable. Bathrooms are extremely small with a shower stall; otherwise, there are enough corridor baths so you'll rarely have to wait. No smoking is allowed in the dining room, where a large English breakfast is served.

Lyndhurst Hotel. 135 Kingsbury Rd., Erdington B24 8QT. ☎ **0121/3735695.** Fax 0121/3735697. 14 units. TV. £56 ($95.20) double. Rates include English breakfast. AE, DC, MC, V. From junction 6 of the M6 motorway, follow A5127; take the right signposted Minworth onto Kingsbury Rd. The hotel is on the right.

Nine miles from the airport, this stone-exterior Victorian hotel in the northern suburbs is convenient to the Convention and City Centres and Aston University. The rooms are well maintained and equipped with everything from a hostess tray to a hair dryer. Most units are a bit small here but well organized for your comfort. Baths are small and only three have a tub and shower combination; the rest with shower. Although the house is Victorian, furnishings are contemporary. Those who have trouble with steep steps may prefer the ground-floor rooms. A bar and homelike dining room serve guests, as does a separate TV lounge. The garden-view restaurant serves standard but very affordable dishes in a relaxed environment.

WHERE TO DINE

A growing phenomenon, which we can only call the **Birmingham Balti Experience,** may interest those who love spicy food. *Balti* literally means bucket, but it refers to a Kashmiri style of cooking over a fast, hot flame. With the city's large Kashmiri population, there are now many *baltihouses* in Birmingham. Most of these restaurants are bare-bones, BYOB affairs. Two of the better ones are **Celebrity Balti,** 44 Broad St. (☎ **0121/6326074**), close to the Convention Centre, which is open daily from 6pm to 2am; and **Eastern Connection,** 884 Old Lode Lane in Solihull (☎ **0121/7437883**), open Sunday to Thursday 6pm to midnight, and Friday and Saturday 5pm to midnight.

Chung Ying. 16 Wrottesley St., City Centre. ☎ **0121/6225669.** Meals around £13 ($22.10) per person. AE, DC, MC, V. Mon–Sat noon–11pm, Sun noon–11:30pm. CHINESE.

There are more than 400 flavorful items on this predominantly Cantonese menu (40 dim sum items alone). Samples include pan-cooked Shanghai dumplings, stuffed crispy duck packed with crabmeat, steamed eel in bean sauce, and a variety of tasty casseroles. If you want to go really authentic and sample some of the dishes the local Chinese community likes, try fried frog's legs with bitter melon, steamed pork pie with dried or fresh squid, or fish cakes.

The **Chung Ying Garden,** another restaurant owned by the same proprietor, is at 17 Thorpe St. (☎ **0121/6666622**).

Leftbank. 79 Broad St., City Centre. ☎ **0121/6434464.** Main courses £11.50–£24.50 ($19.55–$41.65). AE, DC, MC, V. Mon–Fri noon–3pm; Mon–Sat 7–10pm. INTERNATIONAL.

This winning restaurant, in a former bank's premises near the International Convention Centre, occupies the ground floor of a grand Victorian building. It's one of the few places in Birmingham where you can almost be guaranteed a good meal. The bistro has a high, coffered ceiling, with gilt, oil paintings, and seating in wicker chairs. The menu from the talented chef, William Marmion, is eclectic. Some of the more delectable items include confit of duck wrapped in cabbage with caramelized vegetables, and fillet of beef with herb dumplings and foie gras.

Maharaja. 23 Hurst St., near the Hippodrome. ☎ **0121/6222641.** Main courses £6.50–£8.05 ($11.05–$13.70). AE, DC, MC, V. Mon–Sat noon–2pm and 6–11pm. INDIAN.

Set a few doors down from the Birmingham Hippodrome, this rather good restaurant specializes in Mughlai and North Indian dishes. Dining is on two floors, with framed fragments of Indian printed cloth on the walls. The menu features such dishes as *lamb dhansak* (cubes of lamb in thick lentil sauce), *chicken patalia* (chicken cooked in spices, herbs, and fruit), and prawn madras. The kitchen's balanced use of spices, herbs, and other flavorings lends most dishes an aromatic but delicate taste.

Shimla Pinks. 215 Broad St., City Centre. ☎ **0121/6330366.** Main courses £13–£20 ($22.10–$34). AE, DC, MC, V. Mon–Fri noon–2:30pm; daily 6–11pm. INDIAN.

A carefully selected menu featuring mostly Indian and Sri Lankan dishes is served by a very courteous staff in this relaxed, elegant restaurant. Try the achari chicken from Uttar Pradesh, or sample the Karachi dishes from the north. Special buffets complement the main menu on Sunday and Monday nights. Parking is available on Tennent Street behind the restaurant.

Another Shimla Pinks is located at 44 Station Road, Solihull (☎ **0121/7040344**).

BIRMINGHAM AFTER DARK

THE PERFORMING ARTS

Connected to the Convention Centre, **Symphony Hall,** at Broad Street (☎ **0121/2123333**), has been hailed as an acoustical gem since its completion in 1990. Home to the **City of Birmingham Symphony Orchestra,** it also hosts special classical music events.

The **National Indoor Arena,** King Edward's Road (☎ **0121/2002202**), seats 13,000 and is a favorite site for jazz, pop, and rock concerts; sporting events; and conventions.

The **Birmingham Repertory Theatre** on Broad Street at Centenary Square (☎ **0121/2364455**), houses one of the top companies in England. Some of the world's greatest actors have performed with the repertory company over the years, including Lord Olivier, Albert Finney, Paul Scoffield, Dame Edith Evans, and Kenneth Branagh. The widely known "Rep" comprises the **Main House,** which seats 900 theater-goers, and **The Door,** a more intimate 140-seat venue that often stages new and innovative works. The box office is open from 9:30am to 8pm Monday through Saturday. Tickets cost £7.25 to £17.50 ($12.35 to $29.75).

Midlands Arts Centre (MAC) in Cannon Hill Park (☎ **0121/4403838**) is close to the Edgbaston Cricket Ground and reached by car or bus (routes 1, 35, 45, 47, 61, 62, 63). The MAC houses three performance areas and stages a lively range of drama, dance, and musical performances, as well as films. The box office is open daily from 9am to 8:45pm.

The **Alexandra Theatre,** Station Street (☎ **0870/607-7533**), hosts national touring companies, including productions from London's West End. Tickets for all theaters are available through Birmingham visitor offices. The theater serves as a temporary home to many of England's touring companies. Contact the box office for show details.

The **Birmingham Hippodrome,** Hurst Street (☎ **0121/6227486**), is home to the **Birmingham Royal Ballet** and visiting companies from around the world. It hosts a variety of events from the Welsh National Opera and musicals to dance. The box office is open Monday through Saturday from 10am to 5pm.

CLUBS & PUBS

Bobby Brown's The Club, 48 Gas St., along the City Centre canal (☎ **0121/6432573**), is a converted warehouse with several small bars and a disco. **Ronnie Scott's,** 258 Broad St. (☎ **0121/6434525**), lets guests unwind with live jazz in a casual setting. **Liberty's,** 184 Hagley Rd. (☎ **0121/4544444**), is a large, fashionable club featuring French cuisine in the Piano Bar restaurant, champagne, cocktails, and other smaller bars.

The Old Varsity Tavern Public House, 56 Bristol Rd. (☎ **0121/4723186**), is ranked as the third largest pub in England and is popular with university students. Says one local fan and reviewer: It's "good for dodgy music," but another laments that while it is "generally a good pub, there are vast numbers of wasted students."

6 Evesham

99 miles NW of London; 30 miles S of Birmingham; 32 miles SW of Coventry

Evesham sits in the center of the Vale of Evesham, along the banks of the Avon River, and has the traditional atmosphere of a bustling and ancient market town. Rich with gardens and riverside parks, Evesham also has several interesting buildings, including a 16th-century bell tower—the only surviving evidence of the Benedictine abbey that once stood here, commemorating the vision of the Virgin Mary that the swineherd saw around the year 700. The town is located in the middle of a host of small farms and orchards. In the springtime, the blossom trail, which begins in the town, bursts into delightful color and flows over the gently rolling hills, making for a memorable walk.

ESSENTIALS

GETTING THERE Seven days a week, trains run every 2 hours from London's Paddington Station to Evesham. For schedules and information, call ☎ **0345/484950.**

A **National Express** bus departs Victoria Coach Station in London every day at 5:30pm for Evesham. For schedules and information, call ☎ **0990/808080.**

From London by car, take the M40 toward Oxford, where you'll exit onto A44. Follow it straight into Evesham. Give yourself about 3 hours for this drive.

VISITOR INFORMATION The **Evesham Tourist Information Centre,** Almonry Museum, Abbey Gate (☎ **01386/446944**), is open year-round Monday to Saturday from 10am to 5pm and Sunday from 2 to 5pm.

SEEING THE SIGHTS

Other sites include the **Abbey Park,** with its Victorian bandstand (music on Sun afternoons from June to Sept), and the **Bell Tower**—all that is left of the once great abbey that was destroyed when Henry VII closed England's monasteries in 1540.

Almonry Heritage Centre. Abbey Gate. ☎ **01386/446944.** Admission £2 ($3.40) adults, £1 ($1.70) children 16 and over, students, and seniors; free for children under 16. Mon–Sat 10am–5pm, Sun 2–5pm. Closed 2 weeks at Christmas.

This ancient house, built in the 14th century, is a superb example of early English architecture. Once the home of the Abbey's Almoner, the monk responsible for looking after the poor and the sick of the town, it now houses a unique collection of artifacts from the town and the Vale, as well as exhibitions on the history of the great abbey and the defeat of Simon de Montfort at the Battle of Evesham in 1265.

WHERE TO STAY & DINE

The Evesham Hotel. Cooper's Lane, off Waterside, Evesham, Worcestershire WR11 6DA. ☎ **01386/765566.** Fax 01386/765443. 41 units. TV TEL. £98 ($166.60) double. AE, DC, MC, V.

The Jenkinson family that runs the place may be savvy business folk, but they bring lots of tongue-in-cheek humor to their hotel (rubber ducks in the bath, teddy bears attached to room keys, radios and magazines within each of the public toilets, and cartoons that gently satirize themselves and vacations in general). Most guests find it enchanting.

The setting is authentically historic. Built in 1540 as a farmhouse, it was "modernized" in 1810 into the solidly elegant Georgian appearance it maintains today. Half a dozen mulberry trees are believed to have been planted by monks around 1500, and a stately cedar of Lebanon, the hotel's horticultural pride, dates from 1809. Bedrooms are loaded with thoughtful and sometimes quirky touches (playing cards are provided). Most have traditional bedspreads and upholsteries, and many have either the original beams, or carefully maintained antique paneling. Bedrooms, most often midsize, are spotlessly maintained and contain "idiot proof" travel alarm clocks, an iron and ironing board, plus baths with hair dryers and such extras as containers of shampoo and bubble bath.

Dining: The Cedar has a large bay window overlooking the garden, and gracious service that many guests will remember long after their meal. There are special high teas (actually, early suppers) for the children of guests every day from 5:30 to 6:30pm. These are whimsical Christopher-Robin-and-Winnie-the-Pooh–type affairs. The dinner menu, served from 7 to 9:30pm, might start with a warm goat's cheese salad and then move on to breast of pheasant cooked in a tea-flavored sauce with walnuts, grapes and orange. Desserts include "Turkish Flan" which is an intriguing cross between a cream caramel and a cheesecake; or "Ocean Beach" which consists of melon balls poached in a light cointreau syrup with vanilla ice cream.

The Mill at Harvington. Anchor Lane, Harvington (4 miles north of Evesham, via A4188 and A435), Evesham, Worcestershire WR11 5NR. ☎ and fax **01386/870688.** 21 units. TV TEL. £109–£119 ($185.30–$202.30) double. Rates include breakfast. AE, DC, MC, V.

This is the most stately looking hotel in Evesham, with a redbrick Georgian-inspired setting that abuts the verdant bank of the River Avon. Beginning around 1750, it functioned as a bakery, and today, the property retains many of its original features, such as the old bakery's ovens (with ornate iron doors), but is now surrounded with bucolic gardens and a stream with nesting swans and herons. The place has been totally refurbished, the bedrooms redecorated and fitted with comfortable furnishings. Rooms are good size, and six of the most spacious and luxuriously appointed are in a separate annex. Bathrooms have a hair dryer. The real appeal of the place lies in the walks and strolls you'll take around its impressive exterior rather than the time you'll spend inside.

Dining: The restaurant serves an imaginative and well-prepared menu. Lunches are less elaborate than dinners, but everything served here has an international panache hard to find at most nearby establishments. At dinner, you might order breast of chicken with wild mushrooms served with a light Marsala sauce, or grilled sea bass topped with chopped pine nuts, fresh basil and bread crumbs and served with a white-wine sauce.

Riverside Restaurant and Hotel. The Parks, Offenham Rd. (2 miles west of Hereford beside B4510), Worcestershire WR11 5JP. ☎ **01386/446200.** Fax 01386/40021. 7 units. TV TEL. £90 ($153) double. Rates include breakfast. MC, V. Closed 2 weeks in Jan; closed Sun night and all day Mon.

Stately and sprawling, this white-sided Edwardian home set within 3 acres of gardens boasts prominent rows of bay windows overlooking the Avon River and its verdant banks. It's intimate, charming, and very English. Public rooms possess a 19th-century ambience. Rooms are cozy, sunny, individually decorated, and meticulously maintained. They are thoughtfully appointed and good sized, opening onto views over the gardens and terrace to the river. The bathrooms are small but efficiently organized.

Dining: Within the pleasant dining room, imaginative, well-prepared meals are served for lunch and dinner. There are garden and Avon River views from the big bay windows, and the service is sensitive and well timed. Your choices include half crisp-roast duckling with fresh sage and onion stuffing and an apple sauce; and roast rump of English lamb, crisp-roast parsnips, and homemade rosemary jelly.

7 Worcester

124 miles NW of London; 26 miles SW of Birmingham; 61 miles N of Bristol

Awash with some of the most magnificent and lush river scenery in all of Europe, the River Wye Valley contains some of the most charming small villages in west-central England. Where wool used to be the main industry in this area, most of the locals today make their living by fruit growing, dairy farming, and, to an increasing degree, tourism.

Worcestershire has become a household name around the world, thanks to the famous sauce that is used to accent a myriad of dishes and to perk up any respectable Bloody Mary. One of the quaintest of the Midland counties, it covers portions of the rich valleys of the Severn and Avon rivers. Between the two cathedral cities of Hereford and Worcester, the ridge of the Malverns rises from the Severn Plain.

The River Severn flows through the heart of Worcester, a world-famous porcelain center. In medieval times, the river—just a short distance away from the bustling High Street—served as the hub of the city's commercial life. Today, it plays host to more leisurely activities like boat trips, fishing, and rowing. The river's bridge also affords the city's best views of 900-year-old Worcester Cathedral, with its 200-foot-high tower.

ESSENTIALS

GETTING THERE Regular trains depart London's Paddington Station for Worcester, arriving about 2¼ hours later. For schedules and information, call ☎ **0345/484950.**

National Express buses leave throughout the day from London's Victoria Coach Station. For schedules and information, call ☎ **0990/808080.**

Driving from London, take the M5 to Junction 7 toward Worcester. Give yourself about 3 hours. From Hereford, it's a short drive to Worcester. Just take A449 26 miles west.

VISITOR INFORMATION The **Worcester Tourist Information Centre,** in the Queen Anne's Guildhall on High Street (☎ **01905/726311**), keeps hours of 10:30am to 5:30pm Monday to Saturday from mid-March to the end of October, and 10:30am to 5pm Monday to Saturday from November to mid-March.

SPECIAL EVENTS The **Three Choirs Festival** was founded in 1715 by the cathedrals choir of Worcester, Gloucester, and Hereford. The cathedrals rotate every year as hosts, with the other two choirs as guests. In 2000, Hereford will serve as host from August 21 to 27, with a program that will feature the works of Elgar, among others. Ticket prices range from £6 to £30 ($10.20 to $51).

WHAT TO SEE & DO

Bickerline River Trips, 98 Christine Ave., Rushwick (☎ **01905/422499**), lets you see Worcester from the river aboard the 88-passenger *Marianne.* These 45-minute trips set sail every day on the hour from 11am to 5pm and until 6pm on Saturday and Sunday. Light refreshments are served and party bookings are available.

If you're interested in shopping, you might want to take a stroll down the architecturally important **Friar Street,** taking in the eclectic collection of individual timber-framed and brick shops. **G. R. Pratley & Sons,** Shambles (☎ **01905/22678** or 01905/28642), offers a smorgasbord of glass, china, and earthenware; it's an agent for Royal Worcester, Royal Doulton, Wedgwood, Spode, Duchess Fine Bone China, and Wood & Sons Ltd. You can also find finely woven Oriental rugs and carpets and top-quality furniture here.

Bygones of Worcester, 55 Sidbury and Cathedral Square (☎ **01905/23132** or 01905/25388), is actually two shops packed with an intriguing collection of antiques and odds and ends. Wander through this store to find furnishings for your home that range from the bizarre to the decorative and fanciful—all from cottages and castles in England.

Worcester Cathedral. College Yard at High St. ☎ **01905/611002.** Admission free, but adults asked for a £2 ($3.40) donation. Daily 7:30am–6pm.

Historically speaking, the most significant part of Worcester Cathedral is its crypt, a classic example of Norman architecture that dates from 1084. Still in use today, it contains the tombs of King John, whose claim to fame is the Magna Carta, and Prince Arthur, the elder brother of Henry VII. Both tombs can be found near the high altar. The 12th-century chapter house is one of the finest in England and, along with the cloisters, evokes the cathedral's rich monastic past. The cathedral is also known for a distinguished history of fine choral music, and, rotating with the cathedrals of Gloucester and Hereford, hosts the oldest choral festival in Europe, the **Three Choirs Festival.**

Royal Worcester Porcelain Factory. Severn St. ☎ **01905/23221.** Factory tours available Mon–Fri beginning at 10:30am; cost is £5 ($8.50). Call ahead to reserve (for a same-day tour, phone before 10am). Museum admission £3 ($5.10) adults, £2 ($3.40) seniors and children. Museum open Mon–Sat 9am–5:30pm and Sun 11am–5pm. Ticket for tour and museum £8 ($13.60) adults, £6.75 ($11.50) children.

This factory has been achieving its goal of creating "ware of a form so precise as to be easily distinguished from other English porcelain" ever since its founding in 1751. It produces a unique range of fine china and porcelain that remains unsurpassed throughout the world. Behind-the-scenes tours last about 45 minutes and do not accept children under 11, very elderly visitors, or persons with disabilities, because of safety regulations.

The **Retail and Seconds Shops** at the factory are open to all, and offer a unique chance to buy the beauty of Royal Worcester at bargain prices. Many of the pieces are marked as seconds, but most of the time you won't be able to tell why. The **Dyson Perrins Museum** is also located at the factory and houses the world's largest collection of Worcester Porcelain.

The Commandery. Sidbury. ☎ **01905/361821.** Open Mon–Sat 10am–5pm, Sun 1:30–5pm. Admission is £3.60 ($6.10) for adults, £2.50 ($4.25) for children and seniors, and £9.60 ($16.30) for a family ticket. The Commandery is a 3-minute walk from Worcester Cathedral.

Originally the 11th-century Hospital of St. Wulstan, the Commandery was transformed over the years into a sprawling 15th-century, medieval timber-framed building that served as the country home of the Wylde family. This was the headquarters of King Charles II during the Battle of Worcester in 1651, the last battle in the English civil war. The Great Hall has a hammer-beam roof and a minstrel's gallery. England's premier **Civil War Centre** is now situated here. This exciting, interactive, and hands-on museum marvelously incorporates life-size figures, sound systems, and videos to take you through the bloody and turbulent years of England's civil war. You can even try on helmets, handle weapons, and pick up cannon balls. The Commandery also has canal-side tearooms, a picnic area, and a Garden of Fragrance.

Worcester Guildhall. High St. ☎ **01905/723471.** Free admission. Mon–Sat 9am–4:30pm.

The guildhall was built between 1721 and 1723. Here, you'll find statues dutifully erected by the Royalists honoring Charles I and Charles II, as well as one of the most beautifully decorated Queen Anne rooms in England. The tourist office is located here.

Sir Edward Elgar's Birthplace Museum. Crown East Lane, Lower Broadheath. ☎ **01905/333224.** Admission £3 ($5.10) adults, £2 ($3.40) seniors, 50p (85¢) children. Summer Thurs–Tues 10:30am–6pm; winter Thurs–Tues 1:30–4:30pm. Closed mid-Jan to mid-Feb. Drive out of Worcester on the A44 toward Leominster. After 2 miles, turn off to the right at the sign. The house is 3/4 mile on the right.

This charming and inviting redbrick country cottage, stable, and coach house is set on well-tended grounds. Elgar, perhaps England's greatest composer, was born in this early-19th-century house on June 2, 1857. Today, the cottage houses a unique collection of manuscripts and musical scores, photographs, and other personal memorabilia.

WHERE TO STAY

Diglis House Hotel. Severn St., Worcester WR1 2NF. ☎ **01905/353518.** Fax 01905/767772. 30 units. TV TEL. Mon–Fri £90–£105 ($153–$178.50) double, Sat–Sun £70–£85 ($119–$144.50) double; £100–£160 ($170–$272) suite. Rates include breakfast. AE, MC, V.

Set within gardens at the edge of the Severn River, this mansion was built in the 1700s as a guest house for visitors to the nearby cathedral. Later, it was the family home of noted landscape architect Benjamin Williams Leader, whose paintings of bucolic England have graced the cover of many English Christmas cards. The building's interior was upgraded to country-house hotel standards. Bedrooms, though small, are cozily and comfortably arranged, each fitted with twin or double beds. The compact baths have adequate shelf space and a shower stall. There's a restaurant (The Conservatory) on the premises, set within a glass-sided greenhouse-style wing of the stately building.

✪ **The Elms Hotel.** On the A443 (2 miles west of Abberley, near Worcester), Worcester WR6 6AT. ☎ **01299/896666.** Fax 01299/896804. 16 units. TV TEL. £140–£175 ($238–$297.50) double. Rates include breakfast. AE, DC, MC, V. Take the A443 for 6 miles west of Worcester, following the signs to Tenbury Wells.

One of the most impressive hotels in the region was built in 1710 by Gilbert White, a disciple of Sir Christopher Wren. It is chic, fun, sophisticated, and international, and lies on the outskirts of Worcester. Surrounded by 10 acres of field, park, and forest, it's outfitted with what some visitors consider a fantasy version of the best of England, complete with mahogany or walnut 18th- and 19th-century antiques, an intriguing collection of clocks and oil paintings, and log-burning fireplaces. The frequently redecorated bedrooms come in various shapes and sizes, and feature twin or double beds. The bathrooms, though compact, still have adequate shelf space and a hair dryer.

There's a restaurant on the premises that's open daily for lunch and dinner.

Fownes Hotel. City Walls Rd., Worcester WR1 2AP. ☎ **01905/613151.** Fax 01905/23742. 61 units. TV TEL. £95 ($161.50) double; £120–£140 ($204–$238) suite. Weekend packages available £78 ($132.60) double per night (breakfast included). AE, DC, MC, V.

A 5-minute walk west of Worcester's cathedral, this hotel occupies the industrial-age premises of the Fownes Glove Factory (ca. 1892). A civic monument, and source of income for many local residents until glove-wearing went out of fashion, it was converted in the 1980s into Worcester's most interesting large hotel. Public rooms are attractively outfitted and are unified by a decorating theme that includes gilt-edged photographs of the hotel during its glove-making heyday. Bedrooms are cozy and furnished in a conservative English style that includes the wide or tall many-paned windows of the factory's original construction. Each comes with a small bathroom featuring excellent maintenance. Some 32 units are set aside for nonsmokers. There's a cocktail bar on the premises, and a dining room, The King's Restaurant.

The Giffard Hotel. High St., Worcester WR1 2QR. ☎ **01905/726262.** Fax 01905/723458. 103 units. TV TEL. £85 ($144.50) double; £99 ($168.30) suite. Minimum 3 day packages £75 ($127.50) for double bed and breakfast. AE, DC, MC, V. Parking £8 ($13.60).

Although this hotel is located directly across from the city's cathedral, absolutely no effort was made to blend the bland modern architecture of this 1967, six-story hotel into the historic area surrounding it. A member of the Forte chain since its inception, it offers clean, conservatively modern rooms that are favored by tour groups and business conventions. Most rooms are small to mid-size, and contain twin or double beds. There is no smoking in 50 of the accommodations. There's a cocktail bar on the premises, and a restaurant. Room service is available 24 hours a day.

WHERE TO DINE

Across from the cathedral, **The Pub at Ye Old Talbot Hotel,** Friar Street (☎ **01905/23573**), contains lots of Victorian nostalgia and old-fashioned wood paneling that's been darkened by generations of cigarette smoke and spilled beer. It offers predictable pub grub that's a bit better than expected, especially when it's accompanied with a pint of the house's half dozen ales on tap.

One of Worcester's most whimsical pubs is the **Little Sauce Factory,** London Road (☎ **01905/350159**). The entire place is a takeoff on Worcester's famous sauce, with posters advertising food flavorings, all the accessories of an old-fashioned kitchen, and an enormous ceiling map of Britain in ceramic tiles.

Il Pescatore. 34 Sidbury. ☎ **01905/21444.** Reservations recommended. Main courses £8–£16 ($13.60–$27.20). MC, V. Tues–Sat noon–2pm and 6:30–10pm. Closed 2 weeks in late July. TUSCAN.

Set within 200 yards of the cathedral in a half-timbered, 16th-century Elizabethan building, this restaurant has an ambience that's a lot more international and suave than the very English exterior suggests. It's the domain of Giuliano Ponzi, a former resident of L'Aquila, north of Rome. An excellent chef, his menu includes *finocchiona* (Tuscan-style, fennel-flavored sausages) served with cannellini beans; daily homemade pastas, such as crabmeat-stuffed ravioli or smoked salmon and basil tagliatelle; and a delicious osso buco alla Milanese (braised veal shanks).

8 The Malverns

127 miles NW of London; 34 miles SW of Birmingham

Once part of the ancient and formidable kingdom of Mercia, the beautiful and historic Malvern Hills lie just west of Worcester, rising suddenly and drastically from the Severn Valley and stretching for 9 miles. This tranquil area is rich in natural beauty. The towns are especially famous for their healing waters, refreshing air, and inspiring vistas.

Six townships cling to the Malvern Hills, making this an outstanding place to strike out for easy day hikes while you're staying in Worcester or Hereford. You can wander through Great Malvern, Malvern Link, West Malvern, Welldon, Malvern Wells, Little Malvern, and several other hamlets in a day's stroll. Great Malvern is resplendent with Victorian grandeur, much of which was gained from its importance as a 19th-century spa resort. The town boasts the largest priory church in the area, dating from the 15th century and boasting some fine stained-glass windows, as well as a great Gothic tower. The monks' stalls have superb misericords and medieval titles. The greatest and most beloved singer of the 19th century, the wildly talented "Swedish Nightingale" Jenny Lind, as well as that century's greatest English composer, Sir Edward Elgar, both called this area home.

The Malvern hills provide a breathtaking backdrop for hiking and biking. You can take in immense views, eastward to the Cotswolds and westward to the Wye Valley and the Welsh mountains, while exploring the most beautiful countryside in England. The Malverns Tourist Information Centre (see below) can provide you with detailed maps and route descriptions.

St. Wulstan's Church, 2 miles out of Great Malvern on the Ledbury Road, is where the composer Sir Edward Elgar is buried with his wife and daughter. You'll find a bronze bust of the composer in Priory Park, and he lived at Craeglea on the Malvern Wells Road and at Forli in Alexandra Road, where he composed the *Enigma Variations, Sea Pictures,* and the *Dreams of Gerontius.*

ESSENTIALS

GETTING THERE From London, trains leave regularly from Paddington Station for this 2-hour trip. For schedules and information, call ☎ **0345/484950.**

One **National Express** bus departs daily from Victoria Coach Station in London, arriving in Great Malvern 2½ hours later. Call ☎ **0990/808080** for more information.

If you're driving from London, take M5 to A4104 west, then A449 north toward Great Malvern. Depending on traffic, the drive takes about 2 hours.

VISITOR INFORMATION The **Malverns Tourist Information Centre,** 21 Church St., Malvern, Worcestershire WR14 2AA (☎ **01684/892289**), is open from 10am to 5pm daily year-round.

WHERE TO STAY

The Cotford Hotel. Graham Rd., Malvern, Worcestershire WR14 2HV. ☎ **01684/574642.** 17 units. TV TEL. £65–£75 ($110.50–$127.50) double. Rates include breakfast. AE, MC, V.

A 5-minute walk east of Malvern's town center, on an acre of lawns and rock gardens, this towering and stately home was built in 1851 as the local bishop's residence. Constructed of Cotswold stone, and accented with lavish gingerbread, it retains a vaguely ecclesiastical air despite the modern-day furnishings. Views extend over the garden through elaborate windows carved from wood to resemble Gothic tracery. The main appeal of the place derives from its monumental historic premises, the warm welcome, and such Victorian touches as the tile-floored wide entrance hallway. The bedrooms, usually mid-size, have been much improved in recent years, with excellent beds and good baths. Evening meals can be prepared, but are usually restricted to residents and their guests.

✪ **Cottage in the Wood.** Holywell Rd., Malvern Hills, Great Malvern, Worcestershire WR14 4LG. ☎ **01684/575859.** Fax 01684/560662. 20 units. TV TEL. £89.50–£139 ($152.15–$236.30) double. Rates include full English breakfast. AE, MC, V. After leaving Great Malvern on A449, turn right just before the B4209 turnoff on the opposite side of the road. The inn is on the right.

There is indeed a cottage in the woods associated with this hotel (it contains four cozy bedrooms and dates from the 17th century). But most of the inn occupies a nearby Georgian house from the late 1700s. Originally built for the semiretired mother of the lord of a neighboring estate, it's referred to as "The Dower House" and is appropriately outfitted in an attractive Laura Ashley style. The bedrooms are quite small, but this place is so charming and offers such panoramic views that most visitors don't mind. The place is exceedingly well furnished with thoughtfully equipped bedrooms. Your hosts are John and Sue Pattin, whose skill is especially visible within their restaurant (see below).

The Foley Arms. 14 Worcester Rd., Malvern, Worcestershire WR14 4QS. ☎ **01684/573397.** Fax 01684/569665. 28 units. TV TEL. £92–£102 ($156.40–$173.40) double. Rates include breakfast. AE, DC, MC, V.

Home to one of the town's most bustling pubs, the Foley Arms is the oldest hotel in Malvern, with a Georgian pedigree from 1810 when it welcomed the affluent and exhausted for curative sessions at the nearby spa. Close to the town center, it rises from a very steep hillside, which makes it inconvenient for mobility-impaired guests, but also gives it glorious views over the Severn River to the edge of the Cotswolds from many of its bedroom windows. Accommodations contain old, usually antique, furniture and heavy draperies; they have all the modern conveniences but still seem old-fashioned. Bedrooms come in various styles and sizes, and five rooms are set aside for nonsmokers. Bathrooms are small, but tidily arranged. The in-house restaurant has a bay window with views over the valley, thoughtful service, and good-value set meals.

WHERE TO DINE

The Cottage in the Wood. Holywell Rd., Malvern Wells. ☎ **01684/575859.** Reservations recommended. Light set-price lunch Mon–Sat £6.95 ($11.80); set-price Sun lunch £14.95 ($25.40). Main courses £14–£17.50 ($23.80–$29.75). AE, MC, V. Mon–Sat 12:30–2pm and 7–9pm, Sun 7–8:30pm. MODERN BRITISH.

The setting is an 18th-century Georgian-style dower's house, set on a steeply sloping, wooded plot of land with panoramic views over the Herefordshire countryside. The setting manages to be elegant, cozy, and nurturing at the same time, thanks to the hard work and charm of resident owners John and Sue Pattin. They offer modern adaptations of traditional British favorites, including monkfish with five spices served on a mascarpone risotto and a red wine sauce, and grilled lamb kidneys with wild mushrooms, red onions, and Worcestershire sauce butter. English cheeses or such desserts as a Drambuie pot are particularly appealing.

✪ **Restaurant Croque-en-Bouche.** 221 Wells Rd., Malvern Wells. ☎ **01684/565612.** E-mail: croque@globalnet.co.uk. 5-course set menus £25–£32 ($42.50–$54.40) Thurs; £35–£40 ($59.50–$68) Fri–Sat. MC, V. Thurs–Sat 7–9pm. MODERN INTERNATIONAL.

Within a dark and woodsy neo-Victorian setting, the Joneses offer only as many tables as can be personally served by Robin (who waits alone on tables) and Marion (who cooks everything herself, often incorporating salads and vegetables from their garden). Menu items are heavily influenced by the traditions of Italy and Japan, and are likely to include vegetable tempura; vegetarian parcels wrapped in phyllo pastry; a frequently changing list of soups, including cannellini-bean soup with black Tuscan cabbage; roasted leg of Welsh lamb served with braised garlic, Pinot Noir, and glazed shallots; or perhaps Cornish codfish spiced with ginger and coriander on a bed of lentils and exotic greens. For such a small and intimate restaurant, the wine list, containing an estimated 1,500 vintages, is amazingly varied.

9 Ledbury

119 miles NW of London; 14 miles W of Hereford; 16 miles SW of Worcester

A thriving market town since 1120, Ledbury has a wealth of historic black-and-white, half-timbered buildings set against a rustic backdrop, especially in springtime when bluebells and wild daffodils abound and the scent of apple blossoms fills the air. Famous 19th-century poet Elizabeth Barrett Browning spent her childhood in nearby Wellington at Hope End (now a hotel), and the renowned poet laureate John Mansfield was born and reared in Ledbury.

ESSENTIALS

GETTING THERE Six trains depart London's Paddington Station for Ledbury daily (a 2 1/2-hour ride). For schedules and information, call ☎ **0345/484950.**

Two **National Express** buses leave daily from London's Victoria Coach Station for the 3-plus-hour trip to Ledbury. For schedules and information, call ☎ **0990/808080.**

If you're driving from London, take the M50 south toward Wales. Then, take exit NW on A417 toward Ledbury.

VISITOR INFORMATION The **Ledbury Tourist Information Centre** is located at 3 The Homend (☎ **01531/636147**), and is open from 10am to 4:30pm daily year-round; closed Sunday in winter.

SEEING THE SIGHTS

Within easy walking distance of the Tourist Information Centre is the delightfully cobbled **Church Lane,** which is so well preserved it's often used as a movie set. *Little Lord Fauntleroy* and *By the Sword Divided* are two films in which you'll be able to spy Church Lane.

The Painted Room (☎ **01531/632306**), located in the Old Council Offices in Church Lane, features a series of 16th-century frescoes found during a 1991 renovation of the building. It's open from Friday to Wednesday from 11am to 2pm if a staff member is available, or a tour can be arranged by phoning ahead.

Almost every street in town is worth exploring for its unique craft galleries and antique shops. It's a wonderful place for finding quality craft work. Just one example is **Homend Pottery,** 205 The Homend (☎ **01531/634571**), a gallery and showroom featuring beautiful hand-thrown wares made right on the premises.

Eastnor Castle. 2 1/2 miles east of Ledbury on A438. ☎ **01531/633160.** Admission £4. 75 ($8.05) adults, £2.50 ($4.25) children. Easter–Oct Sun and bank holiday Mondays 11am–5pm; July–Aug Sun–Fri 11am–5pm. Closed Oct–Easter.

The castle transports you back to a more romantic time. Built in 1812 by a local aristocrat, Eastnor has undergone a virtual renaissance thanks to the hard work, dedication, and youthful vitality of the Hervey-Bathursts, descendants of the castle's original owner. The many rooms are spectacularly appointed and overflow with early Italian fine art, 17th-century Venetian furniture and Flemish tapestries, plus medieval armor and paintings by Van Dyck, Reynolds, Romney, and Watts. Lunches and teas are also available.

Hellen's Much Marcle. 4 miles southwest of Ledbury in Much Marcle. ☎ **01531/660668.** Admission £3.50 ($5.95) adults, £1.50 ($2.55) children. Guided tours on the hour 2–5pm on Wed, Sat, and Sun from Good Friday to beginning of Oct.

Begun in 1292, Much Marcle was the boyhood home of one of the original Knights of the Garter, a knighthood that is only bestowed upon those men who have accomplished something extraordinarily courageous or exceptional for Great Britain. This ancient manor, brimming with a haunting atmosphere, still houses the great fireplace by which Queen Isabella of England waited for the Great Seal and abdication of King Edward II in 1326, as well as the bedroom prepared for Bloody Mary, Queen of England, in 1554.

Westons Cider Mill. The Bounds, Much Marcle. ☎ **01531/660233.** Tours £3 ($5.10) . Mill open year-round Mon–Fri 9:30am–4:30pm, Sat 10am–1pm. Tours Mon, Wed, and Fri at 2:30pm.

Situated in the middle of apple and pear orchards, this cider mill was established in 1880. Although the tour is long (2 1/2 hours), it's a real treat, including a tasting of ciders and perries (fermented pear juices) in the Visitors Centre and Shop. Tours need to be booked in advance. If your time is limited, skip the tour, but drop into the shop for a free cider tasting. A new restaurant, Scrumpy's House, opened in January 1998, serving sandwiches and salads for lunch Monday to Saturday; dinner, consisting of traditional British fare, is served evenings Thursday to Saturday.

WHERE TO STAY & DINE

The Feathers Hotel. High St., Ledbury, Worcestershire HR8 1DS. ☎ **01531/635266.** Fax 01531/638955. E-mail: feathers@ledbury.kc3ltd.co.uk. 19 units. TV TEL. £89.50–£145 ($152.15–$246.50) double. Rates include breakfast. AE, DC, MC, V.

This is one of the most prominent buildings on Ledbury's High Street, an Elizabethan fantasy of blackened timbers and meticulously maintained stucco. It's the most evocative and charming choice in town. Rooms combine rugged-looking half-timbering with patterned chintz fabrics and upholsteries. Each has an electric kettle and tea, plus the requisite squeaking floors, and is accessible only by somewhat irregular and very old-fashioned staircases. As befits the old structure, rooms come in different shapes and sizes, and one room has a four-poster. Bathrooms are small but up to date. However rustic, the hotel recently completed renovations that added a conference center, a swimming pool, and a gym, complete with a steam room.

At the more appealing of the hotel's two restaurants, Fuggles, you'll find dishes that range from the informal (burgers and hearty soups) to the more elaborate (spinach-and-ricotta tart). The other dining area, Quills, is open only for dinner on Friday and Saturday nights, and is rather staid and stiff.

10 Hereford

133 miles NW of London; 51 miles SW of Birmingham

Situated on the Wye River, the city of Hereford is one of the most colorful towns in England. It was the birthplace of both David Garrick—the actor, producer, and dramatist who breathed life back into London theater in the mid-18th century—and Nell Gwynne, an actress who was the mistress of Charles II. Dating from 1080, the red sandstone Hereford Cathedral contains an eclectic mix of architectural styles from Norman to Perpendicular.

Surrounded by pristine countryside, including orchards and lush pasturelands, Hereford is home to the world-famous, white-faced Hereford cattle and some of the finest cider around, best sampled in one of the city's traditional and atmospheric pubs.

ESSENTIALS

GETTING THERE By train from London's Paddington Station, Hereford is a 3-hour trip. For schedules and information, call ☎ **0345/484950.**

To make the 4-hour-plus trip by bus from London, you'll need to catch a **National Express** bus from Victoria Coach Station. For schedules and information, call ☎ **0990/808080.**

The trip to Hereford makes a scenic 3-hour drive from London. Take M5 to either Ledbury or Romp-on-Wye, then turn onto A49 toward Hereford.

VISITOR INFORMATION Hereford's **Tourist Information Centre** (☎ **01432/268430**) is located at 1 King St., and is open Monday to Saturday from 9am to 5pm and on Sunday from 10am to 4pm in summer, and Monday through Saturday from 9am to 5pm off-season.

EXPLORING THE TOWN

There's interesting shopping within a labyrinth of historic buildings known collectively as **High Town.** Limited only to pedestrians, it's enhanced with street performers and visiting entertainers. Principal shopping streets include Widemarsh Street, Commercial Road, St. Owen's Street, and perhaps the most charming and artfully old-fashioned of them all, Church Street.

Also near the town center is **Hereford Market,** which evokes West Country street fairs of old with its cornucopia of collectibles and junk displayed in an open-air setting. It's conducted throughout the year, every Wednesday and Saturday morning from 8am to 3:30pm. The area literally pulsates with life as vendors sell items ranging from sweatshirts and saucepans to paintings and pet food.

Andrew Lamputt, The Silver Shop, 28 St. Owen St. (☎ **01432/274961**), is the place to pick up the perfect silver gift. It boasts an extensive array of quality silverware and fine gold jewelry, and maintains a stable of skilled craftspeople who restore old pieces.

Hereford Cathedral. Hereford city center. ☎ **01432/359880.** Cathedral open year-round with free admission. Guided tours £2.50 ($4.25) per person. Mappa Mundi and Chained Library exhibition also open Mon–Sat 10:30am–5pm, Sun 12:30–4pm in summer, Mon–Sat 11:30am–3pm, off-season. Admission for exhibitions £4 ($6.80) adults, £3 ($5.10) children and seniors, free for children under 5; family ticket (2 adults and 3 children) £10 ($17).

This is one of the oldest cathedrals in England (its cornerstone was laid in 1080). The cathedral is primarily Norman, and includes a 13th-century Lady Chapel erected in 1220, as well as a majestic "Father" Willis organ, one of the finest in the world. Exhibited together in the new library building at the west end of the Hereford Cathedral are two of Hereford's unique and priceless historical treasures: the Mappa Mundi of 1290, which portrays the world oriented around Jerusalem, and a 1,600-volume library of chained books, with some volumes dating from the 8th century. The cathedral also contains the Diocesan Treasury and the St. Thomas Becket Reliquary.

The Cider Museum and King Offa Cider Brandy Distillery. Pomona Place, Whitecross Rd. (a 5-minute walk from the city center and 1/4 mile from the city ring rd. on the A438 to Brecon). ☎ **01432/354207.** Admission £2.40 ($4.10) adults, £1.90 ($3.25) children. Family ticket £6.60 ($11.20). Museum Apr–Oct daily 10am–3:30pm; Nov–Mar Tues–Sun 11am–3pm.

This museum tells the story of traditional cider making from its heyday in the 17th century right through to modern factory methods. The King Offa Distillery has been granted the first new license to distill cider in the United Kingdom in more than 250 years, and visitors can see it being produced from beautiful copper stills brought from Normandy. The museum shop sells cider, cider brandy, cider brandy liqueur, and Royal Cider, the real wine of old England, as well as a good selection of gifts and souvenirs.

The Old House. High Town. ☎ **01432/260694.** Free admission. Apr–Sept Tues–Sun 10am–4pm; Oct–Mar Tues–Sat 10am–4pm.

This is a completely restored Jacobean-period museum with 17th-century furnishings on three floors. The painstakingly restored half-timbered building was constructed in 1621 and includes a kitchen, hall, and rooms with four-poster beds.

The Churchill Gardens Museum and Hatton Gallery. Venns Lane, at the top of Aylestone Hill, on the outskirts of town (off the main Worcester Rd./A465, a 10-minute walk from the city center). ☎ **01432/260693.** Free admission. Apr–Sept Wed–Sun 2–5pm.

Located in a large park, the museum boasts collections of fine furniture, costumes, and paintings from the 18th and 19th centuries. The Hatton Gallery is devoted to the work of a local artist, Brian Hatton, who was killed in World War I.

WHERE TO STAY

✪ **Ancient Camp Inn.** Ruckhall, Herefordshire HR2 9QX. ☎ **01981/250449.** Fax 01981/251581. 5 units. £55–£70 ($93.50–$119) double. TV TEL. MC, V.

Perched 75 feet above the Wye River, this little inn—known more for its food than its rooms—takes its name from an Iron Age hill fort that originally stood here. East of Hereford, and rather remotely located, it is a real discovery, and worth a visit even if you're not staying here. Filled with charm and character, the inn is the domain of Pauline and Ewart McKie (he's the chef). Bedrooms are roomy but not luxurious, and the beds are comfortable; bathrooms are small.

Dinner is served in a setting of flagstone floors, open fires, and exposed beams. The food is exceptional. The menu is changed daily, but most of it is based on what is fresh and good at the market that day. In season game is a feature, and the good country Welsh lamb is also excellent. Begin with a terrine, and save room for one of the desserts, such as sticky toffee pudding or homemade vanilla ice cream. Meals cost around £25 ($42.50). To reach the site, take the A465 from Hereford. Turn right at the signpost to Ruckhall and Belmont Abbey. The inn is 2½ miles along this road.

The Green Dragon. Broad St., Herefordshire HR4 9BG. ☎ **01432/272506.** Fax 01432/352139. 83 units. TV TEL. £850 ($1,445) double. AE, DC, MC, V.

The Green Dragon is the oldest, most historic hotel in Hereford, and the best. In 1857, this attractive inn, situated near the cathedral, had already been in business for 300 years when the then-owners decided to replace its front with the stately neoclassical facade you see today. Rooms are scattered over three upper floors, and have all the high ceilings, thick walls, and squeaky floors you'd expect from an old treasure like this. Each has reasonably modern furnishings and a tea maker. Rooms are small to mid-size, but are comfortably appointed. There's a cocktail bar on the premises, as well as a rowdier (and more fun) pub, and a restaurant, The Shires, that's recommended below.

Three Counties Hotel. Belmont Rd. (Hwy. A465), Herefordshire HR2 7XB. ☎ **01432/299955.** Fax 01432/275114. 60 units. TV TEL. £79.80–£110 ($135.65–$187) double. Rate includes breakfast. AE, DC, MC, V.

Set 1 mile south of Hereford's center on the opposite bank of the River Wye, this hotel has a distinctive hip-roofed, barnlike design that's more common in central Europe than England. You can't miss its prominent tawny-colored tile roof from a distance. The hotel caters to business travelers and bus tours. Rooms are monochromatic and modern, nothing fussy. Comfort is the keynote here, and some of the small to mid-size bedrooms are suitable for persons with disabilities. Not all of the rooms are in the main building; some lie in separate buildings opening onto the parking lot. Bathrooms are small and compact. Cozier, woodsier, and more British-looking are the ground-level cocktail lounges and in-house restaurant.

WHERE TO DINE

The Ancient Camp Inn (see above) serves some of the best cuisine in the area.

Shires Restaurant. In The Green Dragon Hotel, Broad St. ☎ **01432/272506.** Main lunch courses £8 ($13.60); main dinner courses £13–£21 ($22.10–$35.70). AE, DC, MC, V. Daily 12:30–3pm and 6:30–10pm. ENGLISH/FRENCH.

Set within the street level of the town's most historic and prestigious hotel, this restaurant is sheathed with very old paneling, some of it from the 17th century, carved from Herefordshire oak. Everyone in town considers it the stateliest restaurant around, suitable for formal family celebrations. Main courses at lunchtime are selected from an all-English carvery table, where a uniformed attendant will carve from roasted joints of beef, turkey, or ham, garnished with all the traditional fixings. Dinners are more

French in their flavor, and are conducted with as much fanfare as anything else. Menu items include a pâté of duck meat and wild mushrooms served with a juniper chutney, and pan-fried fillet of salmon with avocado.

A FAVORITE LOCAL PUB

One of the most consistently popular pubs is the **Orange Tree,** 16 King St. (☎ **01432/267698**), attracting beer lovers and tipplers from across the county. There's nothing particularly unusual about this woodsy pub (it's mostly a place to soak up local color), but its beers on tap include Buddington's and a changing roster of ales and lagers sent on spec from local breweries, sometimes as part of local sales promotions.

11 Ludlow

162 miles NW of London; 29 miles S of Shrewsbury

An outpost on the Welsh border during Norman times, this mellow town on the tranquil Teme River is often referred to as "the perfect historic town." Indeed, a tremendous amount of history whispers through its quiet lanes and courts, all lined with Georgian and Jacobean timbered buildings. The two little princes who died in the Tower of London lived here, and it was once the refuge of Henry VIII's first wife, Catherine of Aragon. You can still visit the church where the unhappy queen prayed. The town's most colorful street is the "Broad," which rises from the old Ludford Bridge to Broadgate, the last remains of a wall erected in the Middle Ages. Be sure to visit the Butter Cross and Reader's House, in particular, as well as A. E. Housman's grave in the town cemetery.

ESSENTIALS

GETTING THERE Trains run hourly from Paddington Station in London to Ludlow, with a transfer at Newport. It's approximately a 3-hour journey. For schedules and information, call ☎ **0345/484950.**

National Express buses depart London's Victoria Coach Station for Shrewsbury, where you must change to the local line to reach Ludlow. It's a slow journey, approximately 5½ hours, but for those who are still interested, call ☎ **0990/808080** for the current schedule.

By car, it's a much shorter, 3-hour drive. Follow the M25 out of London to the M40 at Oxford. Take the M40 to Bromsgrove. Once at Bromsgrove, follow the M42 until Kidderminster. From here, take A456 to Ludlow.

VISITOR INFORMATION The **Ludlow Tourist Information Centre,** Castle Street (☎ **01584/875053**), is open November to March, Monday to Saturday from 10am to 1pm and 2 to 5pm; Saturday 10am-5pm; from April to October, it is also open on Sunday from 10:30am to 5pm.

SPECIAL EVENTS The ✪ **Ludlow Festival,** held annually in late June and early July, is one of England's major arts festivals. The centerpiece is an open-air Shakespeare performance within the Inner Bailey of Ludlow Castle. Orchestral concerts, historical lectures, readings, exhibitions, and workshops round out the festival. From March onward, a schedule can be obtained from the box office. Write to The Ludlow Festival box office, Castle Square, Ludlow, Shropshire SY8 1AY, enclosing a self-addressed stamped envelope, or call ☎ **01584/872150.** The box office is open daily beginning in early May.

EXPLORING THE TOWN

Whitcliffe Common was the common land of Ludlow during the Middle Ages. From here, you can enjoy panoramic views of Ludlow as you stroll. Leave town by one of two bridges across the River Teme and follow any of a number of paths through the Common.

A colorful Sunday **flea market** is held on Castle Square on alternate Sundays throughout the year from 9am to approximately 4pm.

In addition, the town is filled with traditional family businesses; of particular interest are the many antiques, book, arts-and-crafts, and gift shops. **The Marches Pottery,** 45 Mill St. (☎ **01584/878413**), produces a wide selection of hand-thrown tableware and individual pieces decorated with subtle Chinese glazes, including a host of terra-cotta flowerpots.

Lower Hundred Craft Workshop, off A49, 7 miles south of Ludlow (☎ **01584/711240**), nestled in peaceful country settings, offers a full range of candles, fabric boxes, and pottery. Tea, coffee, and homemade cakes are also available.

Ludlow Castle. Ludlow Town Centre. ☎ **01584/873355.** Admission £3 ($5.10) adults, £2.50 ($4.25) seniors, £1.50 ($2.55) children, £8.50 ($14.45) family. Jan Sat–Sun only, 10am–4pm; Feb–Apr and Oct–Dec daily 10am to 4pm; May–July and Sept daily 10am–5pm; Aug daily 10am–7pm.

This Norman castle was built around 1094 as a frontier outpost to keep out the as yet unconquered Welsh. The original castle, or the inner bailey, was encircled in the early 14th century by a very large outer bailey and transformed into a medieval palace by Roger Mortimer, the most powerful man in England at the time. After the War of the Roses, the castle was turned into a royal residence, and Edward IV sent the Prince of Wales and his brother (the "Princes in the Tower") to live here in 1472. It was also the seat of government for Wales and the Border Counties. Catherine of Aragon and Mary Tudor and her court also spent time in this 900-year-old home. Norman, Medieval, and Tudor architectural styles can be found throughout the castle. Many of the original buildings still stand, including the Chapel of St. Mary Magdalene, with one of England's last remaining circular naves. Excellent views of the castle can be spied from the banks of the River Teme.

Ludlow Museum. Castle Sq. ☎ **01584/875384.** Admission £1 ($1.70) adults, 50p (85¢) children and seniors. Apr–Oct daily 10:30am–1pm and 2–5pm. Guided tours available.

This museum tells the story of Ludlow town: the construction of its castle 900 years ago, the prosperity gained from wool and agriculture during the Middle Ages, and its rise in political importance. The museum also houses natural-history displays; and the Norton Gallery contains "Reading the Rocks," an exhibit that celebrates Ludlow's unique contribution to international geology. There are several hands-on, interactive displays, including a video microscope that lets you examine geological specimens. Visitors can also try on helmets used in England's civil war. It's a great place for kids.

WHERE TO STAY

Dinham Hall Hotel. Dinham by the Castle, Ludlow, Shropshire SY8 1EJ. ☎ **01584/876464.** Fax 01584/876019. 14 units. TV TEL. £100–£130 ($170–$221) double. Rates include breakfast. AE, MC, V.

Not to be confused with a less desirable competitor, Ludlow's Dinham Weir Hotel, the Dinham Hall Hotel rises in severe gray-stoned dignity, immediately across the road from Ludlow Castle. Built in 1792, it was constructed by the earl of Mortimer, and served through the 1960s and 1970s as a dormitory for the nearby public boys' school.

Many of the comfortable but very simple bedrooms bear the names of that school's former headmasters. The hotel enjoys a well-deserved reputation for the quality of its bedrooms, two of which are in a converted cottage. Some of the rooms have four-poster beds. Especially popular with participants of Ludlow's annual Shakespeare festival, it offers a kind of Georgian-era, stately ambience. On the premises is a worthwhile restaurant that offers relatively formal, well-prepared lunches and dinners every day of the year.

The Feathers at Ludlow. Bull Ring, Ludlow, Shropshire SY8 1AA. ☎ **01584/875261.** Fax 01584/876030. 40 units. TV TEL. £108.50 ($184.45) double; £138.50 ($235.45) suite. Rates include breakfast. AE, DC, MC, V.

The New York Times hailed this as "the most handsome inn in the world," and after a glance at its lavishly ornate half-timbered facade, you might agree. Originally built as a private home in 1603, and enlarged many times since, it boasts a winning combination of formal, high-style plasterwork ceilings as well as rustic, Elizabethan-style half-timbering and exposed stone, especially in the pub (the Comus) and restaurant (the Housman). Only the suite and a few of the rooms have exposed Tudor-style beams; the others are traditional and conservative, but without the medieval vestiges of the building's exterior. Twelve rooms have recently been refurbished in an old Georgian style. Each bedroom is cozy; some of the spacious rooms have massive headboards skillfully fashioned from antique overmantels or mirror frames. Five accommodations are reserved for nonsmokers. Bathrooms are tidily maintained, with hair dryers. The hotel's antique conference rooms and its "Olde-Englandy" pub are favorite meeting places for local civic groups.

WHERE TO DINE

Les Marches. In the Overton Grange Hotel, Overton, near Ludlow. ☎ **01584/873500.** Reservations recommended. Set lunch menus £28.50 ($48.45); set dinner menus £32.50 ($55.25). MC, V. Daily 12:30pm–1:45pm and 7:15–9:30pm. MODERN BRITISH/FRENCH.

This is a well-recommended and rather stylish restaurant with an ambitious menu that usually succeeds with flair. The richly oak-paneled dining room evokes the grand age of private dinner parties. Menu items are prepared by Claude Bosi or his assistants, and make straightforward but intelligent use of fresh ingredients. Examples include roasted Cornish lobster with pan-fried cauliflower and watercress purée and a sweet and sour sauce, or pan-fried squab with fresh dates and a lemon and apricot mousse. The wine list boasts over 250 selections.

✪ **The Merchant House.** Lower Corve St. ☎ **01584/875438.** Reservations required. Set menu £29.50 ($50.15). MC, V. Fri–Sat 12:30–2pm; Tues–Sat 7–9:30pm. MODERN BRITISH.

The Merchant House is the best restaurant in town. In virtually any other city in the world, much attention and fuss would be made over the half-timbered facade of this late–16th-century building (the former home of a wool merchant), but in Ludlow, it blends right in. Within a room where you could imagine Will Shakespeare concocting some of his sonnets, you'll enjoy a view over the River Corve. The only drawbacks are a comparatively small dining room (with seating for only 24) and limited hours.

The creative forces here are Shaun (who prepares the food) and Anja (the manager) Hill, whose cuisine is based on a deep respect for fresh local ingredients. Enjoy roasted venison with celeriac and gnocchi stuffed with fresh goat cheese, or an artfully arranged chunk of brill with perfectly prepared vegetables and drizzled with a watercress-and-vermouth sauce. One of the best desserts is a chocolate-flavored *pativier* that elevates an old-fashioned almond tart to chocoholic heaven.

A FAVORITE LOCAL PUB

The town's most atmospheric and evocative pub, **The Church Inn,** Church Street, Buttercross (☎ **01584/872174**), is everybody's favorite source for beer, gossip, and good cheer. Beer, mead, and wine have flowed here since at least 1446, and according to some historians, even earlier. Meals are served daily from noon to 2pm, and Monday to Saturday from 6:30 to 9pm. Whether you eat informally in the bar or head for the more formal restaurant, the food and prices are exactly the same. Main courses range from £5 to £9.50 ($8.50 to $16.15). Cuisine is straightforward, British, and ribsticking, with traditional pub grub like steak and kidney pie, fried prawns, and omelettes. The bar is open Monday to Saturday from 11am to 11pm, and Sunday from noon to 10:30pm.

12 Shrewsbury

164 miles NW of London; 39 miles SW of Stoke-on-Trent; 48 miles NW of Birmingham

The finest Tudor town in England, Shrewsbury is noted for its black-and-white buildings of timber and plaster, including Abbot's House (dating from 1450), and the tall gabled Ireland's Mansion (ca. 1575) on High Street. These houses were built by the powerful and prosperous wool traders, or drapers. Charles Dickens wrote of his stay in Shrewsbury's Lion Hotel, "I am lodged in the strangest little rooms, the ceilings of which I can touch with my hands. From the windows I can look all downhill and slantwise at the crookedest black-and-white houses, all of many shapes except straight shapes." The town also has a number of Georgian and Regency mansions, some old bridges, and handsome churches, including the Abbey Church of Saint Peter, and St. Mary's Church.

ESSENTIALS

GETTING THERE Shrewsbury-bound trains depart London's Euston Station daily every half hour. There's a change of trains in Birmingham before you arrive in Shrewsbury 3 hours later. For schedules and information, call ☎ **0345/484950.**

Three **National Express** buses depart daily from London's Victoria Coach Station for the 5-hour trip. For schedules and information, call ☎ **0990/808080.**

By car from London, the drive is 2½ hours; take the M1 to the M6 to the M54 to reach A5, which will take you directly to Shrewsbury.

VISITOR INFORMATION From May 26 to September 30, the **Shrewsbury Tourist Information Centre,** The Square (☎ **01743/281200**), is open from 10am to 6pm Monday to Saturday, and 10am to 4pm Sunday. From October to Easter, its hours are 10am to 5pm Monday to Saturday.

SEEING THE SIGHTS

Many tales and stories are locked within Shrewsbury's winding narrow streets and black-and-white buildings. The best way to learn this local lore is to take one of the many walking or coach tours hosted by official Shrewsbury guides. Special themed walking tours such as Ghosts, Brother Cadfael, and the Civil War are also available. A typical tour starts in the town center and lasts 1½ hours. Tickets can be purchased from the Tourist Information Centre (see above).

Shrewsbury Castle. Castle St. ☎ **01743/358516.** Free admission. Feb 4–Mar 15 Thurs–Sat 10am–4:30pm; Mar 18–Dec 19 Tues–Sat 10am–4:30pm; Easter–Sept 26 10am–4:30pm; closed Dec 20–Feb 3.

Built in 1083 by a Norman earl, Roger de Montgomery, this castle was designed as a powerful fortress to secure the border with Wales. The Great Hall and walls were constructed during the reign of Edward I, but 200 years ago, Thomas Telford extensively remodeled the castle. Today, it houses the Shropshire Regimental Museum, which includes the collections of the King's Shropshire Light Infantry, the Shropshire Yeomanry, and the Shropshire Royal Horse Artillery. These collections represent more than 300 years of regimental service, and include a lock of Napoléon's hair and an American flag captured during the seizure and burning of the White House during the War of 1812.

Rowley's House Museum. Barker St. ☎ **01743/361196.** Free admission. Tues–Sat 10am–5pm, plus Sun 10am–4pm Easter–Sept.

This museum is housed in a fine 16th-century timber-frame warehouse and an adjoining 17th-century brick-and-stone mansion dating from 1618. The museum includes displays on art, local history, Roman and prehistoric archaeology, geology, costumes, and natural history. The great treasures include the Hadrianic forum inscription and silver mirror, both from the nearby Roman city of Viroconium (Wroxeter).

Clive House Museum. College Hill. ☎ **01743/354811.** Free admission. Tues–Sat 10am–4pm, plus Sun 10am–4pm May 30–Sept 26.

This Georgian town house, home to Clive of India when he served as mayor and member of parliament for Shrewsbury in the 1760s, contains period rooms and local pottery and porcelain, early watercolors, and textiles, plus displays on the natural historians of 19th-century Shrewsbury such as Charles Darwin. There is also a secluded walled garden.

Attingham Park. Shrewsbury. ☎ **01743/709203.** House admission £4 ($6.80) adults, £2 ($3.40) children, £10 ($17) families. Park and grounds £1.80 ($3.05) adults. House, tearoom, and shop Mar 28–Nov 1 Fri–Tues 1:30–5pm (the tearoom opens an hour earlier for lunch); park and grounds open daily 9am–5pm, until 9pm in summer.

This elegant classical house set on 250 acres of woodlands and landscaped deer park is graced with superbly decorated state rooms, including a red dining room and blue drawing room. Treasures of the house include Regency silver used at 19th-century ambassadorial receptions and elegant Italian furniture. A tearoom and gift shop on the grounds make a pleasant stop before or after you've toured the house.

Shrewsbury Abbey. Abbey Foregate. ☎ **01743/232723.** Admission free, but donations requested for the Abbey Fund. Easter–Oct daily 9:30am–5:30pm, Nov–Easter daily 10:30am–3pm.

Founded in 1083, Shrewsbury Abbey became one of the most powerful Benedictine monasteries in England. It's the setting of the Brother Cadfael tales, a series of mysteries written by Ellis Peters that have recently been adapted for television. The church remains in use to this day, and visitors can see displays devoted to the abbey's history as well as the remains of the 14th-century shrine of St. Winefride.

The Shrewsbury Quest. Abbey Foregate. ☎ **01743/243324** or 01743/355990. Admission £4.25 ($7.25) adults, £3.60 ($6.10) seniors and students, £2.95 ($5) children under 12. Family ticket £13 ($22.10). Apr–Oct daily 10am–5pm; Nov–Mar daily 10am–4pm. Closed Dec 25 and Jan 1.

On the site of the 5-century-old Benedictine Abbey of St. Peter and St. Paul, the world of the medieval monastery comes to life, with busy tradespeople, a great store, sweet sounds of dulcimer, harp, and lute, vespers bells, plus monastic gardens planted with a collection of herbs dating from the 12th century. Visitors can participate in different activities, including making an illuminated manuscript in the Scriptorium, solving mysteries like Ellis Peters's Brother Cadfael, and playing ancient games of skill in the Cloisters.

SHOPPING

The narrow, cobbled streets of Shrewsbury host wonderful, small shops in Tudor-fronted buildings, selling everything from secondhand books and art-deco bric-a-brac to geological specimens, musical instruments, and antiques.

St. Julian's Craft Centre, Wyle Cop (☎ **01743/353516**), housed in a 12th-century tower, has been the place to purchase high-quality, locally made crafts for over 15 years. Shoppers can see artisans at work in the center of the tower, or browse Saturday craft fairs and art exhibitions, which change every 2 weeks.

The staff at **Mansers Antiques,** 53/54 Wyle Cop (☎ **01743/351120**), is always ready to dispense free advice, and offers one of the largest comprehensive stocks of antiques in the United Kingdom. Items for sale include furniture of all periods, silver and plate, china and glass, clocks and metal goods, jewelry, linen, paintings, and Oriental items. There's a restoration department, and the shop will ship purchases.

For secondhand and antiquarian books, head to **Quarry Books** at 24 Clarmemont Hill (☎ **01743/361404**); for prints, the **Victorian Gallery** at 40 St. John's Hill (☎ **01743/356351**), is the place to go.

WHERE TO STAY

✪ **Albright Hussey Hotel.** Ellesmere Rd., Shrewsbury, Shropshire SY4 5TX. ☎ **01939/290571.** Fax 01939/291143. 14 units. TV TEL. £95 ($161.50) double, £95 ($161.50) suite. Rates include breakfast. AE, DC, MC, V. 2 1/2 miles northeast of Shrewsbury along A528.

Its unusual name derives from the feudal family (the Husseys) who occupied it between 1292 and the 1600s. Today, it's one of the best examples of an elaborate Tudor timber-frame building in Shrewsbury. The brick-and-stone wing was added around 1560. The interior contains all the old-world charm and eccentricities you could hope for, including oak panels, fireplaces large enough to roast an ox, and a moated garden with several pairs of fiercely territorial black swans. Most furnishings date from the early 19th century, and contrast well with the dozens of beams that have been artfully exposed in the ceilings and walls of bedrooms and public areas. The rooms in the main house have more character, although those in the new wing are slightly more spacious with more up-to-date furnishings. Three units are set aside for nonsmokers. Most of the rooms open onto views of the landscaped gardens. Bathrooms are small but well organized.

Dining: The owners are Tuscany-born Franco Subbiani and his German/Czech wife, Vera. Together, they produce fine cuisine derived from Italy, France, and England that changes frequently. Dishes might include ravioli with wild mushrooms in a saffron cream sauce, or shredded duck with orange sauce presented in a potato galette on a bed of exotic greens.

The Lion. Wyle Cop, Shrewsbury, Shropshire SY1 1UY. ☎ **01743/353107.** Fax 01743/352744. 59 units. TV TEL. £55 ($93.50) double; £110 ($187) suite. Discounts of £10 ($17) per room Fri–Sun. AE, DC, MC, V.

Housed on the site of a 17th-century coaching inn that claims to have origins in the 14th century, this is easily the most evocative hotel in Shrewsbury. Since then, the rooms have been enlarged, and the setting has been lavishly gentrified with lots of patterned chintz and modern amenities. Only the suite contains artfully gnarled oaken beams—other rooms are comfortable as well, and are being refurbished in a style evocative of the 17th century. Beds are exceedingly comfortable; bathrooms are small and compact. Thirty accommodations are set aside for nonsmokers.

Dining: The pub has all the old England touches you could hope for. A restaurant, The Shires, is open Monday to Saturday from noon to 2pm, and 7 to 9:30pm, and on Sunday from 12:30 to 2:30 and 7 to 9pm. There, you can order elaborate, if not innovative, dishes such as duck breast with Grand Marnier and oranges.

Prince Rupert Hotel. Butcher Row, Shrewsbury, Shropshire SY1 1UQ. ☎ **01743/499955.** Fax 01743/357306. 69 units. Mon–Thurs £85–£95 ($144.50–$161.50) double; suite £120–£160 ($204–$272). Rates include breakfast. AE, DC, MC, V.

Its half-timbered Elizabethan core is one of the most historic structures in this very historic town. In the 17th century, it was the home of the Bohemian-born Prince Rupert, nephew to Charles I, who commanded Royalist forces here during the English civil war. In the 1980s, a modern wing, not inconsistent with the architecture of the original design, was added, transforming the site into a large, somewhat conventional chain hotel. Only about half a dozen of the accommodations contain exposed beams from the building's early origins; the others are conservatively modern and somewhat bland. The bedrooms, small to mid-size, have been upgraded for the most part. Bathrooms are small but have adequate shelf space. In the restaurant, a well-executed cuisine that's roughly 80% British and 20% international is served daily at lunch and dinner. The latest restaurant, Chambers, which opened in 1997, serves both English and continental fare.

WHERE TO DINE

Country Friends. Dorrington (6 miles south of Shrewsbury via A49), Shropshire S45 7JD. ☎ **01743/718707.** E-mail: whittakes@countryfriends.demon.co.uk. Light luncheon platters £2.70–£10 ($4.60–$17); 2-course set menus £27.50 ($46.75); 3-course set menus £29.90 ($50.85). MC, V. Tues–Sat noon–2pm and 7–9pm. MODERN BRITISH.

Originally built in 1673 as a private home, this pleasant restaurant today boasts a much-restored Tudor facade amid attractive gardens. Inside, a hardworking kitchen concocts modern reinventions of such old-fashioned dishes as lamb noisettes roasted in mustard crust with mint hollandaise and fillet steak with a leek and horseradish topping and red wine sauce. Some aspects of the menu change almost every week. They also feature three bedrooms at a rate of £115 ($195.50) double occupancy, including dinner.

The Peach Tree. 21 Abbey Foregate. ☎ **01743/355055.** Reservations recommended on weekends. Main courses £7.95–£14.95 ($13.50–$25.40). AE, MC, V. Tues–Sun 10am–9:30pm. BRITISH/EUROPEAN.

Its name derives from the hundreds of ripe peaches, peach trees, and peach boughs that someone laboriously stenciled onto the walls. The setting dates from the 15th century, when this was a weaver's cottage adjacent to the abbey. The food is based on solid, time-tested recipes made with fresh ingredients and loads of European savoir-faire. It's some of the best in town. Main courses include medallions of venison over caramelized red onion mash, with a robust gingerbread sauce; and such vegetarian dishes as ragout of woodland mushrooms with filo pastry and a basil and crème fraîche. The dessert that keeps everyone coming back for more is homemade meringue with ice cream, traditional butterscotch sauce, and shreddings of roasted coconut. Although the upstairs restaurant is more fancy, you can have any of the platters informally in the street-level bar if you're alone or in a hurry.

SHREWSBURY AFTER DARK

Quench your thirst or have a bite to eat at the **Lion & Pheasant Hotel** bar, 49–50 Wyle Cop (☎ **01743/236288**), where in colder months, an inviting firelight ambience presides. Or check out the **Boat House Pub,** New Street (☎ **01743/362965**), located beside a beautiful old park on the River Severn. In summer, they open up the terrace overlooking the river, and it becomes a popular date place. Couples enjoy a healthy selection of beers and ales, along with a tasty pub grub that ranges from soup and sandwiches to pies.

The **Buttermarket Nightclub** (☎ **01743/241455**), set in the old butter market on Howard Street, caters to the over-25 crowd. It has two theme nights: Saturday (disco) and Thursday (world music).

Other clubs include the **Park Lane Nightclub,** Ravens Meadows (☎ **01743/358786**). **The Music Hall,** The Square (☎ **01743/281281**), hosts musicals, plays, and concerts year-round. Tickets range from £5 to £13 ($8.50 to $22.10).

13 Ironbridge

135 miles NW of London; 36 miles NW of Birmingham; 18 miles SE of Shrewsbury

Ironbridge, located in the Ironbridge Gorge, is famous for kicking off an early stage of the Industrial Revolution. Indeed, this stretch of the Severn River valley has been an important industrial area since the Middle Ages because of its iron and limestone deposits. But the event that clinched this area's importance came in 1709, when the Quaker ironmaster, Abraham Darby I, discovered a method for smelting iron by using coke as a fuel, instead of charcoal. This paved the way for the first iron rails, boats, wheels, aqueducts, and bridge, cast in Coalbrookdale in 1779. So momentous was this accomplishment that the area, originally called Coalbrookdale, was renamed Ironbridge. The area literally buzzed with the new transportation and engineering innovations that soon followed.

Today, you'll find an intriguing complex of museums that documents and brings to life the rich history of Ironbridge Gorge. The gift shops and other stores in town have plenty of unusual souvenirs to help you remember your visit.

ESSENTIALS

GETTING THERE Seven days a week, trains leave London's Euston Station hourly for Telford Central Station in Telford. From here, take a bus or taxi into Ironbridge. The entire journey takes about 3 hours. For schedules and information, call ☎ **0345/484950.**

Three buses depart daily from London's Victoria Coach Station, arriving in Telford about 5 hours later. Call ☎ **0990/808080** for more information. Local buses that leave Telford for the 20-minute ride to Ironbridge include nos. 6, 8, 9, and 99.

If you're driving a car from London, take the M1 to the M6 to the M54, which leads directly to Ironbridge.

VISITOR INFORMATION **The Ironbridge Gorge Tourist Information Centre,** 4 The Wharfage (☎ **01952/432166**), is open Monday through Friday from 9am to 5pm and Saturday and Sunday from 10am to 5pm.

EXPLORING THE AREA

The Ironbridge Valley plays host to seven main museums and several smaller ones, collectively called the **Ironbridge Gorge Museums,** Ironbridge, Telford (☎ **01952/433522** on weekdays and 01952/432166 on Saturday and Sunday). These include the

Coalbrookdale Museum, with its Darby Furnace of Iron and sound-and-light display, as well as restored 19th-century homes of the Quaker ironmasters; the **Iron Bridge,** with its original tollhouse; the **Jackfield Tile Museum,** where you can see demonstrations of tile-pressing, decorating, and firing; the **Blists Hill Open Air Museum,** with its re-creation of a 19th-century town; and the **Coalport China Museum.** A passport ticket to all museums in Ironbridge Gorge is £9.50 ($16.15) for adults, £8.50 ($14.45) for seniors, £5.50 ($9.35) for students and children, and £29 ($49.30) for a family of two adults and up to five children. The sites are open Easter to October daily from 10am to 5pm. The Iron Bridge Tollhouse and Rosehill House are closed from November to March.

There's also some good shopping. You can buy Coalport china at the **Coalport China Museum** and decorative tiles at the **Jackfield Tile Museum.** Another place worth visiting is just beyond the Jackfield Museum: **Maws Craft Workshops** (☎ **01952/883030**) is the site of 25 workshops situated in an old Victorian tile works beside the River Severn. Here, you can browse for porcelain dolls, glass sculptures, dollhouses, original and Celtic art, pictures with frames made while you wait, jewelry, stained glass, and children's clothes. There's also a tearoom on site that's open for lunch and afternoon tea.

WHERE TO STAY

Bridge House. Buildwas, Telford, Shropshire TF8 7BN. ☎ **01952/432105.** Fax 01952/432105. www.smoothhound.co.uk/hotelsbridgehs.html. 4 units. £55 ($93.50) double. Rates include breakfast. AE, MC, V. Closed for 2 weeks at Christmas.

Set 1½ miles west of Ironbridge, on the outskirts of the hamlet of Buildwas, this ivy-draped, half-timbered building originated in 1620 as a coaching inn. Resident proprietor Janet Hedges will tell you unusual stories about the house, such as the 365 nails (one for every day of the year) that hold together the planks of the front door, or the fact that the building's front porch was removed from the nearby abbey. Rooms are genteel and comfortable, sometimes with touches of Edwardian drama (lavishly draped beds, in some cases). Others have exposed beams, and all have creaking floors and uneven walls that testify to the age of the building. Rooms are small but snug, and each is individually decorated, containing such extras as beverage makers. The compact baths are efficiently organized.

The Valley Hotel. Ironbridge, Telford, Shropshire, TF8 7DW. ☎ **01952/432247.** Fax 01952/432308. 35 units. TV TEL. £98 ($166.60) double. Rates include breakfast. AE, DC, MC, V.

Originally built as a private home around 1750, this riverside inn was enlarged over the years into the sprawling, light-brown brick design you see today. The high-ceilinged interior contains hints of its original grandeur, including a worthwhile restaurant, the Chez Maw (see below). Fifteen of the hotel's rooms lie within the original stable, and are accessible via a glass-roofed courtyard. Although rooms in the main house usually have more panoramic views, many visitors prefer the coziness of the former stables. All rooms are clean and modern, and have coffeemakers. The small baths have a hair dryer.

WHERE TO DINE

Restaurant Chez Maw. In The Valley House Hotel. ☎ **01952/432247.** Reservations recommended. Main courses £11–£13 ($18.70–$22.10); fixed-price menu £21 ($35.70). AE, DC, MC, V. Mon–Sat noon–2pm and 9–9:30pm; Sun 7–9:30pm. BRITISH.

The name refers to Arthur Maw, long-ago owner of the house, and founder of a nearby factory that produced decorative tiles during the 19th century. Prized examples of his ceramic creations line the reception area and the monumental staircase. Outfitted with crisp napery, Windsor-style chairs, and a high ceiling, the restaurant serves such updated British food as tortellini laced with cream, herbs, and slices of Parma ham; platters of smoked tuna and marinated salmon; and fillets of pork and beef drizzled with sauce made from Shropshire blue cheese.

A FAVORITE LOCAL PUB

A rebuilt Victorian pub, complete with a chicken coop in the backyard? Yes, it's the **New Inn,** located within the Blists Hill Museum complex (☎ **01952/586063**). It has atmosphere galore, with its gas lamps, sawdust floors, and knowledgeable and friendly staff sporting vintage Victorian garb. You'll find a goodly selection of ales, hearty, rib-sticking home-cooked meals, and plenty of pub games.

14 Stoke-on-Trent: The Potteries

162 miles NW of London; 46 miles N of Birmingham; 59 miles NW of Leicester; 41 miles S of Manchester

Situated halfway between the Irish and the North seas, Staffordshire is a county of peaceful countryside, rugged moorlands, and Cheshire plains. While there are several charming country inns here, pottery is Staffordshire's real claim to fame. Although it's been created in the area since 2000 B.C., it wasn't until the Romans rolled through in A.D. 46 that the first pottery kiln was set up at Trent Vale. Now it's **Stoke-on-Trent,** a loose confederation of six towns (Tunstall, Burslem, Stoke, Fenton, Longton, and Hanley, the most important town) covering a 7-mile area, that's the real center of the pottery trade. During the Industrial Revolution, the area known collectively as Stoke-on-Trent became the world's leading producer of pottery, and today it's become a tourist attraction.

ESSENTIALS

GETTING THERE It's a direct train ride of 2 hours to Stoke-on-Trent from London's Euston Station. Trains make hourly departures daily. For schedules and information, call ☎ **0345/484950.**

Six **National Express** buses leave London's Victoria Coach Station daily for the 4- to 5-hour trip to Stoke. For schedules and information, call ☎ **0990/808080.**

By car from London, drive along the M1 to the M6 to A500 at Junction 15. It will take you 2 to 3 hours by car.

VISITOR INFORMATION The **Stoke-on-Trent Tourist Information Centre,** Quadrant Road, Hanley, Stoke-on-Trent (☎ **01782/236000**), is open Monday through Saturday from 9:15am to 5:15pm. Here, you can pick up a China Experience visitor map, which notes most potteries, shops, and museums in the area.

HISTORY FIRST: TWO WORTHWHILE MUSEUMS

The Potteries Museum and Art Gallery. Bethesda St., Hanley. ☎ **01782/232323.** Free admission. Mon–Sat 10am–5pm, Sun 2–5pm.

Start here for an overview of Stoke-on-Trent history. It houses departments of fine arts, decorative arts, natural history, archaeology, and social history. It also has one of the largest and finest collections of ceramics in the world. It's a great place for training your eyes before exploring the factories and shops of Stoke-on-Trent.

The Gladstone Pottery Museum. Uttoxeter Rd. at Longton. ☎ **01782/319232.** Admission £3.95 ($6.70) adults, £2.95 ($5) seniors and students, £2.50 ($4.25) children £10 ($17) family ticket. Daily 10am–5pm; last admission at 4pm.

This is the only Victorian pottery factory that has been restored as a museum, with craftspeople providing daily demonstrations in original workshops. Various galleries depict the rise of the Staffordshire pottery industry, tile history, and so on (check out the toilets of all shapes, sizes, colors, and decoration). Great hands-on opportunities for plate painting, pot throwing, and ornamental-flower making.

TOURING & SHOPPING THE POTTERIES

With more than 40 factories in Stoke-on-Trent, you'll need to get in shape for this adventure. All have gift shops and seconds shops on site—in fact, some have several shops, selling everything from fine china dinner services to hand-painted tiles.

Seconds are always a great bargain. They're still high-quality pieces with imperfections that only the professional eye can detect. But don't expect bargains on top-of-the-line pieces. Shops discount their best wares once in a while, but most of the time, prices for first-quality items are the same here as they are in London, elsewhere in England, or in America.

During the big January sales in London, many department stores, including Harrods, truck in seconds from the factories in Stoke, so if you're in London then, you don't have to visit here to bring home a bargain.

Each of the factories we discuss below offers shipping and can help you with your value-added tax (VAT) refund. Expect your purchases to be delivered within 1 to 3 months.

Wedgwood Visitor Centre. Barlaston. ☎ **01782/204218.** Tours £7.25 ($12.35) adults, seniors, students, and children 15 and older. Admission to everything else £4.95 ($8.40) adults; £3.95 ($6.70) seniors, students, and children; £9.95 ($16.90) family ticket (up to 2 adults and 3 children). Factory tours Mon–Thurs at 10am and 2pm; they last 2 hours and must be booked in advance. Centre open Mon–Fri 9am–5pm, Sat–Sun 10am–5pm. It's easiest to get here by taxi from the Stoke-on-Trent train station, a 6-mile trip that will cost around £7.50 ($12.75). If you're driving from London, head north along the M1 until you reach the M6. Continue north to Junction 14, which becomes the A34. Follow the A34 to Barlaston and follow the signs to Wedgwood.

The visitor center includes a demonstration hall where you can watch clay pots being formed on the potter's wheel, and witness how plates are turned and fired, then painted. Highly skilled potters and decorators are happy to answer your questions. An art gallery and a gift shop showcase samples of factory-made items that also can be purchased. (Note that the prices at this shop are the same as those found elsewhere.) Tours must be booked in advance.

Also located at the Wedgwood Centre, the **Wedgwood Museum** covers three centuries of design and features living displays including Josiah Wedgwood's Etruria factory and his Victorian showroom. Other room settings can also be seen at the museum. The Josiah Wedgwood Restaurant is the perfect place to relax with a cup of coffee or a full meal.

Wedgwood seconds, which are available at reduced prices, are not sold at the center but are available at the **Wedgwood Group Factory Shop,** King Street, Fenton (☎ **01782/316161**).

Royal Doulton Pottery Factory. Nile St. Burslem, near Stoke-on-Trent. ☎ **01782/292434.** Admission for both tour and Visitor Centre £6.50 ($11.05) adults; £5 ($8.50) children ages 10–16, students, and seniors; £17 ($28.90) family tickets. Admission to just Visitor

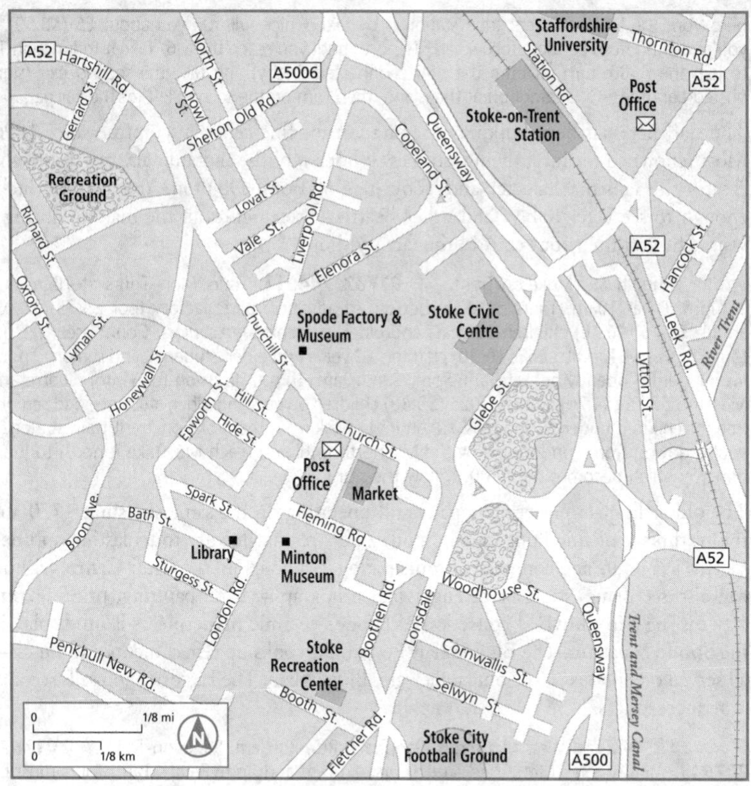

Centre £3 ($5.10) adults; £1 ($1.70) children ages 5–9; £2.25 ($3.80) children ages 10–16, students, and seniors; £7 ($11.90) family tickets. Tours offered Mon–Fri 10:30am–2pm. They must be booked in advance. Visitor Centre open Mon–Sat 9:30am–5pm, Sun 10:30am–4:30pm; shop open Mon–Sat 9am–5:30pm, Sun 10:30am–4:30pm. A taxi from the Stoke-on-Trent train station will cost about £4 ($6.80). If you're driving from London, follow the M1 north until you reach M6. Take it to Junction 15, which becomes the A500. Follow the A500 to its junction with the A527, then follow the brown signs to the factory.

Wear some comfortable shoes if you take the tour here—you'll walk nearly a mile and tackle upward of 250 steps, but you will see exactly how plates, cups, and figures are made from start to finish. Live demonstrations of how figures are assembled from a mold and decorated are given at the **Visitor Centre,** which also has the world's largest collection of Royal Doulton figures. Next door to the Visitor Centre is the **Minton Fine Art Studio,** where plates and pill boxes are hand-painted and richly decorated with gold before your eyes.

The Gallery Restaurant serves cakes and coffee, light lunches, and afternoon tea. Of course, everything is served on the finest bone china. The gift shop is stocked with a full range of Royal Doulton figures and tableware, featuring a selection of bargains.

John Beswick Studios of Royal Doulton. Gold St., Longton, near Stoke-on-Trent. ☎ **01782/291213.** Factory tours Mon–Thurs at 1:30pm. Tours need to be booked in advance by calling 01782/291213; tour price is £3.50 ($5.95) adults, £3 ($5.10) seniors and children 10 and older; free for children under 10. Shop hours Mon–Fri 9am–4:30pm. The easiest way to get here from the Stoke-on-Trent train station is by taxi, which will run you about £5 ($8.50). If you're driving from London, follow the M1 north until you reach the M6. Take it to Junction 15 to join the A500, turn off onto the A50 (signposted Derby) and take the second exit (signposted Longton). Go straight on at the island, then turn on the second left for the car park.

The staff here has been building a reputation for fine ceramic sculpture since 1896. Most renowned for its authentic studies of horses, birds, and animals, the studio also creates the famed Character and Toby Jugs of Royal Doulton. You may be lucky enough to see Peter Rabbit and other Beatrix Potter figures in the making during a visit. The 1½-hour tour ends in the factory shop.

Spode. Church St., Stoke-on-Trent. ☎ **01782/744011.** Tours Mon–Thurs at 10am and 1:30pm, Fri at 10am. Tours must be booked in advance. Basic factory tour £4.75 ($8.05) adults; £3.75 ($6.40) children 12 years and older, students, and seniors. Connoisseur factory tour £7 ($11.90) adults, £6 ($10.20) children 12 years and older, students, and seniors. Spode Visitor Centre open Mon–Sat 9am–5pm, Sun 10am–4pm. Admission for Visitor Centre and Museum £2.75 ($4.70) adults; £2.25 ($3.80) children 5 years and older, students, and seniors; free for children under 5. Spode is a 10-minute walk from the Stoke-on-Trent train station. If you're driving from London, follow the M1 north until you reach M6. Take it north to Junction 15, which becomes the A500. Follow the signs.

The oldest English pottery company still operating on the same site since 1770 and the birthplace of fine bone china, Spode offers regular factory tours lasting approximately 1½ hours and connoisseur tours lasting 2½ hours. In the **Craft Centre,** visitors can also see demonstrations of engraving, lithography, hand painting, printing, and clay casting. An unrivaled collection of Spode's ceramic masterpieces is on display in the **Spode Museum.** The Blue Italian Restaurant cooks up refreshments and lunch—all served on Spode's classic blue tableware, Blue Italian. The Factory Shop sells seconds at reduced prices.

Moorcroft Pottery. West Moorcroft, Sandbach Rd., Burslem, Stoke-on-Trent. ☎ **01782/207943.** Factory tours Mon, Wed, and Thurs at 11am and 2pm; Fri at 11am. Tours must be booked in advance; cost is £2.50 ($4.25) adults, £1.50 ($2.55) seniors and children under 16. Museum and shop open Mon–Fri 10am–5pm, Sat 9:30am–4:30pm. A taxi from the Stoke-on-Trent train station will run about £5 ($8.50). If you're driving from London, follow the M1 north to the M6. Take it north to Junction 15, which becomes the A500. Follow the signs.

Moorcroft is a welcome change from the world-famous names you've just seen. It was founded in 1898 by William Moorcroft, who produced his own special brand of pottery and was his own exclusive designer until his death in 1945. Decoration is part of the first firing here, giving it a higher quality of color and brilliance than, say, Spode. Today, the design is in the hands of William's son, John, who carries on the personal traditions of the family firm, creating floral designs in bright, clear colors (think of it as the art nouveau of the pottery world). There is much to admire and buy in the factory seconds shop. There is always someone around to explain the various processes and to show you around the museum, with its collections of early Moorcroft.

WHERE TO STAY

George Hotel. Swan Sq., Burslem, Stoke-on-Trent ST6 2AE. ☎ **01782/577544.** Fax 01782/837496. 40 units. TV TEL. £85 ($144.50) double. Rates include breakfast. AE, DC, MC, V.

This is one of the most upscale, formal, and dignified hotels in town, the kind of place where the mayor would invite some cronies or a businessperson might bring an important client. Built in 1929 of red brick, it rises three floors from the hamlet of Burslem, one of the six villages comprising the Stoke-on-Trent district. Public areas are outfitted with traditional furniture and large 19th-century oil paintings of the town and region. The conservative but comfortable bedrooms are well furnished and generally spacious, with such extras as tea-making facilities and a trouser press. Each small bathroom comes with a hair dryer. The restaurant serves solid and reliable fare.

Haydon House Hotel. 1–9 Haydon St., Basford, Stoke-on-Trent, Staffordshire ST4 6JD. ☎ **01782/711311.** Fax 01782/717470. www.touristnetuk.com. 30 units. TV TEL. Mon–Thurs £79 ($134.30) double; £120 ($204) suite. Fri–Sun £60 ($102) double; £100 ($170) suite. AE, DC, MC, V.

This imposing late Victorian house has long been the home of the Machin family. They've added a collection of built-in mahogany furniture to the bedrooms, and reconfigured their home and their lives to welcome overnight guests. Today, you'll find many of the original Victorian fittings, an unusual collection of clocks, and many modern amenities that will make your stay comfortable. There are quality beds in the roomy bedrooms, plus a hair dryer in the small bathrooms, most of which have a tub and shower combination. A restaurant on the premises serves lunch and dinner, and suites each have efficiently arranged kitchenettes.

Stoke-on-Trent Moat House. Etruria Hall, Festival Way, Etruria, Stoke-on-Trent, Staffordshire ST1 5BQ. ☎ **01782/609988.** Fax 01782/284500. 143 units. TV TEL. £120 ($204) double; £164 ($278.80) suite. Rates include breakfast. AE, DC, MC, V.

Originally built in the 18th century as the home of Josiah Wedgwood, father of the ceramics company that bears his name today, this redbrick house functioned for many years as an administrative office for British Steel. By the time the Queen's Moat House chain bought it in the late 1980s, many of the architectural nuances had been removed, except for the sweeping staircase and a few remnants. The new owners subsequently began the laborious process of enlarging and restoring the premises. The result is a four-story annex wing—joined to the historic core by a glass-sided corridor—in which the bulk of the accommodations lie. Its redbrick walls more or less match those of the original premises. The result is a modern, chain-style hotel that retains a sense of history, which its hardworking staff strives to maintain. All the mid-size rooms have been redecorated and furnished to a comfortable standard. Bathrooms are small but have adequate shelf space and a hair dryer.

Amenities: On site are two bars and a restaurant, the Viva Brasserie, open daily for lunch and dinner. There's also a heated swimming pool, a health club/gymnasium, and a business center.

WHERE TO DINE

Jeremiah Johnson's. 325 Hartshill Rd., Hartshill. ☎ **01782/634925.** Main courses £4.95–£10.95 ($8.40–$18.60). AE, DC, MC, V. Daily noon–midnight. TEX MEX.

This Spanish tapas and Tex-Mex bar is one of the best value places to eat in Hartshill, and it also serves some of the tastiest food. For lunch try the wrap-and-roll special for £2.75 ($4.70) where you choose the type of tortilla you want and then just add the fillings of your choice. For dinner sample Cajun-style tuna steak, or the ever-popular fajitas. Tapas food is also available, such as gambas al ajillo (prawns in garlic), or tortilla española (traditional Spanish potato and onion omelette). They also offer a reasonable selection of Spanish and South American wines.

15 Stafford

142 miles NW of London, 26 miles N of Birmingham, 17 miles S of Stoke-on-Trent

The county town of Staffordshire was the birthplace of Izaak Walton, the British writer and celebrated fisherman. Long famous as a boot-making center, it contains many historic buildings, notably St. Chad's, the town's oldest church; St. Mary's, with its unusual octagonal tower; and the Ancient High House, the largest timber-frame town house in England.

ESSENTIALS

GETTING THERE To get here from London, take a train from Euston Station for the approximately 2-hour trip. For schedules and information, call ☎ **0345/484950.**

National Express buses depart London's Victoria Coach Station, arriving about 5 hours later. For schedules and information, call ☎ **0990/808080.**

For the 3-hour car trip, take the M40 to the M6, which leads directly to Stafford.

VISITOR INFORMATION Visitor information is available from the **Stafford Tourist Information Centre,** located in the Ancient High House, Greengate Street (☎ **01785/619136**). It is open Monday to Friday from 9am to 5pm and Saturday from 10am to 4pm

EXPLORING THE TOWN

Stafford's **shopping** opportunities run the gamut from dusty antiquarian bookshops to upscale, one-of-a-kind galleries. The **Schott Zwiesel Factory Shop,** Drummond Road, Astonfields Industrial Estate (☎ **01785/223166**), is Europe's largest manufacturer of blown crystal glassware. It combines advanced glass technology with the finest quality and design. You can find plain or fine-cut crystal stemware, giftware, and blown decorative crystal.

Shire Hall Gallery, Market Square (☎ **01785/278345**), housed in the richly restored historic courthouse built in 1798, is an important visual-arts complex that offers a lively program of exhibitions and a craft shop that stocks a wide range of contemporary ceramics, textiles, jewelry, and glass objects. All are chosen for their quality and are displayed in original surroundings.

Ancient High House. Greengate St. ☎ **01785/619619.** Admission £2 ($3.40) adults; £1.20 ($2.05) students, children, and seniors; £4 ($6.80) family ticket for 2 adults, 2 children. Year-round Mon–Fri 9am–5pm; Sat 10am–4pm Apr–Oct, 10am–3pm Nov–Mar.

Reputedly the tallest timber-framed townhouse in England, the Ancient High House, built in 1595, served as living quarters for King Charles I and his nephew Prince Rupert at the start of England's civil war in 1642. The next year, the Parliamentarians turned the house into a prison for Royalist officers. Many of the rooms throughout the house have been restored, and each corresponds with an important period in the house's history.

Stafford Castle. Newport Rd. ☎ **01785/257698.** Admission £2 ($3.40) adults; £1.30 ($2.20) students, children, and seniors; £4 ($6.80) family ticket for 2 adults, 2 children. Apr–Sept Tues–Sun 10am–5pm; Oct–Mar Tues–Sun 10am–4pm.

Built on an easily defensible promontory, Stafford Castle began as a timber fortress in A.D. 1100, a scant 40 years after the Norman invasion. Its long history peaked in 1444 when its owner, Humphrey Stafford, became the duke of Buckinghamshire. In the 17th century, during the English civil war, the castle was defended by Lady Isabel but was eventually abandoned and almost entirely destroyed. In 1813, the ruins of the castle were reconstructed in the Gothic Revival style but nonetheless fell into disarray by the middle of this century. The Visitor Centre has the floor plan of a Norman guardhouse from the 12th century, and, along with its collection of artifacts from on-site excavations, is designed to bring to life the tumultuous history of Stafford Castle. Many programs, events, and reenactments are scheduled throughout the year (during winter, torchlight tours of the castle can be arranged for organized groups). The castle also has a 16-bed herb garden and a host of arms and armor that visitors can try on.

Izaak Walton Cottage. Worston Lane. ☎ **01785/760278.** Admission £1.60 ($2.70) adults; £1 ($1.70) children, students, and seniors; £4 ($6.80) family ticket for 2 adults, 2 children. Apr–Oct Tues–Sun and bank holiday Mondays 11am–4:30pm.

In 1654, after publishing *The Compleat Angler,* Izaak Walton bought a 16th-century, typical mid-Staffordshire cottage that's now open to visitors. To this day, Walton's work is recognized as one of the greatest books on fishing ever written. After a difficult history that's included two fires in the 20th century alone, the cottage has been rethatched and restored to its original condition. A cottage garden and an angling museum can be found on the grounds, too.

WHERE TO STAY

The Garth. Wolverhampton Rd., near Stafford ST17 9JR. ☎ **01785/256124.** Fax 01785/255152. 60 units. TV TEL. Mon–Thurs £87 ($147.90) double; Fri–Sat £55 ($93.50) double. AE, DC, MC, V.

This Edwardian-era house enjoys a garden setting in a peaceful residential area just 2 miles southeast of the center of Stafford. It's been altered and enlarged extensively since the 1950s (the interior was renovated more successfully than the exterior). Additional renovations were made in 1992 and 1996. Today, the only authentic vestige of the building's original turn-of-the-century architecture lies within the richly paneled cocktail lounge. The rest of the hotel is attractively traditional, with well-trained service, but with fewer lush reminders of England's Age of Empire than one might have hoped for. Rooms, which vary in shape and size, have recently been upgraded, with improved mattresses and furnishings of a high standard. Each unit has a beverage maker. The baths, although small, have adequate shelf space and a shower stall. There's a restaurant and bar on the premises.

Tillington Hall. Eccleshall Rd., Stafford ST16 1JJ. ☎ **01785/253531.** Fax 01785/259223. 92 units. TV TEL. £110–£130 ($187–$221). Rates include breakfast. AE, MC, V.

This, along with the Garth, is one of the two best hotels in Stafford, and Tillington Hall lies closer to the town center. Its historic core is a late-19th-century manor house whose severely dignified design was enlarged in the 1980s with a new, brick-built, three-story wing that contains most of the accommodations. These are comfortable, contemporary rooms like those you'd find in any British chain hotel. Most accommodations are mid-size, and all of them have been modernized. You can request a room with a four-poster, but chances are you'll get a king size or double bed. There's a no-smoking policy in 42 units. Each bathroom is compact with adequate shelf space. The hotel offers an indoor swimming pool, gym, and sauna, as well as a nearby tennis court. Favored by business travelers, the hotel has its own cocktail lounge, and a restaurant serving English and international cuisine.

WHERE TO DINE

Spaggos. 13 Bailey St., Woodlings Yard. ☎ **01785/246265.** Reservations recommended. Main courses £6.50 ($11.05). MC, V. Mon–Fri noon–2pm; Mon–Sat 6:30–10pm. ITALIAN.

This place opened in 1997, in a spot previously occupied by another fine Italian restaurant. Despite the changes since the new owner, Andrew Dean, took over, it's still the best choice in town, providing Mediterranean flair from a white-sided Victorian cottage adjacent to downtown Stafford's only cinema. The menu is a welcome relief from British staples. Pastas include succulent spaghetti marinara, Bolognese, or carbonara. Popular choices include chicken stuffed with bacon, mushrooms and gorgonzola sauce; and oven-baked cod on a bed of parsley and mashed potato with roasted red peppers and oregano on top.

PUBS

The Stafford Arms, 43 Railway St. (☎ **01785/253313**), tends to be a very happening place, drawing patrons from all walks of life. It always has a fun, friendly feel. The staff is outgoing, serving a fine array of ales, ever-changing microbrewery specials, and good inexpensive grub.

The Malt & Hops, 135 Lichfield Rd. (☎ **01785/258555**), is more laid-back than the Stafford Arms, though it attracts an energetic young crowd on weekend nights. It, too, has a wise choice of ales and good food.

16 Lichfield

128 miles NW of London, 16 miles N of Birmingham, 30 miles SE of Stoke-on-Trent

Set near the heartland of the English Midlands, Lichfield—which dates from the 8th century—has escaped excessive industrialization. Visitors can reflect on earlier times while strolling down the medieval streets, complete with a mix of Georgian, Tudor, and Victorian architectural styles. Fans of Samuel Johnson take pilgrimages to this historic city to see where the author of the first important English dictionary was born in 1709. The city is noted for its cathedral, whose three spires are known as "Ladies of the Vale." The half-timbered houses in the vicar's close and the 17th-century bishop's palace have survived a tremendous number of sieges down through the years.

ESSENTIALS

GETTING THERE A few direct trains leave daily out of London's Euston Station in the early morning and evening. The trip takes about 2½ hours. For schedules and information, call ☎ **0345/484950.**

To travel here by bus, take the **National Express** from London's Victoria Coach Station to Birmingham, then change to local bus no. 912 to reach Lichfield. Plan on about 4 hours for the bus trip, depending on your connection in Birmingham. (The Birmingham-Lichfield leg takes approximately an hour.) For schedules and information, call ☎ **0990/808080.**

If you plan on making the 3-hour drive from London yourself, take the M1 to the M42 to A38.

VISITOR INFORMATION The **Lichfield Tourist Information Centre,** Donegal House, Bore Street, Lichfield (☎ **01543/308209**), provides visitor information Monday through Saturday between 9am and 5pm from September to May; and Monday through Saturday from 9am to 6pm and Sunday 1 to 5:30pm during the summer months.

SPECIAL EVENTS In summer, Lichfield District is home to many small but fun events. June brings a jazz and blues festival, a real ale festival with more than 50 different brews to sample, and a folk festival. The Lichfield Festival plus Fringe occurs in July and is a music, arts, and drama extravaganza. Contact the Tourist Information Centre for exact dates.

SEEING THE SIGHTS

The Samuel Johnson Birthplace Museum. Breadmarket St. ☎ **01543/264972.** Admission £2 ($3.40) adults, £1.10 ($1.85) children and seniors, £4 ($6.80) family ticket (up to 2 adults, 4 children). Feb–Oct Mon–Sun 10:30am–4:30pm, Nov–Jan Mon–Sat 10:30am–4:30pm. Last admission at 4:15pm.

Dedicated to one of England's most gifted writers, this museum occupies the restored house where Dr. Johnson was born in 1709. Johnson wrote poetry, essays, biographies, and, of course, the first important English dictionary. The museum contains tableaux rooms revealing how the house looked in the early 18th century, four floors of exhibits illustrating Johnson's life and work, a bookshop, a reading room, and displays of Johnson's manuscripts and other personal effects.

Lichfield Heritage Centre. In St. Mary's Centre, Breadmarket St. in Market Square. ☎ **01543/256611.** Across the street from Dr. Johnson's Birthplace Museum stands the Heritage Centre & Treasury. Admission £2 ($3.40) adults; £1.50 ($2.55) children, seniors, and students; £6 ($10.20) family ticket. Viewing platform admission £1 ($1.70) adults, 80p ($1.35) children over 10, students, and seniors. Daily 10am–5pm (last admission at 4:15pm).

The former parish church, which still maintains the Dyott Chapel for worship, has been transformed into a treasury and exhibition room with a coffee shop and a gift shop. And the best panoramic views of the town can be seen from the 40-meter (44-yd.) viewing platforms in the spire of St. Mary's Centre.

Guildhall Cells. Bore St. ☎ **01543/250011.** Admission 30p (50¢) adults, 20p (35¢) seniors and children. Dungeons open May to Sept Sat 10am–4pm; Oct–Apr on the last Sat of every month 10am–4pm.

Just behind the Heritage Centre is the Victorian Gothic Guildhall. Rebuilt in 1846, this former meeting place of the city council is actually built over the medieval city dungeons, where it is reported that a man was imprisoned for 12 years for counterfeiting a sixpence. Many of its prisoners were burned at the stake in Market Square.

Lichfield Cathedral. The Old Registry, The Close. ☎ **01543/306240.** Free admission. Cathedral daily 7:30am–6:30pm (7:30pm in summer); Visitors Study Centre May–Sept daily 9am–5pm.

The west front of Lichfield Cathedral was built around 1280. The entire cathedral was heavily damaged during the civil war but was restored in the 1660s, and later in the 1800s. Thanks to the careful restoration, its three spires, known as the "Ladies of the Vale," can still be seen for miles around, with its tallest spire rising more than 250 feet. The cathedral's many treasures include the illuminated manuscript known as "the Lichfield Gospels"; Sir Francis Chantrey's famous sculpture *The Sleeping Children;* 16th-century Flemish glass in the Lady Chapel; and a High Victorian pulpit and chancel screen by Gilbert Scott and Francis Skidmore.

WHERE TO STAY

Little Barrow Hotel. Beacon St., Lichfield, Staffordshire WS13 7AR. ☎ **01543/414500.** Fax 01543/415734. 25 units. TV TEL. £70–£80 ($119–$136) double. Family room £80–£90 ($136–$153). Rates include breakfast. AE, MC, V.

This place has been enlarged and improved so many times during its lifetime that the exterior today includes everything from half-timbering to relatively modern stucco. This is the largest hotel in Lichfield, and its interior seems like a personalized version of a modern, upscale chain hotel run by a well-trained staff. Bedrooms are warm, clean, and cozy, each with an electric kettle and tea. The modernized rooms, mostly small to mid-size, have recently been refurbished. Baths are small but tidy, with a shower stall. There's a cocktail lounge and a restaurant.

The Swan Hotel. Bird St., Lichfield, Staffordshire WS13 6PT. ☎ **01543/414777.** Fax 01543/411277. 19 units. TV TEL. Mon–Thurs £64.50 ($109.65) double; Fri–Sun £52.50 ($89.25) double. Rates include breakfast. AE, DC, MC, V.

This place has thrived since the 1700s, partly because of its location near the cathedral and its rustic warmth. The heart and soul of the place is its old-fashioned pub, where half a dozen ales and lagers are available on tap, and simple platters of conventional but filling food are served every day at lunch. Eleven of the bedrooms lie within the main building, and in most cases come with all the dark woodwork, ceiling beams, and old-fashioned charm you'd expect. Another eight rooms, in a 1970s-era annex, are comfortable, but have a chain-hotel appearance. The compact baths come with a shower stall. The staff is helpful and cheery.

WHERE TO DINE

Champs-Élysées. Minster House, Pool Walk. ☎ **01543/253788.** Reservations recommended. Fixed-price lunch £7.95 ($13.50); fixed-price dinner £11.95 ($20.30). Main courses £14–£20 ($23.80–$34). AE, MC, V. Daily 12:30–2pm; Mon–Sat 7:30–9:30pm. FRENCH.

Firmly committed to preparing fine French food, this restaurant occupies two floors of a house built around 1760. The setting offers a collection of photographs of Paris in the late 19th century, and the service is provided by a crew that's familiar with the language and customs that prevail on the opposite side of *La Manche.* Menu items include chicken stuffed with crabmeat, served on a bed of lobster bisque and king prawns in a brandy cream and garlic sauce.

Oakleigh House. 25 Chad's Rd. ☎ **01543/262688.** Reservations recommended. Main courses £6.95–£18 ($11.80–$30.60). MC, V. Daily noon–2pm and 7–9pm. INTERNATIONAL.

This place provides warmth, whimsy, and well-prepared food that's less expensive than you might think, considering its quality and finesse. Menu items change according to the seasonality of the ingredients and the inspiration of the chef, but generally include a variety of good meats such as ham steak with mustard sauce, or sausage with mashed potatoes and onion gravy; and the chef's signature version of salmon inlaid with scallops and watercress mousse and set on a fish glaze. Vegetarian choices are always available. Everyone's favorite dessert is an old-fashioned version of English spotted dick with *sauce anglaise.* Look forward to a drink in the bar before your meal, beneath the house's most unusual ceiling, where co-owner Andrew Usher mixes drinks and carries on conversations.

PUBS

The King's Head, Bird Street (☎ **01543/256822**), saw quite a bit of action during the English civil war and has no problem still attracting a noisy, animated, and frenetic crowd. In a 15th-century coaching inn decorated with military memorabilia, the town's under-25 crowd enjoys live music, reasonable ales, good food, and a disco on Friday, Saturday, and Sunday. No cover.

The Shoulder of Mouton, London Road (☎ **01543/263279**), has been recently renovated and has a more relaxed atmosphere and an older crowd than the King's Head. This is a friendly place filled with lots of big comfy chairs just perfect for listening to its Monday-evening live jazz sessions. Traditional pub-style food and drink are available. No cover.

One of the town's most cheerful and comfortably old-fashioned pubs is in the **Swan Hotel,** Bird Street (☎ **01543/414777**). Its interior hasn't changed much since the days of Charles Dickens. Ales on tap (management refers to them as "cask ales") and lagers are served along with pub-style lunches, really simple platters of British staples. *Dance alert:* Disco isn't dead, at least not in Lichfield. Every Friday and Saturday night, from 8pm till the 11pm closing, the site is transformed into a disco. There is no cover charge.

Another good pub choice is the **Pig & Truffle Bar & Bistro,** Tamworth Street (☎ **01543/262312**), where diners and drinkers alike congregate in a wood-paneled, stone-trimmed setting for burgers, stuffed jacket potatoes, and baguettes. Lunches are served daily from noon to 2:30pm, dinner only Monday to Thursday from 6 to 9pm. No cover.

17 Tutbury

132 miles NW of London, 33 miles N of Birmingham, 27 miles SE of Stoke-on-Trent

Once a stronghold of the Anglo-Saxon kings of Mercia, and mentioned in the *Domesday Book,* Tutbury is a small town on the Dove River that lies 4 miles north of Burton-upon-Trent. Over the centuries, this town has borne more than its fair share of violent history. It has been scarred by the armies of Parliamentarians, Royalists, Welsh mercenaries, and marauding Danes. Some of the most famous figures in English history have placed their mark on Tutbury, too, including Ethelred I, John of Gaunt, King John, Henry II and his Queen Eleanor, Henry IV and Henry V, Mary Queen of Scots, James I, Charles I, and even Queen Elizabeth II. It also has a fine Norman church and the ruins of Tutbury Castle.

ESSENTIALS

GETTING THERE There are no direct trains from London to Tutbury. All the London trains arrive in the nearby town of Burton-upon-Trent. And you'll need to take a 15-minute bus ride to complete the trip to Tutbury. Trains depart from two London stations daily. If you leave from Euston Station, you'll have to change in Birmingham. From St. Pancras Station, the change is in Derby. Either way, the train trip takes about 3 hours. For schedules and information, call ☎ **0345/484950.**

National Express buses depart daily from London's Victoria Coach Station for nearby Burton-upon-Trent. The ride takes about 5 hours. For schedules and information, call ☎ **0990/808080.** Once in Burton-upon-Trent, local buses no. 401 and no. 83 will take you to Tutbury. Again, this is about a 15-minute ride.

You can drive from London to Tutbury in approximately 3 hours by taking the M1 to A50.

VISITOR INFORMATION For visitor information on Tutbury, contact the **Burton-upon-Trent Tourist Information Centre,** New Street, Burton-upon-Trent (☎ **01283/516609**). It is open year-round Monday through Friday from 9am to 5:30pm and Saturday from 9am to 4pm.

SEEING THE SIGHTS

Tutbury is an important center for glassblowing and a virtual treasure trove of crystal glassware. Both **Tutbury Crystal,** Burton Street (☎ **01283/813281**), and **Georgian Crystal,** Silk Mill Lane (☎ **01283/814534**), specialize in full lead-crystal manufacturing and have factory shops. There is also any number of crystal shops in town that complement the factory shops by offering their own unique items. For a shop specializing in hand-cut crystal, visit **The Crystal Studio,** 22 High St. (☎ **01283/520917**).

Tutbury Castle. ☎ **01283/812123.** Admission £1.50 ($2.55) adults; 75p ($1.30) students, children, and seniors. Good Friday to Sept Fri–Wed 10am–5:30pm, Sat noon–5:30pm, Sun 10am–6pm.

Built in a motte-and-bailey style, Tutbury Castle has a chapel that dates from the 12th century, even if most of its remaining structures are from the 15th century. Mary Queen of Scots was imprisoned here from 1569 to 1585, before she left for Fotheringhay and eventual execution.

Priory Church of Saint Mary the Virgin. ☎ **01283/813127.** Admission free; however, donations are appreciated. Not open regularly, but appointments to see the church can be made in advance by contacting the vicar.

Originally built in 1089, the church was almost completely destroyed during the Reformation. Only the west door remained intact. This famous west front is 14 feet high and 9 feet wide, and is set in a series of six receding arches and a square table. The size of this church attests to its importance during Norman times. It has a noteworthy Norman nave and unique quatrefoil pillars. Note that the lectern was carved from one piece of bog oak that is at least 6,000 years old.

WHERE TO STAY & DINE

✪ **Ye Olde Dog & Partridge.** High St., Tutbury (near Burton-upon-Trent), Staffordshire DE13 9LS. ☎ **01283/813030.** Fax 01283/813178. 17 units. MINIBAR TV TEL. Mon–Thurs £80–£99 ($136–$168.30), Fri–Sun £70–£99 ($119–$168.30) double. Rates include breakfast. AE, MC, V.

Set within a pair of side-by-side 15th-century buildings on Tutbury's main street, this is one of the most evocative and historic inns in the west of England. It's been wining and dining guests since the outbreak of the Wars of the Roses, and in the 18th and 19th centuries became a coaching inn, servicing the busy traffic between Liverpool and London. Rooms have been upgraded to contemporary standards of elegance, with wall-to-wall carpets, and, in many cases, deep cove moldings. Only three of them (nos. 31, 32, and 33; all within the hotel's Tudor-era main core), are accented with the building's original heavy beams. The remaining rooms are located within the Georgian-style house next door, and have a pleasant mixture of 19th-century styles, always with dignified copies of 18th-century antiques. Bedrooms are small to mid-size, and each comes with a compact bath with a shower stall and adequate shelf space. Notice the wonderful sinuous staircase that winds upward from the ground floor of the hotel's annex.

Dining/Diversions: There's a pub and a slightly more formal cocktail lounge, a brasserie and a carvery-style restaurant where, amid polished brass and copper and the music of a resident pianist, you can enjoy the English country life along with as many as 150 other diners. Menu items include platters of venison sausage, roast beef, ham, and turkey; lamb with wine or mint sauce; roasted pheasant in season; and Dover sole with lemon-butter sauce.

Cambridge & East Anglia

13

The four essentially bucolic counties of East Anglia (Essex, Suffolk, Norfolk, and Cambridgeshire) were an ancient Anglo-Saxon kingdom dominated by the Danes. In part, it's a land of heaths, fens, marshes, and inland lagoons known as "broads." Many old villages and market towns abound, and bird watchers, anglers, walkers, and cyclists are all drawn to the area.

Suffolk and Essex are Constable Country, and boast some of England's finest landscapes. (The little village of Thaxted makes a good base for exploring Essex. Either Long Melford or Lavenham are the most idyllic centers for exploring Suffolk.)

Many visitors drive through Essex on the way to Cambridge. Even though it's close to London and is itself industrialized in places, this land of rolling fields has rural areas and villages, many on the seaside. Essex stretches east to the English Channel, where its major city, Colchester, is known for oysters and roses. Fifty miles from London, Colchester was the first Roman city in Britain and is the oldest recorded town in the kingdom.

Since Colchester is not on the route of most visitors, we have focused instead on tiny villages in the western part of Essex, such as Thaxted, which is just south of Cambridge, and easily explored on your way there from London.

The easternmost county of England, Suffolk is a refuge for artists, just as it was in the day of its famous native sons, Constable and Gainsborough, who preserved its landscapes on canvas. Although a fast train can whisk visitors from London to East Suffolk in approximately $1^1/_2$ hours, its fishing villages, historic homes, and national monuments remain off the beaten track for most tourists. To capture the true charm of Suffolk, you must explore its little market towns and villages. Beginning at the Essex border, we'll head toward the North Sea, highlighting the most scenic villages as we move eastward across the shire.

Seat of the dukes of Norfolk, Norwich is less popular, but those who do venture toward the North Sea will be rewarded with some of England's most beautiful scenery. An occasional dike or windmill makes you think you're in the Netherlands. From here you can branch out and visit the "Broads."

The resort town of Wroxham, capital of the Broads, is easily reached from Norwich, only 8 miles to the northeast. Motorboats regularly take parties on short trips from Wroxham. Some of the best scenery of the Broads is found on the periphery of Wroxham. From Norwich you can also make a trip to Sandringham, the country home of four generations of British monarchs.

1 Cambridge: Town & Gown

55 miles N of London; 80 miles NE of Oxford

The university town of Cambridge is a collage of images: the Bridge of Sighs; spires and turrets; drooping willows; dusty secondhand bookshops; carol-singing on Christmas Eve in King's College Chapel; dancing until sunrise at the May balls; the sound of Elizabethan madrigals; narrow lanes where Darwin, Newton, and Cromwell once walked; the "Backs," where the lawns of the colleges sweep down to the Cam River; the tattered black robe of a hurrying upperclassman flying in the wind.

Along with Oxford, Cambridge is one of Britain's ancient seats of learning. In many ways their stories are similar, particularly the age-old conflict between town and gown. As far as the locals are concerned, alumni such as Isaac Newton, John Milton, and Virginia Woolf aren't from yesterday. Cambridge continues to graduate many famous scientists such as physicist Stephen Hawking, author of *A Brief History of Time.*

In the 1990s, Cambridge became known as a high-tech outpost, or "a silicon fen," if you will. More and more high-tech ventures are installing themselves here to produce new software—thousands of start-up companies producing $3 billion a year in revenues. Even Bill Gates, in 1997, decided to finance an $80 million research center here, claiming that Cambridge was becoming "a world center of advanced technology."

ESSENTIALS

GETTING THERE Trains depart frequently from London's Liverpool Street and King's Cross stations, arriving an hour later. For inquiries, call ☎ **0345/484950.** An off-peak, same-day round-trip is £13.50 ($22.95). A peak-time, same-day round-trip is £16.10 ($27.35). An off-peak, longer stay round-trip (up to 5-day period) is £18.40 ($31.30).

National Express buses run hourly between London's Victoria Coach Station for the 2-hour trip to Drummer Street Station in Cambridge. A one-way or same-day round-trip costs £8 ($13.60). If you'd like to return in a day or two the cost is £11 ($18.70). For schedules and information, call ☎ **0990/808080.**

If you're driving from London, head north on the M11.

VISITOR INFORMATION The **Cambridge Tourist Information Centre,** Wheeler Street (☎ **01223/322640**), is in back of the Guildhall. The center has a wide range of information, including data on public transportation in the area and on different sightseeing attractions. It's open April through June and September, Monday to Friday from 9am to 6pm, Saturday from 9am to 5pm, and Sunday from 10:30am to 5:30pm; July and August, daily from 10am to 6:30pm; October through March, Monday to Friday from 10am to 5:30pm and Saturday from 10am to 5pm.

A tourist reception center for Cambridge and Cambridgeshire is operated by **Guide Friday Ltd.** at Cambridge Railway Station (☎ **01223/362444**). The center, on the concourse of the railway station, sells brochures and maps. Also available is a full range of tourist services, including accommodations booking. Open in summer daily from 9:30am to 6pm (closes at 3pm off-season). Guided tours of Cambridge leave the center daily.

GETTING AROUND The center of Cambridge is made for pedestrians, so leave your car at one of the many parking lots (they get more expensive as you approach the city center) and stroll to some of the colleges spread throughout the city. Follow the

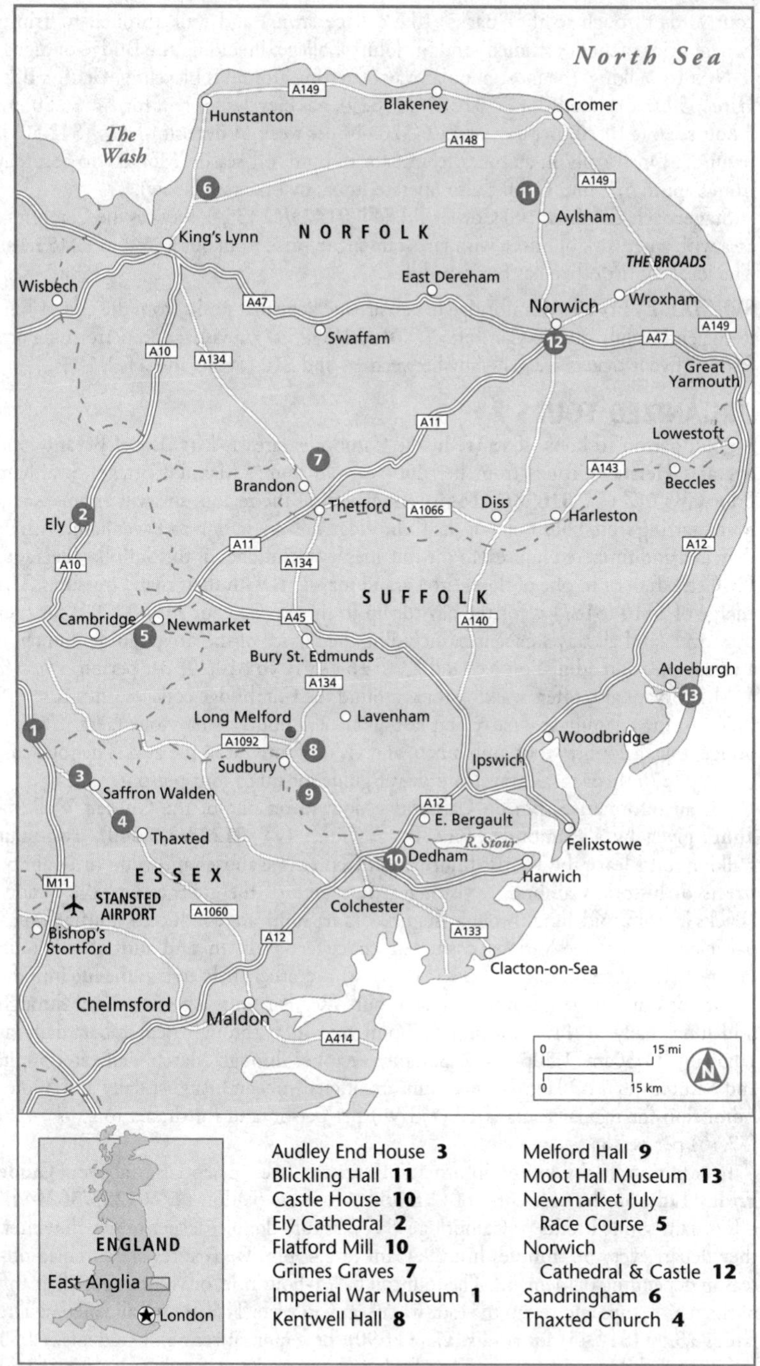
North Sea
The Wash
Hunstanton
A149
Blakeney
Cromer
A148
A149
NORFOLK
King's Lynn
Aylsham
THE BROADS
Wisbech
East Dereham
Norwich
Wroxham
A47
Swaffam
A149
A47
A10
A134
Great Yarmouth
A11
Lowestoft
A143
Beccles
Brandon
Thetford
A1066
Diss
Harleston
Ely
A11
A134
A12
A10
SUFFOLK
Cambridge
Newmarket
A45
A140
Bury St. Edmunds
Aldeburgh
A134
Long Melford
Lavenham
A1092
Woodbridge
Sudbury
Ipswich
Saffron Walden
A12
E. Bergault
Thaxted
R. Stour
Felixstowe
Dedham
ESSEX
Harwich
M11
STANSTED AIRPORT
A1060
Colchester
Bishop's Stortford
A12
A133
Clacton-on-Sea
Chelmsford
Maldon
A414
0
15 mi
0
15 km
N
ENGLAND
East Anglia
London
Audley End House 3
Blickling Hall 11
Castle House 10
Ely Cathedral 2
Flatford Mill 10
Grimes Graves 7
Imperial War Museum 1
Kentwell Hall 8
Melford Hall 9
Moot Hall Museum 13
Newmarket July Race Course 5
Norwich Cathedral & Castle 12
Sandringham 6
Thaxted Church 4

courtyards through to the "Backs" (the college lawns) and walk through to Trinity (where Prince Charles studied) and St. John's College, including the Bridge of Sighs.

Next to walking, the most popular way of getting around is bicycling. **Geoff's Bike Hire,** 65 Devonshire Rd. (☎ **01223/365629**), has bicycles for rent for £4 ($6.80) for 3 hours, £6 ($10.20) per day, or £12 ($20.40) per week. A deposit of £25 ($42.50) is required. Open daily in summer from 9am to 6pm; off-season Monday to Saturday from 9am to 5:30pm. Geoff's also operates tours by bike (see below).

Stagecoach Cambus, 100 Cowley Rd. (☎ **01223/423554**), services the Cambridge area with a network of buses, with fares ranging in price from 50p (85¢) to £2 ($3.40). The local tourist office has bus schedules.

SPECIAL EVENTS Cambridge has an artistic bent that peaks from the end of June to the end of July during **Camfest** (☎ **01223/359547**), a visual and performing arts festival. Event tickets are generally between £4 and £10 ($6.80 and $17).

ORGANIZED TOURS

A good person to know if you're in the Cambridge area is Mrs. Isobel Bryant, who operates **Heritage Tours** from her 200-year-old home, Manor Cottage, Swaffham Prior CB5 0JZ (☎ **01638/741440**). An expert on the region, she will arrange small tours starting from your hotel or the Cambridge railway station to Lavenham, with its thatched and timbered houses, to the fine medieval churches of the Suffolk villages, to Ely Cathedral, or to one of the nearby grand mansions with their many treasures. The charge of £110 ($187) is for the day for up to three people, or £120 ($204) for four passengers and all travel expenses, including the service of the driver-guide. Lunch in a village pub and admission fees add £3 to £6 ($5.10 to $10.20) per person.

Mrs. Bryant also offers walking tours around the Cambridge colleges; they cost £45 ($76.50) for a family-size party and last about 2½ hours. A day tour takes in Cambridge, then a country tour, pub lunch, and visits of interest in the area. The total cost of £120 ($204) covers all travel and driver-guide for up to four persons.

For an informative spin on Cambridge, join in on one of the **Guided Walking Tours** given by a Cambridge Blue Badge Guide (☎ **01223/322640**). Two-hour walking tours leave the Tourist Information Centre (see above) and wind through the streets of historic Cambridge, visiting at least one of the colleges and the famous "Backs." From mid-June through August, drama tours are conducted, during which participants may see various costumed characters walk in and out of the tour. Henry VIII, Queen Elizabeth I, Isaac Newton, and others help to breathe life into the history of Cambridge during the drama tours. Regular tours are given April through mid-June, daily at 11:30am and 1:30pm; mid-June through September, daily at 10:30am, 11:30am, 1:30pm, and 2:30pm; October through March, daily at 1:30pm and Saturday at 11:30am. Drama tours are offered July and August daily at 6:30pm. Admission for regular tours is £7 ($11.90) per person and for drama tours is £4.20 ($7.15) per person.

In addition to its visitor information services (see "Essentials," above), **Guide Friday Ltd.,** on the concourse of Cambridge Railway Station (☎ **01223/362444**), offers daily guided tours of Cambridge via open-top, double-decker buses. In winter, they depart every 30 minutes from 9:45am to 2:45pm. Departures are curtailed off-season depending on demand. The tour can be a 1-hour ride, or you can get off at any of the many stops and rejoin the tour whenever you wish. Tickets are valid all day. The fare is £8.50 ($14.45) for adults, £7 ($11.90) for senior citizens and students, £2.50 ($4.25) for children 5 to 12, and free for kids 4 and under. A family ticket for £19.50 ($33.15) covers two adults and up to three children. Office hours are daily 9:15am to 6:30pm in summer and 9:30am to 3pm during off-season.

Geoff's Bike Hire, 65 Devonshire Rd. (☎ **01223/365629**), has guided bicycle tours on Tuesday, Wednesday, Thursday, and Saturday at 2:30pm. A 10:30am tour on Saturday is also offered. These cost £7.50 ($12.75) including bike rental. Or you can just rent a bike, which is £6 ($10.20).

EXPLORING THE UNIVERSITY

Oxford University predates Cambridge, but by the early 13th century, scholars began coming here, too. Eventually, Cambridge won partial recognition from Henry III, rising or falling with the approval of subsequent English monarchs. Cambridge consists of 31 colleges for both men and women. Colleges are closed for exams from mid-April until the end of June.

A word of warning: Unfortunately, because of the disturbances caused by the influx of tourists, Cambridge has had to limit visitors, or even exclude them altogether, from various parts of the university. In some cases, a small entry fee will be charged. Small groups of up to six people are generally admitted with no problem, and you can inquire with the local tourist office about visiting hours (see above). All colleges are closed during exams and graduation, on Easter and all bank holidays, and at other times without notice.

The following is only a sample of some of the more interesting colleges.

✪ **KING'S COLLEGE** The adolescent Henry VI founded King's College on King's Parade (☎ **01223/331212**) in 1441. Most of its buildings today are from the 19th century, but its crowning glory, the Perpendicular King's College Chapel, dates from the Middle Ages and is one of England's architectural gems. Its most characteristic features are the magnificent fan vaulting, all of stone, and the great windows, most of which were fashioned by Flemish artisans between 1517 and 1531. The stained glass portrays biblical scenes, in hues of red, blue, and amber. The chapel also houses Rubens's *The Adoration of the Magi.* The rood screen is from the early 16th century.

The chapel is open during vacation time, Monday to Saturday from 9:30am to 4:30pm, and on Sunday from 10am to 4:30pm. During the term, the public is welcome to attend choral services Monday to Saturday at 5:30pm and on Sunday at 10:30am and 3:30pm. During the term, the chapel is open to visitors Monday to Saturday from 9:30am to 3:15pm and on Sunday from 1:15 to 2:15pm; it is closed December 23 to January 1. It may be closed at other times for recording sessions, broadcasts, and concerts.

There is an exhibition in the seven northern side chapels showing why and how the chapel was built. Admission to the college and chapel, including the exhibition, is £3.50 ($5.95) for adults, £2.50 ($4.25) for students and children 12 to 17, and free for children under 12.

PETERHOUSE This college, on Trumpington Street (☎ **01223/338200**), is the oldest Cambridge college, founded in 1284 by Hugh de Balsham, the bishop of Ely. Of the original buildings, only the hall remains, but this was restored in the 19th century and now boasts stained-glass windows by William Morris. Old Court, constructed in the 15th century, was renovated in 1754; the chapel dates from 1632. Ask permission to enter at the porter's lodge.

TRINITY COLLEGE On Trinity Street, Trinity College (not to be confused with Trinity Hall) is the largest college in Cambridge. It was founded in 1546 by Henry VIII, who consolidated a number of smaller colleges that had existed on the site. The courtyard is the most spacious in Cambridge, built when Thomas Nevile was master. Sir Christopher Wren designed the library. For entry to the college, apply at the Great Gate, or call ☎ **01223/338400** for information. There is a charge of £1.75 ($3) from March to November.

EMMANUEL COLLEGE On St. Andrew's Street, Emmanuel (☎ **01223/334274**) was founded in 1584 by Sir Walter Mildmay, a chancellor of the exchequer to Elizabeth I. *Harvard grads, take note:* John Harvard, patron of Harvard University, studied here. You can take a nice stroll around its attractive gardens and visit the chapel designed by Sir Christopher Wren and consecrated in 1677. Both the chapel and college are open daily from 9am to 6pm (closed during exam time).

QUEENS' COLLEGE On Queens' Lane, Queens' College (☎ **01223/335511**) is the loveliest of Cambridge's colleges. Dating from 1448, it was founded by two English queens, one the wife of Henry VI, the other the wife of Edward IV. Its second cloister is the most interesting, flanked by the early–16th-century President's Lodge. Admission is £1 ($1.70); free for children under 12 accompanied by parents. A printed guide is issued. From November until March 19, hours are daily 1:45 to 4:30pm; March 20 to May 15, Monday to Friday 1:45 to 4:30pm, Saturday and Sunday 10am to 4:45pm; closed May 17 to June 19. From June 20 to September 19, Monday to Friday 10am to 4:30pm, Saturday and Sunday 10am to 4:45pm; September 20 to October 31, Monday to Friday 1:45 to 4:30pm, Saturday and Sunday 10am to 4:45pm. Entry and exit is by the old porter's lodge in Queens' Lane only. The old hall and chapel are usually open to the public when not in use.

Insider's tip: The Grove fronts the west bank of the River Cam on the north side of the bridge. It's a riot of blossoms in spring. The walk along the riverbank reveals the best view of King's College but ends at a small branch channel in the river. Beyond the lawn on the other side of the river, the high stone wall dividing the two colleges is the last remaining fragment of a Carmelite monastery dissolved in 1538.

ST. JOHN'S COLLEGE On St. John's Street, this college (☎ **01223/338600**) was founded in 1511 by Lady Margaret Beaufort, mother of Henry VII. A few years earlier she had founded Christ's College. Before her intervention, an old hospital had stood on the site of St. John's. The impressive gateway bears the Tudor coat of arms, and Second Court is a fine example of late Tudor brickwork. But its best-known feature is the **Bridge of Sighs** crossing the Cam, built in the 19th century and patterned after the bridge in Venice. It connects the older part of the college with New Court, a Gothic Revival on the opposite bank from which there is an outstanding view of the famous Backs. The Bridge of Sighs is closed to visitors but can be seen from the neighboring Kitchen Bridge. The college is open from March to October daily from 10am to 5:30pm. Admission is £1.75 ($3) for adults and £1 ($1.70) for children. Visitors are welcome to attend choral services in the chapel.

CAMBRIDGE'S OTHER ATTRACTIONS

✪ **The Fitzwilliam Museum.** Trumpington St., near Peterhouse. ☎ **01223/332900.** Free admission. Tues–Sat 10am–5pm, Sun 2:15–5pm. Guided tours Sun 2:30pm. Closed Jan 1, Good Friday, May Day, and Dec 24–31.

One of the finest museums in Britain is worth the trip here. Although it features temporary exhibitions, its permanent collections are noted for their antiquities from ancient Egypt, Greece, and Rome. The Applied Arts section features English and European pottery and glass, along with furniture, clocks, fans, and armor, Chinese jades and ceramics from Japan and Korea, plus rugs and samplers. The museum is also noted for its rare-coin collection. Many rare printed books and illuminated manuscripts, both literary and musical, are also on display.

But the best for last: The paintings include masterpieces by Simone Martini, Domenico Veneziano, Titian, Veronese, Rubens, Van Dyck, Canaletto, Hogarth,

Cambridge

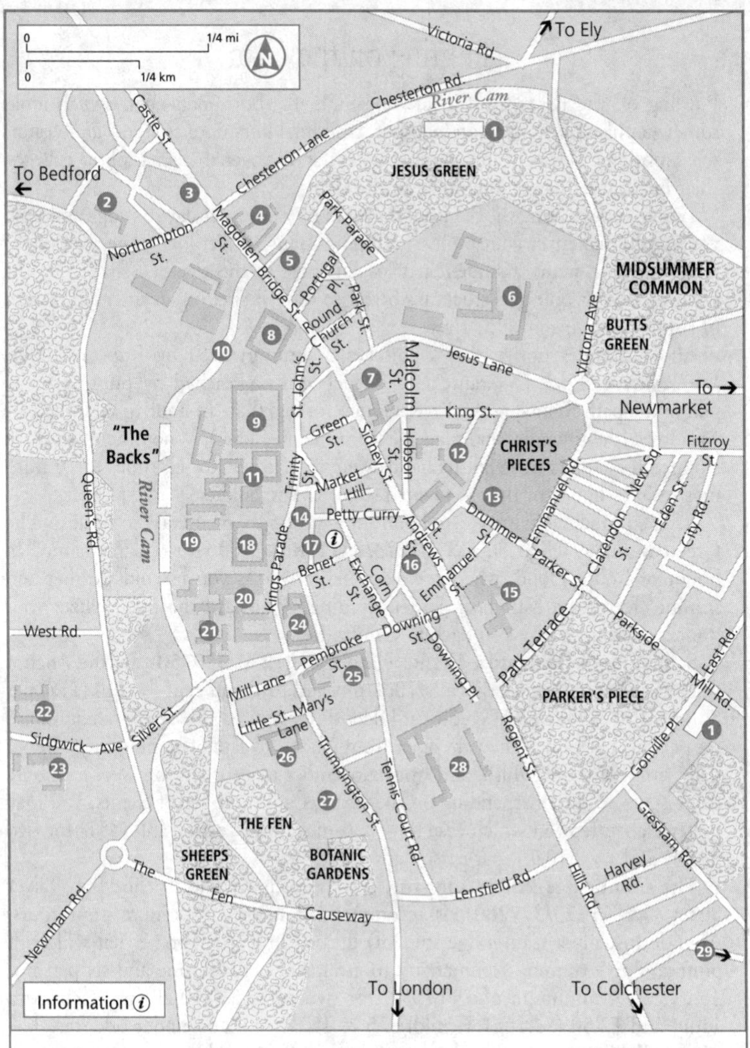

The Bridge of Sighs **10**
British Rail Station **29**
Bus Station **13**
Christ's College **12**
Clare College **19**
Corpus Christi College **24**
Downing College **28**
Emmanuel College **15**
Fitzwilliam Museum **27**
Folk Museum **3**
General Post Office **16**
Gonville & Caius College **11**
Great St. Mary **14**
Jesus College **6**
King's College **18**
Magdalene College **4**
Newnham College **23**
Pembroke College **25**
Peterhouse College **26**
Punts **5**
Queen's College **21**
St. Catharine's College **20**
St. John's College **8**
Selwyn College **22**
Sidney Sussex College **7**
Swimming Pool **1**
Tourist Information Office **17**
Trinity College **9**
Westminster College **2**

Punting on the Cam

Punting on the River Cam in a wood-built, flat-bottomed boat (which looks somewhat like a Venetian gondola) is a traditional pursuit of students and visitors to Cambridge. Downstream, you pass along the ivy-covered "Backs" of the colleges, their lush gardens sweeping down to the Cam.

People sprawl along the banks of the Cam on a summer day to judge and tease you as you maneuver your punt with a pole about 15 feet long. The river's floor is muddy, and many a student has lost his pole in the riverbed shaded by the willows. If your pole gets stuck, it's better to leave it sticking in the mud instead of risking a plunge into the river.

About 2 miles upriver lies Grantchester, immortalized by Rupert Brooke. Literary types flock to Grantchester, which can be reached by punting or by taking the path following the River Granta for less than an hour to Grantchester Meadows (the town lies about a mile from the meadows). When the town clock stopped for repairs in 1985, its hands were left frozen "for all time" at 10 minutes to 3, in honor of Brooke's famed sonnet "The Soldier."

After so much activity, you're bound to get hungry or thirsty, so head to **The Green Man,** 59 High St. (☎ **01223/841178**), a 400-year-old inn named in honor of Robin Hood, where a crackling fire warms you in cold weather and summer features a back beer garden, leading off toward the river, where your punt is waiting to take you back to Cambridge.

Scudamore's Boatyards, Granta Place (☎ **01223/359750**), by the Anchor Pub, has been in business since 1910. Punts and rowboats rent for £10 ($17) per hour. A £50 ($85) cash or credit-card deposit is required. There is a maximum of six persons per punt. They are open from March to late September or October daily from 9am until dusk, and from November to February on weekends only from 10am to dusk, depending on the weather and number of clients. You may prefer a chauffeur, in which case there is a minimum cost of £30 ($51) for two people and £6 ($10.20) per person after that.

The Cambridge Punt Company, working out of The Anchor Pub, Silver Street (☎ **01223/327280**), is recommended for its 45-minute punt tours. A guide (usually a Cambridge student) dressed in a straw boater hat will both punt and give running commentary to groups of between one and six persons. Tours cost a minimum of £30 ($51) for two and £6 ($10.20) per each extra adult, and £2.50 ($4.25) for children 5 to 12. Kids 4 and under ride free. The Anchor Pub's service staff can call a guide over to your table. If you want to row yourself along the Cam, "unchauffeured" boats rent for £10 ($17) per hour. The company is open daily from 9am to dusk, although everyone packs up if it rains or if the winds get too high.

Gainsborough, Constable, Monet, Degas, Renoir, Cézanne, and Picasso. There is also a fine collection of other 20th-century art, miniatures, drawings, watercolors, and prints.

Insider's tip: Occasional musical events, including evening concerts, and some of the best lectures in England are staged here throughout the year. For more details, call ☎ **01223/332900.**

Great St. Mary's. King's Parade. ☎ **01223/350914.** Admission to tower £1.75 ($3) adults, children free. Tower Mon–Sat 10am–4:30pm, Sun 12:30–4:30pm; church daily 9am–6pm.

Cambridge's central church was built on the site of an 11th-century church, but the present building dates largely from 1478. It was closely associated with events of the Reformation. The cloth that covered the hearse of King Henry VII is on display in the church. There is a fine view of Cambridge from the top of the tower.

SHOPPING

Forage around the shops lining St. John's Street, Trinity Street, King's Parade, and Trumpington Street.

Check out **English Teddy Bear Company,** 1 King's Parade (☎ **01223/300908**), which sells teddy bears handmade in cottages all over the United Kingdom—a real British souvenir.

Primavera, 10 King's Parade (☎ **01223/357708**), is a showplace of British crafts, featuring pottery, glass, ceramics, jewelry, ironwork, and fabric crafts ranging from ties to wall hangings. Be sure to explore their basement exhibition of paintings and craft items.

Music buffs will want to visit the **Cambridge Music Shop,** 1-A All Saints Passage (☎ **01223/351786**), which carries stringed instruments, musical scores, music books, and accessories.

Another well-defined shopping district is comprised of Bridge Street, Sidney Street, St. Andrew's Street, and Regent Street. Particularly worth noting in this area is **James Pringle Weavers,** 11 Bridge St. (☎ **01223/361534**), a Scottish haven. You'll find a mind-boggling array of Scottish tartans, kilts, tweeds, fine knitwear, Scottish food, and, of course, postcards.

A posh area of extremely chic, small, and exclusive shops runs between Market Square and Trinity Street and is called **Rose Crescent.** Here, you can buy leather goods, smart women's clothing, fine hats, as well as jewelry and a host of very expensive gift items.

Cambridge's pedestrian shopping district runs between Market Square and St. Andrew's Street and is known as the **Lion Yard. Culpepper the Herbalists,** 25 Lion Yard (☎ **01223/367370**), carries a complete herbal line that includes everything from extracts of plants to jellies, honeys, teas, cosmetics, bath products, pillows, and potpourri.

If you're a book lover, Cambridge's bookstores will truly delight you. **Heffers of Cambridge** is a huge book, stationery, and music store with six branches, all of which can be contacted through their central phone number (☎ **01223/568568**). The main store, at 20 Trinity St., carries academic books; the children's book shop is at 30 Trinity St.; the stationery store can be found at 19 Sydney St.; Heffers's paperback and video shop is at 31 St. Andrews St.; their art-and-graphics shop has an address of 15–21 King St.; and the music store at 19 Trinity St. features classical and popular cassettes, CDs, and choral college music. Heffers also has a shop in the mall at Grafton Centre that carries new fiction and nonfiction titles.

Also owned by Heffers, **Deighton, Bell & Co.,** 13 Trinity St. (☎ **01223/568568**), sells art and architectural books downstairs and antiquarian as well as secondhand books upstairs. **G. David,** 16 St. Edward's Passage (☎ **01223/354619**), hawks secondhand books, publishers' overruns at reduced prices, and antiquarian books. **Dillons,** 22 Sydney St. (☎ **01223/351688**), deals exclusively in new books on a variety of subjects. The **Haunted Bookshop,** 9 St. Edward's Passage (☎ **01223/312913**), specializes in out-of-print children's books and first editions.

WHERE TO STAY

VERY EXPENSIVE

Cambridge Garden House Moat House. Granta Place, Mill Lane, Cambridge, Cambridgeshire CB2 1RT. ☎ **01223/259988.** Fax 01223/316605. 117 units. MINIBAR TV TEL. £165 ($280.50) double; £350 ($595) suite. AE, DC, MC, V.

This modern hotel, the best in Cambridge, is situated between the riverbank and a cobblestone street in the oldest part of town, a short stroll from the principal colleges. Because of its riverside location, we prefer it over its nearest competitor, the University Arms, which is in the center of town. It offers ample parking. You can rent punts at a boatyard next door. Visitors can relax on comfortable sofas and chairs in the bars and lounge. The soundproof bedrooms have glass-topped nightstands, adequate desk space, and private balconies. The expensive units are called premium rooms, and they are very spacious with large sitting areas with face-to-face sofas. The river-view rooms are the most desirable. Bathrooms are large with hair dryers.

Dining/Diversions: Overlooking the river and gardens, the hotel's restaurant called simply "The Restaurant" offers fixed-price and à la carte menus, including vegetarian meals, at lunch and dinner. The Riverside Lounge provides light meals, accompanied in the evening by piano music. The hotel has a series of outdoor terraces where drinks and afternoon tea are served in nice weather.

Amenities: Fitness center with pool, gym, health club, sauna, Jacuzzi, and aerobics; 24-hour room service; laundry/dry cleaning; valet parking; business center.

EXPENSIVE

University Arms Hotel. Regent St., Cambridge, Cambridgeshire CB2 1AD. ☎ **01223/351241.** Fax 01223/315256. www.devere.com. E-mail: devere.uniarms@airtime.co.uk. 116 units. TV TEL. £135–£150 ($229.50–$255) double; £270 ($459) suite. Rates include English breakfast. AE, DC, MC, V. Bus no. 1.

This 1834 hotel maintains much of its antique charm and many of its original architectural features despite discreet modernization over the years. This is the only real rival in town to the Garden House, although it lacks the river location and time-worn Edwardian elegance of the former. Near the city center and the university, it offers tastefully decorated bedrooms. Rooms range from small to mid-size, each with bedside controls and trouser presses; the premium rooms also have slippers and robes. Forty bedrooms have recently been refurbished. Rooms in front are smaller but more up-to-date and have double-glazed windows. Extra touches include a beverage maker, and each room comes with a king or twin beds. Bathrooms have a hair dryer. Suite residents will also find fresh flowers, fruits, and chocolates in their rooms. The porter can arrange a guided tour of the city.

Dining: The Octagon Lounge, with its stained-glass domed ceiling and open log fire, is a popular place to meet for tea. There's also a spacious oak-paneled restaurant.

Amenities: Concierge, 24-hour room service, dry cleaning/laundry, valet parking.

MODERATE

Arundel Hotel. 53 Chesterton Rd., Cambridge, Cambridgeshire CB4 3AN. ☎ **01223/367701.** Fax 01223/367721. 105 units. TV TEL. £69–£96 ($117.30–$163.20) double. Rates include continental breakfast. AE, DC, MC, V. Bus nos. 3 or 5.

The Arundel has a great location. Until recently, it consisted of six identical Victorian row houses, connected many years ago. In 1994, after two additional row houses were purchased from the university, the hotel was enlarged and upgraded into the well-maintained place you'll see today. Rooms overlooking the River Cam and Jesus Green cost more than those facing the other way; and because there's no elevator, rooms on lower floors go for more than those upstairs. Regardless of their location, all accommodations are clean and comfortable, fitted with king or twin beds, plus a compact bathroom with adequate shelf space. A coin-operated launderette is on the premises. There's a bar and restaurant (see "Where to Dine," below) and a garden with outdoor tables for drinks in warm weather; the Arundel offers the best dining of any hotel in town.

Cambridgeshire Moat House. Huntingdon Rd., Bar Hill, Cambridge, Cambridgeshire CB3 8EU. ☎ **01954/249988.** Fax 01954/780010. 134 units. TV TEL. £100–£120 ($170–$204) double. Children 15 and under stay free in parents' room. AE, DC, MC, V. Take A14 5 1/2 miles northwest of the town center.

This place, a more affordable member of the same chain that manages the Cambridge Garden House Moat House (reviewed above), offers the best sports facilities in the Cambridge area. Built around 1977, it has comfortable bedrooms with nice views, a heated indoor swimming pool, a sauna, putting green, and an 18-hole championship golf course where greens fees range from £15 to £30 ($25.50 to $51). The small to mid-size bedrooms are equipped with hair dryers, trouser presses, and beverage makers. The compact bathrooms are fitted with shower stalls. There's a restaurant in the hotel, although the food is just standard stuff. Meals are also served daily in the bar.

Gonville Hotel. Gonville Place, Cambridge, Cambridgeshire CB1 1LY. ☎ **800/528-1234** in the U.S. and Canada, or 01223/366611. Fax 01223/315470. E-mail: gonvillehotel@BTConnect.com. 62 units. TV TEL. £106 ($180.20) double. AE, CB, DC, MC, V.

Only a 5-minute walk from the center of town, this hotel and its grounds are opposite Parker's Piece. The Gonville has been much improved in recent years, and is now better than ever. It's not unlike a country house, with shade trees and a formal car entry, and it attracts businesspeople as well as tourists. The recently refurbished rooms are comfortable and furnished in a modern style. Bedrooms are small to mid-size and well maintained, with a compact bathroom containing a hair dryer. There is air-conditioning in the restaurant.

Post House Hotel. Lakeview, Bridge Rd., Lakeview Bridge, Impington, Cambridge, Cambridgeshire CB4 4PH. ☎ **800/225-5843** in the U.S. and Canada, or 01223/237000. Fax 01223/233426. 165 units. TV TEL. Sun–Thurs £99 ($168.30) double; Fri–Sat £65 ($110.50) double. AE, DC, MC, V. Bus no. 104. Drive 2 miles north of Cambridge on B1049 (Histon Rd.) to the A45 intersection.

Located a short walk from a small artificial lake, which the bedrooms overlook, this modern two-story hotel was vaguely influenced by the designs of nearby country houses. Like the Moat House, it emphasizes leisure facilities (though it doesn't offer golf), and of the two, it has better bedrooms. There's a grassy courtyard partially enclosed by the hotel's wings. Peak-ceilinged public rooms are furnished with scattered clusters of sofas and chairs. The bedrooms have large windows with pleasant views. Bedrooms are a bit small but still quite comfortable, with compact bathrooms containing shower stalls. Facilities include a heated indoor swimming pool, a Jacuzzi, a sauna, and a lobby bar. The restaurant has reproductions of paintings created by Sir Winston Churchill. The hotel has recently enlarged its health-and-fitness room.

Regent Hotel. 41 Regent St., Cambridge, Cambridgeshire CB2 1AB. ☎ **01223/351470.** Fax 01223/566562. www.regenthotel.co.uk. E-mail: reservations@regenthotel.co.uk. 26 units. TV TEL. £85 ($144.50) double. Rates include continental breakfast. AE, DC, MC, V.

This is one of the nicest of the reasonably priced small hotels in Cambridge. Right in the city center, overlooking Parker's Piece, the house was built in the 1840s as the original site of Newham College. It became a hotel when the college outgrew its quarters. The attractive bedrooms have radios, hair dryers, and trouser presses. Many of the small to mid-size bedrooms were recently refurbished. Each comes with a coffeemaker, plus a compact bathroom, most with tub and shower combination. There's a cocktail bar on the street level, and the coffee bar serves breakfast, late snacks, and afternoon tea.

INEXPENSIVE

Hamilton Hotel. 156 Chesterton Rd., Cambridge, Cambridgeshire CB4 1DA. ☎ **01223/365664.** Fax 01223/314866. 26 units, 17 with bathroom (shower only). £45 ($76.50) double without bath, £55–£69 ($93.50–$117.30) double with bath. Rates include English breakfast. AE, DC, MC, V. Bus nos. 3 or 3A.

One of the better and more reasonably priced of the small hotels of Cambridge, this redbrick establishment lies about a mile northeast of the city center, close to the River Cam. A well-run, modestly accessorized hotel, it stands on a busy highway, but there's a parking area out back. The well-furnished bedrooms contain beverage-making equipment and phones, plus reasonably comfortable twins or double beds. Bathrooms are compact with shower stalls. The hotel has a small, traditionally styled licensed bar, offering standard pub food and snacks.

Regency Guest House. 7 Regent Terrace, Cambridge, Cambridgeshire CB2 1AA. ☎ **01223/329626.** Fax 01223/301567. www.guest-house.demon.co.uk. E-mail: regency@guest-house.demon.co.uk. 8 units, 3 with bathroom. TV. £50–£55 ($85–$93.50) double without bathroom, £60–£65 ($102–$110.50) double with bathroom. Rates include continental breakfast. No credit cards. Bus no. 5.

In a desirable location near the town center, overlooking the verdant city park known as Parker's Piece, this hotel was built around 1850. Set behind a stone facade, and similar in design to many of its neighbors, it offers bedrooms with beverage makers and 1950s-style retro furniture. The rooms are painted about every six months and have a bright, fresh look. Most of the rooms are small, and the beds are reasonably comfortable. The compact bathrooms have adequate shelf space and a hair dryer. Breakfast includes ample portions of continental-inspired selections, although cooked English breakfasts can be arranged for a supplement of £3 ($5.10).

WHERE TO DINE

Drop down into the cozy **Rainbow Vegetarian Bistro,** King's Parade, across from King's College (☎ **01223/321551**), for coffee, a slice of fresh-baked cake, or a meal from their selection of whole-food and vegetarian offerings. A main course lunch or dinner goes for only £6.25 ($10.65); if you're around for breakfast, an omelette is just £4.75 ($8.05). Open Monday to Saturday from 11am to 10:30pm. The cafe lies at the end of a lily-lined path.

VERY EXPENSIVE

✪ **Midsummer House.** Midsummer Common. ☎ **01223/369299.** Reservations required. 3-course lunch £19.50 ($33.15); Sun lunch £27.50 ($46.75); 3-course fixed-price dinner £25–£39.50 ($42.50–$67.15). AE, MC, V. Tues–Fri and Sun noon–2pm; Tues–Sat 7–10pm. CONTINENTAL.

Located in an Edwardian-era cottage near the River Cam, the Midsummer House is a real find. We prefer to dine in the elegant conservatory, but you can also find a smartly laid table upstairs. The fixed-price menus are wisely limited, and quality control and high standards are much in evidence here. Daniel Clifford is the master chef, and he has created such specialties as filet of beef Rossini with braised winter vegetables and sauce Perigourdine; and roast squab pigeon, pomme Anna, tart tatin of onions, caramelized endives and jus of morels.

Moderate

Arundel House Restaurant. 53 Chesterton Rd. ☎ **01223/367701.** Reservations required. Main courses £7.75–£16.95 ($13.15–$28.80). AE, DC, MC, V. Daily 12:15–1:45pm and 6:30–9:30pm. Bus nos. 3 or 5. FRENCH/BRITISH/VEGETARIAN.

One of the best and most acclaimed restaurants in Cambridge is in a hotel overlooking the River Cam and Jesus Green, a short walk from the city center. Winner of many awards, it's noted not only for its excellence and use of fresh produce, but also for its good value. The decor is warmly inviting with Sanderson curtains, Louis XV-upholstered chairs, and spacious tables. The menu changes frequently, and you dine both à la carte or from the set menu. Perhaps you'll begin with a homemade golden-pea-and-ham soup or a white-rum-and-passion-fruit cocktail. Fish choices include plaice or salmon; try the pork-and-pigeon casserole, or the Japanese-style braised lamb.

Browns. 23 Trumpington St. (5 minutes from King's College and opposite the Fitzwilliam Museum). ☎ **01223/461655.** Main courses £7.55–£14.95 ($12.85–$25.40). AE, MC, V. Daily 11am–11:30pm. Bus no. 2. ENGLISH/CONTINENTAL.

With a neoclassical colonnade in front, Browns has all the grandeur of the Edwardian era, but inside, it's the most lighthearted restaurant in the city, with wicker chairs, high ceilings, pre–World War I woodwork, and a long bar covered with bottles of wine. The extensive bill of continually varied fare includes pasta, scores of fresh salads, several selections of meat and fish (from charcoal-grilled leg of lamb with rosemary to fresh fish in season), hot sandwiches, and the chef's daily specials posted on a blackboard. If you drop by in the afternoon, you can also order thick milk shakes or natural fruit juices. In fair weather, there's outdoor seating.

✪ **Twenty Two.** 22 Chesterton Rd. ☎ **01223/351880.** Reservations required. Fixed-price menu £23.50–£28.50 ($39.95–$48.45). AE, MC, V. Tues–Sat 7:30–10pm. ENGLISH/CONTINENTAL.

One of the best in Cambridge, this restaurant is located in a quiet district near Jesus Green, and is a secret jealously guarded by the locals. The homelike but elegant Victorian dining room offers an ever-changing fixed-price menu based on fresh market produce. Owners David Carter and Louise Crompton use time-tested recipes along with their own inspirations, offering creations such as white onion soup with toasted goats cheese or sautéed breast of chicken on braised celery with thyme jus.

Inexpensive

Charlie Chan. 14 Regent St. ☎ **01223/361763.** Reservations recommended. Main courses £5.80–£9.95 ($9.85–$16.90); fixed-price menus £13.50–£28 ($22.95–$47.60). AE, MC, V. Daily noon–2pm and 6–11pm. CHINESE.

Most people agree that this is the finest Chinese restaurant in Cambridge. We've always found Charlie Chan reliable and capable, which is remarkable given its huge menu. Downstairs is a long corridorlike restaurant, with pristine decor. The ambience is more lush in the Blue Lagoon upstairs. Most of the dishes here are inspired by the traditional cuisine of Beijing. The specialties we've most enjoyed include an aromatic and crispy duck, lemon chicken, and prawn with garlic and ginger.

CAMBRIDGE AFTER DARK

You can take in a production where Emma Thompson and other well-known thespians got their start at **The Amateur Dramatic Club,** Park Street near Jesus Lane (☎ **01223/359547;** box office 01223/503333). It presents two student productions nightly, Tuesday through Saturday, with the main show tending toward classic and modern drama or opera, and the late show being of a comic or experimental nature. The theater is open 40 weeks a year, closing in August and September, and tickets run from £3.50 to £7 ($5.95 to $11.90).

Then there's the most popular Cantebridgian activity: the pub crawl. There are too many pubs in the city to list them all here, but you might as well start at Cambridge's oldest pub, the **Pickerel,** on Bridge Street (☎ **01223/355068**), which dates from 1432. English pubs don't get more traditional than this. If the ceiling beams or floorboards groan occasionally—well, they've certainly earned the right over the years. Real ales on tap include Bulmer's Traditional Cider, Old Speckled Hen, or Theakston's 6X, Old Peculiar, and Best Bitter. **The Maypole,** Portugal Place at Park Street (☎ **01223/352999**), is the local hangout for actors when they're not in the nearby ADC Theatre. It's known for cocktails instead of ales, but you can get a Tetley's 6X or Castle Eden anyway.

The Eagle, Benet Street off King's Parade (☎ **01223/505020**), will be forever famous as the place where Nobel Laureates Watson and Crick first announced their discovery of the DNA double helix. Real ales include Icebreaker and local brewery Greene King's Abbott, so make your order and raise a pint to the wonders of modern science.

To meet up with current Cambridge students, join the locals at the **Anchor,** Silver Street (☎ **01223/353554**), or **Tap and Spiel (The Mill),** Mill Lane, off Silver Street Bridge (☎ **01223/357026**), for a pint of Greene King's IPA or Abbott. The crowd at the Anchor spills out onto the bridge in fair weather, whereas the Tap and Spiel's clientele lay claim to the entire riverside park.

There's also musical entertainment to be had, and you can find out who's playing by checking out flyers posted around town, or reading the *Varsity.* **The Corn Exchange,** Wheeler Street and Corn Exchange (☎ **01223/357851**), hosts everything from classical concerts to bigger-name rock shows. The **Fresher & Firkin,** 16 Chesterton Rd. (☎ **01223/324325**), a pub located in a former movie theater, has live music or DJs on Friday and Saturday, with no cover charge.

Entertainment in some form can be found nightly at **The Junction,** Clifton Road, near the train station (☎ **01223/511511**), where an eclectic mix of acts take to the stage weeknights to perform all genres of music, comedy, and theater, and DJs take over on the weekend. Cover charges vary from £7 to £13 ($11.90 to $22.10), depending on the event.

5th Avenue, Lion Yard (☎ **01223/364222**), a second-story club, has a huge dance floor and plays everything from house to the latest pop hits, Monday through Saturday from 9pm until 2am. Sometimes they even DJ the old-fashioned way, by taking requests. The cover charge ranges from £4 to £7 ($6.80 to $11.90), depending on what night you're here.

SIDE TRIPS FROM CAMBRIDGE

A Glimpse of Wartime Britain

✪ **Imperial War Museum.** Duxford, on A505, at Junction 10 of M11. ☎ **01223/835000.** Admission £7.40 ($12.60) adults, £5.20 ($8.85) seniors, £3.70 ($6.30) children over 16 and students, children under 16 free. Mid-Mar to Oct daily 10am–6pm; Nov to mid-Mar daily 10am–4pm. Closed Dec 24–26. Bus: Cambus no. 103 from Drummer St. Station in Cambridge. By car, take M11 to Junction 10, 8 miles south of Cambridge.

In this former Battle of Britain station and U.S. Eighth Air Force base during World War II, you'll find a huge collection of historic civil and military aircraft from both world wars, including the only B-29 Superfortress in Europe. Other exhibits include midget submarines, tanks, and a variety of field artillery pieces, as well as a historical display on the U.S. Eighth Air Force.

In the summer of 1997, Elizabeth II opened the American Air Museum here as part of the larger complex. It houses Europe's finest collection of historic American combat aircraft and is the largest precast concrete structure in Europe. Aircraft on show range from a World War I biplane to the giant B-52 jet bomber. A number are dramatically suspended from the ceiling as if in flight.

THAXTED

The nearby village of Thaxted is famous for its well-preserved Elizabethan houses and for hosting the famous **Morris Ring,** the first weekend after Spring Bank Holiday, a processional street dance that attracts more than 300 dancers and culminates with a haunting horn dance as dusk falls.

Thaxted is 5 miles south of Saffron Walden. To get here from Saffron Walden, drive along B184 (the Thaxted Road), following signs to Thaxted and Great Dunmow. A bus follows this route Monday to Saturday five to six times a day.

Thaxted has the most beautiful small church in England, the ✪ **Church of St. John the Baptist, Our Lady and St. Lawrence** (☎ **01371/830221**), whose graceful spire can be seen for miles around. Its belfry has special chimes that call parishioners to church services. Dating from 1340, the church is a nearly perfect example of religious architecture.

Other sights include the **Thaxted Guildhall** (☎ **01371/831339**), located next to the church and the site of a medieval marketplace. It is a fine example of a medieval Guildhall, few of which now remain. It was built between 1393 and 1420, possibly by the Cutlers Guild. Open April through September, Saturday, Sunday, Monday, and bank holidays, from 2 to 6pm.

WHERE TO STAY NEAR THAXTED

Whitehall. Church End, Broxted, Essex CM6 2BZ. ☎ **01279/850603.** Fax 01279/850385. 25 units. TV TEL. £120–£150 ($204–$255) double. AE, DC, MC, V. Take B1052 about 4 miles southwest of Thaxted. If you're driving from Stansted Airport, follow the signs to Broxted for the 7-minute drive.

This hotel lies adjacent to the village church of Broxted, with a garden behind it and lots of open land nearby. It's also very convenient for passengers using Stansted Airport outside London. In the 18th century, this property was attached to almost 28,000 acres of prime farmland. By the 1900s, Daisy, the countess of Warwick, then its mistress, entertained King Edward VII within these baronial walls. One of the renowned hostesses of the Edwardian era, the countess was also the mistress of Victoria's son. Today's guests are still entertained more or less royally. Some of the mostly spacious bedrooms are uniquely furnished in 18th-century style; all have thoughtful extras such as beverage makers and views of the yew trees in the ancient walled garden. Half of the rooms lie within a modern wing that was added in 1985. The new-wing rooms are conservatively traditional, with country-house accessories. Bathrooms, although small, have adequate shelf.

Dining: A medieval brew house with a soaring ceiling is the dining venue for specialties prepared with fresh ingredients, subtle flavors, and imaginative presentation. The specialty fixed-price menu costs £37.50 ($63.75) for a six-course "menu surprise."

2 Ely

70 miles NE of London; 16 miles N of Cambridge

Ely Cathedral is the top attraction in the fen country, outside of Cambridge. After you've seen the cathedral, you can safely be on your way, as Ely is simply a sleepy market town that can't compete with the life and bustle found at Cambridge.

ESSENTIALS

GETTING THERE Ely is a major railway junction served by express trains to Cambridge. Service is frequent from London's Liverpool Street Station. For schedules and information, call ☎ **0345/484950.**

Campus buses run frequently between Cambridge and Ely. Call ☎ **01223/423554** for schedules and information.

If you're driving from Cambridge, take A10 north.

VISITOR INFORMATION The **Tourist Information Centre** is at Oliver Cromwell's House, 29 St. Mary's St. (☎ **01353/662062**); open April through September daily from 10am to 6pm; October through March, Monday to Saturday from 10am to 5pm.

SEEING THE SIGHTS

✪ **Ely Cathedral.** ☎ **01353/667735.** Admission £4 ($6.80) adults; £3.50 ($5.95) seniors, students; free for children under 16. Apr–Oct daily 7am–7pm; Nov–Mar Mon–Sat 7:30am–6pm, Sun 7:30am–5pm.

The near-legendary founder of this cathedral was Etheldreda, the wife of a Northumbrian king who established a monastery on the spot in 673. The present structure dates from 1081. Visible for miles around, the landmark octagonal lantern is the crowning glory of the cathedral. Erected in 1322 following the collapse of the old tower, it represents a remarkable engineering achievement. Four hundred tons of lead and wood hang in space, held there by timbers reaching to the eight pillars.

You enter the cathedral through the Galilee West Door, a good example of the early English style of architecture. The lantern tower and the Octagon are the most notable features inside, but visit the Lady Chapel too. Although its decor has deteriorated over the centuries, it's still a handsome example of the Perpendicular style, having been completed in the mid-14th century. The entry fee goes to help preserve the cathedral. Monday to Saturday, guided tours gather at 11:15am and 2:15pm; in the summer, tours occur throughout the day.

There's also a Brass Rubbing Centre, where a large selection of replica brass is available for you to rub. These can produce remarkable results for wall hangings or special gifts. The center is open year-round in the North Aisle, outside the Cathedral Shop.

Ely Museum. The Old Gaol, Market St. ☎ **01353/666655.** Admission £2 ($3.40) adults; £1.25 ($2.15) children, students, and seniors; free for children 6 and under. Daily 10:30am–4:30pm. Closed Dec 20–Jan 2.

A gallery presents a chronological history of Ely and the Isle from the Ice Age to the present day. Displays include archaeology, social history, rural life, local industry, and military, as well as a tableau of the debtor's cell and condemned cell, which are also on view.

Oliver Cromwell's House. 29 St. Mary's St. (next to St. Mary's Church). ☎ **01353/662062.** Admission £2.70 ($4.60) adults; £2.20 ($3.75) children, seniors, and students; £7 ($11.90) family ticket. Apr–Sept daily 10am–5:30pm; off-season Mon–Sat 10am–5pm, Sun 10:15am–3pm.

This recently restored house was owned by the Puritan Oliver Cromwell, a name hardly beloved by the royals, even today. He rose to fame as a military and political leader during the English civil wars of 1642 to 1649. These wars led to the execution of Charles I, and the replacement of the monarchy by the Commonwealth. In 1653 Cromwell was declared lord protector, and the local farmer became the most powerful man in the land until his death in 1658. Exhibitions, displays, and period rooms offer insight into Cromwell's character and 17th-century domestic life. The tourist center is also located here.

Grimes Graves. On the B1107, 2¾ miles northeast of Brandon, Norfolkshire. ☎ **01842/810656.** Admission £1.75 ($3) adults, £1.30 ($2.20) students and seniors, 90p ($1.55) children 5–15; free for children 4 and under. Apr–Oct daily 10am–1pm and 2–6pm; Nov–Mar Wed–Sun 10am–1pm and 2–4pm. Take the A134 for 7 miles northwest of Thetford, then transfer to B1107.

This is the largest and best-preserved group of Neolithic flint mines in Britain; it produced the cutting edges of spears, arrows, and knives for prehistoric tribes throughout the region. Because of its isolated location within sparsely populated, fir-wooded countryside, it's easy to imagine yourself transported back through the millennia.

A guardian will meet you near the well-signposted parking lot. After determining that you are not physically impaired, he or she will open one or several of the mine shafts, each of which requires a descent down an almost-vertical 30-foot ladder (a visit here is not recommended for very young children, elderly travelers, or those with disabilities). Since the tunnel and shaft have been restored and reinforced, it's now possible to see where work took place during Neolithic times. Although it's not essential, many archaeologists, professional and amateur, bring their own flashlights with them. The mines, incidentally, are situated close to the military bases that housed thousands of American air-force personnel during World War II.

WHERE TO STAY

Lamb Hotel. 2 Lynn Rd., Ely, Cambridgeshire CB7 4EJ. ☎ **01353/663574.** Fax 01353/662023. 32 units. TV TEL. £85 ($144.50) double. Rates include English breakfast. AE, DC, MC, V. Bus no. 109.

Right in the center of town, this hotel is a former 14th-century coaching inn whose ground-floor areas, including the lounge and bars, were completely refurbished in 1996. In the shadow of the cathedral, this hotel offers renovated bedrooms with beverage makers. The bedrooms are furnished traditionally but with modern comfort, and contain good English beds, usually king-size or twin. Bathrooms are efficiently organized with adequate shelf space and a tub and shower combination. In the 1400s, this place was known as the "Holy Lambe," a stopping-off spot for wayfarers, often pilgrims, passing through East Anglia. Rather standard English meals are served.

WHERE TO DINE

Around the corner from St. Mary's Church is **Steeplegate,** 16–18 High St. (☎ **01353/664731**), a tearoom and craft shop with wooden tables and ancient windows. There are tea selections plus light lunch items, scones, and creamy gâteaux. After tea, venture downstairs to the craft shop and have a look at the variety of handmade pottery, glass, and baskets.

An unusual choice is **The Almonry Restaurant & Tea Rooms** in The College, Ely Cathedral (☎ **01353/666360**). Housed in the medieval college buildings on the north side of the Cathedral, this is a comfortable tearoom with table service in a beautiful 12th-century undercroft licensed to sell drinks. You can take your tea out to a garden seat in good weather. It is open for late morning coffee, lunches, and afternoon teas. Meals start at £4.50 ($7.65).

The Old Fire Engine House. 25 St. Mary's St. (opposite St. Mary's Church). ☎ **01353/662582.** Reservations required. Main courses £12–£15.80 ($20.40–$26.85). MC, V. Daily 12:30–2pm; Mon–Sat 7:30–9pm (last entry). Bus no. 109. ENGLISH.

It's worth making a special trip to this converted fire station in a walled garden, within a building complex that includes an art gallery. Soups are served in huge bowls, accompanied by coarse-grained crusty bread. Main dishes include lamb noisettes in pastry with tomato and basil, jugged hare, casseroled pheasant, and rabbit with mustard and parsley. In summer, you can dine outside in the garden and even order a cream tea.

3 Newmarket

62 miles NE of London; 13 miles NE of Cambridge

This old Suffolk town has been famous as a horse-racing center since the time of James I. Visitors can see Nell Gwynne's House, but mainly they come to visit Britain's first and only equestrian museum.

GETTING THERE

Trains depart from London's Liverpool Street Station every 45 to 60 minutes for Cambridge (see above). In Cambridge, passengers change trains and head in the direction of Mildenhall. Three stops later, they arrive at Newmarket.

About eight **National Express** buses depart from London's Victoria Coach Station for Norwich every day, stopping at Stratford, Stansted, and (finally) Newmarket along the way. For schedules and information, call ☎ **0990/808080.**

If you're driving from Cambridge, head east on A133.

OFF TO THE RACES

Britain's most prestigious racecourse lies at Newmarket, a small country town whose main tourist draw is the series of warm-weather horse races whose origins date from the days of James I and Charles II. Charles II was so enthusiastic about racing that he frequently ordered most of his Restoration-era court up from London to attend the races.

The headquarters of British racing, and the venue where precedents and policies are hammered out before being applied to the more formal venue of Ascot, Newmarket is the only racecourse in Britain with two separate racetracks.

The more bucolic of these is the **July Race Course,** where races are held during the heat and glare of June, July, and August. It's the site of the prestigious July Cup. The Rowley Mile, smaller than the other course, is known for its rows of beech trees that shade the saddling boxes and promenade grounds, as well as the thatched roofs that add an old-English charm to the ornamental entranceways and some of the showcase buildings used by investors, owners, and fans. The grandstands, however, have conventional roofs shielding fans from the sun and the rain.

The more industrial-looking racetrack is the **Rowley Mile,** used during the racing season's cooler months (mid-April to late May and early September to November 2). Dress codes are less strictly observed here and at the July Race Course, where men wear jackets and ties, but the venue at Rowley Mile attracts a bigger and brasher crowd. At the Rowley Mile, prestigious races such as the Guineas Races, the Cesarewitch Handicap, and the Champion Stakes are run.

The two courses lie within a half mile of each other, and share the same administration. For more information, contact **The Clerk of the Course,** Westfield House, The Links, Newmarket, Suffolk CB8 0TG (☎ **01638/663482**).

National Horseracing Museum. 99 High St. ☎ **01638/667333.** Admission £3.50 ($5.95) adults, £1.50 ($2.55) children, £2.50 ($4.25) seniors. Tues–Sun 10am–5pm. Closed Nov–Mar.

Visitors can see the history of horse racing over 300 years in this museum housed in the old subscription rooms, early-19th-century rooms used for betting. There are fine paintings of famous horses, paintings on loan from Queen Elizabeth II, and copies of old parliamentary acts governing races. A 53-minute audiovisual presentation shows races and racehorses.

To make history come alive for visitors, they also offer equine tours of this historic town. Guides take you to watch morning gallops on the heath where you'll see bronzes of horses from the past and other points of interest. An optional tour of a famous training establishment is offered, plus a visit to the Jockey Club rooms, known for their fine collection of paintings. Reservations are necessary. Tours depart every day when the museum is open except Sundays and in October. Departures are at 9:20am, costing £15 ($25.50) for adults, £12.50 ($21.25) for seniors, students, and children. There are also free guided tours of the museum daily at 2:30pm.

The National Stud. July Race Course. ☎ **01638/666789.** Admission £4 ($6.80) adults, £3 ($5.10) seniors, £2.50 ($4.25) children 6–12 years. Mar–Aug and Sept–Oct race day only. Guided tours Mon–Sat 11:15am and 2:30pm, Sun 2:30pm. Closed Nov–Feb.

Next to Newmarket's July Race Course, 2 miles southwest of the town, this place is home to some of the world's finest horses, and a renowned breeding stud operation. A tour lasting about 75 minutes lets you see many mares and foals, plus top-class stallions. Reservations for tours must be made at the National Stud office or by phoning the number given above.

WHERE TO STAY & DINE

Heath Court Hotel. Moulton Rd., Newmarket, Suffolk CB8 8DY. ☎ **01638/667171.** Fax 01638/666533. E-mail: quality@heathcourt-hotel.co.uk. 41 units. TV TEL. Mon–Thurs £98–£118 ($166.60–$200.60) double, Fri–Sun £88–£108 ($149.60–$183.60) double. All week £120 ($204) family room for 3; £175 ($297.50) suite. Extra bed £30 ($51). Rates include English breakfast. AE, DC, MC, V.

A member of Queen's Moat House hotel chain, this brick-fronted hotel is near The Gallops, the exercise area for the stables at the Newmarket Heath racetrack, about a 5-minute walk from the center of town. Built in the mid-1970s, it's a favorite of the English horse-racing world and is fully booked during the racing season. It is decorated in an appropriate country-elegant style in its public rooms, including oil portraits of horses and souvenirs of the racing life in its bar and restaurant. The bedrooms are well appointed, conservatively modern, and comfortable. Most of the units are spacious and have such extras as trouser presses and beverage makers. In the more expensive units, called executive rooms, there are also bathrobes and a small refrigerator. Baths are compact and well maintained.

Bertie's Rotisserie is an informal restaurant serving an English and continental menu, ranging from pink-roasted knuckle of lamb to paella, including Newmarket bangers and mash.

Swynford Paddocks. Six Mile Bottom, Cambridgeshire CB8 0UE. ☎ **01638/570234.** Fax 01638/570283. www.swynfordpaddocks.com. 15 units. TV TEL. £128 ($217.60) double. Rates include English breakfast. AE, DC, MC, V. Take A1304 6 miles southwest of Newmarket.

This well-appointed country house, one of the finest in the area, is situated on a 60-acre stud farm surrounded by beautiful grounds. It was once a retreat of Lord Byron, who wrote many of his works at the foot of a now-felled beech. The house then became the home of Lord and Lady Halifax until 1976, when it was converted into a luxury hotel. Many guests use it as a base for exploring not only Newmarket but Cambridge as well. Each of the bedrooms, opening onto scenic views, is decorated with a special character; some have four-poster beds and are quite romantic. Rooms are spacious and contain many amenities such as beverage makers, trouser presses, and hair dryers. The ample bathrooms are handsomely equipped with adequate shelf space and toiletries. For extra-special occasions, there's a suite of rooms or two sumptuous four-posters. The rates are expensive, but the quality is excellent. The restaurant serves a first-rate English, French, and Irish cuisine.

4 Bury St. Edmunds

79 miles NE of London; 27 miles E of Cambridge; 12 miles N of Lavenham

Bury St. Edmunds is "a handsome little town, of thriving and cleanly appearance." That's how Charles Dickens described it in *Pickwick Papers* and it holds true today. This historical town, founded around the powerful Benedictine Abbey in 1020, derives its name from St. Edmund, King of the East Angles in the mid-9th century. It was in the Abbey Church that the barons of England united and forced King John to sign the Magna Carta in 1214. Even though it's sometimes hard to tell, Bury is filled with many original medieval buildings. (Many buildings were given face-lifts in the 17th and 18th centuries; it's only when you step inside that their medieval roots become clear.) During the 18th century, this market town was quite prosperous and had a thriving cloth-making industry. The large number of fine Georgian buildings bear testament to the wealth of the day.

Upon the Vikings' arrival to the area, they dubbed it "The Summer Country." And, indeed, the summer, when the town bursts into bloom, is the best time to visit. Most of the historic sites and gardens open for the season on Easter.

ESSENTIALS

GETTING THERE Trains leave regularly from either Liverpool Street Station or King's Cross Station in London; however, none are direct. Leaving from Liverpool Street, you will change at Ipswich. And from King's Cross Station, you'll have to switch trains at Cambridge. The trip takes approximately 1½ hours. For schedules and information, call ☎ **0345/484950.**

National Express runs several direct buses every day from London's Victoria Coach Station, which reach Bury in 2 hours. For schedules and information, call ☎ **0990/808080.**

By car, take M11 north out of London. As you near Cambridge, get on A45 and continue on to Bury. The drive takes about 1½ hours.

It's also possible to get here by train or bus from Cambridge. Regular trains leave from the Cambridge Rail Station and arrive about 45 minutes later in Bury St. Edmunds. **Cambus Bus Company** runs five buses a day to Bury from the Drummer Street Bus Station in Cambridge, a 1-hour ride. Call ☎ **01223/423554** for information and schedules. By car, simply take A45 directly from Cambridge. It's a 45-minute drive.

VISITOR INFORMATION The **Bury St. Edmunds Tourist Information Centre,** 6 Angel Hill (☎ **01284/764667**), is open November through Easter, Monday to Friday from 10am to 4pm and Saturday from 10am to 1pm; Easter through October, Monday to Saturday from 9:30am to 5:30pm and Sunday from 10am to 3pm.

SPECIAL EVENTS The **Bury St. Edmunds Festival** (☎ **01284/757099**) is held annually in May. The 17-day festival includes performances from leading ensembles and soloists ranging from classical to contemporary. Exhibitions, talks, walks, films, plays, and a fireworks display are integral parts of this internationally renowned festival.

EXPLORING THE TOWN

For a bit of easy and always interesting sightseeing, take one of the hour-long **guided walks** around Bury St. Edmunds. Choices include a Blue Badge Guided Tour and theme tours with Bury's historical monk, Brother Jocelin, or gravedigger William Hunter. Tours leave from the Tourist Information Centre (see above) where tickets can also be purchased.

The normally quiet town center becomes a hub of hustle and bustle on Wednesday and Saturday mornings when the **market** arrives. Weather permitting, hours are approximately 9am to 4pm. You'll find a pleasing mix of family run businesses and High Street names for shopping in and around the town and its pedestrian zones.

The Bury St. Edmunds Art Gallery, Market Cross, Cornhill (☎ **01284/762081**), hosts eight fine art and craft exhibitions each year and serves as a venue for local craftspeople and artists. A craft shop located in the gallery sells ceramics, prints, books, glassware, and jewelry. **The Parsley Pot,** 17 Abbeygate St. (☎ **01284/760289**), sells an assortment of gift items, including china and porcelain.

Several parks are located just outside of town. Seven miles north of Bury is the 125-acre **West Stow Country Park** with heathland, woodland, and a large lake bordered by the River Lark. This diverse area is perfect for the proverbial "walk in the park" with a rustic twist. **The West Stow Anglo-Saxon Village** (☎ **01284/728718**) is part of West Stow Country Park. This reconstructed village is built on the excavated site of an ancient Anglo-Saxon village, and period reenactments take place throughout the year. The park is open October to March daily from 9am to 5pm and April to October daily from 8am to 8pm. Admission is free. The village is open year-round from 10am to 5pm. Admission is £4.50 ($7.65) for adults and £3.50 ($5.95) for children. Family tickets are also available for £13 ($22.10).

Nowton Park (☎ **01284/763666**) is 1½ miles outside of Bury on 200 acres of Suffolk countryside. Landscaped a century ago, the park is typically Victorian and has many country-estate features. In the springtime, walk the avenue of lime trees with its masses of bright yellow daffodils. Marked walking paths snake through the park. Depending on the path, walks take between 20 and 75 minutes. It's open daily from 8:30am to dusk; free admission.

The Abbey. Samson's Tower. ☎ **01284/763110** for Visitor Centre. Free admission. Visitor Centre Easter through Oct daily 10am–5pm. Abbey Gardens and ruins year-round Mon–Sat 7:30am to half hour before dusk, Sun 9am to half hour before dusk.

The **Visitor Centre** is a good starting point for a visit to the entire Abbey precinct. (The Abbey itself is in ruins today and sits in the middle of the Abbey Gardens.) The Visitor Centre is housed in the west front of the Abbey of St. Edmunds's remains and uses a clever series of displays to give the visitor an idea of what life was like in this powerful abbey from its beginnings in 1020 to its dissolution in 1539.

Moving on to the formal **Abbey Gardens** with its flower beds and well-kept lawns, you'll see the ruins of the abbey. When the long shadows cast themselves across the weathered ruins, the landscape becomes surreal and looks much like a Dalí masterpiece. In reality, the abandoned abbey was used as a quarry for the townspeople down through the ages, and that is the reason for the extremely worn condition and melted character of the ruins. A rather interesting tour of the Abbey Gardens is led by medieval monk Brother Jocelin, bookable through the Tourist Information Centre at ☎ **01284/764667.**

Moyse's Hall Museum. Cornhill. ☎ **01284/757488.** Admission £1.60 ($2.70) adults, £1 ($1.70) seniors, children; free admission 4–5pm. Mon–Sat 10am–5pm, Sun 2–5pm.

Located in one of England's last surviving Norman stone houses, this museum has nationally important archaeological collections and local artifacts.

Manor House Museum. Honey Hill. ☎ **01284/757072.** Admission £2.50 ($4.25) adults, £1.50 ($2.55) seniors and children, £7.50 ($12.75) family ticket. Sun–Wed noon–5pm.

Housed in a restored Georgian mansion, this museum uses touch-screen computers to help interpret its displays of fine and decorative art.

The Cathedral Church of St. James. Angel Hill. ☎ **01284/754933.** Free admission. Daily 8:30am–dusk.

This 16th-century church has a magnificent font, beautiful stained-glass windows, and a display of 1,000 embroidered kneelers.

St. Mary's Church. Crown St. ☎ **01284/706668.** Call the church to arrange a tour. Free admission.

St. Mary's was built on the site of a Norman church in 1427. Note its impressive roof and nave. It is also where Henry VIII's sister, Mary Rose, is buried.

Ickworth House. 3 miles south of Bury at Horringer. ☎ **01284/735270.** Admission £5.50 ($9.35) adults, £2.40 ($4.10) children, £9.50 ($16.15) family ticket. Easter–Oct Tues–Wed and Fri–Sun 1–5pm.

This National Trust property was built in 1795 and contains an impressive rotunda, state rooms, and art collections of silver and paintings. An Italian garden surrounds the house, and all is set in a peaceful, landscaped park.

WHERE TO STAY

Angel Hotel. Angel Hill, Bury St. Edmunds, Suffolk IP33 1LT. ☎ **01284/753926.** Fax 01284/750092. www.theangel.co.uk. E-mail: sales@theangel.co.uk. 43 units. TV TEL. £89–£133 ($151.30–$226.10) double; £115–£150 ($195.50–$255) suite. AE, DC, MC, V.

Originally a 1452 coaching inn, the hotel received an exterior face-lift during the Georgian era, and its front facade is now completely covered with lush ivy. The location is ideal for sightseeing and shopping, as both are only a short walk from the hotel. Look out the window of any of the front-facing rooms, and you'll see the romantic Abbey Gardens. Each of the rooms is individually decorated with freestanding furnishings and some have four-poster beds. Room 36 is one of the more popular rooms with its four-poster bed, bold peach-colored walls (a shade you can almost taste), and armchairs. You'll find beverage makers in all the rooms, plus king or twin beds. Ten of the bedrooms have been recently refurbished. Bathrooms are compact but well maintained, with adequate shelf space and a hair dryer.

The hotel runs two restaurants: The Vault, located in the cellar, serves an informal lunch and dinner, and the more formal Abbeygate Restaurant serves imaginative English and continental dishes.

Butterfly Hotel. Symonds Rd., Bury St. Edmunds, Suffolk IP32 7BW. ☎ **01284/760884.** Fax 01284/755476. www.butterflyhotels.co.uk. E-mail: reception@butterflyhotels.co.uk. 66 units. TV TEL. Sun–Thurs £67.50 ($114.75) double, Fri–Sat £49.50 ($84.15) double; £95 ($161.50) suite. AE, DC, MC, V.

This standard, rather ordinary hotel, built relatively recently, is located 10 minutes from Bury on the A14 motorway. The grassy grounds are landscaped, and there is a sunny patio for dining alfresco. All the rooms are decorated in the same bland style with landscape pictures and an armchair or two, along with an accompanying desk. Because of the proximity to the motorway, the windows are double-paned to reduce traffic noise and to help guests get a better night's rest. Beverage-making equipment is provided in every room. Often mid-size, the rooms are well laid out, each containing a king or twins. Ten rooms are rented to nonsmokers. The compact bathrooms come with hair dryers. The Walt, the hotel's restaurant, serves three standard meals a day.

Ravenwood Hall. Rougham, Bury St. Edmunds, Suffolk IP30 9JA. ☎ **01359/270345.** Fax 01359/270788. 14 units. TV TEL. £87–£121 ($147.90–$205.70) double. Rates include breakfast. AE, DC, MC, V.

Located 3 miles outside of town, this Tudor hall dates from the 1500s, and is set in a very peaceful 7-acre park with well-manicured lawns, gardens, and forest. There are also tennis courts and an outdoor swimming pool. This rustic country place has a magnificent fireplace that is the focal point of the restaurant, where diners enjoy an à la carte menu. The individually decorated rooms are full of atmosphere and have tea- and coffeemakers. If you're a fancier of fine beds, check out the Oak Room with its four-poster bed and the bridal suite with its brass bed. Some of the rooms are in the main house, while others are in a converted stable mews, but all are equally comfortable. Bathrooms are exceedingly fine here, with adequate shelf space and a hair dryer. There is also an informal, somewhat cozy bar that offers snacks and drinks.

WHERE TO DINE

Maison Bleve at Mortimer's. 31 Churchgate St. ☎ **01284/760623.** Dinner reservations recommended. Main courses £8.50–£14.50 ($14.45–$24.65); fixed-price lunch £7.50–£14.95 ($12.75–$25.40); 3-course fixed-price dinner £18.50 ($31.45). AE, MC, V. Mon–Sat noon–2:30pm and 6:30–9:30pm (open until 10pm on Friday and Saturday). SEAFOOD.

This restaurant has quickly become the town's best, although a change in management may affect things here during the lifetime of this edition. The open and airy dining room has a nautical theme, in keeping with the fresh seafood that's served here. The same menu is available for both lunch and dinner and changes regularly with the season. Favorites include fillet of sea bass in a fennel sauce; boneless wing of skate with bacon, onion, and mushrooms; and lobster in a cream and brandy sauce. All main courses are presented with new potatoes.

BURY ST. EDMUNDS AFTER DARK

Throughout the centuries, Bury has enjoyed a well-deserved reputation as a small center of arts and entertainment. **The Theatre Royal,** Westgate Street (☎ **01284/769505**), is the oldest purpose-built theater in England. Its Georgian building has been lovingly and richly restored to its original grandeur. Programs include opera, dance, music, and drama from the best touring companies. Tickets are £5 to £15 ($8.50 to $25.50) and can be purchased at the box office (☎ **01284/769505**).

Stop by the 17th-century pub **Dog and Partridge,** 29 Crown St. (☎ **01284/764792**), and see where the bar scenes from the BBC hit series *Lovejoy* were filmed while you sample one of the region's Greene King Ales. Also try wiggling your way into the **Nutshell,** corner of The Traverse and Abbeygate Street (☎ **01284/764867**). This pub has been notoriously dubbed the smallest pub in all of England and is a favorite tourist stop. **The Masons Arms,** 14 Whiting St. (☎ **01284/753955**), features more of a family atmosphere and welcomes children. Home-cooked food is served along with a standard selection of ales. There's a patio garden in use in summer.

A SIDE TRIP TO SUDBURY

Twenty miles south of Bury St. Edmunds along A134 is Sudbury, a town that has prospered through the ages thanks to its sheep (the wool industry) and prime location along the banks of the River Stour. A handful of medieval half-timbered buildings and Georgian homes attest to the town's ripe old age. Its most famous native son is Thomas Gainsborough, who was born in 1727 and went on to become one of England's most well-liked painters.

His birthplace, **Gainsborough's House,** 46 Gainsborough St. (☎ **01787/372958**), is a museum and arts center that has many of his works of art on display. Visitors will notice that several different architectural styles make up the house, and there is a walled garden in back worth seeing. It's open mid-April to October, Tuesday through Saturday from 10am to 5pm and Sunday from 2 to 4pm; November to mid-April, Tuesday through Saturday from 10am to 4pm and Sunday from 2 to 4pm. Admission is £3 ($5.10) during the year, but it is free during the month of December.

WHERE TO STAY

The Mill Hotel. Walnuttree Lane, Sudbury CO10 6BD. ☎ **01787/375544.** Fax 01787/373027. 56 units. TV TEL. £60–£99 ($102–$168.30) double. AE, DC, MC, V.

As its name implies, this hotel is located in the shell of an old mill. In fact, the River Stour, which runs under the hotel, still turns the mill's 16-foot water wheel, now encased in glass and on display in the hotel's restaurant and bar. Rooms vary in size; some have heavy oak beams and massive columns, but all are outfitted with comfortable furnishings, including good king or twin beds. Bathrooms are compact but have generous shelf space and a hair dryer. You may even be able to watch the local cows occasionally pass by the water's edge, as many of the rooms have a river or millpond view. The restaurant and bar areas are welcoming with their polished hardwood floors, stylish Oriental carpets, and antiques.

WHERE TO DINE

Brasserie 47. 47 Gainsborough St. ☎ **01787/374298.** Reservations recommended for dinner. 2-course fixed-price menu £12.50 ($21.25), 3-course fixed-price menu £15.50 ($26.35). AE, DC, MC, V. Tues–Sat noon–2pm and 7–10pm. Closed 5 days during Christmas. INTERNATIONAL.

Right next door to the Gainsborough House, this friendly brasserie, full of pine furnishings and lots of earthy terra-cotta and navy accents, is ideal for lunch or dinner. In fact, the same menu is used for both, along with a host of specials that change daily. Popular main dishes include the pan-fried scallop of salmon with saffron and a white-wine sauce; grilled rib-eye steak with tarragon sauce; and lamb steak in rosemary sauce served with couscous and a leafy salad. Homemade ice creams and exotic sorbets, such as orange caramel and toasted poppy seed, open the dessert selection. But the hot-syrup sponge cake with vanilla custard sauce is hands-down the most deservedly popular dessert.

5 Lavenham

66 miles NE of London; 35 miles SE of Cambridge

Once a great wool center, Lavenham is the classic Suffolk village, beautifully preserved today. It features a number of half-timbered Tudor houses washed in the characteristic Suffolk pink. The town's wool-trading profits are apparent in its guildhall, on the triangular main "square." Inside are exhibits on Lavenham's textile industry, showing how yarn was spun, then "dyed in the wool" with woad (the plant used by the ancient Picts to dye themselves blue), and following on to the weaving process. There is also a display showing how half-timbered houses were constructed.

The Church of St. Peter and St. Paul, at the edge of Lavenham, has interesting carvings on the misericords and the chancel screen, as well as ornate tombs. This is one of the "wool churches" of the area, built by pious merchants in the Perpendicular style with a landmark tower.

ESSENTIALS

GETTING THERE Trains depart London's North Street Station at least once an hour, sometimes more often, for Colchester, where they connect quickly to the town of Sudbury. For schedules and information, call ☎ **0345/484950.** From Sudbury, Beeston's Coaches, Ltd., has about nine daily buses making the short run to Lavenham. The trip from London takes between 2 and 2$^1/_2$ hours.

National Express buses depart from London's Victoria Coach Station, carrying passengers to the town of Bury St. Edmunds, some 9 miles from Lavenham. For schedules and information, call ☎ **0990/808080.** From Bury St. Edmunds, you can take another bus onto Lavenham. The trip takes about 2$^1/_2$ hours.

If you're driving from Bury St. Edmunds, continue south on A134 toward Long Melford, but cut southeast to Lavenham at the junction with A1141.

VISITOR INFORMATION The **Tourist Information Centre** is on Lady Street (☎ **01787/248207**) and is open Monday to Saturday April through September from 10am to 4:45pm; and Monday to Saturday October through March from 10am to 2:45pm.

SHOPPING & TEATIME

Shoppers from all over East Anglia flock to **Timbers,** 13 High St. (☎ **01787/247218**), a center housing 24 dealers specializing in antiques and collectibles, including books, toys, military artifacts, glass, porcelain, and much more. It's open Thursday through Tuesday.

After strolling the medieval streets of Lavenham, stop by **Tickle Manor Tea Rooms,** High Street (☎ **01787/248438**). This two-story timber frame home was built by the son of a priest in 1530 and provides an ample dose of history for patrons to absorb while sipping any one of a selection of teas that are served with English breakfast, sandwiches, or a piece of cake.

WHERE TO STAY

The Great House (see "Where to Dine," below) also rents rooms.

✪ **The Swan.** High St., Lavenham, Sudbury, Suffolk CO10 9QA. ☎ **800/225-5843** in the U.S. and Canada, or 01787/247477. Fax 01787/248286. 50 units. MINIBAR TV TEL. £120–£145 ($204–$246.50) double; £154–£175 ($261.80–$297.50) suite. AE, DC, MC, V.

This lavishly timbered inn, the best accommodation in Suffolk, is one of the oldest and best-preserved buildings in a relatively unspoiled village. It's been so successful that it's expanded into an adjoining ancient wool hall, which provides a high-ceilinged guest house and raftered, second-story bedrooms opening onto a tiny cloistered garden. The bedrooms vary in size, according to the eccentricities of the architecture. Most have beamed ceilings and a mixture of traditional pieces that blend well with the old. The more expensive rooms feature four-poster beds. Fifteen accommodations are rented to nonsmokers. Bathrooms are immaculately maintained, each with a hair dryer. There are nearly enough lounges for guests to try a different one every night of the week.

Dining/Diversions: The Garden Bar opens onto yet another garden, with old stone walls and flower beds. Londoners often visit on weekends for dinner and chamber-music concerts, which are performed in October, December, and March. Meals in the two-story-high dining room, where you sit on leather-and-oak chairs with brass studs, have their own drama. Even if you're not spending the night, you can sample the three-course lunch or an evening table d'hôte dinner. During World War II, Allied pilots made the Swan their second home and carved their signatures into the bar, in a longish room with a timbered ceiling and a fine weapons collection.

WHERE TO DINE

✪ **The Great House.** Market Place. ☎ **01787/247431.** Fax 01787/248007. Reservations recommended. Snacks £3.25–£9.95 ($5.50–$16.90); fixed-price meals lunch £15.95 ($27.10) Tues–Fri, £19.95 ($33.90) Sunday at lunch and at dinner Tues–Fri and Sun. AE, MC, V. Tues–Sun noon–2:30pm and 7–9:30pm. FRENCH.

With its Georgian facade and location near the marketplace, The Great House is the town's finest place to dine, a quintessentially French hotel in a beautiful English town. The interior is also attractively decorated, with Laura Ashley prints, an inglenook fireplace, and old oak beams. Assisted by his wife, Martine, owner Régis Crépy does double duty as the *chef de cuisine.* He is an inventive, quixotic cook, as reflected by such dishes as roasted magret of duck served with wild mushrooms and a green peppercorn sauce; roasted rack of English lamb served with sautéed garnish Provençale, fried garlic and an eggplant and coriander coulis; and stuffed fillet of sea bass perfumed with liquorice and served with aromatic rice.

The house also rents five elegantly decorated suites for £42 to £120 ($71.40 to $204) double, including English breakfast and dinner. The units have TVs, phones, and private bathrooms or showers.

6 Two Stately Homes in Long Melford

61 miles NE of London; 34 miles SE of Cambridge

Long Melford has been famous since the days of the early cloth makers. Like Lavenham, it attained prestige and importance during the Middle Ages. Of the old buildings remaining, the village church is often called "one of the glories of the shire." Along its 3-mile-long High Street—said to boast the highest concentration of antiques shops in Europe—are many private homes erected by wealthy wool merchants of yore. Of special interest are Long Melford's two stately homes, Melford Hall and Kentwell Hall.

ESSENTIALS

GETTING THERE Trains run from London's Liverpool Street Station toward Ipswich and on to Marks Tey. Call ☎ **0345/484950** for information and schedules.

Here, you can take a shuttle train going back and forth between that junction and Sudbury. From the town of Sudbury, it's a 3-mile taxi ride to Long Melford.

From Cambridge, take a Cambus Bus Company coach to Bury St. Edmunds, then change for the final ride into Long Melford. These buses run about once an hour throughout the day and early evening.

If driving from Newmarket, continue east on A45 to Bury St. Edmunds, but cut south on A134 (toward Sudbury) to Long Melford.

VISITOR INFORMATION There is a **Tourist Information** office in the Town Hall, Sudbury (☎ **01787/881320**), that's open Monday through Saturday from 10am to 4:45pm during summer, and Monday through Saturday 10am to 2:45pm during winter.

BEATRIX POTTER'S ANCESTRAL HOME & A TUDOR MANSION

Melford Hall. Long Melford, Sudbury, Suffolk. ☎ **01787/880286.** Admission £4.20 ($7.15) adults, £2.10 ($3.55) children. May–Sept Wed–Sun and bank holiday Mon 2–5:30pm; Apr and Oct Sat–Sun and bank holiday Mon 2–5:30pm.

This is the ancestral home of Beatrix Potter, who often visited. Jemima PuddleDuck still occupies a chair in one of the bedrooms upstairs, and some of her other figures are on display. The house, built between 1554 and 1578, has paintings, fine furniture, and Chinese porcelain. The gardens alone make a visit here worthwhile.

Kentwell Hall. On the A134 between Sudbury and Bury St. Edmunds. ☎ **01787/310207.** Open Mar–Sept. Times and admission costs vary according to the event. It is advisable to call first. The entrance is north of the green in Long Melford on the west side of A134, about 1/2 mile north of Melford Hall.

At the end of an avenue of linden trees, the redbrick Tudor mansion called Kentwell Hall, surrounded by a broad moat, has been restored by its owners, Mr. and Mrs. Patrick Phillips. A 15th-century moat house, interconnecting gardens, a brick-paved maze, and a costume display are of interest. There are also rare-breed farm animals here. Two gatehouses are constructed in 16th-century style. The hall hosts regular re-creations of Tudor domestic life, including the well-known annual events for the weeks of June 16 to July 7 when admission prices tend to escalate slightly.

WHERE TO STAY

✪ **Bull Hotel.** Hall St., Long Melford, Sudbury, Suffolk CO10 9JG. ☎ **01787/378494.** Fax 01787/880307. 25 units. TV TEL. £100–£110 ($170–$187) double; £120–£130 ($204–$221) suite. Leisure breaks (2-night minimum) £75 ($127.50) per person double, including half board. AE, DC, MC, V.

Here is an opportunity to experience life in one of the great old inns of East Anglia. Built by a wool merchant in 1540, this is Long Melford's finest hotel and its best-preserved building, with lots of improvements and modernizations added over the years. The rooms here are a mix of the old and the new. The interior and exterior of the hotel have been refurbished, and the beds are usually a king or twins. Eleven rooms are reserved for nonsmokers. Bathrooms are well kept, each with a hair dryer. A medieval weavers' gallery and an open hearth with Elizabethan brickwork have been incorporated into the hotel's design.

Dining: The Cordell Restaurant is the outstanding part of the Bull, with its high-beamed ceilings, trestle tables, and handmade chairs, as well as a 10-foot fireplace. The English and continental cuisines are worth a stop even if you're not staying here. Menu choices are likely to include poached filet of plaice with white-wine-and-mushroom sauce.

The Countrymen. The Green, Long Melford, Suffolk CO10 9DN. ☎ **01787/312356.** Fax 01787/374557. 9 units. TV TEL. £70–£90 ($119–$153) double; from £105 ($178.50) suite. Rates include English breakfast. AE, MC, V.

There has been some type of inn on this spot since the 1100s. Fourteenth-century documents mention it as the spot where drinks were dispensed to revolutionaries during one of the peasants' revolts. The present building dates from the early 1800s; it has been richly restored by its present owners. Although the Bull (see above) remains the most atmospheric choice here, the Countrymen overlooks one of the loveliest village greens in Suffolk. Each of the individually decorated bedrooms features tea- and coffeemakers. Bathrooms are first rate with good shelf space and a hair dryer.

An added bonus is the hotel's well-patronized Countrymen bistro, which offers lighter meals and a well-chosen wine list. Fixed-price meals are served at both lunch and dinner. Bar lunches are a simpler, cheaper option. Their special is pasta made fresh daily by chefs/owners Stephen and Janet Errington.

WHERE TO DINE

Chimneys. Hall St. ☎ **01787/379806.** Reservations recommended. Main courses £11.50–£18.50 ($19.55–$31.45). MC, V. Daily noon–2pm; Mon–Sat 7–9pm. BRITISH/ CONTINENTAL.

This is the most venerable restaurant in town, with a more refined cuisine than that served at Scutchers Bistro (see below). The building here was erected in the 16th century and retains its original dark-stained oaken beams and mellow brick walls in the dining room. A walled garden is in back. The menus offer a wide choice of foods, influenced by the best modern British cuisine trends. Begin with a warm salad of duck confit and orange, or a gratin of king prawns with chili and cheese. Main courses are equally sumptuous, such as baked fillet of Scottish salmon with a brioche and herb crust, or braised lamb shank with red onion and rosemary. For dessert, try the mango Bavarois set on a forest fruit puree. Chimneys also has one of the most extensive wine lists in town.

Scutchers Bistro. Westgate St. ☎ **01787/310200.** Reservations recommended. Main courses £7.95–£15 ($13.50–$25.50). AE, MC, V. Tues–Sat noon–2pm and 7–9:30pm. BRITISH.

This upscale bistro has earned favorable recommendations from many locals throughout Suffolk. The building was erected in stages between the 1600s and the 1800s and was named after the workers (scutchers) who, in olden days, rendered flax into linen. As The Scutchers Arms, it was a favorite pub—until the new owners painted its facade bright yellow and covered its heavily beamed interior with vivid Mediterranean colors. Menu choices change daily. Your meal might include sautéed tiger prawns with mushrooms, bacon, and garlic; steamed scallops with asparagus and lemon-flavored hollandaise; and a very English version of steamed fruit pudding with custard.

7 Dedham

63 miles NE of London; 8 miles NE of Colchester

Remember Constable's *Vale of Dedham?* The Vale of Dedham lies between the towns of Colchester and Ipswich in a wide valley through which runs the River Stour, the boundary between Essex and Suffolk. It's not only the link with Constable that has made this vale so popular. It is one of the most beautiful, unspoiled areas left in southeast England. In this little Essex village on the Stour River you're in the heart of Constable Country. Flatford Mill is only a mile farther down the river. The village, with its Tudor, Georgian, and Regency houses, is set in the midst of the water meadows of the Stour. Constable painted its church and tower. Dedham is right on the Essex-Suffolk border and makes a good center for exploring both North Essex and the Suffolk border country.

GETTING THERE

Trains depart every 20 minutes from London's Liverpool Street Station for the 50-minute ride to Colchester. For schedules and information, call ☎ **0345/484950.** From Colchester, it's possible to take a taxi from the railway station to the bus station, then board a bus run by the Eastern National Bus Company for the 5-mile trip to Dedham. (Buses leave about once an hour.) Most people take a taxi from Colchester directly to Dedham.

National Express buses depart from London's Victoria Coach Station for Colchester, where you have the choice of taking either another bus or a taxi to Dedham. For schedules and information, call ☎ **0990/808080.**

If you're driving from the London ring road, travel northeast on A12 to Colchester, turning off at East Bergholt onto a small secondary road leading east to Dedham.

VISITING THE PAINTERS' HOMES

Less than a mile from the village center is **The Sir Alfred Munnings Art Museum,** East Lane (☎ **01206/322127**), home of Sir Alfred Munnings, president of the Royal Academy from 1944 to 1949 and painter extraordinaire of racehorses and other animals. The house and studio, which have sketches and other works, are open from early May to early October, on Sunday, Wednesday, and bank holidays (plus Thurs and Sat during Aug) from 2 to 5pm. Admission is £3 ($5.10) for adults, 50p (85¢) for children.

The English landscape painter John Constable (1776–1837) was born at East Bergholt, directly north of Dedham. Near the village is **Flatford Mill,** East Bergholt (☎ **01206/298283**), subject of one of his most renowned works. The mill was given to the National Trust in 1943, and has since been leased to the Field Studies Council for use as a residential center. The center offers more than 170 short courses each year in all aspects of art and the environment. Fees are from £114 ($193.80) for a weekend (Sat and Sun) and from £325 ($552.50) for a full week. The fee includes accommodation, meals, and tuition. Write to Field Studies Council, Flatford Mill Field Centre, East Bergholt, Colchester CO7 6UL.

WHERE TO STAY

Dedham Hall/Fountain House Restaurant. Brook St., Dedham CO7 6AD. ☎ **01206/323027.** Fax 01206/323293. 16 units. TV. £65 ($107.25) double. Rates include English breakfast. MC, V.

A 3-minute walk east of the center of town, this well-managed hotel has flourished since its adoption by Jim and Wendy Sarton in 1991. Set on 5 acres of grazing land whose centerpiece is a pond favored by geese and wild swans, it consists of a 400-year-old brick-sided cottage linked to a 200-year-old home of stately proportions. The older section is reserved for the breakfast room, a bar, and a sitting room for residents of the six second-floor bedrooms. Each cozy room comes with tea makers, and a compact bathroom with a hair dryer. A cluster of three converted barns provides accommodations for many artists who congregate here several times throughout the year for painting seminars and art workshops.

Dining: Beneath beamed ceilings, you can enjoy a fixed-price dinner at the Fountain House Restaurant daily for £21.50 ($35.50). There's a wide selection of dishes with all-fresh ingredients and an abundance of natural flavors.

Maison Talbooth. Stratford Rd., Dedham, Colchester, Essex CO7 6HN. ☎ **01206/322367.** Fax 01206/322752. www.talbooth.com. E-mail: mtreception@talbooth.co.uk. 15 units. MINIBAR TV TEL. £155–£195 ($263.50–$331.50) double. Rates include continental breakfast. AE, DC, MC, V. Take Stratford Rd. 1/2 mile west of the town center.

This small and exclusive hotel is located in a handsomely restored Victorian country house on a bluff overlooking the river valley, with views that stretch as far as the medieval Church of Stratford St. Mary. Accommodations here consist of spacious suites distinctively furnished by one of England's best-known decorators. High-fashion colors abound, antiques are mixed discreetly with reproductions, and the original architectural beauty has been preserved. The sumptuous beds feature deluxe mattresses and fine linens. The luxurious bathrooms include a hair dryer. A super-luxury suite has a sunken bath and a draped bed, and each suite has its own theme. Fresh flowers, fruit, and a private bar are standard amenities in the suites. The restaurant, Le Talbooth, is award-winning (see below).

WHERE TO DINE

Le Talbooth. Gun Hill. ☎ **01206/323150.** Reservations recommended. Main courses £15.50–£20 ($26.35–$34); fixed-price lunch £16.50 ($28.05) for 2 courses and £19 ($32.30) for 3 courses; fixed-price dinner £22 ($37.40) for 2 courses and £27 ($45.90) for 3 courses. AE, DC, MC, V. Daily noon–2pm and 7–9:30pm. ENGLISH/FRENCH.

A hand-hewn, half-timbered weaver's house is the setting for this restaurant standing amid beautiful gardens on the banks of the River Stour. Le Talbooth was featured in Constable's *Vale of Dedham.* You descend a sloping driveway leading past flowering terraces. A well-mannered staff will usher you to a low-ceilinged bar for an aperitif.

Owner Gerald Milsom has brought a high standard of cooking to this rustically elegant place, where a well-chosen wine list complements the good food. An à la carte menu changes six times a year, and special dishes are altered daily, reflecting the best produce available at the market. You'll get off to a fine start with half a dozen native oysters from nearby Colchester. The velvety smooth parfait of foie gras and duck livers is hard to resist. Each night a different roast is featured, ranging from honey-coated ham to leg of lamb. Your main course, inevitably a delight, might be roast breast of guinea fowl with tarragon-scented sausage, shiitake mushrooms and broad beans in a creamy sauce.

8 Woodbridge & Aldeburgh

Woodbridge: 81 miles NE of London; 47 miles S of NorwichAldeburgh: 97 miles NE of London; 41 miles SE of Norwich

On the Deben River, the market town of Woodbridge is a yachting center. Its best-known, most famous resident was Edward FitzGerald, Victorian poet and translator of the "Rubaiyat of Omar Khayyam." Woodbridge is a good base for exploring the East Suffolk coastline, particularly the small resort of Aldeburgh, noted for its moot hall.

On the North Sea, 15 miles from Woodbridge, Aldeburgh is an exclusive resort, and it attracts many Dutch visitors, who make the sea-crossing via Harwich and Felixstowe, both major entry ports for traffic from the Continent. Aldeburgh dates from Roman times, and has long been known as a small port for North Sea fisheries. The Aldeburgh Festival, held every June, is the most important arts festival in East Anglia, and one of the best attended in England.

ESSENTIALS

GETTING THERE Woodbridge is on the rail line to Lowestoft from either Victoria Station or Liverpool Street Station in London. Get off two stops after Ipswich. For schedules and information, call ☎ **0345/484950.** The nearest rail station to Aldeburgh is on the same line, at Saxmundham, six stops after Ipswich. From Saxmundham, you can take a taxi or one of six buses that run the 6 miles to Aldeburgh during the day.

One **National Express** bus a day passes through Aldeburgh and Woodbridge on the way from London's Victoria Coach Station to Great Yarmouth. It stops at every country town and narrow lane along the way, so the trip to Aldeburgh takes a woeful 4½ hours. For schedules and information, call ☎ **0990/808080.** Many visitors reach both towns by Eastern County Bus Company's service from Ipswich. That company's no. 80/81 buses run frequently between Woodbridge and Aldeburgh.

If you're driving from London's ring road, take A12 northeast to Ipswich, then continue northeast on A12 to Woodbridge. To get to Aldeburgh, stay on A12 until you reach the junction with A1094, then head east to the North Sea.

VISITOR INFORMATION The **Tourist Information Centre** is at the Cinema, 51 High St., Aldeburgh (☎ **01728/453637**), and is open Easter through October, Monday to Saturday from 9am to 5:30pm and on Sunday from 9:30am to 5pm.

SPECIAL EVENTS Aldeburgh was the home of Benjamin Britten (1913–76), renowned composer of the operas *Peter Grimes* and *Billy Budd,* as well as many orchestral works. Many of his compositions were first performed at the ✪ **Aldeburgh Festival,** which he founded in 1946. The festival takes place in June, featuring internationally known performers. There are other concerts and events throughout the year. Write or call the tourist office for details. The Snape Maltings Concert Hall nearby is one of the more successful among the smaller British concert halls; it also houses the Britten-Pears School of Advanced Musical Studies, established in 1973.

SEEING THE SIGHTS IN ALDEBURGH

There are two local golf courses, one at Aldeburgh and another at Thorpeness, 2 miles away. A yacht club is situated on the River Alde, 9 miles from the river's mouth. There are also two bird sanctuaries nearby, Minsmere and Havergate Island. Managed by the Royal Society for the Protection of Birds, they are famous for their waterfowl.

Insider's tip: Seek out **Crag Path,** running along Aldeburgh's wild shore. It is unusually attractive, with its two lookout towers built early in the 19th century to keep watch for vessels putting down or needing pilots.

Constructed on a shelf of land at the sea level, the High Street runs parallel to the often-turbulent waterfront. A cliff face rises some 55 feet above the main street. A major attraction is the 16th-century **Moot Hall Museum,** Market Cross Place, Aldeburgh (☎ **01728/453295**). The hall dates from the time of Henry VIII, but its tall twin chimneys are later additions. The timber-frame structure displays old maps, prints, and Anglo-Saxon burial urns, as well as other items of historical interest. It is open July and August daily from 10:30am to 12:30pm and 2:30 to 5pm. It is also open Easter to May Saturday and Sunday from 2:30 to 5pm, and in June, September, and October daily from 2:30 to 5pm. Admission is 50p (85¢) for adults and free for children.

Aldeburgh is also the site of the nation's northernmost martello tower, erected to protect the coast from a feared invasion by Napoléon.

WHERE TO STAY & DINE

NEAR WOODBRIDGE

✪ **Seckford Hall.** On A12 (1½ miles from the Woodbridge rail station), Woodbridge, Suffolk IP13 6NU. ☎ **01394/385678.** Fax 01394/380610. www.seckford.co.uk. E-mail: reception@seckford.co.uk. 32 units. TV TEL. £165 ($280.50) double; £140–£165 ($238–$280.50) suite. Rates include English breakfast. AE, DC, MC, V.

This ivy-covered estate's pure Tudor, crow-stepped gables, mullioned windows, and ornate chimneys capture the spirit of the days of Henry VIII and his strong-willed daughter Elizabeth (the latter may have held court here). Today, it provides some of the finest accommodations in Suffolk, rivaling those at The Swan in Lavenham (see review, above). You enter through a heavy, studded Tudor door into a flagstone hallway with antiques. The butler will show you to your bedroom. Many rooms have four-poster beds, one of them a monumental 1587 specimen. Bedrooms are statements in luxury and elegance, each with the most comfortable beds. Bathrooms are lavish and include a hair dryer.

If you arrive before sundown, you may want to stroll through the 34-acre gardens, which include a rose garden, herbaceous borders, and greenhouses. At the bottom of the garden is an ornamental lake, complete with weeping willows and paddling ducks.

Dining: At 4pm you can enjoy a complete tea in the Great Hall. Sip your brew slowly as you enjoy the atmosphere of heavy beams and a stone fireplace. Dinner will be announced by the butler. Good English meals are served in a setting of linen-fold paneling and Chippendale and Hepplewhite chairs. After-dinner coffee and brandy are featured in the Tudor Bar. (Call ahead for reservations if you're not staying here.)

Amenities: Heated indoor swimming pool, golf course, Jacuzzi, nearby squash and tennis courts.

IN ALDEBURGH

Brudenell Hotel. The Parade, Aldeburgh, Suffolk IP15 5BU. ☎ **01728/452071.** Fax 01728/454082. 47 units. TV TEL. £100–£110 ($170–$187) double. AE, DC, MC, V.

Located on the waterfront, this hotel was built at the beginning of the 20th century and has been remodeled and redecorated to achieve a pleasant interior. Many of the bedrooms face the sea, and each has a radio, tea- and coffeemakers, central heating, and comfortable beds. Rooms, ranging from small to mid-size, are attractively decorated, and eleven of them are rented to nonsmokers only. Bathrooms, although compact, are well equipped. The dining room, with an all-glass wall overlooking the coast, is an ideal spot for lunch; dinner is also served.

Wentworth Hotel. Wentworth Rd., Aldeburgh, Suffolk IP15 5BD. ☎ **01728/452312.** Fax 01728/454343. 38 units, 35 with bathroom. TV TEL. £127–£147 ($215.90–$249.90) double with bathroom. Rates include English breakfast and dinner. AE, DC, MC, V. Closed Dec 27–Jan 9.

A traditional country-house hotel with tall chimneys and gables, the Wentworth overlooks the sea. Built in the early 19th century as a private residence, it was converted into a hotel around 1900. The Pritt family has welcomed the world here since 1920, including Sir Benjamin Britten and the novelist E. M. Forster. In summer, tables are placed outside so guests can enjoy the sun, but in winter the open fires in the lounges, even the cozy bar, are a welcome sight. Many guest rooms, seven of which are reserved for nonsmokers, have panoramic views. There's a 19th-century building across the road from the main house that's a comfortable, seven-room annex. The standards here match those of the main house, though a few singles do not have bathrooms. Bedrooms usually feature twin or king beds, and each bathroom has a hair dryer.

Dining: Many come here just to enjoy the good food and wine. Bar lunches range from £7.50 ($12.75), with a table d'hôte dinner costing £12.95 ($22) Sunday to Friday, rising to £15.50 ($26.35) on Saturday.

9 Norwich

109 miles NE of London; 20 miles W of the North Sea

Norwich still holds to its claim as the capital of East Anglia. Despite its partial industrialization, it's a charming and historic city. In addition to its cathedral, it has more than 30 medieval parish churches built of flint. It's also the most important shopping center in East Anglia and has a lot to offer in the way of entertainment and interesting hotels, many of them in its narrow streets and alleyways. There also is a big open-air market, busy every weekday, where fruit, flowers, vegetables, and other goods are sold from stalls with colored canvas roofs.

ESSENTIALS

GETTING THERE There is hourly train service from London's Liverpool Street Station. The trip takes nearly 2 hours. For schedules and information, call ☎ **0345/484950.**

National Express buses depart London's Victoria Coach Station once each hour for the 3-hour ride. For schedules and information, call ☎ **0990/808080.**

If you're driving from London's ring road, head north toward Cambridge on the M11. Turn northeast at the junction with A11, which will take you all the way to Norwich.

GETTING AROUND Norwich and its surrounding countryside are best seen from the seat of a bicycle. **ABC Anglia Cycles,** 72-A Gloucester St. (☎ **01603/632467**), has the best selection. Bicycles are rented by the day or the week. Hours are Monday to Saturday from 9am to 6pm, and rates are £5 ($8.50) per day. There's a 20% discount for rentals over 7 days as well as a discount for card-carrying students.

VISITOR INFORMATION The **Tourist Information Centre** is located in the Guildhall in Gaol (jail), Norwich, near the marketplace in the center of town. ☎ **01603/666071.** Open May through September Monday to Saturday from 9:30am to 5pm; October through April Monday to Saturday from 9:30am to 4:30pm.

SEEING THE SIGHTS

Norwich Cathedral. 62 The Close. ☎ **01603/764385.** Free admission, but £3 ($5.10) donation suggested. Oct–May daily 7:30am–6pm; June–Sept daily 7am–7pm.

Dating from 1096, and principally of Norman design, Norwich Cathedral is noted primarily for its long nave with lofty columns. Built in the late Perpendicular style, the spire rises 315 feet; together with the keep of the castle, it forms a significant landmark on the Norwich skyline. More than 300 *bosses* (knoblike ornamental projections) on the ceiling depict biblical scenes. The impressive choir stalls with handsome misericords date from the 15th century. Edith Cavell, an English nurse executed by the Germans during World War I, is buried on the cathedral's Life's Green. The quadrangular cloisters, which date from the 13th century, are the largest monastic cloisters in England.

The cathedral visitor center includes a refreshment area and exhibition and film room with tape/slide shows about the cathedral. Inquire at the information desk about guided tours from June through September. A short walk from the cathedral will take you to Tombland, one of the most interesting old squares in Norwich.

✪ Sainsbury Centre for Visual Arts. University of East Anglia, Earlham Rd. ☎ **01603/456060.** Admission £2 ($3.40) adults, £1 ($1.70) children and students. Tues–Sun 11am–5pm. Bus nos. 3, 4, 12, 27, or 76 from Castle Meadow.

The center was the gift of Sir Robert and Lady Sainsbury, who, in 1973, contributed their private collection to the University of East Anglia, 3 miles west of Norwich on Earlham Road. Together with their son David, they gave an endowment to provide a building to house the collection. Designed by Foster Associates, the center was opened in 1978 and has since won many national and international awards. Features of the structure are its flexibility, allowing solid and glass areas to be interchanged, and the superb quality of light, which permits optimum viewing of works of art. Special exhibitions are often presented in the 1991 Crescent Wing extension. The Sainsbury Collection is one of the foremost in the country, including modern, ancient, classical, and ethnographic art. Its most prominent works are those by Francis Bacon, Alberto Giacometti, and Henry Moore.

The Mustard Shop Museum. 3 Bridewell Alley. ☎ **01603/627889.** Free admission. Mon–Sat 9:30am–5pm. Closed bank holidays.

The Victorian-style Mustard Shop displays a wealth of mahogany and shining brass. The standard of service and pace of life reflect the personality and courtesy of a bygone age. The Mustard Museum features exhibits on the history of the Colman Company and the making of mustard, including its properties and origins. There are old advertisements, as well as packages and "tins." You can browse in the shop, selecting whichever mustards you prefer, including the really hot English type. The shop also sells aprons, tea towels, pottery mustard pots, and mugs.

Second Air Division Memorial Library. 71 Ber St. ☎ **01603/215206.** Free admission. Mon–Fri 10am–5pm, Sat 9am–5pm.

A memorial room honoring the Second Air Division of the Eighth U.S. Army Air Force is part of the central library. The library staff will assist veterans who wish to visit their old air bases in East Anglia. At the library, you can find pertinent books, audiovisual materials, and records of the various bomber groups.

Blickling Hall. Blickling, near Aylsham. ☎ **01263/733084.** House and gardens, Tues–Sat £6.50 ($11.05) adults, £2.75 ($4.70) children. Gardens only, Tues–Sat £3.70 ($6.30) adults, £1.85 ($3.15) children. Late Mar–Oct Wed–Sun, bank holiday Mon, 1–4:30pm. (Garden, shop, restaurant, and Plant Centre open Thurs–Sun and bank holiday Mon 10:30am–5:30pm). Blickling Hall lies 14 miles north of the city of Norwich, 1 1/2 miles west of Aylsham on B1354; take A140 toward Cromer and follow the signs. Telephone before visiting to confirm opening arrangements.

Massive yew hedges bordering a long drive frame your first view of Blickling Hall, a great Jacobean house built in the early 17th century, one of the finest examples of such architecture in the country. The long gallery has an elaborate 17th-century ceiling, and the Peter the Great Room, decorated later, has a fine tapestry on the wall. The house is set in ornamental parkland with a formal garden and an orangery.

EXPLORING THE BROADS

Wroxham, 7 miles northeast of Norwich, is the best center for exploring the Broads, mostly shallow lagoons connected by streams. These are fun to explore by boat, of course, but some folks prefer to ride their bikes along the Broads.

To get to Wroxham from Norwich, take bus 51. The 30-minute ride costs £2 ($3.40) for a return ticket. Information about touring the Broads is provided by the **Hoveton Tourist Office,** Station Road (☎ **01603/782281**), open Easter through October daily from 9am to 1pm and 2 to 5pm. At this office you can get a list of boat-rental facilities.

If you don't want to handle your own boat, you can take an organized tour. The best ones are offered by **Broads Tours,** near the Wroxham bridge (☎ **01603/782207**). Their cruises last 1½ to 3½ hours. In summer, most departures are at either 11:30am or 2:30pm. The cost ranges from £4.60 to £6.25 ($7.80 to $10.65) for adults, and £3.40 to £5 ($5.80 to $8.50) for children 5 to 15 years.

SHOPPING

For the best in antiques, books, and crafts, shoppers can search out the historic lanes and alleys of the town center.

Norwich Antiques Centre, 14 Tombland (☎ **01603/619129**), is a three-floor house opposite the cathedral where 60-plus dealers set up shop. The selection is wide and varied and includes everything from small collectibles to antique furniture. There's also a small coffee shop in the house.

Right next to the Antiques Centre, **James and Ann Tillett,** 12–13 Tombland (☎ **01603/624914**), have a marvelous shop specializing in antique silver, barometers, and new as well as antique jewelry.

St. Michael-at-Plea, Bank Plain (☎ **01603/618989**), calls a 13th-century church home. The church's stained-glass windows were stolen by Henry VIII. Here, 30 dealers sell toys, books, linens, ceramics, and furniture, among other things. Browsers can get snacks, sandwiches, and coffee at the small on-site restaurant.

For book fanciers, **Peter Crowe,** 75 Upper St. Giles St. (☎ **01603/624800**), specializes in 17th- and 18th-century scholarly books, well-bound and illustrated 19th-century books, general secondhand books, and modern first editions.

The **Black Horse Bookshop,** 8–10 Wensum St. (☎ **01603/626871**), rates itself the best general bookstore in the city, but its specialty is fine art tomes. This store is also the official agency for British government publications.

If you're into dolls, don't miss the **Elm Hill Craft Shop,** 2 Elm Hill (☎ **01603/621076**), with its custom-made dollhouses and furnishings, plus traditional children's toys, books, and children's jewelry.

WHERE TO STAY

EXPENSIVE

Sprowston Manor Hotel. Sprowston Park, Wroxham Rd., Norwich, Norfolk NR7 8RP. ☎ **01603/410871.** Fax 01603/423911. 94 units. MINIBAR TV TEL. £145 ($246.50) double; £165–£200 ($280.50–$340) suite. Children under 15 stay free in parents' room. Rates include English breakfast. AE, DC, MC, V.

Norfolk's premier hotel had a long and illustrious history as a private home before it became a hotel in the 1970s. Built in 1559 by a Protestant family prominent in the civil war of the 1640s, it was eventually sold to the lord mayor of Norwich in the late 1800s. It wasn't until 1991, however, that a comprehensive redevelopment added 87 new bedrooms and leisure and conference facilities.

The hotel lies in 10 acres of parkland surrounded by the 18-hole Sprowston Park Golf Course. Elegance and informality are its hallmarks. The bedrooms are spacious, quiet, and filled with stylish furniture; some rooms have four-posters. Rooms come in various styles, and all have wonderful views. Bathrooms are of generous size.

Dining: Some of Norfolk's best cuisine is served here, either in The Manor Restaurant, restored with ancient mahogany reed columns, oil paintings, and crystal chandeliers, or else in The Orangery, draped with Gothic arched windows, a wall fountain, and ferns.

Amenities: There's an indoor swimming pool, spa bath, sauna, steam room, beauty salon, gym and solarium, even a guest laundry room. The **La Fontana Health & Beauty Spa** (☎ **01603/788788**) is also located at the Sprowston Hotel and is resplendent with palms and stone balustrades. At the spa, you can balance your mind and your body with a wide range of therapeutic spa treatments. La Fontana also offers a variety of packages.

Moderate

Maid's Head Hotel. Palace St., Tombland, Norwich, Norfolk NR3 1LB. ☎ **01603/209955.** Fax 01603/613688. 84 units. TV TEL. £105 ($178.50) double; £145 ($246.50) suite. AE, DC, MC, V.

In business since 1272, the Maid's Head claims to be the oldest continuously operated hotel in the United Kingdom. Located next to Norwich Cathedral in the oldest part of the city, it has Elizabethan and Georgian architectural styles. The Georgian section has a prim white entry and small-paned windows. Many of the bedrooms, which range from small to midsize, have oak beams evocative of the hotel's earlier days. Each is supplied with bowls of fresh fruit and a complimentary newspaper. Forty bedrooms are rented to nonsmokers. Bathrooms are well maintained. Traditional services such as shoe cleaning, breakfast in bed, and afternoon cream teas are offered. The four-poster Queen Elizabeth I Suite (where the Tudor monarch allegedly once slept) is much sought after.

Meals are served in an indoor/outdoor restaurant called the Courtyard Restaurant. Here, lunch, tea, coffee, and sandwiches are served every day to nonresidents from 9am to 5:30pm. Dinner is a more elaborate fare.

The Swallow Nelson Hotel. 121 Prince of Wales Rd., Norwich, NR1 1DX. ☎ **01603/760260.** Fax 01603/620008. www.swallowhotels.com. E-mail: info@swallowhotels.com. 132 units. TV TEL. £105 ($178.50) double; £124 ($210.80) suite. Rates include breakfast. AE, DC, MC, V.

Located by the water near Thorpe Station and Foundry Bridge, this four-story hotel has the best modern amenities and facilities in town, although it lacks the character and atmosphere of Maid's Head (see above). Each of the bedrooms provides a view of either the river or a pleasant courtyard. All the bedrooms are well furnished, but some are a bit more spacious than others. Four-poster rooms are available, but each has king or twins, with firm mattresses. Bathrooms are excellent.

The Quarterdeck restaurant offers fast, cheerful service and a choice of dishes such as fish and chips or beef-and-beer casserole with mushrooms and noodles. It's open daily for coffee and drinks, lunch, and informal dinners. There's also the more formal Trafalgar dining room. Facilities include a swimming pool, sauna, gym, and beauty salon.

Inexpensive

Pearl Continental Hotel. 116 Thorpe Rd., Norwich, Norfolk NR1 1RU. ☎ **01603/620302.** Fax 01603/761706. 45 units. TV TEL. Sun–Thurs £69 ($117.30) double, Fri–Sat £70 ($119) double. Weekend rates include English breakfast. AE, DC, MC, V. Take Thorpe Rd. 1/2 mile east of city center.

This hotel was originally constructed in the 18th century as a residence for the local lord mayor. The refurbished bedrooms are situated in the main building, as well as in two semidetached cottages. The cottages have bay windows and wooden beams, as well as a private garden. Most bedrooms are midsize, each with a comfortable bed, plus a bathroom with a shower stall.

The reception area's chandeliers light the way to the restaurant, where fixed-price lunches and dinners for £14.95 ($25.40) are served. Meals get off to a promising start with appetizers such as a perfectly prepared terrine of peppers and tomato with baby fennels. Main dish temptations include the likes of roast silverside of beef with Provençal sauce. A special delight is the breast, foie gras, and leg of a duck with the perfect accompaniments of buttered lentils and a red-wine sauce.

Post House Norwich Hotel. Ipswich Rd., Norwich, Norfolk NR4 6EP. ☎ **01603/456431.** Fax 01603/506400. 116 units. MINIBAR TV TEL. Sun–Thurs £70 ($119) double, Fri–Sat £65 ($110.50) double. AE, DC, MC, V. Take A140 (Ipswich Rd.) 2 miles from city center and 1 mile from A11 (London Rd.).

Situated on a sloping hillside about 2 miles from the city center, this redbrick building offers comfortably contemporary accommodations for business travelers and visitors. Although uninspired, it's a good, clean, and safe haven. Many of the bedrooms feature sitting areas with sofas and armchairs. Rooms range from small to mid-size, but each is well appointed. The small bathrooms have a shower stall and adequate shelf space. On the premises is Seasons Bar and Grill, as well as a fitness center with an indoor pool, gym, Jacuzzi and sauna.

WHERE TO DINE

✪ **Adlard's.** 79 Upper St. Giles St. ☎ **01603/633522.** Fax 01603/617733. Lunch main course £12 ($20.40); 3-course dinner £33 ($56.10), 4-course dinner £36 ($61.20). MC, V. Tues–Sat 12:30–1:45pm; Mon–Sat 7:30–10:30pm. MODERN BRITISH.

Chef/proprietor David Adlard and his head chef Aiden Byrne are clearly the culinary stars of Norwich. This stylish dining room has a clean crisp decor of green and white, with candlelit tables and a collection of paintings. David sees to it that service is correct in every way but also relaxed enough to make diners comfortable. The chef specializes in modern British cookery, bringing his own interpretation to every dish. These might include cannelloni stuffed with ratatouille and tomato coulis, or breast of duck with confit of cabbage and wild mushroom.

Brasted's. 8–10 St. Andrews Hill. ☎ **01508/491112.** Reservations required. Main courses £11.50–£18.50 ($19.55–$31.45). AE, DC, MC, V. Mon–Fri noon–2pm; Mon–Sat 7–10pm. ENGLISH/FRENCH.

Within an easy stroll of both the cathedral and the castle, Brasted's is housed in a lovely home with a rather flamboyant interior. Come here to sample the savory cooking of Adrian Coarke, the chef who replaced the restaurant's namesake but who possesses an equal mastery of cooking techniques and innovations. He has a special skill with soufflés. Other dishes, including roast Norfolk pheasant, vegetarian dishes, and desserts, seem equally well prepared.

Greens Seafood Restaurant. 82 Upper St. Giles St. ☎ **01603/623733.** Reservations recommended. Main courses £12.50–£14.80 ($21.25–$25.15); set-price lunches £13–£16 ($22.10–$27.20). MC, V. Tues–Fri 12:15–2pm; Tues–Sat 7–10pm. Closed Christmas, Boxing Day, and New Year's Day. SEAFOOD.

Owner-chef Dennis Crompton's restaurant is painted green inside in honor of its name. Surrounded by sepia-toned engravings of the seafaring life, you'll enjoy the best and freshest fish in the region. Menu choices include both intricate and complicated preparations of fresh seafood influenced by classic European traditions, as well as a wide selection of less complicated grilled fish served with a variety of sauces. There's also a "classic menu" including the likes of pan-roasted fillet of turbot on parsley and garlic mashed potatoes with saffron sauce. A live pianist provides music for about half of each dinner hour from Thursday to Saturday.

The Royal Residence of Sandringham

Some 110 miles northeast of London, 7,000-acre Sandringham has been the country home of four generations of British monarchs, ever since Queen Victoria's son, the Prince of Wales (later King Edward VII), purchased it in 1861. He and his Danish wife, Princess Alexandra, rebuilt the house, which in time became a popular meeting place for British society. The redbrick and stone Victorian-Tudor mansion consists of more than 200 rooms, some of which are open to the public, including two drawing rooms, the ballroom, and a dining room. The atmosphere of a well-loved family home is a contrast to the formal splendor of Buckingham Palace. Guests can also view a loft salon with a minstrel's gallery used as a sitting room by the royal family and full of photographs and mementos.

A **Land Train** designed and built on the estate makes it easy for visitors to reach Sandringham House, which sits at the heart of 60 acres of beautiful grounds. The train's covered carriages have room for wheelchairs.

The **Sandringham Museum** holds a wealth of rare items relating to the history of the royal family's time here, and displays tell the story of the monarchs who have owned the estate since 1862. Visitors can see the big-game trophies in settings that include a safari trail.

Sandringham is some 50 miles west of Norwich and 8 miles northeast of King's Lynn (off A149). King's Lynn is the end of the main train route from London's Liverpool Street Station that goes via Cambridge and Ely. Trains from London arrive at King's Lynn every 2 hours, a trip of 2½ hours. From Cambridge, the train ride takes only 1 hour. Buses from both Cambridge and Norwich run to King's Lynn, where you can catch bus no. 411 to take you the rest of the way to Sandringham.

The grounds and museum of Sandringham (☎ 01553/772675) are open Easter to July 20 and August 5 to October 3 daily from 11am to 5pm. Admission to the house, grounds, and museum is £5.50 ($9.35) for adults, £4.50 ($7.65) for senior citizens, £3.50 ($5.95) for children. Admission to the grounds and museum is £4.50 ($7.65) for adults, £4 ($6.80) for senior citizens, and £3 ($5.10) for children 5 to 15 years.

Marco's. 17 Pottergate. ☎ **01603/624044.** Reservations required. Main courses £10.50–£17.50 ($17.85–$29.75); fixed-price lunch £15 ($25.50). AE, DC, MC, V. Tues–Sat noon–2pm and 7–10pm. NORTHERN ITALIAN.

Norwich's premier Italian restaurant is located in a Regency house, a 2-minute walk from Market Place. It's not the kind of place where Chianti bottles hang from the ceiling and troubadours serenade you. Instead, you'll find one of the smallest dining rooms in town, its six tables decorated with elegant cove moldings. Although smoking is not allowed in the dining room, you can have before- or after-dinner puffs and drinks in a comfortable bar/lounge decorated in the Chinese style (in honor of another Italian, Marco Polo). Try such tasty dishes as veal filled with mushroom and eggplant stuffing with a tomato and basil sauce, or perhaps baked rack of lamb with a wine, mint and berry sauce.

NORWICH AFTER DARK

From fine art to pop art, there's quite a lot happening around Norwich at night. Information on almost all of it can be found at **The Ticket Shop,** Guildhall (☎ **01603/764764**), where you can also pick up tickets to just about any event.

The **Theatre Royal,** Theatre Street (box office ☎ **01603/630000**), hosts touring companies performing drama, opera, ballet, and modern dance. The Royal Shakespeare Company and London's Royal National troupe are among the regular visitors. Ticket prices run £15 to £30 ($25.50 to $51), with senior and student discounts usually available for Wednesday, Thursday, and Saturday matinees. The box office is open Monday through Saturday from 9:30am until 8pm on performance days, and closes at 6pm on nonperformance days.

Hosting productions of classic drama on most evenings, the **Norwich Playhouse,** Gun Wharf, 42–58 St. George's St. (☎ **01603/612580**), offers tickets ranging from £5 to £12 ($8.50 to $20.40). The box office is open daily from 10am until 8pm.

An Elizabethan-style theater, the **Maddermarket Theatre,** 1 St. John's Alley (☎ **01603/620917**), is home to the amateur Norwich Players' productions of classical and contemporary drama. Tickets, ranging from £4 to £12 ($6.80 to $20.40), and schedules are available at the box office, Monday through Saturday from 10am to 9pm and from 10am to 5pm on nonperformance days.

The city's **Theatre in the Parks** (☎ **01603/212137**) includes about 40 outdoor performances every summer in various venues.

Located in a converted medieval church, **Norwich Puppet Theatre,** St. James, Whitefriars (☎ **01603/629921**), offers original puppet shows most afternoons and some mornings in an octagonal studio that holds about 50 people. Tickets are £5 ($8.50) for adults, £3.75 ($6.40) for children, and are available at the box office Monday through Friday from 9:30am to 5pm, and on Saturday on days of performances.

The most versatile entertainment complex in town, the **Norwich Arts Centre,** Reeves Yard, St. Benedict's Street (☎ **01603/660352**), hosts performances of ballet, comedy, poetry, and an emphasis on ethnic music. Tickets are £5 to £10 ($8.50 to $17), and the box office is open Monday through Friday from 10am to 5pm, and Saturday from 11am to 4pm. On days of performances, the box office is open until 9pm.

Before or after your cultural event, check out the local culture at **Adam and Eve,** 17 Bishopgate (☎ **01603/667423**), the oldest pub in Norwich, founded in 1249, which serves a well-kept John Smith's or Old Peculiar. A traditional bare-wood pub, the **Finnesko & Firkin,** 10 Dereham Rd. (☎ **01603/666821**), serves five real ales brewed on the premises, and **The Gardener's Arms,** 2–4 Timberhill (☎ **01603/621447**), pours Boddington's and London Pride to a lively crowd of locals and students. A good place to wait for the next film, **Take 5,** St. Andrew's Street (☎ **01603/763099**), a cafe-bar located next door to Cinema City, is the hangout for the local arts crowd.

14 The East Midlands

This region is a mix of dreary industrial sections and incredible scenery, particularly in the Peak District National Park, centered in Derbyshire. Byron said that the landscapes in the Peak District rivaled those of Switzerland and Greece. In the East Midlands you'll also find the tulip land of Lincolnshire, the 18th-century spa of Buxton in Derbyshire, and the remains of Robin Hood's Sherwood Forest in Nottinghamshire. George Washington looked to Sulgrave Manor in Northamptonshire as his ancestral home. If you have Pilgrims in your past, you can trace your roots to the East Midlands.

Except for Sulgrave Manor and Althorp House, where Princess Di spent her girlhood, Northamptonshire is not on the tourist circuit. If you do decide to stop here, the best place to base yourself is Northampton, the capital.

In Leicestershire, you can use the industrialized county town of Leicester as a base to explore many notable sights in the countryside, including Belvoir Castle, the setting for Steven Spielberg's movie, *Young Sherlock Holmes,* and Bosworth Battlefield, site of one of England's most important battles.

Derbyshire is noted primarily for the Peak District National Park, but it also has a number of historic homes—notably Chatsworth, the home of the 11th duke of Devonshire. The best places to base yourself here are Buxton, Bakewell, and Ashbourne.

In Nottinghamshire, the city of Nottingham is a good center for exploring what's left of Sherwood Forest, the legendary stomping grounds of Robin Hood.

If you're headed for Lincolnshire, the highlight is the cathedral city of Lincoln itself, with stopovers at the old seaport of Boston, which lent its name to the famous American city.

1 Northamptonshire

In the heart of the Midlands, Northamptonshire has been inhabited since Paleolithic times. Traces have been found here of Beaker and other Bronze Age people, and remains of a number of Iron Age hill-forts can still be seen. Two Roman roads—now Watling and Ermine streets—ran through the county, and relics of Roman settlements have been discovered at Towcester, Whilton, Irchester, and Castor. West Saxons and Anglicans invaded in the 7th century. In 655, the first abbey was established at Medehamstede, now Peterborough. In the

The East Midlands

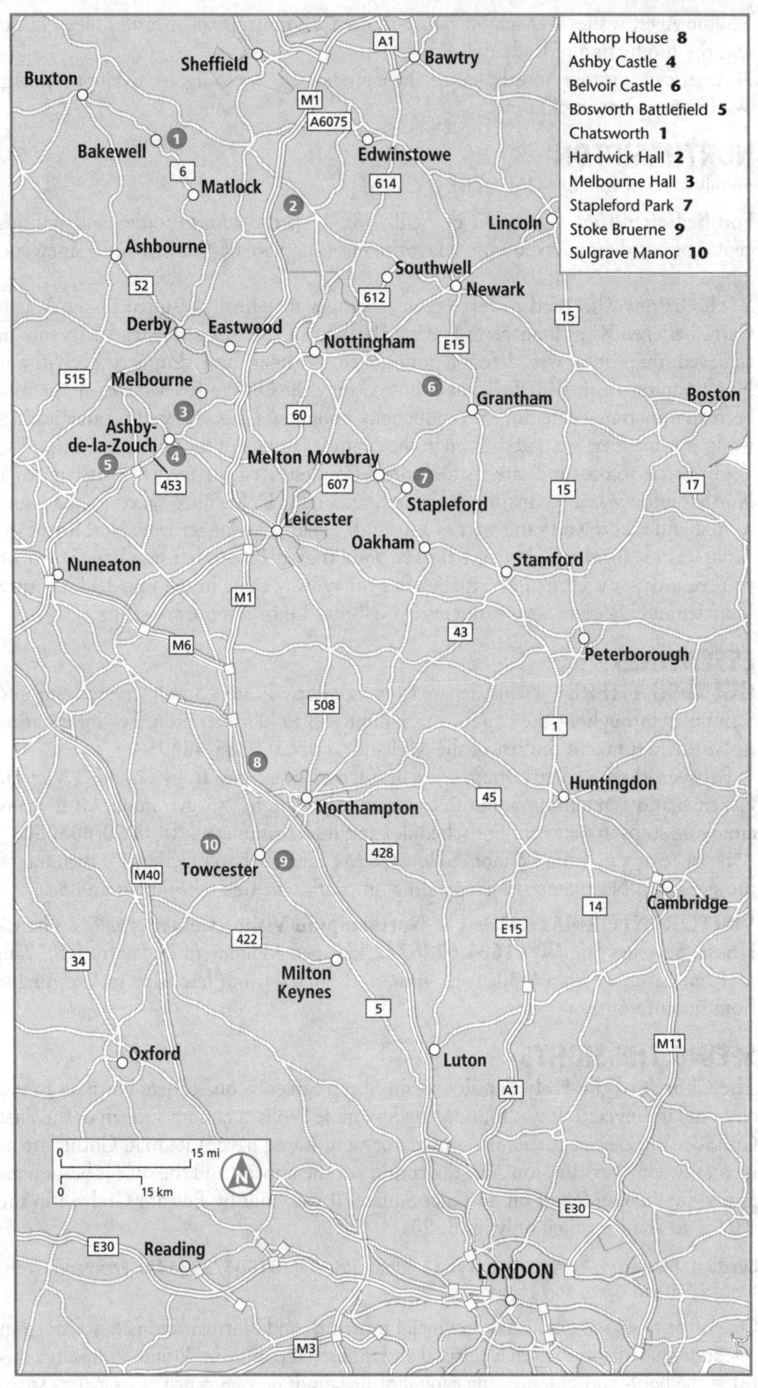

Middle Ages, castles and manor houses dotted a country rich in cattle, sheep farms, and the production of leatherwork.

American visitors mostly come here today to see Sulgrave Manor, George Washington's ancestral home.

NORTHAMPTON

69 miles NW of London; 41 miles NE of Oxford

Fortified after 1066 by Simon de Senlis (St. Liz), the administrative and political center of Northamptonshire was a favorite meeting place of Norman and Plantagenet kings.

The barons who tried to force policy changes that finally resulted in the Magna Carta besieged King John here. During the War of the Roses, Henry VI (before he achieved that title) was defeated and taken prisoner, and during the civil war, Northampton stuck with Parliament and Cromwell. On the River Nene, it has long been an important center for the production of boots and shoes, as well as other leatherwork, pursuits that are traced through the centuries in two of the city's museums.

Historical records indicate that, before a fire destroyed the medieval city in 1675, Northampton was a fascinating town architecturally. Defoe once called it "the handsomest and best town in this part of England." That is no longer true. Nothing of the castle (ca. 1100) where Thomas à Becket stood trial in 1164 is left standing. The town you see today was created essentially after the railway came in the mid-19th century. If ancient architecture is your interest, you'll find Lincoln more appealing.

ESSENTIALS

GETTING THERE Trains depart from London's Euston Station every hour and 5 minutes throughout the day for the 1-hour trip to Northampton. For information in Northampton and the rest of the Midlands, call ☎ **0345/484950.**

Between three and five motor coaches depart every day from London's Victoria Coach Station, requiring about 2 hours for the ride to Northampton, with many annoying stops in between. For schedules and information, call ☎ **0990/808080.**

If you're driving from London, follow the M1 due north to junction 15, then follow the signs into Northampton. Depending on traffic, the trek takes about an hour.

VISITOR INFORMATION The **Northampton Visitor Center** is at Mr. Grant's House, St. Giles Sq. (☎ **01604/622677**). It's open Monday to Friday from 9:30am to 5pm, Saturday from 9:30am to 4pm, and Sunday from late May to late August from noon to 4pm.

SEEING THE SIGHTS

The **Church of the Holy Sepulchre,** on Sheep Street, is one of five Norman round churches in England. It was founded by Simon de Senlis, a famous veteran of the First Crusade. You can see its circular ambulatory and round nave. Victorian Gothic architecture swept Northampton after the coming of the railway, and the style is best exemplified by the **Guidehall** on St. Giles Square. It was built by Edward Godwin in the 1860s, an architect then only in his 20s.

Central Museum & Art Gallery. Guildhall Rd. ☎ **01604/238548.** Free admission. Mon–Sat 10am–5pm, Sun 2–5pm.

One of Britain's most unusual provincial museums and Northampton's key attraction celebrates Northampton's rich cultural and industrial traditions. Proud of the city's status as the boot- and shoe-making capital of Britain, it devotes much of its gallery space to exhibitions of the largest collection of antique shoes in the world, spanning centuries of footwear, with emphasis on the Victorian era. Also on display are artworks from Italy spanning the 15th to the 18th centuries, a wide spectrum from the history of British art, and objects uncovered from nearby archaeological sites dating from the Stone Age.

WHERE TO STAY IN & AROUND NORTHAMPTON

Crossroads Hotel. High St., Weedon, Northamptonshire NN7 4PX. ☎ **01327/340354.** Fax 01327/340849. 45 units. TV TEL. £45.50 ($77.35) double. AE, DC, MC, V. Take the A45 8 miles west of Northampton.

This hotel was acquired in the early 1990s by a competent but unpretentious nationwide chain, which enlarged and renovated it into a simple and rather standard format suited to business travelers. Hints of the building's original antique core are visible in the stone facade, which originally sheltered a tollbooth that taxed travelers between Northampton and nearby Daventry. Bedrooms are boxy and have the standard comforts, such as beverage-makers, plus compact bathrooms with a hair dryer. Set on Weedon's main street, the hotel contains a straightforward restaurant serving English fare.

Northampton Moat House Inn. Silver St., Northampton, Northamptonshire NN1 2TA. ☎ **01604/739988.** Fax 01604/230614. 140 units. TV TEL. £120 ($204) double. AE, DC, MC, V.

The Moat House is often booked by conventioneers and business travelers who appreciate its comfort and its location near the heart of town. Built in the mid-1970s in an efficient, no-nonsense format of concrete and glass, it lies close to the western edge of the Inner Ring Road. The restaurant and bar have exposed stone, flickering candles, and varnished wood trim. The comfortable bedrooms are what you'd expect from an upscale chain hotel. Four units are large enough for families, and 105 bedrooms are for nonsmokers. Bathrooms are well equipped, each with a hair dryer. Overall, it's a fine if not particularly historic choice for an overnight stay.

Swallow Hotel. Eagle Dr., Northampton, Northamptonshire NN4 7HW. ☎ **01604/768700.** Fax 01604/769011. www.swallowhotels.com. E-mail: info@swallowhotels.com. 120 units. MINIBAR TV TEL. Mon–Thurs £130 ($221) double, Fri–Sun £90 ($153) double; £145 ($246.50) suite. Rates include English breakfast. AE, DC, MC, V.

Unlike the Moat House, this 1980s-vintage hotel, 3 miles east of Northampton's center, has a country setting, easy access to a golf course, and an on-site health club with swimming pool, sauna, steam bath, and exercise equipment. It also contains two restaurants—an Italian trattoria and a more formal French and English restaurant—that, for lack of anything better near the town center, are popular local choices. Bedrooms are not excessively large, but comfortably outfitted with monochromatic modern furnishings. Twelve rooms are large enough for families, and 82 units are reserved for nonsmokers. They're better maintained than any other lodgings in town. The Swallow is friendly and competently run.

WHERE TO DINE

The restaurant situation in Northampton's center is pretty dismal. Many visitors prefer to dine at the Swallow Hotel (see above) or head out of town to The Pavilion.

The Pavilion. 160 Kettering Rd. ☎ **01604/621292.** Reservations recommended. Main courses £8–£16 ($13.60–$27.20). AE, DC, MC, V. Daily noon–2pm and 6–11pm. BRITISH/CONTINENTAL.

Up three flights of stairs, this long and narrow dining room overlooks tennis courts, bowling greens, and the rusted hulk of Victorian bleachers surrounding a racecourse that hasn't seen any action since 1870. Scholars of the Industrial Revolution consider the intricate but rusted ironwork comparable to the elaborate structure of Paris's Eiffel Tower, and something of a sightseeing attraction in its own right.

Rich and copious fare is this restaurant's trademark, including salmon *Coullibiac* (prepared with mushrooms, prawns, and lobster sauce, all presented in puff pastry). Rack of New Zealand lamb is served with red currants and mint sauce. "Pavilion smokies" are smoked haddock poached in white wine, herbs, and cream, and topped with English cheddar.

SULGRAVE MANOR: GEORGE WASHINGTON'S ANCESTRAL HOME

Sulgrave Manor. Manor Rd. ☎ **01295/760205.** Admission £4 ($6.80) adults, £2 ($3.40) children ages 5–16; free for children under 5. Apr–July and Sept–Oct Mon–Tues and Thurs–Fri 2–5:30pm, Sat–Sun 10:30am–1pm and 2–5:30pm; Aug Thurs–Tues 10:30am–1pm and 2–5:30pm; Nov–Dec Sat–Sun 10:30am–1pm and 2–4:30pm. Closed Jan–Feb except for schools and prebooked groups. From Northampton, drive 18 miles southwest on A43, then B4525 to Sulgrave. From Stratford-upon-Avon, take A422 via Banbury (whose famous cross entered nursery-rhyme fame) and continue to Brackley; 6 miles from Brackley, leave A422 and join B4525, which goes to the tiny village of Sulgrave. Signs will lead you to Sulgrave Manor.

American visitors will be especially interested in this small mid-16th-century Tudor manor, the ancestral home of George Washington. As part of a plan to dissolve the monasteries, Henry VIII sold the priory-owned manor in 1539 to Lawrence Washington, who had been mayor of Northampton. The Washington family occupied Sulgrave for more than a century, but in 1656, Col. John Washington left for the New World. Born in Virginia, George Washington was a direct descendant of Lawrence (seven generations removed).

A group of English people bought the manor in 1914 in honor of the friendship between Britain and the United States. Beginning with a large donation in 1927, the Colonial Dames have been largely responsible for raising the money for a major restoration to return it as much as possible to its original state. Appropriate furnishings and portraits, including a Gilbert Stuart original of the first president, have been donated on both sides of the Atlantic. The Washington family coat of arms on the main doorway—two bars and a trio of mullets—is believed to have been the inspiration for the Stars and Stripes.

ALTHORP: THE GIRLHOOD HOME & FINAL RESTING PLACE OF PRINCESS DIANA

Althorp. 6 miles northwest of Northampton on A428 in Althorp, near Harlestone. ☎ **01604/592020.** www.althorpe.com. Admission £10 ($17) adults, £7.50 ($12.75) seniors, £5 ($8.50) children 5–17, children under 5 are free. Open only July 1–Aug 30.

Originally built in 1508 by Sir John Spencer, Althorp has brought a sometimes unwelcome dose of fame to the surrounding rural area because it was the girlhood home of Princess Diana. It was glamorously revived by Raine Spencer, Diana's stepmother. At least part of the beauty and historical authenticity of this frequently renovated site is the result of her efforts.

Since the death of Lord Spencer, Diana's father, the house has been under the jurisdiction of Charles Spencer, Diana's older brother, who emigrated to South Africa. The house collection includes paintings by Van Dyck, Reynolds, Gainsborough, and Rubens, as well as an assortment of rare French and English furniture, and porcelain by Sèvres, Bow, and Chelsea.

To visit, *you must book ahead.* Following the tragic death of Princess Diana in August 1997, a ticket to Althorp House became extremely difficult to obtain. More than 200, 24-hour telephone lines handle orders for tickets. Althorp is open to the public only from July 1, Diana's birthday, to August 30, the day before the anniversary of her death.

Diana was buried on an island in an artificial lake on the property. Visitors do not have access to the island, but have a clear view of it across the lake. A museum celebrating Diana's life, complete with schoolgirl letters, her stunning silk wedding dress, and some of her haute couture clothes, also opened here in the summer of 1998.

The museum also shows poignant films of her as a carefree child dancing in the gardens and later as a mother riding with her sons, William and Harry, plus videos that include the moving footage of her funeral. The museum makes no mention of Dodi al-Fayed who died with her in the Paris car crash, and there is certainly no mention of her former lover, James Hewitt. Her estranged husband is also not featured prominently in the exhibition.

Facilities on site include a restaurant and a shop selling a range of souvenirs associated with Diana. The estate states that these souvenirs do not "cheapen her memory in any way." You decide that.

STOKE BRUERNE: HEART OF THE CANAL NETWORKS

Stoke Bruerne is the center of the East Midland canal networks, the waterway equivalent of a modern motorway junction. The canal reached Stoke Bruerne in 1800, and it has played a central role in the canal system ever since. Today, you can visit the Canal Museum and take a cruise on the waterways.

Stoke Bruerne is 9 miles southwest of Northampton near Towcester, just south of the Blisworth Tunnel (take the A508 from the M1 junction 15 or the A5).

SEEING THE SIGHTS

A ride along the canal complements a visit to the Canal Museum. The most convenient operator is **Indian Chief Cruises** (☎ **01604/862428**), at the pub of The Boat Inn (see "Where to Dine," below). Two competitors are **Linda Cruises** (☎ **01604/862107**), from a base adjacent to the museum, and **Blisworth Tunnel Boats** (☎ **01604/858868**), which operates from the village of Blisworth, 3 miles to the north.

Any of the three can arrange daylong rentals of 30-foot "narrows" boats—long, shallow-bottomed motorboats suitable for up to 12 occupants. The companies offer the same loosely scheduled services, hauling groups of passengers up and down the canal for rides that last between 25 minutes and 6 hours depending on the cruise selected. There are no timetables, and the prices vary depending on the company and on the length of the cruise. Indian Chief Cruises charges £1.75 ($3) for adults and £1.25 ($2.15) for children for a 25-minute cruise and as much as £10 ($17) for adults and £6 ($10.20) for children for a 6-hour cruise with a pub stop for a meal. Linda Cruises charges from £2 to £10 ($3.40 to $17) for adults and £1.25 to £7 ($2.15 to $11.90) for children for cruises lasting from a half hour to 6 hours. Blisworth Tunnel Boats rents boats that hold 8 to 12 people for £85 to £100 ($144.50 to $170) for the day. Rentals require a refundable deposit of £30 ($51), and are always accompanied with instruction on how to operate and navigate them. Be warned that the operations are extremely fluid, and depend a lot on the season and the weather.

Canal Museum. Rte. A508, Stoke Bruerne. ☎ **01604/862229.** Admission £3 ($5.10) adults, £2 ($3.40) children under 16 and seniors. Apr–Oct daily 10am–5pm; off-season Tues–Sun 10am–4pm.

Set within a restored corn mill beside the banks of the Grant Union Canal, this organization celebrates 200 years of traditions that developed around the inland canals and waterways of the Midlands. Its exhibits include videos, a collection of horse-drawn barges and motorized vessels from the earliest years of the Industrial Revolution, memorabilia, tools and artifacts, period costumes, and a well-attended museum shop containing posters, postcards, books, and more.

WHERE TO DINE

The Boat Inn. Stoke Bruerne. ☎ **01604/862428.** Reservations recommended for upstairs restaurant, not accepted in street-level bars and bistros. Restaurant, fixed-price menus £12.95–£21.95 ($22–$37.30). Bistro and pubs, main courses £4–£9 ($6.80–$15.30), tea with pastries or sandwiches £4 ($6.80). AE, DC, MC, V accepted in restaurant, MC, V accepted in bars. Restaurant Tues–Sun noon–2pm and daily 7–9:15pm. Street-level bars daily 9am–11pm. BRITISH/FRENCH.

This is the largest and most popular restaurant in Stoke Bruerne, a canal-side complex that manages to incorporate four bars, cocktail lounges, and dining rooms into an interconnected row of 17th-century cottages. Most of the original character resides in the street-level bars, which boast a thatched roof, limestone walls, stone floors, and open fireplaces. You can order platters of simple food along with your beer (which includes lagers and eight kinds of bitter).

More formal meals, with more elaborate service, are offered upstairs in the restaurant, a barn-style extension with lots of exposed wood and a view over the canal. Menu items change with the season but include venison with red-wine sauce, guinea fowl, lobster Thermidor, salmon, trout, and chicken.

✪ **Bruerne's Lock Restaurant.** 5 The Canalside. ☎ **01604/863654.** Reservations recommended. Set-price lunch and dinner £17 ($28.90); dinner main courses £15–£30 ($25.50–$51). AE, MC, V. Tues–Fri and Sun 12:15–2pm; Tues–Sat 7:30–10pm. CONTINENTAL/MODERN ENGLISH.

This is the most sophisticated and, at least in terms of cuisine, elegant restaurant in Northamptonshire, a destination sought out by gastronomes as far away as Birmingham and Manchester. Its present allure dates from 1989, when a trio of Franco-British entrepreneurs took over a thick-walled Georgian building whose foundations were built in the 17th century. Past functions of the building, which is situated near the uppermost of the town's seven canal locks, have included roles as a post office, a surgeon's office, and a nursery.

Within a warm and formal setting you can enjoy the most creative and imaginative cuisine in the region. Examples might include baked goat's cheese served with a herb mousse or breast of wood pigeon in puff pastry served with a flap mushroom sauce. Desserts are equally imaginative and include such treats as poached rhubarb and custard tart flavored with orange and ginger, and sticky toffee pudding laced with a butterscotch sauce.

2 Leicester

107 miles NW of London; 43 miles NE of Birmingham; 24 miles NE of Coventry; 26 miles S of Nottingham

Hang on to your hats, because this county town is definitely no Sleepy Hollow. Leicester, pronounced "*Les*-ter," one of the 10 largest cities in England, overflows with hustle and bustle and is by far the most cosmopolitan city in the East Midlands. This city of firsts—Beethoven's music was first performed here, the BBC's first local radio station was BBC Radio Leicester—thrives on the spirit of discovery and adventure. More recently, it gave birth to genetic fingerprinting.

Although it has some historic attractions, think of Leicester as a base for exploring the surrounding countryside. Its real lure with locals and tourists alike is its shopping, art scene, and nightlife.

ESSENTIALS

GETTING THERE Trains depart from London's St. Pancras Station every 30 minutes throughout the day for Leicester, a trip of about 90 minutes. The fare costs £29 ($49.30) each way Saturday through Thursday and £34.50 ($58.65) on Friday. For schedules and information, call ☎ **0345/484950.**

About 8 buses a day leave London's Victoria Coach Station for Leicester. They call at several secondary stops en route, thus taking 2 hours and 45 minutes each way. The round-trip fare is £17.50 ($29.75) if you stay overnight but only £12 ($20.40) if you return the same day. For schedules and information, call ☎ **0990/808080.**

If you're driving from London, follow the M1 north to junction 21 toward Leicester. The drive takes 2 hours.

VISITOR INFORMATION The main tourist information office is at 7–9 Every St., Town Hall Square (☎ **0116/2998888**). It's open Monday to Wednesday and Friday from 9am to 5:30pm, Thursday from 10am to 5:30pm, and Saturday from 9am to 5pm. They'll supply a useful map. Blue Badge guided walks are offered at ☎ **0116/2862252.**

SPECIAL EVENTS The **Leicester Early Music Festival** (☎ **0116/2707820**) takes place in May and June. Tickets for the whole series cost £19 to £23 ($32.30 to $39.10). Also in June, the **Leicester International Music Festival** (☎ **0116/2473043**) attracts some of the biggest names in classical music. Ticket prices vary, but average about £6 to £15 ($10.20 to $25.50).

EXPLORING THE TOWN

Leicester is worth a look if you have an afternoon to spare. In addition to the sights mentioned below, the town has a boating lake, riverside walks, and ornamental gardens.

An exciting wave of new shops has opened in Leicester. In addition to Victorian-style **Shires Shopping Centre,** with its designer and collectible stores, wide walkways, fountains, and sunny skylights, there's **St. Martins Square** in the city center, which has given new life to old restored buildings, with new retailers, cafes, and tea shops. A wealth of specialty shops—out a quarter mile on either side of the railway station—and several antique stores line Oxford Street and Western Boulevard.

Venture out from the center of town to Belgrave Road and you'll discover the **"Golden Mile."** This neighborhood is home to the largest sari shop outside of India, and the store windows along Belgrave Road overflow with fine Indian silks, organzas, and cottons. Sari shops also generally carry a variety of accessories including bags, jewelry, shoes, and shawls.

Jewry Wall and Archeology Museum. St. Nicholas Circle (about 1/2 mile from the town center, adjacent to the Holiday Inn). ☎ **0116/2473021.** Free admission. Mon–Sat 10am–5pm, Sun 2–5pm.

Set near the excavation of an ancient Roman bath, this museum has nothing at all to do with Jewish history. Its name derives from a corruption of the Norman French "Jurad," which referred to the governing magistrates of an early medieval town, who used to gather in the shadow of this wall for their municipal decisions. More than

40 feet high, the wall is higher than any other piece of ancient Roman architecture in Britain. Exhibits within the museum include a pair of ancient Roman mosaics, the Peacock Pavement and the Blackfriars Mosaic, which are the finest of their kind in the British Midlands. Each was laboriously sliced from the masonry of ancient villas within the district and set into new masonry beds here.

Leicester Abbey. Abbey Park, Abbey Park Rd. ☎ **0116/2221000.** Free admission. Daily dawn to dusk.

Set within a verdant public park that's favored by joggers and picnickers, about 3/4 mile north of Leicester's historic core, these evocative, poetically shattered remains are all that's left of the richest Augustinian monastery in England, built in 1132. In 1530, Cardinal Wolsey came here to die, demoralized and broken after his political and religious conflicts with Henry VIII. The abbey was torn down during the Reformation and stones were used in the construction of Cavendish House next door.

Leicester Guildhall. Guildhall Lane. ☎ **0116/2532569.** Free admission. Mon–Sat 10am–5:30pm, Sun 2–5:30pm.

Built in stages between the 14th and 16th centuries, the city's most prominent public building was Leicester's first town hall and contains one of the oldest libraries in Britain. Plaques commemorate its role as a die-hard last bastion of the Parliamentarians during the civil war. On its ground floor, you'll see a 19th-century police station with a pair of original prison cells, whose mournful effigies afford a powerful testimony to the horrors of the Victorian penal system. Shakespeare's troupe is said to have appeared here.

Leicestershire Museum and Art Gallery. 53 New Walk. ☎ **0116/2554100.** Free admission but donations accepted. Mon–Sat 10am–4:30pm, Sun 1:30–4:30pm. Closed Dec 24–26 and Jan 1.

This multipurpose museum has two distinctly separate features. The street level contains exhibits of archaeology and natural history: a dinosaur bone found in a field near Leicester; a collection of Egyptian mummies and artifacts brought back to the Midlands by Thomas Cook, the 19th-century travel mogul; and geological exhibits. One floor above street level is a collection of paintings by British and European artists (including some by Gainsborough) from the 18th through 20th centuries. The collection of early–20th-century canvasses by German expressionists is one of the largest in Europe.

St. Martin's Cathedral. 1 St. Martin's E. ☎ **0116/2625294.** Free admission. Daily 7:30am–5pm.

It may not have the soaring grandeur of the cathedrals of York or Lincoln, but this is the most venerated and historic church in Leicester. In 1086, it was one of the region's parish churches, and it was enlarged during the 1300s and the 1500s. In 1927, it was designated as the cathedral of Leicester, a nomenclature that adds considerably to its pomp and circumstance. The oak vaulting beneath the building's north porch is one of the most unusual treatments of its kind in England. For walking tours, contact the tourist office.

WHERE TO STAY

Jarvis Grand Hotel. 73 Granby St., Leicester, Leicestershire LE1 6ES. ☎ **0116/2555599.** Fax 0116/2544736. 92 units. TV TEL. Mon–Thurs £114 ($193.80) double; £160 ($272) suite. Fri–Sun £69 ($117.30) double; £130 ($221) suite. Weekend rates include English breakfast. AE, DC, MC, V.

Jarvis Grand is the finest choice in the city itself. When it was built in 1898, no expense was spared. The original oak and mahogany paneling has been retained, even though the building was enlarged in the 1970s, later taken over by the nationwide Jarvis chain, and completely renovated between 1995 and 1996. Bedrooms are more streamlined and contemporary than the semiantique public areas suggest. Each is fitted with a firm mattress on a comfortable English bed, and each comes with a shower stall.

On the premises are the Sports Bar, the slightly more formal Club Bar, a bistro and cafe, and the Club Restaurant, an antique-looking restaurant touting fixed-price dinners.

Rothley Court Hotel. Westfield Lane, Rothley, Leicester, Leicestershire LE7 7LG. ☎ **0116/2374141.** Fax 0116/2374483. 32 units. TV TEL. £95 ($161.50) double; £100 ($170) suite. Rates include breakfast. AE, MC, V. Head 6 miles north of Leicester on the B5328 Rd., just off the A6 between Leicester and Loughborough.

This hotel stands on the edge of Charnwood Forest, a royal hunting ground for centuries. In 1231, Henry III granted the manor and "soke" (right to hold court under feudal law) to the Knights Templar. The chapel erected next to the existing abbey around 1240 is second only to the Temple in London as the best preserved Templar chapel in Britain.

Standing on 6 acres of grounds, the hotel is surrounded by open farmland. Stone fireplaces, oak paneling, and stained-glass windows evoke its rich historical associations. Bedrooms have been handsomely restored and are comfortable, with modern conveniences. Accommodations come in different sizes (some are quite spacious), and many are furnished with antiques. The less desirable rooms with standard furnishings are in a modern annex. Each comes with a compact private bath with adequate shelf space and a shower stall.

The hotel serves some of the finest cuisine in the area (see below).

WHERE TO DINE

Rothley Court Hotel Restaurant. Westfield Lane, Rothley. ☎ **0116/2374141.** Reservations recommended. Set-price lunch £14.95 ($25.40), set-price dinner £22.50 ($38.25); main courses £11.95–£36.50 ($20.30–$62.05). AE, MC, V. Daily 7–9:30am, 12:30–3pm, and 7–9:30pm. ENGLISH.

Part of the fun of dining at this hotel involves a pre- or postmeal visit to one of Britain's best-preserved strongholds of the Knights Templar, a 13th-century semi-fanatical sect that played an important role in the Crusades. Within the venerable walls of a historic manor house surrounded with parks and farmland, you can enjoy a sophisticated blend of modern and traditional English cuisine—say, a medley of monkfish and crayfish with lime juice, coriander, and artichoke hearts; steak Diane with Dijon mustard, shallots, mushrooms, tomatoes, and a cognac sauce; or seared filet of Scottish salmon with nut-brown butter sauce. Not all these dishes reach gastronomic heights, but this is as good as it gets in the Leicester area.

Welford Place. 9 Welford Place. ☎ **0116/2470758.** English breakfast £6.25 ($10.65); main courses £7.50–£17.50 ($12.75–$29.75); set menus £14 ($23.80). AE, DC, MC, V. Mon–Sat 8am–midnight. BRITISH/ITALIAN.

This place serves everything from midmorning coffee to a steaming pot of mid-afternoon tea, as well as drinks and full meals. Menu items include filet of sea bass with butter beans and rosemary; roast guinea fowl with cabbage and bacon; or duck confit with creamed potatoes and a balsamic vinegar sauce. All of it is dispensed with good cheer and an utter lack of pretension by members of the hardworking Hope family. The dignified building within Leicester's center was originally constructed in 1877 as a private men's club, and the interior retains its original shoulder-height oaken paneling and Victorian motifs.

Two Great Country-House Hotels

Outside Melton Mowbray are two of the great country houses of England, and the finest places to stay or dine in Leicestershire itself.

✪ **Stapleford Park,** 5 miles east of Melton Mowbray on Highway B676 (Stapleford Road; ☎ **01572/787522;** fax 01572/787651; www.stapleford.co.uk; E-mail: reservations@stapleford.co.uk) has it all. Capability Brown himself laid out the 500 acres of parkland surrounding the 19th-century mansion, with parts dating from the 16th century. In the 17th century, it functioned as the seat of the earls of Harlborough. It was magnificently renovated by the estate's former owner, the late Bob Payton, founder of the Chicago Pizza Factory chain. The present decor was selected by another pair of former owners, David Hicks and Nina Campbell, who defined the place as a "sporting estate," partly because the site has a school of falconry, colonies of trained hawks and owls, a stable with half a dozen horses, and a group of hunt masters who take guests out on game shoots. The present owner, Peter DeSavary, purchased the property in 1996. The lush bedrooms are outfitted with modern comforts, 18th-century antiques, and have 24-hour room service. Rates for the 51 units, which have televisions and telephones, are £165 to £495 ($280.50 to $841.50) for a double. The bedrooms are truly splendid and eclectic, each designed by a sponsor, including Coca-Cola, MGM, or Land-Rover. Bathrooms are equally sumptuous with deluxe toiletries. Major credit cards are accepted.

With sophisticated and elegant Mediterranean and continental cuisine, the dining room here is opulent and highly acclaimed. The offerings aren't quite on the level of Hambleton Hall, but you'll dine in a lavishly outfitted dining room that's as spectacular as 400 years of British tradition and gobs of money can provide. Even the yellow-painted wall carvings are historically important, carved by Grinling Gibbons, who was to wood carvings what Thomas Chippendale was to furniture. Menu items include Cornish crab cakes, or melted onion and leek tart

LEICESTER AFTER DARK

The **Haymarket Theatre,** Belgrave Gate (☎ **0116/2539797**), one of the nation's leading provincial theaters, has been the launching point for many successful West End productions, including *Hot Stuff, Me and My Girl,* and *Mack & Mabel.* Popular musicals like these are the house specialty, but you'll find anything from contemporary drama to visiting dance companies gracing the stage.

The **Phoenix Arts Centre,** Newarke Street (☎ **0116/2554854**), hosts dance, music, and theatrical productions from around the world, but local dancers, musicians, and actors also entertain from its stage, and there's even an occasional film screening.

On weekends, the area around the **Clock Tower** in the center of town is alive with bustling crowds headed out to the clubs and bars on Church Gate, Silver Street, and High Street. **Kudos,** 97 Church Gate (☎ **0116/2629720**), is a popular club pumping out dance music until the wee hours. Open Monday and Thursday to Saturday only. Free before 10pm; after that the cover ranges from £3 to £6 ($5.10 to $10.20).

As you might expect of a university town, Leicester has a variety of pubs, but the two most favored by locals are the **Pump and Tap,** Duns Lane (☎ **0116/2540324**), and **The Magazine,** Newarke Street (☎ **0116/2228815**). Stop by either to sample ales by Leicestershire's three home brewers: Everards, Ruddles, and Hoskins.

as appetizers. Technically precise main courses may feature roast scallops and langoustine, or oatmeal-crisped fillet of beef. On occasion, roasted venison cutlet with Savoy cabbage and lentils is served. The dining room is open daily from noon to 2:30pm and from 7:30 to 9:30pm. Reservations are required.

✪ **Hambleton Hall,** on A606, 3 miles east of Oldham and 26 miles northeast of Leicester, in the small village of Hambleton, near Oakham, Leicestershire (☎ **01572/756991;** fax 01572/724721; E-mail: hotel@hambletonhall.com) is another great country house, with a fabulous restaurant.

Originally built in 1881 as a hunting lodge by a Victorian industrialist named Walter Marshall, it sits on 12 acres of landscaped park at the edge of an artificial lake, Rutland Water. Everything about the place evokes a Victorian/Edwardian country house, including the many flower arrangements and comfortable but severely dignified furniture. Bedrooms have the chintz curtains and Victorian antiques you'd expect. Each comes with a sumptuous bed and a luxurious bathroom with a hair dryer. Terraced gardens run down to the edge of the lake. Rates for the 15 rooms, which have televisions and telephones, are £185 to £305 ($314.50 to $518.50) for a double, including continental breakfast. Major credit cards are accepted.

Hambleton Hall is widely known for its prestigious formal dining room, which is open to the public. You dine here amid walls upholstered in russet-colored silk and order from a menu that changes according to the practiced but imaginative whims of chef Aaron Patterson, who takes full advantage of the game available from the surrounding countryside and even grows some of the produce in the hotel's walled garden. Menu items include fillet of red mullet with a sweet pepper sauce, a mosaic of game terrine, or ravioli of langoustines. It's open daily from noon to 1:30pm and from 7 to 9:30pm. Reservations are recommended.

HISTORIC SIGHTS NEAR LEICESTER

Bosworth Battlefield Visitor Centre and Country Park. 18 miles southwest of Leicester between the M1 and the M6 (near the town of Nuneaton). ☎ **01455/290429.** Admission £2.80 ($4.75) adults, £1.80 ($3.05) children under 16 and seniors; family ticket £7.40 ($12.60). Battlefield can be visited anytime during daylight hours year-round. Visitor center Apr–Oct Mon–Sat 11am–5pm Sun and bank holidays 11am–6pm.

This site commemorates the 1485 battle that ended one of England's most important conflicts. The Battle of Bosworth ended the War of the Roses between the houses of York and Lancaster. When the fighting subsided, King Richard III, last of the Yorkists, lay dead, and Henry Tudor, a Welsh nobleman who had been banished to France to thwart his royal ambition, was proclaimed the victor. Henry thus became King Henry VII, and the Tudor dynasty was born.

Today, the appropriate standards fly where the opponents had their positions. You can see the whole scene by taking a 1 3/4-mile walk along the marked battle trails. In the center are exhibitions, models, book and gift shops, a cafeteria, and a theater where an audiovisual introduction with an excerpt from the Lord Laurence Olivier film version of Shakespeare's *Richard III* is presented.

Ashby Castle. Ashby-de-la-Zouch (18 miles northwest of Leicester). ☎ **01530/413343.** Admission £2.60 ($4.40) adults, £2 ($3.40) seniors, £1.30 ($2.20) children under 16. Apr–Oct daily 10am–6pm; off-season Wed–Sun 10am–4pm.

If you've read Sir Walter Scott's *Ivanhoe,* you will remember Ashby-de-la-Zouch, a town that retains a pleasant country atmosphere. The main attraction here is the ruined Norman manor house, Ashby Castle, where Mary Queen of Scots was imprisoned. The building was already an antique in 1464 when its thick walls were converted into a fortress.

Melbourne Hall. 8 miles south of Derby on A447, on Church Square. ☎ **01332/862502.** Admission to house and garden £4.50 ($7.65) adults, £3.50 ($5.95) students and seniors, £2.50 ($4.25) children 5–15; free for children 4 and under. House only, £2.50 ($4.25) adults, £2 ($3.40) students and seniors, £1 ($1.70) children 5–15. Gardens only, £3 ($5.10) adults, £2 ($3.40) students, children 5–15, and seniors. House open Aug only, daily 2–5pm (closed the first 3 Mondays). Gardens Apr–Sept Wed, Sat–Sun, and bank holidays 1:30–5:30pm.

Originally built by the bishops of Carlisle in 1133, Melbourne Hall stands in one of the most famous formal gardens in Britain. The ecclesiastical structure was restored in the 1600s by one of the cabinet ministers of Charles I and enlarged by Queen Anne's vice chamberlain. It was the home of Lord Melbourne, who was prime minister when Victoria ascended to the throne. Lady Palmerston later inherited the house, which contains an important collection of antique furniture and artwork. A special feature is the beautifully restored wrought-iron pergola by Robert Bakewell, noted 18th-century iron smith.

Belvoir Castle. 7 miles southwest of Grantham, between the A607 to Melton Mowbray and the A52 to Nottingham. ☎ **01476/870262.** Admission £5.25 ($8.90) adults, £4 ($6.80) seniors, £3 ($5.10) children under 16; £14.50 ($24.65) family ticket (2 adults, 2 children). Apr–Sept Tues–Thurs and Sat–Sun 11am–5pm.

On the northern border of Leicestershire overlooking the Vale of Belvoir (pronounced *Beaver*), Belvoir Castle has been the seat of the dukes of Rutland since the time of Henry VII. Rebuilt by Wyatt in 1816, the castle contains paintings by Holbein, Reynolds, and Gainsborough, as well as tapestries in its magnificent state rooms. The castle was the location of the movies *Little Lord Fauntelroy* and *Young Sherlock Holmes.* In summer, it's the site of medieval jousting tournaments.

3 Derbyshire & Peak District National Park

The most magnificent scenery in the Midlands is found in Derbyshire, between Nottinghamshire and Staffordshire. Some travelers avoid this part of the country because it's ringed by the industrial sprawl of Manchester, Leeds, Sheffield, and Derby. But missing this area is a pity, for Derbyshire has actually been less defaced by industry than its neighbors.

The north of the county, containing the Peak District National Park, contains waterfalls, hills, moors, green valleys, and dales. In the south, the land is more level and you'll find pastoral meadows. Dovedale, Chee Dale, and Millers Dale are worth a detour.

EXPLORING PEAK DISTRICT NATIONAL PARK

✪ **Peak District National Park** covers some 542 square miles, most of it in Derbyshire, with some spilling over into South Yorkshire and Staffordshire. It stretches from Holmfirth in the north to Ashbourne in the south, and from Sheffield in the east to Macclesfield in the west. The best central place to stay overnight is Buxton (see below).

The peak in the name is a bit misleading, since there is no actual "peak"—the highest point is just 2,100 feet. The park has some 4,000 walking trails that cover some of the most beautiful hill country in England.

The southern portion of the park, called **White Peak,** is filled with limestone hills, tiny villages, old stone walls, and hidden valleys. August and September are the best and most beautiful times to hike these rolling hills.

In the north, called **Dark Peak,** the scenery changes to rugged moors and deep gullies. This area is best visited in the spring when the purple heather, so beloved by Emily Brontë, comes into bloom.

Many come to the park not for its natural beauty but for the **"well dressings."** A unique park tradition, this festival with pagan origins is best viewed in the villages of Eyam, Youlgrave, Monyash, and Worksworth, which lie within the park's parameters. Local tourist offices will supply details. The dressings began as pagan offerings to local "water spirits," but later became part of Christian ceremonies. Dressings of the wells take place from early May to August of every year. Designs are pricked on large boards covered in clay. The board is then decorated with grasses, lichens, bark, seeds, and flowers and placed by the spring or well and blessed.

If you're planning an extensive visit to the park, write for details to the **Peak Park Joint Planning Board,** National Park Office, Aldern House, Bakewell, Derbyshire DE45 1AE. A list of publications will be sent to you, and you can order according to your wishes.

GETTING TO THE PARK You can reach Buxton (see below) by train from Manchester. It's also possible to travel by bus, the Transpeak, taking 3½ hours from Manchester to Nottingham, with stops at such major centers as Buxton, Bakewell, Matlock, and Matlock Bath. If you're planning to use public transportation, consider purchasing a **Derbyshire Warfarer,** sold at various rail and bus stations; for £7.25 ($12.35) for adults or £3.65 ($6.20) for children, you can ride all the bus and rail lines within the peak district for a day.

If you're driving, the main route is A515 north from Birmingham, with Buxton as the gateway. From Manchester, route 6 heads southeast to Buxton.

GETTING AROUND THE PARK Many visitors prefer to walk from one village to another. If you're not so hearty, you can take local buses, which connect various villages. Instead of the usual Sunday slowdown in bus service, more buses run on that day than during weekdays because of the increased demand, especially in summer. Call ☎ **01298/23098** daily between the hours of 7am to 8pm for bus information.

Another popular way to explore the park is by bicycle. Park authorities operate six **Cycle Hire Centres,** renting bikes for £9 ($15.30) a day for adults and £6 ($10.20) for children 15 and under, with a £20 ($34) deposit, helmet included. Centers are at Mapleton Lane in Ashbourne (☎ **01335/343156**); near the Fairholmes Information Centre at Derwent (☎ **01433/651261**); near New Mills on Station Road in the Sett Valley at Hayfield (☎ **01663/746222**); near Matlock on the High Peak Trail at Middleton Top (☎ **01629/823204**); at the junction of Tissington and High Peak Trails at Parsley Hay (☎ **01298/84493**); and between Ashbourne and Leek on the A523 near the southern tip of the Manifold Trail at Waterhouses (☎ **01538/308609**).

BUXTON: A LOVELY BASE FOR EXPLORING THE PARK

172 miles NW of London; 38 miles NW of Derby; 25 miles SE of Manchester

One of the loveliest towns in Britain, Buxton rivaled the spa at Bath in the 18th century. Its waters were known to the Romans, whose settlement here was called *Aquae Arnemetiae.* The thermal waters were pretty much forgotten from Roman times until the reign of Queen Elizabeth I, when the baths were reactivated. Mary Queen of Scots was brought here to take the waters by her caretaker, the earl of Shrewsbury.

Buxton today is mostly the result of the 18th-century development carried out under the direction of the duke of Devonshire. Its spa days have come and gone, but it's still the best center for exploring the peak district. The climate is amazingly mild, considering that at 1,000 feet altitude, Buxton is the second highest town in England.

Essentials

GETTING THERE Trains depart from Manchester (see chapter 15) at least every hour during the day. It's a 30-minute trip.

About half a dozen buses also run between Manchester and Sheffield, stopping in Buxton en route, after a 40-minute ride.

VISITOR INFORMATION The **Tourist Office** is at The Crescent (☎ **01298/25106**) and is open between March and October daily from 9:30am to 5pm; off-season daily from 10am to 4pm. It helps arrange a limited roster of 2-hour guided walking tours of the town between June and September. Although they're free, a gratuity to the guide is appreciated. More practical are the self-guided tours that meander through the historic streets of the town, beginning and ending at the tourist office. Most visitors require between 75 and 90 minutes for the circuit. The tourist office also sells pamphlets outlining the town's most remarkable sites for 30p (50¢) a copy.

SPECIAL EVENTS The town hosts a well-known **opera festival** during a 2½-week period in July, followed by a 2½-week **Gilbert and Sullivan festival** that draws people from around the world. The tourist office will supply details.

Seeing the Sights

Water from nine thermal wells is no longer available for spa treatment except in the hydrotherapy pool at the Devonshire Royal Hospital, behind The Crescent. It is also used in the swimming pool at the 23-acre **Pavilion Gardens** (which are open at all times; admission is free). You can purchase a drink of spa waters at the tourist information center or help yourself at the public fountain across the street.

Another sight, **Poole's Cavern,** Buxton Country Park, Green Lane (☎ **01298/26978**), is a cave that was inhabited by Stone Age people, who may have been the first to marvel at the natural vaulted roof bedecked with stalactites. Explorers can walk through the spacious galleries, viewing the incredible horizontal cave, which is electrically lighted. It is open daily from March through October from 10am to 5pm. Admission is £4.75 ($8.05) adults, £3.50 ($5.95) for seniors, £2.50 ($4.25) for children 5 to 15, and free for kids 4 and under. A family ticket costs £12.50 ($21.25).

Set about 1¼ miles south of Buxton's town center is one of the oddest pieces of public architecture in the Midlands, **Solomon's Temple,** whose circular design might remind you of a straight castellated Tower of Pisa as interpreted by the neo-Gothic designers of Victorian England. It was conceived as a folly in 1895, and donated to the city by a prominent building contractor, Solomon Mycock. It sits atop a tumulus (burial mound) from neolithic times. Climb a small spiral staircase inside the temple for impressive views over Buxton and the surrounding countryside. It's open all the time, day and night, and admission is free.

Where to Stay

Lee Wood Hotel. The Park, 13 Manchester Rd. (Hwy. A5004), Buxton, Derbyshire SK17 6TQ. ☎ **800/528-1234** in the U.S. and Canada, or 01298/23002. Fax 01298/23228. www.bestwestern.co.uk. E-mail: leewoodhotel@btinternet.com. 37 units. TV TEL. £95–£116 ($161.50–$197.20) double. Rates include English breakfast. AE, DC, MC, V.

Within a 15-minute walk north of the town center and overlooking Buxton's most popular cricket ground, this hotel was built adjacent to a forest during the Victorian age of Derbyshire limestone. It's the most sophisticated hotel in town. Renovated during the 1990s, it has comfortable bedrooms, each with firm mattresses and tasteful appointments. The small bathrooms come with adequate shelf space.

A glassed-in restaurant, The Conservatory, isn't as cozy and charming as The Columbine restaurant (see below), but its food is almost as good, with more of an emphasis on recipes considered exotic by the locals. Set-price menus range from £18 to £26.50 ($30.60 to $45.05) in the conservatory, and are likely to include breast of French duckling cooked in fennel seed, ginger and garlic, or oven-baked fillet of red mullet topped with a salmon and coriander mousseline nestled on a saffron sauce with heat-shaped vegetables. Less ambitious platters and snacks are served in The Beer Keller, a popular pub.

WHERE TO DINE

The Columbine. 7 Hallbank. ☎ **01298/78752.** Reservations recommended. Main courses £7.50–£12 ($12.75–$20.40). AE, MC, V. Mon–Sat 7–10pm, Thurs–Sat noon–1:45pm May–Oct; Mon and Wed–Sat 7–10pm Nov–April. CONTINENTAL/MODERN ENGLISH.

Here is Buxton's most charming restaurant, serving the town's best food. It's reasonably priced but still rivals some of the more formal and expensive country-house hotels outside the center of town. Set behind a facade of gray Derbyshire stone, it was built during the Victorian age as a private home and retains some of its oldest vestiges within an atmospheric cellar. The place is especially popular during the town's annual music festivals; it sometimes prepares pre- and post-theater suppers. Menu items are straightforward and unpretentious, but fresh and flavorful, served in a bistro-style setting. Dishes might include supreme of chicken stuffed with a sauté of mushrooms served on a sherry vinegar jus, or grilled tuna steak with a black olive, red onion, and fresh basil butter.

THE HISTORIC MARKET TOWN OF ASHBOURNE

146 miles NW of London; 48 miles SE of Manchester; 33 miles NW of Nottingham

Another center for exploring the Peak District, this historic market town has a 13th-century church, a 16th-century grammar school, ancient almshouses, a population that doesn't exceed 5,000, and no fewer than 13 pubs, more than virtually any town its size in the district. The River Dove, which runs nearby, is known for outstanding trout fishing.

ESSENTIALS

GETTING THERE There's no train service to Ashbourne, as the rail lines that used to run into the village have been reconfigured into a walking trail.

The bus connecting Manchester with Derby stops in Ashbourne en route. It runs five times a day, and takes about 1¼ hours.

From Nottingham, you can take the train to Derby, then transfer to the Trent Bus no. 107. The bus takes about an hour and runs hourly from Monday to Saturday.

If you're driving from London, take the M1 motorway north, getting off at Junction 24. Continue east along A50 for the next 10 miles, turning onto A515 north into Ashbourne. From Manchester, take the A6 south as far as Buxton, continuing south along A515 into Ashbourne.

VISITOR INFORMATION The town's **Information Centre** is at 13 Market Place (☎ **01335/343666**) and is open from early March through June and September and

October, Monday to Saturday from 9:30am to 5pm; July and August daily from 9:30am to 5pm; off-season Monday to Saturday from 10am to 4pm.

WHERE TO STAY & DINE

For the best pot of tea around, try **The Old Post Office Tea Room,** Alstonefield, near Ashbourne (☎ **01335/310201**). Ernie and Jean Allen, owners and tea aficionados, offer a set tea menu. They also prepare an assortment of homemade goodies such as baked quiche, soup, and cold roasted meats—all perfect for a light lunch.

Callow Hall. Mappleton Rd., Ashbourne, Derbyshire DE6 2AA. ☎ **01335/300900.** Fax 01335/343624. www.callowhall.demon.co.uk. E-mail: emma@callowhall.demon.co.uk. 16 units. TV TEL. £130–£165 ($221–$280.50) double; £190 ($323) suite. Rates include breakfast. AE, DC, MC, V.

This is by far the most historic, appealing, and comfortable hotel in town, and it also sports Ashbourne's most prestigious restaurant. Originally built in 1848 as a private home, it was transformed into a well-managed hotel in the early 1980s. Most of the 30 acres of land have been leased to neighboring farmers. Set about 1/2-mile northwest of Ashbourne, the Gothic-looking, stone-sided house has been skillfully reincarnated to receive paying guests. Bedrooms are old-fashioned, with hints of the Victorian and Edwardian ages. The comforts, however, are up-to-date, especially the firm mattresses on the English beds, most often twins. Two rooms are large enough for families, and there is no smoking in eight bedrooms. Bathrooms, although small, are well equipped.

Rather pricey meals are served in a trio of dining rooms with flocked wallpaper and views over the garden. Menu items include escalope of veal with Dijon mustard, mustard seeds, and asparagus tips; and steamed halibut steak draped with smoked salmon with a leek and white wine sauce.

Izaak Walton Hotel. Dovedale, near Ashbourne, Derbyshire DE6 2AY. ☎ **01335/350555.** Fax 01335/350–359. 31 units. TV TEL. £105–£135 ($178.50–$229.50) double. Rates include breakfast. AE, DC, MC, V. From Ashbourne, drive north along the A515, following signs to Buxton. Two miles later, turn left and follow signs to Thorpe and Dovedale. The hotel is on the outskirts of Dovedale.

Set adjacent to the River Dove, a stream noted for its springtime trout fishing, this hotel was named after Izaak Walton, the 18th-century sportsman. The hotel occupies the site of a cottage set on the premises of what used to be Half Head Farm, where Walton was born and where in 1653 he wrote *The Compleat Angler,* one of the English language's definitive texts on fly-fishing. Set amid fields of grazing sheep in an isolated position about 1 mile west of Thorpe, it was built in the 17th century as a farmhouse. Today, it's an ivy-covered, overgrown cottage with stone walls and rustic grandeur. Bedrooms lie within both an original and a more recent wing, and each contains tea-making facilities and an iron. All of the rooms were last renovated in 1995. Each has a small bathroom with a shower stall, tidy maintenance, and adequate shelf space.

Even if you're not a resident of the hotel, you'll be welcomed for bar snacks in the cozy lounge or for full-fledged dinners in the dining room.

BAKEWELL

160 miles NW of London; 26 miles N of Derby; 37 miles SE of Manchester; 33 miles NW of Nottingham

Lying 12 miles southeast of Buxton, Bakewell is yet another possible base for exploring the southern Peak District, especially the beautiful valleys of Ashwood Dale, Monsal Dale, and Wyedale. On the River Wey, Bakewell is just a market town, but its old houses constructed from gray-brown stone and its narrow streets give it a picture-postcard look. Its most spectacular feature is a medieval bridge across the river with five graceful arches.

Still served in local tearooms is the famous Bakewell Tart, which was supposedly created by accident. A local chef spilled a rich cake mixture over some jam tarts, and tearoom history was made.

The best time to be here is on Monday, **market day,** when local farmers come in to sell their produce. Entrepreneurs from throughout the Midlands also set up flea market stands in the town's main square, The Market Place. Sales are conducted from 8:30am until 5:30pm in winter and until 7:30pm in summer.

ESSENTIALS

GETTING THERE To reach Bakewell from Derby, take the A6 north to Matlock, passing by the town and continuing on the A6 north toward Rowsley. Just past Rowsley, you'll come to a bridge. Follow the signpost across the bridge into Bakewell.

From London, take the M1 motorway north to Junction 28. Then follow A38 for 3 miles, connecting with the A615 signposted to Matlock. Once you're at Matlock, follow the A6 into Bakewell.

VISITOR INFORMATION The **Bakewell Information Centre** (☎ **01629/813227**) is at the Old Market Hall, Bridge Street. It's open Easter to October daily from 9am to 5:30pm; November to Easter daily 10am to 5pm.

WHERE TO STAY & DINE IN THE AREA

For a look at a working 19th-century flour mill, stop in at **Caudwell's Mill,** Bakewell Road (☎ **01629/733185**). Here, you can have afternoon tea with freshly baked cakes, breads, and pastries made right here at the mill, and then stroll through a variety of shops, including a handcrafted furniture store, glassblowing studio, jewelry shop, and art gallery.

✪ **Cavendish Hotel.** Baslow, Bakewell, Derbyshire DE4 1SP. ☎ **01246/582311.** Fax 01246/582312. www.cavendish-hotel.net. E-mail: info@cavendish–hotel.net. 24 units. MINIBAR TV TEL. £125–£145 ($212.50–$246.50) double; £195 ($331.50) suite. AE, DC, MC, V.

Four miles east of Bakewell, the Cavendish is one of the most stately country hotels of England. The stone-sided building was constructed in the 1780s as the Peacock Inn, and because of its location on the duke of Devonshire's private estate, has remained closely associated with that family.

The duke and duchess took personal charge of the hotel and its lavish restoration in 1975, furnishing the public areas and the more expensive bedrooms with antiques from nearby Chatsworth, a 15-minute walk to the south. The hotel is lavish, aristocratic, and charming. Beds are sumptuous with elegant fabrics and deluxe mattresses. Each room includes a well-designed bathroom with deluxe toiletries. Two rooms are rented to nonsmokers.

On the premises is a woodsy-looking pub, the informal Garden Restaurant, and another rather formal and elegant restaurant.

Riber Hall. Riber, Matlock, Derbyshire DE4 5JU. ☎ **01629/582795.** Fax 01629/580475. www.riber-hall.co.uk. E-mail: info@riber-hall.co.uk. 14 units. MINIBAR TV TEL. £118.50–£162 ($201.45–$275.40) double. Rates include continental breakfast. AE, DC, MC, V.

Directly south of Bakewell along Route 6, this symmetrically gabled structure was built from gray-toned Derbyshire stone around 1450, enlarged and discreetly altered by the Jacobeans, and intricately restored to what you'll see today by the present owners. Public areas are as richly historic and atmospheric as anything in the district. Bedrooms occupy the premises of a converted stable and are charmingly furnished, each with a four-poster bed and tasteful chintzes and antiques. The rooms are beautifully furnished and spacious with comfortable sitting areas. Four are rented to nonsmokers.

Many residents of the shire consider the hotel restaurant their favorite local haunt. It features elaborate table settings, well-informed cuisine, and is rather formal. Menu items include fillet of beef wrapped in bacon and herbs, topped with baked goat cheese with Provençale sauce; lamb served on spinach, tomatoes, and mushroom with garlic and white-wine sauce; and succulent desserts.

Rutland Arms Hotel. The Square, Bakewell, Derbyshire DE45 1BT. ☎ **01629/812812.** Fax 01629/812309. www.bakewell.demon.co.uk. E-mail: rutland@bakewell.demon.co.uk. 35 units. TV TEL. £74–£89 ($125.80–$151.30) double; £95–£105 ($161.50–$178.50) James Austen's bedchamber. Rates include breakfast. AE, DC, MC, V.

A dignified early Georgian building set behind a gray stone facade originally built in 1804, this is a landmark in the town, and a good base for visiting nearby Haddon Hall and Chatsworth House. Jane Austen rewrote part of *Pride and Prejudice* while staying here. Its original owner operated a prosperous livery stable; some of the bedrooms are in the old stable block in back. Last renovated in 1995, the hotel offers cozy, well-maintained bedrooms. Rooms are generally spacious and each has a comfortable English bed. Bathrooms are small; ten come with a tub and shower combination, the rest with shower stalls. Each is equipped with a hair dryer.

The restaurant offers sophisticated and flavorful dishes. Lunch and dinner might include roasted supreme of duck with a pineapple and prawn sauce served on a bed of Soya-flavored peppers; baked eggplant glazed with goats cheese served over curried vegetables; or grilled Dover sole with a champagne and caper butter.

HISTORIC HOMES NEAR BAKEWELL

The tourist office in Bakewell (see above) will provide you with a map outlining the best routes to take to reach each of the attractions below.

✪ **Chatsworth.** 4 miles east of Bakewell, beside the A6 (10 miles north of Matlock). ☎ **01246/582204.** Admission £6.75 ($11.50) adults, £3 ($5.10) children 5–15; free for children 4 and under. Mar 15–Oct 29 daily 11am–4:30pm.

Here stands one of the great country houses of England, the home of the 11th duke of Devonshire and his duchess, the former Deborah Mitford. With its lavishly decorated interior and a wealth of art treasures, it has 175 rooms, the most spectacular of which are open to the public.

Dating from 1686, the present building stands on a spot where the eccentric Bess of Hardwick built the house in which Mary Queen of Scots was held prisoner upon orders of Queen Elizabeth I. Capability Brown (who seems to have been everywhere) worked on the landscaping of the present house. But it was Joseph Paxton, the gardener to the sixth duke, who turned the garden into one of the most celebrated in Europe. Queen Victoria and Prince Albert were lavishly entertained here in 1843. The house contains a great library and such paintings as the *Adoration of the Magi* by Veronese and *King Uzziah* by Rembrandt. On the grounds you can see spectacular fountains, and there is a playground for children in the farmyard.

Hardwick Hall. Doe Lea, 9½ miles southeast of Chesterfield. ☎ **01246/850430.** Admission £6 ($10.20) adults, £3 ($5.10) children, £15 ($25.50) family ticket. House Apr–Oct Wed–Thurs, Sat–Sun, and bank holiday Mon 12:30–4:30pm. Grounds open daily year-round; gardens open daily April–Oct. Take junction 29 from the M1 motorway.

Hardwick Hall was built in 1597 for Bess of Hardwick, a woman who acquired an estate from each of her four husbands. It is particularly noted for its "more glass than wall" architecture. The high great chamber and long gallery crown an unparalleled series of late–16th-century interiors, including an important collection of tapestries, needlework, and furniture. The house is surrounded by a 300-acre country park, featuring walled gardens, orchards, and an herb garden.

MORE ATTRACTIONS AROUND THE REGION

National Tramway Museum. At Crich, near Matlock. ☎ **01773/852565.** Admission £6.70 ($11.40) adults, £5.80 ($9.85) seniors, £3.30 ($5.60) children 5–15; £18.20 ($30.95) family ticket (2 adults, 3 children); Apr–Oct daily 10am–5:30pm; (open until 6:30 weekends Jun, July, and Aug); Nov–Mar Sun 11am–3pm.

The National Tramway Museum is a paradise of vintage trams—electric, steam, and horse-drawn—from England and overseas, including New York. Your admission ticket allows you unlimited rides on the trams, which make the 2-mile round-trip to Glory Mine with scenic views over the Derwent Valley via Wakeridge, where a stop is made to visit the Peak District Mines Historical Society display of lead mining. It also includes admission to various tramway exhibitions.

Peak District Mining Museum. At the Pavilion, Matlock Bath. ☎ **01629/583834.** Admission £2.50 ($4.25) adults, £1.50 ($2.55) seniors and children, £6 ($10.20) family ticket. Apr–Oct daily 10am–5pm; off-season daily 11am–3pm.

This museum traces 2,000 years of Derbyshire lead mining. Its centerpiece is a giant water-pressure engine that used to pump water from a lead mine 360 feet underground in the early 19th century. You can crawl through a simulated mine level and climbing shaft.

The Royal Crown Derby Factory. 194 Osmaston Rd., Derby. ☎ **01332/7128000.** Tours £5.50 ($9.35) adult; £4.95 ($8.40) seniors and children; museum £2.75 ($4.70) adults, £2.25 ($3.80) seniors and children. Tours Mon–Thurs 10:30am and 1:45pm and Fri 10:30am and 1:45pm; museum Mon–Sat 9:30am–4pm and Sun 10am–4pm.

This is the only pottery factory allowed to use both the words *royal* and *crown* in its name, a double honor granted by George III and Queen Victoria. At the end of a 90-minute tour, you can treat yourself to a bargain in the gift shop and visit the Royal Crown Derby Museum.

4 Nottinghamshire: Robin Hood Country

"Notts," as Nottinghamshire is known, lies in the heart of the East Midlands. Its towns are rich in folklore or have bustling markets. Many famous people have come from Nottingham, notably those 13th-century outlaws from Sherwood Forest, Robin Hood and his Merry Men. It also was home to the romantic poet Lord Byron; you can visit his ancestral home at Newstead Abbey. D. H. Lawrence, author of *Sons and Lovers* and *Lady Chatterley's Lover,* was born in a tiny miner's cottage in Eastwood, which he later immortalized in his writings.

NOTTINGHAM

121 miles N of London; 72 miles SE of Manchester

Although it's an industrial center, Nottingham is still a good base for exploring Sherwood Forest and the rest of the shire. Nottingham is known to literary buffs for its association with author D. H. Lawrence and its medieval sheriff, who played an important role in the Robin Hood story.

It was an important pre-Norman settlement guarding the River Trent, the gateway to the north of England. Followers of William the Conqueror arrived in 1068 to erect a fort here. In a later reincarnation, the fort saw supporters of Prince John surrender to Richard the Lionheart in 1194. Many other exploits occurred here—notably Edward III's capture of Roger Mortimer and Queen Isabella, the assassins of Edward II. From Nottingham, Richard III marched out with his men to face defeat and his own death at Bosworth Field in 1485.

With the arrival of the spinning jenny in 1768, Nottingham was launched into the forefront of the Industrial Revolution. It's still a center of industry and home base to many well-known British firms, turning out such products as John Player cigarettes, Boots pharmaceuticals, and Raleigh cycles.

Nottingham doesn't have many attractions, but it's a young and vital city, very student-oriented. Its Hockley neighborhood is as hip as anything this side of Manchester or London. A look at one of the alternative newspapers or magazines freely distributed around town can connect you with the city's constantly changing nightlife scene.

Essentials

GETTING THERE The best rail connection is via Lincoln, from which 28 trains arrive Monday through Saturday, and about eight trains on Sunday. The trip takes about 45 minutes. Trains also leave from London's St. Pancras Station; the trip takes about 2½ hours. For schedules and information, call ☎ **0345/484950.**

Buses from London arrive at the rate of about seven per day. For schedules and information, call ☎ **0990/808080.**

If you're driving from London, the M1 motorway runs to a few miles west of Nottingham. Feeder roads, including the A453, are well marked the short distance into town. The drive takes about 3 to 3½ hours.

VISITOR INFORMATION Information is available at the **City Information Centre,** 1–4 Smithy Row (☎ **0115/9155330**). It's open Easter to the first week in October, Monday through Friday from 8:30am to 5pm, Saturday from 9am to 5pm, and Sunday from 10am to 4pm; the rest of the year, it's open Monday to Friday from 8:30am to 5pm and Saturday from 9am to 5pm.

SPECIAL EVENTS Culturally, Nottingham is on the maps with its **Nottingham Festival,** a premier musical and artistic festival lasting throughout the summer. The tourist office will provide you with complete details.

Exploring the Area

Put on your most comfortable shoes and prepare to tackle the more than 800 shops in and around town—Nottingham boasts some of England's best shopping. Start in the city center, with its maze of pedestrian streets, and work your way out toward the two grand indoor shopping malls, the Victoria and the Broad Marsh, located to the north and to the south of the center of town. Then, head over to Derby Road for your fill of antiques.

Fine Nottingham lace can be found in the **Lace Centre,** Castle Road, across the street from Nottingham Castle (☎ **0115/9413539**), or in the shops around the area known as the **Lace Market** along High Pavement.

Then, to catch up on the hippest and latest in fashion and furnishing trends, explore the many boutiques in the Hockley area, the Exchange Arcade, and the Flying Horse Mall, all in the city center.

The Search for Pilgrim Roots

Many North Americans who trace their ancestry to the Pilgrims come to this part of England to see where it all started.

The Separatist Movement had its origin in a small area north of Nottingham and south of York called Bassettlaw. Hamlets that were the strongholds of the Separatist membership are clustered into a relatively small area interconnected to Nottingham via the A60 and the A614 highways, between 30 and 35 miles north of Nottingham's center. In the order you'll reach them from Nottingham, they include Babworth, Blyth, Scrooby, and Austerfield Bawtry (you'll see it on maps simply as Bawtry).

Pilgrim patriarchs associated with these villages include William Brewster (usually identified with Scrooby) and William Bradford, who was born in a manor house still standing in Austerfield Bawtry. During the Industrial Revolution, Babworth was inhabited mostly by the owners and employees of the region's many coal mines.

Blyth is the most beautiful of the villages. It's no surprise that it looks like a New England town, with a green surrounded by well-kept old houses. The parish church was developed from the 11th-century nave of a Benedictine priory church. On the green is a 12th-century stone building, which was once the Hospital of St. John.

Scrooby is a tiny village of some 160 inhabitants where the Pilgrim leader William Brewster was born in 1566. His father was bailiff of the manor, so the infant Brewster first saw the light of day in the manor house. The original house dated from the 12th century, and the present manor farm, built on the site in the 18th century, has little except its historical association to offer. Brewster Cottage, with its pinfold where stray animals were impounded, lies beside the village church of St. Wilfred, but it's uncertain whether Brewster ever lived in it.

The village also contains Monks Mill on the River Ryton, now almost a backwater but once a navigable stream down which Brewster and his companions may have escaped to Leyden in Holland and on to their eventual freedom.

A turnpike ran through Scrooby in the 18th century, and there are many stories of highwaymen, robberies, and murders. The remains of one John Spencer dangled here for more than 60 years as a reminder of the penalties of wrongdoing. He had attempted to dispose of the bodies of the keeper of the Scrooby tollbar and his mother in the river.

The tourist office at Nottingham can offer advice on exploring these villages.

Of course, in a shopping mecca like Nottingham, unique art items abound. **International Fine Arts,** No. 5, The Poultry (☎ **0115/9412580**), is a prestigious art gallery, selling original oil paintings, watercolors, limited editions, and collections by David Shepherd, Sir William Russell Flint, Gordon King, and L. S. Lowry.

Patchings Farm Art Centre, Oxton Road, near Calverton (☎ **0115/9653479**), is a 60-acre art haven. Restored farm buildings house three galleries, working art and pottery studios, a gift shop, and art and framing shops.

And long known as Britain's first real craft center, **Longdale Craft Centre,** Longdale Lane, Ravenshead (☎ **01623/794858**), is a labyrinth of re-created Victorian streets where professional craftspeople work on a whole range of craft items, including jewelry, pottery, and prints.

Nottingham Castle Museum and Art Gallery. Castle Rd. ☎ **0115/9153700.** Admission Sat–Sun £2 ($3.40) adults, £1 ($1.70) children; free Mon–Fri. Mar–Oct daily 10am–5pm; Nov–Feb Sat–Thurs 10am–5pm.

Overlooking the city, Nottingham Castle was built in 1679 by the duke of Newcastle on the site of an old Norman fortress. After restoration in 1878, it was opened as a provincial museum surrounded by a charmingly arranged garden. Of particular interest is the History of Nottingham Gallery, re-creating the legends associated with the city, plus a rare collection of ceramics and a unique exhibition of medieval alabaster carvings, which were executed between 1350 and 1530. These delicately detailed scenes illustrate the life of Christ, the Virgin Mother, and various saints. Paintings cover several periods but are strong on 16th-century Italian, 17th-century French and Dutch, and the richest English paintings of the past 2 centuries.

The only surviving element of the original Norman castle is a subterranean passage called Mortimer's Hole. The passage leads to **Ye Olde Trip to Jerusalem,** 1 Brewhouse Yard at Castle Rd. (☎ **0115/9473171**), dating from 1189 and said to be the oldest inn in England. King Edward III is said to have led a band of noblemen through these secret passages, surprising Roger Mortimer and his queen, killing Mortimer and putting his lady in prison. A statue of Robin Hood stands at the base of the castle.

Brewhouse Yard Museum. Brewhouse Yard, Castle Rock. ☎ **0115/9153640.** Admission Sat–Sun and bank holidays £1.50 ($2.55) adults, 80p ($1.35) children; free Mon–Fri. Daily 10am–4pm. Closed Christmas Day, Boxing Day, and New Year's Day.

This museum consists of five 17th-century cottages at the foot of Castle Rock, presenting a panorama of Nottingham life in a series of furnished rooms and shops. Some of them, open from cellar to attic, display much local history, and visitors are encouraged to handle the exhibits. The most interesting features are in a series of cellars cut into the rock of the castle instead of below the houses, plus an exhibition of a Nottingham shopping street from around 1919 to 1939. This is not a typical folk museum, but attempts to be as lively as possible, involving both visitors and the Nottingham community in expanding displays and altering exhibitions on a bimonthly basis.

Museum of Costume & Textiles. 51 Castle Gate. ☎ **0115/9153500.** Free admission. Wed–Sun and bank holiday Mon 10am–4pm.

This is one of the half dozen or so best collections of period costumes in Britain, with exhibitions ranging from the 17th century to the Carnaby Street era of the 1960s. Many garments date from the 1700s, and include exhibitions of "fallals and fripperies" (gewgaws and accessories as designated by the disapproving Puritans), as well as lace, weavings, and embroideries, each of them a celebration of the textile industry that dominated part of Nottingham's economy for many generations. Look for the Eyre Map Tapestries, woven in 1632 and depicting the geography of the region.

Historic Homes Near Nottingham

Newstead Abbey. On A60 (Mansfield Rd.), 12 miles north of Nottingham center in Linby. ☎ **01623/455900.** Admission to house and grounds £4 ($6.80) adults, £2 ($3.40) students and seniors, £1 ($1.70) children. Gardens only £2 ($3.40) adults, £1.50 ($2.55) children. House Apr–Oct daily noon–5pm; gardens open year-round daily 9:30am–dusk.

Lord Byron once made his home at Newstead Abbey, one of eight museums administered by the city of Nottingham. Some of the original Augustinian priory, purchased by Sir John Byron in 1540, still survives. In the 19th century, the mansion was given a neo-Gothic restoration. Mementos, including first editions and manuscripts, are displayed inside. You can explore the parkland of some 300 acres, with waterfalls, rose gardens, a Monk's Stew Pond, and a Japanese water garden.

Wollaton Hall. In Wollaton Park, 3 miles from Nottingham center. ☎ **0115/9153900.** Admission on Sat–Sun and bank holiday Mon £1.50 ($2.55) adults, 80p ($1.35) children. Free other days. Apr–Oct daily 11am–5pm; Nov–Mar Sat–Thurs 11am–4pm. Drive southwest along the A609 (Ilkeston Rd.), which will become Wollaton Rd.

This well-preserved Elizabethan mansion, finished in 1588, is the most ornate in England. Today, it houses a natural-history museum with lots of insects, invertebrates, British mammals, birds, reptiles, amphibians, and fish. The hall is surrounded by a deer park and garden. See the camellia house with the world's earliest cast-iron front dating from 1823. The bird dioramas here are among the best in Britain.

Where to Stay

Nottingham Moat House. 296 Mansfield Rd., Nottingham, Nottinghamshire NG5 2BT. ☎ **0115/9359988.** Fax 0115/9691506. 175 units. TV TEL. £70–£120 ($119–$204) double; £100–£140 ($170–$238) suite. Rates include breakfast. AE, MC, V.

If you're driving, you'll appreciate this chain hotel's easy access from the A60 highway, and its location less than a mile north of the city center. It was built in 1968 as a modern alternative to the town's B&Bs. The rooms are standard but are well maintained; most contain twin beds. Most of the bedrooms are mid-size, except for the cramped singles often rented to business travelers. Thirty of the bedrooms are suitable for rental to families, and 130 units are rented to nonsmokers. Business travelers might be comfortable entertaining clients in the Churchill Restaurant.

If this hotel is full, a desk employee will be glad to refer you to the hotel's sibling, the **Royal Moat House Nottingham,** Wollaton Street (☎ **0115/9369988;** fax 0115/947-5888), where 210 units await. Doubles here cost £125 to £135 ($212.50 to $229.50) suites £140 to £200 ($238 to $340). Although the bedrooms are a bit more modern, and although it contains four different restaurants and bars, many travelers prefer to save a few pounds by staying at the Nottingham Moat House.

Strathdon Hotel. 44 Derby Rd., Nottingham, Nottinghamshire NG1 5FT. ☎ **0115/9418501.** Fax 0115/948-3725. 68 units. TV TEL. Mon–Thurs £125 ($212.50) double, Fri–Sun £69 ($117.30) double. AE, DC, MC, V.

This is a solid and unpretentious member of a nationwide chain. Built in the 1970s of gray-colored brick in the heart of town, it has seven floors, neutral public areas, and two bars. The nondescript bedrooms are equipped to a high standard, evocative of a first-class roadside motel. Amenities in the twin-bedded rooms include beverage makers, satellite TVs, in-room feature films, and 24-hour room service. Bathrooms are compact but have adequate shelf space. Forty-six units have a tub and shower combination, the rest shower stalls.

We much prefer the informal Boston Bean Bar, a combination saloon and diner watering hole, to the sedate cocktail lounge. More elaborate meals are served in Bobbins, a well-run but somewhat lackluster restaurant.

Where to Dine

Sonny's. 3 Carlton St. ☎ **0115/9473041.** Reservations required. Main courses £9.75–£12.95 ($16.60–$22). AE, MC, V. Mon–Fri 11am–3:30pm, Sat noon–3:30pm, Sun noon–3pm; Sun–Thurs 7–10:30pm, Fri–Sat 7–11pm. MODERN PACIFIC RIM/BRITISH/FRENCH.

This choice, in the fashionable neighborhood of Hockley, seems almost like a hip London restaurant of the moment. Dishes include charcoal-grilled peppered duck with mango and sesame-seed oil; tomato, fennel and goats cheese tart; and roast rack of lamb with butter bean jus and rosemary. Desserts include an exotic fruit salad with soft cheese flavored with lime juice and ginger and are deliberately conceived to raise eyebrows; many are delicious.

SHERWOOD FOREST

Second only to Germany's Schwarzwald in European lore and legend, ✪ **Sherwood Forest** comprises 450 acres of oak and silver birch trees owned and strictly protected by a local entity, the Thoresby Estate, and maintained by the county of Nottinghamshire. Actually, very little of this area was forest even when it provided cover for Robin Hood, Friar Tuck, and Little John.

Robin Hood, the folk hero of tale and ballad, fired the imagination of a hard-working, impoverished English people, who particularly liked his adopted slogan: "Take from the rich and give to the poor."

Celebrating their freedom in verdant Sherwood Forest, Robin Hood's eternally youthful band rejoiced in "hearing the twang of the bow of yew and in watching the gray goose shaft as it cleaves the glistening willow wand or brings down the king's proud buck." Life was one long picnic beneath the splendid oaks of a primeval forest, with plenty of ale and flavorful venison poached from the forests of an oppressive king. The clever guerrilla rebellion Robin Hood waged against authority (represented by the haughty, despotic, and overfed sheriff of Nottingham) was full of heroic exploits and a desire to win justice for the victims of oppression.

Now, as then, the forest consists of woodland glades, farm fields, villages, and hamlets. But the surroundings are so built up that Robin Hood wouldn't recognize them today.

Sherwood Forest Visitor Centre (☎ **01623/823202**) is in Sherwood Forest Country Park at Edwinstowe, some 18 miles north of Nottingham city off the A614, or 8 miles east of Mansfield on B6034. It stands near the Major Oak, popularly known as Robin Hood's tree, although analysis of its bark reveals that it wasn't around in the 13th century. Many marked walks and footpaths lead from the visitor center through the woodland. There's an exhibition of life-size models of Robin and the other well-known outlaws, as well as a shop with books, gifts, and souvenirs. The center will provide as much information as is known about the Merry Men and Maid Marian, whom Robin Hood is believed to have married at Edwinstowe Church near the visitor center. Little John's grave can be seen at Hathersage (36 miles away), Will Scarlet's at Blidworth (9½ miles away).

The center also contains a visitor information facility and the **Forest Table,** which offers cafeteria service and meals with an emphasis on traditional English country recipes.

Opening times for the country park are dawn to dusk, and for the visitor center, April to October daily from 10:30am to 5pm and November to March from 10:30am to 4:30pm. Entrance to the center is free, and "Robin Hood's Sherwood" exhibition is also free. A year-round program of events is presented, mainly on weekends and during national and school holiday periods. Parking costs £1.50 ($2.50) per car per day from April to October.

An odd and somewhat archaic holdover from medieval times are **The Dukeries,** large country estates that contain privately owned remnants of whatever trees and vales remain of Sherwood Forest. Most lie on the edge of heavily industrialized towns, and may or may not have privately owned houses of historic merit. Very few can actually be visited without special invitations from their owners. On the other hand, **Clumber Park,** a 3,800-acre tract of park and woodland maintained by National Trust authorities, is favored by local families for picnics and strolls. It contains an 80-acre lake at its center, a monumental promenade flanked with venerable lime (linden) trees, and the Gothic-Revival **Clumber Chapel.** Built between 1886 and 1889 as a site of worship for the private use of the seventh duke of Newcastle, it's open from early March until mid-January, daily from 10am to 4pm.

The park itself is open year-round during daylight hours, although its allure and the services it provides are at their lowest ebb during November and December. The gift shop and tearoom are open January through March daily from 10:30am to 4pm, and from April to late October daily from 10am to 6pm. Admission to the park, including the chapel, ranges from £3 to £14 ($5.10 to $23.80), depending on the size of your vehicle.

If you're specifically interested in the botany and plant life, head for the park's **Conservation Centre,** a walled garden with extensive greenhouses. It's open from April 1 to late September on Saturday, Sunday, and bank-holiday Mondays from 1 to 4pm. For information about the park and its features, contact the **Clumber Park Estate Office,** Worksop, Nottingham SKO 3AZ (☎ **01909/476592**).

SOUTHWELL

135 miles NW of London; 24 miles SW of Lincoln; 14 miles NE of Nottingham

If you don't want to stay in Nottingham, the ancient market town of Southwell, England's smallest cathedral town, about a half-hour drive from Lord Byron's Newstead Abbey, is a good center for exploring Robin Hood country. From Nottingham's center, drive northeast along the B686 (the Southwell Road), then transfer onto the A612 for the remaining distance into Southwell. It's a 17-mile drive.

ONE OF ENGLAND'S MOST BEAUTIFUL CHURCHES

✪ **Southwell Minster.** Admission free but a donation is suggested. Daily 8am–dusk.

The old twin-spired cathedral is an unexpected gem in this part of England. James I found that it held up with "any other kirk in Christendom." The Minster is the only cathedral in England to boast three Norman towers. The west front is pierced by a Perpendicular, seven-light window. Interior architectural highlights include a screen built in the mid-1300s and depicting 286 images of gods, men, and devils. Look also for a stunning early English choir and chapter house from 1288, the first single-span, stone-vaulted chapter house in the Christian world. The chapter house is noted for its "Leaves of Southwell," stone foliage so realistic you can distinguish oak from hawthorn, buttercup from ivy.

WHERE TO STAY

Saracen's Head. Market Place, Southwell, Nottinghamshire NG25 0HE. ☎ **01636/812701.** Fax 01636/815408. 27 units. TV TEL. £80 ($136) double. Rates include breakfast. AE, DC, MC, V.

Other than Southwell Minster, this is the town's most famous and historic building. Built during the Elizabethan age, it retains its original Tudor-style, black-and-white, half-timbered facade. Both Charles I and James I dined here, and Charles I was imprisoned here before the Scots handed him over to the Parliamentarians. After he was beheaded, the name of the inn was changed from the King's Arms to the Saracen's Head. Commanding the junction of the main ancient thoroughfares leading into the town, the old inn frequently entertained Byron. Today, you'll find cozy bedrooms strewn with nostalgic reminders of old England. That doesn't mean that modern comforts haven't been installed—they have. Bedrooms come in various shapes and styles, although all are comfortable, and a dozen are reserved for nonsmokers. Each compact bathroom has adequate shelf space. There is a pair of cozy bars with exposed beams and paneling, plus a restaurant serving well-prepared traditional table d'hôte meals.

WHERE TO DINE

Muscrofts Café Restaurant. 12 King St. ☎ **01636/816573.** Reservations recommended. 3-course traditional roast lunch £6.95 ($11.80), 2-course dinner £13.95 ($23.70), 3-course dinner £16.95 ($28.80). Mon–Sat 11am–4pm and 7–9:30pm. MODERN/BRITISH

If you don't dine at Saracen's Head (see above), this new addition is the other fine choice in town. The atmosphere is rustic, with wooden plank floors and low ceilings with beams. The chef, Andrew Ledger, offers fairly traditional British fare with a twist, which generally comes in the form of his creative and imaginative sauces. Try the grilled sirloin steak with a tomato and chestnut sauce, topped with almonds; stilton cheese and sweet corn crêpes with a parsley sauce; or Barbary duck served with a brandy, cream, and walnut sauce.

A SIDE TRIP TO NEWARK CASTLE

While based at Southwell, you can easily visit the ancient riverside market town of **Newark-on-Trent,** 7 miles to the east on the A612 and the A617, which is on the Roman Fosse Way.

King John died in **Newark Castle** in 1216. Constructed between the 12th and 15th centuries, the castle survived three sieges by Cromwell's troops, finally falling in 1646. Now in ruins, all that remains are a series of two watch towers, a gate, and a stretch of wall.

Although the ruins are unsafe to walk on or about, Newark has transformed a nearby building that was conceived in the 1880s as a public library into **The Gilstrap Center,** Castlegate (☎ **01636/78962**), an exhibition center and tourist information office. It commemorates the castle's role in English history. The main allure is an exhibit, *The Newark Castle Story and Crossroads*, and three videos are available for viewing. The center is open from April through September daily from 9am to 6pm. Off-season hours are daily from 9am to 5pm. Admission is free.

The castle gardens are open during the day. Technically, however, open hours are daily from 9am to dusk. Admission is free.

The **Parish Church of Mary Magdalen,** Church Street (☎ **01636/706473**), the town's delicately detailed parish church, is among the finest such structures in the country. Its 252-foot spire overshadows the Market Place. In the interior, seek out its vast transept windows. A stunning wall painting, *Dance of Death,* in the south chantry chapel, dates from around 1520 (exact year of its origin unknown). Open daily from 8:30am to noon and 2 to 4pm. Admission is free, but there is a donation box.

The Millgate Museum of Social and Folk Life, 48 Millgate (☎ **01636/655730**), is housed in a 19th-century oil-seed mill. Today, it contains portrayals of social and industrial life in the area from around 1750 until the dawn of World War II. Agricultural, malting, and printing artifacts are displayed, and a series of rooms depict domestic life in bygone times. The museum is open Monday to Friday from 10am to 5pm and Saturday and Sunday, and bank holidays, from 1 to 5pm. Admission is free.

EASTWOOD: A STOP FOR D. H. LAWRENCE FANS

100 miles N of London; 7½ miles NW of Nottingham

D. H. Lawrence was born in the Nottinghamshire village of Eastwood on September 11, 1885, son of a coal miner who labored in the nearby mines at Brimsley.

The site is commemorated with the **D. H. Lawrence Birthplace Museum,** 8A Victoria St. (☎ **01773/763312**). The memorabilia and furnishings authentically replicate what you might have found in a miner's home in 1885, with an audiovisual presentation that pays tribute to the conditions of the working class during Victorian times.

Admission is £2 ($3.40) for adults, £1.20 ($2.05) for children 5 to 15 and senior citizens, and free for kids 4 and under. Family ticket £8 ($13.60). The museum is open from April to October daily from 10am to 5pm; from November to March daily from 10am to 4pm.

Just down the road from the birthplace museum is the **D. H. Lawrence Heritage Centre,** Mansfield Road, (☎ **01773/717353**) commemorating the life of the author, this center, complete in a Victorian classroom. There is a gift shop, a coffee shop as well as a restaurant serving light meals. Admission times and costs are the same as the museum. However there is a combined ticket for £3.50 ($5.95) adults and £1.50 ($2.55) senior and children, for both venues.

If your interest in Lawrence is still piqued, you might want to stop into **Eastwood's Public Library,** Nottingham Road (☎ **01773/712209**), which devotes a room to folios, manuscripts, and memorabilia associated with the town's famous and iconoclastic writer. It's open Monday, Tuesday, and Thursday from 9:30am to 7pm, Friday from 9:30am to 6pm, and Saturday from 9:30am to 1pm. Admission is free.

Either the museum or the public library can provide a free pamphlet for the town's self-guided "Blue Line Tour." A badly scuffed but still visible blue line will lead you along the village's sites that played a role in Lawrence's life. The museum staff will describe for you a sojourn to the nearby coal mines at Brimsley, where Lawrence's father labored, and an excursion to Cossall, a nearby hamlet that was the home of Lawrence's fiancée and provided the setting for scenes in his novel *The Rainbow.*

To reach Eastwood from Nottingham, go to Victoria Station and board either Bus 231 or R11. Or you can drive for 7 1/2 miles northwest along the A610.

5 Lincoln

140 miles N of London; 94 miles NW of Cambridge; 82 miles SE of York

The ancient city of Lincoln was the site of a Bronze Age settlement, and later, in the 3rd century, was one of the four provincial capitals of Roman Britain. In the Middle Ages it was the center of Lindsey, a famous Anglo-Saxon kingdom. After the Norman conquest, it grew increasingly important and was known throughout the land for its cathedral and castle. Its merchants grew rich by shipping wool directly to Flanders.

Much of the past remains in Lincoln today to delight visitors who wander past half-timbered Tudor houses, the Norman castle, and the towering Lincoln Cathedral. Medieval streets climbing the hillsides and cobblestones re-create the past. Lincoln, unlike other East Midlands towns such as Nottingham and Leicester, maintains somewhat of a country-town atmosphere. But it also extends welcoming arms to tourists, the mainstay of its economy.

ESSENTIALS

GETTING THERE Trains arrive every hour during the day from London's King's Cross Station, a 2-hour trip usually requiring a change of trains at Newark. Trains also arrive from Cambridge, again requiring a change at Newark. For schedules and information, call ☎ **0345/484950.**

National Express buses from London's Victoria Coach Station service Lincoln, a 3-hour ride. For schedules and information, call ☎ **0990/808080.** Once in Lincoln, local and regional buses service the county from the City Bus Station, off St. Mary's Street opposite the train station.

If you're driving from London, take the M1 north to the junction with A57, then head east to Lincoln.

VISITOR INFORMATION The **Tourist Information Centre** is at 9 Castle Hill (☎ **01522/529828**) and is open Monday to Thursday from 9:30am to 5:30pm, Friday from 9am to 5pm, and Saturday and Sunday from 10am to 5pm.

EXPLORING THE CITY

The best lanes for strolling are those tumbling down the appropriately named Steep Hill to the Witham River.

The cathedral is a good starting point for your shopping tour of Lincoln, as the streets leading down the hill (you won't be working against gravity this way) are lined with a mélange of interesting stores. Wander in and out of these historic lanes, down Steep Hill, along Bailgate, around the Stonebow gateway and Guildhall, and then down High Street. Following this route, you'll find all sorts of clothing, books, antiques, arts and crafts, and gift items.

While walking down Steep Hill, stop in the **Harding House Gallery,** 53 Steep Hill (☎ **01522/523537**), to see some of the best local crafts: ceramics, teddy bears, textiles, wood, metal sculptures, and jewelry. You can peek down St. Paul's Lane, just off Bailgate, to investigate **Cobb Hall Centre,** St. Paul's Lane (☎ **01522/527317**), a small cluster of specialty shops selling outdoor gear, candies and gift items, German figures, and antiques.

✪ **Lincoln Cathedral.** ☎ **01522/544544.** Admission £3.50 ($5.95) adults, £3 ($5.10) seniors, students, and children. June–Aug Mon–Sat 7:15am–8pm, Sun 7:15am–6pm; Sept–May Mon–Sat 7:15am–6pm, Sun 7:15am–5pm.

No other English cathedral dominates its surroundings as does Lincoln's. Visible from up to 30 miles away, the central tower is 271 feet high, which makes it the second tallest in England. The central tower once carried a huge spire, which, before heavy gale damage in 1549, made it the tallest in the world at 525 feet.

Construction on the original Norman cathedral was begun in 1072, and it was consecrated 20 years later. It sustained a major fire and, in 1185, an earthquake. Only the central portion of the West Front and lower halves of the western towers survive from this period.

The present cathedral is Gothic in style, particularly the early English and decorated periods. The nave is 13th century, but the black font of Tournai marble originates from the 12th century. In the Great North Transept is a rose medallion window known as the Dean's Eye. Opposite it, in the Great South Transept, is its cousin, the Bishop's Eye. East of the high altar is the Angel Choir, consecrated in 1280, and so called after the sculpted angels high on the walls. The exquisite wood carving in St. Hugh's Choir dates from the 14th century. Lincoln's roof bosses, dating from the 13th and 14th centuries, are handsome, and a mirror trolley assists visitors in their appreciation of these features, which are some 70 feet above the floor. Oak bosses are in the cloister.

In the Seamen's Chapel (Great North Transept) is a window commemorating Lincolnshire-born Capt. John Smith, one of the pioneers of early settlement in America and the first governor of Virginia. The library and north walk of the cloister were built in 1674 to designs by Sir Christopher Wren. In the Treasury is fine silver plate from the churches of the diocese.

Museum of Lincolnshire Life. Burton Rd. ☎ **01522/528448.** Admission £2 ($3.40) adults, 60p ($1) children. Mon–Sat 10am–5:30pm, Sun 2–5:30pm. Closed Good Friday, Dec 24–27, and New Year's Day.

This is the largest museum of social history in the Midlands. Housed in what was originally built as an army barracks in 1857, it's a short walk north of the city center.

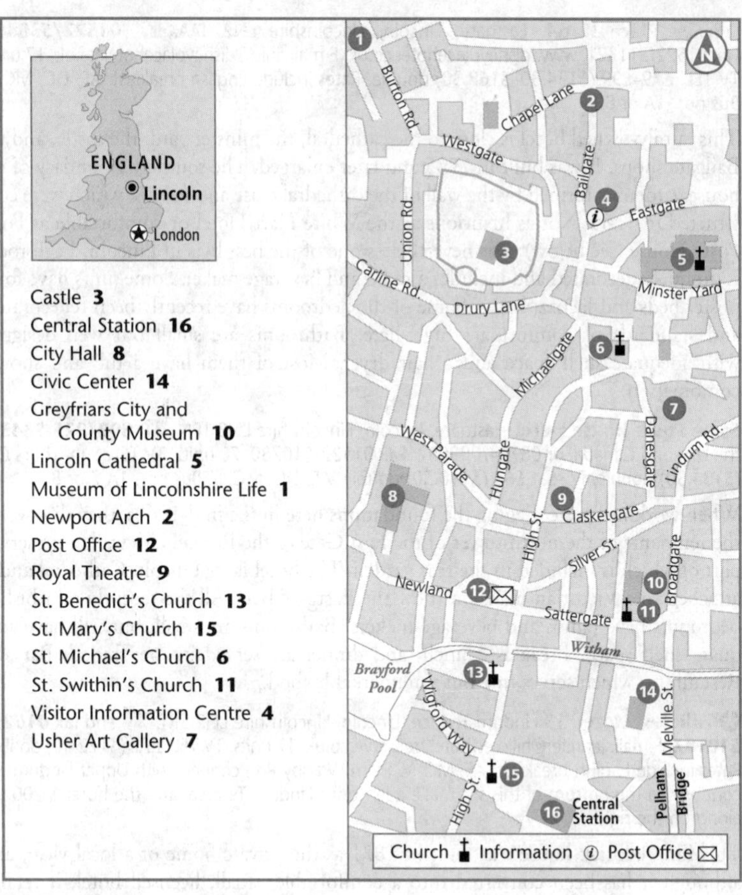

Displays here range from a Victorian schoolroom to a collection of locally built steam engines.

WHERE TO STAY

Castle Hotel. Westgate, Lincoln, Lincolnshire LN1 3AS. ☎ **01522/538801.** Fax 01522/575457. www.castlehotel.net. 20 units. TV TEL. £79 ($134.30) double. Rates include English breakfast and newspaper. DC, MC, V.

This redbrick, three-story, traditional English hotel sited in old Lincoln has been carefully converted from what was the North District National School, dating from 1858. It boasts splendid views of the castle and cathedral, which is just a 3-minute walk away. The bedrooms have been individually decorated and are named after British castles. Amenities include tea- and coffeemakers, radios and a complimentary newspaper. One room is large enough to rent to families. Some bathrooms contain a hair dryer, and most units have a tub and shower combination. Good English-style cooking can be enjoyed by candlelight amid tapestry screens in the oak-paneled Knights restaurant. Children under ten are not permitted.

D'Isney Place Hotel. Eastgate, Lincoln, Lincolnshire LN2 4AA. ☎ **01522/538881.** Fax 01522/511321. www.disneyplacehotel.co.uk. E-mail: info@disneyplacehotel.co.uk. 17 units. TV TEL. £79–£99 ($134.30–$168.30) double. Rates include English breakfast. AE, DC, MC, V. Bus nos. 1A or 8.

This family-owned hotel is close to the cathedral, the minster yard, the castle, and the Bailgate shops. It was built in 1735 and later enlarged. The southern boundary of the house gardens is formed by the wall of the cathedral close and towers, which were constructed in 1285. Not as luxurious as the White Hart Hotel or comfortable as Forte Poste House (see below), it is nevertheless one of the best bets in Lincoln. Each room is uniquely decorated and includes a radio and beverage maker. Some units have four-poster beds and Jacuzzi baths. Some of the bedrooms have recently been redecorated, and standards of comfort are high here. Bathrooms are small but well designed with adequate shelf space and a hair dryer. Most of them have a tub and shower combination.

Forte Poste House Hotel. Eastgate, Lincoln, Lincolnshire LN2 1PN. ☎ **800/225-5843** in the U.S. and Canada, or 08704/009052. Fax 01522/510780. 70 units. TV TEL. Sun–Thurs £79 ($134.30) double, Fri–Sat £65 ($110.50) double. AE, DC, MC, V. Bus nos, 1A 7 or 8.

When workmen were digging the foundations here in the mid-1960s, they discovered the remnants of the north tower of the East Gate of the Roman city wall, a preserved part of which is included in the rear garden. The hotel faces Lincoln Cathedral and is attached to a Victorian mansion (now the Eastgate Bar). All the recently refurbished bedrooms have radios and beverage makers. Bathrooms are small, but still have adequate shelf space. Breakfast, lunch, and dinner are served in the Trader's Bar and Restaurant, which serves fine but unremarkable food.

✪ **Hillcrest Hotel.** 15 Lindum Terrace, Lincoln, Lincolnshire LN2 5RT. ☎ and fax **01522/510182.** E-mail: jennifer@hillcresthotel.freeserve.co.uk. 17 units. TV TEL. £72 ($122.40) double. Rates include English breakfast. AE, MC, V. From Wragby Rd., connect with Upper Lindum St.; continue to the bottom of this st., make a left onto Lindum Terrace, and the hotel is 200 yd. along on the right.

This fine redbrick house was built in 1871 as the private home of a local vicar, and although it has been converted into a comfortable, small, licensed hotel, it retains many of its original features. The Hillcrest offers a cozy atmosphere and tries to accommodate personal requests. It's on a quiet, tree-lined road overlooking 26 acres of parkland, in the old high town and within easy walking distance of Lincoln Cathedral and the Roman remains. All bedrooms are well furnished and kept in shape. Rooms range in size and shape, but each has comfortable twin or double beds; some rooms have a four-poster. Extras include coffeemakers, and nearly all of the rooms open onto a view. The compact bathrooms have shower stalls and a hair dryer. The Terrace Restaurant offers a wide variety of English dishes with a European flavor cooked to order, with special menus for vegetarians and children.

✪ **White Hart Hotel.** Bailgate, Lincoln, Lincolnshire LN1 3AR. ☎ **01522/526222.** Fax 01522/531798. 48 units. TV TEL. £110 ($187) double; £140 ($238) suite. AE, DC,MC, V. $^1/_4$ mile from Lincoln Station.

The White Hart is named after the emblem of Richard II, who visited this region shortly before this hotel was constructed and probably stayed at an inn on the site. A letter written in 1460 by a London woman who paid sixpence for her room complains that her bed was lumpy.

The inn's facade dates from the 1700s, when it was a luxurious private home. Its life as a modern hotel began in 1913 when the live-in owners started accepting paying guests (only if they came with ironclad references). The hotel also hosted several meetings between Churchill and Eisenhower in the darkest days of World War II. Other guests have included David Lloyd George, Edward VIII, and Baroness Margaret Thatcher.

The inn is still going strong today and is still the best choice in town. The lumpy beds are long gone, although the inn does have a superb collection of antiques. Enter through a revolving mahogany door into a large and finely proportioned lounge filled with fine antiques, rare and unusual clocks, and display cabinets of rare silver, glass, and porcelain. Each of the accommodations, many of which were restored in 1995, has some antique furniture, a well-accessorized bathroom, and views of the old city. Opt if possible for an accommodation in the older structure where the units are more spacious and stylish than those in the lackluster annex. Each comes with a double or twin beds. Bathrooms are sparkling new with thick towels, sinks set into marble counters, and power showers over the tubs. You'll have to negotiate a labyrinth of narrow halls and stairways to reach your room. The Georgian-style main dining room has elegant furnishings and well-prepared lunches and dinners.

WHERE TO DINE

Jews House Restaurant. The Jews House, 15 The Strait. ☎ **01522/524851.** Reservations required. Main courses £12.50–£16 ($21.25–$27.20); fixed-price lunch from £6.50 ($11.05), fixed-price dinner £26 ($44.20). AE, DC, MC, V. Tues–Sat noon–1:30pm and 7–9pm. Bus nos. 1A or 8. CONTINENTAL.

Originally constructed around 1150, this stone-fronted building is said by local historians to be the oldest occupied house in Europe. Today, it offers the finest food in Lincoln. The dining room has a low-beamed ceiling, a cast-iron fireplace, and medieval features. Two of the massive ceiling beams are known to date from the construction of the original house. Seating only about 28 diners, the restaurant is run by chef-proprietor Richard Gibbs and his wife, Sally. Their menu features stylish dishes that change weekly according to market ingredients and the inspiration of the chef—perhaps grilled goat cheese served on a bed of fresh spinach with croutons and bacon, or roast rack of lamb with a pesto crust. All these dishes are savory and prepared in an up-to-date, modern style without heavy saucing. No smoking in the main restaurant.

Wig & Mitre. 30 Steep Hill. ☎ **01522/535190.** Reservations recommended. Main courses £5.95–£17 ($10.10–$28.90); sandwiches £3.95–£5 ($6.70–$8.50). AE, DC, MC, V. Daily 8am–11pm. Bus nos. 1A or 8. INTERNATIONAL.

This is not only the best pub in old Lincoln, but it serves fine food, too. Sitting on the aptly named Steep Hill near the cathedral, and loaded with an Old English atmosphere, it operates somewhat like a cafe-brasserie. The main restaurant, behind the bar on the second floor, has oak timbers, Victorian armchairs, and settees. This 14th-century pub has been substantially restored over the years. If the restaurant is full, you can dine in the bar downstairs. Starters are always intriguing, ranging from a salad of smoked mackerel to deep fried salmon, crab, and spring onion fish cakes. The menu is never staid and old-fashioned, but is constantly kept up-to-date, like in a trendy London wine bar.

FAVORITE LOCAL PUBS

Drop by the **Adam & Eve Tavern,** Lindum Hill (☎ **01522/537108**), the oldest pub in Lincoln, dating from 1701, where you can knock back a Magnet, Old Speckled Hen, or Theakston's Best Bitter in a homey, cottage atmosphere complete with gas fires and a large front garden for warm-weather drinking and browsing.

The **Jolly Brewer,** 27 Broadgate (☎ **01522/528583**), dates from 1850, and it's a basic wooden floorboards place where you'll be welcomed into a mixed straight and gay crowd. If you're hungry, there's pub grub at lunchtime only, and draft ales include Spitfire no. 3 and Bass, as well as rotating guests.

If you're looking for a drink and maybe a band in a unique atmosphere, visit **Cornhill Vaults,** Cornhill Exchange, opposite the Central Market (☎ **01522/535113**), a Roman wine cellar converted into a subterranean pub and club full of nooks and crannies scattered with brewery relics. On weekends the place gets packed and smoky.

A SIDE TRIP TO BOSTON

122 miles N of London; 35 miles SE of Lincoln; 55 miles E of Nottingham

New Englanders like to visit this old seaport, which gave its name to the more famous Massachusetts city. But it's ironic that the Pilgrims chose to name their seaport after this English town, for they suffered a great deal here.

In 1607, about a dozen years before their eventual transit to the New World on the *Mayflower,* some Pilgrims arranged for a ship to carry them to new lives in Holland via The Wash and the sea lanes of the North Sea. The captain of the ship betrayed them and absconded with their money; as a result, the group was imprisoned in Boston's guildhall for a month for attempting to emigrate from England without the king's permission. The cells they occupied can still be visited within Boston's guildhall. Also at Scotia Creek, on a riverbank near town, is a memorial to those early Pilgrims.

GETTING THERE

From Lincoln, there are about half a dozen trains a day, each of which requires a transfer in the town of Sleaford. The trip takes about an hour. From London, about 10 trains a day depart from King's Cross Station for the 2½-hour trip. For schedules and information, call ☎ **0345/484950.**

There's no bus service from Lincoln, and perhaps one or two buses a day depart from London's Victoria Coach Station to Boston. For schedules and information, call ☎ **0990/808080.**

If you're driving from Lincoln, take A17 southeast for 35 miles; the trip takes about 45 minutes. From London, take the A1 motorway north to Peterborough, then follow the signs to Boston. It's about a 3½-hour drive.

SEEING THE SIGHTS

The center of Boston is closed to cars, so you will have to walk to visit attractions such as the **Boston Stump,** the lantern tower of the Church of St. Botolph with a view for miles around of the all-encircling fens. As it stands, the tower was finished in 1460. In the 1930s, the people of Boston, Massachusetts, paid for the restoration of the tower, known officially as St. Botolph's Tower. The stairs aren't in good shape, so we don't recommend that you climb the tower. The city officials were going to add a spire, making it the tallest in England, but because of the wind and the weight, they feared the tower would collapse. Therefore, it became known as "the Boston Stump." An elderly gentleman at the tower assured us it was the tallest in England—that is, 272½ feet tall.

The **Boston Guildhall Museum,** South Street (☎ **01205/365954**), is a 15th-century guildhall that contains the courtrooms where the Pilgrims were tried and the cells where they were imprisoned. It is open year-round Monday to Saturday from 10am to 5pm, and Sunday from 10am to 4pm. The admission of £1.25 ($2.15) for adults or 80p ($1.35) for seniors. Children are free. Admission includes a 45-minute audio guided tour. Thursday is free.

Next door to the guildhall, the 1700s **Fydell House** (☎ **01205/351520**) is an adult education center but has a room set aside to welcome visitors not only from

Boston, Massachusetts, but also from the rest of the United States. It is open Monday to Thursday from 9:30am to 12:30pm and 1:30 to 4:30pm, and Friday from 9am to 4pm. Admission is free.

WHERE TO STAY & DINE

Comfort Friendly Inn. Bicker Bar (8 miles southwest of Boston at the junction of A17 and A52), Lincolnshire PE20 3AM. ☎ **01205/820118.** Fax 01205/820228. www.choicehotelseurope.com. E-mail: admin@GB607.u-net.com. 54 units. TV TEL. £57 ($96.90) double. Rate includes breakfast. AE, DC, MC, V.

This 1993 redbrick hotel is the largest hotel in the area. It's run better, and its amenities are more up-to-date, than any of the hotels in Boston's center, although its location southwest of the city is somewhat inconvenient. The comfortable and well-upholstered bedrooms are favored by business travelers, who also appreciate the hotel's many conference facilities and small gym. Beds have firm mattresses, and four of the rooms are spacious enough for families. Some two dozen rooms are set aside for non-smokers. On the premises is a well-managed restaurant where set menus are reasonably priced and a cocktail bar where simple platters of pub-style food, such as stuffed baked potatoes, are offered daily.

New England Hotel. 49 Wide Bargate, Boston, Lincolnshire PE21 6SH. ☎ **01205/365255.** Fax 01205/310597. www.menzies-hotels.co.uk. E-mail: newengland@menzies-hotels.co.uk. 25 units. TV TEL. £75 ($127.50) double. AE, DC, MC, V.

Originally built a century ago as a coaching inn near the Market Square (which at the time was on the outskirts of the city), this is the most appealing hotel in the town center. Its bedrooms were recently renovated into a bland contemporary format that is nonetheless very comfortable. The attractively decorated bedrooms are mostly mid-sized, and each includes a teamaker. Bathrooms are small but have adequate shelf space. Two rooms are large enough for families, and five are set aside for nonsmokers.

Pilgrims is one of the best restaurants in town, offering a fixed-price lunch menu for £9.95 ($16.90) and a fixed-price dinner menu for £13.50 ($22.95). There is also an à la carte menu offering such dishes as grilled salmon topped with cracked black pepper and a lemon butter sauce. There's also a cocktail lounge and a lobby bar, which is a bit grander than a pub.

15 The Northwest

The great industrial shadow of the 19th century cast such a darkness over England's northwest that the area has been relatively neglected by visitors. Most Americans rush through, heading for the Lake District and Scotland. But in spite of its industry and bleak commercial area, the northwest still has a lot to offer, including some beautiful countryside that remains unspoiled.

We will concentrate, however, on only three of its more important cities—Manchester, Liverpool, and Chester—plus a side trip to Blackpool, a huge Coney Island–style resort. You may want to visit it not so much for its beaches but for its kitschy, old-world appeal.

1 Manchester: Gateway to the North

202 miles NW of London; 86 miles N of Birmingham; 35 miles E of Liverpool

The second-largest city in England, ✪ **Manchester** is becoming increasingly important, as major airlines now fly here from North America, making the city a gateway to northern England. In recent years, Manchester has made great strides to shake its image as an industrial wasteland. Although chimneys still spike the skyline, they no longer make the metropolitan sky an ash-filled canopy. Abandoned warehouses are being renovated to provide sleek new loft apartments for yuppies. Rustic factory equipment turns up in museums rather than piling up in salvage yards. Even the old Victorian architecture has been given a facelift. The overall effect is a gritty kind of charm.

Manchester's roots date from A.D. 79, when the Romans settled here. It remained under Roman occupation until A.D. 410 when the empire began its storied fall. The west gate has since been reconstructed upon its original site. Little is known of Manchester's Middle Ages.

But then in the mid-17th century, the city began to capitalize on the wealth of opportunity that the burgeoning textile industry offered. Manchester eventually became the Dickensian paradigm of the industrial complex and the plight of cities. The railways were equally responsible for catapulting the city to the forefront of the industrial movement. England found Manchester both a convenient terminus and refinement center through which raw goods became viable exports. It is apt indeed that the Museum of Science and Technology resides here.

The Northwest

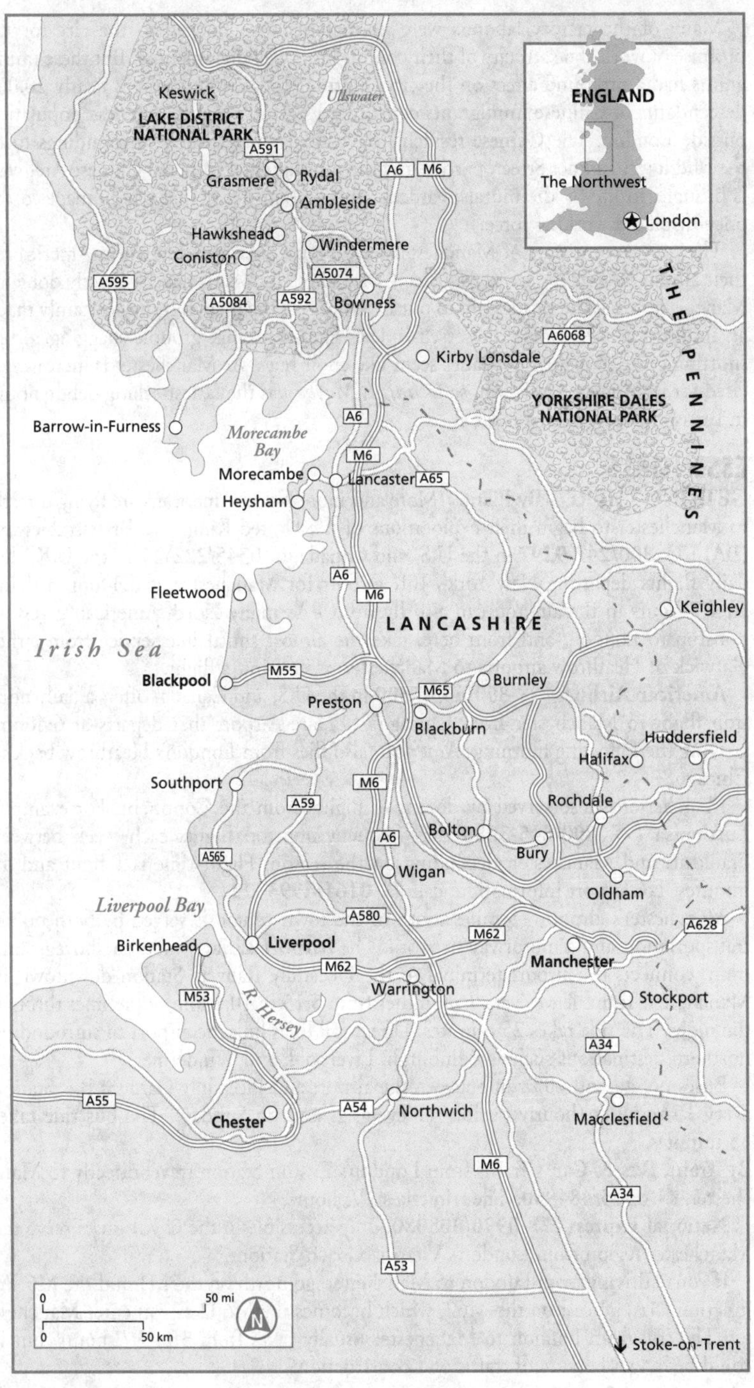
ENGLAND
The Northwest
London
Keswick
Ullswater
LAKE DISTRICT NATIONAL PARK
A591
Grasmere
Rydal
A6
M6
Ambleside
Hawkshead
Windermere
Coniston
A5074
A595
A5084
A592
Bowness
A6068
Kirby Lonsdale
THE PENNINES
YORKSHIRE DALES NATIONAL PARK
A6
Barrow-in-Furness
Morecambe Bay
M6
Morecambe
Lancaster
A65
Heysham
A6
Fleetwood
M6
Keighley
LANCASHIRE
Irish Sea
M55
Blackpool
Burnley
M65
Preston
Blackburn
Huddersfield
Halifax
Southport
M6
A59
Rochdale
Bolton
A6
Bury
A565
Wigan
Oldham
Liverpool Bay
A580
M62
A628
Birkenhead
Liverpool
Manchester
M62
Warrington
M53
Stockport
R. Mersey
A34
A55
A54
Northwich
Chester
Macclesfield
M6
A34
A53
0
50 mi
0
50 km
N
Stoke-on-Trent

Many of the factory laborers were immigrants who flocked to the city for the promise of work. The atrocity of their conditions is well documented. But these immigrants had a profound effect on the city's culture. Today, Manchester's nearly 20,000 descendants of Chinese immigrants constitute England's highest Chinese population outside London. The Chinese residents have amalgamated their surroundings to fit their heritage. Falkner Street, particularly the monumental Imperial Chinese Archway, is brought to life by the murals, gardens, and vibrant decor that pay homage to the once-displaced working force.

The most recent stars of Manchester have been Oasis, best known in America for their album *(What's the Story) Morning Glory.* These rock stars haven't exactly done for Manchester what the Beatles did to put Liverpool on the map, but they certainly made an impression. Of course, these self-styled "hard-drinking, groupie-shagging, drug-snorting geezers" make the Beatles seem like choir boys. As Manchester is increasingly cited for its hipness, Oasis, whose *Definitely Maybe* was the fastest-selling debut album in British history, helped make it so.

ESSENTIALS

GETTING THERE **By Plane** More and more North Americans are flying directly to Manchester to begin their explorations of the United Kingdom. **British Airways (BA)** (☎ **800/247-9297** in the U.S. and Canada, or 0345/222111 in the U.K.) has daily flights departing New York's JFK airport for Manchester at 6:30pm, arriving after 7 hours in the air. You can also fly from BA's many North American gateways nonstop to London, and from here, take the almost shuttlelike service from either Gatwick or Heathrow airports to Manchester, a 50-minute flight.

American Airlines (☎ **800/433-7300** in the U.S. and Canada) offers a daily nonstop flight to Manchester from Chicago's O'Hare Airport that departs at 6:40pm, arriving the following morning. American also flies from London's Heathrow back to Chicago.

Manchester is also served by dozens of flights from the Continent. For example, **Lufthansa** (☎ **800/645-3880**) has frequent nonstop flights each week between Frankfurt and Manchester, depending on the season. Flight time is 1 hour and 45 minutes. For airport information, call ☎ **0161/4993322.**

Manchester's airport, 15 miles south of the town center, is served by both public transportation and a motorway network. The **Airport Link,** a modern aboveground train, connects the airport terminal to the Piccadilly Railway Station downtown in Manchester. Trains leave every 15 minutes from 5:15 to 10:10pm, sometimes through the night. The ride takes 25 minutes. Direct rail lines link the airport to surrounding northern destinations such as Edinburgh, Liverpool, and Windermere.

Buses no. 44 and 105 run between the airport and Piccadilly Gardens Bus Station every 15 minutes (hourly during the evenings and on Sunday). The bus ride takes 55 minutes.

By Train, Bus & Car Trains from London's Euston Station travel directly to Manchester ☎ **0345/484950.** The trip takes 2½ hours.

National Express (☎ **0990/808080,** only accessible in the U.K.) buses serve the Manchester region from London's Victoria Coach Station.

If you're driving from London to Manchester, go north on the M1 and the M6. At junction 21A, go east on the M62, which becomes the M602 as you enter Manchester. The trip from London to Manchester usually takes from 3 to 3½ hours, but it could be longer because of traffic and construction.

VISITOR INFORMATION The **Manchester Visitor Centre,** Town Hall Extension, Lloyd Street (☎ **0161/2343157**) is open Monday to Saturday from 10am to 5:30pm and Sunday and bank holidays from 11am to 4pm. To reach it, take the Metrolink tram to St. Peter's Square. Especially useful are a series of four free pamphlets with information on accommodations, dining, city attractions, and cultural/entertainment options. Alternatively, if you are having trouble getting through to this Visitor Centre, you can try the Manchester North Visitor Centre, Granada service area, west bound M62 junction 18–19 birch (☎ **0161/6430988**). This center is open Monday to Friday from 10am to 4pm and Saturday and Sunday from 9am to 3pm.

GETTING AROUND It's not a good idea to try to hoof it in Manchester. It's better to take the bus and Metrolink. Timetables, bus routes, fare information, and a copy of a helpful leaflet, the *Passenger's Guide,* are available from **The Kiosk,** a general information booth within the Piccadilly Gardens Bus Station, Market Street (☎ **0161/2287811**), open daily from 8am to 8pm.

Buses begin running within Manchester at 6am and operate in full force until 11pm, then continue with limited routes until 3am. Tickets are sold at a kiosk at Piccadilly Gardens Bus Station.

A day pass, the **Wayfarer** (☎ **0161/2287811**) costs £6.60 ($11.20) for adults and £3.30 ($5.60) for children 5 to 15 and is valid for a complete day of public bus travel. Another source of bus information is **Stagecoach** (☎ **0161/2733377**).

Metrolink (☎ **0161/2052000**) streetcars connect the bus stations and provide a useful north-south conduit. Self-service ticket machines dispense zone-based fares. The streetcars operate Monday to Thursday from 6am to 11pm (Friday and Saturday 6am to midnight), and on Sunday from 7am to 11pm. They are wheelchair accessible.

SEEING THE SIGHTS

One of the city's major attractions, the City Art Gallery, will be closed until the spring of 2001. Consult their Web site for further information on the expansion project at http://www.u-net.com/set/mcag/cag.html.

If you're here between Easter and October, consider a visit to **Heaton Hall,** the museum's annex, 4 miles to the east. It's the centerpiece of 650 acres of rolling parkland, and accessible via the Metrolink tram (get off at Heaton Park). Built of York stone in 1772, and filled with furniture and decorative art of the 18th and 19th centuries, it is open only between Easter and October. Opening hours may vary, however are generally Wednesday to Sunday 10am to noon and 1 to 5:30pm. Call the Visitor Centre to confirm. Admission is free.

Manchester Town Hall. St. Peter's Ct. ☎ **0161/2343157.** Free admission. Mon–Fri 10am–5:30pm, Sun 11am–4pm. Closed Dec 25–26 and New Year's Day. Guided tours 2nd and 4th Wed and Sat at 2pm.

Alfred Waterhouse designed this neo-Gothic structure that first opened in 1877, and extensions were added just before World War II. The tower rises nearly 300 feet above the town. The Great Hall and its signature hammer-beam roof houses 12 pre-Raphaelite murals by Ford Madox Brown, commissioned between 1852 and 1856. The paintings chronicle the town's storied past, from the 1st century Roman occupation to the Industrial Revolution of the 19th century.

Manchester Cathedral. Victoria St. Daily 8am–6pm.

Originally just a medieval parish in 1421, Manchester achieved cathedral status in 1847 with the creation of the new diocese. The cathedral's nave, the widest of its kind in Britain, is formed by six bays, as is the choir. The choir stall features unique 16th-century misericord seats—caricatures of medieval life. The choir screen is a wood carving from the same era. Carel Weight provides her 20th-century canvas rendition of the beatitudes and there's also a sculpture by typographer Eric Gill.

The Jewish Museum. Cheetham Hill Rd. ☎ **0161/8349879.** Admission £3.25 ($5.50) adults, £2.50 ($4.25) children, students, and seniors, £8 ($13.60) family. Mon–Thurs 10:30am–4pm, Sun 10:30am–5pm. Closed Jewish holidays. Bus: 21, 56, 59, 89, 134, 135, 167.

The premises here were originally built in the Moorish revival style in 1874 as a Sephardic synagogue. It's one of only two such museums in Britain (the other is in London). It traces the culture and history of Manchester's Jewish community, estimated today at around 27,000. Part of the emphasis is on the experiences of immigrants, many from Eastern Europe, whose recorded voices describe the experience of life in Manchester's Jewish quarter in the years before World War II.

The Pumphouse People's History Museum. Left Bank, Bridge St. ☎ **0161/8396061.** Admission £1 ($1.70) adults Sat–Thurs, free Fri; free for students, seniors, and children. Tues–Sun 11am–4:30pm. Tram: Metrolink to St. Peter's Sq.

Few other museums in Europe catalog and commemorate the social history of the working class as carefully and with as much objectivity as this one. The museum began to take shape in 1990 when this was designated as the archive of Britain's communist party. Despite the fact that every exhibit is carefully couched in apolitical terms, it remains the most controversial museum in the Midlands. Of special note are exhibitions that describe the 1819 Peterloo Massacre of trade union activists by government forces, and the ongoing struggles of the coal miners of Yorkshire in their fight for higher wages and better working conditions.

Manchester Museum. University of Manchester, Oxford Rd., near Booth St. ☎ **0161/2752634.** Free admission. Mon–Sat 10am–5pm. Metrolink tram to St. Peter's Sq., then bus no. 41, 42, or 45.

This venerable museum showcases an eclectic and sometimes eccentric collection of the spoils brought back by local industrialists from their adventurous forays outside of England; there are archaeological finds from all over the world, including England's largest collection of ancient Egyptian mummies outside the British Museum in London. The museum is undergoing major refurbishment over the next two years, which may, at certain times, affect some of its exhibits. Call ahead to check.

EXPLORING CASTLEFIELD

Manchester had its origins in Castlefield, the city's historic core that local authorities have recently designated an "urban heritage park." It comprises the densely populated neighborhood that housed as many as 2,000 civilians beginning in A.D. 79, when Manchester was *Mancestra,* a fortified Roman camp strategically positioned between other Roman outposts, Chester and Carlisle. The roots of modern-day Manchester grew from here, providing the basic goods and services that supplied the soldiers in the nearby fort. After the Romans abandoned their fortress in A.D. 411, the settlement stood alone throughout the Dark Ages.

Castlefield's next major development was the **Bridgewater Canal,** which transferred coal from Worsley. Many other goods passed through this center because of the ease of transportation. Warehouses arose around the wharves, their names suggesting their wares (for example, Potato Wharf). Later, Liverpool Road housed the world's first passenger railway station, today home to the Museum of Science and Technology.

Manchester

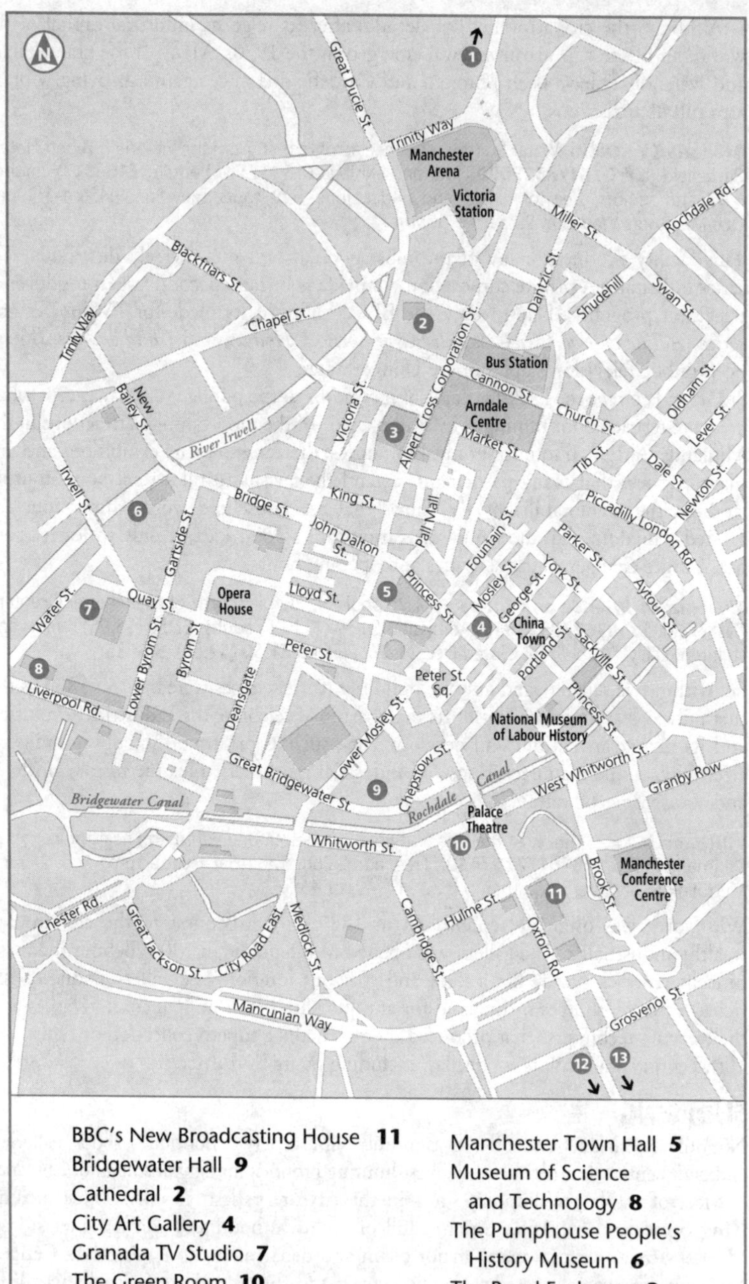

BBC's New Broadcasting House **11**
Bridgewater Hall **9**
Cathedral **2**
City Art Gallery **4**
Granada TV Studio **7**
The Green Room **10**
The Jewish Museum **1**
Manchester Museum **12**
Manchester Town Hall **5**
Museum of Science and Technology **8**
The Pumphouse People's History Museum **6**
The Royal Exchange **3**
Whitworth Art Gallery **13**

Although the city atrophied for decades after its reign as industrial capital of the world, an interest in urban renewal emerged in the 1970s. Many of the grand canals and warehouses have been restored, and Castlefield is once again a thriving, vibrant area full of attractions.

Granada TV Studio. Water St. (tour entrance across the st. from the Victoria & Albert Hotel), Castlefield. ☎ **0161/8329090.** Tour and exhibits £15 ($25.50) adults, £10 ($17) children 6–12 and seniors, free for kids 5 and under. June–Sept tours Tues–Sun 9:45am–5:30pm; Oct–May tours Wed–Sun 9:45am–5:30pm.

This facility produces many of the most popular and most widely distributed TV series in Britain. A private corporation, Granada is Britain's second largest producer of television programs, behind only the BBC. Many of its made-for-TV movies and series *(A Tale of Two Cities, Adventures of Sherlock Holmes,* and *Children's Ward)* have been public television staples in the United States.

Granada opens the backstage area of its studios to the public every day except when areas are restricted for filming. The studio is one of the most popular attractions in the Midlands. Although tours last only 45 minutes, there are so many exhibitions and displays on view that many participants extend their visits to fill several hours touring through the memorabilia of TV shows that are household words throughout the United Kingdom. Advance tour reservations are a good idea, if only to learn about last-minute changes to the activities and opening hours.

Museum of Science and Industry. Liverpool Rd. (1 mile north of Manchester's center), Castlefield. ☎ **0161/8321830.** Admission £6.50 ($11.05) adults, £3.50 ($5.95) seniors and children. Daily 10am–5pm. Closed Dec 24–26. Parking £1.50 ($2.55). Bus: 33.

Set within five separate and antique buildings, the premises were built in 1830 as the first railway station in the world. Its many exhibits celebrate the Industrial Revolution and its myriad inventions and developments, such as printing, the railway industry, electricity, textile manufacturing, and industrial machinery, plus the history of flight and aerospace exploration.

Whitworth Art Gallery. At the University of Manchester, on Oxford Rd., near the corner of Denmark Rd. ☎ **0161/2757450.** Free admission. Mon–Sat 10am–5pm, Sun 2–5pm. Metrolink to St. Peter's Sq., then bus no. 41, 42, or 45.

Whitworth was originally established in 1889 with a bequest to the city from a wealthy industrialist. The gallery was opened to the public in 1908. Behind the magnificent redbrick facade lies a light and spacious interior. The gallery is one of the richest research sources in England for antique patterns of wallpaper and textiles and the weaving techniques that produced them. There's a superb collection of 18th- and 19th-century watercolors on display, including many by Turner.

SHOPPING

Not only does Manchester offer a vast number and variety of boutiques, shops, galleries, and craft centers, but it's one of the best hunting grounds for bargains in all of England.

Most of the larger shopping areas in the city are pedestrian-only. These include **King Street** and **St. Ann's Square,** full of exclusive boutiques and designer stores; **Market Street,** with its many major chain and department stores; **Arndale Centre,** Manchester's largest covered shopping center; and the recently revitalized **Piccadilly** and **Oldham streets,** for fashion, music, and plenty of bargains. **Deansgate Street** is not pedestrian-only but does have a lot of adventure-sports shops.

ANTIQUES & FINE ART Those of you who like to search through dusty stacks of stuff searching for treasures will find Manchester and the greater Manchester area prime hunting grounds.

The Ginnel Antique Centre, 18–22 Lloyd St. (☎ **0161/8339037**), for example, has a massive selection of books, collectibles, art-deco and art-nouveau pottery, glass, and furniture.

More pricey antiques can be found along Bury New Road in Prestwich village, just outside of Manchester.

ART GALLERIES If you're into contemporary art, stop by the artist-run **Castlefield Gallery,** Liverpool Road (☎ **0161/8328034**). **The Gallery Manchester's Art House,** 131 Portland St. (☎ **0161/2373551**), focuses on artists whose work can be classified as being from the Northern School.

ARTS & CRAFTS You can really rack up a lot of one-of-a-kind items while exploring the many shops devoted to craftspeople and their art. For ceramics, glass, textiles, jewelry, toys, dollhouses, and the like, visit the exquisite Victorian building that houses **Manchester Craft Centre,** 17 Oak St. (☎ **0161/8324274**); **The Alexandra Craft Centre,** Upper Mill, Oldham (☎ **01457/876675**); and **St. George's Craft Centre,** St. George's Road, Bolton (☎ **01204/398071**).

FASHION Most of the fashion stores are centered around St. Ann's Square and King Street.

Men's and women's avant-garde clothing can be found at **Flannels,** Police Street (☎ **0161/8349442**). Classic and unisex clothing is sold at **Racing Green,** 33 King St. (☎ **0161/8352022**).

MARKETS Here in the north, markets are a tradition and offer you a chance to jump in and barter with the locals. Tourists tend to steer clear of them, so this is a great chance for a really authentic experience.

Although markets tend to sell everyday items and foodstuff, some stalls are devoted to flea-market goods and "antiques." Market days vary throughout the city, but you're bound to find at least one in full swing each day of the work week.

The major ones include Arndale Market and Market Hall in Manchester Arndale Centre; Grey Mare Lane Market and Beswick District Shopping Centre in Beswick; Moss Side Market and Moss Lane East in Moss Side. For information on Manchester's markets, call ☎ **0161/2341282.**

MILL SHOPS Manchester is an industrial stronghold with lots of textile mills. Most mills used to have a store, or mill shop, on site where customers could come to buy mill goods. Today, more and more of the mills are setting up shop in towns across the country.

Bury New Road in Cheetham Hill, near Boddington's Brewery, has a great selection of factory shops, discount stores, warehouses, cash-and-carry outlets, and street stalls on Sunday mornings. Some of the stores along this road do not sell to the general public and others require a minimum purchase.

The **Jaeger Factory Shop,** Thomas Burnley, Gomersal Mills, Cleakheaton (☎ **01274/852303**), has developed an extensive chain of outlet stores all over England. Jaeger will provide you with a complete list of stores and addresses. Stock includes overruns, damages, and imperfectly colored men's and women's clothing. This is the place to find the best price in the world on cashmere sweaters and factory knit seconds. A good line of Van Heusen shirts is also available.

A. Sanderson & Sons, 2 Pollard St., Ancoats (☎ **0161/2728501**), is one of England's most famous brands. The shop is right outside the heart of downtown and easy to get to. It's clean, modern, and fun to shop for fabrics by the yard, gift items made of Sanderson fabrics, as well as bed linen, carpet, and draperies.

MUSIC Audiophiles take note: There's more than live Britpop to be found in Manchester. The largest secondhand album and CD shop in all of England is the city's **Vinyl Exchange Used Record & CD Shop,** 18 Oldham St. (☎ **0161/2281122**), with recordings from all musical genres split between vinyl on the first floor, and CDs upstairs. With more than 25,000 selections in stock, it's worth setting aside some browsing time. You may just walk out with that single you've been trying to track down for the past few years.

Also check out the secondhand music stalls found near Piccadilly Station along Church Street.

For newer music, go to the **Virgin Megastore,** 52-56 Market St. (☎ **0161/8331111**).

WHERE TO STAY

Expensive to Moderate

Etrop Grange Hotel. Thorley Lane, Manchester Airport M90 4EG. ☎ **0161/4990500.** Fax 0161/499-0790. www.corushotels.com. 64 units. TV TEL. Mon–Thurs £132–£165 ($224.40–$280.50) double; £195 ($331.50) suite. Fri–Sun £90–£130 ($153–$221) double; £145 ($246.50) suite. AE, DC, MC, V.

Of the many hotels near Manchester Airport, this is the most historic; it carefully cultivates its image as an antique manor house. Originally built of red brick in 1760, with a modern wing added in the late 1980s in the same architectural style as the original bedrooms, it lies only a couple of minutes drive east of the airport. Don't expect lush meadows and views of fen and forest: The setting, like those of every other hotel at the airport, is one of sprawling parking lots and industrial-looking warehouses. But inside you'll find open fireplaces, ornate chandeliers, Edwardian windows, and many of the architectural features of the building's original construction. Bedrooms are often small but comfortably appointed; many have antique beds, but all beds are ensconced in brass or else canopied. Extras include beverage-makers, plus black-and-white tiled bathrooms with brass fittings and toiletries. Bathrooms have antique-style tubs without showers or else stalls with cascading showerheads. The gem here is a series of four-poster master bedrooms with sitting areas and baths fitted with whirlpool tubs. There's a bar, plus an informal restaurant with well-prepared food.

Forte Posthouse. Manchester Airport, Ringway Rd. (off Junction 5 of M56 beside Terminal One), Wythenshawe, Manchester M90 3NS. ☎ **0161/4375811.** Fax 0161/4362400. 290 units. MINIBAR TV TEL. Mon–Thurs £99–£119 ($168.30–$202.30) double, Fri–Sun £68–£89 ($115.60–$151.30) double. AE, DC, MC, V.

Among the first of Manchester's many airport hotels, this sprawling, four-story structure was built in 1961. It was refurbished in 1998 and is now quite modern. All bedrooms feature tea- and coffeemakers; TVs that can provide wake-up calls, guest information, room-service menus, and bill viewing; hair dryers; and hospitality trays. Crowned by dark wood headboards, beds are twins or doubles, each with a firm mattress. The tiled baths, though small, have heated towel racks and marble sinks. Extras include trouser presses and soundproofing. Some rooms are set aside for nonsmokers.

Dining: You can dine at Junction's with its modern style and innovative cuisine, or have a light meal at the bar and lounge while eavesdropping on the multilingual conversations going on around you.

Amenities: Health-and-fitness club with indoor swimming pool, gym, and sauna; courtesy bus to and from the airport; 24-hour room service.

Four Seasons Hotel. Hale Rd., Hale Barns, near Altrincham (2 miles from the airport, near Exit 6 of M56), Manchester WA15 8XW. ☎ **0161/9040301.** Fax 0161/980–1787. 147 units.

TV TEL. Mon–Thurs £120–£140 ($204–$238) double; £160–£250 ($272–$425) suite. Fri–Sun £69.50–£79.50 ($118.15–$135.15) double; £100–£150 ($170–$255) suite. AE, DC, MC, V.

Of the many airport accommodations, this one most closely emulates an American-style courtyard hotel, with a verdant oasis surrounded by a two-story block of motel-style bedrooms. The enclosed garden is very attractive, and a health club and indoor pool have been added. Rooms are done in the modern chain-hotel style you'd expect. Each comes with a firm mattress, plus a small tiled bath with showers. It's just fine for a one-night stopover, although you may not want to linger after that. Stiff drinks and filling meals are served in two in-house bars and two restaurants.

Hilton International. Outwood Lane (near Junction 5 of the M56), Manchester Airport, Manchester M90 4WP. ☎ **800/445-8667** in the U.S. and Canada or 0161/435-3000. Fax 0161/435-3040. www.hilton.com. 223 units. A/C MINIBAR TV TEL. Mon–Thurs £150–£175 ($255–$297.50) double, Fri–Sun £75–£118 ($127.50–$200.60) double. AE, DC, MC, V.

This is the best of the many modern hotels that flank Manchester's airport. Built during the mid-1980s, it features conservative but modern bedrooms with soundproofed windows. Plush carpets and pickled pine furnishings are inviting, and padded headboards overlook the comfortable beds. Rooms feature trouser presses, beverage makers, and desk space. Bathrooms have pseudo marble baths with hair dryers. The 60 more expensive "Plaza Club" rooms feature a wider assortment of perks and amenities than the less expensive accommodations.

Dining: Meals are served in both a cheerful and unpretentious carvery and a more formal restaurant, The Portico, where food always seems to be most felicitously preceded with a round of drinks in the Lounge Bar.

Amenities: 24-hour room service, shuttle service to and from the airport. There's a health club with a swimming pool, a garden, and a business center.

Midland Crowne Plaza Hotel. Peter St., Manchester M60 2DS. ☎ **0161/2363333.** Fax 0161/9324100. 303 units. MINIBAR TV TEL. Mon–Thurs £139–£159 ($236.30–$270.30) double, Fri–Sun £99 ($168.30) double; daily £225–£525 ($382.50–$892.50) suite. Breakfast £14.50 ($24.65) Mon–Thurs for doubles, and for occupants of suites all week. Fri–Sun double rates include breakfast. AE, DC, MC, V. Tram: Metrolink to Piccadilly.

This is one of the leading hotels in Manchester, a six-story, redbrick structure originally built in 1903 as the city's railway station hotel. Holiday Inn acquired it in 1985 and radically renovated and upgraded it as one of its top-of-the-line offerings, a Crowne Plaza Hotel. Although comfortable, bedrooms are rather anonymous looking, with none of the Edwardian flair retained in some of the public areas, which have the high ceilings, skylights, arches, and majestic columns of their original construction. Although lacking imagination, bedrooms with double or twin beds are fitted with fine mattresses, and the small tiled baths have shower stalls and adequate shelf space.

Dining: The most formal dining room is the French Restaurant. The more casual and least expensive choice is the Nico's Bar and Grill, offering French and international dishes. Somewhere in the middle is a staid but solid carvery, Trafford Room, which serves British roasts.

✪ **Victoria & Albert Hotel.** Water St., Castlefield, Manchester M3 4JQ. ☎ **0161/8321188.** Fax 0161/834-2484. 156 units. MINIBAR TV TEL. Mon–Thurs £165–£195 ($280.50–$331.50) double, £275–£400 ($467.50–$680) suite; Fri–Sun £99–£145 ($168.30–$246.50) double; £275–£350 ($467.50–$595) suite. Rates include full English breakfast Fri–Sun only. AE, DC, MC, V.

One of the most unusual hotels in Britain occupies a renovated brick-sided pair of warehouses, originally conceived in 1843 to store bales of cotton being barged along the nearby Irwell River and the Manchester Ship Canal to looms and mills throughout the Midlands. About a decade ago, Granada TV transformed the then-decrepit buildings into lodgings for their out-of-town guests, and a showcase for many of their creative ideas.

Bedrooms here are dripping with the authenticity and charm of the Victorian age. Each has exposed brick walls, massive ceiling beams, an individualized shape and themed decor, and in many cases, the ornate cast-iron columns of its earlier warehouse manifestation. Each room carries the name of a Granada TV show or series, all instantly recognizable to millions of Brits. Rooms are well equipped, most often with two armchairs, a dozen channels on TV plus pay films, trouser presses, one double bed, and dressers that form desks. The bathrooms have such touches as yellow duckies ready to float in the tubs with you and generous shelf space. The best and most spacious accommodations are called the Sovereign Rooms. Extras include beverage makers, fruit baskets, bidets, and private safes. Some rooms on the third floor are rented to women only, apparently for security reasons.

Dining: The Sherlock Holmes is one of the most clever restaurants in the Midlands (see "Where to Dine," below). There's also a bar named after Dr. Holmes's sidekick, Dr. Watson, and a French-style brasserie, Café Maigret.

INEXPENSIVE

Kempton House Hotel. 400 Wilbraham Rd., Chorlton-Cum-Hardy M21 0UH. ☎ and fax **0161/881-8766.** 12 units, 5 with bathroom. TV. £34 ($57.80) double without bathroom, £41 ($69.70) double with bathroom. Rates include English breakfast. MC, V.

A large Victorian house located 2½ miles south of the city center, this hotel provides basic, centrally located accommodations at a reasonable rate. You don't get much in the way of grand comfort in the rather smallish rooms here but you do get a good bed for the night, all at a reasonable rate. Rooms that contain private plumbing will have a shower stall. Those who must share a bath will find the corridor baths adequate, and you rarely have to wait in line. Rooms include tea- and coffeemakers. The hotel features a small bar and lounge. Several buses run by the hotel on a regular basis.

New Central Hotel. 144–146 Heywood St., Cheetham, M8 0PD. ☎ and fax **0161/205-2169.** 10 units, 7 with shower. TV. £33 ($56.10) double without shower, £35 ($59.50) double with shower. Rates include English breakfast. MC, V.

Located just off the A665 Cheerham Hill Road, 1½ miles from Victoria Station, this hotel offers simple but comfortable accommodations, each with a tea- and coffeemaker. Rooms are smallish but decently maintained with comfortable beds. You stay here for the price, not any grand luxury. There is a lounge and a bright, pleasant dining room where you can arrange dinner service upon request. Be sure and specify your needs when booking a room, since three rooms share all facilities, and none has private toilet facilities.

WHERE TO DINE

EXPENSIVE

✪ **Market Restaurant.** 19 Edge St. or 104 High St. ☎ **0161/8343743.** Reservations recommended. Main courses £9.95–£15.95 ($16.90–$27.10). AE, DC, MC, V. Wed–Sat 6–9:30pm. Tram: Metrolink to Piccadilly or Victoria Station (best to take a taxi). BRITISH.

The Market offers genuine nostalgia and unpretentious cheerfulness. Set in a 19th-century industrial building, it's outfitted with pieces made between 1930 and 1955. The seasonally changing repertoire is based on sophisticated but earthy interpretations of cuisine from throughout Britain and, to a lesser extent, some of its former colonies.

Examples include fillet of lemon sole stuffed with avocado and smoked salmon with a hollandaise sauce, or roast fillet of lamb with bubble and squeak (potatoes and cabbage) and rosemary gravy. About a third of the dishes are vegetarian, and might include Bulgarian spinach gratin with feta cheese and potato. Desserts are nothing short of splendid, raising syllabubs, puddings, and trifles to levels of bliss rarely experienced by diners of yesteryear. The rhubarb crumble ice cream served with a compote of rhubarb is as delicious as it is British.

Moss Nook. Ringway Rd., Moss Nook, 3/4 mile from the Manchester Airport. ☎ **0161/4374778.** Reservations recommended. 5-course set lunch £18.50 ($31.45), 7-course set dinner £31.50 ($53.55); main courses £19.50–£24 ($33.15–$40.80). AE, MC, V. Tues–Fri noon–1:30pm (last order); Tues–Sat 7–9:30pm (last order). CONTINENTAL.

This restaurant, named after the village of Moss Nook where it is located, is a favorite local choice for an upscale dinner. The setting, complete with red suede wallpaper, hefty cutlery, and elaborate table settings, is rather formal and heavy. The service is professional but warm and friendly. Menu choices include everything from the standard to the exotically imaginative—breast of duckling can be served in an orange sauce, or with red-currant-and-elderflower dressing. Especially good is a soufflé of Swiss cheese with chives and red-pepper sauce or halibut with scallops prepared in a parsley sauce.

Reform Bar & Restaurant. King St. ☎ **0161/399966.** Reservations required. 2-course lunch £12.96 ($22.05), 3-course lunch £16.95 ($28.80). Dinner main courses £12.95–£26.75 ($22–$45.50). AE, DC, MC, V. Mon–Thurs noon–midnight, Fri–Sat 6pm–2am. FRENCH.

Installed in the former headquarters of the Manchester Liberal Party, this Victorian building with Gothic overtones evocative of Venice lies in the old banking area of the city which has been turned into a bastion of the fashion industry. Replacing the politicians of yesterday, today's trendy crowd of models, photographers, and designers enjoy the feeling of a gentleman's club which has been enlivened and updated by Belgian-born designer and restaurateur Bernard Carroll. Large pieces of brass in female shapes and candlestick holders worthy of a haunted manor characterize the décor. An intriguing choice of both warm and cold starters tempt palates, ranging from a terrine of game with fig chutney to woodland mushrooms flavored with olive oil, garlic, fresh parsley, and shallots. A good representation of fish and vegetable dishes keeps the menu light and sophisticated, although there is an equal number of meat and game dishes prepared with competence, understanding, and no gimmicks. Try the partridge roasted in vines leaves and served with honeyed cranberries or the rump of lamb roasted with thyme and rosemary as in the English kitchens of yore. We've seen better dessert lists in our day, although the citrus cheesecake with lemon curd is worth saving room for.

✪ **Sherlock Holmes Restaurant.** In the Victoria & Albert Hotel, Water St. ☎ **0161/8321188.** Reservations recommended. 3-course fixed-price dinner £24 ($40.80); main courses £16–£24 ($27.20–$40.80). AE, DC, MC, V. Mon–Sat 7–9:30pm. BRITISH.

This is the most hip and interesting restaurant in Manchester. The setting—a converted 1843 cotton warehouse—combines soaring brick walls, heavy ceiling beams, dozens of verdant plants, cast-iron columns, and views of the Irwell River with a lively association with Granada, Britain's second-largest TV studio.

Your meal might include what the menu describes as "snobby queen scallops and expensive wild-mushroom stew with layered potatoes," and "mega-trendy terrine of salmon and herbs with lobster-flavored mayonnaise and a prawn and olive-oil dressing in the style of Paris House." Whether you come here to ogle, dine, or both, you'll have lots of company. Anyone from a hopeful job applicant to a media wanna-be from London might be at the next table.

The adjacent bar, Dr. Watson's, is warmly comfortable—a re-creation of the fussy but masculine parlor you might have found within the sleuth's apocryphal Victorian town house on London's Baker Street.

MODERATE

Rhodes & Co. Brasserie & Bar. Water's Beach. Tafford Park. ☎ **0161/681900.** Reservations required. Lunch main courses £3.80–£6.80 ($6.45–$11.55). Dinner main courses £7.50–£14 ($12.75–$23.80). AE, DC, MC, V. Mon–Sat noon–3:30pm and 6:30–9:45pm, Sat 6:30–9:45pm. MODERN BRITISH.

Today the gourmets of Manchester don't have to go all the way to London to sample the superb viands of super-chef and media darling, Gary Rhodes. The celebrity chef has established a northern outpost in Manchester, at the unlikely site of the middle-bracket Quality Hotel. A huge Manchester fan, Mr. Rhodes chose this site with its glass entrance overlooking the city's grand soccer stadium. Sports are put aside once you enter the subdued and elegant setting with candlelight. Although he's most often elsewhere, the menu is pure Gary Rhodes style where England and other classics are reinvented by him.

His interpretation of English cuisine is light and humorous. He's got all the old favorites on the menu but never have fried cod and chips tasted so light and feathery, with a delicate flavor. His smoked haddock comes topped with Welsh rarebit, a wine risotto, and, as a throwback to mama, English mashed potatoes. Delectable vegetarian dishes are also cooked to order. Mr. Rhodes has long been known for his cutting-edge desserts, and his Manchester outpost serves up some of the best of them. Seemingly British puddings have never received such love and care in the kitchen or tasted better.

Yang Sing. 34 Princess St. ☎ **0161/2362200.** Reservations required. Main courses £8–£12 ($13.60–$20.40). AE, MC, V. Daily noon–11pm. Metrolink tram to Piccadilly. CANTONESE.

Manchester has a large population of immigrants from China, Hong Kong, and India. Many of them consider Yang Sing their favorite restaurant, as proven by the cacophony of languages spoken within its basement dining room. It's loud but efficient, with a fast turnover of tables. Dim sum, those delicate dumplings, are served in a blissful array of choices from a pair of oversize carts in the dining room's center. Menu items cover the gamut of the Cantonese repertoire.

In 1996, Yang Sing began offering a street-level "steamboat restaurant," where containers of bubbling broth are brought to your table accompanied with an assortment of raw chicken, fish, chopped vegetables, and beef. Use your chopsticks to dunk the tidbits into the hot broth (think of it as a Chinese version of a Swiss fondue).

MANCHESTER AFTER DARK

THE CLUB & MUSIC SCENE

Above all else, Manchester is known for its recent contributions to pop music. From The Smiths and New Order to Oasis and the Stone Roses, the "Manchester sound" has been known throughout the world for over a decade. Yet surprisingly enough, live music went by the wayside in the early 1990s, and clubs were in short supply until they started making a steady comeback in the last couple of years.

The city's most famous landmark, **The Hacienda,** sadly has closed. It used to book some of the top music groups in England, and fans still come here looking for the site. Hooking up with the same booking agents, the **Boardwalk,** Little Peter Street

(☎ **0161/2283555**), has gained popularity by hosting "Stone Love II," an extension of the former Hacienda's showcase.

Other nights of the week, head to **The Roadhouse,** Newton Street (☎ **0161/2281789**), the hottest small venue in Manchester, which hosts bands up to 7 nights a week. Monday through Saturday check out **Band on the Wall,** 25 Swan St., at Oak Street (☎ **0161/8326625**), where live rock, blues, jazz, and reggae can be heard. For edgier music, check the stage at **Star & Garter,** Farefield Street (☎ **0161/2736726**), on Wednesday through Friday, when harder rock and hard-core acts will get in your face.

Dance clubs have taken over the town in the '90s. Just stroll through the Castlefield district on a weekend night and check out all the bars featuring a DJ. Clubs are everywhere.

On York Street near Oxford Road, **The Holy City Zoo** (☎ **0161/2737467**) offers up everything from garage to house on Thursday through Saturday nights.

Located in the old three-story headquarters of Factory Records, **Paradise Factory,** 112–116 Princess St. (☎ **0161/2735422**), offers up techno and disco to a mainly gay crowd.

A Pub Crawl

Peveril of the Peak, Great Bridgewater Street (☎ **0161/2366364**), is easy enough to find—just look for a 380-year-old triangular building covered in tile from top to bottom. No one seems to know why it was designed or built that way, but you can step inside and enjoy a pint of Wilson's Original, Theakston's Best Bitter, Yorkshire Terrier, or Webster's Best Bitter while you puzzle over it.

Manto, 46 Canal St., behind Chorlton Street Coach Station (☎ **0161/2362667**), is more than a gay pub; it's a major scene, and serves as a sort of clearinghouse of information on the hottest happenings in the gay community. Read the flyers posted around the interior and strike up a conversation with an employee or regular to find out what's what if you're out and about.

A late-Victorian drinking house renowned for its environment as well as its ales, the **Marble Arch,** 73 Rochdale Rd., Ancoats, at the corner of Gould Street (☎ **0161/8325914**), just east of Victoria Station, has high barrel-vaulted ceilings, extensive marble and tile surfaces, a mosaic barroom floor, carved wooden mantelpiece, and glazed brick walls. It's a great place to linger over a pint of Hopwood Bitter, Oak Wobbly Bob, or Titanic Captain Smith. If you like slapstick, the Laurel and Hardy Preservation Society shows old movies here on the 3rd Wednesday of the month. Recent improvements include the opening of their own microbrewery featuring four of their homemade suds.

The Performing Arts

Everyone knows about the rock scene in Manchester, but the fine arts are thriving as well. For information on what's happening when you visit, contact **Arts About Manchester,** 23 New Mount St. (☎ **0161/9534035**).

For drama with an unobstructed view, go to the nation's largest theater-in-the-round, **The Royal Exchange,** St. Ann's Square (☎ **0161/8339833**), which is housed in a futuristic glass-and-steel structure built within the Great Hall of Manchester's former Cotton Exchange, and offers 48 weeks of in-house dramaturgy every year.

Home of the renowned **Halle Orchestra, The Bridgewater Hall,** Lower Mosley Street (☎ **0161/9079000**), is a state-of-the-art, 2,400-seat concert hall. In addition to the orchestra's season, it also presents other classical performances as well as some pop and comedy, too.

The University of Manchester's Department of Music, Dunmark Road (☎ **0161/2754982**), is home to one of the nation's most distinctive classical string quartets, the **Lindsay String Quartet,** which performs a series of eight evening concerts in the department's auditorium during the year. For a real bargain, check on its luncheon recital series, which is free.

The BBC's **New Broadcasting House,** Oxford Road (☎ **0161/2444001**), has free tickets to musical performances that are taped in its Studio Seven for broadcast on BBC Radio 3.

The internationally acclaimed **BBC Philharmonic** performs Saturday-evening concerts 12 times a year at Bridgewater Hall (box office **0161/9079000**).

Presenting new theater, dance, and live art at the local, national, and international levels, **The Green Room,** Whitworth Street West (☎ **0161/9505777,** or 0161/9505900 for the box office), a theater-cafe bar, hosts performances mainly during its two seasons, spring (January through June) and autumn (September through December).

2 Liverpool

219 miles NW of London; 103 miles NW of Birmingham; 35 miles W of Manchester

Liverpool, with its famous waterfront on the River Mersey, is a great shipping port and industrial center. King John launched it on its road to glory when he granted it a charter in 1207. Before that, it had been a tiny 12th-century fishing village, but it quickly became a port for shipping men and materials to Ireland. In the 18th century, it grew to prominence because of the sugar, spice, and tobacco trade with the Americans. By the time Victoria came to the throne, Liverpool had become Britain's biggest commercial seaport.

Recent refurbishing of the Albert Dock, the establishment of a Maritime Museum, and the conversion of warehouses into little stores similar to those in Ghirardelli Square in San Francisco have made this an up-and-coming area once again, with many attractions for visitors. Liverpudlians are proud of their city, with its new hotels, two cathedrals, shopping and entertainment complexes, and parks. And of course, whether they're fans of the Fab Four or not, most visitors to Liverpool want to see where Beatlemania began.

ESSENTIALS

GETTING THERE Liverpool has its own airport (☎ **0151/2884000**), which has frequent daily flights from many parts of the United Kingdom, including London, the Isle of Man, and Ireland.

Frequent express trains depart London's Euston Station for Liverpool, a 2¾-hour trip. For schedules and information, call **0345/484950.** There is also frequent service from Manchester, a 45-minute ride away.

National Express buses depart London's Victoria Coach Station every 3 hours for the 4¼-hour trip to Liverpool. Buses also arrive every hour from Manchester, a 1-hour ride away. For schedules and information, call ☎ **0990/808080.**

If you're driving from London, head north on the M1, then northwest on the M6 to the junction with M62, which heads west to Liverpool.

VISITOR INFORMATION The **Tourist Information Centre** is at the Atlantic Pavilion, Albert Dock (☎ **0151/7088854**), and is open daily from 10am to 5:30pm. There is also a Tourist Information Centre in the City Centre: **Merseyside Welcome Centre,** Clayton Square (☎ **0151/7088838**). It's open Monday through Saturday from 9:30am to 5:30pm.

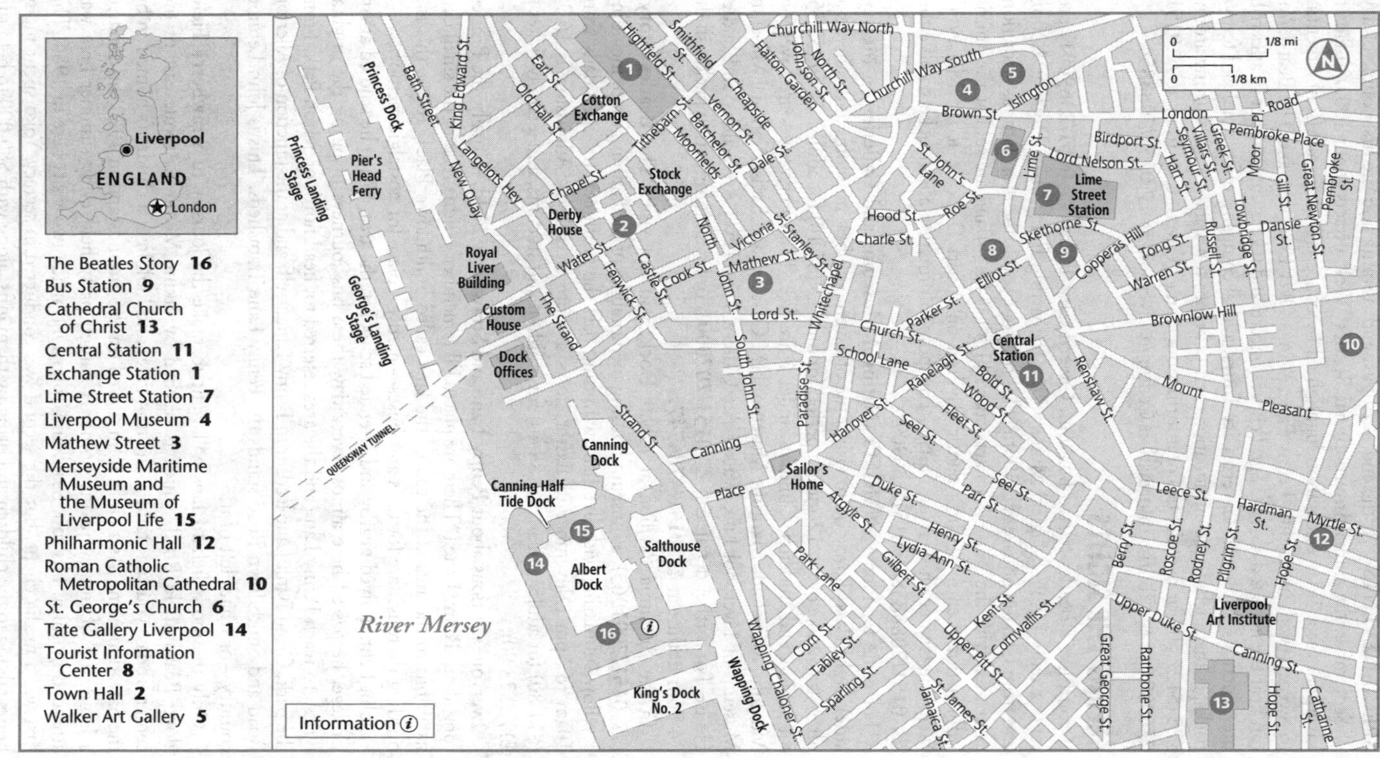
Liverpool
ENGLAND
London
The Beatles Story 16
Bus Station 9
Cathedral Church of Christ 13
Central Station 11
Exchange Station 1
Lime Street Station 7
Liverpool Museum 4
Mathew Street 3
Merseyside Maritime Museum and the Museum of Liverpool Life 15
Philharmonic Hall 12
Roman Catholic Metropolitan Cathedral 10
St. George's Church 6
Tate Gallery Liverpool 14
Tourist Information Center 8
Town Hall 2
Walker Art Gallery 5
Information
River Mersey
0
1/8 mi
0
1/8 km
N
Princess Dock
Bath Street
King Edward St.
Princess Landing Stage
Pier's Head Ferry
George's Landing Stage
QUEENSWAY TUNNEL
Royal Liver Building
Custom House
Dock Offices
Canning Dock
Canning Half Tide Dock
Albert Dock
Salthouse Dock
King's Dock No. 2
Wapping Dock
Cotton Exchange
Stock Exchange
Derby House
Sailor's Home
Central Station
Lime Street Station
Liverpool Art Institute
New Quay
Langelots Hey
Old Hall St.
Earl St.
Chapel St.
Highfield St.
Smithfield St.
Tithebarn St.
Moorfields
Cheapside
Vernon St.
Batchelor St.
Dale St.
Halton Garden
Johnson St.
North St.
Churchill Way North
Churchill Way South
Brown St.
Islington
Lime St.
St. John's Lane
Roe St.
Hood St.
Charle St.
Whitechapel
Stanley St.
Victoria St.
Mathew St.
North John St.
Cook St.
Castle St.
Fenwick St.
Water St.
The Strand
Strand St.
Lord St.
South John St.
Paradise St.
Canning Place
Church St.
Parker St.
School Lane
Hanover St.
Ranelagh St.
Bold St.
Wood St.
Fleet St.
Seel St.
Duke St.
Argyle St.
Park Lane
Parr St.
Henry St.
Lydia Ann St.
Gilbert St.
Corn St.
Tabley St.
Sparling St.
Wapping Chaloner St.
Jamaica St.
St. James St.
Upper Pitt St.
Kent St.
Cornwallis St.
Great George St.
Rathbone St.
Upper Duke St.
Berry St.
Roscoe St.
Rodney St.
Pilgrim St.
Hope St.
Leece St.
Hardman St.
Myrtle St.
Canning St.
Catharine St.
Renshaw St.
Elliot St.
Skethorne St.
Copperas Hill
Warren St.
Tong St.
Brownlow Hill
Mount Pleasant
Lord Nelson St.
Birdport St.
London Road
Hart St.
Seymour St.
Villars St.
Greek St.
Russell St.
Towbridge St.
Moor Pl.
Pembroke Place
Gill St.
Dansie St.
Great Newton St.
Pembroke St.

SPECIAL EVENTS At the end of August and running into the first couple of days of September, the annual **International Beatles Week** attracts about 100,000 fans to Liverpool for a 7-day celebration highlighted by concerts from bands from Argentina to Sweden (with names like Lenny Pane, Wings Over Liverpool, and The Beats). You can hear the news today at the Sgt. Pepper concert, and take in many other Beatles tributes, auctions, and tours. **Cavern City Tours,** a local company, offers hotel and festival packages that include accommodations and tickets to tours and events, starting around £75 ($127.50) for two nights. For information, contact Cavern City Tours at ☎ **0151/2369091** or the Tourist Information Centre in Liverpool at ☎ **0151/7088854.**

SEEING THE SIGHTS

If you'd like a Beatles-related bus tour, **Cavern City Tours** (☎ **0151/2369091**) presents a daily 2-hour Magical Mystery Tour, departing from Albert Dock at 2:20pm and from Clayton Square at 2:30pm. This bus tour covers the most famous attractions associated with the Beatles. Tickets cost £11.50 ($19.55) and are sold at the Tourist Information Centre at the Atlantic Pavilion on Albert Dock or at the Merseyside Welcome Center on Clayton Square. For more information about tickets, call either ☎ **0151/7088838** or 0151/2369091.

For value for money**, NMGM's (National Museums and Galleries on Merseyside) Eight Pass** allows you to visit some of Liverpool's best museums and galleries as often as you like over a 12-month period for only £3 ($5.10) for adults, £1.50 ($2.55) for seniors and students. Children under 6 are free. The eight venues are Liverpool Museum, Merseyside Maritime Museum, HM Customs and Excise National Museum, Museum of Liverpool Life, Walker Art Gallery, Lady Lever Art Gallery and Sudley House. For further details call ☎ **0151/2070001,** or for an information pack, call the 24-hour hotline at ☎ **0151/4784747.**

In the Britannia Pavilion at Albert Dock, you can visit **"The Beatles Story"** (☎ **0151/7091963**), a museum housing memorabilia of the famous group, including a yellow submarine with live fish swimming past the portholes. It's open daily from 10am to 5pm (November to Easter closes at 5pm weekdays). Admission is £6.95 ($11.80) for adults and £4.95 ($8.40) for children and students, and a family ticket is £17 ($28.90).

Everyone's curious about **Penny Lane** and **Strawberry Field.** Actually, the Beatles' song about Penny Lane ("There are places I'll remember") didn't refer to the small lane itself, but to the area at the top of the lane called Smithdown Place. Today, this is a bustling thoroughfare for taxis and buses—hardly a place for nostalgic memories.

John Lennon lived nearby and attended school in the area. When he studied at Art College, he passed here almost every day, these bus journeys inspiring the original lyrics. To reach Penny Lane and the area referred to, head north of Sefton Park. From the park, Green Bank Lane leads into Penny Lane itself, and at the junction of Allerton Road and Smithdown Road stands the Penny Lane Tramsheds. This is John Lennon country—or what's left of it.

Only the most diehard fans will want to make the journey to **Strawberry Field** along Beaconsfield Road, which is reached by taking Menlove Avenue east of the center. Today, you can stand at the iron gates and look in at a children's home run by the Salvation Army. As a child John played on the grounds and in 1970, he donated a large sum of money to the home. A garden party held every summer here was attended by John. His son, Sean, and Yoko Ono made two visits here in 1984. The first was a media circus, but the second was conducted in secrecy. Yoko spent many hours talking to the children and bringing them gifts, along with $80,000 to help run their home.

Since these sights are hard to reach by public transport and lie outside the center, you may want to take one of the Cavern City Tours (see above) which feature both Strawberry Field and Penny Lane.

A fun thing to do is to take the famous **Mersey Ferry** that travels from the Pier Head to both Woodside and Seacombe. Service operates daily from early morning to early evening throughout the year. Special cruises run throughout the summer including trips along the Manchester Ship Canal. For more information, contact **Mersey Ferries,** Victoria Place, Seacombe, Wallasey (☎ **0151/6301030**).

Albert Dock. Albert Dock Co. Ltd. ☎ **0151/7087334.** Free admission. Shops daily 10am–5:30pm. Bars and restaurants daily 11am–11pm. Smart Bus from city center.

Built of brick, stone, and cast iron, this showpiece development on Liverpool's waterfront opened in 1846, saw a long period of decline, and has now been extensively renovated and refurbished. The dockland warehouses now house shops, restaurants, cafes, an English pub, and a cellar wine bar. One pavilion encompasses the main building of the Merseyside Maritime Museum (see below) and another is the home of the Tate Gallery Liverpool, the National Collection of modern art in the north of England (see below). Parking is available.

✪ **Tate Gallery Liverpool.** Albert Dock. ☎ **0151/7093223.** Free admission except special exhibitions, £4 ($6.80) adults, £2.50 ($4.25) children. Tues–Sun 10am–5:50pm. Bus: "Albert Dock Shuttle" from city center.

This museum displays much of the National Collection of 20th-century art, complemented by changing art exhibitions of international standing. Three- and four-month special exhibitions are frequently mounted here, perhaps the prints of Joan Miró or the sculptures of the iconoclastic British sculptress Rachel Whiteread. The tourist office has full details of all special exhibitions, or you can call the museum directly.

✪ **Merseyside Maritime Museum and the Museum of Liverpool Life.** Albert Dock. ☎ **0151/4784499.** Admission with NMGM's Eight Pass (see above) Daily 10am–5pm. Bus: "Albert Dock Shuttle" from city center.

Set in the historic heart of Liverpool's waterfront, this museum provides a unique blend of floating exhibits, craft demonstrations, working displays, and special events. In addition to restored waterfront buildings, exhibitions present the story of mass emigration through Liverpool in the last century, shipbuilding on Merseyside, the Battle of the Atlantic Gallery, and Transatlantic Slavery. There is wheelchair access.

The Conservation Centre. Whitechapel, Liverpool. ☎ **0151/4784999.** Admission via NMGM's Eight Pass (see above). Mon–Sat 10am–5pm, Sun noon–5pm. Closed Dec 23–26 and Jan 1.

The Conservation Centre, in the heart of Liverpool, is the first of its kind in Europe. The Caught in Time exhibition uncovers the secret world of museum conservation and reveals how the 1.2 million artifacts in national museums and galleries on Merseyside collections are kept from the ravages of time. Using state-of-the-art hand-held audio guides, video linkups, demonstrations, behind-the-scenes tours, and interactive displays, visitors can see how everything from fine art and a Beatles gold disc to a mummified crocodile are saved from decay by expert conservators using the most up-to-date techniques.

The McCartney House. 20 Forthlin Rd., Allerton 16. ☎ **0151/708-8574** booking office; 0870/900-0256 information line. Admission £5 ($8.50) adult and £2.60 ($4.40) children. Mar 31–Oct 31 Wed–Sat noon–5pm; Nov–Dec Sat only noon–5pm.

The house where the McCartney's lived in Liverpool before Paul's meteoric rise to superstardom has been purchased by the National Trust. Working from old photographs taken by Paul's brother Michael, the house has been restored to its original 1950s appearance, complete with the patterned brown sofa and armchair with the white linen antimacassars where Paul and John scribbled out their first songs; and the Chinese willow print wallpaper which doesn't reach the corners because the family was too poor to buy enough. Hardly Graceland, it does give an insight into the humble beginnings of one of the world's most famous and influential entertainers. The house is only open to the public through tours organized by the National Trust. Six tours a day depart from Speak Hall, The Walk. Groups are limited to 14 people at any one time. Book well in advance.

✪ **Walker Art Gallery.** William Brown St. ☎ **0151/4784199.** Admission via NMGM's Eight Pass (see above). Mon–Sat 10am–5pm, Sun noon–5pm. Closed Dec 23–26 and Jan 1.

One of Europe's finest art galleries offers an outstanding collection of European art from 1300 to the present day. The gallery is especially rich in European old masters, Victorian and pre-Raphaelite works, and contemporary British art. It also has an award-winning sculpture gallery, featuring works from the 18th and 19th centuries. Seek out, in particular, Simone Martini's *Jesus Discovered in the Temple* and Salvator Rosa's *Landscape with Hermit.* Rembrandt is on show, as is an enticing *Nymph of the Fountain* by Cranach. The work of British artists is strongest here, ranging from *Horse Frightened by a Lion* by Stubbs to *Snowdon from Llan Nantlle* by Richard Wilson. Among the pre-Raphaelites are Ford Madox Brown and W. R. Yeames. French impressionists include the works of Monet, Seurat, and Degas, among others. Modern British paintings include works by Lucian Freud and Stanley Spencer. The admission charged is good for 1 year into any and all of the eight museums and galleries on Merseyside.

✪ **Liverpool Museum.** William Brown St. ☎ **0151/2070001.** Admission via NMGM's Eight Pass (see above). Mon–Sat 10am–5pm, Sun noon–5pm.

One of Britain's finest museums features collections from all over the world—from the earliest beginnings with giant dinosaurs through centuries of great art and inventions. At the Natural History Centre you can use microscopes and video cameras to learn about the natural world. Living displays from the vivarium and aquarium form a large part of the collections, and a planetarium features daily programs covering modern space exploration—an armchair tour toward the beginning of the universe and the far-flung reaches of the cosmos. There is a small charge for the planetarium and temporary exhibitions.

✪ **Cathedral Church of Christ.** St. James Mt. ☎ **0151/7096271.** Admission to cathedral free; tower and embroidery gallery £2 ($3.40) adults, £1 ($1.70) children. Daily 8am–6pm.

The great new Anglican edifice overlooking the River Mersey was begun in 1904 and was largely completed 74 years later; it was the last Gothic-style cathedral to be built worldwide. Dedicated in the presence of Queen Elizabeth II in 1978, it is the largest church in England and the fifth largest in the world. Its vaulting under the tower is 175 feet high, the highest in the world, and its length, 619 feet, makes it one of the longest cathedrals in the world. The organ has nearly 10,000 pipes, the most found in any church. The tower houses the highest (219 ft.) and the heaviest (31 tons) bells in the world, and the Gothic arches are the highest ever built. From the tower, you can see to North Wales.

A Visitor Centre and Refectory features an aerial sculpture of 12 huge sails, with a ship's bell, clock, and light that changes color on an hourly basis. You can enjoy full meals in the charming refectory.

✪ **Roman Catholic Metropolitan Cathedral of Christ the King.** Mt. Pleasant. ☎ **0151/7099222.** Free admission. Daily 9am–6pm (closes 5pm Sun in winter).

Half a mile away from the Anglican cathedral stands the Roman Catholic cathedral—the two are joined by a road called Hope Street. The construction of the cathedral, designed by Sir Edwin Lutyens, was started in 1930, but when World War II interrupted in 1939, not even the granite and brick vaulting of the crypt was complete. At the end of the war it was estimated that the cost of completing the structure as Lutyens had designed it would be some £27 million. Architects throughout the world were invited to compete to design a more realistic project to cost about £1 million and to be completed in 5 years. Sir Frederick Gibberd won the competition and was commissioned to oversee the construction of the circular cathedral in concrete and glass, pitched like a tent at one end of the piazza that covered all the original site, crypt included.

Construction was completed between 1962 and 1967, and today the cathedral provides seating for more than 2,000, all within 50 feet of the central altar. Above the altar rises a multicolored glass lantern weighing 2,000 tons and rising to a height of 290 feet. Called a space-age cathedral, it has a bookshop, a tearoom, and tour guides.

SHOPPING

Pedestrian shopping areas with boutiques, specialty shops, and department stores include Church Street, Lord Street, Bold Street, Whitechapel, and Paradise Street. Right on the river, Albert Dock also houses a collection of small shops.

For shopping centers, go to **Cavern Walks** on Mathew Street, the heart of Beatleland (☎ **0151/2369082**), or **Quiggins Centre,** 12-16 School Lane (☎ **0151/7092462**).

If you want to buy that special piece of Beatles memorabilia, wander through the **Beatles Shop,** 31 Mathew St. (☎ **0151/2368066**), or the **Heritage Shop,** 1 The Colonnades, Albert Dock (☎ **0151/7097474**).

For a huge selection of British crafts, visit **Bluecoat Display Centre,** School Lane (☎ **0151/7094014**), with its gallery of metal, ceramics, glass, jewelry, and wood pieces by some 350 British craftspeople.

Frank Green's, 10 Britannia Pavilion, Albert Dock (☎ **0151/7093330**), is where you'll find prints by this famous local artist who has been capturing the Liverpool scene on canvas since the 1960s. His work includes city secular buildings, churches, and street life.

Two of Liverpool's best bookshops include **Waterstone's,** 52 Bold St. (☎ **0151/7090866**), and **Gallery Shop,** Tate Gallery, Albert Dock (☎ **0151/7093223**). Since the Gallery Shop is located in Tate Gallery, it also carries gallery-related merchandise.

A couple of other specialty shops that warrant a visit include **Sewill Marine,** Cornhill House, 24 Cornhill St. (☎ **0151/7087744**), which has been making nautical

In the Footsteps of the Fab Four

Wherever you turn in Liverpool today, somebody is hawking a Beatles tour. But if you'd like to see a few of the famous spots on your own, stop in at the **Cavern,** 10 Mathew St., now touted as "The Most Famous Club in the World," and pick up a Cavern City Tour map to find famous Beatles locations in the city center. The Beatles played 292 gigs here between 1961 and 1963. Manager Brian Epstein first saw them here on November 9, 1961, and by December 10, he had signed a contract with the band.

instruments longer than anyone in the known world; and **Thornton's,** 16 Whitechapel (☎ **0151/7086849**), where you can choose from a dizzying selection of continental and traditional English chocolates, toffees, and mints.

WHERE TO STAY

EXPENSIVE

Atlantic Tower Thistle. 30 Chapel St., Liverpool, Merseyside L3 9RE. ☎ **800/847-4358** in the U.S., or 0151/2274444. Fax 0151/236–3973. E-mail: liverpool@thistle.co.uk. 226 units. A/C TV TEL. £120 ($204) double; £150 ($255) suite. Weekends £80 ($136) double including breakfast. AE, DC, MC, V.

Showcased in an austere high-rise evoking the bow of a great luxury liner, the Atlantic Tower is one of the top three hotels in the city. It caters largely to business travelers. You check in to a spacious lobby and are shown to one of the well-furnished but pretty standard bedrooms. Many bedrooms, although quite small, provide views of the River Mersey, and you can request a minibar. There is average—not grand—comfort here. The best units are the corner bedrooms, which are triangular in shape and face the river. Bedrooms are frequently renovated as the need arises. Each small bathroom comes with a hair dryer and adequate shelf space.

Dining: You can dine in the Stateroom Restaurant, enjoying drinks in a bar that resembles a Pullman coach.

Liverpool Moat House. Paradise St., Liverpool, Merseyside O1 8JD. ☎ **0151/4719988.** Fax 0151/709-2706. 263 units. A/C TV TEL. Mon–Thurs £130 ($221) double, Fri–Sun £110 ($187) double; daily £150 ($255) suite. Weekend rates include English breakfast. AE, DC, MC, V.

This hotel may have zoomed past the Britannia Adelphi and the Atlantic Tower in the race for the title of Liverpool's best hotel, but that doesn't mean it's a world-class hotel like you'll find in Manchester or even Chester. Located in the center of the city, it is nonetheless one of the most comfortable, efficient hotels in Merseyside. The spacious bedrooms are spread across eight floors, and many have recently been refurbished. An astonishing 200 bedrooms are large enough to be used as family rooms, and 130 units are set aside for nonsmokers. Typically favored by businesspeople, the hotel is also a perfectly nice choice for sightseers.

Dining: A brasserie serves international fare daily from 6am to 10pm. There is also 24-hour room service.

Amenities: Solarium, gym, indoor swimming pool, and garden.

MODERATE

Britannia Adelphi Hotel. Ranelagh Place, Liverpool, Merseyside L3 5UL. ☎ **0151/7097200.** Fax 0151/708-0743. 402 units. TV TEL. £87 ($147.90) double; £120 ($204) suite. Children under 13 stay free in parents' room. AE, DC, MC, V. Parking £10 ($17).

This grand hotel, built in 1914, is known for its fine Edwardian rooms and good cuisine. Past the elegant entrance, you enter an overblown world of marble corridors, molded ceilings, and dark polished wood. These traditional features are complemented by modern amenities, since the hotel has been completely refurbished. Many still view this as the best address in town, but we rank it number three, after the Liverpool Moat House and Atlantic Tower Thistle (see above); given the price differential, however, it's a better buy. Each bedroom is well furnished and attractively appointed. All the bedrooms have recently been refurbished, and each comes with double-glazed windows, beverage-makers, and trouser presses. The mezzanine bedrooms are likely to be noisy. Some two dozen bathrooms are fitted with whirlpool tubs. Facilities include three restaurants, four bars, hair and beauty salons, and a health club with swimming pool, gym, solarium, and Jacuzzi. There is garage space for 100 cars.

✪ **Trials.** 56–62 Castle St., Liverpool, Merseyside L2 7LQ ☎ **0151/2271021.** Fax 0151/236-0110. 20 suites. MINIBAR TV TEL. £85–£140 ($144.50–$238) suite. AE, MC, V.

Although it's small, this rather luxurious hotel has charm and character. It was created in 1986 from a centrally located Victorian structure that had once been a bank. Now beautifully converted, it's often the choice of discriminating visitors. The plush accommodations are all split-level suites with Jacuzzis, trouser presses, and hair dryers. Each offers roomy comfort, plus well-maintained bathrooms with fluffy towels and generous shelf space. Trials Restaurant offers breakfast only, whereas the Trials Bar serves lunch. The hotel has 24-hour room service.

INEXPENSIVE

Feathers Hotel. 119–125 Mt. Pleasant, Liverpool, Merseyside L3 5TF. ☎ **0151/7099655.** Fax 0151/7093838. 74 units. TV TEL. £60–£100 ($102–$170) double. Rates include buffet breakfast. AE, DC, MC, V. Bus: 80 (the airport bus).

This brick-fronted hotel is composed of four separate Georgian-style town houses. It sits in the heart of the city, adjacent to the modern Metropolitan Cathedral. The hotel contains a cocktail lounge (Zach's) serving bar snacks, as well as the Asher's Restaurant. The bedrooms are comfortable, with simple traditional furniture, but don't expect much charm. Each is well maintained nonetheless and offers old-fashioned comfort. Most units have a small bathroom with a shower stall.

WHERE TO DINE

For such a world-famous city, Liverpool has yet to have a world-class restaurant. Here are the best non-hotel restaurants it has to offer.

La Grande Bouffe, 48A Castle St. (☎ **0151/2363375**), is a basement restaurant offering lunches weekdays from noon to 3pm. The steamed monkfish *à la niçoise* places you on the French Riviera, but homemade black pudding returns you squarely to the northwest of England. Dinners are also served Tuesday to Saturday from 5:30 to 10:30pm.

Armadillo. 20 Mathew St. ☎ **0151/2366049.** Reservations required. Main courses £11.50–£17.50 ($19.55–$29.75). AE, MC, V. Tues–Fri noon–3pm and 5–6:30pm; Tues–Sat 7:30–10:30pm. MODERN BRITISH.

With a conservative modern decor and big windows, this restaurant seems to be near the top of everybody's list of favorites in Liverpool. It's housed in the solid stone walls of a converted Victorian warehouse across the street from the site of the famous Cavern, where the Beatles got their start. The menu includes such dishes as seafood gazpacho, sirloin with garlic sauce, pan-fried Dover sole with peppercorn and pomegranate, or roast pheasant with chorizo sausages and lamb kidneys. The cooking has some artful touches, and ingredients are above average.

✪ **Becher's Brook.** 29A Hope St. ☎ **0151/7070005.** Reservations recommended. Main courses £12.50–£21 ($21.25–$35.70); 3-course fixed-price lunch £16 ($27.20). AE, DC, MC, V. Mon–Fri noon–2:30pm; Mon–Sat 5–10pm. Bus 14 or 79. INTERNATIONAL.

Close to both cathedrals, this new restaurant has received a lot of attention locally. A challenge to the old-time favorites, its run by David Cooke and Gerard Mogan, who operate from a restored Georgian townhouse with a bar in the cellar. A rustic look prevails, with bare wood-planked floors and brick walls decorated with clusters of fresh herbs. Flavors are carefully thought out here, and main dishes are full of good taste and freshness. The appetizers are especially satisfying, notably the warm salad of roast quail. Then, it's on to such main courses as fillet of cod baked with langoustines or braised shin of beef on a leek and thyme mash with glazed onions and a Bordelais sauce. Most wines are reasonably priced.

Far East. 27–35 Berry St. ☎ **0151/7096641.** Reservations required. Main courses £7–£20 ($11.90–$34); fixed-price meals £8–£14 ($13.60–$23.80) at lunch, £14.50–£20 ($24.65–$34) at dinner. AE, DC, MC, V. Sun–Thurs noon–11:15pm; Fri–Sat noon–12:45am; Sun noon–11pm. CANTONESE/BEIJING.

Liverpool is famous for its Chinese restaurants—not surprising since the city has one of the largest Chinese populations in Europe and its own Chinatown. Far East is a great Chinese restaurant. You might enjoy a dim sum lunch, later returning in the evening for more haute Chinese fare. You face a vast array of Cantonese specialties, including our favorite chile-flavored large prawns. The chefs also do marvelous things with duck.

Jenny's Seafood Restaurant. Old Ropery, Fenwich St. ☎ **0151/2360332.** Reservations required. Main courses £8.95–£16.95 ($15.20–$28.80); fixed-price lunch or dinner £20.95 ($35.60). AE, MC, V. Mon–Fri noon–2:15pm; Tues–Sat 7–10pm. Closed Aug 5–21 and 2 weeks at Christmas. SEAFOOD.

This restaurant has been a Liverpool staple for as long as anyone can remember. You'll find Jenny's near the harbor, in a big white Victorian building on a cul-de-sac at the lower end of Fenwich Street. Small, cozy, and select, it serves the city's best fresh seafood, which might include grilled Dover sole in Newburgh sauce or in white wine, prawn, and mushroom sauce; at least three different preparations of sea bass, including one baked in a salt crust; and monkfish, flounder, prawns, and North Atlantic lobsters. Sure, the cooking is old-fashioned, but Liverpudlians wouldn't change a thing.

LIVERPOOL AFTER DARK

Liverpool's nightlife is nothing if not diverse. There are several publications and places that will help you get a handle on the entertainment options around town. The evening *Liverpool Echo* is a good source of daily information about larger and fine-arts events; the youth-oriented *L: Scene* magazine will provide you with a thorough calendar of club dates and gigs, and the free *City X Blag,* available in most clubs and pubs, will do the same. Available free in gay clubs and pubs, *Pulse* lists gay activities and events throughout the region.

The **Student Entertainment Office** (☎ **0151/7944143**) at the University of Liverpool can tell you about the range of activities sponsored by the school, or you can stop by the student union on Mount Pleasant and check out the bulletin board. Two other good places for finding out about the underground scene are **The Palace,** Slater Street (☎ **0151/7088515**), and **Quiggins Centre,** School Lane (☎ **0151/7092462**). Each is overflowing with flyers advertising local events.

Open year-round, the **Liverpool Empire,** Lime Street (☎ **08706/063541**), hosts visiting stage productions ranging from dramas and comedies to ballets and tributes. The box office is open Monday through Saturday from 10am until 6pm.

Philharmonic Hall, Hope Street (☎ **0151/2102895**), is home to **The Royal Philharmonic Orchestra,** one of the best orchestras outside of London, which performs twice weekly. When the orchestra is not on, there are often concerts by touring musicians, and films are sometimes shown as well.

Open Monday through Saturday nights, **Lomax,** 34 Cumberland St. (☎ **0151/2982300**), is a good place to catch local and touring indie bands.

Krazy House, Wood Street (☎ **0151/7085016**), hosts live music 2 to 3 nights a week on a small and a larger stage. Within its split-level layout, you can catch everything from unknown locals to popular touring bands.

At the **Zanzibar Club,** 43 Seel St. (☎ **0151/7070633**), DJs spin salsa and other Latin sounds Monday through Saturday nights, and if you like your dancing exotic, the first Friday of each month has a Brazilian Carnival theme, with samba music, costumed dancers, stilt walkers, and a rowdy, party atmosphere.

Cream/Nation, Parr Street, north of Slater Street (☎ **0151/7091693**), is where the Nation, a huge warehouse club, hosts one of England's top-rated dance clubs, Cream, every Saturday night. The last Friday of every month, Cream pulls an all-nighter and attracts club-goers from all over England. Admission to Cream is a pricey £12 ($20.40).

A mixed/gay nightclub, **Garlands,** 8–10 Eberle St., off Dale Street (☎ **0151/2363307**), sometimes hosts bizarre special events, but you can always count on dancing Friday through Saturday, when the cover charge will range from £6 to £15 ($10.20 to $25.50).

A cafe by day, **Baa Bar,** 43–45 Fleet St. (☎ **0151/7070610**), serves an eclectic menu, and free dancing to a DJ brings in a lot of the evening's business.

A pub with a Fab Four spin, **Ye Cracke,** Rice Street (☎ **0151/7094171**), was a favorite watering hole of John Lennon in pre- and early Beatles days (but expect regulars to suggest you quit living in the past if you ask about it). Better just soak up the little-changed atmosphere over a pint of Oak Wobbly Bob, Cains, or Pedigree.

3 The Walled City of Chester

207 miles NW of London; 19 miles S of Liverpool; 91 miles NW of Birmingham

A Roman legion founded Chester on the Dee River in the 1st century A.D. It reached its pinnacle as a bustling port in the 13th and 14th centuries but declined following the gradual silting up of the river. While other walls of medieval cities of England were either torn down or badly fragmented, Chester still has 2 miles of fortified city walls intact. The main entrance into Chester is Eastgate, which dates only from the 18th century. Within the walls are half-timbered houses and shops, although not all of them date from Tudor days. Chester is unusual in that some of its builders used black-and-white timbered facades even during the Georgian and Victorian eras.

Chester today has aged gracefully and is a lovely old place to visit, if you don't mind the summer crowds who overrun the place. It has far more charm and intimacy then either Liverpool or Manchester, and is one of the most interesting medieval cities in England.

ESSENTIALS

GETTING THERE About 21 trains depart London's Euston Station every hour daily for the 2½-hour trip to Chester. Trains also run every hour between Liverpool and Chester, a 45-minute ride. For schedules and information, call ☎ **0345/484950.**

One **National Express** bus runs every hour between Birmingham and Chester; the trip takes 2 hours. The same bus line also offers service between Liverpool and Chester. It's also possible to catch a National Express coach from London's Victoria Coach Station to Chester. For schedules and information, call ☎ **0990/808080.**

If you're driving from London, head north on the M1, then take the M6 at the junction near Coventry. Continue northwest to the junction with A54, which leads west to Chester.

VISITOR INFORMATION The **Tourist Information Centre** is at the Town Hall, Northgate Street (☎ **01244/402385**). It offers a hotel-reservation service as well as information. Arrangements can also be made for coach tours or walking tours of Chester (including a ghost-hunter tour). It's open May through October, Monday to Saturday from 10am to 5pm and Sunday from 10am to 4pm; in the off-season, Monday to Saturday from 9am to 5:30pm.

SPECIAL EVENTS The last 2 weeks of July are an active time in Chester, as the **Chester Summer Music Festival** (☎ **01244/320700** or 01244/341200, Monday through Friday from 9am to 5:30pm, Saturday 10am to 4pm) hosts orchestras and other classical performers from around Britain in lunch concerts, with tickets averaging £5 ($8.50); small indoor evening concerts, where tickets cost between £8 to £20 ($13.60 to $34); and large outdoor shows, with tickets starting at £17 ($28.90). For additional information about the music festival, you can also write to the Chester Summer Music Festival Office, 8 Abbey Square, Chester CH1 2BH.

Occurring simultaneously, the **Chester Fringe Festival** (☎ **01244/340392**) focuses on other musical genres, offering Latin, rock, Cajun, folk, and jazz concerts. Ticket prices vary widely, depending on the performer.

SEEING THE SIGHTS

In a big Victorian building opposite the Roman amphitheater, the largest uncovered amphitheater in Britain, the **Chester Visitor Centre,** Vicars Lane (☎ **01244/319019**), offers a number of services to visitors. A visit to a life-size Victorian street, complete with sounds and smells, helps your appreciation of Chester. The center has a gift shop and a licensed restaurant serving meals and snacks. Admission is free, and the center is open May through October, Monday to Saturday from 9am to 6:30pm, and Sunday 10am to 4pm; November through April, Monday to Saturday 9am to 5:30pm, and Sunday 10am to 4pm. Guided walking tours of the city depart daily at 10:30am in the winter and at 10:30am and 2pm in the summer.

To the accompaniment of a hand bell, the **town crier** appears at the City Cross—the junction of Watergate, Northgate, and Bridge streets—from April to September at noon and 3pm Tuesday to Saturday to shout news about sales, exhibitions, and attractions in the city.

In the center of town, you'll see the much-photographed **Eastgate clock.** Climb the nearby stairs and walk along the top of the **city wall** for a view down on Chester. Passing through centuries of English history, you'll go by a cricket field, see the River Dee, formerly a major trade artery, and get a look at many 18th-century buildings. The wall also goes past some Roman ruins, and it's possible to leave the walkway to explore them. The walk is charming and free.

Eastgate Street is now a pedestrian way, and musicians often perform for your pleasure beside St. Peter's Church and the Town Cross.

The Rows are double-decker layers of shops, one tier on the street level, the others stacked on top and connected by a footway. The upper tier is like a continuous galleried balcony—walking in the rain is never a problem here.

Chester Cathedral. St. Werburgh St. ☎ **01244/324756.** £2 ($3.40) donation suggested. Daily 9am–4:45pm.

The present building, founded in 1092 as a Benedictine abbey, was made an Anglican cathedral church in 1541. Many architectural restorations were carried out in the 19th century, but older parts have been preserved. Notable features include the fine range of monastic buildings, particularly the cloisters and refectory, the chapter house, and

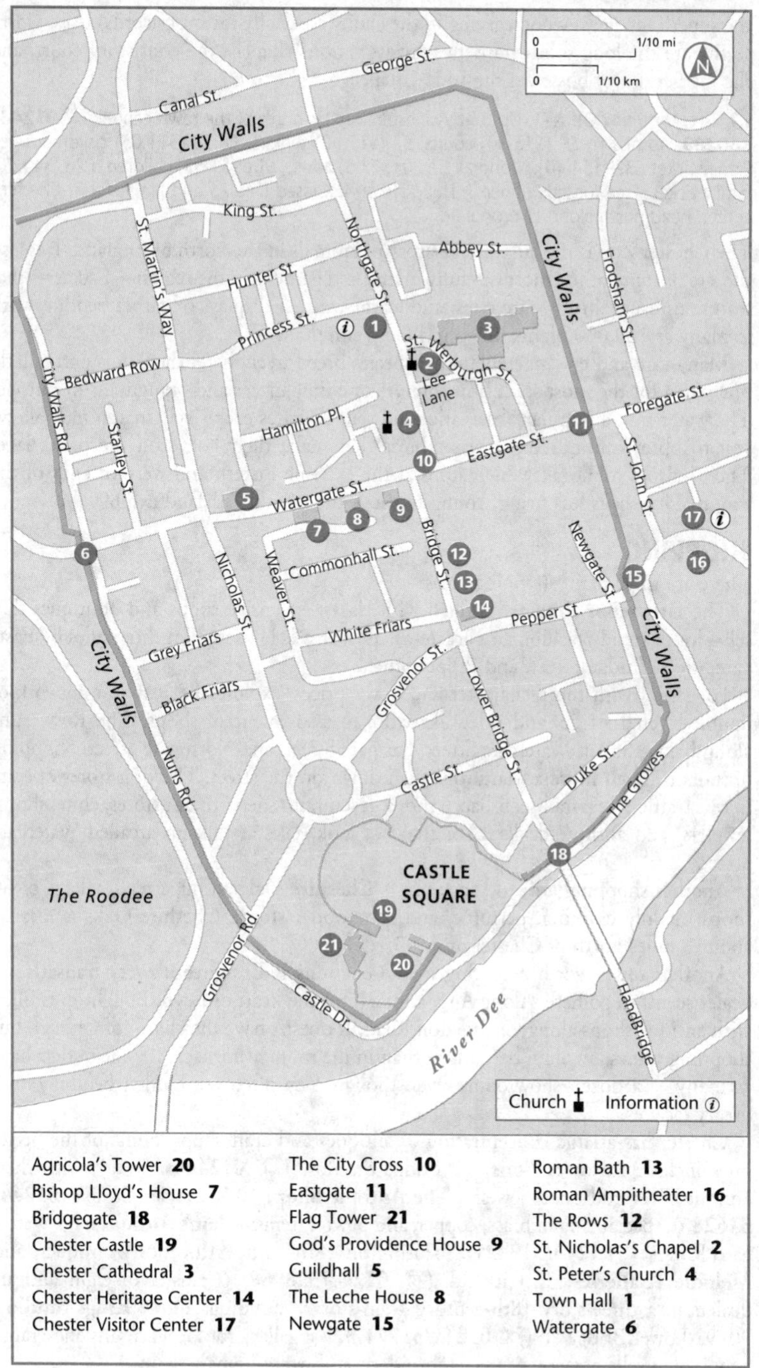
0 1/10 mi
0 1/10 km
N
George St.
Canal St.
City Walls
King St.
St. Martin's Way
Northgate St.
Abbey St.
City Walls
Frodsham St.
Hunter St.
Princess St.
St. Werburgh St.
Bedward Row
Lee Lane
City Walls Rd
Hamilton Pl.
Foregate St.
Stanley St.
Eastgate St.
St. John St.
Watergate St.
Newgate St.
Bridge St.
Commonhall St.
Nicholas St.
Weaver St.
Pepper St.
White Friars
Grey Friars
City Walls
Grosvenor St.
Lower Bridge St.
City Walls
Black Friars
Nuns Rd.
Castle St.
Duke St.
The Groves
CASTLE SQUARE
The Roodee
Grosvenor Rd.
Castle Dr.
River Dee
HandBridge
Church
Information
Agricola's Tower 20
Bishop Lloyd's House 7
Bridgegate 18
Chester Castle 19
Chester Cathedral 3
Chester Heritage Center 14
Chester Visitor Center 17
The City Cross 10
Eastgate 11
Flag Tower 21
God's Providence House 9
Guildhall 5
The Leche House 8
Newgate 15
Roman Bath 13
Roman Ampitheater 16
The Rows 12
St. Nicholas's Chapel 2
St. Peter's Church 4
Town Hall 1
Watergate 6

the superb medieval wood carving in the choir (especially for misericords). Also worth seeing are the long south transept with its various chapels, the consistory court, and the medieval roof bosses in the Lady Chapel.

✪ **Chester Zoo.** Off A41, Upton-by-Chester, 2 miles north of the town center. ☎ **01244/380280.** Admission £9 ($15.30) adults, £7 ($11.90) seniors, £6.50 ($11.05) children 3–15. Family ticket £32 ($54.40). Monorail £1.20 ($2.05) adults, 90p ($1.55) children, £26 ($44.20) family ticket. Free for kids under 3. Daily 10am–4. Closed Dec 25 and Jan 1. From Chester's center, head north along Liverpool Rd.

The Chester Zoo is the largest repository of animals in the north of England. It is also the site of some of the most carefully manicured gardens in the region—110 acres that feature unusual shrubs, rare trees, and warm-weather displays of carpet bedding with as many as 160,000 plants timed to bloom simultaneously.

Many rare and endangered animal species breed freely here; the zoo is particularly renowned for the most successful colonies of chimpanzees and orangutans in Europe. The water bus, a popular observation aid that operates exclusively in summer, allows you to observe hundreds of water birds that make their home on the park's lake. There's also a monorail, which stops at the extreme eastern and western ends of the zoo, making visits less tiring. Youngsters love the Monkey's Island exhibit.

SHOPPING

There are three main shopping areas.

The **Grosvenor Precinct** is filled with classy, expensive shops and boutiques that sell a lot of trendy fashion and art items. This area is bordered on three sides by Eastgate Street, Bridge Street, and Pepper Street.

For stores with more character and lower prices, explore **the Rows,** a network of double-layered streets and sidewalks with an assortment of shops. The Rows runs along Bridge Street, Watergate Street, Eastgate Street, and Northgate Street. Shopping upstairs is much more adventurous than down on the street. Thriving stores operate in this traffic-free paradise: tobacco shops, restaurants, department stores, china shops, jewelers, and antique dealers. For the best look, take a walk on arcaded Watergate Street.

Another shopping area to check out is **Cheshire Oaks,** a huge retail village of 60 shops, mainly clothing, perfume, and shoe outlet stores. Cheshire Oaks is located about 8 miles north of Chester on M53.

Another town worth exploring in the environs is **Boughton;** every transatlantic dealer seems to go here. Along A41, a mile from the heart of town, Boughton is filled with antique shops along Christledon Road. It doesn't have the charm of Chester, but shopping values are often better here than in the more historic city. Some outlets have as many as a dozen showrooms, even though they often are hidden behind rather dreary facades.

Chester has a large concentration of antiques and craft shops. Some of the better ones include **Lowe & Sons,** 11 Bridge St. Row (☎ **01244/325850**), with their antique silver and estate jewelry; **The Antique Shop,** 40 Watergate St. (☎ **01244/316286**), specializing in brass, copper, and pewter items; **Adam's Antiques,** 65 Watergate Row (☎ **01244/319421**), focusing on 18th- and 19th-century antiques; and **Melodies Galleries,** 32 City Rd. (☎ **01244/328968**), a cluster of eight antique dealers in a three-story 18th-century grain-storage building. **Three Kings Studios,** 90–92 Lower Bridge St. (☎ **01244/317717**), is a gallery for local artisans and craftspeople that sells pottery, prints, embroidery, and wood items.

Weekly antiques shows and auctions are held on Thursday at the Guildhall in Chester. Call the **Tourist Information Board** in Chester at ☎ **01244/402111.**

One of the better shops for jewelry is **Boodle and Dunthorne,** 52 Eastgate St. (☎ **01244/326666**). Since the days of George III, **Brown's of Chester,** Eastgate Street (☎ **01244/350001**), has carried women's fashions and perfumes.

For a good selection of cheeses, chutneys, olives, pastas, and English fruit wines, seek out **The Cheese Shop,** 116 Northgate St. (☎ **01244/346240**).

WHERE TO STAY

VERY EXPENSIVE

✪ **Chester Grosvenor Hotel.** Eastgate, Chester, Cheshire CH1 1LT. ☎ **01244/324024.** Fax 01244/313246. 82 units. A/C MINIBAR TV TEL. Mon–Thurs £185 ($314.50) double, Fri–Sun £160 ($272) double; Mon–Thurs £350–£450 ($595–$765) suite, Fri–Sun £240–£320 ($408–$544) suite (weekend rates include breakfast). Children under 15 stay free in parents' room. AE, DC, MC, V.

This fine, half-timbered, five-story building in the heart of Chester is one of the most luxurious hotels in northern England. Its reputation is well deserved. It is owned and named after the family of the dukes of Westminster, and its origin can be traced from the reign of Queen Elizabeth I. Started as a Tudor inn, it became a political headquarters in Hanoverian days, was later transformed into a glittering mecca for the Regency and Victorian set, and continued to be a social center during the Edwardian era. It's hosted its share of royalty, including Prince Albert, Princess Diana, and Prince Rainier.

The high-ceilinged, marble-floored foyer of the hotel, with its 200-year-old chandelier, carved wooden staircase, and antiques, sets the tone. The large, well-furnished bedrooms have radios and hair dryers. Each bedroom is individually styled, and there are silks from France and handmade furnishings from Italy. Extras include huge closets, trouser presses, and private safes. Some of the bathrooms are marble, but, regrettably, others are still a sorry sight with white laminate and linoleum. Each comes with heated towel racks and deluxe toiletries.

Dining: This grand hotel has the finest dining rooms in the county. See "Where to Dine," below, for details about its formal restaurant, Arkle, and the more informal La Brasserie.

Amenities: 24-hour room service, laundry, sauna, gym, Jacuzzi, solarium, business center.

✪ **Crabwall Manor.** Parkgate Rd., Mollington, Chester, Cheshire CH1 6NE. ☎ **01244/851666.** Fax 01244/851400. www.crabwall.com. E-mail: sales@crabwall.com. 48 units. TV TEL. Mon–Thurs £140 ($238) double; from £185 ($314.50) suite; Fri–Sun £120 ($204) double, £140 ($238) suite. Weekend rates include breakfast. AE, DC, MC, V. Bus: 22 or 23. Take A540 2 1/4 miles northwest of Chester.

Chester's premier country-house hotel, the imposing crenellated Crabwall Manor traces its origins from the 16th century, although most of the present building dates from the early 1800s. It has a more peaceful location than the Chester Grosvenor, although it lacks the facilities and the top-notch service of its more highly rated competitor. Standing amid 11 acres of private grounds and gardens, the capably managed hotel rents well-furnished bedrooms. Most rooms are quite large and show a certain flair in their decoration. The bathrooms are first class; most have bidets and separate showers.

Dining: The finest of contemporary English and French dishes are offered in a conservatory restaurant overlooking the gardens. Nonresidents are also welcome to enjoy the harmonious flavors, the subtle sauces, and the well-chosen menu.

Amenities: Health club, Jacuzzi, sauna, 24-hour room service, laundry, and dry cleaning.

MODERATE

Blossoms Hotel. St. John's St., Chester, Cheshire CH1 1HL. ☎ **800/225-5843** in the U.S. and Canada, or 01244/323186. Fax 01244/346433. 64 units. TV TEL. £105 ($178.50) double; £125 ($212.50) minisuite; £140 ($238) full suite. AE, DC, MC, V.

Blossoms Hotel has been in business since the mid-17th century, although the present structure was rebuilt late in Victoria's day. An old open staircase in the reception room helps set the tone here, but otherwise the public rooms are uninspired. Bedrooms are fitted with dark wood pieces, firm beds, and extras such as beverage-makers. Many of the rooms have recently been refurbished. Bathrooms are carpeted and beautifully maintained with luxury toiletries and generous shelf space. Maintenance could be a bit better. Lunch and dinner are served in the Brooks Restaurant, and there's also the Malt Shop bar.

Mollington Banastre. Parkgate Rd., Chester, Cheshire CH1 6NN. ☎ **800/528-1234** in the U.S. and Canada, or 01244/851471. Fax 01244/851165. 63 units. TV TEL. £112–£122 ($190.40–$207.40) double; £140 ($238) family unit (2 adults and up to 4 children), £157 ($266.90) suite for 2. Children 15 and under stay free in parents' room. AE, DC, MC, V. Take A540 2 miles northwest of the center of Chester. Or take Junction 16 of the M56 and continue for 1½ miles.

This Victorian mansion, surrounded by gardens, has been successfully converted into one of the leading country-house hotels in Cheshire, now affiliated with the Best Western reservation system. A gabled house, it offers a health club complex, along with two dining rooms and well-furnished bedrooms. Bedrooms come in a range of sizes and shapes; 8 are spacious enough for families. Rooms have comfortable doubles or twin beds equipped with firm mattresses. Seven rooms are set aside for nonsmokers. It's not the most opulent choice in town, but it's a great value for the money, especially with all its facilities, including 24-hour room service, a sauna, solarium, indoor swimming pool, and a gym. There's also a beauty salon and a coffee shop.

Rowton Hall Hotel. Whitchurch Rd., Rowton, Chester, Cheshire CH3 6AD. ☎ **01244/335262.** Fax 01244/335464. 38 units. TV TEL. £105–£200 ($178.50–$340) double. Rates include English or continental breakfast. AE, DC, MC, V. Take A41 2 miles from the center of Chester.

This stately home stands on the site of the Battle of Rowton Moor, which was fought in 1643 between the Roundheads and the Cavaliers. Built in 1779, with a wing added later, the house has an 8-acre garden, with a formal driveway entrance. Rowton Hall has comfortable traditional and contemporary furnishings. The better and more stylish rooms are in the old house. An adjoining wing contains more sterile and uninspired units, which some readers have complained about. Regardless of room assignment, each has a firm mattress on a comfortable bed. Four rooms are large enough for families. Bathrooms are small.

Good English meals are served in an oak-paneled dining room with a Tudor fireplace. Fresh vegetables and herbs are supplied by the hall's kitchen garden. Overlooking the garden, the conservatory-style Hamilton Lounge is an ideal venue for coffee, afternoon tea, or drinks. Special features include the hotel's swimming pool and its gym, which offers massages, aerobics classes, and a personal trainer.

WHERE TO DINE

✪ **Arkle Restaurant.** In the Chester Grosvenor Hotel, Eastgate. ☎ **01244/324024.** Reservations required. 2-course fixed-price menu £40 ($68), 3-course fixed-price menu £48 ($81.60); fixed-price menu gourmand £50 ($85). AE, DC, MC, V. Tues–Sun noon–2:30pm; Mon–Sat 7–9:30pm. BRITISH/CONTINENTAL.

Arkle is the premier restaurant in this part of England. The 45-seat formal, gourmet restaurant has a superb *chef de cuisine* and a talented 40-strong team that uses the freshest ingredients to create modern British and continental dishes prepared with subtle touches and a certain lightness. Main courses include langoustine ravioli, and Welsh black beef fillet topped with fresh horseradish. Desserts are equally luscious and tempting. Arkle has an award-winning cheese selection and a choice of at least six unique breads daily.

Elliot's Restaurant. 2 Abbey Green, off Northgate St. ☎ **01244/329932.** Reservations not needed. Lunch specials £3.50–£3.95 ($5.95–$6.70). Dinner main courses £9.50–£11.85 ($16.15–$20.15). MC, V. BRITISH.

In the heart of Chester, this family-run old English restaurant buys local produce and the best of regional products. It is concerned with free range, organic, and natural products which it fashions into good-tasting and time-tested recipes. All its vegetables are steam cooked and served crisp. The lunch menu is abbreviated, but includes a homemade soup of the day with freshly made bread, a selection of both hot and cold sandwiches, along with a cheese platter (a choice of four British cheeses), and daily specials posted on the board. For appetizers at night, select such delights as a seafood cocktail or venison sausages. Main dishes evoke England at its best, including a traditional roast beef dinner with Yorkshire pudding or free-range turkey pie flavored with fresh herbs. Vegetarian dishes are also served. Homemade pies make an excellent dessert.

La Brasserie. In the Chester Grosvenor Hotel, Eastgate St. ☎ **01244/324024.** Main courses £8–£25 ($13.60–$42.50). AE, DC, MC, V. Mon–Sat noon–10:30pm, Sun noon–10pm. ENGLISH/FRENCH.

This is perhaps the best all-around dining choice in Chester for convenience, price, and quality. In a delightful art-nouveau setting, the Brasserie offers an extensive à la carte menu to suit most tastes and pocketbooks. You get robust flavors and hearty ingredients. Main dishes include fried fish cakes with a hot Greek salad and crumbled feta; baked chicken with potato pancakes and garlic cheese; and other hearty brasserie food.

CHESTER AFTER DARK

If you want to relax in a pub, grab a pint of Marston's at the **Olde Custom House,** Watergate Street (☎ **01244/324435**), a 17th-century customhouse with many original features still intact. The **Pied Bull,** Northgate Street (☎ **01244/325829**), is an 18th-century coaching inn where you can still eat, drink, or rent a room. Real ales on tap include Flowers, and Greenall's Bitter and Traditional. At **Ye Olde King's Head,** Lower Bridge Street (☎ **01244/324855**), ales are not the only spirits you might encounter. This B&B pub, built in 1622, is said to be haunted by three ghosts; a crying woman and baby in room no. 6, and the ghostly initials "ST" that appear in steam on the bathroom mirror of room no. 4. If you prefer your spirits in a glass, stick to the pub, where you can sip on a Boddington's Bitter, or Greenall's Original or Local.

Live Irish music and atmosphere can be sampled at **Scruffy Murphy's,** 59 Northgate St. (☎ **01244/321750**), where you can hear traditional music on Wednesday and Sunday nights for the price of a pint of Guinness. **Alexandre's,** Rufus Court off Northgate Street (☎ **01244/340005**), offers more varied entertainment.

For dancing, head to **Raphael's,** Love Street off Foregate (☎ **01244/340754**).

4 Blackpool: Playground of the Midlands

246 miles NW of London; 88 miles W of Leeds; 56 miles N of Liverpool; 51 miles NW of Manchester

This once-antiquated Midlands resort is struggling to make a comeback by marketing itself to a new generation of vacationers. The result may remind you of Atlantic City or even Las Vegas (with a weird Victorian twist). The city has a midwinter population of 125,000 that swells to three or four times that in midsummer.

The country's largest resort makes its living from conferences, tour groups, families, and couples looking for an affordable getaway. Its 7 miles of beaches, 6 miles of colored lights, and dozens of Disney-like attractions and rides make Blackpool one of the most entertaining (and least apologetic) pieces of razzle-dazzle in England.

Disadvantages include unpredictable weather that brews over the nearby Irish Channel; a sandy, flat-as-a-pancake landscape that's less than inspiring; and a (sometimes undeserved) reputation for dowdiness. But some people love the brisk sea air, the architectural remnants of Britain's greatest Imperial Age, the utter lack of pretentiousness, and the poignant nostalgia that clings to the edges of places like Coney Island, where people look back fondly on the carefree fun they had in a simpler time.

ESSENTIALS

GETTING THERE Two trains from Manchester pull in every hour (trip time: $1^1/_2$ hours), and there's one every hour from Liverpool (trip time: $1^1/_2$ hours). For schedules and information, call ☎ **0345/484950.**

National Express buses arrive from Chester at the rate of three per day (trip time: 4 hours); Liverpool at the rate of six per day (trip time: $3^1/_2$ hours); Manchester, five per day (trip time: 2 hours; and London, six per day (trip time: $6^1/_2$ hours). For schedules and information, call ☎ **0990/808080.**

If you're driving from Manchester, take M61 north to M6 then M55 toward Blackpool. The trip takes about 1 hour.

VISITOR INFORMATION The helpful **Tourist Office** staff is at 1 Clifton St. (☎ **01253/478222**). The office is open November through March Monday to Saturday from 9am to 4:30pm; April through October, Monday to Saturday from 9am to 5pm, and Sunday from 10am to 3:30pm.

WHERE TO PLAY

Blackpool is famous for the **Illuminations,** an extravaganza of electric lights affixed to just about any stationary object along the Promenade. It features hundreds of illuminated figures, including Diamonds Are Forever, Santa's Workshop, Lamp Lighters, and Kitchen Lites. The tradition began in 1879 with just eight electric lights, and has grown with time and technology to include 6 miles of fiber optics, low-voltage neon tubes, and traditional lamps. The illuminations burn bright into the night from the end of August to the beginning of November. Take a tram ride down the Promenade for a great view of these tacky but festive lights.

Without a doubt, the most famous landmark in this town is the **Tower** along the Central Promenade (☎ **01253/622242**). In 1891, during the reign of Queen Victoria, a madcap idea started floating around to construct a 518-foot tower that resembled a half-size version of Paris's Eiffel Tower. The idea was first formerly presented to the town leaders of Brighton, who laughed at the idea, thinking it was a joke. But the forward-thinking leaders of Blackpool, when presented the plan, immediately saw the advantages of having such an attraction, and quickly approved the tower's construction. You be the judge.

Lighted by more than 10,000 bulbs, this landmark has become a tower of fun. It is truly an indoor entertainment complex both day and night and features the Tower Ballroom (one of the great Victorian ballrooms of Britain), the Tower Circus, the Hornpipe Galley, and the Dawn of Time dinosaur ride for kids, as well as the Tower Aquarium. An elevator takes visitors to the top of the Tower for a 60-mile view. The Tower is open from Easter to May Sunday to Friday 10am to 6pm and Saturday 10am to 11pm; and June through October daily from 10am to 11pm. The circus has two shows daily (except Friday evening) at 2:30pm and 7:30pm. Tower admission is £5 to £9 ($8.25 to $14.85).

WHERE TO STAY

De Vere Blackpool. E. Park Dr., Blackpool, Lancashire FY3 8LL. ☎ **01253/838866.** Fax 01253/798800. www.devere.com. 164 units. TV TEL. £140 ($238) double; £230 ($391) suite. AE, DC, MC, V.

This hotel symbolizes the renewal of Blackpool. It was erected on 236 flat and sandy acres in 1992, adjacent to the town's zoo and Stanley Park. Designed in a postmodern style that some visitors liken to a mansard-roofed French château, it evokes Las Vegas with a Midlands accent, partly because of the cheerful razzle-dazzle its hardworking staff throw into their jobs, and partly because of the many diversions on hand right here. These include an 18-hole golf course, pool tables, squash courts, a health spa and exercise room, and a large indoor swimming pool. There are also three bars and three restaurants, the most upscale of which is The Grill. Bedrooms are traditional but modern, done with light woods, and despite their relative youth, were renovated early in 1997. Most rooms open onto views of a golf course, and each offers the most comfortable beds in Blackpool hoteldom. Eight rooms are large enough to rent to families, and 95 are set aside for nonsmokers. Bathrooms have first-rate toiletries and generous shelf space.

The Imperial Hotel. N. Promenade, Blackpool, Lancashire FY1 2HB. ☎ **01253/623971.** Fax 01253/751784. 181 units. £150 ($255) double; £250 ($425) suite. Rates include breakfast. AE, DC, MC, V.

Noted as a stylish venue for group conferences, this hotel was built by the Victorians as a massive redbrick pile. It's still a major landmark in town. Recent renovations added vestiges of 19th-century country-house stateliness to the public areas and some of the bedrooms, and a scattering of artwork related to such genteel pleasures as "the hunt." Accommodations come in various shapes and sizes, but each is well appointed. Most bathrooms have a tub and shower combination, and each offers tidy maintenance and adequate shelf space. There's also the occasional touch of color that relieves an otherwise heavy use of beige and neutral tones. Everything is pretty anonymous and standard. There are two bars and a restaurant, The Palm Court, plus 24-hour room service.

The Savoy Hotel. Queens Promenade, Blackpool FY2 9SJ. ☎ **01253/352561.** Fax 01253/500735. 131 units. TV TEL. £55–£120 ($93.50–$204) double; £200 ($340) suite. AE, DC, MC, V.

The roots of this hotel stretch back to the late 19th century, when its redbrick tower and bay windows beckoned vacationers to its seaside location near the North Pier. Since then, ongoing refurbishment has kept the place well carpeted, well painted, and well upholstered. Bedrooms are conservatively up to date and restful. Most rooms are quite spacious, many offering sea views, although individual shape and size can vary considerably. Fourteen are large enough to rent to families. Each room has twin or double beds. Most rooms have a tub and shower combination, and each is fitted with a hair dryer. On the premises is an attractive restaurant, Gilbert's, whose paneled interior attracts its own rather active bar trade.

WHERE TO DINE

September Brasserie. 15–17 Queen St. ☎ **01253/623282.** Reservations recommended. Main courses £10.50–£13 ($17.85–$22.10); 2-course set-price dinner £16.90 ($28.75), 3-course set-price dinner £18.90 ($32.15). AE, DC, MC, V. Tues–Sat noon–2pm and 7–10pm. MODERN BRITISH/INTERNATIONAL.

Set within a three-story building that originally functioned as a Victorian-era haberdashery, this noteworthy restaurant developed from the core of a hairdressing salon that still flourishes on the street level today. Both elements of the place are the domain of the Golowicz family, which maintains (with a smile) that the staff that works inside are probably the best-coifed restaurant employees in the west of England. The restaurant prides itself on its sophisticated, modern, British cuisine (a step up from the pub grub and fish-and-chip parlors that proliferate in the surrounding neighborhood). Menu items include roasted organic salmon fillet with tapenade noodles and saffron sauce; and breast of local pheasant and teal with creamed mushrooms and mashed potato.

The Lake District

16

The Lake District, one of the most beautiful parts of Great Britain, is actually quite small, measuring about 35 miles wide. Most of the district is in Cumbria, although it begins in the northern part of Lancashire.

Bordering Scotland, the far-northwestern part of the shire is generally divided geographically into three segments: the Pennines, dominating the eastern sector (loftiest point at Cross Fell, nearly 3,000 feet high); the Valley of Eden; and the lakes and secluded valleys of the west, which are by far the most interesting.

So beautifully described by the romantic poets, the area enjoys many literary associations with William Wordsworth, Samuel Taylor Coleridge, Charlotte Brontë, Charles Lamb, Percy Bysshe Shelley, John Keats, Alfred Lord Tennyson, and Matthew Arnold. In Queen Victoria's day, the Lake District was one of England's most popular summer retreats.

The largest town is Carlisle, up by the Scotland border, which is a possible base for exploring Hadrian's Wall (see chapter 17)—but for now, we will concentrate on the district's lovely lakeside villages. **Windermere** is the best base for exploring the Lake District.

WALKS & RAMBLES

Driving in the wilds of this scenic shire is fine for a start, but the best way to take in its beauty is by walking—an art best practiced here with a crooked stick. There is a great deal of rain and heavy mist, and sunny days are few. (Pack some good waterproof hiking boots and a lightweight rain jacket—even if you set out on a nice morning, you need to be prepared for changing conditions.) When the mist starts to fall, do as the locals do and head for the nearest inn or pub, where you can drop in and warm yourself beside an open fireplace. You'll be carried back to the good old days, since many places in Cumbria have valiantly resisted change.

If you want to make hiking in the Lake District a focus of your entire vacation, you might prefer an organized outing. **Countrywide Holidays,** Grove House, Wilmslow Road, Didsbury, Manchester M20 2HU (☎ **01942/823430**), has offered walking and special-interest vacations for more than 100 years. Safe and sociable guided walks are led by experienced guides for all ages and abilities. It's ideal for independent walkers, with boot-drying rooms provided. They have four comfortable, informal, and welcoming guest houses set in beautiful Lakeland locations.

1 Kendal

270 miles NW of London; 64 miles NW of Bradford; 72 miles NW of Leeds; 9 miles SE of Windermere

The River Kent winds its way through a rich valley of limestone hills and cliffs, known as "fells," and down through the "Auld Grey Town" of Kendal, whose moniker refers to the large number of gray stone houses found in and about the town. Many visitors to the Lake District simply pass through Kendal on their way to more attractive destinations—the town is a gateway rather than a true stopping place. It's never depended entirely on the tourist dollar. This fact should not deter you, however, from taking a bit of time to discover some of this market town's more intriguing areas.

Kendal contains the ruins of a castle where Catherine Parr, Henry VIII's last wife, was allegedly born. Recent speculation about her actual birthplace has led to a clouding of the historic record. Even if she wasn't born here, it is still said that she most likely lived at the castle at some time in her life. Among other historic sites, Kendal has a 13th-century parish church that merits a visit.

Today, Kendal is famous for its mint cake and its surrounding limestone fells, which offer excellent vistas of the area and make for great hikes.

ESSENTIALS

GETTING THERE Trains from London's Euston Station do not go directly to Kendal; seven daily trains arrive in Oxenholme, about 1½ miles away. From here, you'll be able to take a cab or board one of the local trains that leave approximately every hour to Kendal proper (total trip time: 3½ hours). For train schedules and information, call ☎ **0345/484950.**

To Kendal from London by bus, take one of the three daily National Express buses (trip time: 7 hours). For schedules and information, call **National Express** at ☎ **0990/808080.**

If you're driving, follow the M1 out of London, then the M6 to Kendal (trip time: 5 hours).

VISITOR INFORMATION The **Tourist Information Centre,** Town Hall, Highgate (☎ **01539/725758**), is open November to Easter, Monday to Saturday from 9am to 5pm; Easter through October, Monday to Saturday from 9am to 5pm, and Sunday from 10am to 4pm.

SEEING THE SIGHTS

Kendal Museum. Station Rd. ☎ **01539/721374.** Admission £3 ($5.10) adults, £2.80 ($4.75) seniors, £1.50 ($2.55) children; £7.50 ($12.75) family. Mid-Feb to Mar and Nov–Dec 24 daily 10:30am–4pm; Apr–Oct daily 10:30am–5pm. Closed Dec 24 to mid-Feb.

One of England's oldest museums takes visitors on a journey of discovery from Roman times to the present. A natural-history section includes a nature trail from mountaintop to lakeside, on which visitors are brought face to face with many of the inhabitants of the area. The World Wildlife Gallery displays a vast collection of exotic animals. One of the exhibitions introduces visitors to the fell-tops' best-known visitor, Alfred Wainwright, who walked, talked, and wrote with a passion and flair about the region. Wainwright worked diligently until his death in 1991.

Museum of Lakeland Life and Industry. Kirkland. ☎ **01539/722464.** Admission £3 ($5.10) adults, £2.80 ($4.75) seniors, £1.50 ($2.55) children. Mid-Feb to Mar and Nov–Dec daily 10:30am–4pm; Apr to Oct daily 10:30am–5pm. Closed Jan to mid-Feb.

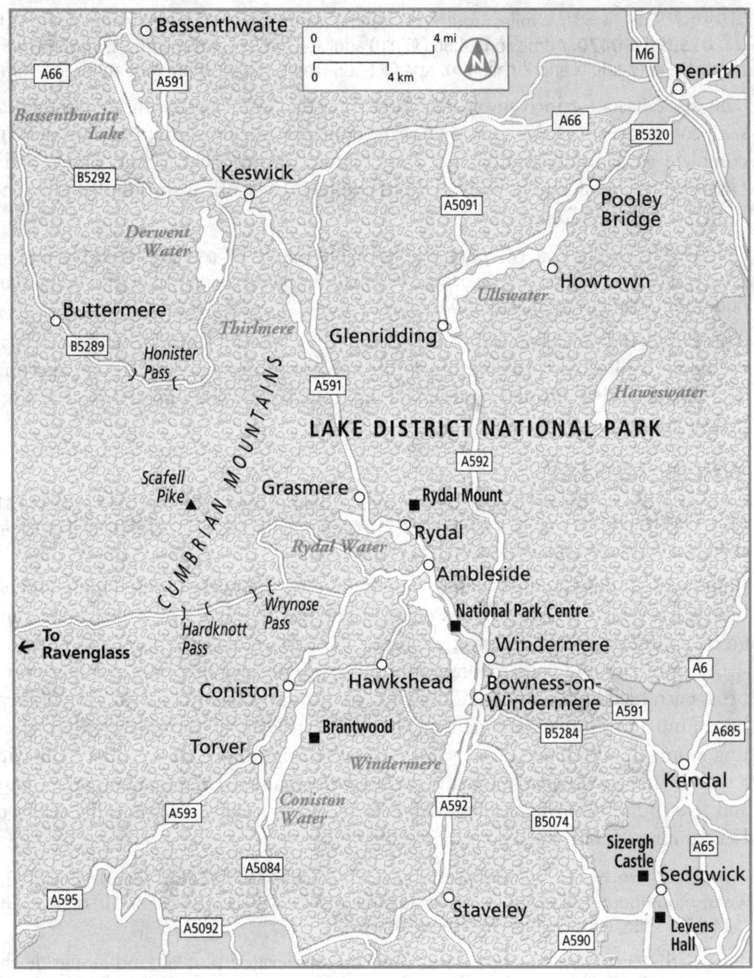

From the re-creation of a Victorian Kendal street, complete with pharmacy and market, the visitor can discover the lost craft and trades of the region and the ways of life that accompanied them.

Abbot Hall Art Gallery. Kirkland. ☎ **01539/722464.** Admission £3 ($5.10) adults, £2.80 ($4.75) seniors, £1.50 ($2.55) children. Mid-Feb to Mar daily 10:30am–4pm; Apr to late Dec daily 10:30am–5pm.

The Georgian elegance of Kendal's Abbot Hall Art Gallery has created an ideal setting for its display of fine art. Paintings by the town's famous son, 18th-century portrait painter George Romney, fill the walls of rooms furnished by Gillows of Lancaster. A major display of work by 20th-century British artists such as Graham Sutherland, John Piper, and Ben Nicholson are on permanent display. Visitors can see the region through the eyes of the many painters who have been inspired by the landscapes in another of the gallery's permanent exhibitions housed in The Peter Scott Gallery.

Sizergh Castle. 3 1/2 miles south of Kendal (northwest of interchange A590/591). ☎ **015395/60070.** Admission £4.60 ($7.80) adults, £2.30 ($3.90) children, £11.50 ($19.55) family ticket (2 adults and 2 children). Apr–Oct Sun–Thurs 1:30–5:30pm (last admission 5pm).

The castle has a fortified tower that dates from the 14th century. Inside, visitors can see a collection of Elizabethan carvings and paneling, fine furniture, and portraits. The complete garden, largely from the 18th century, incorporates a rock garden and a famous planting of hardy ferns and dwarf conifers. The castle is surrounded by a show of fiery colors in autumn.

Levens Hall. Levens Park, Levens (4 miles south of Kendal). ☎ **015395/60321.** Admission £5.50 ($9.35) for house and gardens; £4 ($6.80) for gardens only. Apr–Oct 14 Sun–Thurs noon–5pm (gardens open at 10am).

This Elizabethan mansion was constructed in the 1500s by James Bellingham. Today, the house is filled with Jacobean furniture and a working model of steam collection. The estate also has a **topiary garden** dating from 1692, with a host of yews and box hedges clipped into a variety of intriguing shapes.

WHERE TO STAY

Garden House Hotel. Fowling Lane, Kendal, Cumbria LA9 6PH. ☎ **01539/731131.** Fax 01539/740064. 11 units. TV TEL. £75 ($127.50) double. £6 ($10.20) extra bed or cot for child. Rates include English breakfast. AE, DC, MC, V.

Built in 1812, this Georgian country house was once a convent for local nuns, and has been a hotel for the past 30 years or so. It's nestled in 2 acres of walled garden and green pastureland, and is perfectly serene. The guest rooms are decorated in pastels with lots of lace and contemporary furnishings; some have fireplaces and four-poster beds. Each tiled bathroom, quite compact, comes with a hair dryer, and most of them have a tub and shower combination. The public areas include a somewhat formal sitting room, an informal lounge bar with lots of seating, an elegant breakfast room with a dark mahogany fireplace, and a restaurant conservatory. The restaurant serves four- and five-course dinners, or guests can take an easy 5-minute walk into the center of Kendal for an interesting choice of restaurants.

Lane Head House. Helsington, Kendal LA9 5RJ. ☎ **01539/731283.** Fax 01539/721023. www.smoothhound.co.uk/hotels/landhead.html. 6 units. TV TEL. £75 ($127.50) double; £85 ($144.50) suite. Rates include English breakfast. V.

This 17th-century manor house was built on an elevated plot of land alongside the ruins of a fortified tower, a fortress used during battles between the English and Scots centuries ago. The guest rooms have their original oak beams and are appointed with period-style reproductions. All rooms have romantic arch windows with views of the landscaped gardens, including an Elizabethan knot garden and an orchard of apple, pear, and plum trees, with glimpses of the River Kent and pastureland beyond. Beds are twins or a double, each draped or canopied. If prearranged, an à la carte dinner can be served.

WHERE TO DINE

Déjà Vu. 124 Stricklandgate. ☎ **01539/724843.** Reservations recommended. Main courses £8.95–£12.95 ($15.20–$22). DC, MC, V. Daily 7–10:30pm. FRENCH.

The interior of this small and cozy French cabaret was inspired by one of van Gogh's landscape paintings. People come for good food and a fun time. A wide range of appetizers evoke a taste of Paris, featuring fresh scallops mille feuille with a basil cream sauce, or St. Marcellin cheese soufflé with caramelized mango and red onions. Follow with such mains as fresh monkfish filet on eggplant with a basil and fennel sauce, or Aberdeen Angus filet of beef with a port and pink peppercorn mousse. Desserts feature many classic French favorites, including the delicious peach tartlet with ice cream and peach liqueur.

Moon. 129 Highgate. ☎ **01539/729254.** Main courses £9.25–£13 ($15.75–$22.10). MC, V. Tues–Sun 6–10pm. INTERNATIONAL.

This bistro cooks up the best food in Kendal. Set in a building that's more than 250 years old, and was once a grocery store, the dining room offers patrons a close, friendly, and informal environment. The food is interesting without being gimmicky. The owners take pride in offering market-fresh ingredients when available. Main courses include lamb shank with either a mustard and Soya sauce, or a cream, leek, and white wine sauce; or for vegetarians, goat's cheese, red pepper, and mango wrapped in filo pastry with an apple, gooseberry, and honey sauce.

2 Windermere & Bowness

274 miles NW of London; 10 miles NW of Kendal; 55 miles N of Liverpool

The largest lake in England is Windermere, whose eastern shore washes up on the town of Bowness (or Bowness-on-Windermere), with the town of Windermere 1½ miles away. From either town, you can climb **Orrest Head** in less than an hour for a panoramic view of the Lakeland. From that vantage point, you can even view **Scafell Pike,** rising to a height of 3,210 feet—it's the tallest peak in all of England.

ESSENTIALS

GETTING THERE Trains to Windermere meet the main line at Oxenholme for connections to both Scotland and London. Information about rail services in the area can be obtained by calling the railway information line at ☎ **0345/484950.** Frequent connections are possible throughout the day. To get to Bowness and its ferry pier from Windermere, turn left from the rail terminal and cross the center of Windermere until you reach New Road, which eventually changes its name to Lake Road before it approaches the outskirts of Bowness. It's about a 20-minute walk downhill. The CMS Lakeland Experience bus also runs from the Windermere Station to Bowness every 20 minutes.

The **National Express** bus link, originating at London's Victoria Coach Station, serves Windermere, with good connections also to Preston, Manchester, and Birmingham. For schedules and information, call ☎ **0990/808080.** Local buses operated mainly by **Stagecoach** (☎ **01946/63222**) go to Kendal, Ambleside, Grasmere, and Keswick. Call for information on various routings within the Lake District.

If you're driving from London, head north on the M1 and M6 past Liverpool until you reach the A685 junction heading west to Kendal. From Kendal, A591 continues west to Windermere.

VISITOR INFORMATION The **Tourist Information Centre** at Windermere is on Victoria Street (☎ **015394/46499**). From September to June, it's open daily from 9am to 6pm, and until 7:30pm in July and August. The **Tourist Information Centre** at The Glebe in Bowness (☎ **015394/42895**) is open April through October daily from 9:30am to 5:30pm.

EXPLORING THE AREA

There is regular **steamer service** around ✪ **Windermere,** the largest of the lakes, about 10½ miles long. It's also possible to take a steamer on Coniston Water, a small lake that Wordsworth called "a broken spoke sticking in the rim." Coniston Water is a smaller and less heavily traveled lake than Windermere.

There are launch and steamer cruises from Bowness daily throughout the year operated by **Windermere Lake Cruises Ltd.** (☎ **015394/43360**). Service is available from Bowness to Ambleside and to Lakeside at rates ranging from £5.80–£10 ($9.85–$17) for adults and £2.90–£5 ($4.95–$8.50) for children. There is a 45-minute Island Cruise for £4.50 ($7.65) for adults and £2.25 ($3.80) for children.

At Lakeside you can ride a steam train to Haverthwaite. A combination boat/train ticket is £4 ($6.80) for adults and £2 ($3.40) for children. An attraction at Lakeside, near Newby Bridge, is the **Aquarium of the Lakes** (☎ **015395/30153**), with an exhibit of fish and wildlife. Combination boat/admission tickets are £9.25 ($15.75) for adults, £6.50 ($11.05) for children, and £37 ($62.90) for a family ticket from Ambleside; and £8.75 ($14.90) for adults, £5.15 ($8.75) for children, and £29 ($49.30) for a family ticket from Bowness.

Directly south of Windermere, **Bowness** is an attractive old lakeside town with lots of interesting architecture, much of it dating from Queen Victoria's day. This has been an important center for boating and fishing for a long time, and you can rent boats of all descriptions to explore the lake.

Windermere Steamboat Museum. Rayrigg Rd. ☎ **015394/45565.** Admission £3.25 ($5.50) adults, £2 ($3.40) children, £8 ($13.60) family ticket. Daily 10am–5pm. Closed Nov–Mar 18.

This museum houses the finest collection of steamboats in the world. Important examples of these elegant Victorian and Edwardian vessels have been preserved in working order. The steamboats are exhibited in a unique wet dock where they are moored in their natural lakeside setting. The fine display of touring and racing motorboats in the dry dock links the heyday of steam with some of the most famous names of powerboat racing and the record-breaking attempts on Windermere, including Sir Henry Segrave's world water-speed record set in 1930.

All the boats have intriguing stories, including the veteran SL *Dolly,* built around 1850 and probably the oldest mechanically driven boat in the world. The vessel was raised from the lake bed of Ullswater in 1962 and, following restoration, ran for 10 years with its original boiler. The *Dolly* is still steamed on special occasions.

The SL *Osprey* (1902) is steamed most days and visitors can make a 50-minute trip on the lake, at a cost of £5 ($8.50) for adults and £4 ($6.80) for children, with the crew serving tea or coffee made using the Windermere steam kettle.

The World of Beatrix Potter. The Old Laundry, Bowness-on-Windermere. ☎ **015394/88444.** Admission £3.25 ($5.50) adults, £2 ($3.40) children. Easter–Sept daily 10am–5:30pm; rest of year daily 10am–5pm. Take A591 to Lake Rd. and follow the signs.

This exhibit uses the latest technology to tell the story of Beatrix Potter's fascinating life. A video wall and special film describe how her tales came to be written and how she became a pioneering Lakeland farmer and conservationist. There is also a shop with a wealth of top-quality Beatrix Potter merchandise, from Wedgwood ceramics to soft toys. It's mobbed on summer weekends; try to come at any other time.

WHERE TO STAY

VERY EXPENSIVE

Holbeck Ghyll. Holbeck Lane (on the A591 3½ miles northwest of town center), Windermere, Cumbria LA23 1LU. ☎ **015394/32375.** Fax 015394/34743. www.slh.com. E-mail: accommodation@holbeck-ghyll.co.uk. 20 units. TV TEL. £65–£85 ($110.50–$144.50) per person double; £95 ($161.50) per person suite, with English breakfast; £80–£100 ($136–$170) per person double; £115 ($195.50) per person suite with breakfast and dinner. Children under 17 stay for half price when sharing parents' room. AE, DC, MC, V.

This country-house hotel was once a 19th-century hunting lodge owned by Lord Lonsdale, one of the richest men in Britain. Overlooking Lake Windermere, this hotel has a high price tag, but offers a lot for the money. An inglenook fireplace welcomes visitors. The most elaborate room is a honeymoon and anniversary room that has a four-poster and a bathroom with a spa bath for two. But each unit is fitted with a luxury bed, often crowned by a canopy or a padded headboard. Rooms are individually designed, coming in various shapes and sizes, and most of them open onto a view of the lake. Six rooms are in a separate cottage added in 1998, and these are even finer than the rooms in the main building. Lodge rooms are inter-connecting with panoramic lake views, ground floor access, and individual balcony or patio areas. Luxurious bathrooms have separate shower cubicles, as well as a tub. Six rooms are set aside for nonsmokers.

Dining: The hotel's primary dining room is one of the finest restaurants in the Lake District. The menu changes daily and is never repeated. Appetizers are likely to include seared scallops with split pea purée and hollandaise. That might be followed by Gressingham duck, cooked two ways, with rösti potatoes and baby vegetables. A second restaurant now offers lunch.

Amenities: The property includes woods with walking paths, streams, ponds, an all-weather tennis court, and a health spa.

Langdale Chase Hotel. On the A591 (2 miles north of town, toward Ambleside), Windermere, Cumbria LA23 1LW. ☎ **015394/32201.** Fax 015394/32604.www.langdalechase.co.uk. E-mail: sales@langdalechase.co.uk. 27 units. TV TEL. £75–£100 ($127.50–$170) per person double. Rates include breakfast and dinner. AE, DC, MC, V. Bus: 555.

A grand old lakeside house, this hotel resembles a villa on Italy's Lake Como. It has better rooms than Miller Howe (see below), although the food is not as good. The bedrooms have excellent furniture, and many were recently refurbished. Most of the bedrooms open onto panoramic views of the lake. Five bedrooms are in a converted cottage on the grounds, and these are equal in comfort to those units in the main building. Another bedroom lies over the boathouse on the lake, and this one is often requested. Bathrooms are tiled and come with adequate shelf space. The interior of the Victorian stone château, with its many gables, balconies, large mullioned windows, and terraces, is a treasure trove of antiques. The main lounge hall looks like a setting for one of those English drawing-room comedies. On the walls are distinctive paintings, mostly Italian primitives, although one is alleged to be a Van Dyck.

Dining: The dining room ranks among the finest in the Lake District, with tables offering a view of the lake. The cuisine is highly personal, mostly updated English fare, supported by a fine wine list.

Amenities: There's waterskiing, rowing, swimming in the lake, tennis, croquet, and fishing.

Lindeth Fell Hotel. Lyth Valley Rd. (on the A5074 1 mile south of Bowness), Bowness-on-Windermere, Cumbria LA23 3JP. ☎ **015394/43286.** Fax 015394/47455. www.lindethfell.co.uk. E-mail: kennedy@lindeth. 14 units. TV TEL. £100–£172 ($170–$292.40) double. Rates include breakfast and dinner. MC, V. Closed Jan–Feb 14.

High above the town is this traditional large Lakeland house, built of stone and brick in 1907. Many of its rooms overlook the handsome gardens and the lake. The owners, the Kennedys, run the place more like a country house than a hotel, achieving an atmosphere of comfort in pleasingly furnished surroundings. Bedrooms open onto beautiful views, and many are quite spacious, others snug, each with comfortable beds and beverage makers. Bathrooms come with a hair dryer.

Lake District National Park

Despite the reverence with which the English treat the Lake District, it required an act of Parliament in 1951 to protect its natural beauty. Sprawling over 885 square miles of hills, eroded mountains, forests, and lakes, the **Lake District National Park** is the largest and one of the most popular national parks in the United Kingdom, with 14 million visitors a year. Its scenery and literary references (Wordsworth, Beatrix Potter, John Ruskin, and Samuel Taylor Coleridge were among its most ardent fans) add an academic gloss to one of the most idealized regions of Britain. Lured by descriptions from the romantic lake poets, visitors arrive to take in the mountains, wildlife, flora, fauna, and secluded waterfalls. Much of the area is privately owned, but landowners work with national park officers to preserve the landscape and its 1,800 miles of footpaths.

Alas, the park's popularity is now one of its major drawbacks. Hordes of weekend tourists descend, especially in summertime and on bank-holiday weekends. During mild weather in midsummer, Windermere, Keswick, and Ambleside are likely to be among the most crowded towns of their size in England. But despite the crowds, great efforts are made to maintain the trails that radiate in a network throughout the district. Rigid building codes manage to accommodate the scores of tourist-industry facilities, while preserving the purity of a landscape that includes more than 100 lakes and countless numbers of grazing sheep.

Before setting out to explore the lake, stop in at the **National Park Visitor Centre** (☎ **015394/46601**), located on the lakeshore at Brockhole, on the A591 between Windermere and Ambleside. It can be reached by bus or by one of the lake launches from Windermere. Here, you can pick up useful information and explore 30 acres of landscaped gardens and parklands; lake cruises, exhibitions, and

Dining: Local produce is used whenever possible to prepare a variety of Lakeland and traditional English dishes, including noisettes of border lamb with mint and onion purée, and poached Scottish salmon with chive and lemon-butter sauce.

Amenities: The Kennedys offer tennis, croquet, and putting on the lawn, as well as a private tarn for fishing.

✪ **The Linthwaite House Hotel.** Crook Rd., Bowness-on-Windermere, Cumbria LA23 3JA. ☎ **015394/88600.** Fax 015934/88601. www.linthwaite.com. E-mail: admin@linthwaite.com. 26 units. TV TEL. £135–£250 ($229.50–$425) double. Rates include English breakfast. AE, DC, MC, V.

This hotel, built in 1900 and surrounded by woodlands and gardens, has a panoramic view of Lake Windermere, Bell Isle, and the distant mountains. The bedrooms are beautifully decorated and offer many amenities, including bathrobes, satellite TVs, tea- and coffeemakers, and hair dryers. As befits its former role as an Edwardian gentleman's house, this hotel offers individually decorated bedrooms that come in various shapes and sizes. All are fitted with sumptuously comfortable beds. Twelve rooms are rented to nonsmokers.

Dining: Since chef Ian Bravery has numerous requests for his secrets, the hotel has decided to produce its own cookbook containing some of the most sought-after recipes, such as sticky toffee pudding, bread-and-butter pudding, gin-and-tonic sorbet, and Lakeland lamb rosemary and thyme jus.

film shows are also offered. Lunches and teas are served in Gaddums tearooms with terrace seating. Normally there is free admission, except for special events staged here. Parking costs £3 ($5.10) for 3 hours or £4 ($6.80) for a full day.

When setting out anywhere in the Lake District, it's wise to take adequate clothing and equipment, including food and drink. Weather conditions can change rapidly in this area, and in the high fells it can be substantially different from that found at lower levels. A **weather** line (☎ **017687/75757**) provides the latest conditions.

Tourist information offices within the park are richly stocked with maps and suggestions for several dozen bracing rambles—perhaps a 4-mile loop around the town of Windermere; a long (7-mile) or short (3¹/₂-mile) hike between Ambleside and Grasmere; or a boat ride from Windermere to the southern edge of the town's lake, followed by a trek northward along the lake's scenic western shore. Regardless of the itinerary you select, you'll spot frequent green-and-white signs, or their older equivalents in varnished pine with Adirondack-style routed letters, announcing FOOTPATH TO. . . .

Be aware before you go that the Lake District receives more rainfall than any other district of England, and that sturdy walking shoes and rain gear are essential. Hiking after dark is not recommended under any circumstances.

Any tourist information office within the park can provide leaflets describing treks through the park. The **Windermere Tourist Information Centre,** Victoria Street, Windermere, Cumbria LA23 1AD (☎ **015394/46499**), is especially helpful.

See also section 5 of this chapter, "Coniston & Hawkshead," for additional details about boating in the national park.

Amenities: The rates include complimentary use of the nearby leisure spa, which has a pool, sauna, steam room/plunge pool, spa bath, and gym.

✪ **Miller Howe Hotel.** Rayrigg Rd. (on A592 between Windermere and Bowness), Windermere, Cumbria LA23 1EY. ☎ **015394/42536.** Fax 015394/45664. www.millerhowe.com. E-mail: lakeview@millerhowe.com. 12 units. TV TEL. £70–£125 ($119–$212.50) per person per night. Rates include English breakfast and 4-course dinner. AE, DC, MC, V. Closed mid-Dec to end of Jan.

International guests come to this inn, which bears the unique imprint of its creator, former actor John Tovey, who treats his guests as if they had been invited to a house party. His country estate overlooks Lake Windermere (with views of the Langdale Pikes), and offers stylish accommodations and exquisite cuisine. The house was built in 1916 in the Edwardian style, sitting on 4¹/₂ acres of statue-dotted garden and parkland. The large, graciously furnished rooms have names (not numbers), and each is supplied with binoculars to help guests fully enjoy the view. Beds are sumptuous, often canopy-draped, each with colorful spreads, soft comfortable mattresses, and padded headboards. Bathrooms are furnished with hair dryers and generous shelf space. There are even copies of *Punch* from the 1890s.

Dining: Dinner at Miller Howe is worth the drive up from London. Susan Elliott, the head chef, has introduced lighter dishes; she uses hot and cold vinaigrettes rather than rich cream sauces, cutting out many of the garnishes and getting back to basics. Even if you can't stay overnight, at least consider a meal here, for which you must make a reservation.

MODERATE

Cedar Manor. Ambleside Rd. (A591), Windermere, Cumbria LA23 1AX. ☎ **015394/ 43192.** Fax 015394/45970. www.cedarmanor.co.uk. E-mail: cedarmanor@fsbdial.co.uk. 12 units. TV TEL. £78–£106 ($132.60–$180.20) double. Half board £47–£58 ($79.90–$98.60) per person. Rates include breakfast. MC, V.

One of the most desirable country-house hotels in the area is Cedar Manor. Originally built in 1860, with gables and chimneys, it was the summer getaway home for a wealthy industrialist from Manchester. But since those times, it has been converted into a small hotel of exceptional merit, with well-furnished bedrooms. Each of the spacious bedrooms is individually designed and the beds have soft mattresses and fluffy pillows. Furnishings are tasteful and fabrics often flowery. Extras include beverage makers. Bathrooms are small and compact with hair dryers and mainly tub and shower combinations. The hotel takes its name from a cedar tree, perhaps from India, which has grown in the garden for some two centuries.

Meals are good and wholesome. Typical dishes include pot roasted lamb rumps or Barbary duck breasts with chestnut stuffing.

Lindeth Howe. Longtail Hill, Storrs Park, Bowness-on-Windermere, Cumbria LA23 3JF. ☎ **015394/45759.** Fax 015394/46368. www.lakes-pages.co.uk. E-mail: lindeth.howe@ lakes-pages.co.uk. 36 units. TV. £42.50–£52.50 ($72.25–$89.25) per person double with breakfast; £61–£71 ($103.70–$120.70) per person double with breakfast and dinner. MC, V. Take B5284 south of Bowness.

This is a country house in a scenic position above Lake Windermere, with 6 acres of grounds. Part stone and part red brick, with a roof of green Westmoreland slate, the house was built for a wealthy mill owner in 1879, but its most famous owner was Beatrix Potter, who installed her mother here while she lived across the lake at Sawrey. The present owner, John A. Tiscornia, has furnished it in fine style. Most of the bedrooms have lake views and are comfortably furnished, with in-house movies, beverage makers, and central heating. Four rooms have handsome four-poster beds and some rooms have spa baths. Rooms come in various shapes and sizes, but most of them have twin or double beds. Three rooms are large enough for families, and another three are set aside for nonsmokers.

The dining room has two deep bay windows overlooking the lake, and there is a lounge featuring a brick fireplace. The hotel has a sauna and solarium and access to the Leisure Club opposite the beautiful grounds which includes a swimming pool, steam room, and Jacuzzi.

INEXPENSIVE

Beaumont Hotel. Holly Rd., Windermere, Cumbria LA23 2AF. ☎ and fax **015394/47075.** www.lakesbeaumont.co.uk. E-mail: the beaumonthotel@btinternet.com. 10 units. TV. £60–£90 ($102–$153) double. Rates include English breakfast. MC, V.

This stone-sided Lakeland villa, originally built in the 1850s, is on a quiet residential street about a minute's walk from Windermere's commercial center. Mr. and Mrs. James C. Casey massively upgraded what had been a rather dowdy interior. Each of the bedrooms is named after one of the characters in the Beatrix Potter sagas (our favorite is Jemima PuddleDuck) and contains either some kind of elaborate canopy or a four-poster bed, fitted with a quality mattress. All the accommodations have recently been refurbished, with new towels, carpets, and curtains; each room has a tea maker. No meals are served other than breakfast, so the owners keep local restaurant menus on hand for their guests to consult.

Fir Trees. Lake Rd., Windermere, Cumbria LA23 2EQ. ☎ and fax **015394/42272.** www.firtrees.com. E-mail: firtreeshotel@msn.com. 8 units. TV. £44–£66 ($74.80–$112.20) double. Rates include English breakfast. AE, MC, V. No smoking.

This is one of the finest guest houses in Windermere. It's very well run, essentially providing hotel-like standards at B&B prices. Opposite St. John's Church, halfway between the villages of Bowness and Windermere, Fir Trees is a Victorian house furnished with antiques. Proprietors Geoff and Kay Todd offer a warm welcome and rent well-furnished and beautifully maintained bedrooms, each with a beverage maker and other thoughtful amenities. The tiled bathrooms are beautifully maintained, and have hair dryers. Some units are large enough for families. The Todds can provide their guests with detailed information on restaurants, country pubs, or where to go and what to see.

WHERE TO DINE

✪ **Miller Howe Café.** Lakeland Plastics, Station Precinct. ☎ **015394/46732.** Main courses £6.95–£7.95 ($11.80–$13.50). MC, V. Mon–Fri 9am–6pm, Sat 10am–5pm, Sun 10am–4pm. INTERNATIONAL.

This restaurant was opened by former actor John Tovey, the celebrated owner of the Miller Howe Hotel (see "Where to Stay," above). Now owned by his former head chef, Ian Dutton, this charming little café lies at the back of a shop that is known as one of the largest retailers of "creative kitchenware" in Britain. Amid a very modern decor, clients place their food orders at a countertop, then wait until the dishes are brought to their tables by waitresses. The cuisine draws upon culinary traditions from around the world, and includes such dishes as diced and curried beef in a spicy sauce, filet of salmon with a fresh garden herb sauce, macaroni baked with heavy cream and red Cheddar cheese, and breast of chicken served in a red wine gravy. The restaurant is adjacent to the town's railway station.

Porthole Eating House. 3 Ash St. ☎ **015394/42793.** Reservations recommended. Main courses £10.75–£18 ($18.25–$30.60). AE, DC, MC, V. Sun–Fri noon–3pm, Wed–Mon 6:30–11pm. FRENCH/ITALIAN/ENGLISH.

In a white-painted Lakeland house near the center of town, this restaurant, owned and operated by Gianni and Judy Barten for the last quarter of a century, serves French, English, and Italian cuisine inspired by Italian-born Gianni. Amid a decor enhanced by rows of wine and liqueur bottles and nautical accessories, you can enjoy well-flavored specialties that change with the seasons. Examples include lobster-and-crab bisque; vegetarian lasagna made with mixed vegetables, fresh herbs, and a fresh tomato coulis and basil sauce; and filet of beef lightly grilled and served with a reduction of butter, fresh herbs, and a touch of white wine.

FAVORITE LOCAL PUBS

Drive a short distance south of Windermere to Cartmel Fell, situated between A592 and A5074, and you'll find a pub-lover's dream. The **Mason Arms,** Strawberry Bank (☎ **01539/568486**), is a Jacobean pub with original oak paneling and flagstone floors. There's sturdy, comfortable wooden furniture spread through a series of five rooms in which you can wander or settle. The outside garden, attractive in its own right, offers a dramatic view of the Winster Valley beyond. The pub offers so many beers that they have a 24-page catalog to help you order, plus a creative, reasonable menu that includes several tasty vegetarian options.

Southeast of the village, off A5074 in Crosthwaithe, the **Punch Bowl** (☎ **015395/68237**) is a 16th-century pub; the central room features a high-beamed ceiling with upper minstrel galleries on two sides. Outdoors, a stepped terrace on the hillside offers a tranquil retreat. Theakstons Best, Jennings Cumberland, or Cocker Hoop are available on tap.

A popular 17th-century pub, **The Queens Head,** on A592 north of Windermere (☎ **015394/32174**), uses a gigantic Elizabethan four-poster bed as its serving counter, and has an eclectic mix of antiques strewn in with basic bar furnishings. There are half a dozen rooms in which you can settle with a pint of Mitchells Lancaster Bomber, Tetleys, or Buddington's.

Established in 1612, the **Hole in t' Wall,** Lowside (☎ **01539/443488**), is the oldest pub in Bowness, a real treasure for its character and friendliness. The barroom is decorated with a hodgepodge of antiquated farming tools, and there's a large slate fireplace lending warmth on winter days plus a good selection of real ales on tap. The menu is determined daily and there's real ingenuity illustrated in an eclectic mix of vegetarian, seafood, and local game dishes. There's a small flagstoned terrace in the front for lingering on warmer days and evenings.

3 Ambleside & Rydal

278 miles NW of London; 14 miles NW of Kendal; 4 miles N of Windermere

An idyllic retreat, Ambleside is just a small village, but it's one of the major places to stay in the Lake District, attracting pony trekkers, hikers, and rock climbers. It's wonderful in warm weather, and even through late autumn, when it's fashionable to sport a mackintosh. Ambleside is perched at the north end of Lake Windermere.

Between Ambleside and Wordsworth's former retreat at Grasmere is Rydal, a small village on one of the smallest lakes, Rydal Water. The village is noted for its sheep-dog trials at the end of summer. It's 1½ miles north of Ambleside on A591.

ESSENTIALS

GETTING THERE Take a train to Windermere (see above), then continue the rest of the way by bus.

Stagecoach Cumberland (☎ **01946/63222**) has hourly bus service from Grasmere and Keswick (see below) and from Windermere. All these buses into Ambleside are labeled either no. 555 or no. 557.

If you're driving from Windermere, continue northwest on A591.

VISITOR INFORMATION The **Tourist Information Centre** is at Market Cross Central Building, in Ambleside (☎ **015394/32582**), and is open daily from 9am to 5:30pm.

EXPLORING THE AREA

Lakeland Safari Tours, 23 Fisherbeck Park, Ambleside (☎ **015394/33904**), help you discover the Lakeland's hidden beauty, heritage, and traditions. The owner, a qualified Blue Badge Guide, provides an exciting selection of full-day and half-day safaris in his luxury six-seat vehicle. A half-day safari is £19 ($32.30) per person; a day-long trek is £29 ($49.30) per person.

✪ **Rydal Mount.** Off the A591, 1½ miles north of Ambleside. ☎ **015394/33002.** Admission £3.75 ($6.40) adults, £3 ($5.10) seniors and students, £1.25 ($2.15) children ages 5–16; free for kids 4 and under. Entrance to the garden is £1.75 ($3). Mar–Oct daily 9:30am–5pm; Nov–Feb Wed–Mon 10am–4pm.

This was the home of William Wordsworth from 1813 until his death in 1850. Part of the house was built as a farmer's lake cottage around 1575. A descendant of Wordsworth now owns the property, which displays numerous portraits, furniture, and family possessions, as well as mementos and the poet's books. The 4½-acre garden, landscaped by Wordsworth, is filled with rare trees, shrubs, and other features of interest.

WHERE TO STAY & DINE

EXPENSIVE

Kirkstone Foot. Kirkstone Pass Rd., Ambleside, Cumbria LA22 9EH. ☎ **015394/32232.** Fax 015394/32805. 27 units. TV. Apr–Oct £78–£98 ($132.60–$166.60) double; Nov–Mar £70–£86 ($119–$146.20) double. Rates include English breakfast. MC, V. Closed 1st 2 weeks in Dec. Take Rydal Rd. north, turning right onto Kirkstone Pass Rd.

This country house is one of the finest places to stay in the area. There's the main 17th-century manor house plus several self-catering apartments in the surrounding parklike grounds. The original building is encircled by a well-tended lawn, whereas the interior is cozily furnished with overstuffed chairs and English paneling. The comfortable accommodations—11 in the main house and 16 in the less desirable outlying units—are tastefully decorated. The rooms that face the front are the most sought after. Bedrooms have quality mattresses on each of the twins or doubles. One room is spacious enough for rental to families.

Dining: The restaurant offers home-cooked English meals. Fresh produce is used whenever possible. A five-course dinner costs £22.95 ($39).

Amenities: Laundry, baby-sitting, room service.

Nanny Brow Hotel. Clappersgate (on A593 about 1 mile west of Ambleside), Ambleside, Cumbria LA22 9NF. ☎ **015394/32036.** Fax 015394/32450. www.nannybrow.co.uk. E-mail: reservations@nannybrowhotel.demon.co.uk. 18 units. TV TEL. £150 ($255) double; £220 ($374) suite for 2. Rates include English breakfast and dinner. AE, DC, MC, V.

Situated on a hill, this former private home, built in 1904, has been turned into one of the most successful hotels in the area, a worthy competitor of Rothay Manor (see below). The Tudor-style gabled house is reached via a steep tree-lined drive. Once you arrive, you'll find a country-house setting containing a lovely sitting room with intricate cove moldings and a log fire. The rooms are in both the main house and a garden wing (the latter offers the best accommodations). Each room is thoughtfully designed and furnished in a traditional style. The bedrooms have recently been refurbished, including the small and efficiently organized private baths that come with a hair dryer. Some of the suites have half-tester beds.

Dining: The food is well prepared, using fresh ingredients.

Amenities: Solarium and whirlpool bath, plus free access to the pool, sauna, and gym at the nearby local time-share complex.

✪ **Rothay Manor.** Rothay Bridge, Ambleside, Cumbria LA22 0EH. ☎ **015394/33605.** Fax 015394/33607. www.rothaymanor.co.uk. E-mail: hotel@rothaymanor.co.uk. 18 units. TV TEL. £110–£135 ($187–$229.50) double; £170 ($289) suite. Rates include English breakfast. AE, DC, MC, V. Take A593 ½ mile south of Ambleside.

At this spot, which is reminiscent of a French country inn, the stars are the cuisine, the well-chosen French wines, and comfortable, centrally heated bedrooms and suites. It's our top choice in an area where the competition is stiff in the country-house race. Each of the bedrooms is individually decorated (two are wheelchair accessible). Most have shuttered French doors opening onto a sun balcony and a mountain view. Each spacious room is fitted with many amenities including hair dryers and beverage makers. Five rooms are large enough to rent to families. Throughout the estate you'll find an eclectic combination of antiques (some Georgian blended harmoniously with Victorian), flowers, and enticing armchairs.

Dining: The manor is also a restaurant open to nonresidents, serving the finest cuisine in Ambleside. The spacious dining room is decked with antique tables and chairs. The flawless appointments include fine crystal, silver, and china. A traditional Sunday lunch always features a whole sirloin of roast beef with Yorkshire pudding. Dinners are more ambitious. The chef is likely to prepare everything from a savory loin of pork roasted with rosemary and onion to chicken stuffed with peppers, onions, tomatoes, and crisp bacon sautéed and flamed with brandy, then roasted.

Wateredge Hotel. Borrans Rd. (on A591, 1 mile south of Ambleside), Waterhead, Ambleside, Cumbria LA22 0EP. ☎ **015394/32332.** Fax 015394/31878. www.wateredgehotel.co.uk. E-mail: contact@wateredgehotel.co.uk. 23 units. TV TEL. £114–£210 ($193.80–$357) double. Rates include breakfast and dinner. AE, MC, V. Closed mid-Dec to early Jan.

The center of this hotel was formed long ago from two 17th-century fishing cottages. Wateredge was, in fact, listed as a lodging house as early as 1873, and further additions were made in the early 1900s. Situated in a beautiful garden overlooking Lake Windermere, the hotel also serves some of the best food in the area. Public rooms have many little nooks for reading and conversation, and there is a cozy bar. However, on sunny days guests prefer to relax in the chairs on the lawn. The rooms vary in size and appointments; some are spacious, others much smaller. Furnishings are continually renewed and upgraded as the need arises, and each of the units is fitted with a beverage maker and a hair dryer. Bathrooms are tiled and compact; most come with a tub and shower combination.

Dining: A six-course, well-balanced, fixed-price dinner is offered to nonresidents nightly if hotel guests don't take all the tables. Fresh produce is used, and the quality of cooking is high—self-styled as a "traditional farmhouse cuisine."

Amenities: Access to nearby health club and tennis courts, room service, concierge, laundry.

Moderate to Inexpensive

Glen Rothay Hotel. On A591, Rydal, Ambleside, Cumbria LA22 9LR. ☎ **015394/34500.** Fax 015394/34505. 8 units. TV TEL. £69–£88 ($117.30–$149.60) double; from £100 ($170) suite for 2. Rates include English breakfast. MC, V. On A591 1 1/2 miles northwest of Ambleside.

Built in the 17th century as a wayfarer's inn, this hotel adjoins Dora's Field, immortalized by Wordsworth. Set back from the highway, it has a stucco-and-flagstone facade. Inside, the place has been modernized, but original details remain, including beamed ceilings and paneling. The comfortable bedrooms upstairs have central heating and coffeemakers. Most rooms have twin or double beds, but a few offer four-posters. The tiled bathrooms are small and compact. There is a popular street-level pub, plus a more formal cocktail lounge with a fireplace and comfortable armchairs, as well as a dining room serving solid English food.

Queens Hotel. Market Place, Ambleside, Cumbria LA22 9BU. ☎ **015394/32206.** Fax 015394/32721. 26 units. TV TEL. Mon–Thurs £50–£58 ($85–$98.60) double, Fri–Sun £54–£66 ($91.80–$112.20) double. AE, DC, MC, V.

In the heart of this area is the Queens, an old-fashioned family run hotel where guests are housed and fed well. It began as a private home in the Victorian era, and was later transformed into a hotel, with some restoration completed in 1992. It's centrally heated in winter. Bedrooms are a bit smallish but reasonably comfortable. The small baths have shower stalls.

Since the hotel has two fully licensed bars and restaurants, you may want to dine here. The food is good and hearty. Locals and tourists alike gravitate to the hotel bar. Bar meals are served throughout the day.

Riverside Hotel. Near Rothay Bridge, Under Loughrigg, Ambleside, Cumbria LA22 9LJ. ☎ **015394/32395.** Fax 015394/32395. 4 units. TV TEL. £65 ($110.50) double; £70 ($119) suite. Rates include breakfast. MC, V. Closed Nov–Feb. From Windermere on the A591, take the left fork at Waterhead toward Coniston. Follow Coniston Rd. for about a mile until you come to the junction at Rothay Bridge. Turn left across the bridge and then immediately make a sharp right along the small lane signposted Under Loughrigg.

Secluded on a quiet lane, this small country hotel was formed by combining three adjoining riverside houses dating from the 1820s. It has the solid slate-block walls and slate roof common to Cumbria and, despite its peaceful location, lies a few minutes' walk from the center of Ambleside. Each of the painstakingly decorated rooms has a hair dryer and central heating—two feature four-poster beds, and the suite has a Jacuzzi. Rooms contain double or twin beds with firm mattresses. Two of the bedrooms have spa baths. Other extras in the rooms include a beverage maker. Guests have access to a nearby health club.

Riverside Lodge Country House. Near Rothay Bridge, Ambleside, Cumbria LA22 0EH. ☎ **015394/34208.** Fax 015394/31884 E-mail: alanrhone@riversidelodge.freeserve.co.uk. 5 units. TV. £26–£35 ($44.20–$59.50) per person per night. Rates include English breakfast. MC, V. From Ambleside, take A593, which crosses Rothay Bridge.

This early Georgian house is set on a riverbank, a short walk from the town center, near the foot of Loughrigg Fell, on 3 acres of grounds. The property is run by Alan and Gillian Rhone. The lodge has some beamed ceilings and offers well-furnished bedrooms, some with river views. The charming bedrooms have been refurbished to a high standard, each bed fitted with soft mattresses and fluffy pillows. The tiled compact bathrooms have a hair dryer. Other room amenities include a beverage maker. The breakfast room overlooks the river, and there's an intimate lounge with an open fire.

WHERE TO DINE

Glass House. Rydal Rd. ☎ **015394/32137.** Reservations recommended. Lunch main courses £4,25–£7.75 ($49.30–$13.15); dinner main courses £8.95–£15 ($15.20–$25.50). AE, DC, MC, V. Daily 10am–10pm. MODERN BRITISH/MEDITERRANEAN.

In the early 1990s, the owners of this popular restaurant renovated what had originally been built in the 1400s as a water-driven mill for the crushing of wheat into flour. Today, you'll find a split-level combination of medieval and postmodern architecture, with big sunny windows, interior views of the mill's original cogs and gears, lots of oaken interior trim, and on the building's outside, a moss-covered, full-scale replica of the original water wheel. Menu items are more sophisticated and elegant than what's served within any of its competitors. Examples include a rolled-up version of spinach ricotta with pasta, served with deep-fried sage and white truffle oil; locally smoked, locally caught salmon with oyster beignets and eggplant in puff pastry; and a tantalizing warm feta cheese and polenta tart with rocket, French beans, beetroot, and fig-based salsa.

WHERE TO SHARE A PINT

The friendliest pub in Ambleside is the **Golden Rule,** Smithy Brow (☎ **01539/433363**), named for the brass yardstick mounted over the bar. There's a country hunt theme in the barroom, which features comfortable leather furniture and cast-iron tables. You can step into one side room and throw darts, or go into the other for a quiet, contemplative pint. Behind the bar, a small but colorful garden provides a serene setting in warm weather. There's inexpensive pub grub if you get hungry.

Located 3 miles west of town, off the A593 in Little Langdale, **Three Shires** (☎ **015394/37215**), a stone-built pub with a stripped timber-and-flagstone interior, offers stunning views of the valley and wooded hills. You can get good pub grub here, as well as a pint of Black Sheep Bitter, Ruddles County, or Websters Yorkshire. Malt whiskies are well represented.

4 Grasmere

282 miles NW of London; 18 miles NW of Kendal; 43 miles S of Carlisle

On a lake of the same name, ✪ **Grasmere** was the home of Wordsworth from 1799 to 1808. He called this area "the loveliest spot that man hath ever known."

ESSENTIALS

GETTING THERE Take a train to Windermere (see above) and continue the rest of the way by bus.

Cumberland Motor Services (☎ **01946/63222**) runs hourly bus service to Grasmere from Keswick (see below) and Windermere (see above). Buses running in either direction are marked no. 555 or no. 557.

If you're driving from Windermere (see above), continue northwest along A591.

VISITOR INFORMATION The summer-only **Tourist Information Centre** is on Red Bank Road (☎ **015394/35245**), and is open April through October daily from 9:30am to 5:30pm; and from November through March Saturday and Sunday only 10am to 3:30pm.

A LITERARY LANDMARK

Afternoon tea is served in the **Dove Cottage Tearoom and Restaurant** (☎ **015394/35268**). A good selection of open sandwiches, scones, cake, and tea breads is offered along with Darjeeling, Assam, Earl Grey, and herbal teas. The tearoom is open daily from 10am to 5pm and the restaurant from 6:30 to 9pm Wednesday to Saturday.

✪ **Dove Cottage/The Wordsworth Museum.** On A591, south of the village of Grasmere on the road to Kendal. ☎ **015394/35544.** Admission to both Dove Cottage and the adjoining museum £4.80 ($7.90) adults (£4.50/$7.65 low season); £2.40 ($4.10) children (£2.25/$3.80 low season). Daily 9:30am–5:30pm. Closed Dec 24–26 and Jan 6–Feb 2.

Wordsworth lived with his writer-and-diarist sister, Dorothy, at Dove Cottage, which is now part of the Wordsworth Museum and administered by the Wordsworth Trust. Wordsworth, the poet laureate, died in the spring of 1850 and was buried in the graveyard of the village church at Grasmere. Another tenant of Dove Cottage was Thomas De Quincey *(Confessions of an English Opium Eater)*. The Wordsworth Museum houses manuscripts, paintings, and memorabilia. There are also various special exhibitions throughout the year that explore the art and literature of English romanticism.

WHERE TO STAY & DINE

VERY EXPENSIVE

✪ **Michael's Nook.** 1/4 mile east of A591, Grasmere, Cumbria LA22 9RP. ☎ **800/544-9941** in the U.S., or 015394/35496. Fax 015394/35645. E-mail: m-nook@wordsworth-grassmere.co.uk. 14 units. TV TEL. £192–£300 ($326.40–$510) double; £410 ($697) suite. Rates include English breakfast and 5-course dinner. AE, DC, MC, V.

This country-house hotel, once a private residence, is situated on its own secluded 3-acre garden and provides the finest and most tranquil stopover in Grasmere. The name honors a hill shepherd, Michael, subject of a Wordsworth poem. A Lakeland home of stone, it is adorned with fine mahogany woodwork and paneling, especially its elegant staircase. Throughout the house, which is owned by Grasmere antique dealer Reg Gifford and his wife, Elizabeth, are many fine antiques. Amenities include hair dryers and sandalwood sachets in drawers; one room has a four-poster bed. Rooms are generally spacious, and some have recently been redecorated. Typical of an 1850s house, rooms come in various shapes and sizes, each individually decorated. Two rooms are large enough for families. During some peak weekends, a minimum 3-night stay is requested, but shorter bookings are accommodated whenever possible.

Dining: Only about 20 people can be served in the intimate dining room, which accepts reservations from nonresidents for both lunch and dinner. Additional seating is available in the Oak Room. Meals are carefully prepared, with menus changing daily. Michael's Nook is now recognized by the British AA as being the best hotel restaurant in the north of England, and it's been awarded four rosettes (out of a possible five) for its cuisine. Room service is available.

White Moss House. On A591 (1 1/2 miles south of town), Rydal Water, Grasmere, Cumbria LA22 9SE. ☎ **015394/35295.** Fax 015394/35516. www.whitemoss.com. E-mail: dixon@whitemoss.com 7 units. TV TEL. £120–£190 ($204–$323) double. Rates include breakfast and dinner. MC, V. Closed Dec–Jan.

This 1730 Lakeland cottage, once owned by Wordsworth, overlooks the lake and the fells. You'll be welcomed here by Peter and Susan Dixon, who will pamper you with morning tea in bed, turn down your bedcovers at night, and cater to your culinary preferences. The rooms are individually decorated, comfortably furnished and well heated in nippy weather. All units have trouser presses and such amenities as herbal bath salts. Rooms range in size from small to spacious, each with comfortable twins or doubles. All the bathrooms are furnished with a hair dryer. There's also Brockstone, their cottage annex, a 5-minute drive along the road, where two, three, or four guests can be accommodated comfortably in utter peace.

Dining: Dinner is a leisurely affair in a little cottage-style room. You're served five courses, which might include roast of lamb with an orange-and-red-currant sauce or quail with a chicken and brown-rice stuffing. For dessert, hope that Mrs. Beeton's chocolate pudding is featured. You must reserve a table early. Room service is available.

Amenities: Access to nearby health club and swimming pool, room service, dry cleaning/laundry.

Wordsworth Hotel. Stock Lane, Grasmere, Cumbria LA22 9SW. ☎ **015394/35592.** Fax 015394/35765. E-mail: enquiry@wordsworth-grasmere.co.uk. 37 units. TV TEL. £130–£170 ($221–$289) double; from £210 ($357) suite. Rates include English breakfast. AE, DC, MC, V. Turn left on A591 at the Grasmere Village sign and follow the road over the bridge past the church, and around an S-bend; the Wordsworth is on the right.

This choice, located in the heart of the village, is situated in a 3-acre garden next to the churchyard where Wordsworth is buried. An old stone Lakeland house that was once the hunting lodge of the earl of Cadogan, the Wordsworth has been completely refurbished to provide luxuriously appointed bedrooms with views of the fells, as well as modern baths and trouser presses. Three rooms have four-poster beds. The original master bedroom contains a Victorian bathroom with a brass towel rail and polished pipes and taps. Rooms vary widely in size and configurations. Bedrooms come with character and comfort, and the canopied beds are rather sumptuous, with excellent mattresses under the chintzy bedspreads. Three rooms are spacious enough for families. All contain beautifully maintained baths with a hair dryer.

Dining/Diversions: There are several lounges, with comfortable armchairs. A buffet lunch is served in the cocktail lounge, including the chef's hot dish of the day. The cuisine is modern English, and local produce, deftly handled by the kitchen staff, is used whenever possible.

Amenities: 24-hour room service, laundry service, large swimming pool, sauna, and minigym.

EXPENSIVE TO MODERATE

Red Lion Hotel. Red Lion Sq., Grasmere, Cumbria LA22 9SS. ☎ **015934/35456.** Fax 015394/35579. 46 units. TV TEL. £108 ($183.60) double. Rates include English breakfast. AE, DC, MC, V.

This 200-year-old coaching inn is only a short stroll from Wordsworth's Dove Cottage, and it's assumed that the poet often stopped here for a meal, drink, or to warm himself by the fire. Recently refurbished, the hotel offers comfortably furnished bedrooms, half with spa baths. In 1999, the hotel opened eight rather snug new bedrooms. The older rooms are fine as well, each fitted with firm mattresses. Four rooms are spacious enough for families. Extras include beverage makers, and each comes with a well-maintained bath with a hair dryer and adequate shelf space. A fitness room includes Nautilus weights, sauna, steam room, Jacuzzi, and solarium. Enjoy a drink or lunch in the airy surroundings of the Easdale Bar, or try the Lamb Inn and Buttery for a more traditional pub atmosphere. In the dining room, The Courtyard Restaurant, you'll be served some of the finest fare in the district.

Swan Hotel. On A591 (on the road to Keswick, 1/2 mile outside Grasmere), Grasmere, Cumbria LA22 9RF. ☎ **800/225-5843** in the U.S. and Canada, or 015394/35551. Fax 015394/35741. www.heritagehotels.com. E-mail: heritagehotelsgrasmere.swan@sorte-hotels.com. 36 units. TV TEL. £120–£138 ($198–$227.70) double. Apr–Aug leisure-break packages available Fri–Sun, £82 ($135.30) per person. Rates include breakfast and dinner. AE, DC, MC, V.

This is one of the best moderately priced choices. Sir Walter Scott used to slip in for a secret drink early in the morning, and Wordsworth mentioned the place in "The Waggoner." In fact, the poet's wooden chair is in one of the rooms. Many bedrooms are in a modern wing, added in 1975, that fits gracefully onto the building's older core (only the shell of the original 1650 building remains). Bedrooms are comfortably furnished, each twin or double bed fitted with a firm mattress. Twenty rooms are rented to nonsmokers.

INEXPENSIVE

Riversdale. Grasmere, Cumbria LA22 9RQ. ☎ **015394/35619.** 3 units. TV. £48–£60 ($81.60–$102) double. Rates include English breakfast. No credit cards. No smoking. Drive 10 miles north of Windermere along A591 (signposted to Keswick), then turn left by the Swan Hotel. In 400 yd., you'll find the inn on the left side of the rd. facing the river.

This lovely old house, built in 1830 of traditional Lakeland stone, is situated on the outskirts of the village of Grasmere along the banks of the River Rothay. The bedrooms are tastefully decorated and offer every comfort, including hair dryers, toiletries, tea- and coffeemakers, and hospitality trays, as well as views of the surrounding fells. Bedrooms, most often mid-size, have quality furnishings. Each unit has a small bathroom, most with a tub and shower combination. Mrs. Joyce Edwards and her sister Jean Newnes are gracious, witty, and full of fun. They are a wealth of information on day trips, whether by car or hiking. Their breakfasts, which are a delight, are served in a dining room overlooking Silver How and the fells beyond Easdale Tarn.

5 Coniston & Hawkshead

263 miles NW of London; 52 miles S of Carlisle; 19 miles NW of Kendal

At Coniston, you can visit the village famously associated with John Ruskin. It's also a good place for hiking and rock climbing. The Coniston "Old Man" towers in the background, at 2,633 feet, give mountain climbers one of the finest views of the Lake District.

Just 4 miles east of Coniston, discover for yourself the village of Hawkshead, with its 15th-century grammar school where Wordsworth studied for 8 years (he carved his name on a desk that is still there). Nearby, in the vicinity of Esthwaite Water, is the 17th-century Hill Top Farm, former home of author Beatrix Potter.

ESSENTIALS

GETTING THERE Take a train to Windermere (see above) and proceed the rest of the way by bus.

Stagecoach Cumberland (☎ **01946/63222**) runs two buses from Windermere to Hawkshead and Coniston from Monday to Saturday, two on Sunday. Take bus no. 505 from Windermere.

By car from Windermere, proceed north on A591 to Ambleside, cutting southwest on B5285 to Hawkshead.

Windermere Lake Cruises Ltd. (☎ **015394/43360**) operates a ferry service in summer from Bowness, directly south of Windermere, to Hawkshead. It reduces driving time considerably (see "Windermere & Bowness," above).

VISITOR INFORMATION The **Tourist Information Centre** (☎ **015394/36525**) is at Hawkshead in the Main Car Park and is open year round daily from 9:30am to 5:30pm.

EXPLORING THE AREA

Of the many places to go boating in the Lake District, Coniston Water in the Lake District National Park may be the best. Coniston Water lies in a tranquil wooded valley between Grisedale Forest and the high fells of Coniston Old Man and Wetherlam. The **Coniston Boating Centre,** Lake Road, Coniston LA21 (☎ **015394/41366**), occupies a sheltered bay at the northern end of the lake. The center provides launching facilities, boat storage, and parking. You can rent row boats that carry from two to six people, sailing dinghies carrying up to six passengers, or Canadian canoes that transport two. There is a picnic area and access to the lakeshore. From the gravel beach you may be able to spot the varied water birds and plants that make Coniston Water a valuable but fragile habitat for wildlife.

You can also cruise the lake in an original Victorian steam-powered yacht, the Gondola. Launched in 1859, and in regular service until 1937, this unique boat was rescued and completely restored by the National Trust. Since 1980 it has become a familiar sight on Coniston Water, and sailings to Park-a-Moor and Brantwood run throughout the summer. Service is subject to weather conditions, of course. For more information, call **015394/41288.**

Coniston Launch is a traditional timber boat that calls at Coniston, Monk Coniston, Torver, and Brantwood. (Discounts are offered in combination with admission to Brantwood house; see below.) This exceptional boating outfitter offers special cruises in summer (a "Swallows and Amazons" tour was inspired by Arthur Ransome's classic story). For more information, call or fax ☎ **015394/36216.**

Summitreks operates from the lakeside at Coniston Boating Centre, offering qualified instruction in canoeing and windsurfing. A wide range of equipment can be rented from the nearby office at Lake Road (☎ **015394/41212**).

In Hawkshead, the **Beatrix Potter Gallery** (☎ **015394/36355**) has an annually changing exhibition of Beatrix Potter's original illustrations from her children's storybooks. The building was once the office of her husband, the solicitor William Heelis, and the interior remains largely unaltered since his day. To get here, take bus 505 from Ambleside-Coniston to the square in Hawkshead.

Brantwood. Coniston. ☎ **015394/41396.** Admission £4 ($6.80) adults, £2.80 ($4.75) students, £1 ($1.70) children 5–16. Nature walk £2 ($3.30) adults, £1 ($1.65) children. Mid-Mar to mid-Nov daily 11am–5:30pm; mid-Nov to mid-Mar Wed–Sun 11am–4:30pm. Closed Christmas Day and Boxing Day.

John Ruskin, poet, artist, and critic, was one of the great figures of the Victorian age and a prophet of social reform, inspiring such diverse men as Proust, Frank Lloyd Wright, and Gandhi. He moved to his home, Brantwood, on the east side of Coniston Water, in 1872 and lived here until his death in 1900. The house today is open for visitors to see his memorabilia, including some 200 of his pictures.

Part of the 250-acre estate is open as a nature trail. The Brantwood stables, designed by Ruskin, have been converted into a tearoom and restaurant, the Jumping Jenny. Also in the stable building is the Coach House Craft Gallery, which follows the Ruskin tradition of encouraging contemporary craft work of the finest quality.

Literary fans may want to pay a pilgrimage to the graveyard of the village church, where Ruskin was buried; his family turned down the invitation to have him interred at Westminster Abbey.

John Ruskin Museum. Yewdale Rd., Coniston. ☎ **015394/41164.** Admission £3 ($5.10) adults, £1.75 ($3) children. Easter–Oct daily 10am–5:30pm. Closed Nov–Easter.

At this institute, in the center of the village, you can see Ruskin's personal possessions and mementos, pictures by him and his friends, letters, and his collection of mineral rocks.

WHERE TO STAY

Coniston Sun Hotel. Brow Hill (off the A593), Coniston, Cumbria LA21 8HQ. ☎ **015394/41248.** Fax 015395/41219. www.smoothhound.co.uk/hotels/sun.html. E-mail: elson@btinternet.com. 11 units. TV TEL. £60–£70 ($102–$119) double. Rates include English breakfast. MC, V.

This is the most popular, traditional, and attractive pub, restaurant, and hotel in Coniston. It's a country-house hotel of much character, dating from 1902, although the inn attached to it is from the 16th century. Situated on beautiful grounds above the village, 150 yards from the town center, it lies at the foot of the Coniston "Old Man." Each bedroom is decorated with style and flair, and two of them have four-posters. Rooms range from small to mid-size, each with a firm mattress on a comfortable bed. Seven of the rooms contain a tub and shower combination. Other amenities include a beverage maker in each room.

Fresh local produce is used whenever possible in the candlelit restaurant. Log fires take the chill off a winter evening, and guests relax informally in the library-like lounge. Many outdoor activities can be arranged, including water sports, pony rides, and mountain biking.

Highfield House. Hawkshead Hill (3/4 mile east of Hawkshead, on the road to Coniston), Hawkshead, Ambleside, Cumbria LA22 0PN. ☎ **015394/36344.** Fax 015394/36793.

www.lakes-pages.co.uk. E-mail: highfield.hawkshead@btinternet.com. 11 units. TV. £80–£90 ($136–$153) double. Rates include English breakfast. MC, V.

This solidly built stone-sided house sits on the side of a hill and on clear days enjoys sweeping views over the Lake District. Constructed around 1870, it is surrounded by 2½ acres of its own land. Operated by members of the Bennett family, it has cozy bedrooms, either with pastel colors or wallpaper inspired by the turn-of-the-century designs of William Morris. Rooms were recently refurbished. It's the thoughtful extras here that make the difference to occupants of the mid-size bedrooms, each with such amenities as bottled water and beverage makers. Most of the bathrooms have a tub and shower combination, and each comes with a hair dryer.

A four-course dinner with such dishes as pork fillet baked with poppy seeds, or grilled salmon with dill and cucumber sauce is always available, but advance notice is recommended.

WHERE TO DINE

Grizedale Lodge. Grizedale, Hawkshead. ☎ **015394/36532.** Fax 015394/36572. Reservations required. Bar lunches £3.50–£9.50 ($5.95–$16.15); fixed-price dinner £23.50 ($39.95). AE, MC, V. Daily 12:30–1:30pm and 7–8pm. From Hawkshead take Newby Bridge Rd. for about 500 yd., then turn right (signposted Grizedale & Forest Fark Center) and follow this road for 2 miles. ENGLISH/FRENCH.

The best place for food in the area is this country *restaurant avec chambres,* which was built in 1902 as a hunting lodge for the chairman of the Cunard Line. Many people come here just to dine because the cuisine is top-notch. During the day, guests order bar lunches, but at night they can enjoy a memorable five-course meal in a tranquil setting. Service is personable.

Mr. and Mrs. Dawson offer nine handsomely furnished bedrooms for guests, each with a private bathroom and TV. For half board, charges are £65 ($110.50) per person per night.

WHERE TO ENJOY A PINT

A display case of fishing lures is the first tip-off, then there's the pond itself—yes, it's true, you can fish while you drink at the **Drunken Duck,** Barnsgate (☎ **01539/436347**). Or you can just sit on the front porch and gaze at Lake Windermere in the distance. Inside, you can choose from an assortment of cushioned settles, old pews, and tub or ladder-back chairs, then order a wild-boar steak or minted lamb casserole to go with a pint of Mitchells Lancaster Bomber, Yates Bitter, or Yates Drunken Duck Bitter, brewed especially for the pub. If you want stronger spirits, there are more than 60 malt whiskies to choose from.

Overlooking the central square of the village, the **Kings Arms** (☎ **01539/436372**) offers a pleasant front terrace or lots of plush leather-covered seating inside the cozy barroom. Traditional pub grub is supplemented with a few pasta dishes, and ales include Greenall's Original, Tetleys, and Theakstons XB. Malt whiskies are also well represented.

6 Keswick

22 miles NW of Windermere; 294 miles NW of London; 31 miles NW of Kendal

Keswick opens onto Derwentwater, one of the loveliest lakes in the region, and the town makes a good base for exploring the northern half of Lake District National Park. Keswick has two landscaped parks, and above the small town is a historic stone circle thought to be some 4,000 years old.

St. Kentigern's Church dates from A.D. 553, and a weekly market held in the center of Keswick can be traced from a charter granted in the 13th century. It's a short walk to Friar's Crag, the classic viewing point on Derwentwater. The walk will also take you past boat landings with launches that operate regular tours around the lake.

Around Derwentwater there are many places with literary associations that evoke memories of Wordsworth, Robert Southey, Coleridge, and Hugh Walpole. Several of Beatrix Potter's stories were based at Keswick. The town also has a professional repertory theater that schedules performances in the summer. There's a swimming pool complex, plus an 18-hole golf course at the foot of the mountains 4 miles away.

ESSENTIALS

GETTING THERE Take a train to Windermere (see above) and proceed the rest of the way by bus.

Stagecoach Cumberland (☎ **01946/63222**) has a regular bus service from Windermere and Grasmere (bus no. 555).

From Windermere, drive northwest on A591.

VISITOR INFORMATION The **Tourist Information Centre,** at Moot Hall, Market Square (☎ **017687/72645**), is open daily April to September from 9:30am to 6pm, and from October through March daily from 9:30am to 4:30pm. It's closed Christmas and New Year's days.

SEEING THE SIGHTS

Internationally known for its unique handmade teapots, **The Teapottery,** off Heads Road (☎ **017687/73983**), now has a branch in Keswick open to visitors who can watch the craftspeople at work. You can experience the history of tea and see the whole range of wild and wonderful teapots in this shop. To get here, go to Keswick's central car park, off Heads Road. It's by the entrance to the car park.

Mirehouse. On the A591, 3 1/2 miles north of Keswick. ☎ **017687/72287.** Admission to house and gardens plus a lakeside walk £4 ($6.80) adults, £2 ($3.40) children and seniors; family ticket (2 adults plus 4 kids ages 5–16) £11.50 ($19.55). Gardens alone £1.70 ($2.90) adults, £1 ($1.70) children. House open Apr–Oct, Sun and Wed (also Fri in Aug), 2–4:30pm. Tearoom and grounds Apr–Oct daily 10am–5:30pm.

A tranquil Cumbrian family home that has not been sold since 1688, Mirehouse has unusually wide-ranging literary and artistic connections. The piano is played on afternoons when guests stop by to visit. The park around it stretches to Bassenthwaite Lake, and has extensive gardens, plus woodland adventure playgrounds. It is in easy reach of the ancient lakeside church and the Old Sawmill Tearoom, which is known for its generous Cumbrian cooking.

WHERE TO STAY

Grange Country House. Manor Brow, Ambleside Rd. (on the southeast side of Keswick, overlooking the town, just off A591), Keswick, Cumbria CA12 4BA. ☎ **017687/72500.** 10 units. TV TEL. £61–£77 ($103.70–$130.90) double. Rates include English breakfast. MC, V. Closed Nov to mid-Feb.

A tranquil retreat, this charming hotel and its gardens are situated on a hilltop. Dating from the 1840s, it is furnished in part with antiques. Guests enjoy the crackling log fires in chilly weather. Many of the attractively furnished, well-kept rooms open onto scenic views of the Lakeland hills. There is continual upgrading of the bedrooms, which come in various shapes and sizes; each is individually decorated and most have double or twin beds. Rooms are mainly mid-size, and each comes with a beverage maker. The compact bathrooms are well organized, each equipped with a hair dryer.

The hotel, run by Jane and Duncan Miller, also offers first-rate cuisine from a varied dinner menu.

Skiddaw Hotel. Market Sq., Keswick, Cumbria CA12 5BN. ☎ **017687/72071.** Fax 017687/74850. 40 units. TV TEL. £70–£90 ($119–$153) double. Rates include English breakfast. AE, CB, DC, DISC, MC, V.

This hotel has an impressive facade and entrance marquee built right onto the sidewalk in the heart of Keswick at the market square. The owners have refurbished the interior, retaining the best features. Bedrooms are compact and eye-catching, have beverage makers, and are gradually being refurbished. Bedrooms are mainly mid-size, and each is well-appointed with comfortable beds. Seven rooms are large enough for families, and 10 are rented to nonsmokers. Bathrooms come with a hair dryer. Guests may use the pool and spa at Armathwaite Hall and golf at Keswick Golf Club during the week.

Folks gather in the lounge or the popular cocktail bar, with its art-nouveau ambience. The meals at Gillespies feature well-prepared English and continental cuisine, available à la carte all day. In addition, a chef's special, such as Cumbria hot pot, is offered at lunch, and afternoon teas are served in the restaurant and in the lounge bar. There is a wide selection of wines.

✪ **Swinside Lodge.** Grange Rd., Newlands, Cumbria CA12 5UE. ☎ and fax **01768/772948.** 7 units. TV. £139–£167 ($236.30–$283.90) double. Rates include dinner and breakfast for two occupants. AE, MC V. Closed Dec–Jan. From Keswick, take the A66 SW for 3 miles, following the signs to Portinscale and to Grange.

Isolated on a knoll that overlooks Lake Derwentwater, and solidly built in the 1850s as a home for the manager of the enormous estate that surround it at the time, this is a cozy, well-managed bed and breakfast hotel where evening meals are better than the norm. The venue belongs to Graham Taylor, with cuisine prepared by Chris and Lisa Asteley. Bedrooms are outfitted with painted, cream-colored furniture, and pastel-colored fabrics that deliberately don't convey a sense of the Edwardian age. Several public rooms and lounges contain shelves of books and diversionary games that will take the boredom off any rainy day. Children under 12 are not encouraged on the premises. Nonresidents who phone in advance can share in the nightly meal for around £25 ($42.50) per person. The food is among the finest in the area.

A NEARBY PLACE TO DINE

The Yew Tree Restaurant. Seatoller. ☎ **017687/77634.** Reservations recommended. Main courses £7.95–£12.95 ($13.50–$22). Tues–Sun 10:30am–11pm. Closed Jan. Take the B5289 8 miles south of Keswick. BRITISH.

This restaurant in the Borrowdale region lies in the hamlet of Seatoller. Named after the 500-year-old yew that broods timelessly near the front entrance, this restaurant occupies an interconnected pair of stone-sided cottages that were built in 1628 as the home of two German-born miners. If you've been out hiking, fortify yourself with simple but nourishing dishes that include soup, Cumberland sausages with salads, and lamb cobbler. Evening meals tend to be more elaborate, and include local trout with almonds. The interior of the place, loaded with oaken beams and memorabilia, is about as evocative as it gets.

SIDE TRIPS FROM KESWICK

BORROWDALE

One of the most scenic parts of the Lake District, Borrowdale stretches south of Derwentwater to Seathwaite in the heart of the county. The valley is walled in by fell sides, and it's an excellent center for exploring, walking, and climbing. Many use it as a center for exploring **Scafell,** England's highest mountain, at 3,210 feet.

This resort is in the Borrowdale Valley, the southernmost settlement of which is Seatoller. The village of Seatoller, at 1,176 feet, is the terminus for buses to and from Keswick. It's also the center for a **Lake District National Park Information Centre** at Dalehead Base, Seatoller Barn (☎ **01768/777294**).

After leaving Seatoller, B5289 takes you west through the Honister Pass and Buttermere Fell, one of the most dramatic drives in the Lake District. The road is lined with towering boulders. The lake village of Buttermere also merits a stopover.

Where to Stay & Dine

Borrowdale Gates Hotel. Grange-in-Borrowdale, Keswick CA12 5UQ. ☎ **01768/777204.** Fax 01768/777254. www.borrowdalegates.com. E-mail: hotel@borrowdale-gates.com. 29 units. TV. £125–£166 ($212.50–$282.20) double. Rates include English breakfast and dinner. AE, MC, V. From Keswick, take B5289 4 miles south to Grange, go over the bridge and the inn sits on the right, just beyond the curve in the road.

The proprietors of this hotel, Terry and Christine Parkinson, have welcomed John Major here for afternoon tea. It was quite the affair around these parts. Their 1860 Victorian country house, built of Lakeland stone, has just received a new addition of nine rooms that faithfully matches the Victorian style. All the rooms range in size from medium to large, and are decorated with rich Victorian colors and period reproductions. Every year some rooms are upgraded and refurbished. All contain beverage makers, excellent mattresses, and quality linens. The place is warm, cozy, and inviting, and the bathrooms have a hair dryer. The public areas, with their antiques and open-log stone fireplaces, sprawl along the ground floor and include a bar, restaurant and dining area, and four sitting lounges. They are all airy and bright with views of the surrounding gardens. Amenities include dry cleaning/laundry and access to health club 4 miles away.

The kitchen is the domain of chef Michael Heathcote, whose passion for good food accounts for the excellence of the cuisine, which relies on the fresh local produce. You can dine here every night and always have a different menu to choose from. Try such delights as a tartar of an avocado pear and Devon crabmeat, followed by a supreme of Bowland pheasant with roasted root vegetables. The kitchen leans heavily on British favorites, but also has a continental flair.

Borrowdale Hotel. Borrowdale Rd. (B5289), Borrowdale, Keswick, Cumbria CA12 5UY. ☎ **017687/77224.** Fax 017687/77338. www.theborrowdalehotel.co.uk. E-mail: theborrowdalehotel@yahoo.com. 33 units. TV TEL. £56–£75 ($95.20–$127.50) per person double. Rates include English breakfast and dinner. MC, V. On B5289, 3½ miles south of Keswick.

When the weather is damp, log fires welcome guests in this Lakeland stone building, which was originally a coaching inn (ca. 1866). The rooms are comfortable and many have fine views. All have intercom units and beverage makers. Each of the mid-size to spacious bedrooms is well designed and furnished; some rooms contain four-poster beds. Bathrooms are well maintained, most often with a tub and shower combination, plus a hair dryer. Amenities include free access to a health club and golf course.

The restaurant fusses over the presentation of its dishes. From Monday to Saturday, lunches are served in the bar, and feature a choice of at least 20 main courses that range from soup and sandwiches to chicken Kiev. Sunday lunch is a more formal, fixed-price affair. At dinner, the restaurant serves six-course set menus with a choice of at least six different dishes. Cuisine from all parts of the globe is offered, and the menu changes daily. If you would like to have the daily roast, the chef will carve it at your table from a silver cart.

Stakis Lodore Swiss Hotel. Borrowdale Rd. (B5289), Borrowdale, Keswick, Cumbria CA12 5UX. ☎ **017687/77285.** Fax 017687/77343. 75 units. MINIBAR TV TEL. £112–£169 ($190.40–$287.30) double. Rates include breakfast. Winter discounts available. AE, DC, MC, V. Indoor parking £4 ($6.80); outdoors, free. On B5289 3 1/2 miles south of Keswick.

The Stakis hotel chain runs this hotel, which overlooks Derwentwater from fields where cows graze. With its spike-capped mansard tower, symmetrical gables, and balcony-embellished stone facade, it seems straight out of the Swiss Alps. (Ironically, the Swiss owners who built this place in the 19th century were named England. Their tradition of good rooms, food, and service continues today.) The interior has been completely modernized, and each of the well-furnished bedrooms has a hair dryer and coffee-maker. Bedrooms vary in size, and it's worth opting for one of the larger ones. Each comes with a comfortable bed fitted with a firm mattress. The tiled baths are small. There is 24-hour room service, an indoor swimming pool and garden, and laundry service.

Dining: The food here is exceptional for the area, with fixed-price meals available to nonresidents. Dishes include roast magret of duck presented on a pear and potato risotto with hazelnut and orange jus; grilled fresh trout with roast Mediterranean vegetables and a warm balsamic and olive dressing; and pan-fried medallions of pork on caramelized apple with a sage and cider cream sauce. Call for a reservation, especially at dinner.

BASSENTHWAITE

In the Lake District National Park, 6 miles north of Keswick, Bassenthwaite is one of the most beautiful of Lakeland villages, and makes the best center for exploring the woodlands of Thornthwaite Forest and Bassenthwaite Lake nearby. Bassenthwaite Lake is the northernmost and only true "lake" in the Lake District, and it's visited yearly by many species of migratory birds from the north of Europe.

Where to Stay

✪ **Armathwaite Hall Hotel.** Bassenthwaite Lake (on B5291, 7 miles northwest of Keswick, 1 1/2 miles west of Bassenthwaite), Keswick, Cumbria CA12 4RE. ☎ **017687/76551.** Fax 017687/76220. www.armathwaite-hall.com. 43 units. TV TEL. £116–£190 ($197.20–$323) double; £210 ($357) suite. Rates include English breakfast. AE, DC, MC, V.

Rich in history, this hotel was originally built in the 1300s as a house for Benedictine nuns. During the Middle Ages, it was plundered frequently, leaving the sisters wretchedly poor. By the 17th century, a series of wealthy landowners had completed the severe Gothic design of its stately facade, and an architecturally compatible series of wings were added in 1844. It was converted into a hotel during the 1930s. Sir Hugh Walpole, who once stayed here, found it "a house of perfect and irresistible charm." Ringed with almost 400 acres of woodland (some bordering the lake), the place offers a magnificent entrance hall sheathed with expensive paneling; the bedrooms are also handsomely furnished. There is a continual refurbishment of the bedrooms, most of which range from mid-size to spacious. Bedrooms are sumptuous with half-canopied beds or padded headboards crowning comfortable beds fitted with firm mattresses and fine linen. Baths are excellently maintained, and equipped with a hair dryer. A Victorian billiard room is lined with old engravings.

There's a small but diverting attraction on its premises: a minizoo featuring unusual breeds of both barnyard and wild animals. The collection includes potbellied pigs, llamas, goats, rabbits, and owls. They also have a reptile house, bird of prey center, animated display, tearoom, and wet-weather facilities. Only a 5-minute walk from the hotel, **Trotters World of Animals** is open February to October daily from 10am to

5:30pm, and on weekends only from November to January. Adults pay £3.75 ($6.40); children age 3 to 14, £2.75 ($4.70). Kids 3 and under enter free.

A first-class restaurant offers a view of the lake. Amenities include an indoor swimming pool, which is ringed with stone walls and sheltered from the rain by a roof of wooden trusses. The hotel also provides the finest equestrian center in the area.

The Castle Inn Hotel. Bassenthwaite (6 miles north of Keswick on A591), Cumbria CA12 4RG. ☎ and fax **017687/76401.** Fax 017687/76604. 48 units. TV TEL. £88–£115 ($149.60–$195.50) double; £106–£145 ($180.20–$246.50) suite. Rates include English breakfast. AE, DC, MC, V. From Keswick, take the A591 6 miles north of town; the inn is on the left.

Don't expect a castle. Although this place plays up its historical importance, you'll find there is an "old" core (no one on the staff is sure of how old), with many newer additions that don't exactly gracefully merge into a unified whole. The result is a hotel that's neither whimsically antique nor strikingly modern—but it is not dowdy. Bedrooms come in various shapes and sizes, including some beautifully appointed and spacious "superior" units. Six are large enough for families, and 14 are set aside for nonsmokers. The more modern but equally comfortable rooms are in a new wing. Many of the old-fashioned rooms contain a four-poster. There is a bar and restaurant on the premises. The hotel also contains both a solarium and a gymnasium/health club.

Overwater Hall. Overwater, Ireby, near Keswick CA5 1HH. ☎ **01768/776566.** www.theaa.co.uk/region2/444.html. E-mail: welcome@overwaterhall.demon.co.uk. 12 units. TV TEL. £85 ($144.50) double. Rates include English breakfast. MC, V.

Built in the late 18th century, this Georgian mansion had battlements added to it by the Victorians, and is reminiscent of a castle and comes complete with a tragic ghost story. When the house was still new, its owner became involved with an alluring Jamaican mistress who became too much of an embarrassment to him. So in a fit of desperation, he threw her to the depths of the nearby lake, cutting off her hands so she could not climb back into the boat. According to all reports, her handless spirit wanders the guest rooms during the night in a harmless manner.

Despite its sad past, this B&B is anything but somber. All the bedrooms, though standard in size, are extremely ritzy (which may be why Overwater's phantom has chosen to stay), having been furnished with top-quality antiques. Some rooms have oak-paneled four-poster beds. Most of the tiled bathrooms have a tub and shower combination, and each is equipped with a hair dryer. Guests can enjoy the regal surroundings of the public rooms with their intricate and rich cove molding and formal Victorian antiques. The drawing room is a great place for afternoon tea, and the piano bar actually has a baby grand piano. The restaurant's elegant dining room serves breakfast and a five-course dinner. Overwater Hall also offers guests the use of their own putting green and abundant fishing for pike on Overwater Tarn.

The Pheasant. Bassenthwaite Lake, Cockermouth, Cumbria CA13 9YE. ☎ **017687/76234.** Fax 017687/76002. 20 units. £98–£104 ($166.60–$176.80) double. MC, V.

Set amid conifers near the northwestern tip of Bassenthwaite Lake, this place originated in the 17th century as a coaching inn; a series of extensions were later added. Everything about it evokes old-fashioned English coziness. Fireplaces warm a moderately eccentric bar area, a mishmash of antique and merely old-fashioned furniture, and bedrooms whose smallish windows overlook 60 acres of forest and parkland associated with the hotel. Three of the rooms are in a separate bungalow. Try if possible for a room in the main building, as those in the bungalow are more impersonal. Room size ranges from small to medium, and each comes with a good mattress. Bathrooms are small with shower stalls. The restaurant is open for breakfast and dinner daily serving traditional English fare.

Where to Dine

The Sun. Bassenthwaite Village. ☎ **017687/76439.** Reservations not accepted. Main courses £6–£8.50 ($10.20–$14.45). No credit cards. Daily noon–1:30pm; Mon–Sat 6–11pm, Sun 7–11pm. BRITISH.

Originally built in the 16th century as a farmhouse, and now Bassenthwaite Village's only pub, this place has oaken beams, squeaking floors, and as much old-world charm as you can digest at a single sitting. It offers the products from a nearby brewery (Jennings), selling ample amounts of such brand names as Jennings Bitter and Jennings Old Smoothie. Menu items are as traditional as the architecture itself: ham or beefsteaks, squid, sausages, salads, ploughman's lunches, and steaming bowls of Lancashire hot pot. Everybody's favorite dessert is sticky toffee pudding. Lunch in winter often is not available; call ahead before you visit.

7 Ullswater

296 miles NW of London; 26 miles SE of Keswick

Set in a region that is home to contrasting vistas of gently rolling fields and dramatic mountain rises, Ullswater is a favorite with those who enjoy spectacular natural beauty. Ullswater itself is a 9-mile expanse of water, stretching from Pooley Bridge to Patterdale and is the second-largest lake in the district. It is a magnet for outdoor types of all levels of ability, offering activities that range from walks and hikes around the shore to rock climbing, mountain biking, canoeing, sailing, and even windsurfing.

This part of the Lakeland, where the majesty of nature tends to entrance and envelope, has always held a special attraction for artists and writers. The area gained most of its fame from writings by the likes of Wordsworth during the early 19th century. It was on the shores of Ullswater that Wordsworth saw his "host of golden daffodils." Aira Force waterfall, near the National Trust's Gowbarrow, inspired both Wordsworth and Coleridge by its beauty. While using this area as a base for outdoor activities, you can also easily explore the many places of prehistoric and historic significance, from the times of the ancient Celts right through to modern day. Two noteworthy sites include Long Meg and her "daughters," an ancient stone circle near Penrith, and Hadrian's Wall, marking the northern extent of the Roman empire, east of Carlisle (see chapter 17).

In Ullswater, two 19th-century **steamers** provide the best way to see the area's panoramic mountain scenery around the lake. In season, there are two scheduled services daily between Glenridding, Howtown, and Pooley Bridge as well as five shorter 1-hour cruises. Passengers may choose to walk back along the lakeside path or break for lunch at either end of the lake. The steamers run from the end of March to the beginning of November and cost £1.95 to £5.30 ($3.30 to $9)per person. For more information, call ☎ **01539/721626.** Glenridding is on A592 at the southern end of Ullswater. Pooley Bridge is 5 miles from the M6 junction 40 Penrith.

ESSENTIALS

GETTING THERE About three trains from London's Euston Station arrive daily in Penrith, this region's main rail junction. Usually, a change of trains isn't necessary. For schedules and information, call ☎ **0345/484950.** Once in Penrith, passengers usually take a taxi to Ullswater.

Two buses operated by **Stagecoach Cumberland** (☎ **01946/63222**) stop at the Penrith Bus Station daily on their way between Carlisle and Keswick. Passengers must take a taxi from Penrith to Ullswater.

If you're driving from Penrith, go southeast on B5320.

VISITOR INFORMATION The summer-only **Tourist Information Centre** for the lake is at The Square, Pooley Bridge (☎ or fax **017684/86530**); it's open daily Easter through November from 10am to 5pm.

WHERE TO STAY & DINE

Gowbarrow Lodge. Watermillock, Ullswater, Cumbria CA11 0JP. ☎ **01768/486286.** 8 units. TV. £55 ($93.50) double. Rates include English breakfast. MC, V.

Named for the large limestone fell running behind the hotel, Gowbarrow Lodge was a filling station a few years ago—and you never could tell it today from looking at its stone facade. The lodge affords views of the green fields, large lake, and distant fells across the road. This view was part of the reason the Whitehead family decided to convert their filling station, which people often described as being "the best filling station around simply because of its view." The bedrooms upstairs are decorated with contemporary, functional furnishings. The tiled baths are small and compact, each with a shower stall. Downstairs, the public rooms, including a small restaurant, lounge, and bar, are full of dark, polished wood with local maps and photographs adorning the walls. The restaurant serves good home-cooked meals.

✪ **Sharrow Bay Country House Hotel.** Howtown Rd., Lake Ullswater, near Penrith, Cumbria CA10 2LZ. ☎ **01768/486301.** Fax 017684/86349. www.sharrow-bay.com. E-mail: inquiries@sharrow-bay.com. 28 units. TV TEL. £300–£390 ($510–$663) double; £360–£390 ($612–$663) suite for 2. Rates include half board. MC, V. Howtown Rd. 2 miles south of Pooley Bridge.

This was Britain's first country-house hotel and is the oldest British member of Relais & Châteaux. It's an unusual Victorian house with a low angled roof and wide eaves. It was a private home until purchased by Francis Coulson in 1948. Realizing its potential, Coulson restored the structure, sleeping on the floor while work was in progress. Three years later he was joined by Brian Sack, and together they turned Sharrow into one of England's finest places to dine. Today, the hotel offers 28 antique-filled bedrooms, 17 of them in the gatehouse and cottages. Individually decorated, each is named after one or another of the glamorous (and often famous) women who have swept in and out of the lives of the articulate owners. Some of the rooms offer views of the lakes, trees, or Martindale Fells. Beds are sumptuous with soft mattresses, cushiony pillows, and quality linen. Each bathroom is well appointed with deluxe toiletries and generous shelf space. Other amenities include room service and laundry/dry cleaning.

In the dining room, the 6-course, fixed-price menu offers a formidable list of choices, all of them made with ultrafresh ingredients and superb vegetables, many of them homegrown. Choices might include medallions of local lamb on braised red cabbage with a cannelloni of wild mushrooms and a juniper berry and dill sauce.

8 Penrith

290 miles NW of London; 31 miles NE of Kendal

This one-time capital of Cumbria, in the old Kingdom of Scotland and Strathclyde, takes its name, some say, from the Celts who called it "Ford by the Hill." The namesake hill is marked today by a red-sandstone beacon and tower. Because of Penrith's central location right above the northern Lake District and beside the Pennines, this thriving market center was important to Scotland and England from its very beginning, eventually prompting England to take it over in 1070.

The characteristically red-sandstone town has been home to many famous and legendary figures through the ages, including Richard, duke of Gloucester; William Cookson, the grandfather of William and Dorothy Wordsworth. Today, Penrith still remains best known as a lively market town.

ESSENTIALS

GETTING THERE Trains from London's Euston Station arrive in Penrith four times a day. The trip takes 4 hours. For train schedules and information, call ☎ **0345/484950.**

To take a bus from London to Penrith, hop on one of the two daily National Express buses to Carlisle and then take a Stagecoach Cumberland bus to Penrith, a total journey of 8 hours. The Stage Coach Cumberland buses leave every hour. For schedules and information, call **National Express** at ☎ **0990/808080** and **Stagecoach Cumberland** at ☎ **01946/63222.**

To drive, take the M1 out of London, getting on the M6 to Penrith. The trip should take no more than 6 hours.

VISITOR INFORMATION The **Tourist Information Centre,** Robinson's School, Middlegate, Penrith (☎ **01768/867466**), is open November to Easter, Monday to Saturday from 9:30am to 5pm; Easter through May and the month of October, Monday to Saturday from 9:30am to 5pm and Sunday from 1 to 5pm; June through September, Monday to Saturday from 9:30am to 6pm and Sunday from 1 to 5pm.

EXPLORING THE AREA

It's a small town of 12,500 people, but there are lots of shops to explore. Major shopping areas include the covered **Devonshire Arcade** with its name-brand stores and boutiques, the pedestrian-only **Angel Lane** and **Little Dockray,** with an abundance of family run specialty shops, as well as **Angel Square** just south of Angel Lane.

For handmade earthenware and stoneware from the only remaining steam-powered pottery in Britain, stop by **Wetheriggs Country Pottery,** Clifton Dykes, 2 miles south of Penrith on the A6 (☎ **01768/892733**).

In the 130-year-old **Briggs & Shoe Mines,** Southend Road (☎ **01768/899001**), you'll have a shoe-shopping extravaganza. It is the largest independent shoe shop in the Lakelands, carrying famous names and offering great bargains, including sportswear, walking boots, clothing, and accessories.

The **Eden Valley Woollen Mill,** Armathwaite, along the M6 heading toward Carlisle (☎ **016974/72457**), is where Steve Wilson and his small and talented team design and weave using restored looms dating from the early 1900s. Their wares include jackets and skirts in traditional and modern tweeds, rugs, throws, ruanas, hats, ties, and scarves. The showroom also carries individual knitwear and yarns.

Penrith Museum. Robinson's School, Middlegate. ☎ **01768/212228.** Free admission. June–Sept Mon–Sat 10am–5pm, Sun 1:30–5pm; Oct–May Mon–Sat 10am–5pm.

For perspective on Penrith and the surrounding area, a visit here isn't a bad idea. Originally constructed in the 1500s, the museum building was turned into a poor-girls school in 1670. Today, the museum offers a survey of the archaeology and geology of Penrith and the Eden Valley, which was a desert millions of years ago.

Penrith Castle. Just across from the train station along Ullswater Rd. No phone. Free admission. Always accessible.

This park contains the massive ruins of the castle, whose construction began in 1399, ordered by William Strickland, the bishop of Canterbury. For the next 70 years, the castle continued to grow in size and strength until it finally became the royal castle and oftentimes residence for Richard, duke of Gloucester.

Acorn Bank Garden. Temple Sowerby, 6 miles east of Penrith on A6. ☎ **017683/61893.** Admission £2.30 ($3.90) adults, £1.20 ($2.05) children; family ticket (2 adults, 2 children) £5.80 ($9.85). Daily 10am–5:30pm (last admission at 5pm). Closed Nov–Good Friday.

For a stroll in an English garden, see the Acorn Bank Garden with its varied landscape of blooming bulbs, plants, and walled spaces. Its claim to fame is its extensive herb garden, said to be the best in all of northern England. The Acorn Bank Garden is part of an estate dating from 1228 and is now owned by the National Trust. Buildings on the estate include a partially restored water mill, parts of which also date from the 13th century, and a red-sandstone primarily Tudor house, which is presently not open to the public.

WHERE TO STAY

George. Devonshire St., Penrith, Cumbria CA11 7SU. ☎ **01768/862696.** Fax 01768/868223. 34 units. TV. £64–£70 ($108.80–$119) double, £80–£110 ($136–$187) suite. Rates include full Cumbrian breakfast. V.

This 300-year-old coaching inn, built right in the heart of town, welcomed Bonnie Prince Charlie in 1745. The front of the George looks out on a street of small specialty shops, and the guest rooms are spread among three floors, and are individually decorated with light colors and up-to-date furnishings. The owners are gradually upgrading all the bedrooms, so standards here will be higher than before. Amenities include beverage makers and hair dryers. Each small bathroom has a tub and shower or else a shower stall. Full of oak beams and paneling, the lounge, two bars, and restaurant with dining room provide everything guests will need during their stay.

North Lakes Hotel. Ullswater Rd., Penrith, Cumbria CA11 8QT. ☎ **01768/868111.** Fax 01768/868291. 84 units. TV TEL. £125 ($212.50) double; £160 ($272) suite. Rates include English breakfast. AE, DC, MC, V.

The exterior may lack character, but you'll find compensation inside. A member of the Shire Inns chain, this hotel is designed to meet the needs of businesspeople during the week and vacationers on weekends. Rooms are bright and spacious, decorated with classic wood furniture, large couches, and soft pastel accents. Each bedroom comes with the finest comfortable beds in town. Six rooms are large enough for rentals to families, and some two dozen are set aside for nonsmokers. Bathrooms have a hair dryer. Guests enjoy an inviting lobby sitting area with a grand, barn-style, open ceiling with rustic beams, and a huge stone fireplace.

There's an intimate bar and a comfortable restaurant specializing in English and French dishes. The hotel's leisure club has a large indoor pool, whirlpool, sauna, solarium, two squash courts, and a gym.

WHERE TO DINE

Passepartout. 51 Castlegate. ☎ **01768/865852.** Main courses £10–£15 ($17–$25.50). MC, V. Tues–Sun 7–10pm. FRENCH/ENGLISH.

Housed in a 400-year-old building, this cozy, candlelit dining room is set among painted stone walls. The chef has designed an imaginative menu around fresh local items, and dishes may include loin of pork with a caraway-and-port-wine sauce on a bed of fennel, tomato and cheese. Desserts range from homemade butterscotch ice cream to an oyster amaretto soufflé with a chocolate sauce. In warmer months, folks relax with drinks in a Spanish-style open courtyard in back of the dining room.

Yorkshire & Northumbria

17

Yorkshire, known to readers of *Wuthering Heights* and *All Creatures Great and Small,* embraces both the moors of North Yorkshire and the dales.

Across this vast region came the Romans, the Anglo-Saxons, the Vikings, the monks of the Middle Ages, kings of England, lords of the manor, craftspeople, hill farmers, and wool growers, all leaving their own mark. You can still see Roman roads and pavements, great abbeys and castles, stately homes, open-air museums, and craft centers, along with parish churches, old villages, and cathedrals.

Some cities and towns still carry the taint of the Industrial Revolution, but there's also wild and remote beauty to be found—limestone crags, caverns along the Pennines, mountainous uplands, rolling hills, chalk land wolds, heather-covered moorlands, broad vales, and tumbling streams. Yorkshire offers not only beautiful inland scenery, but also 100 miles of shoreline, with rocky headlands, cliffs, and sandy bays, rock pools, sheltered coves, fishing villages, bird sanctuaries, former smugglers' dens, and yachting havens. And in summer, the moors in North York Moors National Park bloom with purple heather. You can hike along the 110-mile Cleveland Way National Trail, encircling the park.

Yorkshire's most visited city is the walled city of York. York Minster, part of the cathedral circuit, is noted for its 100 stained-glass windows. In West Yorkshire is the literary shrine of Haworth, the home of the Brontës.

On the way north to Hadrian's Wall, we suggest you spend the night in the ancient cathedral city of Durham. This great medieval city is among the most dramatically sited and most interesting in the north.

Northumbria is made up of the counties of Northumberland, Cleveland, and Durham. The Saxons, who came to northern England centuries ago, carved out this kingdom, which at the time stretched from the Firth of Forth in Scotland to the banks of the Humber in Yorkshire. Vast tracts of that ancient kingdom remain natural and unspoiled. Again, this slice of England has more than its share of industrial towns, but you should explore the wild hills and open spaces and cross the dales of the eastern Pennines.

The whole area evokes ancient battles and bloody border raids. Space constraints don't permit us to cover this area in great detail, and it's often overlooked by the rushed North American visitor. But we suggest that you at least venture to see Hadrian's Wall, a Roman structure that was one of the wonders of the Western world. The finest stretch of the wall lies within the Northumberland National Park, between the stony North Tyne River and the county boundary at Gilsland. And about 40 miles of the 150-mile Pennine Way meanders through the park; the Pennine Way is one of Britain's most challenging hiking paths.

1 York

203 miles N of London; 26 miles NE of Leeds; 88 miles N of Nottingham

Few cities in England are as rich in history as York. It is still encircled by its 13th- and 14th-century city walls, about 2½ miles long, with four gates. One of these, Micklegate, once grimly greeted visitors coming up from the south with the heads of traitors. To this day, you can walk on the footpath of the medieval walls.

The crowning achievement of York is its minister, or cathedral, which makes the city an ecclesiastical center equaled only by Canterbury. It can easily be seen on a drive up to Edinburgh. Or, after visiting Cambridge, you can make a swing through the great cathedral cities of Ely, Lincoln, York, and Ripon.

There was a Roman York (Hadrian came this way), then a Saxon York, a Danish York, a Norman York (William the Conqueror slept here), a medieval York, a Georgian York, and a Victorian York (the center of a flourishing rail business). Today, a large amount of 18th-century York remains, including Richard Boyle's restored Assembly Rooms.

At some point in your exploration, you may want to visit the Shambles; once the meat-butchering center of York, it dates from before the Norman Conquest. The messy business is gone now, but the ancient street survives, filled today with jewelry stores, cafes, and buildings that huddle so closely together that you can practically stand in the middle of the pavement, arms outstretched, and touch the houses on both sides of the street.

ESSENTIALS

GETTING THERE British Midland flights arrive at Leeds/Bradford Airport, a 50-minute flight from London's Heathrow Airport. For schedules and fares, call the airline at ☎ **0870/6070555.** Connecting buses at the airport take you east and the rest of the distance to York.

From London's King's Cross Station, York-bound trains leave every 30 minutes. The trip takes 2 hours. For schedules and information, call ☎ **0345/484950.**

Four **National Express** buses depart daily from London's Victoria Coach Station for the 4½ hour trip to York. For schedules and information, call ☎ **0990/808080.**

If you're driving from London, head north on M1, cutting northeast below Leeds at the junction with A64, heading east to York.

VISITOR INFORMATION The **Tourist Information Centre** at De Grey Rooms, Exhibition Square (☎ **01904/621756**), is open Monday to Saturday from 9am to 5pm, and Sunday from 9:30am to 3pm.

SEEING THE SIGHTS

The best way to see York is to go to Exhibition Square (opposite the Tourist Information Centre), where a volunteer guide will take you on a **free 2-hour walking tour** of the city. You'll learn about history and lore through numerous intriguing stories. Tours are given April through October, daily at 10:15am and 2:15pm, plus 7pm from June to August; from November to March, a daily tour is given at 10:15am. Groups

The Northeast: Yorkshire & Northumbria

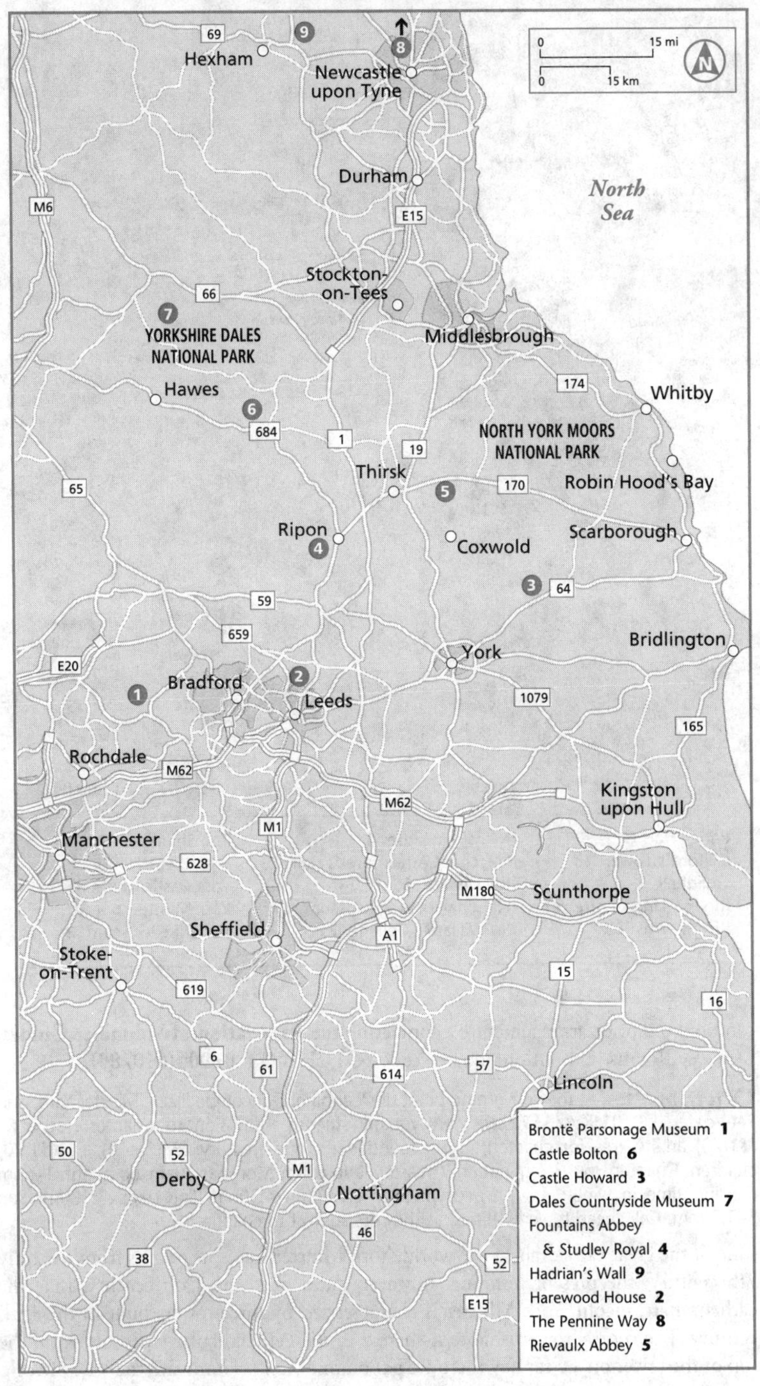

York

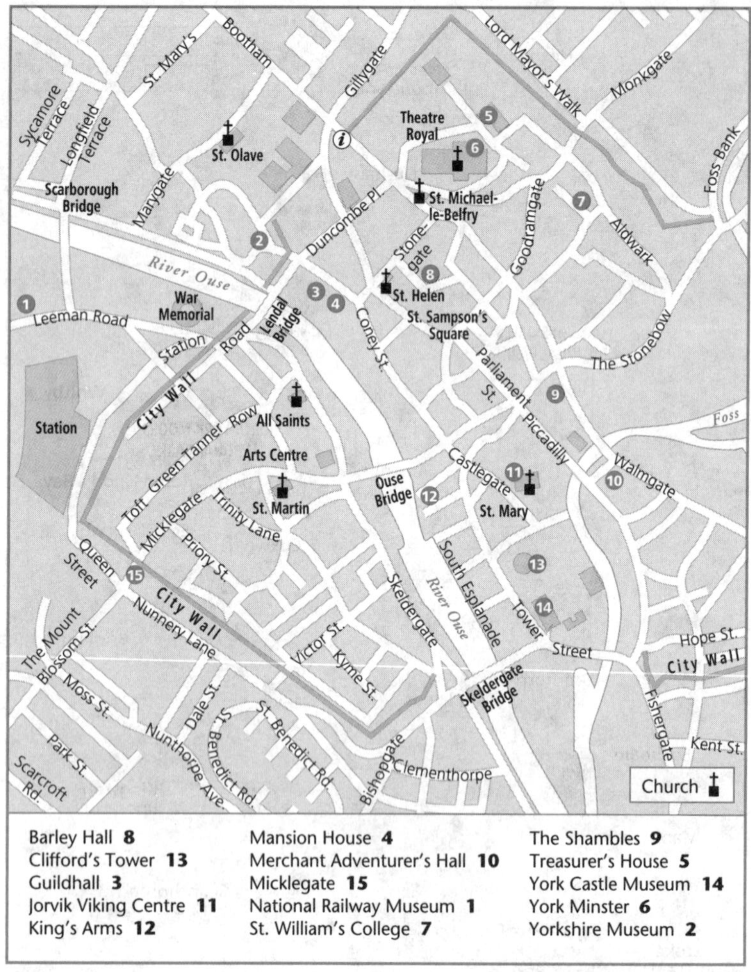

can book by prior arrangement by contacting the **Association of Volunteer Guides,** De Grey Rooms, Exhibition Square, York YO1 2HB (☎ **01904/640780**).

✪ **York Minster.** At the converging point of Deangate, Duncombe Place, Minster Yard, and Petergate. ☎ **01904/557216;** www.yorkminister.org Admission to Chapter House £1 ($1.70) adults, free for children; crypt, foundations, and treasury £3 ($5.10), £1 ($1.70) children. Chapter House, foundations, treasury, and tower Mon–Sat 10am–6pm, Sun 1–6pm (closing time in winter 4:30pm). Crypt Mon–Fri 10am–4:30pm, Sat 10am–3:30pm, Sun 1–3:30pm. Call ahead to verify times, as they are subject to change.

One of the great cathedrals of the world, York Minster traces its origins from the early 7th century; the present building, however, dates from the 13th century. Like the cathedral at Lincoln, York Minster is characterized by three towers built in the 15th century. The central tower is lantern-shaped in the Perpendicular style, and from the top of the tower on a clear day there are panoramic views of York and the Vale of York.

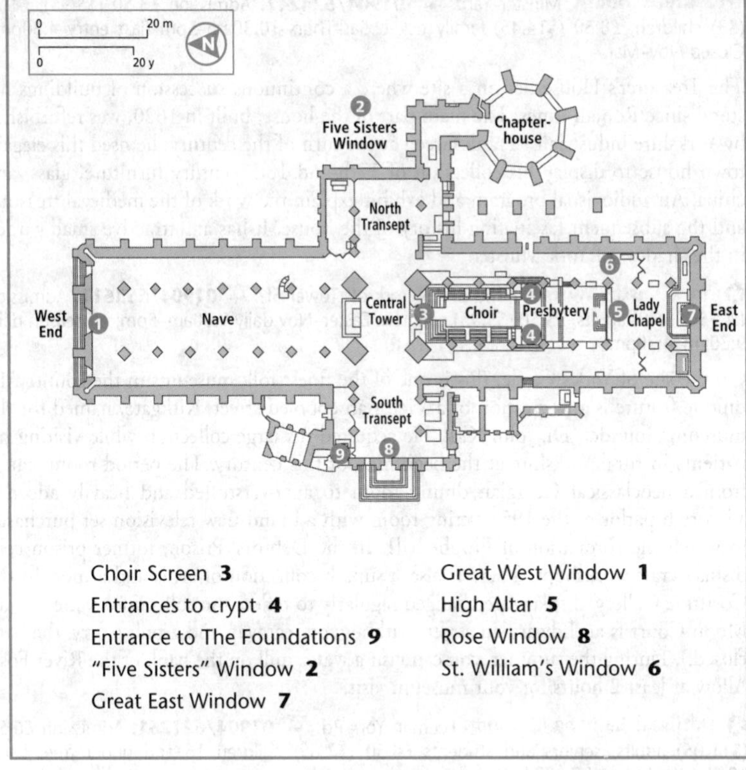

The climb up a stone spiral staircase is steep and not recommended for very elderly or very young visitors, or anyone with a heart condition or breathing difficulties.

The outstanding characteristic of the cathedral is its **stained glass** from the Middle Ages, in glorious Angelico blues, ruby reds, forest greens, and honey-colored ambers. See especially the Great East Window, the work of a 15th-century Coventry-based glass painter. In the north transept is an architectural gem of the mid-13th century: the Five Sisters Window, with its five lancets in grisaille glass. The late–15th-century choir screen in its Octagonal Chapter House has an impressive lineup of historical figures—everybody from William the Conqueror to the overthrown Henry VI.

At a reception desk near the entrance to the minster, groups can arrange a guide, if one is available. Conducted tours are free but donations toward the upkeep of the cathedral are requested.

Insider's tip: Check out **St. William's Restaurant** at the front of St. William's Cottage (☎ **01904/634830**), close to the east end of the minster. This splendid timbered building provides a setting daily for coffee, an affordable lunch, or tea. Here you can get tasty quiches, homemade soups, and luscious desserts. Not only that, if you can arrange for a party of 35 or more, you can have a medieval banquet staged on your behalf, complete with minstrels, jesters, and jugglers. One way to do this is to post a notice at your hotel and get people to sign up and invite their newly made acquaintances. In one day our party swelled to nearly 50 and we were regally fed and entertained. For more information, call ☎ **01904/634830.**

Treasurer's House. Minster Yard. ☎ **01904/624247.** Admission £3.50 ($5.95), £1.75 ($3) children, £8.50 ($14.45) family ticket. Sat–Thurs 10:30am–5pm (last entry 4:30pm). Closed Nov–Mar.

The Treasurer's House lies on a site where a continuous succession of buildings has stood since Roman times. The main part of the house, built in 1620, was refurbished by Yorkshire industrialist Frank Green at the turn of the century; he used this elegant town house to display his collection of 17th-and 18th-century furniture, glass, and china. An audiovisual program and exhibit explain the work of the medieval treasures and the subsequent fascinating history of the house. It has an attractive small garden in the shadow of York Minster.

✪ **York Castle Museum.** The Eye of York off Tower St. ☎ **01904/653611.** Admission £4.95 ($8.40) adults, £3.50 ($5.95) children. Easter–Nov daily 9:30am–5pm; off-season daily 9:30am–4:30pm.

On the site of York's Castle, this is one of the finest folk museums in the country. Its unique feature is a re-creation of a Victorian cobbled street, Kirkgate, named for the museum's founder, Dr. John Kirk. He acquired his large collection while visiting his patients in rural Yorkshire at the beginning of this century. The period rooms range from a neoclassical Georgian dining room to an overstuffed and heavily adorned Victorian parlor to the 1953 sitting room with a brand-new television set purchased to watch the coronation of Elizabeth II. In the Debtors' Prison, former prison cells display craft workshops. There is also a superb collection of arms and armor. In the Costume Gallery, displays are changed regularly to reflect the collection's variety. Half Moon Court is an Edwardian street, with a gypsy caravan and a pub (sorry, the bar's closed!). During the summer, you can visit a water mill on the bank of the River Foss. Allow at least 2 hours for your museum visit.

✪ **National Railway Museum.** Leeman York Rd. ☎ **01904/621261.** Admission £6.50 ($11.05) adults, seniors and students £4.50 ($7.65) children 16 and under free. Daily 10am–6pm. Closed Dec 24–26.

This was the first national museum to be built outside London, and it has attracted millions of train buffs. Adapted from an original steam-locomotive depot, the museum gives visitors a chance to see how Queen Victoria traveled in luxury, and to look under and inside steam locomotives. In addition, there's a collection of railway memorabilia, including an early-19th-century clock and penny machine for purchasing tickets on the railway platform. More than 40 locomotives are on display. One, the *Agenoria,* dates from 1829 and is a contemporary of Stephenson's well-known *Rocket.* Of several royal coaches, the most interesting is Queen Victoria's Royal Saloon; it's like a small hotel, with polished wood, silk, brocade, and silver accessories.

Jorvik Viking Centre. Coppergate. ☎ **01904/643211.** Admission £5.35 ($9.10) adults, £4 ($6.80) children 5–15 years, £4.60 ($7.80) seniors and students. Family ticket £17 ($28.90). Apr–Oct daily 9am–5:30pm; Nov–Mar Sun–Fri 9am–3:30pm, Sat 9–4:30pm.

This Viking city, discovered many feet below present ground level, was reconstructed as it stood in 948. In a "time car," you travel back through the ages to 1067, when Normans sacked the city, and then you ride slowly through the street market peopled by faithfully modeled Vikings. You also go through a house where a family lived and down to the river to see the ship chandlers at work and a Norwegian cargo ship unloading. At the end of the ride, you pass through the Finds Hut, where thousands of artifacts are displayed. The time car departs at regular intervals.

SHOPPING

Several of the main areas to explore include **Gillygate** for antiques dealers, **St. Mary's Square** and its **Coppergate** pedestrian mall for name brands and chain stores, and **Newgate Marketplace** for local vendors selling a variety of wares Monday through Saturday.

Several specialty shops that have ideal gift items include **Maxwell and Kennedy,** 79 Low Petergate (☎ **01904/610034**), a candy store specializing in both Belgian chocolate and Cambridge Wells dark, milk, and white chocolate; **Mulberry Hall,** 17 Stonegate (☎ **01904/620736**), housed in a medieval house from 1436, with 16 showrooms on three floors devoted to the best in British and European porcelain, fine china, crystal, and some antiques; and **Wooden Horse,** 9 Goodramgate (☎ **01904/626012**), featuring an eclectic mixture of ethnic items such as shirts, tops, jewelry, cushions, rugs, and throws from Africa, India, China, and Mexico.

WHERE TO STAY

EXPENSIVE

✪ **Dean Court Hotel.** Duncombe Place, York, N. Yorkshire YO1 2EF. ☎ **800/528-1234** in the U.S., or 01904/625082. Fax 01904/620305. www.deancourt-york.co.uk. E-mail: info@deancourt-york.co.uk. 39 units, some with shower only. TV TEL. £100–£170 ($170–$289) double. £15 ($25.50) children under 17 in parent's room. Rates include English breakfast. AE, DC, MC, V.

This 1850 building lies right beneath the towers of the minster. It was originally constructed to provide housing for the clergy of York Minster and then converted to a hotel after World War I. It may not be the most atmospheric choice in York, but recent refurbishments have vastly improved the accommodations. The rooms are very comfortable, with firm mattresses and quality linens on the beds. Two rooms are spacious enough for use by families, and a dozen are set aside for nonsmokers.

Dining: Snacks are served in a coffee lounge from 9:30am to 6:30pm. The Dean Court Restaurant serves both traditional English and international dishes at lunch and dinner.

Amenities: Concierge, room service, dry cleaning/laundry, baby-sitting, access to nearby health club.

✪ **Middlethorpe Hall Hotel.** Bishopthorpe Rd. (on the A64, 1 1/2 miles south of town), York, N. Yorkshire 4023 2GB. ☎ **800/260-8338** in the U.S., or 01904/641241. Fax 01904/620176. www.middlethorpe.com. E-mail: info@middlethorpe.u-net.com. 30 units. TV TEL. £145–£225 ($246.50–$382.50) double; £185–£250 ($314.50–$425) suite. AE, MC, V.

Set on a 26-acre park, this hotel is on the outskirts of York, near the racecourse and away from the traffic. It's clearly York's leading hotel. Built in 1699, the stately, red-brick William-and-Mary country house was purchased by Historic House Hotels and beautifully restored, both inside and out. Fresh flowers are displayed profusely and lots of antiques create the ambience of a classic manor house. The rooms are located in the main house and restored outbuildings. Accommodations in the wing have less drama and flair, although you can enjoy greater privacy there. Rooms have such niceties as homemade cookies and bottles of mineral water, as well as bathrobes. All the bedrooms, from decorations to antiques and fine pictures, have been styled to evoke the aura of a country house, although all the modern comforts have been installed as well. Each bedroom is decorated individually with four-poster beds, or padded or canopied headboards. Trouser presses and beverage makers are offered, and each bathroom has a hair dryer.

Is York Haunted?

After London, York has been the site of more beheadings, medieval tortures, and human anguish than any other city in Britain. Psychics and mystics insist that dozens of lost souls wander among the city's historic core reliving the traumatic moments of their earthly lives. Ghost walks are held every evening in York, allegedly England's most haunted city.

Several outfits conduct these tours, but the most charming one, **"The Ghost Hunt of York,"** leaves at 7:30pm every night from The Shambles. The 1½-hour tour costs £3 ($5.10) for adults, £2 ($3.40) for children. Be prepared for lively commentary and more ghoulishness than you might expect. Call (☎ **01904/608700**) for more information.

Dining: Distinguished meals are served in two restaurants, one oak-paneled and one a grill room. A choice of either international or English traditional meals is offered.

Amenities: Concierge, car-rental desk, dry cleaning/laundry.

Viking Moat House. North St., York, N. Yorkshire YO1 1JF. ☎ **01904/459988.** Fax 01904/641793. www.moathousehotels.com. 200 units. TV TEL. £135 ($229.50) double; £165 ($280.50) suite. AE, DC, MC, V. Parking £6 ($10.20).

Within the ancient city walls, this modern hotel overlooks the River Ouse and is the leading hotel within the center of York. Built in the 1970s, the hotel is the largest in town and is conveniently located for sightseeing. The well-furnished and modern bedrooms, many with views looking toward the minster, have trouser presses, hair dryers, and beverage makers. Many of the mid-size bedrooms have fine views of the city. Seven rooms are spacious enough for families.

Dining/Diversions: The hotel's waterfront restaurant offers fixed-price lunches and dinners daily. The hotel also has two bars, both providing a warm and welcoming atmosphere.

Amenities: 24-hour room service, a dance studio, sauna, solarium, gym, dry cleaning/laundry, baby-sitting.

MODERATE

Hudson's Hotel. 60 Bootham, York, N. Yorkshire YO3 7BZ. ☎ **01904/621267.** Fax 01904/654719. www.freepages.co.uk/hudsonshotel/. 34 units. TV TEL. £90–£115 ($153–$195.50) double; £100 ($170) triple. Rates include English breakfast. AE, DC, MC, V.

Just a short walk from the minster, this hotel offers personal service. The owner converted two Victorian houses into the main hotel building in 1981 and later added an extension in the Victorian style. All accommodations are comfortably furnished and have tea- and coffeemakers. Rooms, equally comfortable, are divided between a Victorian section where smoking is allowed and a more modern wing where smoking is not permitted. Those in the Victorian section are decorated in a period style, but have modern beds. Hudson's has its own large parking lot. Both bar food and an English/French menu are offered.

The Judges Lodging. 9 Lendal, York, N. Yorkshire YO1 2AQ. ☎ **01904/638733.** Fax 01904/679947. E-mail:judgeshotel@aol.com 14 units. TV TEL. £100–£175 ($170–$297.50) double. Rates include English breakfast. AE, DC, MC, V.

The earliest historical fact about this charming house is that it was the home of a certain Dr. Wintringham in 1710. It is listed as having been a judges' lodging at the beginning of the 19th century. To get to your room, you'll climb a circular wooden staircase, the only one of its type in the United Kingdom. Some bedrooms have four-poster beds. If you want to spoil yourself, book the large Prince Albert room, a twin-bedded room with three large windows overlooking the minster (Prince Albert actually slept in the room once). Each room has a different decor and is named accordingly. Bedrooms, ranging from small to mid-size, have been thoughtfully renovated. The tiled bathrooms are equipped with a hair dryer. Many rooms have a view of York Minster.

There are two dining rooms. Candles flicker and the carefully trained staff attends to your every need. All meat, fish, and vegetables are fresh. You'll find a cocktail bar, open to the public. A private bar that serves simple meals is also open to guests only.

Mount Royale Hotel. 119 The Mount, York, N. Yorkshire YO2 2DA. ☎ **01904/628856.** Fax 01904/611171. www.mountroyale.co.uk. E-mail: stuart@mountroyale.co.uk. 23 units. TV TEL. £95–£105 ($161.50–$178.50) double; £140 ($238) suite. Rates include English breakfast. AE, DC, MC, V.

A short walk west of York's city walls, in a neighborhood known as The Mount, this hotel is the personal statement of two generations of the Oxtaby family. They work hard to create a friendly, homelike atmosphere. The main house was built as a private home in 1833, although several years ago the owners merged a neighboring house of the same era into the original core. Accommodations and public rooms are furnished with both antiques and modern pieces. Some bedrooms have private terraces leading into the garden. Bedrooms come in a wide variety of shapes and sizes, and two are large enough to rent to families. The bathrooms are small but well organized. Room service, laundry, and an outdoor swimming pool are available.

The restaurant features roasts with interesting accompaniments. There's also an extensive fixed-price menu. Reservations are recommended. The dining room opens onto an attractive garden.

Inexpensive

Beechwood Close Hotel. 19 Shipton Rd. (on the A19 north of the city), Clifton, York, N. Yorkshire YO30 5RE. ☎ **01904/658378.** Fax 01904/647124. www.beechwood-close.co.uk. E-mail: bch@dial.selcom.co.uk. 14 units. TV TEL. £70 ($119) double. Rates include English breakfast. AE, DC, MC, V.

Beechwood is a large house surrounded by trees, a garden with a putting green, and a parking area. Mr. and Mrs. Blythe run the small hotel, which offers comfortable bedrooms with central heating and beverage makers. Each small bath has a hair dryer; most have a tub and shower combination. Good dinners or bar meals are served in the dining room overlooking the garden. The hotel is a 15-minute walk to the minster, either by road or along the river.

Cottage Hotel. 3 Clifton Green, York, N. Yorkshire YO3 6LH. ☎ **01904/643711.** Fax 01904/611230. 20 units. TV TEL. £50–£65 ($85–$110.50) double. Rates include English breakfast. AE, DC, MC, V.

About a 10-minute walk north of York Minster, this hotel comprises two refurbished and extended Victorian houses overlooking the village green of Clifton. The hotel offers cozy, small bedrooms with simple furnishings and hot-beverage makers. Each comes with a well-maintained bath with a shower stall. Some 400-year-old timbers rescued from the demolition of a medieval building in one of the city's historic streets (Micklegate) grace the restaurant and bar, which does a thriving business in its own right. The hotel provides secured parking for its guests.

Grasmead House Hotel. 1 Scarcroft Hill, York, N. Yorkshire Y024 1DF. ☎ and fax **01904/629996.** www.uktourism.com/yk-grasmead. E-mail: stansue@grasmeadhouse.freeserve.co.uk 6 units. TV. £60–£75 ($102–$127.50) double. Rates include English breakfast. AE, MC, V.

This house was built in 1896 on a narrow strip of land between an ancient drover's road leading to the walled center of York and a residential street. It was converted to a small hotel in 1951, and has been thriving ever since. A 15-minute walk south of the town center, this lovely B&B features antique four-poster beds in each of its six rooms, with the oldest bed dating from 1750. It's perfect for a romantic getaway, but families are welcome as well; two rooms are large suites with an extra single bed. The hotel is the home of proprietors Stan and Sue Long, and their guests are extended family, so just ask for anything from advice to aspirin. Each room, individually decorated with antiques and in a Victorian style, has its own small bathroom, heating, alarm clock, and beverage makers. Bedrooms are all no-smoking, and the comfort level is high. There's also a sitting room, complete with a licensed bar for guests, and a full English breakfast is served every morning in the Tea Room dining room.

Heworth Court. 76 Heworth Green, York, N. Yorkshire YO3 7TQ. ☎ **01904/425156.** Fax 01904/415290. www.heworth.co.uk. E-mail: hotel@heworth.co.uk. 27 units. TV TEL. £58–£90 ($98.60–$153) double. Rates include English breakfast. AE, DC, MC, V. Take the A1036 to the east side of the city.

Just a 10- to 15-minute walk east of the city center is this 3-story redbrick Victorian structure (many of its bedrooms are located in a modern extension added during the 1980s). The rooms are agreeably furnished and some open onto the court-yard. Each comes with a comfortable bed, plus a compact bath with a shower stall and adequate shelf space. The hotel also offers really fine food.

WHERE TO DINE

Oscar's Wine Bar & Bistro, 8A Little Stonegate (☎ **01904/652002**), offers heaping plates of meats and salads, attracting a young crowd (often because of the inexpensive beer). There's a courtyard and a large menu. A DJ spins dance music on Friday and Saturday. Open daily from 11am to 11pm, Sunday noon to 10:30pm.

The best place for afternoon tea is **Betty's Café & Tea Rooms,** 6–8 St. Helen's Sq. (☎ **01904/659142**). We also recommend **St. William's College Restaurant,** 3 College St. (☎ **01904/634830**), and **Theatre Royal Café Bar,** St. Leonard's Place (☎ **01904/632596**).

The Ivy/The Seafood Bar/The Brasserie. In the Grange Hotel, 1 Clifton (off Bootham Rd.), York, N. Yorkshire YO3 6AA. ☎ **01904/644744.** Fax 01904/612453. Reservations recommended in The Ivy and The Seafood Bar; not necessary in The Brasserie. Fixed-price 3-course menu in The Ivy £25 ($42.50); main courses in The Seafood Bar £8.95–£10.25 ($15.20–$17.45); main courses in The Brasserie £7.50–£10.50 ($12.75–$17.85). AE, DC, MC, V. The Ivy Mon–Fri noon–2pm, daily 7–10pm; Seafood Bar daily 7–10pm; The Brasserie Mon–Sat noon–2:30pm and 6–10:30pm, Sun 7–10pm. FRENCH/ENGLISH.

A 10-minute walk west of York Minster, this dining complex is one of the most appealing in town. It's housed within an ivy-covered Regency town house that's also a 30-room hotel.

The least formal venue is The Brasserie, a paneled, candlelit hideaway in the cellar. The hearty menu items include steaks, fish, and ale. It's the most crowded of the complex's three restaurants.

On the building's street level, The Ivy restaurant and The Seafood Bar are set adjacent to one another. Cuisine in The Ivy is more upscale than that in the cellar, and includes dishes such as monkfish on pearl barley risotto, with mussel and saffron nage.

A few steps away, The Seafood Bar has a great trompe l'oeil panoramic mural of York's Racecourse, complete with views of the city's skyline. The menu here features mostly seafood prepared in many ways. Examples include grilled sea scallops, with sesame, soya, and a spring onion dressing.

Kites. 13 Grape Lane. ☎ **01904/641750.** Reservations required. Main courses £10.50–£15.95 ($17.85–$27.10). AE, DC, DISC, MC, V. Mon–Sat noon–2pm and 6:30–10:30pm. INTERNATIONAL.

About a 5-minute walk from the minster, this restaurant is in the heart of York, on a small street near Stonegate (walk up a narrow staircase to the second floor). This is a simple York bistro where the food is good and the atmosphere and service are unpretentious. Kites's many fans are attracted to its eclectic brand of cooking. One recipe might have been a dish served in the Middle Ages in England (perhaps with adaptations); the next might come from Thailand. Meals may feature trout, game, tuna, or pork depending on what the hunters and gatherers return with. Fondues, fresh salads, and vegetarian meals are also available.

✪ **Melton's Restaurant.** 7 Scarcroft Rd. ☎ **01904/634341.** Reservations required. Main courses £10.50–£14.50 ($17.85–$24.65); fixed-price menu (Mon–Sat) £20 ($34). MC, V. Tues–Sun noon–2pm; Mon–Sat 5:30–10pm. Closed Aug 25–Sept 2 and Dec 24–Jan 11. CONTINENTAL/ENGLISH.

Some local food critics claim that Michael and Lucy Hjort serve the finest food in York, and we agree. Their small and unpretentious restaurant is approximately 1 mile from the heart of the city. Mr. Hjort trained with the famous Roux brothers of Le Gavroche in London, but he doesn't charge their astronomical prices. His cuisine reflects his own imprint.

In what has always been known as a culinary backwater town, the Hjorts have created some local excitement with this family friendly place. Their menu changes frequently, but could include a medley of seafood with garlic and rosemary; roast confit of duck with bitter leaves and a warm potato salad; or a trio of lamb with a zucchini and onion ragout and lemon and mint couscous. Vegetarian meals are also available, and families with children are welcome.

19 Grape Lane. 19 Grape Lane. ☎ **01904/636366.** Reservations recommended for dinner. Main courses £9.95–£14.50 ($16.90–$24.65). MC, V. Tues–Sat noon–2pm and 6–11pm. ENGLISH.

In the heart of York, on a cobbled lane off Petergate, this restaurant occupies two floors of a timbered building with a wealth of its original features. With such a name, you would expect a very British restaurant and it is, but with a very contemporary touch. You can begin with a Jamaican cocktail, which is their own blend of poached salmon, banana, prawns and pineapple served with a spiced mayonnaise; follow with filets of trout stuffed with crabmeat and wrapped in lettuce leaves. The menus are wisely limited to about 10 main courses, so that every dish will be fresh. The cooking is without needless adornment. The wine list is ever-growing, and service is thoughtful and considerate.

A YORK PUB CRAWL

One of the city's oldest inns, **The Black Swan,** Peaseholme Green (☎ **01904/686911**), is a fine, timbered, frame house that was once the home of the lord mayor of York in 1417; the mother of Gen. James Wolfe of Québec also lived here. You can enjoy pub meals in front of a log fire in a brick inglenook. There are fish and chips, burgers and steak. This is one of York's "musical pubs," featuring live folk music on Thursday, with a small cover charge.

Situated at the base of the Ouse Bridge, a few steps from the edge of the river, the 16th-century **Kings Arms Public House,** King's Staith (☎ **01904/659435**), is boisterous and fun. A historic monument in its own right, it's filled with charm and character and has the ceiling beams, paneling, and weathered brickwork you'd expect. In summer, rows of outdoor tables are placed beside the river. Your hosts serve a full range of draft and bottled beers, the most popular of which (Samuel Smith's) is still brewed in Tadcaster, only 10 miles away. The ghost walk we recommend leaves here every night at 8pm (see box above).

On a pedestrian street in Old York, **Ye Olde Starre Inne,** 40 Stonegate (☎ **01904/623063**), dates from 1644 and is York's oldest licensed pub. An inn (of one kind or another) has stood on this spot since 900. In a pub said to be haunted by an old woman, a little girl, and a cat, you enter into an atmosphere of cast-iron tables, an open fireplace, oak Victorian settles, and time-blackened beams. Recently, the owners have added a year-round glassed-in garden. In all types of weather, guests can enjoy the plants and the view of the minster from their tables here.

2 Leeds

204 miles NW of London; 75 miles NE of Liverpool; 43 miles NE of Manchester; 74 miles N of Nottingham

The foundations for a permanent community were laid nearly 2,000 years ago when the Romans set up a small camp here called Cambodunum, but the next step toward modern Leeds didn't come until the 7th century, when the Northumbrian King Edwin established a residence. Kirkstall Abbey was founded in 1152, and in 1207 Leeds finally obtained its charter and laid out the grid pattern still evident in the streets today.

During the medieval era, Leeds took the Golden Fleece as its coat of arms, representative of its growth and importance as a wool town. In time, it became the greatest center of cloth trade in the region. Industrial advancements have played a great role in the development of the city, with the introduction of steam power leading to the development of the coal fields to the south. Other innovations allowed the continued growth of its textile industry, as well as the rapid development of such upstart industries as printing, tailoring, and engineering. The Victorian era marked the city's glory days.

After languishing for years and being dismissed for its industrial blight, the city is moving progressively forward again today. It's experiencing some economic growth, and many of the great Victorian buildings have been renovated in its bustling central core: The Corn Exchange, The Grand Theatre, and the Victoria Quarter. Add to this the recently passed "24-Hour City Initiative," making it the only U.K. location to not only allow but encourage around-the-clock work and entertainment options, and you've got an up-and-coming city with a lot of new energy.

ESSENTIALS

GETTING THERE **Leeds-Bradford International Airport** (☎ **0113/2509696**), has daily flights to and from London and Manchester, with air transport taking less than an hour. There is also a 24-hour direct rail link between Manchester airport and Leeds.

Trains from London's King's Cross Station arrive hourly during the day, with the trip taking about 2 hours. For schedules and information, call ☎ **0345/484950.**

Leeds is also serviced daily by **National Express** buses from London. For schedules and information, call ☎ **0990/808080.**

Leeds lies at the crossroads of the North/South M1 and East/West M62 routes, making it easily accessible by car from anywhere in England or Scotland.

VISITOR INFORMATION The **Gateway Yorkshire Regional Travel & Tourist Information Centre,** The Arcade, City Station (☎ **0113/2425242**), is open Monday through Saturday from 9:30am to 6pm and Sunday from 10am to 4pm. Leeds also has a Web site (www.leeds.gov.uk) with information on transportation, lodging, dining, shopping, and entertainment in the city.

Information on local bus and train routes and times is available by calling **Metroline** at ☎ **0113/2457676.**

SPECIAL EVENTS In July, more than 40,000 opera lovers turn out at **Temple Newsam,** Temple Newsam Road, off Selby Road (☎ **0113/2425242**), for the single performance of Opera in the Park, the largest free outdoor opera concert in the United Kingdom. The gargantuan **Party in the Park** (☎ **0113/2478222**), also held at Temple Newsam, is one of the largest free pop and rock concerts in the United Kingdom. It's usually held the day following Opera in the Park, and features some of the hottest acts in rock music.

Film buffs turn out in droves for the annual **Leeds International Film Festival** (☎ **0113/2478308**). Screened in October at cinemas throughout Leeds, it's the only theme-based film festival in the United Kingdom. It regularly features British as well as world-premiere films, and hosts film-related lectures, seminars, and workshops.

EXPLORING LEEDS

Despite its longtime reputation as a grimy northern industrial city, Leeds will surprise you with the beauty and diversity of its **City Centre,** where £400 million ($640 million) has been invested in both new construction and renovation of warehouses and landmark Victorian structures into homes, lodging, shops, and restaurants along The Waterfront and in the central shopping district.

✪ **Leeds City Art Gallery.** The Headrow. ☎ **0113/2478248.** Free admission. Mon–Tues and Thurs–Sat 10am–5pm, Wed 10am–8pm, Sun 1–5pm.

Spread over three floors, this gallery, founded in 1888, houses England's best collection of 20th-century art outside of London, including impressive collections of French postimpressionist paintings, contemporary British sculpture, prints, watercolors, and drawings. Throughout the year it also hosts visiting exhibits, enhanced by workshops, talks, and other related events.

Located within the gallery, the **Craft Centre and Design Gallery** (☎ **0113/2478241**), showcases contemporary ceramics, jewelry, prints, textiles, and applied arts from around the world, as well as hosts openings and exhibits by local and regional artists working within these mediums.

The Henry Moore Institute. 74 The Headrow. ☎ **0113/2343158.** Mon–Tues and Thurs–Sun 10am–5:30pm, Wed 10am–9pm.

Located next door to the City Art Gallery, this is the largest sculpture gallery in Europe, as well as the first devoted to the display, study, and research of sculpture from all periods and cultures. The institute is named after the greatest British sculptor of the 20th century, Henry Moore (1898–1986), who was a Yorkshireman. This center shows the range of his accomplishments, from his early *Reclining Figure* (1929) to his most powerful postwar statements like *Meat Porters.* The works of many of Moore's contemporaries are also displayed. Lectures throughout the year supplement the institute's exhibitions.

Leeds

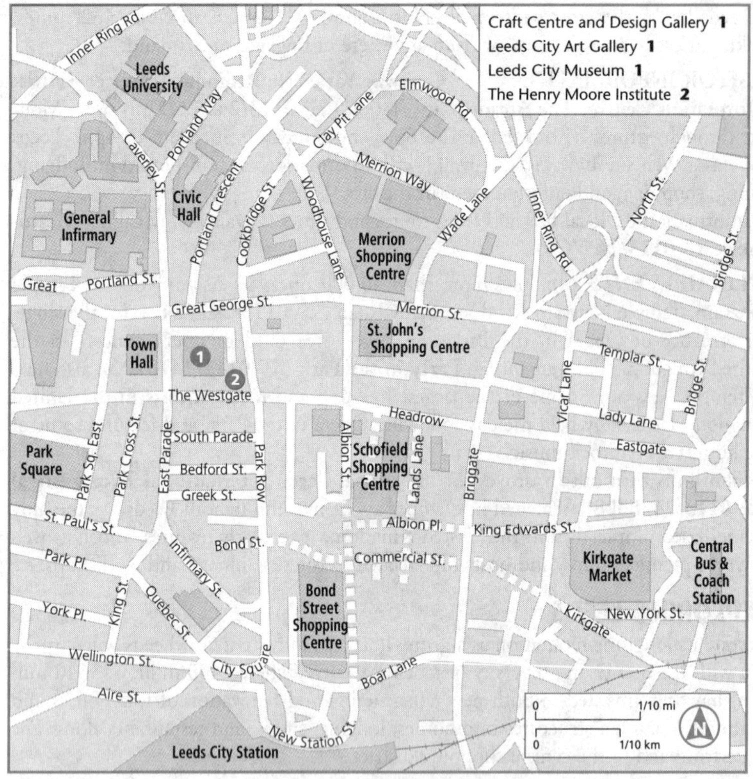

Royal Armouries Museum. Armouries Dr. ☎ **0113/2201999.** Admission £7.95 ($13.50) adults, £6.95 ($11.80) seniors and students, £4.95 ($8.40) children, £23.95 ($40.70) family ticket. Mar 4–Nov 8 daily 10:30am–5:30pm; off-season Mon–Fri 10:30am–4:30pm, Sat–Sun 10:30am–5:30pm. Closed Dec 24–25.

A notable construction along The Waterfront, this £42 million facility is the home of London Tower's Royal Armouries, England's oldest museum, dating from the working arsenal of the medieval kings. It is designed to exhibit the many pieces that have been in perpetual storage because of inadequate facilities in London. The museum illustrates the development and use of arms and armor for war, sport, hunting, self-defense, and fashion.

Temple Newsam House. Temple Newsam Rd. (off Selby Rd.; 4 miles from Leeds City Centre off the A63). ☎ **0113/2647321.** Admission £2 ($3.40) adults, £1 ($1.70) seniors and students, 50p (85¢) for children accompanied by adult. Summer Tues–Sat 10am–5pm, Sun 1–5pm; Winter Tues–Sat 10am–4pm, Sun noon–4pm.

This was the birthplace, in 1545, of the ill-fated Lord Darnley, husband of Mary Queen of Scots. Construction began on this Tudor-Jacobean mansion in 1521, and substantial remodeling occurred in both the 17th and late 18th centuries. It stands as an odd but beautiful tribute to several eras of architecture. Today, it houses a splendid collection of silver and Chippendale furniture. The surrounding 1,200 acres of parkland includes the popular Home Farm, a breeding ground for rare farm animals, and the annual venue for Opera in the Park.

WHERE TO STAY

If you'd like advice on local lodging, or if you'd just like to tell someone your price range and requirements and let them book you a room, contact the **Gateway Yorkshire Accommodation Booking Line** (☎ **0800/808050** or 0113/2425242). For a £2 ($3.40) handling fee and a refundable deposit of 10% of your first night's stay, they'll find you a bed for the night.

Aragon Hotel. 250 Stainbeck Lane, Leeds LS7 2PS. ☎ **0113/2759306.** Fax 0113/2757166. 12 units. TV TEL. £53.90 ($91.65) double. Rates include English breakfast. AE, DC, MC, V. From Leeds, follow A61 Harrogate signs out of the city. This becomes Scott Hall Rd. (A61). Take the 2nd roundabout, turning left onto Stainbeck Lane, and follow it down one hill and up another. The hotel is on the right. It is also conveniently located about 200 yd. from a bus stop with routes to Leeds and the surrounding area.

Located only 2 miles from City Centre, this small family-run hotel is set well back from the road on an acre of gardens. The surrounding properties stretch out in open fields and woods. Accommodations, while not luxurious, are neat and comfortable, and each room includes tea- and coffeemaking facilities. Bedrooms range from small to mid-size, each with a small bath with a shower stall. There's a pleasant lounge for resident's that features a large marble fireplace, as well as a full bar, both of which look out over the gardens. When you get hungry, dinner is available in the 22-seat dining room. (The hotel is completely no-smoking)

✪ **42 The Calls.** 42 The Calls, Leeds LS2 7EW. ☎ **0113/2440099.** Fax 0113/2344100. www.42thecalls.co.uk. E-mail: hotel@42thecalls.co.uk. 41 units. MINIBAR TV TEL. £128–£150 ($217.60–$255) double; from £185 ($314.50) suite. AE, DC, MC, V.

Overlooking the River Aire in the heart of Leeds, this is a small but deluxe hotel. It's the most tranquil and elegant choice in Leeds, created from an 18th-century grain mill in a once dilapidated waterfront area that's all high-tech and high-comfort now. Each room is individually designed with its own fabrics and color scheme, ranging from more traditional rooms to the Black Room, with a huge black bed and black-striped walls, or Room 303, with an original winch hanging from the ceiling—a nod to the building's origins. Business travelers will appreciate the three phones in every room, the full-size work desk, an individual fax machine on request, and dictation by arrangement. Each room includes a CD player, satellite TV, a quality mattress, a coffeemaker, a hair dryer, and a trouser press. Baths feature deluxe toiletries, plush towels, and bathrobes. There's a comfortable small bar tucked away in a corner of the lobby, and a nice selection of CDs and videos are available in the lobby.

You can order breakfast in, and have it passed into your room without disturbance via an ingenious "two-way pass" system, or you can enjoy excellent meals at the neighboring Brasserie 44 or Pool Court at 42. Amenities include access to nearby health club, car-rental desk, concierge, dry cleaning/laundry, baby-sitting, secretarial services, courtesy car.

Haley's Hotel & Restaurant. Shire Oak Rd. (2 miles from Leeds City Centre and 7 miles from Leeds/Bradford International Airport), Headingley, Leeds LS6 2DE. ☎ **0113/2784446.** Fax 0113/2753342. www.haley's.co.uk. 29 units. TV TEL. £130–£150 ($221–$255) double; from £210 ($357) suite. Rates include English or continental breakfast. AE, DC, MC, V.

Located in a quiet, tree-lined cul-de-sac just off the main Otley-Leeds road (A660), this town-house hotel, set up in a Victorian mansion, makes it easy to forget you're in the suburbs of a major metropolitan area. The hotel's rooms are comfortably laid out and opt for tasteful individuality, each with its own fabrics and period-specific, polished, natural wood antiques. Features include a work desk with telephone, a trouser press, an iron and ironing board, a hair dryer and tea-and coffeemakers. As for the beds, management accurately quotes Charles Dickens, "It would make anyone go to sleep, that bedstead would, whether they wanted to or not." The staff is diligent, accommodating guests with such options as a late supper or shoe-cleaning service. The hotel also offers 24-hour room service and dry cleaning/laundry.

Haley's Restaurant offers modern British table d'hôte and à la carte options so enticing that it's earned two AA rosettes for cuisine. In fact, it's so popular you'd better make your dinner reservations when you book a room. See "Where to Dine," below for a review.

✪ **Oulton Hall.** Rothwell Lane (5 1/2 miles from Leeds by A61 and A639), Oulton, Leeds LS26 8HN. ☎ **0113/2821000.** Fax 0113/2828066. 152 units. MINIBAR TV TEL. £160 ($272) double; £205–£245 ($348.50–$416.50) suite. Rates include English breakfast. AE, DC, MC, V.

A painstakingly restored 1850s Italianate mansion, this hotel has an atmosphere of pure elegance, from the black-and-white tiled front entrance and the damask-hung walls of the public rooms with their great crystal chandeliers, to the library with its mahogany wall paneling and window seat. You can enjoy butler service in the drawing room, a drink in the plush red-leather interior of the Calverley Bar, or stroll through formal gardens re-created to the original 19th-century plans. Most of the well-furnished bedrooms are in the modern wing; the grand suites are in the original house. Two rooms are equipped for persons with disabilities. Bedrooms, midsize to spacious, enjoy views of the well-manicured grounds and championship golf course. There is a no-smoking policy in 128 bedrooms. Baths have a hair dryer.

In the Brontë Restaurant, which was awarded an AA rosette for its cuisine, the service is impeccable and the wine list will please any palate. Amenities include championship 9- and 18-hole golf courses and driving range, croquet lawn, squash courts, full gym, indoor heated pool, Jacuzzi, sauna, steam room, aerobics classes, and beauty therapy.

WHERE TO DINE

Haley's Restaurant. In Haley's Hotel, Shire Oak Rd., Headingley. ☎ **0113/2784446.** Reservations required well in advance. Main courses £18–£22 ($30.60–$37.40); fixed-price Sun lunch £15.95 ($27.10) for 3 courses. AE, DC, MC, V. Mon–Sat 7:15–9:45pm, Sun 12:15–2pm. Closed Dec 26–30. BRITISH.

This hotel restaurant, in a beautifully restored Victorian mansion, is so popular among locals that even the guests have to reserve long in advance. The understated browns and creams of the restaurant's decor contribute to a relaxed atmosphere.

Chef John Vennell changes his à la carte dinner menu monthly to use the freshest, best market ingredients. Starters might include a warm cheese fondue, or a terrine of chicken, ham and rabbit; followed by a succulent pork confit served with apples, smoked bacon, and an onion sauce, or a duo of lemon sole and sea bass with a shallot and red wine confit and watercress sauce; finished with orange delice in a hazelnut tulip served with a tangy lime coulis. The wine cellar has interesting offerings from around the world.

Leodis Brasserie. Victoria Mill, Sovereign St. ☎ **0113/2421010.** Reservations recommended. Main courses £8.90–£15.90 ($15.15–$27.05); fixed-price lunch £14.95 ($25.40). AE, DC, MC, V. Mon–Fri noon–2pm and 6–10pm, Sat 6–11pm. BRITISH.

Another fine choice in the revitalized canal district, Leodis is housed in an artfully renovated old mill. You dine in a comfortable dining space created from the mill's original cast-iron columns and new glass screens.

The menu here changes weekly. At lunch, there are four three-course set meals to choose from, plus several à la carte options. Dishes are often quite simple, yet incredibly well prepared. Starters might include fish cakes in tomato-lime salsa, followed by a main course of roast cod with warm Italian dressing, finished with caramelized burnt orange crème or a chocolate marquise. There's a full bar and a lengthy wine list as well.

✪ **Pool Court at 42.** 42–44 The Calls. ☎ **0113/2444242.** Reservations recommended. Fixed-price 3-course lunch £19 ($32.30), Fixed-price 3-course dinner £35 ($59.50). AE, DC, MC, V. Mon–Fri noon–2pm; Mon–Thurs 7–10pm, Fri–Sat 7–10:30pm. CONTINENTAL.

This small, elegant restaurant with its popular riverside terrace is built into the lodging at 42 The Calls, but functions independently and has a private street entrance. It's an intimate space, seating only 38 diners, and the modern decor is stylish and refined. It's a comfortable spot, with great attention to detail and delectable food.

The menu is entirely a set-price affair, though you'll have a few choices for each course. Chef Jeff Baker scours the markets to see what's freshest and most abundant, then updates his menu often, with creations such as roast scallops of peppered duck foie gras, or sea scallops with braised fennel in a red wine and lobster sauce. You can finish with one of the *assiettes,* a combination of three desserts, usually with a central theme, such as assiette of chocolate. There are some unusual selections on the wine list as well.

Rascasse. Canal Wharf, Water Lane. ☎ **0113/2446611.** Reservations recommended. Fixed-price 2-course lunch £13.50 ($22.95), £18 ($30.60) for 3 courses; main courses £10.50–£18.50 ($17.85–$31.45). AE, DC, MC, V. Mon–Fri noon–2pm; Mon–Thurs 6:30–10pm, Fri–Sat 6:30–10:30pm. CONTINENTAL.

When you step into this airy, light restaurant, you might forget that you're setting foot in an early-19th-century extension of a granary. Located in the revitalized canal district, Mark Nesbitts restaurant has taken what's best about its surroundings—a large, solid room and waterfront location—and reworked them into a stylish modern restaurant.

The same can be said of his menu, a seasonal offering of classic dishes and ingredients. He reinterprets golden oldie recipes with flavor and flair. Examples include starters like risotto of English lobster, tarragon and essence of lobster, or a salad of fresh figs, Parma ham, and purple basil. Main courses include filet of Scotch beef, roast polenta, wild mushrooms and essence of flap mushrooms; or old-smoked haddock, bubble and squeak (cabbage and potatoes) and sauce Béarnaise. A tempting dessert is the citrus parfait with gin and tonic sorbet.

LEEDS AFTER DARK

Thanks to a recently passed city initiative aimed at relaxing licensing restrictions and increasing late-night entertainment options, it's safe to say that Leeds now rocks around the clock. It was already humming with classical concerts, opera, jazz, dance, theater, cinema, rock and dance clubs, cafes, and pubs.

THE CLUB & MUSIC SCENE Leeds has a thriving rock scene, with recent bands like Sisters of Mercy and The Mission rising out of the music scene at The Warehouse. Today's up-and-coming music scene is, not surprisingly, very influenced by the Manchester scene, but innovative bands like Black Star Liner, Bedlam A Go Go, and Embrace show that Leeds still has a musical voice all its own.

The **Cockpit,** Bridge House, Swinegate (☎ **0113/2441573**), can host about 600 fans, who turn out to hear the latest indie bands in a converted railway arch setting. Open Thursday to Saturday night with a cover charge ranging from £3 to £5 ($5.10 to $8.50).

For real intimacy, you can't beat the **Duchess of York,** Vicar Lane (☎ **0113/2453929**), the city's most famous music pub, unrivaled in its nightly schedule of up-and-coming bands.

When you'd rather groove to the beat than watch the guitarist, you can head to a vast array of dance clubs around town. Leeds' dance-music scene is thriving, as is evident by the presence of such internationally acclaimed clubs as **The Warehouse,** Somers Street (☎ **0113/2461033**), on Saturday, with admission for £10 ($17).

You'll find the jazz you're looking for at **Arts Café,** 42 Call Lane (☎ **0113/2438243**), a European-style cafe bar that offers tapas, bottled beers, and coffees to accompany its occasional live jazz. **The Underground,** Cookridge Street, at the back of the Town & Country Club (☎ **0113/2443403**), offers lunch and evening jazz, featuring Thursday-night salsa and other Latin music.

Considering its size, there is a substantial gay scene in Leeds. The most popular club at the moment is **Queens Court,** Lower Briggate (☎ **0113/2459449).** Downstairs is a restaurant and bar which is open daily from 11am to 11pm; after which, head upstairs for the disco which is open Monday to Sunday from 11pm to 2am. The other hot spot at the moment is **The Bridge Inn,** 1–5 Bridge Inn (☎ **0113/2444734**), which has a friendly local pub atmosphere and becomes increasingly clubby as the night progresses. There is a cover of £3 ($5.10).

PUBS Stop by **Whitelocks,** Turks Head Yard (☎ **0113/2453950**), in the alley of Briggate, opposite Marks and Spencers. There's a copper-topped bar with a handmade ceramic-tile front, a marble sandwich bar, old advertising mirrors, and stained-glass windows. Locals keep the conversation flowing in a thick, northern accent. If you get hungry, there's cheap traditional pub grub. Tap selections are varied and quite good, including McEwans 80, Youngers IPA, Scotch, and Theakston's Old Peculiar.

Hearkening back to Leeds' glory days, **Victoria,** Great George Street (☎ **0113/2451386**), is every bit as Victorian as its name suggests, with ornate globe lamps, etched mirrors, and a well-adorned bar. Politicians and lawyers frequent the place. Join in the conversation or sit back and listen while you enjoy a pint of Tetley's Mild and maybe a bar snack or two.

THE PERFORMING ARTS **Leeds Town Hall,** The Headrow (☎ **0113/2477985,** or box office 0113/2476962), hosts orchestras from around the globe as part of the city's annual **International Concert Season,** and is also home to the world-famous **Leeds International Pianoforte Competition,** held every 3 years, with the next scheduled competition in 2000. Opera North offers on average three to four productions during its October-through-April seasonal run at the **Leeds Grand Theatre and Opera House,** New Briggate (☎ **0113/2226222**), featuring a beautifully renovated 1,500-seat auditorium behind its original 1878 Victorian facade.

Theatergoers are much impressed by the facilities at the £12 million ($19.2 million) **West Yorkshire Playhouse,** Playhouse Square, Quarry Hill (☎ **0113/2137700**), home to the "national theatre of the north." Playhouse artistic director Jude Kelly started out strong in the early inaugural seasons, with 17 productions, including eight British or world premieres. There's been no slowing down since then, and you can find a dramatic offering at most any time in either The Playhouse's Quarry Auditorium, which seats 750, or The Courtyard, seating 350. The Playhouse, which is the cornerstone of a proposed £70 million ($112 million) Quarry Hill arts complex, also hosts other events throughout the year, including the annual Jazz at the Playhouse series.

The **Yorkshire Dance Centre,** St. Peters Building, York Street (☎ **0113/2439867**), is home of the internationally renowned **Phoenix Dance Troupe.**

3 Bradford

212 miles N of London; 32 miles NE of Manchester; 9 miles W of Leeds

This city of nearly half a million souls retains a rich ethnic heritage from the succession of immigrants who came to work the mills beginning in the mid-19th century. Generations of Irish, German, Italian, Eastern European, and later, Asian and African Caribbean immigrants, today give this West Yorkshire town an international flavor.

Bradford boosters like to say the town is one of the best-kept secrets in the United Kingdom. High-tech firms, galleries, and museums have displaced many of the textile factories of the past. Centrally located between the Yorkshire Dales and the Pennines, Bradford provides a nice diversion and is convenient to a historic countryside where the Brontës once dwelled and armor-covered soldiers clashed in the Wars of the Roses.

ESSENTIALS

GETTING THERE Bradford is readily reached by car via the M62 and M606.

Most rail links go through nearby Leeds (see section 2, above), but at least one direct train each day connects London's Kings Cross Station with Bradford (a 3-hr. trip). Train travel from Manchester takes about 1 hour; it's 3 hours from Birmingham.

Leeds/Bradford Airport (☎ **0113/2509696**) is located about 10 miles from Bradford, and a number of scheduled flights connect to London's Heathrow and Gatwick airports and most major regional U.K. airports. A taxi from the airport to town costs about £10 ($16.50). Bus service schedules and Day Rover discounted tickets are available through the tourist office.

VISITOR INFORMATION The **Bradford Tourist Information Centre** (☎ **01274/753678**). The center assists visitors in selecting accommodations or purchasing tickets, and provides public-transit timetables and city guides. Hours are Monday through Friday from 9am to 5:30pm and Saturday from 9am to 5pm. If you need to make a personal visit, call the number above for the address which will be shifted in the lifetime of this edition, although the phone number will remain the same.

EXPLORING BRADFORD

Bradford's museums, mill shops, and restaurants provide the main attractions for tourists. The city also boasts Bradford University, one of the better regional universities in the United Kingdom.

The Industrial Museum and Horse at Work, Moorside Mills, Moorside Road (☎ **01274/631756**), depicts mill life for worker and owner in the 1870s and offers Shire horse rides for kids. The **Saltaire,** Salt's Mill, is the restored model factory-community developed in the mid-19th century by mill owner and philanthropist Titus Salt. The **1853 Gallery** at Saltaire (☎ **01274/531163**) exhibits more than 400 works of local artist David Hockney, among other works.

Visitors can travel by steam-driven train on the **Keighley & Worth Valley Railway** (☎ **01535/647777**) for a tour of Brontë Country in Haworth, through Oakworth's Edwardian station, and Damen's Station, billed as Britain's smallest rail station. A Day Rover ticket costs £8 ($13.20).

The **National Museum of Photography, Film, and Television,** Pictureville (☎ **01274/727488**), captures the history of photography, film, and television in audiovisual presentations that span the past 150 years. The 5-story-high IMAX screen, the largest in England, explores a dazzling variety of cinematic images in a series of new and continuing exhibitions. Admission to the museum is free; the IMAX movie costs £5.80 ($9.85) and advance booking is recommended. Open Tuesday through Sunday from 10am to 6pm.

Bradford's textile industry is still represented in dozens of area mill shops where bargain hunters may find a great variety of mohair, pure-wool yarns, fabrics, sportswear, and other clothing and accessories. Some mill shops provide tours of factory spinning, weaving, and textile finishing.

Listers Mill Shop, Manningham Hills, Heaton Road (☎ **01274/542222**), specializes in made-to-measure services for upholstered furniture, curtains, cushions, and other furnishings. **Suit Length & Fabric Centre,** Wakefield Road, Dudley Hill (☎ **01274/729103**), will customize suits and garments for the individual tastes and fit of shoppers. **British Mohair Spinners,** Valley Road (☎ **01274/728456**), showcases the art of spinning hair and cotton into the heavy, shiny mohair fabric.

WHERE TO STAY

Restaurant Nineteen (see "Where to Dine," below) also rents rooms.

The Guide Post Hotel. Common Rd. (3 miles from Junction 26 of M62), Low Moor, Bradford, W. Yorkshire BD12 OST. ☎ **01274/607866.** Fax 01274/671085. 43 units. TV TEL. Mon–Thurs £72.50 ($123.25) double, Fri–Sat £47.50 ($80.75) double. Rates include breakfast. AE, DC, MC, V.

Welcoming both business and leisure travelers, this is a winning little choice. You get a warm welcome as you're shown to your spacious, well-furnished room, filled with all the amenities needed, including beverage-making equipment and satellite TV. The more expensive executive rooms have a spacious lounge area and include trouser-pressing facilities. Three rooms are large enough for families; seven rooms are set aside for nonsmokers. The hotel is known for its restaurant, serving a good English Anglo/Gaelic cuisine, with an affordable wine list. There's also a spacious bar area.

Victoria Hotel. Bridge St., Bradford, W. Yorkshire BD1 1JX. ☎ **01274/728706.** Fax 01274/736358. Email: admin@gb6540-net.com. 60 units. TV TEL. £90–£108 ($153–$183.60) double; £120 ($204) suite. AE, DC, MC, V. From the M62, take Junction 26 to the M606, then to A6177 and A611, and exit at roundabout to Hallings; turn right at traffic light and hotel is at left.

Built in 1875, the Victoria in the City Centre has been entirely restored since 1995. Once the showpiece of the Lancashire and Yorkshire Railway, the hotel provides stylish accommodations at affordable rates. The well-furnished bedrooms all have stereos, VCRs, trouser presses, hair dryers, and superb bathrooms with power showers and thick towels. Bedrooms come in various shapes and sizes, each with a quality mattress. Forty bedrooms are rented to nonsmokers, and there are three family rooms. Vic and Bert's restaurant is a modern interpretation of a Parisian brasserie (see "Where to Dine," below). Facilities include the Pie Eyed Parrot Pub, and a gym and sauna.

WHERE TO DINE

Bradford is called "the curry capital of the U.K.," boasting a vast array of Asian restaurants featuring dishes from Kashmir, Gujerat, the Punjab, and beyond.

Bombay Brasserie. Simes St. ☎ **01274/737564.** Main courses £5.75–£9.95 ($9.80–$16.90); set-price menu for 4 £13.75 ($23.40) per person. MC, V. Mon–Sat noon–2pm; Mon–Thurs 6pm–midnight, Fri–Sat 6pm–1am. NORTH INDIAN/BANGLADESHI.

Here you'll find a variety of curry dishes, from mild versions such as *korma* (with nuts and cream) and *bhoona* to medium-strength curries like *dhansak* (lentil-based curry) and *jal-frezi* (dry curried meat cooked in onion slices). For those who like their curry hot, there's *madras* and *very* hot *phal* dishes. The restaurant also caters to vegetarian tastes.

Restaurant Nineteen. N. Park Rd., Heaton. ☎ **01274/492559.** Fax 01274/483827. Reservations recommended. 3-course fixed-price dinner £12.95–£19.95 ($22–$33.90). AE, MC, V. Tues–Fri noon–2:30pm; Tues–Sat 6:30–10pm, Sat 7–10pm. Closed 2 weeks in Dec–Jan. ENGLISH/CONTINENTAL.

This highly rated, classic restaurant—the best in Bradford—takes up the main floor of a onetime mill-owner's Victorian mansion that overlooks Lister Park. Main course samplings include seafood bass with a potato cake, marinated venison, and roast leg of rabbit stuffed with foie gras purée. Even the soups have imagination and flair—witness the pumpkin and smoked haddock or the zucchini and sweet corn flavored with cream of coconut. The cooking is light and deft, and the service is of a high standard.

If dessert, perhaps a chocolate pot filled with frozen coffee parfait and served with a pear compote, has got you too stuffed to move, you can also stay here. It's a rather elegant B&B, renting four classy rooms, all with bathroom, shower, TV, and phone, at rates from £89 ($146.85) for a double, including breakfast. Many English stars such as Derek Jacobi, appearing at the nearby Alhambra Theatre, often stay here.

Vic and Bert's. In the Victoria Hotel, Bridge St. ☎ **01274/728706.** Reservations recommended. Main courses £12.95–£14.95 ($22–$25.40); fixed-price 3-course menu £14.50 ($24.65). AE, DC, MC, V. Mon–Fri noon–2pm; daily 7–10pm. CONTINENTAL.

This elegant brasserie offers wood-grill cooking with an Oriental flavor. The clever chefs here have managed to lighten and modernize many dishes, although still showing a respect for traditional favorites. Their eclectic menu borrows liberally from around the world, and may include tuna steak marinated in Thai fish sauce and served over noodles, Japanese sushi rolls, and prawn and curried vegetables. For the heartier appetite, guests may select from courses featuring beef bourguignonne, deep-fried duck pancakes, or the popular "bottomless" bowl of spaghetti.

BRADFORD AFTER DARK

The **Alhambra Theatre,** Morley Street (☎ **01274/752000**), offers a variety of presentations ranging from amateur to professional. At certain times of the year, leading actors of the English stage and screen may appear here. You can also see children's theater, ballet, and musicals. Ticket prices vary depending upon the type of performance. The theater is closed for a few weeks in August.

But perhaps you're just looking for a local pub. In the city center, the **Shoulder of Mutton,** 28 Kirkgate (☎ **01274/726038**), has a beer garden that comes complete with flower beds and hanging baskets. The oldest brewery in Yorkshire, it was originally Samuel Smith's Old Brewery. Lunch is available, and they also sell real ale here. As many as 200 drinkers can crowd in here on a summer night.

As an alternative choice, try the old-fashioned ale house, the **Fighting Cock,** 21–23 Preston St. (☎ **01274/726907**), with its bare floors and 12 different bitters. The best ales are Exmoor Gold, Timothy Taylors, Black Sheep, and Green King Albert, but they also sell foreign-bottled beers and farm ciders. On nippy nights, coal fires keep the atmosphere mellow. Bar snacks are among the most reasonable in town, and the house specialty is chili (the chef guards the recipe).

4 Haworth: Home of the Brontës

45 miles SW of York; 21 miles W of Leeds

✪ **Haworth,** a village on the high moor of the Pennines, is famous as the home of the Brontës, the most visited literary shrine in England after Stratford-upon-Avon.

ESSENTIALS

GETTING THERE To reach Haworth by rail, take the West Yorkshire Metrotrain from Leeds City Station to Keighley (it leaves approximately every 30 min.). Change trains at Keighley and take the Keighley and Worth Valley Railway to Haworth and Oxenhope. Train services operate every weekend throughout the year, with 7 to 12 departures. From late June to the beginning of September, trains also run four times a day Monday through Friday. For general inquiries, call ☎ **01535/645214;** for a 24-hour timetable, dial ☎ **01535/647777.**

Yorkshire Rider, a private company, offers bus service between Hebden Bridge (which has rail links to Leeds and York) and Haworth. Bus no. 500 makes the trip between Hebden Bridge and Haworth, four trips per day Sunday through Friday and five on Saturday. For information, call ☎ **01422/365985.**

If you're driving from York, head west toward Leeds on A64 approaching the A6120 Ring Road to Shipley; then take A650 to Keighley, and finally link up with the B6142 south to Haworth.

VISITOR INFORMATION The **Tourist Information Centre** is at 2–4 West Lane in Haworth (☎ **01535/642329**). It's open April through October daily from 9:30am to 5:30pm; November through March daily from 9:30am to 5pm (closed December 24–26).

LITERARY LANDMARKS

Anne Brontë wrote two novels, *The Tenant of Wildfell Hall* and *Agnes Grey;* Charlotte wrote two masterpieces, *Jane Eyre* and *Villette,* which depicted her experiences as a teacher, as well as several other novels; and Emily is the author of *Wuthering Heights,* a novel of passion and haunting melancholy. Charlotte and Emily are buried in the family vault under the **Church of St. Michael.**

While in Haworth, you'll want to visit the **Brontë Weaving Shed,** Townend Mill (☎ **01535/646217**). The shop is not far from the Brontë Parsonage, and features the famous Brontë tweed, which combines browns, greens, and oranges to evoke the look of the local countryside.

Brontë Parsonage Museum. Church St. ☎ **01535/642323.** Admission £3.80 ($6.45) adults, £1.20 ($2.05) children; free for children under 5; £8.80 ($14.95) family ticket (2 adults and 3 children). Apr–Sept daily 10am–5pm, Oct–Mar daily 11am–4:30pm. Closed mid-Jan to early Feb and at Christmastime.

The parsonage where the Brontë family lived has been preserved as this museum, which houses their furniture, personal treasures, pictures, books, and manuscripts. The stone-sided parsonage, originally built near the top of the village in 1777, was assigned for the course of his lifetime as the residence of the Brontë's father, Patrick, the Perpetual Curator of the Church of St. Michael and All Angel's Church. Regrettably, the church tended by the Brontës was demolished in 1870; it was rebuilt in its present form the same year. The parsonage contains a walled garden very similar to the one cultivated by the Brontës, five bedrooms, and a collection of family furniture (some bought with proceeds from Charlotte's literary success), as well as personal effects, pictures and paintings, and original manuscripts. It also contains the largest archive of family correspondence in the world.

The museum is maintained by a professional staff selected by the Brontë Society, an organization established in 1893 to perpetuate the memory and legacy of Britain's most famous literary family. Contributions to the society are welcomed. The museum tends to be extremely crowded in July and August.

WHERE TO STAY

Old White Lion Hotel. 6 West Lane, Haworth near Keighley, W. Yorkshire BD22 8DU. ☎ **01535/642313.** Fax 01535/646222. www.oldwhitelionhotel.com. E-mail: inquiries@oldwhitelionhotel.com. 14 units. TV TEL. £60–£68 ($102–$115.60) double. Rates include English breakfast. AE, DC, MC, V.

At the top of a cobblestone street, this hotel was built around 1700 with a solid stone roof. It's almost next door to the church where the Reverend Brontë preached, as well as the parsonage where the family lived. Paul and Christopher Bradford welcome visitors from all over the world to their warm, cheerful, and comfortable hotel. Although full of old-world charm, all rooms are completely up-to-date. Room size varies considerably, but each is attractively furnished and has a comfortable bed and a small bathroom. Three rooms are large enough to rent to families.

Meals feature fresh vegetables and are table d'hôte in the evenings. Bar snacks include the usual favorites: ploughman's lunch, hot pies, fish, and sandwiches.

WHERE TO DINE

Weaver's Restaurant. 15 West Lane. ☎ **01535/643822.** Reservations recommended. Main courses £8.95–£15.95 ($15.20–$27.10) 3-course fixed-price dinner £13.50 ($22.95). AE, DC, MC, V. Tues–Sat 7–9:30pm. MODERN BRITISH.

The best restaurant in the Brontë hometown, this spot is British to the core. It not only has an inviting, informal atmosphere, but it serves excellent food made with fresh ingredients. Jane and Colin Rushworth are quite talented in the kitchen. Dinners might include such classic dishes as slow-cooked Yorkshire lamb. If available, try one of the Gressingham ducks, which are widely praised in the United Kingdom. For dessert, try a British cheese or one of the homemade delicacies. The restaurant is likely to be closed for vacation for a certain period each summer, so call in advance to check. They also rent four bedrooms of high caliber that cost £75 ($127.50) for a double.

5 Yorkshire's Country Houses, Castles & More

Yorkshire's battle-scarred castles, Gothic abbeys, and great country manor houses (from all periods) are unrivaled anywhere in Britain. Here are some of the highlights.

IN NORTH YORKSHIRE

✪ **Castle Howard.** Malton (15 miles northeast of York, 3 miles off A64). ☎ **01653/648333.** Admission £7 ($11.90) adults, £6.50 ($11.05) seniors and students, £4.50 ($7.65) children. Mid-Mar to late Oct, grounds daily 10am–5pm, house daily 11am–5pm (with last admission at 4:30pm).

In its dramatic setting of lakes, fountains, and extensive gardens, Castle Howard, the 18th-century palace designed by Sir John Vanbrugh, is undoubtedly the finest private residence in Yorkshire. The principal location for the TV miniseries *Brideshead Revisited,* this was the first major achievement of the architect who later created the lavish Blenheim Palace near Oxford. The Yorkshire palace was begun in 1699 for the third earl of Carlisle, Charles Howard.

The striking facade is topped by a painted and gilded dome, which reaches more than 80 feet into the air. The interior boasts a 192-foot-long gallery, as well as a chapel with magnificent stained-glass windows by the 19th-century artist Sir Edward Burne-Jones. Besides the collections of antique furniture, porcelains, and sculpture, the castle has many important paintings, including a portrait of Henry VIII by Holbein and works by Rubens, Reynolds, and Gainsborough.

The seemingly endless grounds around the palace also offer the visitor some memorable sights, including the domed Temple of the Four Winds, by Vanbrugh, and the richly designed family mausoleum, by Hawksmoor. There are two rose gardens, one with old-fashioned roses, the other featuring modern creations.

✪ **Fountains Abbey & Studley Royal.** At Fountains, 4 miles southwest of Ripon off B6265. ☎ **01765/608888.** Admission £4.30 ($7.30) adults, £2.10 ($3.55) children, £10.50 ($17.85) family ticket. Oct–Mar daily 10am–5pm; Apr–Sept daily 10am–7pm. Closed Dec 24–25, Fri in Nov–Jan. It's best to drive, although it can be reached from York by public transportation. From York, take bus no. 143 leaving from the York Hall Station to Ripon, 23 miles to the northwest (A59, A1, and B6265 lead to Ripon). From Ripon, it will be necessary to take a taxi 4 miles to the southwest, although some prefer to take the scenic walk.

On the banks of the Silver Skell, the abbey was founded by Cistercian monks in 1132 and is the largest monastic ruin in Britain. In 1987, it was awarded World Heritage status. The ruins provide the focal point of the 18th-century landscape garden at Studley Royal, one of the few surviving examples of a Georgian green garden. It's known for its conservation work in the water gardens, ornamental temples, follies, and vistas. The garden is bounded at its northern edge by a lake and 400 acres of deer park. The Fountains Hall and Elizabethan Mansion are undergoing restoration.

IN WEST YORKSHIRE

✪ **Harewood House & Bird Garden.** At the junction of A61 and A659, midway between Leeds and Harrogate, at Harewood Village. ☎ **0113/2886331.** House, grounds, bird garden, and the terrace gallery £6.95 ($11.80) adults, £6.25 ($10.65) seniors, £4.75 ($8.05) children, family ticket £22.50 ($38.25). Grounds only: £5.75 ($9.80) adults, £4.75 ($8.05) seniors, £3.25 ($5.50) children 15 and under, family ticket £17.50 ($29.75). House, bird garden, and adventure playground Mar–Oct daily 11am–6pm. Terrace gallery 10am–6pm. From York, head west along B1224 toward Wetherby and follow the signs to Harewood from there.

Twenty-two miles west of York, the home of the earl and countess of Harewood is one of England's great 18th-century houses. It has always been owned by the Lascelles family. The fine Adam interior has superb ceilings and plasterwork and furniture made especially for Harewood by Chippendale. There are also important collections of English and Italian paintings and Sèvres and Chinese porcelain.

The gardens, designed by Capability Brown, include terraces, lakeside and woodland walks, and a 4½-acre bird garden with exotic species from all over the world, including penguins, macaws, flamingos, and snowy owls. Other facilities include an art gallery, shops, a restaurant, and cafeteria. Parking is free, and there is a picnic area, plus an adventure playground for the children.

6 Yorkshire Dales National Park

The national park consists of some 700 square miles of water-carved country. In the dales you'll find dramatic white limestone crags, roads and fields bordered by dry-stone walls, fast-running rivers, isolated sheep farms, and clusters of sandstone cottages.

Malhamdale receives more visitors annually than any dale in Yorkshire. Two of the most interesting historic attractions are the 12th-century ruins of Bolton Priory and the 14th-century Castle Bolton, to the north in Wensleydale.

Richmond, the most frequently copied town name in the world, stands at the head of the dales and, like Hawes (see below), is a good center for touring the surrounding countryside.

EXPLORING THE DALES

For orientation purposes, head first for **Grassington,** 10 miles north of Skipton and 25 miles west of Ripon. Constructed around a cobbled marketplace, this is a stone-built village that's ideal for exploring Upper Wharfedale, one of the most scenic parts of the Dales. In fact, the Dales Way footpath passes right through the heart of the village.

Drop in to the **National Park Centre,** Colvend, Hebdon Rd. (☎ **01756/752774**), which is open April through October daily from 9:30am to 5:30pm. From November through March, hours are Wednesday and Friday to Sunday 10am to 4pm. Maps, bus schedules through the dales, and a choice of guidebooks are available here to help you navigate your way. If you'd like a more in-depth look than what you can do on your own, you can arrange for a qualified guide who knows the most beautiful places and can point out the most interesting geological and botanical features of the wilderness.

Ten miles west of Grassington (reached along the B6265), **Malham** is a great place to set out on a hike in summer. Branching out from here, you can set out to explore some of the most remarkable limestone formations in Britain. First, it's best to stop in for maps and information at the **National Park Centre** (☎ **01729/830363**), which is open Easter through October daily from 9:30am to 5pm; off-season, only Saturday and Sunday from 10am to 4pm. Amazingly, this village of 200 or so souls receives a half million visitors annually. May or in September is the time to come, as the hordes descend from June through August.

The scenery in this area has been extolled by no less an authority than Wordsworth, and it's been painted by Turner. A trio of scenic destinations, **Malham Cove, Malham Tarn,** and **Gordale Scar,** can be explored on a circular walk of 8 miles that takes most hikers 5 hours. If your time (and your stamina) is more limited, you can take a circular walk from the heart of the village to Malham Cove and Gordale Scar in about two hours. At least try to walk 1 mile north of the village to Malham Cove, a large natural rock amphitheater. Gordale Scar is a deep natural chasm between overhanging limestone cliffs, and Malham Tarn is a lake in a desolate location.

Another interesting center, **Kettlewell,** lies 8 miles northwest of Malham and 6 miles north of Grassington. This is the main village in the Upper Wharfedale and is a good base for hiking through the local hills and valleys, which look straight out of *Wuthering Heights.* Narrow pack bridges and riverside walks characterize the region, and signs point the way to **The Dales Way** hiking path.

After Kettlewell, you can drive for 4 miles on B6160 to the hamlet of **Buckden,** the last village in the Upper Wharfedale. Once here, follow the sign to **Kidstone Pass,** still staying on B6160. At Aysgarth, the river plummets over a series of waterfalls. This is one of the dramatic scenic highlights of the Yorkshire Dales.

HAWES: A BASE FOR EXPLORING YORKSHIRE DALES NATIONAL PARK

About 65 miles northwest of York, on A684, Hawes is the natural center of Yorkshire Dales National Park and a good place to stay. On the Pennine Way, it's England's highest market town and the capital of Wensleydale, which is famous for its cheese. There are rail connections from York taking you to Garsdale, which is 5 miles from Hawes. From Garsdale, bus connections will take you into Hawes.

While you're there, you might want to check out the **Dales Countryside Museum,** Station Yard (the old train station; (☎ **01969/667494**), which traces folk life in the Dales, a story of 10,000 years of human history. Peat cutting and cheese making, among other occupations, are depicted. The museum is open April through October daily from 10am to 5pm. Winter opening hours vary; you'll have to check locally. Admission is £2 ($3.40) for adults and £1 ($1.70) for children, students, and senior citizens.

WHERE TO STAY

Cockett's Hotel & Restaurant. Market Place, Hawes, North Yorkshire DL8 3RD. ☎ **01969/667312.** Fax 01969/667162. E-mail: cocketts@callnetuk.com. 8 units. TV TEL. £46–£59 ($78.20–$100.30) double. Rates include English breakfast. AE, DC, MC, V.

Charming, with reminders of its age, this 1668 building has the date of its construction carved into one of its lintels. Set in the center of town, it's a 2-story, slate-roofed, stone cottage whose front yard is almost entirely covered with flagstones. Accommodations are done in an old-world style with exposed wooden beams; they're snug, cozy, and well maintained, each with a good mattress and a small bath.

A table d'hôte evening meal (three courses plus coffee) costs £15.95 ($27.10) per person. Lunches from £3.95 ($6.70) are served Easter through October, as well as substantial mid-afternoon cream teas at £2.60 ($4.40) per person.

Simonstone Hall. 1½ miles north of Hawes on the road signposted to Muker, Hawes, North Yorkshire DL8 3RD. ☎ **01969/667255.** Fax 01969/667741. 18 units. TV TEL. £70–£105 ($119–$178.50) per person double. Rates include half board. MC, V.

Just north of Hawes, you can stay and dine at Simonstone Hall. Constructed in 1733, this building has been restored and converted into a comfortable family run, country-house hotel. It's the former home of the earls of Wharncliffe. Both the public rooms and the bedrooms are ideal for relaxation and comfort. Most bedrooms are spacious, and all are furnished tastefully with antiques. The rooms are prettily decorated and kept in immaculate order by the helpful young staff. Each comes with a quality bed, and an efficiently organized bath.

You can have drinks in The Game Tavern and enjoy good food in the hotel's dining room. Nonresidents can enjoy home-cooked bar meals or order a two- or four-course dinner. Dinner can be complemented with good wines from the extensive cellar.

7 North York Moors National Park

The moors, on the other side of the Vale of York, have a wild beauty all their own, quite different from that of the dales. This rather barren moorland blossoms in summer with purple heather. Bounded on the east by the North Sea, it embraces a 554-square-mile area, which has been preserved as a national park.

If you're looking for a hot, sunny beach vacation where the warm water beckons, the North Yorkshire Coast isn't for you—the climate here is cool because of the brisk waters of the North Sea. Even the summer months aren't extremely hot. Many Britons do visit North Yorkshire for beach vacations, however, so you will find a beach town atmosphere along the coast. Brightly colored stalls line the seafront and the people seem to be a bit more relaxed than their inland counterparts.

The beauty and history of the area are the real reasons to visit North Yorkshire. The national park is perfect for solitary strolls and peaceful drives. For remnants of the area's exciting days of smugglers and brave explorers, visitors can follow the Captain Cook Heritage Trail along the coast. The fishing industry is still very much alive in the area, although the whaling ships of yesteryear have been anchored and the fishmongers now concentrate on smaller trappings.

Because the park sprawls over such a large area, you can access it from five or six different gateways. Most visitors enter it from the side closest to York, by following either the A19 north via the hamlet of **Thirsk,** or by detouring to the northeast along the A64 and entering via **Scarborough.** You can also get in through **Helmsley,** where the park's administrative headquarters are located; just follow the roads from York that are signposted Helmsley. Gateways along the park's northern edges, which are less convenient to York, include the villages of **Whitby** (accessible via A171), and **Stokesley** (accessible via A19).

For information on accommodations and transportation before you go, contact **North York Moors National Park,** The Old Vicarage, Bondgate, Helmsley, York YO6 5BP (☎ **01439/770657**). Advice, specialized guidebooks, maps, and information can be obtained at the **Sutton Bank Visitor Centre,** Sutton Bank, near Thirsk, North Yorkshire YO7 2EK (☎ **01845/597426**). Another well-inventoried information source is **The Moors Centre,** Danby Lodge, Lodge Lane, Danby, near Whitby YO21 2NB (☎ **01287/660540**).

EXPLORING THE MOORS

Bounded by the Cleveland and Hambleton hills, the moors are dotted with early burial grounds and ancient stone crosses. **Pickering** and **Northallerton,** both market towns, serve as gateways to the moors.

The North York Moors will always be associated with doomed trysts between unlucky lovers, and ghosts who wander vengefully across the rugged plateaus of their lonely and windswept surfaces. Although the earth is relatively fertile in the river valleys, the thin, rocky soil of the heather-clad uplands has been scorned by local farmers as wasteland, suitable only for sheep grazing and healthy (but melancholy) rambles. During the 19th century, a handful of manor houses were built on their lonely promontories by moguls of the Industrial Revolution, but not until 1953 was the 554-square-mile district designated the North York Moors National Park.

Encompassing England's largest expanse of moorland, the park is famous for the diversity of heathers, which thrive between the sandstone outcroppings of the uplands. If you visit between October and February, you'll see smoldering fires across the landscape—deliberately controlled attempts by shepherds and farmers to burn the omni-present heather back to stubs. Repeated in age-old cycles every 15 years, the blazes encourage the heather's renewal with new growth for the uncounted thousands of sheep that thrive in the district.

Although public bridle and footpaths take you to all corners of the moors, there are two especially noteworthy, clearly demarcated trails that comprise the most comprehensive moor walks in Europe. The shorter of the two is the **Lyle Wake Walk,** a 40-mile east-to-west trek that connects the hamlets of Osmotherly and Ravenscar. It traces the rugged path established by 18th-century coffin bearers. The longer trek (the **Cleveland Walk**) is a 110-mile circumnavigation of the national park's perimeter. A good section of it skirts the edge of the Yorkshire coastline; other stretches take climbers up and down a series of steep fells in the park's interior.

Don't even consider an ambitious moor trek without good shoes, a compass, an ordinance survey map, and a detailed park guidebook. With descriptions of geologically interesting sites, safety warnings, and listings of inns and farmhouses (haunted or otherwise) offering overnight stays, they sell for less than £4 ($6.60) each at any local tourist office.

The isolation and the beauty of the landscape attracted the founders of **three great abbeys:** Rievaulx near Helmsley, Byland Abbey near the village of Wass, and Ampleforth Abbey. Nearby is **Coxwold,** one of the most attractive villages in the moors. The Cistercian Rievaulx and Byland abbeys are in ruins, but the Benedictine Ampleforth still functions as a monastery and well-known Roman Catholic boys' school. Although many of its buildings date from the 19th and 20th centuries, they do contain earlier artifacts.

BASING YOURSELF IN THIRSK

You can drive through the moorland while based in York, but if you'd like to be closer to the moors, there are places to stay in and around the national park.

The old market town of Thirsk, in the Vale of Mowbray, 24 miles north of York on A19, is near the western fringe of the park. It has a fine parish church, but what makes it such a popular stopover is its association with the late James Herriot (1916–95), author of *All Creatures Great and Small.* Mr. Herriot used to practice veterinary medicine in Thirsk.

WHERE TO STAY

✪ **Sheppard's Hotel Restaurant & Bistro.** Front St., Sowerby, near Thirsk, N. Yorkshire YO7 1JF. ☎ **01845/523655.** Fax 01845/524720. E-mail: sheppards@thirskny.freeserve.co.uk. 12 units, 9 with bathroom. TV. £40 ($68) double without bathroom, £50–£85 ($85–$144.50) double with bathroom; £88 ($149.60) 4-poster room. Rates include English breakfast. MC, V. Closed 1st week of Jan.

The late James Herriot treated his last horse on these premises, but now the Sheppard family has turned the complex into one of the finest lodging choices in the area. This family-run concern operates out of an old stable block and granary (now restaurant and bistro, with well-furnished bedrooms overhead). A country atmosphere prevails, and the decor often consists of nailed horse brasses on the beams. Many guests request the "fat bedroom," so named because of its oversized double bed. The private bathrooms are small, with shower stalls. Otherwise, corridor baths are adequate for those who must share. All the buildings in the complex are grouped around a cobbled courtyard.

Many visitors come here just for a meal. The restaurant operates out of the old stables; a garden-room bistro was opened in the granary. Guests dine informally by candlelight in a setting of potted plants and palms. Mr. Herriot used to entertain his American publisher here. Main-course dishes, served with a choice of fresh vegetables, might include supreme of duckling lightly grilled and fanned over a kumquat glaze. Filet of Moors lamb is oven-roasted with rosemary.

EXPLORING THE NORTH YORKSHIRE COAST

Along the eastern boundary of the park, North Yorkshire's 45-mile coastline shelters such traditional seaside resorts as Filey, Whitby, and Scarborough, the latter claiming to be the oldest seaside spa in Britain, located supposedly on the site of a Roman signaling station. The spa was founded in 1622, when mineral springs with medicinal properties were discovered. In the 19th century, its Grand Hotel, a Victorian structure, was acclaimed the best in Europe. The Norman castle on the big cliffs overlooks the twin bays.

It's easy to follow the main road from Bridlington north to Scarborough and on to Robin Hood's Bay and Whitby. As you drive up the coast, you'll see small fishing ports and wide expanses of moorland.

BRIDLINGTON

18 miles SE of Scarborough

Bridlington is a good starting point for a trip up the North Yorkshire Coast. A fishing port with an ancient harbor, the wide beach and busy seafront markets draw crowds who enjoy relaxing on the sand or browsing through the gift shops and stalls that line the streets. Flamborough Head is one of the most distinguishable features on England's east coast.

Jutting out into the North Sea, it features an 85-foot-tall lighthouse that stands atop a chalk cliff towering 170 feet above the sea. A path that winds up the cliffs ends at

Bempton, site of a bird sanctuary that is one of the finest reserves on the coast. You can enjoy watching the seabirds or simply take in the view of the sea off Flamborough, the final resting place of more than a few ships. Bridlington also has many country houses that are open for tours, in addition to Pickering and Helmsley castles and the deserted village of Wharram Percy.

Where to Stay

The Manor House. Flamborough, Bridlington, E. Yorkshire, YO15 1PD. ☎ and fax **01262/850943.** www.manorhouse.clara.net. E-mail: manorhouse@clara.co.uk. 2 units. TV. £31–£36 ($52.70–$61.20) per person double; £8 ($13.60) single supplement. Rates include English breakfast. AE, MC, V.

The current manor house of Flamborough was built around 1800. It was fully restored by local craftspeople and now boasts comfortable accommodations and a friendly atmosphere. Bedrooms are tastefully appointed with a fine bed. The small baths have showers and adequate shelf space. Many visitors come to the house to browse through the variety of antiques sold in the converted stable block or to purchase a Gansey sweater. (These intricate fishermen's sweaters are handmade in the traditional way, an almost-lost process that has been revived by Lesley Berry, the house's proprietor.) For guests who choose to stay at the house, dinners can be arranged. These often feature local seafood and cost £21 ($35.70) per person.

SCARBOROUGH

18 miles NW of Bridlington; 34 miles NE of York; 253 miles N of London

Scarborough, one of the first seaside resorts in Britain, has been attracting visitors for more than three centuries. A mineral spring discovered in the early 17th century led to the establishment of a spa that lured clients with promises of its water's healing benefits. In the 18th century, swimmers were attracted to the waters off the coast—sea bathing had come in vogue, and the beaches of England swarmed with tourists taking part in the craze.

The city of Scarborough is divided into two unique districts separated by a green headland that holds the remains of Scarborough Castle, which dates from Norman times. South of the headland, the town conforms to its historical molds. High cliffs and garden walks interspersed with early Victorian residences dominate the landscape. The north side is more touristy; souvenir shops and fast-food stands line the promenade. "Rock" (brightly colored hard candy that can be etched with the saying of your choice) and cotton candy ("candy floss" to Britons) satisfy even the most die-hard sweet tooth.

For more information about what to see and do while you're in Scarborough, call or visit the **Tourist Information Centre,** Pavillion House, Valley Bridge Road, (☎ **01723/373333**), open May to September daily from 9:30am to 6pm; the rest of the year it's open from 10am to 4:30pm.

Trains leave London's Victoria Station approximately every hour headed for York, where you'll have to transfer to another train. The entire trip takes just under 3 hours. For more information on schedules and prices, call ☎ **0345/484950.** One bus a day leaves London heading for York, another will take you from York to Scarborough. If you're taking the bus, plan on spending most of a day riding. **National Express** bus service can be reached at ☎ **0990/808080.**

Exploring the Town

The ruins of **Scarborough Castle,** Castle Road (☎ **01723/372451**), stand on the promontory near a former Viking settlement. From the castle, you can look out over the North Bay, the beaches, and the gardens along the shore. Throughout the summer, there are fairs and festivals that celebrate days of yore with mock battles, pageantry, and falconry displays. The castle is open April to September daily from 10am to 6pm; in October it closes at 5pm. From November to March, Scarborough Castle is open Wednesday through Sunday only from 10am to 4pm. Admission is £2.30 ($3.90) for adults, £1.70 ($2.90) for senior citizens and persons with disabilities, and £1.20 ($2.05) for children. Children under 5 years are free.

Nearby is the medieval **Church of St. Mary,** Castle Road (no phone), where Anne Brontë, the youngest of the three sisters of literary fame, was buried in 1849. She died in Scarborough after being brought from her home in Haworth in hopes that the sea air would revive her health.

Wood End Museum, The Crescent (☎ **01723/367326**), was once the vacation home of writers Edith, Osbert, and Sacheverell Sitwell. It now houses a library of their works as well as the collections of the **Museum of Natural History.** The house is open from May to mid-October, Tuesday through Sunday from 10am to 5pm. The rest of the year it opens Wednesday, Saturday, and Sunday from 11am to 4pm. Admission is £3 ($5.10) adults, £1.50 ($2.55) seniors and children, £7 ($11.90) family ticket. Children under 5 are free. This ticket also allows entry to the Art Gallery and the Rotunda Museum.

Also located at The Crescent is **The Art Gallery** (☎ **01723/374753**). The gallery's permanent collection features pieces ranging from 17th-century portraits to 20th-century masterworks. Many of the works relate to the Scarborough area. Changing exhibitions by young artists and local craftspeople are also displayed. If you're interested in learning how to create your own works of art, you may want to spend a while at the **Crescent Arts Workshop,** which is located in the basement of the gallery. Local artists offer courses and demonstrations in their respective mediums. The Art Gallery is open May to mid-October, Tuesday to Sunday from 10am to 5pm. The rest of the year it opens Thursday through Saturday from 11am to 4pm. Admission is £3 ($5.10) adults, £1.50 ($2.55) seniors and children, £7 ($11.90) family ticket. Children under 5 are admitted free. This ticket also allows entry to the Wood End Museum and the Rotunda Museum. For information about workshop offerings, call ☎ **01723/351461.**

Local history collections as well as displays of important archaeological finds can be found at the **Rotunda Museum,** Vernon Road, just down the street from Wood End (☎ **01723/374839**). The museum is housed in a circular building originally constructed in 1829 for William Smith, the "Father of English Geology," to display his collection; it was one of the first public buildings in England to be constructed specifically for use as a museum. The Rotunda is open from May to mid-October, Tuesday through Sunday from 10am to 5pm; mid-October to April, Tuesday to Saturday and Sunday from 11am to 4pm. Admission is £3 ($5.10) adults, £1.50 ($2.55) seniors and children, £7 ($11.90) family ticket. Children under 5 are free. This ticket allows admission to the Wood End Museum and the Art Gallery.

More than 70 species of sea creatures are housed at the **Sea Life Centre,** Scalby Mills, North Bay (☎ **01723/376125**). An acrylic tunnel passes under the watery habitat of rays and sharks and feeding pools; hands-on displays encourage interaction with the animals. A favorite of children and adults alike is the Seal Rescue and Rehabilitation Centre, which takes in and cares for stray pups and provides a haven for resident adult gray seals. The center is open daily from 10am to 7pm in the summer and from 10am to 5pm the rest of the year. Admission is £5.50 ($9.35) adults, £4 ($6.80) children.

Of course, Scarborough still has the springs that established its popularity. **The Spa,** South Bay (☎ **01723/376774**), no longer offers guests the opportunity to partake of the waters; it is now an entertainment and conference center in the midst of elegant gardens and buildings dating from several eras. In the summer months, there is a concert of some kind every day (usually classical and often held outdoors). Unless you just want to wander through the grounds, which is entertaining in itself, you may want to call ahead for concert times and prices.

Where to Stay

The Crown Hotel. Esplanade, Scarborough, N. Yorkshire YO11 2AG. ☎ **01723/373491.** Fax 01723/362271. 78 units. TV TEL. £85 ($144.50) double. AE, DC, MC, V.

This hotel overlooks South Bay and the castle headland from its setting atop Scarborough's South Cliff. In recent years extensive renovations have brought everything up-to-date. The accommodations are comfortable, with many rooms offering pleasant views over the sea. Most of the rooms, ranging from mid-size to spacious, have been rejuvenated, and include roomy baths. Nine bedrooms are rented to nonsmokers, and 7 are large enough for families. The bar is a popular meeting place for both guests and locals, many of whom enjoy sampling locally brewed beers. There is also a game room with a snooker table.

Palm Court Hotel. St. Nicholas Cliff, Scarborough, N. Yorkshire YO11 2ES. ☎ **01723/368161.** Fax 01723/371547. 47 units. TV TEL. £64–£84 ($108.80–$142.80) double. Rates include English breakfast. AE, DC, MC, V.

The Palm Court provides guests with modern amenities in an elegant, old-world atmosphere. Inviting common areas, such as the lounge and cocktail bar, provide ideal settings for sharing a drink with friends. Rooms are tastefully furnished and among the most comfortable at the resort. Most accommodations are generally spacious, and seven are rented to families. Bathrooms are well organized. There's also a sauna and an indoor heated pool where guests can take a dip. Table d'hôte dinners are served in the dining room for £13.50 ($22.95). On Saturday nights guests can enjoy dinner and dancing as the resident band plays catchy, toe-tapping tunes in the ballroom.

Wrea Head Country House Hotel. Barmoor Lane, Scalby, Scarborough, N. Yorkshire YO13 0PB. ☎ **01723/378211.** Fax 01723/355936. 20 units. TV TEL. £115–£170 ($195.50–$289) double. Rates include breakfast. AE, DC, MC, V.

This Victorian country house is situated just north of Scarborough on 14 acres of beautifully kept grounds. There are several very compelling common rooms, such as a library and comfortable bar, that entice guests to sit and relax. The rooms vary in size and are individually styled with tasteful furnishings, including first-rate beds. Two rooms are ideal for families. The hotel restaurant, the Four Seasons, serves appealing meals prepared with locally grown produce. Guests often spend part of their stay strolling through the well-tended gardens or participating in a game of croquet with friends.

Where to Dine

Lanterna. 33 Queen St. ☎ **01723/363616.** Reservations recommended. Main courses £9.50–£19 ($16.15–$32.30). MC, V. Mon–Sat 6:30–11pm. ITALIAN.

The Alessio family runs this small Italian restaurant, which is well known for its tasty, straightforward dishes featuring local seafood. Small scallops called "Queenies" are sweet tasting—perfect in the light marinara sauce served over homemade pasta. Many diners end their meal with one of the decadent desserts, such as zabaglione or baked tiramisu.

Scarborough After Dark

Alan Ayckbourn, a popular contemporary playwright, calls Scarborough home. **The Stephen Joseph Theatre,** Westborough, performs many of his plays as well as other favorites. Call the box office at ☎ **01723/370541** for information about shows and prices.

The Hole in the Wall, Vernon Road (☎ **01723/373746**), is a well-stocked, lively pub where both locals and visitors gather to share drinks. Sheppard Neome's Master Brew, Fuller's ESB, and Durham's Margus are among the ales served at the long bar, and basic meals are served at lunch.

Robin Hood's Bay

13 miles NW of Scarborough

Although Robin Hood's Bay was once a notorious port for smugglers, there is no connection with the well-known outlaw who shares the village's name. The tiny fishing port is tucked into a deep ravine; in fact, space is so limited that cars can't enter the village center. The villagers live in cottages precariously balanced on the steep cliffs, where narrow roads curve between the dwellings.

Where to Stay

Raven Hall Hotel. Ravenscar, N. Scarborough, YO13 0ET. ☎ **01723/870353.** Fax 01723/870072. www.ravenhall.co.uk. E-mail:inquiries@ravenhall.co.uk 53 units. TV TEL. £70–£130 ($119–$221) double. Rates include English breakfast. AE, DC, MC, V.

Many guests never leave the grounds of the hotel for entertainment, though Raven Hall makes a good base from which to venture out into Strasbourg and nearby Robin Hood's Bay. The rooms have pleasant views of the water, the moors, or the garden. Each of the traditionally furnished bedrooms comes with a comfortable bed. Twenty-two rooms are large enough for families. Bathrooms are well maintained with adequate shelf space.

In the restaurant, diners enjoy dishes such as roast guinea fowl with red wine, bacon, and onion sauce or lamb cutlets with honey-and-rosemary glaze. Amenities include a 9-hole golf course, two tennis courts, a heated indoor pool and sauna, putting green, lawn bowling.

Whitby

7 miles NW of Robin Hood's Bay; 350 miles NE of London

The resort town of Whitby, which lies at the mouth of the River Esk, has a rich and interesting history. It began as a religious center in the 7th century when Whitby Abbey was first founded. Later, Whitby became a prominent whaling port and eventually, like most coastal towns, it was an active participant in the smuggling trade.

Several famous explorers have pushed off from the beaches of Whitby, including Capt. James Cook. Captain Cook, as the king's surveyor, circumnavigated the globe twice in ships constructed by local carpenters and craftsmen. He also claimed Australia and New Zealand for Great Britain.

Literary references to Whitby add intrigue to the town. Herman Melville paid tribute to William Scoresby, captain of some of the first ships that sailed to Greenland and inventor of the crow's nest, in his novel *Moby Dick,* and Bram Stoker found his inspiration for *Dracula* in the quaint streets of Whitby.

Whitby Tourist Centre, Langborne Road (☎ **01947/602674**), is open daily from May through September from 9:30am to 6pm. The rest of the year it opens daily from 10am to 12:30pm and 1 to 4:30pm.

There is one bus a day that travels between London and Whitby. The trip takes approximately 7 hours and is a direct route. Call the **National Express** bus service at ☎ **0990/808080** for more details. To get to Whitby from London by train, you'll have to ride to Middlesborough or Scarborough then transfer to the train to Whitby. The number of trains to Whitby varies, so call ahead. The number for rail information is ☎ **0345/484950**.

Seeing the Sights

The ruins of **Whitby Abbey,** Abbey Lane (☎ **01947/603568**), lie high on the East Cliff, where they are visible from almost everywhere in town. The abbey dates from the 12th century and adjoins the site of a Saxon Monastery that was established in A.D. 657 Caedmon, the first identifiable English-language poet, was a monk here. It was on this site in A.D. 664 that the date for Easter was decided. The abbey is open Easter to September daily from 10am to 6pm; October from 10am to 5pm, and the rest of the year it closes at 4pm. Admission is £1.80 ($3.05) for adults, £1.40 ($2.40) for senior citizens, and 90p ($1.55) for children.

Another religious sight is the uniquely designed **Church of St. Mary** (**01947/603421**). Stairs leading to the church (there are 199 of them) begin at the end of Church Street. If you have the stamina to climb them, you can walk through the rather spooky churchyard; it was here that Lucy was taken as Dracula's victim in Bram Stoker's novel. The church itself is an eclectic mix of architectural styles.

The **Whitby Museum,** Pannett Park (☎ **01947/602908**), features exhibits that center around the city's history. Of course, ship models and details of Captain Cook's adventures are essential to the museum, but there are also displays about the archaeology and natural history of the area. The Pannett Art Gallery (same address and phone) has a permanent collection featuring paintings by George Weatherill. There are also constantly changing special exhibits. The museum and gallery are open from May 1 to September 30, from 9:30am to 5:30pm Monday to Saturday and from 2 to 5pm Sunday. From October 1 to April 30, they're open Tuesday from 10am to 1pm, Wednesday through Saturday from 10am to 4pm, and Sunday from 2 to 4pm. Admission to the museum is £2 ($3.40) for adults, £1 ($1.70) for children; and £5 ($8.50) for a family ticket; there is no charge for the gallery.

Captain Cook Memorial Museum, Grape Lane (☎ **01947/601900**), deals more specifically with the life and achievements of the famous explorer James Cook. It is open weekends in March from 11am to 3pm and daily from April through October from 9:45am to 5pm. Last entry is 15 minutes before closing. Admission is £2.60 ($4.40) for adults, £2.20 ($3.75) for senior citizens, £1.90 ($3.25) for children, and £7.80 ($13.25) for a family ticket.

Whitby Tourist Information Centre (☎ **01947/602674**) can give anglers information about fishing along the town's coastline. Fishing is free all along the Whitby shore. If you'd rather go out to sea to reel in a big one, there are boats for hire at points throughout the city. The cost usually includes tackle and bait.

Golfers should visit the **Whitby Golf Club,** Low Straggleton (☎ **01947/602768**). The 6,134-yard course is open to visiting golfers daily. **Raven Hall Hotel Golf Course,** Ravenscar (☎ **01723/870353**), is open to nonguests all day, every day. The 9-hole course is well tended and offers panoramic views of the moors and the sea. Raven Hall is also the best place in the area for tennis.

Where to Stay

Dunsley Hall. Dunsley, Whitby, N. Yorkshire YO21 3TL. ☎ **01947/893437.** Fax 01947/893505. www.dunsleyhall.com. 18 units. TV TEL. £54.85 ($93.25) per person double; £64 ($108.80) per person 4-poster room; £74.85 ($127.25) per person minisuite. Rates include breakfast. AE, MC, V.

Just outside of Whitby in a small hamlet, Dunsley Hall was built at the turn of the century by a Newcastle shipping magnate who lived here with his family until 1940. Some of the original carpets and furnishings remain, and now add historical charm to the well-appointed hotel. There are carefully tended gardens around the house where guests can enjoy a stroll; there's also a fitness room and an indoor heated swimming pool. The rooms are all equipped with beverage makers and hair dryers. Two of the spacious bedrooms are set aside for families, and four are rented to nonsmokers. Bathrooms are small but well maintained. In the Terrace Dining Room, traditional dishes are prepared with locally grown produce.

Stakesby Manor. Manor Close, High Stakesby, Whitby, N. Yorkshire YO21 1HL. ☎ **01947/602773.** Fax 01947/602140. www.stakesby-manor.co.uk. E-mail: relax@stakesby-manor.co.uk. 13 units. TV. £76 ($129.20) double. Rate includes breakfast. AE, MC, V.

From your room at Stakesby Manor, a converted 1710 Georgian manor, you'll have a view of either the old town of Whitby or of the surrounding moorland. The guest house is located within 1 mile of the beach, the golf course, and the town center. Although bedrooms vary in shape and size, each is modernized with comfortable mattresses. Two are large enough for families, and five are reserved for nonsmokers. Each small bath comes with adequate shelf space. Rod and Jill Hodgson are responsible for the day-to-day running of the hotel and are happy to arrange theater bookings or other entertainment for their guests. The Oak Room restaurant serves traditional English fare, and packed lunches are available on request.

Where to Dine

Many hotels in the area offer half-board plans (with dinner) in addition to bed-and-breakfast rates; it may save you time and money if you take advantage of these. If you don't, or if you're looking for lunch, try **Trencher's,** New Quay Road (☎ **01947/603212**), for terrific fish-and-chips. Fresh Filets of haddock or cod are fried in a crispy batter and served with thick-cut fries. For good food in an even better atmosphere, stop by **White House and Griffin,** Church Street (☎ **01947/604857**). While surrounded by the character of the 18th-century structure, you might enjoy pan-fried herring or Whitby bouillabaisse.

8 Durham

250 miles N of London; 15 miles S of Newcastle upon Tyne

This medieval city took root in 1090 after the Normans, under William the Conqueror, took over and began construction of Durham's world-renowned cathedral and castle on a peninsula surrounded by the River Wear. The cathedral, "Half Church of God, half Castle 'gainst the Scots," was built as a shrine to protect the remains of St. Cuthbert, while also providing a sturdy fortress against the warring Scots to the north.

The cathedral castle thrust Durham into its role as a protective border post for England. For centuries, Durham Castle was the seat of the prince bishops—kings of the wild northern territories in all but name—and a pilgrimage site for Christians coming to pay tribute to St. Cuthbert, a monk on Lindisfarne. His life of contemplation and prayer led to his consecration as a bishop in 685, and his sainthood after death.

Today, Durham boasts a university (built on the cornerstone of the castle), and is an excellent base for exploring this stretch of the North Sea coast, as well as the unspoiled rolling hills and waterfalls of the Durham Dales in the North Pennines.

ESSENTIALS

GETTING THERE Trains from London's King's Cross Station arrive hourly during the day, with the trip taking about 3 hours, and trains from York leave every hour, arriving approximately an hour later. Durham lies on the main London-to-Edinburgh rail line. For schedules and information, call ☎ **0345/484950.**

Blue Line buses from London arrive twice daily, with the trip taking about 5 hours. For schedules and information, call ☎ **0990/808080.**

If you're driving from London, follow the A1/A1(M) north to Durham.

VISITOR INFORMATION The **Durham Tourist Office** is at Market Place (☎ **0191/3843720**), and is open July and August, Monday through Saturday from 9:30am to 6pm and Sunday from 2 to 5pm; June and September, Monday through Saturday from 10am to 5:30pm; October through May, Monday through Saturday from 10am to 5pm.

SPECIAL EVENTS At the **Durham Folk Festival,** held the last weekend in July, you can sing, clog, or just cavort to music; almost every event is free. The weekend also includes free camping along the River Wear, though you'd better arrive early on Friday if you want to get a choice spot. In mid-June, crowds swarm along the riverbank to cheer the crew racing the **Durham Regatta,** and the first weekend of September brings the sodden celebration of the nation's second-largest **beer festival.**

SEEING THE SIGHTS

✪ **Durham Cathedral.** Palace Green. ☎ **0191/3864266.** Free admission to cathedral; tower £2 ($3.40) adults, £1 ($1.70) children; treasury £2 ($3.40) adults, 50p (85¢) children; Monk's Dormitory 80p ($1.35) adults, 20p (35¢) children; audiovisual Visitors' Exhibition 80p ($1.35) adults, 20p (35¢) children. Cathedral May–Aug daily 9:30am–8pm; Sept–Apr Mon–Sat 9:30am–6pm, Sun 12:30–5pm. Guided tours May to mid-Sept Mon–Sat at 10:30am, and 2pm (also 11:30am during Aug). £2.50 ($4.25) requested donation. Treasury Mon–Sat 10am–4:30pm, Sun 2–4:30pm. Monk's Dormitory Apr–Oct Mon–Sat 10am–3:30pm, Sun 12:30–3pm. Audiovisual Visitors' Exhibition Mar–Oct Mon–Sat 10am–3pm.

Under construction for more than 40 years, the cathedral was completed in 1133, and today is Britain's largest, best-preserved Norman stronghold and one of its grandest surviving Romanesque palaces. The structure is not only breathtaking to view, it is also architecturally innovative, the first English building to feature ribbed vault construction. It is also the first stone-roofed cathedral in Europe, an architectural necessity because of its role as a border fortress.

The treasury houses such relics as the original 12th-century door knocker, St. Cuthbert's coffin, ancient illuminated manuscripts, and more. You can still attend daily services in the sanctuary.

Durham Castle. Palace Green. ☎ **0191/3743800.** Admission £3 ($5.10) adults, £2 ($3.40) children, £6.50 ($11.05) family ticket. Guided tours April–June daily 2–4pm, and July–Sept daily 10am–noon and 2–4:30pm; other times of the year, Mon, Wed, and Sat 2–4:30pm. Closed during university Christmas breaks.

Adjoining the cathedral, the castle was the seat of the prince bishops of Durham for more than 800 years. In 1832, it became the first building of the fledgling local college, now Durham University, and today still houses University College. During university breaks, it offers unique bed-and-breakfast accommodations to the public.

Oriental Museum. Elvet Hill off South Rd. ☎ **0191/3747911.** Admission £1.50 ($2.55) adults, 75p ($1.30) children and seniors. Mon–Fri 9:30am–5pm, Sat–Sun 2–5pm.

This is the nation's only museum devoted entirely to Eastern culture and art. It covers all major periods of art from ancient Egypt through India, as well as relics from Tibet, China, and Japan. The attractions are displayed in a way designed to make them understandable to the nonspecialist.

OUTDOOR PURSUITS

Fishing is a good sport all along the Rivers Tees and Wear, as well as in the several reservoirs and ponds scattered throughout the county. Boating is also available, and **Brown's Boat House,** Elvet Bridge (☎ **0191/3869525**), rents rowboats for pulls up or down the Wear, as well as offering short cruises from April through October, at the price of £3 ($5.10) for adults and £1.50 ($2.55) for children.

Hikers can either take the challenge provided by the 270 miles of trails (40 miles of which are in the county) along the **Pennine Way,** the **Weardale Way's** 78-mile course along the River Wear from Monkwearmouth in Sunderland to Cowshill in County Durham, or the **Teesdale Way,** running 90 miles from Middleton in Teesdale to Teesmouth in Cleveland. Rambles in town along public footpaths have recently been supplemented by more than 50 miles of former railway. Seven such trails make use of interlinked routes and range from the 4½-mile **Auckland Walk** to the 10½-mile **Derwent Walk.** If you don't feel like going it alone, there are also more than 200 guided walks throughout the county, providing background on the history, culture, and plant and animal life of the surrounding area; contact the tourist office (see "Visitor Information," above).

Cyclists can opt for road biking along quiet country lanes and converted railway routes, or mountain biking in **Hamsterley Forest.** The acclaimed **C2C national cycle route** passes through the Durham Dales and North Durham, along a 140-mile sign-posted route. Both road- and mountain-bike rentals are available at several locations, including **Cycle Force,** 29 Claypath St. (☎ **0191/3840319**), open Monday to Wednesday and Friday 9am to 5:30pm, Thursday 9am to 7pm, and Saturday from 9am to 5pm. A bike rental costs £15 ($25.50) day, with a £35 ($59.50) deposit.

WHERE TO STAY

✪ **Georgian Town House.** 10 Crossgate, Durham DH1 4PS. ☎ and fax **0191/3868070.** 7 units. TV. £60 ($102) double. Rates include breakfast. No credit cards.

This is the most desirable B&B in Durham, an unusually decorated place lying on a steep cobbled Georgian terrace street, close to everything, including the cathedral. It is a wonder of decoration, especially the reception hallway with its stenciled pillars and leaf patterns. It's almost like entering an arbor in sunny Sicily. In the lounge, "stars" twinkle on the walls. Sofas are placed around the fireplace where guests can mingle. Rooms, except for a cramped single, are tastefully decorated and are light and airy. The small bathrooms include showers. Maintenance is very high here. The house has a panoramic view of the cathedral and castle. The grilled English breakfast is a hearty way to start the day.

Royal County Hotel. Old Elvet, Durham DH1 3JN. ☎ **0191/3866821.** Fax 0191/3860704. www.swallowhotels.com. E-mail: royal.country@swallow-hotels.co.uk. 151 units. MINIBAR TV TEL. From £145 ($246.50) double; from £195–£225 ($331.50–$382.50) suite. AE, DC, MC, V.

This is where we prefer to stay. Although some critics consider this an anonymous chain hotel (it's part of the Swallow chain), it has many winning features in its three Georgian buildings, plus a convenient location right in the heart of Durham. Skillfully converted from a row of riverside houses, it was once the family home of the Queen Mother before being turned into one of the region's premier hotels. Many of its original details have been retained, including an oak staircase that was transported here from Loch Leven, the Scottish castle where Mary Queen of Scots was held prisoner. The bedrooms all maintain a high standard of comfort and furnishings, although they vary in size. Room features include tea- and coffeemakers, trouser press, iron and ironing board, and a hair dryer. Four rooms are large enough to rent to families, and 62 are reserved for nonsmokers. Bathrooms for the most part come with tub and shower combinations. Other hotel amenities include a heated indoor swimming pool, fitness room, solarium, steam room, and sauna.

On the premises, the County Restaurant offers traditional English dishes. The service is the most attentive in Durham, and you can enjoy piano music in the evening, while taking in the crisp linen, fresh flowers, and sparkling silver. You can also dine more informally in the Brasserie, which is open all day.

Three Tuns Hotel. New Elvet, Durham DH1 3AQ. ☎ **0191/3864326.** Fax 0191/3861406. www.swallowhotels.com. E-mail: threetons@swallowhotels.co.uk 50 units. TV TEL. £115–£140 ($195.50–$238) double. Rates include breakfast. AE, DC, MC, V.

The second-best property in town was formerly a 16th-century coaching inn, housing travelers headed north to Scotland. Almost all traces of its former role are gone today, and the property is run by the Swallow chain, which also operates the Royal County Hotel (see above). In fact, Three Tuns is only 200 yards from the Royal County and lodgers here are allowed to use the health-club facilities there. Bedrooms have been completely modernized and furnished to a high, if not exciting, standard. Each room has satellite TV, beverage makers, a hair dryer, and an iron and ironing board; many also offer trouser presses and minifridges. The best and most spacious rooms are the executive units, but each room has a good mattress on the double or twin beds. Two rooms are large enough for families, and 30 are reserved for nonsmokers. Bathrooms are roomy. The public rooms have more character and are roomy and inviting. Acceptable English and French meals are efficiently served in the hotel dining room.

WHERE TO DINE

Bistro 21. Aykley Heads House, Aykley Heads. ☎ **0191/3844354.** Reservations recommended. Main courses £9–£18 ($15.30–$30.60); fixed-price lunch £14.50 ($24.65). AE, DC, MC, V. Tues–Sat noon–2pm and 6–10:30pm. INTERNATIONAL.

A big hit locally, this is a bright, farm-themed bistro. Chef Adrian Watson's cuisine is precise and carefully prepared, with market-fresh ingredients that are allowed to keep their natural essence without being overly sauced or disguised. We especially recommend trying the blackboard specials. The food is full of flavor and rather forceful, borrowing from all over Europe-certainly the Mediterranean, but also offering traditional British fare at times, such as deep-fried plaice and chips. You can finish with one of the rich desserts, including double chocolate truffle cake. But if you want to be terribly old-fashioned and very English, you'll ask for the toffee pudding with butterscotch sauce. If you go in for this type of thing, it's prepared to perfection here.

DURHAM AFTER DARK

Much of Durham's nightlife revolves around its university students. When school is in session, **The Hogs Head,** 58 Saddler St. (☎ **0191/3864134**), is a popular traditional English-style pub. It's open Monday through Saturday 11am to 11pm, and Sunday from noon until 10:30pm. **Coach and Eight,** Bridge House, Framwellgate Bridge (☎ **0191/3863284**), has disco Thursday through Sunday nights, and is open Monday through Saturday from 11am to 11pm, and Sunday from 11am to 10:30pm.

SIDE TRIPS TO THE DURHAM DALES, BARNARD CASTLE & BEAMISH

This densely populated county of northeast England was once pictured as a dismal, forbidding place, with coalfields, ironworks, mining towns, and shipyards. Yet the **Durham Dales,** occupying the western third of the county, is a popular panorama of rolling hills, valleys of quiet charm, and wild moors. **Teesdale** is particularly notable for its several waterfalls, including **High Force,** the largest waterfall in England, which drops a thundering 70 feet to join the River Tees. It is equally known for the rare wildflowers that grow in the sugar limestone soil of the region; they have helped it earn protection as a National Nature Reserve.

Also notable is **Weardale,** once the hunting ground of Durham's prince bishops, with its idyllic brown sandstone villages. For more information on the wide range of options the area has to offer, contact the **Durham Dales Centre,** Castle Garden, Stanhope, Bishop Auckland, County Durham DL13 2SJ (☎ **01388/527650;** fax 01388/527461). Hours are November through March, Monday through Friday from 10am to 4pm and Saturday and Sunday 11am to 4pm; and April through October daily from 10am to 5pm.

The 12th-century **Barnard Castle** (☎ **0183/3638212**) is an extensive Norman ruin overlooking the River Tees. It is open daily, April through September, from 10am to 6pm; daily in October, 10am to 5pm; and Wednesday through Sunday, November through March, 10am to 1pm and 2 to 4pm. Admission is £2.30 ($3.90) adults, £1.20 ($2.05) children under 16.

Barnard Castle is also home to the **Josephine and John Bowes Museum** (☎ **0183/3690606**), a sprawling French-style château housing one of Britain's most important collections of European art, including paintings from Goya to El Greco, plus tapestries, ceramics, costumes, musical instruments, and French and English furniture. There is also a children's gallery. The museum is open November through March daily from 11am to 5pm, and April through October daily from 10am to 5pm. Admission is £3.90 ($6.65) for adults and £2.90 ($4.95) for children and senior citizens, and £12 ($20.40) for a family ticket. Buses run from Durham several times daily.

✪ **North of England Open Air Museum.** Just off the A693 in Beamish. ☎ **0120/7231811.** Admission spring and summer £10 ($17) adults, £6 ($10.20) children; winter £3 ($5.10) for all. Free for children under 5. Spring and summer daily 10am–5pm (to 6pm mid-July to Aug); off-season Sat–Sun and Tues–Thurs 10am–4pm. Closed Dec 13–Jan 4.

West of Chester-le-Street, 8 miles southwest of Newcastle upon Tyne, and 12 miles northwest of Durham City, this is a vivid re-creation of a turn-of-the-century village. A costumed staff goes through the motions of daily life in shops, houses, pubs, a newspaper office, and garage, as well as a Methodist chapel, village school, home farm, and railway station. An average summer visit takes around 4 hours, and a winter visit, including the town and railway only, takes about 2 hours.

9 Hexham, Hadrian's Wall & the Pennine Way

304 miles N of London; 37 miles E of Carlisle; 21 miles W of Newcastle upon Tyne

Above the Tyne River, the historic old market town of Hexham has narrow streets, an old market square, a fine abbey church, and a moot hall. It makes a good base for exploring Hadrian's Wall and the Roman supply base of Corstopitum at Corbridge-on-Tyne, the ancient capital of Northumberland. The tourist office has lots of information on the wall, whether you're hiking, driving, camping, or picnicking.

ESSENTIALS

GETTING THERE Take one of the many daily trains from London's King's Cross Station to Newcastle upon Tyne. At Newcastle, change trains and take one in the direction of Carlisle. The fifth or sixth (depending on the schedule) stop after Newcastle will be Hexham. For schedules and information, call ☎ **0345/484950.**

Hexham lies 14 miles southeast of Hadrian's Wall. If you are primarily interested in the wall (rather than in Hexham), get off the Carlisle-bound train at the second stop (Bardon Mill) or at the third stop (Haltwhistle), which are 4 miles and 2½ miles, respectively, from the wall. At either of these hamlets, you can take a taxi to whichever part of the wall you care to visit. Taxis line up readily at the railway station in Hexham, but less often at the other villages. If you get off at one of the above-mentioned villages and don't see a taxi, call ☎ **01434/344272** and a local taxi will come to get you. Many visitors ask their taxi drivers to return at a prearranged time (which they gladly do) to pick them up after their excursion on the windy ridges near the wall.

Stagecoach coaches to Newcastle and Carlisle connect with Northumbria bus service 685. Trip time to Hexham from Carlisle is about 1½ hours and from Newcastle about 1 hour. For schedules and information, call ☎ **01946/63222.** Local bus services connect Hexham with North Tynedale and the North Pennines.

If you're driving from Newcastle upon Tyne, head west on A69 until you see the cutoff south to Hexham.

VISITOR INFORMATION The **Tourist Information Centre** at Hexham is at the Manor Office, Hallgate (☎ **01434/605225**). It's open Easter to September daily from 9am to 6pm; November through March, Monday to Saturday from 9am to 5pm.

HADRIAN'S WALL & ITS FORTRESSES

✪ **Hadrian's Wall,** which extends for 73 miles across the north of England, from the North Sea to the Irish Sea, is particularly interesting for a stretch of 10 miles west of Housesteads, which lies 2¾ miles northeast of Bardon Mill on B6318. Only the lower courses of the wall have been preserved intact; the rest were reconstructed in the 19th century using original stones. From the wall, there are incomparable views north to the Cheviot Hills along the Scottish border and south to the Durham moors.

The wall was built in A.D. 122 after the visit of the emperor Hadrian, who was inspecting far frontiers of the Roman Empire and wanted to construct a dramatic line between the empire and the barbarians. Legionnaires were ordered to build a wall across the width of the island of Britain, stretching 73½ miles, beginning at the North Sea and ending at the Irish Sea.

The wall is one of Europe's top Roman ruins. The western end can be reached from Carlisle, which also has an interesting museum of Roman artifacts; the eastern end can be reached from Newcastle upon Tyne (where some remains can be seen on the city outskirts; there's also a nice museum at the university).

From early May to late September, the Tynedale Council and the Northumberland National Park run a **bus service** that visits every important site along the wall, then turns around in the village of Haltwhistle and returns to Hexham. Buses depart Saturday and bank holidays from a point near the railway station in Hexham four times a day, and Sundays twice a day. From April to late September, the tours are given daily. Call ☎ **01434/605225** for more information. The cost is £5 ($8.50) for adults, £3 ($5.10) for children, and £10 ($17) for a family ticket. Many visitors take one bus out, then return on a subsequent bus, 2, 4, or 6 hours later. Every Sunday, a national-park warden leads a 2½-hour walking tour of the wall, in connection with the bus service. The Hexham tourist office (see "Visitor Information," above) will provide further details.

Housesteads Fort and Museum. 3 miles northeast of Bardon Mill on B6318. ☎ **01434/344363.** Admission £2.80 ($4.75) adults, £2.10 ($3.55) seniors and students, £1.40 ($2.40) children. Apr–Sept daily 10am–6pm; Oct–Mar daily 10am–4pm. Closed Dec 24–26 and Jan 1.

Along the wall are several Roman forts, the most important of which was called *Vercovicium* by the Romans. This substantially excavated fort, on a dramatic site, contains the only visible example of a Roman hospital in Britain.

✪ **Vindolanda.** Just west of Housesteads, on a minor road 1 1/4 miles southeast of Twice Brewed off the B6318. ☎ **01434/344277.** Admission £3.80 ($6.45) adults, £3.20 ($5.45) seniors and students, £2.80 ($4.75) children. Last 2 weeks of Feb and first 2 weeks of Nov 10am–4pm, Mar and Oct 10am–5pm, Apr and Sept 10am–5:30pm, May–June 10am–6pm, July–Aug 10am–6:30pm.

This is another well-preserved fort south of the wall; the last of eight successive forts to be built on this site. There is also an excavated civilian settlement outside the fort with an interesting museum of artifacts of everyday Roman life.

Roman Army Museum. At the junction of A69 and B6318, 18 miles west of Hexham. ☎ **01697/747485.** Admission £3 ($5.10) adults, £2.60 ($4.40) seniors and students, £2.40 ($4.10) children. Last 2 weeks of Feb and first 2 weeks of Nov 10am–4pm, Mar and Oct 10am–5pm, Apr–Sept 10am–5:30pm, May–June 10am–6pm, July–Aug 10am–6:30pm.

Near Vindolanda at the garrison fort at Carvoran, close to the village of Greenhead, the Roman Army Museum traces the growth and influence of Rome from its early beginnings to the development and expansion of the empire, with special emphasis on the role of the Roman army and the garrisons of Hadrian's Wall. A barracks room depicts basic army living conditions. Realistic life-size figures make this a strikingly visual museum experience.

Within easy walking distance of the Roman Army Museum is one of the most imposing and high-standing sections of Hadrian's Wall, **Walltown Crags,** where the height of the wall and magnificent views to the north and south are impressive.

HIKING THE PENNINE WAY IN NORTHUMBERLAND NATIONAL PARK

Northumberland National Park, established in 1956, encompasses the borderlands that were a buffer zone between the warring English and Scots during the 13th and 14th centuries. Today, the park comprises almost 400 square miles of the least-populated area in England and is noted for its rugged landscape and associations with the northern frontier of the ancient Roman Empire.

Touching on the border with Scotland, the park covers some of the most tortured geology in England, the Cheviot Hills, whose surfaces have been wrinkled by volcanic pressures, inundated with sea water, scoured and gouged by glaciers, silted over by rivers, and thrust upward in a complicated series of geological events. Much of the heather-sheathed terrain here is used for sheep grazing; woolly balls of fluff adorn hill-sides ravaged by high winds and frequent rain.

Northumberland Park includes the remains of Hadrian's Wall, one of the most impressive classical ruins of northern Europe. Footpaths run alongside it and there are a variety of walks in the country to the north and south of the monument. One of the most challenging hiking paths in Britain, the ✪ **Pennine Way,** snakes up the back-bone of the park. The 80 miles of the 250-mile path that are in the park are clearly marked; one of the most worthwhile (and safest) hikes is between Bellingham and the Hamlet of Riding Wood.

A map of the trails, priced at 50p (85¢), can be purchased for these and other hiking trails at almost any local tourist office in the district. There are **National Park Centres** at Once Brewed (☎ **01434/344396**), Rothbury (☎ **01669/620414**), and Ingram (☎ **01665/578248**). The Head Office is at Eastburn, South Park, Hexham, Northumberland NE46 1BS (☎ **01434/605555**).

NEARBY PLACES TO STAY & DINE

Anchor Hotel. John Martin St. (on the A69, 7 miles west of Hexham), Haydon Bridge, Northumberland NE47 6AB. ☎ **01434/684227.** Fax 01434/684586. www.freespace.virgin.net/alanmcjannet4/index.html. 10 units. TV TEL. £60 ($102) double. Rates include English breakfast. MC, V.

This is the social center of the village. Ideally situated for visitors to the wall and its surroundings, between Haltwhistle (9 miles away) and Hexham (7 miles), this riverside village pub was once a coaching inn on the route from Newcastle to Carlisle. The building, which was constructed in 1700 near the edge of the North Tyne River (which still flows within a few feet of its foundations), sits in the heart of the tiny village of Haydon Bridge. The cozy bar is a local hangout. In the country dining room, wholesome evening meals are served. The bedrooms are comfortably furnished, albeit a bit small, and each comes with a cozy bed. Bathrooms are also small with shower stalls.

George Hotel. Chollerford, Humshaugh, near Hexham, Northumberland NE46 4EW. ☎ **01434/681611.** Fax 01434/681727. www.swallowhotels.com. 47 units. MINIBAR TV TEL. £120 ($204) double. Rates include English breakfast. AE, DC, MC, V. Take A6079 5 miles north of Hexham.

Standing on the banks of the Tyne, this country hotel has gardens leading to the riverbank. It's a convenient base for visiting Hadrian's Wall. The hotel dates from the 18th century, when the original structure was built of Roman stone. It has been extensively refurbished to a high standard, and has conference facilities and a health club. All bedrooms are comfortably furnished and equipped with such amenities as minibars with fresh milk daily for the beverage maker, an iron and ironing board, and a hair dryer. Rooms range from small to mid-size, and each is fitted with firm mattresses. Bathrooms are a bit cramped and are equipped with shower stalls.

The Fisherman's Bar is where locals gather for a traditional pub welcome and bar snacks served at lunch.

Hadrian Hotel. Wall, near Hexham, Northumberland NE46 4EE. ☎ and fax **01434/681232.** 6 units. TV. £49 ($83.30) double. Rates include English breakfast. DC, MC, V.

Ideal for a stopover along Hadrian's Wall, the Hadrian lies on the only street of the hamlet of Wall, 3½ miles north of Hexham. It's an ivy-covered 18th-century building erected of stones gathered long ago from the site of the ancient wall. The owners have carefully refurbished the place, which now has two Jacobean-style bars serving bar meals. There is also a restaurant, serving à la carte lunches and dinners. Each attractive bedroom has a beverage maker. All the rooms have been modernized and offer comfortable double or twin beds. Baths are small but have a shower stall and adequate shelf space. The hotel has a private garden and a beer garden that serves as a warm-weather extension of its pub.

Langley Castle Hotel. Langley-on-Tyne, Hexham, Northumberland NE47 5LU. ☎ **01434/688888.** Fax 01434/684019. www.langleycastle.com E-mail: langley@dial.pipek.com. 18 units. TV TEL. £105 ($178.50) double; £155 ($263.50) suite. Rates include English breakfast. AE, DC, MC, V. From Hexham, go west on A69 to Haydon Bridge, then head south on A686 for 2 miles.

To experience a stately home, we recommend this hotel located on 10 acres of woodlands at the edge of Northumberland National Park, southwest of Haydon Bridge and about 7 miles west of Hexham. It's the only medieval fortified castle home in England that receives paying guests. The castle, built in 1350, was largely uninhabited after being damaged in 1400 during an English-Scottish war, until it was purchased in the late 19th century by Cadwallader Bates, a historian, who spent the rest of his life carefully restoring the property to its original beauty. Medieval features here include the 14th-century spiral staircase, stained-glass windows, huge open fireplaces, 7-foot-thick walls, and many turrets. The luxuriously appointed bedrooms vary in size; some have whirlpools or saunas. An adjacent building has extra accommodations, including four new suites, as well as a small conference room with a view of the castle. A number of bedrooms have been recently redecorated, and the comfort level is high in all the rooms. Each unit comes with a beverage maker and hair dryer.

The hotel has an elegant drawing room, with an adjoining oak-paneled bar. Local specialties are served in the intimate restaurant.

England in Depth

1 History 101

FROM MURKY BEGINNINGS TO ROMAN OCCUPATION Britain was probably split off from the continent of Europe some 8 millennia ago by continental drift and other natural forces. The early inhabitants, the Iberians, were later to be identified with stories of fairies, brownies, and "little people." These are the people whose ingenuity and enterprise are believed to have created Stonehenge, but despite that great and mysterious monument, little is known about them.

They were replaced by the iron-wielding Celts, whose massive invasions around 500 B.C. drove the Iberians back to the Scottish Highlands and Welsh mountains, where some of their descendants still live today.

In 54 B.C. Julius Caesar invaded England, but the Romans did not become established there until A.D. 43. They went as far as Caledonia (now Scotland), where they gave up, leaving that land to "the painted ones," or the warring Picts. The wall built by Emperor Hadrian across the north of England marked the northernmost reaches of the Roman Empire. During almost four centuries of occupation, the Romans built roads, villas, towns, walls, and fortresses; they farmed the land and introduced first their pagan religions, then Christianity. Agriculture and trade flourished.

Dateline

- **54 B.C.** Julius Caesar invades England.
- **A.D. 43** Romans conquer England.
- **410** Jutes, Angles, and Saxons form small kingdoms in England.
- **500–1066** Anglo-Saxon kingdoms fight off Viking warriors.
- **1066** William, duke of Normandy, invades England, defeats Harold II at the Battle of Hastings.
- **1154** Henry II, first of the Plantagenets, launches their rule (which lasts until 1399).
- **1215** King John signs the Magna Carta at Runnymede.
- **1337** Hundred Years' War between France and England begins.
- **1485** Battle of Bosworth Field ends the War of the Roses between the Houses of York and Lancaster; Henry VII launches the Tudor dynasty.
- **1534** Henry VIII brings the Reformation to England and dissolves the monasteries.
- **1558** The accession of Elizabeth I ushers in an era of exploration and a renaissance in science and learning.

continues

- **1588** Spanish Armada defeated.
- **1603** James VI of Scotland becomes James I of England, thus uniting the crowns of England and Scotland.
- **1620** Pilgrims sail from Plymouth on the Mayflower to found a colony in the New World.
- **1629** Charles I dissolves Parliament, ruling alone.
- **1642–49** Civil War between Royalists and Parliamentarians; the Parliamentarians win.
- **1649** Charles I beheaded, and England is a republic.
- **1653** Oliver Cromwell becomes Lord Protector.
- **1660** Charles II restored to the throne with limited power.
- **1665–66** Great Plague and Great Fire decimate London.
- **1688** James II, a Catholic, is deposed, and William and Mary come to the throne, signing a bill of rights.
- **1727** George I, the first of the Hanoverians, assumes the throne.
- **1756–63** In the Seven Years' War, Britain wins Canada from France.
- **1775–83** Britain loses its American colonies.
- **1795–1815** The Napoleonic Wars lead, finally, to the Battle of Waterloo and the defeat of Napoléon.
- **1837** Queen Victoria begins her reign as Britain reaches the zenith of its empire.
- **1901** Victoria dies, and Edward VII becomes king.
- **1914–18** England enters World War I and emerges victorious on the Allied side.
- **1936** Edward VIII abdicates to marry an American divorcée.
- **1939–45** In World War II, Britain stands alone against Hitler from the fall of France in 1940 until America enters

continues

FROM ANGLO-SAXON RULE TO THE NORMAN CONQUEST When the Roman legions withdrew, around A.D. 410, they left the country open to waves of invasions by Jutes, Angles, and Saxons, who established themselves in small kingdoms throughout the former Roman colony. From the 8th through the 11th centuries, the Anglo-Saxons contended with Danish raiders for control of the land.

By the time of the Norman conquest, the Saxon kingdoms were united under an elected king, Edward the Confessor. His successor was to rule less than a year before the Norman invasion.

The date 1066 is familiar to every English schoolchild. It marked an epic event, the only successful military invasion of Britain in history, and one of England's great turning points: King Harold, the last Anglo-Saxon king, was defeated at the Battle of Hastings, and William of Normandy was crowned William I.

One of William's first acts was to order a survey of the land he had conquered, assessing all property in the nation for tax purposes. This survey was called the *Domesday Book*, or "Book of Doom," as some pegged it. The resulting document was completed around 1086 and has been a fertile sourcebook for British historians ever since.

Norman rule had an enormous impact on English society. All high offices were held by Normans, and the Norman barons were given great grants of lands, and they built Norman-style castles and strongholds throughout the country. French was the language of the court for centuries—few people realize that heroes such as Richard the Lionheart probably spoke little or no English.

FROM THE RULE OF HENRY II TO THE MAGNA CARTA In 1154 Henry II, the first of the Plantagenets, was crowned (reigned 1154–89). This remarkable character in English history ruled a vast empire—not only most of Britain but Normandy, Anjou, Brittany, and Aquitaine in France.

Henry was a man of powerful physique, both charming and terrifying. He reformed the courts and introduced the system of common law, which still operates in moderated form in England today, and also influenced the American legal system. But Henry is best remembered for ordering the infamous murder of Thomas à Becket, Archbishop of Canterbury. Henry, at odds with his archbishop, exclaimed, "Who will rid me of this turbulent priest?" His knights, overhearing and taking him at his word, murdered Thomas in front of the high altar in Canterbury Cathedral.

Henry's wife, Eleanor of Aquitaine, the most famous woman of her time, was no less of a colorful character. She accompanied her first husband, Louis VII of France, on the Second Crusade, and it was rumored that she had a romantic affair at that time with the Saracen leader, Saladin. Domestic and political life did not run smoothly, however, and Henry and Eleanor and their sons were often at odds. The pair have been the subject of many plays and films, including *The Lion in Winter, Becket,* and T. S. Eliot's *Murder in the Cathedral.*

Two of their sons were crowned kings of England. Richard the Lionheart actually spent most of his life outside England, on crusades, or in France. John was forced by his nobles to sign the Magna Carta at Runnymede, in 1215—another date well known to English schoolchildren.

The Magna Carta guaranteed that the king was subject to the rule of law and gave certain rights to the king's subjects, beginning a process that eventually led to the development of parliamentary democracy as it is known in Britain today, a process that would have enormous influence on the American colonies many years later. The Magna Carta became known as the cornerstone of English liberties, though it only granted liberties to the barons. It took the rebellion of Simon de Montfort half a century later to introduce the notion that the boroughs and burghers should also have a voice and representation.

THE BLACK DEATH & THE WARS OF THE ROSES In 1348, half the population died as the Black Death ravaged England. By the end of the century, the population of Britain had fallen from four million to two million.

England also suffered in the Hundred Years' War, which went on intermittently for more than a century. By 1371, England had lost much of its land on French soil. Henry V, immortalized by Shakespeare, revived England's claims to France, and his victory at Agincourt was notable for making obsolete the forms of medieval chivalry and warfare.

After Henry's death in 1422, disputes arose among successors to the crown that resulted in

the war in 1941. Dunkirk is evacuated in 1940; bombs rattle London during the blitz.

- **1945** Germany surrenders. Churchill is defeated; the Labor government introduces the welfare state and begins to dismantle the empire.
- **1952** Queen Elizabeth II ascends the throne.
- **1973** Britain joins the European Union.
- **1979** Margaret Thatcher becomes prime minister.
- **1982** Britain defeats Argentina in the Falklands War.
- **1990** Thatcher is ousted; John Major becomes prime minister.
- **1991** Britain fights with Allies to defeat Iraq.
- **1992** Royals jolted by fire at Windsor Castle and marital troubles of their two sons. Britain joins the European Single Market. Deep recession signals the end of the booming 1980s.
- **1994** England is linked to the Continent by rail via the Channel Tunnel or Chunnel. Tony Blair elected Labour party leader.
- **1996** The IRA breaks a 17-month cease-fire with a truck bomb at the Docklands that claims two lives. Charles and Di divorce. The government concedes a possible link between mad-cow disease and a fatal brain ailment afflicting humans; British beef imports face banishment globally.
- **1997** London swings again. The Labour party ends 18 years of Conservative rule with a landslide election victory. The tragic death of Diana, Princess of Wales, prompts worldwide outpouring of grief.

continues

- **1998** Prime Minister Tony Blair launches "New Britain"—young, stylish, and informal.
- **1999** England rushed toward the 21st century with the Millennium Dome at Greenwich.
- **2000** London "presides" over millennium celebration; gays allowed to serve openly in the military, and hereditary peers in House of Lords get boot from Blair.

a long period of civil strife, the Wars of the Roses, between the Yorkists, who used a white rose as their symbol, and the Lancastrians with their red rose. The last Yorkist king was Richard III, who got bad press from Shakespeare, but who is defended to this day as a hero by the people of the city of York. Richard was defeated at Bosworth Field, and the victory introduced England to the first Tudor, the shrewd and wily Henry VII.

THE TUDORS TAKE THE THRONE The Tudors were unlike the kings who had ruled before them. They introduced into England a strong central monarchy with far-reaching powers. The system worked well under the first three strong and capable Tudor monarchs, but began to break down later when the Stuarts came to the throne.

Henry VIII is surely the most notorious Tudor. Imperious and flamboyant, a colossus among English royalty, he slammed shut the door on the Middle Ages and introduced the Renaissance to England. He is best known, of course, for his treatment of his six wives and the unfortunate fates that befell five of them.

When his first wife, Catherine of Aragon, failed to produce an heir, and his ambitious mistress, Anne Boleyn, became pregnant, he tried to annul his marriage, but the pope refused, and Catherine contested the action. Defying the power of Rome, Henry had his marriage with Catherine declared invalid and secretly married Anne Boleyn in 1533.

The events that followed had profound consequences and introduced the religious controversy that was to dominate English politics for the next four centuries. Henry's break with the Roman Catholic Church and the formation of the Church of England, with himself as supreme head, was a turning point in English history. It led eventually to the Dissolution of the Monasteries, civil unrest, and much social dislocation. The confiscation of the church's land and possessions brought untold wealth into the king's coffers, wealth that was distributed to a new aristocracy that supported the monarch. In one sweeping gesture, Henry destroyed the ecclesiastical culture of the Middle Ages. Among those executed for refusing to cooperate with Henry's changes was Sir Thomas More, humanist, international man of letters, and author of *Utopia*.

Anne Boleyn bore Henry a daughter, the future Elizabeth I, but failed to produce a male heir. She was brought to trial on a trumped-up charge of adultery and beheaded; in 1536, Henry married Jane Seymour, who died giving birth to Edward VI. For his next wife, he looked farther afield and chose Anne of Cleves from a flattering portrait, but she proved disappointing—he called her "The Great Flanders Mare." He divorced her the same year and next picked a pretty young woman from his court, Catherine Howard. She was also beheaded on a charge of adultery but, unlike Anne Boleyn, was probably guilty. Finally, he married an older woman, Catherine Parr, in 1543. She survived him.

Henry's heir, sickly Edward VI (reigned 1547–53), did not live long. He died of consumption—or, as rumor has it, overmedication. He was succeeded by his sister, Mary I (reigned 1553–58), and the trouble Henry had stirred up with the break with Rome came home to roost for the first time. Mary restored the Roman Catholic faith, and her persecution of the adherents of the Church of England earned her the name of "Bloody Mary." Some 300 Protestants were executed, many burned alive at the stake. She made an unpopular and unhappy marriage to Philip of Spain; despite her bloody reputation, her life was a sad one.

Elizabeth I (reigned 1558–1603) came next to the throne, ushering in an era of peace and prosperity, exploration, and a renaissance in science and learning. An entire age was named after her: the Elizabethan age. She was the last great and grand monarch to rule England, and her passion and magnetism were said to match her father's. Through her era marched Drake, Raleigh, Frobisher, Grenville, Shakespeare, Spenser, Byrd, and Hilliard. During her reign, she had to face the appalling precedent of ordering the execution of a fellow sovereign, Mary, Queen of Scots. Her diplomatic skills kept war at bay until 1588, when at the apogee of her reign, the Spanish Armada was defeated. She will be forever remembered as "Good Queen Bess."

CIVIL WAR ERUPTS The Stuarts ascended the throne in 1603, but though they held it through a century of civil war and religious dissension, they were not as capable as the Tudors in walking the line between the demands of a strong centralized monarchy and the rights increasingly demanded by the representatives of the people in Parliament.

Charles I, attracted by the French idea of the divine right of the king, considered himself above the law, a mistake the Tudors had never made (Elizabeth, in particular, was clever and careful in her dealings with Parliament). Charles's position was a fatal response to the Puritans and other Dissenters who sought far more power. In 1629, Charles dissolved Parliament, determined to rule without it.

Civil War followed, and the victory went to the Roundheads under Oliver Cromwell. Charles I was put on trial and was led to his execution, stepping onto the scaffold through the window of his gloriously decorated Banqueting House. His once-proud head rolled on the ground.

Oliver Cromwell, the melancholy, unambitious, clumsy farmer, became England's first and only virtual dictator. He saw his soldiers as God's faithful servants, and promised them rewards in heaven. The English people, however, did not take kindly to this form of government, and after Cromwell's death, Charles II, the dead king's son, returned and was crowned in 1660, but was given greatly limited powers.

FROM THE RESTORATION TO THE NAPOLEONIC WARS The reign of Charles II was the beginning of a dreadful decade that saw London decimated by the Great Plague and destroyed by the Great Fire.

His successor, James II, attempted to return the country to Catholicism, an attempt that so frightened the powers that be that Catholics were for a long time deprived of their civil rights. James was deposed in the "Glorious Revolution" of 1688 and succeeded by his daughter Mary (1662–1694) and William of Orange (1650–1702). (William of Orange was the grandson of Charles I, the tyrannical king whom Cromwell helped to depose). This secured a Protestant succession that has continued to this day. These tolerant and levelheaded monarchs signed a bill of rights, establishing the principle that the monarch reigns not by divine right but by the will of Parliament. William outlived his wife, reigning until 1702.

Queen Anne then came to the throne ruling from 1702 until her own death in 1714. She was the sister of Mary of Orange and was another daughter of James II. The last of the Stuarts, Anne marked her reign with the most significant event, the 1707 Act of Union with Scotland. She outlived all her children, leaving her throne without an heir.

Upon the death of Anne, England looked for a Protestant prince to succeed her, and chose George of Hanover who reigned from 1714–1727. Although he spoke only German and spent as little time in England as possible, he was chosen because he was the great-grandson of James I. Beginning with this "distant cousin" to the throne, the reign of George I marked the beginning of the 174-year rule of the Hanoverians who preceded Victoria.

George I left the running of the government to the English politicians and created the office of prime minister. Under the Hanoverians, the powers of Parliament were extended, and the constitutional monarchy developed into what it is today.

The American colonies were lost under the Hanoverian George III, but other British possessions were expanded: Canada was won from the French in the Seven Years' War (1756–63), British control over India was affirmed, and Captain Cook claimed Australia and New Zealand for England. The British became embroiled in the Napoleonic Wars (1795–1815), achieving two of their greatest victories and acquiring two of their greatest heroes: Nelson at Trafalgar and Wellington at Waterloo.

THE INDUSTRIAL REVOLUTION & THE REIGN OF VICTORIA

The mid- to late-18th century saw the beginnings of the Industrial Revolution. This event changed the lives of the laboring class, created a wealthy middle class, and transformed England from a rural, agricultural society into an urban, industrial economy. England was now a world-class financial and military power. Male suffrage was extended, though women were to continue under a series of civil disabilities for the rest of the century.

Queen Victoria's reign (1837–1901) coincided with the height of the Industrial Revolution. When she ascended the throne, the monarchy as an institution was in considerable doubt, but her 64-year reign, the longest tenure in English history, was an incomparable success.

The Victorian era was shaped by the growing power of the bourgeoisie, the queen and her consort's personal moral stance, and the perceived moral responsibilities of managing a vast empire. During this time, the first trade unions were formed, a public (state) school system was developed, and railroads were built.

Victoria never recovered from the death of her German husband, Albert. He died from typhoid fever in 1861, and the queen never remarried. Although she had many children, she found them tiresome, but was a pillar of family values nonetheless. One historian said her greatest asset was her relative ordinariness.

Middle-class values ruled Victorian England and were embodied by the queen. The racy England of the past went underground. Our present-day view of England is still influenced by the attitudes of the Victorian era, and we tend to forget that English society in earlier centuries was famous for its rowdiness, sexual license, and spicy scandal.

Victoria's son Edward VII (reigned 1901–10) was a playboy who had waited too long in the wings. He is famous for mistresses, especially Lillie Langtry, and his love of elaborate dinners. During his brief reign, he, too, had an era named after him: the Edwardian age. Under Edward, the country entered the 20th century at the height of its imperial power, and at home the advent of the motorcar and the telephone radically changed social life, and the women's suffrage movement began.

World War I marked the end of an era. It had been assumed that peace, progress, prosperity, empire, and even social improvement would continue indefinitely. World War I and the troubled decades of social unrest, political uncertainty, and the rise of Nazism and fascism put an end to these expectations.

THE WINDS OF WAR World War II began in 1939, and soon thereafter Britain found a new and inspiring leader, Winston Churchill. Churchill led the nation during its "finest hour." From the time the Germans took France, Britain stood alone against Hitler. The evacuation of Dunkirk in 1940, the blitz of London, and the Battle of Britain were dark hours for the British people, and Churchill is remembered for urging them to hold onto their courage. Once the British forces were joined by their American allies, the tide finally turned, culminating in the D-Day invasion of German-occupied Normandy. These bloody events are still remembered by many with pride, and with nostalgia for the era when Britain was still a great world power.

The years following World War II brought many changes to England. Britain began to lose its grip on an empire (India became independent in 1947), and the Labour government, which came into power in 1945, established the welfare state and brought profound social change to Britain.

QUEEN ELIZABETH RULES TO THE PRESENT DAY Upon the death of the "wartime king," George VI, Elizabeth II ascended the throne in 1953. Her reign has seen the erosion of Britain's once-mighty industrial power, and, in recent years, a severe recession.

Political power has seesawed back and forth between the Conservative and Labour parties. Margaret Thatcher, who became prime minister in 1979, seriously eroded the welfare state and was ambivalent toward the European Union. Her popularity soared during the successful Falklands War, when Britain seemed to recover some of its military glory for a brief time.

Although the queen has remained steadfast and punctiliously performed her ceremonial duties, rumors about the royal family abounded, and in the year 1992, which Queen Elizabeth labeled an *annus horribilis,* a devastating fire swept through Windsor Castle, the marriages of several of her children crumbled, and the queen agreed to pay taxes for the first time. Prince Charles and Princess Diana agreed to a separation, and there were ominous rumblings about the future of the House of Windsor. By 1994 and 1995, Britain's economy was improving after several glum years, but Conservative prime minister John Major, heir to Margaret Thatcher's legacy, was coming under increasing criticism.

The IRA, reputedly enraged at the slow pace of peace talks, relaunched its reign of terror across London in February 1996, planting a massive bomb that ripped through a building in London's Docklands, injuring more than 100 people and killing two. Shattered, too, was the 17-month cease-fire by the IRA, which brought hope that peace was at least possible. Another bomb went off in Manchester in June.

Headlines about the IRA bombing gave way to another big bomb: the end of the marriage of Princess Diana and Prince Charles. The Wedding of the Century had become the Divorce of the Century. The lurid tabloids had been right all along about this unhappy pair. But details of the $26 million divorce settlement didn't satisfy the curious: Scrutiny of Prince Charles's relationship with Camilla Parker-Bowles, as well as gossip about Princess Diana's love life, continued in the press.

But in 1997, everyone's attention shifted to the parliamentary election. John Major's support had been steadily eroding since the early nineties, but the public's confidence in him seemed to hit an all-time low with his handling of the mad-cow disease crisis. Although scientists now claim the epidemic will end naturally by 2001, many British voters blamed Major and the Tories for it.

The political limelight now rested on the young Labour Leader Tony Blair. From his rock-star acquaintances to his "New Labour" rhetoric, which is chock-full of pop-culture buzzwords, he is a stark contrast to the more staid Major. His media-savvy personality obviously registered with the British electorate. On May 1, 1997, the Labour Party ended 18 years of Conservative rule with a landslide election victory. At age 44, Blair became Britain's youngest prime minister in 185 years, following in the wake of the largest Labour triumph since Winston Churchill was swept out of office at the end of World War II.

Blair's election—which came just at the moment when London was being touted by the international press for its renaissance in art, music, fashion, and dining—had many British entrepreneurs poised and ready to take advantage of what they perceived as enthusiasm for new ideas and ventures. Comparisons to Harold Macmillan and his reign over the Swinging Sixties were inevitable, and insiders agreed that something was in the air.

However, events took a shocking turn in August 1997 when Princess Diana was killed—along with her companion, Harrods heir Dodi al-Fayed—in a high-speed car crash in Paris.

"The People's Princess" still continued to dominate many headlines in 1998 with bizarre conspiracy theories about her death. But the royal family isn't the real force in Britain today. The spotlight remains on Tony Blair, who is moving ahead in streamlining the government.

Blair continues to lead Britain on a program of constitutional reform without parallel in this century. Critics fear that Blair will one day preside over a "dis-united" Britain, with Scotland breaking away and Northern Ireland forming a self-government.

Of course, the future of the monarchy still remains a hot topic of discussion in Britain. There is little support for doing away with the monarchy in Britain today in spite of wide criticism of the royal family's behavior in the wake of Diana's death. Apparently, if polls are to be believed, some three-quarters of the British populace want the monarchy to continue. Prince Charles is even making a comeback with the British public and has appeared in public—to the delight of the paparazzi—with his longtime mistress, Camilla Parker-Bowles. At the very least the monarchy is good for the tourist trade, on which Britain is increasingly dependent. And what would the tabloids do without it?

At the dawn of the millennium, major social changes occurred in Britain. No sooner had the year 2000 begun than Britain announced a change of its code of conduct for the military, allowing openly gay men and women to serve in the armed forces. The action followed a European court ruling in the fall of 1999 that forbade Britain to discriminate against homosexuals. This change brings Britain in line with almost all other NATO countries, including France, Canada, and Germany. The United States remains at variance with the trend.

Tony Blair continues to shake up the House of Lords—that is, in expelling the hereditary peers from the 1,200-member chamber. For the first time in their political careers, members of the House of Lords may have to face the unthinkable—an election.

2 Pies, Pudding & Pints: The Lowdown on British Cuisine

The late British humorist George Mikes wrote that "the Continentals have good food; the English have good table manners." But the British no longer deserve their reputation for soggy cabbage and tasteless dishes. Contemporary London—and the country as a whole—boasts many fine restaurants and sophisticated cuisine.

There's a lot more to British food today than the traditional roast, which has been celebrated since long before the days of Henry VIII. Of course, parsnip soup is still served, but now it's likely to graced with a dollop of walnut salsa verde. In contemporary England, the chef of the 1990s has taken on celebrity status. The creator of breast of Gressingham duck topped with deep-fried seaweed and served with a passion-fruit sauce is honored the way rock stars were in the 1970s. Some restaurants are so popular that they are demanding reservations 2 weeks in advance, if not more.

If you want to see what Britain is eating today, just drop in at Harvey Nichol's Fifth Floor in London's Knightsbridge for its dazzling display of produce from all over the globe.

The new buzzword for British cuisine is *magpie,* meaning borrowing ideas from global travels, taking them home, but improving on the original.

Be aware that many of the trendiest, most innovative restaurants are mind-blowingly expensive, especially in London. We've pointed out some innovative but affordable choices in this book, but if you're really trying to save on dining costs, you'll no doubt find yourself falling back on the traditional pub favorites (or better still, turning to an increasingly good selection of ethnic restaurants).

WHAT YOU'LL FIND ON THE MENU On any pub menu you're likely to encounter such dishes as the **Cornish pasty** and **shepherd's pie.** The first, traditionally made from Sunday-meal leftovers and taken by West Country fishers for Monday lunch, consists of chopped potatoes, carrots, and onions mixed together with seasoning and put into a pastry envelope. The second is a deep dish of chopped cooked beef mixed with onions and seasoning, covered with a layer of mashed potatoes, and served hot. Another version is cottage pie, which is minced beef covered with potatoes and also served hot. Of course, these beef dishes are subject to availability. In addition to a pasty, Cornwall also gives us "Stargazy Pie"—a deep-dish fish pie with a crisp crust covering a creamy concoction of freshly caught herring and vegetables.

The most common pub meal, though, is the **ploughman's lunch,** traditional farm-worker's fare, consisting of a good chunk of local cheese, a hunk of homemade crusty white or brown bread, some butter, and a pickled onion or two, washed down with ale. You'll now find such variations as pâté and chutney occasionally replacing the onions and cheese. Or you might find **Lancashire hot pot,** a stew of mutton, potatoes, kidneys, and onions (sometimes carrots). This concoction was originally put into a deep dish and set on the edge of the stove to cook slowly while the workers spent the day at the local mill.

Among appetizers, called **"starters"** in England, the most typical are potted shrimp (small buttered shrimp preserved in a jar), prawn cocktail, and smoked salmon. You might also be served pâté or "fish pie," which is very light fish pâté. Most menus will feature a variety of soups, including cock-a-leekie (chicken soup flavored with leeks), perhaps a game soup that has been doused with sherry, and many others.

Among the best-known traditional English meals is **roast beef** and **Yorkshire pudding** (the pudding is made with a flour base and cooked under the roast, allowing the fat from the meat to drop onto it). The beef could easily be a large sirloin (rolled loin), which, so the story goes, was named by James I when he was a guest at Houghton Tower, Lancashire. "Arise, Sir Loin," he cried, as he knighted the leg of beef before him with his dagger. (Again, because of the mad-cow crisis, beef dishes may not be available or advisable.) Another dish that makes use of a flour base is toad-in-the-hole, in which sausages are cooked in batter. Game, especially pheasant and grouse, is also a staple on British tables.

On any menu, you'll find **fresh seafood:** cod, haddock, herring, plaice, and Dover sole, the aristocrat of flatfish. Cod and haddock are used in making British **fish-and-chips** (chips are fried potatoes or thick French fries), which the true Briton covers with salt and vinegar. If you like **oysters,** try some of the famous Colchester variety. On the west coast, you'll find a not-to-be-missed delicacy: **Morecambe Bay shrimp.** Every region of England has its seafood specialties. In Ely, lying in the marshy fen district of East Anglia, it might be fenland eel pie with a twiggy seaweed as your green vegetable. Amphire also grows here in the salt marshes and along the Norfolk Coast. It's pickled in May and June and appears as a delicacy on many summer menus.

The **East End of London** has quite a few interesting old dishes, among them tripe and onions. In winter, Dr. Johnson's favorite tavern, the Cheshire Cheese on Fleet Street, offers a beefsteak-kidney-mushroom-and-game pudding in a suet case; in summer, there's a pastry case. East Enders can still be seen on Sunday at the Jellied Eel stall by Petticoat Lane, eating eel, cockles (small clams), mussels, whelks, and winkles—all with a touch of vinegar.

The British call desserts "sweets," although some people still refer to any dessert as **"pudding." Trifle** is the most famous English dessert, consisting of sponge cake soaked in brandy or sherry, coated with fruit or jam, and topped with cream custard. A "fool," such as gooseberry fool, is a light cream dessert whipped up from seasonal fruits. Regional sweets include the **northern "flitting" dumpling** (dates, walnuts, and syrup mixed with other ingredients and made into a pudding that is easily sliced and carried along when you're "flitting" from place to place). Similarly, **hasty pudding,** a Newcastle dish, is supposed to have been invented by people in a hurry to avoid the bailiff. It consists of stale bread, to which some dried fruit and milk are added before it is put into the oven.

Cheese is traditionally served after dessert as a savory. There are many regional cheeses, the best known being cheddar, a good, solid, mature cheese. Others are the semismooth Caerphilly, from a beautiful part of Wales, and Stilton, a blue-veined crumbly cheese that's often enjoyed with a glass of port.

ENGLISH BREAKFASTS & AFTERNOON TEA Britain is famous for its enormous breakfast of bacon, eggs, grilled tomato, and fried bread. Some places have replaced this cholesterol festival with a continental breakfast, but you'll still find the traditional morning meal available.

Kipper, or smoked herring, is also a popular breakfast dish. The finest come from the Isle of Man, Whitby, or Lock Fyne, in Scotland. The herrings are split open, placed over oak chips, and slowly cooked to produce a nice pale-brown smoked fish.

Many people still enjoy afternoon tea, which may consist of a simple cup of tea or a formal tea that starts with tiny crustless sandwiches filled with cucumber or watercress and proceeds through scones, crumpets with jam, or clotted cream, followed by cakes and tarts—all accompanied by a proper pot of tea. The tea at Brown's, in London, is quintessentially English, whereas the Ritz's tea is an elaborate affair, complete with orchestra and dancing.

In the country, tea shops abound, and in Devon, Cornwall, and the West Country you'll find the best cream teas; they consist of scones spread with jam and thick, clotted Devonshire cream. It's a delicious treat, indeed. People in Britain drink an average of four cups of tea a day, although many younger people prefer coffee.

WHAT TO WASH IT ALL DOWN WITH English pubs serve a variety of cocktails, but their stock-in-trade is beer: brown beer, or bitter; blond beer, or lager; and very dark beer, or stout. The standard English draft beer is much stronger than American beer and is served "with the chill off," because it doesn't taste good cold. Lager is always chilled, whereas stout can be served either way. Beer is always served straight from the tap, in two sizes: half-pint (8 oz.) and pint (16 oz.).

One of the most significant changes in English drinking habits has been the popularity of wine bars, and you will find many to try, including some that turn into discos late at night. Britain isn't known for its wine, although it does produce some medium-sweet fruity whites. Its cider, though, is famous—and mighty potent in contrast to the American variety.

Whisky (spelled without the *e*) refers to scotch. Canadian and Irish whiskey (spelled with the *e*) are also available, but only the very best-stocked bars have American bourbon and rye.

While you're in England, you may want to try the very English drink called **Pimm's,** a mixture developed by James Pimm, owner of a popular London oyster house in the 1840s. Although it can be consumed on the rocks, it's usually served as a Pimm's Cup—a drink that will have any number and variety of ingredients, depending on which part of the world (or empire) you're in. Here, just for fun, is a typical recipe: Take a very tall glass and fill it with ice. Add a thin slice of lemon (or orange), a cucumber spike (or a curl of cucumber rind), and 2 ounces of Pimm's liquor. Then finish with a splash of either lemon or club soda, 7-Up, or Tom Collins mix.

The English tend to drink everything at a warmer temperature than Americans are used to. So if you like ice in your soda, be sure to ask for lots of it, or you're likely to end up with a measly, quickly melting cube or two.

Index

Index

Index

Notes

Notes

p.16 Cotswolds, marshes near Brum

Frommer's® Complete Travel Guides

Alaska
Amsterdam
Arizona
Atlanta
Australia
Austria
Bahamas
Barcelona, Madrid & Seville
Beijing
Belgium, Holland & Luxembourg
Bermuda
Boston
British Columbia & the Canadian Rockies
Budapest & the Best of Hungary
California
Canada
Cancún, Cozumel & the Yucatán
Cape Cod, Nantucket & Martha's Vineyard
Caribbean
Caribbean Cruises & Ports of Call
Caribbean Ports of Call
Carolinas & Georgia
Chicago
China
Colorado
Costa Rica
Denmark
Denver, Boulder & Colorado Springs
England
Europe
European Cruises & Ports of Call
Florida
France
Germany
Greece
Greek Islands
Hawaii
Hong Kong
Honolulu, Waikiki & Oahu
Ireland
Israel
Italy
Jamaica
Japan
Las Vegas
London
Los Angeles
Maryland & Delaware
Maui
Mexico
Miami & the Keys
Montana & Wyoming
Montréal & Québec City
Munich & the Bavarian Alps
Nashville & Memphis
Nepal
New England
New Mexico
New Orleans
New York City
New Zealand
Nova Scotia, New Brunswick & Prince Edward Island
Oregon
Paris
Philadelphia & the Amish Country
Portugal
Prague & the Best of the Czech Republic
Provence & the Riviera
Puerto Rico
Rome
San Antonio & Austin
San Diego
San Francisco
Santa Fe, Taos & Albuquerque
Scandinavia
Scotland
Seattle & Portland
Singapore & Malaysia
South Africa
Southeast Asia
South Pacific
Spain
Sweden
Switzerland
Thailand
Tokyo
Toronto
Tuscany & Umbria
USA
Utah
Vancouver & Victoria
Vermont, New Hampshire & Maine
Vienna & the Danube Valley
Virgin Islands
Virginia
Walt Disney World & Orlando
Washington, D.C.
Washington State

Frommer's® Dollar-a-Day Guides

Australia from $50 a Day
California from $60 a Day
Caribbean from $70 a Day
England from $70 a Day
Europe from $60 a Day
Florida from $60 a Day
Hawaii from $70 a Day
Ireland from $60 a Day
Italy from $70 a Day
London from $85 a Day
New York from $80 a Day
Paris from $85 a Day
San Francisco from $60 a Day
Washington, D.C., from $60 a Day

Frommer's® Portable Guides

Acapulco, Ixtapa & Zihuatanejo
Alaska Cruises & Ports of Call
Bahamas
Baja & Los Cabos
Berlin
California Wine Country
Charleston & Savannah
Chicago
Dublin
Hawaii: The Big Island
Las Vegas
London
Maine Coast
Maui
New Orleans
New York City
Paris
Puerto Vallarta, Manzanillo & Guadalajara
San Diego
San Francisco
Sydney
Tampa & St. Petersburg
Venice
Washington, D.C.

Frommer's® National Park Guides

Family Vacations in the National Parks
Grand Canyon
National Parks of the American West
Rocky Mountain
Yellowstone & Grand Teton
Yosemite & Sequoia/Kings Canyon
Zion & Bryce Canyon

Frommer's® Memorable Walks

Chicago
London
New York
Paris
San Francisco
Washington, D.C.

Frommer's® Great Outdoor Guides

New England
Northern California
Southern California & Baja
Southern New England
Washington & Oregon

Frommer's® Born to Shop Guides

Born to Shop: China
Born to Shop: France
Born to Shop: Italy
Born to Shop: London
Born to Shop: New York
Born to Shop: Paris

Frommer's® Irreverent Guides

Amsterdam
Boston
Chicago
Las Vegas
London
Los Angeles
Manhattan
New Orleans
Paris
San Francisco
Seattle & Portland
Vancouver
Walt Disney World
Washington, D.C.

Frommer's® Best-Loved Driving Tours

America
Britain
California
Florida
France
Germany
Ireland
Italy
New England
Scotland
Spain
Western Europe

The Unofficial Guides®

Bed & Breakfasts in California
Bed & Breakfasts in New England
Bed & Breakfasts in the Northwest
Beyond Disney
Branson, Missouri
California with Kids
Chicago
Cruises
Disneyland
Florida with Kids
Golf Vacations in the Eastern U.S.
The Great Smoky & Blue Ridge Mountains
Inside Disney
Hawaii
Las Vegas
London
Miami & the Keys
Mini Las Vegas
Mini-Mickey
New Orleans
New York City
Paris
Safaris
San Francisco
Skiing in the West
Walt Disney World
Walt Disney World for Grown-ups
Walt Disney World for Kids
Washington, D.C.

Special-Interest Titles

Frommer's Britain's Best Bed & Breakfasts and Country Inns
Frommer's Britain's Best Bike Rides
The Civil War Trust's Official Guide to the Civil War Discovery Trail
Frommer's Caribbean Hideaways
Frommer's Food Lover's Companion to France
Frommer's Food Lover's Companion to Italy
Frommer's Gay & Lesbian Europe
Frommer's Exploring America by RV
Hanging Out in Europe
Israel Past & Present
Mad Monks' Guide to California
Mad Monks' Guide to New York City
Frommer's The Moon
Frommer's New York City with Kids
The New York Times' Unforgettable Weekends
Places Rated Almanac
Retirement Places Rated
Frommer's Road Atlas Britain
Frommer's Road Atlas Europe
Frommer's Washington, D.C., with Kids
Frommer's What the Airlines Never Tell You